The Encyclopedia of Philosophy

SUPPLEMENT

The ENCYCLOPEDIA *of* PHILOSOPHY

SUPPLEMENT

DONALD M. BORCHERT, *Editor in Chief*

MACMILLAN REFERENCE USA
Simon & Schuster Macmillan
NEW YORK

SIMON & SCHUSTER AND PRENTICE HALL INTERNATIONAL
LONDON MEXICO CITY NEW DELHI SINGAPORE SYDNEY TORONTO

Simon & Schuster Macmillan
1633 Broadway
New York, NY 10019

Library of Congress Catalog Card Number: 95-47988

Printed in the United States of America

printing number
2 3 4 5 6 7 8 9 10

Library of Congress Cataloging-in-Publication Data
Encyclopedia of Philosophy Supplement/Donald M. Borchert, editor in chief

p. cm.
Includes bibliographical references and index.
ISBN 0-02-864629-0
1. Philosophy—Encyclopedias. I. Borchert, Donald M., 1934–
B41.E5 1996 95-47988
103-dc20 CIP

This paper meets the requirements of ANSI-NISO Z39.48-1992 (Permanence of Paper).

Editorial Board

Consulting Editors

Contents

Editorial and Production Staff

Hélène G. Potter: *Project Editor*

David L. Severtson: *Copy Editor*

Jessica Hornik Evans: *Proofreader*

AEIOU, Inc.: *Indexer*

Rose Capozzelli: *Production Manager*

Debra Alpern, Alison Avery, Jessica Brent: *Editorial Assistants*

MACMILLAN REFERENCE
Elly Dickason, *Publisher*
Paul Bernabeo, *Editor in Chief*

Preface

THIS volume is a supplementary companion to the eight-volume *Encyclopedia of Philosophy,* which was published almost three decades ago under the aegis of the Macmillan Publishing Company. Paul Edwards, the editor in chief for the 1967 *Encyclopedia,* along with his editorial board assembled a multivolume work that became, not only a standard reference work on the shelves of virtually every college and public library, but also a frequently consulted resource in the personal libraries of countless professors and graduate students. The *Encyclopedia* will, no doubt, continue to be a valuable asset to students and scholars in years to come because it contains so many fine articles that have become classic pieces.

Yet much has happened in the discipline of philosophy since 1967. Intense and intellectually powerful discussions have taken place in almost every domain of the discipline, resulting in exciting discoveries, fresh insights, and even the flourishing of entirely new subfields such as feminist philosophy and applied ethics. Early in the 1990s Macmillan decided that the *Encyclopedia of Philosophy* needed updating and began planning for the publication of a single-volume *Supplement.*

It would be no easy task, however, to survey in one volume three decades of robust philosophical debate. The *Supplement* of necessity would have to be selective. And it would have to provide balanced accounts that reflected the fact that a consensus among philosophers concerning the philosophical issues discussed has seldom emerged. In addition, the *Supplement* would have to include personal entries that acknowledged the contributions of major thinkers.

In early 1992 Macmillan appointed an editor in chief and an editorial board of eight scholars to help guide the project from planning to publication. To assist in shaping the *Supplement* as a selective yet balanced work, recommendations were solicited from contributors to the *Encyclopedia* of 1967. More than one hundred responses were received. All of them provided helpful, detailed suggestions, and the vast majority of them took the opportunity to encourage Macmillan in the production of the *Supplement,* calling it a welcome and timely addition to an outstanding encyclopedia.

Having reviewed carefully the suggestions of the former contributors, the board of editors decided to plan the *Supplement* primarily in terms of major subfields within philosophy. Overview articles were prepared to review the significant post-1967 developments in each subfield, thereby providing the reader with useful summaries. In addition, break-out entries were written for each subfield in which specific issues germane to that subfield are treated separately in some detail. Many of these break-out entries are cross-referenced in the overview articles to provide the reader with direction for further study.

The subfields selected for inclusion are as follows:

- Aesthetics
- Applied Ethics
- Continental Philosophy, including overviews of
    - *Critical Theory*
    - *Deconstruction*
    - *Existentialism*
    - *Hermeneutic Phenomenology*
    - *Poststructuralism*
- Epistemology
- Ethical Theory
- Feminist Philosophy
- Logic, including overviews of
    - *Mathematical Logic*
    - *Philosophical Logic*
- Metaphysics
- Philosophy of Language
- Philosophy of Mind
- Philosophy of Religion
- Philosophy of Science
- Social and Political Philosophy

As in the original *Encyclopedia,* all the entries in the *Supplement* (the overviews as well as the break-outs) have been arranged in alphabetical order for easy location.

Some readers might wish to explore a subfield in detail. For them we have provided, in the front matter, an outline of contents listing each subfield with its relevant break-out entries. This table of contents will be particularly useful to those professors who might wish to use the *Supplement* as a textbook for courses focusing on one or more of the specific subfields. The overview article and its pertinent break-out entries prepared by a cluster of scholars in the field offer students a range of diverse expert voices. Also, almost all of the entries include bibliographies that focus on key works that facilitate further advanced study.

In addition to this treatment of the subfields of philosophy, the *Supplement* contains about sixty-five entries on specific philosophers, about one-half of which are updates of personal entries appearing in the *Encyclopedia.* Also included in the *Supplement* are several articles, such as "Philosophy of Medicine," that are not easily subsumed under any of the major subfields singled out for overview entries.

Where appropriate, entries in the *Supplement* are cross-referenced to other entries in the *Supplement* as well as to entries that first appeared in the 1967 *Encyclopedia.* Cross-references are indicated by words set in small caps and are followed by brackets [ ] containing the volume or volumes where the cross-referenced entry appears. An S within brackets [S] indicates that the cross-referenced entry appears in the present volume. Arabic numerals refer to entries contained in one of the *Encyclopedia*'s original volumes. Such cross-referencing reminds us that this volume presupposes and builds on the work embodied in the *Encyclopedia.*

As editor in chief of the *Supplement,* I am grateful for the assistance of many people without whom a project of this magnitude could never have been accomplished. A special note of gratitude must be sounded for the yeoman service of the board of editors: K. Danner Clouser, Paul Horwich, Jaegwon Kim, Joseph J. Kockelmans, Helen E. Longino, Louis Pojman, Ernest Sosa, and Michael Tooley. Each devoted many hours to selecting the *Supplement*'s 350 entries, generating scope descriptions to guide the authors, recruiting able and respected scholars to prepare the entries, and then carefully reviewing the entries when written. Also, I am deeply grateful to Vann McGee, who joined the board of editors as a special consultant on logic; to Robert Audi and Bernard Gert, who provided invaluable advice as the project was taking shape; and to the fine group of philosophers who consented to serve as consulting editors.

Each one of my colleagues in the Philosophy Department at Ohio University merits a special word of appreciation for providing the kind of environment in which a person can pursue a project such as this. In particular, I am grateful to John Bender, H. Gene Blocker, Philip Ehrlich, Albert Mosley, and Arthur Zucker for the countless ways in which they assisted me during the course of many months. The Philosophy Department secretaries, Alice Donohoe, Christina Dalesandry, and Penny Schall, with their clerical and computer skills, lifted many burdens from my shoulders. In addition, I am grateful for the generous grant from the 1804 Endowment of Ohio University that partially underwrote my expenses associated with this project.

To the entire staff at Macmillan Reference, the board of editors and I wish to express our gratitude, especially to Elly Dickason, the Associate Publisher of Macmillan Reference, who conceived the project, masterfully launched it, and skillfully piloted it into print; to Philip Friedman, the Publisher of Macmillan Reference, who backed the project; and to Hélène Potter, the project editor, who ensured day after day that no detail important for the success of the project was overlooked; to these fine professionals at Macmillan Reference we convey a hearty vote of thanks.

Finally, all of us who use and are enriched by the *Supplement* owe a debt of gratitude to the more than 300 scholars who have written the entries and signed their names to the articles appearing in this volume. To them belong much praise and appreciation for the benefits we derive from using this resource.

Ohio University
March 1996

Donald M. Borchert
EDITOR IN CHIEF

List of Articles

List of Contributors

Peter Achinstein
Johns Hopkins University

Ernest W. Adams
Soquel, California

Robert M. Adams
Yale University

Prudence Allen
Concordia University, Loyola Campus

Francis J. Ambrosio
Georgetown University

Brad Armendt
Arizona State University

David Armstrong
The University of Sydney

Robert Audi
University of Nebraska, Lincoln

Bruce Aune
University of Massachusetts, Amherst

Robert J. Baum
University of Florida, Gainesville

George Bealer
University of Colorado, Boulder

Tom L. Beauchamp
Georgetown University

John W. Bender
Ohio University, Athens

Robert Bernasconi
Memphis State University

Simon Blackburn
University of North Carolina, Chapel Hill

Ned Block
Massachusetts Institute of Technology

H. Gene Blocker
Ohio University, Athens

Margaret Boden
University of Sussex, England

Paul Artin Boghossian
New York University

Stephen Braude
University of Maryland Baltimore County, Baltimore

Phillip Bricker
University of Massachusetts, Amherst

Susan J. Brison
Dartmouth College

Justin Broackes
Brown University

Dan W. Brock
Brown University

Sylvain Bromberger
Massachusetts Institute of Technology

Anthony Brueckner
University of California, Santa Barbara

John P. Burgess
Princeton University

Panayot Butchvarov
University of Iowa

Duane L. Cady
Hamline University

Keith Campbell
The University of Sydney

Claudia F. Card
University of Wisconsin, Madison

Albert Casullo
University of Nebraska, Lincoln

Thomas Christiano
University of Arizona

K. Danner Clouser
Milton S. Hershey Medical Center

Lorraine Code
York University

L. J. Cohen
Queen's College, Oxford University, England

Earl Conee
University of Rochester

Daniel W. Conway
Pennsylvania State University

David Copp
University of California, Davis

Michael Corrado
University of North Carolina, Chapel Hill

Richard Creath
Arizona State University

Ann E. Cudd
University of Kansas, Lawrence

Fred B. D'Agostino
University of New England, Armidale, Australia

Omar Dahbour
Ohio University, Athens

Arleen B. Dallery
La Salle University

Arthur C. Danto
Columbia University

Stephen L. Darwall
University of Michigan, Ann Arbor

Martin Davies
Corpus Christi College, Oxford University, England

Stephen J. Davies
University of Auckland, New Zealand

Martin Davis
New York University

Michael DePaul
University of Notre Dame

Keith DeRose
Rice University

Keith Devlin
St. Mary's College of California, Moraga

Cora Diamond
University of Virginia, Charlottesville

George T. Dickie
University of Illinois, Chicago

Martin C. Dillon
State University of New York at Binghamton

James Dreier
Brown University

Michael A. Dummett
Oxford, England

Gerald Dworkin
University of British Columbia

John Earman
University of Pittsburgh

Frances Egan
Rutgers University

Catherine Z. Elgin
Lexington, Massachusetts

Charles Elkan
University of California, San Diego

Parvis Emad
University of Wisconsin, La Crosse

Steven M. Emmanuel
Virginia Wesleyan College

Herbert B. Enderton
University of California, Los Angeles

Ronald P. Endicott
Arkansas State University

Robert Ewin
University of Western Australia

Gertrude Ezorsky
New York, New York

Solomon Feferman
Stanford University

Joel Feinberg
University of Arizona, Tucson

Richard Feldman
University of Rochester

Owen Flanagan
Duke University

Thomas R. Flynn
Emory University

Richard Foley
Rutgers University

Lois Frankel
Ewing, New Jersey

R. G. Frey
Bowling Green State University

Elizabeth Fricker
Magdalen College, Oxford University, England

Alan E. Fuchs
College of William and Mary

Richard Fumerton
University of Iowa

Daniel Garber
University of Chicago

Richard Garner
Ohio State University, Columbus

Don J. Garrett
University of Utah

Alexander George
Amherst College

Bernard Gert
Dartmouth College

Marcus Giaquinto
University College London, England

Roger F. Gibson
Washington University, St. Louis

Clark Glymour
University of Pittsburgh

Alan H. Goldman
University of Miami

Roger Gottlieb
Worcester Polytechnic Institute

Richard E. Grandy
Rice University

John Greco
Fordham University

Anil Gupta
Indiana University, Bloomington

Susan Haack
University of Miami

Michael Hand
Texas A & M University

Valerie Gray Hardcastle
Virginia Polytechnic Institute and State University

Gilbert Harman
Princeton University

Sterling V. Harwood
San Jose State University

William Hasker
Huntington College

Richard Healey
University of Arizona

John Heil
Davidson College

Hilde Hein
College of the Holy Cross

Virginia Held
City University of New York

John Hick
Birmingham, England

James Higginbotham
Somerville College, Oxford University, England

Wilfrid A. Hodges
Queen Mary and Westfield College, University of London, England

Ted Honderich
University College London, England

Terence E. Horgan
University of Memphis

Nathan Houser
Indiana University–Purdue University

Paul Hoyningen-Huene
Zurich, Switzerland

Bruce Hunter
University of Alberta

Don Ihde
State University of New York at Stony Brook

David Ingram
Loyola University of Chicago

Frank C. Jackson
Australian National University

Robert N. Johnson
University of Missouri, Columbia

Michael Jubien
University of California, Davis

Pierre Kerszberg
Pennsylvania State University

Peter King
Ohio State University, Columbus

Theodore J. Kisiel
Northern Illinois University

Eva F. Kittay
State University of New York at Stony Brook

Richard Kraut
Northwestern University

Sonia Kruks
Amherst, Massachusetts

Henry E. Kyburg
University of Rochester

Will Kymlicka
University of Ottawa, Canada

Berel Lang
State University of New York at Albany

Joseph Levine
North Carolina State University, Raleigh

Jerrold Levinson
University of Maryland at College Park

Peter Lipton
University of Cambridge, England

Barry Loewer
Rutgers University

Lawrence B. Lombard
Wayne State University

Robert B. Louden
University of Southern Maine

Peter Ludlow
State University of New York at Stony Brook

William Lyons
University of Dublin, Ireland

Cynthia Macdonald
University of Manchester, England

Ruth Macklin
Bronx, New York

Donald Marquis
University of Kansas, Lawrence

Robert Matthews
Rutgers University

Thomas A. McCarthy
Northwestern University

John J. McDermott
Texas A & M University

Vann McGee
Rutgers University

Robert McKim
University of Illinois, Urbana-Champaign

Brian P. McLaughlin
Rutgers University

Alfred Mele
Davidson College

Susan Sauvé Meyer
University of Pennsylvania

Carl Mitcham
Pennsylvania State University

Jitendra N. Mohanty
Temple University

James H. Moor
Dartmouth College

Kathryn Pauly Morgan
University of Toronto, Canada

Paul K. Moser
Loyola University of Chicago

Albert Mosley
Ohio University, Athens

Jan Narveson
University of Waterloo, Canada

Stephen Neale
University of California, Berkeley

Thomas Nenon
University of Memphis

Graeme Nicholson
Trinity College, Toronto, Canada

Harold W. Noonan
University of Birmingham, England

Andrea Nye
University of Wisconsin, Whitewater

Eileen O'Neill
University of Massachusetts, Amherst

Graham Oddie
University of Colorado, Boulder

Richard Palmer
MacMurray College

David Papineau
King's College London, England

George S. Pappas
Ohio State University, Columbus

Rohit Parikh
City University of New York

Charles Parsons
Stanford University

Barbara H. Partee
University of Massachusetts, Amherst

Adriaan Peperzak
Loyola University of Chicago

John Perry
Stanford University

Philip Pettit
Australian National University

Charles R. Pigden
University of Otago, New Zealand

Robert Pippin
University of Chicago

Joseph C. Pitt
Virginia Polytechnic Institute and State University

Graham G. Priest
University of Queensland, Australia

Phillip L. Quinn
University of Notre Dame

Diana Raffman
Ohio State University, Columbus

Peter A. Railton
University of Michigan, Ann Arbor

Bjorn T. Ramberg
Simon Fraser University

Tom Regan
North Carolina State University, Raleigh

Mark E. Richard
Tufts University

William J. Richardson
Boston College

Grace G. Roosevelt
New York University

Gideon Rosen
Princeton University

Alex Rosenberg
University of Georgia

William Rowe
Purdue University

Michael Ruse
University of Guelph, Canada

Wesley Salmon
University of Pittsburgh

Virginia Sapiro
University of Wisconsin, Madison

Dennis J. Schmidt
Villanova University

Lawrence Schmidt
Hendrix College

Frederick Schmitt
University of Illinois, Urbana-Champaign

Alan D. Schrift
Grinnell College

Daniel Schulthess
Université de Neuchâtel, Switzerland

R. Barton Schultz
University of Chicago

Dion Scott-Kakures
Scripps College

Krister Segerberg
Uppsala University, Sweden

Charlene Haddock Seigfried
Evanston, Illinois

Gila Sher
University of California, San Diego

Sanford Shieh
Wesleyan University

Richard M. Shusterman
Temple University

Alan Sidelle
University of Wisconsin, Madison

Hugh J. Silverman
State University of New York at Stony Brook

Anita Silvers
San Francisco State University

Peter M. Simons
Universität Salzburg, Austria

Walter Sinnott-Armstrong
Dartmouth College

Lawrence Sklar
University of Michigan, Ann Arbor

Robert C. Sleigh, Jr.
University of Massachusetts, Amherst

Michael Slote
University of Maryland

Barry Smith
University of London, England

Nicholas D. Smith
Michigan State University, East Lansing

P. Christopher Smith
Portsmouth, New Hampshire

Quentin Smith
Western Michigan University

Paul F. Snowdon
Exeter College, University of Oxford, England

Miriam Solomon
Temple University

Roy Sorensen
New York University

Joan Stambaugh
Hunter College

James P. Sterba
Notre Dame University

Kathleen Sullivan
Stanford University

Frederick Suppe
Indiana University

Marshall Swain
Ohio State University, Columbus

Richard Tieszen
San Jose State University

Mark Timmons
University of Memphis

James Tomberlin
California State University, Northridge

Michael Tooley
University of Colorado, Boulder

Charles Travis
Sterling University, Scotland

Michael Tye
Temple University

Margaret Van de Pitte
University of Alberta

Peter van Inwagen
Notre Dame University

Rineke Verbrugge
University of Göteborg, Sweden

William J. Wainwright
University of Wisconsin, Milwaukee

Mary Ellen Waithe
Cleveland State University

Kendall L. Walton
University of Michigan, Ann Arbor

Wayne Waxman
Princeton, New Jersey

Vivian Weil
Illinois Institute of Technology

Peter S. Wenz
Sangamon State University

Patricia Werhane
University of Virginia, Charlottesville

Charles C. West
Princeton Theological Seminary

Henry R. West
Macalester College

Robin West
Georgetown University

Michael Williams
Northwestern University

Timothy Williamson
The University of Edinburgh, England

Deirdre Wilson
University College London, England

Kwasi Wiredu
University of South Florida, Tampa

Michael J. Wreen
Marquette University

Alison Wylie
University of Western Ontario, Canada

John W. Yolton
Piscataway, New Jersey

Palle Yourgrau
Brandeis University

Günter Zöller
Harvard University

Arthur Zucker
Ohio University, Athens

Outline of Contents

This Outline of Contents provides an alphabetized list of the entries appearing in the *Supplement* arranged according to major subfields. In addition, at the end of the Table there are two sections: one listing special topics not easily subsumed under one of the subfields and another listing all of the personal entries contained in the *Supplement.* In the subfield of "Continental Philosophy" personal entries are also included in order to cluster under the name of a specific philosopher the topical entries that focus primarily on that philosopher. (BE) signifies a Blind Entry that is cross-referenced to another entry. An asterisk [*] indicates that the entry has been listed under more than one subfield.

The Encyclopedia of Philosophy

SUPPLEMENT

ABORTION. The claims to which partisans on both sides of the abortion issue appeal seem, if one is not thinking of the abortion issue, close to self-evident, or they appear to be easily defensible. The case against abortion (Beckwith, 1993) rests on the proposition that there is a very strong presumption that ending another human life is seriously wrong. Almost everyone who is not thinking about the abortion issue would agree. There are good arguments for the view that fetuses are both living and human. ('Fetus' is generally used in the philosophical literature on abortion to refer to a human organism from the time of conception to the time of birth.) Thus, it is easy for those opposed to abortion to think that only the morally depraved or the seriously confused could disagree with them.

Standard prochoice views appeal either to the proposition that women have the right to make decisions concerning their own bodies or to the proposition that fetuses are not yet persons. Both of these propositions seem either to be platitudes or to be straightforwardly defensible. Thus, it is easy for prochoicers to believe that only religious fanatics or dogmatic conservatives could disagree. This explains, at least in part, why the abortion issue has created so much controversy. The philosophical debate regarding abortion has been concerned largely with subjecting these apparently obvious claims to the analytical scrutiny philosophers ought to give to them.

Consider first the standard argument against abortion. One frequent objection to the claim that fetuses are both human and alive is that we do not know when life begins. The reply to this objection is that fetuses both grow and metabolize and whatever grows and metabolizes is alive. Some argue that the beginning of life should be defined in terms of the appearance of brain function, because death is now defined in terms of the absence of brain function (Brody, 1975). This would permit abortion within at least eight weeks after conception. However, because death is, strictly speaking, defined in terms of the irreversible loss of brain function, the mere absence of brain function is not a sufficient condition for the absence of life. Accordingly, the claim that the presence of brain function is a necessary condition for the presence of life is left unsupported. Also, the standard antiabortion argument is criticized on the ground that we do not know when the soul enters the body. However, such a criticism is plainly irrelevant to the standard, apparently secular, antiabortion argument we are considering.

The Thomistic premise that it is always wrong intentionally to end an innocent human life is used by the Vatican to generate the prohibition of abortion. This premise is often attacked for presupposing 'absolutism'. This Vatican principle seems to render immoral active euthanasia, even when a patient is in excruciating, unrelievable pain or in persistent coma; it even seems to render immoral ending the life of a human cancer-cell culture. In none of these cases is the individual whose life is ended victimized. Thus, the Vatican principle seems most implausible.

Opponents of abortion are better off appealing to the weaker proposition that there is a very strong presumption against ending a human life (Beckwith, 1993). Because this presumption can be overridden when the victim has no interest in continued life, use of this premise provides a way of dealing with the above counterexamples. However, this tactic provides room for another objection to the antiabortion argument. Some prochoicers have argued that insentient fetuses have no interest in continued life. Because what is insentient does not care about what is done to it and because what does not care about what is done to it cannot have interests, insentient fetuses cannot have an interest in living. Therefore, abortion of insentient fetuses is not wrong (Steinbock, 1992; Sumner, 1981; and Warren, 1987).

If this argument were sound, then it would also show that patients who are in temporary coma, and therefore insentient, do not have an interest in living. M. A. Warren (1987) attempts to avoid this counterexample by making the neurological capacity for sentience a necessary condition for having any interests at all and, therefore, for having an interest in living. This move does not solve the problem, however. Because the argument in favor of permitting the abortion of insentient fetuses generated an untenable conclusion, that argument must be rejected. Because the argument rests on an equivocation between what one takes an interest in and what is in one's interest, there are even better reasons for rejecting it. Accordingly, this objection to the standard antiabortion argument is unsupported.

The classic antiabortion argument is subject to a major theoretical difficulty. Antiabortionists have tried vigorously to avoid the charge that they are trying to force their religious views upon persons who do not share them. However, the moral rule to which the standard antiabortion argument appeals obtains its particular force in the abortion dispute because it singles out members of the species *Homo sapiens* (rather than persons or sentient beings or beings with a future like ours, for example). It is difficult to imagine how the *Homo sapiens* rule could be defended against its competitors without relying upon the standard theological exegesis of the Sixth Commandment and upon the divine-command theory on which its moral standing rests. This leads to two problems. First, arguments against divine-command ethical theory seem compelling. Second, when arguments based on divine-command theory are transported into the Constitutional realm, First Amendment problems arise.

The philosophical literature contains two major kinds of prochoice strategies. The personhood strategy appeals to the proposition that no fetuses are persons. If this is so, then, because a woman plainly has the right to control her own body if she does not directly harm another person, abortion is morally permissible. However, Judith Thomson (1971) has argued that a woman's right to control her own body can justify the right to an abortion in some situations even if fetuses are persons. This second strategy rests on the claim that no one's right to life entails the right to a life-support system provided by another's body even if use of that life-support system is the only way to save one's life. Thus, even if opponents of abortion are successful in establishing that fetuses have the right to life, they have not thereby established that any fetus has the right to anyone else's uterus.

It is widely believed that Thomson's strategy can justify abortion in cases of rape and in cases where the life of a pregnant woman is threatened by pregnancy (Warren, 1973). There is much less unanimity concerning other cases, because it is generally believed that, if we create a predicament for others, we have special obligations to help them in their predicament. Furthermore, let us grant that A's right to life does not entail A's right to B's body even when A needs B's body to sustain life. Presumably, by parity of reasoning, B's right to B's body does not entail B's right to take A's life even if A's continuing to live severely restricts B's choices. Thus, we have a standoff, and the winner from the moral point of view will be that individual with the strongest right. Although Thomson's strategy has been widely discussed and raises interesting questions about the duty of beneficence, questions both about its philosophical underpinnings and about its scope suggest that philosophically inclined prochoicers would be better off with a personhood strategy.

No doubt, this is why personhood strategies have dominated the prochoice philosophical literature. Such strategies come in many varieties (Engelhardt, 1986; Feinberg, 1986; Tooley, 1972, 1983, and 1994; and Warren, 1973, 1987). Warren's 1973 version is most famous. She argued that reflection on our concept of person suggests that in order to be a person one must possess at least more than one of the following five characteristics: consciousness, rationality, self-motivated activity, the capacity to communicate, and the presence of a concept of self. Since no fetus possesses any of these characteristics, no fetus is a person. If only persons have full moral rights, then fetuses lack the full right to life. Therefore, abortion may never be forbidden for the sake of a fetus.

One might object to such a strategy on the ground that, since fetuses are potential persons, the moral importance of personhood guarantees them a full place in the moral community. The best reply to such an objection is that the claim that *X*'s have a right to *Y* does not entail that potential *X*'s have a right to *Y* (think of potential voters and potential presidents; Feinberg, 1986).

Although personhood theorists (like antiabortionists) tend to say little about the moral theories on which their views rest (Engelhardt, 1986, is an interesting exception), presumably most personhood theorists will turn out to be, when driven to the wall, social-contract theorists. Such theories, according to which morality is a self-interested agreement concerning rules of conduct among rational agents, tend to have problems accounting for the moral standing of those who are not rational agents—beings such as animals, young children, the retarded, the psychotic, and the senile. Thus, the personhood defense of the prochoice position tends to have problems that are the inverse of those of the classic antiabortion argument (*see* ANIMAL RIGHTS AND WELFARE; RIGHTS [7; S]).

Both standard antiabortion and personhood accounts appeal, in the final analysis, to the characteristics fetuses manifest at the time they are fetuses as a basis for their arguments concerning the ethics of abortion. This appeal may be a mistake both defenses share. My premature death would be a great misfortune to me because it would deprive me of a future of value. This is both generalizable and arguably the basis for the presumptive wrongness of ending human life. Such a view seems to imply that abortion is seriously immoral, seems to have a defensible intuitive basis, and seems to avoid the counterexamples that threaten alternative views (Marquis, 1989). However, this view is subject to two major objections. One could argue that the difference between the relation of fetuses to their futures and the relation of adults to their futures would explain why adults are wronged by losing their futures but fetuses are not (McInerney, 1990). One might also argue that because human sperm and ova have valuable futures like ours, the valuable future criterion for the wrongness of killing is too broad (Norcross, 1990). Not everyone believes these objections are conclusive. (SEE ALSO: *Biomedical Ethics* [S])

Bibliography

Beckwith, F. J. *Politically Correct Death: Answering Arguments for Abortion Rights.* Grand Rapids, MI, 1993.

Brody, B. *Abortion and the Sanctity of Human Life: A Philosophical View.* Cambridge, MA, 1975.

Dworkin, R. *Life's Dominion: An Argument about Abortion, Euthanasia, and Individual Freedom.* New York, 1993.

Engelhardt, Jr., H. T. *The Foundations of Bioethics.* New York, 1986. An attempt to place the personhood strategy in the context of an ethical theory and other issues in bioethics.

Feinberg, J., ed. *The Problem of Abortion.* Belmont, CA, 1984. An excellent anthology.

———. "Abortion," in Tom Regan, ed., *Matters of Life and Death: New Introductory Essays in Moral Philosophy,* 2d ed. (New York, 1986). The best account of the personhood strategy in a single essay.

Kamm, F. M. *Creation and Abortion: A Study in Moral and Legal Philosophy.* New York, 1992. A defense of Thomson's strategy.

Marquis, D. "Why Abortion Is Immoral," *Journal of Philosophy,* Vol. 86 (1989), 183–202.

McInerney, P. "Does a Fetus Already Have a Future-Like-Ours?" *Journal of Philosophy,* Vol. 87 (1990), 265–68.

Norcross, A. "Killing, Abortion, and Contraception: A Reply to Marquis," *Journal of Philosophy,* Vol. 87 (1990), 268–77.

Pojman, L. J., and F. J. Beckwith, eds. *The Abortion Controversy: A Reader.* Boston, 1994. An excellent anthology.

Steinbock, B. *Life before Birth: The Moral and Legal Status of Embryos and Fetuses.* New York, 1992. A sentience strategy.

Sumner, L. W. *Abortion and Moral Theory.* Princeton, NJ, 1981. A sentience strategy.

Thomson, J. J. "A Defense of Abortion," *Philosophy and Public Affairs,* Vol. 1 (1971), 47–66. A classic paper.

Tooley, M. "Abortion and Infanticide," *Philosophy and Public Affairs,* Vol. 2 (1972), 37–65. A classic paper.

———. *Abortion and Infanticide.* New York, 1983.

———. "In Defense of Abortion and Infanticide," in L. P. Poman and F. J. Beckwith, eds., *The Abortion Controversy: A Reader* (Boston, 1994). Tooley's most recent account of his views.

Warren, M. A. "On the Moral and Legal Status of Abortion," *Monist,* Vol. 57 (1973), 43–61. A classic paper.

Warren, M. A. "The Abortion Issue," in D. VanDeVeer and T. Regan, eds., *Health Care Ethics: An Introduction* (Philadelphia, 1987). A sentience strategy combined with a personhood strategy.

DON MARQUIS

ACTION THEORY. Action theory's primary concerns are the nature and explanation of human action. The explanatory concern emerged early and prominently in philosophy, in PLATO's [6; S] and ARISTOTLE's [1; S] ethical writings. In the 1960s action theory came to be seen as a philosophical discipline in its own right, with connections to ethics, METAPHYSICS [5; S], and the PHILOSOPHY OF MIND [S]. Two questions were central to it then: (1) what is an action? (2) how are actions to be explained? The latter eventually became paramount.

The first question suggests two others: (1a) how do actions differ from nonactions? (1b) how do actions differ from one another (the question of "action individuation")? According to a leading causal position on (1a), actions are like sunburns in an important respect. The burn on Ann's back is a sunburn partly in virtue of its having been caused by direct exposure to the sun's rays; a burn that looks and feels just the same is not a sunburn if it was caused by a heat lamp. Similarly, on the view in question, a certain event is Ann's raising her right hand—an action—partly in virtue of its having been suitably caused by mental items. On an influential version of this view, reasons, constructed as belief/desire complexes, are causes of actions, and an event counts as an action partly in virtue of its having been suitably caused by a reason. Alternative conceptions of action include an "internalist" position, according to which actions differ experientially from other events in a way that is essentially independent of how, or whether, they are caused; a conception of actions as composites of nonactional mental events or states (e.g., intentions) and pertinent nonactional effects (e.g., an arm's rising); and views identifying an action with the causing of a suitable nonactional product by an appropriate nonactional mental event or state—or, instead, by an agent.

By the end of the 1970s a lively debate over (1b) had produced a collection of relatively precise alternatives on action individuation: a fine-grained view, a coarse-grained view, and componential views. The first treats *A* and *B* as different actions if, in performing them, the agent exemplifies different act properties. Thus, if Al illuminates the room by flipping the switch, his flipping the switch and his illuminating the room are two different actions, since the act properties at issue are distinct. The second counts Al's flipping the switch and his illuminating the room as the same action under two different descriptions. Views of the third sort regard Al's illuminating the room as an action having various components, including his moving his arm, his flipping the switch, and the light's going on. Where proponents of the other two theories find, alternatively, a single action under different descriptions or a collection of related actions, advocates of the various component views locate a "larger" action having "smaller" actions among its parts.

Most philosophers agree that actions are explicable at least partly in terms of mental items and that we at least sketch an explanation of an intentional action by identifying the reasons for which the agent performed it. However, whether reasons can provide causal explanations is a contested issue. In 1963 Donald DAVIDSON [S] challenged anticausalists about "reasons-explanations" to provide an account of the reasons for which we act—effective reasons—that does not treat (our having) those reasons as causes of relevant actions. The challenge is particularly acute when an agent has more than one reason for doing *A* but does it only for some subset of those reasons. For example, Al has a pair of reasons for mowing his lawn this morning. First, he wants to mow it this week and he deems this morning the most convenient time. Second, he has an urge to repay his neighbor for rudely awakening him recently with her early morning mowing, and he believes that mowing his lawn this morning would constitute repayment. As it happens, Al mows his lawn this morning only for one of these reasons. In virtue of what is it true that he mows it for this reason, and not for the other, if not that this reason (or his having it), and not the other, plays a suitable causal role in his mowing his lawn? Although no one has demonstrated that Davidson's challenge cannot be met, the most detailed attempts to meet it are revealingly problematic.

The causal view of action explanation faces problems of its own. It typically is embraced as part of a naturalistic stand on agency, according to which mental items that play causal/explanatory roles in action bear some important relation to physical states and events. Relations that have been explored include identity (both type-type and token-token) and various kinds of supervenience. Each kind of relation faces difficulties, and some philosophers have argued that anything less than type-type identity (which many view as untenable) will fail to avert an unacceptable epiphenomenalism.

Action theorists have fruitfully scrutinized psychological states and events alleged to play crucial causal/explanatory roles in intentional action. At one time belief and desire were assumed to shoulder this burden. By the late 1980s intentions had gained a prominent place in action theory. Some theorists focused on proximal intentions—intentions for the specious present—as the primary link between reasons and action. Others concentrated on the roles of distal intentions—intentions for the nonimmediate future—in guiding practical reasoning and in coordinating one's own behavior over time and interaction with other agents. A lively debate occurred over whether intentions are reducible to belief/desire complexes or, instead, are irreducible states of mind; and the project of constructing a causal analysis of intentional action gained new momentum. Some theorists fruitfully appealed to intentions in attempting to avoid problems that "deviant causal chains" posed for attempted analyses of intentional action featuring reasons (belief/desire complexes) as causes. Briefly, the general alleged problem is this: whatever psychological causes are deemed necessary and sufficient for a resultant action's being intentional, cases can be described in which, owing to an atypical causal connection between the favored psychological antecedents and a pertinent resultant action, that action is not intentional. For example, Ann wants to frighten a prowler away and she believes that she may do so by making a deafening noise. Motivated (causally) by this desire and belief, Ann may search for a suitable object and, in her search, accidentally knock over her aquarium—producing a deafening crash. In so doing, she might frighten the prowler away; but her frightening the prowler is not an intentional action. The task for those who wish to analyze intentional action causally is to specify not only the psychological causes of actions associated with their being intentional but also the pertinent roles played by these causes (e.g., guidance).

Action theorists want to know both what it is that explanations of actions explain and how actions are properly explained. A full-blown theory of action's nature and explanation would not only tell us how actions differ from nonactions and from one another, it would also solve part of the MIND–BODY PROBLEM [5]. Further, such a theory would bear directly on the issues of FREEDOM [3] of action and moral RESPONSIBILITY [7].

Bibliography

Audi, R. *Action, Intention, and Reason.* Ithaca, NY, 1993.

Brand, M. *Intending and Acting.* Cambridge, MA, 1984.

Bratman, M. *Intention, Plans, and Practical Reason.* Cambridge, MA, 1987.

Davidson, D. *Essays on Actions and Events.* Oxford, 1980. Includes his 1963 essay, "Actions, Reasons, and Causes."

Ginet, C. *On Action.* Cambridge, 1990.

Goldman, A. *A Theory of Human Action.* Englewood Cliffs, NJ, 1970.

Hornsby, J. *Actions.* London, 1980.

Mele, A. *Springs of Action.* Oxford, 1992.

ALFRED R. MELE

AESTHETIC ATTITUDE. The aesthetic attitude is the supposed mental state or perspective necessary for aesthetic experience, the mental state in which it is said that human beings are capable of experiencing and enjoying the BEAUTY [1; S] and symbolic significance of art and natural objects and without which such experiences cannot occur. The aesthetic attitude was therefore understood as the key to the analysis of "aesthetic experience," the central problem of philosophical aesthetics since the early eighteenth century. Although there were isolated discussions by Greek, Roman, and medieval philosophers of topics relating to art and beauty, the idea of an independent science or discipline of aesthetics did not appear until around 1730, when BAUMGARTEN [1] proposed a division of philosophical psychology into "logic" and "aesthetic." Logic dealt with all the cognitive, analytic operations of thinking, while aesthetics would deal with all the intuitive, sensuous areas of human experience, including the experience and enjoyment of natural beauty and art.

The key question was, therefore, What is the nature or essence of aesthetic experience, and how does it differ from other sorts of experiences, especially "logical" experiences? Although various answers were proposed over the next centuries, most aestheticians agreed that there was a peculiar aesthetic point of view or stance that, when directed toward works of art or objects of nature, would yield an aesthetic experience of those objects. A tree, lake, or mountain, for example, could be perceived or considered from other points of view or attitudes—pragmatically, ecologically, and so on, in ways that did not reveal the aesthetic qualities of the object. But by shifting one's attention ("attitude"), looking at an object in a different way, one could become aware of its aesthetic qualities (beauty, charm, and symbolic significance).

The major concern, then, was the nature or essence of the "aesthetic attitude." Again, although answers varied considerably, there was general agreement among aestheticians since the early eighteenth century that the aesthetic attitude differed from other mental attitudes in being "disinterested," "detached," and "distanced" from practical and self-interested concerns of real life. This problem of defining the psychological state of mind of the aesthetic observer dominated aesthetics from the early eighteenth century through the early twentieth century. In the twentieth century, however, the interests of aestheticians broadened to include questions of creativity, art history, art institutions, and, generally, the social and political background to art, and interest in the nature of the aesthetic attitude of the perceiver waned. As aestheticians such as Joseph Margolis attempted in the late 1950s and early 1960s to bring aesthetics more firmly within analytic philosophy, problems in clarifying the concept of the aesthetic attitude in terms of "disinterestedness" became increasingly daunting. In the 1960s George Dickie argued against the very existence of an aesthetic attitude. In this same period Arthur Danto argued that it was not adopting the aesthetic attitude that made the appreciation of contemporary art possible but rather art institutions, the "artworld," as he called it, that explained and made possible aesthetic experience (*see* ARTWORLD [S]). More recently, feminists (*see* FEMINIST AESTHETICS AND CRITICISM [S]), "postcolonialists," and others concerned with the marginalization of minority perspectives have wondered if the assumption of a single, monolithic, "normal" aesthetic attitude was not simply the biased, acculturated perspective of a well-educated European male. Despite efforts by Jerome Stolnitz and others to clarify aesthetic-attitude theories, "postmodern" interest in art has tended to reject any monolithic psychological or "intentional" accounts in favor of greater "reader" (observer) participation, diversity, and freedom from supposed norms, emphasizing an institutional, sociological, or political rather than psychological perspective (*see* MODERNISM AND POSTMODERNISM [S]).

(SEE ALSO: *Aesthetics, History of,* and *Aesthetics, Problems of* [1; S])

Bibliography

Danto, A. *The Philosophical Disenfranchisement of Art.* New York, 1986.

Dickie, G. *Art and the Aesthetic.* Ithaca, NY, 1974.

Ecker, G. *Feminist Aesthetics,* H. Anderson, trans. Boston, 1985.

Margolis, J., ed. *Philosophy Looks at the Arts.* New York, 1987.

Showalter, E., ed. *The New Feminist Critics: Essays on Women, Literature, and Theory.* New York, 1985.

Silverman, H., ed. *Postmodernism: Philosophy and the Arts.* New York, 1989.

Stolnitz, J. *Aesthetics and Philosophy of Art Criticism.* Boston, 1960.

H. GENE BLOCKER

AESTHETIC AUTONOMY. That art should be autonomous has its source in the belief that the value of art lies in the aesthetic, a realm disconnected from practical concerns. This eighteenth century idea departs from antiquity's positioning of art as instrumental for cultural and social life.

KANT [4; S] is the main authority for those who characterize the aesthetic as irreducible to instrumental terms and hence autonomous. For him, each instance of aesthetic gratification is unique and unpredictable because occasioned by the free play of the imagination and understanding. Being not rule governed, aesthetic valuation cannot be equated with cognitive, moral, political, practical, or prudential judgment. In the twentieth century, formalists such as Bell and Adorno further Kant's view by insisting that aesthetic significance consists solely in how the elements of the aesthetic object relate to one another, not in how these elements represent the world external to the aesthetic object.

If aesthetic experience is responsive solely to the perceived aesthetic object and is free of external determinants, its significance must be exclusively aesthetic. However, the definitive demarcation of the aesthetic from the nonaesthetic has proven elusive, not in the least because contemporary art strives to demonstrate that, given the right context, anything can be an aesthetic object. Fascism and POSTMODERNISM [S] even aestheticize political objectives. And scientific and moral experience both contain the intuitive and analogical elements Kant reserved to aesthetic experience. All these considerations challenge the view that the aesthetic is distinct from and undetermined by other realms.

Furthermore, if the aesthetic is autonomous, two implausible conclusions are entailed: first, the aesthetic is thoroughly detached *from* the moral, social, and political environment; second, the aesthetic should be thoroughly detached *about* the moral, social, and political environment. As to the first, recent critical analysis is replete with demonstrations of how aesthetic evaluation is reflective of its environment. As to the second, from antiquity aesthetic significance has been understood to be amplified by rather than detracted from objects' success in celebrating, condemning or otherwise reflecting on the environment from which they emerge.

(SEE ALSO: *Aesthetics, History of*, and *Aesthetics, Problems of* [1; S])

Bibliography

Adorno, T. W. *Aesthetische Theorie.* Frankfurt am Main, 1970.

Bell, C. *Art* [London, 1914], 3rd ed. Oxford, 1987.

Kant, I. *The Critique of Judgement.* Oxford, 1928.

Krukowski, L. "Contextualism and Autonomy in Aesthetics," *Journal of Aesthetic Education,* Vol. 24 (1990), 123–34.

Sankowski, E. "Art Museums, Autonomy, and Canons," *Monist,* 75:4 (October 1993), 535–55.

ANITA SILVERS

AESTHETIC PROPERTIES. Although philosophers in the eighteenth and nineteenth centuries concentrated on BEAUTY [1; S] and sublimity almost to the exclusion of every other aesthetic property, late-twentieth-century philosophers have done their best to redress the balance and have concentrated on almost every aesthetic property except the two just mentioned. Or at least so it might seem. In truth, their attention has turned from understanding the nature of, or providing criteria of application for, these two admittedly important aesthetic properties to investigating the nature and importance of aesthetic properties as such.

Aesthetic properties include unity, balance, integration, lifelessness, delicacy, dumpiness, loveliness, restlessness, and powerfulness, among many others. Nonaesthetic properties include, again among many others, redness, squareness, noisiness, weighing 50 pounds, being in Philadelphia, and taking up wall space. While lists such as these can be continued almost indefinitely, and there is an intuitive feel to the aesthetic/nonaesthetic property distinction, as well as considerable agreement concerning whether a given property (properly understood) is aesthetic or nonaesthetic, a central philosophical question is what the distinction amounts to or is based on. The problem lies on the aesthetic property side of the distinction.

One way to define 'aesthetic property' is epistemologically, in the way such properties are known, or in the manner in which we become acquainted with them. Epistemological definitions can invoke and have invoked special modes of aesthetic perception, but they need not. Frank Sibley, for instance, speaks of the need to see (experience) aesthetic properties, but he does not think that any special perceptual faculty or sensory modality is involved in such perception. What distinguishes aesthetic perception from nonaesthetic perception, he thinks, is that taste is required for the former but not the latter. Given that taste is, according to Sibley, the ability to discern aesthetic qualities, circularity would seem to threaten: aesthetic properties are defined in terms of taste and taste in terms of aesthetic properties.

A different tack is to define 'aesthetic property' semantically or semiotically. Very roughly speaking, the view is that an aesthetic property is one that involves a reference by an object to something else. The object becomes, because it possesses the aesthetic property, a "presentational symbol" of that something else. More precisely, property A of object X is an aesthetic property if and only if X exemplifies A, in the sense that it possesses A and refers to A (inspired by GOODMAN [3; S], 1968). A certain passage of Walter Pater's prose, for example, may be languid and refer to languidness in general. Aesthetic properties, on this view, function in a direct symbolic fashion in a way that nonaesthetic properties do not.

A semiotic or 'symbolic' definition of this sort works well with many literary works and many works of visual art. It does not fare as well, however, with musical compositions (most seem to involve no reference to anything outside themselves), or with natural objects (they do not seem to function symbolically at all), or with many artifacts and human actions (e.g., a perfume may be cloying, or a person's walk graceful). All seem to be about, or refer to, nothing at all, not even themselves. And there are problems in the other direction. A swatch of cloth—one of Goodman's own examples—may well exemplify kelly green, but kelly greenness is not an aesthetic property.

Another alternative is to define 'aesthetic property' in terms of a connection with aesthetic value. An aesthetic property, Monroe Beardsley thinks, is one that contributes, or contributes directly, to the aesthetic value (goodness) or disvalue (badness) of an object (1982). There are two principal problems with this definition, however. One is that some aesthetic properties—austerity or detachedness, for example—seem to be neutral, to count neither for nor against a judgment of aesthetic value, or to be variable, to count positively in one context, negatively in a second, and neither positively nor negatively in a third. The second problem is that unless the notion of aesthetic value, or the aesthetic concept it is defined in terms of, can itself be defined in nonaesthetic terms, circularity would again threaten. Even so, these difficulties may not be insurmountable. Beardsley thinks that the neutrality of certain aesthetic properties is only apparent and evaporates when the vagueness of the corresponding aesthetic term is eliminated; and he has attempted to define (or ground) the aesthetic in nonaesthetic terms.

Another major issue concerning aesthetic properties is their relation to nonaesthetic properties. Speaking in terms of features and terms rather than properties, Sibley has argued that "there are no sufficient conditions, no non-aesthetic features such that the presence of some set or number of them will beyond question logically justify or warrant the application of an aesthetic term" (1979, p. 546). (There are nonaesthetic sufficient conditions for an aesthetic term's not applying, Sibley thinks—for example, a painting that consists solely of two bars of pale blue and one of a very pale gray could not be gaudy.) This is stronger than saying that aesthetic concepts are defeasible, according to Sibley, since defeasible concepts have conditions that are normally sufficient (that apply if they are not 'defeated' because other conditions obtain), and we can be sure they apply if we know that those conditions hold and no 'voiding' conditions do. No such assurance is possible with aesthetic concepts, since the exercise of taste is always required in order to know that they apply. (It should also be noted that Sibley and virtually everyone else hold that there are no nonaesthetic necessary conditions for an aesthetic term's applying. Both a painting and a musical composition may be energetic and yet not share any [interesting] nonaesthetic features.)

As might be expected, Sibley has had his critics. Some have offered counterexamples to his thesis; some have alleged that his arguments are question begging; some have even questioned the existence of a philosophically neutral aesthetic/nonaesthetic property distinction. Putting these issues to the side, there is another matter to consider: aesthetic properties depend on nonaesthetic properties, but not vice versa. A painting may be foreboding (in part) because it has ashen grays that gradually twist into dark browns and deep blacks, but a painting could not be composed of whites and pastel blues because it is joyful: aesthetic properties supervene on nonaesthetic ones (*see* SUPERVENIENCE [S]). In some cases aesthetic properties may also supervene on other aesthetic properties—a symphony could be triumphant (in part) because it is fiery, for example—but, ultimately, all aesthetic properties are, it is claimed, based on nonaesthetic ones.

What exactly the relation of supervenience is, is not altogether clear. Nor is it clear whether aesthetic supervenience differs from other kinds of supervenience, such as moral supervenience (the moral rightness of an act, for example, supervening on various nonmoral characteristics of it, such as bringing about the most pleasure possible in the circumstances) and mental supervenience (the belief of a person supervening on certain of his/her brain states, for instance). Aestheticians have, however, argued for a number of theses in relation to supervenience. On the skeptical side some have claimed that some aesthetic properties, such as gracefulness, are not supervenient at all, while others have argued that supervenience is not a fruitful notion to use to explain the aesthetic properties of great works of art. More positively, attempts have been made to distinguish between weak and strong supervenience and to argue for (or against) the supervenience relation being causal, logical, or quasi-logical in nature. Efforts have also been made to quell the skeptical doubts just mentioned by arguing that aesthetic properties, including gracefulness, do indeed supervene on nonaesthetic properties, but the determination of such properties also depends on an object's being perceived in the right category, such as fugue or impressionist painting. Supervenience is indeed a useful notion to employ, it is claimed, but its importance may not be fully appreciated if the concept of an artistic category is not brought into play. (SEE ALSO: *Aesthetics, History of,* and *Aesthetics, Problems of* [1; S])

Bibliography

Beardsley, M. "What Is an Aesthetic Quality?" in *The Aesthetic Point of View,* edited by M. J. Wreen and D. Callen (Ithaca, NY, 1982).

Bender, J. "Supervenience and the Justification of Aesthetic Judgments," *Journal of Aesthetics and Art Criticism,* Vol. 46 (1987), 31–40.

Casebier, A. "The Alleged Special Logic for Aesthetic Terms," *Journal of Aesthetics and Art Criticism,* Vol. 31 (1973), 357–64.

Cohen, T. "Aesthetic/Non-aesthetic and the Concept of Taste: A Critique of Sibley's Position," *Theoria,* Vol. 39 (1973), 113–52.

Currie, G. "Supervenience, Essentialism, and Aesthetic Properties," *Philosophical Studies,* Vol. 58 (1990), 243–57.

Eaton, M. "The Intrinsic, Non-Supervenient Nature of Aesthetic Properties," *Journal of Aesthetics and Art Criticism,* Vol. 52 (1994), 383–97.

Goldman, A. "Aesthetic Qualities and Aesthetic Value," *Journal of Philosophy,* Vol. 87 (1990), 23–37.

Goodman, N. *Languages of Art.* Indianapolis, 1968. Chap. 2.

Hermeren, G. "Aesthetic Qualities, Value, and Emotive Meaning," *Theoria,* Vol. 39 (1973), 71–100.

Kivy, P. *Speaking of Art.* The Hague, 1973. Esp. chaps. 1–3.

———. "Aesthetic Concepts: Some Fresh Considerations," *Journal of Aesthetics and Art Criticism,* Vol. 37 (1979), 423–32.

Levinson, J. "Aesthetic Supervenience," *The Southern Journal of Philosophy,* Vol. 22 (1983), Supp., 93–110.

Sibley, F. "Aesthetic and Nonaesthetic," *Philosophical Review,* Vol. 74 (1965), 135–59.

———. "Symposium: About Taste, Part II," *British Journal of Aesthetics,* Vol. 6 (1966), 55–69.

———. "Objectivity and Aesthetics," *Proceedings of the Aristotelian Society,* Vol. 42 (1968), Supp., 31–54.

———. "Aesthetic Concepts," in W. E. Kennick, ed., *Art and Philosophy,* 2d ed. (New York, 1979).

Wicks, R. "Supervenience and Aesthetic Judgment," *Journal of Aesthetics and Art Criticism,* Vol. 46 (1988), 509–11.

Zangwill, N. "Long Live Supervenience," *Journal of Aesthetics and Art Criticism,* Vol. 50 (1992), 319–22.

Zemach, E. "The Ontology of Aesthetic Properties," *Iyyun,* Vol. 42 (1993), 49–66.

MICHAEL WREEN

AESTHETIC RELATIVISM. "There's no disputing about tastes" is a common expression of aesthetic relativism, and indeed, it captures the spirit of relativism, if not the letter. It may be misleading in several respects, however. First, in speaking of "taste," it suggests only a relativism of judgments of aesthetic value (aesthetic goodness or badness). Relativism need not be so confined. Many art critics and philosophers think that all judgments that attribute AESTHETIC PROPERTIES [S] to objects behave relativistically and/or that interpretive judgments that say a work of art means or refers to, behave relativistically. Second, the remark suggests individual relativism, the view that judgments are relativized to the individual. Again, relativism need not be so confined. The great majority of relativists hold that judgments are relativized to a group, usually a culture, or to a set of principles, even if there are many sets of such principles within a single culture. Finally, the expression "no disputing," especially in being coupled with "taste," suggests that mere liking is in question. Few relativists hold that. Sophisticated relativists all leave a great deal of room for reason-giving, and almost all insist that a genuine judgment requires support with reasons.

Still, the maxim captures the important kernel of relativism. To focus only on judgments of aesthetic value: relativism is the view that there are two or more equally true (valid) standards, or sets of standards, of aesthetic value. Just as MORAL RELATIVISM [S] is the view that there is no one true morality, so aesthetic relativism is the view that there is no one true aesthetic. Instead, there is a variety of incompatible aesthetics, no one of which can claim truth to the exclusion of others. So understood, relativism entails that aesthetic goodness and badness are not properties that objects have independent of human beings. In that sense, relativism is a form of subjectivism, the view that aesthetic value is subjective, or mind dependent. Relativism requires more than subjectivism, however, for if aesthetic value is a function of the objective properties of objects as filtered through, or operated on by, subjective but universal features of the human mind (as KANT [4; S] thought), aesthetic value would be subjective, but there would be only one true aesthetic. If relativism is true, there is no such subjective but universal backing for judgments of aesthetic value.

Actually, relativism, if it is to be interesting, requires even more than that. If there are no such universal features of the human mind involved in judgments of aesthetic value, and if evaluative standards are conventional (and so mind dependent) and variable (meaning that there is more than one set of true or valid standards), relativism would be true. It might still be the case, however, that judgments that attribute aesthetic value to objects are fixed and not variable; it might be that there is only one true answer to the question, How much and what kind of aesthetic value (positive or negative) does this object have? Facts about the object, such as what category (e.g., sonata) or categories (e.g., painting, abstract expressionist painting) it is in, could settle which particular set of evaluative principles is the correct one to use in evaluating it. Or, eschewing the notion of categories, other facts about the object might settle the matter. For example, where and when a novel was composed, or what evaluative criteria were operative in the culture or subculture in which it was created, might determine which standards of evaluation are the correct ones to use in evaluating it. What is the right set of principles in one case, for one object, might well be the wrong set of principles in another case, for another object; and yet there is only one correct attribution of aesthetic value in each case. To be interesting, to allow for genuine competing and incompatible judgments of aesthetic value, relativism would have to rule this possibility out as well.

The main argument in favor of relativism has always been the diversity of judgments of aesthetic value. Poetry that one person or culture judges excellent, another thinks mediocre, and a third poor. Moreover, such judgments vary over time, even with a single person or within a culture. A painting judged superior at one time might fall from favor only to regain its place as a superb work of art. In and of itself, such diversity proves nothing, antirelativists are quick to point out, since all it shows is that people disagree. Widespread disagreement is possible about anything, including objective matters, such as the shape of the Earth or the existence of the Loch Ness monster. The best explanation of such disagreement, they think, is that judging aesthetic value is a delicate matter and a difficult business—and also that critics, like everyone else, invest their egos in their pronouncements and thus find it difficult to view matters dispassionately or to change their minds, once made up.

The relativist response to this is usually twofold. First, since disagreement over aesthetic matters is not only widespread but has shown and continues to show no sign of abating, it differs markedly from disagreement over objective matters. The best explanation of such continuing, irresolvable disagreement is that, at base, what is in question are differing sets of subjective concerns. Second, regardless of how such disagreement is best explained, the burden of proof is on the antirelativist, who must provide an ontology of aesthetic value that makes it a real, mind-independent property of objects or a real, universally underwritten mind-dependent property of objects; and he or she must provide an epistemology of aesthetic value, one that shows how human beings have access to such a property when it obviously differs radically from objective properties such as shape or size or even 'secondary qualities' such as color or odor.

Antirelativists may see things differently, however. Some, at least, think that the burden of proof is on the relativist. As Monroe Beardsley puts it, relativists hold that what looks like the attribution of a simple, nonrelational property is really an attribution of a two-or-more place relation (Beardsley, 1983). 'This is aesthetically good' is appearance; the reality is 'This is aesthetically good relative to standards A'. Goodness is never simple; it is always goodness in relation to such-and-such standards. Relativists have to complicate matters this way, according to Beardsley, for otherwise they underwrite contradictions: if goodness and badness were simple properties, 'This is aesthetically good' would be logically incompatible with 'this is aesthetically bad.' Thus, since the relational properties the relativist is committed to are more complex than the nonrelational ones we pre-theoretically attribute to objects, the burden of proof is on the relativist; he or she must show that such complex, covertly attributed properties are required. Worse still, Beardsley thinks, that burden can never be met. It is always possible to say, in the face of the widespread disagreement that the relativist cites as evidence (for the need to relativize attributions), that the aesthetic value of an object simply is inaccessible to a person or culture. The critic or culture may not be sufficiently sensitive to the language of a poem, for example, or for other reasons be unable to gauge aesthetic value accurately.

As might be expected, there are a number of relativist responses to this argument. One is to deny that judgments of aesthetic value are covertly relational, but to avoid the contradictions waiting in the wings by also denying that such judgments can be true or false. Rather, they are plausible or implausible, probable or improbable, reasonable or unreasonable, but never true or false. Denying truth to judgments of aesthetic value is a radical move, however, and one that plays havoc with a large number of concepts central to art criticism.

A second response allows such judgments to be true or false but claims that they are not covertly relational in the way alleged. Contradictions are avoided by claiming that the relativizing in question is to an assumed and unstated framework. Just as 'Coughlin Hall is to the left of LaLumiere Hall' is true when one framework (e.g., facing north) is assumed but 'LaLumiere Hall is to the left of Coughlin Hall' is true when another (e.g., facing south) is assumed, so, too, for judgments of aesthetic value. In neither case is the framework, that which is relativized to, part of the predicate of the judgment made. Genuine competing and incompatible judgments of aesthetic value are thus possible, according to this response, because 'aesthetically good' and 'aesthetically bad' are univocal and not telescoped relational terms.

A third response to the antirelativist argument attempts to discharge the burden of proof that (Beardsley and others claim) the relativist bears, and also attempts to show that relativism is required to explain widespread, continuing disagreement. This response notes that, as the antirelativist argument has it, disagreement about aesthetic value can be diminished if people are sensitized to a culture or to the properties of (say) a poem. The problem is that such sensitizing is more like enculturation, or internalizing an ideology, than it is like learning a new science or mastering a new technique of objective inquiry. Relativism is required, then, not just because widespread disagreement is best explained by relativism, but also because the most plausible explanation of how such disagreement is diminished involves an educational process that is itself inherently relativistic.

Another antirelativist argument worth considering is that if widespread disagreement about judgments of aesthetic value shows that such judgments are not objectively true, or true in any universalistic but subjectively underwritten way, so, too, should widespread disagreement about aesthetic relativism show that it is not objectively true, or true in any universalistic but subjectively underwritten way. Indeed, all the arguments and counterarguments the aesthetic relativist marshals in relation to judgments of aesthetic value would seem to apply, mutatis mutandis, in relation to the judgment that aesthetic relativism is true. Aesthetic relativism is, on this argument, hoisted by its own petard.

This, however, is far from the entirety of the debate over relativism. Many of the arguments for or against moral relativism also apply, mutatis mutandis, to aesthetic relativism, although precisely which arguments do apply is itself a matter of dispute.

(SEE ALSO: *Aesthetics, History of,* and *Aesthetics, Problems of* [1; S])

Bibliography

Beardsley, M. "Can We Dispute about Tastes?" In M. Singer and R. Ammerman, eds., *Introductory Readings in Philosophy* (New York, 1960).

———. "The Refutation of Relativism," *Journal of Aesthetics and Art Criticism,* Vol. 41, (1983), 265–70.

Crawford, D. "Causes, Reasons, and Aesthetic Objectivity," *American Philosophical Quarterly,* Vol. 8 (1971), 266–74.

Goldman, A. "Aesthetic Qualities and Aesthetic Values," *Journal of Philosophy,* Vol. 87 (1990), 23–27.

Hume, D. "On the Standard of Taste," in G. Dickie and R. Sclafani, eds., *Aesthetic: A Critical Introduction* (New York, 1977).

Kant, I. *Critique of Judgment* [1790], translated by Werner Pluhar. Indianapolis, 1987. Part 1.

Lewis, C. I. *An Analysis of Knowledge and Valuation.* La-Salle, IL, 1946. Book 3, esp. chaps. 12–15.

MacIntyre, A. "Colors, Cultures, and Practices," *Midwest Studies in Philosophy,* Vol. 17 (1992), 1–23.

Mackie, J. L. "Aesthetic Judgments—a Logical Study," in *Selected Papers,* Vol. 2, *Persons and Values* (Oxford, 1985).

McDowell, J. "Aesthetic Value, Objectivity, and the Fabric of the World," in E. Schaper, ed., *Pleasure, Preference, and Value* (Cambridge, 1983).

Olen, J. "Theories, Interpretations, and Aesthetic Qualities," *Journal of Aesthetics and Art Criticism,* Vol. 35 (1977), 425–31.

Pettit, P. "The Possibility of Aesthetic Realism," in E. Schaper, ed., *Pleasure, Preference, and Value* (Cambridge, 1983).

Stolnitz, J. "On Objective Relativism in Aesthetics," *Journal of Philosophy,* Vol. 57 (1960), 261–76.

Walton, K. "Categories of Art," *Philosophical Review,* Vol. 79 (1970), 334–67.

MICHAEL WREEN

AESTHETICS, HISTORY OF. Despite the problems of such general classifications, contemporary aesthetic theory may be divided into the following major approaches: analytic, pragmatist, Marxist, structuralist and poststructuralist, postmodernist, and feminist. As the first two derive directly from Anglo-American philosophy, the others have been largely inspired by European thought. Though some of the European theories treated here were published before 1960, their influence on Anglo-American aesthetics is more recent and was not previously covered by the Encyclopedia.

ANALYTIC AESTHETICS

Analytic aesthetics arose against the tradition of transcendental idealism that dominated early twentieth-century aesthetics through CROCE and COLLINGWOOD [2]. Assuming that all art shared a common essence, they argued that this essence is intuition-expression and that artworks are therefore all mental or ideal. Croce thus scorned all empirical distinctions between the different arts and their genres. Analytic aesthetics was an attempt to render philosophy of art more empirical and concrete by rejecting metaphysical speculation and adopting the general methods and presumptions of analytic philosophy. Though the different analysts shared a respect for empirical facts and a fervent commitment to conceptual analysis as the proper method of philosophy, they disagreed as to what analysis was. One form of analysis (associated with "ordinary language" philosophy) aims at simply clarifying our actual concepts without trying to revise or reject them. A second form (advocated by RUSSELL [7], CARNAP [2; S], and GOODMAN [3; S]) sees the goal of clarificational analysis as the replacing of a confused concept by other related concepts that will be more philosophically useful and less problematic—either by breaking down the original concept to more basic ones or by rationally reconstructing the concept to make it more precise and systematic. Both forms are found in analytic aesthetics: most preferred the former, though Goodman was influential in employing the latter in his notational definitions of works of art.

Nonessentialism about art has been a dominant theme in analytic aesthetics and is in part a product of its quest for clarity. The confusions of traditional aesthetics were imputed to its assumption that all art must share a common essence whose discovery could be used as an evaluative standard. This assumption, the analysts argued (relying on WITTGENSTEIN [8; S]), was mistaken. It led philosophers to ignore, conflate, and homogenize important differences between the arts and propose formulas of putative essence that were distortive, vague, and uninteresting. Thus, Passmore (as also Hampshire, Kennick, Gallie, Weitz [see bibliography]) saw the murky "dreariness" of traditional aesthetics "as arising out of the attempt to impose a spurious unity on things" that are quite different. Rather than generalizations for all art, this analytic current advocated "special study of the separate arts" with real respect for their differences (Passmore, 1954, pp. 44, 55). Nonessentialism also adduced the fact that the subsumption of these various forms under our current general concept of art is only a product of modern history, effected in the eighteenth century. It is then argued by Wollheim, Margolis, Weitz, and others that art has no essence because it is constituted by its changing history and such history is always open to further change. Viewing art as an open concept whose objects exhibited no common essence but only "strands of similarities," Morris Weitz (1956) argued that aesthetics should eschew impossible attempts to define art (or any of its developing genres) in terms of essence. Theory should instead focus on analyzing the logic of the concept of art (and its genre concepts), in which he distinguished two different logical uses: description (or classification) and honorific evaluation.

Three major analytic aestheticians resisted nonessentialism. Monroe Beardsley (1958) defined all art in terms of its essential use for aesthetic experience. George Dickie (1971) proposed an institutional essence for works of art, defining art (in the nonevaluative sense) as any artifact that is conferred the status of candidate for appreciation by an agent on behalf of the ARTWORLD [S]. Art's essence is not in exhibited properties but in genesis, and this allows for openness to any historical development the artworld will allow. Arthur Danto, from whom Dickie took the notion of artworld, rejects Dickie's view because it presumes the omnipotence of artworld agents without recognizing the historical constraints that structure their actions. His own form of essentialism identifies art with what art is historically interpreted to be in the artworld. Future history will not upset this definition, since, Danto argues, art's history (though not its actual practice) has reached its end in the recognition that anything can be art if it is so interpreted (Danto, 1981, 1986). These analytic appeals to history and social institutions are, however, rather abstract, "internal," and formal in comparison to Marxist, pragmatist, poststructuralist, and postmodernist theorizing, which emphasize also the wider socioeconomic forces and political struggles that shape the artworld's history.

Central to analytic aesthetics was its self-conception as philosophy of criticism. Rather than offering revisionary manifestos of what art and criticism should be, it sought to elucidate, systematize, and refine the principles of art and criticism as reflected in established practice to make them more logical and scientific. Analytic aesthetics thus got impetus from the growth of scientific art criticism in the academy.

One consequence of this metacriticism was an overwhelming preoccupation with art rather than natural BEAUTY [1; S]. Another was greater interest in issues of interpretation rather than aesthetic experience. Indeed, despite some early attempts to define the aesthetic (Sibley, Urmson), the dominant recent trend has been to criticize traditional notions of aesthetic experience and AESTHETIC ATTITUDE [S] (Dickie, 1964, 1965). Goodman and Danto even denounce the aesthetic as an oppressive ideology that trivializes art as sensual, emotive pleasure rather than cognition. Another consequence of analytic aesthetic's self-conception as metacriticism was a tendency to avoid evaluative issues, typically by relegating them to the first-order level of criticism itself. Just as academic criticism focused on interpretation rather than evaluation, so did analytic aesthetics. Goodman voiced this attitude in arguing that traditional "concentration on the question of excellence has been responsible . . . for . . . distortion of aesthetic inquiry" (1969, pp. 261–62). It is also expressed in Dickie's attempt to define art in a purely nonevaluative, classificational sense, leaving all normative decisions to the artworld and assuming that the very idea of a candidate for appreciation does not presuppose that art is, in some holistic sense, an evaluative concept, even though not all artworks may be valuable.

Intense preoccupation with the objects (rather than experience) of art was also fostered by the paradigm of metacriticism. Devoted to objective critical truth, it sought to define with great precision the objects of criticism, the exact ontological status and identity of particular works, and the authenticity of their alleged manifestations. Goodman, for example, offers strict notational definitions for works of music and literature, in which, because of the transitivity of identity, one changed letter or note would automatically result in the change of the work's identity.

PRAGMATISM

After an influential debut DEWEY'S [2; S] pragmatist aesthetics of *Art as Experience* (1934) was soon eclipsed by analysis. While analysis emphasized distinctions and objects, Dewey emphasized continuities and transformative aesthetic experience; while analysis privileged clarification of established practice, Dewey advocated progressive reform. If analysts typically followed MOORE [5] in thinking of aesthetic qualities as nonnatural and art as disinterested, privileged, and free from practical function, Dewey insisted that the aesthetic is a natural emergence of our animal feelings and practical interests and is designed to serve as well as refine them. Dewey's pragmatist influence is salient in two major analysts. Beardsley's highlighting and account of aesthetic experience (in terms of intensity, harmony, development, and integration) owes much to Dewey. Goodman, like Dewey, insists that art and science are continuous, serving human interests through "their common cognitive function." Despite his own strict definitions of works of art, Goodman insists with Dewey that what matters aesthetically is not what the object is but how it functions in dynamic experience, urging that we replace the question "What is art?" with that of "When is art?" (Goodman, 1978, p. 70; 1984, pp. 142–44). Richard Rorty, Joseph Margolis, and Richard Shusterman continue the Deweyan critique of the reified artwork by showing how interpretation can be transformative of the texts they interpret without thereby depriving us of shared objects to study and discuss. The democratic impulse of PRAGMATISM [6; S] has been developed in Shusterman's aesthetic defense of popular art. Stanley Cavell, who resists the pragmatist label, connects with pragmatist aesthetics, not only in his sympathetic analyses of popular film, but in the insistence on art's practical functionality as an ethical tool in the perfectionist project of self-improvement.

MARXIST AND HERMENEUTIC THEORIES

Contemporary Marxist aesthetics has its most influential expression in the Frankfurt school tradition of Adorno, Marcuse, and Benjamin that was influenced by LUKACS [5] and in the French blend of structuralist Marxism forged by Althusser. Though Adorno recognizes that art is socially conditioned, he nonetheless insists that its struggle for autonomy and promise of pleasure represents a crucial utopian moment and a critique of the dismal reality from which it seeks to distinguish itself. Criticism must deal with this dialectic between the work's autonomous form and the ideological and historical factors that shape it. Herbert Marcuse probed a related dialectic of art's tendency to affirm our culture even in criticizing it. Adorno (with Horkheimer) influentially condemned popular art as "the culture industry" because it refused the austere autonomy, distance, and demanding formal novelty of high art. Benjamin instead saw popular art as a potentially democratic product of our changing aesthetic sensibilities, which change through material changes in our world. Mechanical reproduction, he argued, has eroded the aura of uniqueness and distance that gave art its sense of monumental autonomy and consequent "cultic" value.

In France Louis Althusser created an original, if problematic, blend of MARXISM [S] and structuralism. Though faithful to Marxist insistence on the priority of the material base of production, he argued that the ideological superstructure (including education, art, and culture) must also have an essential role in sustaining that base (e.g., as "ideological state apparatus"), since one is dealing with a structural totality, all of whose parts affect each other. His disciples include Pierre Macherey and the influential Anglophone critics Fredric Jameson and Terry Eagleton. All three provide interesting studies of literature in terms of symbolic production and ideological conflict (which the artwork both embodies and tries to displace or fictionally resolve).

The influential hermeneutics of HEIDEGGER [3; S] and GADAMER [S] not only provides new holistic accounts of interpretation but, like pragmatism and Marxism, insists that art's experience be fully linked to the historical praxis of life and valued for its truth and not simply for autonomous formal pleasure.

STRUCTURALISM AND POSTSTRUCTURALISM

Structuralist theory, deriving from Saussure's linguistics, contains three central premises. First, literature is a systematic whole that is more than the sum of its parts, and its underlying rules or structures are more important to study than the particular meanings of individual works, since these basic structures are what are responsible for generating these meanings. Second, linguistic or literary elements are essentially relational or differential, whose meaning is defined in terms of their combination and contrast with each other. Third, these elements are merely conventional, their meaning determined not by inherent qualities but only by the conventional functions they have in the structural system. This holism eventually leads structuralism away from narrow concern with particular artworks toward the larger totality of a culture's codes of social communication (a development we can see in Roman Jakobson, Jan Mukarovsky, Claude Lévi-Strauss, and Roland Barthes). Structuralism thus goes against the traditional attempts at isolating a separate aesthetic domain, just as it resists traditional criticism's concentration on the interpretation and evaluation of particular artworks and their authors. These works are seen more as the rule-governed products of textuality than the expression of an individual creative genius. Even the unconscious was held to be structured like language, according to the influential structuralist psychoanalyst Jacques Lacan.

By the time structuralism gained influence in American aesthetics it was already being eclipsed by POSTSTRUCTURALISM [S], whose leading figures (Barthes, FOUCAULT, DERRIDA [S]) shared a structuralist background. Poststructuralism (one of whose varieties is DECONSTRUCTION [S]) agrees that all elements get their meaning from their functional and differential relations to each other, that these relations are conventional rather than natural, and that the systemic meanings are always more than the sum of the individual parts. But by insisting that history and change affect language, it denies the structuralist presumption that the system or structure is ever closed or complete. If language is constantly changing, through new combinations of its elements, so must the meaning of any of its member elements, which raises problems of how any text could have a fixed meaning that would guarantee the possibility of true interpretation. As the work's fixity of meaning is threatened, so is the notion of its organic unity, an explicit target of Foucault, Derrida, and Paul de Man. Deconstructionist flux and relational identity also challenge the firmness of genre distinctions, including the distinction between philosophy and literature; everything is part of the dynamic, generative general text that lacks the closure of a system in the structuralist sense.

POSTMODERNISM AND FEMINISM

Though already used in reference to architecture (in the late 1940s) and literature (by the 1960s), postmodernism emerged as a general trend of aesthetic theory only after the advent of poststructuralism. Like poststructuralism, its heightened sense of flux challenges the stabilities of unity, meaning, and rule-governed structure central to traditional aesthetics. Like postmodern art, postmodern aesthetics challenges the modernist idea of AESTHETIC AUTONOMY [S], purity, and distance. Arguing that we cannot compartmentalize art from political and social issues to achieve pure aesthetic experience, it also challenges the strict division between legitimate art and popular culture. Jean-François Lyotard, who made the term famous in philosophy, described the postmodern attitude as an incredulity toward grand metanarratives, toward monolithic unitary views of a topic.

Though independent of postmodernism and not as generally skeptical, feminist aesthetics has most flourished in the climate of postmodern theory, for it represents a challenge to what it sees as the grand metanarrative of "phallogocentric" theory. Like postmodernism, feminism challenges traditional ideas of aesthetic autonomy and distance that support patriarchal culture through the traditional male gaze, which subordinates the female as an object of aesthetic delight. Not surprisingly, embodiment or "writing with the body" is stressed by many feminist theorists, most notably Julia Kristeva, Hélène Cixous, and Luce Irigaray. Feminist and postmodernist perspectives are now making their way into mainstream Anglo-American aesthetics through the work of Elaine Showalter and others (see Korsmeyer & Brand, 1990).

(SEE ALSO: *Aesthetics, History of* [1], and *Feminist Aesthetics and Criticism* [S])

Bibliography

Adorno, T. W. *Aesthetic Theory.* London, 1984.

Althusser, L. *For Marx.* London, 1969.

Barthes, R. *Image-Meaning-Text.* New York, 1977.

Beardsley, M. C. *Aesthetics.* New York, 1958.

Benjamin, W. *Illuminations.* New York, 1968.

Cavell, S. *Pursuits of Happiness.* Cambridge, MA, 1981.

Cixous, H. *"Coming to Writing" and Other Essays.* New York, 1991.

Danto, A. *The Transfiguration of the Commonplace.* Cambridge, MA, 1981.

———. *The Philosophical Disenfranchisement of Art.* New York, 1986.

De Man, P. *Blindness and Insight.* Minneapolis, 1983.

Derrida, J. *Of Grammatology.* Baltimore, 1967.

———. *Writing and Difference.* Chicago, 1977.

Dewey, J. *Art as Experience.* New York, 1934.

Dickie, G. *Aesthetics.* New York, 1971.

Eagleton, T. *Criticism and Ideology.* London, 1976.

Foucault, M. *Language, Counter-Memory, Practice.* Ithaca, NY, 1977.

Gadamer, H.-G. *Truth and Method.* New York, 1982.

Gallie, W. B. "The Function of Philosophical Aesthetics," in W. Elton, ed., *Aesthetics and Language* (Oxford, 1954).

Goodman, N. *Languages of Art.* Oxford, 1969.

———. *Ways of Worldmaking.* New York, 1978.

———. *Of Mind and Other Matters.* Cambridge, MA, 1984.

Heidegger, M. *Being and Time.* New York, 1962.

———. *Poetry, Language, Thought.* New York, 1971.

Irigaray, L. *This Sex Which Is Not One.* Ithaca, NY, 1985.

Jameson, F. *Marxism and Form.* Princeton, NJ, 1971.

Kennick, W. E. "Does Traditional Aesthetics Rest on a Mistake?" *Mind,* Vol. 47 (1958).

Korsmeyer, C., and P. Brand. *Feminist Aesthetics.* Special issue of *Journal of Aesthetics and Art Criticism* (1990).

Kristeva, J. *The Kristeva Reader,* edited by T. Moi. New York, 1986.

Lacan, J. *Ecrits: A Selection.* New York, 1977.

Lukacs, G. *History and Class Consciousness.* New York, 1971.

Lyotard, J.-F. *The Postmodern Condition.* Minneapolis, 1984.

Macherey, P. *A Theory of Literary Production.* London, 1978.

Marcuse, H. *Negations.* Harmondsworth, Middlesex, 1972.

Margolis, J. *Philosophy Looks at the Arts.* Philadelphia, 1978.

———. *Interpretation: Radical But Not Unruly.* Berkeley, 1994.

Moi, T. *Sexual/Textual Politics: Feminist Literary Theory.* London, 1985.

Rorty, R. *Contingency, Irony, and Solidarity.* Cambridge, MA, 1989.

Showalter, E. *The New Feminist Criticism.* New York, 1985.

Shusterman, R. M. *Pragmatist Aesthetics.* Oxford, 1992.

———, ed. *Analytic Aesthetics.* Oxford, 1989.

Sibley, F. "Aesthetic Concepts," in J. Margolis, ed., *Philosophy Looks at the Arts* (Philadelphia, 1978).

Urmson, J. O. "What Makes a Situation Aesthetic?" in F. J. Coleman, ed., *Contemporary Studies in Aesthetics* (New York, 1968).

Weitz, M. "The Role of Theory in Aesthetics," *Journal of Aesthetics and Art Criticism,* Vol. 16 (1956), 27–35.

Wollheim, R. *Art and Its Objects.* New York, 1968.

RICHARD M. SHUSTERMAN

AESTHETICS, PROBLEMS OF. Aesthetics is the branch of philosophy studying concepts and issues related to art and aesthetic experience. The range of the aesthetic is wider than that of art, since not only works of art but natural objects are objects of aesthetic experience and judgment and display aesthetic qualities. Though different, the concepts of art and the aesthetic have been closely related in modernity, when the specific philosophical discipline of aesthetics was first established, along with the very concept of the aesthetic and the rise of autonomous art. In terms of modernity's tripartite differentiation of cultural spheres (reflected in KANT's [4; S] three Critiques), art and the aesthetic were linked together in opposition to the domains of pure cognition and practical reason. Much twentieth-century aesthetics is concerned with explaining (or challenging) this differentiation of art and the aesthetic by trying to determine the precise nature of these concepts, often attempting to define art in terms of the aesthetic and vice versa. Besides the issues of art and the aesthetic, this article will treat the problems of art's interpretation and evaluation. Other important issues, not reviewed in this article, include: the ontological status of artworks; the nature of representation in the arts; the nature of fiction, metaphor, and authenticity; the role of emotion in aesthetic appreciation; and the distinction between high and popular art (*see* ARTWORKS, ONTOLOGICAL STATUS OF IN HEIDEGGER; ART, REPRESENTATION IN; and AUTHENTICITY REGARDING THE ARTIST AND THE ARTWORKS [S]).

THE AESTHETIC AND AESTHETIC EXPERIENCE

Diverse attempts have been made to distinguish the aesthetic from other domains—for example, in terms of a special kind of property (such as beauty), a special kind of attitude, judgment, or experience. Some try to define the property of BEAUTY [1; S] (Mothersill, Savile), while others try to distinguish aesthetic from nonaesthetic properties in terms of the aesthetic's use of a nonrule-governed logic of application (Sibley). But general skepticism about the robust reality and objectivity of aesthetic properties (Do they exist at all? Are they simply supervenient on more basic physical properties?) has encouraged most recent thinkers to define the aesthetic through the subject-centered notions of attitude and experience. Let us concentrate on aesthetic experience, whose nature has been widely theorized and critiqued in both Anglo-American and Continental philosophy.

Aesthetic experience has, through its history, developed the following rough profile. Dynamic, enjoyable, and valuable, it is vividly felt and phenomenologically savored experience, powerfully absorbing us in its immediate presence. Aesthetic experience is also meaningful experience, not mere sensation. In standing out from the ordinary flow of experience by its vividness, pleasure, and greater meaning and unity, it is closely identified with the distinction of autonomous fine art and represents art's prime, autonomous aim. The idea of "art for art's sake" is thus construed as for the sake of art's own experience. Contemporary criticism of aesthetic experience often focuses on its alleged immediacy and its link to the compartmentalizing ideology of art for art's sake.

DEWEY'S [2; S] *Art as Experience* concentrates on attacking art's compartmentalization precisely by arguing that art be defined in terms of aesthetic experience and that such experience transcends the institutional boundaries of fine art—for example, in the appreciation of nature and festival. Opposing the fetishization of art's elite objects, Dewey argued that art's essence and value are not in its artifacts but in the dynamic, developing activity through which they are created and perceived. Aesthetic experience, hence art, can be achieved in any domain of human activity; it is distinguished by its vividness, dynamic development, and integrated satisfying form that makes it stand out from ordinary experience as "*an* experience." It is "directly fulfilling" and, in this sense, immediate, though involving the mediacy of developmental process. Dewey's definition of art as aesthetic experience can be criticized for failing to reflect the actual usage of our established concept of art, even if his real aim was probably instead to transform it radically.

Building on Dewey's theory (but not its critique of differentiation), Monroe Beardsley (1958, 1982) defines art as a function class whose defining function is the production of aesthetic experience. Art's value depends on the basic value and intrinsic pleasure of that experience; better works are those capable of producing aesthetic experiences of "greater magnitude." Aesthetic experience, for Beardsley, is an intrinsically enjoyable, unified, affective, and comparatively intense experience, where the subject's attention is firmly and actively focused on some phenomenal field. Analytic colleagues rejected Beardsley's theory on three grounds: subjective experiences are not the sorts of things that can have unity; aesthetic experience often lacks unity, pleasure, intensity, and affect; and it cannot be defined in positive terms, since some aesthetic experience is bad (e.g., with bad art). The first ground has led some to deny the existence of Beardsley's aesthetic experience (Dickie, 1965) while suggesting that aesthetic experience (conceived as having intrinsic value and positive affect) cannot define art, since such a definition must allow for bad art as well.

To resolve such difficulties, Nelson GOODMAN (1968, 1978, 1984 [3; S]) offers a definition of aesthetic experience that is nonevaluative and not based on the immediate phenomenological feel of experience. Instead, stressing how aesthetic experience is mediated through symbols, he defines it in purely semiotic terms as "cognitive experience distinguished by the dominance of certain symbolic characteristics": syntactic and semantic density, relative repleteness, exemplification, multiple and complex reference. If an object's "functioning exhibits all these symptoms, then very likely the object is a work of art" (1989, p. 199). However, as Goodman admits, these symptoms do not strictly constitute necessary and sufficient conditions for defining a work of art.

Turning to the Continental critique of aesthetic experience, one may begin with HEIDEGGER'S [3; S] denial that art is for mere "appreciation" divorced from the goal of truth. An artwork is not a gadget for enjoyable experience. "To be a work means to set up a world" and, in setting up a world, to reveal the truth of being. "Art then is the becoming and happening of truth" (1971, pp. 44, 71). GADAMER [S] develops these insights into a critique of aesthetic experience's alleged immediacy and radical differentiation from life. Only by such differentiation can art's appreciation be reduced to an immediate experience, but this does not do justice to art's enduring impact on our lives and world, its roots and effects in our cultural tradition, and its claim to truth. Art's meaning is not immediately given but a developing product of history that reaches beyond compartmentalized aesthetic contexts. True aesthetic experience "becomes an experience changing the person experiencing it" (1982, p. 92); nor is this experience a private subjectivity but the intersubjectively structured play of the work itself. As a game "plays" its players who must follow its rules, so the artwork submits those who want its meaning to the intersubjective structures that guide its experience.

Agreeing that "real aesthetic experience" requires submission "to the objective constitution of the work," Theodor Adorno concludes that it demands a "self-abnegation" inconsistent with immediate, facile pleasure (1984, pp. 474, 476). Art's experience must also go beyond immediate understanding (*Verstehen*), requiring critical "secondary reflection" of its ideological meaning and the sociohistorical conditions that shape it. Though Adorno insists that art's capacity for critical emancipatory truth depends on its distance from the unjust world, he recognizes that art's relative autonomy is only the product of social forces that ultimately condition the nature of aesthetic experience. Since changes in the nonaesthetic world affect our very capacities for experience, aesthetic experience cannot be a fixed natural kind.

This is central to Walter Benjamin's critique of aesthetic experience as immediate *Erlebnis*. Because of the fragmentation and shocks of modern life, immediate experience is no longer capable of any meaningful unity, becoming but a jumble of sensations merely lived through (*erlebt*). Benjamin instead advocates a notion of experience (*Erfahrung*) that requires the mediated, temporally cumulative accretion of coherent transmittable wisdom, though he doubts whether it can still be achieved. Modernization and technology (with its modes of mechanical reproduction) have also eroded aesthetic experience's transcendent "aura" of uniqueness and differentiation from ordinary reality; hence, the aesthetic comes into the world of politics and popular culture. Despite the dangers of the use of aesthetics in fascism, Benjamin, like Dewey, sees the loss of aura and aesthetic compartmentalization as potentially emancipatory.

THE DEFINITION OF ART

The difficulty of defining art through aesthetic experience and through other familiar criteria (e.g., form, expression, etc.) intensified doubts that art could be adequately defined in any strict sense—that is, in terms of an essence or set of necessary and sufficient conditions. Relying on WITTGENSTEIN [8; S], Morris Weitz (1955) and others (e.g., Gallie, Kennick) argue that art's essence could not in principle be defined because it simply had none. If we examine the class of artworks, we find they exhibit no set of properties that is common, peculiar, and essential to all of them. Nor is such essence necessary for the shared meaning of the concept 'art'; the network of similarities and family resemblances among artworks is enough to govern the concept's application. Indeed, art can have no defining essence because it is an intrinsically open, complex, contested, and mutable concept, a field that prides itself on originality and innovation. Thus, any definition that might seem to work would spur art to transcend it. Part of the conceptual complexity of 'art' is having both a mere classificational use and a use that is evaluative, hence contested.

To overcome these problems, a new style of definition was proposed. If evaluative issues make any definition contestable, then definition should be confined to the classificatory sense of art. If artworks exhibit no set of shared properties, then perhaps art's defining essence is not in exhibited properties but in its generative process. Moreover, the notion of family resemblance already implies a common generative core or history. These arguments led to George Dickie's institutional theory of art, which defines an artwork (in a purely classificational sense) as "an artifact ... upon which some person or persons acting on behalf of a certain social institution (the artworld) has conferred the status of candidate for appreciation" (1971, p. 101).

Though defining art in terms of necessary and sufficient conditions, this influential theory is purely formal or procedural and thus would neither foreclose on innovation nor prejudice with respect to evaluative criteria. Such foreclosures and prejudices are conveniently left to the artworld, as are all other substantive matters. The theory has the merit of highlighting the social context through which art is generated and given properties that are not directly perceived by the senses. Moreover, its flexible formalism can be used to cover whatever the artworld determines to be art. But the theory has problems as well. Though Dickie is right to insist that being an artwork does not entail being valuable, it is wrong to think that art can be defined without reference to value. Indeed, his definition presupposes evaluation in its notion of appreciation, but it provides no substantive insight that would explain *why* art is appreciated and that would enrich our understanding of it. Further, there are problems with seeing the artworld as an institution, since institutions typically involve roles, structures, and practices that are much more clearly codified and strictly administered than in the artworld. To respond that the artworld is a very informal institution is to merge this theory into a far more influential one: that art is a cultural tradition or sociohistorical practice.

Arthur Danto, who propounds this view and whose "discovery" of the ARTWORLD [S] inspired Dickie, rejects the institutional theory because of its lack of historical depth. Ignoring Wöllflin's insight that not everything is possible at every time, it gave artworld agents an unlimited power without considering the historical constraints that structure the artworld and thus limit its agents' actions. Even if it could explain how Andy Warhol's Brillo boxes could be art today, it could not explain why such a proposal would not have been accepted in quattrocento Florence. Such acceptance depends on the state of art's history and theory. Nothing, Danto argues, is art unless it is so interpreted, and the artworld "required a certain historical development" to make it possible to interpret the Brillo boxes as art. Since the artworld is but an abstraction from the artistic, critical, curatorial, and theoretical practices that constitute art's history, art is essentially a complex historical practice or tradition best defined historically. Richard Wollheim also asserts that "art is essentially historical," and Adorno concurs that art cannot be defined by any "invariable principle," since it is a historically changing constellation of moments whose constitutive unity is best defined by its concrete development as a distinct practice, at once socially embedded and resistantly autonomous. A new generation of analytic aestheticians (Carroll, Levinson, Wolterstoff) has likewise insisted on defining art by its history as a practice.

Though this strategy has many merits, some pragmatists (such as Shusterman, 1992) find it too quietistic and limited. In defining art as a practice defined by its art-historical narrative, it leaves all decisions as to what counts *as* art or *in* art to the backward-looking practice of art history but does not directly confront such issues. Philosophy of art thus becomes a representation of art history's representation of art, an imitation of an imitation that shirks normative engagement. Moreover, equating art with its historically defined practice involves the shrinking of art's extension, since art as defined by its established historical narrative amounts, in modern times, to the fine art that makes art history, thus essentially limiting art to elite fine art (*see* ART, DEFINITION OF [S]).

INTERPRETATION AND EVALUATION

The logic of interpretation and evaluation involves two different but related issues: the logical status of interpretive or evaluative statements (i.e., Are they propositions having truth value of some sort, or are they more like performative, creative acts?) and the role of reasons and arguments (i.e., Are they evidence, principles, or merely perceptual or rhetorical devices of persuasion?). Let us concentrate on the first, more basic issue.

In the quest for interpretive truth, authorial intention long served as the aim and criterion, an artwork meaning what its creator intended in creating it. Since correct evaluation should depend on correct understanding, intention thus seemed important for evaluation as well. This standard was successfully challenged in the second half of the twentieth century by analytic philosophers associated with the New Criticism, structuralist and poststructuralist thinkers, and several neopragmatists. Monroe Beardsley opposed what he (with New Critic Wimsatt) called "the intentional fallacy" by arguing that the concept of work-meaning could not be identical with author's meaning, since works can change their meaning without authorial agency (e.g., in the changes of meaning that occur after an author's death). It is the work's meaning that interpretation should seek, since this meaning is available by the norms of language, while access to the author is often not available. Defenders of intentionalism (such as Hirsch) argue that anti-intentionalists fail to distinguish between meaning and significance. Only the latter can change, while meaning must remain fixed to preserve the work's identity. The anti-intentionalists reply that the text itself provides identity enough, while Hirsch says the text itself remains too ambiguous to fix identity without a disambiguating intention.

Both Hirsch and Beardsley agree, however, that valid interpretations are true propositions about the meaning of an artwork that preclude the validity of conflicting interpretations. Margolis opposes this with a relativist position, asserting that interpretive statements express cognitive claims having some sort of truth value but that this value is weaker than in standard bivalent logic (involving plausibility, not strict truth). Thus it can allow conflicting interpretations to be valid, as plausible though not as true. For him (as for Ingarden) the ontologically indeterminate status of elements in an artwork provides gaps that can be differently filled in by interpretation. Here, as in critical pluralism, intentionalist interpretation can take its place along with other modes without special privilege.

Like New Critics and pluralists, structuralists and poststructuralists proclaim "the death of the author" as the privileged locus and determiner of work-meaning. Instead, meaning is seen as the product of structural relations among the work's elements and the features of the more general linguistic-cultural sphere. Poststructuralists (including deconstructionists such as DERRIDA [S]) then argue that meaning is always changing, since these relations of elements are always changing with the changing play of language. Hence, interpretation can never return to recapture the original meaning. Its very use of language to do so involves activity that changes the meaning by changing linguistic relations. Hence, all readings are misreadings. They can nonetheless be productive because of the interesting, insightful meanings they produce (*see* DECONSTRUCTION and POSTSTRUCTURALISM [S]).

This theory of interpretation clearly puts its emphasis on productive performativity rather than propositional truth. Harold Bloom, for example, urges that good interpretations are strong, innovative misreadings that help transform the work's meaning into the critic's own. Such a doctrine clearly suits the academy's pressures of constantly producing new interpretations for the professional advancement of its members. Influential pragmatists such as Richard Rorty and Stanley Fish likewise identify the right way of reading with distinctive, novel interpretation, for they argue that, in any case, all reading, like all experience, is always transformative interpretation. But without resorting to foundationalism, Richard Shusterman (1992) argued that we can and often do make a pragmatic distinction between mere acts of reading (or understanding) and interpretations. Such more ordinary (albeit often vague and implicit) understandings remain a necessary background and initial though not apodictic base for innovative interpretation.

Evaluation has received, in recent times, less philosophical attention than interpretation. For Beardsley the standard of artistic value was an artwork's capacity to produce aesthetic experience of some magnitude, but since such experience was subjective he also offered three "objective" canons of critical judgment evaluation: unity, intensity, and complexity. Goodman identifies artistic value with cognitive value achieved through the functioning of aesthetic symbol systems. Anthony Savile has reconstructed Samuel Johnson's theory that an artwork's value is proved by the test of time, while Barbara Smith offers a more complex sociohistorical account of how value is neither intrinsic nor merely subjective but rather the product of social forces and agendas locked in a continuing struggle for greater legitimacy and hegemony. (SEE ALSO: *Aesthetics, Problems of* [1]; and *Aesthetic Atti-*

tude; Aesthetic Autonomy; Aesthetic Properties; Aesthetic Relativism; Art, End of; Art, Interpretation of; Art as Performance; and *Feminist Aesthetics and Criticism* [S])

Bibliography

Adorno, T. *Aesthetic Theory.* London, 1984.
Barthes, R. *Image-Meaning-Text.* New York, 1977.
Beardsley, M. C. *Aesthetics.* New York, 1958.
———. *The Possibility of Criticism.* Detroit, 1973.
———. *The Aesthetic Point of View.* Ithaca, NY, 1982.
Benjamin, W. *Illuminations.* New York, 1968.
Bloom, H. *A Map of Misreading.* New York, 1975.
———. *Agon: Towards a Theory of Revisionism.* New York, 1982.
Budd, M. *Music and the Emotions.* London, 1985.
Carroll, N. "Art, Practice, and Narrative," *The Monist,* Vol. 71 (1988), 140–56.
———. *Philosophy of Horror.* New York, 1991.
Cavell, S. *The World Viewed.* Cambridge, MA, 1979.
Danto, A. *The Transfiguration of the Commonplace.* Cambridge, MA, 1981.
———. *The Philosophical Disenfranchisement of Art.* New York, 1986.
Derrida, J. *Of Grammatology.* Baltimore, 1967.
———. *Writing and Difference.* Chicago, 1977.
Dewey, J. *Art as Experience.* New York, 1934.
Dickie, G. "Beardsley's Phantom Aesthetic Experience," *Journal of Philosophy,* Vol. 62 (1965), 129–36.
———. *Aesthetics.* New York, 1971.
Fish, S. *Doing What Comes Naturally.* Durham, NC, 1989.
Gadamer, H.-G. *Truth and Method.* New York, 1982.
Gallie, W. B. "The Function of Philosophical Aesthetics," in W. Elton, ed., *Aesthetics and Language* (Oxford, 1954).
Goodman, N. *Languages of Art.* Oxford, 1968.
———. *Ways of Worldmaking.* Indianapolis, 1978.
———. *Of Mind and Other Matters.* Cambridge, MA, 1984.
Heidegger, M. *Poetry, Language, Thought.* New York, 1971.
Hirsch, E. D. *The Aims of Interpretation.* Chicago, 1978.
Ingarden, R. *The Literary Work of Art.* Evanston, IL, 1973.
Iseminger, G., ed. *Interpretation, Intention, and Truth.* Philadelphia, 1992.
Kennick, W. E. "Does Traditional Aesthetics Rest on a Mistake?" *Mind,* Vol. 47 (1958),
Kivy, P. *The Corded Shell.* Princeton, NJ, 1980.
Levinson, J. *Music, Art, and Metaphysics.* Ithaca, NY, 1990.
Margolis, J. *Art and Philosophy.* Brighton, 1980.
———. *Interpretation: Radical but Not Unruly.* Berkeley, 1994.
Mothersill, M. *Beauty Restored.* New York, 1984.
Novitz, D. *Knowledge, Fiction, and Imagination.* Philadelphia, 1987.
Rorty, R. *Objectivity, Relativism, and Truth.* Cambridge, MA, 1991.
Savile, A. *The Test of Time.* Oxford, 1982.
Shusterman, R. M. *The Object of Literary Criticism.* Amsterdam, 1984.
———. *Pragmatist Aesthetics.* Oxford, 1992.
Sibley, F. "Aesthetic Concepts," in J. Margolis, ed., *Philosophy Looks at the Arts* (Philadelphia, 1978).
Smith, B. *Contingencies of Value.* Cambridge, MA, 1988.
Weitz, M. "The Role of Theory in Aesthetics," *Journal of Aesthetics and Art Criticism,* Vol. 16 (1956), 27–35.
Walton, K. *Mimesis as Make-Believe.* Cambridge, MA, 1990.
Wollheim, R. *Art and Its Objects.* New York, 1968.
Wolterstorff, N. *Works and Worlds of Art.* Oxford, 1980.
———. "Philosophy after Analysis and Romanticism," in R. Shusterman, ed., *Analytic Aesthetics* (Oxford, 1989).

RICHARD M. SHUSTERMAN

AFFIRMATIVE ACTION. An understanding of affirmative action requires that we distinguish two kinds of discrimination: first, overt discrimination, which always involves prejudice by a perpetrator against a victim; second, institutional discrimination, which occurs when procedures such as selection through personal connections, qualification requirements, and seniority status, although they may be administered by unprejudiced persons, nevertheless have disproportionately adverse impact on minorities and women. While institutional and overt discrimination are distinct concepts, in reality they work together. For example, minorities and women tend to lack seniority protection against layoff because in the past prejudiced supervisors refused to hire them. Also, in large part because of race prejudice, African-Americans are excluded from relations of friendship and intimacy with whites; hence, they lack the personal connections to better jobs where whites predominate.

Affirmative action, a remedy for institutional discrimination, is exemplified, not in passive nondiscrimination, but in efforts to reduce the disparate impact of selection through personal connections, qualification requirements, and seniority status by actively recruiting and promoting significant numbers of minorities and women to positions in employment and as students in universities and professional schools.

Two important affirmative-action measures are, first, ensuring that qualification requirements having disparate impact are relevant to job performance and, second, establishing numerical goals for recruiting and promoting significant numbers of minorities and women. Where underrepresentation is severe, fulfilling a numerical goal may require "preference"—that is, selection of "basically qualified" minorities or women over more qualified white males.

Some critics claim that affirmative action has helped only a few fortunate minorities. But proponents claim that it has brought significant numbers of minority persons from low-status background into professional schools and employment as, for example, police, firefighters, textile workers, and teachers.

Moral critics of affirmative action suggest that preferential treatment is unjust because it undermines our current system of merit selection. Proponents argue that, while being the best candidate is one way to get the job, merit standards are currently ignored in several ways—children of alumni receive preferential admission to elite schools, war veterans are preferred to those without experience in the armed forces, tests that are irrelevant to job performance are used to select employees, and many jobs are filled through personal connections (probably the most widely used recruitment system in American employment).

Moral critics have also argued that preference is unfair to males who are singled out to bear the burden of remedying past discrimination. Some proponents deny that such treatment is unjust, while others, granting that these white males are unfairly singled out, suggest that they be given monetary awards to compensate for their loss.

(SEE ALSO: *Racism* [7; S], and *Social and Political Philosophy* [S])

Bibliography

Boxill, B. *Blacks and Social Justice.* Totowa, NJ, 1984.

Cohen, M., T. Nagel, and T. Scanlon, eds. *Equality and Preferential Treatment.* Princeton, NJ, 1977.

Ezorsky, G. *Racism and Justice: The Case for Affirmative Action.* Ithaca, NY, 1991.

Goldman, A. *Justice and Reverse Discrimination.* Princeton, NJ, 1979.

Wilson, W. J. *The Truly Disadvantaged.* Chicago, 1987.

GERTRUDE EZORSKY

AFRICAN PHILOSOPHY. As a habit of thought, philosophy is a primeval component of African culture. However, its academic cultivation, although also native to some parts of Africa, has been conducted in Western-style educational institutions in many parts of Africa, on account of the accident of colonization. These two circumstances account, in large measure, for the present character of African philosophy as a discipline.

Flowing directly from the circumstances just alluded to have been two imperatives of philosophical research in postcolonial Africa. They might be called the imperatives of reclamation and of reconstruction. The objective of the first has been to bring out, by means of a firsthand knowledge of African culture and, more especially, of African languages, the true character of the philosophical thought of precolonial Africa, which had suffered neglect or distortion during the colonial period; that of the second to evaluate the results of the first enterprise and, using the insights that might be derived from them in combination with the resources of modern knowledge and reflection, to construct philosophies suitable for present-day existence.

On the first front, available accounts already reveal oral traditions rich in ethical, political, and metaphysical ideas. They reveal, moreover, fundamental contrasts between African and Western conceptions, at least regarding predominant tendencies. Perhaps the most basic of these ideas and also the most illustrative of the contrasts is the idea of human personality. African notions of a human person frequently see human individuality as presupposing the existence of society rather than the other way around. (Good sense, by the way, forbids unqualified universals about the entire continent of Africa.) Two of arguably the most famous quotations in the literature of contemporary African philosophy are about exactly this point. Senghor, the African statesman-philosopher, contrasts the African orientation with the Cartesian one by epitomizing it as "I feel, I dance the other; I am" (1964, p. 73). Mbiti maintains, for his part, that the African individual can only say, "I am because we are, and since we are, therefore I am" (1990, p. 106). The point here is not just that the existence of a person presupposes at least the minimal society of a parental couple. The idea is rather that the notion of a person is intrinsically social; so that a totally unsocialized being replicating human morphology to perfection would still not be a person. But socialization is only a necessary condition. A person, according to this way of thinking, is a human individual who has matured into a responsible member of the community. Thus, as Menkiti (1984) points out, personhood is not something that one is born with but rather something that one may or may not achieve, and the achievement is susceptible of degree (*see* PERSONS [6]).

Of the various implications of this conception of personhood one of an especial philosophical significance is that the notion has both descriptive and normative components. Normatively, it is indicative of the communalistic ethic of many African societies. In such societies the understanding of the necessity for the adjustment of the interests of the individual to those of the community is developed through bonding to large circles of kinship groups. The multitude of obligations and rights—note the order—that thus emerge go well beyond the province of morality in the strict sense, but this contextualization of the moral sense gives rise, as a rule, to a pragmatic, as opposed to a supernaturalistic, conception of the basis of morality. Contrary to frequent suggestions, in the earlier literature, of the dependency of morality on religion in African thought, recent distinctively philosophical analyses of ethics in various African societies, such as those by Wiredu (1983), Gyekye (1987, chap. 8), and Gbadegesin (1991, chap. 3), converge in the finding that morality is viewed as conceptually grounded on practical and rational considerations about the harmonization of human interests in society rather than on any beliefs of a religious character.

In connection with the descriptive dimension of human personhood a very basic fact about much of African ontological thinking becomes apparent—namely, that sharp cleavages are eschewed in the ontological taxonomy of personhood and of reality in general. Thus, a person is commonly conceived to consist of the visible assemblage of flesh, bones, and nerves together with a set of rarefied, not normally visible, constituents of a quasi-material likeness. The number of these subtle components and their exact characterization differ from place to place. But, generally, there are at least two, and they are postulated to account, first, for the fact of animation and, second, for the uniqueness of human individuality.

The Yorubas, for example, attribute life in the human frame to a principle emanating directly from God, which they call 'emi'. (See, e.g., Gbadegesin, 1991, chap. 2.) But they associate the pattern of contingencies of character and circumstance that differentiate one person from another with the 'ori-inu', literally, the inner head, which is supposed to receive the summation of that destiny from God just before earthly incarnation. Two additional constituents are invoked to account for the power of thought. There is the 'okan', literally, the heart, which is regarded as the seat of emotion, and there is the 'opolo', the brain, to which is ascribed the basis of the capacity for ratiocinative thought. It is clear, though easily unnoticed, that if mind is construed, as it so often is in Western thought, as a kind of substance, there is nothing in the Yoruba analysis of personhood that corresponds to it and its associated perplexities. Nor, relatedly, is there any counterpart of the soul of Western dualistic metaphysics (*see* MIND-BODY PROBLEM [5]). The same is true, mutatis mutandis, of the conceptions of personhood entertained among various African peoples such as the Akans of Ghana and the Banyarwandas of Rwanda.

From the point of view of ontology an even more interesting fact is that, in view of the activities and susceptibilities attributed to the nonbodily constituents of human personality, the difference between them and the physical body is one not of a categorical chasm but only of the degree of materiality. They are only relatively less material than the body in that, although not subject to the grosser limitations of ordinary material bodies, they belong essentially to the general framework of material existence. Ironically, this is more unmistakable from African portrayals of life after death. (See Wiredu, 1992.) The conceptual similarities between African worlds of the dead and the living are so pronounced that they have escaped few students of African thought. This ontological continuity can be seen writ large in the speculative cosmologies of many African peoples. Typically, there is a cosmic order occupied at the apex by a supreme being with, next below him, a variety of extrahuman forces and beings of variable capabilities and virtue. Between this domain and the world of the lesser animals, plants, and inanimate matter is the race of homo sapiens. African ideas of the continual interactions among these orders of being provide little rational incentive for the application to this cosmic picture of metaphysical distinctions familiar in Western philosophy such as those between the natural and the supernatural and the temporal and the nontemporal.

The traditional communal thought of various African peoples owes its origin to the cogitations of individual philosophers, even if usually unnamed. Such indigenous thinkers, practically untouched by Western influences, still exist in Africa. Attention to their views, long overdue, is now being stimulated by works such as Oruka (1991) and, a little indirectly, Hallen and Sodipo (1986). Philosophical thinkers of much longer standing are, of course, known in some parts of Africa. One does not have to go as far as to Pharaonic Egypt for such discoveries. Claude Sumner's five-volume work on Ethiopian philosophy (1974–84), for instance, showcases, among other things, the written philosophy of Za'ra Ya'eqob, who in the seventeenth century propounded an indigenous rationalistic philosophy sterner, perhaps, in its subjection of religious dogma to the canons of reason than DESCARTES's [2; S] philosophy. One might mention also earlier leading lights in philosophy in Africa such as TERTULLIAN (160–230; [8]) and ST. AUGUSTINE (354–430; [1; S]).

An urgent question, however, that has arisen for contemporary Africans faced with the challenges of postcolonial reconstruction in philosophy is, How can philosophizing deeply impregnated by foreign ideas or methods, such as the Christ-intoxicated meditations of Tertullian and Augustine or, for that matter, the scientifically oriented analyses of a Western-trained African philosopher of the last half of the twentieth century, lay just claims to African authenticity? The immediate post-independence rulers of Africa, with little spare time for methodological niceties, made their own syntheses of the foreign and the indigenous and in the 1960s produced political philosophies for national reconstruction still worthy of study. (See, for example, Mutiso & Rohio, 1975). Inevitably, African academic philosophers have been especially prone to methodological soul searching, and controversy on the question of the authenticity of African philosophy has absorbed a considerable proportion of their attention, as may be seen in Serequeberham (1991). Still, work in African philosophy sensitive to insights from Western philosophy is being done. Eventually, the imperatives of reclamation and reconstruction will merge (*see* PHILOSOPHY [6; S]).

Bibliography

Appiah, K. A. *In My Father's House: Africa in the Philosophy of Culture.* New York, 1992.

Gbadegesin, S. *African Philosophy: Traditional Yoruba Philosophy and Contemporary African Realities.* New York, 1991.

Gyekye, K. *An Essay on African Philosophical Thought: The Akan Conceptual Scheme.* New York, 1987.

Hallen, B., and J. O. Sodipo. *Knowledge, Belief, and Witchcraft: Analytic Experiments in African Philosophy.* London, 1986.

Hountondji, P. *African Philosophy: Myth and Reality.* Bloomington, IN, 1976. Principal catalyst of the contemporary controversy on the best way of approaching the study of African traditions in relation to the tasks of African philosophy in the world today.

Masolo, D. A. *African Philosophy in Search of Identity.* Bloomington, IN, 1994.

Mbiti, J. *African Religions and Philosophy.* London, 1990.

Menkiti, I. "Person and Community in African Traditional Thought," in R. A. Wright, ed., *African Philosophy: An Introduction* (New York, 1984). Note the bibliography appended to this book.

Mudimbe, V. Y. *The Invention of Africa: Gnosis, Philosophy, and the Order of Knowledge.* Bloomington, IN, 1988. Note the bibliography.

Mutiso, G.-C., and S. W. Rohio. *Readings in African Political Thought.* London, 1975.

Oruka, O. H. *Sage Philosophy: Indigenous Thinkers and the Modern Debate on African Philosophy.* Nairobi, 1991.

Senghor, L. S. *On African Socialism.* New York, 1964.

Serequeberhan, T., ed. *African Philosophy: The Essential Readings.* New York, 1991.

———. *The Hermeneutics of African Philosophy.* New York, 1994.

Sumner, C. *Ethiopian Philosophy,* 5 vols. Addis Ababa, 1974–84. Vol. 2 (1976) is subtitled *The Treatise of Za'ara Ya'eqob and of Walda Heywat, Text and Authorship.*

———. *Classical Ethiopian Philosophy.* Los Angeles, 1994.

Tempels, P. *Bantu Philosophy.* Paris, 1959. Much-discussed philosophical study of an African people by a Belgian missionary. Regarded by some contemporary African philosophers as the paradigm of how not to do African philosophy.

Wiredu, K. *Philosophy and an African Culture.* Cambridge, 1980.

———. "Morality and Religion in Akan Thought," in H. O. Oruka and D. A. Masolo, *Philosophy and Cultures* (Nairobi, 1983).

———. "Death and the Afterlife in African Culture," in K. Wiredu and K. Gyekye, eds., *Person and Community: Ghanaian Philosophical Essays* (Washington, DC, 1992).

KWASI WIREDU

ANALYTIC FEMINISM. Analytic feminism applies analytic concepts and methods to feminist issues and applies feminist concepts and insights to issues that traditionally have been of interest to analytic philosophers. Analytic feminists, like analytic philosophers more generally, value clarity and precision in argument and use logical and linguistic analysis to help them achieve that clarity and precision. Unlike nonfeminists, they insist on recognizing and contesting SEXISM [S] and androcentrism (practices that take males or men and their experiences to be the norm or the ideal for human life). Analytic feminism holds that the best way to counter sexism and androcentrism is through forming a clear conception of and pursuing truth, logical consistency, objectivity, rationality, justice, and the good while recognizing that these notions have often been perverted by androcentrism throughout the history of philosophy. Analytic feminists engage the literature traditionally thought of as analytic philosophy but also draw on other traditions in philosophy as well as work by feminists working in other disciplines, especially the social and biological sciences.

Analytic feminists assert the distinction between the biological concept of sex and the socially constructed concept of gender (nonisomorphic to sex), though they may disagree widely on how this distinction is to be drawn and what moral or political implications it has. Although they share the conviction that the social constructions of gender create a fundamentally unjust imbalance in contemporary social and political arrangements, there is no other political thesis generally held by them. Many analytic feminists are not political philosophers, but those who are defend political views that reflect progressive positions found in contemporary nonfeminist political philosophy, from LIBERALISM [4; S] (Okin, 1989) to SOCIALISM [7] (Jaggar, 1983). They also draw on views of previous generations of feminist political philosophers from John Stuart MILL [5; S] and Mary WOLLSTONECRAFT [S] to Friederich ENGELS [2], Emma Goldman, and Charlotte Perkins Gilman. Analytic feminists, like nonanalytic feminists, have written much about social and political issues such as ABORTION [S], pornography, prostitution, rape, sexual harassment, surrogacy, and violence against women. What characterizes analytic feminism here is the use of logical analysis and, sometimes, decision-theoretic analysis (Cudd, 1993).

Analytic feminists often defend traditional analytic methods and concepts against criticisms from many nonanalytic feminists who charge (in various ways) that the notions of reason, truth, and objectivity or the methods of logical and linguistic analysis are hopelessly masculinist and cannot be reclaimed for feminist purposes. They criticize canonical philosophers, including ARISTOTLE [1; S], DESCARTES [2; S], KANT [4; S], ROUSSEAU [7; S], FREGE [3; S], QUINE [7; S], and RAWLS [S], as sexist or at least androcentric, and at times they suggest that these philosophers have nothing useful to say to women. But analytic feminists argue that to reject philosophers on those grounds would indict similarly almost the entire history of philosophy. The question analytic feminists ask is whether those androcentric or sexist writings can be corrected and rescued by an enlightened critical reader. Annette Baier's work on HUME [4; S] (in Baier, 1994), Marcia Homiak's (1993) work on Aristotle, and Barbara Herman's (1993) work on Kant exemplify such attempts.

Analytic feminism holds that many traditional philosophical notions are not only normatively compelling, but also in some ways empowering and liberating for women. While postmodern feminism rejects the universality of truth, justice, and objectivity and the univocality of "women," analytic feminism defends these notions. It recognizes that to reject a view because it is false or oppressive to women one needs some rational, objective ground from which to argue that it is in fact false or oppressive. An important task for analytic feminism involves investigating the objectivity of science. Helen Longino's *Science as Social Knowledge* (1990) was the first such analytic feminist work. Elizabeth Anderson's "Feminist Epistemology: An Interpretation and a Defense" (1995) shows how a carefully aimed feminist critique can improve the objectivity of science by distinguishing and illustrating four ways that feminist critiques have corrected the distorted lenses of masculinist science: by critiquing gendered structures in the social organization of science, by analyzing gendered symbols in scientific models, by exposing sexism in scientific practices and aims, and by revealing androcentrism in its concepts and theories. In its analysis of traditional philosophical topics such as objectivity and new topics such as sexism in language (Vetterling-Braggin, 1981), analytic feminism reveals the blurriness of the distinction between metaphysics, epistemology, and social/political philosophy.

(SEE ALSO: *Feminist Philosophy* [S])

Bibliography

Anderson, E. "Feminist Epistemology: An Interpretation and a Defense," *Hypatia,* Vol. 10 (Summer 1995).

Antony, L. M., and C. Witt, eds. *A Mind of One's Own: Feminist Essays on Reason and Objectivity.* Boulder, CO, 1993.

Baier, A. C. *Moral Prejudices.* Cambridge, MA, 1994.

Cudd, A. E. "Oppression by Choice," *Journal of Social Philosophy,* Vol. 25 (1994).

Cudd, A. E., and V. Klenk, eds. *Hypatia,* Vol. 10 (Summer 1995). A special issue devoted to analytic feminism.

Grimshaw, J. *Philosophy and Feminist Thinking.* Minneapolis, 1986.

Herman, B. "Could It Be Worth Thinking about Kant on Sex and Marriage?" in L. M. Antony and C. Witt, eds., *A Mind of One's Own: Feminist Essays on Reason and Objectivity* (Boulder, CO, 1993).

Homiak, M. "Feminism and Aristotle's Rational Ideal," in L. M. Antony and C. Witt, eds., *A Mind of One's Own: Feminist Essays on Reason and Objectivity* (Boulder, CO, 1993).

Jaggar, A. M. *Feminist Politics and Human Nature.* Totowa, NJ, 1983.

Longino, H. *Science as Social Knowledge.* Princeton, NJ, 1990.

Nelson, L. H. *Who Knows: From Quine to a Feminist Empiricism.* Philadelphia, 1990.

Okin, S. M. *Justice, Gender, and the Family.* Boston, 1989.

Vetterling-Braggin, M., ed. *Sexist Language: A Modern Philosophical Analysis.* Lanham, MD, 1981.

ANN E. CUDD

ANALYTICITY. The idea of analyticity—or truth by virtue of meaning—can be understood in two different ways. On the one hand, it might stand for an epistemic notion, for the idea that mere grasp of the meaning of a sentence suffices for knowledge that it is true. On the other hand, it might stand for a metaphysical notion, for the idea that a statement owes its truth value completely to its meaning, and not at all to "the facts." We may call the first notion "epistemic analyticity" and the second "metaphysical analyticity." On the face of it, these are distinct notions that subserve distinct philosophical programs. Willard Van Orman QUINE [7; S], whose writings are largely responsible for the contemporary rejection of analyticity, failed to distinguish between them; as a result, many philosophers came to assume that the two notions stand or fall together. However, it is the moral of recent work in this area that this assumption is mistaken: epistemic analyticity can be defended even while its metaphysical cousin is rejected.

The metaphysical concept of analyticity is presupposed by the logical positivist program of reducing all necessity to linguistic necessity. Guided by both the fear that objective, language-independent necessary connections would be metaphysically odd, and that no empiricist epistemology could explain our knowledge of them, philosophers like Rudolf CARNAP [2; S] (1947) and A. J. AYER [1] (1946) attempted to show that all necessary truths are simply disguised decisions concerning the meanings of words. According to this view, there is no more to the truth of, say, "Either snow is white or it is not" than a decision concerning the meaning of the word "or." On this view, linguistic meaning by itself is supposed to generate necessary truth; a fortiori, linguistic meaning by itself is supposed to generate truth. Hence the play with the metaphysical notion of analyticity.

However, it is doubtful that this makes a lot of sense. What could it possibly mean to say that the truth of a statement is fixed exclusively by its meaning and not by the facts? Is it not in general true that for any statement **S**,

S is true if and only if (iff) for some **p**, **S** means that **p** and **p**?

How could the mere fact that **S** means that **p** make it the case that **S** is true? Doesn't it also have to be the case that **p** (see Harman, 1960)?

The proponent of the metaphysical notion does have a comeback, one that has perhaps not been sufficiently addressed. What he will say instead is that, in some appropriate sense, our meaning **p** by **S** makes it the case that **p**.

But this line is itself fraught with difficulty. For how are we to understand how our meaning something by a sentence can make something or other the case? It is easy to understand how the fact that we mean what we do by a sentence determines whether that sentence expresses something true or false. But as Quine (1951) points out, that is just the normal dependence of truth on meaning. What is not clear is how the truth of what the sentence expresses could depend on the fact that it is expressed by that sentence, so that we would be entitled to say that what is expressed would not have been true at all had it not been for the fact that it is expressed by that sentence. But are we really to suppose that, prior to our stipulating a meaning for the sentence

"Either snow is white or it is not"

it was not the case that either snow was white or it was not? Is it not overwhelmingly obvious that this claim was true *before* such an act of meaning, and that it would have been true even if no one had thought about it, or chosen it to be expressed by one of our sentences?

There is, then, very little to recommend the linguistic theory of necessity and, with it, the metaphysical notion of analyticity that is supposed to subserve it. Epistemic analyticity, by contrast, is not involved in that futile reductive enterprise. Its role, rather, is to provide a theory of a priori knowledge (*see* KNOWLEDGE, A PRIORI [S]).

Intuitively speaking, it does seem that we can know certain statements—the truths of logic, mathematics, and conceptual analysis, most centrally—without recourse to empirical experience. The problem has always been to explain how.

The history of philosophy has known a number of answers to this question, among which the following has been very influential: We are equipped with a special evidence-gathering faculty of intuition, distinct from the standard five senses, that allows us to arrive at justified beliefs about the necessary properties of the world. By exercising this faculty, we are able to know a priori such truths as those of mathematics and logic.

The central impetus behind the analytic explanation of the a priori is to explain the possibility of a priori knowledge without having to postulate any such special faculty of "intuition," an idea that has never been adequately elaborated.

This is where the concept of epistemic analyticity comes in. If mere grasp of **S**'s meaning by **O** were to suffice for **O**'s being justified (with a strength sufficient for knowledge—henceforth, we will take this qualification to be understood) in holding **S** true, then **S**'s apriority would be explainable without appeal to a special faculty of intuition: the very fact that it means what it does for **O** would by itself explain why **O** is justified in holding it to be true.

How could mere grasp of a sentence's meaning justify someone in holding it true? Clearly, the answer to this question has to be semantical: something about the sentence's meaning, or about the way that meaning is fixed, must explain how its truth is knowable in this special way. What could this explanation be?

In the history of the subject, two different sorts of explanation have been especially important. Although these, too, have often been conflated, it is crucial to distinguish between them.

One idea was first formulated in full generality by Gottlob FREGE [3; S] (1884). According to this view, a statement's epistemic analyticity is to be explained by the fact that it is transformable into a logical truth by the substitution of synonyms for synonyms. We may call statements that satisfy this semantical condition 'Frege-analytic'.

Quine's enormously influential "Two Dogmas of Empiricism," (1951) complained that there couldn't be any Frege-analytic statements because there couldn't be any synonymies. But, as Herbert P. GRICE [S] and Peter F. STRAWSON [8; S] showed (1956), the arguments for this claim are highly disputable. And Paul Boghossian (1995) has added to this by arguing that Quine's negative arguments cannot plausibly stop short of his radical thesis of the indeterminacy of meaning, a thesis that most philosophers continue to reject.

The real problem with Frege-analyticity is not that there are not any instances of it, but that it is limited in its ability to explain the full range of a priori statements. Two classes remain problematic: a priori statements that are not transformable into logical truths by the substitution of synonyms for synonyms, and a priori statements that are trivially so transformable.

An example of the first class is the sentence "Whatever is red all over is not blue." Because the ingredient descriptive terms do not decompose in the appropriate way, this sentence is not transformable into a logical truth by substitution of synonyms.

The second class of recalcitrant statements consists precisely of the truths of logic. These truths satisfy, of course, the conditions on Frege-analyticity. But they satisfy them trivially. And it seems obvious that we cannot hope to explain our entitlement to belief in the truths of logic by appealing to their analyticity in this sense: knowledge of Frege-analyticity presupposes knowledge of logical truth and so cannot explain it.

How, then, is the epistemic analyticity of these recalcitrant truths to be explained? The solution proposed by Carnap (1947) and the middle WITTGENSTEIN [8; S] (1974) turned on the suggestion that such statements are to be thought of as 'implicit definitions' of their ingredient terms. Applied to the case of logic (a similar treatment is possible in the case of the other class of recalcitrant truths), this suggestion generates the semantical thesis we may call:

> Implicit definition: It is by arbitrarily stipulating that certain sentences of logic are to be true, or that certain inferences are to be valid, that we attach a meaning to the logical constants. A particular constant means that logical object, if any, which makes valid a specified set of sentences and/or inferences involving it.

The transition from this sort of implicit definition account of grasp to an account of the apriority of logic can then seem immediate, and the following sort of argument would appear to be in place:

1. If logical constant **C** is to mean what it does, then argument-form **A** has to be valid, for **C** means whatever logical object in fact makes **A** valid.

2. **C** means what it does.
Therefore,
3. **A** is valid.

Quine's "Truth by Convention" (1936) and "Carnap and Logical Truth" (1976) raised several important objections against the thesis of implicit definition: first, that it leads to an implausible CONVENTIONALISM [2] about logical truth; second, that it results in a vicious regress; and third, that it is committed to a notion—that of a meaning-constituting sentence or inference—that cannot be made out.

Even the proponents of implicit definition seem to have agreed that some sort of conventionalism about logical truth follows from implicit definition. However, Nathan Salmon (1994) and Boghossian (1995) have argued that this is a mistake: no version of conventionalism follows from the semantical thesis of implicit definition, provided that a distinction is observed between a sentence and the claim that it expresses.

Quine's second objection is also problematic in relying on a defective conception of what it is for a person to adopt a certain rule with respect to an expression, according to which the adoption of a rule always involves explicitly stating in linguistic terms the rule that is being adopted. On the contrary, it seems far more plausible to construe **x**'s following rule **R** with respect to **e** as consisting in some sort of fact about **x**'s *behavior* with **e**.

In what would such a fact consist? Here there are at least two options of which the most influential is this: **O**'s following rule **R** with respect to **e** consists in **O**'s being disposed, under appropriate circumstances, to conform to rule **R** in his employment of **e**.

According to this view, then, the logical constants mean what they do by virtue of figuring in certain inferences and/or sentences involving them and not in others. If some expressions mean what they do by virtue of figuring in certain inferences and sentences, then some inferences and sentences are constitutive of an expression's meaning what it does, and others are not.

Quine's final objection to implicit definition is that there will be no way to specify systematically the meaning-constituting inferences, because there will be no way to distinguish systematically between a meaning constituting inference and one that is not meaning-constituting but simply obvious. However, although this is a serious challenge, and although it remains unmet, there is every reason for optimism (see, for example, Peacocke, 1994, and Boghossian, 1995).

Quine helped us see the vacuity of the metaphysical concept of analyticity and, with it, the futility of the project it was supposed to underwrite—the linguistic theory of necessity. But those arguments do not affect the epistemic notion of analyticity, the notion that is needed for the purposes of the theory of a priori knowledge. Indeed, the analytic theory of apriority seems to be a promising research program, given reasonable optimism about the prospects both for a conceptual role semantics and for the idea of Frege-analyticity.

Bibliography

Ayer, A. J. *Language, Truth and Logic*. London, 1946.

Boghossian, P. A. "Analyticity," in C. Wright and B. Hale, eds., *A Companion to the Philosophy of Language* (Cambridge, Eng., 1995).

Carnap, R. *Meaning and Necessity*. Chicago, 1947.

Dummett, M. *Frege: The Philosophy of Mathematics*. Cambridge, MA, 1991.

Frege, G. *Die Grundlagen der Arithmetik: eine logisch-mathematische Untersuchung uber den Begriff der Zahl* [1884], translated by J. L. Austin as *The Foundations of Arithmetic*. Oxford, 1953.

Grice, H. P., and P. Strawson. "In Defense of a Dogma," *Philosophical Review*, Vol. 65 (1956), 141–58.

Harman, G. "Quine on Meaning and Existence I," *Review of Metaphysics*, Vol. 21 (1960), 124–51.

Pap, A. *Semantics and Necessary Truth*. New Haven, 1958.

Peacocke, C. *A Study of Concepts*. Cambridge, MA, 1992.

———. "How are A Priori Truths Possible?" *European Journal of Philosophy*, Vol. 1 (1993), 175–99.

Putnam, H. *Mind, Language and Reality—Philosophical Papers*, Vol. 2. Cambridge, MA, 1975.

Quine, W. V. O. "Truth by Convention," in O. H. Lee, ed., *Philosophical Essays for A. N. Whitehead* (New York, 1936; reprinted in *The Ways of Paradox*, Cambridge, MA, 1976).

———. "Two Dogmas of Empiricism," *Philosophical Review*, 1951; reprinted in *From a Logical Point of View* (Cambridge, MA, 1953).

———. "Carnap and Logical Truth," [1954]; reprinted in *The Ways of Paradox* (Cambridge, MA, 1976).

———. *Word and Object*. Boston, 1960.

Salmon, N. "Analyticity and Apriority," *Philosophical Perspectives*, 1994.

Wittgenstein, L. J. J. *Philosophical Grammar* [1932–34]. Los Angeles, 1974.

PAUL ARTIN BOGHOSSIAN

ANAPHORA. The study of *anaphora* (from Greek, "carry back") is the study of the ways in which occurrences of certain expressions, particularly pronouns, depend for their interpretations upon the interpretations of occurrences of other expressions. Problems of anaphora are of interest to philosophy and logic because of their intersection with problems of ONTOLOGY [5; S], quantification, and LOGICAL FORM [S].

REFERENTIAL ANAPHORA

Pronouns understood as anaphoric on referential noun phrases are plausibly viewed as referring to the same things as their antecedents. Sentences (1)–(3) permit such readings (coindexing will be used to indicate an intentional anaphoric connection):

(1) Jim_1 respects students who argue with him_1.
(2) Jim_1 loves his_1 mother.
(3) Jim_1 is here. He_1 arrived yesterday. I think he_1's asleep right now.

We might call these pronouns 'referential anaphors'.

It is sometimes suggested (see, e.g., Soames, 1994) that anaphoric pronouns in such constructions can be understood in a second way. For example, although (2) might be understood as equivalent to 'Jim loves Jim's mother', it might seem to admit of another interpretation that makes it equivalent to 'Jim is a self's-mother-lover', the logical form of which is given by (2′):

(2′) λx(*x* loves x's mother)Jim.

The contrast between the two readings emerges when (2) is embedded, as in

(4) Mary believes that Jim_1 loves his_1 mother.

Certainly, many of the traditional problems involved in interpreting proper names recur for pronouns anaphoric on names.

BOUND-VARIABLE ANAPHORA

Pronouns anaphoric on quantified noun phrases cannot be treated as straightforwardly referential. Consider the following:

(5) Every man_1 thinks he would be a good president_1.
(6) No man_1 respects his_1 brothers' friends.

There is no point inquiring into the referents of the pronouns in examples like these. Following QUINE [7; S] (1960) and Geach (1962), philosophers have tended to treat such pronouns as the natural-language analogs of the variables of quantification theory. Certainly, the logical forms of quantified sentences of the form 'every F is G' and 'some Fs and Gs' can be captured using the standard first-order quantifiers '∀' and '∃'. But a comprehensive semantic theory must treat sentences containing noun phrases formed using 'no', 'the', 'exactly one', 'most', 'few', and so on. This fact highlights two problems. Using the identity sign '=' and the negation sign '¬', it is possible to use '∀' and '∃' to represent sentences containing 'no', 'the', 'exactly one', 'exactly two', and so forth, but the resulting formulae obscure the relationship between the surface syntax of a sentence and its logical form. For example, if RUSSELL [7] is right that 'the F is G' is true if and only if every F is G and there is exactly one F, then the logical form of this sentence is as follows:

(7) $(\exists x)((\forall y)(Fy \equiv y = x)\ \&\ Gx)$.

A more serious problem is that there are sentences that cannot be dealt with in first-order logic—for instance, sentences of the form 'most Fs are Gs'.

Both of these problems are solved if quantification in natural language is viewed as *restricted.* The basic idea here is that determiners combine with their complements (noun complexes) to form restricted quantifiers. So, for example, 'every', 'some', 'most', 'the', and so on combine with simple nouns such as 'pig' (or 'pigs'), 'man' (or 'men'), and so forth (or complex nouns such as 'man who owns a pig', etc.) to form restricted quantifiers such as 'some man', 'most men', 'every man who owns a pig', and so forth. We can represent a restricted quantifier 'every man' as '[every x: man x]'. This quantifier may combine with a predicate phrase such as 'is mortal' (which we can represent as 'x is mortal') to form the sentence 'every man is mortal', which we can represent as

(8) [every x: man x]x is mortal.

Now consider sentences (5) and (6) again. If we treat the anaphoric pronouns in these examples as bound variables, their logical forms will be (abstracting somewhat):

(5′) [every x: man x](x thinks x would be a good president).
(6′) [no x: man x](x respects x's brothers' friends).

VARIABLE BINDING AND SCOPE

Evans (1977) has argued that not all pronouns anaphoric on quantified noun phrases are bound variables. Consider the following examples.

(9) Jim bought some pigs and Harry vaccinated them.
(10) Just one man ate haggis and he was ill afterwards.

A bound-variable treatment of the occurrence of 'them' in (9) yields the wrong result. On such an account, the logical form of the sentence will be

(9′) [some x: pigs x](Jim bought x & Harry vaccinated x).

But (9′) can be true even if Harry did not vaccinate *all* of the pigs Jim bought, whereas (9) cannot. (If Jim bought ten pigs and Harry vaccinated only two of them, (9′) would be true whereas (9) would not.) And if the pronoun 'he' in (10) is treated as a bound variable, the logical form of the sentence will be

(10′) [just one x: man x](x ate haggis and x was ill afterwards).

This is also incorrect; if two men ate haggis and only one was ill afterwards, (10′) will be true whereas (10) will be false.

There is a plausible syntactic explanation of these facts. In both (9) and (10), the pronoun is located outside the smallest sentence containing the quantifier upon which it is anaphoric and hence lies outside its scope, according to the most promising syntactic characterization of this notion. The scope of an expression α in a sentence of a natural language appears to correspond to the first branching node dominating α at the syntactic level relevant to semantic interpretation. If this is correct, and contemporary syntactic theory suggests it is, then syntactic theory explains why the pronouns in (9) and (10) are not understood as bound variables. There seem to be, therefore, anaphoric pronouns that are neither bound nor straightforwardly referential.

UNBOUND ANAPHORA

A plausible paraphrase of (9) is (9″):

(9″) Jim bought some pigs and Harry vaccinated the pigs Jim bought.

In view of this, Evans (1977) suggests that the pronoun 'them' in (9) is understood in terms of the plural description 'the pigs Jim bought', as what he calls an "E-type" pronoun. An E-type pronoun has its reference fixed by description (in KRIPKE's [S] sense) and is therefore a rigid designator. On this account, in (9) the pronoun 'them' is taken to refer to those objects satisfying 'pigs Jim bought'.

Similarly where the antecedent is singular. A plausible paraphrase of (11) is (11′):

(11) Jim bought a pig and Harry vaccinated it.
(11′) Jim bought a pig and Harry vaccinated the pig Jim bought.

According to Evans, the pronoun 'it' in (11) refers to the unique object satisfying 'pig Jim bought'.

This idea forms the basis of Evans's general account of the semantic content of unbound anaphors. The pronoun 'he' in (10) has its reference fixed by 'the man who ate haggis'; and in (12) 'they' has its reference fixed by 'the philosophers who came':

(12) A few philosophers came. They drank far too much.

Evans's proposal can be summarized thus: if *P* is an unbound pronoun anaphoric on a quantified noun phrase '[DET x: ϕ]' occurring in a sentence '[DET x: ϕ]ψ', then the referent of *P* is fixed by the description '[the x: ϕ & ψ]'.

Examination of more complex cases reveals weaknesses in Evans's theory (see below). The problems uncovered have tended to steer semanticists in one of two directions. First, there have been attempts to modify or refine Evans's framework (Davies, 1981; Neale, 1990). Second, there have been attempts to replace the entire framework with a uniform, discourse-based approach (Kamp, 1981; Heim, 1982). Both approaches will now be examined.

DESCRIPTIVE ANAPHORA

Evans rejected the view that unbound anaphors go proxy for descriptions (in favor of the view that they have their referents fixed by description) on the grounds that such pronouns, unlike overt descriptions, do not give rise to ambiguities of scope. But consider the following:

(14) A man murdered Smith, but Jim doesn't think he did it.
(15) A man murdered Smith. The police have reason to think he injured himself in the process.

If 'he' goes proxy for 'the man who murdered Smith', there will be two readings for each of the anaphor clauses in these examples—the so-called *de re* and *de dicto* readings—according as the description for which the pronoun goes proxy is given large or small scope:

(14a) [the x: man x & x murdered Smith]
(Jim doesn't believe that x murdered Smith)
(14b) Jim doesn't believe that
[the x: man x & x murdered Smith](x murdered Smith)

It is natural to interpret (14) as attributing to Jim a noncontradictory belief concerning the murderer to the effect that he is not the murderer. On the proxy view this is captured by the *de re* reading of the second conjunct. The *de dicto* reading is technically available to the proxy theorist but is obviously not the preferred interpretation. But with (15) the *de dicto* reading of the second sentence is actually the more natural; yet Evans's theory explicitly precludes its existence.

Further support for the proxy rather than reference-fixing approach comes from examples containing modal expressions:

(16) Mary wants to marry a rich man. He must be a banker.

The first sentence in (16) may be read either *de re* or *de dicto.* Moreover, the pronoun 'he' can be anaphoric on 'a rich man' on either reading. But as Karttunen (1976) points out, the modal expression has to be there for the anaphora to work if the antecedent sentence is to be interpreted *de dicto.* That is, in

(17) Mary wants to marry a rich man. He is a banker.

it is not possible to get the *de dicto* reading for the antecedent clause if 'he' is anaphoric on 'a rich man'. This contrast between (16) and (17) is explicable on the assumption that the anaphoric pronoun in (16) goes proxy for the description 'the man Mary marries' and may therefore take large or small scope with respect to the modal expression. On the *de dicto* reading of the antecedent clause, the *de re* reading of the anaphor clause is infelicitous because an implication of existence results from giving the description large scope. But the *de dicto* reading of the anaphor clause is fine because on such a reading the description is within the scope of the modal expression. In (17), on the other hand, since there is no modal operator with respect to which the pronoun can be understood with small scope, the sentence has no felicitous reading when the antecedent clause is read *de dicto*.

DONKEY ANAPHORA

Kamp (1981) and Heim (1982) have explored alternative approaches that aim to treat all anaphoric pronouns in a unitary fashion. One motivation is the problem of so called donkey anaphora, typified by sentences like (18) and (19), originally discussed by Geach (1962):

(18) If a man buys a donkey he vaccinates it.
(19) Every man who buys a donkey vaccinates it.

Both Evans's theory and the simple proxy theory seem to fail here. For example, if the pronoun 'it' in (19) is analyzed in terms of the singular description 'the donkey he buys' (with 'he' bound by 'every man who buys a donkey') the sentence will be true just in case every man who buys a donkey vaccinates the unique donkey he buys. Consequently, it will be false if any man buys more than one donkey. But this is incorrect; the truth of (19) is quite compatible with some men owning more than one donkey, as long as every man who buys a donkey vaccinates *every* donkey he buys. It would appear, then, that the indefinite description 'a donkey'—which can normally be treated as an existentially quantified phrase—has the force of a *universally* quantified phrase in (19). And in (18) both 'man' and 'a donkey' appear to have universal force.

A common explanation of the "universalization" of the indefinite descriptions in such examples has been proposed by Kamp. The idea (roughly) is that noun phrases introduce variables to which common nouns and predicates supply "conditions" within a "discourse representation" (DR). Typically, the variable is bound by an existential quantifier taking scope over the entire discourse. On this account, an indefinite description is not inherently quantificational; rather, it introduces a variable with conditions on it imposed by, among other things, the predicative material it contains. The DR for (18) might be represented as:

(18′) [man(x) & donkey(y) & buys(x,y)] IFTHEN [vaccinates(x,y)].

Kamp proposes that (18′) is true if and only if every assignment of values to x and y that makes the antecedent true also makes the consequent true. The apparent universalization of the indefinite descriptions 'a man' and 'a donkey' is thus explained as a consequence of a general analysis of conditionals.

In the light of the equivalence of (18) and (19), Kamp suggests that, although (18) is not actually a conditional, because the subject quantifier is universal we get a DR in which the indefinite 'a donkey' has universal force. That is, the DR for (19) is given by

(19′) [man(x) & donkey(y) & buys(x,y)] EVERY [vaccinates(x,y)].

Like (18′), (19′) is true if and only if every assignment of values to x and y that makes '[man(x) & donkey(y) & buys(x,y)]' true, also makes '[vaccinates(x,y)]' true.

One problem with this proposal is that it does not predict that indefinite descriptions "universalize" when they are embedded in *other* quantifiers and thus leads to the so-called proportion problem. Consider

(20) Most men who buy a donkey vaccinate it.

By analogy with (18′) and (19′), the DR for (20) will be

(20′) [man(x) & donkey(y) & buys(x,y)] MOST [vaccinates(x,y)]

which is true just in case *most* assignments of values to x and y that make '[man(x) & donkey(y) & buys(x,y)]' true also make '[vaccinates(x,y)]' true. But on its most natural reading, the truth of (20) requires that most men who buy a donkey vaccinate *every* donkey they buy, whereas (20′) can be true as long as most of the donkeys that are bought by men are vaccinated by their respective buyers. Suppose Alan buys five donkeys, Bill buys one donkey, Clive buys one donkey, and no other man buys any donkeys. Sentence (20′) will come out true if Alan vaccinates at least four of his donkeys, even if Bill and Clive do not vaccinate their respective donkeys; but in such a situation (20) would be false. (It has been suggested that there is another reading of (20), which requires that most men who buy at least one donkey vaccinate most of the donkeys they buy; but (20′) does not capture this reading either.)

From this brief overview it should be clear that both the simple descriptive theory and the simple DR theory need to be refined if they are to do justice to the full range of antecedent/anaphor relations in natural language. For example, the descriptive approach needs to be modified if it is to handle donkey anaphora, perhaps allowing for the possibility of interpreting some donkey pronouns in terms of 'all of the' rather than 'the' (Davies, 1981; Neale 1990). And the DR approach needs to be modified to

avoid the proportion problem and also permit pronouns to be understood with various scopes. At the time of writing, more sophisticated versions of these theories are being developed, as are alternatives to both.
(SEE ALSO: *Philosophy of Language* [S])

Bibliography

Davies, M. *Meaning, Quantification, Necessity.* London, 1981.

Evans, G. "Pronouns, Quantifiers, and Relative Clauses (I)," *Canadian Journal of Philosophy,* Vol. 7 (1977), 467–536. (Reprinted in Evans [1985], 76–152.)

———. "Pronouns," *Linguistic Inquiry,* Vol. 11 (1980), 337–62. (Reprinted in Evans [1985], 214–48.)

———. *The Collected Papers.* Oxford, 1985.

Geach, P. *Reference and Generality.* Ithaca, NY, 1962.

Heim, I. *The Semantics of Definite and Indefinite Noun Phrases.* Amherst, MA, 1982.

Kamp, H. "A Theory of Truth and Semantic Interpretation," in J. Groenendijk et al., eds., *Formal Methods in the Study of Natural Language* (Amsterdam, 1981).

Karttunen, L. "Discourse Referents," in J. McCawley, ed., *Syntax and Semantics,* Vol. 7, *Notes from the Linguistic Underground* (New York, 1976).

Kripke, S. "Naming and Necessity," in D. Davidson and G. Harman, eds., *Semantics of Natural Language* (Dordrecht, 1972).

Neale, S. *Descriptions.* Cambridge, MA, 1990.

Quine, W. V. O. *Word and Object.* Cambridge, MA, 1960.

Soames, S. "Attitudes and Anaphora," *Philosophical Perspectives,* Vol. 8 (1994), 251–72.

STEPHEN NEALE

ANIMAL RIGHTS AND WELFARE. Although all the major moral philosophers in the Western tradition have had something to say about the moral status of animals, they have commented infrequently and for the most part only in brief. This tradition of neglect changed dramatically during the last quarter of this century, when dozens of works in ethical theory, hundreds of professional essays, and more than a score of academic conferences were devoted to the moral foundations of our treatment of nonhuman animals.

Two main alternatives—animal welfare and animal rights—have come to be recognized. Animal welfarists accept the permissibility of human use of nonhuman animals as a food source and in biomedical research, for example, provided such use is carried out humanely. Animal rightists, by contrast, deny the permissibility of such use, however humanely it is done.

Differ though they do, both positions have much in common. For example, both reject DESCARTES's [2; S] view that nonhuman animals are *automata.* Those animals raised for food and hunted in the wild have a subjective presence in the world; in addition to sharing sensory capacities with human beings, they experience pleasure and pain, satisfaction and frustration, and a variety of other mental states. There is a growing consensus that many nonhuman animals have a mind that, in Charles DARWIN's [2] words, differs from the human "in degree and not in kind."

Proponents of animal welfare and animal rights have different views about the moral significance of our psychological kinship with other animals. Animal welfarists have two options. First, they can argue that we ought to treat animals humanely because this will lead us to treat one another with greater kindness and less cruelty. On this view we have no duties to animals, only duties involving them; and all those duties involving them turn out to be, as KANT [4; S] wrote, "indirect duties to Mankind." Theorists as diverse as Kant, St. Thomas AQUINAS [8], and John RAWLS [S] favor an indirect-duty account of the moral status of nonhuman animals.

Second, animal welfarists can maintain that some of our duties are owed directly to animals. This is the alternative favored by utilitarians, beginning with Jeremy BENTHAM [1] and John Stuart MILL [5; S] and culminating in the work of Peter Singer. Animal pain and pleasure count morally in their own right, not only indirectly through the filter of the human interest in having humans treated better. The duty not to cause animals to suffer unnecessarily is a duty owed directly to them.

Of the two options the latter seems the more reasonable. It is difficult to understand why the suffering of animals should count morally only if it leads to human suffering in the future. Imagine that a man sadistically tortures a dog and dies of a heart attack as a result of his physical exertion; what he does seems clearly wrong even though he does not live long enough to mistreat a human being. If this is true, then we have at least some direct duties to animals.

Animal welfarists who are utilitarians (Singer is the most notable example) use utilitarian theory to criticize how animals are treated in contemporary industries (animal agriculture and biomedical research, for example; *see* UTILITARIANISM [8]). For in these industries animals are made to suffer and, Singer alleges, to suffer unnecessarily.

Other animal welfarists who are utilitarians disagree. Government and industry leaders agree that some animals sometimes suffer in the course of being raised for food or used in biomedical research; but they deny that they are made to suffer unnecessarily.

Consider organ transplant research. Research on animals in this quarter involves transplanting some internal organ from one healthy animal to another; the "donor" animal, who is under anesthetic, is killed, but the "receiver" animal is permitted to recover and doubtless experiences no small amount of postoperative pain before being humanely killed.

Is the pain unnecessary? In one sense it clearly is. For since the organ was not transplanted for the good of the recipient animal, all the pain that animal experienced was unnecessary. However, this is not the real question, given the utilitarian perspective. The pain caused to this particular animal is only one part of the overall calculation that needs to be carried out. We need also to ask about the possible benefits for humans who are in need of organ transplants, the value of the skills surgeons acquire carrying out animal organ transplants, the value of knowledge for its own sake, and so on. After these questions have been answered and the overall benefits impartially calculated, then an informed judgment can be made about whether organ transplant research involving nonhuman animals does or does not cause unnecessary suffering.

As this example illustrates, animal welfarists who are utilitarians can disagree about when animals suffer unnecessarily. As such, these animal welfarists can differ in judging whether animals are being treated humanely and, if not, how much reform is called for.

Advocates of animal rights advance a position that avoids the always daunting, frequently divisive challenge of carrying out uncertain utilitarian calculations. Central to their view is the Kantian idea that animals are never to be treated merely as a means to human ends, however good these ends might be. The acquisition of knowledge, including biological knowledge, is surely a good end, as is the promotion of human health. But the goodness of these ends does not justify the utilization of nonhuman animals as means. Thus, even if animal-model organ transplant research can be justified on utilitarian grounds, animal rights advocates would judge it immoral.

Of the two main options—animal welfare and animal rights—it is the latter that attempts to offer a basis for a radical reassessment of how animals are treated. Animal welfare, provided the calculations work out a certain way, enables one to call for reforms in human institutions that routinely utilize nonhuman animals. But animal rights, independent of such calculations, enables one to call for the abolition of all forms of institutional exploitation. (SEE ALSO: *Speciesism* [S])

Bibliography

Clark, S. S. L. *The Moral Status of Animals.* Oxford, 1977.

Frey, R. G. *Interests and Rights: The Case against Animals.* Oxford, 1980.

Magel, C. R. *Keyguide to Information Sources in Animal Rights.* Jefferson, NC, 1989.

Midgley, M. *Animals and Why They Matter.* New York, 1983.

Rachels, J. *Created from Animals: The Moral Implications of Darwinism.* Oxford, 1990.

Regan, T. *The Case for Animal Rights.* Berkeley, 1983.

Regan, T., and P. Singer, eds. *Animal Rights and Human Obligations,* 2d ed. Englewood Cliffs, NJ, 1991.

Rollin, B. *Animal Rights and Human Morality.* Buffalo, NY, 1981.

Sapontzis, S. *Morals, Reason, and Animals.* Philadelphia, 1987.

Singer, P. *Animal Liberation,* 2d ed. New York, 1990.

TOM REGAN

ANOMALOUS MONISM. Originated by Donald DAVIDSON [S], anomalous monism is a nonreductive, token physicalist position on the relation between the mental and the physical. According to it, each mental event is a physical event, although mental descriptions are neither reducible to nor nomologically correlated with physical ones. In terms that are ontologically more robust than those used by Davidson, the position asserts identities between individual mental and physical events while denying that mental types or properties are either identical with, or nomologically connected with, physical ones. The position specifically concerns intentional mental phenomena such as beliefs and desires, although it is arguable that it can be extended to cover other mental phenomena such as sensations.

Davidson's argument for this position results from an attempt to reconcile three apparently inconsistent principles, two of which he finds independently plausible and the third of which he defends at length. The first is the principle of causal interaction (PCI), which states that mental events cause physical events and vice versa, causality being understood as relating events in extension. The second is the principle of the nomological character of causality (PNCC), which states that events that are causally related have descriptions under which they instantiate strict causal laws. The third is the principle of the anomalism of the mental (PAM), which states that there are no strict laws in which mental terms figure. The principles appear to conflict in that the first two imply what the third seems to deny—namely that there are strict laws governing causal interactions between mental and physical events.

Davidson argues that the principles can be reconciled by adopting the thesis that each mental event has a physical description and so is a physical event. He further suggests that a sound argument can be constructed from these principles to this thesis. Suppose a mental event, *m,* causes a physical event, *p.* Then, by the PNCC, *m* and *p* have descriptions under which they instantiate a strict causal law. By PAM this cannot be mental in that it cannot contain mental terminology. Therefore *m* must have a physical description under which it instantiates a strict causal law, which is to say that it is a physical event. Although the argument is formulated in terms of events and their descriptions, it can be formulated equally effectively in the terminology of events and their properties.

Davidson does not take PAM to be obvious. His defense of it involves the idea that laws bring together terms from the same or similar conceptual domains. Using this idea he argues that the constraints that govern the application of mental terms and their associated concepts to things are normative in nature, involving "constitutive" principles of rational coherence, deductive and inductive consistency, and the like. These principles constitute the distinctive rationalistic normativity that is the earmark of the intentional domain; and Davidson argues that they have no place in physical theory.

The argument for anomalous monism appears to work because of the extensionality of the causal relation and the intensionality of nomologicality. Events are causally related no matter how described; but they are governed by laws only as they are described one way rather than another. This opens up a conceptual space between causality and nomologicality that makes it possible to hold both that mental events that interact causally with physical ones are governed by laws and that there are no strict psychological or psychophysical laws.

Davidson's argument has had a profound effect on discussions of MENTAL CAUSATION [S] and token physicalism. Many have found either the PNCC or the PAM questionable and have taken issue with it. However, the main objection to the argument is that, on a certain conception of the relation between causality and laws, it leads either to inconsistency or to epiphenomenalism. According to this conception, laws link events causally by linking certain, but not all, of their descriptions or properties, the causally relevant ones. The question now arises, In virtue of which of their properties do mental events interact causally with physical ones? If the answer is the mental ones, then anomalous monism is threatened with inconsistency since this implies that there are laws in which mental descriptions/properties figure. If the answer is the physical ones, then anomalous monism is threatened with epiphenomenalism since it is in virtue of their physical properties that mental events are causally efficacious. Since PAM is a crucial premise in the argument for anomalous monism, it is the epiphenomenalism charge that poses the real threat to the position.

There is a general question of whether nonreductive token physicalist theories count as proper forms of physicalism since they recognize the existence of irreducibly mental properties. Davidson himself favors supplementing his position with some sort of SUPERVENIENCE [S] thesis, according to which, necessarily, if things (events) are the same with regard to their physical descriptions/properties, then they are the same with regard to their mental descriptions/properties. The principal difficulty in formulating such a thesis is in specifying a dependency relation strong enough to ensure that physical properties determine mental ones without leading to reducibility and hence to type PHYSICALISM [S].

(SEE ALSO: *Philosophy of Mind* [S])

Bibliography

Davidson, D. "Thinking Causes," in J. Heil and A. Mele, eds., *Mental Causation* (Oxford, 1993). Responds to the charge that anomalous monism leads to the causal inefficacy of the mental.

———. "Mental Events," in L. Foster and J. W. Swanson, eds., *Experience and Theory* (Amherst, MA, 1970). Reprinted in D. Davidson, *Essays on Actions and Events* (Oxford, 1980). The classic statement of the argument for anomalous monism.

———. "Psychology as Philosophy," in S. C. Brown, ed., *Philosophy of Psychology* (London, 1974). Reprinted in D. Davidson, *Essays on Actions and Events* (Oxford, 1980). Discusses anomalous monism and the argument against psychophysical laws.

Honderich, T. "The Argument for Anomalous Monism," *Analysis,* Vol. 42 (1982). Classic statement of the inconsistency-or-epiphenomenalism objection to anomalous monism.

Kim, J. "The Myth of Nonreductive Materialism," *Proceedings of the American Philosophical Association,* Vol. 63 (1989), 31–47. Argues that nonreductive materialism leads to epiphenomenalism.

———. "Psychophysical Laws," in E. LePore and B. McLaughlin, eds., *Actions and Events: Perspectives on the Philosophy of Donald Davidson* (Oxford, 1985). Discusses and defends an interpretation of Davidson's argument against psychophysical laws.

LePore, E., and B. Loewer. "Mind Matters," *Journal of Philosophy,* Vol. 84 (1987), 630–41. Discusses the causal efficacy of the mental within the context of physicalism.

LePore, E., and B. McLaughlin, eds. *Actions and Events: Perspectives on the Philosophy of Donald Davidson.* Oxford, 1985. Articles on Davidson's argument for anomalous monism.

Macdonald, C. *Mind–Body Identity Theories.* London, 1989. Surveys various type–type and token identity theories, and defends a version of nonreductive monism.

Macdonald, C., and G. Macdonald. "Mental Causes and Explanation of Action," *Philosophical Quarterly,* Vol. 36 (1986), 145–58. Reprinted in L. Stevenson, R. Squires, and J. Haldane, eds., *Mind, Causation, and Action* (Oxford, 1986). Defends anomalous monism against the charge of epiphenomenalism.

McLaughlin, B. "Type Epiphenomenalism, Type Dualism, and the Causal Priority of the Physical," in *Philosophical Perspectives,* Vol. 3 (1989). Discusses the problem of mental causation for anomalous monism.

CYNTHIA MACDONALD

ANSCOMBE, GERTRUDE ELIZABETH MARGARET, English philosopher, was born in 1919 and was educated at Sydenham High School and St. Hugh's College, Oxford, where she read *Literae Humaniores* (Greats). She went as a research student to Cambridge, where she became the pupil of Ludwig WITTGENSTEIN [8; S]. He and ARISTOTLE [1; S] have been the most important influences on her philosophical thought. Anscombe became a Roman Catholic while in her teens, and her Catholicism has also been a shaping influence. She was a Fellow for many years of Somerville College, Oxford, and held the Chair of Philosophy at Cambridge from 1970 until 1986. A philosopher of great range, she has made important contributions to ethics, PHILOSOPHY OF MIND, METAPHYSICS [S], and philosophy of logic. Much of her most interesting work has been in the history of philosophy; her discussions of ancient, medieval, and modern philosophers combine illuminating accounts of challenging texts with penetrating treatment of the philosophical problems themselves. As one of Wittgenstein's literary executors, as an editor and translator of his writings, and as a writer and lecturer about Wittgenstein, she has done more than anyone else to make his work accessible. Her *Introduction to Wittgenstein's Tractatus* (1959) is a superb introduction to the central themes of that work, making clear the character of the problems (like that of negation) treated in it.

Long before it became fashionable in the 1970s for moral philosophers to concern themselves with practical problems, Anscombe was writing about them. Her first published essay, in 1939, concerned the justice of the European war. She has discussed closely related topics in connection with the honorary degree Oxford University awarded Harry Truman in 1957 and with the policy of nuclear deterrence. She has also written on contraception and EUTHANASIA [S]. All her writings on such questions reflect her belief in the importance for ethics of the concepts of action and intention, in connection especially with questions about our responsibility for the consequences of our actions. She has explained and defended the doctrine of double effect, arguing that its denial "has been the corruption of non-Catholic thought and its abuse the corruption of Catholic thought" (1981, 3:54). Her interest in war and in the concept of murder led her also to more general philosophical questions about political authority. "Modern Moral Philosophy" (1981) has been the most influential of her papers on ethics. In it she defended three theses: that moral philosophy cannot profitably be done until we have an adequate philosophical psychology; that the concepts of moral obligation, moral duty, and the moral "ought" are survivals from a now largely abandoned conception of ethics, are incoherent outside that framework and should therefore if possible be abandoned; and that English moral philosophers from SIDGWICK [7; S] on differ only in superficial ways. In explaining the third thesis Anscombe introduced the term CONSEQUENTIALISM [S] for what modern moral philosophers shared, and she argued that consequentialism is a corrupt and shallow philosophy.

In the monograph *Intention* (1957) Anscombe raised and discussed questions about INTENTION [4], action, and practical thought (practical reasoning and practical knowledge). The prevalent philosophical ideas about intention treat it as some special kind of mental state or event, and Anscombe departed radically from that tradition, beginning with an account of intentional action in terms of the applicability to it of a kind of question asking for the agent's reason. It is thus possible to show the importance of conceptions of good in practical thought. The questions with which she is concerned frequently straddle metaphysics, philosophy of logic, and philosophy of mind, as for example in "The First Person" (1981), in which she explains how we are led into confusion by misunderstandings of "I" on the model of a proper name. In "The Intentionality of Sensation: A Grammatical Feature" (1981) she draws on philosophy of language in explaining grammatical analogies between intention and sensation, and is able to give a very interesting and original account of what is right in sense-impression philosophy and of what is misleading in it.

Anscombe has explored the topic of CAUSATION [2; S] in several papers, questioning in them widely held assumptions. "Causality and Determination" (1981) begins by formulating two such assumptions: that causality is some kind of necessary connection and that it involves a universal generalization connecting events of two kinds. One or other or both of the assumptions is accepted by virtually all writers on causation, but Anscombe questioned both, together with the related idea that, if two courses of events appear similar but have different outcomes, there must be some further relevant difference. She argued that the root idea in all our causal notions is that of derivativeness of one thing from another, and that this need not involve necessitation. In "Times, Beginnings and Causes" (1981) she challenges also two widely accepted views of HUME's [4; S], that causal relations never involve logical necessity and that something can, logically, begin to exist without being caused to do so. Questions about time figure centrally in other papers as well, including "The Reality of the Past," which treats a problem raised by PARMENIDES [6] and shows how attempts to explain the concept of the past by reference to memory must fail; it also contains one of the best short discussions of Wittgenstein's later approach to philosophy.

Bibliography

WORKS BY ANSCOMBE

Intention. Oxford, 1957.

An Introduction to Wittgenstein's Tractatus. London, 1959.

Three Philosophers (with Peter Geach). Oxford, 1963.

Collected Philosophical Papers. Vol. 1: *From Parmenides to Wittgenstein;* Vol. 2: *Metaphysics and the Philosophy of Mind;* Vol. 3: *Ethics, Religion and Politics.* Oxford, 1981.

"Murder and the Morality of Euthanasia: Some Philosophical Considerations," in L. Gormally, ed., *Euthanasia, Clinical Practice and the Law* (London, 1994).

WORKS ON ANSCOMBE

Diamond, C., and J. Teichman, eds. *Intention and Intentionality: Essays in Honour of G. E. M. Anscombe.* Brighton, 1979. Contains a bibliography, not complete, of writings by Anscombe up to 1979.

Haber, J. G., ed. *Absolutism and Its Consequentialist Critics.* Lanham, MD, 1994.

CORA DIAMOND

ANTIREALISM. See: Realism [7; S]

APPLIED ETHICS. Moral philosophers have traditionally aspired to normative theories of what is right or wrong that are set out in the most general terms. But a practical price is paid for generality in ETHICAL THEORY [S]: it is often unclear whether and, if so, how theory is to be applied in specific cases and contexts. The terms applied ethics and practical ethics came in vogue in the 1970s, when philosophical ethics began to address issues in professional ethics as well as social problems such as capital punishment, ABORTION [S], environmental responsibility, and AFFIRMATIVE ACTION [S]. Philosophers interested in applying their training to such problems share with persons from numerous other fields the conviction that decision making in these areas is fundamentally moral and of the highest social importance.

Philosophers working in applied ethics sometimes do more than teach and publish articles about applications of ethical theory. Their work involves actual applications. They serve as consultants to government agencies, hospitals, law firms, physician groups, business corporations, and engineering firms. Branching out further, they serve as advisers on ethics to radio and educational television, serve on national and state commissions on ethics and policy, and give testimony to legislative bodies. Occasionally, they draft public policy documents, some with the force of law.

Controversies have arisen about whether philosophers have an ethical expertise suited to such work and also about whether the work is philosophical in any interesting sense. Enthusiasm about applied ethics is mixed in academic philosophy. It has been criticized as lacking in serious scholarship, and many philosophers regard it as reducing ethics to engineering—a mere device of problem solving. Some philosophers are not convinced that philosophical theories have a significant role to play in the analysis of cases or in policy and professional contexts, and others are skeptical that philosophical theories have direct practical implications.

DEFINITIONAL PROBLEMS

'Applied ethics' has proved difficult to define, but the following is a widely accepted account: applied ethics is the application of general ethical theories to moral problems with the objective of solving the problems. However, this definition is so narrow that many will not recognize is as reflecting their understanding of either the appropriate method or content. 'Applied ethics' is also used more broadly to refer to any use of philosophical methods critically to examine practical moral decisions and to treat moral problems, practices, and policies in the professions, technology, government, and the like. This broader usage permits a range of philosophical methods (including conceptual analysis, reflective equilibrium, phenomenology, etc.) and does not insist on problem solving as the objective. BIOMEDICAL ETHICS [S], political ethics, journalistic ethics, legal ethics, ENVIRONMENTAL ETHICS, and BUSINESS ETHICS [S] are fertile areas for such philosophical investigation. However, 'applied ethics' is not synonymous with 'professional ethics' (a category from which business ethics is often excluded). Problems such as the allocation of scarce social resources, just wars, abortion, conflicts of interest in surrogate decision making, whistleblowing, the entrapment of public officials, research on animals, and the confidentiality of tax information extend beyond professional conduct, but all are in the domain of applied ethics. Likewise, professional ethics should not be viewed as a part of the wider domain of applied ethics. The latter is usually understood as the province of philosophy, the former as reaching well beyond philosophy and into the professions themselves.

HISTORY

Philosophers from SOCRATES [7; S] to the present have been attracted to topics in applied ethics such as civil disobedience, suicide, and free speech; and philosophers have written in detail about practical reasoning. Nonetheless, it is arguably the case that there never has been a genuine practical program of applied philosophy in the history of philosophy (the casuists possibly qualifying as an exception). Philosophers have traditionally tried to account for and justify morality, to clarify concepts, to examine how moral judgments and arguments are made, and to array basic principles—not to use either morality or theories to solve practical problems.

This traditional set of commitments began to undergo modification about the time the *Encyclopedia of Philosophy* was first published in 1967. Many hypotheses can be invoked to explain why. The most plausible explanation is that law, ethics, and many of the professions—including medicine, business, engineering, and scientific research—were profoundly affected by issues and concerns in the wider society regarding individual liberties, social equality, and various forms of abuse and injustice. The issues raised by civil rights, women's rights, the consumer movement, the environmental movement, and the rights of prisoners and the mentally ill often included ethical issues that stimulated the imagination of philosophers and came to be regarded by many as essentially philosophical problems. Teaching in the philosophy classroom was influenced by these and other social concerns, most noticeably about unjust wars, dramatic ethical lapses in institutions, domestic violence, and international terrorism. Increases in the number of working women, affirmative action programs, escalation in international business competition, and a host of other factors heightened awareness. Classroom successes propelled the new applied ethics in philosophy throughout the 1970s, when few philosophers were working in the area but public interest was increasing.

It is difficult to identify landmark events that stimulated philosophers prior to *Roe v. Wade* (the U.S. Supreme Court decision on abortion in 1973), which deeply affected applied philosophical thinking. But at least one other landmark deserves mention. Research ethics had been poorly developed and almost universally ignored in all disciplines prior to the Nuremberg Trials. This apathy was shaken when the Nuremberg Military Tribunals unambiguously condemned the sinister political motivation and moral failures of Nazi physicians. The ten principles constituting the "Nuremberg Code" served as a model for many professional and governmental codes formulated in the 1950s and 1960s and eventually influenced philosophers as well.

In the late 1960s and early 1970s there emerged a rich and complex interplay of scholarly publications, journalism, public outrage, legislation, and case law. The 1970s and 1980s saw the publication of several books devoted to philosophical treatments of various subjects in applied ethics, concentrating first on biomedical ethics and second on business ethics. Virtually every book published in these applied fields prior to 1979 was organized topically; none was developed explicitly in terms of moral principles or ethical theory. Philosophers had by this time been working in areas of applied ethics for several years with an interest in the connection between theory, principles, practical decision making, and policy. However, in retrospect, it appears that these connections and their problems were not well understood prior to the mid-1980s.

MODELS OF APPLICATION, REASONING, AND JUSTIFICATION

When applied ethics began to receive acceptance in philosophy, it was widely presumed that the "applied" part involves the application of basic moral principles or theories to particular moral problems or cases. This vision suggests that ethical theory develops general principles, rules, and the like, whereas applied ethics treats particular contexts through less general, derived principles, rules, judgments, and the like. From this perspective applied ethics is old morality or old ethical theory applied to new areas. New, derived precepts emerge, but they receive their moral content from the old precepts. Applied work need not, then, generate novel ethical content. Applied ethics requires only a detailed knowledge of the areas to which the ethical theory is being applied (medicine, engineering, journalism, business, public policy, court cases, etc.).

Many philosophers reject this account because it reduces applied ethics to a form of deductivism in which justified moral judgments must be deduced from a preexisting theoretical structure of normative precepts that cover the judgment. This model is inspired by justification in disciplines such as mathematics, in which a claim is shown to follow logically (deductively) from credible premises. In ethics the parallel idea is that justification occurs if and only if general principles or rules, together with the relevant facts of a situation (in the fields to which the theory is being applied) support an inference to the correct or justified judgment(s). In short, the method of reasoning at work is the application of a norm to a clear case falling under the norm.

This deductive model is sometimes said to be a top-down "application" of precepts. The deductive form in the application of a rule is the following:

1. Every act of description A is obligatory. (rule)
2. Act b is of description A. (fact)

Therefore,

3. Act b is obligatory. (applied moral conclusion)

This structure directs attention from particular judgments to a covering level of generality (rules and principles that cover and justify particular judgments) and then to the level of ethical theory (which covers and warrants rules and principles).

This model functions smoothly whenever a fact circumstance can be subsumed directly under a general precept, but it does not adequately capture how moral reasoning and justification proceed in complicated cases. The failure to explain complex moral decision making and innovative moral judgment has led to a widespread rejection of deductivism as an appropriate model for applied ethics. Among the replacements for deductivism as a model of application, two have been widely discussed in the literature: case-based reasoning and reflective equilibrium.

Case-Based Reasoning (a Form of Casuistry). This approach focuses on practical decision making about particular cases, where judgments cannot simply be brought under general norms. Proponents are skeptical of principles, rules, rights, and theory divorced from history, circumstances, and experience: one can make successful moral judgments of agents and actions, they say, only when one has an intimate understanding of particular situations and an appreciation of the record of similar situations. They cite the use of narratives, paradigm cases, analogies, models, classification schemes, and even immediate intuition and discerning insight.

An analogy to the authority operative in case law is sometimes noted: when the decision of a majority of judges becomes authoritative in a case, their judgments are positioned to become authoritative for other courts hearing cases with similar facts. This is the doctrine of precedent. Defenders of case-based reasoning see moral authority similarly: social ethics develops from a social consensus formed around cases, which can then be extended to new cases without loss of the accumulated moral wisdom. As a history of similar cases and similar judgments mounts, a society becomes more confident in its moral judgments, and the stable elements crystallize in the form of tentative principles; but these principles are derivative, not foundational.

In addition to having a history dating from medieval casuistry, the case method, as it is often called, has long been used in law schools and business schools. Training in the case method is widely believed to sharpen skills of legal and business reasoning as well as moral reasoning. One can tear a case apart and then construct a better way of treating similar situations. In the thrust-and-parry classroom setting, teacher and student alike reach conclusions about rights, wrongs, and best outcomes in cases. The objective is to develop a capacity to grasp problems and to find novel solutions that work in the context: knowing how to reason and act is more prized then knowing that something is the case on the basis of a foundational rule.

The case method in law has come to be understood as a way of learning to assemble facts and judge the weight of evidence—enabling the transfer of that weight to new cases. This task is accomplished by generalizing and mastering the principles that control the transfer, usually principles at work in the reasoning of judges. Use of the case method in business schools springs from an ideal of education that puts the student in the decision-making role after an initial immersion in the facts of a complex situation. Here the essence of the case method is to present a situation replete with the facts, opinions, and prejudices that one might encounter and to find a way of making appropriate decisions in such an environment.

Reflective Equilibrium (a Form of Coherence Theory). Many now insist that the relationship between general norms and the particulars of experience is bilateral (not unilateral). Moral beliefs arise both by generalization from the particulars of experience (cases) and by making judgments in particular circumstances by appeal to general precepts. John RAWLS's [S] celebrated account of 'reflective equilibrium' has been the most influential model of this sort. In developing and maintaining a system of ethics, he argues, it is appropriate to start with the broadest possible set of considered judgments about a subject and to erect a provisional set of principles that reflects them. Reflective equilibrium views investigation in ethics (and theory construction) as a reflective testing of moral principles, theoretical postulates, and other relevant moral beliefs to make them as coherent as possible. Starting with paradigms of what is morally proper or morally improper, one then searches for principles that are consistent with these paradigms as well as one another. Widely accepted principles of right action and considered judgments are taken, as Rawls puts it, "provisionally as fixed points" but also as "liable to revision."

'Considered judgments' is a technical term referring to judgments in which moral beliefs and capacities are most likely to be presented without a distorting bias. Examples are judgments about the wrongness of racial discrimination, religious intolerance, and political conflict of interest. By contrast, judgments in which one's confidence level is low or in which one is influenced by the possibility of personal gain are excluded from consideration. The goal is to match, prune, and adjust considered judgments so that they coincide and are rendered coherent with the premises of theory. That is, one starts with paradigm judgments of moral rightness and wrongness and then constructs a more general theory that is consistent with these paradigm judgments (rendering them as coherent as possible); any loopholes are closed, as are all forms of incoherence that are detected. The resultant action guides are tested to see if they too yield incoherent results. If so, they are readjusted or given up, and the process is renewed, because one can never assume a completely stable equilibrium. The pruning and adjusting occur by reflection and dialectical adjustment, in view of the perpetual goal of achieving reflective equilibrium.

This model demands the best approximation to full coherence under the assumption of a never-ending search for defects of coherence, for counterexamples to beliefs, and for unanticipated situations. From this perspective moral thinking is analogous to hypotheses in science that are tested, modified, or rejected through experience and experimental thinking. Justification is neither purely deductivist (giving general action guides preeminent status), nor purely inductivist (giving experience and analogy preeminent status). Many different considerations provide reciprocal support in the attempt to fit moral beliefs into a coherent unit. This is how we test, revise, and further specify moral beliefs. This outlook is very different from deductivism, because it holds that ethical theories are never complete, always stand to be informed by practical contexts, and must be tested for adequacy by their practical implications.

METHOD AND CONTENT: DEPARTURES FROM TRADITIONAL ETHICAL THEORY

In light of the differences in the models just explored and the enormously diverse literature in applied philosophy it is questionable whether applied ethics has a special philosophical method. Applied philosophers appear to do what philosophers have always done: they analyze concepts, examine the hidden presuppositions of moral opinions and theories, offer criticism and constructive accounts of the moral phenomena in question, and criticize strategies that are used to justify beliefs, policies, and actions. They seek a reasoned defense of a moral viewpoint, and they use proposed moral frameworks to distinguish justified moral claims from unjustified ones. They try to stimulate the moral imagination, promote analytical skills, and weed out prejudice, emotion, misappropriated data, false authority, and the like.

Differences between ethical theory and applied ethics are as apparent over content as over method. Instead of analyzing general terms such as 'good', 'rationality', 'ideals', and 'virtues', philosophers interested in applied ethics attend to the analysis of concepts such as confidentiality, trade secrets, environmental responsibility, euthanasia, authority, undue influence, free press, privacy, and entrapment. If normative guidelines are proposed, they are usually specific and directive. Principles in ethical theory are typically general guides that leave considerable room for judgment in specific cases, but in applied ethics proponents tend either to reject principles and rules altogether or to advance precise action guides that instruct persons how to act in ways that allow for less interpretation and discretion. Examples are found in literature that proposes rules of informed consent, confidentiality, conflict of interest, access to information, and employee drug testing.

However, in philosophy journals that publish both applied and theoretical work no sharp line of demarcation is apparent between the concepts and norms of ethical theory and applied ethics. There is not even a discernible continuum from theoretical to applied concepts or principles. The applied/theoretical distinction therefore needs to be used with great caution.

COMPETING THEORIES AND PROBLEMS OF SPECIFICITY

One reason theory and application are merged in the literature is that several different types of ethical theories have been employed in attempts to address practical problems. At least the following types of theories have been explicitly invoked: (1) UTILITARIANISM [8], (2) Kantianism (*see* DEONTOLOGICAL ETHICS [2; S]), (3) RIGHTS [S] theory, (4) contract theory, (5) virtue theory (*see* VIRTUE ETHICS [S]), (6) COMMUNITARIANISM [S], (7) casuistry, and (8) PRAGMATISM [6; S]. Many proponents of these theories would agree that specific policy and practical guidelines cannot be squeezed from appeals to these philosophical ethical theories and that some additional content is always necessary.

Ethical theories have rarely been able to raise or answer the social and policy questions commonplace in applied ethics. General theories are ill suited for this work, because they address philosophical problems and are not by their nature practical or policy oriented. The content of a philosophical theory, as traditionally understood, is not of the right sort. Philosophical theories are about morality, but they are primarily attempts to explain, unify, or justify morality, not attempts to specify the practical commitments of moral principles in public policy or in particular cases. In applied ethics, ethical theory is often far less important than moral insight and the defense and development of appropriate guidelines suited to a complex circumstance.

Every general ethical norm contains an indeterminacy requiring further development and enrichment to make it applicable in a complex circumstance. To have sufficient content, general theories and principles must be made specific for contexts; otherwise, they will be empty and ineffectual. Factors such as efficiency, institutional rules, law, and clientele acceptance must be taken into account to make them more specific. An ethics useful for public and institutional policies needs to prove a practical strategy that incorporates political procedures, legal constraints, uncertainty about risk, and the like. Progressive specification of norms will be required to handle the variety of problems that arise, gradually reducing dilemmas, policy options, and contingent conflicts that abstract theory and principle are unable to handle.

Some philosophers view this strategy of specification as heavily dependent upon preexistent practices. They maintain that major contributions in philosophical ethics have run from "applied" contexts to "general" theory rather than the reverse. In examining case law and institutional practices, they say, philosophers have learned about morality in ways that require rethinking and modifying general norms of truth telling, consenting, confidentiality, JUSTICE [4; S], and so forth. To the extent that sophisticated philosophical treatments of such notions are now emerging, they move, not from theory application (including specification), but from practice to theory. Traditional ethical theory, from this perspective, has no privileged position and has more to learn from "applied contexts" than the other way around.

Nonetheless, there are problems with attempts to base applied ethics entirely in practice standards. A practice standard often does not exist within the relevant field, group, or profession. If current standards are low, they could not legitimately determine what the appropriate standards should be. Most moral problems present issues that have to be thought through, not issues to which good answers have already been provided, which explains why many in the professions have turned to philosophers for help in developing professional ethics. Applied philosophers are often most useful to those with whom they collaborate in other fields when practice standards are defective or deficient and a vacuum needs filling by reflection on, criticism of, and reformulation of moral viewpoints or standards.

Bibliography

Beauchamp, T. L. "On Eliminating the Distinction between Applied Ethics and Ethical Theory," *The Monist,* Vol. 67 (1984), 514–31.

Brock, D. W. "Truth or Consequences: The Role of Philosophers in Policy-Making," *Ethics,* Vol. 97 (1987), 786–91.

Caplan, A. L. "Ethical Engineers Need Not Apply: The State of Applied Ethics Today," *Science, Technology, and Human Values,* Vol. 6 (Fall 1980), 24–32.

DeGrazia, D. "Moving Forward in Bioethical Theory: Theories, Cases, and Specified Principlism," *Journal of Medicine and Philosophy,* Vol. 17 (1992), 511–39.

Encyclopedia of Bioethics, 2d ed., edited by Warren Reich. New York, 1995.

Feinberg, J. *The Moral Limits of the Criminal Law,* 4 vols. New York, 1984–87.

Fullinwider, R. K. "Against Theory, or: Applied Philosophy—a Cautionary Tale," *Metaphilosophy,* Vol. 20 (1989), 222–34.

Gert, B. "Licensing Professions," *Business and Professional Ethics Journal,* Vol. 1 (1982), 51–60.

———. "Moral Theory and Applied Ethics," *The Monist,* Vol. 67 (1984), 532–48.

Jonsen, A., and S. Toulmin. *The Abuse of Casuistry: A History of Moral Reasoning.* Berkeley, 1988.

MacIntyre, A. "What Has Ethics to Learn from Medical Ethics?" *Philosophic Exchange,* Vol. 2 (1978), 37–47.

———. "Does Applied Ethics Rest on a Mistake?" *The Monist,* Vol. 67 (1984), 498–513.

Noble, C. "Ethics and Experts," *Hastings Center Report,* Vol. 12 (June 1982), 7–10, with responses by four critics.

Professional Ethics, Vol. 1, nos. 1–2 (Spring-Summer 1992). Special issue on applied ethics.

Rawls, J. *A Theory of Justice.* Cambridge, MA, 1971.

Regan, T., ed. *Matters of Life and Death,* 3d ed. New York, 1992.

Richardson, H. "Specifying Norms as a Way to Resolve Concrete Ethical Problems," *Philosophy and Public Affairs,* Vol. 19 (1990), 279–310.

Singer, P. *Practical Ethics,* 2d ed. New York, 1993.

Winkler, E. R., and J. R. Coombs, eds. *Applied Ethics: A Reader.* Oxford, 1993.

TOM L. BEAUCHAMP

ARCHAEOLOGY. Developed by Michel FOUCAULT [S] in the writings of his early period of scholarly activity, archaeology is a method of historical investigation. The subject matter investigated by the archaeologist is the discourse of the human sciences, by which Foucault means, not only the explicit language of scientific disciplines, but also the background structures and practices that determine the form and content of scientific language. As an archaeologist Foucault ascribed primary agency, not to the experts who claim to conduct scientific inquiry, but to the "anonymous field of practices" embedded within the discourse itself. He consequently ignored the truth value and meaning of the propositions produced by the discourse, attending instead to the internal coherence that unifies its constituent practices. He thus intended his archaeological investigations to reveal the epistemic principles governing a period of discursive convergence.

The guiding aim of the archaeologist is twofold: (1) to identify historical periods of epistemic convergence across a cluster of sciences and disciplines and (2) to chart the transformation, and eventual disintegration, of epistemic coherence within the discursive practices of science. Foucault introduced the term 'episteme' to designate the epistemic coherence of various discursive practices within a single historical period. The sciences and disciplines clustered within an episteme all share a common epistemic framework and specialized vocabulary; they consequently exhibit general agreement on the conditions and criteria of truth, knowledge, and certainty.

An archaeology of knowledge is possible only when an episteme begins to disintegrate, as the clustered sciences and disciplines become conscious of the nature—and limitations—of the common epistemic framework they share. Discursive practices become visible to the archaeologist only when they manifest their internal instabilities, as evidenced by the mounting failures of their defining epistemic projects. At the conclusion of an episteme, the archaeologist is able to detect the internal incoherencies, which, when hidden, enabled the epistemic convergence of discursive practices in the first place. The episteme of the classical age, for example, disintegrated at the end of the eighteenth century, when it became clear that its governing trope, representation, could not account for the very activity of representing.

Foucault designed his archaeologies to yield purely descriptive results. He neither claimed nor expected to derive from them a critical appraisal of the discourse or episteme under investigation. While archaeology afforded him the critical distance he sought from the discursive practices he wished to investigate, it did not enable him to address the concrete social problems that concerned him. In order to supplement his archaeological expeditions with a critical, political dimension, Foucault developed the method of historical investigation known as "genealogy." Although he never abandoned his archaeological method, he eventually came to rely on genealogy to expose the subtle transformations that signal the movement of power toward totalization.

(SEE ALSO: *Order of Things* [S])

DANIEL CONWAY

ARENDT, HANNAH, American philosopher and political scientist, was born in 1906 in Hanover, Germany. In 1928 she completed her Ph.D. under Karl JASPERS [4] at the University of Heidelberg, having previously studied with Martin HEIDEGGER [3; S] at the University of Marburg. Upon immigrating to the United States in 1941, she became director of several Jewish organizations and served as chief editor of Schocken Books before being appointed to the Committee on Social Thought at the University of Chicago in 1963. She taught at the New School for Social Research in New York from 1967 until her death in 1975. Her most famous disciple and critic is the German social theorist Jürgen HABERMAS [S], who traces his own theory of communicative action back to her belief in the existential centrality of communication that she herself had inherited from Jaspers (see COMMUNICATIVE ACTION [S]).

FREEDOM AND ACTION

Arendt's chief concern throughout her life was politics and political action. As the quintessential appearance of human FREEDOM [3; S], political action, she argued, must be distinguished from both work and cultural fabrication. Laboring to procure life's necessities is unfree; and the freedom of artistic creation is at best hidden and derivative. As distinct from the solitary application of means in pursuit of ends, true freedom must be communicated publicly, in political deeds and words. For this there must be a public space—exemplified by the Greek *polis* and such modern-day equivalents as the worker council and town-hall meeting—wherein equals representing diverse opinions meet and deliberate together.

SECULARIZATION AND THE CRISIS IN CULTURE

Most of Arendt's famous studies—on totalitarianism, evil (*see* EVIL, THE PROBLEM OF [3; S]), revolution, and the Jewish question—document the decline of the public space in the wake of modern secularization. Although she did not blame secularization for this decline (indeed, in her opinion, the glory of the American Revolution resided in its freely enacting a new order without benefit of any traditional precedent), she nonetheless believed that the destruction of the old Roman trinity of religion, tradition, and authority contributed to a crisis of culture that undermined essential differences—between public and private, political and economic, action and work—on which the survival of this space depended. Transcendent authority anchored the autonomy of the public realm as a sacred, if indeed secular, space for manifesting immortal deeds in beautiful words, unsullied by the profane preoccupation with biological self-preservation; the waning of authority diminishes that autonomy, thereby enabling the assimilation of both culture and politics to economics.

Arendt's diagnosis of the crisis in culture bears directly on her political concerns. Like Heidegger, she appealed to the Greek conception of culture as an aesthetic revelation of community that memorializes political actions. In the absence of tradition, art provides perduring standards of judgment so that without it the public space wherein judging and acting complement one another would cease to be meaningful. Political life is thus jeopardized whenever culture becomes the private preserve of elites. Conversely, culture intended for mass consumption loses its enduring authority to memorialize the beauty of deeds and words.

TOTALITARIANISM AND RADICAL EVIL

According to Arendt, the culture and politics of mass society reflect the loss of purpose experienced by individuals isolated in their lonely pursuit of self-preservation. Under these conditions it is the state, not the individual, that assumes responsibility for integrating the life of the community. In this connection Arendt banefully observed that the subordination of political life to economic administration substitutes the totalitarian fatalism of work for the spontaneous plurality of action. Ultimately, the administrative organization of masses into a single will and identity must view political dissent as an obstacle to the achievement of social welfare.

However, in Arendt's opinion, what really distinguishes modern totalitarianism from absolute despotism is not suppression of dissent but the total administration of a mass for whom private and political life has ceased to be meaningful. In lieu of constitutionally protected freedom, totalitarianism offers ideological determinism, which conceives history as the necessary realization of some abstract idea. This abandonment of commonsense realism in deference to dogmatic idealism subsequently leads to a permanent revolution hostile to any constitutional stability.

By engendering a system in which human life is made totally superfluous, totalitarianism represents the epitome of "radical evil." Contrary to popular opinion, however, such evil is seldom if ever motivated by diabolical intentions. Eichmann's evil, Arendt observed, simply consisted in his banal "thoughtlessness." Like most persons living in mass society, he confused moral duty of citizenship with doing one's job well, as authority commands. However, Arendt also believed that the "absolute goodness" and violence born of idealism (as personified in Melville's Billy Budd) are as pernicious as the radical evil and destructiveness born of any workmanlike devotion to order.

(SEE ALSO: *Ricoeur: Evil, Problem of* [S])

MORAL JUDGMENT AND POLITICAL ACTION

Arendt's own IDEALISM [4] clashed with her REALISM [7; S]. The "inner dialogue" of moral thought, she noted, is at one remove from the real, *vita activa*; indeed, its critical autonomy depends on maintaining this contemplative distance. Accordingly, she held, following KANT [4; S], that the integrity of judgment depends on imaginatively representing things from the standpoint of all others, not as they actually represent them, but as they might represent them, were they to communicate their thoughts and feelings disinterestedly, in abstraction from the real limitations that normally prejudice their sensibilities. Counterbalancing this contemplative idealism, however, is Arendt's conviction that judgment must be cultivated in real political action, where persons are free to communicate their thoughts to one another. But this too accords with Kant's belief that freedom from prejudice—the hallmark of moral autonomy—requires the critical check of engaged interlocutors (*see* JUDGMENT AND ACTION [S]).

Bibliography

WORKS BY ARENDT

The Human Condition. Chicago, 1958.

The Origins of Totalitarianism, enlarged ed. New York, 1958.

On Revolution. New York, 1963.

Eichmann in Jerusalem: A Report on the Banality of Evil. New York, 1965.

Men in Dark Times. New York, 1968.

On Violence. New York, 1970.

Crisis of the Republic. New York, 1972.

Rahel Varnhagen: The Life of a Jewish Woman. New York, 1974.

Between Past and Future: Eight Exercises in Political Thought. New York, 1978.

The Jew as Pariah: Jewish Identity and Politics in the Modern Age. Ron Feldman, ed. New York, 1978.

The Life of the Mind, 2 vols. Mary McCarthy, ed. New York, 1978.

Lectures on Kant's Political Philosophy. R. Beiner, ed. Chicago, 1982.

WORKS ON ARENDT

Bernauer, J., ed. *Amor Mundi: Explorations in the Faith and Thought of Hannah Arendt.* Dordrecht, 1987.

Bowen-Moore, P. *Hannah Arendt's Philosophy of Natality.* New York, 1989.

Bradshaw, L. *Acting and Thinking: The Political Thought of Hannah Arendt.* Toronto, 1989.

Carnovan, M. *The Political Thought of Hannah Arendt.* New York, 1974.

———. *Hannah Arendt: A Reinterpretation of Her Thought.* New York, 1992.

Garner, R. ed. *In the Realm of Humanitas: Responses to the Writings of Hannah Arendt.* New York, 1990.

Gottsegen, M. G. *The Political Thought of Hannah Arendt.* Albany, NY, 1994.

Hill, M. A., ed. *Hannah Arendt: Recovery of the Public World.* New York, 1979.

Hinchman, L. P., and K. Sandra, eds. *Hannah Arendt: Critical Essays.* Albany, NY, 1994. Contains essays by Arendt.

Kateb, G. *Hannah Arendt, Politics, Conscience, Evil.* Totowa, NJ, 1984.

Kohn, J., and L. May. *Hannah Arendt: Twenty Years Later.* Cambridge, MA, 1996.

Parekh, B. C. *Hannah Arendt and the Search for a New Political Philosophy.* Atlantic Highlands, NJ, 1981.

Watson, D. *Hannah Arendt.* London, 1992.

Young-Bruehl, E. *Hannah Arendt: For Love of the World.* New Haven, 1982. Contains a bibliography.

DAVID INGRAM

ARISTOTLE. Kerferd's 1967 *Encyclopedia* article considers ARISTOTLE [1] in the context of Werner Jaeger's proposal that Aristotle developed gradually from a committed Platonist to an empirically minded anti-Platonist, and that the chronology of his works (and indeed of passages within individual works) may be determined according to the degree of PLATONISM [6] and EMPIRICISM [2] displayed therein. Philosophical discussion of Aristotle is no longer dominated by Jaeger's developmental hypothesis. While questions of chronology and development continue to interest Aristotelian scholars, the dominant goal of post-Jaegerian studies of Aristotle is to elucidate, examine, and criticize the philosophical problems and arguments that Aristotle poses and addresses. The present brief update cannot summarize fully the wide range of questions at issue in Aristotelian studies, but some especially important and interesting areas of consensus and disagreement are described below. For a fuller guide to the issues, the extensive annotated and analytical bibliography in the *Cambridge Companion to Aristotle* (Barnes, 1995) is a valuable resource.

PHILOSOPHICAL METHOD

Aristotle's *Posterior Analytics* describes scientific knowledge (episteme) as a hierarchical axiomatized system whose characteristic method is demonstration: syllogistic proof from the first principles of a science of all its derivative truths. It is generally recognized that in Aristotle's own scientific and philosophical treatises he employs not this method but one he describes as inductive or dialectical. Aristotle describes his dialectical method as involving three stages: (1) The inquirer begins by collecting the "appearance" (*phainomena*)—a category that includes not only empirical observations but also widely accepted views and the theories of reputable authorities. (2) Next, one generates puzzles (*aporiai*) from the "appearances"—pointing to difficulties and contradictions that result from combining these initially plausible views. (3) In the final, constructive stage of dialectical argument, one resolves the puzzles by revising the "appearances" that give rise to them—maintaining some, rejecting or revising others—with a view to retaining most of the initial appearances, and especially the most important ones (cf. *Nicomachean Ethics* VII, 1145b2–7). It is disputed whether Aristotle thinks the sort of knowledge yielded by dialectical inquiry can be objective, given its tie to "appearances" (M. Nussbaum has argued for the negative answer, T. H. Irwin and others for the affirmative). Such disagreement notwithstanding, it is generally agreed that Aristotle's written works typically do employ, if not always explicitly, the dialectical strategy he describes. One must therefore read Aristotle carefully and consider whether a given passage articulates (1) an appearance he is enumerating but not necessarily endorsing, (2) a puzzle that will dissolve once the appearances have been suitably revised, or (3) an appearance that he is endorsing after resolving the puzzles.

NATURAL PHILOSOPHY

The philosophical innovation of which Aristotle was arguably most proud is his view that there are four different types of cause or explanation. These are generally referred to by scholars as the material, formal, efficient, and final (or teleological) causes. In the case of natural things, Aristotle argues, the formal, final, and efficient causes coincide, so the most basic causal distinction in these cases is between matter and form. Aristotle's use of this distinction to analyze natural and psychological phenomena is sometimes referred to as his *hylomorphism* (from *hyle,* 'matter', and *morphe,* 'form'). The ontological implications of his hylomorphism have been much disputed. Aristotle typically illustrates the distinction between matter and form by citing artifacts. In these examples, the distinction is easy to grasp. The matter of a wall is bricks and mortar, while the form is the shape or arrangement that makes the bricks and mortar into a wall. Artificial examples also make it easy to agree that the form is not an extra element, analogous to the bricks and mortar, that needs to be added to the matter in order to make a wall. Rather, form appears to relate to matter as its shape, arrangement, or proportion. Hylomorphism as applied to natural things is, however, more complicated. Aristotle thinks natural things are significantly different from artifacts in that they have an internal source of growth, development, and activity. He identifies this internal source with form rather than matter. Given the coincidence of formal and final causation in natural things, Aristotle articulates his preference for formal over material explanation via his thesis of natural teleology: natural processes are to be explained with reference to the final rather than the material cause. Some commentators (including J. Cooper, A. Gotthelf, and S. Waterlow) have concluded that the forms of natural things, for Aristotle, involve more than simple arrangements, or proportions, or the like, of the material constituents; forms must be *sui generis* elements whose presence, in addition to matter and its arrangements, is necessary for natural activity to occur. Other scholars (including D. Charles, S. Meyer, and M. Nussbaum) have resisted this conclusion, proposing that Aristotle finds not that the material elements are incapable of constituting natural entities or of causing their natural activities, but rather that the simple invocation of matter, without mention of form or function, does not explain natural processes. On the latter interpretation, the ontological status of form is analogous in the artificial and the natural cases.

PSYCHOLOGY

The interpretation of Aristotle's hylomorphism becomes increasingly difficult and disputed in its application to psychology. Aristotle's *De Anima* gives an account of the soul (*psyche*) or principle of life. While the body of a living thing is its material cause, the soul of a living thing is its formal, final, and efficient cause. The life activities of which the soul is the principle include some that Aristotle also classifies as natural (nutrition and growth), but his list also includes activities (sensation, desire, and thought) that modern philosophers would classify as mental, and to which the application of the hylomorphic model is not straightforward. To David Wiggins, Aristotle's hylomorphism yields a promising account of personal identity over time. Others (e.g., R. Sorabji) have understood it as an alternative both to dualism and to the cruder aspects of some versions of materialism about the mental. Aristotle has been hailed by some (M. Nussbaum, and H. PUTNAM [S]) as a nonreductive materialist or even a proto-functionalist. Dissenters typically argue that Aristotle's conception of matter (that is, the material cause) has little in common with the post-Cartesian conception assumed by modern forms of MATERIALISM [5] (M. F. Burnyeat, W. F. R. Hardie, and H. Robinson).

METAPHYSICS

The central books of the *Metaphysics* (Zeta, Eta, and Theta) have received much attention. Here Aristotle considers whether sensible individuals, such as particular people or animals, are substances—a question he answers in the affirmative in the *Categories.* The question arises because the hylomorphic analysis of natural substances (which is absent from the *Categories*), together with the *Categories'* criterion that substance is what underlies other things, invites the challenge that not Callias' form but his matter is substance, and so (since Callias is identified with his form rather than with his matter) Callias is not a substance. In Zeta 3 Aristotle addresses this issue by asking whether Callias' form, or his matter, or the compound of the two, is substance. The ensuing discussion ranks among the most intractably difficult of his writings. There is no scholarly consensus about the extent to which Aristotle allows that matter and the compound may be substance, or about whether he retains the criterion that substance is what underlies. While there is agreement that Aristotle's main project in Zeta is to defend the substantial status of forms, it is disputed whether the forms to which he attributes substantial status are individuals (e.g., Callias) or universals (e.g., the species Man). (Proponents of the former view include M. Frede and T. H. Irwin; defenders of the latter include M. Furth and M. Loux.)

ETHICS

Aristotle's moral psychology, particularly his conception of reason's role in morality, is generally recognized as an alternative both to Humean and to Kantian views. In contrast to the Kantian picture, Aristotle requires that the proper moral motivation involves having appropriate desires and emotions in addition to the correct judgment. In contrast with HUME [4; S], Aristotle allows that reason is not purely instrumental, but may (and should) be exercised to determine one's ultimate ends. Within this consensus, there are still many open questions about the role of reason. For example, it is disputed exactly how reason functions in the decision making (*prohairesis*) of the virtuous agent. One school of thought supposes that the virtuous person has a more or less explicit conception of happiness (*eudaimonia*) to which he or she appeals in making choices and decisions, and that this conception is reflected in the dispositions of desire and emotion that are his or her moral virtues. Others reject this supposition, pointing to Aristotle's remarks that ethical matters belie formulation in general rules, and to his emphasis on the role perception plays in the virtuous person's decision making. The issue comes to a head in the interpretation of Aristotle's account of *akrasia* (weakness of will). One of the most forceful proponents of the latter position (J. McDowell) goes so far as to claim that advocates of the former are thereby committed to a Humean interpretation of practical reason in Aristotle. Yet those sympathetic to the former position (e.g., J. Cooper and T. H. Irwin) typically reject a Humean account of Aristotle.

Another issue of continuing interest concerns Aristotle's apparent indecision (or inconsistency) on the question of whether happiness, properly understood, includes practical activity (this seems to be implied by the attention he devotes, in his ethical writing, to the moral virtues) or whether it involves only pure theoretical reason (this appears to be the import of his remarks on happiness in Book X of the *Nicomachean Ethics*). While the former interpretation has been dominant, the latter is defended anew by Richard Kraut (1989).

Bibliography

TRANSLATIONS AND COMMENTARIES

The old 12-volume Oxford translation has been revised and improved in:

Barnes, J., ed. *The Complete Works of Aristotle: The Revised Oxford Translation,* 2 vols. Princeton, NJ, 1984.

Ancient commentaries:

The enormous extant body of ancient commentary on Aristotle, collected and published in Greek by the Berlin Academy (1882–1909), is being translated into English as the series, *The Ancient Commentators on Aristotle,* whose general editor is Richard Sorabji. For a general account of the commentary tradition, see:

Sorabji, R. *Aristotle Transformed: The Ancient Commentators and Their Influence.* London and Ithaca, NY, 1990.

Modern commentaries:

The Clarendon Aristotle Series (1963–) offers generally excellent translations into English, with detailed philosophical notes for the Greekless reader, of many of Aristotle's texts.

Other modern translations and commentaries:

Frede, M., and G. Patzig. *Aristoteles Metaphysik Z.* Munich, 1988.

Furth, M. *Aristotle: Metaphysics Books VII-X.* Indianapolis, 1985.

Irwin, T. H. *Aristotle: Nicomachean Ethics.* Indianapolis, 1985.

Nussbaum, M. C. *Aristotle's De Motu Animalium.* Princeton, NJ, 1978. Includes general essays on Aristotle's teleology.

General books:

Introductory articles on many aspects of Aristotle's philosophy, together with an extensive annotated and analytical bibliography (covering both European and English-language works) are in

Barnes, J., ed. *The Cambridge Companion to Aristotle.* Cambridge, 1995.

A short general account of Aristotle's philosophy is

Ackrill, J. L. *Aristotle the Philosopher.* Oxford, 1981.

COLLECTIONS OF PAPERS

The proceedings of the triennial *Symposium Aristotelicum* (1957–present) provide excellent examples of post-Jaegerian Aristotelian scholarship by European, British, and North American scholars. The bibliography in Barnes (1995) lists the individual titles.

Other collections include:

Barnes, J., M. Schofield, and R. Sorabji, eds. *Articles on Aristotle,* 4 vols. London, 1975–79.

Frede, M. *Essays on Ancient Philosophy.* Minneapolis, 1987.

Gotthelf, A., and J. Lennox, eds. *Philosophical Issues in Aristotle's Biology.* Cambridge, 1987.

Judson, L., ed. *Aristotle's "Physics."* Oxford, 1991.

Keyt, D., and F. D. Miller, eds. *A Companion to Aristotle's Politics.* Oxford, 1991.

Nussbaum, M. C., and A. O. Rorty, eds. *Essays on Aristotle's de Anima.* Oxford, 1992.

Owen, C. E. L. *Logic, Science, and Dialectic,* edited by M. C. Nussbaum. Cambridge, 1986.

Rorty, A. O., ed. *Essays on Aristotle's Ethics.* Berkeley, 1980.

———, ed. *Essays on Aristotle's "Poetics."* Princeton, NJ, 1992.

MONOGRAPHS

Broadie, S. *Ethics with Aristotle.* New York, 1991.

Charles, D. *Aristotle's Philosophy of Action.* London and Ithaca, NY, 1984.

Cooper, J. M. *Reason and Human Good in Aristotle.* Cambridge, MA, 1975.

Fine, G. *On Ideas: Aristotle's Criticism of Plato's Theory of Forms.* Oxford, 1993.

Halliwell, S. *Aristotle's Poetics.* Chapel Hill, NC, 1986.

Hardie, W. F. R. *Aristotle's Ethical Theory,* 2nd ed. Oxford, 1980.

Hartman, E. *Substance, Body, and Soul.* Princeton, NJ, 1977.

Irwin, T. H. *Aristotle's First Principles.* Oxford, 1988.

Kraut, R. *Aristotle on the Human Good.* Princeton, NJ, 1989.

Loux, M. *Primary Ousia: An Essay on Aristotle's "Metaphysics" Z.* Ithaca, NY, 1991.

Pellegrin, P. *La Classification des animaux chez Aristote.* Paris, 1982. Revised edition translated into English by A. Preus as *Aristotle's Classification of Animals* (Berkeley, 1986).

Sorabji, R. *Necessity, Cause, and Blame: Perspectives on Aristotle's Theory.* London, 1980.

Waterlow, S. *Nature, Change, and Agency in Aristotle's "Physics."* Oxford, 1982.

SUSAN SAUVÉ MEYER

ARMSTRONG, DAVID M., was born in 1926 in Melbourne, Australia. He was a student of John Anderson's at the University of Sydney and was one of the first of many Australian philosophers to take the B.Phil. degree at Oxford (in 1954). He taught briefly at Birkbeck College, London, before returning to Australia to teach at the University of Melbourne. In 1964 he moved to Sydney, succeeding J. L. MACKIE [S] in Anderson's chair.

Armstrong has made influential contributions to a remarkable range of major topics in epistemology and metaphysics, including perception, materialism, bodily sensations, belief and knowledge, laws, universals, and possibility. Recurrent themes have been the need to reconcile what the philosopher says with the teachings of science and a preference for realist over instrumentalist theories.

Armstrong is best known for his *A Materialist Theory of the Mind.* He was originally a behaviorist but was converted to the mind–brain identity theory, the view that mental states are states of the brain, by another Australian philosopher, J. J. C. SMART [S]. In this book he argues that mental states are defined by what they do, in particular by what they do by way of mediating between inputs, outputs, and other mental states. His view was thus an early version of FUNCTIONALISM [S]. Therefore, for him, the question of the identity of a given mental state is simply the (empirical) question of what plays the causally intermediate role distinctive of that state. He observes that it will most likely turn out in each case to be some state or other of the brain that plays the distinctive role. Thus, Armstrong derives the identity theory from a view about what is definitive of a mental state combined with a view about what most likely satisfies the definition.

In the philosophy of perception he argued that we must move away from the tradition that seeks to understand perception as an acquaintance with a special, mental item sometimes called a sense datum and adopt an account that analyzes perception as the acquisition of belief—an account that has the signal advantage of making sense of the role of perception in our traffic with the world.

His treatment of belief follows a suggestion of F. P. RAMSEY's [7] that belief is like a map by which we steer. His account of knowledge is a version of RELIABILISM [S]: *S*'s true belief that *p* is knowledge if it is an empirically reliable sign that *p*. His account of bodily sensations is in terms of the putative perception of goings on in the body and associated attitudes toward those goings on. To give the rough idea: pain is the putative perception of a bodily disturbance combined with a negative attitude toward that perception.

Armstrong is a realist about universals without being a Platonic realist: universals exist, they are not reducible to sets of particulars, they serve as the "truth makers" for predication, but there are no uninstantiated universals. He draws on his realism about universals in his account of laws of nature and of possibility. He rejects any kind of regularity or neo-Humean account of laws in favor of one in terms of relations of nomic necessitation between universals: roughly, "Every *F* is *G*" is a fundamental law if being *F* necessitates being *G*. Armstrong's account of possibility is a combinatorial one. We can think of how things are as a huge arrangement of particulars and universals. The various possibilities can then be thought of as all the combinations and recombinations of these particulars and universals according to various rules for combining them.

Bibliography

Armstrong, D. M. *Belief, Truth and Knowledge.* Cambridge, 1973.

———. *Berkeley's Theory of Vision.* Melbourne, 1960.

———. *Bodily Sensations.* London, 1962.

———. *A Combinatorial Theory of Possibility.* Cambridge, 1989.

Armstrong, D. M., with N. Malcolm. *Consciousness and Causality: A Debate on the Nature of Mind.* Oxford, 1984.

———. *A Materialist Theory of the Mind.* London, 1968.

———. *Perception and the Physical World.* London, 1961.

———. *Universals: An Opinionated Introduction.* Boulder, CO, 1989.

———. *Universals and Scientific Realism,* 2 vols. Cambridge, 1973.

———. *What Is a Law of Nature?* Cambridge, 1983.

FRANK JACKSON

ART, DEFINITION OF. Traditionally, the definition of "art" has been the focal point of theorizing about art and has functioned as a kind of summary of a theory of art. Ideally, such a definition is supposed to specify the necessary and sufficient conditions for being a work of art. Traditionally, the conditions given are themselves supposed to be specifiable independently of the notion of art in order to avoid circularity.

What class of objects should be focused on in trying to define art in terms of necessary and sufficient conditions? First, the class must include everything that is generally regarded as an artwork. Second, the class's members must be artifacts, because philosophers of art have always theorized about a subset of human artifacts; artifactuality is a built-in necessary feature. Finally, should all the members of the class be valuable? That is, should the definition be evaluational or simply classificatory? This is a controversial issue, but this article will be concerned with classificatory definitions.

In the mid-1950s Paul Ziff, Morris Weitz, and others claimed that defining art is impossible because art is a "family resemblance" concept, one that picks out a class the members of which share no common, essential feature. Instead, they claimed such a class's members merely have overlapping resemblances. They even claimed that a natural object (nonartifact) can be art if it resembles an established artwork. These antiessentialists were so persuasive that for about fifteen years philosophers lost interest in defining art.

The antiessentialists were finally challenged by Arthur Danto (1964) and Maurice Mandelbaum (1965). Danto, ignoring the antiessentialists, claimed that the art theory prevailing at a particular time makes art possible. Danto thus attempted to specify one necessary condition of art. Mandelbaum did not try to specify the conditions of art. He did argue that the antiessentialists focused only on easily noted characteristics and ignored the nonexhibited, relational properties of art that connect it to its producers and appreciators. Mandelbaum claimed that nonexhibited properties are more promising for defining. Danto's visually-indistinguishable-pairs argument (1964, 1973, 1974) also called attention to nonexhibited properties (*see* INDISCERNIBLES [S]). This argument focuses on indiscernible pairs of objects, one of which is an artwork and one of which is not. One of Danto's examples of such a pair is *The Polish Rider,* which is an artwork, and an accidentally produced canvas and paint object that exactly resembles it, which is not an artwork. Another pair of indiscernibles is Duchamp's artwork *Fountain* and a urinal that looks just like it. *Fountain*'s context of (nonexhibited) relations to its producer and appreciators in the artworld makes it art, and the urinal's lack of such a context prevents it from being art.

Once antiessentialism had been challenged, philosophers returned to the task of defining art. But whereas philosophers in the pre-antiessentialist period had used psychological notions such as the expression of emotion and aesthetic emotion, philosophers in the post-antiessentialist period have almost all tried to define art in terms of cultural notions.

Danto's idea of a prevailing art theory is a cultural concept quite unlike the earlier psychological notions. Nelson GOODMAN (1968; [3; S]) claimed that the arts are symbol systems and defined an artwork as a symbol that functions in an aesthetic way. A symbol system is a cultural notion involving the coordinated interaction of group members. Danto (1973, 1974) changed his view of the kind of cultural context that is necessary for art, claiming that being about something is necessary for being art. In Danto's later view the necessary cultural phenomenon is a linguistic one and resembles to a degree Goodman's notion of art as a symbol (*see* ARTWORLD [S]).

In 1969 George Dickie began developing a cultural-context theory called the institutional theory of art. His efforts culminated with this definition: "A work of art is an artifact of a kind created to be presented to an artworld public" (1984, p. 80). The definition's circularity is thought by many to be a difficulty, but Dickie has argued that it is a virtue because of the interconnectedness of the elements that make up the artworld and because these related elements are understood from early childhood.

Monroe Beardsley is one of the few post-antiessentialist theorists to attempt to define art in psychological terms, and he did so self-consciously in the face of the prevailing trend. Beardsley wrote, "an artwork can be usefully defined as an intentional arrangement of conditions for affording experiences with marked aesthetic character" (1979, p. 729). The main difficulty of this approach is that it cannot account for nonaesthetic art such as Dadaist works and the like.

As a final example of a cultural account of art, consider the following historical definition offered by Jerrold Levinson (1979, p. 234): "a work of art is a thing intended for regard-as-a-work-of-art: regard in any of the ways works of art existing prior to it have been correctly regarded." As Levinson noted in 1993, the primary problem for such a theory is accounting for the first artwork(s). Cultural theories of art continue to proliferate.

(SEE ALSO: *Aesthetics, Problems of* [S])

Bibliography

Beardsley, M. "In Defense of Aesthetic Value," *Proceedings and Addresses of the American Philosophical Association,* Vol. 52, (1979), 723–49.

———. "Redefining Art," in M. J. Wreen and D. M. Callan, eds. *The Aesthetic Point of View* (Ithaca, NY, 1982).

Binkley, T. "Deciding about Art," in L. Aagaard-Mogensen, ed., *Culture and Art* (Atlantic Highlands, NJ, 1976).

Carroll, N. "Historical Narratives and the Philosophy of Art," *Journal of Aesthetics and Art Criticism,* Vol. 51 (1993), 313–26.

Danto, A. "The Artworld," *Journal of Philosophy,* Vol. 61 (1964), 571–84.

———. "Artworks and Real Things," *Theoria,* Vol. 39 (1973), 1–17.

———. "The Transfiguration of the Commonplace," *Journal of Aesthetics and Art Criticism,* Vol. 33 (1974), 139–48.

———. *The Transfiguration of the Commonplace,* Cambridge, MA, 1981.

Davies, S. *Definitions of Art.* Ithaca, NY, 1991.

Dickie, G. "Defining Art," *American Philosophical Quarterly,* Vol. 6 (1969), 253–56.

———. *Art and the Aesthetic.* Ithaca, NY, 1974.

———. *The Art Circle.* New York, 1984.

Eaton, M. *Art and Nonart.* East Brunswick, NJ, 1983.

Krukowski, L. *Art and Concept.* Amherst, MA, 1987.

Levinson, J. "Defining Art Historically," *British Journal of Aesthetics,* Vol. 19 (1979), 232–50.

———. "Extending Art Historically," *Journal of Aesthetics and Art Criticism,* Vol. 51 (1993), 411–23.

Mandelbaum, M. "Family Resemblances and Generalization Concerning the Arts," *American Philosophical Quarterly,* Vol. 2 (1965), 219–28.

Margolis, J. "Works of Art as Physically Embodied and Culturally Emergent Entities," *British Journal of Aesthetics,* Vol. 14 (1974), 187–96.

Weitz, M. "The Role of Theory in Aesthetics," *Journal of Aesthetics and Art Criticism,* Vol. 15 (1956), 27–35.

Ziff, P. "The Task of Defining a Work of Art," *Philosophical Review,* Vol. 62 (1953), 58–78.

GEORGE DICKIE

ART, END OF. "End of art" is a concept based on HEGEL'S [3; S]) claim that art, the first stage in the realization of Absolute Spirit, is now, because of the increasing self-consciousness to which art has itself contributed, a "thing of the past . . . [which] has lost for us genuine truth and life" (Hegel, [1835] 1975, p. 11). On this account art is superseded historically by religion and then philosophy—a progression anticipated in the "symbolic," "classical," and "romantic" stages of art history as the proportions there shift between the sensuous form and the "idea" comprising the individual work. In the last of these stages idea or content "triumphs over" form, and art then loses its efficacy to a more abstract medium. (The phrase "end of art" and its variant, "death of art," are both glosses on Hegel's own words.)

Attempts to reconcile the pronouncement of the end of art with art's apparent persistence have sometimes interpreted the "end" as a recurrent, not a one-time, event, thus as part of an alternating pattern of normalization and obsolescence. On either analysis, however, art is historically contingent and linked to other elements of the social and intellectual context; this contention, together with the related Hegelian claim that the individual stages of art history follow an internal logic, has, although with many variations, greatly influenced modern stylistics and the historiography of art.

The historicist premises of the end of art thesis underlie the recent postmodernist and institutional or "ARTWORLD" [S] critiques of essentialist definitions of art, which view the phenomenon of art as humanly or culturally fixed and atemporal (see ART, DEFINITION OF [S]). The radical displacement of art is, however, only one possible outcome of art's contingent status; in any event the question of what medium would supersede art depends at least in part on the causal factors identified as bringing about the end.

(SEE ALSO: *Aesthetics, History of,* and *Aesthetics, Problems of* [1; S])

Bibliography

Danto, A. *The Disenfranchisement of Art.* New York, 1986.

Harris, H. S. "The Resurrection of Art," *Owl of Minerva,* Vol. 16 (1984), 5–20.

Hegel, G. W. F. *Aesthetics: Lectures on Fine Art* [1835], 2 vols. T. M. Knox, trans. Oxford, 1975.

Lang, B., ed. *The Death of Art.* New York, 1984.

BEREL LANG

ART, EXPRESSION IN. The expressive power of art has long drawn the attention of aestheticians no less than it has beguiled artists and appreciators of art alike. In the late nineteenth and early twentieth centuries the so-called expression theory of art was, in one or another of its forms, widely endorsed (by Leo TOLSTOY [8], Eugene Veron, Benedetto CROCE [2], R. G. COLLINGWOOD [2], George SANTAYANA [7], C. J. DUCASSE [2], and John DEWEY [2; S]) and constituted one of the main tenets of ROMANTICISM [7] in aesthetics. This theory defined art in terms of the expressive act of the artist, the embodying or objectifying of the artist's affect or thought in a communicable medium. Gradually, however, it became clear that the expressive properties of art objects are not necessarily the effects of the artist's experiencing the homonymous (i.e., same-named) psychological state: works expressing anguish need not be expressive of an anguished state of the artist. Consequently, philosophical interest largely turned from the creative or expressive act to the puzzles surrounding the idea that art objects are artifacts with expressive properties. The two most important areas of concern became the semantics of expressive predicates and the ontology of expressive properties.

In the 1960s and 1970s a variety of philosophical techniques were applied to the semantics of artistic expression. For example, Guy Sircello (1972) employed ordinary-language philosophy and argued that artworks differ in important ways from natural signs and from nonexpressive symbols (expression involving a peculiar "showing" or "standing out" relation) and that their expressive import is not determined conventionally. Sircello claimed that anthropomorphic predicates apply to artworks in virtue of the specific "artistic acts" (such as portraying, presenting, inveighing, etc.) that the artist performs "in" the work.

In contrast, Nelson GOODMAN [3; S], in his influential *Languages of Art* (1968), treated artworks as symbols and defined expression in terms of the semantic relations of reference and denotation. A work expresses ø if and only if the work is a member of the metaphorical denotation of the predicate 'ø' and the work "refers back" to that predicate. Less nominalistically stated, expression is a form of property exemplification for Goodman. A work exemplifies a property if it not only possesses but "highlights" that property, much as a tailor's swatch highlights the texture and design of the material, because of the conventions surrounding its use. Expression is exemplification of properties that a work actually but metaphorically possesses.

Others have wanted to distinguish clearly between, for example, a work's being expressive of anguish and the work's possessing the property of anguish, even metaphorically. Alan Tormey (1971) has proposed that expressive properties are those properties of artworks whose names also designate intentional states of persons. He further suggests that a work's expressive properties are revealed through its perceivable nonexpressive properties, rather as a person's intentional states are revealed through behavior. This area has yet to produce much philosophical consensus, excepting only the conclusion that our language of artistic expression has complex and varied uses.

The ontological problem surrounding expressive properties is to clarify how such properties are related to the more mundane nonaesthetic features of artworks. Most philosophers hold that a work's expressive properties are dependent or supervenient upon, but are not reducible or identical to, its nonexpressive properties. (Tormey offers a different thesis, viz., that expressive properties are wholly but ambiguously constituted by a work's nonexpressive properties.) The difficulty has been to clarify the nature of this dependency, especially in light of the rather widespread acceptance of an idea of Frank Sibley, that no set of nonexpressive features provides logically necessary and sufficient conditions for the possession of an expressive property. Some—for example, Monroe Beardsley—have suggested that the dependency relation is better construed as a causal and psychological fact about our reactions to artwork rather than a conceptual, quasi-logical connection between aesthetic and nonaesthetic descriptions of artworks.

The 1980s and 1990s, in fact, brought renewed discussion of the nature of our reactions to expressive qualities of works of art. It was part of the romanticist theory of expression, or at least certain versions of it, that a work expressive of ø caused its audience to feel ø in the course of their aesthetic appreciation of the work. Peter Kivy, Goodman, and other "cognitivists" have denied that appreciating a work's expressive properties involves arousal of the homonymous emotion. For Kivy (1989) and the case of music such appreciation is a matter of cognitively grasping the way expressive features function "syntactically" in the musical structure. Although it seems clear that artworks expressive of sadness do not necessarily evoke sadness, it is equally obvious that they sometimes do arouse this emotion. The debate between the cognitivist and the emotivist may finally be resolving into the realization that philosophers of art can profitably examine the emotional impact as well as the cognitive and symbolic functions of the expressive properties of art.

(SEE ALSO: *Aesthetics, History of,* and *Aesthetics, Problems of* [1; S])

Bibliography

Beardsley, M. "The Descriptivist Account of Aesthetic Attributions," *Revue internationale de philosophie*, Vol. 28 (1974), 336-52.

Goodman, N. *Languages of Art.* Indianapolis, 1968.

Kivy, P. *Sound Sentiment.* Philadelphia, 1989.

Levinson, J. "Aesthetic Supervenience," *Southern Journal of Philosophy,* Vol. 22 (1983), Supplement, 93–110.

Sibley, F. "Aesthetic Concepts," *Philosophical Review,* Vol. 68 (1959), 42–50.

Sircello, G. *Mind and Art.* Princeton, NJ, 1972.

Tormey, A. *The Concept of Expression.* Princeton, NJ, 1971.

JOHN W. BENDER

ART, INTERPRETATION OF. Traditionally, artworks were thought to be about something, to indirectly refer, symbolize, or mean, and interpreters used ordinary language to open up their meanings. This view is no longer common, in part because of the failure of the dominant critical approaches to give a coherent and workable account of interpretation.

For example, the New Critics suppose understanding literary works to provide the model for all interpretation of artworks. Literary texts are taken to be uniquely and autonomously meaningful, irreducible to extrinsic meanings and ordinary (nonliterary) discourse (cf. Wimsatt & Beardsley, 1954). This position disarms the critic, who must use a language inappropriate to its object—ordinary language and its shared senses. The New Critics, according to their critics, are condemned to silence or to systematic falsification of the sense of the work.

The structuralists suppose that poetic discourse has structural laws of its own analogous to the laws of ordinary discourse. The difference is that poetic meanings are a function of context whereas ordinary meanings are not (cf. Barthes, 1966). According to structuralism's critics, the structuralist then comes to the same end as does the New Critic, to silence or falsification, because to recast contextual meanings as lexical meanings is grossly to distort them.

The hermeneuticists develop the notion that all meaning, poetic and ordinary, is contextual. Poetic texts provide the model for all meaningful domains; the way they are understood provides the model for every kind of understanding. The problem of having to allow as many interpretations as critics, cultures, or historical periods is avoided by postulating some limiting principle (e.g., tradition). This principle conditions any new interpretation, which is understood as the last remark in a dialogue over time (cf. GADAMER, 1975 [S]). Hermeneuticism's critics note that this limits the relativism of understanding by contradicting the basic insight that there is no first, foundational principle limiting the subjectivity of understanding.

Poststructuralists and deconstructionists, in various ways, simply accept the inherent relativity of understanding and license criticism for a variety of pragmatic reasons (*see* DECONSTRUCTION and POSTSTRUCTURALISM [S]). They provide a negative but still informative reading of works by unearthing the hidden assumptions, beliefs, cultural fashions, aesthetic influences, and political ideologies that inform and constitute the work. Works can be deconstructed for destructive or playful reasons, or for constructive and even moral purposes (cf. DERRIDA, 1967 [S]). Postcolonial, new historicist, feminist, and Marxist critics may suppose an objective understanding of works is possible; more likely, they understand the force of the idea that meaning is contextual and constituted, and they criticize art to promote the personal, social, or political changes they desire.

It is natural that theory of interpretation has gone from the quest for objectivity to relativism and pragmatism, this being a small chapter in the critique of MODERNISM [S]. Abandoning key concepts of modern philosophy, such as REALISM [7; S], representationalism, and correspondence truth theory (*see* CORRESPONDENCE THEORY OF TRUTH [2]), profoundly affects interpretive theory. So does the transformation of art. Nonphysical works, nonart artifacts, natural objects, accidental art, minimal art, and art (including the literary) intended to be minimally meaningful, indefinitely meaningful, meaningless, or merely self-referring, all these bedevil the classical interpreter intent upon meaning and truth. The same is true if one takes the work itself to be an interpretation subject to second-order (i.e., normal) interpretations (cf. Danto, 1981) or to be identifiable as art only in terms of second-order characteristics (cf. Dickie, 1984). Some of these theories contain no implications for interpretive theory (or a theory of evaluation) and suggest none are forthcoming. Not all theorists agree with this general line, (e.g., Rosen, 1987), and critics often write as though artworks are intelligible and their remarks helpful to those seeking to understand them.

(SEE ALSO: *Aesthetics, Problems of* [S])

Bibliography

Barthes, R. *Critique et vérité.* Paris, 1966.

Berman, A. *From the New Criticism to Deconstruction: The Reception of Structuralism and Post-Structuralism.* Chicago, 1988. A critical overview, typical of a large literature on the evolution of theory of interpretation. Useful bibliography.

Danto, A. C. *The Transfiguration of the Commonplace.* Cambridge, MA, 1981.

Derrida, J. *L'écriture et la différence.* Paris, 1967.

Dickie, G. *The Art Circle.* New York, 1984.

Gadamer, H.-G. *Wahrheit und Methode.* Tübingen, 1975.

Parrinder, P. "Having Your Assumptions Questioned," in R. Bradford, ed., *The State of Theory* (London, 1993). Survey and deconstructive analysis of books on theories of interpretation.

Rosen, S. *Hermeneutics as Politics.* New York, 1987.

The Monist, Vol. 73 (1990), 115–330. Special issue edited by J. Hospers and J. Margolis on "The Theory of Interpretation." Contains eleven articles on the fate of interpretation after the advent of deconstruction.

Wimsatt, W., and M. Beardsley. "The Intentional Fallacy," in W. Wimsatt and M. Beardsley, *The Verbal Icon: Studies in the Meaning of Poetry* (Lexington, KY, 1954).

MARGARET VAN DE PITTE

ART, NATURE OF, IN HEIDEGGER.

Martin HEIDEGGER [3; S] distinguishes three factors involved in aesthetics: the artist, the work of art, and art. Contrary to the traditional interpretations he states that art is the origin of both the artist and the artwork. Like everything that is, a work of art is in the broadest sense of the word a thing. Proceeding to differentiate between a mere thing in the ordinary sense and an artwork, Heidegger enumerates three paradigms that philosophers have come up with to analyze a thing. He is satisfied with none of these traditional interpretations, stating that they are not adequate to characterize the artwork. Analyses of useful things or equipment also fail to get at the nature of the work of art. Taking Vincent van Gogh's painting of a pair of peasant shoes as his example, Heidegger states that it reveals the world of the peasant woman. He concludes that art is the setting-into-work of truth, where truth as the unconcealing of the strife between world and earth is at once the subject and object of the setting.

(SEE ALSO: *Aesthetics, Problems of* [S])

Bibliography

Heidegger, M. *Poetry, Language, Thought.* Translated into English by A. Hofstadter. New York, 1971.

JOAN STAMBAUGH

ART, REPRESENTATION IN.

Both the method (or means) and the values of representations vary across the different artforms and media. Literature represents characters, situations, and events by describing fictional worlds—by generating fictional truths through its descriptions, or prescribing what readers are to imagine is the case. Music sometimes represents sounds in nature or human society by duplicating or imitating those sounds, and it sometimes represents situations or characters through conventional association with its motifs. More often, musical representation shades into expression of emotional states. This is accomplished both by imitating in its pitch, volume, and rhythmic and melodic contours the natural expressions of emotion in voice, demeanor, and behavior and by arousing related emotions in listeners (by harmonic means as well). For example, sad music tends to be slow, low, soft, and in minor keys.

The means by which a painter achieves pictorial representation or depiction, or the criterion for a painting's being a depiction of a particular object or kind of object, is controversial. Of seeming relevance are the artist's intention to depict a certain object, the causal context of the painting's production, conventions for representing certain kinds of objects, and some sort of resemblance relation between the painting and the object represented (*see* ART, RESEMBLANCE IN [S]). Artistic intention is necessary both for depiction in general, since accidental likenesses are not depictions, and for picking out from among the possibilities the actual object represented in a painting. A particular causal relation to its object is not required for a pictorial representation (in this respect paintings differ from photographs), since artists do not necessarily represent the models from which they paint. But the causal context (i.e., marking a surface with paint) is relevant, since photographs and fabric samples do not depict, although they resemble and represent (in a broader sense) their objects (*see* AUTHENTICITY REGARDING THE ARTIST AND THE ARTWORK [S]).

Aestheticians differ over the roles of convention and resemblance. In general we do not need to know semantic and syntactic conventions for interpreting parts of paintings and putting those parts together in order to interpret the paintings as depictions. We do so by seeing the objects in the paintings, in virtue of being able to recognize both the objects and the resemblance between our visual experience of the paintings and that of the objects. It is important to emphasize that the relevant resemblance is between visual experiences and not objects themselves; painters must painstakingly learn how to create such resemblances through two-dimensional cues. Convention supplements ordinary recognitional capacities in the depiction of characters or objects that are not (or no longer) recognizable from real life.

We may combine these factors into the following criterion: a painting represents an object when it realizes an artist's intention to mark a surface so as to make the visual experience of it resemble that of the object. This criterion is similar to that first suggested by PLATO [6; S]) in the earliest writings in aesthetics, when he held that painters imitate the appearances of objects. This claim raised for him the problem of value in representation: how could a mere imitation possess value approaching the experience of the original?

Kendall Walton has suggested in reply that representations function as props in imaginative games. By imagining ourselves in the fictional worlds of artworks we can try out different roles, learn new responses, and broaden our cognitive and emotional repertoires. If such games of make believe are more common in relation to literature, expression and representation in music and painting serve other aesthetic functions. When music is intensely expressive of emotions it tends to engage us completely, and such experience can be its own reward. Viewing representational paintings can alter the ways we view real objects. Representation in painting can also create higher-order formal structures and intensify the sensuous beauty of pure color and form.

(SEE ALSO: *Aesthetics, History of,* and *Aesthetics, Problems of* [1; S])

Bibliography

Plato. *The Republic,* translated by A. Bloom. New York, 1968. Book 10.

Schier, F. *Deeper into Pictures.* Cambridge, 1986.

Walton, K. *Mimesis as Make-Believe.* Cambridge, MA, 1990.

ALAN H. GOLDMAN

ART, RESEMBLANCE IN.

When a painting depicts a certain object, it seems intuitively that some sort of resemblance enters into that relation of representation. It is easy to show that resemblance is not sufficient for pictorial representation, since, for example, virtually every painting resembles every other painting more than it resembles the objects it represents (see ART, REPRESENTATION IN [S]). But this leaves open the possibility that resemblance is necessary, and it seems so from the fact that an artist's intention and the causal relation between the object and the act of painting do not suffice for depiction. Nor do we need to learn a conventional symbol system before being able to interpret paintings as pictures of objects.

The sort of resemblance that is necessary for depiction is that between visual experience of the object and that of the painting. Painters must learn how to produce such similarity through two-dimensional visual cues. Similarity of shape in the visual field is normally important, but not always crucial (as in the depiction of a leaf by a bright green dot).

If a threshold of such resemblance is necessary for depiction, we may also suppose that the greater its degree, the more true-to-life is the painting.

(SEE ALSO: *Aesthetics, History of,* and *Aesthetics, Problems of* [1; S])

Bibliography

Neander, K. "Pictorial Representation: A Matter of Resemblance," *British Journal of Aesthetics,* Vol. 27 (1987), 213–26.

Peacocke, C. "Depiction," *Philosophical Review,* Vol. 96 (1987), 383–410.

ALAN H. GOLDMAN

ART AS PERFORMANCE.

Drama, music, and dance are the primary performing arts. In these, executants typically display their skills to an audience. Performances might be freely improvised, but many aim to instance a work, such as a tragedy or symphony, created by an artist.

The artist often supplies a work-specification recorded as instructions (scripts, scores) addressed to performers. The interpretation of the specification presupposes an awareness of the relevant performance tradition, since some things required of the performer may not be indicated and not all aspects of the notation are to be read literally. An accurate rendering of a work-specification results in an instance of the given work; frequently, a work also remains recognizable despite some performance errors or other departures from the artist's specification. The work is completed when its designation is, so a work for performance might have no instances. But such pieces are intended for performance, usually more than once.

Alternatively, the artist might provide a model instance of the work, this being imitated in subsequent presentations. Which features of the model are work properties and which performance properties depends on the relevant genre and conventions. Only the attributes that characterize the work are mandated for its future performances.

Performance is creative because the artist's instructions or model leave much to the performers' discretion. As a result, performances possess finer detail than do the works they exemplify; also, accurate performances of a given piece can differ considerably. A particular manner of realizing a work is an interpretation; this might be repeated in many performances. The audience is as likely to be interested in the interpretation and the talents displayed as in the work itself, especially where the work is well known.

In some arts, such as cinema, performers are employed in the creation of the work. Such works, when finished, are not for performance but for showing.

(SEE ALSO: *Aesthetics, History of,* and *Aesthetics, Problems of* [1; S])

Bibliography

Alperson, P. "On Musical Improvisation," *Journal of Aesthetics and Art Criticism,* Vol. 43 (1984), 17–30.

Callen, D. "Making Music Live," *Theoria,* Vol. 48 (1982), 139–68.

Carlson, M. *Theories of the Theatre: A Historical and Critical Survey from the Greeks to the Present.* Ithaca, NY, 1984.

Davies, S. "Authenticity in Musical Performance," *British Journal of Aesthetics,* Vol. 27 (1987), 39–50.

Sparshott, F. *Off the Ground: First Steps to a Philosophical Consideration of the Dance.* Princeton, NJ, 1988.

Thom, P. *For an Audience: A Philosophy of the Performing Arts.* Philadelphia, 1993.

STEPHEN DAVIES

ARTIFICIAL INTELLIGENCE. Artificial intelligence (AI) tries to enable computers to do the things that minds can do. Although AI research covers cognition, motivation, and emotion, it has focused primarily on cognition.

Some AI researchers seek solutions to technological problems, not caring whether these solutions resemble human psychology. Others want to understand how human (or animal) minds work or even how intelligence in general is possible. The latter approach is more relevant for the philosophy of mind and is central to COGNITIVE SCIENCE [S] and the COMPUTATIONAL MODEL OF MIND [S]. Its practitioners generally accept some form of FUNCTIONALISM [S] (for example, the physical symbol system hypothesis of Newell and Simon).

The things that minds can do include abilities not normally regarded as requiring intelligence, such as seeing pathways, picking things up, and learning categories from experience—all of which many animals can do. Thus, human intelligence is not the sole focus of AI. Even terrestrial psychology is not since some use AI to explore the range of possible minds.

There are four major AI methodologies: symbolic AI, CONNECTIONISM [S], situated robotics, and evolutionary programming. Symbolic AI (also known as classical AI) models thinking on the step-by-step processing of digital computers. Thinking is seen as symbol manipulation, as (formal) computation over (formal) representations. Folk psychological categories (*see* PROPOSITIONAL ATTITUDE [S]) are explicitly modeled in the processing. This type of AI is defended by Fodor, who sees connectionism as concerned merely with how symbolic computation can be implemented.

Connectionism, which became widely visible in the mid-1980s, is often said to be opposed to AI. But connectionism has been part of AI from its beginnings in the 1940s and is opposed, rather, to symbolic AI. Connectionism defines associative networks of simple computational units that can tolerate imperfect data and (often) learn patterns from experience. Most philosophical interest is in the type known as PDP (parallel distributed processing), which employs subsymbolic units whose semantic significance cannot be easily expressed in terms of propositional content. (Some classical AI programs employ subsymbolic units too.) PDP representations are embodied as equilibrated activity patterns of the whole network, not as activations of single units or entries in single memory locations.

These two AI methodologies have complementary strengths and weaknesses. For instance, symbolic AI is better at modeling hierarchy and "strong" constraints, whereas connectionism copes better with pattern recognition, especially if many conflicting constraints must be considered. But neither can illuminate all of psychology. Both have been criticized by Searle as being concerned only with syntax, not semantics: neither approach, he argues, possesses (or explains) intentionality. He allows, however, that connectionism shows that semantically appropriate inferences can be drawn without the formal symbol manipulations favored by Newell, Simon, and Fodor.

The third AI methodology is situated robotics. Situated robots are described as autonomous systems embedded in their environment (HEIDEGGER [3; S] is sometimes cited). Instead of planning their actions, as classical robots do, they react directly to environmental cues. Although they contain no objective representations of the world, they may construct temporary, subject-centered (deictic) representations.

In evolutionary programming, a program makes random variations (like biological mutations and crossovers) in its own rules. The most successful rules are automatically selected and (probably) varied again. Eventually, the system is well adapted to its task. This AI method is used within both symbolic and connectionist systems and for both abstract problem solving and evolutionary robotics—wherein the brain and sensorimotor anatomy of robots evolve within a specific task environment.

AI is closely related to artificial life (A-Life). A-Life employs computer simulation to study the emergence of complexity in self-organizing, self-reproducing, adaptive systems. Situated and evolutionary robotics are forms of AI commonly seen as lying within A-Life. However, since psychological properties arise in living things, the whole of AI could be regarded as a subarea of A-Life.
(SEE ALSO: *Philosophy of Mind* [S])

Bibliography

Boden, M. A., ed. *The Philosophy of Artificial Intelligence.* Oxford, 1990.

———. *Artificial Intelligence and Natural Man,* 2d ed. London, 1987.

Clark, A. J. *Associative Engines: Connectionism, Concepts, and Representational Change.* Cambridge, MA, 1993.

———. *Microcognition: Philosophy, Cognitive Science, and Parallel Distributed Processing.* Cambridge, MA, 1989.

Dreyfus, H. L. *What Computers Can't Do: The Limits of Artificial Intelligence,* 2d ed. New York, 1979.

Fodor, J. A. *Psychosemantics: The Problem of Meaning in the Philosophy of Mind.* Cambridge, MA, 1987.

Holland, J. H., K. J. Holyoak, R. E. Nisbet, and P. R. Thagard. *Induction: Processes of Inference, Learning, and Discovery.* Cambridge, MA, 1986.

Rich, E., and K. Knight. *Artificial Intelligence,* 2d ed. New York, 1991.

Searle, J. R. *The Rediscovery of the Mind.* Cambridge, MA, 1993.

MARGARET BODEN

ARTWORKS, ONTOLOGICAL STATUS OF, IN HEIDEGGER. The most striking feature of the ontological status of artworks for Martin HEIDEGGER [3; S] is that they have to do not so much with the traditional concept of BEAUTY [1; S], but with the happening of TRUTH [S]. Truth is conceived, not as the correspondence between idea and thing, but as the unconcealing of the strife between earth and world. Setting up a world and setting forth the earth create a clearing (*Lichtung*) that grants and guarantees to humans a passage to those beings that they are not and access to the beings that they themselves are. This constitutes an interim stage on the way to the theme of the FOURFOLD [S] developed in later works. The fact of createdness belongs emphatically to the ontological status of the work of art. But what is significant about createdness is not the N. N. *Fecit* (x created it) but the *factum est* (it was created). Not the artist but the "*that* it is" of createdness is important.
(SEE ALSO: *Aesthetics, Problems of* [S])

Bibliography

Heidegger, M. *Poetry, Language, Thought.* Translated into English by A. Hofstadter. New York, 1971.

JOAN STAMBAUGH

ARTWORLD. "Artworld" designates that complex of individuals and institutions involved in the production and presentation of works of visual art—artists, dealers, collectors, critics, curators, journalists, and the like. The expression achieved philosophical status in Arthur C. Danto's 1964 "The Art World," where it was invoked specifically to explain how certain objects, like Duchamp's ready-mades, get accepted as works of art: "To see something as art requires something the eye cannot descry—an atmosphere of artistic theory, a knowledge of history of art: an artworld." This formulation inspired George Dickie's initial formulations of the institutional theory of art.
(SEE ALSO: *Aesthetics, Problems of* [S])

Bibliography

Danto, A. C. "The Artworld," *Journal of Philosophy,* Vol. 61 (1964), 571–84.

Dickie, G. *Art and the Aesthetic: An Institutional Analysis.* Ithaca, NY, 1974.

ARTHUR C. DANTO

AUGUSTINE, ST., continues to elicit scholarly discussions of theological issues, but there is an ever-growing number of studies devoted to historical and philosophical issues in their own right. Recent philosophical work has concentrated on deepening our understanding of his arguments, assessing the adequacy of his positions, and contextualizing them in a historically informed way.

P. Brown, *Augustine of Hippo: A Biography* (London, 1967), is a masterful work that situates Augustine in his social and historical surroundings. Accessible overviews of Augustine's life and thought are provided in J. J. O'Donnell, *Augustine* (Boston, 1985), and H. Chadwick, *Augustine* (Oxford, 1986). Our understanding of Augustine's autobiography has been greatly advanced by the fine commentary given in J. J. O'Donnell, *Augustine: Confessions* (3 vols., Oxford, 1992).

Augustine is seen against the background of classical philosophy in J. Rist, *Augustine: Ancient Thought Baptized* (Cambridge, 1994), which provides a guide to Augustine's philosophical views. Another introduction to Augustine as a philosopher is C. Kirwan, *Augustine* (London, 1989), which takes up selected topics in detail. The bibliographies of both these works should be consulted as a guide to the literature. Articles on a variety of topics are usefully collected in R. A. Markus (ed.), *Augustine: A Collection of Critical Essays* (London, 1972); there has been no anthology for philosophers since.

Turning now to particular aspects of Augustine's philosophy, G. J. P. O'Daly, *Augustine's Philosophy of Mind* (London, 1987), and G. Matthews, *Thought's Ego in Augustine and Descartes* (Ithaca, NY, 1992), deal with his philosophical psychology. Epistemology and the theory of illumination are the primary focus of R. H. Nash, *The Light of the Mind: St. Augustine's Theory of Knowledge* (Lexington, KY, 1969); B. Bubacz, *St. Augustine's Theory of Knowledge: A Contemporary Analysis* (New York, 1981); U. Wienbruch, *Erleuchtete Einsicht: Zur Erkenntnislehre Augustins* (Bonn, 1989). Metaphysical problems as well as the issue of Augustine's indebtedness to Plotinus are treated in R. J. O'Connell, *The Origin of the Soul in St. Augustine's Later Works* (New York, 1987). Augustine's account of time is analyzed in R. Sorabji, *Time, Creation, and the Continuum* (Ithaca, NY, 1983), and subjected to a wide-ranging examination in J. Pelikan, *The Mystery of Continuity: Time and History, Memory and Eternity in the Thought of Saint Augustine* (Charlottesville, VA, 1986). Philosophy of language is discussed by M. Burnyeat, "Wittgenstein and Augustine *de Magistro*," in *Proceedings of the Aristotelian Society* (1987, supp. vol.). Augustine's ethical theory is the subject of J. Wetzel, *Augustine and the Limits of Virtue* (Cambridge, 1992), and discussed in G. R. Evans, *Augustine on Evil* (Cambridge, 1982). A recent philosophical study of Augustine's views on freedom, weakness of will, and voluntary action is T. Chappell, *Aristotle and Augustine on Freedom* (New York, 1995). R. Coles, *Self/Power/Other: Political Theory and Dialogical Ethics* (Ithaca, NY, 1992), offers a Foucaultian account of Augustine's political philosophy.

A bibliography of works through 1970 is provided in C. Andresen, *Bibliographia Augustiniana* (Darmstadt, 1973); the next decade of Augustinian studies is covered in T. Miethe, *Augustinian Bibliography, 1970–1980* (Westport, CT, 1982).

(SEE ALSO: *Augustine, St.* [1])

PETER KING

AUTHENTICITY. If there is a single existentialist virtue, it is authenticity (Martin HEIDEGGER's [3; S] *Eigentlichkeit* and Jean-Paul SARTRE's [7; S] *l'authenticité*). It functions as a kind of ethical gyroscope in a Nietzschean world of moral free-fall. For Heidegger the term denotes my "ownmost" way of being-in-the-world. In *Being and Time* Heidegger advocates resolutely affirming my most authentic possibility, namely, my being-unto-death, and disvalues my prevailing tendency to flee this anguished condition in favor of the average everyday world in which "one dies" (as in Tolstoy's *The Death of Ivan Ilych*). But only I can know how to respond authentically to this fact of my radical finitude because that finitude is most properly my own and not another's. Heidegger introduced the concept to facilitate access to the meaning of being, which was his project in *Being and Time*. Resolutely affirming that I will not be, he argued, reveals what it means to be at all. This use of "authenticity" is ontological and epistemic. Heidegger denied that the term carried moral significance, a claim reinforced by his refusal to write an ethics. But Sartre insisted that it was as moral a concept for Heidegger as it was for him. And so it came to be regarded in the vintage days of EXISTENTIALISM [3; S]).

Sartre added a footnote to *Being and Nothingness,* promising to write "an ethic of deliverance through authenticity." He wrote hundreds of pages in fulfillment of that promise. But until the posthumous publication of *Notebooks for an Ethics,* his most extended definition of authenticity appeared in *Anti-Semite and Jew:* "Authenticity . . . consists in having a true and lucid consciousness of the situation, in assuming the responsibilities and risks that it involves, in accepting it in pride or humiliation, sometimes in horror and hate" (Sartre, 1948, p. 90). This seemed to yield an ethical style rather than a content.

The publication of *Notebooks* provides the content for this ethics of authenticity by discussions of such concepts as good faith, gift-appeal, generosity, and positive reciprocity. This important text modifies the common conception of Sartre as the prophet of inevitable inauthenticity (see BAD FAITH [S]). It establishes the historical and socioeconomic context in which his more pessimistic assessments are said to apply. To be authentic still includes the acceptance of our human project as simultaneously gratuitous and reflectively appropriated. And it continues to entail a double aspect of unveiling and creation: unveiling of its radical contingency and creation of a reflective relation to this contingency. But authenticity now assumes a social dimension wherein I commit myself to modify others' situations so that they too may act in an authentic manner. Authenticity implies living the tension that arises from appropriating the truth about the human condition: that it is a finite, temporalizing flux, that this fluidity entails profound responsibility for whatever permanence we sustain within that flux, and that mutual recognition among freedoms enhances this concrete freedom even as it increases that lived tension.

Although it is common to read "authenticity" as equivalent to "genuineness," "truthfulness to self," and even "self-realization," these terms are inapplicable to the existentialist use of the term. As the defining maxim of existentialism, "existence precedes essence," implies, there is no pregiven self, essence, or type to realize in one's creative choices. "Truthfulness to one's condition" might better translate "authenticity," provided one respected the contingency, lack of identity, "inner distance," and temporal spread denoted by the term "condition" (see EXISTENTIAL PSYCHOANALYSIS [3; S]).

Authenticity is often criticized on three grounds: individualism, relativism, and NIHILISM [5]. Taylor (1991) sketches a nonexistentialist answer to such objections. The existentialist response would note that Heidegger speaks of "authentic being-with" (*Mitsein*) and that Sartre, especially in his later work, emphasizes the concepts of mutual recognition and common action as integral to authentic existence. The charges of relativism and nihilism are answered by the positive value each thinker places on the revelation of Being and the fostering of concrete freedom respectively. "Authenticity" does imply an individuating decision, as does any moral choice. That it is neither the application of a principle nor the following of a rule, but a creative choice, does not leave it arbitrary or random.

Bibliography

Heidegger, M. *Sein und Zeit.* Tübingen, 1927. Translated by J. Macquarrie and J. Robinson as *Being and Time.* New York, 1962.

Martin, M. *Self-Deception and Morality.* Lawrence, KS, 1986.

Santoni, R. E. *Bad Faith, Good Faith and Authenticity in Sartre's Early Philosophy.* Philadelphia, 1995.

Sartre, J.-P. *Cahiers pour une morale.* 1983. Translated by D. Pellauer as *Notebooks for an Ethics.* Chicago, 1992.

———. *L'Etre et le néant.* 1943. Translated by H. E. Barnes as *Being and Nothingness.* New York, 1956.

———. *Réflexions sur la question juive.* 1946. Translated by G. J. Becker as *Anti-Semite and Jew.* New York, 1948.

Taylor, C. *The Ethics of Authenticity.* Cambridge, 1991.

Trilling, L. *Sincerity and Authenticity.* Cambridge, 1972.

THOMAS R. FLYNN

AUTHENTICITY REGARDING THE ARTIST AND THE ARTWORK. In the main sense of the term an artwork is authentic if it is the artwork it is thought to be—if it has the history of production it is represented as having or gives the impression of having, if it was created where, when, how, and by whom it is supposed or appears to have been created. Thus, a work may be inauthentic in virtue of being a forgery, or a misattribution, or a replica not identified as such. A reproduction (e.g., in an art book) is inauthentic only in a weaker sense: though not the artwork it reproduces, it does not purport to be and runs no danger of being confused with it.

The chief issue concerning the authenticity of artworks has been the extent to which a work's aesthetic properties, artistic value, and proper appreciation legitimately depend on questions of authenticity in the above sense. The issue is often framed in terms of a challenge: What is wrong with a forgery? or What privileges an original artistically?

Broadly speaking, there are two opposed views on this issue. On one view an artwork is merely a perceivable structure—for example, a constellation of colors and shapes, a set of notes, a string of words, or the like. Furthermore, this structure is the entire source of its aesthetic and artistic properties and is the only thing relevant to its appreciation and evaluation as art. Thus, anything preserving the artwork's perceivable structure, so as to be perceptually indiscernible from it, is equivalent to it artistically and even ontologically. Such a view underlies the formalism of Clive Bell and Roger Fry, the literary stance of the New Critics, and to some extent the aesthetics of Monroe Beardsley. By these lights there is nothing much wrong with a forgery—provided, of course, that it is a perfect one, not detectably different from the original.

On the other view perceivable structure is not the sole determinant of a work's aesthetic complexion or its artistic character. Rather, a work's context of origination, including the problematic from which it issues, partly determines how the work is rightly apprehended and experienced and thus its aesthetic and artistic properties. Aspects of the context or manner of creation arguably enter even into the identity of the work of art, as essential to its being the particular work it is. By these lights there is quite a lot wrong with a forgery. It differs from the original in numerous respects, both aesthetic and artistic, and as a human product—a making, an achievement, an utterance—it is of an entirely different order, however similar it appears on superficial examination.

If the second view sketched above is sound, then any artwork, *pace* GOODMAN [3; S]), can be forged—that is, represented as having a provenance and history other than its own, though how this will be effected differs from artform to artform, especially when one crosses from particular arts (such as painting) to type arts in which structure may be notationally determined (such as music). And this is because, in all artforms, the identity of a work is partly a matter of the historical circumstances of its emergence.

Goodman famously argued, against the aesthetic equivalence of an original painting and an ostensibly perfect forgery, that the possibility of discovering a perceptual difference between the former and the latter constitutes an aesthetic difference between them. Unfortunately, this argument seems to trade on conflating an aesthetic difference and an aesthetically relevant difference between two objects. However, as suggested above, the aesthetic and artistic differences between originals and forgeries, which are ample, rest securely on quite other grounds.

AUTHENTICITY OF ARTWORK INSTANCE

In cases of multiple or type arts an instance of a work—a copy, impression, casting, performance, staging, screening, and so forth—may be denominated authentic or inauthentic insofar as it is or is not a correct or faithful instance of the work. And this, according to different accounts, is a matter of its adequately instantiating and representing the structure thought definitive of the work in question, a matter of its having the right sort of causal or intentional relations to the work in question or of being produced in a certain manner, a matter of its conveying the aesthetic or artistic properties believed crucial to the work—or some combination of these.

AUTHENTICITY OF ARTIST

Finally, authenticity is sometimes considered a predicate of the artist, describing laudatorily the artist's characteristic mode of creating or the relation between the artist and the content of the works the artist creates. An authentic artist is one thought, variously, to be sincere in expression, pure in motivation, true to self, honest about medium, rooted in a tradition, resistant to ideology yet reflective of society—or all of these. There seems to be only a passing relation between authenticity in this sense and the authenticity of work or instance canvased above. (SEE ALSO: *Aesthetics, History of,* and *Aesthetics, Problems of* [1; S])

Bibliography

Bailey, G. "Amateurs Imitate, Professionals Steal," *Journal of Aesthetics and Art Criticism,* Vol. 47 (1989), 221–28.

Baugh, B. "Authenticity Revisited," *Journal of Aesthetics and Art Criticism,* Vol. 46 (1988), 477–87.

Currie, G. *An Ontology of Art.* New York, 1989.

Danto, A. *Transfiguration of the Commonplace.* Cambridge, MA, 1981.

Davies, S. "Authenticity in Musical Performance," *British Journal of Aesthetics,* Vol. 27 (1987), 39–50.

———. "The Ontology of Musical Works and the Authenticity of Their Performances," *Noûs,* Vol. 25 (1991), 21–41.

Dutton, D., ed. *The Forger's Art.* Berkeley, CA, 1983.

Godlovitch, S. "Authentic Performance," *The Monist,* Vol. 71 (1988), 258–77.

Goodman, N. *Languages of Art,* 2d ed. Indianapolis, 1976.

———. *Of Mind and Other Matters.* Cambridge, MA, 1984. Chap. 4.

Kennick, W. E. "Art and Inauthenticity," *Journal of Aesthetics and Art Criticism,* Vol. 44 (1985), 3–12.

Levinson, J. *Music, Art, and Metaphysics.* Ithaca, NY, 1990.

Levinson, J. "Art, Work of," in *The Dictionary of Art* (London, 1995).

Sagoff, M. "Historical Authenticity," *Erkenntnis,* Vol. 12 (1978), 83–93.

———. "On Restoring and Reproducing Art," *Journal of Philosophy,* Vol. 75 (1978), 453–70.

Sartwell, C. "Aesthetics of the Spurious," *British Journal of Aesthetics,* Vol. 28 (1988), 360–67.

Savile, A. "The Rationale of Restoration," *Journal of Aesthetics and Art Criticism,* Vol. 51 (1993), 463–74.

Thom, P. *For an Audience: A Philosophy of the Performing Arts.* Philadelphia, 1992.

Walton, K. "Categories of Art," *Philosophical Review,* Vol. 79 (1970), 334–67.

Wollheim, R. *Art and Its Objects,* 2d ed. Cambridge, 1980.

JERROLD LEVINSON

B

BAD FAITH. The most common form of inauthenticity in the EXISTENTIALISM [3; S]) of Jean-Paul SARTRE [7; S]), bad faith is paradoxically a lie to oneself. For such self-deception to be possible, the human being must be divided against itself, one level or aspect concealing from the other what it in some sense "knows." The paradox arises from the condition that this operation occurs within the unity of a single consciousness.

The root of Sartrean bad faith is a twofold dividedness of the human being, psychological and ontological. As conscious, humans are prereflectively aware of what they may not reflectively know. Such prereflective awareness or "comprehension," as he will later call it, functions in Sartre's psychology in a manner similar to FREUD's [3; S] UNCONSCIOUS [8], a concept that Sartre notoriously rejected (see EXISTENTIAL PSYCHOANALYSIS [S]). The project of bad faith—to keep oneself in the dark about certain matters—is itself in bad faith since prereflective consciousness "chooses" not to acknowledge on reflection what it is concealing from reflective consciousness.

There can be an entire Weltanschauung of bad faith: the habits, practices, objects, and institutions that one employs to maintain oneself in a state of "perpetual distraction." Sartre's analysis of Second Empire French society in his work on Flaubert is a study in collective bad faith. But the root of the moral responsibility that this term carries lies in the self-translucency of prereflective consciousness: individuals, alone or together, are prereflectively *aware* of more than they reflectively allow themselves to *know*.

The ontological basis of bad faith is the dividedness of the human situation. Every human exists in-situation. Situation is an ambiguous mix of facticity (the given) and transcendence (the surpassing of the given by our projects). Bad faith is our way of fleeing the anguish that this ambiguity causes either by collapsing our transcendence into facticity (as in various forms of DETERMINISM [2]) or by volatilizing our facticity into transcendence (like the dreamer who refuses to acknowledge the facts of his or her life). Though the details of bad faith are as singular as our self-defining choices, its moral significance is the same in each instance. Bad faith is basically flight from our freedom-in-situation.

As Sartre's concept of situation expanded to include and even place a premium on socioeconomic conditions, the relation between bad faith and class struggle became more pronounced. He later argued that good faith, which in *Being and Nothingness* he dismissed as a form of bad faith, was fostered by socioeconomic equality and that scarcity of material goods made bad faith almost inevitable. The anti-Semite was in bad faith, but so too was his or her liberal assimilationist defender; likewise the neocolonialist and the industrial capitalist, both of whom fled their responsibility for subscribing to and sustaining a system that made exploitation of others "necessary."

Only in his posthumously published *Notebooks for an Ethics* does Sartre discuss the nature and possibility of good faith at any length. This presumes a "conversion" in which one chooses to live one's anguished dividedness while fostering via generous cooperation a situation that enables others to do likewise (see AUTHENTICITY [S]).

Bibliography

Beauvoir, S. de. *Pour une morale de l'ambiguité.* Paris, 1947. Translated by B. Frechtman as *The Ethics of Ambiguity.* New York, 1948.

Fingarette, H. *Self-Deception.* London, 1969.

Martin, M. W. *Self-Deception and Morality.* Lawrence, KS, 1986.

Mirvish, A. "Bad Faith, Good Faith, and the Faith of Faith," in R. Aronson and A. van den Hoven, eds., *Sartre Alive* (Detroit, 1991).

Morris, P. "Self-Deception: Sartre's Resolution of the Paradox," in H. J. Silverman and F. A. Elliston, eds., *Jean-Paul Sartre: Contemporary Approaches to His Philosophy* (Pittsburgh, 1980).

Santoni, R. E. *Bad Faith, Good Faith and Authenticity in Sartre's Early Philosophy*. Philadelphia, 1995.

Sartre, J.-P. *Cahiers pour une morale*. Paris, 1983. Translated by D. Pellauer as *Notebooks for an Ethics*. Chicago, 1992.

———. *L'Etre et le néant*. Paris, 1943. Translated by H. E. Barnes as *Being and Nothingness*. New York, 1956.

THOMAS R. FLYNN

BAYESIANISM. Bayesianism holds that in their cognitive interactions with the world rational agents can be represented as having degrees of belief that are regimented according to the PROBABILITY [6; S] calculus. Over time an agent's degrees of belief will change as a result of learning experiences. In the case where such an experience can be characterized as having a propositional content E, it is assumed that the new degrees of belief Pr_{new} are related to the old Pr_{old} by the rule of strict conditionalization: $Pr_{new}(\bullet) = Pr_{old}(\bullet/E)$, where Pr(X/Y) is the conditional probability of X on Y. A more sophisticated rule that allows for uncertain learning has been proposed by Jeffrey (1983).

One justification for regarding the axioms of probability as rationality constraints comes from the demonstration that the failure to conform degrees of belief to the axioms leads to Dutch book: a finite series of bets, each of which the agent regards as fair, with the net result that the agent is guaranteed to lose money. Similarly, diachronic Dutch book arguments have been offered as justifications for the rule of strict conditionalization. Despite their surface appeal, the import of these arguments is controversial (see Maher, 1993).

The subjectivist version of Bayesianism holds that there are no other constraints on rational belief. By such lights the Rev. Thomas Bayes was not himself a pure subjectivist. Bayes's theorem, a result not explicitly stated in Bayes's (1764) original paper, says that Pr(H/E&B) = (Pr(H/B)xPr(E/H&B))/Pr(E/B). It is helpful to think of H as the hypothesis under investigation, B as the background knowledge, and E as the evidence acquired by observation or experiment. The theorem says that the posterior probability Pr(H/E&B) of H is equal to the product of the prior probability Pr(H/B) of H and the posterior likelihood Pr(E/H&B) of E, divided by the prior likelihood Pr(E/B) of E. Bayes thought that the principle of sufficient reason imposes constraints on the prior probability Pr(H/B). This and other attempts to objectify priors run into notorious difficulties. The subjectivists hold that the objectivity of belief is to be gained not by constraints on priors but by the washing out of priors with accumulating evidence. Whether or not mathematical theorems on washing out of priors are applicable to typical cases of scientific inference is a matter of debate (see Earman, 1992).

With conditional probability defined by Pr(X/Y) = Pr(X&Y)/Pr(Y) (which assumes that $Pr(Y) \neq 0$), Bayes's theorem is a triviality. Alternatively, if conditional probability is taken as primitive, the theorem is an easy consequence of the multiplication axiom Pr(X&Y/Z) = Pr(X/Y)xPr(Y/X&Z). Although trivial to prove, Bayes's theorem has profound implications for the confirmation of scientific hypotheses. Suppose, for example, that H and B together entail E, as is assumed in the hypothetico-deductive (HD) method. Then an application of Bayes's theorem shows that if $0 < Pr(H/B) < 1$ (one was not certain about H to begin with) and $0 < Pr(E/B) < 1$ (one was not certain that the observation or experiment would yield E or a result incompatible with E), then $Pr(H/E\&B) > Pr(H/B)$. That is, H is incrementally confirmed by E, showing that there is a kernel of truth to the much criticized HD method.

The same machinery can be used to illuminate Hempel's ravens paradox. *Pace* Hempel, it can be shown that, under appropriate background assumptions, the observation of a nonblack nonraven does incrementally confirm the hypothesis that all ravens are black. But it can also be shown that, given plausible assumptions about the relative sizes of the classes of ravens and of nonblack things, the observation of a black raven confirms the ravens hypothesis more than does the discovery of a white shoe.

The Bayesian approach to confirmation must contend with Glymour's (1980) problem of old evidence, the most virulent form of which occurs when the evidence E was known before the hypothesis H was even formulated. Thus, for example, the anomalous advance of the perihelion of Mercury was known to astronomers long before EINSTEIN [2] formulated his general theory of RELATIVITY [7]. A naive application of Bayes's theorem would seem to imply that no incremental confirmation takes place, despite the fact that physicists uniformly claim that general relativity receives strong confirmation from its explanation of the perihelion advance.

Bibliography

Bayes, T. "An Essay Towards Solving a Problem in the Doctrine of Chances," *Philosophical Transaction of the Royal Society (London)*, Vol. 53 (1764), 370–418.

Earman, J. *Bayes or Bust? A Critical Examination of Bayesian Confirmation Theory*. Cambridge, MA, 1992.

Glymour, C. *Theory and Evidence*. Princeton, NJ, 1980.

Howson, C., and P. Urbach. *Scientific Reasoning: The Bayesian Approach*, 2d ed. La Salle, IL, 1993.

Jeffrey, R. C. *The Logic of Decision*, 2d ed. Chicago, 1983.

Maher, P. *Betting on Theories*. Cambridge, 1993.

JOHN EARMAN

BEAUTY. While it is true that BEAUTY [1] is the central idea of aesthetics from the origins of metaphysics in PLATO [6; S] to the eighteenth century, it is equally true that the attempt to understand the significance of the demotion of the idea of beauty from aesthetic theory in most aesthetic treatises written since the time of Baumgarten in both the rationalist and empiricist traditions has been a dominant concern of reflections on art and nature since that time. By the mid-twentieth century art had followed suit: art no longer takes its kinship with the feeling of beauty as its definitive impulse. Moving into the realm of cultural critique, and taking its task to be more concerned with an exploration of the nature and forms of representation in general than the production of beautiful objects, the divorce of artworks from their traditional marriage to beauty is now a commonplace. However, while artworks no longer seem to define themselves by their relation to beauty, it is now the case that aesthetic theories are finding themselves increasingly interested in asking about the prospects of beauty in the contemporary world. Thus, while HEGEL [3; S] can write that beauty is passé from the standpoint of truth, and NIETZSCHE [5; S] can write that art should no longer be judged according to the category of beauty, Heidegger [3; S], writing in 1935, can suggest that this question of the status of beauty is among the most pressing questions of our age.

Many of the most innovative efforts in the Continental tradition to reopen the question of beauty in contemporary aesthetics have done so by taking reference to the major text of eighteenth-century aesthetics, Kant's *Critique of Judgment* (*see* KANT [4; S]). Thus, one finds Adorno, ARENDT, GADAMER, DERRIDA [S], and Lyotard all taking up Kant's text where the question of aesthetics is divided into natural and artistic beauty, and where any claim about beauty is understood as a subjective judgment of taste laying claim to universality. Recent discussions of aesthetic experience frequently follow the Kantian matrix discussing beauty; namely, it is discussed in its difference from the other form of aesthetic experience found in sublimity, in its different significance as natural and artistic beauty, and in the form of subjectivity that is called into play in the judgment of taste.

(SEE ALSO: *Aesthetics, History of,* and *Aesthetics, Problems of* [1; S])

Bibliography

Arendt, H. *Lectures on Kant's Political Philosophy.* Chicago, 1982.

Derrida, J. *Truth in Painting.* Chicago, 1987.

Gadamer, H.-G. *Truth and Method.* New York, 1975. Part 1.

Harries, K. *The Meaning of Modern Art.* Evanston, IL, 1968.

DENNIS J. SCHMIDT

BEAUVOIR, SIMONE DE, French existentialist feminist, was born in Paris in 1908 and died in 1986, after a prolific career as a philosopher, essayist, novelist, and political activist. Her writings were, by her own accounts, heavily influenced by the philosophy of Jean-Paul SARTRE [7; S], her intellectual companion for half a century, leading some critics to dismiss her as philosophically unoriginal. Even de Beauvoir, in a 1979 interview, said that she did not consider herself to be a philosopher. In her view, however, "a philosopher is someone like SPINOZA [7; S], HEGEL [3; S], or like Sartre, someone who builds a grand system" (quoted in Simons, 1986, p. 168), a definition that would exclude most contemporary professional philosophers. Furthermore, as several recent commentators have argued, de Beauvoir seems to have underestimated her influence on the discipline in general and on Sartre in particular. Although she incorporated Sartrean ideas such as his existentialist conception of freedom in her ethical and political writings, her critiques of Sartre's work-in-progress helped shape his philosophy, which she then extended and transformed in significant ways.

In *The Ethics of Ambiguity,* de Beauvoir attempted to develop an existentialist ethics out of the ontological categories in Sartre's *Being and Nothingness* (*see* EXISTENTIALISM [3; S]). In Sartre's view, there is no God and therefore no God-given human nature. Nor is human nature determined by biological, psychological, economic, cultural, or any other factors. People are "condemned to be free," and in the course of existing and making choices they construct their own natures (which are continually revisable). Human consciousness is such that, although it is being-for-itself (the being of free and transcendent subjects), it vainly tries to turn itself into being-in-itself (the being of objects, things trapped in their immanence). De Beauvoir called this doomed attempt to synthesize the for-itself and the in-itself the "ambiguity" of the human condition, and she argued that it is because of this inability of human beings to "coincide with" themselves that an ethics is both possible and required. She attempted to ground ethics in individual freedom by asserting that "To will oneself free is also to will others free" (73), but her defense of this claim appears to slip both Kantian and Hegelian presuppositions about human nature into a philosophy that denies that there is such a thing.

In *The Ethics of Ambiguity* de Beauvoir moved beyond Sartrean existentialism in acknowledging certain constraints on freedom, including political oppression and early socialization, that Sartre did not recognize until much later. In her memoirs de Beauvoir recalled conversations she had with Sartre in 1940 about his account of freedom as an active transcendence of one's situation. She had maintained that not every situation offered the same scope for freedom: "What sort of transcendence could a woman shut up in a harem achieve?" Sartre had insisted that even such a limiting situation could be lived in a variety of ways, but de Beauvoir was not persuaded. To defend her view, though, she would "have had to abandon the plane of individual, and therefore idealistic, morality" on which they had set themselves (1962, p. 346).

In *The Second Sex* de Beauvoir continued to move away from a purely metaphysical view of freedom in developing an account of how women's oppression limits their freedom. Although in arguing that "One is not born, but rather becomes, a woman" de Beauvoir applied the existentialist tenet that "existence precedes essence" to the situation of women, she was also influenced by Marxist accounts of the material constraints on our freedom to create ourselves. In addition, she described the ways the socialization of girls and the cultural representations of women perpetuate the view of women as other, thereby limiting their potential for transcendence.

Critics of de Beauvoir's feminism have pointed out tensions between her existentialist premises and her account of the relation between embodiment and oppression. Although, according to existentialism, anatomy is not destiny (nor is anything else), de Beauvoir's discussion of female sexuality at times suggests that women's reproductive capacities are less conducive than men's to the achievement of transcendence. De Beauvoir has also been criticized for advocating (in 1949) that women assume men's place in society, although in interviews (in the 1970s and 1980s) she urged a transformation of both men's and women's roles.

Even de Beauvoir's critics, however, acknowledge her enormous impact on contemporary feminism. Her analysis of what has become known as the sex/gender distinction set the stage for all subsequent discussions. In drawing on philosophy, psychology, sociology, biology, history, and literature in *The Second Sex* and other essays she anticipated the interdisciplinary field of women's studies. Her concern with autobiography, with self-revelation as "illuminating the lives of others" (1962, p. 8), prefigured feminism's preoccupation with the personal as political. It also drew on a philosophical tradition as old as Socrates; her relentless scrutiny of herself and others exemplified, to an extent unmatched by any other twentieth-century philosopher, the maxim that "the unexamined life is not worth living."

In her fiction as well as in her essays and memoirs de Beauvoir discussed numerous philosophical themes—for example, freedom, choice, responsibility, and the other—and she also explored the political issues and conflicts of the day, so much so that she has been described as "witness to a century." But she was more than a mere chronicler of events; she was a powerful social critic and an internationally known "public intellectual" whose influence will continue to be felt for a long time.

Selected Works by de Beauvoir

(For a comprehensive bibliography of the publications of de Beauvoir from 1943 to 1977, see Claude Francis and Fernande Gontier, *Les Écrits de Simone de Beauvoir* [Paris, 1979].)

ESSAYS

Pyrrhus et Cinéas. Paris, 1944.

Pour une morale de l'ambiguïté. Paris, 1947. Translated by B. Frechtman as *The Ethics of Ambiguity.* New York, 1948.

Le Deuxième sexe. Paris, 1949. Translated by H. M. Parshley as *The Second Sex.* New York, 1953.

La Vieillesse. Paris, 1970. Translated by P. O'Brien as *The Coming of Age.* New York, 1972.

FICTION

L'Invitée. Paris, 1943. Translated by Y. Moyse and R. Senhouse as *She Came to Stay.* New York, 1954.

Les Mandarins. Paris, 1954. Translated by L. M. Friedman as *The Mandarins.* New York, 1956.

MEMOIRS

Mémoires d'une jeune fille rangée. Paris, 1958. Translated by James Kirkup as *Memoirs of a Dutiful Daughter.* New York, 1959.

La Force de l'âge. Paris, 1960. Translated by P. Green as *The Prime of Life.* New York, 1962.

La Force des choses. Paris, 1963. Translated by R. Howard as *Force of Circumstance.* New York, 1965.

Tout compte fait. Paris, 1972. Translated by P. O'Brien as *All Said and Done.* New York, 1974.

Selected Works on de Beauvoir

Brosman, C. S. *Simone de Beauvoir Revisited.* Boston, 1991.

Dietz, M. G. "Introduction: Debating Simone de Beauvoir," *Signs,* Vol. 18 (1992), 74–88.

Gatens, M. "Woman as Other," in *Feminism and Philosophy* (Cambridge, 1991).

Le Doeuff, M. "Simone de Beauvoir and Existentialism," translated from the French by C. Gordon, *Feminist Studies,* Vol. 6 (1980), 277–89.

Mackenzie, C. "Simone de Beauvoir: Philosophy and/or the Female Body," in C. Pateman and E. Gross, eds., *Feminist Challenges: Social and Political Theory* (Boston, 1986).

McCall, D. K. "Simone de Beauvoir, *The Second Sex,* and Jean-Paul Sartre," *Signs,* Vol. 5 (1979), 209–23.

Simons, M. A. "Beauvoir and Sartre: The Philosophical Relationship," in H. V. Wenzel, ed., *Simone de Beauvoir: Witness to a Century,* special volume of *Yale French Studies,* No. 72 (1986), 165–79.

Tong, R. "Existentialist Feminism," in *Feminist Thought* (Boulder, CO, 1989).

Whitmarsh, A. *Simone de Beauvoir and the Limits of Commitment.* Cambridge, 1981.

SUSAN J. BRISON

BEING-PROCESS. This term has been used by English-language commentators and translators to call attention to deeper currents in the later thought of HEIDEGGER [3; S] concerning Being.

First of all, it warns us against substantivizing. We err if we suppose Being to be an object, a thing, or a structure rather than an event or process. English-language writers have sometimes suggested this point by inserting a hyphen before the suffix: Be-ing. Heidegger sometimes made a similar point in German by substituting for the infinitive verb *sein* the much less common infinitive *wesen.* Spelled with a capital W, this is a noun, *das Wesen,* which we translate "essence." Spelled with a lowercase w, it signifies the event or process, Be-ing. Heidegger connected the verb *wesen* to the verb *waehren,* to last or endure, thus hearing in the verb the echo of time. In *Beiträge zur Philosophie,* published many years after Heidegger's death, he resorted to a more radical measure still, writing the impossible word *die Wesung,* from which all traces of the substantive have been erased.

In the second place this term signifies the separation of Be-ing from beings: the entities that have being, the things that are. In his lectures in the 1920s Heidegger called this the ontological difference, inviting us thereby not only to pay heed to beings but to their Being, the Being-process so often neglected by science and philosophy. In his later period he found still further complexities that required new terms. Thinking the ontological difference, we may still apprehend Being as the ground for beings and thereby perpetuate the traditional pathway of thinking that approaches Being only by way of beings. Failure to release Being from the grounding of beings perpetuates a reverse movement that grounds Being in its very grounding function, failing to ask about Being in its own truth. For this theme Heidegger came to use an archaic spelling favored by Friedrich HÖLDERLIN [4]—*das Seyn*—and this too has been rendered Being-process in English. It means the absolute event of *Seyn* and also the interplay of that event with the Being of beings. For *das Seyn* is not utterly unknown to humanity or utterly abstracted from the Being of beings; it is what has ordained different destinies for Being in different epochs.

The interplay of *Seyn* with the Being of beings is at work in the phenomenon of presence, and this too has been signified by the term Being-process. From his earliest publications to his latest, Heidegger defended the interpretation that in Greek and other languages "being present" was the primary sense of all the verbs for "be." The things that are are present: present to the mind, to themselves, to God, and their very being affords them unconcealment as well as concealment. From this, however, Heidegger himself infers (in *On Time and Being*) that Being is *not* the presence that they enjoy (*parousia, die Anwesenheit*) but rather the event of coming-into-presence (*das Anwesen*), which first accounts for every case of presence. Indeed, he infers further that Being is precisely the letting them come into presence: *das Anwesen-lassen.* This is the Being-process: letting beings be. It is interwoven at the profoundest level with time and history, for it is only in the reaching over of future and past time into each other that *Anwesen-lassen* occurs. Every epoch is destined to admit some variant of presence, excluding others—the *Geschick* that marks the tie of Being to time. Heidegger traces all our awareness, knowledge, and truth to the Being-process, to the unconcealment that is granted by *Anwesen-lassen.*

Bibliography

Heidegger, M. *Beitraege zur Philosophie [Vom Ereignis] (1936–1938)*, edited by F. W. von Herrmann. Frankfurt, 1989.

———. *Zur Sache des Denkens.* Tübingen, 1969. Translated by J. Stambaugh as *On Time and Being.* New York, 1972.

Richardson, W. J. *Heidegger: Through Phenomenology to Thought.* The Hague, 1963.

GRAEME NICHOLSON

BEITRÄGE ZUR PHILOSOPHIE (VOM EREIGNIS). Written between 1936 and 1938 and published in 1989, this text presents Martin HEIDEGGER's [3; S] first major work after *Being and Time.* This work articulates the main directives for thinking Being's historical/epochal unfoldings. Considering its language and structure, it is unlike any other work of Heidegger's. Moreover, it completely abandons the familiar styles of philosophical writing. Consisting of 281 consecutively numbered sections, *Beiträge* opens with a "Preview," goes through six parts called "joinings"/*Fügungen,* and ends with a final part entitled "Seyn."

The language of *Beiträge* bespeaks a pristine experience of being and shapes an extraordinary philosophical utterance. The structure of this work requires that it have both a "public" title, *Beiträge zur Philosophie* (Contributions to Philosophy), and a "more appropriate heading," *Vom Ereignis* (On Appropriating Event).

Each of the six parts stands for itself, but only so that the Appropriating Event that joins them becomes more penetratingly manifest. *Ereignis* unfolds from the depth of what Western metaphysics, in its first historical/epochal beginning, calls BEING [1]. This beginning is distinguished by the breakthrough of the difference between Being and beings. *Beiträge* aims at a transition to "another" beginning that may arrive in the opening made by that breakthrough.

Philosophical thinking in each beginning is grounded in an attunement: in the first beginning in wonder, and in "another" beginning in reservedness (*Verhaltenheit*). This attunement holds what is to arrive in reserve for thinking. Thus reserved and preserved, arrival of "another" beginning resounds/echoes in the first beginning. However, this echo is not the same as the arrival of "another" beginning in the first beginning.

Elaboration of this "echo" is the task of the first part, called "Echo." The task of the second part is to show "The Inter-Play," the playing between the first historical/epochal unfolding of Being and the other possible future beginning. This interplay occurs in accord with the "echo" of *Ereignis.* The task of the third part is to indicate

"The Leap" that claims thinking and may lead it to "another" beginning. The place where this leap occurs is *Dasein.* This is the theme of the fourth part, which is called "Founding."

Dasein is to be "founded" as a temporal-spatial jointure wherein the historical/epochal throw (*Wurf*) of Being is received and projected. The founding of Dasein and the overcoming of the notion of the human being as rational animal are one and the same event. The fifth part names such "founders" "The Future Ones," because they belong to "another" beginning. The sixth part is called "The Last God." *Beiträge* speaks of the "passage" of the last God. The word "passage" is intended to set this God apart from the metaphysical agent of *creatio ex nihilo,* from *summum bonum, ens realissimum, causa sui,* and *deus sive natura.* The passage of the last God is to be thought as a historical/epochal moment of both unconcealment and withdrawal.

Central to a discussion of *Beiträge,* however brief, are at least three terms: *Ereignis, Wesen,* and *Wesung.*

EREIGNIS

As future Dasein unfolds, it reveals the coming together in *Ereignis* of the ensuing manifestness of Being. Such coming together is manifest as the future Dasein hears the "echo" of Being; such coming together is at play in the playing within the first historical unfolding of Being; such coming together invites thinking to undertake the leap from the metaphysical thinking of Being to this thinking's nonmetaphysical ground; finally, this coming together transforms the rational animal and opens the way for passage of the last God.

WESEN

With this word, *Beiträge* indicates the abiding, enduring, and unfolding of beings in the first as well as in "another" beginning. This word does not mean *essence* of beings, because *Beiträge* distinguishes the ontological difference between beings in the first and in "another" beginning: in the domain of the first beginning beings are abandoned by Being and their relation to Being is forgotten so that they become characterizable by fixed essences. Hence, the epochs of the first beginning are the epochs of abandonment and oblivion of Being. By contrast, in "another" beginning, beings abide, endure, and unfold as sheltered in Being.

WESUNG

This word names Being's abiding and unfolding as *Ereignis:* it indicates Dasein's being appropriated by Being while receiving its "throw" and "projecting" it.

(SEE ALSO: *Being-Process; Language and Heidegger; Poetizing and Thinking;* and *Fourfold, the* [S])

Bibliography

PRIMARY SOURCE

Heidegger, M. *Beiträge zur Philosophie (Vom Ereignis).* Frankfurt, 1989.

SECONDARY SOURCES

Emad, P. "The Echo of Being in *Beiträge zur Philosophie*—Der Anklang: Directives for Its Interpretation," *Heidegger Studies,* Vol. 7 (1991), 15–35.

Fédier, F. "Traduire les *Beiträge zur Philosophie (Vom Ereignis),*" *Heidegger Studies,* Vol. 9 (1993), 15–33.

Gander, H.-H. "Grund- und Leitstimmungen in Heideggers *Beiträge zur Philosophie,*" *Heidegger Studies,* Vol. 10 (1994), 15–31.

Herrmann, F. W. von. *Wege ins Ereignis: zu Heideggers "Beiträge zur Philosophie."* Frankfurt, 1994.

Kovacs, G. "The Leap *(Der Sprung)* for Being in Heidegger's *Beiträge zur Philosophie (Vom Ereignis),*" *Man and World,* Vol. 25 (1992), 39–59.

Maly, K. "Soundings of *Beiträge zur Philosophie (Vom Ereignis),*" *Research in Phenomenology,* Vol. 21 (1991), 169–83.

Richardson, W. J. "Dasein and the Ground of Negativity: A Note on the Fourth Movement of the *Beiträge*-Symphony," *Heidegger Studies,* Vol. 9 (1993), 35–52.

Stenstad, G. "The Last God: A Reading," *Research in Phenomenology,* Vol. 24 (1994), 172–84.

PARVIS EMAD

BELIEF ATTRIBUTIONS. Belief attributions are uses of sentences of the form *N* believes that *s* (where *N* is a noun phrase, *s* a sentence). Their semantic and logical properties have been debated under the assumption that an account of "believes" will carry over to other propositional attitudes such as desire, knowledge, and fear. Most of the debate focuses on two issues: does "believe" pick out a relation, and how do so-called *de re* and *de dicto* attributions differ?

IS "BELIEVES" RELATIONAL?

The obvious hypothesis is that in

(1) Maggie believes that Twain lives.

"believes" has the semantic status of a transitive verb, picking out a relation between a believer and something (a proposition) provided by the verb's complement,

(2) that Twain lives.

Grammatical evidence suggests this: "believes" can be followed by names and demonstratives ("I believe Church's thesis," "she believes that") as well as expressions that behave like (nominal) variables ("whenever the Pope says something I believe it").

Gottlob FREGE [3; S] and Bertrand RUSSELL [7], whose work inspires most subsequent debate about belief attribution, agreed on the obvious hypothesis. Frege held that expressions embedded within "believes that" shift their reference to a way of thinking, or sense, of what they refer to unembedded. Russell held that no such semantic shift occurs; the proposition that *s* is determined by what *s*'s parts pick out when used unembedded.

Since "Twain" and "Clemens" refer to the same author, the Russellian approach seems committed to the identity of the propositions, that Twain lives and that Clemens does, and thus to (1)'s implying

(3) Maggie believes that Clemens lives.

Russell would avoid this by saying that "Twain" and "Clemens" typically function as truncated definite descriptions. This last suggestion is widely thought to have been discredited by Saul KRIPKE ([S]; see Kripke, 1979).

One problem Fregean views face is that sense is idiosyncratic: different people associate with a name different ways of thinking of the referent. It is implausible that when I utter (1) I speak truly only if Maggie thinks of Twain as do I. But if (2) in (1) named Maggie's sense for "Twain lives," the argument "Maggie believes that Twain lives; Seth believes what Maggie does; so Seth believes that Twain lives" would be invalid.

Contemporary Russellians such as Nathan Salmon and Scott Soames hold that to believe a proposition involves grasping or representing it and its constituents; thus, belief is a three-place relation among a believer, a Russellian content, and a representation. Salmon and Soames nonetheless hold that (1) tells us only that Maggie believes ("under some representation") the Russellian proposition that Twain lives; the appearance that (1) and (3) may disagree in truth value results from mistaking a conversational or pragmatic implicature, about the representation under which a belief is held, for part of what a belief attribution, strictly speaking, says.

John Perry and Mark Crimmins have suggested that a belief attribution involves implicit reference to the Russellian's representations or modes of grasping: the complement of "believes" determines a Russellian proposition, but the verb has an "implicit argument place" for representations. A use of (1) makes a claim along the lines of *Maggie believes the Russellian proposition that Twain lives under representation r,* with the representation referred to differing across occasions of use. A problem with this view is that it renders the argument mentioned two paragraphs above invalid.

Some think belief attributions implicitly quotational. The simplest version of such a view sees *that s* as a quotation name of *s,* "believes" naming a relation to sentence types. To this it may be objected that different uses of "Seth thinks I am sad" may have different truth values. Another view sees a "that" clause as picking out a fusion of linguistic items with their interpretations—for example, the result of combining a sentence with the semantic values of its expressions.

Mark Richard's version of this view has *that s* pick out a fusion of the sentence *s* and its Russellian content. In belief attribution, such fusions are offered as "translations" of the believer's thoughts, where a thought is the result of combining a representation that realizes a belief with its Russellian content: (1) is true if the "that" clause provides a translation of a thought of Maggie's. Standards of translation shift from context to context: "Twain" may represent a representation of Maggie's in some but not all contexts. Thus, on this view, the truth of (1) does not demand that of (3).

Donald DAVIDSON [S] denies that (2) is a semantically significant part of (1). "Believes" is a predicate whose second argument is the demonstrative "that"; its referent is the ensuing utterance of "Twain lives." The overall force of (1) is roughly some belief state of Maggie's agrees in content with that utterance. (Davidson made such a proposal for "says" but clearly intended to generalize.) Yet more radical views deny that "believes" is a predicate. Arthur N. PRIOR [S] took "believes" to combine with a name and sentence to form a more complex sentence; W. V. O. QUINE [7; S] has entertained the idea that "believes that Twain lives" is a predicate without semantically significant structure. A problem for Quine is to explain how infinitely many (semantically unstructured) belief predicates acquire their meanings; Prior thought little useful could be said on such issues.

DE RE AND *DE DICTO*

There seem to be two ways of interpreting sentences like

(4) Sam believes that Melinda's husband is unmarried.

Sam believes that some Frenchman is not French.

One interpretation attributes to Sam necessarily false beliefs; the other, suggested by

(4′) Of Melinda's husband, Sam believes he is unmarried.

Of some Frenchman, Sam believes he is not French.

does not. Note that (4′) ascribes to Sam beliefs in some sense about particular individuals, while this is not true of the interpretation of (4).

The interpretations seem to correspond to different scopes that may be assigned to the quantifier phrases "Melinda's husband" and "some Frenchman." In a *de re* attribution, an expression functioning as a variable within the scope of "believes" is bound by a quantifier outside its scope (and the scopes of other verbs of propositional attitudes). Interpreting the sentences in (4) as in (4′) is *de re* attribution: "he" and "she" are bound to "Melinda's husband" and "some women," which are not in the scope of "believes." An attribution that is not *de re* is *de dicto.* If we accept a relational account of "believes," we will say that a *de dicto* interpretation of *N* believes that *s* attributes to *N* a belief in the proposition expressed by *s.* (An attribution might also count as *de re* if it has a term anaphoric on a name outside of the attribution, as in the natural understanding of

(5) Twain was an author, but Seth believes that he was president.)

Not everyone would characterize the *de re–de dicto* distinction as above. Quine held that it is impossible for a quantifier to bind a variable that occurs opaquely—that is, inside a construction, like "believes," which causes failures to substitutivity. If Quine were correct, some other account of the two understandings of (4) is needed. (Quine himself suggested that "believes" is ambiguous.) Quine's view is not widely shared. (See Kaplan, 1986, for discussion.)

The relations between *de re* and *de dicto* attributions are of interest in good part because *de re* attributions are anomalous on some views. A *de re* attribution identifies a belief in terms of the objects it is about, not in terms of how those objects are conceptualized. For a Russellian this is the norm: all there is to belief attribution is identifying the state of affairs believed to obtain. For a Fregean, (4′) is at best an aberration, lacking information about sense, which belief attribution is supposed to convey. *De re* belief attributions provide a focus for the debates among Russellians, Fregeans, and others.

(SEE ALSO: *Epistemology* [S])

Bibliography

Crimmins, M. *Talk about Beliefs.* Cambridge, MA, 1992.

Davidson, D. "On Saying That," in *Essays on Truth and Interpretation* (Oxford, 1984).

Frege, G. "Uber Sinn und Bedeutung," *Zeitschrift fur Philosophie and Philosophische Kritik,* Vol. 100 (1892), 25–50. Translated by P. Geach and M. Black as "On Sense and Reference," in Geach and Black, eds., *Translations from the Philosophical Writings of Gottlob Frege* (Cambridge, 1952).

Higginbotham, J. "Belief and Logical Form," *Mind and Language,* Vol. 6 (1991), 344–69.

Kaplan, D. "Quantifying In," in D. Davidson and G. Harman, eds., *Words and Objections* (Dordrecht, 1969).

———. "Opacity," in L. Hahn and P. Schlipp, eds., *The Philosophy of W. V. Quine* (La Salle, IL, 1986).

Kripke, S. "A Puzzle about Belief," in A. Margalit, ed., *Meaning and Use* (Dordrecht, 1979). Also in Salmon and Soames, 1988.

Perry, J. and M. Crimmins. "The Prince and the Phone Booth," *Journal of Philosophy,* Vol. 86 (1989), 685–711.

Prior, A. N. *Objects of Thought.* Oxford, 1971.

Quine, W. V. "Quantifiers and Propositional Attitudes," *Journal of Philosophy,* Vol. 53 (1956), 177–87.

———. *Word and Object.* Cambridge, MA, 1960.

Richard, M. *Propositional Attitudes.* Cambridge, 1990.

Salmon, N. *Frege's Puzzle.* Cambridge, MA, 1986.

Salmon, N., and S. Soames, eds. *Propositions and Attitudes.* Oxford, 1988.

MARK RICHARD

BERKELEY, GEORGE, believed that there are only minds and ideas. The existence of minds (or spirits or souls), BERKELEY [1] tells us, consists in perceiving, whereas the existence of ideas (including sensations) consists in being perceived. Minds, which are the only substances, are active, and ideas are passive. The existence of physical objects consists in their being perceived: this is so because such objects consist of qualities, and qualities are sensations. Thus, Berkeley endorses the idealist view that the physical world is kept in existence by being perceived and therefore depends upon the mind. Consequently, there is no need for material substance. Indeed, the very concept of material substance is incoherent.

The ideas or sensations that constitute the physical world are given to us by God. Since God is their source we are in intimate contact with God, and we ought therefore always to be assured of God's existence.

That the foregoing claims are central to Berkeley's philosophy is uncontroversial. However, disagreement persists about Berkeley's views in many areas, including the following.

ABSTRACTION AND IMMATERIALISM

Berkeley devotes most of the introduction to *A Treatise concerning the Principles of Human Knowledge,* Part 1, to a refutation of the Lockean belief in abstract ideas (see LOCKE [4; S]). He seems to understand the case against abstraction to be central to his case for thinking that physical objects may not exist apart from PERCEPTION [6; S]. But how is the case against abstraction supposed to contribute to the case against mind-independent physical objects?

One strand in his thinking may be that it is wrong to believe things that are incapable of existing apart to exist apart. Physical objects are incapable of existing apart from perception. Hence, it is wrong to believe them to do so. That is, we cannot conceive of, or have an idea of, *a* and *b* as existing apart if *a* and *b* are incapable of existing apart; and since there cannot be existence apart from perception, we are unable to conceive of existence without perception. On this reading the case against abstracting existence from perception requires that it has already been shown that there cannot be existence apart from perception; and the case against abstraction contributes nothing to the defense of Berkeley's philosophy.

Perhaps the idea is that we are incapable of conceiving of sensible things, which are nothing but the sensible ideas we perceive, as existing apart from perception: thus, just as pain is felt pain, so taste is perceived taste, color is perceived color, shape is observed shape, and so forth. Hence, it is impossible for us to believe that physical things exist apart from perception. However, this is not exactly an argument against mind-independent existence. It is closer to being an argument against believing in mind-independent existence; but it really amounts merely to an assertion that we are incapable of believing in this sort of existence.

On this reading the case against abstract ideas is not a premise in an argument against mind-independent existence. At most it is a diagnosis or illumination of the sort of error that is involved in believing that there are unperceived objects, or at least of the sort of error involved in thinking that one is believing in mind-independent existence, since we are told that it is impossible to so believe. Indeed, it seems that the case against abstraction is irrelevant to, and unnecessary for, this line of thought. For if the idea of unperceived existence is contradictory, as Berkeley insists, then even if there were abstract ideas we would still be incapable of conceiving of existence apart from perception, just as we would still be incapable of conceiving of married bachelors or round squares or any other manifestly contradictory concepts even if there were abstract ideas. A further difficulty for this line of thought is that Berkeley actually states that the belief in mind-independent existence is prevalent.

MINDS AND BODIES

How did Berkeley conceive of the relationship between the mind and the body? A human body, like any other physical object, is—or at least is in part—a set of ideas. Are the ideas that constitute, or partly constitute, physical objects bestowed on finite minds by God? If so, when a human arm is moved, one set of ideas produced by God is followed by another such set. Berkeley says that we move our own limbs and that on this issue he differs from MALEBRANCHE [5]. But how can he account for our moving our limbs? (And if he is unable to account for our doing so, on what basis does he think that one finite mind may reasonably conclude that there are other such minds?) Are we able to produce some sensations? Or are we "active beings" who are actually inactive in the world: is the claim that we are able to move our limbs to be reduced to the view that certain sequences of ideas that we produce serve as the occasion for God to grant us certain sensations? Or is it to be reduced to the view that certain sensations (in particular those that constitute, or partially constitute, states of affairs or events that we wish to obtain or occur) can be thought of as being produced by us?

IDEAS AND THE PERCEPTION OF IDEAS

How did Berkeley conceive of the relationship between ideas and their perception? Are there two things, an object and an act, which stand in a certain relationship to each other? (Are there at any rate an object and a process in the mind to be related? For Berkeley says that in sense perception the mind is passive, which incidentally is a view that needs to be reconciled with his idea of the mind as an active, indivisible entity.) Berkeley says that the existence of an idea is identical with its being perceived. His model for the relation between an idea and its perception is the relation between a pain and its perception. That relation is one of numerical identity. If an idea is identical with its being perceived, and if the perception of an idea is a private event in the mental life of an individual, it follows that an idea is something private to the mind in which it occurs.

On the other hand it is natural to think of the qualities of objects, such as the redness of an apple, as something public that different people can perceive. Berkeley would want to preserve this commonsense belief. Yet if qualities are ideas, and an idea is identical with its being perceived, how can different perceivers perceive the same quality?

Perhaps Berkeley should say that different people may perceive numerically the same quality even though they may not perceive numerically the same idea, thereby abandoning his identification of ideas and qualities. Or perhaps he should abandon the view that qualities are public and argue that physical objects are public even though they consist of qualities that are private to the mind that has the ideas with which they are identical.

THE EXISTENCE OF GOD

Berkeley thought that we can know that God exists because our sensations come to us from an external source. He thought too that since some physical objects continue to exist while unperceived by us, there must be some other mind that perceives them while we do not perceive them; and Berkeley also presents this line of thought as the basis for a case for God's existence. Further, he thought that since the ideas we perceive have an external source, they (or their archetypes) exist apart from us in some other mind that exhibits them to us. Does Berkeley intend to offer three distinct arguments (one that appeals to the source of our ideas, a second that appeals to the continued existence of unperceived objects, and a third that appeals to the independent existence of our ideas or their archetypes), or are these best understood as three strands in a single argument? However Berkeley may have conceived of the connections among these considerations, a case can be made for regarding the appeal to continuity as subsidiary to the appeal to the independent existence of our ideas or their archetypes. For if at all times at which they exist, including times at which we perceive them and times at which we do not perceive them, the objects we perceive by sense exist in another mind, by whom they are exhibited to us, then the fact that they exist when we do not perceive them seems fairly incidental. That is, their existence at times when we are not perceiving them is just a function of the fact that they have an independent existence, an existence that they have both while we perceive them and at times at which we do not perceive them but during which they continue to exist. Yet another argument for God's existence derives from Berkeley's thought that visual sensations are a language in that, for example, they tell us what other sensations we may receive and in that our sensations are often combined in complex patterns. The use of a language requires a mind.

IMMEDIATE PERCEPTION OF OBJECTS

Are physical objects the immediate objects of sense perception, or do we perceive them indirectly by directly perceiving various sensations such as sensations of light, colors, sounds, and odors? Berkeley frequently says that, strictly speaking, nothing is seen but light and colors, nothing is heard but sounds, nothing tasted but tastes, and so on for the other sensory modes. However, if objects consist, or even partly consist, of ideas of sense, perhaps we may perceive them immediately by perceiving some of the ideas that constitute them. It would not be reasonable to object that since, on this view, we immediately perceive them only in part, we do not immediately perceive them: this would be to rule out the direct perception of objects on any conception of an object. Berkeley accepts that there are ideas that are among the constituents of objects that are only suggested to us by the ideas we perceive directly. Thus, the shape and figure of a coach are suggested to us by the sound of the coach. But why think of the object as a whole as being mediately perceived because some of the ideas that are among its components are mediately perceived? Why not think of the object as immediately perceived because ideas that are among its components are immediately perceived?

IDEAS AND OBJECTS

Berkeley sometimes seems to say that physical objects are just collections of sensations. But he also seems to explain the continued existence of objects that are not currently perceived by us by appealing to God's perceptions and to God's volitions. In addition, as noted above, he says that the ideas we perceive exist apart from our minds at all times at which they exist. But if objects can exist *qua* divine ideas or volitions, or if they have any sort of existence independent of our perception, then they are not just collections of sensations. They are not just families of ideas produced in us by God. Further, God can perceive a great deal more than we can: God can perceive objects from all angles at once and can perceive the interiors of physical objects whose surface alone we can see. It seems that if objects consist of our ideas along with God's ideas, our ideas are in danger of being second-class counterparts of God's. But even if Berkeley were to accept that our ideas are second-class counterparts of God's, he need not also accept that the real objects are in God's mind; and he need not be committed to a representative theory of perception.

Bibliography

ABSTRACTION AND IMMATERIALISM

Bolton, M. B. "Berkeley's Objection to Abstract Ideas and Unconceived Objects," in E. Sosa, ed., *Essays on the Philosophy of George Berkeley* (Dordrecht, 1987).

Pappas, G. S. "Abstract Ideas and the Esse Is Percipi Thesis," in D. Berman, ed., *George Berkeley: Essays and Replies* (Dublin, 1986).

MINDS AND BODIES

Taylor, C. C. W. "Action and Inaction in Berkeley," in J. Foster and H. Robinson, eds., *Essays on Berkeley: A Tercentennial Celebration* (Oxford, 1985).

Tipton, I. *Berkeley*. London, 1974.

IDEAS AND THE PERCEPTION OF IDEAS

McCracken, C. J. "Berkeley on the Relation of Ideas to the Mind," in P. D. Cummins and G. Zoeller, eds., *Minds, Ideas, and Objects: Essays on the Theory of Representation in Modern Philosophy* (Atascadero, CA, 1992).

Pitcher, G. *Berkeley*. London, 1977.

THE EXISTENCE OF GOD

Ayers, M. R. "Divine Ideas and Berkeley's Proofs of God's Existence," in E. Sosa, ed., *Essays on the Philosophy of George Berkeley* (Dordrecht, 1987).

Kline, A. D. "Berkeley's Divine Language Argument," in E. Sosa, ed., *Essays on the Philosophy of George Berkeley* (Dordrecht, 1987).

IMMEDIATE PERCEPTION OF OBJECTS

Pappas, G. S. "Berkeley and Immediate Perception," in E. Sosa, ed., *Essays on the Philosophy of George Berkeley* (Dordrecht, 1987).

Pitcher, G. *Berkeley*. London, 1977.

IDEAS AND OBJECTS

Foster, J. "Berkeley on the Physical World," in J. Foster and H. Robinson, eds., *Essays on Berkeley: A Tercentennial Celebration* (Oxford, 1985).

McKim, R. "Berkeley on Perceiving the Same Thing," in P. D. Cummins and G. Zoeller, eds., *Minds, Ideas, and Objects: Essays on the Theory of Representation in Modern Philosophy* (Atascadero, CA, 1992).

OTHER WORKS

Atherton, M. *Berkeley's Revolution in Vision*. Ithaca, NY, 1990.

Berkeley, G. *A Treatise concerning the Principles of Human Knowledge,* edited by C. M. Turbayne. Indianapolis, 1970. With critical essays.

Berman, D. *George Berkeley: Idealism and the Man*. Oxford, 1994.

Dancy, J. *Berkeley: An Introduction*. Oxford, 1987.

Grayling, A. C. *Berkeley: The Central Arguments*. La Salle, IL, 1986.

Jesseph, D. *Berkeley's Philosophy of Mathematics*. Chicago, 1993.

Muehlmann, R. *Berkeley's Ontology*. Indianapolis, 1992.

Winkler, K. *Berkeley: An Interpretation*. Oxford, 1989.

Robert McKim

BIOMEDICAL ETHICS. Biomedical ethics, as it is currently known, began in the mid-1960s, around the time of the publication of the *Encyclopedia of Philosophy*. Some date the beginning from the first kidney dialysis unit (1962, in Seattle). Many more people were in need of dialysis than the unit could accommodate; so a committee of community and medical representatives decided who among their kidney-impaired fellow citizens would receive the life-saving procedure. In an important sense this launched the era of biomedical ethics, the thrust of which was to open up moral issues in medicine to public scrutiny. In 1971 the term bioethics was coined, whose connotation was inclusive of but broader than medical ethics (Reich, 1995). "Bioethics" encompassed moral concerns in and about science, scientific research, the treatment of animals, and environmental matters, though it had its beginnings in the concerns of medicine and medical research. Solidifying these moral concerns as a public endeavor were the appointment of national commissions that were constituted to deliberate, analyze, and recommend with respect to selected issues. The terminology gradually shifted from medical ethics to bioethics. As the breadth of bioethics unfolded, "biomedical ethics" was used to distinguish that portion of bioethics devoted to medically related concerns. Eventually, "bioethics" came to be used interchangeably with "biomedical ethics" in denoting this enlarged field of medical ethics. To add to the confusion, "bioethics" and "APPLIED ETHICS" [S] are often used interchangeably, though applied ethics is the more inclusive term.

Medical ethics is, of course, a subject probably as old as medicine itself. Nevertheless, the resurgent interest generated in the 1960s was sufficiently strong and different enough to be considered a new era. A confluence of societal forces and events contributed to this rebirth. There was a strong emphasis on individual rights (the civil rights movement), as well as an increasing distrust of authority and institutions. The public no longer showed unquestioning deference to the experts in fields such as medicine, engineering, education, law, and government. Value assumptions were uncovered and questioned. Consumerism was on the rise. Many new medical technologies and therapies were becoming available and more were promised by the "new biology." Inasmuch as there was no clear societal consensus on values, there was considerable need for public discussion of these issues. Though biomedical ethics was the core of this minirevolution, other disciplinary ethics were taking shape—for example, BUSINESS ETHICS, ENGINEERING ETHICS, and ENVIRONMENTAL ETHICS [S].

It is hard to overstate the societywide impact of biomedical ethics. Many articles began to appear, especially in medical journals; new journals devoted to such matters were established; courses in biomedical ethics and then in bioethics at the undergraduate level were developed at most colleges and universities (usually within the religion or the philosophy department); week-long summer workshops in bioethics and professional ethics were attended by persons (totaling thousands) from a wide variety of professional backgrounds. Public discourse of moral issues and scholarly investigation of those issues were well launched by the 1980s.

Many disciplines were involved in the emergence of biomedical ethics. The fields of medicine, religion, journalism, law, social sciences, history, nursing, and others, as well as philosophy, were active in giving shape and substance to this new field. Two important organizations in this development were the Society of Health and Human Values and the Hastings Center. The former, a successor organization to a group called Ministers in Medical Education (mid-1950s), was originally affiliated with the Association of American Medical Colleges, and its members were mostly medical educators. Though continuing to be closely related to the education of health professionals, its membership has become a diverse group from such fields as sociology, nursing, religion, philosophy, law, medicine, literature, and history. The Hastings Center (originally more descriptively named the Institute of Society, Ethics, and the Life Sciences), founded in 1969, similarly had a diverse membership with a core of elected Fellows, most of whom were in the fields of religion, law, medicine, and philosophy. As increasing numbers engaged in clinical ethical consultations, there was a felt need to understand, develop, and assess the emerging phenomenon of bioethical consultation. To meet that need the Society for Bioethics Consultation was created in 1986–87. The American Association of Bioethics, a professional society for bioethics composed primarily of philosophers and lawyers, was organized in 1992–93. The AAB sought to ensure the soundness and continuation of bioethics as an academic discipline, to provide a forum for exchange of ideas and information, and to meet a perceived need for an official organization to engage the issues of bioethics at the national and international level, particularly on matters of policy.

PHILOSOPHY AND BIOMEDICAL ETHICS

Many disciplines have contributed to and continue to contribute to the development of biomedical ethics—religion, law, medicine, journalism, social sciences, literature. This entry, however, will focus only on philosophy's involvement. There has been a complicated, reciprocal relationship between philosophy and biomedical ethics. Each has been changed somewhat by the encounter (Clouser, 1989).

Though traditionally ethics has been a major field within philosophy, during roughly the first half of the twentieth century philosophical ethics focused primarily on highly theoretical and metaethical matters. Nevertheless, it may well have been that theoretical orientation that recommended philosophy as a participant in the public moral discourse of biomedical ethical issues, theories, and methods. Neither a professional medical ethic nor a sectarian, religious ethic seemed appropriate as a framework for the public discussion of medically related moral issues. Rather, it was philosophical ethics that appeared to provide the neutrality necessary to nurture the public discussion of practical moral issues in a pluralistic society (Jonsen, 1995).

There is no canonical view of philosophy's involvement. If such a view emerges at all, it will happen only after some histories of this period have been written and debated. Philosophy as a whole did not embrace the new challenge of biomedical ethics, but there were individual philosophers who were drawn to the task. The sheer practicality of the enterprise seemed antithetical to the tradition of philosophy; on the other hand, there were many intriguing issues and dilemmas that called for philosophy's traditional skills of conceptual analysis. For many philosophers it seemed out of character for philosophers to ponder practical moral decision making in medical clinics and hospitals.

SOME ISSUES

Philosophy's engagement with biomedical ethics took many forms. Primarily it was a matter of individuals trained in philosophy and serving in a variety of different capacities: as teachers of undergraduates; as teachers in medical, nursing, and other healthcare professional schools; as staff members of organizations dealing with bioethics issues, including some appropriate government commissions; as ethics consultants on hospital staffs or in private practice; as providers of educational opportunities in bioethics in venues such as workshops, continuing education, and conferences; as researchers on special projects involving bioethical issues. There was no formal engagement and no party line coming from philosophy as such. As is typical of philosophy and philosophers, the philosophical input into bioethics was individualistic.

Yet there was a common core of moral issues that, at least in the beginning, were addressed by biomedical ethics and were of particular interest to philosophers. What follows is not a substantive discussion of the issues but a summary revealing those structures of particular interest to philosophers.

From the beginning ABORTION [S] has been of interest to philosophers. Even after the 1973 *Roe v. Wade* Supreme Court decision, which diminished the urgency of discussion by establishing legal guidelines for practice, the concept of abortion still had many component issues that were natural for philosophy. When does life begin? What constitutes personhood? Does humanity have an essence? Does that essence "enter" at some point in embryonic development? Is there a difference between a potential being and a possible being? Under what circumstances can a right to one's own body justify taking a life? Is one responsible for known but unintended consequences of an action? It was only natural that philosophy would be drawn into this subject matter, which turned more on conceptual analysis than on facts.

EUTHANASIA [S] is another major concern addressed by biomedical ethics. This bundle of concerns would be better labeled, as it frequently is, "decisions near the end of life." Until the 1990s the focus was seldom on actively killing the patient; rather, the focus was on "allowing the patient to die." The search for moral differences between various methods of "allowing to die" provided many conceptual problems that were ideal for philosophical treatment. For example, is choosing not to save a patient from death (e.g., from a heart attack or a respiratory emergency) the moral equivalent of killing him? Is withdrawing a life-saving therapy (such as a ventilator) from a patient morally the same as not beginning it in the first place? Is there a moral difference between the types of life-saving therapy that are withheld or withdrawn: the patient's regular maintenance medications (e.g., insulin or antihypertensives) versus acute care therapies (e.g. CPR or antibiotics) versus nutrition and hydration? Physicians (and society) had come to recognize that the patient had a right to refuse treatment, and they were equally certain that the physician could not legally acquiesce in the patient's request to kill him directly. But they were unsure whether a patient could refuse the very treatments that, if discontinued, would result in his death, since if withdrawing treatment were morally equivalent to killing the physician would then be killing at the request of the patient (for contrasting views see Clouser, 1977, and Rachels, 1975). Many of these conceptual problems were circumvented by legislation, state by state, establishing the legality of advance directives (originally called "living wills") whereby an individual, while competent, could give directions for his own care to be followed when he was no longer competent to speak for himself. However, advance directives brought their own ambiguities and conceptual problems, especially with respect to the conditions necessary to activate the advance directive. During the early 1990s several states attempted, by voter referendum, to establish laws allowing physicians to assist patients in committing SUICIDE [8]. Suicide and assisted suicide are matters of longstanding interest to philosophers.

The doctor–patient relationship has generated moral issues for philosophical consideration. It is a given that a physician owes it to her patient always to act in the patient's best interest, but there are varying accounts of why this is so. There are also questions that arise as to the extent of this "fiduciary" obligation. For example, when and under what conditions may the doctor, in order to do "the best" for her patient, violate that which morality generally requires? This is the issue of PATERNALISM [S], which has been a philosophical topic for many years. Precisely what it is and what would justify it has been a significant concern of biomedical ethics. A closely related issue has been a main thrust of the era of biomedical ethics, namely, establishing the self-determination (or autonomy) of patients. This was provoked by a combination of society's strong insistence on individual rights and the quantum leap of medical progress that entails many more therapeutic options, each with its own inherent advantages and disadvantages. With such a smorgasbord of risk–benefit trade-offs among appropriate therapies, it became prudent for the patient to choose her own therapy.

However, there are ambiguities concerning autonomy, such as determining when a decision is "truly" autonomous. KANT [4; S] thought a decision to commit suicide could never be an autonomous decision, yet most bioethicists believe that a terminally ill, competent patient's decision to be allowed to die, or even to be killed, is the epitome of an autonomous decision. An inevitable inquiry that emerges from the prominence given autonomy concerns what limits may or must be placed on autonomy. It is argued that the well-being of an individual's family or community have some claim against the autonomous decision. A moral view called COMMUNITARIANISM [S] arose as if in response to unfettered autonomy. Its emphasis is to give voice to the interests and rights of others affected by an individual's decisions.

Among the more interesting philosophical aspects to emerge from the focus on the doctor–patient relationship is the concept of duty. Though duty has often been understood among philosophers simply as a general moral obligation that everyone has toward each other, it is arguable that duties are more helpfully and accurately understood as limited to those moral requirements established by virtue of one's role or relationship to others. Duties thus understood are established through tradition, law, codes, and societal expectations and have important legal and moral implications for how one must, may, and must not act toward the one to whom the duty is owed.

Experimentation on humans for medical and behavioral research constitutes a major area of concern. It was the matter of experimentation with all its attendant moral issues that especially triggered the era of bioethics and brought such matters to public attention. The National Commission for the Protection of Human Subjects of Biomedical and Behavioral Research, established in 1972, was charged with making recommendations for federal regulations to protect the rights and welfare of human subjects of research sponsored by the federal government and to determine the ethical and moral principles governing research with human subjects. This undertaking and the attention it brought to moral concerns in research had far-reaching effects: extensive studies of consent and the conditions necessary for its moral validity (such as the subject's being competent and his decision being informed, free, and voluntary); investigations of the morality of using various populations as research subjects—fetuses, children, prisoners, the senile, the elderly, and the mentally retarded; the establishment of review boards in every institution in the country that uses federal funds for research (a board's function being to assess the moral acceptability of every proposal for research that uses human subjects); and an equally intense parallel concern for the use of animals in research, spawning a new specialty in animal ethics as well as review committees to determine the moral acceptability of research proposals using animals as subjects, known as Institutional Animal Care and Utilization Committees (IACUCs; *see* ANIMAL RIGHTS AND WELFARE [S]). The major emphasis given to the importance of informed consent for research carried over to informed consent for therapy as well. Analyzing what makes a consent (or refusal) valid, and if and when it can be overridden, has been of keen interest to philosophers.

Distributive justice in the world of health care has been a continuing theme in biomedical ethics. In the real world of needy people and limited resources there is pressure to find moral methods or principles for resource distribution. This issue is relevant from the most concrete level (Who should get the next available bed in the intensive care unit? Who should receive the next available organ for transplant?) to the policy level dealing with how goods should be allocated among, for example, hospitals, museums, schools, and road construction. Debated criteria for distribution on the concrete level include equal shares, equal outcome, merit, age, need, health, and personal responsibility for the health deficit (e.g., whether alcoholics should receive liver transplants).

Justice, including distributive justice, has been an issue within philosophy since its inception (see JUSTICE [4; S]). During the early years of bioethics the most reflected-upon philosophical work in this context was John RAWLS's [S] *Theory of Justice*. Though not originally intended to deal with matters of justice in health care, the book become a paradigm and resource in that area. Rawlsian theory has been ingeniously squeezed for every implication it might have for health-care ethics in general as well as health-care distribution in particular (Daniels, 1985). Another matter dealt with under the rubric of justice is the question of a right to health care: is it a natural human right, or one granted by the government, or one implicit in the U.S. constitution (e.g., following from a guarantee of equal opportunity)?

Reproductive technologies and genetics, though always of concern, rose to prominence in the 1980s, boosted by the increase in related scientific and medical research. The creation of the National Center for Human Genome Research at the National Institutes of Health (1989), dedicated to the mapping and sequencing of the human genome, has especially initiated substantial moral deliberations in and around genetics. Whereas all the other biomedical ethical issues focus especially on weighing harms and benefits and protecting individuals, reproductive technologies and genetics have an additional component. For many the issues are morally challenging because they appear to involve more of an interference with a basic order of nature. Whereas most moral deliberation begins with human nature as a given, genetic engineering raises the possibility of changing that very human nature, either by deleting certain qualities and characteristics or by enhancing them. There are those who regard the creation of human beings as a special and basic order of nature with which no one should tamper. Such metaphysical, religious, or quasi-religious considerations go beyond simply lessening the amount of harm in the world; they entail world views on which it may become very difficult to reach consensus. Meanwhile, practical moral problems must be decided—for example, ownership of preserved sperm or ova or embryos, limits on what may be done with them, and the best policy for handling the various possible combinations of sperm, ova, and hired gestational "mothers." Other issues in genetics pivot around the control and management of knowledge about an individual's genetic makeup, which, in effect, will be significantly predictive of the health status of that individual and thus have important implications concerning privacy, insurability, and life plans (*see* GENETICS AND REPRODUCTIVE TECHNOLOGIES [S].

PHILOSOPHICAL REFLECTIONS

Certain questions especially of interest to philosophers are provoked by involvement in the very practical world of biomedical ethics. The following are a few of the matters that, though not necessarily new, have been highlighted for philosophers in the era of bioethics.

"Stretching" Morality. Inevitably, when confronted with new and unusual circumstances, one questions whether a new ethics is needed in order to deal with such new and different circumstances, or whether somehow the old morality can be "stretched" to cover the new circumstances. Van Rensselaer Potter, who was the first to use the term bioethics (Potter, 1971), believed that what was needed was a more scientifically based ethic, achieved by combining biological knowledge with the knowledge of human value systems. The goal was the survival of the human species. It is not clear that this combination would produce a new ethic, but the scientific aspect, in the service of human values, might sufficiently alert humans to the facts that would both motivate and, by virtue of understanding better the causes and effects in the biological world, give direction to their actions for survival. The idea of inventing new ethics is odd. What would be its justification? Could the new ethics approve of killing a certain group of persons, or causing others pain, or taking away their freedom? It seems that the ethics would have to be fundamentally the same as always, though, given newly discovered facts, capabilities, and causal relationships, the means to a given end may be different. That is, there may be new ways of causing or preventing harm or a new realization that certain actions would result in harms that humans had not realized. Nevertheless, the moral admonition not to cause harm to anyone (unless the moral agent is willing for everyone to know that it would be acceptable for them also to do the same thing in the same morally relevant circumstances) remains the same as ever. Though much has been made of the new ethics, more likely what has happened is a more intense investigation of the "old ethics" to gain insight and clarity for dealing with situations and problems that had not been encountered.

Theory and Its Application. One of the surprises of bioethics was how little the ethical theories of philosophy seemed to help in solving the real and complex moral problems of medicine. Philosophy was consulted by those in the medical world seeking help, because philosophy was the traditional academic home for ethics and because philosophy appeared more neutral and nonsectarian, which was an essential feature for an ethic that was becoming a public discussion. But the theories of philosophical ethics were not much help. There was more a chasm between the theory and its use in solving real moral problems than had been suspected. The relentlessness of real circumstances with all their complications seemed more than theory could handle. The early textbooks of biomedical ethics were anthologies, and samples from MILL [5; S] Kant, and Rawls constituted the usual fare. Such use of anthologies implicitly suggested either that the reader simply choose whichever she found preferable or that each theory individually was inadequate, but taken all together they might provide enough guidance for making practical moral decisions. One difficulty with the latter interpretation is that there was no overarching theory to resolve conflicts between the individual theories.

The apparent inadequacy of moral theories to deal with practical moral problems produced at least three responses. One was to conclude that moral theories were not helpful because they were too general for the particularity of the circumstances. This led to an antitheory movement (see Clarke & Simpson, 1989). Another response was to conclude that the theories in question were flawed because they were too simple and a more complex theory was needed. Gert (1988), for example, developed a general moral theory showing the integral relationship of applied ethics (biomedical ethics, in particular) to general morality and a procedure for using the theory in dealing with substantive moral problems. A middle position was to limit one's theorizing to the biomedical sphere, wherein the generalities were more immediately related to the particulars of the practice. Among the theoretical frameworks so developed the most popular were "principle based" ethics and "virtue based" ethics (*see* VIRTUE ETHICS [S]). The former was particularly influential and was clearly articulated by Beauchamp and Childress (1994), the latter by Pellegrino and Thomasma (1993). Casuistry also was revisited and renewed in general response to the inadequacy of theory for practical moral problems (Jonsen & Toulmin, 1988).

How Many Moralities? While working in bioethics one quickly becomes aware of all the coexisting moral practices and codes of ethics. Not only do we have engineering ethics, business ethics, environmental ethics, dental ethics, nursing ethics, medical ethics, sports ethics, and so forth, but within each of these there are many different groups, each with its own "moral code." Of course it is no surprise to a philosopher that morality may vary from culture to culture, though what constituted a "culture" in this context was never precisely clear. In the practical world of bioethics there are hundreds of moral codes, each designed for the guidance of a particular—usually professional—group. This multiplicity of codes existing side by side in the "same" culture should trouble the cultural relativist. Just as important, this multiplicity of moral practices and codes of ethics raises the question: can a moral code simply be invented by any group or any individual? Certainly that is what has happened through the years. Some of the codes (or aspects thereof) are quite self-serving of the group itself rather than concerned with those with whom they come in professional contact.

The unavoidable awareness of the multiplicity of moralities and moral codes inevitably provokes a basic question: how many moralities are there? Do all the "different moralities" have something in common such that that commonality constitutes "general morality"? If there is just one general morality, what accounts for these various manifestations? These many and various manifestations of morality impel one to search for a system that underlies them and compel one to take the notion of moral system seriously. A traditional, necessary element of morality is IMPARTIALITY [S], and that requires a system such that what is moral for one person is moral for anyone else in the same circumstances. Awareness of the multiplicity of "moralities" in the everyday world makes the search for system ever more urgent.

These are important philosophical questions, stimulated by applied ethics inasmuch as applied ethics takes seriously the everyday practical manifestations of morality. Applied ethics has paid more attention to morality as lived and practiced than has traditional philosophical ethics, which tended more to invent ideal moralities.

The Scope of Ethics. Scope is a major issue, primarily provoked by applied ethics. The scope of ethics refers to the domain over which ethics has relevance or control. Animals, the environment, fields and streams, fetuses, the senile, and so on, all would fall outside our ordinary scope of morality, whose domain generally is limited to rational agents. But the breadth of bioethics has brought into its circle of concern animals, forests, fields, and streams. This is an enigma to some strands of traditional ethics that have assumed the participants in morality to be rational beings who could reason together and understand what was to their mutual benefit.

How the scope of morality is expanded to be more inclusive takes various forms. Some argue that these other entities have rights in and of themselves. Thus, one's actions toward these entities must be guided by considerations of what is for the entities' own good, fulfilling whatever internal goals or purposes that are attributed to them. On the other hand, some argue that the only way such rights can make sense is if the rights are granted by humans in a manner that is ultimately for the benefit of humans. That is, granting such rights may be a heuristic device (e.g., for the protection of aspects of nature, the protecting of which might be seen as ultimately important to humankind).

Many would limit the scope to sentient beings. In general it would be argued that though many sentient beings may not be rational and hence not capable of being held responsible for their own behavior, nevertheless, inasmuch as they are capable of suffering, rational agents have a moral obligation to avoid causing that suffering as well as to prevent it. If the goal of morality is (as many would argue) to reduce the amount of harm incurred in the world, then this extension in scope would seem entirely appropriate.

Scope could even be understood to have an aspect of temporal inclusiveness or exclusiveness. The "problem of future generations" would be an example. In this case it is not the nature of the "beings" or "entities" that is in question, but how far into the future they are owed moral consideration (*see* DISTANT PEOPLES AND FUTURE GENERATIONS [S]). This was a frequently argued issue in the 1970s and 1980s. Matters of genetic manipulation and the environment would obviously raise these future-oriented reflections. If humans would suffer as a result of actions taken now, then the moral implications of those actions need to be taken seriously. Naturally there is increased uncertainty about the consequences of actions in the distant future; causal chains are difficult enough to estimate even into the much closer future. Furthermore, the seriousness of effects on future generations (for example, of the extinction of a species of plants or animals) often cannot be convincingly argued. Thus, consequences to humans are susceptible to too many "fudge" factors, and, accordingly, other bases for moral judgment are found by those anxious to preserve animals, plants, and the environment in general. It may be that a metaphysical worldview is necessary to set the scope of ethics. That is, it seems that beliefs about the purpose of the world and about the roles and relationships of its inhabitants will inevitably be assumed in arguing for the "proper" behavior of rational agents toward the totality of the planet.

Real Cases. One of the significant contributions of bioethics is bringing to center stage real moral problems in all their fullness. These are very different from the traditional hypothetical cases offered by philosophers. The former are rich in practical detail and seem relentless in admitting no easy solutions; the latter are usually concocted with a single point in mind to illustrate a theoretical point. The hardness of real cases may be one reason philosophy was slow to acknowledge bioethics. Real cases are often messy; they cannot be dealt with cleanly and decisively; conflicts of claims, rules, and principles abound. It was in the face of these hard cases that many began to suspect that traditional moral philosophies could not help and indeed may even be irrelevant to moral problems in the real world.

The combination of complicated real cases and theories of minimal help led to a focus on facts rather than on theory. Considerable attention had to be given to the facts and their context, because the cases were arising from a variety of complex fields of endeavor such as medicine, engineering, environment, law, and genetics. In order to see the moral issues one had to grasp the nuances, relationships, understandings, and practices within these fields. Thus, the primary work of bioethics was really in gathering and comprehending facts rather than in delving deep into moral theory. Correspondingly, most "moral" disagreements in these areas of bioethics turned out to be disagreements over the facts of the case rather than over morality or moral theory. In clinical settings, for example, once there was a consensus on the facts, there was far more agreement than disagreement on the moral lines of action.

The considerably increased focus on the facts led to two interesting philosophical moves that turned out to be closely related. One was a focused concern for determining which of the infinity of facts were of moral relevance; the other was a realization that there were conceptual clarifications necessary before the moral relevance of some facts could be established.

Though the importance of facts to moral deliberation has never been doubted, perhaps the necessity of establishing criteria for the moral relevance of the facts was not clearly realized until facts became a central focus in bioethics' work with real, concrete cases. The importance of such criteria goes beyond simply trying to sort through the multitude of facts being presented around each case. Such criteria become necessary in making sense of that critical and pivotal phrase "in the same morally relevant circumstances." Without it one situation cannot be compared with another; it is crucial in order to make moral decisions consistent from one time and place to the next. Morality is a system and as such requires uniformity and consistency throughout. If the action of one person is moral (or immoral) in a certain situation, then that action is moral (or immoral) for everyone to do "in the same morally relevant circumstances." Thus, a lot turns on precisely what factors in a situation are morally relevant. One philosopher who has worked explicitly on this matter is Gert (1988), and he continues to do so (Clouser & Gert, 1994; Gert et al., 1996).

The other philosophical move initiated by applied ethics' immersion in facts was the need for conceptual analysis. Of course, conceptual analysis is as old as philosophy, but bioethics was necessarily more focused on conceptual analysis than on ethics. Most of its work was on "preparing" the facts of the case for moral judgment. The ethics was relatively uncomplicated once the facts were properly understood. Is withdrawing life supports the same as killing? Is withholding life supports the same as withdrawing? Is a particular behavior of the physician paternalistic? If it is, must it be morally justified? Does the physician have a duty to act always in the best interest of the patient? All the time? What is duty? How is one's duty determined? Is it a breach of patient confidentiality when a physician gives a patient record to a secretary to type or to a student to study? What is competence to consent and how is it determined? What is the definition of death? When does life begin? What is the moral status of frozen embryos and how is ownership determined? These are simply a sampling of the kinds of conceptual issues that occupy applied ethics (in these instances, biomedical ethics). Notice that traditional moral theories would have little to say about them, yet these are the kinds of issues that bioethics must work through in order to deal with the moral issues at stake.

CONTRIBUTIONS OF PHILOSOPHY TO BIOMEDICAL ETHICS

Philosophy has contributed significantly to biomedical ethics. For all the failure of philosophical theories of ethics to connect with the moral dilemmas of the medical world, the forced dialogue between the theories and the dilemmas has been crucial in helping to systematize, to focus, and to pose the fruitful, organizing questions. Until the late 1960s medical ethics was hardly even an individuated discipline. It was a mixture of religion, tradition, exhortation, legal precedents, miscellaneous rules, epithets, and slogans. It is arguable that philosophy provided the push toward systematization, consistency, and clarity by asking probing and organizing questions, by directing informed attention to assumptions, implications, and foundations, and by locating and analyzing pivotal concepts. Though many disciplines have participated in the recent revival of biomedical ethics, philosophy has provided the framework within which the discussion takes place and within which the contributions of the other disciplines play their part.

Bibliography

Beauchamp, T. L., and J. F. Childress. *Principles of Biomedical Ethics,* 4th ed. New York, 1994. Earlier editions were more characteristically examples of principlism.

Brody, B. A. *Life and Death Decision Making.* New York, 1988.

Callahan, D. "Bioethics," in *Encyclopedia of Bioethics,* edited by W. Reich, Vol. 1, 2d ed. (New York, 1995).

Clarke, S. G., and E. Simpson. *Anti-Theory in Ethics and Moral Conservatism.* Albany, NY, 1989.

Clouser, K. D. "Allowing or Causing: Another Look," *Annals of Internal Medicine,* Vol. 87 (1977), 622–24.

———. "Bioethics," in *Encyclopedia of Bioethics,* edited by W. Reich, Vol. 1 (New York, 1978).

———. "Ethical Theory and Applied Ethics: Reflections on Connections," in B. Hoffmaster, B. Freedman, and G. Fraser, eds., *Clinical Ethics: Theory and Practice* (Clifton, NJ, 1989).

———, and B. Gert. "Morality vs. Principlism," in R. Gillon, ed., *Principles of Health Care Ethics* (Chichester, England, 1994).

———, and L. Kopelman, eds. "Philosophical Critique of Bioethics," *Journal of Medicine and Philosophy,* Vol. 15 (1990).

Engelhardt, H. T., Jr. *The Foundations of Bioethics.* New York, 1986.

Gert, B. *Morality: A New Justification of the Moral Rules.* New York, 1988.

——— et al. *Morality and the New Genetics.* Boston, 1996.

Jonsen, A. R. "Theological Ethics, Moral Philosophy, and Public Moral Discourse," *Kennedy Institute of Ethics Journal,* Vol. 4 (1994), 1–11.

———, and S. Toulmin. *The Abuse of Casuistry: A History of Moral Reasoning.* Berkeley, 1988.

Mason, C. S., ed. "Theories and Methods in Bioethics: Principlism and Its Critics," *Kennedy Institute of Ethics Journal,* Vol. 5 (1995).

Pellegrino, E. D., and D. C. Thomasma. *The Virtues in Medical Practice.* New York, 1993.

Potter, V. R. *Bioethics: Bridge to the Future.* Englewood Cliffs, NJ, 1971.

Rachels, J. "Active and Passive Euthanasia," *New England Journal of Medicine,* Vol. 292 (1975), 78–80.

Rawls, J. *A Theory of Justice.* Cambridge, MA, 1971.

Reich, W. T., ed. *Encyclopedia of Bioethics.* 5 vols. 2d ed. New York, 1995.

"The Word 'Bioethics': The Struggle over Its Earliest Meanings,"*Kennedy Institute of Ethics Journal,* Vol. 5 (1995), 19–34.

Veatch, R. M. *A Theory of Medical Ethics.* New York, 1981.

K. Danner Clouser

BUSINESS ETHICS. The study of ethics and economics and the analysis of ethical decision making in business are traditions as old as philosophy itself, and the development of reasonable standards for business behavior is part of every culture. Yet the process of integrating and applying ethical standards to management decision making appears to be difficult, because economic goals and exigencies often seem to override other considerations. But ethical issues are part of economics, management, accounting, finance, marketing, and other business disciplines, just as management, marketing, accounting, and so forth are part of business. Not to take into account normative considerations in economic affairs is itself a normative decision that ignores some elementary facts: (1) economic decisions are choices in which the decision makers could have done otherwise; (2) every such decision or action affects people, and an alternative action or inaction would affect them differently; and (3) every economic decision or set of decisions is embedded in a belief system that presupposes some basic values or their abrogation.

Although ethical issues in business are age-old problems, it is an academic discipline that has developed in the latter half of this century, primarily in North America. The discipline of business ethics traces its roots to earlier developments in other areas of APPLIED ETHICS [S] and to the interest in what was labeled "social issues in management" that developed in the 1950s. During that decade some business schools began to offer courses in "business and society," "corporate social responsibility," or "sociolegal studies" in which emphasis is on the relationship between corporations and society or government. This focus shifted, however, when in 1961, as part of his doctoral work at Harvard, Raymond C. Baumhart did a landmark study of the attitudes of business people toward ethics in their business decision making. The work expanded the study of business ethics to include individual managerial as well as corporate decision making and extended its purview to all normative aspects of business, including issues in management, marketing, finance, accounting, operations, employment, research, technology, multicultural relationships, corporate governance, the environment, and community and government relationships. Although the study of business ethics began in the United States and Canada, the discipline has spread to Europe, Russia, Australia, New Zealand, and Japan and has begun to be taken seriously in other countries as well.

Technically defined, business ethics is the study of codes, rules, or principles that govern business conduct; it seeks to understand business practices, institutions, and actions in light of what is right and good. Business ethics is also descriptive: it engages in behavioral and sociological studies of what in fact managers and companies do. Business ethics analyzes the moral development of managers and how they behave, it studies how corporate culture affects managerial behavior, and it describes the interactions between corporations and government, the environment, and the community. These studies are important descriptions of the causal interrelationships between individuals, corporations, and society and of how those relationships affect individual and corporate choices and actions (Goodpaster, 1992).

Most important, business ethics is normative: it evaluates business and business practices in light of standards elucidating what is right and good, and it offers recommendations and solutions to ethical dilemmas. From this point of view business ethics is defined as a set of normative rules of conduct, a code, a standard, or a set of principles that govern what one ought to do in the practical context of business when the well-being, rights, or integrity of oneself, of other people, of a corporation, or even a nation is at stake.

The subject for business ethics extends beyond individual decision making to include questions about corporate moral responsibility and issues arising from the interrelationships between corporations and society (Goodpaster, 1992). On the individual level questions of managerial character, rights and responsibilities of employees, affirmative action, comparable worth, conflict of interest, and whistleblowing are some of the focal points for analysis and evaluation. Yet most of these issues entail relationships between the individual and the corporation or business.

On the corporate level one central topic is whether and how a corporation or a corporate culture is a moral agent and thus morally responsible. While one must be careful not to anthropomorphize institutions such as corporations, at some level we do hold corporations as well as individuals morally liable. How this is possible is still much in debate, but the literature on collective moral agency is helpful in framing a kind of secondary moral agency for corporations that is unique to collectives (May, 1987; Werhane, 1985). Issues confronting corporations include product safety, marketing and advertising practices, downsizing, mergers, plant relocation, product safety, consumer and company liability, insider trading, pollution, and corporate governance. These issues concern and affect individuals, other corporations, and society. Business ethics also examined social, economic, and political systems that define property arrangements and frame the legal and regulatory environment for commerce.

Milton Friedman (1962) has contended that the primary responsibility of business is its fiduciary responsibility to its shareholders or owners. However, a number of philosophers and management theorists now argue that any good business decision, and thus any ethical decision in business, must weigh the positive and negative consequences to each affected stakeholder, and these consequences are not merely material but involve issues of rights and fairness as well (Evan & Freeman, 1992). So, for example, a decision to downsize a company affects employees, customers, suppliers, shareholders, and the community in which the company is based, and it affects the rights of employees and shareholders as well as their economic interests.

Finally, despite its roots in North America, business ethics is multicultural, and there is a new and growing area of international business ethics in which the emphasis is on multicultural decision making in the context of business. Issues such as exporting unacceptable products, dumping hazardous waste, discriminatory pay of expatriates and nationals, use of indigenous national resources, manufacturing in developing countries, regulatory inconsistencies, demands for sensitive payments to foreign officials, and international trade barriers further complicate decision making. But there is no separate field of "international ethics" that we apply to multinational business. Rather, like business ethics, international business ethics engages in an exploration of the normative dimensions of (cross-cultural) economic activities. These normative dimensions are embedded in these business processes and integral to them.

Bibliography

Beauchamp, T., and N. Bowie, eds. *Ethical Theory and Business,* 4th ed. Englewood Cliffs, NJ, 1992.

Boatright, J. R. *Ethics and the Conduct of Business.* Englewood Cliffs, NJ, 1993.

Bowie, N., and R. Duska. *Business Ethics.* Englewood Cliffs, NJ, 1990.

Bowie, N., and R. E. Freeman, eds. *Ethics and Agency Theory.* New York, 1992.

De George, R. *Business Ethics,* 2d ed. New York, 1991.

Donaldson, T. *Corporations and Morality.* Englewood Cliffs, NJ, 1983.

Donaldson, T., *The Ethics of International Business.* New York, 1989.

Donaldson, T., and P. H. Werhane, eds. *Ethical Issues in Business,* 4th ed. Englewood Cliffs, NJ, 1992.

Evan, W., and R. E. Freeman. "A Stakeholder Theory of the Modern Corporation: Kantian Capitalism," in T. Beauchamp and N. Bowie, eds., *Ethical Theory and Business,* 4th ed. (Englewood Cliffs, NJ, 1992).

Friedman, M. *Capitalism and Freedom.* Chicago, 1962.

Goodpaster, K. "Business Ethics," in *Encyclopedia of Ethics* (New York, 1992).

Hoffman, M., and J. Moore, eds. *Business Ethics,* 3d. ed. New York, 1994.

May, L. *The Morality of Groups.* Notre Dame, IN, 1987.

Sen, A. *On Ethics and Economics.* Oxford, 1987.

Solomon, R. C. *Ethics and Excellence.* Oxford, 1992.

Velasquez, M. *Business Ethics,* 3d ed. Englewood Cliffs, NJ, 1992.

Walton, C. *The Moral Manager.* New York, 1988.

Werhane, P. *Persons, Rights, and Corporations.* Englewood Cliffs, NJ, 1985.

———. *Adam Smith and His Legacy for Modern Capitalism.* New York, 1991.

PATRICIA WERHANE

C

CARE. Care is the comprehensive "existential" concept of HEIDEGGER's [3; S] *Sein und Zeit.* Formally indicated by ex-sistence and the understanding *of* BEING [1], care develops the formal structural totality schematizing the intentionality of the individual human situation (*Dasein*) as a whole: ahead-of-itself—already-being-in-(the-world)—as being-amid (beings encountered within the world). As this unity of existentiality, facticity, and fallenness corresponding to future, past, and present, care receives its ontological sense from the unifying whole of original temporality. Care is first care of the self in its being, which, as being-in-the-world, is "equally original" with solicitude for others and preoccupied concern with things.

Since the very being of Dasein "is" its understanding of Being, care in the later Heidegger becomes the care *of* Being itself. The self "out-standing" toward Being in its full temporality becomes "in-standing" in the unconcealing truth of Being, its "clearing," which as a "projective reach" still traces the future's "leeway" dominating Dasein's "temporal play-space."

Care can be regarded as Heidegger's temporalizing of Greek *eros,* the desire to be (whole), the "want" that conjoins being and nonbeing in the erotetic question *of* Being. Proximate sources in choosing "caring" to identify "the basic (relational) sense of life's movement" are the biblical θλλĩψψις ("thlipsis": need, affliction, trouble) and AUGUSTINE's [1; S] *cura.* Seeking to exclude ontic connotations such as "trouble and toil" from its formality, Heidegger nevertheless explicates care ontologically as caretaking, holding truth in trust (troth), and, later, as a "shepherding" that seeks and guards the truth of Being.

Bibliography

Heidegger, M. *Basic Writings: From "Being and Time" (1927) to "The Task of Thinking" (1964).* New York, 1977, 2nd revised ed., 1992.

———. *Sein und Zeit* [1927]. 16th ed., Tübingen, 1986. Translated by J. Macquarrie and E. Robinson as *Being and Time.* New York, 1962. §§ 41, 65.

Kisiel, T. *The Genesis of Heidegger's "Being and Time."* Berkeley, 1993.

THEODORE KISIEL

CARNAP, RUDOLF (1891–1970), remained philosophically active throughout his life. Most of his research in his final decade continued to focus on PROBABILITY [6; S], but two other volumes devoted substantially to other issues also came out. The first of these, *The Philosophy of Rudolf Carnap,* appeared in early 1964, though dated 1963. This 1,100-page volume was the result of ten years of work and contains a substantial autobiography, a detailed bibliography (through 1961), as well as twenty-six critical essays (with Carnap's replies) on all aspects of his work. A second nonprobability volume, *Philosophical Foundations of Physics: An Introduction to the Philosophy of Science,* appeared in 1966 (and in very slightly revised form under its less formidable subtitle in 1974). This is essentially a transcript of one of Carnap's seminars edited into very readable form by Martin Gardner.

Carnap's final body of work on probability comprises a very substantial revision (or more accurately the beginnings of such a revision) of the research done twenty years earlier, which had culminated in *Logical Foundations of Probability.* CARNAP [2] had agreed in the preface to the second edition of this book that primitive predicates having logical structure were admissible, even though the apparatus therein was unable to cope with them. In various places he had also agreed that, not only was the function c^* too narrow, but so was the whole continuum of inductive methods as well as the first attempts to broaden that continuum. Meanwhile, Carnap concluded that it would be significantly more convenient to treat probabilities as applying to propositions rather than, as he had in earlier work, to sentences. The (revisable) foundation of these changes was to be "A Basic System of Inductive Logic," which Carnap had all but finished at the time of his death on September 14, 1970. This long (284 pages) article was a progress report in both senses: first, as an announcement of substantial advances on the problems noted and, second, as an interim statement on the way to something better. Perhaps he would have been pleased to have all of his works so viewed: as substantial advances in clarity, power, and generosity to opposing views and as interim statements on the way to something better.

CARNAP'S REPUTATION: DECLINE AND RESURGENCE

Carnap and the other logical empiricists never dominated philosophy to the extent that some have recalled. But beginning perhaps about 1960 their collective reputations began to decline to the point that, twenty years later, discussion of their views was regularly consigned to crude caricatures in the opening paragraphs of works in the PHILOSOPHY OF SCIENCE [6; S]. No doubt there are many causes of this decline: continued attacks by POPPER [6], QUINE [7; S], and KUHN [S], Carnap's technical and often inaccessible writing style, his refusal to engage in polemics with his critics, and even the inevitable swings of fashion. In the late 1970s, however, there arose a group of historically minded philosophers who, armed with massive and newly available archival evidence, began reassessing the work of Carnap and other logical empiricists. This work was further spurred by numerous conferences, journal issues, and other activities surrounding the centennial, on May 18, 1991, of Carnap's birth.

Among the emphases of this reappraisal has been a fuller recognition of the important role that Kantianism plays in Carnap's intellectual context, in his own early work, and particularly in such work as the *Aufbau,* which is now seen as focused not on ontology but on the semantics of intersubjective meaning. *The Logical Syntax of Language,* too, has been reappraised and its sophisticated conventionalism and pragmatism more fully understood. Of particular note is the discovery that the program of syntax was broad enough to include a Tarski-type truth theory and that indeed Carnap had himself developed even within that book what we would now call a semantical theory astonishingly close to Tarski's result (*see* TARSKI [8]). Similar reexaminations of Carnap's views on observation, ANALYTICITY [S], REALISM [7; S], and probability have shown that many of the standard criticisms were predicated on misunderstandings of these views. Certainly, as the historical reassessment of Carnap and other logical empiricists proceeds, a richer picture of their work emerges, as does a fuller understanding of the extent to which ongoing work both arises out of theirs and can continue to benefit from studying it.

(SEE ALSO: *Logical Positivism* [5])

Bibliography

WORKS BY CARNAP

Philosophical Foundations of Physics: An Introduction to the Philosophy of Science, edited by M. Gardner. New York, 1966.

"A Basic System of Inductive Logic," Part 1, in R. Carnap and R. C. Jeffrey, eds., *Studies in Inductive Logic and Probability,* Vol. 1 (Berkeley, 1971).

"A Basic System of Inductive Logic," Part 2, in R. C. Jeffrey, ed., *Studies in Inductive Logic and Probability,* Vol. 2 (Berkeley, 1980).

"On Protocol Sentences," *Noûs,* Vol. 21 (1987), 457–70.

With W. V. O. Quine, *Dear Carnap, Dear Van: The Quine–Carnap Correspondence and Related Work,* edited by R. Creath. Los Angeles, 1990.

WORKS ON CARNAP

Coffa, J. A. *The Semantic Tradition from Kant to Carnap: To the Vienna Station.* Cambridge, 1991. The pioneering study in the area.

Creath, R. "The Unimportance of Semantics," in A. Fine, M. Forbes, and L. Wessels, eds., *PSA 1990,* Vol. 2 (East Lansing, MI, 1990). All these papers by Creath are on analyticity, especially in connection with Quine.

"Every Dogma Has Its Day," *Erkenntnis,* Vol. 35 (1991), 347–89. See this issue for other valuable essays.

———. "Functionalist Theories of Meaning and the Defense of Analyticity," in W. Salmon and G. Wolters, eds., *Logic, Language, and the Structure of Scientific Theories* (Pittsburgh, 1994).

Friedman, M. "Carnap and A Priori Truth," in D. Bell and W. Vossenkuhl, eds., *Science and Subjectivity: The Vienna Circle and Twentieth-Century Philosophy* (Berlin, 1992). This and Goldfarb and Ricketts's paper (see below) are important papers on the a priori and on mathematics.

———. "Epistemology in the *Aufbau,*" *Synthese,* Vol. 93 (1992), 15–57. This and Richardson's essay (see below) are valuable essays on Carnap's early Kantianism; other valuable essays appear in this issue.

"Geometry, Convention, and the Relativized A Priori: Reichenbach, Schlick, and Carnap," in W. Salmon and G. Wolters, eds., *Logic, Language, and the Structure of Scientific Theories* (Pittsburgh, 1994).

Goldfarb, W., and T. Ricketts. "Carnap and the Philosophy of Mathematics," in D. Bell and W. Vossenkuhl, eds., *Science and Subjectivity: The Vienna Circle and Twentieth-Century Philosophy* (Berlin, 1992).

Richardson, A. W. "Logical Idealism and Carnap's Construction of the World," *Synthese,* Vol. 93 (1992), 59–92.

RICHARD CREATH

CAUSAL OR CONDITIONAL OR EXPLANATORY-RELATION ACCOUNTS. Edmund Gettier attacked the traditional analysis of knowledge by showing that inferring a true belief from a false but justified belief produces a justified true belief that does not qualify as knowledge. Subsequent analyses of knowledge were motivated in large part by the wish to avoid examples of the type Gettier used. One way to do so is to insist that a belief must be connected in some proper way to the fact that makes it true in order for it to count as knowledge. In Gettier's examples beliefs are only accidentally true since there are no proper connections between them and the facts that make them true. Analyses that require such connections may either retain or drop the justification condition from the traditional analysis. Without it they are thoroughly externalist analyses since they require only that a belief be externally connected with the fact that makes it true, not that the subject be able to specify this connection.

One intuitive way to specify the proper connection is to say that it is causal: the fact that makes a belief true must help cause the belief in the subject if the subject is to have knowledge. When this causal relation holds, the truth of the belief is nonaccidental. The causal analysis of knowledge therefore excludes standard Gettier-type cases, but it seems on reflection to be both too weak and too strong: too strong in that knowledge of universal propositions, mathematical truths, and logical connections seems to be ruled out if these cannot enter into causal relations, too weak in allowing knowledge when a subject cannot distinguish a fact that causes her belief from relevant alternatives. Suppose, for example, that a subject *S* cannot tell red expanses from green ones but believes that there is a red expanse before her whenever either a red or a green expanse is there. Then, on an occasion in which a red expanse is before *S* the usual sort of perceptual causal connection will hold, but knowledge that the expanse is red will be lacking.

A different way to specify the necessary connection that handles the sort of case just cited is provided by the conditional account. According to this account, *S* knows that *p* only if *S* would not believe that *p* if *p* were not true. In close possible worlds in which *p* is not true, it must be the case that *S* does not believe it. This rules out the case of the red and green expanses since, in a close world in which the expanse is not red but green, *S* continues to believe it is red. A further condition required by this account is that in close worlds in which *p* continues to be true but other things change, *S* continues to believe that *p*.

The conditional account handles both Gettier's cases and those that require the distinction of relevant alternatives. But once again there are examples that seem to show it both too weak and too strong. That the first condition is too strong can be shown by a variation on the color expanse example. Suppose that *S* cannot tell red from green but is very good at detecting blue. Then, on the basis of seeing a blue expanse *S* can come to know that there is not a green expanse before her. But if this proposition were false (if there were a green expanse before her), she would still believe it true (she would think she was seeing red). That the second condition is too strong seems clear from the case of a very old person whose mental capacities are still intact but soon will fail him. That there are close worlds in which he does not continue to believe as he does now by exercising those capacities does not mean that he cannot know various facts now through their exercise.

That these conditions are too weak can perhaps be shown by cases in which someone intentionally induces a Gettier-type belief in *S*. In this case, if the belief were not true, it would not have been induced in *S*, and yet *S* does not know. Such a case might or might not be ruled out by the second condition, depending on how it is specified and on how the second condition is interpreted. But there are other cases that seem more certainly to indicate that the conditions are too weak. If *S* steadfastly believes every mathematical proposition that she entertains, then the conditions will be met, but she will not know all the true mathematical propositions that she entertains.

An analysis of knowledge should not only accommodate various intuitions regarding examples; it should also be useful to the normative epistemologist in reconstructing the structure of knowledge and addressing skeptical challenges. The conditional account, as interpreted by its main proponent, Robert Nozick, has interesting implications regarding skepticism. According to it, I can know various ordinary perceptual truths, such as that I am seated before a fire, even though I cannot know that there is no Cartesian demon always deceiving me. This is because in the closest possible worlds in which I am not before the fire, I do not believe that I am (I am somewhere else with different perceptual evidence). But in the closest world in which there is a Cartesian demon, I do not believe there is one (since all my perceptual evidence remains the same). These implications are welcome to Nozick but are troubling to other philosophers. My knowledge of being before the fire depends on the demon world not being among the closest in which I am not before the fire. But, according to the conditional account, I cannot know that this last clause is true. Hence, I cannot show that my knowledge that I sit before the fire is actual, as opposed to merely being possible, and it seems that I ultimately lack grounds for being convinced that this is so. Furthermore, implications regarding more specific claims to knowledge and skeptical possibilities are counterintuitive as well. For example, according to this account I cannot know that my son is not a robot brilliantly constructed by aliens, although I can know that I do not have a brilliantly constructed robot son.

A third way of specifying the required connection that makes beliefs true is to describe it as explanatory. If *S* knows that *p*, then the fact that *p* must help to explain *S*'s belief. To see whether this account handles the sorts of cases cited, we would need to define the notion of explanation being used here. One way to do so is in terms of a certain notion of probability: roughly, *p* explains *q* if the probability of *q* given *p* is higher than the probability of *q* in the relevant reference class (reflecting relevant alternatives); put another way, if the ratio of (close) possible worlds in which *q* is true is higher in the worlds in which *p* obtains than in the relevant contrasting set of worlds. Given this interpretation, the analysis handles the perceptual discrimination case. In it *S* does not know there is a red expanse before him because its being red does not raise the probability of his belief that it is relative to those possible worlds in which this belief is based on its being green. The analysis also allows knowledge in the variation that defeats the conditional account. In it *S* knows that there is not a green expanse before her since the fact that the expanse is not green (i.e., it is blue) explains her belief that it is not green. Since the account must allow explanatory chains, it can be interpreted so as to include knowledge of mathematical propositions, which do not enter into causal relations. In the usual case in which *S* has mathematical knowledge that *p* her belief must be explanatorily linked to *p* via some proof. The truth of *p* makes a proof possible, and the ratio of close worlds in which *S* believes *p* must be higher in worlds in which there is a proof than in the overall set of worlds.

The explanatory account needs to be filled out further if it is to accommodate cases involving intentionally produced beliefs resembling Gettier's examples since in such cases the fact that *p* helps to explain why the belief that *p* is induced in *S*. As an externalist account, it would also need to provide defense for the claim that *S* can know that *p* even when, from his point of view, he has no good reasons for believing *p*. The analysis does suggest an approach to answering the skeptic different from that suggested by the conditional account. A proponent of this analysis would answer the skeptic by showing that nonskeptical theses provide better explanations of our ordinary beliefs than do skeptical theses.

(SEE ALSO: *Epistemology* [S])

Bibliography

Dretske, F. "Conclusive Reason," *Australasian Journal of Philosophy,* Vol. 49 (1971), 1–22.

Gettier, E. "Is Justified True Belief Knowledge?" *Analysis,* Vol. 23 (1963), 121–23.

Goldman, A. H. *Empirical Knowledge.* Berkeley, 1988.

Goldman, A. I. "A Causal Theory of Knowing," *Journal of Philosophy,* Vol. 64 (1967), 357–72.

———. "Discrimination and Perceptual Knowledge," *Journal of Philosophy,* Vol. 73 (1976), 771–91.

Luper-Foy, S., ed. *The Possibility of Knowledge: Nozick and His Critics.* Totowa, NJ, 1987.

Nozick, R. *Philosophical Explanations.* Cambridge, MA, 1981.

ALAN H. GOLDMAN

CAUSATION. Among the questions that any adequate account of the nature of CAUSATION [2] must answer, the following are especially crucial. First, how are causal states of affairs—including both causal laws and causal relations between events—related to noncausal states of affairs? Second, which are more basic—causal laws or causal relations? Third, how should the direction of causation be defined?

Since David HUME'S [4; S] time, reductionist answers have held sway, and philosophers have generally maintained that all causal relations between events are logically supervenient upon causal laws and noncausal states of affairs, that causal laws are supervenient upon noncausal facts, and that the direction of causation is definable in noncausal terms. Since the 1970s, however, these antireductionists have challenged all of these reductionist claims.

REDUCTIONISM

Reductionist approaches are of three main types: first, accounts that analyze causation in terms of conditions that in the circumstances are nomologically necessary, sufficient, or both; second, accounts in which subjunctive conditionals play the crucial role; and third, accounts based upon probabilistic relations (*see* REDUCTIONISM [S]).

Causes and Nomological Conditions. This first reductionist approach comes in different forms. According to perhaps the most common version, a cause is a condition that is necessary in the circumstances for its effect. To say that event *c* is necessary in the circumstances for event *e* is roughly to say that there is some law, *l,* and some circumstance, *s,* such that the nonoccurrence of *c,* in circumstance *s,* together with law *l,* logically entails the nonoccurrence of *e.*

It may be held instead that a cause is a condition that is sufficient in the circumstances for its effect. To say that event *c* is sufficient in the circumstances for event *e* is to say that there is some law, *l,* and some circumstance, *s,* such that the occurrence of *c,* in circumstance *s,* together with law *l,* logically entails the occurrence of *e.*

Finally, it has also been suggested that for one event to cause another is for its occurrence to be both necessary and sufficient in the circumstances for the occurrence of the other event.

What problems do such approaches encounter? Perhaps the most serious difficulty concerns the direction of causation. Suppose that our world were a Newtonian one, in which the basic laws are time-symmetric. Then the total state of the universe in 1950 would have been both necessary and sufficient not only for the total state in 2050 but also for the total state in 1850. It would therefore follow that events in 1950 had caused events in 1850.

Less general objections are also important. First, if a cause is necessary in the circumstances for its effect, this precludes cases of causal preemption, in which event *d* would have caused event *e* were it not for the presence of event *c,* which both caused *e* and prevented *d* from doing so. In such a case *c* is not necessary for *e* since, if *c* had not occurred, *e* would have been caused by *d.* Second, cases of causal overdetermination are also ruled out. For if both *c* and *d* are causally sufficient to bring about *e,* and both do so, then neither *c* nor *d* was necessary in the circumstances for the occurrence of *e.*

These objections can be avoided if one holds instead that a cause is sufficient in the circumstances for its effect. But then other objections emerge. In particular it follows that there can be no causal relations if all the laws of nature are probabilistic. This is a serious difficulty, especially given the indeterministic nature of quantum mechanics.

Subjunctive Conditional Approaches. A second important reductionist approach attempts to analyze causation using subjunctive conditionals. One way of arriving at this approach is by analyzing causation in terms of necessary or sufficient conditions (or both) but then interpreting the latter, not as nomological connections, as above, but as subjunctive conditionals. Thus one can say that *c* is necessary in the circumstances for *e* if, and only if, had *c* not occurred *e* would not have occurred, and that *c* is sufficient in the circumstances for *e* if, and only if, had *e* not occurred *c* would not have occurred.

John L. MACKIE [S] took this tack in developing a more sophisticated analysis of causation in terms of necessary and sufficient conditions. Thus, after defining an INUS condition of an event as an insufficient but necessary part of a condition which is itself unnecessary but exclusively sufficient for the event, and then arguing that *c*'s being a cause of *e* can then be analyzed as *c*'s being at least an INUS condition of *e,* Mackie asked how necessary and sufficient conditions should be understood. For general causal statements, Mackie favored a nomological account, but for singular causal statements he argued for an analysis in terms of subjunctive conditionals.

The most fully worked-out subjunctive conditional approach is that of David Lewis. His basic strategy involves analyzing causation using a narrower notion of causal dependence and then analyzing causal dependence counterfactually: (1) an event *c* causes an event *e* if, and only if, there is a chain of causally dependent events linking *e* with *c;* (2) an event *g* is causally dependent upon an event *f* if, and only if, had *f* not occurred *g* would not have occurred.

Causes, so construed, need not be necessary for their effects because counterfactual dependence, and hence causal dependence, are not necessarily transitive. Nevertheless, Lewis's approach is closely related to necessary-condition analyses of causation since the more basic relation of causal dependence is a matter of one event's being counterfactually necessary in the circumstances for another event.

What problems arise for such approaches? One is circularity. Classical analyses of subjunctive conditionals refer to causal laws, and so the question is whether any adequate, alternative analysis can avoid such reference.

Second, Lewis's account falls prey to both overdetermination cases and certain carefully constructed preemption cases, and Mackie's approach, while avoiding the problem of preemption, also rules out overdetermination.

Third, there is once again the problem of explaining the direction of causation. One possibility is to define the direction of causation as the direction of time, but neither Mackie nor Lewis favors that approach: both think that backward causation is logically possible. Mackie's main proposal appeals to the direction of irreversible processes involving the transmission of order—such as with outgoing concentric waves produced by a stone hitting a pond—and Lewis advances a somewhat related proposal, in which the direction of counterfactual dependence, and hence causal dependence, is based upon the idea that events in this world have many more effects than they have causes. But the problem with both of these suggestions is that the relevant features are at best contingent ones, and it would seem that, even if the world had neither of these features, it could still contain causally related events.

Probabilistic Approaches. Among the more significant developments in the philosophy of causation since the time of Hume is the idea, motivated in part by quantum mechanics, that causation is not restricted to deterministic processes. This has led several philosophers to propose that causation itself should be analyzed in probabilistic terms.

The central idea is that causes must make their effects more likely. This idea can, however, be expressed in two rather different ways. The traditional approach, developed by Hans REICHENBACH [7], I. J. Good, and Patrick Suppes, focuses upon types of events and involves the notion of positive statistical relevance. According to this notion, an event of type *C* is positively relevant to an event of type *E* if and only if the conditional probability of an event of type *E,* given an event of type *C,* is greater than the unconditional probability of an event of type *E.* The basic idea, then, is that for events of type *C* to be direct causes of events of type *E,* a necessary condition is that the former be positively relevant to the latter.

Other philosophers, including David Lewis, have suggested an alternative approach that focuses instead upon individual events and is formulated in terms of subjunctive conditionals concerning objective chances. The basic idea is that a necessary condition for *c*'s being a direct cause of *e* is that the objective chance of *e*'s occurring was greater, given that *c* occurred, than it would have been had *c* not occurred.

But do causes necessarily make their effects more likely? Consider two diseases, *A* and *B,* governed by the following laws. First, disease *A* causes death with probability 0.1, while disease *B* causes death with probability 0.8. Second, contracting either disease produces complete immunity to the other. Third, in condition *C*, an individual must contract either disease *A* or disease *B*. (Condition *C* might be a weakening of the immune system.) Finally, assume that individual *m* is in condition *C* and contracts disease *A*, which causes his death. Given these conditions, what if *m*, though in condition *C*, had not contracted disease *A*? Then *m* would have contracted disease *B*. But if so, then *m*'s probability of dying had he not contracted disease *A* would have been 0.8—higher than his probability of dying given that he had contracted disease *A*. So the claim that lies at the heart of probabilistic approaches—that causes necessarily make their effects more likely—does not appear to be true.

REALISM

Varieties of Realism. Traditional antireductionist approaches have generally held that the concept of causation is primitive and that causal relations are immediately observable. Both these claims, however, seem problematic. Regarding the first, the concept of causation appears to enter into various necessary truths—for example, that causation is irreflexive, asymmetric, and transitive—and if the concept of causation were analytically basic, no explanation of such necessary truths would be forthcoming. As for the second claim, it appears to be incompatible with an empiricist epistemology since the traditional argument from hallucination would seem to show that one cannot have noninferentially justified beliefs about causal states of affairs.

A very different form of causal realism holds, however, that causation is a theoretical relation between events. On this view, all knowledge of causal states of affairs is inferential knowledge, and the concept of causation stands in need of analysis. But unlike reductionist accounts, the relevant anlaysis does not imply that causal states of affairs are logically supervenient upon noncausal states of affairs.

Singularism and Causal Laws. Realist approaches to causation have generally rejected the claim that causal relations between events are reducible to causal laws and to noncausal states of affairs. But in addition, realism frequently has been combined with a singularist concept of causation, according to which events can be causally related even without falling under any causal law. But what reasons are there for accepting this view? The main traditional argument is that causation is directly observable, which would be impossible if causal relations presupposed causal laws—an argument that, as just indicated, involves a dubious premise. But other arguments can be offered, such as the following. Assume that indeterministic laws are logically possible and that, in particular, it is a basic law both that an object's acquiring property *P* causes it to acquire either property *Q* or property *R*, and that an object's acquiring property *S* also causes it to acquire either property *Q* or property *R*. Suppose now that some object simultaneously acquires both property *P* and property *S* and then immediately acquires both property *Q* and property *R*. The problem now is that, given that the relevant laws are basic, there cannot be any noncausal facts that will determine which causal relations obtain. Did the acquisition of *P* cause the acquisition of *Q*, or did it cause the acquisition of *R*? On a reductionist approach, no answer is possible. So it would seem that causal relations between events cannot be logically supervenient upon causal laws plus noncausal states of affairs.

Reductionism and the Direction of Causation. What determines the direction of causation? Reductionists have advanced various suggestions, but some arguments seem to show that no reductionist account can work. One such argument appeals to the idea of a very simple world—consisting, say, of a single particle, or of two particles rotating endlessly about one another. Such simple worlds would still involve causation since the identity over time of the particles, for example, requires causal relations between their temporal parts. But since such worlds are time-symmetric, the events in them will not exhibit any noncausal patterns that could provide the basis for a reductionist account of the direction of causation.

A second argument turns upon the idea of possible universes that are temporally inverted twins. Thus, given an instantaneous slice of any Newtonian universe, there could be another universe in which the spatial arrangement of the particles at some instant was the same but with all the velocities reversed. In one universe the direction of causation would agree with the direction of the propagation of order in irreversible processes, the direction of increase in ENTROPY [2], the direction of open forks, and so on, but in the inverted twin the direction of causation would be opposite. Accordingly, no reductionist account of the direction of causation can generate the correct answer for all possible worlds. It would seem, then, that only a realist account of causation will do. (SEE ALSO: *Metaphysics; Philosophy of Science* [S])

Bibliography

Anscombe, G. E. M. *Causality and Determination.* Cambridge, 1971. A defense of a realist view of causation, arguing that causation is directly observable.

Eells, E. *Probabilistic Causality.* Cambridge, 1991. A detailed exposition of a probabilistic approach, although with sparse discussion of objections.

Fales, E. *Causation and Universals.* London, 1990. A realist approach to causation, defending the view that causation is immediately observable.

Good, I. J. "A Causal Calculus," Parts 1 and 2, *British Journal for the Philosophy of Science,* Vol. 11 (1961), 305–18, and

Vol. 12 (1962), 43–51. An early exposition of a probabilistic approach; advocates introducing quantitative causal relations.

Lewis, D. "Counterfactual Dependence and Time's Arrow," *Noûs,* Vol. 13 (1979), 455–76. Reprinted, with postscripts, in *Philosophical Papers,* Vol. 2 (Oxford, 1986). Addresses the problem of the direction of counterfactual dependence.

———. "Causation," *Journal of Philosophy,* Vol. 70 (1973), 556–67. Reprinted, with postscripts, in *Philosophical Papers,* Vol. 2 (Oxford, 1986). An exposition and defense of a counterfactual approach.

Mackie, J. L. *The Cement of the Universe.* Oxford, 1974. A careful exposition of a reductionist approach to causation.

———. "Causes and Conditions," *American Philosophical Quarterly,* Vol. 2 (1965), 245–64. An exposition of the INUS condition account.

Reichenbach, H. *The Direction of Time.* Berkeley, 1956. The earliest exposition of a probabilistic approach to causation.

Salmon, W. C. *Scientific Explanation and the Causal Structure of the World.* Princeton, 1984. A reductionist approach that combines the idea of causal processes with a probabilistic account of causal interaction.

———. "Probabilistic Causality," *Pacific Philosophical Quarterly,* Vol. 61 (1980), 50–74. A critical examination of probabilistic approaches to causation.

Sosa, E., and M. Tooley, eds. *Causation.* Oxford, 1993. An anthology containing contemporary discussions of causation, plus a bibliography.

Strawson, G. *The Secret Connexion: Causation, Realism, and David Hume.* Oxford, 1989. Defends realism and challenges the standard reductionist interpretation of David Hume's approach.

Suppes, P. *A Probabilistic Theory of Causality.* Amsterdam, 1970. An accessible exposition of a probabilistic approach.

Tooley, M. "The Nature of Causation: A Singularist Account," in D. Copp, ed., *Canadian Philosophers, Canadian Journal of Philosophy,* Suppl., Vol. 16 (1990), 271–322. A defense of a singularist approach to causation.

———. *Causation: A Realist Approach.* Oxford, 1987. A defense of a realist view, arguing that causation is a theoretical relation between events.

Von Wright, G. H. *Explanation and Understanding.* Ithaca, NY, 1971. A defense of the view that the concept of causation is to be analyzed in terms of the idea of action.

MICHAEL TOOLEY

CENSORSHIP. Censorship is the suppression of speech or symbolic expression for reason of its message. Liberal Western constitutionalism has traditionally condemned censorship on both instrumental and intrinsic grounds, classically articulated by John Stuart MILL [5; S] in *On Liberty* (*see* LIBERTY [S]). In this traditional liberal view, freedom of speech instrumentally serves the ends of truth and self-government. Censorship, by entrenching orthodoxy and suppressing dissent, impedes the advancement of truth and the processes of democratic change (*see* DEMOCRACY [2; S]). Freedom of speech is also intrinsically valuable, in this view, as an aspect of human autonomy. Censorship illegitimately interferes with that autonomy, because speech, unlike action, typically causes others no harm. The proper response to bad speech is more speech, not government regulation.

Late-twentieth-century critics have challenged both the instrumental and the intrinsic justifications for freeing speech from censorship. First, some suggest that the power to speak is so unequally distributed that free competition in the marketplace of ideas is unlikely to produce either truth or democracy. For example, advocates of regulating campaign advertisements argue that wealthy voices dominate and thus distort political debate, and advocates of hate-speech regulation argue that racial epithets and invective perpetuate a form of cultural white supremacy in which minority voices are effectively silenced. These critics would turn the traditional free-speech principle on its head. In their view freedom of speech helps to entrench the existing status quo while government regulation of the speech of powerful groups can level the playing field. Redistribution of speaking power would advance truth and political equality better than a regime of laissez-faire.

Second, some critics argue that the defense of free speech on autonomy grounds undervalues the harms that speech causes. On this view speech regulation ought to be more widely allowed to protect the countervailing autonomy interests of listeners or bystanders. Liberal constitutional democracies generally permit censorship only to avert a narrow range of material harms. For example, incitement to riot may be forbidden, as may publication of the movements of troops at war. But censorship is rarely permitted on the ground that speech will cause disapproval, anger, alarm, resentment, or offense on the part of the audience. American constitutional law categorically forbids such justifications. Legal systems that permit them do so only in exceptional contexts: for example, British law forbids expressions of racial hatred, and some international human rights laws forbid advocacy of genocide.

Free-speech critics argue that such exceptions should be more the rule. First, some argue, government should be free to prevent injury, not only to bodies, but also to hearts and minds, including the injury caused by expressions of caustic opinion. Second, others argue, speech should be regulable for its social impact, even in the absence of immediate physical harm. On this view speech is not self-regarding but rather helps to structure social life. Thus, for example, pornography, hate speech, and graphic television violence inculcate attitudes that make society more immoral, sexist, racist, lawless, or violent than it would be if a different rhetoric prevailed. Speech helps construct society by socializing behavior, and reconstructing society, in this view, requires regulating speech.

At stake in these debates is whether speech will continue to be understood, like religious and reproductive practices, as presumptively a matter for private resolution, or instead will be subject to greater government regulation in the pursuit of social ends, including that of maximizing the quantity or diversity of speech itself.

Bibliography

Bork, R. "Neutral Principles and Some First Amendment Problems," *Indiana Law Journal,* Vol. 49 (1971), 1.

Dworkin, R. "The Coming Battles over Free Speech," *New York Review of Books,* June 11, 1992, 55.

Gates, H. L., Jr. "Let Them Talk," *New Republic,* Sept. 20 & 27, 1993, 37.

MacKinnon, C. A. *Only Words.* Cambridge, MA, 1993.

Matsuda, M. J., et al. *Words That Wound: Critical Race Theory, Assaultive Speech, and the First Amendment.* Boulder, CO, 1993.

Meiklejohn, A. *Free Speech and Its Relation to Self-Government.* New York, 1948.

Mill, J. S. *On Liberty.* 1859.

Scanlon, T. "A Theory of Free Expression," *Philosophy and Public Affairs,* Vol. 1 (1972), 204.

Strossen, N. *Defending Pornography: Free Speech, Sex, and the Fight for Women's Rights.* New York, 1995.

Sunstein, C. R. *Democracy and the Problem of Free Speech.* New York, 1993.

KATHLEEN M. SULLIVAN

CHISHOLM, RODERICK M., is a twentieth-century American philosopher who has made major contributions in almost every area of philosophy but most notably epistemology and metaphysics. He was an undergraduate at Brown University from 1934 to 1938 and a graduate student at Harvard from 1938 to 1942. He served in the military from 1942 to 1946, and then, after briefly holding a teaching post with the Barnes Foundation and the University of Pennsylvania, he returned in 1947 to Brown University, where he remained until his retirement.

EPISTEMOLOGY

In epistemology Chisholm is a defender of FOUNDATIONALISM [S]. He thinks that any proposition that is justified gets at least part of its justification from basic propositions, which are justified but not by anything else. Contingent propositions are basic insofar as they correspond to self-presenting states, which for Chisholm are states such that whenever one is in the state and believes that one is in it, then one's belief is maximally justified. There are two types of self-presenting states, intentional states (ways of thinking, hoping, fearing, desiring, wondering, intending, etc.) and sensory states (ways of being appeared to by the various senses). A noncontingent proposition is basic if understanding it is sufficient for understanding that it is true and hence also sufficient for making it justified. "2 + 3 = 5" and "If Jones is ill and Smith is away, then Jones is ill" are examples of such propositions, says Chisholm.

Self-presentation and understanding are among the sources of epistemic justification, but according to Chisholm there are other sources as well. The principal of these are perception, memory, belief coupled with a lack of negative coherence (e.g., no inconsistencies among the propositions believed), and belief coupled with positive coherence (i.e., mutual support among the propositions believed). For each of these sources, Chisholm forwards an epistemic principle that describes the precise conditions under which the source produces justified beliefs.

Despite his thinking that there are many sources of epistemic justification, Chisholm is rightly regarded as a foundationalist because all the sources are such that they can produce justified beliefs only because some propositions are justified basically. For example, Chisholm's principles concerning perception and memory make reference to propositions that are justified because they correspond to self-presenting states. In the case of perception the relevant states are sensings, and for memory the relevant states are beliefs (specifically, beliefs to the effect that one remembers something). In a similar spirit, Chisholm says that coherence relations among propositions are not capable of generating justification for propositions that have nothing else to recommend them; their role instead is to increase the degree of justification that propositions have by virtue of being supported by basic propositions.

Chisholm is also a proponent of INTERNALISM [S] in epistemology, in two senses of the term. First, he thinks that epistemic justification supervenes on our conscious states; thus, whether one's beliefs are justified is determined by one's own internal states rather than by conditions obtaining in one's external environment. Second, he thinks that the conditions, if any, that justify one's beliefs are accessible to one; thus, one can determine, if one reflects carefully enough, whether one's beliefs are justified.

Chisholm's epistemology is resolutely antiskeptical. Indeed, he says that the proper way to begin doing epistemology is by presupposing that some of our beliefs are justified and some constitute knowledge. Epistemology, so conceived, becomes primarily a search for the conditions that account for these beliefs being justified. A second task is to define the conditions that turn a true belief into knowledge. Chisholm's approach to this latter task is to defend a nondefeasibility account to knowledge. We know a proposition *p,* he says, whenever we believe *p, p* is true, and *p* is nondefectively evident for us, where *p* is nondefectively evident for us (some details aside) just in case there is a set of basic propositions that justify *p* and nothing false for us.

METAPHYSICS

Chisholm has well-worked-out views on almost every major issue in metaphysics, but his most influential views have been concerned with thought and language, ontology, action, and material bodies.

With respect to thought and language, Chisholm is a defender of the primacy of thought; the intentionality of language is to be understood in terms of the intentionality of thought, he says, rather than conversely. He develops this idea in his direct attribution theory of REFERENCE [S]. At the heart of the theory is a proposal that we are able to refer to things other than ourselves by directly attributing properties to them and that we indirectly attribute properties to them by directly attributing properties to ourselves. For example, if you are the only person in a room with me and you are wearing a blue sweater, then by directly attributing to myself the property of being a person *X* such that the only other person in the room with *X* is wearing a blue sweater, I indirectly attribute to you the property of wearing a blue sweater and thereby refer to you. Using these notions of direct and indirect attribution, Chisholm provides an account of various semantic notions including sense and reference.

In ontology, Chisholm's view is that there are only two kinds of entities, attributes and the individual things that have these attributes. Everything else, including propositions, states of affairs, possible worlds, and sets, can be understood in terms of two categories. Attributes are possible objects of thought—more specifically, what we are able to attribute, either directly (to ourselves) or indirectly (both to ourselves and other things). Thus, in ontology, Chisholm once again is a defender of the primacy of thought in that he uses the phenomenon of intentionality to identify and understand what kinds of entities there are.

His theory of action is an indeterministic one (*see* ACTION THEORY [S]). The fundamental notions are those of undertaking and causing, and with respect to the latter notion he carefully distinguishes among necessary causal conditions for an event, sufficient causal conditions, and causal contributions. With these notions in hand, he opposes compatibilist attempts to understand what it is for a person to be free to undertake something, insisting that one has undertaken to do something freely only if there was no sufficient causal condition for one to undertake it (although there may have been extensive causal contributions to the undertaking).

Much of Chisholm's work on bodies is concerned with puzzles about the PERSISTENCE [S] of physical bodies through time, and most of these puzzles, in turn, are concerned with apparent violations of Leibniz's principle of the indiscernibility of identicals. According to this principle, if *X* and *Y* are identical, then whatever is true of *X* is also true of *Y*. One famous puzzle, for example, is the ship of Theseus. Even if one plank of the ship is replaced at a time *t*, it is the same ship, namely Theseus's, that exists before *t* and after *t*, and yet the ship might appear to have different properties before *t* and after *t*. Chisholm attempts to solve this and other puzzles about the identity of physical bodies through time by using his fundamental ontological categories, attributes and individual things, to make precise the seventeenth-century distinction between substances and their modes.

Bibliography

Bogdan, R., ed. *Roderick M. Chisholm.* Dordrecht, 1986. Critical essays on Chisholm and a helpful self-profile.

Chisholm, R. *The First Person: An Essay on Reference and Intentionality.* Minneapolis, 1981. A detailed defense of the direct attribution theory of reference.

———. *Theory of Knowledge.* Englewood Cliffs, NJ, 1st ed., 1966; 2d ed., 1977; 3d ed., 1987. His most influential work in epistemology; the later editions contain important modifications of his earlier views.

———. *Person and Object: A Metaphysical Study.* London, 1976. Most of his metaphysical positions are defended in this volume.

———. *Human Freedom and the Self.* Lawrence, KS, 1964. A defense of his indeterministic account of human freedom.

———. *Perceiving: A Philosophical Study.* Ithaca, NY, 1957. His first major work on epistemology.

Lehrer, K., ed. *Analysis and Metaphysics: Essays in Honor of R. M. Chisholm.* Dordrecht, 1975. Critical essays on Chisholm's metaphysics and epistemology.

RICHARD FOLEY

CHOMSKY, NOAM, born in 1928, is the foremost linguistic theorist of the postwar era, an important contributor to philosophical debates, and a notable radical activist. His influence is felt in many other fields, however, most notably, perhaps, in the area of cognitive studies.

Chomsky's main achievement was to distinguish linguistic competence from its manifestations in performance and to characterize competence as a system of explicit rules for the construction and interpretation of sentences. Indeed, this achievement provided a model for investigations, in this and other cognitive domains, that replaced then-dominant models based on the notion of analogy and oriented to the causal explanation of behavior.

The competence of individuals to use their language is constituted, on Chomsky's account, by their (tacit) knowledge of a formal grammar (or system of rules); their linguistic performance, involving the deployment of such knowledge, may be influenced by a host of extraneous factors that need not be accounted for by the grammar itself but, instead and if possible, by subsidiary theories (e.g., of perceptual processing, etc.). Furthermore, knowledge of such a system of rules permits a kind of creativity in performance that exhibits itself in the novelty, in relation to speakers' prior linguistic experiences, of (many of) the sentences they actually produce. (Crudely put, they can understand and produce sentences they have never before encountered.)

The competence/performance distinction reflects Chomsky's preference for 'Galiean' theorizing (i.e., for a 'modular' approach), and its introduction was tremendously liberating. A direct attack on performance, under broadly behavioristic auspices, had proved barren, for reasons Chomsky identified with devastating clarity in his review of B. F. Skinner's *Verbal Behavior* (*see* BEHAVIORISM [1]). Also pertinent was Chomsky's analysis of linguistic creativity in a second, distinct sense: the appropriateness and yet stimulus-independence (and therefore causal inexplicability) of much of what a speaker says in concrete circumstances. Shifting the linguist's problematic from behavior to the system underlying behavior was probably Chomsky's most important contribution to the development of 'scientific' studies of social phenomena. (Of course, the competence/performance distinction owes much to Ferdinand de Saussure's earlier distinction between *langue* and *parole.* But Saussure did not think of the system underlying behavior as primarily rule-based, and so his distinction proved less fertile than Chomsky's.)

In a series of works beginning with *Cartesian Linguistics,* Chomsky took up what he came to call "Plato's problem"—that of explaining how the gap is bridged between individuals' limited opportunities, as children, for acquiring knowledge of their (native) language(s) and the competence to make many subtle and complex discriminations that, as mature speakers, they do indeed possess. He solved this problem, siding with classical rationalists such as LEIBNIZ [4; S], by assuming the existence, as an innate species-wide attribute, of a 'universal grammar'. During the course of language acquisition, limited data fixes the values of free 'parameters' associated with this grammar, thus providing a basis for full-blown knowledge of the language that far exceeds the ordinary 'inductive' implications of these data.

Chomsky has also been a notable advocate, very significantly in a discipline previously marked by instrumentalist assumptions about theorizing, of a realist perspective on theoretical entities and processes. In early work deep structures were postulated as sources, via transformations, of familiar superficial structures of sentences. So, for instance, a superficially passive sentence was said to be derived from the same deep structure as its active counterpart. And while it might have been more in line with then-contemporary practice to treat these so-called deep structures as pure postulates, useful in simplifying the description and taxonomization of the superficial sentences of our 'experience', Chomsky advocated, instead, that they be treated as having psychological reality and thereby fostered many profound psycholinguistic studies intended to bear out or refute this contention. A topic of continuing importance is whether it is only structures or, instead, derivational processes as well that are to be treated as 'real'.

Less noticed by commentators is Chomsky's profoundly individualistic approach to linguistic phenomena. For him, language itself is a secondary phenomena; primacy is accorded to an individual's competence, a purely psychological phenomenon. Indeed, Chomsky explains the coordination of linguistic interaction, not by reference to any transpersonal system of conventions (as might be thought appropriate in relation to other social phenomena), but, instead, to a harmony—between the competence of the speaker and the marginally different competence of the hearer—that depends largely on the innate constraints on their (typically) quite separate episodes of language acquisition. Even if each learns in isolation from the other, and has quite (though not 'too') different experiential bases for learning, each will acquire an 'idiolect' that is accessible to the other: otherwise rather different data-sets fix the free parameters of the universal grammar in sufficiently similar ways to permit mutual intelligibility.

Other philosophically important themes in Chomsky's work include: (1) his identification of the ideological interests that are served by certain allegedly 'scientific' approaches to the study of human behavior; (2) his argument for treating the capacity for language as species-specific and thus as an aspect of the human 'essence'; (3) his speculations about the possibility that there are innate limitations on the human capacity for knowledge of the world; and (4) his continued defense, in the face of broadly 'postmodernist' opposition (*see* POSTMODERNISM [S]), of the role of reason in understanding and improving the human condition and of the viability of the notion of 'progress' in relation to these projects.

Bibliography

WORKS BY CHOMSKY

Syntactic Structures. The Hague, 1957.

"A Review of B. F. Skinner's *Verbal Behavior,*" in J. A. Fodor and J. J. Katz, eds., *The Structure of Language* (Englewood Cliffs, NJ, 1964).

Cartesian Linguistics. New York, 1966.

Language and Mind. New York, 1972.

For Reasons of State. London, 1973.

Language and Problems of Knowledge. Cambridge, MA, 1988.

WORKS ON CHOMSKY

D'Agostino, F. *Chomsky's System of Ideas.* Oxford, 1986.

Harman, G., ed. *On Noam Chomsky.* Garden City, NY, 1974.

Kasher, A., ed. *The Chomskyan Turn.* Oxford, 1991.

Sampson, G. *Liberty and Language.* Oxford, 1979.

FRED D'AGOSTINO

CLASSICAL FOUNDATIONALISM. Classical foundationalism maintains that all knowledge and justified belief rest ultimately on a foundation of noninferential knowledge and noninferentially justified belief. Because the classical foundationalist typically assumes an account of knowledge in terms of justified or rational true belief, this entry will focus on the distinction invoked between inferentially and noninferentially justified beliefs.

If we think about most of the beliefs we take to be justified and ask ourselves what justifies them, it seems natural to answer in terms of other justified beliefs. One's justification for believing that it will rain, for example, may consist in part of one's justifiably believing that the barometer is dropping rapidly. But under what conditions can one justifiably infer the truth of one proposition *p* from another *e*? The classic foundationalist typically answers this question with what might be called the principle of inferential justification. To be justified in believing *p* by inferring it from *e*, one must be (1) justified in believing *e* and (2) justified in believing that *e* confirms (makes probable) *p*.

The principle of inferential justification is a crucial premise in the famous regress argument for foundationalism. If the principle is correct, then to be justified in believing some proposition *p* on the basis of some other evidence, e_1, one would need to be justified in believing e_1. But if all justification were inferential, then to be justified in believing e_1, one would need to infer it from something else e_2, which one justifiably believes, and so on ad infinitum. This first regress is generated by clause (1) of the principle of inferential justification. If clause (2) is correct, the potential regresses proliferate endlessly. To be justified in inferring *p* from e_1, one must justifiably believe not only e_1 but also that e_1 makes *p* likely, and one must infer this from something else, f_1, which one must justifiably infer from some other proposition, f_2, which one justifiably infers. . . . But one must also justifiably believe that f_1 makes likely that e_1 makes likely *p*, so one must justifiably infer that from some other proposition, g_1, which one justifiably infers. . . . If all justification were inferential, then to justifiably believe any proposition *p* we would need to complete not one but an infinite number of infinitely long chains of reasoning. The human mind is finite and cannot complete infinitely long chains of reasoning. To avoid the absurd conclusion that we have no reason for believing anything whatsoever, we must suppose that some beliefs are justified without inference and that these noninferentially justified beliefs ground the justification of all other justified beliefs.

Classical foundationalists refer to the foundations of knowledge and justified belief in a variety of ways—noninferentially justified beliefs, self-evident truths, directly evident truths, incorrigible beliefs, infallible beliefs—but there is no consensus on what confers foundational status on a belief. Some, following René DESCARTES [2; S], seek foundations in beliefs that do not admit the possibility of error. As we shall see, the possibility in question can be interpreted in a number of different ways, but classical foundationalists invoke a very strong concept of possibility—if a belief is foundational, it must be inconceivable that the belief is false. Having the belief must somehow entail its truth.

Many other classical foundationalists sought the source of foundational knowledge in some relation (other than belief) between a believer and the truth conditions of what is believed. One often-invoked metaphor is the concept of acquaintance. When one believes that one is in pain when one is in pain, one is directly acquainted or confronted with the pain itself (the very state that makes true the proposition believed). The knower's direct confrontation with the relevant aspect of reality to which the truth in question corresponds obviates the need for any inference.

There might also be direct acquaintance with logical relations holding between propositions, states of affairs, or properties, direct acquaintance with which yields direct knowledge of necessary truths. On such a view, then, one might locate the source of both a priori and a posteriori foundational knowledge in the same relation of acquaintance. The difference between the two kinds of knowledge might lie more on the side of the relata of the acquaintance relation than on the source of the knowledge.

Classical foundationalism has come under considerable attack from many different directions. Some would argue that the search for infallible beliefs as the foundations of knowledge is both fruitless and misguided, at least if infallibility is understood in terms of a belief's entailing the truth of what is believed. First, it has been pointed out that if one believes a necessary truth, one's belief will trivially entail the truth of what is believed. But surely such a belief would not constitute knowledge if the person held the belief as a matter of pure whimsy. Once one sees that the entailment between belief and the truth of what one believes is not sufficient for any kind of knowledge, one might begin to wonder whether it is ever getting at the heart of any interesting epistemic concept. Still other philosophers have pointed out that beliefs that entail their truth are few and far between and, if knowledge rests on a foundation of these, the foundation is precarious indeed. Consider a favorite example of a foundational belief offered by classical foundationalists—the belief one has that one is in pain. Believing that one is in pain seems to be a state logically distinct from the pain. As such it seems always at least conceivable that the belief could occur (perhaps produced by some evil demon) without the pain.

Some contemporary philosophers are sympathetic to the idea of direct knowledge, understood in terms of beliefs that cannot be false, but have understood the relevant possibility in causal or nomological terms. Thus, the circumstances that produce my belief that *p* may be causally sufficient for the truth of *p*. It is not easy to spell out in an interesting way how one specifies the relevant circumstances causally responsible for a belief, but this approach does succeed in calling into question the classical foundationalists' emphasis on conceivability or logical possibility as the relevant concept to employ in defining epistemically interesting concepts of infallibility.

Reliance on the concept of acquaintance to define the concept of foundational knowledge has not fared much better when it comes to contemporary philosophical fashion. The standard line most often taken is that there is no such relation and, even if there were, it would be of no epistemic interest. Foundational knowledge must be knowledge of propositions if it is to yield the premises from which we can infer the rest of what we justifiably believe. But acquaintance with a fact seems to be a relation that has nothing to do with anything that has a truth value. Facts are not the kinds of things that can be true or false. How does acquaintance with a fact yield access to truth? Indeed, can one even make sense of reference to facts independently of truth? Some philosophers would argue that referring to a fact is just another way of referring to a proposition's being true. If facts are reducible to truths, it would clearly be uninformative to locate the source of noninferential knowledge of truths in terms of acquaintance with facts to which truths correspond.

To attack various versions of foundationalism is not, of course, to respond to the regress argument for foundationalism. It has already been noted that some contemporary foundationalists accept the fundamental idea that there are foundations to knowledge but reject classical accounts of what those foundations consist in. Many externalists, for example, identify justificatory conditions for belief with the circumstances producing the belief (*see* EXTERNALISM [S]). Reliabilists, for example, count a belief as justified if it is reliably produced and allow that a belief might be reliably produced even if the input producing the belief involves no other beliefs (*see* RELIABILISM [S]). Such reliable belief-independent processes can end a regress of beliefs justified by reference to other beliefs.

The other main alternative to classical foundationalism is the coherence theory of justification (*see* COHERENTISM [S]). The coherentist rejects the classical foundationalist's assumption that justification is linear in structure. According to the coherentist, there is no escape from the circle of one's beliefs—nothing can justify a belief but other beliefs. But one doesn't justify a belief by reference to other prior justified beliefs. Rather, each belief is justified by reference to its "fit" in an entire system of beliefs.

(SEE ALSO: *Epistemology* [S])

Bibliography

Descartes, R. *Discourse on Method and Meditations*, translated by L. Lafleur. Indianapolis, 1960.

Lehrer, K. *Knowledge*, Chap. 4–6. Oxford, 1974.

Price, H. H. *Perception*, Chap. 1, London, 1950.

Russell, B. *The Problems of Philosophy*, Chap. 5, Oxford, 1959.

RICHARD FUMERTON

COGNITIVE SCIENCE. Cognitive science is the interdisciplinary study of mind in which the concepts and methods of ARTIFICIAL INTELLIGENCE (AI) [S] are central. The most prominent subdisciplines are AI, psychology, philosophy, and linguistics. Howard Gardner (1985) includes anthropology and sociology, and Mark Turner (1991) adds English studies. Not everyone working in these disciplines is a cognitive scientist; only those taking a computational approach to questions about mind can be given this designation. Relevant subfields include the psychology of human–computer interaction and computational musicology. Nonhuman minds are studied by cognitive and computational ethology and by parts of artificial life (A-Life). Computational neuroscience, which studies computational functions in the brain, also falls within cognitive science.

Cognitive science includes cognitive psychology: the study of language, memory, perception, problem solving, and creativity. Most research has focused on individual human adult cognition, but some research has focused on other aspects of mind: motivation, emotion, development, psychopathology, interpersonal phenomena, motor control, and animal (and artificial) psychology. Cognitive science is not concerned only with cognition.

Cognitive science employs COMPUTATIONAL MODELS OF MIND [S], in two senses. First, the substantive concepts in its theories are computational. The mind is seen as some sort of computational system (just what sort is disputed), and mental processes are described accordingly. Second, computer modeling is often used to clarify and test those theories. If a program produces a given performance, we know that it suffices to do so. Whether real minds use similar processes to produce equivalent performance is another question that must also be addressed.

Many philosophical disputes arise within cognitive science. One concerns the relative merits of two AI approaches: classical (symbolic) AI and CONNECTIONISM [S]. Some researchers champion only one of these, while others admit both because of their complementary strengths and weaknesses. Another debate concerns the nature and importance of various kinds of internal representation and whether thought requires language. A third asks whether (and if so, how) MEANING [5; S] (intentionality) can be grounded in the real world. And a fourth concerns whether consciousness could be explained in computational (or any other scientific) terms.

Some recent work opposes orthodox (neo-Cartesian) cognitive science, preferring the phenomenological tradi-

tion. It rejects both symbolic and connectionist AI, and the concept of representation. It highlights embodied systems (not abstract simulations) that are embedded in their environments and respond directly to them. Examples include situated robotics in AI, dynamical systems theory, ecological psychology, and A-Life studies of evolution and coevolution.
(SEE ALSO: *Philosophy of Mind* [S])

Bibliography

Boden, M. A., ed. *The Philosophy of Artificial Intelligence.* Oxford, 1990.

———. *Computer Models of Mind: Computational Approaches in Theoretical Psychology.* Cambridge, 1988.

Dennett, D. C. *Consciousness Explained.* Boston, 1991.

Fodor, J. A. *Psychosemantics: The Problem of Meaning in the Philosophy of Mind.* Cambridge, MA, 1987.

Gardner, H. *The Mind's New Science: A History of the Cognitive Revolution.* New York, 1985.

Johnson-Laird, P. N. *The Computer and the Mind: An Introduction to Cognitive Science.* London, 1988.

Turner, M. *Reading Minds: The Study of English in the Age of Cognitive Science.* Princeton, NJ, 1991.

Varela, F. J., E. Thompson, and E. Rosch. *The Embodied Mind: Cognitive Science and Human Experience.* Cambridge, MA, 1991.

MARGARET BODEN

COHERENTISM. One of the three major views of the nature of epistemic justification, the coherence theory (or coherentism) experienced a revival during the 1970s and 1980s after its near total eclipse earlier in the century. Although its origins can be traced to idealists, including Francis BRADLEY, Bernard BOSANQUET, and Brand BLANSHARD [1], the coherence theory has more recently been espoused by empiricist-minded contemporary philosophers such as Wilfrid SELLARS [S], Nicholas Rescher, Keith Lehrer, Gilbert Harman, and Laurence Bonjour. The coherence theory of justification stands as an alternative to both the more traditional foundations theory (*see* CLASSICAL FOUNDATIONALISM [S]) and the view called RELIABILISM [S]. It should not be confused with a COHERENCE THEORY OF TRUTH [2]. A coherence theorist about justification can acknowledge a fact that cripples the coherence theory of truth, namely, that there are instances of coherent, hence justified, beliefs in falsehoods.

Although the details of different versions of the coherence theory vary widely, all versions share a positive thesis and a resulting negative claim. The coherence theory's positive thesis is that a belief is justified or warranted for a person to the degree that that belief coheres with the rest of that person's belief system. As a fabric derives its strength from the reciprocal ties and interconnections among its constitutive threads, so, for the coherentist, beliefs derive their justification from their interconnectedness with one's other beliefs. The negative claim endorsed by all coherentists is that FOUNDATIONALISM [S] is in error when it asserts that some of our justified beliefs are privileged or basic—that is, their justification is at least partly independent of their connectedness with other held beliefs.

The coherentist's picture of mutual support or fit among our beliefs departs (to varying degrees) from the strictly linear image of justification that classical foundationalism endorses. For the foundationalist epistemic justification is transmitted to nonbasic beliefs, from those that are basic or foundational, along lines of inference and explanation. Inferred beliefs are justified by those from which they are inferred. For the coherentist the belief's justificatory status has less to do with the grounds on which a belief is based and more to do with the whole cluster of relations (of consistency, implication, probability, explanation, and the like) that more or less strongly fix that belief within the network of other held beliefs.

The exact nature of epistemic coherence, however, is very difficult to clarify, and disagreements occur even among coherentists. Some have argued that coherence is always and ultimately explanatory coherence, a question of whether a belief is a member of the best overall explanatory account accessible to an individual. Others claim that there are justificatory relations of comparative reasonableness of competing beliefs that reflect concerns wider than explanation alone, including measures of subjective probability and the relative informativeness of the proposition believed. Logical consistency seems to be a minimal necessary condition for maximal coherence, but some have argued that at least certain inconsistencies are unavoidable but do not so undermine coherence as to prevent beliefs from being justified. Speaking generally, coherence is a property of a belief system that is determined by the (various) connections of intelligibility among the elements of the system. Most agree that these include deductive, inductive, and abductive relations, as well as other explanatory and probabilistic connections. Some writers, especially pragmatists, are prepared to add relations such as the relative simplicity or the power of the explanations contained in one's belief system as contributors to overall coherence.

Motivation for the coherence theory comes most directly from finding foundationalism unworkable and believing as a consequence that some version of coherence must be correct. Another motivation comes from the observation that it seems apt and possible to ask about any belief what a person's reasons are for holding it. The theory also appears particularly compatible with the realization that all instances of epistemic justification are defeasible—that is, the justification of a given belief is always liable to undermining by other held beliefs, no matter how strong the initial grounds or evidential basis of the belief might be. Since undermining can come from any element of one's system that might be negatively relevant to a specific belief, it appears that complete epistemic justification, the kind necessary to support claims of knowledge, is sensitive to all of the connections among our beliefs, precisely as the coherence theorist urges. This argument for the coherence theory is not decisive, however, since foundationalists can freely admit that warrant is undermined by a lack of coherence while still rejecting the coherentist's positive claim that coherence is the source of all epistemic justification.

In addition to the unclarities surrounding measuring degrees of coherence, numerous objections have been offered to coherentism. Four have been particularly prominent.

THE CIRCULARITY OBJECTION

If there are no foundational beliefs that act as the ultimate source of epistemic justification, and if the lines of justification transmission are not infinitely long (which appears absurd given the finitude of our mental capacities), then the coherence theory seems forced to claim that justification can be ultimately but not viciously circular. It is not immediately clear how circularity of this sort is anything but vicious, no matter how wide the circle may be, even though some have argued that wideness of a justificatory circle immunizes against viciousness. But if A is the source of justification for B, how can B be the source of justification for A? The coherentist can reply that the "source" of justification is the entire belief system. The linear model of justification on which the circularity objection is based may not be forceful against a more holistic construal of the relation. Taken as a holistic and higher-order relation constituted by lower-order reciprocal relations (at least some of which are asymmetric, such as "explaining" and "being explained by"), coherence might be able to avoid the problem of vicious circularity.

THE PROBLEM OF PERCEPTUAL BELIEFS

Certain simple and apparently immediate perceptual beliefs seem to be justified for us on the basis of the perceptual experience we currently are having rather than on any considerations about how that belief coheres with the rest of our belief system. Experience often seems to warrant beliefs that are anomalous—that is, do not cohere with already-held beliefs. In such cases we do not think that we are justified in rejecting the new belief on grounds of incoherence but often concede that revision of some previously held beliefs is appropriate. Coherentists have replied to this objection by arguing that the justification of even the most immediate perceptual belief requires that that belief cohere with our metabeliefs regarding how reliable or trustworthy we take our perceptual processes to be in the particular conditions. It is such metabeliefs that make it more reasonable to accept the anomalous perceptual experience than it is for us to conclude that we are hallucinating or have been deceived in some fashion. The introduction of metabeliefs into the explanation why immediate perceptual beliefs are often justified for us has struck many, however, as overintellectualizing our epistemic situation, as well as possibly reintroducing foundational principles into the theory of justification.

THE ISOLATION OBJECTION

This objection, closely related to the problem of perceptual beliefs, begins with the observation that coherence is a cognitively internal relation, relating belief to belief. But might not a thoroughly coherent system of beliefs nonetheless fail to be justified because they are not properly linked to the external perceptual circumstances? Would acceptance of a coherent fiction be justified if it were entirely the product of wishful thinking? The continual perceptual input we receive from the world must be assimilated into our belief system or else the justification for those beliefs will often suffer from undermining. The coherence theory seems too internalist to be a complete theory of epistemic justification, the objection concludes. Since coherence does not necessarily serve the epistemic goals of pursuing truth and avoiding error in our belief system, further constraints seem necessary if our notion of justification is to relate appropriately to knowledge. Coherentists respond in a number of ways to the isolation objection.

One alternative is to admit the objection's force and add a requirement that all justified systems include the belief that certain kinds of spontaneously occurring beliefs such as perceptual and memory beliefs are reliable or likely to be true. Demonstrating that this constraint is not an ad hoc amendment to coherentism is a difficult matter. A similar requirement applied to acceptances based on spontaneous wishful thinking would be obviously ad hoc and unacceptable. Some have suggested that metabeliefs about the trustworthiness of our perceptual beliefs in certain circumstances are not ad hoc and are important and legitimate members of our belief system, justified, as all beliefs are, through their coherence with our other beliefs. Whether such beliefs can be noncircularly defended, whether they constitute a sort of foundational belief, and whether they are realistically necessary for epistemic justification are each open matters.

THE INFERENTIAL-STRUCTURE OBJECTION

The foundationalist's traditional view—that whether one is epistemically justified in believing some proposition depends crucially upon the actual course of inference taken in arriving at a belief—is not easily relinquished. Coherence, however, is a relation determined only by the contents of beliefs and not by the order in which they have been inferred. Consequently, it appears possible that a series of beliefs inferred one from the other in a wholly fallacious manner might nevertheless cohere maximally with a background system of beliefs as long as there is another valid (but unused) course of inference that does connect them. This leads to the conclusion that, even if the coherence theory adequately captures the concept of epistemically justifiable beliefs relative to a system, it fails to explicate the notion of being justified in believing a proposition. Coherentists have responded to this challenge by relying once more on metabeliefs, claiming that when we infer A from B and B from C we also accept or believe that A follows from B, and not, for example, that C follows from A. Incorrect metabeliefs will, on some versions of coherentism, cause incoherence and loss of justification, keeping blatantly fallacious reasoning from ending in justified beliefs. This response, however, may generate an infinite regress of metabeliefs. Not all uses of inference schemes contain premises stating that the scheme is valid. One can infer B from A without first having to infer that B follows from A. Some coherentists answer this and other objections by admitting that their proposed conditions for coherence constitute ideals to which human knowers should aspire but seldom in actuality achieve. Debate over the merits of the coherence theory promises to continue unabated.

(SEE ALSO: *Epistemology* [S]; and *Epistemology, History of* [3])

Bibliography

Audi, R. "Foundationalism, Coherentism, and Epistemological Dogmatism," in J. Tomberlin, ed., *Philosophical Perspectives,* Vol. 2, 1988.

Bender, J. W., ed. *The Current State of the Coherence Theory.* Philosophical Studies, Vol. 44. Dordrecht, 1989.

Bonjour, L. *The Structure of Empirical Knowledge.* Cambridge, MA, 1985.

Lehrer, K. *Theory of Knowledge.* Boulder, CO, 1990.

Plantinga, A. *Warrant: The Current Debate.* Oxford, 1993.

Pollock, J. *Contemporary Theories of Knowledge.* Totowa, NJ, 1986.

JOHN W. BENDER

COLORS.

The phenomena of color pose a special puzzle to philosophers characterizing the mind, the world, and the interaction of the two. In various ways, both subjective and objective, both appearance and reality, color has been the subject of wide disagreement. Besides the extreme view that colors are literally sensations—which would imply that they are not in the category of properties and that they last precisely as long as sensations—the main views are these.

PHYSICALISM

D. M. ARMSTRONG, J. J. C. SMART [S], and others have suggested that red (or being red), for example, is a physical property—perhaps a surface physical characteristic (like Boyle's "textures")—or a propensity to reflect some kinds of light more than others. The threat that physical science might be unable to find a predicate coextensive with "red" seems small; but there are challenges to the idea that any such property can be identified with red. First, will a physical property have the same higher-level properties as red does? Red is a "unique" color—there is a "pure" shade of red with no hint of any other color (unlike orange, every shade of which evidently contains red and yellow); however, it seems nonsense to say that some reflectance characteristic is "unique." The physicalist may perhaps reply: a reflectance characteristic can indeed have the property of "uniqueness"—if that is understood as the property of *suggesting to a normal observer no hint of any other color.* (That higher-level property will no doubt be the subject of a later reduction.) A second challenge is this: ordinary people surely know, for example, that red is more similar to orange than to blue, but if colors are properties whose true nature is revealed only in science, then (until they know more science) they should be in no position to know this. The physicalist may have a reply: this kind of knowledge is of phenomenal similarity, not physical similarity—and on that ordinary perceivers are authoritative. Both challenges suggest an important point, however—that physicalism can at best be a theory about properties that we think of initially without any thought of physical science.

DISPOSITIONAL VIEWS

The view that colors are dispositions to produce experiences has long been nearly an orthodoxy in the field. Proposed by BOYLE [1] and LOCKE [4; S], it has seemed a perfect way to capture the connections between color concepts and color experience. You cannot, it seems, grasp the idea of red unless things sometimes look red to you. And you cannot have a full grasp of the idea unless you realize that your color judgments will be defeasible if it turns out that either you or the conditions are abnormal. The proposal may be strengthened by adding an actuality operator: to be red, an object needs to look red to such observers and in such conditions as *actually* count as normal. This last phrase shall be abbreviated as "to look red [etc.]."

A preliminary worry can perhaps be met. Are there any such things as "normal conditions" and "normal observers"? Normal conditions vary hugely with the nature of the object and with our interests; in some cases (e.g., bioluminescent fish) there may be no clear answer to the question what normal conditions are. "Normal observers" pose a further problem: even when we rule out "color-blind" people, there is surprising disagreement among the remainder (e.g., over which shade of green is "unique"). These problems may not be fatal. If there is indeterminacy in the truth of "x is disposed to look red to normal observers under normal conditions," there may be an exactly corresponding indeterminacy in the truth of "x is red"—the moral may be that some things have no determinate color, not that color is mischaracterized by the dispositional thesis.

Dispositional views vary according to whether they take the experience of a thing's looking red to be a sensation or a representation. The sensationalist version faces the suspicion that the required "sensations of red" (or the "red′ regions of the visual field" in Peacocke's language) are mythical creatures of a modern-day sense-datum theory. (For some of this debate, *see* QUALIA [S].) The view also implies that when an object looks red, it looks disposed to produce red′ regions in the visual field. And that seems excessively sophisticated.

The representational version has a related problem: if "red" literally means "disposed to look red [etc.]," then "looks red" will have to mean "looks disposed to look red [etc.]"—which is surely false. This—like related objections about circularity—shows that "red" cannot mean "disposed to look red [etc.]"; but it may not rule out a nonobvious identity of redness and the disposition to look red [etc.], or an a priori necessary coextensiveness.

A final challenge—for both versions of the dispositional view—is more serious. Imagine a yellow object that also emits death rays, so that anyone who looks at it is killed before he can see its color. The object will be yellow but have no disposition to produce experiences as of yellow in normal observers. (The example is due to KRIPKE [S].) One can indeed insist that the object would look yellow to normal observers if only we masked the death rays. But we need to mask the death rays without masking or changing the color. And there is no knowledge of what that amounts to, independent of a substantial conception of what color is. We may believe, for example, that the color of a surface is a matter of the way it reflects incident light; so we can change and mask anything that leaves intact the object's *way of changing incident light.* But if we have that belief, it is no thanks to the definition of yellow as simply "the disposition to look yellow [etc.]." Our prime conception of color must have a different source.

VIEWS AVAILABLE

If the physicalist and dispositional views can at best be true with respect to properties first identified by some other route, then we need a new account of our thought about color and of the object of that thought. If color thinking contains an error, the options are projectivism and eliminativism; more easily overlooked is the possibility that color thinking may contain no error and a nonreductive simple realism be the appropriate view.

PROJECTIVISM

GALILEO [3] and (at times) DESCARTES [2; S] and Locke are the first of many to treat colors as properties of experiences, which we wrongly 'project' onto external objects. Attractive though the view is, it faces two tasks. It must establish its right to a sensational conception of color vision; and it must clarify what exactly is meant by "projecting" a sensation. The difficulty is to find a precise account of projection that does not make the process so absurd that humans could not commit it or so innocent that it is not actually a mistake.

REPRESENTATIONAL ERROR THEORY AND ELIMINATIVISM

Some have suggested that color vision is representational—color vision involves the apparent representation of properties of external objects, but there is in fact no suitable external referent. C. L. Hardin has a related view: colors are properties neither of external objects nor of experiences. Colors are to be "eliminated," though there remain "chromatic perceptual states," which are to be reduced to neural states.

The strengths of these views must lie in the careful analysis of what is involved in naive thought about color. If naive thought makes fundamental assumptions that are false, then error theory must be the right conclusion. But an everyday commitment to the notions of normal observers and normal conditions may (as we have seen) not be disastrous. Incoherence in everyday color thought may have to be sought elsewhere.

AUTONOMY VIEWS

If color experience apparently represents features of physical objects, what is to prevent us from saying that (in ordinary cases) it correctly represents features of those things, namely colors? These colors would need to be supervenient upon physical properties, though they might or might not be reducible to them. (The model might be DAVIDSON's [S] or Fodor's view of mental properties.) Colors would have their place in a scheme of explanation that was autonomous with respect to physics, in that its legitimacy was not dependent upon ratification by physics. And that explanatory scheme would no doubt make connections between the colors we see and the contingencies of our perceptual system—thus making those colors not only genuine features of external objects but also in a certain way subjective and relative.

The view needs to overcome the suspicions that the only genuine properties are those recognized in physics, or those intelligible from an "absolute" point of view. A defense is needed of the idea that the world (and not just the mind) can contain subjective items, and an account of the mind's thought about such items. Until these tasks are achieved the autonomy view will at best be programmatic. If they cannot be achieved, the option seems to be an error theory. They are large tasks, central in the PHILOSOPHY OF MIND and METAPHYSICS [S], and it is a measure of the difficulty of the topic that they have taken so long to come clearly to light.

Bibliography

Armstrong, D. M. *A Materialist Theory of the Mind.* London, 1968. Chap. 12.

Boghossian, P., and J. D. Velleman. "Colour as a Secondary Quality," *Mind* (1989), 81–103.

Hardin, C. L., *Color for Philosophers: Unweaving the Rainbow.* Indianapolis, 1988.

Hilbert, D. R. *Color and Color Perception: A Study in Anthropocentric Realism.* Stanford, CA, 1987.

Peacocke, C. *Sense and Content.* Oxford, 1983. Chap. 2.

Westphal, J. *Colour.* Oxford, 1987. 2d ed., 1991.

JUSTIN BROACKES

COMMUNICATIVE ACTION. "Communicative action" is the central concept in Jürgen HABERMAS'S [S] attempt to displace the subject-centered approaches to reason characteristic of modern Western philosophy with an approach based in a theory of communication. His version of the linguistic turn leads to a 'universal pragmatics' that seeks to reconstruct the 'universal core' of language-in-use or speech. The guiding idea is that not only linguistic competence but 'communicative competence' admits of theoretical representation. Speaker/hearer competence must include, not only an ability to produce and understand grammatical sentences, but also an ability to establish and understand the connections to the world that make situated utterances meaningful. The act of utterance places sentences in relation to the 'external world' of objects and events, the 'internal world' of the speaker's own experiences, and a 'social world' of shared normative expectations. From this pragmatic perspective it becomes clear that mutual understanding in language involves raising and recognizing a variety of 'validity claims'—claims to the truth of assertions in relation to the external world, to the rightness of actions in relation to a shared social world, and to the sincerity of expressions of one's own intentions, feelings, desires, and the like. Naturally, claims of these sorts can be contested and criticized. One way of settling disputed claims, weighing reasons pro and con, appealing to no force but the force of the better argument, has traditionally been regarded as fundamental to the idea of rationality, and is by Habermas as well.

The idea of 'communicative rationality' also serves to develop the categorical framework and normative foundations of Habermas's social theory: "If we assume that the human species maintains itself through the socially coordinated activities of its members and that this coordination is established through communication . . . then the reproduction of the species also requires satisfying the conditions of rationality inherent in communicative action" (Habermas, 1984, p. 397). By stressing that the goal-directed actions of individuals have to be socially coordinated, Habermas directs attention to the broader social contexts of instrumental actions. Thus, the idea of the LIFEWORLD (*Lebenswelt*) [S]—the taken-for-granted, indeterminate, and inexhaustible background of all our activities—is introduced as a necessary dimension of communicative interaction.

In the course of social and cultural rationalization, the use of reasons or grounds to gain intersubjective recognition for contestable validity claims has taken an increasingly reflective turn in certain domains. Modes of argumentation have been differentiated and discursive institutions established that permit sustained, organized discussions of specific types of validity claims. And this has made learning processes possible in such dimensions as science and technology, law and morality. That means, Habermas argues, that cultural and social changes cannot be understood solely in terms of external, contingent factors; they often evince features that have to be grasped in terms of the differentiation, development, and institutionalization of specific dimensions of communicative reason. It is from this perspective as well that the selectivity of capitalist modernization becomes evident. Habermas argues that many of the problems and paradoxes of modernity are rooted in a one-sidedly instrumental rationalization of culture and society—that is, in our failure to develop and institutionalize in a balanced way all the different dimensions of communicative reason. In his view the Enlightenment project has not failed but remains unfinished.

(SEE ALSO: *Discourse Ethics* [S])

Bibliography

WORKS BY HABERMAS

Communication and the Evolution of Society, translated by T. McCarthy. Boston, 1979.

The Theory of Communicative Action, 2 vols., translated by T. McCarthy. Boston, 1984–87.

Postmetaphysical Thinking, translated by W. Hohengarten. Cambridge, MA, 1992.

WORKS ON HABERMAS

Cooke, M. *Language and Reason: A Study of Habermas's Pragmatics.* Cambridge, MA, 1994.

Honneth, A., and H. Joas, eds. *Communicative Action.* Cambridge, MA, 1991.

White, S. *The Recent Work of Jürgen Habermas.* Cambridge, 1988.

THOMAS MCCARTHY

COMMUNITARIANISM. In the 1980s communitarians displaced Marxists as the most prominent critics of liberal political theory (*see* LIBERALISM [4; S], MARXISM [S]). Communitarians share a belief that liberalism is excessively "individualistic" or "atomistic," ignoring people's dependence on communal relationships. They differ in where they locate this flaw. Some criticize the liberal ideal of freedom of choice, arguing that people's ends in life are defined by their communal ties, not freely chosen (Sandel, 1984). Others accept the ideal of freedom of choice but criticize liberalism for ignoring its social and cultural preconditions (Taylor, 1989). Yet others argue that moral reasoning is dependent on communal traditions, so that liberal claims to universal validity are illegitimate (Walzer, 1983; MacIntyre, 1988).

Bibliography

MacIntyre, A. *Whose Justice? Which Rationality?* London, 1988.

Mulhall, S., and A. Swift. *Liberals and Communitarians.* Oxford, 1992.

Sandel, M., ed. *Liberalism and Its Critics.* New York, 1984.

Taylor, C., "Cross-Purposes: The Liberal-Communitarian Debate," in N. Rosenblum, ed., *Liberalism and the Moral Life* (Cambridge, MA, 1989).

Walzer, M. *Spheres of Justice: A Defense of Pluralism and Equality.* New York, 1983.

WILL KYMLICKA

COMPUTATION. The growth of LOGIC [S] in computer science since the late sixties has been explosive. Several conferences are either devoted to logic or rely heavily on it. Given the enormous body of literature thus produced, a comprehensive survey is out of the question. What follows, therefore, is merely a sampling, with some pointers to other topics and to the literature.

LOGIC PROGRAMMING

Let the letters *F, M,* and *A* stand respectively for the predicates "father of," "mother of," and "ancestor of." Then the implications $F(x,y) \rightarrow A(x,y)$, $M(x,y) \rightarrow A(x,y)$ and $A(x,z) \& A(y,z) \rightarrow A(x,z)$ all hold. These implications, written with a backward arrow $\leftarrow$ and "," replacing "&" become the logic program (1) $A(x,y) \leftarrow F(x,y)$ (2) $A(x,y) \leftarrow M(x,y)$ (3) $A(x,y) \leftarrow A(x,z), A(z,y)$.

It turns out that a proof rule called SLD-resolution allows us to compute all true instances $A(a,b)$ using (1)–(3) if all true instances of F and M are given. This technique, implemented in the programming language Prolog, turns many definitions into programs and is much used in ARTIFICIAL INTELLIGENCE [S].

However, we cannot derive true instances $\neg A(a,b)$ this way, even if all true instances of $\neg F$ and $\neg M$ are given. Reiter suggests adding the "closed world assumption" (CWA), which intuitively amounts to adding "and these are all the ancestors" to (1)–(3). However, the CWA cannot be effectively implemented. An effectively implementable alternative is to add the "negation as failure" rule, which says in effect that if the search for a justification of $A(a,b)$ is completed and does not succeed, then we should conclude $\neg A(a,b)$. Unfortunately, infinite but futile searches cannot be handled this way and so this alternative is incomplete.

LOGICS OF PROGRAMS

One writes programs to accomplish a task. However, programs do not always accomplish their goals. Hence the need for logics to prove their correctness—that is, that they accomplish the desired goals.

Hoare Logic. One strength of Hoare Logic is that it respects modularity. A program is usually made up of simpler parts, and it helps to be able to derive properties of programs from those of their subparts. Another feature of Hoare Logic is that it splits up program correctness into two issues: termination—showing that the program does end, and partial correctness—showing that if the program does end, it yields correct results. The partial correctness statement (PCA) $\{A\}\alpha\{B\}$ says that if the property A holds at the start of the program α then on termination the property B will hold. The properties A and B are usually expressed by first order formulas. One of Hoare's rules is: from $\{A\}\alpha\{B\}$ and $\{B\}\beta\{C\}$ derive $\{A\}\alpha;\beta\{C\}$, where $\alpha;\beta$ is the program: "first do α and then do β." (There are similar rules for the other program constructs such as "if A holds then do α else β" and "while A holds do α"). Now if we want to prove a true assertion $\{A\}\alpha;\beta\{C\}$, we will need to find a B such that $\{A\}\alpha\{B\}$ and $\{B\}\beta\{C\}$ both hold. Unfortunately, though the requisite B always exists, it might not be expressible in first order logic even if A and C are, so that the Hoare rule cannot be used.

Dynamic Logic. Pratt's solution to the Hoare rule problem is to extend the language of first order logic by allowing program modalities $[\alpha]$. $[\alpha]B$ means that B will hold if and when α terminates. Thus $\{A\}\alpha\{B\}$ holds if and only if A implies $[\alpha]B$. Also, to prove $\{A\}\alpha;\beta\{C\}$, the formula $[\beta]C$ will work as the intermediate B whose absence was a problem above. Propositional dynamic logic can be effectively axiomatized, a fact shown independently by Gabbay and Parikh. Dynamic logic also allows us to express dispositions—for example, a substance is fragile if, when thrown, it will break. So we can write $Fragile(x) \leftrightarrow [thrown]Broken(x)$. Thus dynamic logic may well have a domain of applications even larger than intended. An extension of dynamic logic is game logic, which can be used to show that many-person interactions have certain desired properties—for example, that an algorithm for sharing something among n people is fair.

Temporal Logic. An alternative to dynamic logic, followed by Pnueli and others, is to abandon modularity, and reason about one program at a time using temporal reasoning, focusing on the passage of time as a program runs. Thus one will use temporal operators such as "the property A will hold sometime in the future," or "A will hold until B does." The time structure may be linear or it may be branching. The latter case arises if the course of the program is not determined but depends on random events, such as coin tosses, or on external influence.

NON-MONOTONIC LOGICS

TARSKI'S [8] monotonicity condition for the notion of consequence is that if a set of propositions T implies *A* and $T \subset T'$ then T′ also implies *A*. However, there are many situations where this condition fails, especially if *A* is not certain but only very likely given T. A standard example given is that if Tweety is a bird, then Tweety flies, but if we know in addition that Tweety is a penguin, then we conclude that she does not fly. Non-monotonicity occurs in many areas: in default logic, in circumscription, in the logic of knowledge, in the logic of conditionals, and in belief revision. Space limitations prevent us from giving details.

KNOWLEDGE AND BELIEF

Formal treatments of knowledge and belief have acquired a great deal of importance in computer science. The TARK (Theoretical Aspects of Reasoning about Knowledge) conferences are devoted to the applications of the logics of knowledge and belief in computer science, economics and artificial intelligence. These logics tend to be multi-modal S4 or S5 logics with several necessity operators, one for each knower, so that interesting questions such as, "does Jill know that Bob does not know that Jill likes tennis?" can be posed and dealt with. Common or mutual knowledge has been a particularly interesting notion. It turns out that if *i* and *j* are individuals and *p* is some fact then the statements "*i* knows *p*", "*j* knows that *i* knows *p*", "*i* knows that *j* knows that *i* knows *p*" are strictly increasing in logical strength. The conjunction of all these infinitely many statements is *mutual knowledge of p* between *i* and *j*. Another important problem is dealing with the lack of logical omniscience, which arises because people fail to know the logical consequences of other facts that they know.

OTHER TOPICS

Other issues not touched on here include "denotational semantics," which arises out of the work of Scott, Plotkin, and others on models for the λ-calculus; "non-well-founded sets," a variant of usual SET THEORY [7; S], in which a set can contain itself as an element, or where two sets can have each other as elements; and "zero knowledge proofs," whereby I can convince you that I have certain information, perhaps the proof of some theorem, but without actually giving it to you. Computer science has been a rich lode of ideas in logic, and also a user of ideas in logic from philosophy and mathematics. This fruitful interchange promises to continue for quite some time.

Bibliography

Aezel, P. *Non-well-founded Sets.* Stanford, CA, 1988.

Fagin, R., J. Halpern, Y. Moses, and M. Vardi. *Reasoning About Knowledge.* Cambridge, MA, 1995. (Logic of knowledge)

Goldwasser, S., S. Micali, and C. Rackoff. "The Knowledge Complexity of Interactive Protocols," *Society for Industrial and Applied Mathematics Journal of Computing,* Vol. 18 (1989), 186–208. (Zero-knowledge proofs)

Kozen, D., and R. Parikh. "An Elementary Completeness Proof for PDL," *Theoretical Computer Science,* Vol. 14 (1981), 113–18. (Dynamic logic)

Lloyd, J. W. *Foundations of Logic Programming,* 2nd ed. New York, 1987. (Logic programming)

Marek, W., and M. Truszynski. *Non-monotonic Logic.* New York, 1991.

Parikh, R. "The Logic of Games," *Annals of Discrete Mathematics,* Vol. 24 (1985), 111–40. (Game logic)

———. "Logical Omniscience, in D. Leivant, ed., *Logic and Computational Complexity* (New York, 1995).

Plotkin, G. "A Powerdomain Construction," *Society for Industrial and Applied Mathematics Journal of Computing* (1976), 452–87. (Denotational semantics)

Pnueli, A. "The Temporal Logic of Programs," *Proceedings of the 18th Annual IEEE Symposium on Foundations of Computer Science* (1977), 46–57. (Temporal logic)

Pratt, V. "Semantical Considerations on Floyd-Hoare Logic," *Proceedings of the 17th Annual Symposium on Foundations of Computer Science* (1976), 109–21. (Dynamic logic)

Scott, D. "Data Types as Lattices," *Society for Industrial and Applied Mathematics Journal of Computing,* Vol. 5 (1976), 522–87. (Denotational semantics)

van Leeuwen, J., ed. *Handbook for Theoretical Computer Science,* Vol. B. Cambridge, MA, 1980.

ROHIT PARIKH

COMPUTATIONAL MODEL OF MIND, THE.

Computer science has been notably successful in building devices capable of performing sophisticated intellectual tasks. Impressed by these successes, many philosophers of mind have embraced a computational account of the mind. Computationalism, as this view is called, is committed to the literal truth of the claim that the mind is a computer: mental states, processes, and events are computational states, processes, and events.

But what exactly are computational states, processes, and events? Traditionally, computational processes have been understood as rule-governed manipulations of internal symbols or representations (what computer scientists call data structures). Though these representations have meaning (i.e., semantic content), the rules apply to them solely in virtue of their structural properties, in the same way that the truth-preserving rules of formal logic apply to the syntax or formal character of natural-language sentences, irrespective of their semantic content. Developments in computer science in the 1980s, in particular the construction of connectionist machines—devices capable of performing cognitive tasks but without fixed symbols over which their operations are defined—have necessitated a broadening of the notion of computation (*see* CONNECTIONISM [S]). Connectionist processes are not naturally interpretable as manipulations of internal symbols. Connectionist devices notwithstanding, philosophers committed to the computational model of mind tend to interpret computation in classical terms, claiming that mental processes are manipulations of symbols in an internal code or language of thought (Fodor, 1974).

Computationalism has been the predominant paradigm in cognitive psychology since the demise of BEHAVIORISM [1] in the early 1960s. The failure of behaviorism can be traced in no small part to its refusal to consider the inner causes of behavior, in particular the capacity of intelligent organisms to represent their environment and use their representations in controlling and modulating their interactions with the environment. Computationalism avoids this failing, explaining intelligent behavior as the product of internal computational processes that manipulate (construct, store, retrieve, etc.) symbolic representations of the organism's environment.

Many philosophers of mind find computationalism attractive for two reasons. First, it promises a physicalistic account of mind (*see* PHYSICALISM, MATERIALISM [S]); specifically, it promises to explain mental phenomena without positing any mysterious nonphysical substances, properties, or events. Computational operations, which apply to the structural properties of objects in their domain (that is, symbols), are physically realized in the computer. Second, it promises a nonreductive account of mind. Although computational processes are physically realized, to describe a device as a computer is not to say anything specific about how the posited computational processes are realized in the device. So too with the mind. If mental processes are computational processes, then these processes are physically realized, but computationalism entails nothing as regards the specific nature of the realization. Indeed, nothing requires that the realization of mental processes be neural. Computationalists take it to be a contingent fact about human mental processes that they are realized in neural matter; these same processes might in other creatures or devices be realized in other ways (e.g., in a silicon-based circuitry). In this respect, computational explanation is a species of functional explanation: it provides an analysis of a cognitive capacity in terms of the organized interaction of distinct components of the system, which are themselves functionally characterized—that is, described in terms of what they do rather than what they are made of.

As a hypothesis about the nature of mind, computationalism is not uncontentious. Important aspects of the mental have so far resisted computational analysis. Computational theorists have had very little to say about the nature of conscious experience. While computers perform many intellectual tasks impressively, no one has succeeded in building a computer that can plausibly be said to feel pain or experience joy. It is quite possible that consciousness requires an explanation in terms of the biochemistry of the brain. In other words, the computationalist strategy of prescinding from the neural details of mental processes may mean that conscious phenomena will escape its explanatory net.

If conscious mental phenomena resist computational analysis, then the computational model of mind cannot be said to provide a general account of the human mind; however, the model might still provide the basis for a theory of those cognitive capacities that do not involve consciousness in any essential way. Cognitive psychologists have applied the computational model to the study of human language processing, memory, vision, and motor control, often with impressive results. Domain-specific processes such as syntactic processing and early vision, about which it might plausibly be argued that the information available to the process is tightly constrained, have proved most amenable to computational analysis. Domain-general or "central" processes such as decision making and rational revision of belief in response to new information have so far resisted computational treatment. Their intractability is due in part to the fact that general constraints on the information that might be relevant to solutions are difficult, if not impossible, to specify. Characterizing how an agent is able to continuously update its knowledge store as the world around it changes is a formidable technical problem known as the "frame problem" in the field of ARTIFICIAL INTELLIGENCE [S] (AI). Unless it can be solved, or otherwise sidestepped, computationalism has a slim chance of providing a general account of human cognitive capacities, even those not essentially involving consciousness.

Computationalism also requires a psychosemantics—that is, an account of how the internal representations it postulates acquire their meaning. In virtue of what fact does a particular data structure mean Snow is white rather than Snow is red? The meanings of natural-language sentences are fixed by public agreement, but inner symbols must acquire their meaning in some other way. Though there have been several proposals, none enjoys consensus in the field.

A related difficulty for computationalism has been raised by John Searle, who argues that understanding cannot be a computational process. The manipulation of symbols according to rules that operate only on their structural properties is, according to Searle, a fundamentally unintelligent process. The argument, which many have found unconvincing, is formulated explicitly for classical or rule-based computational models, but if Searle is right it would apply to any mechanical model of the mind, hence to connectionist models as well.

(SEE ALSO: *Philosophy of Mind* [S])

Bibliography

Fodor, J. *The Language of Thought.* New York, 1974.

Haugeland, J. *Artificial Intelligence: The Very Idea.* Cambridge, MA, 1985.

Posner, M., ed. *Foundations of Cognitive Science.* Cambridge, MA, 1989.

Pylyshyn, Z. W. *Computation and Cognition.* Cambridge, MA, 1984.

Searle, J. "Minds, Brains, and Programs," *Behavioral and Brain Sciences,* Vol. 3 (1980), 417–24. Published with critical commentaries.

Sterelny, K. *The Representational Theory of Mind.* Oxford, 1990. A useful introduction to basic issues in computationalism.

FRANCES EGAN

COMPUTER ETHICS. Computer ethics is a branch of APPLIED ETHICS [S] that considers ethical issues raised by computing technology. Computing technology, which includes hardware, software, and networks, is both flexible and powerful. Computers can be programmed or trained to perform a wide range of functions, and because of their logical malleability computers have numerous and diverse applications in our society. Computing technology is revolutionizing society, and ethical issues abound.

Computer ethics is philosophically interesting, not merely because computing technology is widely used, but because computing technology raises intriguing conceptual issues and serious ethical problems for society. What rights do people have to use computer technology and to be protected from it? When computing technology is deployed in a novel way, clear ethical guidelines for its use may not exist. Such policy vacuums are often accompanied by conceptual confusion about how to understand the computerized situation adequately. Hence, computer ethics involves more than simply applying ethical theory to ethical issues in computing. Computer ethics requires a philosophical analysis of the nature and impact of developing computing technology and the corresponding formulation and justification of policies for the ethical use of such technology. Traditionally, computer-ethics research has been trained on at least four broad areas of investigation: privacy, property, power, and professionalism.

Privacy is a central concern of computer ethics because computers rapidly store and search vast amounts of information. Personal information in medical documents, criminal records, and credit histories is easily retrieved and transmitted to others electronically. Individuals are vulnerable to the improper disclosure of sensitive information and to the unwitting introduction of errors into their records. Philosophically, the development of computing technology has necessitated an analysis and expansion of the concept of privacy. Now privacy is routinely understood in terms of protection and control of information as well as the protection against intrusion. Debates about the boundaries of privacy continue, because technological innovations create new informational opportunities and risks.

Property protection is a major issue within computer ethics. To what extent, for example, should computer programs be protected as intellectual property? Computer programs are algorithmic and hence mathematical in nature. Perhaps computer programs, like the Pythagorean theorem, should not be owned at all. However, many computer programs are lengthy, original human expressions and as such are entitled to copyright protection. In their operation on machines computer programs are processes, and, when they are novel, useful, nonobvious processes, they may be properly patentable. How, or even whether, computer programs should be protected depends largely on a philosophical analysis of the nature of computer programs and on a philosophical justification of protecting intellectual property. The issues of protecting computerized property extend well beyond computer programs. Computers process all kinds of data. The information stored on computers, manipulated with computers, displayed by computers, and forwarded on networks to other computers generates complex disputes about what aspects of computerized information can be owned, stolen, and regulated.

Powerful computers and networks allow us to perform tasks more easily and to accomplish some activities that we could never do without them. Those who have access to computers have access to power. One feature of this power is that computer users can act from a distance over networks and thereby accomplish goals without being observed. Like the shepherd with the ring of Gyges, a computer user may act invisibly with an elevated level of protection from harmful consequences. What are the ethical boundaries of actions performed over computer networks and how can they be enforced? And what is the proper distribution of computer power among people? Inequalities in the distribution of computing technology among age groups, sexes, races, and nations raise ethical questions. Unequal distribution of power may require ethical countermeasures to ensure fairness. To what extent, for example, should disabled citizens be assured of equal access to computing technology? Moreover, when computers are introduced into a situation, the balance of power frequently shifts among groups, sometimes quite dramatically. Workers may find themselves no longer needed for their jobs or may become easy targets of surveillance by their own computer tools. Children may find pornography readily accessible on computer networks. To what extent, if any, do rights and responsibilities change with this shifting balance of power?

Many who design and operate computing systems regard themselves as computing professionals. But, given that anyone, regardless of educational background, can be hired to do computing, what does it mean to claim that someone is a computing professional? To what standards, including ethical standards, should computing professionals adhere? Although several debated codes of ethics have been offered to clarify what duties and responsibilities computer professionals have, professional responsibility has been difficult to establish for at least two reasons. First, unlike medicine and law, the field does not have a tradition of professional qualifying examinations and licensing, and therefore enforcement of any code of ethics is difficult. Second, the nature of computing itself makes the assessment of responsibility difficult. Computer programs are often enormously complex, written by dozens of people, and incomprehensible to any one person. Such large computer programs may be brittle in that a tiny, obscure error can shatter the performance of the entire system under certain conditions. To what extent should computing professionals be regarded as liable when such difficult-to-predict errors lead to major failures or even catastrophic results?

Computation and ethics intersect in yet another way. Although most of computer ethics concerns ethical examinations of computing situations, a philosophically rich subfield is computational ethics, which reflects on the impact computing has or theoretically may have on ethics itself. Philosophical issues in this area include questions such as: In what ways can ethical decision making be properly assisted by computational methods? In principle, could a computer ever make appropriate ethical decisions? Could a computer, or perhaps a robot, ever have rights or moral responsibilities?

Bibliography

Bynum, T. W., ed. *Computers and Ethics.* Special issue of *Metaphilosophy,* Vol. 16 (1985).

Forester, T., and P. Morrison. *Computer Ethics,* 2d ed. Cambridge, MA, 1994.

Gould, C. G., ed. *The Information Web.* Boulder, CO, 1989.

Johnson, D. G. *Computer Ethics,* 2d ed. Englewood, Cliffs, NJ, 1994.

Johnson, D. G., and H. Nissenbaum. *Computers, Ethics, and Social Values.* Englewood Cliffs, NJ, 1995.

JAMES H. MOOR

CONDITIONALS. In the 1960s the problem of conditionals was thought to concern so-called counterfactuals such as "If the match had been struck it would have burned," as contrasted with an indicative conditional such as "If the match was struck it burned," which was thought could be false only if the match was struck but did not burn—that is, was thought to be equivalent to a material conditional (cf. GOODMAN, 1954 [3; S]). Since then, while the counterfactual has continued to be a subject of controversy, there has been increasing concern with the 'material conditional analysis' of the indicative (MatCond), and no fewer than fifteen books and a hundred scholarly papers on the topic, in fields as disparate as formal logic, ARTIFICIAL INTELLIGENCE [S], psychology, and linguistics, appeared between 1967 and 1994. This article will attempt to explain this surge of interest and to outline recent currents of thought, especially on indicatives.

Dissatisfaction with MatCond stems in large part from the fact that it entails 'fallacies' such as that the intuitively absurd inference

I_1 Today is not Tuesday; therefore, if today is Tuesday then tomorrow is Thursday.

is valid because its conclusion must be true if its premise is true. Some of these fallacies have long been known, but more recently other fallacies have been the subject of attention, and new ones have come to light, even apparent counterexamples to the rule of *modus ponens,* one being a variant of counterexamples due to V. McGee (1985):

I_2 If that is a dog, then, if it weighs 500 pounds, it is a 500-pound dog. That is a dog. Therefore, if that weighs 500 pounds it is a 500-pound dog.

While these kinds of examples have been disputed, it is not implausible that a person could assert both premises but deny the conclusion, thinking that whatever 'it' is, if it weighs 500 pounds, it can only look like a dog.

Responses to these challenges to MatCond have tended to be of three kinds: (1) to argue that the theory is right, and seeming fallacies can be explained by reference to what GRICE (1989 [S]) called the logic of conversation, as explained below; (2) to advance alternative accounts of the truth conditions of conditional statements; (3) to argue that the concept of truth does not apply to conditionals but that another kind of 'rightness', namely probability, does apply to them, and the premises of inferences such as I_1 have this kind of rightness but their conclusions do not.

The first response distinguishes the truth conditions of ordinary-language statements from what can reasonably be inferred on the assumption that the persons who assert them conform to 'maxims of conversational quality'. Thus, Grice explains the seeming absurdity of inference I_1 by arguing that, while the truth of its premise guarantees the truth of its conclusion, it would violate maxims of conversational quality to assert its conclusion when its premise can be asserted. Others, including Lewis (1974) and Jackson (1987), have followed this general approach while disagreeing with Grice on points of detail. It is noteworthy, incidentally, that many persons who reject this defense of MatCond nevertheless accept the validity and importance of the distinction between truth-conditional logic and 'conversational logic'.

Most of the alternative theories of the truth of "If P then Q" reject the idea that its truth value is determined by the truth values of P and Q, and a more complicated account is required. The best known of these are based on modal concepts, especially that of truth in a world (ModCond). The version due to Stalnaker (1968), variations of which have been proposed by Lewis (1974—for counterfactuals), Nute (1980), and others, holds that "If P then Q" is true in a world w if Q is true in the world 'nearest' to w in which P is true. The notion of nearness of worlds is difficult to explicate, but it can be represented geometrically quite simply. In figure 1 P-worlds and Q-worlds—that is, worlds in which P and Q are true—are pictured as occupying rectangles in a 'universe of possible worlds', and w is pictured as a point in this universe (*see* POSSIBLE WORLDS [S]). Most important, the figure represents "not P" as being true in world w, while "If P then Q" is false, because Q is not true in the world nearest to w in which P is true. It follows that, according to ModCond, inferences of the form of I_1 are invalid, which accords better with intuition than with MatCond.

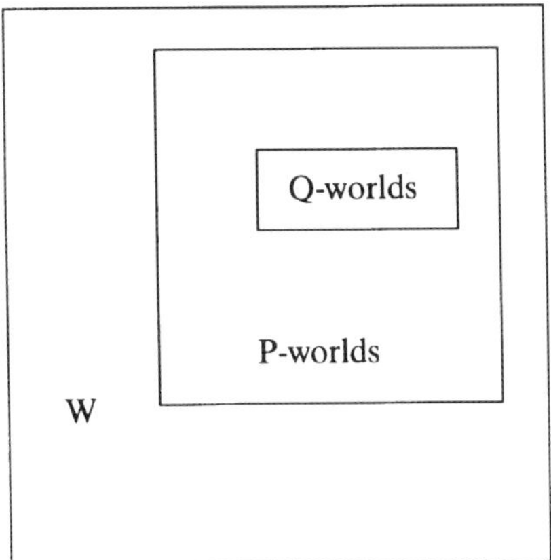

Figure 1

In application to other patterns of inference, ModCond has the surprising consequence that many inferences that are not usually questioned are invalid. For instance, the reader can easily see that figure 1 pictures contraposition as invalid, because "If P then not Q" is true but "if Q then not P" is false in world w. Moreover, there are ordinary-language examples that confirm this, such as:

I_3 If it rained it didn't rain hard. Therefore, if it rained hard it didn't rain.

In contrast, ModCond does imply the validity of all 'traditionally valid' inferences that do not involve conditionals, as well as such conditional inferences as *modus tollens* and *modus ponens.* Of course, that it implies the validity of the latter means that it cannot account for the seeming invalidity of inference I_2, which is one instance of a general problem that arises in connection with conditionals that are embedded in larger sentences, which will be discussed following comments on the third approach.

This approach, originally proposed independently by Adams (1965), Ellis (1969), and Jeffrey (1964), has many similarities to ModCond, but it considers not the truth-in-worlds of conditionals but their probabilities (ProbCond), and it argues that what is wrong with inferences such as I_1–I_3 is that their premises can be probable while their conclusions are improbable, not that their premises can be true while their conclusions are false. This is intuitively obvious in I_3, since it can be highly probable that if it rained it didn't rain hard, but it would be absurd to claim that if it rained hard it didn't rain. Figure 1 can also be interpreted to picture this, assuming that "It rained" corresponds to region P, "It rained hard" corresponds to region Q, and the probability of "if it rained it rained hard" corresponds to the probability that if a world chosen at random lies inside P then it lies inside Q. This is the same as the proportion of P that lies inside Q, and, similarly, the probability of "if it rained it didn't rain hard" corresponds to the proportion of P that lies outside Q. Assuming this, "If it rained it didn't rain hard" is pictured as probable because most of P lies outside Q, while "If it rained hard it didn't rain" is pictured as totally improbable since all of Q lies inside P.

Given the foregoing, it will not surprise the reader that there is a kind of 'congruence' between the ModCond and ProbCond theories of the conditional. This has been made precise by Adams (1977) and Gibbard (1981), who proved, assuming a precise definition of 'probabilistic validity', that inferences like I_1 and I_3 that do not involve embedded conditionals are valid according to one theory if and only if they are valid according to the other.

But the above congruence is limited because, while ModCond applies to embedded conditionals, the ProbCond theory does not. This is brought out in application to the controversial principle of the conditional excluded middle, which concerns propositions such as

P_1 Either, if it rained it rained hard, or if it rained it didn't rain hard.

which is true in all possible worlds according to Stalnaker's version of ModCond but not according to Lewis's (1974) version (with the qualification that Lewis applies this only to counterfactuals, which is inessential to the present point). In contrast, ProbCond does not even apply to sentences with embedded conditionals, as in P_1 and, ipso facto, it does not apply to ones such as "If that is a dog, then, if it weighs 500 pounds, it is a 500-pound dog," which enters into I_2. This is explained by some very striking discoveries concerning the ProbCond theory, namely Lewis's (1976) triviality results, which can be pictured intuitively in figure 1.

The probability of a factual proposition such as "It rained" is represented in the figure by the area of the region that corresponds to it, namely rectangle P, and it can be interpreted as the probability of being in a world in which "It rained" is true. On the other hand, the probability of the conditional "If it rained it rained hard" is represented not by an area but by the proportion of rectangle P that lies inside Q. This is a ratio of areas, and it cannot be interpreted as the probability of being in a world in which something is true. Ipso facto, the probability of a disjunction of conditionals as in P_1 cannot be the probability of being in a world in which one of its disjuncts is true. Using the precise mathematical concept of conditional probability, Lewis showed that if ProbCond is right then no 'standard' kind of probability can apply to sentences with embedded conditionals. However, it is noteworthy that a number of writers, including Appiah (1985), Jackson (1987), McGee (1989), and van Fraassen (1976), who accept different versions of the ProbCond theory, have attempted to extend it in 'nonstandard' ways to embeddings of various kinds. Necessarily, all of these extensions are either partial, in the sense that they do not apply to all grammatical sentences with embedded conditionals, or they give up certain basic laws in these applications. Thus, McGee gives up *modus ponens* as applied to I_2, and van Fraassen gives up a basic law of 'probability dynamics'. The latter is important because of its connection with counterfactuals.

The most notable development in the theory of counterfactuals is the application to them of the new 'models' of the indicative, similar to ModCond and ProbCond. For instance, while "If that match had been struck it would have burned" and "If that match was struck it burned" are not equivalent, they can both be diagrammed in the same way as "If it rained it rained hard." Assuming this, Stalnaker argues that if distances between worlds are measured 'counterfactually' the first is right, while if they are measured 'indicatively' the second is right, and Adams (1975, chap. 4) and Skyrms (1981) argue that something very like this holds for probabilities measured counterfactually and indicatively. Thus, probabilities and distances between worlds are 'perspectively-dependent', unlike material truth values, and, in the case of probabilities at least, the counterfactual perspective at one time is often the same as an indicative perspective at another. For instance, the probability that attaches to "If that match had been struck it would have burned" *now* is, plausibly, equal to the probability that *would have* attached to the indicative "If that match is struck it will burn" at some prior time.

But the intertwining of conditionals with 'perspectives' on distance and probability raises complicated issues connected with a still deeper one with which this article will close. Much current controversy centers on the question of whether "If it rained it didn't rain hard" can have the same kind of perspective-independent 'correspondence with the facts' that "It rained" has (cf. Edgington, 1991). ModCond and ProbCond suggest that this is not the case, and, more fundamental, ProbCond's suggestion that perspective-dependent probabilities are logically 'more important' in the evaluation of conditionals than are perspective-independent truth values raises the question of what the values of TRUTH [S] and PROBABILITY [6; S] are. That the controversy concerning conditionals raises this question, which goes to the heart of all of logical theory, shows how much is at stake in it.

(SEE ALSO: *Philosophy of Language* [S])

Bibliography

Adams, E. W. "On the Logic of Conditionals," *Inquiry,* Vol. 8 (1965), 166–97.

———. *The Logic of Conditionals.* Dordrecht, 1975.

———. "A Note on Comparing Probabilistic and Modal Logics of Conditionals," *Theoria,* Vol. 43, No. 3 (1977), 186–94.

Appiah, A. *Assertion and Conditionals.* Cambridge, 1985.

Edgington, D. "The Mystery of the Missing Matter of Fact," *Aristotelian Society Supplementary Volume,* Vol. 65 (1991), 185–209.

Ellis, B. D. "An Epistemological Concept of Truth," in R. Brown and C. D. Rollins, eds., *Contemporary Philosophy in Australia* (London, 1969).

Gibbard, A. "Two Recent Theories of Conditionals," in W. Harper, G. Pearce, and R. Stalnaker, eds., *Ifs* (Dordrecht, 1980).

Goodman, N. *Fact, Fiction, and Forecast.* London, 1954.

Grice, H. P., "Indicative Conditionals," in *Studies in the Way of Words* (Oxford, 1989).

Jackson, F. *Conditionals.* Oxford, 1987.

Jeffrey, R. C. "If" (abstract), *Journal of Philosophy,* Vol. 61 (1964), 702–3.

Lewis, D. *Counterfactuals.* Cambridge, MA, 1974.

———. "Conditional Probabilities and Probabilities of Conditionals," *Philosophical Review,* Vol. 76 (1976), 297–315.

McGee, V. "A Counterexample to Modus Ponens," *Journal of Philosophy,* Vol. 82 (1985), 462–71.

———. "Conditional Probabilities and Compounds of Conditionals," *Philosophical Review,* Vol. 98 (1989), 484–542.

Nute, D. *Theories of Conditionals.* Dordrecht, 1980.

Pollock, J. L. *Subjunctive Reasoning.* Dordrecht, 1976.

Skyrms, B. "The Prior Propensity Account of Counterfactuals," in W. Harper, G. Pearce, and R. Stalnaker, eds., *Ifs* (Dordrecht, 1981).

Stalnaker, R. C. "A Theory of Conditionals," in N. Rescher, ed., *Studies in Logical Theory.* American Philosophical Quarterly monograph series, no. 2 (Oxford, 1968).

van Fraassen, B. "Probabilities of Conditionals," in W. Harper and C. Hooker, eds., *Foundations of Probability Theory, Statistical Theory, and Statistical Theories of Science,* Vol. 1 (Dordrecht, 1976).

ERNEST ADAMS

CONFIRMATION THEORY. Confirmation theory seeks to describe normative relations between hypotheses and evidence, relations that measure or indicate whether and how much any body of evidence warrants belief or lends credence to any hypothesis. A related enterprise, DECISION THEORY [2; S], seeks (among other things) to describe normative methods for deciding whether to reject or to accept hypotheses. Still another related enterprise—variously called estimation theory (in statistics), or learning theory, or reliability analysis (in computer science)—seeks to describe strategies for conjecturing hypotheses from data that under specified assumptions reliably converge to the correct hypothesis. All three methodological strands are represented in philosophy and in statistics.

In statistics, Ronald Fisher developed the most influential confirmation theory in this century. Fisher's work on the testing of statistical hypotheses, on the design and analysis of experiments and their outcomes, and on "fiducial inference" to the probabilities of hypotheses, gave an account of scientific method largely unified by his use of the concept of "information." Biologists, psychologists, medical scientists, and social scientists of every kind continue to be influenced by Fisher's writings, in part because of the wealth of concrete applications he provided and because of the comparative ease with which his calculations can be executed in suitably idealized circumstances. Fisher's views have been debated at length in the statistical literature and examined, defended, or criticized by a number of philosophical writers. Bruno De Finetti proposed a quite different account of confirmation, founded on the idea that PROBABILITY [6; S] measures a (rational) individual's degree of belief and that as evidence is acquired, the degree of belief should change by forming the conditional probability on the new evidence. Under the misnomer Bayesian statistics, De Finetti's viewpoint has found an increasing following among economists, social scientists, and others, especially since digital computers have made possible the computation of conditional probability distributions appropriate to many applied issues. Jerzy Neyman and Egon Pearson developed a decision theoretic approach in which a decision is made whether to reject a hypothesis in the light of evidence, and decision rules are justified by the limiting frequency of errors they produce in an infinite sequence of such tests. Corrupted versions of Neyman and Pearson's ideas are widely used in applications. Modern statistical estimation theory also owes a great deal to Fisher, who introduced concepts of likelihood, consistency, bias, sufficiency, and efficiency. Estimation theory seeks rules (functions from data to hypotheses) for conjecturing hypotheses—usually hypotheses about the values of a parameter—such that under appropriate assumptions the rules can be shown to converge to the correct hypothesis as the size of samples increases without bound, and so that the rules have other virtues. Although estimation theory is an investigation of a restricted class of procedures for scientific discovery, the mainstream of the statistical community has adamantly opposed the investigation of rules for discovery in broader contexts, for example rules for conjecturing from data "statistical models" or parametrized causal hypotheses. Nonetheless, such procedures have been repeatedly proposed in the statistical literature—factor analysis and stepwise multiple regression are examples—but without any rigorous study of their reliability.

A number of philosophical proposals have attempted to analyze confirmation as a logical relation between evidence, represented by a body of propositions, and hypotheses. Carl G. HEMPEL'S [3] well-known proposal held that a body of singular evidence statements confirms a hypothesis statement if the hypothesis statement is true in every domain in which the evidence is true and each member of the domain is named in the evidence. Ludwig WITTGENSTEIN [8; S], and later and more successfully, Rudolf CARNAP [2; S], developed confirmation theories in which hypotheses were given probability measures determined by syntactical relations between hypotheses and evidence. Carnap's theories were restricted to rather simple first order, monadic languages, but later alternatives developed by Richard Jeffrey and Jaakko Hintikka were not so limited. None of these proposals have had much influence on scientific practice, perhaps because they assumed the data to be consistent with the true, nonstatistical, hypothesis, and in most sciences no data are consistent with any interesting hypotheses of that kind. After mid-century, several philosophical writers proposed accounts of confirmation as change of subjective degree of belief measured by probabilities and effected by forming conditional probability distributions given the evidence. Clark Glymour provided a series of puzzles for Bayesian confirmation theory, the most discussed of which, the problem of old evidence, asks how accepted data can confirm a novel theory (*see* BAYESIANISM [S]).

Isaac Levi, Patrick Maher, and others have combined subjective probability with decision theory to represent scientific inference as a series of decision problems involving adjustments of probabilities and utilities for features of hypotheses such as truth, simplicity, and informativeness. The same idea has been pursued by some Bayesian statistical writers. Levi's account includes a carefully developed theory of belief change in which hypotheses may become so accepted that they determine (literally) truth but may nonetheless be abandoned in favor of other, contradictory beliefs that in turn determine a new set of truths.

A standard problem for confirmation theory has been to explain how evidence given under a description bears on hypotheses that are stated in different terms. Hypothetico-deductive accounts of confirmation appear to entail that arbitrary and irrelevant hypotheses are confirmed by data. Herman WEYL [8], Rudolf Carnap, and Hans REICHENBACH [7] suggested that certain hypotheses connecting evidence descriptions and more theoretical language are stipulations that specify (partly) the "meanings" of theoretical terms, and that these stipulations function as tacit premises in relating theory to evidence. Clark Glymour proposed a related "bootstrap" account in which evidence is relevant to a hypothesis only relative to a theory, including possibly a theory that entails the evidence. The latter feature of the proposal was refuted in a series of papers by various authors, principally in issues of the journal *Philosophy of Science.*

The most interesting challenge to the very idea of confirmation theory comes from a literature on reliability analysis that developed from papers in the *Journal of Symbolic Logic* by Hilary PUTNAM [S] and E. Mark Gold in the 1960s, but which traces a philosophical heritage to PLATO's [6; S] *Meno.* Reliability analysis takes the goal of inquiry to be to settle upon the truth, eventually, and the aim of methodology to study methods by which that may be done reliably. Reliability requires that, no matter which of some collection of hypotheses is true, a method converge to the truth. Methods of inference may be subject to a variety of constraints, for example, constraints on memory, or computability, or number of hypothesis revisions, or amount of data required to succeed, or experimental powers of the inquirer. The sense in which inquiry gets to the truth may also be varied—successful inquiry may be required to reach the truth with certainty at some point; may instead be required only to make at most a finite number of errors; or may be required to assign numerical values (between 0 and 1) to hypotheses in such a way that the sequence of values assigned to true hypotheses, and only true hypotheses, approaches 1 in the limit. Roughly in the spirit of Karl POPPER's [6] philosophy of science, or Hans Reichenbach's, an inquirer or scientist is viewed as producing a sequence of hypotheses in response to changing evidence rather than a sequence of confirmations or disconfirmations. Daniel Osherson, Scott Weinstein, and Michael Stob provided the first book-length introduction to the subject, and have also produced a series of methodological results in related papers. The best introduction to the subject now available is Kevin Kelly's *The Logic of Reliable Inquiry* (1995).

The relations between confirmation theory and reliability theory are intricate and interesting. If no limits are imposed on the mathematical powers of a Bayesian inquirer, then for every discovery problem that can be reliably solved in the limit by a Putnam/Gold-style learner, there is a prior probability distribution for which the Bayesian reliably converges to the truth as well. The converse is obviously true. The equivalence fails, however, if both learners must be computable, in the sense that they calculate functions from data to hypotheses (or from data to degrees of belief) that could be computed by some Turing machine. In that case the reliability of Bayesian methods is dominated by that of computable Putnam/Gold-style learners. Other methodological principles championed by philosophers of science are subject to similar criticism; there are discovery problems, for example, that can be solved reliably by computable procedures, but not by any computable procedures that output only hypotheses consistent with the data and background assumptions; Popper's method of generating a hypothesis and testing and holding it until the data conflict can be shown to be suboptimal.

From a Bayesian or confirmation theoretic perspective, reliable Putnam/Gold learners may be irrational and arbitrary and fail to measure the weight of finite evidence. From the reliabilist point of view, confirmation theories, Bayesian or otherwise, are a codification of prejudices that can interfere with the principal goal of inquiry—finding out something interesting. Reliability analysis challenges the view that confirmation relations and philosophical methodology have any normative force when the aim of inquiry is to discover informative truths. If, further, "ought" implies "can," and humans and their inference devices are all Turing computable, the normative basis for Bayesian and other methodologies is still more dubious. On the other hand, it is easy to show that reliability is impossible to obtain in many contexts without very strong background assumptions, and reliability analysis provides no account of how such assumptions can be justified.

Philosophical confirmation theory has found few applications. One exception is computer science, where machine learning methods as early as the 1960s implemented various confirmation functions as cogs in hypothesis-assessment schemes. Thus Hempel's confirmation theory was used in the Dendral and Meta-Dendral programs designed to infer chemical structure from mass spectroscopy data, and some early programs for medical diagnosis used Bayesian confirmation theory. A Popperian machine learning scheme was developed by Ehud Shapiro. Patrick Langley and his collaborators used bootstrap techniques in some of their programs for reproducing historical scientific discoveries. Reliability analysis has been applied in cognitive psychology to produce constraints on procedures by which children can possibly learn the grammars of natural languages. Most recently, the reliability framework has been applied to study inference strategies in cognitive neuropsychology.

Bibliography

Earman, J., ed. *Testing Scientific Theories.* Minneapolis, 1983.

Glymour, C. *Theory and Evidence.* Princeton, NJ, 1980.

Howson, C., and P. Urbach. *Scientific Reasoning: The Bayesian Approach.* Chicago, 1989.

Kelly, K. *The Logic of Reliable Inquiry.* Oxford, 1995.

Langley, P., et al. *Scientific Discovery.* Cambridge, MA, 1985.

Kotz, S. *Breakthroughs in Statistics.* New York, 1992.

Levi, I. *The Fixation of Belief and Its Undoing: Changing Beliefs Through Inquiry.* Cambridge, 1991.

Maher, P. *Betting on Theories.* Cambridge, 1993.

Osherson, D., M. Stob, and S. Weinstein. *Systems that Learn.* Cambridge, MA, 1985.

Fisher, R. *Statistical Methods for Research Workers*. Oxford, 1990.

Seidenfeld, T. *Philosophical Problems of Statistical Inference: Learning from R. A. Fisher*. Theory & Decision Library, no. 22 (Norwell, MA, 1979).

CLARK GLYMOUR

CONNECTIONISM. Connectionism is an approach within COGNITIVE SCIENCE [S] that employs neural networks, rather than computer programs, as the basis for modeling mentality. A connectionist system, or neural network, is a structure of simple neuronlike processors called nodes or units. Each node has directed connections to other nodes, so that the nodes send and receive excitatory and inhibitory signals to and from one another. The total input to a node determines its state of activation. When a node is on, it sends out signals to the nodes to which it has output connections, with the intensity of a signal depending upon both (1) the activation level of the sending node and (2) the strength or "weight" of the connection between it and the receiving node. Typically at each moment during processing, many nodes are simultaneously sending signals to others.

When neural networks are employed for information processing, certain nodes are designated "input" units and others as "output" units, and potential patterns of activation across them are assigned interpretations. (The remaining nodes are called "hidden units.") Typically a "problem" is posed to a network by activating a pattern in the input nodes; then the various nodes in the system simultaneously send and receive signals repeatedly until the system settles into a stable configuration; the semantic interpretation of the resulting pattern in the output nodes is what the system currently represents, hence its "answer" to the problem. Connectionist systems are capable of "learning" from "experience" by having their weights changed systematically in a way that depends upon how well the network has performed in generating solutions to problems posed to it as a training regimen. (Typically the device employed is not an actual neural network but a simulation of one on a standard digital computer.)

The most striking difference between such networks and conventional computers is the lack of an executive component. In a conventional computer the behavior of the whole system is controlled at the central processing unit (CPU) by a stored program. A connectionist system lacks both a CPU and a stored program. Nevertheless, often in a connectionist system certain activation patterns over sets of hidden units can be interpreted as internal representations with interesting content, and often the system also can be interpreted as embodying, in its weighted connections, information that gets automatically accommodated during processing without getting explicitly represented via activation patterns.

Connectionist models have yielded particularly encouraging results for cognitive processes such as learning, pattern recognition, and so-called multiple-soft-constraint satisfaction (i.e., solving a problem governed by several constraints, where an optimal solution may require violating some constraints in order to satisfy others). For example, Terry Sejnowski and Charles Rosenberg trained a network they called NETtalk to convert inputs that represent a sequence of letters, spaces, and punctuation constituting written English into outputs that represent the audible sounds constituting the corresponding spoken English. (The phonetic output code then can be fed into a speech synthesizer, a device that actually produces the sounds.)

Philosophical discussion of connectionism has largely centered on whether connectionism yields or suggests a conception of mentality that is importantly different from the conception of mind-as-computer at the core of classical cognitive science. Several different nonclassical alternatives have been suggested; each has been alleged to fit well with connectionism, and each has been a locus of debate between fans and foes of connectionism. Three proposed interpretations of connectionism deserve specific mention.

On one view, the key difference between classical models of mental processes and connectionist models is that the former assume the existence of languagelike mental representations that constitute a so-called LANGUAGE OF THOUGHT (LOT) [S], whereas the latter supposedly favor representations that are alleged to be inherently non-languagelike in structure: namely, activation patterns distributed over several nodes of a network, so-called activation vectors. On this interpretation connectionism shares with classicism the assumption that cognition is computation over mental representations—that cognitive transitions conform to rules for transforming representations on the basis of their formal structure, rules that could be formulated as an explicit computer program. (In connectionist systems the rules are wired into the weights and connections rather than being explicitly represented. In classical systems some rules must be hard wired; and there may be—but need not be—other rules that are explicitly represented as stored data structures.) The key difference allegedly turns on the languagelike or non-languagelike structure of mental representations.

This construal of connectionism fits naturally with the idea that human cognition involves state transitions that are all essentially associative—in the sense that they reflect statistical correlations among items the system can represent and can be analyzed as the drawing of statistical inferences. Many fans of connectionism, including Patricia Churchland and Paul Churchland, evidently see things this way and tend to regard connectionism as breathing new life into associationism. Prominent foes of connectionism, notably Jerry Fodor and Zenon Pylyshyn, also see things this way; but they regard the link with associationism as grounds for maintaining that connectionism is bound to founder on the same general problem that plagued traditional associationism in psychology: namely, inability to account for the rich semantic coherence of much human thought. To overcome this problem, Fodor and Pylyshyn maintain, cognitive science must continue to posit both (1) mental representations that encode propositional information via languagelike syntactic structure and (2) modes of processing that are suitably sensitive to syntactic structure and are thereby sensitive to propositional content.

A second interpretation of connectionism claims that connectionist models do not really employ internal representations at all in their hidden units (and, a fortiori, do not employ internal representations with languagelike structure). This view has been defended—by Rodney Brooks, for example—on the grounds that putative representations in connectionist systems play no genuine explanatory role. It has also been defended—for instance, by Hubert Dreyfus and Stuart Dreyfus—on the basis of a Heideggerian critique of the notion of mental representation itself. The approach goes contrary to the views of most (but not all) practicing connectionists, who typically posit internal representations in connectionist models and assign them a central explanatory role.

A third interpretation assumes the existence of internal mental representations; and it does not deny—indeed, the version defended by Terence Horgan and John Tienson resolutely affirms—that mental representations often have languagelike structure. It focuses instead on the classical assumption that cognition is computation (see above). This third approach maintains (1) that much of human cognition is too rich and too subtle to conform to programmable rules and (2) that connectionism has theoretical resources for potentially explaining such nonalgorithmic cognitive processing. The approach stresses that there is a powerful branch of mathematics that applies naturally to neural networks: dynamical systems theory. According to this anticomputational construal of connectionism, there can be cognitive systems—subservable mathematically by dynamical systems, which in turn are subservable physically by neural networks—whose cognitive state transitions are not tractably computable. In other words, mental activity in these systems is too refined and too supple to conform to programmable rules. Humans are alleged to be such cognitive systems, and connectionism (so interpreted) is held to yield a more adequate picture of the mind than the classical computational picture.

One objection to this third interpretation of connectionism alleges that cognitive state transitions in a connectionist system must inevitably conform to programmable rules, especially since neural networks are simulable on standard computers. Another objection, directed specifically at the version that retains languagelike representations, alleges that the LOT hypothesis is intelligible only on the assumption that cognition is computation.

In much of the early philosophical debate between proponents and opponents of connectionism, the first interpretation was largely taken for granted. But as competing interpretations get articulated, defended, and acknowledged, philosophical discussion of connectionism and its potential implications becomes richer.

(SEE ALSO: *Philosophy of Mind* [S])

Bibliography

Aizawa, K. "Representations without Rules, Connectionism, and the Syntactic Argument," *Synthese,* Vol. 101 (1994), 465–92.

Bechtel, W., and A. Abrahamsen. *Connectionism and the Mind: An Introduction to Parallel Distributed Processing.* Oxford, 1991.

Brooks, R. "Intelligence without Representation," *Artificial Intelligence,* Vol. 47 (1991), 139–59.

Churchland, P. M. *The Engine of Reason, the Seat of the Soul: A Philosophical Inquiry into the Brain.* Cambridge, MA, 1995.

Churchland, P. S. *Neurophilosophy: Toward a Unified Science of the Mind/Brain.* Cambridge, MA, 1986.

Clark. A., and J. Toribo. "Doing without Representing?" *Synthese,* Vol. 101 (1994), 404–31.

Dreyfus, H., and S. Dreyfus. "Making a Mind versus Modelling the Brain: Artificial Intelligence Back at a Branch-Point," in S. Graubard, ed., *The Artificial Intelligence Debate: False Starts, Real Foundations* (Cambridge, MA, 1988).

Fodor, J., and Z. Pylyshyn. "Connectionism and Cognitive Architecture: A Critical Analysis," *Cognition,* Vol. 28 (1988), 3–71.

Garson, J. "No Representations without Rules," *Mind and Language,* Vol. 9 (1994), 25–37.

Horgan, T., and J. Tienson, "Representations without Rules," *Philosophical Topics,* Vol. 17 (1989), 27–43.

———. "A Nonclassical Framework for Cognitive Science," *Synthese,* Vol. 101 (1994), 305–45.

———, eds., *Connectionism and the Philosophy of Mind.* Dordrecht, 1991.

McLaughlin, B., and T. A. Warfield. "The Allure of Connectionism Reexamined," *Synthese,* Vol. 101 (1994), 365–400.

Ramsey, W., S. Stich, and D. Rumelhart, eds. *Philosophy and Connectionist Theory.* Hillsdale, NJ, 1991.

Sejnowski, T., and C. Rosenberg. "Parallel Networks That Learn to Pronounce English Text," *Complex Systems,* Vol. 1 (1987), 145–68.

Tienson, J. "Introduction to Connectionism," in J. Garfield, ed., *Foundations of Cognitive Science: The Essential Readings* (New York, 1990).

van Gelder, T. J. "What Might Cognition Be if Not Computation?" in R. Port and T. J. van Gelder, eds., *Mind as Motion: Dynamics, Behavior, and Cognition* (Cambridge, MA, 1995).

TERENCE E. HORGAN

CONSCIOUSNESS IN ANGLO-AMERICAN PHILOSOPHY. Thomas H. HUXLEY [4] said, "How it is that anything so remarkable as a state of consciousness comes about as a result of irritating nervous tissue, is just as unaccountable as the appearance of Djin when Aladdin rubbed his lamp." We have no conception of our physical or functional nature that allows us to understand how it could explain our subjective experience, or so says one point of view on CONSCIOUSNESS [2]. This issue has dominated the discussion of consciousness in recent years.

THE EXPLANATORY GAP

Neuroscientists have hypothesized that the neural basis of consciousness is to be found in certain phase-locked 40 Hz neural oscillations. But how does a 40 Hz neural oscillation explain what it is like (in Nagel's memorable phrase) to be us? What is so special about a 40 Hz oscillation as opposed to some other physical state? And why could not there be creatures with brains just like ours in their physical and functional properties, including their 40 Hz oscillation patterns, whose owners' experiences were very unlike ours, or who had no subjective experiences at all? One does not have to suppose that there really could be creatures with brains just like ours who have different experiences or no experiences to demand an account of why not. But no one has a clue about how to answer these questions. This is the heart of the MIND–BODY PROBLEM [5].

Consciousness, in the sense discussed, is phenomenal consciousness. "What's that?," you ask. There is no noncircular definition to be offered; the best that can be done is the offering of synonyms, examples, and one or another type of pointing to the phenomenon. For example, "subjective experience" and "what it is like to be us" were used earlier as synonyms. In explaining phenomenal consciousness, one can also appeal to conscious properties or qualities, e.g., the ways things seem to us, or immediate phenomenological qualities. Or one can appeal to examples: the ways things look or sound, the way pain feels, and more generally the experiential properties of sensations, feelings and perceptual experiences. One could also add that thoughts, wants, and emotions often have characteristic conscious aspects, and that a difference in representational content can make a phenomenal difference. Seeing something as a cloud differs from seeing it as a part of a painted backdrop. What it is like to hear Bulgarian spoken depends on whether one understands the language.

We gain some perspective on the explanatory gap if we contrast the issue of the physical/functional basis of consciousness with the issue of the physical/functional basis of thought. In the case of thought, we do have some theoretical proposals about what thought is, or at least what human thought is, in scientific terms. Cognitive scientists have had some success in explaining some features of our thought processes in terms of the notions of representation and COMPUTATION [S]. There are many disagreements among cognitive scientists; especially notable is the disagreement between connectionists and classical LANGUAGE OF THOUGHT [S] theorists. However, the fact is that in the case of thought, we actually have more than one substantive research program, and their proponents are busy fighting it out, comparing which research program handles which phenomena best. But in the case of consciousness, we have nothing worthy of being called a research program, nor are there any substantive proposals about how to go about starting one. Researchers are stumped. There have been many tantalizing discoveries recently about neuropsychological syndromes in which consciousness seems to be in some way missing or defective, but no one has yet come up with a theoretical perspective that uses these data to narrow the explanatory gap, even a little bit.

PERSPECTIVES ON THE EXPLANATORY GAP

There are many different attitudes toward this problem, but five of them stand out. First, we might mention eliminativism (*see* ELIMINATIVE MATERIALISM, ELIMINATIVISM [S]), the view that consciousness as understood above simply does not exist (P. S. Churchland, 1983; Dennett, 1988; Rey, 1983). So there is nothing for there to be an explanatory gap about. Second, we have various forms of reductionism (*see* REDUCTION, REDUCTIONISM [S]), notably FUNCTIONALISM [S] and physicalism (*see* PHYSICALISM, MATERIALISM [S]). According to these views, there is such a thing as consciousness, but there is no singular explanatory gap, that is, there are no mysteries concerning the physical basis of consciousness that differ in kind from run-of-the-mill unsolved scientific problems about the physical/functional basis of liquidity, inheritance or computation. On this view, there is an explanatory gap, but it is unremarkable (Dennett, 1991, flirts with both this position and eliminativism). A third view is what Flanagan (1992) calls the new mysterianism. Its most extreme form is transcendentalism, the view that consciousness is simply not a natural phenomenon and is not explainable in terms of science at all. A less extreme form of new mysterianism is that of McGinn (1991), which concedes that consciousness is a natural phenomenon but emphasizes our problem in understanding the physical basis of consciousness. McGinn argues that there are physical properties of our brains that do in fact explain consciousness, but though this explanation might be available to some other type of being, it is cognitively closed off to us. A fourth view, NATURALISM [5; S] (Flanagan, 1992; Searle, 1992), holds that though there may be important differences between a naturalistic explanation of consciousness and naturalistic explanations of other phenomena, there is no convincing reason to regard consciousness as non-natural or unexplainable in naturalistic terms. This view is suggested by Nagel's remark that we are like the person ignorant of relativity theory, who is told that matter is a form of energy but who does not have the concepts to appreciate how there could be chains of reference-links leading from a single phenomenon to both "matter" and "energy." The explanatory gap exists—and we cannot conceive of how to close it—because we lack the scientific concepts. But future theory may provide those concepts. A fifth view says the gap is unclosable, but not because we cannot find the right physical concepts. Rather, it is unclosable because reductive explanation requires an a priori functional analysis of the phenomenon to be explained, and no such analysis can be given of our concepts of conscious experience (Levine, 1993). The unavailability of these functional analyses is no accident: if our only concept of consciousness were one that could be analyzed functionally, we would need a different concept of consciousness to capture the features of experience that give rise to the explanatory gap.

OTHER CONCEPTS OF CONSCIOUSNESS

There are other concepts of consciousness—cognitive, or intentional, or functional concepts of consciousness—that are often not distinguished from it, and it is common for deflationists or reductionists about phenomenal consciousness to slide tacitly from phenomenal consciousness to one or another of these cognitive, or intentional, or functional concepts (see Dennett, 1991, and Block, 1995). Three such concepts of consciousness will be mentioned: self-consciousness, monitoring-consciousness, and access-consciousness.

(1) Self-consciousness is the possession of the concept of the SELF [S] and the ability to use this concept in thinking about oneself. There is reason to think that animals or babies can have phenomenally conscious states without employing any concept of the self. To suppose that phenomenal consciousness requires the concept of the self is to place an implausible intellectual condition on phenomenal consciousness. Perhaps phenomenally conscious states have a nonconceptual content that could be described as "experienced as mine," but there is no reason to think that this representational aspect of the state exhausts its phenomenal properties. After all, if both my experience as of blue and my experience as of red are experienced as mine, we still need to explain the difference between the two experiences; the fact that they are both experienced as mine will not distinguish them. (The "as of" terminology is intended to preclude cases in which red things don't look red.)

(2) Monitoring-consciousness takes many forms. One form is "internal scanning," but it would be a mistake to conflate internal scanning with phenomenal consciousness. As Rey (1983) notes, ordinary laptop computers are capable of internal scanning, but it would be silly to think of one's laptop as conscious. Rey favors supposing that internal scanning is sufficient for consciousness, if there is such a thing, and so he concludes that consciousness is a concept that both includes and precludes laptop computers being conscious, and hence that the concept of consciousness is incoherent. But even if we acknowledge "internal scanning consciousness," we should drop the idea that internal scanning is sufficient for phenomenal consciousness, and so we get no incoherence.

Another form of monitoring consciousness is that of accompaniment by a higher-order thought. That is, a conscious state is one that is accompanied by a thought (grounded noninferentially and nonobservationally) to the effect that one is in that state. If one favors a liberal terminological policy, then there should be no objection to this idea as a concept of consciousness. But one may object to the idea (Rosenthal, 1986) that phenomenal consciousness should be identified with higher-order-thought consciousness. One way to see what is wrong with that view is to note that even if one were to come to know about states of one's liver noninferentially and nonobservationally—as some people just know what time it is—that would not make the states of one's liver phenomenally conscious (see Dretske, 1995). Another objection is that phenomenal consciousness does not require the intellectual apparatus that is required for higher-order thought. Thus, the identification of phenomenal consciousness with higher-order thought shares the over-intellectualism of the identification of phenomenal consciousness with self-consciousness. Dogs and babies may have phenomenally conscious pains without thoughts to the effect that they have those pains.

A distinction is often made between state consciousness—or intransitive consciousness—and consciousness-of, or transitive consciousness (Rosenthal, 1986). For example, saying "I'm nauseous," ascribes a kind of intransitive consciousness to oneself, and if one says one is now seeing something as a mosquito, one ascribes transitive consciousness. The higher-order thought view purposely collapses these notions. According to the higher-order thought view, a conscious state (intransitive consciousness) is simply a state that one is conscious of (transitive consciousness), and consciousness-of is simply a matter of accompaniment by a thought to the effect that one is in that state. So what it is for a state to be conscious (intransitively) is for it to be accompanied by a thought that one is in that state.

This intentional conflation has an element of plausibility to it, which can be seen by comparing two dogs, one of which has a perceptual state whereas the other has a similar perceptual state plus a representation of it. Surely the latter dog has a conscious state even if the former dog does not! Quite so, because consciousness-of brings consciousness with it. But it is the converse that is problematic. State consciousness makes less in the way of intellectual demands than consciousness-of, and so the first dog could be conscious without being conscious of anything.

(3) Access-consciousness does not make the intellectual demands of self-consciousness or higher-order-thought

consciousness, and for that reason, reductionists about phenomenal consciousness would do better to identify phenomenal consciousness with access-consciousness. A state is access-conscious if it is poised for global control. To add more detail, an access-conscious representation is poised for free use in reasoning and for direct control of action and speech. An access-conscious state is one that consists in having an access-conscious representation.

A good way to see the distinction between access-consciousness and phenomenal consciousness is to note cases of one without the other. Consider a robot with a computer brain that is behaviorally and computationally identical to ours. The question arises as to whether what it is like to be that robot is different from what it is like to be us, or, indeed, whether there is anything at all that it is like to be that robot. If there is nothing it is like to be that robot, the robot is a zombie. If zombies are conceptually possible, they certainly illustrate access-consciousness without phenomenal consciousness. But there is widespread opposition to the conceptual coherence of zombies (see Shoemaker, 1975, 1981; Dennett, 1991). So for illustrating access-consciousness without phenomenal consciousness, one would rather rely on a very limited sort of partial zombie.

Consider blindsight, a neurological syndrome in which subjects seem to have "blind" areas in their visual fields. If the experimenter flashes a stimulus to one of those blind areas, the patient claims to see nothing at all. But if the experimenter insists that the subject guess, and the experimenter supplies a few alternatives, the blindsight patients are able to "guess" reliably about certain features of the stimulus—features having to do with motion, location, direction—and they are able to discriminate some simple forms. Consider a blindsight patient who "guesses" that there is an 'X' rather than an 'O' in his blind field. The patient has no access-consciousness of the stimulus (because, until he hears his own guess, he cannot use the information freely in reasoning or in rational control of action), and it is plausible that he has no phenomenal consciousness of it either. Now imagine something that does not exist, what we might call super-blindsight. A real blindsight patient can only guess when given a choice among a small set of alternatives ('X'/'O', horizontal/vertical, and so forth). But suppose (apparently contrary to fact) that a blindsight patient could be trained to prompt himself at will, guessing what is in the blind field without being told to guess. Visual information from the blind field simply pops into his thoughts the way that solutions to problems sometimes pop into ours, or (to use an example given earlier) the way some people just know what time it is without any special perceptual experience. The super-blindsight patient says there is something it is like to see an 'X' in his sighted field, but not in his blind field, and we believe him. This would be a case of access-consciousness without phenomenal consciousness, a sort of partial zombie.

Here is an example of the converse of the zombie cases, namely phenomenal consciousness without access-consciousness. It appears that some areas of the brain specialize in reasoning and rational control of action, whereas other areas subserve sensation. If a person's brain has the former areas destroyed, he is unable to use the deliverances of the senses to control action rationally, to reason or to report sensibly, but he can still have experiences. Such a person has phenomenal consciousness without access consciousness.

Here is a different sort of example. Suppose that you are engaged in intense conversation when suddenly, at midnight, you realize that there is now and has been for some time a deafening pounding noise going on. You had raised your voice in response to the noise, but you had not noticed the noise or that you had raised your voice. You were aware of the noise all along, but only at midnight were you consciously aware of it. That is, you were phenomenally conscious of the noise all along, but only at midnight did you become access-conscious of it. The period before midnight illustrates phenomenal consciousness without access-consciousness. 'Conscious' and 'aware' are roughly synonomous, so it is natural to use one for the period before midnight, and both for the period after midnight, when there are two kinds of consciousness present. The Freudian sense of UNCONSCIOUS [8] means access-unconscious. Suppose a person was tortured in a red room and represses that fact; Freudian theory allows visual images of the red room that lead to desperate flight when the person is in a similarly colored room, but mechanisms of repression can prevent thought, reasoning, and reporting about the torture and the room. The vivid visual image would be phenomenally conscious but access-unconscious.

The cases mentioned earlier of phenomenal consciousness without access-consciousness are also counterexamples to the higher-order-thought theory of phenomenal consciousness. If the subject has no access to the phenomenal state, he cannot think about it either. Before midnight, you have a phenomenally conscious state caused by the noise but no thought to the effect that you are in such a state. The victim of repression has a phenomenally conscious state that he is unable to think about.

Akins (1993) has argued against the distinction between a phenomenal and a representational aspect of experience. She keys her discussion to Nagel's (1974) claim that we cannot know what it is like to be a bat, challenging the reader to imagine that what it is like to be a bat is just what it is like to be us—only all those experiences represent totally different things. Correctly, she says that you cannot imagine that. That is because, as mentioned earlier, representational differences of a certain sort make a phenomenal difference. What it is like to hear a sound as coming from the left is different from what it is like to hear a sound as coming from

the right. But from the fact that some representational differences make a phenomenal difference, one should not conclude that the phenomenal character of a conscious state is exhausted by its representational content. Note, for example, that there are phenomenal states that arguably have little or no representational content, orgasm for example (but see Tye, 1995, for the opposite view).
(SEE ALSO: *Philosophy of Mind* [S])

Bibliography

Akins, K. "A Bat Without Qualities," in M. Davies and G. Humphreys, eds., *Consciousness* (Oxford, 1993).

Block, N. "On a Confusion about a Function of Consciousness," *The Behavioral and Brain Sciences,* Vol. 18, No. 2 (1995), 227–47.

Churchland, P. S. "Consciousness: The Transmutation of a Concept," *Pacific Philosophical Quarterly,* Vol. 64 (1983), 80–93.

Dennett, D. "Quining Qualia," in A. Marcel and E. Bisiach, eds., *Consciousness in Contemporary Society* (Oxford, 1988).

———. *Consciousness Explained.* New York, 1991.

Dretske, F. *Naturalizing the Mind.* Cambridge, MA, 1995.

Flanagan, O. *Consciousness Reconsidered.* Cambridge, MA, 1992.

Levine, J. "On Leaving Out What It Is Like," in M. Davies and G. Humphreys, eds., *Consciousness* (Oxford, 1993).

Lycan, W. *Consciousness.* Cambridge, MA, 1987.

McGinn, C. *The Problem of Consciousness.* Oxford, 1991.

Nagel, T. "What Is It Like to Be a Bat?" *Philosophical Review* (1974).

Rey, G. "A Reason for Doubting the Existence of Consciousness," in R. Davidson, G. Schwartz, and D. Shapiro, eds., *Consciousness and Self-Regulation,* Vol. 3 (New York, 1983).

Rosenthal, D. "Two Concepts of Consciousness," Vol. 3 *Philosophical Studies,* Vol. 49 (1986), 329–59.

Searle, J. *The Rediscovery of the Mind.* Cambridge, MA, 1992.

Shoemaker, S. "Functionalism and Qualia," *Philosophical Studies,* Vol. 27 (1975), 291–315.

Shoemaker, S. "Absent Qualia Are Impossible—A Reply to Block," *Philosophical Review,* Vol. 90, No. 4 (1981), 581–99.

Tye, M. *Ten Problems of Consciousness: A Representational Theory of the Phenomenal Mind.* Cambridge, MA, 1995.

NED BLOCK

CONSCIOUSNESS IN PHENOMENOLOGY: HUSSERL. For HUSSERL [4; S], the two basic features of consciousness are INTENTIONALITY [4] and temporality. Intentionality means that all consciousness is directed to some object. The thesis that consciousness is temporal means, not only that all conscious states have a temporal location, but that each of them has within itself a temporal structure and that the temporal structure of consciousness is the basis for all other determinations of consciousness and its objects.

Husserl's philosophical method proceeds through an analysis of conscious life. However, since all consciousness is intentional, the analysis of the forms and structures of various kinds of consciousness (including volitional, emotional, and evaluative as well as theoretical) is also the appropriate way to analyze the essential forms and structures of various kinds of objects. Since Husserl also believes that consciousness involves at least implicit self-consciousness of one's own mental states, the focus on consciousness shifts the analysis to a sphere that is immediately and directly given in reflection and is therefore the source of apodictic certainty, the transcendental ego. In later works Husserl qualifies this assertion by pointing out that self-givenness even for ideal objects never necessarily involves absolute certainty, so that all purported givenness requires reconfirmation. He also turns his attention to the sphere of passive synthesis, whose results may be directly given to us, while the operations that originally generate them are not, so that a phenomenological reconstruction or intentional analysis is necessary to reveal sedimented or initially hidden and prepredicative elements of consciousness.
(SEE ALSO: *Intentionality in Husserl, Temporality and Time,* and *Time Consciousness*)

Bibliography

Husserl, E. *Cartesianische Meditationen. Husserliana,* Vol. 1, edited by S. Strasser. The Hague, 1950. Translated by D. Cairns as *Cartesian Meditations.* The Hague, 1960. See especially secs. 6–22 regarding intentionality and reflection. See secs. 30–41 regarding the temporal nature of consciousness and passive genesis.

———. *Formale und transzendentale Logik. Husserliana,* Vol. 17, edited by P. Jannsen. The Hague, 1974. Translated by D. Cairns as *Formal and Transcendental Logic.* The Hague, 1969. Secs. 58ff. distinguish between self-givenness and infallibility.

———. *Ideen zu einer reinen Phänomenologie und phänomenologischen Philosophie, Buch 1. Husserliana,* Vol. 3. The Hague, 1976. Translated by F. Kersten as *Ideas Pertaining to a Pure Phenomenology and Phenomenological Philosophy. First Book.* The Hague, 1982. See especially secs. 34–62 regarding the intentionality of consciousness and its accessibility to pure reflection.

THOMAS NENON

CONSCIOUSNESS IN PHENOMENOLOGY: SARTRE. Jean-Paul SARTRE [7; S] considered himself a philosopher of CONSCIOUSNESS [2] during the first half of his career. He subscribed to the Cartesian ideal of the cogito as the starting point of philosophy and placed a premium on the apodictic evidence it yielded (*see* DESCARTES, RENÉ [2; S]). But he valued consciousness as much for its freedom and spontaneity as for its epistemological translucency. In fact, it was the relevance of translucency to moral responsibility that led him to deny both a transcendental ego and the Freudian UNCONSCIOUS [8] and to posit a "prereflective *Cogito.*"

In his *The Psychology of Imagination* he describes imaging consciousness as the locus of "negativity, possibility, and lack." Because we are able to "hold the world at bay" and "derealize" perceptual objects imagistically, he argues, we are free. Imaging consciousness becomes paradigmatic of consciousness in general (being-for-itself) in *Being and Nothingness.* Adopting Edmund HUSSERL's [4; S] thesis that all consciousness is intentional, he insists that this INTENTIONALITY [4] is primarily practical, articulating a fundamental project that gives meaning/direction (*sens*) to our existence.

Sartre makes much of the prereflective self-awareness that accompanies our explicit awareness of any object, including our egos as reflective objects. Since we are always implicitly self-aware, it is unnecessary to seek self-consciousness in an endless infinity of reflections on reflections or to chase after a subject that cannot be an object (the transcendental ego). The unblinking eye of prereflective consciousness makes possible both BAD FAITH [S] and its overcoming through what he calls "purifying reflection," the authentic "choice" to live at a creative distance from one's ego (see AUTHENTICITY [S]).

Bibliography

Sartre, J.-P. *L'Etre et le néant.* Paris, 1943. Translated by H. E. Barnes as *Being and Nothingness.* New York, 1956.

———. *L'Imaginaire.* Paris, 1940. Translated by B. Frechtman as *The Psychology of Imagination.* New York, 1966.

———. *La Transcendence de l'ego.* Paris, 1937. Translated by R. Kirkpatrick and F. Williams as *The Transcendence of the Ego.* New York, 1957.

THOMAS R. FLYNN

CONSEQUENTIALISM. As a name for any ETHICAL THEORY [S] or for the class of ethical theories that evaluate actions by the value of the consequences of the actions, consequentialism thus refers to classical UTILITARIANISM [8] and other theories that share this characteristic.

Classical utilitarianism, in the philosophies of Jeremy BENTHAM [1], John Stuart MILL [5; S], and Henry SIDGWICK [7; S], was consequentialist, judging actions right in proportion as they tended to produce happiness, wrong as they tended to produce pain. In the nineteenth and early twentieth centuries much of the criticism of utilitarianism was directed at the hedonistic value theory on which the ethical theory was founded (*see* HEDONISM [3]). Some philosophers, such as G. E. MOORE [5], agreed with the claim of utilitarianism that acts are right insofar as they produce good consequences, wrong as they produce bad consequences, but put forward a richer theory of value, claiming that other things besides pleasure and pain are of intrinsic value and disvalue. Such theories were sometimes labeled ideal utilitarianism. The term consequentialism is now used in a generic sense to include both hedonistic and nonhedonistic theories.

The term was probably introduced into usage by Elizabeth ANSCOMBE [S] in "Modern Moral Philosophy" (1958), an essay in which she claims that there is little difference between strictly consequentialist theories and other moral theories from Sidgwick on that permit forbidden acts to be overridden by consequentialist considerations. For example, W. D. ROSS [7], who was an intuitionist in opposition to utilitarianism, even "ideal" utilitarianism, believed that a prima facie wrong action, such as the deliberately unjust punishment of an innocent person, could be outweighed by some consequentialist consideration such as the national interest. One contrast with consequentialism, then, is absolutism, the claim that there are some actions that are never right, whatever the consequences.

In the most usual usage of "consequentialism" as a term for ethical theories, however, it is contrasted, not only to absolutism, but to any theory, such as Kantianism, intuitionism, VIRTUE ETHICS, RIGHTS [S] theories, and so on, that does not in some way make consequences the determinant of right and wrong. The consequences may be considered indirectly. Distinctions have been made between act utilitarianism, which judges acts right or wrong according to the consequences of the particular act, case by case, rule utilitarianism, which judges acts right or wrong according to whether the acts are in accord with or in violation of a useful rule—that is, a rule whose general practice would have good consequences (or better consequences than any feasible alternative rule)—and motive utilitarianism, which judges acts right or wrong if stemming from a motive that, as a motive for action, generally has good consequences. These distinctions carry over to consequentialism as a generic category of ethical theories, and one can speak of act consequentialism, rule consequentialism, and so on. Consequentialist theories can also have a place for virtues and for rights, if the inculcation of certain virtues or the respect for certain rights has good consequences. But for the consequentialist the virtues or rights are not ultimate. Their value is dependent upon their contribution to good consequences.

Abstracting from the alternative theories of value, there are still important controversies regarding consequentialist theories. Some are problems of measuring consequences or making interpersonal comparisons, whatever the theory of value, but these cannot be addressed in the abstract. Another is the theory of responsibility. One prominent criticism of consequentialism, stated, for example, by Bernard Williams (1973), is that it does not adequately distinguish between positive and negative responsibility. The claim is that consequentialism is indifferent between states of affairs that are produced by what an agent does and those that occur because of what someone else would do that the agent could prevent. It becomes an agent's responsibility to prevent someone else from doing harm as well as not to do harm oneself. Related to this is the claim that consequentialism undermines agent integrity. For example, someone opposed to research in chemical and biological warfare might be required to engage in such research to prevent someone else from doing it more zealously. Another criticism is that if it is formulated as a "maximizing" theory, requiring the maximization of best consequences, consequentialism goes beyond the limits of obligation. For example, one would be morally obligated to spend one's wealth and income on others as long as there is anyone who could benefit more than oneself.

There are four basic kinds of responses that the consequentialist can make to these criticisms. One is to stick to the theory, saying that these things are morally demanded, even if not generally recognized in our selfish and self-centered society, as Peter Singer (1972) argues concerning famine relief. Another is to challenge the implications of the examples, claiming that for moral agents to focus energy and attention on their own lives with integrity to their own principles has better consequences than doing otherwise. A third strategy for a nonhedonist is to attempt to avoid some of these objections by enriching the theory of value, such as to claim that integrity is something that is intrinsically valuable. A fourth strategy is to modify the structure of the theory. Michael Slote (1984) has argued in favor of a "satisficing" rather than a maximizing theory. Samuel Scheffler (1982) has proposed a "hybrid" theory that permits an agent either to maximize best consequences or to pursue the "agent-centered prerogative" of not always doing so.

(SEE ALSO: *Deontological Ethics* [2; S])

Bibliography

Anscombe, G. E. M. "Modern Moral Philosophy," *Philosophy,* Vol. 33 (1958), 1–19.

Bennett, J. "Whatever the Consequences," *Analysis,* Vol. 26 (1965–66), 83–102.

Brandt, R. B. "Utilitarianism and Moral Rights," *Canadian Journal of Philosophy,* Vol. 14 (1984), 1–19.

Kagan, S. "Does Consequentialism Demand Too Much? Recent Work on the Limits of Obligation," *Philosophy and Public Affairs,* Vol. 13 (1983–84), 239–54.

Pettit, P., ed. *Consequentialism.* Brookfield, VT, 1993.

Scheffler, S. *The Rejection of Consequentialism.* Oxford, 1982.

Singer, P. "Famine, Affluence, and Morality," *Philosophy and Public Affairs,* Vol. 1 (1971–72), 229–43.

Slote, M. "Satisficing Consequentialism," *The Aristotelian Society,* Vol. 43 (1984), suppl. vol., 139–63.

Smart, J. J. C. "An Outline of a System of Utilitarian Ethics," in J. J. C. Smart and B. Williams, eds., *Utilitarianism: For and Against* (Cambridge, 1973).

Williams, B. "A Critique of Utilitarianism," in J. J. C. Smart and Bernard Williams, eds., *Utilitarianism: For and Against* (Cambridge, 1973).

HENRY R. WEST

CONSTITUTION IN HUSSERL. From his earliest work on the foundation of mathematics, up through his final work on the legitimacy of modern science's claim to be the exclusive arbiter of objectivity and legitimacy, a central issue for Edmund HUSSERL [4; S] concerned the question of the origin of various kinds of entities. Even before the notion of "constitution" was systematically introduced in his *Ideen I* (1913), Husserl's analyses pointed to the origins of different kinds of objects in subjective operations or "acts" that are involved in the emergence of these specific kinds of entities for consciousness, in what he comes to call "meaning bestowing" or "meaning establishing" acts in his *Logische Untersuchungen* (1900–01; *see* CONSCIOUSNESS IN PHENOMENOLOGY: HUSSERL [S]). Accordingly, in *Ideen I,* Husserl describes the problem of the "constitution of objectivities" for consciousness as the central problem of phenomenology. In adopting the term "constitution" for the process by which objects come to be present as intended for consciousness, Husserl seeks to avoid causal terms that would imply a dependency relationship between two existing things, namely consciousness and objects, yet at the same time he stresses the necessary role of specific cognitive operations if various kinds of objects are to become present for consciousness. The term is therefore closely connected to Husserl's explicit turn to transcendental philosophy, in which the structures of various forms of objectivity—noemetic structures—are traced back to the structures of cognition in the broadest sense (including feeling, desiring, willing, and knowing)—their noetic structures.

Already in his first extensive work, *Philosophie der Arithmetik* (1891), Husserl had shown how the very concept of number involved the operations of abstraction and combination. He also showed how the symbolic representation of numbers is essential for the science of arithmetic. One can thus describe Husserl's early work on mathematics in terms of constitutional analysis, even though he does not yet employ the term. In the subsequent *Logische Untersuchungen,* Husserl indicates that all objects are intentional objects and shows how they are essentially related to acts of meaning intention or meaning bestowal that may or may not find fulfillment in intuition; and he shows specifically how categorial objects such as propositions are constituted as the correlates of complex categorial intentions that are constructed on the basis of lower-order simpler intention of the objects of sense perceptions. To this extent *LU* may also be read as an early version of constitutive phenomenology. (Some commentators have taken a realist stance toward this work and maintained that the emphasis upon acts as the source of objectivity is an error, just as the analysis of numbers in terms of operations in Husserl's earlier work had not been sufficiently purged of PSYCHOLOGISM [6], as Husserl himself admitted. This tradition of Husserl interpretation, known as realist phenomenology, accordingly also views Husserl's explicit turn to constitutive phenomenology and his concurrent acceptance of transcendental idealism in the works that follow as a mistake.)

During the first decade of this century another problem that becomes particularly significant for Husserl is the constitution of TIME CONSCIOUSNESS [S]. He first shows how objective time can be traced back to internal time-consciousness, then ultimately to the elements involved in the very constitution of internal time-consciousness itself. This represents the most basic level of constitutional analysis, the study of primary constitution (*Urkonstitution*), since temporality turns out to be the most basic structure of consciousness itself, within which all other forms of objectivity are constituted. At first, the temporal structure of consciousness is seen only as an isolated problem, and the implications for all regions of beings are not made clear.

In *Ideen I,* Husserl identifies constitution primarily with the activities of consciousness that organize sense perceptions into material objects; he also shows how further operations of consciousness allow for the emergence of other kinds of nonphysical, higher-order objects. At this stage constitution is still thought of in terms of the cognitive activities of individual subjects and is conceived statically—that is, in terms of identifying invariant a priori laws for the constitution of various kinds of objects. However, already during this period Husserl's focus begins to shift from the necessary structures of individual acts that constitute different kinds of objects to the attitudes (*Einstellungen*) that allow the same object to be viewed in different ways, for instance as an object of natural science or as a culturally constituted object of use in our everyday life. Husserl's analyses thus show how shifts in attitudes allow whole new kinds of entities such as scientific objects, objects of use, or ideal objects to emerge.

This sets the stage for the final developments in which Husserl moves from static analyses of constitution to genetic constitution analysis and from constitution as an individual activity to the constitution of intersubjectivity and thereby to the intersubjective constitution of a common lifeworld. In his genetic approach to the problem of constitution, several of Husserl's earlier themes are brought together as he attempts to make explicit the temporal dimension involved in the constitution of all objects, including seemingly nontemporal objects such as numbers and logical principles. This leads to the contrast between an original genesis, in which all of the constitutive elements were actually present to the constituting subject, and the sedimentations of this genesis in habitualities, in which the subject no longer has all these elements consciously present but acts and thinks on the basis of sedimentations that may be either individual or common. Constitutive analysis therefore comes to concern itself, not only with that which can be made immediately present to the consciousness of the individual through reflection, but also with those elements that intentional analysis shows must have been involved in the genesis of the objectivity in question. Husserl's later works center on genetic analyses of constitution, which can be seen as a kind of a priori reconstruction of the history of the constitution of an object, a history that involves passive as well as active elements and an intersubjective component that forms the backdrop for the conscious activities of the individual subject.

(SEE ALSO: *Life-World in Husserl* [S])

Bibliography

Husserl, E. *Logische Untersuchungen.* Tübingen, 1968. Translated by J. N. Findlay as *Logical Investigations.* New York, 1970. Esp. the I. Investigation regarding meaning-bestowing acts and the VI. Investigation regarding the constitution of categorial objects.

———. *Philosophie der Arithmetik. Husserliana,* Vol. 12, edited by L. Eley. The Hague, 1970.

———. *Ideen zu einer reinen Phänomenologie und phänomenologischen Philosophie, Buch 1. Husserliana,* Vol. 3. The Hague, 1976. Translated by F. Kersten as *Ideas Pertaining to a Pure Phenomenology and Phenomenological Philosophy. First Book.* The Hague, 1982.

Sokolowski, R. *The Formation of Husserl's Concept of Constitution.* Phaenomenologica 18. The Hague, 1964. Clear description of the issues that led to the development of the concept of constitution for Husserl.

THOMAS NENON

CONSTRUCTIVISM, CONVENTIONALISM.

CONVENTIONALISM [2] and constructivism are kindred, often overlapping positions, asserting that the subject matter of some area of inquiry is not fully mind-independent. "Conventionalism" and "constructivism" are not well-defined names of positions but labels adopted—as often by critics as by advocates—to emphasize one positive aspect of positions in a wide range of areas; consequently, these terms group together a variety of positions with varying motivations. In general, the label "conventionalism" is applied to positions that claim the truths in some area are so in virtue of the conventions of a linguistic or conceptual scheme, while "constructivism" emphasizes that a position assigns to the cognitive faculties of humans some role in "making" the objects or facts in the area in question.

CONVENTIONALISM

Conventionalists claim either that the truths of some subject matter—such as mathematics or logic, or of a certain sort, such as necessary truths, or some dispute, such as whether Euclid's parallel postulate holds of our physical world—are matters of convention rather than of how the world is independent of mind. Some extreme versions of conventionalism take the fact that it is a matter of convention what our words mean (we could have used *cat* to designate Napoleon) to show that all truth is conventional. However, its being a convention that "Napoleon" names Napoleon hardly makes it conventional that Napoleon was defeated at Waterloo. An interesting conventionalism must assert something more than the conventionality of word meaning and must rest on something more than wild inference from it.

One area in which conventionalism is familiar, though controversial, is necessary truth. This was one cornerstone of LOGICAL POSITIVISM [5]; from the seeming a priori nature of necessary truths, the positivists argued (some would say claimed) that since a priori knowledge cannot be of (mind-independent) facts, necessary truths must be analytic, which they understood as true by definition. Given that mathematics is also a priori, their argument was applied there as well. This sort of epistemological argument is typical of conventionalist views: arguing that our methods for ascertaining what is so in some area could not give us knowledge of a mind-independent world, they claim that this knowledge would not be problematic on the assumption that what is fundamentally under investigation are our conventions. Some sorts of conventionalism are also supported by metaphysical considerations such as naturalistic concerns about what, in the mind-independent world, could make for the relevant sort of truth. This sort of argument is common to necessary truths, mathematics, ethics, and other areas with normative import; plainly, such arguments need to be supplemented with an account of how it is that conventions can provide the relevant features.

Saul KRIPKE'S [S] arguments that there are necessary truths that are a posteriori—and, so, not analytic—seemed to some to undermine conventionalism about necessity (Kripke, 1980). It has, however, been argued that conventions could explain the necessity of these truths without the truths themselves being analytic—that is, true by convention (Sidelle, 1989). This may indicate that in general conventionalism, with respect to a subject matter, does not require that all target truths themselves be analytic but only that conventions be responsible for the features that purportedly cannot be adequately handled within a realistic interpretation.

Aside from the claim that certain truths are so by convention, another common conventionalist position is that some dispute is a conventional rather than factual matter. POINCARÉ'S [6] famous conventionalism about geometry is of this sort. He claims that the choice among systems of geometry, for describing the physical world, is not an issue of which is true but of which is most convenient or useful. By adopting any of them, we could modify our physics so as to have equally full and correct descriptions of the world; indeed, this last claim is the basis for his view that the issue is conventional rather than factual. CARNAP [2; S] offers a similar view about ontological disputes between, for instance, phenomenalists and materialists. Both of these views illustrate that "conventional" does not as such imply 'arbitrary', as pragmatic differences may be quite genuine; we can also see that the plausibility of conventionalism in some area depends largely on how implausible it is to claim that the issue, or truth in question, is a matter of mind-independent fact.

On a more local level, some disputes can appear "purely verbal," as perhaps whether some politician is conservative. When this is plausible, the issue may be said to be a matter of convention or choice rather than fact. The conventionalism of Poincaré, Carnap, and others is akin to this, only in a wider application. In book 3, chapters 7 and 11, of his *Essay,* LOCKE [4; S] speculates that many of the "great disputes" are of this sort.

As applied to areas in which the truths are well established (mathematics or logic, for instance), conventionalism is fundamentally a deflationary interpretive position, urging that we not mistake the metaphysical status of these truths. Applied to areas of controversy—ontological or essentialist claims, or whether whales are fish—conventionalism claims that disputes here can only be over what our conventions in fact are, or what they should be, either pragmatically or perhaps morally. In either case, if conventionalism is right, our focus and methods of investigation—and certainly our understanding of what is at stake—for the questions at hand would probably require alteration.

CONSTRUCTIVISM

Thomas KUHN [S], by virtue of his *The Structure of Scientific Revolutions,* may be considered constructivism's leading protagonist of the mid-to-late twentieth century, despite not adopting the label himself and expressing unease at having it assigned to him. He writes of scientists within different paradigms—roughly, methodological and theoretical traditions or frameworks—as studying different worlds and of their paradigms as in "a sense . . . constitutive of nature" (Kuhn, 1970, p. 110, chaps. 10, 13), at least suggesting a constructivism about the world studied by science. Kuhn's major concerns are epistemological; he argues that scientific procedure is deeply theory laden and encodes ontological and theoretical commitments that it is incapable of testing. How, then, can such a method give us knowledge of the world? Those who see a constructivist in Kuhn have him answer that the world under investigation is itself partly a product of the investigating paradigm. This puts Kuhn in the tradition of KANT [4; S], except that the features we "impose" upon the phenomenal world are not (as for Kant) necessary for the possibility of experience, but, rather, contingent features of current science. It is important to note that, even as interpreted, this constructivism does not have scientists making the world out of whole cloth with their paradigms; rather, there is something mind-independent that "filters through" the conceptual apparatus of the paradigm. This is a central difference between constructivism and idealism. The object of scientific study is, however, not this mind-independent world, but rather that which results "through the filter."

Other philosophers, as well as historians and sociologists of science, have taken the supposedly arational or nonobjective features guiding scientific judgment to establish that scientific truth is relative to one's background theory or paradigm. This is sometimes then articulated as the view that these theories or paradigms in part "make" the objects of study—that is, as constructivism. Indeed, many positions that formerly would have simply been called relativist have come, in the late twentieth century, to be called constructivist by their protagonists; arguments in their support tend to be of the familiar relativist sort and thus have the same strengths and problems. It should be noted that neither constructivism nor conventionalism need take a relativistic form.

Another philosopher associated with constructivism is Nelson GOODMAN [3; S], due largely to his *Ways of Worldmaking.* Goodman argues that no sense can be made of the notion "the (one) way the world is"; rather, there are lots of ways the world is, depending on the conceptual apparatus one brings. This sort of position is found in many philosophers since Kant, often argued on the trivial ground that one cannot describe or investigate the world without using a system of representation, therefore (*sic*) the world investigated is not mind-independent but partly constructed by our conceptual scheme. This is sometimes added to, or confused with, the relativistic considerations mentioned above. What needs to be explained is how we are supposed to get this substantive conclusion from the banal premise. Why can't the objects represented by the elements of a system of representation—by the name "Tabby," say—be wholly and utterly mind-independent? And even if we add the fact that there can be different schemes of representation, why can it not simply be that they pick out different features of a mind-independent reality? What gives Goodman his special place is that he supplements this argument with the claim that different schemes may be such that their claims conflict with each other, but there can be no grounds for maintaining that one is correct and the other not. Goodman uses as examples the claims that the planets revolve around the sun and that the sun and other planets revolve around the earth. Both, he claims, must be judged as correct (within the appropriately formulated total systems), but they cannot simply be seen as two notationally different descriptions of a single world (thus differing from Poincaré's conventionalism). The success of this argument depends on whether one can simultaneously make out that these claims genuinely do conflict with each other and that, so understood, neither of them can be judged to be true while the other is false.

PROSPECTS

While both Kuhn and Goodman offer relatively global constructivist positions, there are constructivists about essences, moral and aesthetic properties, mathematical objects, and in principle anything. The same is true of conventionalism. Both conventionalism and constructivism are motivated primarily by negative considerations against a realistic understanding of the subject matter in question; this is sometimes supplemented with positive arguments that by understanding the matter as concerning our conventions or choices we can get a better explanation of the phenomena at hand. Often, the negative arguments are very quick and fail to fully consider the range of options available to realists (Sheffler, 1966, presents good discussion), and sometimes they fail to consider whether their positive proposals actually fare any better. Plainly, the plausibility of these positions depends on how well these arguments can be made out, and this may vary drastically across the different subject matters for which conventionalist and constructivist proposals have been offered. Additionally, if these positions are even to be candidates for serious consideration, defenders must be prepared to offer further proof. Conventionalists must specify some sense in which that which is purportedly so by convention would have been otherwise had our conventions been different, and constructivists must describe some sense in which the purportedly constructed objects would not have existed without our input.

Bibliography

Carnap, R. "Empiricism, Semantics, and Ontology," in *Meaning and Necessity* (Chicago, 1947). A classic exposition of the conventionalist's treatment of apparently ontological questions as fundamentally linguistic.

Dummett, M. *Frege: Philosophy of Language,* 2d ed. Cambridge, 1981. Chap. 16, esp. pp. 560–83. An interesting presentation of what may be seen as a constructivist position on objects or a conventionalist position on identity criteria.

Goodman, N. *Ways of Worldmaking.* Indianapolis, 1978. For useful discussion, see C. G. Hempel, "Comments on Goodman's *Ways of Worldmaking,*" and I. Scheffler, "The Wonderful Worlds of Goodman," both in *Synthese,* Vol. 45 (1980), 193–209.

Horwich, P. "A Defence of Conventionalism," in G. MacDonald and C. Wright, eds., *Fact, Science and Morality* (Oxford, 1986).

Knorr-Cetina, K. "The Ethnographic Study of Scientific Work: Towards a Constructivist Interpretation of Science," in K. Knorr-Cetina and M. Mulkay, eds., *Science Observed: Perspectives on the Social Study of Science* (London, 1983).

Kripke, S. *Naming and Necessity.* Cambridge, 1980.

Kuhn, T. S. *The Structure of Scientific Revolutions,* 2d ed. Chicago, 1970.

Kyburg, H. E. "A Defense of Conventionalism," *Noûs,* Vol. 11 (1977), 75–95.

Latour, B., and S. Woolger, *Laboratory Life: The Social Construction of Scientific Facts,* 2d ed. Princeton, NJ, 1986.

Lewis, D. *Convention.* Cambridge, 1969. Argues that sense can be made of the idea of nonexplicit conventions, *contra* Quine (1953).

Locke, J. *An Essay Concerning Human Understanding.* 1689. Locke's discussion of substance in book 3, chap. 7, classically expounds his conventionalism about essence and kinds.

Niiniluoto, I. "Realism, Relativism, and Constructivism," *Synthese,* Vol. 89 (1991), 135–62. Critical discussion of constructivism in the social sciences.

Pap, A. *Semantics and Necessary Truth.* New Haven, 1958. An extended argument against conventionalism about necessity.

Poincaré, H. *Science and Hypothesis.* London, 1905.

Putnam, H. "The Refutation of Conventionalism," in *Mind, Language, and Reality* (Cambridge, 1975).

Quine, W. V. O. "Two Dogmas of Empiricism," in *From a Logical Point of View* (Cambridge, 1953). Classical argument against the analytic–synthetic distinction and so against truth by convention.

———. "Truth by Convention," in *The Ways of Paradox and Other Essays* (Cambridge, 1966). A classic argument against the possibility of truth by convention alone.

Reichenbach, H. *Experience and Prediction.* Chicago, 1938.

Scheffler, I. *Science and Subjectivity.* Indianapolis, 1966. Responds to arguments based on the history of science against objectivity in science, particularly Kuhn's, which are often used to bolster constructivist positions about the objects of scientific study.

Sidelle, A. *Necessity, Essence, and Individuation: A Defense of Conventionalism.* Ithaca, NY, 1989.

ALAN SIDELLE

CONSTRUCTIVISM, MORAL. Moral constructivism is a metaethical view about the nature of moral truth and moral facts (and properties), so called because the intuitive idea behind the view is that such truths and facts are human constructs rather than objects of discovery. More precisely, constructivism involves both a semantic thesis about moral sentences and a two-part metaphysical thesis about the existence and nature of moral facts and properties. According to the semantic thesis, ordinary moral sentences purport to be fact-stating sentences and thus purport to be genuinely true or false. And, according to the metaphysical thesis, there are moral facts whose existence and nature are in some sense dependent upon human attitudes, agreements, conventions, and the like. Thus, constructivism represents a metaethical view in partial agreement with versions of MORAL REALISM [S]. Like the realist, the constructivist is a so-called cognitivist (descriptivist)—moral sentences have descriptive content and thus purport to be genuinely fact stating. Again, like the realist, the constructivist accepts the view that there are moral facts that serve as the truth makers of true moral sentences. But unlike the realist, the constructivist rejects the idea that there are moral facts (and properties) that are independent of human attitudes, conventions, and the like.

It is useful to distinguish between simple and sophisticated versions of constructivism as well as between nonrelativist and relativist versions. Simple versions of constructivism are represented by certain views that would construe moral truth in terms of the actual attitudes of individuals or actual agreements within cultures about matters of moral concern. More sophisticated versions of constructivism construe moral truths (and associated moral facts and properties) in terms of the hypothetical attitudes of individuals or perhaps hypothetical agreements among members of a group reached under suitably constrained circumstances. Nonrelativist versions of constructivism maintain that all individuals and groups whose attitudes, agreements, and so forth provide the basis for moral truths and facts do or would accept the same set of basic moral norms with the result that there is a single set of moral truths and facts. Usually, such views are wedded to some version or other of sophisticated constructivism. Thus, a version of the ideal-observer view of moral truth—according to which basic moral truths are represented by the moral norms that would be accepted by an ideal observer, where the notion of an ideal observer is so characterized that all ideal observers will agree on the same set of basic moral norms—is a version of sophisticated nonrelativist constructivism. Relativist versions of constructivism allow that there may be more than one individual or group with differing attitudes and agreements that serve as the basis for different (and conflicting) sets of basic moral norms. Versions of MORAL RELATIVISM [S], according to which moral truths and facts are a matter of what basic moral norms a culture in fact accepts, represent versions of simple, relativistic constructivism; versions of relativism, according to which moral truths and facts are a matter of what would be accepted under conditions that are ideal for choosing such norms, represent sophisticated relativistic versions of constructivism. Versions of the ideal-observer view are relativistic if they allow that there can be ideal observers who would accept different (and conflicting) sets of moral norms. So-called Kantian constructivism of the sort recently elaborated and defended by John RAWLS [S], which appeals to choices made by hypothetical individuals behind a veil of ignorance (a version of contractarianism), is yet another sophisticated and apparently nonrelativistic constructivist view.

Constructivism, at least in its sophisticated versions, is supposed to capture what is plausible about moral realism, leaving behind what is problematic about realist views. Thus, constructivism can accommodate quite well certain 'objective pretensions' of commonsense moral thinking. Some of these pretensions have to do with the form and content of moral discourse. A good many moral sentences are in the declarative mood (e.g., "Abortion, except in cases of rape and incest, is wrong") and are thus naturally interpreted as genuinely fact-stating sentences. Moreover, some such sentences appear to make references to (putative) moral facts and properties (e.g., "The evil of American slavery was partly responsible for its demise as an institution"). Other objective pretensions have to do with such activities as moral deliberation, debate, and argument. These critical practices are seemingly aimed at arriving nonarbitrarily at true or correct moral views, ones that would ideally resolve intrapersonal and interpersonal conflict and uncertainty about moral issues. Like realism, constructivism is attractive in apparently being able to accommodate such objective pretensions of ordinary moral discourse. Moreover, it attempts to accommodate these features without endorsing the sorts of metaphysical commitments to independently existing moral properties and facts countenanced by the realist. In short, at least certain versions of constructivism boast a robust notion of moral objectivity without problematic metaphysical commitments.

One serious challenge to constructivism is represented by the argument from moral error. According to constructivism, moral truths and associated facts are to be understood in terms of the attitudes and agreements of individuals and groups. However, if we take ordinary moral discourse and argument seriously, then since such discourse and argument presuppose that there are right answers to moral questions whose correctness outstrips any actual or even ideal set of attitudes or agreements, the constructivist view cannot be correct. To understand this objection more clearly, it will be useful to distinguish between basic and nonbasic moral truths and facts. Basic moral truths and facts are of a quite general sort, properly expressed by moral principles, and are the direct objects of choice by those under ideal conditions of moral thought and deliberation. Nonbasic moral truths and facts are those truths and facts that, in some sense, follow from the basic ones together with nonmoral information. Now the constructivist can allow for certain sorts of errors in moral judgment. For instance, simple moral relativism can allow that individuals and groups can be mistaken about particular moral judgments owing to misinformation about particular cases or perhaps to faulty reasoning from basic moral principles to concrete cases. However, this kind of moral relativism cannot allow for error at the level of actual agreements, since such agreements constitute basic moral truths. The sophisticated constructivist can allow for error at the level of communal agreement, since it is possible on such views that the actual agreements of actual groups are at odds with those hypothetical choices constitutive of moral truth on this sort of view. However, the sophisticated constructivist cannot allow for error at the level of choice made under ideal conditions—call this 'deep moral error'. After all, the constructivist construes such choice as constitutive and not just evidence of basic moral truths and facts. But, so the objection goes, given our critical practices, we can sensibly raise questions about the truth of those moral principles and norms that are chosen under ideal circumstances. This indicates that moral truth is one thing and the norms and principles chosen even under the most ideal of circumstances is another. Hence, constructivism, in both its simple and sophisticated versions, is not acceptable.

In response, the constructivist can perhaps block the argument from moral error in the following way. First, the constructivist can note that it is dubious that our critical practices presuppose that deep moral error—error at the level of choice under ideal conditions—is possible. After all, our commonsense critical practices are not finely tuned to subtle differences in metaethical positions, and, in particular, common sense does not (so the constructivist might plead) make any distinction between the sort of realist objectivity that presupposes the possibility of deep moral error and a kind of constructivist objectivity that denies this possibility. Can we, for instance, really make sense of the idea that we might be mistaken about such basic moral principles as one that prohibits torture for fun? Furthermore, the constructivist can question the basic move featured in the argument from moral error—that is, the move from (1) it is quite sensible to raise questions about choices that purport to be made under ideal conditions to (2) an explanation of this phenomenon requires moral realism. Granted, the supposed gap between the truth of moral principles on the one hand and choice of such principles under ideal conditions on the other is one way to explain how we can sensibly raise questions about the truth of moral judgments made under ideal conditions, but this is not the only way to make sense of such critical stances. The constructivist can note that in the context of everyday discussion where we have to judge whether or not to accept the moral judgments of others, one can sensibly raise questions about some judgment by raising questions about the judger herself. After all, whatever is involved according to the constructivist in being ideally well situated for choosing basic moral principles, it is not likely to involve features of the judger and her situation that are easy to detect. For example, part of being ideally well situated would seem to require having all sorts of factual information, being free from certain forms of bias, and properly weighing the interests of parties affected by the choice of principles. But it is difficult to determine that someone has satisfied these and other relevant desiderata for being well situated. So, even if it is not possible for someone who really is well situated to be mistaken in moral judgment, it is possible for critics who acknowledge that such error is not possible to raise sensible questions about the truth of a person's moral judgment. Hence, although the constructivist cannot allow for the possibility of deep moral error, she can plausibly argue that our commonsense critical practices do not presuppose that deep moral error is possible. Moreover, she can go on to accommodate the idea that it makes sense to criticize those who are ideally situated. The constructivist, it would appear, can plausibly

respond to the argument from moral error.
(SEE ALSO: *Ethical Theory* [S])

Bibliography

Brink, D. O. *Moral Realism and the Foundations of Ethics.* Cambridge, 1989. In chapter 2 Brink uses the argument from moral error against constructivism. Appendix 4 is a critical discussion of Rawlsian constructivism.

Firth, R. "Ethical Absolutism and the Ideal Observer," *Philosophy and Phenomenological Research,* Vol. 12 (1952), 317–45. A classic statement of the ideal-observer version of constructivism.

Milo, R. "Skepticism and Moral Justification," *The Monist,* Vol. 76 (1993), 379–93. Milo defends a contractarian version of constructivism.

O'Neill, O. "Constructivisms in Ethics," in *Constructions of Reason* (Cambridge, 1990). O'Neill criticizes Rawls's version of constructivism and sketches what she takes to be a more plausible version of the view inspired by Kant's writings.

Rawls, J. "Kantian Constructivism in Moral Theory," *Journal of Philosophy,* Vol. 77 (1980), 515–72. An elaboration of a constructivist view that centrally involves a Kantian conception of persons.

Timmons, M. "Irrealism and Error in Ethics," *Philosophia,* Vol. 22 (1993), 373–406. A critical discussion of the argument from moral error.

Wong, D. *Moral Relativity.* Berkeley, 1984. Wong both criticizes various versions of moral relativism and defends his own version.

MARK TIMMONS

CONTENT, MENTAL. Beliefs, desires, perceptions, and other mental states and events are said to possess content. We attribute such states and events with sentences such as

(1) Arabella believes that the cat is crying.

(1) contains a PROPOSITIONAL ATTITUDE [S] verb ("believes") and a sentence complement ("the cat is crying"). The verb specifies a type of mental state (belief), and the complement sentence indicates the content of the state. On most accounts this content is the proposition expressed by that sentence. Propositions have been variously conceived as abstract entities composed of modes of presentation, sets of possible worlds, sets of synonymous sentences, and structured entities containing individuals and properties. All these accounts agree that propositions determine truth conditions. Some mental states and events (e.g., desiring to visit Paris) seem to have contents that are not propositions. However, for most of the current discussion, contents will be identified with propositions and contentful mental states with mental states that possess truth conditions.

Both natural-language sentences and mental states possess contents. The relation between content properties of the two items is controversial. Some philosophers think that natural-language expressions derive their contents from mental states, while others hold that, at least in some cases, the dependency goes the other way. In any case, it is plausible that there are mental states whose contents cannot be expressed or cannot be completely expressed by sentences of English (or other natural languages). For example, the full propositional content of a person watching the sun set is only partially captured by an attribution such as "*A* sees that the sun is setting." Also, some of the states posited by cognitive psychology and the mental states of animals plausibly have contents that fail to correspond to any contents expressible in English.

Content apparently endows mental states with a number of remarkable features. First, they or their constituents refer to extra mental reality. When a person perceives that the sun is setting her perception refers to and thus puts her into contact with the sun. Second, they seem to be essentially normative. For example, a person ought to believe that the sun is setting only if the sun is setting, and if she believes that the sun is setting she ought not believe that the sun is not setting. Third, they apparently cause other mental states and behavior in virtue of their contents. For example, Arabella's belief that the cat is crying causes her to feed it. Fourth, a person can apparently know the contents of her own thought a priori and with an authority available only to her.

It is difficult to see how anything can exemplify all these features. The problem is especially difficult for philosophers who endorse NATURALISM [5; S], the view that all genuine properties are constituted by or realized by properties that are mentioned in true theories of the natural sciences. Content properties are prima facie so different from physical and biological properties as to raise the question of whether they are natural properties.

Hilary PUTNAM [S] (1975) and Tyler Burge (1979) described thought experiments that have been taken to have important consequences for the nature of mental contents. Putnam imagined two thinkers, Oscar and twin-Oscar, who are identical with respect to their intrinsic neurophysiological properties but whose environments differ. Specifically, Oscar shares our environment, but twin-Oscar lives on twin-earth where the abundant substance that quenches thirst, fills the twin-earth oceans, and so forth is not H_2O but XYZ. H_2O's and XYZ's superficial properties are identical, and the two substances are indistinguishable without chemical analysis. Putnam claims that, while Oscar's sentence "Water is wet" and the thought he expresses with it are about H_2O, the same sentence in twin-Oscar's language and the thought he expresses with it are about XYZ. The two thoughts differ in their propositional contents, since one is true if and only if (iff) H_2O is wet and the other iff

XYZ is wet. Putnam supports these conclusions with the intuition that, were Oscar and twin-Oscar to learn that the substances each refers to with the word water differ in their chemical natures, they would agree that their utterances of "Water is wet" possessed different truth conditions.

Putnam's thought experiment has been taken to establish the truth of content externalism, the thesis that the individuation conditions of mental content are partially external to the thinker. The point generalizes to other mental states whose contents are the same as the contents of sentences containing natural-kind terms such as water. Burge described further thought experiments that he thinks show that practically all thoughts expressible in natural language are externally individuated, and others have argued that all mental states that express extra-mental truth conditions are externally individuated (LePore & Loewer, 1986).

Some philosophers (Fodor, 1987; Loar, 1987) react to content externalism by granting that mental states possess externally individuated contents but adding that they also possess narrow contents that are not externally individuated. Oscar's and twin-Oscar's beliefs possess the same narrow content. Philosophers sympathetic to narrow contents raise a number of considerations. One is the Cartesian intuition that thinkers in the same intrinsic state have the same mental lives. It seems essential to our conception of a mental life that it possess content, so there must be some kind of content that such thinkers share. The other consideration is that the causal powers of Oscar's and twin-Oscar's mental states seem to be, in an important way, the same. Fodor (1987) claims that if these causal powers involve the states' contents, then that content must be narrow.

Whether or not these considerations are persuasive, it has proved difficult to formulate a satisfactory notion of narrow content. If natural-language sentences express only externally individuated contents, then we do not attribute narrow content with sentences such as (1). While identity of intrinsic neurophysiological states is sufficient for identity of narrow content, it is not a plausible necessary condition. To adopt it as such would make it enormously unlikely that two people have ever shared the same narrow content state and impossible for a state to maintain its content in the course of reasoning. While some proposals for necessary and sufficient conditions for identity of narrow content have been forthcoming (Fodor, 1987), there is little agreement concerning whether they are correct or, for that matter, whether a notion of narrow content is even needed.

EXTERNALISM [S] seems to be in tension with our having a priori knowledge of the contents of our thoughts (Boghossian, 1989). If the content of the thought (e.g., that water is wet) is individuated in part by external factors, then it seems that a person could know that she is thinking this thought only if she knows that those external factors obtain, and thus it is implausible that such knowledge is a priori. One response to this is to grant that we have a priori knowledge only of narrow contents. But a number of philosophers (Burge, 1988; Warfield, 1994) have responded that the tension is only apparent. Burge claims that judgments of the form "I am now thinking that water is wet" are self-verifying, since one cannot make the judgment without thinking the thought that the judgment is about. If this is correct, then externalism and a priori knowledge of content are not always incompatible. But such self-verifying thoughts seem to be a very special case of the thoughts whose contents we seem able to know a priori. It is likely that little progress concerning the epistemology of content can be made without an account of the nature of contentful mental states *(see* KNOWLEDGE, A PRIORI [S]).

The dominant view in the PHILOSOPHY OF MIND [S] is that contentful mental states are functionally individuated internal states. Some philosophers (Dretske, 1981; Fodor 1987) posit that these states are partially constituted by mental representations that are the bearers of propositional content. Mental representations are conceived of as picturelike (mental images), maps, or linguistic expressions. One view (Fodor, 1979) is that mental representations are expressions in a language of thought, Mentalese. On this account thinking that the cat is crying involves tokening a Mentalese sentence with the content that the cat is crying. The thought inherits its content from the semantic properties of its constituent sentence, which in turn obtains its content from the semantic properties of its constituent expressions. Fodor identifies concepts with Mentalese expressions. So, for example, possessing the concept cat is being able to token a Mentalese expression that refers to cats. Some philosophers (Peacocke, 1986) have argued that the contents of perceptual states are nonconceptual. If so, then the contents of these states are not borne by Mentalese expressions.

The nature of the bearers of mental content is best seen as an empirical issue. Fodor (1987) cites the fact that thought is productive and systematic as support for the language-of-thought hypothesis. Productivity is the capacity to produce complicated thoughts by combining simpler thoughts, and systematicity involves being able to think thoughts that are systematically related to each other, as are the thoughts that Bill loves Newt and that Newt loves Bill. Fodor argues that the LANGUAGE-OF-THOUGHT [S] hypothesis provides the best explanation of these phenomena, since languages are productive and systematic. Further, cognitive scientists have constructed theories of cognitive processes, language comprehension (Pinker, 1994), perception (Marr, 1982), and so forth that involve subpersonal contentful mental representations. For example, on one such theory understanding a natural-language sentence involves tokening a representation of its grammatical structure. These representations are not accessible to consciousness and have contents that are not usually available as the contents of a person's beliefs.

There have been various attempts to specify conditions in virtue of which mental states or mental representations possess their contents. Some of these are attempts to naturalize content properties. Following are brief descriptions of the main proposals.

According to interpretationist theories (ITs; Davidson, 1984; Lewis, 1974) our practices of interpreting one another partially constitute the contents of mental states. On DAVIDSON'S [S] approach interpretation is constrained by principles of rationality and charity. These principles say, roughly, that a person's mental states are generally rational and her beliefs are generally true. According to Davidson the evidential base for an assignment of contentful mental states to a person consists of her dispositions to hold true sentences under various conditions. She believes that *p* (desires that *p*, etc.) iff assignments of content to her sentences and to her mental states that systematize these holding true dispositions and that conform to the principles of charity and rationality assign to her the belief that *p* (desire that *p*, etc.).

On ITs, content properties are holistic, since whether or not a person exemplifies a particular contentful mental state depends on what other mental states she exemplifies and on their relations to each other and to environmental conditions. Davidson's IT is externalist, since a state's content is partially determined by relations to environmental conditions. But his account does not provide a naturalistic account of content, since it explains content in terms that presuppose content: holding true, rationality, truth. The primary difficulty with extant ITs is their vagueness. No one has formulated the principles of rationality and charity with sufficient clarity to permit an evaluation of proposed ITs.

According to conceptual role semantics (CRS), the content of a mental representation (or mental state) is determined by the inferential relations among representations and causal relations between representations and extramental events (Block, 1986; Loar, 1981; Sellars, 1963). In this respect CRS is similar to IT. The difference is that, whereas ITs employ holistic principles of interpretations (rationality and charity), CRS attempts to spell out inferential patterns associated with particular concepts. CRS seems plausible for the logical connectives. For example, if a thinker is disposed to infer the representation A#B from A and B and vice versa, then # is the thinker's conjunction concept. Some philosophers (Peacocke, 1992) have attempted to formulate conditions that are necessary and/or sufficient for possessing certain predicate concepts. It appears that any such account is committed to a substantial analytic–synthetic distinction, since it will hold that certain inferences involving a concept are necessary to having the concept (Fodor & LePore, 1992). QUINE'S [7; S] arguments (1960) that there are no analytic inferences poses an important problem for CRS.

Another approach is informational semantics (Dretske, 1981; Stalnaker, 1984). These theories are supposed to provide naturalizations of content; that is, they specify naturalistic properties that are claimed to be sufficient for possessing content. Informational theories claim that the content of a belief is constituted by the information the belief state carries under certain conditions. A state S carries the information that a property P is instantiated just in case the occurrence of S is caused by and nomically implies the instantiation of P. Informational theories have difficulty accounting for the possibility of error, since if a belief state has the content that *p* it carries the information that *p*. To solve this problem Dretske proposed that the content of a belief is the information that it carries during what he calls "the learning period." A different suggestion (Stalnaker, 1984) is to identify belief content with the information the belief state carries under epistemically optimal conditions. Loewer (1987) has argued that these accounts are not successful as naturalizations, since they appeal to notions—learning, epistemic optimality—that themselves presuppose semantic notions.

Fodor has developed a sophisticated variant of informational theories that applies to the reference of Mentalese predicates. On this account, asymmetric dependency theory (ADT), a Mentalese predicate C refers to, for example, the property of being a cow if it is a law that cows cause Cs, and any other causal relation between something other than cows and Cs depends on this law but not vice versa. That is, if the other causal relations were to fail, it would still be a law that cows cause cows, but if the law were to fail, so would the other causal relation.

ADT is an atomistic account of content in that, contrary to CRS and ITs, it implies that the property of possessing a particular reference is metaphysically independent of inferential connections among thoughts and, indeed, independent of the existence of any other items with content. Whether or not one sees this as an advantage will depend on how one views the analytic–synthetic distinction. Obviously, ADT makes heavy use of metaphysical notions that are less than perspicacious, so one may wonder about its naturalistic credentials. It has also been argued (Boghossian, 1991) that it is equivalent to an optimal-conditions account and is subject to the objections that show that account not to be a naturalization.

Teleological theories of content ground the contents of mental states in biological functions. The biological functions of a system in an organism are those of its features that increased the organism's fitness. Teleological accounts are quite elaborate, but the basic idea (Millikan, 1984; Papineau, 1992) is that there are desire-producing and belief-producing biological systems with certain biological functions. The desire-producing system has the function of producing states that tend to bring about certain effects. The effect associated with a particular desire is its content. The belief-producing systems have the function of producing states that tend to be tokened when certain states of affairs obtain. The state of affairs thus associated with a belief is its content.

Teleological accounts are appealing, since they are naturalistic, assign biological significance to contentful states, and seem to supply them with a kind of normativity. But various serious objections have been raised to teleological theories of content (Fodor, 1992). The most serious is that it is doubtful that teleological considerations are sufficient to assign determinate contents to mental states. A desire state will typically tend to bring about a number of different advantageous effects. Natural selection does not select any one of these effects as the content of the desire. Similarly, natural selection will not single out one of the states of affairs a belief state will typically be associated with as its unique content.

Whether or not content properties can be naturalized is an open question. Some consider it a very important question, since they think that if content properties cannot be naturalized then they are unsuitable to appear in scientific theories or, even worse, that they do not exist or are uninstantiated (Stich, 1983). The unsuitability of content properties for science would be a blow to the emerging cognitive sciences. But the nonexistence of content properties would be devastating to the way we think about ourselves and others, since these ways are permeated with attributions of contentful states. In fact, it has been argued (Boghossian, 1990) that the thesis that there are no content properties is incoherent. Fortunately, no dire consequences strictly follow from the failure of naturalization. It may be that content properties are natural but not naturalizable (McGinn, 1991). It is possible that, while content properties are natural, connections between them and properties that occur in the natural sciences are too unsystematic or too complicated for us to discern. But whether or not this is so is also an open question.

Bibliography

Block, N. "Advertisement for a Semantics for Psychology," in *Midwest Studies in Philosophy,* Vol. 10. Minneappolis, 1986.

Boghossian, P. "The Status of Content," *Philosophical Review,* Vol. 99 (1990), 157–84.

———. "Naturalizing Content," in B. Loewer and G. Rey, eds., *Meaning and Mind* (Oxford, 1991).

———. "Content and Self-Knowledge," *Philosophical Topics*, Vol. 17 (1989), 5–26.

Burge, T. "Individualism and the Mental," *Midwest Studies in Philosophy,* Vol. 4. Minneapolis, 1979.

———. "Individualism and Self-knowledge," *Journal of Philosophy,* Vol. 85 (1988), 644–58.

Davidson, D. *Inquiries into Truth and Interpretation.* Oxford, 1984.

Dretske, F. *Knowledge and the Flow of Information.* Cambridge, MA, 1981.

Fodor, J. *The Language of Thought.* Cambridge, MA, 1979.

———. *Psychosemantics.* Cambridge, MA, 1987.

———. *A Theory of Content and Other Essays.* Cambridge, MA, 1990.

———. *Theory of Content and Other Essays.* Cambridge, MA, 1992.

Fodor, J., and E. LePore. *Holism: A Shopper's Guide.* Oxford, 1992.

Grice, P. "Meaning," *Philosophical Review,* Vol. 66 (1957), 377–88.

LePore, E., and B. Loewer. "Solipsistic Semantics," *Midwest Studies in Philosophy* (1986).

Lewis, D. *Convention.* Cambridge, MA, 1969.

———. "Radical Interpretation," *Synthese,* Vol. 23 (1974), 331–44.

Loar, B. *Mind and Meaning.* Cambridge, 1981.

———. "Social Content and Psychological Content," in R. Grimm and D. Merrill, eds., *Contents of Thought* (Tucson, 1986).

Loewer, B. "From Information to Intentionality," *Synthese,* Vol. 70 (1987), 287–317.

Marr, D. *Vision.* San Francisco, 1982.

McGinn, C. *The Limits of Philosophy.* Oxford, 1991.

Millikan, R. *Language, Thought, and Other Biological Categories.* Cambridge, MA, 1984.

Papineau, D. *Naturalism.* Oxford, 1992.

Peacocke, C. *Thoughts: An Essay on Content.* Cambridge, MA, 1986.

———. *A Study of Concepts.* Cambridge, MA, 1992.

Pinker, S. *The Language Instinct.* New York, 1994.

Putnam, H. "The Meaning of Meaning," in *Mind, Language, and Reality* (Cambridge, 1975).

Quine, W. V. O. *Word and Object.* Cambridge, MA, 1960.

Schiffer, S. *Meaning.* Cambridge, MA, 1972.

Sellars, W. *Science, Perception, and Reality.* London, 1963.

Stalnaker, R. *Inquiry.* Cambridge, MA, 1984.

Stich, S. *From Folk Psychology to Cognitive Psychology.* Cambridge, MA, 1983.

Warfield, F. "Externalism and Self-Knowledge," *Analysis* (1994).

BARRY LOEWER

CONTEXTUALISM. Varying standards seem to govern our practices of attributing knowledge to subjects. In certain contexts we'll say a subject knows provided only that she has a true belief and is in a reasonably strong epistemic position with respect to the proposition in question. In other contexts—when, for instance, a lot rides on whether the subject is right—we may deny that the subject knows unless we think she's in a very strong epistemic position with respect to the proposition in question. Thus, for instance, if over coffee someone asks me merely out of idle curiosity whether I know if my colleague Thelma was in her office on a particular day about a week ago, I'll answer affirmatively if I have a clear recollection of a trustworthy source telling me on the day in question that Thelma was in. But if I were asked the same question in a trial at which Thelma is being charged with committing a murder at the office on the day in question, I'd probably deny that I know that she was in her office, testifying, "I think she was in her office because I remember so-and-so telling me she was in there. But, no, I don't know that she was in." Multiple examples would show that our practices of ascribing knowledge are sensitive to a wide variety of contextual factors that govern the standards a subject must live up to before we'll credit her with having knowledge. Similarly subject to contextually varying standards are our practices of saying that subjects' beliefs are or are not justified.

That such shifting standards govern whether we'll say that a subject knows or doesn't know, or is justified or unjustified in her belief, is not controversial. But invariantists believe that, lying behind the ever-shifting standards that govern whether we'll say that someone knows (is justified in believing), are constant, unchanging standards that govern whether they really know (are justified). Thus, the invariantist will hold that, supposing that Thelma was in fact in her office, since I'm in an equally strong epistemic position with respect to that fact in each of the two situations imagined above, either my claim to know in the first case or my admission in the second case that I don't know must be false, however warranted or conversationally useful this false assertion may be. The contextualist, on the other hand, can hold that both of my assertions are true, for the contextualist believes that the standards that govern whether I can be truthfully credited with knowledge—and not just those that govern whether speakers will in fact credit me with knowledge—vary with context.

Contextualism comes in two basic varieties. Contextualists of the first type tend to focus their attention on the context of the putative subject of knowledge, stressing that the epistemic standards to be applied to that subject depend on various features of her context: What form of inquiry is she engaged in? What are the standards of the relevant social group she's a member of? What questions or doubts have been raised in the conversation she's participating in? Contextualists of the second type tend to express their contextualist thesis metalinguistically, saying that the truth conditions, meaning, or content of sentences ascribing knowledge to subjects vary with the context in which those sentences are uttered. These contextualists therefore tend to focus on the conversational context of the speaker—the person uttering the sentence ascribing knowledge to the subject—rather than on the context of the subject herself, in locating what it is that sets the epistemic standards in force. Of course, in the case of first-person knowledge claims, the speaker and the putative subject of knowledge are one and the same. But the distinction becomes important in treating third-person attributions of knowledge (or in treating first-person claims to have known something in the past: here contextualists of the second type will look to the speaker's context at the time of utterance, and not at the past time being talked about, for what sets the standards).

Suppose you and I are discussing whether Thelma was in her office on the day of the murder, and we're in a context governed by very high standards—so high that I've denied knowing that she was in her office, even though I remember the trustworthy source telling me she was there. You then ask me whether Louise might know if Thelma was in her office. I know that Louise heard the same report I did from the trustworthy source but, like me, has nothing else to go by in the matter. But I also know that Louise is discussing the murder at the local tavern—a place renowned for the low epistemic standards that govern all conversations within its walls. Here it seems clear that I should say that, like me, Louise doesn't know that Thelma was in her office. The standards are set here by features of the speaker's conversational context, and not by the context of the putative subject of knowledge. Of course, for certain purposes, and especially in cases where we're judging whether a subject's belief is justified, we may wish to evaluate her belief relative to standards set by features of her context. But there's nothing in the second version of contextualism to rule this out: among the many standards a speaker's context may select are those relevant to the subject's context.

This case illustrates an important feature of contextualist theories of the second type. On these views, one speaker may truthfully ascribe knowledge of a fact to a subject, while another speaker may truthfully deny that the same subject knows that very fact. Thus, Louise may truthfully say she knows that Thelma was in her office, while at the same time I may truthfully deny that Louise knows that very thing.

Most contextualists hold that, in addition to such factors as the speaker's setting and the importance of being right, epistemic standards are sensitive to what's been said in a given conversation and can change as a conversation progresses. Such sensitivity makes possible one of the most important applications of contextualist theories, which is to the problem of SKEPTICISM [7; S].

Certain skeptical arguments threaten to show that we know nothing or very little and are therefore wrong whenever, or almost whenever, we claim to know anything. While few are really tempted to accept such skeptical conclusions, many find the arguments for them very powerful. Contextualist theories can sometimes explain the power of these skeptical arguments while at the same time protecting the truth of most of our claims to know. For the contextualist can claim that the skeptic, in presenting his argument, manipulates the standards for knowledge, raising them to such a level as to make his conclusion (that we don't know) true. The skeptic may do this by injecting into the conversation, and thereby making conversationally relevant, certain ordinarily irrelevant alternatives to what we claim to know—alternatives we cannot rule out even if we usually don't have to rule them out to be truthfully credited with knowledge. Or the skeptic's denials that we know may trigger what David

Lewis calls a "rule of accommodation"—a rule according to which the "conversational score" tends to adjust to make what's said true—which will raise the standards to the level needed to validate his skeptical denials of knowledge (Lewis, 1979). Whatever conversational mechanism is manipulated, if the skeptical arguments work by raising the standards for knowledge, then, while the skeptic may be able to truthfully state his conclusion, this will not show that we're wrong in other contexts, when, with no pesky skeptics around raising the standards, we claim to know the very things the skeptic truthfully says we don't know. For the fact that we fail to satisfy the skeptic's unusually inflated epistemic standards does not imply that we fall short of meeting the lower standards that govern our other conversations and debates.
(SEE ALSO: *Epistemology* [S])

Bibliography

Annis, D. "A Contextual Theory of Epistemic Justification," *American Philosophical Quarterly,* Vol. 15 (1978), 213–19.

Cohen, S. "Knowledge, Context, and Social Standards," *Synthese,* Vol. 73 (1987), 3–26.

———. "How to Be a Fallibilist," *Philosophical Perspectives,* Vol. 2 (1988), 91–123.

DeRose, K. "Contextualism and Knowledge Attributions," *Philosophy and Phenomenological Research,* Vol. 52 (1992), 913–29.

———. "Solving the Skeptical Problem," *The Philosophical Review,* Vol. 104 (1995), 1–52.

Dretske, F. "The Pragmatic Dimension of Knowledge," *Philosophical Studies,* Vol. 40 (1981), 363–78.

Hambourger, R. "Justified Assertion and the Relativity of Knowledge," *Philosophical Studies,* Vol. 51 (1987), 241–69.

Lewis, D. "Scorekeeping in a Language Game," *Journal of Philosophical Logic,* Vol. 8 (1979), 339–59.

Unger, P. *Philosophical Relativity.* Minneapolis, 1984.

———. "The Cone Model of Knowledge," *Philosophical Topics,* Vol. 14 (1986), 125–78.

Williams, M. *Unnatural Doubts: Epistemological Realism and the Basis of Scepticism.* Cambridge, MA, 1991.

Wittgenstein, L. *On Certainty.* New York, 1969.

KEITH DEROSE

CONTINENTAL PHILOSOPHY. *The treatment of Continental Philosophy in the* Supplement *focuses primarily upon the following philosophers: Hannah Arendt, Simone de Beauvoir, Jacques Derrida, Michel Foucault, Hans-Georg Gadamer, Jürgen Habermas, Martin Heidegger, Edmund Husserl, Emmanuel Levinas, Maurice Merleau-Ponty, Paul Ricoeur, and Jean-Paul Sartre. Please refer to the personal entries for each of these philosophers. In addition, most of these personal entries are cross-referenced to discussions of key concepts that are central to the thought of these philosophers. For a complete listing of these philosophers and their key concepts, as well as other important entries in Continental Philosophy, please refer to the "Outline of Contents" that appears in the front matter of this volume.*

CONWAY, ANNE (Anne Finch, Viscountess Conway, 1631–79), English philosopher, was born in London. Her education was primarily informal and self-directed. Her associates included Henry MORE [5], Ralph CUDWORTH [2], Francis Mercury Van Helmont, William HARVEY [3], and Robert BOYLE [1], the latter two as physicians for her serious headaches. Later in life she scandalized More by becoming a Quaker.

WORK AND INFLUENCE

Conway's sole published work, *The Principles of the Most Ancient and Modern Philosophy,* published posthumously in 1690, shows the influence of the CAMBRIDGE PLATONISTS [2], Kabbalism, and NEOPLATONISM [5]. It criticized HOBBES [4; S], SPINOZA [7; S], and DESCARTES [2; S], and influenced LEIBNIZ [4; S], who, during the year he was introduced to her work by Van Helmont in 1696, adopted her term 'monad' and used it in a quite similar way (Merchant, 1979). A notable difference between their uses of the term is that, while Leibniz's monads are purely spiritual, Conway's are both physical and spiritual. Leibniz refers directly to Conway in his *New Essays* (book 1, chap. 1) as one of the better advocates of VITALISM [8].

METAPHYSICS

Conway begins the *Principles* by asserting without proof the existence of a perfect God, the description of which is influenced by neoplatonism and Kabbalism. Conway's God is one of three kinds of substance, each with its own essence. God is a complete, self-sufficient fountain that necessarily emanates Christ, the second kind of substance, and through the mediation of Christ, who shares some attributes with God, others with creatures, necessarily emanates creatures—the third kind of substance. Because emanative creation is creation 'out of' God rather than 'out of' nothing, creatures have a share of the divine attribute of life. Since all creatures are of the same kind of substance, they have a single essence, differing only modally from one another. Thus, spirit or mind and body are not 'really distinct'. There are many degrees of corporeity, and thus "a Thing may more or less approach to, or recede from the State and Condition of a body or a Spirit" (Conway, 1982, p. 192). Conway draws the further conclusion that creatures are interconvertible: a horse, for example, can turn into a bird and spirits can turn into bodies (p. 177).

Not only God's creative act, but all of God's actions flow automatically from God's nature. Thus, God does whatever does not involve a contradiction. Conway's deity, like Leibniz's, is timeless. Both Conway and Leibniz consider time to be relative to succession and motion; they consider succession and motion to be inferior analogues of eternity and the divine will, respectively, and thus to belong only to creatures (Conway, 1982, p. 161).

Conway employs the concept of mediation, introduced in her account of creation, to explain action at a distance as well as causation betwen bodies and spirits. All created substances, in addition to sharing an essence, are interconnected by means of "Subtiler Parts," which are the "Emanation of one Creature into another." These mediated connections facilitate action at a distance and form "the Foundation of all Sympathy and Antipathy which happens in Creatures" (Conway, 1982, p. 164). Conway offers, by contrast to the mechanical philosophy, a fairly direct account of the intelligibility of causation based on the concepts of similarity (or sympathy) and mediation. Similarity between cause and effect, as in the case of causation among bodies, renders causation directly intelligible, "because Things of one, or alike Nature, can easily affect each other." Mediation is required in the case of mind–body causation, because a soul is a "Spiritual Body" (pp. 214–15).

Since Conway regards interconnection as primitive, she requires no detailed explanations of causal interactions. Here she contrasts markedly with mechanistic philosophers' demands for explanations using motion and passive matter as primitives. Conway nonetheless incorporates causation by motion into her overall account of CAUSATION [2; S]: motion, especially vital motion, and divine emanation do not differ intrinsically from one another but are analogically related.

Bibliography

Conway, A. *The Principles of the Most Ancient and Modern Philosophy,* edited by P. Lopston. The Hague, 1982.

Duran, J. "Anne Viscountess Conway: A Seventeenth-Century Rationalist," *Hypatia,* Vol. 4 (1989), 64–79.

Frankel, L. "Anne Finch, Viscountess Conway," in M. E. Waithe, ed., *A History of Women Philosophers,* Vol. 3 (Dordrecht, 1991).

———. "The Value of Harmony," in S. Nadler, ed., *Causation in Early Modern Philosophy* (University Park, PA, 1993).

Merchant, C. "The Vitalism of Anne Conway: Its Impact on Leibniz's Concept of the Monad," *Journal of the History of Philosophy,* Vol. 17 (1979), 255–69.

Nicolson, M. H. *Conway Letters.* New Haven, 1930.

LOIS FRANKEL

COUNTERPART THEORY.

See: MODALITY, PHILOSOPHY and METAPHYSICS OF [S]

CRITERIOLOGY.

"Science of criteria" or criteriology is a term, originally neoscholastic, for a theory of knowledge in which judgments are warranted or justified simply by conforming to certain criteria for correct judgment. These criteria are general principles that specify what sorts of considerations ultimately confer warrant on some judgments and that tend (tacitly) to guide self-reflective persons in checking and correcting their judgments. The epistemologist's task is to formulate these principles by reflecting on the considerations present and absent in various judgments we intuitively think of as warranted and unwarranted.

Different criteria may deal with different subject matters, degrees, and sources of warrant (e.g., in perception, memory, inference). Ultimately, there must be warranting considerations other than inferability from other warranted judgments. These must be internally accessible through introspection or reflection without relying on further warranted judgments. They won't be considerations such as whether nature designed us to be reliable judges but ones such as whether we ostensibly see or recall something or intuitively grasp or clearly and distinctly conceive something.

Many epistemologists argue that critical considerations needn't guarantee truth or confer certainty, and whatever warrant they confer may be defeated. For instance, if one ostensibly sees something red, one is prima facie or defeasibly warranted in judging that one actually sees something red. The judgment might not be warranted when, despite ostensibly seeing something red, one has evidence that the illumination makes everything look red. We need additional principles specifying what considerations defeat warrant.

However, if criterial considerations don't guarantee truth, what makes a set of principles genuinely warranting? Putative common contingent features such as their overall reliability rest warrant on something beyond mere conformity to these principles and may allow for alternative principles. Criteriologists (e.g., Pollock, 1974, 1986) often appeal to controversial, nonscholastic, views about concepts and truth influenced by WITTGENSTEIN [8; S]. Criteria are internalized norms (rules) about when to make and correct judgments ascribing a concept. They characterize what persons must, in order to have a particular concept, tacitly know how to do in their judging and reasoning and be tacitly guided by. Criteria individuate our concepts and thus are necessarily correct. Although warranted judgments needn't be true, we have no idea of their truth completely divorced from what undefeated criterial considerations warrant. Critics often respond: surely this norm conformity must have a purpose beyond itself, like accurately representing the world?

(SEE ALSO: *Epistemology* [S])

Bibliography

CRITERIOLOGIES

Coffey, P. *Epistemology or the Theory of Knowledge: An Introduction to General Metaphysics,* 2 vols. London, 1917.

Pollock, J. *Knowledge and Justification.* Princeton, 1974.

———. *Contemporary Theories of Knowledge*. Totowa, NJ, 1986.

CRITICAL DISCUSSIONS

Lycan, W. G. "Non-inductive Evidence: Recent Work on Wittgenstein's 'criteria,'" *American Philosophical Quarterly*, Vol. 8 (1971), 109–25.

Millikan, R. "Truth Rules, Hoverflies, and the Kripke-Wittgenstein Paradox," *Philosophical Review*, Vol. 99 (1990), 323–53.

Plantinga, A. *Warrant: The Current Debate*. Oxford, 1993.

Wright, C. J. G. "Second Thoughts about Criteria," *Synthese*, Vol. 58 (1984), 383–405.

BRUCE HUNTER

CRITICAL THEORY. "Critical theory" is used to refer to the diverse body of work produced by members and associates of the Frankfurt Institute for Social Research after Max Horkheimer became its director in 1930. The first generation of what came to be called the Frankfurt school included, in addition to Horkheimer, such prominent figures as Theodor Adorno, Herbert Marcuse, Walter Benjamin, Erich Fromm, Leo Löwenthal, Franz Neumann, Otto Kirchheimer, and Frederick Pollock. The most influential members of the second generation are Jürgen HABERMAS [S], Karl-Otto Apel, and Albrecht Wellmer. As the variety of backgrounds and interests might suggest, critical social theory was conceived as a multidisciplinary program linking philosophy to history and the human sciences in a kind of "philosophically oriented social inquiry," as Horkheimer put it. Though very strongly influenced by KANT [4; S] and NEO-KANTIANISM [5], HEGEL [3; S] and German idealism, WEBER [8] and FREUD [3; S], it was understood as a renewal of MARXISM [S] inspired in part by the earlier work of Georg LUKÁCS [5] and Karl Korsch. This updated Marxism would take account of the altered historical realities of advanced capitalism and integrate areas of inquiry neglected by traditional Marxism, such as philosophy and political theory, cultural studies (including studies of mass culture), and social psychology (appropriating psychoanalysis for social theory). With the rise of National Socialism (*see* GERMAN PHILOSOPHY AND NATIONAL SOCIALISM [3]), the institute moved briefly to Geneva and Paris in 1933 and then in 1934 to Columbia University in New York, where its journal, the *Zeitschrift für Sozialforschung*, continued to be published until 1941, the last volume in English. Early in the 1950s, Horkheimer and Adorno reestablished the institute in Frankfurt. Habermas became an assistant there in 1955.

The original project of a critical social theory advanced by Horkheimer was a version of MARX's [5] *Aufhebung* of philosophy in social theory and practice. Philosophy was to become a sociohistorical, practically oriented critique of reason and its claimed realizations. While the dominant forms of reason were often distorted in the interests of dominant classes, the aim of critical theory was, not simply to negate them, but, by examining their genesis and functions, to transform them and enlist them in the struggle for a better world. The insistence on the 'truth content' of the 'bourgeois ideals' of freedom, truth, and justice, the refusal to abandon them as mere ideology, was severely tested by the horrors of World War II. Early in the 1940s, in their collaborative reflections on the 'dialectic of enlightenment,' Horkheimer and Adorno offered a much more pessimistic view of the history of reason. Keying on a tendency that Weber had emphasized, the relentless spread of "instrumental" rationality, they reversed Marx's positive evaluation of scientific-technological progress. It was now seen as the core of a domination that had spread to all spheres of life and, in the process, had immobilized the potential agents of social change. In this 'totally administered society' with what Marcuse later called its "one-dimensional man," critical theory could at best reveal the unreason at the heart of what passed for reason, without offering any positive account of its own.

Habermas's work since the 1960s might be viewed as an attempt to avoid this impasse by introducing into critical theory a fundamental shift in paradigms from the philosophy of the subject to the theory of communication and from means-ends rationality to communicative rationality (*see* COMMUNICATIVE ACTION [S]). This serves as the basis for an altered diagnosis of the ills of modernity—as rooted, not in rationalization as such, but in a one-sided rationalization driven by economic and administrative forces—and an altered prescription for their cure, the democratization of public opinion and will formation in an effectively functioning public sphere, where issues of general concern are submitted to rational, critical public debate.

Bibliography

Arato, A., and E. Gebhardt, eds. *The Essential Frankfurt School Reader*. New York, 1978.

Bronner, S., and D. Kellner, eds., *Critical Theory and Society: A Reader*. New York, 1989.

Ingram, D., and J. Simon-Ingram, eds. *Critical Theory: The Essential Readings*. New York, 1990.

Jay, M. *The Dialectical Imagination*. Boston, 1973.

Wiggershaus, R. *The Frankfurt School*, translated by M. Robertson. Cambridge, MA, 1994.

THOMAS McCARTHY

D

DAVIDSON, DONALD, Willis and Marion Slusser Professor of Philosophy at the University of California at Berkeley, was born in 1917 in Springfield, Massachusetts, and graduated from Harvard in 1939. After serving in the United States Navy, Davidson returned to Harvard, writing his doctoral dissertation on PLATO's [6; S] *Philebus*. Receiving his Ph.D. in 1949, Davidson went on to do extensive work in DECISION THEORY [S], in collaboration with Patrick Suppes and others. The methodological challenges of giving empirical application to rational-choice theory have had a lasting influence on Davidson, apparent in his formulation of philosophical questions regarding action, the mental, and linguistic meaning. Davidson's views have come gradually to articulation through series of papers presenting detailed arguments pertaining to specific problems in each of these areas of philosophy, elaborating a set of closely interconnected and highly influential doctrines. This entry looks briefly at each area in turn, emphasizing certain general features characteristic of Davidson's approach, and then concludes with a glance at the key themes of Davidson's more explicitly metaphilosophical work of the 1980s and 1990s.

THE CAUSAL THEORY OF ACTION

Davidson's view, first set out in print in *Actions, Reasons, and Causes* (1963, see 1980a), is that we must consider the reasons for our actions—combinations of propositional attitudes, paradigmatically belief-desire pairs—to be also their causes (1980a). In this and related papers Davidson grants a main premise of the anti-causalist view prevailing at the time, that the teleological form of action-explanation makes such explanation irreducibly different from the nomological form characteristic of explanation in the natural sciences. What is distinctive about action-explanation is that it identifies the events involved (the action and its explanatory antecedent) in terms that reveal them to be part of a rational pattern. Davidson goes on to challenge anti-causal orthodoxy, however, by arguing that it does not follow from this irreducible difference that action explanation is not a species of causal explanation.

A striking aspect of Davidson's view is the claim that the appeal to reason on which action explanations turn will be genuinely explanatory only insofar as the particular events thus rationally related are also related as cause and effect, and hence, for Davidson, may also be characterized by nomologically related descriptions. But Davidson insists that the explanatory efficacy of the reason-explanation in no way depends on our possessing the explanation that nomologically relates the particular events in question. Indeed, in the typical case we enjoy the full benefits of effective action explanation without the slightest idea of what the descriptions might be of the relevant events under which they are subsumed by causal law. Davidson thus reconciles the following three fundamental claims. First, when an event is cited in successful explanation of another event, the former is a cause of the latter. Second, causal relations between events entail nomological relations between them. Third, *explanans* and *explanandum* in action explanations are captured in terms that cannot be subsumed under strict law. This reconciliation trades on a particular conception of the relation between cause and law. If two events are causally related, they are so related no matter how described. The nomological relation, however, obtains between kinds of events; laws, as Davidson says, are linguistic, and so while causal relations are extensional, and causally related events necessarily fall under what he terms strict law (that is, law "free from caveats and *ceteris paribus* clauses" [1993, p. 8]), they instantiate such law only under some appropriate description. Hence, the descriptions under which two causally related events appear in successful action explanation may be such that no amount of knowledge of strict causal law would allow us to infer the action from knowledge of the conditions cited in the explanation of it (1980a, 1993).

ANOMALOUS MONISM

A crucial element in Davidson's account of action is the distinction between a particular event and the descriptions that sort particular events under kinds. This same distinction is central also to his claims about the nature of the mental and its relation to the physical. In "Mental Events" and subsequent papers (1980a; 1993), Davidson argues that what it is to be a mental event is to be an event that falls under a mental predicate, that is to say, for Davidson, an intentional term. Correspondingly, what it is to be a physical event is to fall under a physical predicate, a predicate suitable for making nomological relations perspicuous. Ultimately, physical predicates are those of developed physics, a vocabulary the constitutive purpose of which is to track the causal structure of the world.

Since Davidson conceives of events as extensionally identified spatio-temporal particulars constituting nodes in the causal network, W. V. O. QUINE's [7; S] basic ontological dictum expresses also for Davidson an important truth; it is the unique business of physics to aim for full coverage. What this means for Davidson is that all events, qua nodes in the causal network, must be describable in the terms of physics. Yet some events are also mental, and Davidson argues that his physicalism supports no reductivist or eliminativist conclusions. For while all particular mental events are also particular physical events, no particular kind of mental event is a particular kind of physical event. The reason for this is that the intentionality, which for Davidson is the mark of the mental, is constituted, in his view, by our efforts to characterize fellow creatures as rational according to an intersubjective standard. We are able to view fellow language users thus because we have at our disposal not only the conceptual resources required to keep track of each other by keeping tabs on objective environmental relations in which we are all embroiled in various and changing ways, but also a set of concepts—of belief, desire, and so on—which allow us to construct accounts of how things seem to someone to be. This system of double bookkeeping allows us to absorb a great deal of variation and irregularity in human behavior by accounting for objective anomalies in terms of subjective variables. But this strategy remains informative and useful only insofar as the essential discrepancies between subjective perspective and objective reality that interpretation exploits are prevented from becoming arbitrary or chaotic—were that to happen, the subjective would lose its explanatory purpose, it would simply mark the place where explanation ends. This is why the interpretive construction of the subjective perspective must be tightly constrained; as Davidson says, making sense of others "we will try for a theory that finds [them] consistent, believer[s] of truths, and lover[s] of the good (all by our own lights, it goes without saying)" (1980a, p. 222). This constraint on the application of intentional terms is often referred to as the "principle of charity." It reflects the fact that only the attitudes (though not only the rational attitudes) of a recognizably rational subject may be invoked in a genuinely explanatory way to account for the subject's behavior. Moreover, as Davidson recently has emphasized, because rationality considerations govern our application of propositional-attitude concepts, these concepts are irreducibly causal, "identified in part by the sorts of action they are prone to cause, given the right conditions" (1991b, p. 162). As he further points out, "the right conditions" are themselves not independently characterizable. The phrase, marking the interdependence of the application conditions of mental predicates, remains an ineliminable qualification of the sort of platitudinous generalizations that express the content of our psychological terms. By contrast, Davidson argues, the application of the predicates of physics—aimed at the formulation of strict causal law—cannot itself depend on causal concepts (1991b). The application conditions of terms related by strict empirical law must be independently specifiable. The real difference, then, between the mental and the physical, and the reason for the irreducibility of one to the other, stems from the fact that the vocabulary of physics and the vocabulary of psychology have evolved under the pressure of distinctively different interests. What we want from the former are modes of description that allow us to interact with each other as persons. What we want from the latter are laws "as complete and precise as we can make them; a different aim" (1991b, p. 163).

TRUTH AND MEANING

In the PHILOSOPHY OF LANGUAGE [S], Davidson is associated with the view that we may account for linguistic competence by appropriately characterizing the evidence available to and resources required by an idealized interpreter (1984a). There are two fundamental aspects to this position. First, what, Davidson asks, might we know such that by knowing it we would be able to say what a speaker of a given language meant by some arbitrary utterance? His answer is a theory of truth for that language, of the sort which Alfred TARSKI [8] showed us how to construct. The condition of adequacy for such a theory is an adaptation of what Tarski called "convention T." We have, Davidson proposes, a theory of meaning for a given language L provided we have a theory that entails for each sentence of L an instance of the schema, 's is true in L if and only if p'. In this schema, 's' would be replaced by an expression that mentions a sentence of L (for example by means of quotation marks), and 'p' is replaced with any sentence of the language in which the theory is stated that is true if and only if the sentence mentioned in 's' is true. Such a theory then provides, based on finite resources, a recursive characterization of the truth conditions for any sentence of L. While all that is demanded by convention T is that the theorems of the theory—known as T-sentences—capture co-extensionality, "the hope," as Davidson says, "is that by putting appropriate formal and empirical restrictions on the theory as a whole, individual T-sentences will in fact serve to yield interpretations" (1984, p. 134). This proposal has spawned a great deal of work in formal SEMANTICS [7; S], guided by the aim of accounting for natural-language idioms in terms of their deep structure, or LOGICAL FORM [S], which makes explicit their truth-theoretical composition. For Davidson, the notion of logical form is extremely powerful; constrained on the one hand by our intuitions concerning entailment relations, and on the other by the logical resources of Tarskian truth-theory, the uncovering of logical form functions as a crucible within which crystallize the ontological categories our language commits us to. So for example, support for an ontology of events takes the form of an argument that we cannot account for the entailment relations intuitively characteristic of action sentences within the logical confines of a Tarskian theory of truth for a language unless we are willing to see such sentences as quantifying over events (cf., "The Logical Form of Action Sentences," 1980a).

If a theory of TRUTH [S] is to serve as a theory of MEANING [5; S] for a language, we need to know how an interpreter may arrive at such a theory for a language she does not know. What is required for a recursive truth-theory to have empirical application? This question directs us to the other main aspect of Davidson's position, where Quine's influence is most apparent. Observing the utterances of a speaker but knowing neither what the speaker means nor what she believes, the interpreter can construct a theory of truth for the speaker by proceeding inductively on the assumption that the speaker's responses to her environment are rational, indeed that her mental life constitutes a rational whole (1984a). This assumption of RATIONALITY [S] is, of course, defeasible with respect to the attribution of any one particular attitude, within the context of the construction of a theory of the meaning of someone's words and the contents of her thoughts. Davidson's point is that irrationality is conceptually parasitic, and can be diagnosed only against a background of reason. Thus, in what Davidson dubs radical interpretation, the principle of charity is methodologically indispensable. Even while minimizing irrationality, however, an idealized interpreter will be able to generate for the speaker different theories of belief and meaning that comport equally well with the empirical evidence (i.e., with the speaker's utterances and their contexts). This indeterminacy Davidson regards as innocuous; the salient facts about meaning and mind are what such differing theories have in common (1984a, 1990b, 1991b).

CHALLENGES

With respect to Davidson's view of action (*see* ACTION THEORY [S]), the most serious objection is probably the claim that it fails to illuminate the feature by virtue of which action explanation actually is explanatory. Critics thus doubt the possibility of reconciling the three fundamental claims regarding explanation, cause, and law to which Davidson is committed (see above). One claim—advanced, for example, by Jerry Fodor—is that informative action explanation must somehow draw on the explanatory power of nomic relations, in which case Davidson's irreducibility–claim will be threatened. An alternative view—defended by anti-causalists like George Wilson—is that the explanatory force of reason-explanation is *sui generis,* and does not depend on reasons being causes. This would jeopardize Davidson's conception of event monism.

With regard specifically to ANOMALOUS MONISM [S], Jaegwon Kim and others have argued that Davidson's view renders the mental causally inert. Partly because of their different views on the individuation of events, this conflict is difficult to assess. However, if we grant Davidson his fundamental claims—that is, that the difference between the mental and the physical is a matter of vocabulary of description, and that events should be extensionally conceived—then his concept of SUPERVENIENCE [S] ensures that a change in the truth value of the relevant kind of mental predicate ascription will entail some difference or other in causal relations. Naturally, alternatives to Davidson's Humean conceptions of causality and of the relations betwen causality and law are frequently at play in criticisms of both anomalous monism as well as Davidson's reconciliation of the irreducibility of action-explanation to nomic explanation with a causal view of action.

As for Davidson's philosophy of language, there have been objections at various levels to the idea that a theory of meaning for a language must take the form of a Tarskian truth-theory. Even while accepting the proposal that a theory of meaning should take the form of a theory of truth, one may ask, for example, why we should restrict ourselves, in producing a formal semantics for a language, to the resources of first-order predicate calculus. And many critics have doubted the prospects of accounting for natural language in purely extensional terms.

METAPHILOSOPHY

It is important to note that Davidson's commitment to the specific contention that theories of truth as Tarski defined them give the structure of theories of meaning is a pragmatic methodological commitment. What supports Davidson's most innovative philosophical conclusions is the more general point that we must understand meaning in terms of truth, in conjunction with his insistence—following Quine—on a third-person perspective to meaning and mind which makes the conditions of interpretation constitutive of content. Together, these commitments yield an account of the concept of truth constrained by the methodological requirements of interpretation (1990b). This account contrasts both with traditional correspondence theories and with epistemic accounts of the sort advanced, for example, by Hilary PUTNAM [S], and is distinct from disquotationalist theories such as that of Paul Horwich (1990b).

The significance of these core commitments is readily apparent also in Davidson's argument aimed to discredit the duality of representational scheme and empirical content on the grounds that it presupposes the notion of an untranslatable language ("On the Very Idea of a Conceptual Scheme," 1984a). If truth and meaning are interlocking concepts whose features are illuminated by an account of the methodology of an ideal interpreter, the idea of alternative representations of reality that are mutually semantically impenetrable is not coherent. This argument also marks a dividing line between Davidson and Quine. For the metaphysical opposition between what is given to the mind on the one hand, and the processes brought to bear on that given, on the other, is the very duality in terms of which EMPIRICISM [2] faces its defining challenge, namely to articulate a coherent notion of sensory evidence (1982). On this fundamental score, Quine has remained within the bounds of empiricism (1990c). Davidson, on the other hand, has gone on explicitly to reject the basic metaphor of mind as inner space on which empiricism rests. For Davidson the hold of this metaphor reveals itself in the persistence of the interdependent notions of mental states as representational and of truth as correspondence (*see* CORRESPONDENCE THEORY OF TRUTH [2]), which, in turn, inextricably entangle us in the problems of relativism and SKEPTICISM [7; S] (1986b, 1987a, 1989a, 1990b).

Davidson's alternative to the representational view of mind is most succinctly expressed in the thesis that there is thought only when there is actual communication (1989b, 1989c, 1991a, 1991b, 1992a). On this controversial view, knowledge of our own mental states, knowledge of the so-called external world, and knowledge of the mental states of others appear mutually interdependent (1991b). This forecloses the very possibility of a skeptical or relativist challenge, insofar as these are typically constructed around arguments that purport to show the impossibility of deriving any one of the three kinds of knowledge from either or both of the other two. This impossibility is something Davidson accepts—indeed insists on. Against the skeptic or relativist his claim is simply that the three forms of knowledge stand or fall together; denying one is to deny all, and to deny all is just to deprive our intentional concepts of any application. This position rests on two key claims. One is that shared linguistic understanding is a prerequisite for any standard of objectivity (1991b). Such a standard gives content to the very distinction exploited by the propositional attitude verbs between what is and what seems from some perspective to be, and hence, on Davidson's conception, is a prerequisite of thought. The other is the claim that the idea of shared linguistic understanding presupposes actual communication (1986c). The mental is thus what we reveal when we subject a certain vaguely delimited range of causal relations to a particular kind of description, the terms of which presuppose the mutual recognition of subjects interacting in a shared world.

This view carries with it the commitments to event monism, to the constitutive role of rationality for content, and to a view of human agents as an integral part of the natural world, that have always been evident in Davidson's work. The distinction between extensionally conceived particulars and their descriptions remains pivotal. But the upshot is fundamentally at odds with the governing metaphors of modern epistemology-centered philosophy: "A community of minds," Davidson concludes, "is the basis of all knowledge: it provides the measure of all things." And he adds: "It makes no sense to question the adequacy of this measure, or to seek a more ultimate standard" (1991b, p. 164). However we assess the plausibility of the considerations Davidson offers in support of this position, cognizance of the through-going externalism on which it is based should lead us to see it not as a species of antirealism or idealism, but as a fundamental rejection of foundationalist aspirations and as expressing a commitment to a recognizably pragmatist view of the nature of philosophy.

Bibliography

WORKS BY DAVIDSON

Essays on Action and Events. Oxford, 1980a.

"Towards a Unified Theory of Meaning and Action," in *Grazer Philosophische Studien,* Vol. 11 (1980b).

"Empirical Content," in *Grazer Philosophische Studien,* Vol. 16/17 (1982), reprinted in LePore, 1986.

Enquiries into Truth and Interpretation. Oxford, 1984a.

Expressing Evaluations (The Lindley Lecture). Lawrence, KS, 1984b.

"First Person Authority," *Dialectica,* Vol. 38 (1984c).

"Judging Interpersonal Interests," in J. Elster and A. Hylland, eds., *Foundations of Social Choice Theory* (Cambridge, 1986a).

"A Coherence Theory of Truth and Knowledge," in E. LePore, ed., *Truth and Interpretation* (Oxford, 1986b). Reprinted, with "Afterthoughts, 1987," in A. Malichowski, ed., *Reading Rorty* (Oxford, 1987).

"A Nice Derangement of Epitaphs," in E. LePore, ed., *Truth and Interpretation* (Oxford, 1986c).

"Knowing One's Own Mind," American Philosophical Association Presidential Address, in *Proceedings and Addresses of the American Philosophical Association,* Vol. 61 (1987a).

"The Myth of the Subjective," in M. Krausz, ed., *Relativism,* (Bloomington, IN, 1989a).

"What is Present to the Mind?" in J. Brandl and W. Gombocz, eds., *The Mind of Donald Davidson* (Amsterdam, 1989b).

"The Conditions of Thought," in J. Brandl and W. Gombocz, eds., *The Mind of Donald Davidson.* (Amsterdam, 1989c).

Plato's "Philebus." New York, 1990a.

"The Structure and Content of Truth," *Journal of Philosophy,* Vol. 87 (1990b).

"Meaning, Truth, and Evidence," in R. Barrett and R. Gibson, eds., *Perspectives on Quine* (Oxford, 1990c).

"Turing's Test," in K. A. Mohyeldin Said, W. H. Newton-Smith, R. Viale, and K. V. Wilkes, eds., *Modelling the Mind* (Oxford, 1990d).

"Representation and Interpretation," in K. A. Mohyeldin Said, W. H. Newton-Smith, R. Viale, and K. V. Wilkes, eds., *Modelling the Mind* (Oxford, 1990e).

"Epistemology Externalized," *Dialectica,* Vol. 45 (1991a).

"Three Varieties of Knowledge," in A. Phillips Griffiths, ed., *A. J. Ayer Memorial Essays,* Vol. 30 (Cambridge, 1991b).

"The Second Person," in P. French, T. Uehling, and H. Wettstein, eds., *Midwest Studies in Philosophy: The Wittgenstein Legacy,* Vol. 17 (Minneapolis, 1992a).

"Thinking Causes," in J. Heil and A. Mele, eds., *Mental Causation* (Oxford, 1993).

WORKS ON DAVIDSON

Brandl, J., and W. Gombocz, eds. *The Mind of Donald Davidson.* Amsterdam, 1989.

Evnine, S. *Donald Davidson.* Palo Alto, CA, 1991.

LePore, E., and B. McLaughlin, eds. *Actions and Events.* Oxford, 1985.

LePore, E., ed. *Truth and Interpretation.* Oxford, 1986.

Malpas, G. *Donald Davidson and the Mirror of Meaning.* Cambridge, 1992.

Preyer, G., F. Siebelt, and A. Ulfig, eds. *Language, Mind and Epistemology: On Donald Davidson's Philosophy.* Dordrecht, 1994.

Ramberg, B. *Donald Davidson's Philosophy of Language: An Introduction.* Oxford, 1989.

Stoecker, R., ed. *Reflecting Davidson.* Berlin, 1993.

Vermazen, B., and M. Hintikka, eds. *Essays on Davidson: Action and Events.* Oxford, 1985.

BJØRN T. RAMBERG

DECISION THEORY.

DECISION THEORY. Along direct and indirect paths contemporary normative DECISION THEORY [2] exerts influence on moral theory, political philosophy, epistemology, and the philosophy of science. The subject is a large one with many recent developments, a few of which can be addressed here.

EXPECTED UTILITY

The expected utility of an action with uncertain outcomes is a weighted average of the utilities of the outcomes, where the weight attached to each is the probability that the act will yield it. $EU(A) = \Sigma_i pr(A$ yields $O_i)$ $U(O_i)$. The proposal that A's value is measured by its EU is consequentialist, in that A's utility depends on the utilities of its outcomes. The consequentialism need not be strict, since "outcome" can be construed broadly enough to include A itself. The probability that doing A yields outcome O_i typically depends on unknown states of the world; this is handled by using weights pr(when S_j, A yields O_i) in a suitable way. Subjective expected utility theory takes pr to reflect the decision maker's beliefs, rather than some objective probability, and takes U to measure value in the eyes of the decision maker rather than some objectively correct value. Such decision theories are meant to explicate subjective practical rationality, the rationality of a decision maker doing the best she can given her information and desires. They leave open the possibility that an account of objective value might be attached to expected utility theory, but normative decision theories as such tend either to embrace subjective utility, or to remain silent on the nature of objectively correct values. The subjective beliefs are often, though not always, taken to be partial beliefs. Bayesians in particular think of beliefs as action-guiding dispositions that come in varying degrees, and they use decision-theoretic arguments to defend this conception of belief. The theories of F. P. Ramsey, Bruno de Finetti, and L. J. Savage are classic examples of that approach (*see* BAYESIANISM [S]).

Controversy has long surrounded the concept of utility in philosophy and economics. Decision theorists base their use of the concept of subjective utility on axiomatic treatments of preference. Suppose an agent with a (rich) collection of preferences that meets the standards of rationality. The idea is to show that she can be interpreted as evaluating the objects she prefers in a way that is nonarbitrarily measured by the quantitative utility.

EVIDENTIAL DECISION THEORY

The main idea of evidental decision theory (EDT) is that action A's value is measured by the EU that weights each possible outcome O_i by its probability conditional on A, $pr(O_i/A)$. Richard Jeffrey (1965) developed an axiomatic decision theory incorporating this approach. The theory avoids the often questionable objects of preference employed by earlier theories, and it avoids requiring that descriptions of states and acts be so fine-grained that each combination of them deterministically fixes an outcome. The theory takes the objects of an agent's preferences to be (the truth of) propositions; the suggestion is that preferring A to B can be understood as preferring getting the news that A to getting the news that B. For a variety of reasons, including the avoidance of objections to previous theories, the familiarity of the propositional algebra it uses, the generality and elegance of the theory, and the company of Jeffrey's important principle of belief revision for cases of uncertain learning, his theory became well known and influential among philosophers. It is the standard formulation of *EDT*.

NEWCOMB'S PROBLEM

Statistical correlations often indicate causal connections, but not always. EDT pays attention to the former, but in our deliberations we are most interested in the latter (what will our actions bring about?). EDT was soon confronted with examples where correlations between states and actions on one hand, and outcomes on the other, do not appropriately reflect the causal influence of actions over outcomes. Best known and much debated is Newcomb's problem, introduced by Robert Nozick (1969). A reliable predictor forecasts which of two options the agent will choose: to take the contents of an opaque box (A1), or the contents of both the opaque box and a transparent box that is seen to contain a thousand dollars (A2). On a prior forecast of A1 the predictor places a million dollars in the opaque box; upon forecasting A2 the predictor leaves the opaque box empty. The forecasts are made and the money arranged before the agent makes her choice, and the agent is confident that the problem is as described, with no cheating. EDT straightforwardly applied recommends A1, since the predictor's reliability makes the probability of a filled opaque box conditional on doing A1 high, so A1's evidential *EU* is also high. This supports the reasoning "most one-boxers get rich and most two-boxers do not, so I will be one of the former." On the other hand, dominance reasoning recommends A2: "The million dollars is there or it is not, and either way it is better also to take the thousand." It is a strange decision problem, but there are other less bizarre examples (e.g., the twin prisoner's dilemma, the smoking gene problem), and the conflict between dominance and evidential reasoning in these cases is real.

CAUSAL DECISION THEORY

Dominance reasoning is unreliable when acts and states are not independent, and in Newcomb's problem the predictions (and the contents of the opaque box) are correlated with the actions. But there is no causal influence from the action to those states, and that is what really matters. Causal decision theory (CDT) is designed fully to employ the agent's beliefs about relevant causal influences; it has been offered in three versions with much in common by Allan Gibbard and William Harper (1978), Brian Skyrms (1980), and David Lewis (1981). In Gibbard and Harper's theory, the *EU* worth maximizing employs the weights $pr(A \square\!\!\rightarrow O_i)$, where $A \square\!\!\rightarrow O_i$ is a causal conditional: $A \square\!\!\rightarrow B$ holds when B is a causal consequence of A, or when B is unavoidable whatever the agent does. When M ("the opaque box contains a million") is not under the agent's influence the probabilities of $A1 \square\!\!\rightarrow M$ and $A2 \square\!\!\rightarrow M$ are equal, dominance reasoning is appropriate, and the theory recommends *A2*. Skyrms's theory avoids causal conditionals by presupposing a partition of states K_j relevant to the problem at hand and outside the influence of the agent. An expanded *EU* calculation by EDT would employ weights $pr(K_j/A)$. Skyrms's similar calculation uses $pr(K_j)$ instead, since K_j is not under the causal influence of A; this gives results in general agreement with Gibbard and Harper's. Lewis extends the Gibbard and Harper theory by employing causal conditionals with chancy consequents. Notable further developments on CDT are in Ellery Eells (1982), Jeffrey (1983), and Brad Armendt (1988).

PRISONER'S DILEMMA

Each of two isolated prisoners is invited to confess the guilt of both. The jailers offer these incentives: if both confess (defect from cooperation with the other prisoner), they receive long sentences of nine years; if both refuse to confess (each cooperates), they receive light sentences of one year on trumped-up charges; if just one confesses he goes free and the other is sentenced to ten years. What should they do? Assuming the sentences represent the total relevant payoffs, each prisoner's dominance reasoning recommends confession by each, but that pair of choices yields a much worse outcome for both than would joint cooperation. This two-person game, attributed to A. W. Tucker, has received much attention from game theorists, philosophers, political scientists, and biologists. The symmetry of the problem, and the tension between the individual incentives to defect and the social optimality of joint cooperation, make it a frequently discussed model for many kinds of interaction.

Interactions may be repeated, and, like other games, the PD (with revised payoffs) can be iterated. The iterated PD is one of the games that has most figured in studies of cooperation among rational agents in society, and among populations of biological organisms. When players expect to reencounter their opponents and expect their present play to be remembered on future occasions, the present payoffs and their deliberations become much more complex. Alternatively, organisms with no capacity to deliberate and limited memory of past encounters in iterated PD-like interactions can nevertheless stimulate and be stimulated by the play of others, leading to interesting "strategic play." Influential studies are Robert Axelrod (1981), which includes discussion of his well-known computer tournaments, and John Maynard Smith's work (presented in his 1982 book) on evolutionarily stable strategies. The descendent field of evolutionary game theory is now very active and rapidly growing.

OTHER DEVELOPMENTS

Some of the many significant further topics in current philosophical work on decision theory include: modeling deliberation; the stability of decision; planning and strategic choice; the justification of game-theoretic solution concepts; convention and the coordination of choice; generalized *EU* and weakened preference principles; and the empirical observations of descriptive decision theory.

Bibliography

Armendt, B. "Conditional Preference and Causal Expected Utility," in W. Harper and B. Skyrms, eds., *Causation in Decision, Belief Change, and Statistics* (Dordrecht, 1988).

Axelrod, R. "The Emergence of Cooperation among Egoists," *American Political Science Review,* Vol. 75 (1981), 306–18.

Broome, J. *Weighing Goods.* Oxford, 1991.

Eells, E. *Rational Decision and Causality.* Cambridge, 1982.

Gauthier, D. *Morals by Agreement.* Oxford, 1986.

Gibbard, A., and W. Harper. "Counterfactuals and Two Kinds of Expected Utility," in C. Hooker, ed., *Foundations and Applications of Decision Theory* (Dordrecht, 1978).

Jeffrey, R. *The Logic of Decision.* New York, 1965. 2nd ed., Chicago, 1983.

Lewis, D. "Causal Decision Theory," *Australasian Journal of Philosophy,* Vol. 59 (1981), 5–30.

Machina, M. "Decision-Making in the Presence of Risk," *Science,* Vol. 236 (1987), 537–43.

Maynard Smith, J. *Evolution and the Theory of Games.* Cambridge, 1982.

Nozick, R. "Newcomb's Problem and Two Principles of Choice," in N. Rescher, ed., *Essays in Honor of Carl G. Hempel* (Dordrecht, 1969).

Ramsey, F. P. "Truth and Probability" [1926], in D. H. Mellor, ed., *Foundations* (London, 1978).

Skyrms, B. *Causal Necessity.* New Haven, 1980.

———. *The Dynamics of Rational Deliberation.* Cambridge, 1990.

BRAD ARMENDT

DECONSTRUCTION. To deconstruct a work of philosophy is to give an immanent reading of its conceptual scheme to the point that one begins to locate within the work a certain 'outside' that the scheme excludes but whose traces are nevertheless marked in the text. The term "deconstruction" was introduced by Jacques DERRIDA [S] in 1967 as a translation of Martin HEIDEGGER'S [3; S] word *Destruktion,* but it became clear almost immediately that with it he intended a major modification of the Heideggerian project. Although deconstruction has spread across the academy, it is with reference to Derrida's relation to Heidegger that the deconstruction of philosophy can be made precise.

Heidegger introduced the term *Destruktion* in *Being and Time* (1927) as part of his attempt to combat the degeneration of tradition into a series of dogmas and categories that had come to be regarded as self-evident by virtue of their longevity. Heidegger's aim was to expand the range of future possibilities by reopening the past and finding what was left unthought, particularly by the Greeks. Derrida's appropriation of the early Heidegger was less favorable to the Greeks because it was mediated by the later Heidegger's project of overcoming metaphysics (*see* METAPHYSICS, OVERCOMING OF [S]). However, Derrida also questioned the later Heidegger's account on the grounds that it relied on the idea of the end of philosophy, a notion Derrida dismissed as preeminently metaphysical because it reinscribed classic notions of teleology, unity, and the opposition of inside and outside. In other words, Derridean deconstruction is a response to a fundamental aporia in Heidegger. Heidegger proclaimed the end of metaphysics but was still metaphysical.

In his early works Derrida also took over from Heidegger the latter's identification of Western philosophy with the privileging of presence. Derrida found by a close reading of the texts of metaphysics that, although they embodied this privilege within their evaluation of the terms of the binary oppositions that structure metaphysical thought, they were unable to sustain it consistently in this hierarchization. That is why the first deconstructive step of reversing the hierarchy is followed by a second step in which the opposition is displaced in favor of a term that is undecidable between the terms of the opposition.

So, for example, although the overriding value that Western philosophy places on presence leads speech to be privileged over writing, Derrida argued that its articulation has recourse to the model of writing. A text like Plato's *Phaedrus,* which is standardly held to denigrate writing, can also be read as saying the reverse. By interweaving both readings, deconstruction avoids simply deepening the founding concepts of metaphysics, like the early Heidegger, or stepping outside its confines, as the later Heidegger sometimes seems to propose. The principal lesson of deconstruction, that what escapes metaphysics is within the metaphysical text and only accessible through it, has not only negotiated the Heideggerian aporia, it has also led to a more profound reading of Heidegger, in which elements of the early Heidegger are found in the later Heidegger and vice versa.

Bibliography

Derrida, J. "La Pharmacie de Platon," *Tel Quel,* No. 32 (1969), 3–48; No. 33 (1969), 18–59. Translated by B. Johnson as "Plato's Pharmacy," in *Dissemination* (Chicago, 1981).

———. "Lettre à un ami japonais," *Psyché* (Paris, 1987), 387–93. Translated by D. Wood and A. Benjamin as "Letter to a Japanese Friend," in D. Wood and R. Bernasconi, eds., *Derrida and Différance* (Evanston, IL, 1988).

Gasché, R. *The Tain of the Mirror.* Cambridge, MA, 1986.

Madison, G. ed. *Working through Derrida.* Evanston, IL, 1993.

ROBERT BERNASCONI

DEDUCTION. How might one learn a previously unknown proposition *q* via deduction? A tempting reply: construct a proof of *q*. But what exactly is the appropriate sense of 'proof' at stake here? A widely accepted answer is that in philosophical discourse any sound and noncircular agrument constitutes a proof of its conclusion. (See, e.g., Cornman, Lehrer, & Pappas, 1982). And yet it is noteworthy that this orthodox view of proofs seems mistaken. For consider the following pair of arguments:

(1) (a) (Washington, D.C., is the capital of the United States) ⊃ (God exists) [where one must read 'A ⊃ B' as 'It is false that (A is true but B is false)']
(b) Washington, D.C., is the capital of the United States.
(c) Thus, God exists.

(2) (d) (God exists) ⊃ (Atlanta, Georgia, is the capital of the United States)
(e) Atlanta, Georgia, is not the capital of the United States.
(f) Thus, God does not exist.

By propositional logic, both (1) and (2) are valid and noncircular. Independently, the second premise of each argument is true. Next, observe that the disjunction of premise (1a) with premise (2d) is a tautology in classical propositional logic. It follows, then, that one of (1) and (2) is a sound and noncircular argument. According to the orthodox account of proofs, therefore, one of these two arguments counts as a proof of its conclusion. And the latter result appears just wrong: offered as philosophical proofs of theism and atheism, respectively, both (1) and (2) are decidedly lame. And the reason this is so seems straightforward. Because a material conditional is false if and only if its antecedent is true and the consequent is false, you cannot know which one of (1) and (2) has all true premises unless you already know which argument has the true conclusion. This in turn suggests a crucial agent-and-time-relativized epistemic requirement for the requisite sense of 'proof'—if a sound and noncircular argument *a* is to constitute a proof of its conclusion for a person *S* at a time *t*, then *S* must be able at *t* to know the premises of *a* without already knowing the conclusion.

Bibliography

Cornman, J. W., K. Lehrer, and G. S. Pappas, *Philosophical Problems and Arguments,* 3d ed. New York, 1982.

JAMES E. TOMBERLIN

DEMOCRACY. It is generally agreed that people live best in societies regulated by laws. Laws and policies help people cooperate, coordinate their activities, and establish justice in society. 'DEMOCRACY' [2] refers to a method in which all minimally competent members of a society can participate in deciding on the laws and policies that regulate the society. The people decide as a single body, and there is some provision for equality in the means to participate. This method contrasts with decentralized methods of decision making such as markets as well as with monarchy, aristocracy, oligarchy, and dictatorship. Theoretical debates about democracy concern its proper range, the nature and strength of the equality that is required, as well as the nature and basis of its worth.

RANGE

What decisions ought to be made democratically? Some think the people have a right to make decisions on all matters that affect people's lives in society (Walzer, 1981). Others would severely limit it to choices about how to preserve order in society, leaving other matters to private individuals and associations (Hayek, 1960). Most (Christiano, 1996) defend an intermediate position that the people have a right to make decisions on all matters that affect them in common but not to intrude in the lives of individuals. Civil liberties such as freedom of conscience, freedom of association, and freedom from arbitrary treatment by the state ought to be protected against the majority's intrusion. On these grounds some (Arneson, 1993) argue that the people ought to be limited by a constitution that is interpreted by a court with the authority to strike down legislation deemed incompatible with civil liberty. Some (Buchanan & Tullock, 1962) assert that the power of the majority should be tempered by dividing legislative power into two or more branches to make it more difficult to do what it wants. Others (Christiano, 1996) argue that democratic rule can be trusted to limit itself to its appropriate range.

STRENGTH OF EQUALITY

Some (Buchanan & Tullock, 1962) argue that each person has a right to an equally weighted vote in elections of representatives to assembly and no more. Others defend a more robust equality requiring public subsidies for political parties and even interest groups to ensure that a broad range of interests and points of views are represented in the political process (Beitz, 1989).

WORTH

What, if anything, is worthwhile about democracy? Instrumentalists argue that it is desirable to the extent that it results in more just legislation or efficient policy than other methods. If rule by one person or a small group could produce the same or superior results, they would be just as good or better, but since human beings are naturally inclined to be concerned with themselves first, power must be dispersed so as to avoid abuse (Arneson, 1993). Others (Nelson, 1980) argue that the people as a whole are likely to be wiser than select, even if individually superior, persons. Instrumentalism has implications regarding the proper range of democracy as well as the nature and proper strength of equality. Those arrangements are best which produce the best results.

Two other approaches attribute intrinsic merits to democracy, in addition to its instrumental virtues. One view is that each has a fundamental right to equal liberty. Individuals are free in a society regulated by law to the extent that they voluntarily make the laws in the democratic process. This approach emphasizes deliberation and consensus, without which many individuals must live under laws to which they are opposed (Cohen, 1989). A different approach makes equality the central ideal of democracy. When people disagree as to how they should order their society, and they must make some decision, the only just way is to give each an equal voice in the decision making. This view emphasizes voting (and access to the relevant information) and majority rule (Christiano, 1996). These two approaches can help us discern the proper range of democratic decision making as well as the appropriate strength of equality among citizens by appeal to the requirements of the underlying ideals of LIBERTY [S] and equality (*see* EQUALITY, MORAL AND SOCIAL [3].

Bibliography

Arneson, R. "Democratic Rights in National and Workplace Levels," in D. Copp, J. Hampton, and J. Roemer, eds., *The Idea of Democracy* (New York, 1993).

Beitz, C. *Political Equality: An Essay in Democratic Theory.* Princeton, NJ, 1989.

Buchanan J., and G. Tullock. *The Calculus of Consent: Logical Foundations of Constitutional Democracy.* Ann Arbor, MI, 1962.

Christiano, T. *The Rule of the Many: Fundamental Issues in Democratic Theory.* Boulder, CO, 1996.

Cohen, J. "Deliberation and Democratic Legitimacy," in A. Hamlin and P. Pettit, eds., *The Good Polity: Normative Analysis of the State* (Oxford, 1989).

Hayek, F. A. *The Constitution of Liberty.* Chicago, 1960.

Nelson, W. *On Justifying Democracy.* London, 1980.

Walzer, M. "Philosophy and Democracy," *Political Theory,* Vol. 9 (1981), 379–99.

THOMAS CHRISTIANO

DEMONSTRATIVES. *See:* INDEXICALS [S]

DEONTOLOGICAL ETHICS. No single idea captures all of the features in virtue of which an ETHICAL THEORY [S] may deserve the name deontology. In one sense of the term a deontology is simply an account of duty, something most ethical theories have. Yet the term normally conveys more than this when it is used to characterize an ethical theory. Very roughly, a deontological view denies that the good, or what is of value, takes priority over the right or duty. What this denial means depends on whether the deontology is a normative theory or a metaethical theory. Deontological normative theories argue that at least sometimes it is one's duty to perform an action, or follow a rule, that would not produce the best overall consequences of the available alternatives. Theories holding that there are absolute rights or duties, for instance, are deontological, since they claim that there are some rights or duties that we must not violate even if doing so would bring about the best overall consequences. Sometimes ethicists refer to such prohibitions as agent-relative or deontological constraints, or moral constraints that apply to an agent regardless of whether they bring about the most overall good.

To the extent that a normative theory such as CONSEQUENTIALISM [S] holds the view that deontologies deny, it is a teleological theory. But hybrid views are possible. For instance, a rule consequentialist might claim that one should follow those rules of behavior that would produce the best overall consequences if everyone were to follow them. Yet she might also claim that one should follow those rules even when one's individual actions would not bring about the best consequences of the available alternatives. Thus, a normative view could have a teleological theory of the rules we ought to follow but a deontological theory of the actions we ought to perform.

The term deontology may also be used to characterize a metaethical theory. Metaethics includes accounts of moral justification, the nature of moral properties, and the meaning and logic of moral statements. Thus, used in this way, the term may imply several different ideas. A theory may be called a deontology, for instance, because it denies that judgments about what is right are justified only if they are inferred from judgments about what is good, together with judgments about the effects of available actions. Or it may earn the name because it denies that the property of rightness is dependent on the property of causing the most overall good. A deontology in this metaphysical sense insists that rightness is an intrinsic, rather than an extrinsic, property of some actions. A theory may also be viewed as deontological because it denies that statements about what it is right to do can be defined or analyzed in terms of statements about what things are good together with statements about the effects of available actions. Again, at the metaethical level, to the extent that a theory holds a view denied by deontologies, it is teleological.

The positive views deontologists hold are diverse. Some hold that doctrines of the right are fundamental. Thus, to take one metaethical dimension as an example, a deontologist may claim that judgments about what is good are justified only when they are inferred from judgments about what it is right to do (e.g., she may claim that the judgment that a state of affairs is good is justified only when it is inferred from the judgment that it was brought about by a right action). Thus, these sorts of deontologies claim that the good is dependent on (in one of the above metaethical senses) the right. Other deontologists claim that neither the right nor the good are fundamental. For example, deontologists who are also intuitionists may claim that judgments neither about what is good nor about what is right need to be inferred from any other judgments in order to be justified, claiming instead that both are self-justifying or intuited. A deontologist need not be an intuitionist about judgment of right, however. Some argue that, in order to be justified, judgments of right must be inferred from or cohere with some other kinds of judgments. For instance, a divine-command deontologist may hold that judgments about what it is right to do are justified only if inferred from judgments about content of NATURAL LAW [5] or the will of God. And Kantian deontologists often argue that judgments of right are justified only if derived from a theory of practical reason.

How metaethical and normative theories interrelate is a complex and controversial issue, and so it is with the relationships between deontological theories of both kinds. Some normative deontologists remain quiet on metaethical questions, but others believe that their views have substantial metaethical implications. For instance, they may argue that, if there are any absolute rights or duties, then rightness must be an intrinsic property of actions. On the other hand, some metaethical deontologists remain silent on normative questions, while others argue that their views have normative implications. And some philosophers may pair a normative deontology with a nondeontological metaethics. For instance, an emotivist may claim that judgments of right are mere expressions of noncognitive attitudes and so are not susceptible to rational justification yet also hold the normative view that one must never torture innocents no matter how good the overall consequences of doing so might be.

(SEE ALSO: *Deontological Ethics* [2]; *Ethics, History of,* and *Ethics, Problems of* [3])

Bibliography

Donagan, A. *The Theory of Morality.* Chicago, 1977.

Finnis, J. *Natural Law and Natural Rights.* Oxford, 1980.

Fried, C. *Right and Wrong.* Cambridge, MA, 1978.

Gewirth, A. *Human Rights: Essays on Justifications and Applications.* Chicago, 1982.

Herman, B. *The Practice of Moral Judgment.* Cambridge, MA, 1993.

Hill, T. E. *Autonomy and Self-Respect.* Cambridge, 1991.

Nagel, T. *The View from Nowhere.* New York, 1986.

Nozick, R. *Anarchy, State, and Utopia.* Oxford, 1974.

O'Neill, O. *Constructions of Reason.* Cambridge, 1990.

Rawls, J. *A Theory of Justice.* Cambridge, MA, 1971.

Scheffler, S. *The Rejection of Consequentialism.* Oxford, 1982.

ROBERT NEAL JOHNSON

DERRIDA, JACQUES. Jacques Derrida's name is synonymous with DECONSTRUCTION [S]. Derrida was born in El-Biar, near Algiers, in 1930. In 1949 he left for Paris and in 1952 began study at the École Normale Supérieure, where he taught from 1964 until 1984. Since 1975 Derrida has spent a few weeks each year teaching in the United States. It was while at Yale University that Derrida collaborated with Paul de Man (1919–1983), leading to the extraordinary impact that deconstruction has had on the study of literature in the United States, an impact that quickly spread to other disciplines and countries.

Derrida's record of publications is remarkable. In 1962 he wrote an introduction to a translation of Husserl's *Origin of Geometry* that in many respects anticipates the later works. In 1967 he published a further study of HUSSERL [4; S], *Speech and Phenomena;* a collection of essays, *Writing and Difference;* and a reading of Saussure, Levi-Strauss, and Jean-Jacques ROUSSEAU [7; S], *Of Grammatology.* Since then there has been a rapid succession of publications, among the most important of which are *Dissemination* (1972), *Glas* (1974), *The Post Card* (1980), and *Psyché* (1987). He has also published extensively on an increasingly broad range of subjects from literature and politics to art and architecture.

STYLES OF DECONSTRUCTION

Deconstruction is neither a method nor a negative critique. It might be better understood as a strategy for reading texts under the influence of Edmund Husserl, Martin HEIDEGGER [3; S], Friedrich NIETZSCHE [5; S], Sigmund FREUD [3; S], Saussure, and Emmanuel LEVINAS [S]. In the early years of deconstruction many of the most important readings were devoted to these thinkers, all of whom, except for Husserl, were the focus of Derrida's 1968 lecture "Différance." Derrida justified this cross-fertilization of disparate authors by saying that their names served to define contemporary thought. This practice came to be generalized as intertextuality and is most pronounced in the cumulative layering of Derrida's writing, whereby he draws heavily on his previous readings. Because Derrida's language is both cumulative and parasitic on the texts that he is reading, attempts to formulate Derridean doctrines are often misleading. It is more appropriate to focus on his strategies.

Most of Derrida's writings operate by close reading, and their impact depends on the capacity of this reading to account for details that more conventional readings either ignore or explain away. In clear contrast, not only with most modern trends in philosophy, but also with a widespread image of him, Derrida is immersed in the history of philosophy. For Derrida this is the only way to avoid unwittingly repeating the most classic gestures of philosophy, a danger that threatens every attempt to ignore that history and begin philosophy anew. Deconstruction locates itself within traditional conceptuality in order to find the radical fissures that it believes can be traced in every work of philosophy. Derrida is drawn to the apparent contradictions of the tradition and makes them the starting point of his analysis, whereas a more conventional treatment tends to stop short as soon as a contradiction is identified. Much that is strange, and to some even offensive, about Derrida's analyses arises from the fact that he is attempting to uncover the structures that organize and so transcend conventional reason.

There is, however, another style of deconstruction that is no less representative of Derrida's thought. It proceeds by the analysis of logico-formal paradoxes. This style is particularly prominent in his treatment of ethics, where he finds a duty to go beyond one's duty. The extent to which this enterprise still reflects the interests of the more textual approach to deconstruction is clear. Sometimes, however, Derrida seems to give to the aporias he investigates a universal status, which suggests that in these cases the deconstruction of philosophy no longer depends on the conception of the history of Western metaphysics that is so prominent in his textual readings of philosophy. However, Derrida does not consider these two styles of deconstruction as independent of each other, so that it would be a mistake to suppose that he had compromised the genealogical component of his work.

EQUIVOCITY

If deconstruction's initial impact within the United States has been strongest in literature departments, this is in part because Derrida's conviction that absolute univocity is impossible is more readily welcomed by literary critics, who have always celebrated the multiplicity of meaning, than by philosophers, whose discipline has tended to encourage the reduction or controlling of equivocity. Whereas the dominant tendency in philosophy has been to mark different uses of a term in an effort to control the ambiguity, the deconstructive approach is to question the basis of any attempt to limit the associations of language. This approach has sometimes been confused with an invitation to so-called free play, in the sense of arbitrariness in interpretation, although Derrida has often rejected this interpretation of his work. In exploring equivocity, Derrida is recognizing and not ignoring the ambiguity of words. In the literary context the constraints of deconstruction are sometimes neglected for the freedom of literary experimentation. This is less common in Derrida than in some of his followers, but it has given ammunition to the critics of deconstruction.

CRITICISMS AND RESPONSES

The most persistent criticism of Derrida arises from his claim in *Of Grammatology* that "there is nothing outside the text." This has sometimes been understood to mean that all reference to the social and historical context is ruled out, and even that the text has no referent. It is easy to show that Derrida has never practiced such an extreme aestheticization of the text. What he did mean is explained in "Living On," in which he sets out the concept of a text as a differential network that overruns all the limits assigned to it. This, the so-called general text, is not conceived as a totality. It does not have an outside, anymore than it has an inside. As Derrida explained in the 1988 afterword to *Limited Inc,* there is nothing outside context, which is almost the opposite of what he is often accused of saying by many who do not share his philosophical background in PHENOMENOLOGY [6; S], psychoanalysis, or structural linguistics and yet fail to make allowance for that fact.

(SEE ALSO: *Supplement; Trace* [S])

Bibliography

A complete list of works by Derrida in French and English up to 1992, established by Albert Leventure and Thomas Keenan, is available in D. Wood, ed., *Derrida: A Critical Reader* (Oxford, 1992).

MAJOR PHILOSOPHICAL WORKS

Introduction to *L'Origine de la géométrie* by E. Husserl. Paris, 1962. Translated by J. Leavey, Jr., as *Edmund Husserl's "Origin of Geometry."* Lincoln, NE, 1989.

L'Écriture et la différance. Paris, 1967. Translated by A. Bass as *Writing and Difference.* Chicago, 1978.

De la grammatologie. Paris, 1967. Translated by G. Spivak as *Of Grammatology.* Baltimore, 1976.

La voix et le phénomène. Paris, 1967. Translated by D. Allison as *Speech and Phenomena.* Evanston, IL, 1973.

La Dissémination. Paris, 1972. Translated by B. Johnson as *Dissemination.* Chicago, 1981.

Marges de la philosophie. Paris, 1972. Translated by A. Bass as *Margins of Philosophy.* Chicago, 1982.

Glas. Paris, 1974. Translated by J. Leavey, Jr., and R. Rand as *Glas.* Lincoln, NE, 1986.

La Carte postale. Paris, 1980. Translated by A. Bass as *The Post Card.* Chicago, 1987.

Psyché: Inventions de l'autre. Paris, 1987.

WORKS ON DERRIDA

Bennington, G., and J. Derrida. *Jacques Derrida.* Paris, 1991. Translated by Geoffrey Bennington as *Jacques Derrida.* Chicago, 1993.

Gasché, R. *The Tain of the Mirror.* Cambridge, MA, 1986.

Lawlor, L. *Imagination and Chance.* Albany, NY, 1992.

Lawlor, L., ed. *Derrida's Interpretation of Husserl.* Southern Journal of Philosophy, Vol. 23 (1993), Supplement.

Llewelyn, J. *Derrida on the Threshold of Sense.* London, 1986.

ROBERT BERNASCONI

DESCARTES, RENÉ [*The following bibliographical notes are provided to update the lengthy overview of Descartes' life and thought appearing in volume 2 of* The Encyclopedia of Philosophy.]

The current best original-language text of Descartes' writings is *Oeuvres de Descartes,* edited by Charles Adam and Paul Tannery, 11 vols., originally published in Paris, 1897–1913, and revised, with the addition of a considerable amount of new material (Paris, 1964–74). There is in preparation a new edition for the Bibliothèque de la Pléiade, which will include new and in many cases improved texts of Descartes' French writings, and translations into French of his Latin writings.

The current best English translation of Descartes' writings is *The Philosophical Writings of Descartes,* edited and translated by John Cottingham, Robert Stoothoff, Dugald Murdoch, and Anthony Kenny, 3 vols. (Cambridge, 1984–1991). Vol. 1 contains the *Rules for the Direction of the Mind,* selections from *Le Monde,* the *Discourse on the Method,* selections from the *Principles of Philosophy,* and the *Passions of the Soul.* Volume 2 contains the *Meditations* and the *Objections and Replies,* as well as the dialogue, *The Search after Truth.* Volume 3 contains a generous selection of Descartes' philosophical correspondence, and is an expansion and revision of *Descartes: Philosophical Letters,* edited and translated by Anthony Kenny (Oxford, 1970).

Important recent literature includes Harry Frankfurt, *Demons, Dreamers, and Madmen* (Indianapolis, 1970); Geneviève Rodis-Lewis, *L'oeuvre de Descartes* (Paris, 1971); Jean-Luc Marion, *Sur l'ontologie grise de Descartes* (Paris, 1975); Margaret Wilson, *Descartes* (London, 1978); Jean-Luc Marion, *Sur la théologie blanche de Descartes* (Paris, 1981); Daniel Garber, *Descartes' Metaphysical Physics* (Chicago, 1992); John Cottingham, ed., *The Cambridge Companion to Descartes* (Cambridge, 1992); and Stephen Gaukroger, *Descartes: An Intellectual Biography* (Oxford, 1995).

DANIEL GARBER

DETERMINISM AND FREEDOM. DETERMINISM [2] is the family of theories that take our choices and the other antecedents of our actions, and our actions themselves, as effects of certain causal sequences. These theories understand effects in the standard way, as necessitated events. An account of choices and actions resting on weaker ideas of CAUSATION [2; S], perhaps the ideas that effects are merely probable events or events that would not have occurred in the absence of earlier events, would not usually count as a determinism. Indeed, the weaker ideas have sometimes been introduced precisely in order to avoid determinism.

The most discussed theories of determinism (sometimes spoken of in the past as physical determinism and psychological determinism) are philosophies of mind (*see* PHILOSOPHY OF MIND [S]). That is, they give or assume answers to the questions of how mental events are related to neural events, how mental events come about, and how actions come about. Most other philosophies of mind, worked out as a result of interest in the mind and without concern for the question of determinism and FREEDOM [3; S], are in fact also deterministic in nature. It can presumably be assumed, as once it was not, that there do exist conceptually adequate theories of determinism—clear, consistent, and complete.

Is any such theory true? Despite the support of neuroscience, many or most think not, because of interpretations of quantum theory. According to these interpretations there are microlevel things that are not effects. This opposition to determinism is not strengthened by the embarrassing fact, too often glossed over, that no satisfactory interpretation of quantum theory's application to reality has ever been achieved. Are the supposedly undetermined things in fact events? Determinism has no concern with anything other than events, for example, propositions or numbers, that are irrelevant to it. Would a microlevel indeterminism entail macrolevel indeterminism—a denial of theories of the kind with which we are concerned, which take actions and such antecedents as choices and neural events, all macrolevel, to be effects? It is arguable but not settled that the answer to both questions is no.

Philosophers continue to be more concerned with another matter, that of what follows if determinism is true.

Compatibilists, undaunted by the want of success of their predecessors over centuries, have persisted in arguing that our ordinary idea of freedom, or our only important idea, connected with moral responsibility is that of voluntariness, which evidently is logically compatible with determinism. At bottom a choice or an action is voluntary if it has certain causes rather than others—it is in accordance with the desires and nature of the agent, not compelled or constrained.

Much renewed effort has gone into attempting to prove that our idea of freedom *is* of just voluntariness by elaborating or varying the idea of voluntariness. One elaboration rests on the idea of desires that are themselves desired (Frankfurt, 1988). Another elaboration has to do with the extent and character of the control of our own lives that is consistent with determinism and also with the mistake of thinking that only less is possible because of too-simple models of deterministic behavior (Dennett, 1984).

Incompatibilists, equally undaunted by the fate of their predecessors, have stuck to the redoubtable conviction that our idea of freedom, or our only important idea, connected with moral responsibility is of a choice or action that is both voluntary and originated and hence something incompatible with determinism. A choice or action is originated if it is not the effect of such a causal sequence as supposed by determinists but nevertheless is within some sort of control of the agent.

Perhaps a majority of philosophers are now skeptical about the possibility of making much or sufficient or satisfactory sense of this talk of control. One takes it to involve a hopeless infinite regress (G. Strawson, 1986). Still, a brave attempt has been made to clarify origination in terms of a kind of medley of determined and undetermined events (Kane, 1985). Other incompatibilists, perhaps a majority, have been less ready to try actually to explain origination but have offered arguments designed to show that determinism is *not* compatible with freedom as we ordinarily conceive it. One line of argument is that in order for me to be free in this way today, if determinism were true, I would have to be able to change the past (Ginet, 1990; van Inwagen, 1986).

Other less traditional work on determinism has questioned common assumptions of both the compatibilist and the incompatibilist traditions. One such assumption is that determinism's threat to holding people morally responsible for actions, or crediting them with responsibility for them, is of unique importance. It is said instead that this moral approval and disapproval is one kind of affected attitude among others (P. F. Strawson, 1968; *see* STRAWSON, PETER F. [S]). Determinism's consequences for our hopes, our nonmoral feelings about other people, and our confidence in our beliefs are as important, and study of them is less distorted by philosophical habits and investments.

A more fundamental assumption of both compatibilism and incompatibilism has also been disputed. It is that we do have only one conception of freedom, or one important conception, and hence that either compatibilism or incompatibilism must be true. If we have two conceptions of freedom, one as voluntariness and one as voluntariness together with origination, then compatibilism and incompatibilism are both false, and the problem of determinism and freedom must be regarded very differently and, so to speak, less intellectually. It is no longer the problem of analyzing correctly our one conception of freedom. On the assumption that determinism is true it is the problem of giving up attitudes, each of them including desires, that rest on the inconsistent idea of origination (Honderich, 1988, 1993). Against all this, and much else, it has also been maintained that we have no respectable idea of freedom at all but only a kind of mess of inconsistent notions (Double, 1991). Not all have been persuaded.

So much for mainstreams of discussion of freedom and determinism. There have also been side streams, eddies, small whirlpools, and maybe stagnant ponds. They get attention in longer surveys (Clarke, 1995).

Bibliography

Clarke, R. "Freedom and Determinism," *Philosophical Books,* Vol. 36 (1995).

Dennett, D. *Elbow Room: The Varieties of Free Will Worth Wanting.* Cambridge, MA, 1984.

Double, R. *The Non-Reality of Free Will.* New York, 1991.

Frankfurt, H. *The Importance of What We Care About.* Cambridge, 1988.

Ginet, C. *On Action.* Cambridge, 1990.

Honderich, T. *A Theory of Determinism: The Mind, Neuroscience, and Life-hopes.* Oxford, 1988.

———. *How Free Are You?* Oxford, 1993.

Kane, R. *Free Will and Values.* Albany, NY, 1985.

Strawson, G. *Freedom and Belief.* Oxford, 1986.

Strawson, P. F. *Studies in the Philosophy of Thought and Action.* Oxford, 1968.

van Inwagen, P. *An Essay on Free Will.* Oxford, 1986.

TED HONDERICH

DEWEY, JOHN, has undergone an extraordinary renaissance of scholarly and public concern with his thought. Dewey (1859–1952) was encyclopedic in both his interests and achievements (see original entry [2]). The full and startling range of his written reflections is now apparent with the completed publication of his *Works* in a critical edition of thirty-seven volumes. Commentaries and critical interpretations have followed apace.

In the mediated public mind, prior discussion of Dewey's thought for the most part was devoted to his work on education, both in theory and practice. Unfortunately, these discussions of Dewey's approach to pedagogy and to schooling as an institution in a democratic society were often disconnected from his metaphysics, aesthetics, and social and political philosophy. This interpretive mishap is now being rectified with the appearance of many perceptive studies of Dewey's thought, including his previously neglected thoughts on religion and logic.

Fundamentally, John Dewey is an unregenerate philosophical naturalist, one for whom the human journey is constitutive of its own meaning and is not to be rescued by any transcendent explanations, principles of accountability, or posthumous salvation. Obviously, this position of Dewey is both liberating and baleful, in that it throws us back on our own human resources, for better and for worse. In effect, we are responsible for our actions, for the course of human history, and we are called upon to navigate between the shoals of supine obeisance and arrogant usurpation. In *A Common Faith* (1934), Dewey warns of the danger to human solidarity when we do not accept this responsibility. "Weak natures take to reverie as a refuge as strong ones do to fanaticism. Those who dissent are mourned over by the first class and converted through the use of force by the second."

Leaving no philosophical stone unturned, Dewey addresses the pitfalls and possibilities of the human condition from a wide array of vantage points. His central text is *Experience and Nature,* in which he probes the transactions of the human organism with the affairs of nature. These transactions are to be understood and diagnosed as experiential oscillations between the "precarious" and the "stable." The settings for this trenchant discussion include communication, mind, art, and value. In retrospect, Dewey offered that he should have titled this work *Culture and Nature,* an appropriate reconsideration, for it is helpful to read Dewey as a philosopher of culture, with an eye toward his grasp of human institutions, social, political, and educational.

In the past decade the focus of commentaries on the work of Dewey has been directed to his social and political philosophy, particularly his writings between 1927 and 1935, namely, *The Public and Its Problems, Individualism Old and New,* and *Liberalism and Social Action.* Although Dewey's thought was indigenous to American culture, it is nonetheless remarkable that themes found in Marxist and existentialist traditions are present in these writings, cast differently but equally telling. Of special note is the renewed admiration for Dewey's philosophy of community and his deep grasp of the complex relationships of individuals in communities. For Dewey the irreducible trait of human life is found in the activity of face-to-face communities. Their quality is the sign of how we are faring, humanly. At the end of *Human Nature and Conduct,* he writes a message for his time and for our time as well.

> Within the flickering inconsequential acts of separate selves dwells a sense of the whole which claims and dignifies them. In its presence we put off mortality and live in the universal. The life of the community in which we live and have our being is the fit symbol of this relationship. The acts in which we express our perception of the ties which bind us to others are its only rites and ceremonies.

Bibliography

WORKS BY DEWEY

Works of John Dewey, edited by J. A. Boydston. Carbondale, IL, 1969–90. Divided into Early Works (5 vols.), Middle Works (15 vols.), and Later Works (17 vols.). This is a critical edition.

The Philosophy of John Dewey, edited by J. J. McDermott. Chicago, 1981. Complete selections from Dewey's major writings.

WORKS ON DEWEY

Campbell, J. *Understanding John Dewey.* Chicago, 1995. The most intelligent and accurate interpretation of Dewey's thought overall.

Hickman, L. A. *John Dewey's Pragmatic Technology.* Bloomington, IN, 1990.

Rockefeller, S. C. *John Dewey: Religious Faith and Democratic Humanism.* New York, 1991.

Ryan, A. *John Dewey and the High Tide of American Liberalism.* New York, 1995.

Schilpp, P. A., and L. E. Hahn, eds. *The Philosophy of John Dewey.* Carbondale, IL, 1989. Contains a bibliography of Dewey's publications with entries and corrections until 1989.

Sleeper, R. S. *The Necessity of Pragmatism: John Dewey's Conception of Philosophy.* New Haven, 1986. An insightful presentation of the relationship between Dewey's thought and major currents in contemporary philosophy.

Welchman, J. *Dewey's Ethical Thought.* Ithaca, NY, 1995.

Westbrook, R. *John Dewey and American Democracy.* Ithaca, NY, 1991. A synoptic and especially perceptive book on Dewey's social thought.

JOHN J. MCDERMOTT

DISCOURSE ETHICS. "Discourse ethics" refers to an approach to moral theory developed by Jürgen HABERMAS [S]. It is a reconstruction of Immanuel KANT's [4; S] idea of practical reason that turns on a reformulation of his categorical imperative: rather than prescribing to others as valid norms which I can will to be universal laws, I must submit norms to others for purposes of discursively testing their putative universality. "Only those norms may claim to be valid that could meet with the approval of all those affected in their capacity as participants in practical discourse" (Habermas, 1990, p. 66). Normative validity, construed as rational acceptability, is thus tied to argumentation processes governed by a principle of universalization: "For a norm to be valid, the consequences and side effects of its general observance for the satisfaction of each person's particular interests must be acceptable to all" (p. 197). Furthermore, by requiring that perspective taking be general and reciprocal, discourse ethics builds a moment of empathy or 'ideal role-taking' into the procedure of practical argumentation.

Like Kant, Habermas distinguishes the types of practical reasoning and the corresponding types of 'ought' connected with questions concerning what is pragmatically expedient, ethically prudent, or morally right. Calculations of rational choice furnish recommendations relevant to the pursuit of contingent purposes in the light of given preference. When serious questions of value arise, deliberation on who one is and wants to be yields insight into the good life. If issues of justice are involved, fair and impartial consideration of conflicting interests is required to judge what is right or just. Again like Kant, Habermas regards questions of the last type, rather than specifically ethical questions, to be the proper domain of theory. (Thus, discourse ethics might properly be called discourse morality.) This is not to deny that ethical discourse is rational or that it exhibits general structures of its own; but the irreducible pluralism of modern life means that questions of self-understanding, self-realization, and the good life do not admit of universal answers. In Habermas's view, that does not preclude a general theory of a narrower sort, namely a theory of JUSTICE [4; S]. Accordingly, the aim of his discourse ethics is solely to reconstruct the moral point of view from which questions of right can be fairly and impartially adjudicated.

By linking discourse ethics to the theory of COMMUNICATIVE ACTION [S], Habermas means to show that our basic moral intuitions are rooted in something deeper and more universal than particularities of our tradition, namely in the intuitive grasp of the normative presuppositions of social interaction possessed by competent social actors in any society. Members of our species become individuals in and through being socialized into networks of reciprocal social relations. The mutual vulnerability that this interdependence brings with it calls for guarantees of mutual consideration to preserve both the integrity of individual persons and the web of their interpersonal relations. In discourse ethics respect for the individual is built into the freedom of each participant in discourse to accept or reject the reasons offered as justifications for norms, and concern for the common good is built into the requirement that each participant take into account the needs, interests, and feelings of all others affected by the norm in question. Hence, the actual practice of moral discourse depends on forms of socialization and social reproduction that foster the requisite capacities and motivation.

Bibliography

Habermas, J. *Moral Consciousness and Communicative Action,* translated by C. Lenhardt and S. Nicholsen. Cambridge, MA, 1990.

———. *Justification and Application: Remarks on Discourse Ethics,* translated by C. Cronin. Cambridge, MA, 1993.

Rehg, W. *Insight and Solidarity: The Discourse Ethics of Jürgen Habermas.* Berkeley, 1994.

THOMAS McCARTHY

DISTANT PEOPLES AND FUTURE GENERATIONS. Only recently have philosophers begun to discuss the question of whether we can meaningfully speak of distant peoples and future generations as having rights against us or of our having corresponding obligations to them. Answering this question with respect to distant peoples is much easier than answering it with respect to future generations. Few philosophers have thought that the mere fact that people are at a distance from us precludes our having any obligations to them or their having any rights against us. Some philosophers, however, have argued that our ignorance of the specific membership of the class of distant peoples does rule out these moral relationships. Yet this cannot be right, given that in other contexts we recognize obligations to indeterminate classes of people, such as a police officer's obligation to help people in distress or the obligation of food producers not to harm those who consume their products.

Of course, before distant peoples can be said to have rights against us, we must be capable of acting across the distance that separates us. Yet as long as this condition is met—as it typically is for people living in most technologically advanced societies—it would certainly seem possible for distant peoples to have rights against us and us corresponding obligations to them.

By contrast, answering the above question with respect to future generations raises more difficult issues. One concerns whether it is logically coherent to speak of future generations as having rights now. Of course, no one who finds talk about rights to be generally meaningful should question whether we can coherently claim that future generations *will* have rights at some point in the future (specifically, when they come into existence and are no longer future generations). But what is questioned, since it is of considerable practical significance, is whether we can coherently claim that future generations have rights now when they do not yet exist.

Let us suppose, for example, that we continue to use up the earth's resources at present or even greater rates, and as a result, it turns out that future generations will face widespread famine, depleted resources, insufficient new technology to handle the crisis, and a drastic decline in the quality of life for nearly everyone. If this were to happen, could persons living in the twenty-second century legitimately claim that we in the twentieth century violated their rights by not restraining our consumption of the world's resources? Surely it would be odd to say that we violated their rights more than one hundred years before they existed. But what exactly is the oddness?

Is it that future generations generally have no way of claiming their rights against existing generations? While this does make the recognition and enforcement of rights much more difficult (future generations would need strong advocates in the existing generations), it does not make it impossible for such rights to exist. After all, the recognition and enforcement of the rights of distant peoples is also a difficult task, but obviously such rights can exist.

Perhaps what troubles us is that future generations do not exist when their rights are said to demand action. But how else could persons have a right to benefit from the effects our actions will have in the distant future if they did not exist just when those effects would be felt? Our contemporaries cannot legitimately make the same demand, for they will not be around to experience those effects. Only future generations could have a right that the effects our actions will have in the distant future contribute to their well-being. Nor need we assume that, for persons to have rights, they must exist when their rights demand action. Thus, to say that future generations have rights against existing generations, we can simply mean that there are enforceable requirements upon existing generations that would benefit future generations or prevent harm to them.

Most likely what really bothers us is that we cannot know for sure what effects our actions will have on future generations. For example, we may, at some cost to ourselves, conserve resources that will be valueless to future generations who may develop different technologies. Or, because we regard them as useless, we may destroy or deplete resources that future generations will find to be essential to their well-being. Nevertheless, we should not allow such possibilities to blind us to the necessity of a social policy in this regard. After all, whatever we do will have its effect on future generations. The best approach, therefore, is to use the knowledge we have and assume that future generations will also require those basic resources we now find to be valuable. If it turns out that future generations require different resources to meet their basic needs, at least we will not be to blame for acting on the basis of the knowledge we have.

Assuming then that we can meaningfully speak of distant peoples and future generations as having rights against us and us corresponding obligations to them, the crucial question that remains is exactly what rights they have against us and what obligations we have to them. While the answer to this question obviously depends on a substantial social and political theory, the expectation is that the rights and obligations that morally bind us to distant peoples and future generations will be quite similar to those that morally bind us to near people and existing generations.

(SEE ALSO: *Rights* [7; S])

Bibliography

Elfstrom, G. *Ethics for a Shrinking World.* New York, 1990.

Hardin, G. *Promethean Ethics.* Seattle, 1980.

Partridge, E. *Responsibilities to Future Generations.* Buffalo, NY, 1981.

JAMES P. STERBA

DUMMETT, MICHAEL ANTHONY EARDLEY,

DUMMETT, MICHAEL ANTHONY EARDLEY, is the most important philosopher of logic of the second half of the twentieth century. Born on 27 June 1925 in London, Dummett completed his formal education at Christ Church, Oxford, and served for many years on the faculty of that university. A fellow of All Soul's College, from 1979 to 1992, Dummett was the Wykeham Professor of Logic. His influential work has made the claim commonplace (though not uncontroversial) that philosophical matters concerning logic and truth are central to metaphysics, understood in roughly the traditional sense. Dummett has profoundly and permanently shifted the ground of debates concerning metaphysical REALISM [7; S].

Much of Dummett's work has taken place in the context of his commentaries on Gottlob FREGE [3; S], at whose hands, Dummett claims, epistemology was supplanted by the philosophy of language as the fundamental field of philosophical investigation. Frege's reorientation of philosophy, comparable to the Cartesian installation of epistemology as the foundation of philosophical thinking, finally directed philosophers' attention at the proper focus: the relation of language to reality. Dummett is thus a leading advocate of the "linguistic turn." He is heavily influenced by Ludwig WITTGENSTEIN's [8; S] later work and by INTUITIONISM [S] in the philosophy of mathematics.

Dummett claims to have articulated a common structure embodied in a number of disputes pitting realists on a given subject matter against opponents of realism on that subject matter. For example, the medieval debate over universals consisted of realists, who held the existence of mind-independent objective properties, against various denials of realism (conceptualism, nominalism). Realism about material objects contrasts with varieties of IDEALISM [4], all of which share the general view that material objects do not exist mind-independently and objectively (absolute idealism, PHENOMENALISM [6]). In general, these positions antagonistic toward the positing of a given objective, mind-independent realm can be called antirealistic positions. Dummett holds that the proper way to represent the realist/antirealist dispute on a given realm of discourse, a way of understanding the dispute that is deeper than talking about mind independence or objectivity, is to investigate what logical principles that are valid on the realistic view must be abandoned by antirealism. In particular Dummett claims that the law of bivalence, according to which every meaningful statement is determinately either true or false, is the mark of realism.

According to Dummett, the route to antirealism must be a meaning-theoretical one and thus focuses on the role of the notion of truth in explicating meaning. His position on the theory of MEANING [5; S] has been called verificationism but, more properly, should be called neo-verificationism to distinguish him from the logical positivists. Dummett argues that TRUTH [S] cannot be the fundamental notion of a theory of meaning, if truth is conceived realistically—that is, as satisfying the principle of bivalence. He recommends abandoning this classical notion of truth. His positive proposal can be put either of two ways: he sometimes suggests that the classical notion of truth must be replaced by a different concept of truth, one that does not include the bivalence principle. Other times he suggests that truth be replaced by verification as the central meaning-theoretical notion.

The theory of meaning is concerned with the relationships of truth, meaning, and use. Holding to a sophisticated reading of the "meaning is use" idea, Dummett argues that a theory of meaning based on the classical notion of truth cannot successfully analyze the ability of speakers to use their language. That is, the meaning of a sentence cannot be identified (or, more weakly, sufficiently intimately connected) with the sentence's truth conditions if truth is conceived classically, because the resultant theory of meaning will not be able to explain the speaker's linguistic abilities as dependent upon her

Dummett's key arguments to this conclusion have been called the acquisition and manifestation arguments. Because some of the sentences of the language in question are undecidable (their truth or falsity cannot be recognized by means of "decision procedures"), it is inexplicable how a speaker is able to learn their truth-conditional meanings through training. The truth conditions of these sentences transcend the abilities of finite beings to teach them. Similarly, since a grasp of a sentence's meaning must be conclusively manifestable in one's actions, it is inconceivable that a speaker could display competence in the language if this means demonstrating her grasp of a sentence's recognition-transcendent truth conditions. Because of this sensitivity of the theory of meaning to such epistemological concerns, Dummett concludes that the central explanation notion of a theory of meaning cannot be epistemically transcendent. Thus, a notion of truth must be adopted that is responsive to the cognitive limitations of language users. This leads to the intuitionistic concept of truth, whereby bivalence fails and certain sentences cannot be said to possess a truth value despite being meaningful. Examples of such sentences include some past-tense and future-tense sentences, attributions of dispositional properties to no-longer-existent objects that never displayed possession or lack of the dispositions in question, and, crucially, sentences involving unrestricted quantification over infinite domains. Further pursuit of this line leads Dummett into consideration and rejection of meaning-theoretical holism and to an emphasis on the role of logical inference in verification.

Dummett thus rests metaphysical questions upon meaning-theoretical ones and in particular argues that the choice concerning which notion of truth is appropriate, and consequently which logic correctly formalizes the corresponding notion of valid or truth-preserving inference, must depend on a prior investigation in the theory of meaning.

Dummett's importance to philosophy lies in his demonstration of the delicate sensitivity of metaphysics to the philosophy of logic and of both to matters belonging squarely to PHILOSOPHY OF LANGUAGE [S].

Bibliography

"What Is a Theory of Meaning?" in S. Guttenplan, ed., *Mind and Language* (Oxford, 1974).

"What Is a Theory of Meaning? (II)" in G. Evans and J. MacDowell, eds., *Meaning and Truth* (Oxford, 1974).

"The Justification of Deduction," in *Truth and Other Enigmas* (Cambridge, MA, 1978).

"The Philosophical Basis of Intuitionistic Logic," in *Truth and Other Enigmas* (Cambridge, MA, 1978).

"The Significance of Quine's Indeterminacy Thesis," in *Truth and Other Enigmas* (Cambridge, MA, 1978).

Frege: Philosophy of Language, 2d ed. Cambridge, MA, 1981.

The Interpretation of Frege's Philosophy. Cambridge, MA, 1981.

"Frege on the Third Realm," in *Frege and Other Philosophers.* Oxford, 1991.

The Logical Basis of Metaphysics. Cambridge, MA, 1991.

Frege: Philosophy of Mathematics. Cambridge, MA, 1993.

The Seas of Language. Oxford, 1993.

MICHAEL HAND

E

EFFECTIVE HISTORY. Effective historical consciousness *(wirkungsgeschichtliches Bewußtsein),* a term introduced by Hans-Georg GADAMER [S], names human CONSCIOUSNESS [2; S] as embedded within effective history *(Wirkungsgeschichte).* Effective history is the continual and continuing sedimentation of previous human experience in human activities, especially language. Two senses of effective historical consciousness are distinguishable. In one sense every person's consciousness is an effective historical consciousness, even if one is unaware of the conditioning effect of history. So, although one may believe consciousness to be autonomous, its cognitions are nevertheless co-effected by history. In this case they occur naively without the possibility of questioning their source and indebtedness to the past. In the second sense effective historical consciousness is aware of history's effect upon it and its role in affecting history.

History conditions consciousness during one's acculturation, especially in learning language, by bestowing one with a set of prejudices. (Here, 'prejudices' has a neutral, not a negative, meaning.) These prejudices, both consciously and unconsciously held, constitute a person's horizon of possible meaning. They situate one within temporal, linguistic tradition(s). Since one may become aware of and actively call into question only some of these prejudices, human consciousness can never become self-transparent. There are always unknown elements of effective history that predetermine, not only what questions may be asked, but also the range of possible answers. In this sense we belong to history more than history belongs to us. The conditioning effect of history undercuts any claims of method or the reflective power of self-consciousness to escape the hermeneutic situation to a supposed absolute and independent position. Since consciousness is embedded in effective history, it cannot be understood as a Cartesian subject. The experience of consciousness deconstructs the telos of the Hegelian dialectic since any resolution remains preconditioned by effective history and points to the truth of experience, human fallibility.

Effective historical consciousness also affects history. The building and FUSION OF HORIZONS [S] are the accomplishments of effective historical consciousness. In projecting and considering the horizon of the other in the fusion of horizons, consciousness actively establishes an openness into which a perspective of the subject matter may shine forth as hermeneutically true. This constitutes the active, critical role of effective historical consciousness. By means of the applicative moment present in all cases of understanding, elements of the inheritance are taken up into the horizon of the present and possibly modified. These are then projected into the future affecting the history of that tradition. Since the continuation and modification of the effect of effective history depends upon the active, critical application of the experienced hermeneutic truth to the projected future, effective history cannot itself be considered substantial or teleological. It is language, as the continuing conversation that we are, that preserves and modifies the past in projecting a future.

Bibliography

Gadamer, H.-G. *Gesammelte Werke.* Tübingen, 1985ff.

———. *Truth and Method,* 2nd revised ed., translated by J. Weinsheimer and D. Marshall. New York, 1989.

Grondin, J. *Hermeneutische Wahrheit? Zum Wahrheitsbegriff Hans-Georg Gadamers.* Königstein, 1982.

Hoy, D. C. *The Critical Circle: Literature and History in Contemporary Hermeneutics.* Berkeley, 1978.

Matika, E. *Gadamer—Bibliographie.* Frankfurt a. M., 1995.

Schmidt, L. K. *The Epistemology of Hans-Georg Gadamer. An Analysis of the Legitimization of 'Vorurteile'.* Frankfurt a. M., 1987.

———, ed. *The Specter of Relativism: Truth, Dialogue, and 'Phronesis' in Philosophical Hermeneutics.* Evanston, IL, 1995.

Wachterhauser, B., ed. *Hermeneutics and Truth.* Evanston, IL, 1994.

Warnke, G. *Gadamer: Hermeneutics, Tradition and Reason.* Stanford, CA, 1987.

Weinsheimer, J. C. *Gadamer's Hermeneutics.* New Haven, 1985.

LAWRENCE K. SCHMIDT

EGALITARIANISM. *See:* SOCIAL AND POLITICAL PHILOSOPHY [S]

ELIMINATIVE MATERIALISM, ELIMINATIVISM. Eliminative materialism espouses the view that our commonsense way of understanding the mind is false, and that, as a result, beliefs, desires, consciousness, and other mental events used in explaining our everyday behavior do not exist. Hence, the language of our "folk" psychology should be expunged, or eliminated, from future scientific discourse.

Two routes have been taken to get to the eliminativist's position. The first and less popular stems from a linguistic analysis of mentalistic language. Paul Feyerabend argues that the commonsense terms for mental states tacitly assume some version of dualism. Insofar as MATERIALISM [5] is true, these terms cannot refer to anything in the physical world. Thus they should not be used in discussing ourselves or our psychologies since we are purely physical beings.

The second and better-developed approach comes out of the philosophies of science developed by Feyerabend, David Lewis, Willard van Orman QUINE [7; S] and Wilfrid SELLARS [S]. Two suppositions are important for eliminativism. (1) There is no fundamental distinction between observations (and our observation language) and theory (and our theoretical language), for previously adopted conceptual frameworks shape all observations and all expressions of those observations. All observations are "theory-laden." These include observations we make of ourselves; in particular, observations we make about our internal states. There are no incorrigible phenomenological "givens." (2) The meaning of our theoretical terms (which includes our observational vocabulary) depends upon how the terms are embedded in the conceptual scheme. Meaning holism of this variety entails that if the theory in which the theoretical terms are embedded is false, then the entities that the theory posits do not exist. The terms would not refer.

Two more planks complete the eliminative argument. (3) Our way of describing ourselves in our everyday interactions comprises a rough and ready theory composed of the platitudes of our commonsense understanding. The terms used in this folk theory are defined by the platitudes. (4) FOLK PSYCHOLOGY [S] is a radically false theory.

In support of this position, Patricia Churchland and Paul Churchland argue that belief-desire psychology wrongly assumes sentential processing; moreover, belief-desire psychology is stagnant, irreducible to neuroscience, and incomplete. Stephen Stich argues that our very notion of belief and, by implication, the other propositional attitudes is unsuitable for cognitive science. Patricia Churchland, Daniel Dennett, Georges Rey, Richard Rorty, and others argue that our notion of CONSCIOUSNESS [2; S] is confused. They all conclude, as do other eliminativists, that folk psychology should be replaced by something entirely different and more accurate, though views differ on what this replacement should be.

Attacks on eliminative materialism generally have come from four fronts, either on premise two, premise three, or premise four of the second approach, or on the eliminativist position itself, without regard to the arguments for it. Premise two asserts meaning holism and a particular theory of REFERENCE [S]. If that theory were false, then the eliminativist's second argument would be undermined. There are alternative approaches to reference that do not assume holism; for example, causal-historical accounts do not. If meaning is not holistic, then even if folk psychology were incorrect, the terms used in that theory could still refer, and elimination of folk psychological terms would not be warranted.

Arguments that our folk psychology is not a true theory deny premise three. Here some detractors point out that even if a completed psychology did not rely on the propositional attitudes or consciousness, that fact would not entail that those sorts of mental states do not exist; instead, they just would not be referred to in scientific discourse. Nevertheless, they could still be used as they are now, in our everyday explanations of our behavior.

Others charge that premise four is false; folk psychology might be a rudimentary theory, but it is not radically false. While agreeing that belief-desire explanations or explanations involving conscious events might not be entirely empirically adequate or complete, champions of folk psychology argue that no other theory is either. In addition, our folk psychology has developed over time, is coherent, and its status with respect to neuroscience is immaterial. These arguments are generally coupled with the claim that no other alternative, either real or imagined, could fulfill the explanatory role that the propositional attitudes play in our understanding of ourselves. And until the eliminativist's promise of a better conceptual scheme is fulfilled folk psychology is here to stay. At least some properly revised version of folk psychology would remain.

Lastly, some supporters of folk psychology argue that any eliminativist program would be fatally flawed, regardless of whatever particular arguments are given, for the very statement of eliminative materialism itself is incoherent. In its simplest form, the argument runs as follows: Eliminative materialism claims that beliefs do not exist. Therefore, if eliminative materialism were true, we could not believe it. Therefore, no one can believe eliminative materialism on pain of inconsistency.

Replies to the four sorts of attacks are ubiquitous. However, answering the first three turns on (primarily empirical) issues yet to be settled. Which theory of reference is correct, whether folk psychology is actually a theory, and what revisions are required to make it adequate depend upon facts we do not yet know about ourselves or our linguistic practices.

The last point is more conceptual. In responding to it, eliminative materialists hold that something else will replace "belief," or some instances or aspects of "belief." Call this "schmelief." It is true that eliminative materialists cannot believe that eliminative materialism is true on pain of inconsistency. But, eliminativists maintain, they can "schmelieve it." Defenders of a revised folk psychology answer that, as used in this context, "schmelief" seems to be some other intentional operator or relation, a mere revision of belief. Without better exposition of what the replacement for folk psychology will be (and how it will be radically different), we simply cannot tell what the future holds for our commonsense theory of self: simple revision, peaceful co-existence, or outright replacement.

(SEE ALSO: *Philosophy of Mind* [S])

Bibliography

Baker, L. R. *Saving Belief: A Critique of Physicalism.* Princeton, NJ, 1987.

Boghossian, P. "The Status of Content," *Philosophical Review,* Vol. 99 (1990), 157–84.

Churchland, P. "Eliminative Materialism and the Propositional Attitudes," *Journal of Philosophy,* Vol. 78 (1981), 67–90.

Feyerabend, P. "Mental Events and the Brain," *Journal of Philosophy,* Vol. 60 (1963), 295–96.

Horgan, T., and J. Woodward. "Folk Psychology Is Here to Stay," *Philosophical Review,* Vol. 94 (1985), 197–225.

Rey, G. "A Reason for Doubting the Existence of Consciousness," in R. Davidson, S. Schwartz, and D. Shapiro, eds., *Consciousness and Self-Regulation,* Vol 3. (New York, 1982).

Rorty, R. "Mind-Body Identity, Privacy, and Categories," *Review of Metaphysics,* Vol. 19 (1965), 24–54.

Stich, S. *From Folk Psychology to Cognitive Science: The Case Against Belief.* Cambridge, MA, 1983.

VALERIE GRAY HARDCASTLE

ENGINEERING ETHICS. Philosophers began to do scholarly work in the area of engineering ethics in the late 1970s; there has been a modest but steady flow of philosophical essays on a variety of issues since that time. Most of the work done by philosophers has been in the United States, although a few philosophers in other countries have begun to contribute to the literature.

As a subfield of APPLIED ETHICS [S], the philosophical study of engineering ethics has evolved out of and built on previous philosophical work in areas such as BIOMEDICAL ETHICS, BUSINESS ETHICS, and the PHILOSOPHY OF TECHNOLOGY [S]. More general works on professional ethics (such as Gert, 1992; Hare, 1992) are of direct value to work in engineering ethics.

A good example of a sustained application to engineering of a topic originally developed in the fields of medical and research ethics appears in a book coauthored by a philosopher. Mike W. Martin and engineer Roland Schinzinger (1983) argue effectively in support of the thesis that most engineering projects involve what can be characterized as social experiments, which for this reason require following informed-consent procedures similar to those used for other experimentation involving human subjects. The most difficult aspect of this approach is the set of complexities associated with identifying the affected parties, providing appropriate information to these parties, and obtaining uncoerced consent from them (*see* INFORMED CONSENT [S]).

In addition to borrowing from related fields, engineering ethics has contributed to these fields. One of the earliest philosophical essays on engineering ethics, De George's (1981) analysis of the Pinto gas-tank case in which he proposes necessary and sufficient conditions for justifying whistleblowing, has been widely discussed and reprinted in the literature of business ethics and other fields. Other work on more general topics (e.g., Davis, 1991; Ladd, 1982; Whitbeck, 1992) displays the positive results of interactions between engineering ethics and related fields.

The professional activities of engineers have significant effects—both direct and indirect—on the health of large numbers of persons and other life forms. Bad engineering work (whether at the design, construction/manufacture, or maintenance level) on an automobile, airplane, chemical process, or nuclear power plant could cause serious injury or death to many individuals. Good engineering work can have substantial positive effects in terms of extending the length and improving the quality of the lives of humans and others. The indirect consequences (especially the negative ones) are more difficult to identify but are often more serious in the long run. The general problems of identifying and evaluating the consequences of engineering activities are among the main topics in the philosophy of technology.

Engineering itself evolved as a separate profession during the nineteenth century. National professional societies representing the major fields of engineering (civil, mechanical, electrical, etc.) were well established by 1900. A number of efforts have been made over the past century to establish a single professional organization representing engineers in all fields, but a variety of factors has prevented the lasting success of all such efforts. (Layton, 1986, provides an excellent historical account up to World War II of the political conflicts within and among the major engineering societies and the impact on their ethics activities.)

Most of the engineering societies had formulated and adopted codes of ethics by 1915. As was the case for many professions evolving at the time, the ethics codes of the engineering societies were modeled to a significant degree on the code of medical ethics of the time, with the term "patient" systematically replaced with "employer" or "client."

The ethics codes of the various engineering societies have changed substantially over the years. The most significant change has been in the specification of the "paramount" responsibility of engineers, which was originally identified as the protection of the employer/client's interests. Revisions of the codes in the 1940s required that engineers balance the interests of the employers/clients with the interests of the general public. In the 1970s the paramount responsibility was narrowed to only the public welfare in many (but not all) engineering codes. Although the problematic degree of PATERNALISM [S] in this formulation has been fairly widely discussed in the literature, this element of the codes has not been changed. In fact, the first international model code of engineering, promulgated by the World Federation of Engineering Organizations in 1993, includes the explicit assertion that professional engineers shall "hold paramount the safety, health and welfare of the public."

A feature of the practice of engineering that once set the field apart from many other professions is that most engineers are employees of large organizations and they work as members of teams in which moral responsibility is not clearly assigned to specific individuals. Engineering now provides a model for many other professions, including medicine, law, and accounting, whose members are increasingly employed in large organizations. A related issue that recurs in the literature is that the boundary between professional roles and managerial roles is increasingly blurred (see Werhane, 1991).

Engineers remain different from other professionals such as physicians, nurses, accountants, and lawyers in at least one ethically significant way in that very few engineers (most of them in civil engineering) are required to be licensed. Since only licensed engineers are governed by any legally enforceable code of ethics, the codes of the various engineering societies are essentially statements of ideals.

Engineering ethics has a "gold mine" of resources for doing case studies that is not available for many other professional fields. Because of the public, large-scale nature of many engineering projects, the occurrence of some failures is widely publicized and openly investigated. Congressional hearings (and even presidential commissions, as in the case of the Challenger explosion) have been conducted on a number of important cases, and the published reports are readily accessible. Even when the government has not been the immediate client, regulatory bodies have had sufficient interest to conduct inquiries and publish substantial reports. (In contrast, hearings before state licensing boards for physicians, lawyers, accountants, and other professionals are often held in closed sessions with the transcripts being sealed.) Philosophers have done thoughtful and balanced analyses of a number of cases that provide important insights into the complexities, subtleties, vaguenesses, and ambiguities of situations in which engineers operate and of the ethical issues that arise in those situations (good examples are Fielder, 1988; Fielder & Birsch, 1992; Harris et al., 1995; and Werhane, 1991).

While much of the literature in engineering ethics is concerned with cases involving "disasters" such as the DC-10 case (only a portion of which is included in Fielder & Birsch, 1992), a few important studies have concentrated on the organizational policies and procedures that have been successful in minimizing harm and maximizing benefits of engineering projects (see Flores, 1982).

As with most other professions, engineering ethics still contains much unexplored territory. This is often due (in part, at least) to the fact that certain legal parameters have been created by legislatures and courts; it is then tacitly assumed that the legal principles are also the ethical norms, and no serious examination is made of the issues. For example, until 1976 almost all engineering codes of ethics contained explicit proscriptions against any form of advertising of professional services. After the U.S. Supreme Court ruled in 1976 that such restrictions violate antitrust laws, the proscriptions were dropped from the codes; some codes substituted recommendations that the advertising should not be misleading or in bad taste, but other codes are still completely silent on the matter. There has been no philosophical discussion of the subtle complexities—such as the problem of determining when even accurate quantitative statements may be misleading to potential clients—associated with this aspect of engineering practice. Of an incomplete list of twenty-five issues in engineering ethics in need of philosophical analysis (Baum, 1980, pp. 47–48), most have received little if any attention from philosophers as of the mid-1990s. Some of the topics have received considerable philosophical attention at a more general level (e.g., in Weil & Snapper, 1989), but the specific issues related to engineering have yet to be examined in detail.

Bibliography

Baum, R. J. *Ethics and Engineering Curricula.* Hastings-on-Hudson, NY, 1980.

Baum, R. J., and A. Flores, eds. *Ethical Problems in Engineering,* 2 vols., 2d ed. Troy, NY, 1980.

Davis, M. "Thinking Like an Engineer: The Place of a Code of Ethics in the Practice of a Profession," *Philosophy and Public Affairs,* Vol. 20, No. 2 (1991), 150–67.

De George, R. "Ethical Responsibilities of Engineers in Large Organizations," *Business and Professional Ethics Journal,* Vol. 1, No. 2 (1981), 1–17.

Fielder, J. H. "Give Goodrich a Break," *Business and Professional Ethics Journal,* Vol. 7, No. 1 (1988), 3–25.

Fielder, J. H., and D. Birsch, eds. *The DC-10 Case: A Study in Applied Ethics, Technology, and Society.* Albany, NY, 1992.

Flores, A., ed. *Designing for Safety: Engineering Ethics in Organizational Contexts.* Troy, NY, 1982.

Gert, B. "Morality, Moral Theory, and Applied and Professional Ethics," *Professional Ethics,* Vol. 1, Nos. 1 & 2 (1992), 3–24.

Hare, R. M. "One Philosopher's Approach to Business and Professional Ethics," *Business and Professional Ethics Journal,* Vol. 11, No. 2 (1992), 3–19.

Harris, C. E., Jr., M. S. Pritchard, and M. J. Rabins. *Engineering Ethics: Concepts and Cases.* Belmont, CA, 1995.

Johnson, D., ed. *Ethical Issues in Engineering.* Englewood Cliffs, NJ, 1991.

Ladd, J. "Collective and Moral Responsibility in Engineering: Some Questions," *IEEE Technology and Society Magazine,* Vol. 1, No. 2 (1982), 3–10.

Layton, E. T., Jr. *The Revolt of the Engineers: Social Responsibility and the American Engineering Profession.* Baltimore, 1986.

Martin, M. W., and R. Schinzinger. *Ethics in Engineering.* New York, 1983.

Schaub, J. H., and K. Pavlovic, eds. *Engineering Professionalism and Ethics.* New York, 1983.

Weil, V., and J. Snapper, eds. *Owning Scientific and Technical Information: Value and Ethical Issues.* New Brunswick, NJ, 1989.

Werhane, P. H. "Engineers and Management: The Challenge of the Challenger Incident," *Journal of Business Ethics,* Vol. 10 (1991), 605–16.

Whitbeck, C. "The Trouble with Dilemmas: Rethinking Applied Ethics," *Professional Ethics,* Vol. 1, Nos. 1 & 2 (1992), 119–42.

ROBERT J. BAUM

ENVIRONMENTAL ETHICS. Spurred by growing environmental concern in the 1960s, philosophers paid increasing attention to environmental ethics in the 1970s and 1980s. The field is dominated by several dichotomies: anthropocentrism versus nonanthropocentrism, individualism versus holism, environmental ethics versus environmental philosophy, organic versus community metaphors, and scientific versus social scientific justifications.

Traditional Western ethics is anthropocentric, as only human beings are considered of moral importance. Because people can help or harm one another indirectly through environmental impact, such as by generating pollution, destroying marshes, and depleting resources, environmental ethics can be pursued as a form of applied ethics in an anthropocentric framework.

Viewed anthropocentrically, environmental ethics is a fertile testing ground for ethical and other theories. Issues of resource depletion, nuclear waste, and population policy, for example, raise questions about the present generation's obligations to future generations. Do future people have rights? Can a meaningful distinction be made between future people and possible people? Why should we care about future people if they can neither harm nor help us? Utilitarian and contractarian theories of ethics are tested in part by their replies to such questions (*see* DISTANT PEOPLES AND FUTURE GENERATIONS [S]).

In the anthropocentric tradition environmental ethics also includes criticism of cost-benefit analysis (CBA). Translating all values into monetary terms not only jeopardizes future generations (through use of a discount rate that renders impacts 500 years from now insignificant) but also treats present people exclusively as consumers. Ideals of individual excellence and civic virtue are improperly ignored.

Opposed to anthropocentrism are those who consider many nonhuman animals to be worthy of moral consideration in their own right (see ANIMAL RIGHTS AND WELFARE [S]). These views extend some traditional ethical theories, such as UTILITARIANISM [8] and neo-Kantianism, to include nonhuman individuals. Paul Taylor advocates further extension, according equal moral consideration to every living individual, amoeba included.

Many environmental philosophers consider moral extensionism too human-centered and individualistic. It is too human-centered because it justifies valuing nonhumans on the basis of similarities to human beings, such as sentience, consciousness, or merely life itself. Human traits remain the touchstone of all value. Moral extensionism is too individualistic for environmental ethics because some matters, such as species diversity, concern collectives, not individuals. From an individualist perspective, saving ten members of a common species is better than saving one member of an endangered species, other things being equal. Environmentalists concerned to maintain species diversity reject individualism for this reason.

They reject individualism also as ecologically unrealistic. Ecology teaches that ecosystems depend on individuals eating and being eaten, killing and being killed. For example, predators must kill enough deer to avoid deer overpopulation, which would threaten flora on which deer feed. Reduced flora threatens soil stability and the land's ability to support life. So protecting individual deer from untimely death, which valuing deer as individuals may suggest, is environmentally harmful. Such harm threatens natural ecosystems, such as wilderness areas, that foster biological evolution, which is the focus of value for some environmentalists.

Tom Regan calls holistic views "environmental fascism." Sacrificing individuals for evolutionary advance or the collective good resembles Hitler's program, especially when human beings may be among those sacrificed. Human overpopulation threatens species diversity, ecosystemic complexity, and natural evolutionary processes, so consistent environmental holism may be misanthropic.

Holists reply that human individuals, as well as environmental wholes and evolutionary processes, are intrinsically valuable, so individual humans should not be sacrificed to promote the corporate good. However, the casuistry of trade-offs among individuals and corporate entities of various species and kinds is not well developed by the holists. On the other hand, Regan has not shown how all individual nonhuman mammals, for example, could not be accorded the equivalent of human rights without obliterating wilderness areas and causing the extinction of many carnivorous species.

Because they value not only nonhumans but holistic entities, many environmental philosophers believe their discipline calls for thorough review of the place of human beings in the cosmos. They reject the title "environmental ethics" in favor of "environmental philosophy" or "ecosophy" to emphasize that their views are not applications of traditional ethics to environmental problems but fundamental metaphysical orientations.

Holistic views tend to compare the environmental wholes they consider valuable in themselves with either communities or organisms. Aldo Leopold's 'land ethic', for example, leans toward the community metaphor. Just as the benefits people derive from their human communities justify loyalty to the group, benefits derived from complex ecological interdependencies justify loyalty to ecosystemic wholes. J. Baird Callicott maintains that community loyalty is emotionally natural to humans, as our ancestors' survival during evolution depended on sentiments of solidarity. Ethics is here based on Humean sentimentalism rather than Kantian rationality or utilitarian calculation.

The Gaia hypothesis and deep ecology stress the similarity of holistic entities to individual organisms, thereby attempting to reconcile individualism with environmentalism. The Gaia hypothesis maintains that life on earth operates as if it were a single organism reacting to altered conditions so as to preserve itself. Deep ecology questions the separateness of any individual from the environmental whole and suggests identifying one's real self with nature. Either way, if life on earth, or nature in general, is an individual, an ethic concentrating on the good of individuals can support concern for environmental entities that are commonly considered wholes.

Whereas the land ethic and Gaia hypothesis rely primarily on information drawn from science, other environmentalists stress social scientific information. Using the results of anthropological studies, especially of foraging (hunter-gatherer) societies, some environmentalists maintain that human life is better where people do not attempt to master nature in the human interest. Many indigenous societies practice an environmental ethic, similar to the land ethic, of reciprocal exchange with nonhuman environmental constituents such as water, sun, trees, and game animals. This enriches human life and preserves the environment.

Ecofeminists emphasize the relationship between mastering nature in the supposed human interest and the oppression of women. In Western culture men are often associated with heaven, mind, reason, and culture, whereas women are associated with earth, body, emotion, and nature. This explains traditional exclusions of women from high religious offices and from professions emphasizing the use of abstract reason. Because women are associated with nature, the mastery of nature celebrated in modern science and industry involves the oppression of women, from witch trials to the feminization of poverty.

Ecofeminists claim that women tend to think more relationally, organically, and holistically than men, who favor individual rights, commercial success, and mechanistic processes. Whereas typical male patterns of thought and action precipitate ecocrises, typical female patterns ameliorate them. Empowering women can save ecosystems and species diversity.

Because environmental ethics/philosophy questions basic assumptions in economics, technology, metaphysics, ethical theory, moral epistemology, and gender relations, it approaches religion in its attention to the fundamental concerns of human existence.

(SEE ALSO: *Applied Ethics* [S]

Bibliography

Des Jardins, J. R. *Environmental Ethics.* Belmont, CA, 1993. Excellent introduction for the general reader.

Environmental Ethics is the leading journal in this area.

Hargrove, E. C. *The Animal Rights/Environmental Ethics Debate: The Environmental Perspective.* Albany, NY, 1992.

Partridge, E., ed. *Responsibilities to Future Generations.* Buffalo, NY, 1981.

Passmore, J. *Man's Responsibility for Nature.* New York, 1974. Maintains anthropocentrism.

Sagoff, M. *The Economy of the Earth.* New York, 1988. Critiques economics and CBA.

Zimmerman, M. E. *Environmental Philosophy.* Englewood Cliffs, NJ, 1993. Contains seminal articles and essays by P. Singer, T. Regan, P. Taylor, A. Leopold, J. Baird Callicott, A. Naess, C. Merchant, and K. Warren and is an excellent source of information on animal rights, biocentrism, the land ethic, deep ecology, social ecology, and ecofeminism.

PETER S. WENZ

EPISTEMOLOGY. There have been numerous exciting developments in EPISTEMOLOGY [3] since 1960. The publication of one brief critical article, Edmund Gettier's "Is Justified True Belief Knowledge?," brought about a flurry of activity (Roth & Galis, 1970). Gettier refuted the traditional analysis of knowledge as justified true belief. He showed that a person can have justifying evidence for a belief that happens to be true as a result of a fortunate accident unrelated to that evidence. Such a proposition would not be known. Gettier concluded that justified true belief is not sufficient for knowledge.

With few exceptions, epistemologists responded to Gettier's work by seeking a fourth condition for knowledge. The search for this fourth condition dominated epistemology from the publication of Gettier's paper in 1963 until the mid-1970s. Some philosophers proposed that in any case of knowledge the justification for the belief is "undefeated," meaning roughly that there is no truth that would undermine the believer's evidence for the proposition. Others suggested that in cases of knowledge the justification never involves any falsehood. Others proposed that in cases of knowledge there is an appropriate causal connection between the person's evidence and the truth of the known proposition. Still others claimed that the knower "tracks the truth" of the known proposition, meaning that the person would believe the proposition if it were true and would not believe it if it were false. Counterexamples falsified the original versions of these analyses, increasingly complex analyses replaced the originals, and new sorts of counterexamples cast doubt on the new analyses. Epistemologists learned much about knowledge from these investigations, but they did not reach a consensus on a fourth condition.

In the 1970s epistemology focused on the justifying condition itself. Epistemologists developed and refined COHERENTISM [S] and FOUNDATIONALISM [S], the two traditional theories of justification. Foundationalists realized that they need not require that foundational beliefs be absolutely certain or infallible. They developed the idea that foundational beliefs need have only some degree of initial justification that is not supplied by other beliefs. Coherentists gave increasing attention to explanatory relations among beliefs as the basis for coherence. A popular coherentist position was that one gets justification by achieving reflective equilibrium—a mutual adjustment of beliefs about particular cases and beliefs about general principles covering these cases that maximizes explanatory relationships among them.

In his seminal paper, "What Is Justified Belief?," Alvin Goldman introduced a new approach to justification, RELIABILISM [6] (Moser, 1986). In its simplest version reliabilism holds that a belief is justified if and only if it is the product of a type of belief-forming process that generally leads to true beliefs. This view has been subject to intense critical scrutiny since its introduction in 1979. Critics identified two main sorts of problems. The first is that of adequately specifying the types of belief-forming processes to which the theory appeals. The second problem stems from the fact that seemingly unjustified beliefs can result from truth-conducive processes. In response to these and other problems, Goldman and others have revised and transformed reliabilism, sometimes drastically. In some of these theories justification depends upon other epistemic virtues in addition to reliability.

The 1980s also saw extensive discussion of the contrast between internalistic and externalistic accounts of justification (*see* INTERNALISM VERSUS EXTERNALISM [S]). Internalists hold that justification is determined by factors internal to the mind, while externalists impose no such restriction. A typical internalist theory is EVIDENTIALISM [S], which holds that the evidence the believer possesses determines the epistemic status of beliefs. Reliability theories exemplify the externalist viewpoint since they maintain that the external and contingent propensity toward truth of the process or mechanism leading to a belief helps to determine the belief's justification. Several philosophers have argued that the central epistemological considerations on both sides of this dispute can be reconciled.

NATURALISM [5; S] was another prominent topic among epistemologists in the 1980s and 1990s. The most frequently cited source of this trend is W. V. O. QUINE'S [7; S] 1969 paper, "Epistemology Naturalized" (Kornblith, 1994). A common reading of Quine's position takes him to advocate abandoning traditional epistemology and replacing it with the closest empirical discipline, cognitive psychology. Few philosophers defend this extreme view. However, many urge tying epistemology closely to empirical studies of human cognition. Those who think that epistemology is primarily devoted to recommending ways in which people can improve their reasoning contend that the empirical study of how people actually reason plays a crucial role in developing useful recommendations. Philosophers who believe that the primary role of epistemology is to analyze the concepts of knowledge, justification, and the like usually see less room for empirical input. But some epistemologists in this last group also advocate a form of NATURALIZED EPISTEMOLOGY [S] that requires analyzing central epistemic concepts in terms that they deem naturalistically legitimate.

Since 1960 philosophers have continued traditional debates about skepticism. Several new arguments appeared, each having its origin in work in the PHILOSOPHY OF LANGUAGE [S] or the PHILOSOPHY OF MIND [S]. One argument, due to Hilary PUTNAM [S], is an attempt to refute the much-discussed "brain-in-a-vat argument. A background assumption of this argument is that a human brain suspended in a vat of nutrients that keep it alive might receive computer-controlled electrical stimulation that duplicates the neural impulses to a brain in an ordinary head in an ordinary world (cf. Descartes's evil demon). The possibility of being such a brain in a vat is a premise in prominent arguments for SKEPTICISM [7; S]. The rest of the argument typically asserts that we cannot know anything about the external world because we cannot rule out the possibility of being a brain in a vat. On one interpretation, Putnam attacks these arguments by a special application of a causal view about reference. He thereby defends the thesis that what envatted brains, lacking all normal environmental interaction, would express by "I am a brain in a vat" would be a falsehood. What people in normal circumstances express by that sentence is also false. The sentence, therefore, does not express a truth, no matter what our actual situation. Thus, the sentence cannot serve as a premise in a successful argument for skepticism. Some critics dispute Putnam's use of the causal theory and deny that this attack refutes any argument for skepticism. Others contend that it refutes only skeptical arguments that are based on certain extreme versions of the brain-in-a-vat hypothesis.

A second new antiskeptical argument is due to Donald DAVIDSON [S], who argues that the possibility of interpretation rests on the assumption that most of what the interpreted person believes is true, or at least that the interpreted beliefs must mostly coincide with what the interpreter believes. Since it is possible for there to be an omniscient interpreter, any interpreted beliefs must largely coincide with those of such an interpreter. Thus, any interpreted believer must have mostly true beliefs. Consequently, skepticism cannot be defended on the basis of the possibility of massive error. Again, some critics deny that this argument is sound. Others reply that it refutes only skeptical arguments relying on the possibility of massive error, leaving untouched defenses of skepticism that rely on the possibility, with respect to each individual belief, that it is in error.

A new defense of a skeptical position derives from Saul KRIPKE's [S] interpretation of WITTGENSTEIN's [8; S] views concerning rules and private languages. Kripke contends that Wittgenstein in effect, if not by intention, offers a powerful skeptical argument. It threatens our knowledge of the meaning of our own expressions by casting doubt on the existence of the sort of meaning that those expressions otherwise seem to have. The central work of the argument is an attempt to show by an exhaustion of the plausible candidates that there can be no determinate fact as to the extension of any expression beyond its actual application. Critical responses to this argument propose candidates for meanings that do determine the full intuitive extension of our terms. No solution to the problem has been established.

Since 1960 formal work in epistemology has also advanced. Especially notable in this area is the development of and debate over Bayesian epistemology (*see* BAYESIANISM [S]). This approach defends the requirement that rational belief change proceed in accordance with the probability calculus, prominently including the constraint that Bayes's theorem imposes on processing new information.

Several new areas within epistemology emerged in the 1980s and 1990s. Feminist epistemologists contended that traditional epistemology would be enhanced, if not replaced, as a result of attending to feminist insights (*see* FEMINIST EPISTEMOLOGY [S]). Social epistemologists focused on the ways in which social factors affect knowledge and justification. Some philosophers even argued for the "death" of epistemology, contending that its traditional problems or concepts rely on false presuppositions. But the vigor of work, the proliferation of issues, and the liveliness of disputes in a field show its continuing life. A death notice for epistemology therefore seems premature.

(SEE ALSO: *Moral Epistemology; Pragmatist Epistemology; Subjectivist Epistemology;* and *Virtue Epistemology* [S])

Bibliography

Alcoff, L., and E. Potter, eds. *Feminist Epistemologies.* London, 1993.

Alston, W. *Epistemic Justification: Essays in the Theory of Knowledge.* Ithaca, NY, 1989.

BonJour, L. *The Structure of Empirical Knowledge.* Cambridge, MA, 1985.

Chisholm, R. *The Theory of Knowledge.* Englewood Cliffs, NJ, 1966; 2d. ed., 1977; 3d ed., 1989.

Davidson, D. "A Coherence Theory of Truth and Knowledge," in D. Henrich, ed., *Kant oder Hegel?* (Stuttgart, 1983).

Dretske, F. *Knowledge and the Flow of Information.* Cambridge, MA, 1981.

French, P., T. Uehling, and H. Wettstein, eds. *Studies in Epistemology,* Midwest Studies in Philosophy, Vol. 5 (Minneapolis, 1980).

Goldman, A. *Epistemology and Cognition.* Cambridge, MA, 1986.

Harman, G. *Change in View: Principles of Reasoned Revision.* Cambridge, MA, 1986.

Kornblith, H., ed. *Naturalizing Epistemology,* 2d ed. Cambridge, MA, 1994. Includes Quine's "Epistemology Naturalized."

Kripke, S. *Wittgenstein on Rules and Private Language.* Cambridge, MA, 1982.

Moser, P., ed. *Empirical Knowledge.* Savage, MD, 1986. Includes Gettier's "Is Justified True Belief Knowledge?" and Goldman's "What Is Justified Belief?

Nozick, R. "Epistemology," in *Philosophical Explanations* (Cambridge, MA, 1981).

Pappas, G., and M. Swain, eds. *Essays on Knowledge and Justification,* Ithaca, NY, 1978.

Plantinga, A. *Warrant: The Current Debate.* Oxford, 1992.

Putnam, H. "Brains in a Vat," in *Reason, Truth, and History* (Cambridge, 1981).

Rorty, R. *Philosophy and the Mirror of Nature.* Princeton, NJ, 1979.

Roth, M. D., and L. Galis, eds. *Knowing: Essays in the Analysis of Knowledge.* New York, 1970. Includes Gettier's "Is Justified True Belief Knowledge?"

Shope, R. K. *The Analysis of Knowing: A Decade of Research.* Princeton, NJ, 1983.

Sosa, E. *Knowledge in Perspective.* Cambridge, MA, 1991.

Stich, S. *The Fragmentation of Reason.* Cambridge, MA, 1990.

Tomberlin, J. E., ed. *Philosophical Perspectives,* Vol. 2 (1988). Special issue.

RICHARD FELDMAN
EARL CONEE

EPISTEMOLOGY, RELIGIOUS. The epistemology of religion, as practiced by philosophers, is seldom concerned with the sorts of epistemological questions that emerge on a practical level in ordinary religious life, such as how to determine the correct interpretation of a scriptural text or how to know whether someone's claim to special divine guidance is to be credited. Rather, it tends to focus on the epistemic evaluation of the most basic tenets of the religious worldview in question—the existence of God, the creation of the world and God's relation to it, and the possibility of recognizing divine action in the world and divine revelation. From the 1960s through the early 1990s, religious epistemology has been characterized by a marked decline of fideism, with a renewal of interest in evidentialism and an even more pronounced upsurge of what may be termed experientialism.

FIDEISM [3] is best characterized as the view that one's basic religious beliefs are not subject to independent rational evaluation. It is defended by urging that religious convictions are the most basic part of a believer's worldview and thus more fundamental than anything else that might be used to evaluate them. It is also said that to evaluate religious beliefs by standards other than the internal standards of the religious belief system itself is in effect to subject God to judgment and is thus a form of idolatry. In the mid-twentieth century fideism took two main forms, existentialism and Wittgensteinian fideism. In the succeeding decades philosophical EXISTENTIALISM [3; S] has suffered a massive decline, as has its theological counterpart, neo-orthodoxy. Wittgensteinian fideism, on the other hand, arose largely in response to the positivist contention that God-talk is cognitively meaningless; with the defeat of POSITIVISM [6] it has lost much of its relevance. Many religious thinkers, freed from the need to defend religion's cognitive meaningfulness, have felt a renewed impulse to contend for the truth of their faith. And on the other hand, critics of religion have moved readily from the contention that belief in God is meaningless to the logically incompatible assertion that it is false and/or lacking in evidential support.

Evidentialism is the view that religious beliefs, in order to be rationally held, must be supported by other things one knows or reasonably believes to be true. Evidentialist defenses of religion typically rely heavily on theistic arguments, and all of the classical arguments have seen renewed interest in the late twentieth century. Versions of the ONTOLOGICAL ARGUMENT [5] propounded by Charles Hartshorne, Norman Malcolm, and Alvin Plantinga are clearly valid, though their premises remain controversial. William Rowe's work has directed renewed attention to the Clarke-Leibniz version of the COSMOLOGICAL ARGUMENT [2], and new versions of the design argument (*see* TELEOLOGICAL ARGUMENT FOR THE EXISTENCE OF GOD [8]), focusing on God as the source of the basic laws of nature, have been developed by Richard Swinburne and others. Even the MORAL ARGUMENT [5] (Robert Adams) and the argument from RELIGIOUS EXPERIENCE [7; S] (Gary Gutting) have come in for renewed attention. Two new arguments, or versions of arguments, are keyed to developments in cosmology. The "kalam cosmological argument" (William Craig) uses big-bang cosmology to argue that the physical universe as a whole has a temporal beginning and thus is in need of an external cause. And the anthropic cosmological principle is used by John Leslie, among others, to support a new version of the design argument: the apparent fact that the basic laws and initial conditions of the universe are "fine tuned" for life, with no apparent scientific explanation for this fact, is taken as evidence of intelligent design. Both of these arguments benefit from their association with cutting-edge science but also in consequence become vulnerable to future changes in scientific thinking on cosmology.

Evidentialist arguments against religion take a variety of forms. Most basically, evidentialists argue that the theistic arguments are unsuccessful and that theism fails for lack of evidential support. There are various challenges to the coherence and logical possibility of the traditional divine attributes. In most cases, however, these arguments, if successful, lead to a reformulation of the attributes in question rather than to the defeat of THEISM [8] as such. But by far the most active area of consideration for antireligious evidentialism has been the problem of evil; the volume of writing on its various forms, by both critics and believers, has probably exceeded that on all of the theistic arguments taken together (*see* EVIL, PROBLEM OF [3; S]).

Along with the renewed consideration of the various arguments there have been reflections on the requirements for a successful argument. Traditional natural theology claimed to proceed from premises known or knowable to any reasonable person (e.g., "Some things are in motion") by means of arguments any reasonable person could see to be valid. By these standards it is not difficult to show that all of the arguments fail. But the standard is clearly too high; it is difficult to find significant arguments in any area of philosophy that meet it. No doubt a good argument should not be circular or question begging, and its premises must enjoy some kind of support that makes them at least plausible. But what seems plausible, or even evidently true, to one person may not seem so to another, equally rational, person; thus, the recognition emerges that arguments and proofs may be "person-relative" (Mavrodes, 1970). Furthermore, even a good argument is not necessarily decisive by itself, so it is necessary to consider the ways in which a number of arguments, none of them in itself conclusive, can lend their combined weight to establishing a conclusion. One model for this has been developed by Basil Mitchell, who compares arguments for religious beliefs to the kinds of cumulative-case arguments found in fields such as history and critical exegesis as well as in the choice between scientific paradigms. Richard Swinburne, on the other hand, builds a cumulative case for divine existence using the mathematical theory of PROBABILITY [6; S]. While it is not possible to assign precise numerical probabilities to the propositions involved in theistic argumentation, Bayes's theorem does provide insight into the way in which evidence contributes in a cumulative fashion to the support or defeat of a hypothesis such as theism (*see* BAYESIANISM [S]. On the other hand, John L. MACKIE [S] and Michael Martin have developed what are in effect cumulative-case arguments for ATHEISM [1].

EXPERIENTIALISM

The most significant development in the epistemology of religion during the 1980s and early 1990s was the rise of a new type of theory distinct from both fideism and evidentialism. This theory, found in the writings of Richard Swinburne, Alvin Plantinga, and William Alston, lacks a generally recognized label (the term "Reformed epistemology" properly applies only to Plantinga's version) but may be termed experientialism in view of its emphasis on the grounding of religious belief in religious experience. Experientialism differs from fideism in that it does not seek to insulate religious belief from critical epistemic evaluation; rather, it affirms that religious experience can provide a sound epistemic basis for such beliefs. Experientialism is also importantly different from the evidentialist "argument from religious experience" in the following respect: the religious experience is not first described in ontologically neutral terms and then made the basis for an inference to the existence of the religious object. On the contrary, the religious belief is grounded directly in the religious experience, without mediation by inference, just as perceptual beliefs are grounded directly in perceptual experience. This difference is important for a couple of reasons. For one thing it is more faithful to the phenomenology of both religious and perceptual belief: in typical cases neither form of belief involves such an inference. But more important, the direct grounding of belief in experience offers better prospects of a favorable epistemic status for the resulting beliefs than does the inferential approach. This is readily apparent in the case of perceptual experience: attempts at a "proof of the external world" have been notably unsuccessful, yet only those in the grip of philosophical theory doubt that we do in fact acquire a great deal of knowledge about the world through our perceptual experience. In the same way it is at least conceivable that believers acquire knowledge of God experientially even if no compelling inferential argument from religious experience is available.

Swinburne, Plantinga, and Alston share what may be termed a weak foundationalist approach to epistemology. That is to say, they accept the distinction between "basic" beliefs, which do not derive their rational acceptability from other beliefs, and "derived" beliefs, which gain their support from the basic beliefs. But they do not accept the traditional foundationalist restriction of basic beliefs to those that are nearly or entirely immune to doubt—beliefs that are self-evident, evident to the senses, or incorrigible. Each of them, furthermore, includes some religious beliefs in the category of basic beliefs. The epistemological task, then, is to show that this inclusion is epistemically proper—to show that such religious beliefs are among our "properly basic beliefs." (The terminology is Plantinga's, but the issue is the same for all three thinkers.) Each of them approaches this issue in a different way, though the approaches are ultimately compatible. Plantinga argues, following Roderick CHISHOLM [S], that the proper approach to the question of which beliefs are properly basic is inductive: one first conducts an inventory of the beliefs one takes oneself to hold rationally, then eliminates those that derive their epistemic support from other beliefs, and those that remain will be taken as properly basic. The typical Christian believer, Plantinga thinks, will find that she considers her belief in God to be rational but does not ground it inferentially on other beliefs she holds; thus, she will conclude that this is a properly basic belief. To be sure, atheists or believers in other religions will not concur in this, but Plantinga finds this to be unproblematic: "Followers of Bertrand Russell and Madalyn Murray O'Hair may disagree; but how is that relevant? Must my criteria, or those of the Christian community, conform to their examples? Surely not. The Christian community is responsible to *its* set of examples, not to theirs" (in Plantinga and Wolterstorff, 1983, p. 78).

In contrast with Plantinga's "internal" justification of the rationality of belief, both Swinburne and Alston attempt to show that religious experiences should have some epistemic weight, even for those who do not share the belief system the experiences ostensibly support. Swinburne appeals to the "principle of credulity," which states that "(in the absence of special considerations) if it seems (epistemically) to a subject that x is present, then probably x is present; what one seems to perceive is probably so" (1979, p. 254). He argues that a general denial of this principle lands us in a "sceptical bog" and that there is no justification for excluding religious experience from its scope. Alston, on the other hand, develops a "doxastic practice" approach to epistemology (indebted to both REID [7; S] and WITTGENSTEIN [8; S]), which holds that all socially established doxastic practices are "innocent until proved guilty"; "they all deserve to be regarded as prima facie rationally engaged in . . . pending a consideration of possible reasons for disqualification" (1991, p. 153). Alston's delineation of the "Christian mystical practice" and his defense of its epistemic status constitute a systematic, detailed, and highly sophisticated presentation of experientialism.

One major difficulty for experientialism is the existence of incompatible experientially grounded beliefs in different religions—in Alston's terms, the existence of a plurality of mutually incompatible mystical practices. Alston concludes that religious experience alone probably cannot resolve this ambiguity and that "the knowledgeable and reflective Christian should be concerned about the situation . . . [and] should do whatever seems feasible to search for common ground on which to adjudicate the crucial differences between the world religions, seeking a way to show in a non-circular way which of the contenders is correct. What success will attend these efforts I do not presume to predict. Perhaps it is only in God's good time that a more thorough insight into the truth behind these divergent perspectives will be revealed to us" (1991, p. 278). (*See* RELIGIOUS PLURALISM [S])

Critics, however, have urged more far-reaching objections to the experientialist program. According to Richard Gale, the analogy between religious experience and sense perception is weak, with the dissimilarities far outweighing the similarities. He also argues that religious experience could not be cognitive—that is, could not provide independent grounds for belief in the existence of its object—and that religious objects such as God or the One are not possible objects of perceptual experience, even if they exist. Alston, on the other hand, has argued in detail that the phenomenological structure of religious experience is perceptual and that "mystical perception" constitutes a genuine species of perception along with sense perception.

(SEE ALSO: *Philosophy of Religion; Theism, Arguments for and Against* [S])

Bibliography

Alston, W. P. *Perceiving God: The Epistemology of Religious Experience.* Ithaca, NY, 1991.

Gale, R. M. *On the Nature and Existence of God.* Cambridge, 1991.

Mackie, J. *The Miracle of Theism: Arguments for and against the Existence of God.* New York, 1982.

Martin, M. *Atheism: A Philosophical Justification.* Philadelphia, 1990.

Mavrodes, G. *Belief in God: A Study in the Epistemology of Religion.* New York, 1970.

Mitchell, B. *The Justification of Religious Belief.* New York, 1981.

Plantinga, A., and N. Wolterstorff, eds. *Faith and Rationality: Reason and Belief in God.* Notre Dame, IN, 1983.

Swinburne, R. *The Existence of God.* Oxford, 1979.

WILLIAM HASKER

EREIGNIS. *See:* BEITRÄGE ZUR PHILOSOPHIE (VOM EREIGNIS) [S]

ERROR THEORY. An error theory of ethics is the view that the ordinary user of moral language is typically making claims that involve a mistake. The concepts of ethics introduce a mistaken, erroneous, way of thinking of the world or of conducting practical reasoning. The theory was most influentially proposed by John L. MACKIE [S] in his book *Ethics: Inventing Right and Wrong* (1977). Mackie believed that ordinary moral claims presuppose that there are objective moral values, but there are no such things. Hence, the practice of morality is founded upon a metaphysical error.

Mackie's arguments against the existence of objective values are of two main kinds. One is the argument from relativity, which cites the familiar phenomenon of ethical disagreement. Another is the argument from 'queerness'. The moral values whose existence Mackie denies are presented as metaphysically strange facts. They are facts with a peculiar necessity built into them: their essence is that they make demands or exist as laws that 'must' be obeyed. In Kantian terms, the demands made by morality are thought of as categorical, "not contingent upon any desire or preference or policy or choice." The foundation of any such demands or laws in the natural world is entirely obscure. Hence, the right response of a naturalist is to deny that there can be such things. It should be noticed that this is not supposed to be an argument against any particular morality, for instance, one demanding honesty or fidelity, but against the entire scheme of thought of which particular ethical systems are examples.

Another influential theorist whose work bears some resemblance to Mackie's is Bernard Williams, whose *Ethics and the Limits of Philosophy* (1985) equally raises the doubt that ethics cannot possibly be what it purports to be, although Williams's own arguments are more specifically targeted on the morality of duty and obligation.

Responses to the error theory have taken several forms. Both the argument from relativity and that from queerness have been queried, the former on the grounds that, even if ethical opinions differ fundamentally, this does not prevent one from being right and the others wrong, and the latter mainly on the grounds that Mackie suffered from an oversimple, "scientistic" conception of the kind of thing a moral fact would have to be. Perhaps more fundamentally, it is not clear what clean, error-free practice the error theorist would wish to substitute for old, error-prone ethics. That is, assuming that people living together have a need for shared practical norms, then some way of expressing and discussing those norms seems to be needed, and this is all that ethics requires. Mackie himself saw that ethics was not a wholly illegitimate branch of thought, for he gave a broadly Humean picture of its function in human life. Even projectivists maintain that our need to express attitudes, coordinate policies, and censure transgressions is a sufficient justification for thinking in terms of ethical demands. Ethics does not invoke a strange world of metaphysically dubious facts but serves a natural human need.

(SEE ALSO: *Ethical Theory* [S])

Bibliography

Mackie, J. L. *Ethics: Inventing Right and Wrong.* Middlesex, 1977.

Blackburn, S. "Errors and the Phenomenology of Value," in *Essays in Quasi-Realism* (New York, 1994).

Williams, B. *Ethics and the Limits of Philosophy*. Cambridge, MA, 1985.

SIMON BLACKBURN

ESP PHENOMENA, PHILOSOPHICAL IMPLICATIONS OF. Since the original *Encyclopedia* article was written, the empirical landscape in parapsychology has changed substantially. For one thing, that article dealt extensively with S. G. Soal's ESP experiments, some of which have since been tainted by evidence of fraud and all of which now must be treated as nonevidential. Since that time, however, parapsychological researchers have introduced some ingenious methodological innovations and research initiatives, and they have amassed a provocative body of new evidence.

Probably the most impressive recent research into ESP has been the "ganzfeld" experiment, pioneered by the late Charles Honorton. This type of experiment evolved from dream telepathy experiments conducted at Maimonides Hospital in Brooklyn. Unlike the forced-choice experiments that characterized the research of Rhine and Soal, in which the subject's task was to make simple target identifications from a fixed set of presented alternatives (as in card-guessing tests), the ganzfeld experiment is a free-response test. In this type of test the subject does not know what the possible targets are, and instead of mere target identifications the subject's task is to describe the target or reproduce it (say, by drawing).

Subjects in ganzfeld experiments, located in an acoustically isolated room, have Ping-Pong ball halves taped over their eyes, and they listen to white noise through stereo headphones. This state of moderate sensory deprivation presents subjects with a relatively homogeneous visual and auditory field, the purpose of which is to quiet major sources of sensory stimulation or distraction and thereby allow other mental processes (including those produced by psychic functioning) to emerge more clearly. After describing their mental imagery for about thirty minutes, subjects view a set of pictures randomly selected from a larger target pool for the entire experimental series, one of which was viewed during the experiment by a remote "sender." The subject then tries to identify which picture was the target for that experiment by ranking all of the pictures in the set. In some cases outside judges also rank transcripts of the subject's mentation reports against the possible targets.

Beginning in the 1980s the ganzfeld experiments were subjected to a series of meta-analyses. Although these have not silenced debate about whether the experiments demonstrate the existence of ESP, even some well-known critics of parapsychology have conceded that the meta-analyses demonstrates a rather robust effect across the entire body of experiments. In one analysis Honorton examined twenty-eight studies using only the direct-hit method of scoring (in which the target picture is ranked first out of the set presented to the subject). These twenty-eight experiments included a total of 835 ganzfeld trials conducted in ten different laboratories, and 43 percent produced significant results. The odds against that result occurring by chance are greater than one billion to one. Honorton also addressed what psychologist Robert Rosenthal has called the "file drawer problem," by estimating how many unreported nonsignificant studies there would have to be in order to cancel out this effect. Honorton found that the total number of direct-hit experiments would have to be 451 (rather than twenty-eight), 423 of which were unknown to parapsychologists. Considering that only a small number of scientists work in the field of parapsychology, only some of whom do ganzfeld experiments, and considering also that the ganzfeld experiment is a time-consuming process, it seems likely that there is no file-drawer problem in this case. Honorton and critic Ray Hyman agreed on a set of stringent standards for future ganzfeld work, and the initial results of automated ganzfeld experiments adhering to those standards showed an effect size similar to that found in the original data base of experiments.

Research in psychokinesis (PK) has also charted a new direction during this period. The problem with experiments on tossed dice, coins, and other objects is that it is not clear to what extent those processes are random. For example, the outcome of falling dice depends on many factors that cannot be adequately controlled and are too obscure or complex to permit an accurate assessment of the statistical properties of a series of such falls. These include the physical properties of the tumbler, the initial position of the dice, the material out of which the dice are made, and the number of times the dice are shaken and allowed to tumble. So the "new wave" of PK research looked for effects on simple random processes whose statistical properties were well known. The leading figure in this body of work is physicist Helmut Schmidt, who initially conducted a series of successful experiments using radioactive decay, and then thermal noise, as sources of randomness.

Predictably, Schmidt's work was criticized. Hansel argued that Schmidt's experiments should be dismissed simply because they did not eliminate all possibility of fraud. But even other critics of parapsychology (such as Hyman) have noted that this standard of acceptability would lead to the rejection of virtually every scientific experiment. The more relevant issue is whether there are good reasons for thinking that fraud actually occurred, and no one has supported that charge in connection with Schmidt's work. A more frequent criticism (echoed by Gardner) is that Schmidt's work has not been replicated. But in 1989, Radin and Nelson published a careful meta-analysis of this so-called "micro-PK" work, which covered 597 experimental studies and 235 control studies from sixty-eight different investigators. According to their calculations, the odds of the robust effect they found occurring by chance are approximately 10^{35} to 1.

Perhaps the most philosophically intriguing micro-PK research concerns tests (again pioneered by Schmidt) using prerecorded targets and appearing (at least on the surface) to demonstrate a form of retrocausality. The form for a typical experiment of this sort is as follows. Suppose that on day 1 a binary random generator is automatically activated (in the absence of anyone present) to record sequences of heads and tails onto audio cassettes, heads in the right channel and tails in the left. Suppose twenty such cassettes are recorded, and also that a duplicate record of heads and tails is simultaneously produced on paper punch tape for the purpose of a permanent record. Then on day 2, half of the cassettes are selected by a random process to be test tapes, and the other cassettes are then designated as control tapes. At this point no one knows the contents of any of the tapes. On day 3, the ten test tapes are played back to a subject who thinks he is taking a normal PK test with spontaneously generated targets. The numbers of heads and tails are added up (and a duplicate record again made on punch tape), and it turns out that the test tapes contain a statistically signficant excess of heads over tails. Then the control tapes are examined for the first time, and it turns out that they contain only chance levels of heads and tails (and also that they match the punch-tape record for day 1). But the only difference between the test and control tapes is that the test tapes were played for a subject making a PK effort. So it appears that the subject's effort on day 3 biased the random generator on day 1 to produce an excess of heads only for the test tapes (whose selection as test tapes, recall, was not decided until later). (SEE ALSO: *ESP Phenomena, Philosophical Implications of* [3])

Bibliography

Braude, S. E. *ESP and Psychokinesis: A Philosophical Examination.* Philadelphia, 1979.

———. *The Limits of Influence: Psychokinesis and the Philosophy of Science.* London, 1991.

Gardner, M. *Science: Good, Bad, and Bogus.* Buffalo, NY, 1981.

Hansel, C. E. M. *ESP and Parapsychology: A Critical Reevaluation.* Buffalo, NY, 1980.

Honorton, C. "Meta-Analysis of Psi Ganzfeld Research: A Response to Hyman," *Journal of Parapsychology,* Vol. 49 (1985), 51–91.

———, et al. "Psi Communication in the Ganzfeld: Experiments with an Automated Testing System and a Comparison with a Meta-Analysis of Earlier Studies," *Journal of Parapsychology,* Vol. 54 (1990), 99–140.

Hyman, R. "Further Comments on Schmidt's PK Experiments," *Skeptical Inquirer,* Vol. 5 (1981), 34–40.

———. "The Ganzfeld Psi Experiment: A Critical Appraisal," *Journal of Parapsychology,* Vol. 49 (1985), 3–49.

———, and C. Honorton. "A Joint Communiqué: The Psi Ganzfeld Controversy," *Journal of Parapsychology,* Vol. 50 (1986), 351–64.

Markwick, B. "The Soal-Goldney Experiments with Basil Shackleton: New Evidence of Data Manipulation," *Proceedings of the Society of Psychical Research,* Vol. 56 (1978), 250–77.

Radin, D. I., and R. D. Nelson. "Consciousness-Related Effects in Random Physical Systems," *Foundations of Psychics,* Vol. 19 (1989), 1499–1514.

Rosenthal, R. "Meta-Analytic Procedures and the Nature of Replication: The Ganzfeld Debate," *Journal of Parapsychology,* Vol. 50 (1986), 315–36.

Schmidt, H. "PK Effect on Pre-Recorded Targets," *Journal of the American Society for Psychical Research,* Vol. 70 (1976), 267–91.

Scott, C. "Comment on the Hyman–Honorton Debate," *Journal of Parapsychology,* Vol. 50 (1986), 349–50.

STEPHEN E. BRAUDE

ETHICAL EGOISM. Generally defined as the view that one ought to do whatever and only whatever is in one's own maximum interest, benefit, advantage, or good, ethical egoism contrasts with (1) psychological egoism, which says that people do in fact, perhaps necessarily, act in that way; and from (2) alternative ethical theories, which claim that we have other fundamental obligations such as to act for the sake of others, even at ultimate cost to ourselves, or in ways having no necessary relation to anyone's benefit.

Egoism strikes many as cutting through pretenses and getting down to fundamentals. This appearance soon dissipates when we make essential distinctions. Foremost is that due to the classic work of Bishop BUTLER [1] (1692–1752). Is "self-interest" in that theory to be understood as one's interest in certain states unique to one's own self—as distinct from certain states of other people? Or is it merely interests of one's own self—the interests one happens to have, whatever they may be? Since action is necessarily motivated by interests of the agent motivated by them, the second interpretation is trivial: whatever we do, we are somehow interested in doing it. But the first interpretation is implausible: people are notoriously capable of sacrificing themselves—for friends, loved ones, or causes.

Ethical egoism would also be vacuous if it said only that whatever we ought to do, we ought to do it only if we are motivated to do it. Only when self-interest is construed in the narrow sense, as describing certain of our interests—those focused specifically on oneself—but not others, does it make sense to say that we ought to act self-interestedly. Then the question "Why?" arises, for we have our choice.

This brings up the question of what is the ultimate good or interest of an agent. Alas, we must leave this important issue open in the present discussion. The next question, however, is crucial. What is meant by "ethical"? Here we must distinguish between a wide sense in which "ethical" means something like "rational" and a narrower sense in which specifically moral requirements are intended. I should choose Bordeaux 1989, but that isn't a moral matter; that I should refrain from cheating is.

If ethical egoism is understood in the wider sense, it is a theory about rational behavior; and construing self-interest in Butler's second way, egoism says that a rational agent acts so as to maximize the realization of whatever she or he is interested in attaining. This highly plausible idea is noncommittal about the content of our interests.

Now turn to the moral version. Moral rules call upon us all to do or refrain from certain things, whether we like it or not. Can there be a rational egoistic morality, then?

But the interests of different persons can conflict. This leads to a problem, which becomes clear when we distinguish two possible interpretations of moral egoism:

1. "First-person" egoism appraises all actions of all persons on the basis of the interests of the propounder alone. What Jim Jones thinks, if he is this kind of an egoist, is not only that Jim Jones ought to do whatever, and only whatever, conduces to Jim Jones's best interests—but that everyone else should, too. This is consistent, to be sure, but from the point of view of anyone except Jim or his devotees, it is evidently irrational, if they too are self-interested.
2. "General" egoism, on the other hand, says that each person ought to do whatever is in that person's interests. If Jim is an egoist of this type, he believes that Jim ought to do whatever is in Jim's interests, but Sheila ought to do whatever is in Sheila's interests, and so on.

Serious conceptual problems arise with general egoism. Suppose that Jim's interests conflict with Sheila's: realizing his frustrates hers. Does Jim tell Sheila that it is Sheila's duty to do what's in Sheila's interests? Or what's in Jim's interests? Or both? Every answer is unacceptable! The first is unacceptable to Jim himself: how can he, as an exclusively self-interested person, support actions of Sheila's that are detrimental to himself? The second is unacceptable to Sheila: If she is exclusively self-interested, why would she take Jim's "advice"? And the third is flatly inconsistent: for their interests to "conflict" means that they cannot both do what is in their own best interest.

A standard reply is to hold that egoism tells each of the differing parties merely to try to do what is in their interests. But this is either just wrong or turns the theory into something else: "Here, all you ought to do is try to bring about your best interests—but it doesn't matter whether you succeed!" But self-interested agents are interested in results.

Or it might be held that the good life consists not in succeeding but in striving. This turns egoism into a game, and in conflict situations, a competitive game. And games are interesting, but also very special, requiring players to abide by certain game-defining rules. True chess-players do not cheat, even if they can—cheating is not really playing the game. They want opponents to do their best, even if they themselves lose. Of course, they prefer to win, but even if they do not, the game is worthwhile. This defense lacks generality. Ethical egoism is not about games, it is about life. Some people may make life into a game, but most people do not. They want results, not just effort; in conflicts, they are not about to cheer for the other side.

So egoism seems to be self-defeating. What to do? The answer requires, first, that we utilize the vital distinction between egoism as (1) a theory of rationality—of what is recommended by reason; and (2) as a theory of morality. The latter is interpersonal, and concerns rules for groups. Such rules require that people sometimes curtail their passions and conform to the rules.

If we view egoism as a theory of rationality, then whether agent A should aim only at bringing about certain states of A is an open question. But that A should aim at bringing about only those states of affairs that A values is not: we can act only on our own values—in acting, we make them our own.

But when we turn to the subject of formulating specifically moral principles, we must attend to the facts of social life. From the point of view of any rational individual, moralities are devices for securing desirable results not attainable without the cooperation of others. To do this, mutual restrictions must be accepted by all concerned. They will be accepted only if they conduce to the agent's interests. Therefore, moral principles, if rational, must be conducive to the interests of all, those to whom they are addressed as well as those of the propounder herself. Thus, egoism leads to contractarianism (qv): moral principles are those acceptable to each person, given that person's own interests, if all comply. Undoubtedly, some will not; but noncompliance, as Hobbes observed, leads to war, which is worse for all.

Rational egoism, then, leads to the abandonment of moral egoism. Sensible people will condemn egotism, and regard selfishness as a vice: we do better if we care about each other, engage in mutually beneficial activity, and thus refrain from one-sided activity that tramples upon others, such as killing, lying, cheating, stealing, or raping. The core of truth in egoism leads to a fairly familiar morality, whose principles must cash out in terms of the good of every agent participating in society. Narrowly egoistic moral principles cannot do this, and thus are the first to be rejected by rational egoists—another of those fascinating paradoxes of which philosophy is full.

(SEE ALSO: *Egoism and Altruism* [2])

Bibliography

Baier, K. *The Moral Point of View*. Ithaca, NY, 1958. Chapter 8, sections 1–4.

Butler, J. *Sermons* [London, 1726], Preface, I, and XI.

Hobbes, T. *Leviathan* [London, 1651], Chapters VI, XIII–XV.

Fumerton, R. A. *Reason and Morality: A Defense of the Egocentric Perspective*. Ithaca, NY, 1990.

Gauthier, D. *Morals by Agreement.* Oxford, 1986. Chapters I, II, VI, VII.

Kalin, J. "Two Kinds of Moral Reasoning: Ethical Egoism as a Moral Theory," *Canadian Journal of Philosophy* 5 (1975), 323–56.

Medlin, B. "Ultimate Principles and Ethical Egoism," *Australian Journal of Philosophy,* Vol. 35 (1957), 111–18.

Plato. *Republic.* Books 1, 2.

JAN NARVESON

ETHICAL THEORY. In the decades leading up to the 1960s, the main focus of analytical moral philosophy was not on normative ethical issues of the GOOD [3] and the right but on 'second order', metaethical questions about ethical discourse and thought. Philosophers by and large accepted a distinction between questions concerning ethical concepts, which can be investigated by analyzing the meanings of ethical language, and (normative) ethical issues posed with those concepts and vocabulary. This analytic turn was stimulated, first, by G. E. MOORE's [5] influential argument in *Principia Ethica* (1903) that clarity about what ethical questions ask is necessary before attempting to answer them and, second, from the 1930s on, by a Wittgensteinian conception of philosophy as conceptual and linguistic analysis (*see* WITTGENSTEIN, LUDWIG J. J. [8; S]). Reinforcing these was the fact that the ascendant metaethical view during this latter period was NONCOGNITIVISM [S], the position that ethical discourse is not fact stating but expressive of states of mind that lack truth values: pro- and con- attitudes, desires, preferences, or feelings. The apparent consequence was that moral philosophy could itself be cognitive only by being restricted to metaethics.

In the 1950s and 1960s various challenges arose to the dominance of noncognitivism as well as to the paradigm of conceptual analysis. On the former front, Elizabeth ANSCOMBE [S] and Philippa Foot argued that ethical language cannot float entirely free of naturalistic criteria. Peter Geach pointed to difficulties noncognitivism faces in accounting for ethical discourse's apparently fact-stating logical structure. W. D. Falk, Kurt Baier, and Stephen Toulmin argued that ethical judgments express convictions about which attitudes are warranted by reasons, not attitudes themselves. Richard Brandt and Roderick Firth maintained along similar lines that ethical discourse is conceptually tied to *idealized* attitudes—those an "ideal observer" would have. Finally, and also to a similar effect, John RAWLS [S] argued that consensus about the characteristics of good ethical judges permits treating their considered judgments as evidence for normative ethical propositions and theories.

At the same time the general dominance of conceptual analysis in philosophy was being shaken by forceful arguments of W. V. O. QUINE [7; S] and Nelson GOODMAN [3; S] that no principled distinction exists between conceptual, definitional issues and substantive ones. Restricting moral philosophy to metaethics began to look arbitrary at best.

The momentum created by these events increased exponentially (in the United States, especially) with the publication of John Rawls's *A Theory of Justice* in 1971. Although primarily a work in political philosophy, Rawls's book was also read as a general program for normative ethical theory. Following Quine and Goodman, the rejection of a sharp theory/observation distinction in the PHILOSOPHY OF SCIENCE [6; S], and his own earlier work on ethical judgment, Rawls argued that the test of a normative theory should be whether it can be held in "reflective equilibrium" with considered ethical judgments as well as with other relevant beliefs, including empirical theory and other philosophical convictions. The normative theorist's task is thus to articulate principles and ideals that organize and explicate considered convictions.

Rawls's own normative theory, 'justice as fairness', was an impressive example. It had two ordered principles: one mandating a system of equal basic liberties and a second requiring that the social distribution of other 'primary goods' work to the greatest benefit of the least advantaged. Rawls argued that these principles fit better than any traditional theory (specifically, better than utilitarianism) with considered judgments about justice as well as with a compelling underlying philosophical rationale—namely, that they would be rationally chosen over utilitarianism and other rivals from a perspective (the 'original position') in which hypothetical choosers were deprived of information about themselves (the 'veil of ignorance'), except interests they have as 'free and equal moral persons' (*see* JUSTICE [4; S]).

A Theory of Justice thus represented a major systematic, deontological alternative to UTILITARIANISM [8], at least so far as questions of justice are concerned. Utilitarianism's critics had usually been content to lodge specific objections, or to defend some set of specific deontological principles, saying little about how these might fit together or be unified by some underlying rationale. By arguing that his principles were rationally choiceworthy from a perspective expressing an ideal of moral persons as free and equal, moreover, Rawls initiated a 'constructivist' interpretation of Kant's ethics that both reinvigorated serious interest in KANT [4; S] and articulated themes of equal dignity and autonomy that resonated profoundly in normative ethical thought of the period, both in the academy and in the wider culture (see CONSTRUCTIVISM, MORAL [S]).

Throughout the next decade, normative ethics flourished in a way unprecedented in this century. But, much as analytical metaethics had driven out normative theory earlier, so during the 1970s was normative theory frequently practiced with little thought of metaethics. No doubt this was due in part to pent-up demand and to reaction against what was increasingly viewed as the sterile and misguided project of conceptual analysis. Encouraged by the method of reflective equilibrium, writers explored specific, 'applied' normative issues no less than general theory by appeal to considered convictions they hoped their readers would share.

Still, even if conceptual analysis remained mostly a dead letter, fundamental questions concerning the metaphysical and epistemological status of ethics could not be wished away. One nagging question, posed pointedly by Philippa Foot, concerned morality's normative force. Even if we accept a particular theory of justice on reflection, we can nonetheless ask why we should be just. Common sense may agree with Kant that morality (justice included) binds categorically, but it can still be asked whether or why this is so. And, Foot replied, the most plausible response is to hold that moral imperatives do *not* bind categorically; their force is only hypothetical, conditional on their furthering the agent's concerns. Philosophers such as Thomas Nagel, David Gauthier, and Kurt Baier argued to the contrary, but more of this below.

By the end of the decade, a number of events transpired to put metaethical concerns back at the center of philosophical discussion, although by no means to the exclusion of normative theory. J. L. MACKIE [S] argued startlingly that rejecting noncognitivism—a step with which he agreed—leads ultimately to the 'ERROR THEORY' [S]: the conclusion that all ethical judgments are false. Ethical judgments, he held, attribute properties that are simply too "queer" to exist, since they would have simultaneously to be actual and intrinsically action guiding. How, he asked, could 'to-be-doneness' be part of the "furniture of the universe"? It is we who *project* ethical properties onto the world: we see things *as* having these properties, though they do not in fact. According to Mackie, ethical discourse and practice can proceed despite the massive error it is committed to, but many doubted that this could be so. For them, Mackie's argument from "queerness" stood as a challenge to the viability of ethics itself.

In a not dissimilar vein, Gilbert Harman argued that ethics faces a "problem" that empirical theory does not. Empirical observations can count as evidence of postulated theoretical properties and entities because the relevant theories provide the best explanation of these very observations. A scientist who takes her visual experience before a laboratory monitor as evidence of the existence of a proton, for example, is likely to believe that the proton's existing explains, because it causes, her having the visual experience she does. But it is hard to see how a similar relation could hold between considered ethical convictions and the ethical theories they might be thought to confirm. Which ethical convictions we have appears to have more to do with facts about us than with which ethical propositions, if any, are actually true. But if that is so, what justifies treating considered convictions as evidence?

Worries of these sorts, coupled with the concern, raised by Brandt and R. M. HARE [S], that ethical 'intuitions' are especially susceptible to infection by prejudice, ideology, and superstition, led to an emerging sense that the viability of normative theory rested ultimately on metaethical issues that could not be indefinitely postponed. The fifteen years that followed saw a reinvigoration of metaethics, although less of conceptual analysis than of more directly metaphysical and epistemological inquiry. Normative theory has thrived also, but especially through the attempt to connect it to issues of fundamental philosophical rationale. This entry's subject, however, is primarily the former phenomenon.

This new life in metaethics has tended to take two different forms dictated by different responses to the problem of placing ethics in relation to the realm of natural fact and empirical method. One trend accepts the challenge in these terms. It holds that ethical methods are continuous with those of science; ethical theories can fit the ethical facts no less than a theory in natural science can fit the facts of nature. Better: ethical facts *are* natural facts, even if ethics is a distinct discipline from, say, psychology. The second insists that the methods and object of ethics are fundamentally different from those of empirical theory but denies that this makes ethics problematic. Prominent among the first trend have been various forms of realist ethical naturalism, both reductionist and nonreductionist (*see* MORAL NATURALISM [S]). The second trend has collected a wide diversity of approaches: practical reasoning theories (*see* PRACTICAL REASON APPROACHES [S]), less rationalist forms of constructivism, SENSIBILITY THEORIES [S], and new forms of noncognitivism.

ETHICAL NATURALISM [3] had been a prominent casualty early in the century of Moore's arguments in *Principia Ethica,* as well as of the noncognitivist lines of thought these inspired. Naturalism commits the naturalistic fallacy, Moore influentially charged, although it was never clear how any logical error could be involved. More persuasive was what became known as the "open question" argument. Intrinsic value cannot be a natural property, Moore argued, since, for any natural property, it always remains an "open question" whether something having it is good. Later, noncognitivists such as STEVENSON [S] and Hare also deployed forms of this thought. The reason that ethical questions remain logically open even when no issue of natural fact remains, Hare argued, is that the former directly engage noncognitive attitudes of commendation and prescription. What is at issue is noncognitive—what to commend or prescribe, not what is the case.

With the undermining of confidence in the analytic/synthetic distinction and in the project of conceptual analysis it underwrote, however, stock in the "open question" argument began to fall. At the same time, important new work in the PHILOSOPHY OF LANGUAGE [S] of Hilary PUTNAM and Saul KRIPKE [S] appeared to show that different terms can refer to the same substance or property even if they have different meanings to ordinary speakers. The function of a term such as 'water', for example, is to refer to whatever it is that flows in the rivers and streams. And it can be a later, substantial discovery that 'H_2O' refers to the very same stuff. From the fact that, at some point, whether water is H_2O is not closed by ordinary meaning it can hardly follow that they are not the same thing. Maybe the same relation could hold between ethical properties and other natural features.

Once these insights were imported into metaethics, ethical naturalism began to find new defenders and new life. There had already been significant movements in this direction. In the late 1950s, for example, Foot had begun to work out a neo-Aristotelian naturalistic alternative to noncognitivism. The new naturalists, however, were characterized by a closer tie to contemporary philosophies of science and language and a desire to use these tools to exhibit a continuity between ethics and the natural sciences.

Thinkers within this broad category include Richard Boyd, Nicholas Sturgeon, David Brink, Gilbert Harman, Richard Brandt, and Peter Railton. They are united by a commitment to metaphysical and methodological naturalism and, with the possible exception of Brandt, to MORAL REALISM [S]. In this context, realism differs from cognitivism—the thesis that ethical claims admit of truth value—or even from the additional proposition that some ethical claims are true. Like scientific realism, moral realism holds that ethical facts exist independently of any access we might have to them and that ethical claims and theories are true when they fit the ethical facts. Naturalist moral realism holds, traditionally, that these ethical facts are natural facts.

The new naturalist realists divide on the issue of the reducibility of ethical properties. One group, represented by Boyd, Sturgeon, and Brink, argue from postpositivist theses in the philosophies of science and language to the conclusion that ethical properties can be both natural and irreducible to properties confirmable by any natural science (other than ethics). Only by discreditable positivist criteria, they claim, does ethics itself not qualify as a natural science. The second group holds, by contrast, that ethical properties must earn objectivity and existence "the old-fashioned" (not to say positivist) way—by some form of reducibility to properties confirmable by the (other) natural sciences. Harman, Railton, and Brandt are in this group.

An important area of debate between these two groups concerns the epistemological status of considered ethical convictions or 'intuitions'. While the postpositivist nonreductionists believe that only by discreditable positivist criteria do ethical intuitions not count as genuine observations, the reductive naturalists take Harman's problem seriously. A nonreductionist such as Sturgeon responds to Harman's problem by saying that ethical facts can indeed explain ethical "observations" in the same way such explanations work in science. For example, that moral opposition to slavery arose only in the eighteenth and nineteenth centuries, despite slavery's long previous history, and then primarily in anglophone and francophone countries, is explainable by the fact that the chattel slavery practiced in English- and French-speaking parts of the New World was worse than earlier and other forms. It is, Sturgeon insists, this ethical fact that best explains the difference in opposition, and, as well, differences in ethical observations or considered judgments people were disposed to make at the time. To this it can be objected that there must have been features of chattel slavery that made it worse than other forms and that it is these, and not the fact of their being worse-making, that explain the differential judgment and opposition. However, the latter explanations may not drive out the former.

This line of thought may help to establish the reality of properties to which ethical vocabulary can refer, but do these exhaust the content of ethical thought and discourse? If, like 'water', ethical terms refer to natural kinds, then the force of Moore's open-question argument is blunted. However, the open question has shown remarkable staying power among philosophers. And the explanation may be that ethical terms have a normative content that is intrinsically regulative of action, feelings, and attitudes. While the function of 'water' is to refer to a natural kind in the causal order, the most general ethical terms, at least, seem less to concern what or how things are in fact than how to respond or act in the face of that.

Reductionist naturalists divide the tasks of securing ethical properties' reality and of establishing their normativity, giving the latter a weight the nonreductionists tend not to. And they generally attempt to do the latter by identifying ethical qualities with natural properties that guarantee an *internalist* connection to motivation or various affective states. In this way they seek to capture the action-, desire-, or emotion-*guiding* character of ethical properties. Taking off from an idea of Brandt's, for example, Peter Railton identifies a person's intrinsic good with what a maximally knowledgeable, experienced, and imaginative extension of that person *would want* for her actual self. Such a claim can be taken either as a synthetic identity thesis or, as Brandt and Railton propose, as a linguistic reform that both satisfies ("old fashioned") naturalist scruples and also secures the normativity of ethical thought and discourse—or, at least, that accomplishes the latter to its closest naturalistic approximation.

A distinctive mark of philosophers who see ethics as fundamentally discontinuous with science is that they deny that ethical properties can be both normative and naturalistic. Recent practical-reasoning theorists, for example, see a discontinuity between the natural and the intrinsically action guiding as arising because of a fundamental difference of perspective—that between the point of view of an observer aiming to describe and understand an independent natural order and the practical perspective of an agent deliberating about what to do. One group, which includes Thomas Nagel, Alan Gewirth, Stephen Darwall, and Christine Korsgaard, have attempted to work out Kantian versions of this approach, arguing that ethical norms are norms of free practical reason. A second, including Kurt Baier and David Gauthier, have pursued a more Hobbesian line. All agree, however, that because it is essentially practical, ethical discourse's truth and objectivity conditions differ fundamentally from those for theoretical disciplines; they must be somehow internal to practical reasoning itself.

For example, Nagel initially argued that any discourse that is not solipsistic must satisfy the constraint that a person be able to make the same judgment of herself from an objective standpoint that she can from her own egocentric point of view. When, however, this is combined with the practical character of deliberative ethical judgments—their intrinsic connection to motivation—Nagel argued that there follows a formal constraint on admissible reasons for acting. Any valid reason must be agent-neutral (e.g., that this will be in someone's interest) rather than agent-relative (that this will be in my—or, indeed, in your—interest); its applicability must not shift with a shift in the agent's point of view. More recently, Nagel has retreated from this strong claim and in a direction that is arguably even more Kantian. Autonomous agency, he now argues, involves an agent's acting on reasons he can reflectively endorse from an objective standpoint, and such a set of reasons can include both agent-relative and agent-neutral ones.

Common to all these Kantian approaches has been the idea that free practical reasoning has a formal structure, with its own internal standards or constraints, and that these provide the truth and objectivity conditions for ethical thought and discourse. Thus, Gewirth maintains that fundamental moral principles are derivable from propositions to which a rational agent is committed from within her deliberative standpoint in acting. And Korsgaard argues that even those who advance "Humean," instrumental theories must believe that practical reasoning requires at least this much form. Once this is admitted, the Kantians hope, debate can take place on a new plane: Is means/end reasoning sufficient for the deliberation of genuine agents? Since, as agents, we regard ourselves as free to adopt and renounce ends, and since what lies behind instrumental reasoning—the hypothetical imperative—is simply a consistency constraint that can be realized as well by renouncing any particular end as by taking means to achieve it, they argue that free practical reasoning requires a formal principle regulating the choice of ends no less than that of means. Agents do things for (and not just because of) reasons and in doing so commit themselves to principles as valid for all. But such a commitment is not, the Kantians claim, a hypothesis about some independently existing order of normative fact to which we might have (theoretical) cognitive access. So the standards to which deliberation is subject must be internal to free practical reasoning itself. But this is possible, they argue, only if practical reasoning is regulated by the categorical imperative: a rule requiring action only on principles that can be willed to regulate the deliberations of all.

Gauthier and Baier reject Kantianism's formalism and apriorism. Both start with the premise that practical rationality must work to the agent's benefit but deny that any purely instrumental or egoistic theory follows from this. Baier argues this is so because a correct theory of RATIONALITY [S] cannot be collectively self-defeating, and everyone's acting according to unrestricted self-interest would be mutually disadvantageous. Gauthier rejects this constraint but puts forward another: a theory of rationality cannot be individually self-defeating. The correct theory is one a rational agent would regulate herself by, where a rational agent is one whose rational character—her dispositions to be guided by deliberative principles—is best suited to benefit her. To the extent that our characters are translucent to each other, it will be advantageous to be disposed to constrain self-interest by the requirements of mutually advantageous agreements, since only then will others enter into such agreements with us. This gives Gauthier an opening to argue that at least some aspects of morality are objective, categorical constraints. However, it may be asked of these Hobbesian approaches what the source of their respective self-defeat conditions can be if not some prior account of (free) rational agency?

T. M. Scanlon's constructive contractualism represents another attempt to establish morality's objectivity as a regime of practical reasoning, but without Kantian ambitions. What stands behind morality, Scanlon holds, is "the desire to be able to justify one's actions to others on grounds they could not reasonably reject." An action is wrong if it is contrary to rules no one could reasonably reject to govern their mutual relations. The authority of this moral category, its normative force, derives from the fact that to do what is wrong is to go against the deep desire to be able to justify oneself to others. It follows, however, that although someone having this desire may still apply moral terms to anyone who lacks it, the normative force of this attribution will remain unsecured—there may be no reason why the other person should avoid what one judges to be wrong.

Constructivist and practical-reasoning approaches lay great stress on the role of freely chosen principle, more, it may seem, than ethics can possibly bear. Frequently we discover our ethical convictions, not so much in recognizing principles to which we are or should be committed but through sentiment and response. For sensibility theorists, such as David Wiggins and John McDowell, the epistemology of ethics is modeled more on perception than on anything like working out what rules satisfy various formal or material constraints. Following a broadly Aristotelian outlook, they argue that ethical aspects of situations are there to be seen, at least when these are viewed in the light of the affective responses that virtuous persons have to them.

Perceiving ethical properties is not like detecting aspects of the causal structure of the world. Rather, like color and other so-called secondary qualities, ethical properties are tied to specific human sensibilities, sensibilities we might have lacked without any loss of rationality or capacity to detect causal structure. But, sensibility theorists argue, this does not mean that ethical judgment is noncognitive or that ethical properties are not real, any more than it does in the case of color. Only a "scientistic" view of reality would have these consequences.

Sensibility theory provides a vantage point for arguing simultaneously against noncognitivism and against various forms of intuitionism. Ethical sensibilities and properties come in matched pairs, it holds. As against noncognitivism, it is of the nature of the relevant sentiments that they implicitly involve attribution of the relevant ethical property. We would not understand a sentiment as moral disapprobation, for example, unless it involved seeing something *as wrong*. But neither can we understand ethical properties independent of their relation to the relevant sentiments, as part of a freestanding order.

Just as there can be better or worse judgments of color, so can there be better or worse discrimination of ethical properties. And, McDowell argues, we should not suppose that this is independent of the ethical properties of the perceiver herself. A virtuous person, for example, may be able to see that another person's shyness and sensitivity calls for certain treatment, even if others are oblivious to this. Moreover, because her seeing the situation in this light involves affective response, she must be moved by her perception; she may take it as a reason for acting and, indeed, act for that reason. Tying ethical properties and their detection to sentiment thus gives ethical qualities an internal connection to the will.

Any close analogy between ethical and secondary qualities is bound to break down at some point, however. One disanalogy sensibility theorists themselves admit is that although something counts as having a given color if, and only if, it is such as to elicit the relevant color impression in normal human observers, ethical properties are tied to appropriate or merited response. It is in relation to just such normative notions as these that the most contentious metaethical issues have traditionally arisen, however. Also, to guarantee objectivity to color judgments, it is necessary to "rigidify" the description 'normal human observers' to something like 'normal human observers as they now are'. But although this assures that there are properties to be tracked by our sensibilities, its arbitrariness seems insufficient to support the idea that ethical properties are what should regulate our choices.

These objections recall a fact/value distinction of the sort that fueled earlier versions of noncognitivism. Noncognitivism fell from its dominant position in the 1960s, not least because of the problems Geach had raised concerning the apparently fact-stating logical structure of ethical discourse. Recently, however, Simon Blackburn and Allan Gibbard have breathed new life into noncognitivism, showing how it can take more sophisticated and plausible forms. Blackburn argues that it is because we need terms not only to express emotive attitudes but also to engage in "reflective evaluative practice," and thus "to express concern for improvements, implications, and coherence of attitudes," that we need the objective-looking emotive predicates that are the ethical vocabulary. Within our use of these terms we employ such notions as truth, logical consequence, and so on, as if we were making claims about real properties. Our use is 'quasi-realistic', but not really so. Ethical claims have no cognitive content; their function is not to represent real aspects of the world. Rather, they project our attitudes onto the world, but not in a way that expresses the false belief that the world really has the projected properties.

Gibbard's form of noncognitivism is a norm expressivism rather than an emotivism (*see* EMOTIVE THEORY OF ETHICS [2]). The distinctive normative core of ethical notions is the idea of something's being warranted, rational, and supported by reasons; or, in Gibbard's favored phrase, of its "making sense." No real property answers to this idea, Gibbard holds. This can be shown, he argues, by marking what is ultimately at issue between people who disagree about normative questions. For example, theorists may differ over what a person should do in a decision- or game-theoretic situation (*see* DECISION THEORY [S]) even when they are completely agreed about the facts of the case, and even when the issue is only what would be most rational in light of the agent's ends. Since there is no disagreement over the facts, Gibbard argues, the remaining disagreement must concern something else. Its source, he suggests, is that the disputants accept conflicting norms of decision or action and that their conflicting judgments express their acceptance of these conflicting norms. Gibbard claims that the mental state of accepting a norm is not a representational state. So to express this state is not to say anything true or false.

Like sensibility theorists, Gibbard agrees that many normative judgments are tied to feelings, but not in the way that either the sensibility theorists or traditional emotivists believed. Gibbard agrees with sensibility theory in rejecting emotivism's view that moral judgments directly *express* feeling; such judgments claim rather that a feeling or sentiment is *warranted.* But, as against sensibility theory, Gibbard maintains that this latter claim is noncognitive; it expresses the acceptance of norms. For example, the judgment that some action is morally wrong expresses the acceptance of norms that warranted feeling impartial anger toward it.

Despite this renewed interest in metaethics, it would be a great mistake to suppose that normative theory has receded into the background in recent years. On the contrary, the area has shown at least as much vitality as metaethics. However, normative theorists have been less than fully satisfied to anchor their theories in a "narrow" reflective equilibrium with considered ethical judgments. More fundamental considerations of rationale and coherence with theory in such areas as MORAL PSYCHOLOGY [S], theory of action (*see* ACTION THEORY [S]), and the metaphysics of PERSONAL IDENTITY [6; S] have come to play a larger role than they did in the "great expansion" of normative theory in the 1970s. In this light the classic debate between CONSEQUENTIALISM [S] and deontology (*see* DEONTOLOGICAL ETHICS [2; S]) has been re-energized. New forms of consequentialism have arisen with more sophisticated theories of the good and accounts of the relation between theories of conduct and theories of moral motivation. The traditional consequentialist complaint that deontology is but a set of "intuitions in search of a foundation" has been given a distinctive form in Samuel Scheffler's charge that no compelling rationale exists for the agent-relative character of deontological constraints—for example, for a requirement not to break one's promise rather than, say, to promote promise keeping in general. After all, if it's bad (in itself) that a promise be broken, it must be worse that several be.

New support for (agent-neutral) consequentialism has also come from Derek Parfit's challenging and influential reductionist theory of personal identity. If no "further fact" of being the same person over time exists beyond a messy set of facts concerning to what degree various relations hold between mental and physical states at various times, then this may tell against deontological theories that apparently require a more robust conception of personal identity and the distinctness of persons.

Thus, if utilitarianism and consequentialism were in retreat after the appearance of Rawls's *A Theory of Justice* in the 1970s, they have managed to gain new ground and go on the offensive more recently. Not that deontology has been on the defensive; far from it. But with a new concern to press fundamental philosophical issues, deontology has been unable to rest on being the theory of moral common sense and has had to seek more deeply satisfying forms.

The deontology/consequentialism debate is rooted in an orthodox tradition of modern moral philosophy that goes back in some form or other to the eighteenth century. One of the more important developments of the 1980s and early 1990s has been a radical critique of this tradition and of the sort of moral theory of which consequentialism and deontology are paradigm examples. Alasdair MacIntyre has argued, for example, that the modern "enlightenment project" of defending universal principles of right without appeal to an essential human aim or *telos* was doomed to failure and that, while we can hardly return to an Aristotelianism that assumes natural final causes, ethics must find foundation in conceptions of virtue and goods that are internal to going traditional practices. It was not necessary to accept MacIntyre's rejection of modern moral theory, however, to agree that, as Philippa Foot put it, "the subject of the virtues and vice" had been "strangely neglected" by analytical moral philosophy. Foot's observation has resonated widely in recent years, and it has combined with the sense of a similar neglect of the moral emotions and sentiments to produce a steadily growing body of work in these areas.

One particularly important development within this general trend has been an investigation of the ethical dimensions of various forms of human relationships together with a radical, sometimes self-consciously feminist critique of orthodox moral theory as distorting the way ethical issues inevitably arise, not in a general or universal context, but within relationships of concern for *particular* others. Annette Baier's work on trust and a variety of writings on the ethics of care, love, and other forms of particularistic concern, much of it inspired by the psychologist Carol Gilligan, have been especially significant here. Finally, some philosophers have argued that morality itself, and not just moral theory, either has (or should have) a more restricted sphere than orthodox theory supposes or that it is actually worthy of abolition since it embodies an irredeemably defective way of conceiving the ethical life. Susan Wolf is prominent in the first group and Bernard Williams in the second. Partly what worries Williams is, again, that morality's universalism cannot be made fully compatible with the forms of particularistic concern that must take root in a good human life. But equally important is the neo-Nietzschean thought that the 'morality system' involves a form of obligation that requires insupportable metaphysical assumptions about human freedom and that threatens to become a form of bondage, shackling human beings to a profoundly less valuable life. (SEE ALSO: *Ethical Egoism* [S]; *Evolutionary Ethics* [S]; *Moral Relativism* [S]; *Moral Skepticism* [S]; *Nondescriptivism* [S]; *Projectivism* [S]; and *Virtue Ethics* [S])

Bibliography

Brandt, R. *A Theory of the Good and the Right.* Oxford, 1979.

Foot, P. "Morality as a System of Hypothetical Imperatives," *Philosophical Review,* Vol. 81 (1972), 305–16. Reprinted in P. Foot, *Virtues and Vices* (Los Angeles, 1978).

Gauthier, D. *Morals by Agreement.* Oxford, 1986.

Gibbard, A. *Wise Choices, Apt Feelings.* Cambridge, 1990.

Harman, G. *The Nature of Morality: An Introduction to Ethics.* New York, 1977.

Mackie, J. L. *Ethics: Inventing Right and Wrong.* Harmondsworth, Eng., 1977.

Nagel, T. *The Possibility of Altruism.* Oxford, 1978.

Rawls, J. *A Theory of Justice*. Cambridge, 1971.

Scanlon, T. M. "Contractualism and Utilitarianism," in A. Sen and B. Williams, *Utilitarianism and Beyond* (Cambridge, 1982).

Wiggins, D. *Needs, Values, Truth: Essays in the Philosophy of Value*. Oxford, 1987.

STEPHEN DARWALL

ETHICAL THEORY IN GADAMER.

Hans-Georg GADAMER [S] meant his hermeneutics to be a theory of interpretation of artworks and of the written and spoken word, not interpretation of ethical principles. Still, two principal sources for his hermeneutics are the ethical thought of PLATO [6; S] and ARISTOTLE [1; S], and yet another source is KIERKEGAARD's [4; S] dialectical transformation of aesthetic subjectivity into ethical engagement. Thus, Gadamer's thinking inevitably has an important, if implicit, ethical dimension.

From Plato's dialogues Gadamer takes the priority of the question over the answer in our reasoning with each other and in reaching an understanding about what is right, decent, and good. Here, in yielding idiosyncratic beliefs tenaciously held, we become willing participants in a conversation and investigation that lead us each time to good passage (*euporia*) through perplexity, even as it also dead-ends at a temporary impasse (*aporia*). Listening to the other, readiness to follow where the argument leads us, and acceptance of indeterminacy and inclusiveness thus displaces rigid dogmatism. Surely this is not only a model for the dialogue of the intrepreter with the text but also for ethical deliberation.

From Aristotle Gadamer appropriates the ethical vocabulary of *phronesis, sunesis,* and *epieikeia* (discernment, understanding shown for someone, and clemency). Phronesis is that combination of tact and reasonableness that guides us to good decisions concerning what we ourselves are to do, while sunesis and epieikeia guide us to fair judgments about what another has done. They all exemplify a kind of knowing that is not methodological in the scientific sense but valid in the historical realm of human affairs, and thus they provide paradigms for anyone who would understand and interpret artworks and texts. But here too Gadamer's use of these terms has inescapable consequences for a theory of ethical understanding.

Finally, Kierkegaard's critique of aesthetic consciousness and dialectical development of the ethical existence shows us how artworks and texts might be understood, not as a stimulus and catalyst for some sort of private experience, but as the conversation between an "I" of stabilized character and a "you" to whom this "I" relates with constancy and loyalty. The transcendence of self-gratification implied here is of the greatest ethical significance too.

The result of Gadamer's work for ethics is that ethical deliberation turns out to be uncertain discursive reasoning from within the historical authority of a given language tradition, in the process of which we continue to get clearer about what is to be done. Ethical deliberation turns out to be discursive reasoning of which only those who have transcended the sophist's and aesthete's self-centeredness and are ready to yield to communal obligation are capable of this kind of discursive reasoning.

Bibliography

WORKS BY GADAMER

Wahrheit und Methode. Tübingen, 1960. Revised translation by D. G. Marshall and J. C. Weinsheimer as *Truth and Method*. London, 1993.

Platos dialektische Ethik. Hamburg, 1968. Translated by R. M. Wallace as *Plato's Dialectical Ethics*. New Haven, 1993.

Die Idee des Guten zwischen Plato und Aristoteles. Heidelberg, 1978. Translated by P. C. Smith as *The Idea of the Good in Platonic-Aristotelian Philosophy*. New Haven, 1986.

"Ich und Du (K. Löwith)" [1929], in *Gesammelte Werke,* Vol. 4, *Neuere Philosophie,* pt. 2 (Tübingen, 1987).

"Begegnung mit dem Sein (H. Kuhn)" [1954], in *Gesammelte Werke,* Vol. 4, *Neuere Philosophie,* pt. 2 (Tübingen, 1987).

"Über die Möglichkeit einer philosophischen Ethik" [1963], in *Gesammelte Werke,* Vol. 4, *Neuere Philosophie,* pt. 2 (Tübingen, 1987).

"Das ontologische Problem des Wertes" [1971], in *Gesammelte Werke,* Vol. 4, *Neuere Philosophie,* pt. 2 (Tübingen, 1987).

"Was ist Praxis? Die Bedingungen gesellschaftlicher Vernunft" [1974] in *Gesammelte Werke,* Vol. 4, *Neuere Philosophie,* pt. 2 (Tübingen, 1987).

"Wertethik und praktische Philosophie" [1982], in *Gesammelte Werke,* Vol. 4, *Neuere Philosophie,* pt. 2 (Tübingen, 1987).

WORK ON GADAMER

Smith, P. C. *Hermeneutics and Human Finitude: Toward a Theory of Ethical Understanding*. Bronx, 1991.

P. CHRISTOPHER SMITH

ETHICAL THEORY IN RICOEUR.

See: RICOEUR, PAUL [S]

EUTHANASIA.

Euthanasia used to refer to an easy and gentle death, but it now refers to methods of inducing that kind of death or, more precisely, methods of bringing about death sooner and usually with less pain and suffering than would have occurred otherwise. Euthanasia used to be limited to patients in the terminal stage of an illness, but it is now thought to be appropriate in some cases of nonterminal patients—for example, those in a persistent vegetative state and those suffering from an incurable and very painful chronic disease.

Voluntary active euthanasia (VAE) is when a physician accedes to a rational request of an adequately informed competent patient for the physician to kill him, with a lethal intravenous injection of pentothal, for example.

Physician-assisted suicide (PAS) is when a physician, at a rational request of an adequately informed competent patient who plans to commit SUICIDE [8], knowingly provides that patient with the medical means to commit suicide and the patient uses those means to commit suicide.

Voluntary passive euthanasia (VPE) is when a physician abides by a valid rational refusal of treatment by an adequately informed competent patient knowing that doing so will result in the patient's dying—for example, complying with the refusal of a ventilator-dependent patient with motor neuron disease to receive further mechanical ventilatory support. Abiding by patient refusal of hydration and nutrition (PRHN) is another example of VPE, as is abiding by such refusals given in advance directives, either living wills or durable powers of attorney for health care, even though the patient is incompetent at the time the treatment is withheld or withdrawn.

Patients are competent to make a decision about their health care if they have the capacity to understand and appreciate all the information necessary to make a rational decision. They are adequately informed when they have been given all the information necessary to make a rational decision. Patient competence, the receipt of adequate information from the physician, and no coercion by the health care team are the elements of valid (informed) consent or refusal of treatment.

A decision by a patient is irrational if he knows it will result in harm—for example, death, pain, or disability—to him and he does not have an adequate reason, such as avoiding suffering an equal or greater harm, for that decision. Only those decisions count as irrational that result in the person's suffering harm and for which almost no one in the person's culture would rank the benefit gained or harm avoided as providing an adequate reason. Often, however, rational people rank harms in different ways. It is rational to rank immediate death as worse than several months of suffering from a terminal disease, and it is also rational to rank that suffering as worse than death.

Involuntary active euthanasia (IAE) is when, out of concern for the patient, a physician kills a permanently incompetent patient—for example, one in a permanent vegetative state. Involuntary passive euthanasia (IPE) is when, in the absence of an advance directive, but out of concern for the patient, a physician ceases treatment of a permanently incompetent patient, knowing that doing so will result in the patient's dying.

At the present time PAS, VAE, and IAE are illegal in the United States, but some people have begun to argue for their legalization, especially PAS, in carefully controlled circumstances. IPE is also illegal, except when continuing treatment is considered futile, but some have recommended that the definition of futility be broadened so that all treatment of permanently unconscious patients be classified as futile.

VPE has been declared acceptable by the U.S. Supreme Court and is approved by the American Medical Association and all other medical and legal organizations. Thus, there have been many attempts by philosophers to provide an account of VPE that explains its almost universal acceptance. All of these attempts have identified VAE with killing and VPE with allowing to die. Two of the most common ways of distinguishing between VAE (killing) and VPE (allowing to die) are (1) acts versus omissions and (2) withholding versus withdrawing.

The philosophical distinction between acts and omissions seems a natural way to distinguish between killing and allowing to die. If a physician does something, performs an action—for example, injects an overdose of morphine or turns off the respirator—that action counts as VAE, is considered killing, and is prohibited. If the physician does nothing, but rather simply fails to do something—for example, does not turn on the respirator or does not provide essential antibiotics—that omission counts as VPE, is considered allowing to die, and is permitted. However, it seems pointless to distinguish between an authorized physician who turns a knob that stops the flow of life-sustaining antibiotics and one who omits filling the bag when it runs out of those antibiotics. Those who have used the distinction between acts and omissions to distinguish between VAE (killing) and VPE (allowing to die) have usually concluded that the distinction has no moral significance.

The distinction between withholding and withdrawing treatment seems to have great appeal for some doctors as a way of distinguishing VAE and VPE. Some doctors maintain that if a patient validly refuses to start life-saving treatment, they do not have a duty to force it on him and so are only allowing him to die. However, once treatment is started, if discontinuing would lead to the patient's death, they have a duty to continue, and it is killing not to. Doctors are not required to force a patient to go on the ventilator if the patient refuses, but once the patient has accepted going on the ventilator, they have a duty to keep him on if taking him off would result in his death, even if he has changed his mind.

Like the previous distinction between acts and omissions, there seems to be no morally significant difference between withholding and withdrawing treatment. Physicians do not have a duty to continue treatment if an adequately informed competent patient rationally refuses to have it continued. Imagine two unconscious patients who are going to be put on a respirator; one becomes conscious before she is put on and the other after she is put on, but both are competent, adequately informed, and rationally refuse treatment. This accident of timing is morally irrelevant. Further, this way of distinguishing between active and passive euthanasia may create serious practical problems. Patients who had not been adequately evaluated (often at the scene of an accident) were sometimes judged inappropriate for rescue efforts because the doctors believed that once the patient was on a ventilator they could not legitimately withdraw him from it.

The inadequacy of these two attempts to distinguish between VAE and VPE has led many to doubt that there is a morally relevant distinction between them. However, closer attention to the way the distinction is actually made, both in law and medicine, shows that what was overlooked is the crucial role played by the patient. When a patient rationally and validly refuses what is offered, the physician is legally and morally required not to overrule that refusal. Abiding by a valid rational refusal, knowing that death will result, counts as VPE, whether this involves (1) an act or an omission or (2) withholding or withdrawing. That everyone acknowledges that a physician must abide by a valid refusal of treatment, whether this involves an action or is a case of withdrawing, explains why VPE is almost universally considered to be morally acceptable.

If a patient requests the physician to do something, however, the physician is not morally required to do it if in his judgment it is inappropriate for him to do so, regardless of the kind of treatment. Physicians may accede to patient requests if they regard them as appropriate, but rarely are they required to do so. If a patient requests that they do something illegal or that they consider immoral, they are never required to do so. Killing patients at their rational request is VAE. It is illegal, and even if it were to be legalized many physicians would still consider it to be immoral. Even if it is sometimes morally acceptable for physicians to kill patients at their request, it should never be legally or morally required for them to do so. This is sufficient to distinguish VAE from VPE, for it is legally and morally required for physicians not to overrule the rational valid refusals of their patients.

Confusion sometimes arises when a patient's refusal is framed in terms resembling a request. For example, a patient's "request" that no cardiopulmonary resuscitation (CPR) be attempted on him is actually a refusal of permission for CPR. Similarly, written advance directives "requesting" the cessation of other therapies or of hydration and nutrition are really refusals of treatment.

Using valid refusal versus requests as the way of distinguishing VPE from VAE, while it explains the moral acceptability of VPE, does not make VAE morally unacceptable. Given present knowledge and technology, one can kill a patient absolutely painlessly within a matter of minutes. If patients have a rational desire to die, why wait several months for them to die, why not kill them quickly and painlessly in a matter of minutes? If there were no way for patients to shorten the time of their dying, or for their pain to be controlled, VAE would seem to be clearly morally acceptable. However, PRHN, which contrary to common belief does not cause suffering, allows patients to become unconscious within a week and to die within another week, and medication is available to control their other pain during that time. Further, all proposals to employ VAE involve at least a two-week waiting period. Thus, it seems pointless to employ VAE, which is controversial, rather than VPE, which is already universally accepted.

Abiding by the refusal in an advance directive of a competent patient, when that patient becomes incompetent, is usually regarded as similar in all moral respects to abiding by the refusal of a currently competent patient. If competent patients explicitly state in an advance directive that, should they become permanently incompetent, they want life-prolonging treatments to be discontinued, then the physician is morally required to abide by that refusal. However, this view is challenged by those claiming that the views of the competent person who filled out the advance directive are not always the same as the views of the incompetent person to whom they are being applied.

Some hold that advance directives need not be followed if the physician believes that the incompetent person would not choose to have life-prolonging treatment withdrawn. One must judge a public policy, however, in terms of the effects that this policy would have on everyone involved if all knew of the policy. Competent persons who fill out advance directives refusing life-prolonging treatment if they become permanently incompetent consider it distasteful and devoid of dignity to live as a permanently incompetent person. The now-incompetent person, however, having no sense of dignity, does not view her life with distaste.

If everyone knew that advance directives would not be honored in these cases, some permanently incompetent persons would live longer than they would if such advance directives were honored. This might be a positive result, but it is not clear whether the incompetent person views it in that way. However, it is clear that another result of having everyone know that their advance directives would not be honored would be anxiety, anger, and other unpleasant feelings. This could result in an increase in deaths of such competent persons in order to avoid the unwanted prolongation of their lives as incompetent persons. The consequences of a public policy of not honoring such advance directives seem to be worse than those of the present policy of honoring them.

(SEE ALSO: *Biomedical Ethics, Informed Consent,* and *Paternalism* [S])

Bibliography

Bernat, J. L., B. Gert, and R. P. Mogielnicki. "Patient Refusal of Hydration and Nutrition: An Alternative to Physician Assisted Suicide or Voluntary Euthanasia," *Archives of Internal Medicine,* Vol. 153 (Dec. 27, 1993), 2723–28.

Brock, D. W. *Life and Death.* Cambridge, 1993. Esp. pp. 95–232.

Clouser, K. D. "Allowing or Causing: Another Look," *Annals of Internal Medicine,* Vol. 87 (1977), 622–24.

Dresser, R. S., and J. A. Robertson. "Quality of Life and Nontreatment Decisions for Incompetent Patients," *Law, Medicine, and Health Care,* Vol. 17, no. 3 (Fall 1989), 234–44.

Gert, B. *Morality: A New Morality of the Moral Rules.* New York, 1988.

The Hastings Center. *Guidelines on the Termination of Life-Sustaining Treatments and Care of the Dying.* Bloomington, IN, 1987.

Lynn, J., ed. *By No Extraordinary Means.* Bloomington, IN, 1986.

President's Commission for the Study of Ethical Problems in Medicine and Biomedical and Behavioral Research. *Deciding to Forgo Life-Sustaining Treatment.* Washington, DC, 1983.

Rachels, J. *The End of Life: Euthanasia and Morality.* New York, 1986.

Van er Maas, P. J., et al. *Euthanasia and Other Medical Decisions concerning the End of Life.* Lancet, 1991.

Wanzer, S. J., et al. "The Physician's Responsibility toward Hopelessly Ill Patients: A Second Look," *New England Journal of Medicine,* Vol. 320 (1989), 844–49.

Weir, R. F. *Abating Treatment with Critically Ill Patients.* New York, 1989.

BERNARD GERT

EVENT THEORY. An event is anything that happens, an occurrence. The idea of an event began to take on a philosophical life of its own in the twentieth century, due to a reawakening of interest in the concept of change, to which the concept of an event seems inextricably tied, and to the growing use of the concept of an event in scientific and metascientific writing (see Broad, 1933, 1938; McTaggart, 1927; and Whitehead, 1929). Interest in events has also been sparked by versions of the mind–body identity thesis formulated in terms of events and by the idea that a clearer picture of events will facilitate discussion of other philosophical issues.

Discussions of events have focused on whether there are events and, if so, what the nature of events is. Since whether there are events depends in part on what they would be like if there were any, the two issues have usually been treated together.

Some philosophers (e.g., J. J. Thomson) simply assume that there are events; others argue for that assumption. Donald DAVIDSON [S] has asserted that there are events (and actions) by arguing that, to explain the meanings of claims involving adverbial modifiers (e.g., "Jones killed Smith in the kitchen") and singular causal claims (e.g., "the short circuit caused the fire"), we should suppose that such claims implicitly quantify over, or posit, actions and events (e.g., killings, short circuits, and fires). Opponents of Davidson's analyses (e.g., Terence Horgan) have argued that alternative semantic theories, which do not posit events, are able to explain the semantic features of Davidson's target sentences.

While some singular terms purporting to refer to events are proper names (e.g., "World War I"), many are definite descriptions (e.g., "the killing of Caesar by Brutus"). The semantics of singular descriptions for events has been studied by Zeno Vendler and Jonathan Bennett. Of particular interest is the distinction between perfect nominals, like "Quisling's betraying of Norway," which refer to events (or actions or states), and imperfect nominals, like "Quisling's betraying Norway," which refer to fact-like entities. Bennett has argued that much of what is wrong in Jaegwon Kim's theory of events can be traced to confusions involving these two sorts of nominals and to expressions (e.g., "the betrayal") that are ambiguous and can refer either to events or to facts.

Most philosophers take events to be abstract particulars: particulars in that they are nonrepeatable and spatially locatable, abstract in that more than one event can occur simultaneously in the same place. Some philosophers who think this way (e.g., Lombard) take events to be the changes that objects undergo when they alter. (Others, such as Bennett, have doubts about this; others, like Kim and David Lewis, deny it outright.) Thus, the time at which an event occurs is the (shortest) time at which the subject of that event changes from the having of one to the having of another, contrary property. Since no object can have both a property and one of its contraries simultaneously, there can be no instantaneous events.

Events inherit their spatial locations from the spatial locations, if any, of the things in which those events are changes. Events do not get their spatial locations by occupying them; if they did, then distinct events, like distinct physical objects, could not occur in the same place simultaneously. But more than one event apparently can occur at the same time and place. However, some philosophers (e.g., QUINE [7; S]) hold that events are concrete and that events and physical objects do not belong to distinct metaphysical kinds.

Though it seems clear that some events are composed of others, it is not clear what the principles are that determine when events compose more complex events.

Some views of events (perhaps WHITEHEAD's [8]) seem compatible with there being subjectless events, events that are not changes in anything whatsoever. However, subjectless events could not be changes, for it seems absurd to suppose that there could be a change that was not a change in or of anything.

Theories about the nature of entities belonging to some metaphysically interesting kind must address the issue of what properties such entities essentially have. In the case of events, the issue is made pressing by the fact that certain theories concerning causation (e.g., David Lewis's) require that judgments be made about whether certain events would occur under certain, counterfactual circumstances.

In the literature on events, attention has been given to four essentialist issues. The first is whether the causes (or effects) of events are essential to the events that have them; Peter van Inwagen has suggested that an event's causes are essential to the events that have them, while Lombard has argued that neither the causes nor the effects of events are essential to them. The second concerns the subjects of events; Bennett and Lewis suggest that the subjects of events are not essential, while Lombard and Kim argue that they are. The third is whether an event's time of occurrence is essential to it. Lombard has argued in favor of this essentialist claim, while Bennett and Lewis have argued against it. And the fourth is whether it is essential that each event be a change with respect to the properties to which it is in fact a change. Though the first three issues have received some attention, the fourth has attracted the most, due to the prominence given to debates between the defenders and opponents of Kim's and Davidson's views on the identity of events.

Theories about events typically contain, as a chief component, a "criterion of identity," a principle giving necessary and sufficient conditions for an event *e* and an event *e′* to be identical. Though there is no general agreement on this, such a principle is sought because, when it satisfies certain constraints, it becomes a vehicle for articulating a view about what it is to be an event and how events are related to objects belonging to other kinds.

Quine holds that events are the temporal parts of physical objects and thus that events and physical objects share the same condition of identity: sameness of spatiotemporal location.

Kim's interest in events centers in part on the idea that they are the objects of empirical explanations. Since what is typically explained is an object's having a property at a certain time, Kim takes an event to be the exemplification of a property (or relation) by an object (or objects) at a time. This idea, combined with some others, led him to hold that an event *e* is the same as an event *e′* if and only if *e* and *e′* are the exemplifications of the same property by the same object(s) at the same time. Kim's view has been criticized, principally by Lombard and Bennett, on the grounds that what it says about events is more plausibly seen as truths about facts. Kim's view has also been criticized by those whose intuitions concerning the identity of events more closely match Davidson's.

Davidson once proposed that events, being essentially the links in causal chains, are identical just in case they have the same causes and effects. He has since abandoned this position in favor of Quine's.

Another view that places causation at the heart of the idea of an event is due to David Lewis, who has tried to construct a theory in which events have just those features that would allow them to fit neatly into his counterfactual analysis of causation. In some respects, Lewis's view is like Myles Brand's in that both are moved in part by the idea that more than one event can occur simultaneously in the same place. Lewis takes an event to be a property-in-intension of a spatio-temporal region, so that events that in fact occur simultaneously in the same place but could have had different spatio-temporal locations are distinct.

Bennett thinks that the concept of an event is not precise enough to withstand much critical examination on its own and that events should be thought to be (only) whatever they need to be in order to make constructive use of them in the discussion of other philosophical issues. Like Lewis, Bennett takes an event to be a property; but, for Bennett, the property seems to be a property-in-extension and is a particular. That is, Bennett thinks that events are tropes.

Lombard's view is, like Kim's, a variation on a property exemplification account. Lombard's version is derived from the idea of events as the changes that objects undergo when they alter, and it takes events to be the exemplifyings of "dynamic" properties at intervals of time. Such alterations are the "movements" by objects from the having of one to the having of another property through densely populated quality spaces, where each quality space is a class of contrary properties, the mere having of any member of which by an object does not imply change. (SEE ALSO: *Metaphysics* [S])

Bibliography

Bennett, J. *Events and Their Names.* Indianapolis, 1988.

Brand, M. "Particulars, Events, and Actions," in M. Brand and D. Walton, eds., *Action Theory* (Dordrecht, 1976).

Broad, C. D. *An Examination of McTaggart's Philosophy.* Cambridge, 1933.

Davidson, D. *Essays on Actions and Events.* New York, 1980.

———. "Reply to Quine on Events," in E. LePore and B. P. McLaughlin, eds., *Actions and Events: Perspectives on the Philosophy of Donald Davidson* (Oxford, 1985).

Horgan, T. "The Case Against Events," *Philosophical Review,* Vol. 87 (1978), 28–47.

Kim, J. "Events and Their Descriptions: Some Considerations," in N. Rescher et al., eds., *Essays in Honor of Carl G. Hempel* (Dordrecht, 1969).

———. *Supervenience and Mind,* Chaps. 1, 3. New York, 1993.

Lewis, D. "Events," in *Philosophical Papers,* Vol. 2 (New York, 1986).

Lombard, L. B. *Events: A Metaphysical Study.* London, 1986.

McTaggart, J. M. E. *The Nature of Existence,* Vol. 2. Cambridge, 1927.

Quine, W. V. O. "Things and Their Place in Theories," in *Theories and Things* (Cambridge, MA, 1981).

———. "Events and Reification," in E. LePore and B. P. McLaughlin, eds., *Actions and Events: Perspectives on the Philosophy of Donald Davidson* (Oxford, 1985).

Thomson, J. J. *Acts and Other Events.* Ithaca, NY, 1977.

van Inwagen, P. "Ability and Responsibility," *Philosophical Review,* Vol. 87 (1978), 201–24, esp. 207–9.

Vendler, Z. "Facts and Events," in *Linguistics and Philosophy* (Ithaca, NY, 1967).

Whitehead, A. N. *The Principles of Natural Knowledge.* Cambridge, 1919.

———. *Process and Reality.* Cambridge, 1929.

LAWRENCE BRIAN LOMBARD

EVIDENTIALISM. Evidentialism is the view about epistemic justification that identifies the extent to which a person is justified in believing a proposition with the extent to which the evidence the person has supports the truth of the proposition. Other doxastic attitudes such as withholding judgment and denying are also justified by the character of the person's evidence.

A full-scale evidentialist theory would explain what constitutes evidence, what it means to have a certain body of evidence, and what it means for a body of evidence to support a proposition to any given extent. Ordinarily, people count as evidence external things such as fingerprints and bank records. However, according to evidentialists, our fundamental evidence is constituted by our perceptual experiences, our apparent memories, and other mental states. A full-scale theory requires an account of what we have as this ultimate sort of evidence: it is unclear, for example, whether someone's unactivated memories are part of the person's current evidence. The evidential support relation to which evidentialists appeal is not a familiar logical relation. Perceptual states can support beliefs about the external world, yet there is no familiar logical relation between those states and the beliefs they support. Furthermore, one's evidence on its own does not support its distant and unnoticed logical consequences. A complete evidentialist theory would clarify the justifying connection between a body of evidence and a proposition.

Leading skeptical controversies are usefully understood to concern what sort of evidence is required for knowledge (*see* SKEPTICISM [7; S]). For example, if knowledge requires complete epistemic justification, and this requires having entailing evidence, then skeptics can cogently argue that we have no such evidence for any empirical proposition and that therefore we have no empirical knowledge. On the other hand, standard skeptical arguments fail if nonentailing evidence can completely justify belief. An evidentialist theory can resolve this dispute either way.

Diverse theories of justification can be understood as evidentialist views that differ on the nature of evidence, its possession, and how it supports belief. For instance, a typical coherentist theory in effect holds that a person has her beliefs as evidence and that support by evidence consists in coherence with it (*see* COHERENTISM [S]). A typical foundationalist theory in effect holds that justified beliefs must include some that are defended by a foundational sort of evidence—for example, by perceptual states—and that this evidence is had by the person by being consciously accessible (*see* FOUNDATIONALISM [S]).

Evidentialism entirely discounts factors that figure centrally in some theories of justified belief. These factors include the intellectual pedigree of the belief, the believer's capacity or intention to fulfill intellectual duties or to exemplify cognitive virtues, and the normal functioning of the operative belief-forming mechanism. Justifying evidence for a belief might happen to arise in an irresponsibly haphazard inquiry with no attempt to fulfill any epistemic duty, as a fluke result of some abnormal cognitive activity lacking in intellectual virtue. The evidentialist view is that regardless of all this, belief is justified because the evidence possessed supports the proposition.
(SEE ALSO: *Epistemology* [S])

Bibliography

Chisholm, R. "A Version of Foundationalism," in *The Foundations of Knowing* (Minneapolis, 1982).

Feldman, R., and Earl Conee. "Evidentialism," *Philosophical Studies,* Vol. 48 (1985), 15–34.

Goldman, A. *Epistemology and Cognition.* Cambridge, MA, 1986. Pp. 87–93.

Haack, S. *Evidence and Inquiry.* Oxford, 1993.

Moser, P. *Knowledge and Evidence.* Cambridge, 1989.

Plantinga, A. *Warrant and Proper Function.* Oxford, 1993. Pp. 185–93.

EARL CONEE
RICHARD FELDMAN

EVIL, PROBLEM OF. Many people feel that the evils that occur in our world, particularly the amount and severity of human and animal suffering, make it difficult to believe in the existence of God, where God is understood to be the perfectly good, infinitely powerful, all-knowing creator of the world. This difficulty for belief in God is held by some to be logical, by others to be evidential, depending on whether one believes that such evils logically preclude the existence of God or that such evils, although perhaps logically consistent with the existence of God, nevertheless constitute evidence against his existence.

LOGICAL PROBLEM OF EVIL

The proponent of the logical problem of evil asserts that it is logically impossible both that God (the infinitely powerful, perfectly good, all-knowing creator of the world) exists and that the world contains the evils we observe. But how can this be proved? If it were necessarily true that God would prevent some of the evils we observe in our world, and we knew that this was so, we could then prove that it is logically impossible both that God exists and that the world contains the evils we observe. But is it necessarily true that God would prevent some of the evils in our world? Presumably God would prevent evils only if he could do so without losing goods that outweigh those evils. So if it is necessarily true that God would prevent some of the evils that occur in the world, it is necessarily true that he could prevent those evils without losing any outweighing goods. Since God is omnipotent, one might think that he must be able to prevent those evils without losing any outweighing goods. But what if God's permitting those evils is itself logically required for outweighing goods? If this were so, then, since most philosophers think power extends only to what is logically possible, few would think that God's omnipotence implies that he could prevent those evils without losing any outweighing goods. Furthermore, even if it is necessarily true that God could prevent some evils we observe in the world without losing any outweighing goods, how could we come to know that this is so? For unless we know that it is so, we cannot prove that God's existence is logically inconsistent with the evils we observe. Consideration of these difficulties has led many philosophers to conclude that the efforts to prove that God's existence is logically inconsistent with the existence of the evils we observe have not been successful. In addition, on the assumptions that our world is a good world and that an act is free only if it is undetermined, a formidable argument (the free-will defense) has been developed by Alvin Plantinga to show that it is logically possible that God could not create a world better than ours that contains less evil. If it is logically possible that God could not create a world better than ours that contains less evil, God's existence is not logically inconsistent with the evils we observe in the world.

EVIDENTIAL PROBLEM OF EVIL

The proponent of the evidential problem of evil holds that, although the evils we observe may be logically consistent with the existence of God, they (or what we know about them) provide us with evidence against the existence of God. If we think of a pointless evil as an evil that God would not be justified in permitting, it is clear that if God exists no pointless evils exist. One popular evidential argument from evil claims that we have good reasons to believe that our world contains pointless evils. Proponents of this argument point to particular cases of horrendous evils—a fawn's being severely burned in a forest fire and undergoing several days of terrible agony before death relieves its suffering, a five-year-old girl being savagely beaten, raped, and strangled—as examples of evils they believe to be pointless. They argue that, when we consider particular instances of horrendous, apparently pointless evil, or reflect on the magnitude of severe human and animal suffering, it is simply staggering to suppose that an omnipotent, omniscient, and perfectly good being is in charge. What could possibly justify his permitting such monstrous evils? When we try to envisage goods whose realization might justify God (if he exists) in permitting these evils, we encounter one or the other of the following difficulties. First, it is clear that many of the goods we can envisage are not good enough to justify God in permitting such horrendous evils. Second, when we envisage goods that do seem to outweigh these horrendous evils, it is reasonable to believe that these goods are realizable by an omnipotent being without his having to permit these horrendous evils. Of course, it is logically possible that there are some outweighing goods beyond our comprehension whose realization by God requires him to permit these horrendous evils. But in the absence of any special reason to think that God would not make himself and his realization of such goods known to us, it is claimed that what we know of the magnitude of horrendous evils we observe in our world gives us reason to think that some of these evils are pointless and that, therefore, the God of traditional THEISM [8] does not exist.

Theistic responses to this line of argument take various forms. Some theists tend to agree that we cannot envisage goods whose realization by God would justify him in permitting many of the evils we observe, but they argue that this is just what we should expect if the theistic hypothesis is true. Since God's knowledge is infinite and his power unlimited, they believe that the goods that justify God in permitting many of the evils we observe would be goods we cannot comprehend. Just as an infant or very young child cannot grasp the good purposes for which the loving parent may allow the child to suffer, so we with our limited minds cannot possibly be aware of the goods that justify God (if he exists) in permitting the multitude of horrendous evils we observe. Other theists reject the view that we are unable to envisage goods whose realization would justify God in permitting so many horrendous evils. They advance theodicies that purport to single out various kinds of goods whose realization by God may justify him in permitting these evils. They suggest that horrendous evils need to occur if human beings are to acquire knowledge of how to do great harm. They also think that the knowledge of how to do great harm is essential if humans are to be free to choose between good and evil and to develop into morally praiseworthy beings. Still other theists argue that, given the human cognitive situation, we are in no position to conclude that no good we know of justifies God in permitting horrendous evils. As opposed to those theists who claim that we can see that some goods we know of could be God's justification for permitting the evils we observe, these theists argue that we are in no position to make an affirmative or negative judgment about whether these goods could be God's justification for permitting the evils we observe. We must remain agnostics about this matter. Finally, it should be noted that a theist may grant that the evidential argument from evil makes God's existence significantly less likely than it would otherwise be, but the theist would argue that the reasons, whether propositional or nonpropositional, in support of the existence of such a being outweigh the evidence against provided by the argument from evil.

These objections and various responses to them are indicative of an ongoing debate between theists and nontheists over one form of the evidential problem of evil. Another form of the evidential argument seeks to undermine the theistic hypothesis by showing that there are naturalistic hypotheses that far more adequately explain certain facts about good and evil. For example, it is known that much pleasure and pain serves a biological function in that it is useful for survival and reproduction. It is argued that this known fact is a good deal more likely on the hypothesis that sentient creatures did not come to be as the result of the good or bad intentions of a supernatural person than it is on the theistic hypothesis. For on the theistic hypothesis one would expect that pain and pleasure would serve distinctly moral purposes. Thus, since the competing hypothesis to theism better explains the known facts about pleasure and pain, it is more likely than the theistic hypothesis relative to the evidence we have concerning the function of pleasure and pain in sentient life. Against this argument, theists have urged that it is a mistake to view theism as an explanatory hypothesis whose justification rests on evidence. Moreover, even if theism is treated as an explanatory hypothesis, theists may argue that certain data often confirm one hypothesis over its competitor, while other data do just the opposite. The question then would be whether the total data is better explained by theism than by its competitors.

(SEE ALSO: *Evil, the Problem of* [3]; and *Philosophy of Religion* [S])

Bibliography

Adams, R. M. "Middle Knowledge and the Problem of Evil." *American Philosophical Quarterly,* Vol. 14 (1977), 109–17.

Alston, W. P. "The Inductive Problem of Evil and the Human Cognitive Condition," in J. E. Tomberlin, ed., *Philosophical Perspectives,* Vol. 5, *Philosophy of Religion* (Atascadero, CA, 1991).

Draper, P. "Pain and Pleasure: An Evidential Problem for Theists," *Noûs,* Vol. 23 (1989), 331–50.

Mackie, J. L. "Evil and Omnipotence," *Mind,* Vol. 64 (1955), 200–212.

Pike, N. "Hume on Evil," *Philosophical Review,* Vol. 72 (1963), 180–97.

Plantinga, A. "God, Evil, and the Metaphysics of Freedom," in *The Nature of Necessity* (Oxford, 1974).

———. "The Probabilistic Argument from Evil," *Philosophical Studies,* Vol. 35 (1979), 1–53.

Rowe, W. L. "The Problem of Evil and Some Varieties of Atheism," *American Philosophical Quarterly,* Vol. 16 (1979), 335–41.

———. "Evil and the Theistic Hypothesis: A Response to Wykstra," *International Journal for Philosophy of Religion,* Vol. 16 (1984), 95–100.

———. "William Alston on the Problem of Evil," in T. Senor, ed., *The Rationality of Belief and the Plurality of Faith* (Ithaca, NY, 1995).

Russell, B. "The Persistent Problem of Evil," *Faith and Philosophy,* Vol. 6 (1989), 121–39.

Swinburne, R. "The Problem of Evil," in *The Existence of God* (Oxford, 1979).

Tooley, M. "The Argument from Evil," in J. E. Tomberlin, ed., *Philosophical Perspectives,* Vol. 5, *Philosophy of Religion* (Atascadero, CA, 1991).

van Inwagen, P. "The Problem of Evil, the Problem of Air, and the Problem of Silence," in J. E. Tomberlin, ed., *Philosophical Perspectives,* Vol. 5, *Philosophy of Religion* (Atascadero, CA, 1991).

Wykstra, S. J. "The Humean Obstacle to Evidential Arguments from Suffering," *International Journal for Philosophy of Religion,* Vol. 16 (1984), 73–93.

WILLIAM L. ROWE

EVIL, PROBLEM OF IN RICOEUR. *See:* RICOEUR, PAUL [S]

EVOLUTIONARY ETHICS. Evolutionary theory came of age with the publication of Charles DARWIN's [2] *Origin of Species* in 1859, where he argued that all organisms, living and dead, including humans, are the end result of a long, slow, natural process of development from one or a few simple forms. Believing this new world history to be the death knell of traditional ways of thinking, many were inspired to extrapolate from the science a deeper meaning for life. Attempts were made to find within the process of evolution appropriate guides for proper human conduct ("substantive ethics"), as well as the justificatory foundations for all such social behavior ("metaethics").

At the substantive level the evolutionary ethicist's usual move was from Darwin's own suggested mechanism of change—the "natural selection" of the "fittest" organisms in life's struggle for existence—to some analogous process supposedly operating in the world of humans. Although this philosophy became known as social DARWINISM [2], its widespread popularity, especially in America, owed less to Darwin himself and more to the voluminous writings of his fellow countryman Herbert SPENCER [7]. Notoriously, Spencer was an enthusiast for an extreme libertarian *laissez-faire,* although today scholars realize that Spencer's beliefs owe at least as much to the self-help philosophy of his nonconformist Christian childhood as to anything to be found in biology.

In later writings Spencer tempered the harshness of his philosophy, seeing a definite role for cooperation in society, and (since he was not much given to retraction) this ambiguity about what was his real position led to his followers, claiming quite contradictory things, all in the name of the same philosophy. At one end of the spectrum there were conservative businessmen like John D. Rockefeller and supporters like the sociologist J. B. Sumner, who saw a place only for the success of the successful, and at the other end were the American Marxists (not to mention all of the would-be reformers in prerevolutionary China), who likewise saw in biology, as mediated by Spencer, the true rules of moral conduct. Softer and more subtle forms of social Darwinism tried to combine social responsibility with enlightened capitalism. Most influential was the iron and steel magnate Andrew Carnegie, who devoted much of his fortune to the founding of public libraries, where the poor but "fit" children might raise themselves in life's struggles.

In this century the debt to Spencer is ignored and unknown, and the term social Darwinism, burdened by history, is avoided. Nevertheless, particularly among biologists and politicians, the tradition has continued of seeking the rules of conduct in what are believed to be the sound principles of the evolutionary process. At the beginning of the century there was the exiled Russian anarchist, Prince Peter KROPOTKIN [4], arguing that all animals are subject to a cooperating tendency toward "mutual aid" and that this can and will function once we dismantle the apparatus of the modern state. Later, the English biologist Julian Huxley operated as the first director general of UNESCO according to a biologically based religion of humanity directed toward the survival of the species. And today we have the Harvard entomologist and sociobiologist Edward O. Wilson, who urges the preservation of the rain forests else humans, who live in symbiotic relation with the rest of nature, fade and die. It is less than obvious, from a historical or conceptual point of view, that some of the more vile racist ideologies of this century owe much to evolutionary biology. The Nazis, for instance, shrank from the implication that all humans have a common origin, ultimately simian.

Evolutionary ethics has long fallen from favor in philosophical circles, chiefly because of its supposed metaethical inadequacy. In his *Principia Ethica* (1903), G. E. MOORE [5] penned the classic critique, complaining that systems like that of Spencer commit the "naturalistic fallacy" trying to define the nonnatural property of goodness in terms of natural properties, in Spencer's case the happiness supposedly produced by the evolutionary process. Psychologically, however, enthusiasts for evolutionary ethics find this critique most unconvincing. It is therefore more effective to point to the earlier attack of Thomas Henry HUXLEY ([4] Julian's grandfather), who argued that systems deriving morality from evolution invariably rely on the hidden—and dubious—premise that evolution is in some sense progressive and that value is thus increased as one goes up the scale. As Huxley noted, in a post-Darwinian world, where fitness is a relative concept, the old picture of evolution "from monad to man" owes more to the Christianized Chain of Being than to the history of the organic world. It may be true that humans value humans and their well-being more than we do that of other organisms, but this is something we read into evolution.

Recently, with the increased biological interest in the evolution of animal social behavior ("sociobiology"), there has been renewed interest by philosophers in the possibility of fruitful connections between biology and morality. In his influential *A Theory of Justice,* John RAWLS [S] suggested that SOCIAL CONTRACT [7] theorists might explore fruitfully the possibility that in real life morality is the end result of the evolutionary process rather than the construct of a hypothesized group of rational beings. In support Rawls drew attention to the similarities between his own beliefs in "justice as fairness" and the results of such sociobiological mechanisms as "reciprocal altruism."

At the metaethical level also there has been renewed thought. Since the search for foundations seems so misguided, could it not be that the evolutionist is directed toward some noncognitivist "ethical skepticism," where there simply are no foundations at all? This is the approach taken by Wilson collaborating with the philosopher Michael Ruse. Following up on the thinking of the late John L. MACKIE [S], they suggest that ethics (at the substantive level) might be simply a collective illusion of our genes, put in place by natural selection to make humans into good cooperators. To this they add the related suggestion that the reason ethics works is that our biology makes us "objectify" our moral sentiments; thus, we are psychologically convinced that morality, despite its lack of real foundation, is more than mere subjective sentiment. Whether these and related suggestions will bear fruit will probably owe as much to developments in human biology as to refined philosophical analysis.

(SEE ALSO: *Ethical Theory* [S])

Bibliography

Huxley, T. H. *Evolution and Ethics* [1894]. Princeton, NJ, 1989.

Mackie, J. L. "The Law of the Jungle," *Philosophy,* Vol. 53 (1978), 553–73.

Moore, G. E. *Principia Ethica.* Cambridge, 1903.

Richards, R. J. *Darwin and the Emergence of Evolutionary Theories of Mind and Behavior.* Chicago, 1987.

Ruse, M. *Taking Darwin Seriously.* Oxford, 1986.

Ruse, M., and E. O. Wilson. "Moral Philosophy as Applied Science," *Philosophy,* Vol. 61 (1986), 173–92.

Spencer, H. *The Principles of Ethics.* 2 vols. London, 1892.

Wilson, E. O. *On Human Nature.* Cambridge, MA, 1978.

MICHAEL RUSE

EXISTENTIALISM. The development of EXISTENTIALISM [3] in the last years of its leading French proponents, Jean-Paul SARTRE [7; S] and Maurice MERLEAU-PONTY

[5; S], occurred in the areas of social philosophy and EXISTENTIAL PSYCHOANALYSIS [3; S]) in the case of Sartre and the philosophy of language and fundamental ontology for Merleau-Ponty (*see* ONTOLOGY AND FUNDAMENTAL ONTOLOGY [S]). Partly in response to the latter's critiques, but chiefly as a result of his own political commitment, Sartre constructed a social ontology and a theory of history in his *Critique of Dialectical Reason.* Faithful to his existentialist emphasis on the primacy of the individual, but replacing his earlier philosophy of consciousness with one of *praxis* (roughly, purposive human activity in its historical and socioeconomic context), Sartre formulated a set of concepts, especially praxis, seriality, and the practico-inert, that respected the power of social forces to countermand, deviate, and reverse our undertakings without totally robbing the organic individual of existentialist freedom and responsibility (*see* AUTHENTICITY [S]). He allowed far greater play to the force of circumstance in assessing human action and underscored the determining power of family and early childhood experience in his massive existential biography of Flaubert, *The Family Idiot.* This last, combining the discourse of *Being and Nothingness* with that of the *Critique,* forms a kind of synthesis of Sartre's work.

At the time of his death in 1961 Merleau-Ponty was at work on a manuscript that has come to be known as *The Visible and the Invisible,* a work that some consider his version of Heidegger's "What Is Metaphysics?" It reveals a growing interest in an ontology that avoids the pitfalls of "philosophies of consciousness," with their subject–object relation, which has defined and limited philosophy in the West for centuries. Inspired by the painter's articulation of the world and building on the concepts of chiasm and flesh, introduced in his earlier *The Phenomenology of Perception,* Merleau-Ponty was moving beyond the boundaries of PHENOMENOLOGY [6; S] to elaborate an "indirect ontology" in which language questioning being questions itself.

THOMAS R. FLYNN

EXISTENTIAL PSYCHOANALYSIS. Toward the conclusion of *Being and Nothingness* Jean-Paul SARTRE [7; S] proposes EXISTENTIAL PSYCHOANALYSIS [3] as an alternative to the Freudian version that he had criticized (*see* Sigmund FREUD [3; S]; PSYCHOANALYTIC THEORIES, LOGICAL STATUS OF [6]). Respecting individual FREEDOM [3] and responsibility, its basic principle is that "man is a totality and not a collection" of drives and complexes. By a comparative hermeneutic of the complex, multilevel symbolic expressions of an agent's actions it uncovers BAD FAITH [S] and ferrets out that fundamental project that gives unity and direction to our lives. It thereby renders possible "conversion" to an authentic existence, in which one can resist the need to create a substantialized self (*see* AUTHENTICITY [S]). Rejecting the hypothesis of an UNCONSCIOUS [8], this method relies heavily on prereflective consciousness and the distinction between what we prereflectively comprehend and reflectively know. The analyst's empathetic understanding helps bring this comprehension to knowledge. Since all CONSCIOUSNESS [2] is practical, for Sartre, this transformation involves a reorientation of one's way of being-in-the-world. Unfortunately, he concedes, "this psychoanalysis has not yet found its Freud."

It has been observed that Sartrean analysis deals with a set of human needs that have nothing to do with Freudian drives, namely "relational needs for holding, mirroring, positive regard, and emotional responsiveness, and needs for the development of a coherent and flexible sense of 'self' " (Cannon, 1991, p. 1). Sartre's later work underscores the enabling power of the third to mediate our identity and social efficacy. In social ensembles some third parties objectify and alienate, whereas others generate practical unity and effectiveness. Sartre argues that consciousness is intentional, not only in the traditional phenomenological sense that it constitutes objects, but in the existential sense that it sets goals and strategies to obtain them. Psychoanalytic interpretation unmasks these goals and strategies.

Sartre has been accused of writing as if the human were born adult. But, in trying to understand Flaubert, he claims that "everything took place in childhood" and devotes several volumes of *The Family Idiot* to chart the "spiral of personalization" by which the individual interiorizes and reexteriorizes the structural relations into which it is born (its protohistory), the experiences of infancy and early childhood (its prehistory), and resultant "constitution" of its character and dispositions. At each stage the individual is in process of "making something out of what he or she has been made into." Sartrean metatheory respects the objective possibilities of this individual's situated being as it establishes "the way in which the child lives his or her family relations inside a given society." The approach is familial.

Sartrean psychoanalysis assumed a social orientation in the 1950s and 1960s, as did his thought generally. It became a form of social critique, linked to the thesis that entire societies could suffer from "objective neurosis," making it extremely difficult for its members to live authentic lives. His psychobiographies were prolonged instances of existentialist psychoanalysis conjoined to a kind of HISTORICAL MATERIALISM [4], which he called the "progressive-regressive method."

Although the concepts of bad faith and authenticity have entered popular discourse, Sartre's psychoanalytic metatheory has yet to be adopted by professionals the way Heideggerian categories have been employed by Ludwig BINSWANGER [1], Medard Boss, and others.

Bibliography

Bugental, J. F. *The Search for Authenticity: An Existential-Analytic Approach to Psychotherapy.* New York, 1989.

Cannon, B. *Sartre and Psychoanalysis: An Existentialist Challenge to Clinical Metatheory.* Lawrence, KS, 1991.

Frankl, V. E. *Psychotherapy and Existentialism: Selected Papers on Logotherapy.* New York, 1985.

Laing, R. D. *The Divided Self.* New York, 1979.

Sartre, J.-P. *L'Idiot de la famille,* 3 vols. Paris, 1971–72. Translated by Carol Cosman as *The Family Idiot,* 5 vols. Chicago, 1981–93.

Van Kaam, A. *Existential Foundations of Psychology.* Garden City, NY, 1969.

THOMAS R. FLYNN

EXPERIENCE AND JUDGMENT. Compiled from a number of separate manuscripts left by Edmund HUSSERL [4; S] in the later part of his career, *Experience and Judgment* introduces a marked difference from his other works. Whereas in his previous works Husserl had described the mind's activity in such a way that it implied the bracketing of the world, a new fundamental character of human intelligence is that it is essentially always in the world. Prepredicative experience is a direct relation to the individual worldly object, rooted in simple sensuous awareness. As such, this experience supplies in advance the most original building stones of the LIFEWORLD [S], or pure universal nature. Subsequent cognitive activity is based on these primitive elements, which at first are objects given only to an ego; any such activity generates a garb of ideas (such as found in the idealizations of science) that mask the original lifeworld—that is, the world in which we are always already living and that provides the foundation for all cognitive performance. But a certain minimal activity, which is the lowest level of judgment, takes place even at the level of the ego. This prepredicative experience is an act of objectification: in turning toward an existent, an active believing cognizance is involved, whereby something is identified as one and the same. Furthermore, even though it is prelinguistic, the passive reception of the basic core of what is truly given as "itself-there" also involves a minimum of meaning-bestowal: that is, the lowest level of experience has its own horizon of sense. The specific forms of judgment in formal logic are founded on these prepredicative conditions of predication. All forms of conceptual thought that lead to true knowledge are detached from these pregiven elements of experience.

(SEE ALSO: *Psychology and Logic*; and *Transcendental Logic* [S])

Bibliography

Bell, D. "Reference, Experience, and Intentionality," in L. Haaparanta, ed., *Mind, Meaning and Mathematics.* Essays on the philosophical views of Husserl and Frege (Dordrecht and Boston, 1994).

Husserl, E. *Experience and Judgment,* translated by J. S. Churchill and K. Ameriks. Evanston, IL, 1973.

Landgrebe, L. "The Phenomenological Concept of Experience," *Philosophy and Phenomenological Research,* 34 (1973), 1–13.

PIERRE KERSZBERG

EXPLANATION, THEORIES OF. Although explanations of many sorts occur in daily life, philosophical theories of explanation have dealt mainly with scientific explanation. EXPLANATION IN SCIENCE [3] in the *Encyclopedia of Philosophy* focused on Carl G. HEMPEL's [3] covering law theory of explanation, which included the deductive-nomological (D-N) model as expounded in Hempel and Oppenheim, (1948) and the inductive-statistical (I-S) model as presented in Hempel (1962). It qualified as "the orthodox view" during most of the 1960s and 1970s.

This approach received a definitive statement in Hempel's essay, "Aspects of Scientific Explanation" (1965), published too late for mention in the *Encyclopedia of Philosophy.* Here Hempel discussed many of the objections that had been brought against the D-N model, offered a much-improved version of the I-S model, and articulated for the first time the deductive-statistical (D-S) model. This article was the major point of departure for discussions of scientific explanation for about three decades.

THE ORTHODOX VIEW

According to the orthodox view, all legitimate scientific explanations fall into one of four categories, depending on the type of phenomenon to be explained (a particular fact or a general law) and on the type of law used in the explanation (universal or statistical), as shown in Table 1 (see p. 166). Every explanation is a logically correct deductive or inductive argument, and every explanation requires a general law in its premises; thus, every explanation represented in this table qualifies as a covering-law explanation. Statistical laws, it should be noted, are just as general as universal laws. "All tritium atoms have a probability of one-half of decaying within 12.32 years" applies to all tritium atoms just as "All green plants contain chlorophyll" applies to all green plants.

The D-S model of explanation differs little from the D-N model as applied to explanations of general laws. Both types explain general laws by deduction from other general laws; the only difference is whether the law to be explained is statistical or universal. Since no statistical law can be deduced from universal laws alone, every

		Type of phenomenon to be explained	
		Particular fact	General law
Type of	Universal law	Deductive-Nomological	Deductive-Nomological
Law	Statistical law	Inductive-Statistical	Deductive-Statistical

Table 1. Types of scientific explanation

D-S explanation contains at least one statistical law among its premises.

Hempel and Oppenheim attempted to offer a precise explication of D-N explanation but had to admit failure regarding explanations of general laws. As they point out (Hempel & Oppenheim, 1948, n. 33), a derivation of KEPLER's [4] laws of planetary motion from NEWTON's [5] laws of gravitation and motion has genuine explanatory value, but a derivation of Kepler's laws from the conjunction of Kepler's laws and BOYLE's [1] law (obviously a valid deduction) has no explanatory merit. They can offer no explicit criterion for distinguishing worthy from worthless explanations of generalizations. The same problem plagues the D-S model. It has received little attention in the philosophical literature and has not been solved (in Hempel, 1965, it is not addressed). Therefore, both types of explanation in the second column stand under a cloud.

The explanations in the first column are explanations of particular facts or events. In each case, deductive or statistical, the explanation is an argument to the effect that the event to be explained was to be expected by virtue of the explanatory facts. This means that, had we possessed the explanatory facts early enough, we could have predicted the explanandum event. In the D-N case, given the explanans, we could have predicted the event with deductive certainty; in the I-S case, given the explanans, we could have predicted the event with high inductive probability.

PROBABILISTIC/STATISTICAL EXPLANATION

Richard Jeffrey (Salmon et al., 1971) and Wesley Salmon (ibid.) severely criticized the I-S model of explanation. According to this model, an event can be explained only if it has a high PROBABILITY [6] relative to a suitable body of background knowledge. Jeffrey argued that events having low probabilities can sometimes be explained in terms of the stochastic mechanisms that give rise to them. The magnitude of the probability has no bearing on the value of the explanation. A run of ten heads with a fair coin is improbable (1/1024) but is fully comprehensible as an outcome of that chance process. Thus, statistical explanations of individual events need not be inductive arguments that render their conclusions highly probable.

Arguing that statistical relevance rather than high probability is the key to statistical explanation, Salmon rejected the I-S model and offered the statistical-relevance (S-R) model instead. Suppose that Mary Smith suffers from a psychological problem; she undergoes extensive psychiatric treatment and recovers. Suppose, further, that the probability of recovery from that problem with such treatment is 90 percent. Does the psychotherapy explain her recovery? If the spontaneous remission rate is also 90 percent, the answer is no, because the treatment has no bearing on the chance of recovery. This example fits the I-S model, but it does not constitute a genuine explanation. If, however, she had been afflicted with a different problem, for which the rate of recovery under psychotherapy is 40 percent but the spontaneous remission rate is 1 percent, the psychotherapy would explain her recovery even though the probability is not high. In this case the psychotherapy is statistically relevant; it makes a significant difference to the chance of recovery. These examples show that high probability is neither necessary nor sufficient for sound statistical explanation. According to the S-R model, a statistical explanation is not an argument, but rather an assemblage of factors relevant to the occurrence of the event to be explained.

When Salmon pointed out the problem of irrelevance in connection with I-S explanation, Henry E. Kyburg, Jr., observed that the same problem arises regarding D-N explanation. The following patently misguided explanation satisfies the D-N pattern: John Jones (a male) avoided becoming pregnant last year because he regularly consumed his wife's birth control pills, and any man who regularly takes oral contraceptives will avoid pregnancy. Thus, because of problems of relevancy, both patterns in the first column of Table 1 are undermined. Although the orthodox view retained its popularity for some time, it had been seriously shaken by the early 1970s. Three major approaches emerged as successors: the causal/mechanical view, the unification view, and the pragmatic view.

Explanation and Causation. Michael Scriven has maintained that to give an explanation of an occurrence is simply to cite its cause, and this squares well with our intuitions. Hempel's orthodox theory, while not denying the existence of causal relations, deliberately avoids allowing them any role in explanation. One suspects that the main reason many philosophers adopt this view lies in David HUME's [4; S] critique of causality. Those philosophers who claim that at least a major subset of explanations are causal take two different lines. One group, including Michael Scriven and Larry Wright, maintains that causal relations are among the givens of experience, and that causality needs no analysis. The other group, including James Fetzer, Paul Humphreys, and Salmon, among many others, have tried to furnish satisfactory analyses. These proffered explications differ markedly from one another.

Reflection on the S-R model also indicates the need for causality in explanation. For example, white spots on the inside of the cheek (known as Koplik spots) invariably accompany measles and appear before the other symptoms of the disease. The appearance of Koplik spots does not explain the occurrence of measles because they do not cause it; they are only a symptom. They are, however, strongly correlated with the occurrence of measles. This example shows that statistical relevance is insufficient for scientific explanation; causal relevance is what matters.

In discussing the role of causality in explanation we must remember that statistical explanation and causal explanation are not mutually exclusive; indeed, a number of authors have promulgated theories of probabilistic causality (see Patrick Suppes, 1970; Fetzer, 1981; Salmon, 1984; Humphreys, 1989; Ellery Eells, 1991). No consensus has developed regarding which analysis is correct.

Explanation and Unification. The Newtonian synthesis is a stunning achievement in the history of science. Three simple laws of motion and one law of gravitation suffice to unify, and thereby explain, a tremendous variety of phenomena—e.g., planetary motions, falling bodies, tides, and comets. According to Michael Friedman (1974) this case exemplifies a general principle—our understanding is increased when we can subsume diverse phenomena under a small number of basic assumptions. Friedman's technical account proved defective (see Salmon, 1989). Philip Kitcher (1989), though critical of Friedman's theory, subsequently developed a different version of the unification approach in which types of argument forms, rather than scientific laws, are the instruments of unification.

Pragmatics and Explanation. PRAGMATICS [S] is the study of contextual factors associated with the uses of language. Although advocates of the orthodox theory, the causal/mechanical approach, and the unification view all recognize that explanations have contextual features, they focus on such objective factors as laws of nature, causal relations, and logical entailments. Philosophers who deal with the pragmatics of explanation emphasize aspects like the interests and background knowledge of people who seek and who give explanations. Sylvain Bromberger did pathbreaking work in this area in the 1960s (see Salmon, 1989), but much greater attention has been drawn to this topic by Bas van Fraassen (1980).

According to van Fraassen, explanations are answers to why-questions. Questions arise in contexts and have presuppositions; if the presuppositions are not fulfilled the question cannot be answered but must be rejected. A why-question has three aspects, a topic, a contrast class, and a relevance relation. When Willie Sutton, the notorious bank robber, was asked by a reporter, "Why do you rob banks?" he replied, "Because that's where the money is." The topic of this question is the fact to be explained, "You rob banks." The question, as stated, is ambiguous because two different contrast classes are available. The journalist presumably had in mind the class {being a bank robber, being a doctor, being a plumber, . . .}. Sutton's answer involved a different class {robbing banks, robbing liquor stores, robbing private homes, . . .}. The humor in his answer plays on his ambiguity. The relevance relation on either interpretation is motivational.

Van Fraassen claims that attention to pragmatic features enables us to avoid the traditional problems surrounding the concept of explanation. His critics hold that he has failed to specify adequately what constitutes an explanatory relevance relation, and that to do so would involve precisely the problems faced by those who focused on the noncontextual aspects of explanation. No doubt investigation of the pragmatics of explanation is illuminated, but objective factors seem indispensable to an adequate theory of explanation.

(SEE ALSO: *Causation* [2; S]; *Explanation, Types of* [S]; and *Philosophy of Science* [S])

Bibliography

Eells, E. *Probabilistic Causality.* Cambridge, 1991.

Feigl, H., and G. Maxwell, eds. *Scientific Explanation, Space, and Time,* Vol. 3, *Minnesota Studies in the Philosophy of Science.* Minneapolis, 1962. Contains Hempel's first article on statistical explanation (superseded by his "Aspects of Scientific Explanation") and articles on explanation by M. Brodbeck, P. Feyerabend, and M. Scriven.

Fetzer, J. H. *Scientific Knowledge.* Dordrecht, 1981.

Friedman, M. "Explanation and Scientific Understanding," *Journal of Philosophy,* Vol. 71 (1974), 5–19.

Hempel, C. G. *Aspects of Scientific Explanation and Other Essays in the Philosophy of Science.* New York, 1965. Contains Hempel's "Aspects of Scientific Explanation," and a reprint of Hempel and Oppenheim, "Studies in the Logic of Explanation" (1948).

Humphreys, P. *The Chances of Explanation.* Princeton, NJ, 1989.

Kitcher, P., and W. C. Salmon. *Scientific Explanation,* Vol. 13, *Minnesota Studies in the Philosophy of Science.* Minneapolis, 1989. Contains nine articles by well-known experts, including Kitcher's "Explanatory Unification and the Causal Structure of the World," and Salmon's "Four Decades of Scientific Explanation." A rich source of bibliographical information, especially Salmon's contribution.

Salmon, W. C. *Scientific Explanation and the Causal Structure of the World.* Princeton, NJ, 1984.

———, et al. *Statistical Explanation and Statistical Relevance.* Pittsburgh, 1971. Contains Jeffrey, "Statistical Explanation vs. Statistical Inference," and Salmon, "Statistical Explanation."

Suppes, P. *A Probabilistic Theory of Causality.* Amsterdam, 1970. The classic work on probabilistic causality.

van Fraassen, B. C. *The Scientific Image.* Oxford, 1980.

WESLEY C. SALMON

EXPLANATION, TYPES OF. Various types of explanation appear in the natural and social sciences. How these are understood depends considerably on one's overall theory of scientific explanation. Deductive and statistical theories such as those of HEMPEL [3] and Salmon attempt to reduce scientific explanation to one or two basic forms. ARISTOTLE's [1; S] theory, which postulates different kinds of explanatory factors in nature, is nonreductionistic. So are pragmatic theories of the sort proposed by Achinstein and van Fraassen, which recognize many nonreducible types of questions that scientific explainers can answer. In what follows three important categories of explanation will be considered.

CAUSAL EXPLANATION

What Is a Causal Explanation? For Aristotle, who held a broad view, a causal explanation is one that cites one or more of the four causes or determining factors that exist in nature and correspond to the meanings of the question Why?: the material cause (the matter or constituents of which something is composed); the formal cause (the form or structure); the efficient cause (an external source of motion or change); and the final cause (the end, purpose, or function of something).

Many contemporary philosophers focus on a concept of cause corresponding roughly to Aristotle's efficient cause, with the idea that this is central in science, other types of causes being reducible to it. Since the 1940s the most influential of these accounts is the deductive-nomological model due to Hempel. To explain a particular event, on this account, one cites universal laws and facts about specific conditions that obtain, from which a statement describing the event is derivable. Such an explanation is causal if all the specific conditions cited occurred prior to the event being explained. This accords with HUME's [4; S] definition of CAUSATION [2; S], which requires the cause to precede the effect. Salmon has provided a more complex Humean account of causal explanation that involves distinguishing three aspects of causation: causal processes (e.g., the motion of a missile through space), causal interaction (e.g., the projection of the missile by a firing device), and conjunctive forks (the projection of several missiles together by a common firing device). Achinstein's pragmatic theory analyzes causal explanation by offering a semantical account of the kinds of questions causal explanations answer.

Are All Explanations Causal? For Aristotle all explanations are causal, since by an explanation he means something that gives one or more of his four causes. Some contemporary philosophers who do not champion such a broad notion of cause nevertheless answer the question affirmatively. David Lewis holds that to explain an event is to provide some information about its causal history. Depending on the context, this might include just one prior event or maximally and ideally a complete causal chain starting from the big bang.

Other writers deny that explanations, including scientific ones, are always causal. For Hempel, noncausal deductive-nomological explanations are possible in which the events cited in the explanans (the explaining sentences) occur cotemporaneously with, or even after, the event being explained. Achinstein characterizes several types of noncausal scientific explanations, including those that explain a regularity (e.g., a projectile continuing in motion) by bringing it under a more general noncausal law (e.g., the law of inertia) and those that explain why something has a given property (e.g., why this gas has the temperature it does) by citing an identical theoretical property (e.g., its mean molecular kinetic energy). Cases of the latter sort are also explored by Ruben.

STATISTICAL EXPLANATION

Some events are explained by citing conditions statistically but not universally associated with the event to be explained. We may say that Jim recovered from strep throat because he took penicillin, even though not all people recover under such conditions. For Hempel these explanations are inductive, not deductive, arguments (by contrast to the deductive-nomological cases). They contain premises describing conditions that obtained (e.g., "Jim had strep throat and took penicillin") together with probabilistic laws (e.g., "the probability of recovery from strep, given a penicillin injection, is such and such"); and they make the conclusion describing the event to be explained ("Jim recovered") probable.

Hempel's statistical model requires laws with high probabilities for the events being explained. Salmon and Railton develop contrasting statistical models that permit laws assigning any probabilities—high or low—to the event in question. On Salmon's statistical relevance model, for example, one can explain why a certain atom decayed when it did by citing the fact that the atom is an atom of radioactive element E and the statistical law that the probability of an atom of element E decaying at a given time is p, where the latter may be low but not zero. For Salmon, unlike Hempel, a statistical explanation cites facts and PROBABILITY [6; S] laws that do not necessarily make the event to be explained probable but show with what probability such an event can be expected. Railton defends what he calls a deductive-nomological-probabilistic (d-n-p) model of statistical explanation. First, from a theory supplying some causal mechanism, a law of the following form is derived deductively: at any time anything that has property F has a probability p to have property G. Second, a fact is cited concerning the event e to be explained—namely, that e has property F at time t. From this and the previous law we deduce: e has a probability p to have property G at time t. Finally, we add, parenthetically, according to what transpired: e did (not) have G at time t. This will constitute a d-n-p explanation of why e did (not) have G at t.

FUNCTIONAL EXPLANATION

A functional explanation is one that explains the existence of some item (e.g., the heart, the rain dance in some society) by citing its function (e.g., to pump the blood, to promote group solidarity). Such explanations frequently occur in biology as well as the social sciences.

What Are Functions? Most philosophical accounts fall into four categories. First is a "good consequence" doctrine, according to which doing y is x's function if and only if doing y confers some good. For biological functions the good is "survival and reproduction" (Ruse; Woodfield). Second, there is a "goal" doctrine, which states that y is x's function if any only if doing y contributes to some goal-state associated with x, the latter usually being defined causally (Nagel). Third, there is an "explanation" doctrine, according to which y is x's function if and only if x exists because it does y and y is a consequence of x's existing (Wright; Cummins and Millikan offer other versions). Fourth is a "means" doctrine that distinguishes various types of functions—including design, use, and service—all of which involve a means-end relationship; for example, "the function that x was designed to serve is to do y" is true if x was designed to serve as a means of doing y (Achinstein).

Are Functional Explanations Legitimate in Science? For Hempel a functional explanation to be scientifically legitimate would have to conform either to the deductive-nomological or the inductive-statistical model of explanation. But this is usually impossible, Hempel claims. Suppose we seek to give a functional explanation of the existence of the heart in mammals. To do so we must cite universal or statistical laws that either entail or make probable the heart's existence. So we might say: (1) mammals exist; (2) mammals exist only if their blood is circulated; (3) their blood is circulated only if they have hearts. But, says Hempel, (3), understood as a law, is false, since it is possible for devices other than (natural) hearts to circulate the blood. We could transform (3) into a truth by changing "only if" to "if." But with this change (1), (2), and the revised (3) would not entail or make probable that hearts exist in mammals. According to Hempel, the problem with functional explanations, whether in biology or the social sciences, is that they usually offer no basis for inferring the existence of the item with the function rather than any other item that could also have served that function.

Hempel's claims are rejected by Wright, who maintains that one can give a functional explanation of the existence of an item without also showing that only that item could serve the function. According to Wright, a functional explanation is a certain type of causal explanation: it explains the existence of an item x with a function y by saying that doing y in the past has been a cause or an important part of the cause of x's existence. Part of the cause of the heart's existing in mammals is that hearts have circulated the blood and continue to do so, even if in principle other blood circulators could have existed.

Both Hempel's attack on functional explanations and Wright's defense of them are based on the idea that teleological claims involving functions, to be legitimate in science, must be reducible to causal or lawlike assertions. This is in fundamental opposition to Aristotle's position that teleological claims are *sui generis* (final causes are not reducible to efficient ones). Achinstein's "means" doctrine of functions is a contemporary representative of the latter tradition. One can explain why hearts exist in mammals not only by answering (1) what caused them to exist (what evolutionary, chemical, or other processes were involved) but also by answering (2) what ends are served by means of hearts for which they exist? Answers to (1) and (2) may be independent.

EXPLANATORY REDUCTIONISM

Philosophers such as Hempel, Salmon, and Railton, who provide "models" of explanation, attempt to show that various types of explanations in the sciences conform to one of these models. But their models have counterexamples. One, to which the models of Hempel and Railton are subject, involves an intervening cause. Suppose that Jones eats a pound of arsenic and that it is a law that anyone who does so dies within twenty-four hours. For Hempel and Railton a correct explanation of Jones's death is his arsenic feast, even if there was an unrelated intervening cause such as a truck accident that killed poor Jones. Modelists generally build two features into their models: first, the presumption that, except for the truth of the explanans, whether or not the conditions required by the model are in fact met can be decided a priori; and second, a requirement that the description of the particular events invoked in the explanans does not by itself, without invoking laws, entail the event to be explained. Achinstein argues that models having both these features are always subject to counterexamples and hence that explanations in science cannot be reduced to the basic types demanded by modelists. For example, in the arsenic case, to avoid the problem noted and satisfy the a prior condition, one could add to the explanans the sentence "Jones's eating a pound of arsenic caused his death"; but this violates the second condition, since, without explicitly invoking laws, it entails the event to be explained.

(SEE ALSO: *Explanation in Science* [3]; *Explanation, Theories of* [S]; and *Philosophy of Science* [S])

Bibliography

Achinstein, P. *The Nature of Explanation.* New York, 1983.

———. "A Type of Non-Causal Explanation," in P. A. French, T. E. Uehling, and H. K. Wettstein, eds., *Causation and Causal Theories,* Midwest Studies in Philosophy, Vol. 9 (Minneapolis, 1984).

Aristotle. *Physica,* Book 2.

Cummins, R. "Functional Analysis," *Journal of Philosophy,* Vol. 72 (1975), 741–65.

Hempel, C. G. *Aspects of Scientific Explanation.* New York, 1965.

Lewis, D. "Causal Explanation," in D.-H. Ruben, ed., *Explanation* (Oxford, 1993).

Milliken, R. *Language, Thought, and Other Biological Categories.* Cambridge, MA, 1984.

Nagel, E. *Teleology Revisited and Other Essays in the Philosophy and History of Science.* New York, 1979.

Pitt, J. C., ed. *Theories of Explanation.* New York, 1988.

Railton, P. "A Deductive-Nomological Model of Probabilistic Explanation," *Philosophy of Science,* Vol. 45 (1978), 206–26.

Ruben, D.-H., ed. *Explanation.* Oxford, 1993.

Ruse, M. *The Philosophy of Biology.* London, 1973.

Salmon, W. C. *Scientific Explanation and the Causal Structure of the World.* Princeton, NJ, 1984.

———. *Four Decades of Scientific Explanation.* Minneapolis, 1989.

———, et al. *Statistical Explanation and Statistical Relevance.* Pittsburgh, 1971.

van Fraassen, B. *The Scientific Image.* Oxford, 1980.

Woodfield, A. *Teleology.* Cambridge, 1976.

Wright, L. *Teleological Explanations.* Berkeley, 1976.

PETER ACHINSTEIN

EXTERNALISM. *See:* CONTENT, MENTAL, and INTERNALISM VERSUS EXTERNALISM [S]

EXTRINSIC AND INTRINSIC PROPERTIES. An intrinsic property is one whose possession by an object at a time involves nothing other than the object (and its parts) at that time; an extrinsic property is one whose possession at a time involves something else. We might say, therefore, that the properties of being red and round are intrinsic to this ball, but the properties of being in Rhode Island, being less than five feet away from a tree, and having once been owned by my sister are extrinsic to it.

Geach has made a corresponding distinction among changes. There is change whenever 'F(x) at time t' is true and 'F(x) at time t″ is false. Socrates will change when he puts on weight; he will also change when he comes to be shorter than Theaetetus merely in virtue of Theaetetus' growth. Changes of the second kind—intuitively less genuine—Geach calls "mere Cambridge changes," without proposing a rigorous criterion. We might define a mere Cambridge property as a property, change in an object's possession of which is a mere Cambridge change. Mere Cambridge properties are plausibly taken to be the same as extrinsic properties.

The matter is important, among other things, for the clear statement of a Humean view of the world (*see* HUME [4; S]). For a Humean there is in principle a description in intrinsic terms of the state of the world at any one time that is both complete and free of implications for the state of the world at any other time. "Solidity, extension, motion; these qualities are all complete in themselves, and never point out any other event which may result from them" (Hume, *Enquiry,* sec. 8, 1) It is not clear, however, that what Hume says can be true: the motion of an object is hardly free of implications about the state of the world at other times. (If an object at place *p* is said to be moving at time *t*, this is standardly in the sense that, at other times more or less near to *t*, the object is in other places more or less near to *p*.) We may have to decide between complete description and a purely intrinsic one.

Two extreme views are that all properties are really intrinsic and that all properties are really extrinsic. LEIBNIZ [4; S] holds the first: "There are no purely extrinsic denominations." His insistence resulted in the drastic denial of the reality of relations and, most notably, of space and time; it has not been widely accepted. A moderate version of the opposite view, that all properties are really extrinsic, might be held by someone, like POPPER [6], who believes that physical properties are essentially dispositional. Both extremes, in different ways, represent a sense that the nature of one thing cannot be divorced from the nature of others. Confidence in a firm distinction between the intrinsic and the extrinsic, on the other hand, is more characteristic of an optimistic Humean.

It is not easy to give a precise characterization of intrinsic properties, and there may not even be a unique idea, so to speak, waiting to be characterized. We might try saying that extrinsic properties are relational properties and intrinsic properties nonrelational. But many intuitively intrinsic properties still in some way involve a relation—squareness involves a relation among the sides of an object. Can we say that intrinsic properties are those that do not involve a relation to anything that is not a part of the object? This is perhaps the clearest criterion, but it may still be incapable of capturing all our intuitions at once. The power to open locks of kind k, for example, apparently involves a relation to external things of a certain kind—which would seem to make it extrinsic. Yet it is a property that a key can have if it is, so to speak, alone in the world—which would seem to make it intrinsic.

It may be helpful to invoke a distinction between relational descriptions of a property and descriptions of a relational property. But that distinction is itself perplexing. Is 'possessing what is actually Jane's favorite intrinsic property' a relational description of a first-order property or a description of second-level relational property?

Philosophers have argued in many cases that apparently intrinsic properties are in fact extrinsic. Terms such as *old, great,* and *imperfect,* LOCKE [4; S] says, "are not looked on to be either relative or so much as external denominations," but they conceal a tacit relation (*Essay*). More worrying are challenges even to the idea that primary qualities, like size and shape, are intrinsic. The size of the ball is, we may think, intrinsic to it. We can describe a scenario where everything else in the universe is twice its actual size while the ball remains the same. But can we properly distinguish this from a scenario where the rest of the world is the same but the ball is half its actual size? Some will argue that length is relational, and the two scenarios make a distinction without a difference: size, after all, is extrinsic. Others will argue instead that even if our descriptions of size are relative, for example, to standard measures, what is described is still an absolute and intrinsic property.

Are any or all of a person's mental properties intrinsic to her? The question is in part about the limitations of methodological solipsism. (See INTERNALISM VERSUS EXTERNALISM [S].) If Jane could not possess the property of thinking of Bertrand Russell if Russell did not exist, then that property must be extrinsic to her. Some will try to segment referential thought into an internal and an external component; but if that proposal fails, referential thought will typically be extrinsic to the thinker. (Another option is that the thinker, or her mind, extends more widely than her body—and actually includes Russell.) One might argue a similar point with respect to thought about properties as well as about individuals. (A brain that has never been out of a vat does not know what a meter is.) Maybe there are very few mental properties intrinsic to a person; or maybe we should think again about what the notion of the intrinsic is, and what exactly it is supposed to do for us.

(SEE ALSO: *Metaphysics* [S])

Bibliography

Geach, P. T. *God and the Soul.* London, 1969.

Leibniz, G. W. "Primary Truths" and "Letters to Des Bosses," in *Philosophical Essays,* translated by R. Ariew and D. Garber. Indianapolis, 1989. See esp. pp. 32, 203.

Lewis, D. K. *On the Plurality of Worlds.* Oxford, 1986. Chaps. 1.5, 4.2.

Lewis, D. K. "Extrinsic Properties," *Philosophical Studies,* Vol. 44 (1983), 197–200.

Locke, J. *Essay concerning Human Understanding.* Bk. 2, Chaps. 25, 28.

Popper, K. *The Logic of Scientific Discovery.* London, 1959. Pp. 424–25.

JUSTIN BROACKES

F

FEMINISM AND CONTINENTAL PHILOSOPHY. Feminism, as a philosophy and a political movement, has been greatly enriched by the existentialist/phenomenological tradition of Jean-Paul SARTRE [7; S], Maurice MERLEAU-PONTY [5; S], and Simone de BEAUVOIR [S]. But the historical conjunction of current feminism with poststructuralist and postmodern philosophy (FOUCAULT [S], DERRIDA [S], Lyotard, Deleuze) has been an uneasy and wary alliance. (*See* MODERNISM AND POSTMODERNISM, and POSTSTRUCTURALISM [S])

American feminists welcomed the phenomenological emphasis on women's lived experience not only to give an authentic voice to the common meanings of their shared experiences but also to "raise political consciousness" of their shared oppression. Feminist philosophers have created rich, phenomenological accounts of female, lived experience, inspired by de Beauvoir's earlier accounts in the *Second Sex* of women's life-experiences in patriarchal societies (Allen & Young, 1989). Critical of the disguised, gender bias of traditional phenomenological categories and its essentialist tendencies, some feminist theorists no longer privilege a "foundational" reality of women's lived experiences. Appropriating Foucault's analysis of power and bodies, contemporary feminist philosophers have shown how women's bodies and identities have been inscribed and shaped by various cultural, signifying practices (Bartky, 1990; Bordo, 1994; Butler, 1989). Taking the cue from Derrida's critique of the phallocentrism of Western philosophy, feminism seeks to dislodge any totalizing dualism of man/woman or essentializing category of woman to focus on differences among women, the multiple ways of being women (Butler).

In its appropriation of continental philosophy, postmodern feminism in the United States and Western Europe may be described according to Derrida's notion of the double gesture: (1) de-constructing binary identities of man/woman, heterosexual/lesbian, to multiply differences in a nonhierarchical and nonoppositional manner; and 2) constructing sexual difference and the feminine by a "new" discourse of women's voices and feminine writing ("l'écriture feminine"). Feminist philosophers have resourcefully used Derrida's tools of DECONSTRUCTION [S] and Foucault's method of genealogical critique to subvert "natural" ontologies of gender, sexual difference, and identity. Yet they have clearly signaled the political impasses to which these practices might lead in the hands of the masters: (1) the destabilizing of a subject; (2) the indifference to sexual difference; (3) blindness to gender oppression; (4) erasure of the feminine; and (5) the impossibility of social and political change and liberatory ideals. It should be noted that feminist thinkers rather robustly debate whether the texts of Foucault and Derrida do pose barriers to feminist political struggles (Cornell, 1991; Sawicki, 1991). Nevertheless, feminist thinkers seek to transcend the impasses that they have discovered in postmodern continental philosophy.

SEXUAL DIFFERENCE

The most well-known French feminist thinkers, Luce Irigaray and Hélène Cixous, have been strongly influenced by Derrida's and Lacan's critiques of the phallologocentrism of Western thought. Irigaray in her own "fling with the philosophers" of the Western tradition has subverted the gender neutrality or humanism of Western philosophy to disclose a male subject *and* a male libidinal economy as the subject of the discourses of philosophy, epistemology, and science. According to Western phallocratic thought or the "symbolic code of the father," women can only be represented as "sameness," as mirror or complement, or contrast to man or male desire; feminine desire and pleasure are unrepresentable within the discourses of phallologocentrism. Irigaray and Cixous accept the dismantling of the Western tradition of man, the "truth and the logos," but they reject postmodernism's repetition of the tradition, the repression of feminine specificity or difference. Moreover, to make matters worse, the feminine becomes appropriated as metaphor by Derrida (and Deleuze) to describe their own philosophic practices of destabilizing binary dualisms, multiplying meanings, and resisting identities.

Cixous and Irigaray have sought to deconstruct the economy of sexual indifference or sameness to enunciate an autonomous construction of feminine, sexual difference, and feminine identities. This notion directly contradicts Derrida's dream of a "choreography of sexual differences," which breaks down the binary of heterosexuality to proliferate undecidable genders and innumerable sexual differences. The symbolic representations of women's bodily geography and pleasures, independent of heterosexual norms of male desire—speaking and writing the body—are taken to be forms of political praxis. Irigaray calls for the construction of a feminine "imaginary." This symbolics of a feminine imaginary is a cultural politics of difference, which projects the becoming of woman, the "not-yet," both discursively and materially. For Irigaray and Cixous the grammar of culture must be changed to create social and economic changes in a patriarchal society.

SUBJECT

Several American feminist theorists (Bartky 1990; Bordo, 1994; Butler, 1989; and Sawicki, 1991, among others) have appropriated Foucault's genealogical method to show how disciplinary practices have constructed (normalized) women's bodies and gender identities in the late twentieth century. Other feminist theorists have criticized this genealogical analysis and the use of Foucauldian methods because they mask forms of patriarchal or gender oppression and do not seemingly engage or promote a politics of liberation. How can women resist these disciplinary and normalizing regimes of bodily inscription, when there is no autonomous agency of female subjects?

GENDER

Debates over essentialism (a universal essence of woman) have called for the strategic uses of woman for political purposes. Some American feminists have staunchly supported the concept of positionality of women according to the differences of race, class, sexual preference, age, eschewing any commonality of woman per se. Essentialism, whether naturally or culturally construed, is a politically regressive category, leading back to social inequality or to praising the virtues of the oppressed.

Is the category of gender dangerous or liberating? Susan Bordo (1994) has reflected on this gender-skepticism as one of the legacies of postmodernism: women's refusal to be Other. Can there be a politics of identity? Contemporary feminism has also been influenced by Derrida's deconstructive critique of the binary man/woman and any unitive totalizing category of woman. These logical categories (logocentrism) presuppose a hierarchical division of male over female, yet the first term paradoxically depends on the second for its definition and completion. Any definition of woman will necessarily exclude other women and reduce the real differences among women.

Rosi Braidotti (1991) has argued that minority women, especially postcolonial and subaltern women, need to claim their own symbolic agency in constructing their own identity, a multiplicity of alternative forms of feminist subjectivity. These differences are not rooted in discursive identities but in the specificity of lived female bodily experience.

The feminist appropriation of both Derridian deconstruction and Foucault's genealogical methods has created these two counterpoints in the movement of contemporary feminism. Postmodern feminists may offer a new conceptual start for the political agendas of the feminist movement. A poetics of the body and sexual difference, the becoming of woman ("devenir femme") in all her multiple identities, may be the prelude to political change.

The field of inquiry cannot be limited to these two movements, however, since postmodernist Habermasian feminists have also opposed Lyotard's rejection of a grand narrative and the ideal of rational consensus in politics. Young and others posit emancipatory ideals in their philosophies. Fraser and Nicholson in their influential book, *Feminism/Postmodernism* (1993), call for local narratives of historical periods, and criticize poststructuralist discourse theory for its neglect of material social praxis and counterhegemonic discourses and voices. These theorists have been influenced by HABERMAS's [S] critique of the postmodern in which he claims that postmodernism leads to conservatism and to NIHILISM [5]. Benhabib seeks to save the subject by placing herself in a specific, historical/social situation, and by leaving open the possibility of a communicative ethics.

(SEE ALSO: *Feminist Philosophy* [S])

Bibliography

Allen, J., and I. Young. *The Thinking Muse.* Bloomington, IN, 1989. General discussion of feminism and continental philosophy.

Bartky, S. *Femininity and Domination.* New York, 1990.

Braidotti, R. *Patterns of Dissonance.* New York, 1991.

Bordo, S. *Unbearable Weight.* Berkeley, 1994.

Butler, J. *Gender Trouble.* New York, 1989.

Cornell, D. *Beyond Accommodation.* New York, 1991.

———. *Philosophy of the Limit.* New York, 1993.

Nicholson, L. *Feminism/Postmodernism.* New York, 1990.

Sawicki, J. *Disciplining Foucault.* New York, 1991.

Young, I. *Throwing Like a Girl and Other Essays*. Bloomington, IN, 1990.

ARLEEN B. DALLERY

FEMINISM AND PRAGMATISM. Feminism and PRAGMATISM [6; S] are theoretically and historically related. Among the pragmatist positions that provide support for a variety of feminist analyses are the following: EXPERIENCE [3], rather than SKEPTICISM [7; S], as both the starting point and test of understanding; individuals and society as dynamically related and interactively constituted; knowledge as the outcome of inquiry that is perspectival and pluralistic; ethics as both a personally and historically developmental process held accountable to actual outcomes; and social democracy as a model of the most empowering relationship between individual development and a just society. As a post-Darwinian philosophy that recognizes the continuity of organism and environment, pragmatism rejects the epistemological turn for a concrete analysis of the interactive process of understanding as a transformative practice. Whereas pragmatism holds that selective interests account for the known world and develops methods both to question and incorporate these pluralistic perspectives into inquiry, feminism focuses on the multiplicity of women's experiences and needs and demonstrates how negative stereotypes have historically masqueraded as nonperspectival, neutral judgments. Beginning with a concrete analysis of the temporality and contingency of the human condition, the goals of philosophy for pragmatists are (1) emancipation from distorting beliefs and practices that hinder personal growth and prevent the elimination of natural and social ills, and (2) development of experimental, consensual strategies for solving problematic situations. Feminists have explicitly identified SEXISM [S], RACISM [7; S], classism, and heterosexism as actually distortive perspectives that are pervasive in everyday life and theoretical explanations. Both pragmatists and many feminists reject the exaggerated individualism of classical liberal theory in their understanding of persons as multiply related and socially and historically situated. Some feminists and most pragmatists also analyze RATIONALITY [S] as an evolutionary developmental process that includes embodiment, emotions, and sociality.

Historically, pragmatism was influenced by women and blacks, some of whom used it to develop feminist and antiracist analyses. According to Charlotte Perkins Gilman's use of evolutionary theory, progress is inevitable, whereas other pragmatists emphasize the randomness of spontaneous variations and the contingency of human intervention. However, she was more explicit about the androcentrism of social and cultural developments and demonstrated the economic basis of women's oppression. Research on sexual differences by Helen Thompson (Wooley) and Jessie Taft at the beginning of the twentieth century was encouraged by pragmatists in the multidisciplinary department of philosophy, psychology, and education at the University of Chicago. John DEWEY's [2; S] earliest formulations of pragmatist philosophy were influenced by both the experiments in developmental education carried out by Alice Chipman Dewey, Ella Flagg Young, and other women at the Laboratory School and by the community-based activist model of Jane Addams, Alice Hamilton, Florence Kelley, Julia Lathrop, and other women of Hull House.

The pragmatist understanding of knowledge as the outcome of experimentation according to ends-in-view is antidogmatic, social, and contextual. W. E. B. Du Bois and Alain Locke showed the effects of racial prejudice on the actual way experimentation was carried out in the social sciences and the theoretical and practical transformations required in response to the experiences and perspectives of blacks. Pragmatism rejects the standpoint of the neutral observer as both epistemologically bankrupt and morally pernicious. Experimentation is transactive, changing both the investigator and the object of investigation. The women of Hull House took this premise one step further by choosing to live among the most needy members of the community and learn with them how to transform oppressive conditions. They uniquely combined the pragmatist theses of learning from experience, perspectival views of knowledge, and anti-elitism into a multicultural, cooperative approach to social problems. Pragmatists argue that the violent overthrow of social and political institutions leaves old habits unchanged. They therefore emphasize lifelong education and experimental method because they can radically reorient those feelings, dispositions, and attitudes that constitute dominant habits of mind and character and thus provide the means as well as the ends of continuing radical transformation.

(SEE ALSO: *Feminist Philosophy* [S])

Bibliography

Addams, J. *Twenty Years at Hull House* [1910]. New York, 1981.

———. *The Social Thought of Jane Addams,* edited by C. Lasch. Indianapolis, 1965. Reprint, New York, 1982.

Dewey, J. *Democracy and Education,* in *Middle Works, Volume 9: 1916*. Carbondale and Edwardsville, IL, 1980.

———. "Philosophy and Democracy," pp. 41–53, in *Middle Works, Volume 11: 1918–1919*. Carbondale and Edwardsville, IL, 1982.

———. "Context and Thought," pp. 3–28; "Education and Birth Control," pp. 146–48; "Senate Birth Control Bill," pp. 388–89; and "Address to the National Association for the Advancement of Colored People," pp. 224–30, in *Later Works, Volume 6: 1931–1932*. Carbondale and Edwardsville, IL, 1985.

Du Bois, W. E. B. *Darkwater: Voices from Within the Veil* [1920]. Reprinted with an introduction by H. Aptheker. Millwood, NY, 1975.

Gilman, C. P. *Women and Economics: A Study of the Economic Relation Between Men and Women as a Factor in Social Evolution* [1898]. Reprinted with an introduction by C. N. Degler. New York, 1966.

———. *The Man-Made World or, Our Androcentric Culture* [1911]. Minneapolis, 1971.

Radin, M. J. "The Pragmatist and the Feminist," *Southern California Law Review,* Vol. 63 (Sept., 1990), 1699–1726. Reprinted in J. Arthur and W. H. Shaw, eds., *Readings in the Philosophy of Law* (Englewood Cliffs, NJ, 1993).

Rorty, R. "Feminism and Pragmatism," *Michigan Quarterly Review,* Vol. 30 (Spring, 1991), 231–58.

Rosenberg, R. *Beyond Separate Spheres: The Intellectual Roots of Modern Feminism.* New Haven, 1982.

Seigfried, C. H., ed. "Special Issue on Feminism and Pragmatism," *Hypatia,* Vol. 8 (1993).

———. *Pragmatism and Feminism: Reweaving the Social Fabric.* Chicago, 1996.

Taft, J. *The Woman Movement from the Point of View of Social Consciousness.* Menasha, WI, 1915.

CHARLENE HADDOCK SEIGFRIED

FEMINIST AESTHETICS AND CRITICISM. Feminist aesthetics is a radical revision of philosophical aesthetic theory that emanates from a feminist perspective. It is fundamentally critical of philosophical orthodoxy, which takes male experience and judgment as normative. Feminist aesthetics addresses the bias implicit in characterizations of art, art creation and evaluation, aesthetic experience, and pleasure. The prototypical artist is male, as are his audience and critics. A feminist analysis begins by doubting the pretension to universality.

Typically, feminist critics first sought to "fill in" the missing subjective orientation by adding a feminine complement to aesthetic concepts still held to be basically sound. But this approach failed to acknowledge that normativity extends to the tools of discourse as well as to its objects. By the prevailing standards those forgotten by history merited their oblivion; and so a related task for feminists was to explain women's nonconformity to those standard in terms of social and political constraints. Linda Nochlin's 1971 article "Why Have There Been No Great Women Artists?" marked a scholarly turning point.

Challenging the masculinist bias directly, feminists next contemplated the universe unapologetically from a woman-centered perspective. This strategy of reversal is essentially reactive and preserves the basic dualisms of conventional theory. Practically, it leads to cultural and political isolation. Epistemologically, however, it encouraged deep questioning of gender concepts that allied feminism with other socially displacing philosophical theories. Driven by the celebration of difference, yet skeptical of a demeaning essentialism, feminists sought validation that would transform the conditions of inclusiveness. This meant reassessing such basic concepts as truth, value, selfhood, and community: for aestheticians it entailed reflection on the historic meanings of BEAUTY [1; S], art, artist, and the ARTWORLD [S].

A feminist transformation of the artworld meant creating alternative exhibition and performance spaces, new venues for artistic expression, new scholarship and critical criteria, new media and outlets for exposure. Feminism required unprecedented interdisciplinary, interprofessional, and intergenerational communication that ultimately also overcame barriers of race and class and undermined the dualisms upon which the aesthetic enterprise had been grounded. Feminism repudiated the dominator view of human nature that depicts the artist as demigod imposing form on recalcitrant matter. Likewise, feminism denied the identity of the work of art, dropped inviolate from the hand of its creator, yet, paradoxically, an object to be sold and bought, publicly scrutinized and privately adored, albeit with "disinterested" affection. Feminists pointed to the voyeurism implicit and theoretically legitimized in conventional aesthetic appreciation, which presumes that the contemplation and delight of the spectator is the final end of all creation. The very concept of beauty was shown to be genderized. Feminist theory reveals the part of the aesthetic in naturalizing the power inequity between subject and object.

The condition of being objectified and thereby implicitly passive is well understood by oppressed people, but that state is not invariably aestheticized as it is for women. It is a task of particular feminist interest to detach beauty from dominating power and to disengender aesthetic pleasure. Feminists are not alone in striving to achieve these aims, but they remain conceptually distinct from their political collaborators.

The positive core of feminist theory and thus a feminist aesthetics is the explicit acknowledgment that gender, however historically constituted, conditions experience and therefore conditions act and judgment. At this juncture feminist theory is obliged to look both backward and forward; (1) to explain present circumstances with the help of the newly validated tool of gender analysis; (2) to project artforms and modes of aesthetic expression that are reconcilable with a feminist worldview (this objective does not invariably entail replacement of traditional works of art with new ones); (3) to devise theory that legitimizes unprecedented modes of expression and experience, releasing the hold of conventional concepts without devaluing what women have always done.

Aesthetic theorizing, especially in the United States, has yoked classical speculation about the beautiful and sublime to eighteenth-century reflections on creativity and the judgment of taste and linked these, in turn, to twentieth-century conceptual analysis of expression, valuation, and the language of criticism. Seeking both the root of their own exclusion and that which detaches philosophical aesthetics from the lived world of aesthetic experience, feminists have exposed the incoherency of prevailing aesthetic doctrine. Some feminists are also striving to realize an aesthetic that draws upon female embodiment, language, and consciousness. Feminist aestheticians, along with feminist artists and critics, are undertaking now to reconnect theory with practice and to address the full range of their application. Whether a theory that is consciously engendered will ultimately satisfy the philosophical quest for universality remains to be determined.

(SEE ALSO: *Feminist Philosophy* [S])

Bibliography

Battersby, C. *Gender and Genius: Towards a Feminist Aesthetics.* Bloomington, IN, 1989.

Brand, P. Z., and C. Korsmeyer. *Feminism and Tradition in Aesthetics.* University Park, PA, 1995.

Broude, N., and M. Gerrard. *Feminism and Art History: Questioning the Litany.* New York, 1982.

Felski, R. *Beyond Feminist Aesthetics: Feminist Literature and Social Change.* Cambridge, MA, 1989.

Hein, H., and C. Korsmeyer. *Aesthetics in Feminist Perspective.* Bloomington, IN, 1993.

Mulvey, L. "Visual Pleasure and Narrative Cinema," *Screen,* Vol. 16, no. 3 (1975), 6–18.

Nochlin, L. "Why Have There Been No Great Women Artists?" in T. B. Hess and E. C. Baker, eds., *Art and Sexual Politics* (New York, 1971).

———. *Women, Art, and Power and Other Essays.* New York, 1988.

HILDE HEIN

FEMINIST EPISTEMOLOGY AND ONTOLOGY. Feminist epistemologists take issue with the (often tacit) universalist pretensions of mainstream (i.e., post-positivist, empiricist, Anglo-American) epistemologies and their exclusionary effects. Conceiving of 'the epistemological project' as an a priori, normative endeavor to determine necessary and sufficient conditions for the possibility of knowledge 'in general', mainstream epistemologists have tended to assume that they can realize these goals only by transcending the particularities of human experiences, locations, and circumstances, to produce and analyze knowledge from a disinterested, dislocated, neutral position. Correlatively, they have conceived of knowledge acquisition as an individual project in which knowers are separately confronted with and accountable to the evidence. These 'individuals' are the abstract, interchangeable individuals of liberal social/political theory. Their interchangeability is crucial to the success of the project of developing normative analyses of objective knowledge, unsullied by the vagaries and uncertainties of subjectivity. Personal idiosyncrasies could not be accorded epistemic salience without compromising or thwarting these universalistic goals.

Feminist epistemologists have, to some extent, made common cause with other critics of the Enlightenment legacy with respect to these two issues: its universalistic—hence nonsituated—claims and the individualism that is integral both to its substantive conclusions and to the ontology that informs them. But feminists part company with these other critics to the extent that they focus on the androcentrism of mainstream epistemologies, even as they acknowledge that androcentrism manifests itself variously across racial, ethnic, economic, religious, and class lines, to mention only some of the pertinent axes (Alcoff & Potter, 1993).

Androcentrism derives from the fact that the producers and promulgators of the Western philosophical canon have, overwhelmingly, been male; and the claim that philosophies are shaped by the gender of their makers is integral to feminist contestations of individualism and universalism. For on a universalist-interchangeability analysis, 'truths' would pass untainted through the minds that come to know them; hence, it would be merely an irrelevant coincidence that philosophies were made by men, for the implication would be that anyone who used his *or her* reason well would have arrived at precisely the same results. Yet feminist charges of androcentricity contest this fundamental claim. They maintain that philosophies—and hence epistemologies—are made, not found, and indelibly bear the mark of their makers. Mainstream epistemologies are androcentric in that they derive from and hence explicate typically male (and white, prosperous, educated) experiences, even though those experiences, too, come across as generic rather than individuated. These epistemologies assume a 'knowing subject' whose autonomous and self-sufficient knowledge seeking attests to a developmental process fostered to sustain the exemplary status of the authoritative masculine values upheld within the affluent middle classes of white Western societies.

DUALIST ONTOLOGY

Equally integral to the presuppositions of mainstream epistemologies is the mind–body dualism (*see* MIND-BODY PROBLEM [S]) that is best known from the writings of DESCARTES [2; S] but is continuous with a veneration of the mind and a denigration of the body that pervades white Western (Judeo-Christian) philosophy and culture. The belief that it is RATIONALITY [S] that distinguishes 'man' from other creatures, coupled with the belief that "reason is alike in all men," fuels the universalistic hopes of philosophy, especially in its epistemological endeavors, and in the moral-political conclusions they inform. The 'subjects' of mainstream epistemology, thus, are rational subjects, whose knowledge—and knowledge-informed action—is produced, ideally at least, by their reason alone (in the rationalist tradition) or by those parts of their perceptual/observational apparatus (in the empiricist tradition) that are common from knowerto knower and hence most amenable to objective, dispassionate verification. Their bodily being—their gendered or racial specificity—has no epistemological significance and is merely incidental to the production and analysis of knowledge properly—objectively—conceived.

Feminist epistemologists have argued, however, that embodiment is not a mere accident of human being but is constitutive of subjectivity and agency and hence of possibilities of knowledge production; it is in consequence of 'different' (from affluent white male) embodiment that people are assigned to marginal epistemic positions. Often in productive dialogue with the phenomenological tradition of 'Continental' philosophy and French feminist theory, many feminists have argued that an adequate epistemology needs to be as cognizant of bodily experiences as it is of rational endeavor, especially if its aim is to enable people to negotiate their circumstances well (Lennon & Whitford, 1994). The point of these arguments is not the simplistic one that there are separate men's and women's ways of knowing. Rather, it is that gender, race, ethnicity, age, class, and other analogous factors position people so as to produce experiential variations that cannot—and should not—simply be eradicated in the cleansing processes of epistemic justification, especially if the knowledge analyzed is to retain continuity with the lives of those who need to act knowledgeably. Epistemologies that tacitly assimilate all experiences to a single norm tend to work from the assumption that all embodied human beings have access to the same experiences and command the epistemic authority that is in fact available only to a privileged and powerful few. Differences from this tacit norm come out as aberrations, to be eradicated from rather than factored into epistemological analysis. Feminist commitments to honoring differences actively contest this tendency.

REASON AND PASSION

This dualist ontology has contributed to producing a conception of knowledge as a purely intellectual, rational product and of knowers as worthy of the title only to the extent that they rely on reason to the exclusion of emotion or affect. These assumptions denigrate the emotions/passions as merely subjective, idiosyncratic, and whimsical; as forces whose onslaught overwhelms and ultimately eradicates objectivity.

Efforts to dissolve the reason/passion dichotomy have figured centrally in feminist projects, and on good grounds. The Western philosophical tradition is marked by a persistent alignment between reason and maleness and between emotion/passion and femaleness: an alignment apparent from folkloric claims to the effect that men are 'more' rational and women 'more' emotional, to philosophical assumptions about the nature of reason both in itself and as it contrasts with emotion and passion (Lloyd, 1993). The alignment manifests itself in conceptions of appropriately gendered divisions of intellectual labor and of the proper hierarchical structuring of the social order. It represents the emotions/passions as fundamentally irrational and sustains public denigrations of emotion and of women because of their alleged emotionality. Moreover, it suppresses the common and frequently trustworthy prephilosophical insight that emotions and passions are cognitive, in that they often function as knowledgeable responses to situations, and rational, in that they are often the most appropriate and reasonable ways of responding. In short, feminists have argued that the epistemologies of modernity tend to celebrate a style of reasoning that is neither the best nor the only available style; and that the dispassionate instrumental rationality that claims the highest respect in Western societies serves no one's interests well, even as it sustains the exemplary status of traditional (middle-class) masculine ways of being.

STANDPOINT THEORIES

Drawing on Marxist analyses, feminists such as Nancy Hartsock (1983) and Sandra Harding (1986) have constructed analogies between the epistemic position of women in patriarchal societies and the economic position of the proletariat in capitalist societies. Just as the subordination of the proletariat of the capitalist class is 'naturalized' by the theoretical assumptions of capitalism, so the subordination of women is 'naturalized' by the theoretical assumptions of patriarchy. And just as analyses that take the lives of the proletariat as their starting point work to denaturalize these assumptions, so, too, starting from women's lives can denaturalize the assumptions on which the patriarchal order rests.

A feminist standpoint, which is distinct from a 'women's standpoint' because of its achieved feminist consciousness, is more than just another perspective on the world. It is a hard-won product of consciousness raising and social-political engagement, designed to reveal the false presuppositions on which patriarchal hierarchies are built and to counter the forms of alienation they produce. Starting from the material realities of women's lives and analyzing their oppressions as structural effects of an unjust social order, standpoint theorists contend that the knowledge the oppressed have had to acquire just to survive under oppression can become a resource for transforming the social order. Critics are often skeptical about the apparent call for a single, representative, or inclusive feminist standpoint, but standpoint theorists contend that such reductivism has no place on their agendas. Multiple standpoints, often united around common issues, are both possible and necessary. Patricia Hill Collins (1990) argues that the 'outsider-within' positioning of a black feminist standpoint can yield an Afrocentric epistemology that shows how subordinate groups produce knowledge that fosters resistance. And Maria Lugones (1988) advocates "world travelling and loving perception" as strategies for breaking out of the confines of a too particular, self-satisfied location.

FEMINISM/POSTMODERNISM

The very act of posing questions about the identities and locations of knowers is postmodern in its contestation of the universalistic and individualistic assumptions of modernity. Yet the label postmodern commonly attaches to projects that do rather more than this: indeed, POSTMODERNISM [S] is often represented as inimical to epistemological inquiry as such, for its rejection of foundationalism is regarded as tantamount to a claim that knowledge is impossible; and its insistence on the instability of subjectivity seems to erase the very possibility of epistemic agency.

These nihilistic consequences are by no means the necessary result of postmodern critiques, however. Many postmodern theorists believe that better, more politically sensitive epistemological strategies can be developed once the stranglehold of oppressive master narratives is broken and once the fiction of a unified, dislocated knowing subject is abandoned. Drawing upon the hermeneutic and genealogical techniques of thinkers such as NIETZSCHE [5; S], GADAMER [S], and FOUCAULT [S], feminists such as Kathy Ferguson (1993) and Joan Scott (1992) have argued that all knowledge-producing projects are politically invested yet open to ongoing critical analyses generated out of an anti-imperialist politics of difference. Such analyses may never yield final or universal conclusions; but they do afford critical tools for debating and negotiating the knowledge claims that are the necessary prerequisite for action. And informed by the psychoanalytic theories of FREUD [3; S] and Lacan—as well as by Marxist-derived materialist theories of subjectivity and Derridean deconstructions of traditional ontologies (*see* DECONSTRUCTION; DERRIDA [S])—feminists such as Denise Riley (1988), Teresa de Lauretis (1987), and Judith Butler (1990) contest mainstream conceptions of a unified subjectivity to work from recognitions of a multiplicity of subjectivities and strategic identities.

SOCIAL ANALYSES OF KNOWLEDGE

One of the principal feminist responses to individualism is the contextual empiricism of Helen Longino (1990), who argues that communities, not individuals, are the primary knowers. Background assumptions always infuse and shape individual cognitive projects and are as epistemologically pertinent as any specific set of knowledge claims. In detailed accounts of experiments in genetic research that work from fundamentally different background assumptions, Longino demonstrates the necessity of analyzing processes of discovery as rigorously as processes of justification have traditionally been analyzed, in order to understand the power relations that contribute to the production of knowledge. Such analyses address epistemological and ontological assumptions at once, for they show that subjectivity is conditioned and formed in social contexts and that a subject's observations will, in consequence, always be assumption (that is, value) laden. The very possibility of an unconditioned, unified subjectivity and of theory-neutral knowledge is called into question by such analyses; yet community standards of respect for empirical evidence are maintained, as are possibilities for accountable cognitive agency, enacted in collaborative, social contexts.

Donna Haraway's (1991) discussion of "situated knowledges" takes up the issue of social analyses of knowledge to argue against the dislocatedness—the "god trick"—of the mainstream tradition and for a relocation of epistemic projects within the multiple structures of power and privilege that situate all human efforts to develop knowledgeable ways of dealing with the world. Haraway recasts both the subject and the object of knowledge as radically located and unpredictable and the knowledge-construction process as one of learning how to see—from below, from the margins, from positions that have been discredited in the dominant accounts of knowledge and reality that have claimed epistemic authority in Western capitalist societies. Her emphasis on learning to see responsibly amounts to a claim that epistemological and moral-political issues cannot reasonably be kept separate: a claim that is implicit in most of the feminist analyses discussed here.

FEMINIST REREADINGS

It would be a mistake to imply that feminists have simply turned their backs on the Western philosophical canon, for productive rereadings of traditional philosophy figure prominently in feminist epistemological enquiry. Annette Baier (1993), for example, proposes that HUME [4; S] could be read as a "reflective women's epistemologist," in part because his is a social/cultural epistemology, and in part because he makes no artificial split between reason and imagination or passion. Lisa Heldke (1989) draws feminists' attention to affinities between DEWEY's [2; S] work and some feminist projects; and Charlene Haddock Seigfried (1993) makes a more comprehensive case for PRAGMATISM [6; S] as a resource for feminist work in epistemology, particularly because of a common emphasis within pragmatist philosophies on the ultimately practical nature of knowing, and because of a recurring pragmatist conception of knowing as a communal activity. Lynn Nelson (1990) and Jane Duran (1991) turn to Quinean 'naturalized epistemology' as a principal resource out of which they variously develop neoempiricist feminist epistemologies that are anti-individualistic yet indebted to the impressive achievements of modern empirical science (see QUINE [7; S]). And Naomi Scheman (1993) offers innovative readings of WITTGENSTEIN's [8; S] later philosophy as consonant in some useful respects with feminist antifoundationalist projects and endeavors to displace individualist ontologies and as a locus for productive disagreement. None of these rereadings uncritically appropriates the theoretical stance it draws upon, nor is this an exhaustive sample. But these minings of the tradition locate feminist enquiry in ongoing dialogue with philosophers of the past in potentially fruitful collaborations.

WOMEN'S COGNITIVE EXPERIENCES

Feminists whose work attests to the multiple influences already detailed in this article draw on women's experiences as a resource for theory. Evelyn Fox Keller's biography of geneticist Barbara McClintock makes visible an approach to scientific investigation that is, above all, attuned to differences and fully engaged with the objects of study. Although McClintock disclaimed any connection between her femaleness and her scientific practice, Keller discerns in her cognitive style a way of constructing the subject/object relation that, by its very divergence from the research methods of the mainstream, contests the hegemony of disinterested objectivism. Lorraine Code (1991, 1995) examines the structures of epistemic power and privilege that produce differently gendered standards of epistemic authority in medical knowledge, in the experiences of welfare recipients in an affluent society, in attempts to establish testimonial credibility, and in women's efforts to demonstrate their rational competence in response to sexist and racist challenges. She works with a conception of subjectivity in which persons are essentially "second persons" and advocates knowing other people as a kind of knowledge at least as vital, and as worthy of epistemological investigation, as knowledge of medium-sized physical objects. Her concentration on issues of epistemic responsibility affirms the moral-political implications of all cognitive activity. And Patricia Williams (1991), drawing on her experiences as a black feminist lawyer, uses a model of inductive empiricism in an endeavor to reveal the intersubjectivity of legal constructions that requires her reader to participate self-consciously and reflexively in the construction of meanings. In so doing she contests received conceptions of legal discourse as an impersonal and purely objective body of knowledge with ultimate authority, just as science-centered analyses contest analogous claims that are upheld for scientific knowledge.

In drawing explicitly on women's cognitive experiences, these theorists break away from the individualist and universalist presuppositions of mainstream theories of knowledge. They examine specifically located experiences in projects where theory and practice are reciprocally constitutive and human beings are diversely positioned within and in relation to them, even as they are active and self-critical participants in their construction.

Bibliography

Alcoff, L., and E. Potter, eds. *Feminist Epistemologies.* New York, 1993.

Baier, A. "Hume: The Reflective Women's Epistemologist?" in L. Antony and C. Witt, eds., *A Mind of One's Own: Feminist Essays on Reason and Objectivity* (Boulder, CO, 1993).

Butler, J. *Gender Trouble: Feminism and the Subversion of Identity.* New York, 1990.

Code, L. *What Can She Know?: Feminist Theory and the Construction of Knowledge.* Ithaca, NY, 1991.

———. *Rhetorical Spaces: Essays on (Gendered) Locations.* New York, 1995.

Collins, P. H. *Black Feminist Thought: Knowledge, Consciousness, and the Politics of Empowerment.* New York, 1990.

de Lauretis, T. *Technologies of Gender.* Bloomington, IN, 1987.

Duran, J. *Toward a Feminist Epistemology.* Totowa, NJ, 1991.

Ferguson, K. E. *The Man Question: Visions of Subjectivity in Feminist Theory.* Berkeley, 1993.

Haraway, D. "Situated Knowledges: The Science Question in Feminism and the Privilege of Partial Perspective," in *Simians, Cyborgs, and Women: The Reinvention of Nature* (New York, 1991).

Harding, S. *The Science Question in Feminism.* Ithaca, NY, 1986.

Hartsock, N. *Money, Sex, and Power: Toward a Feminist Historical Materialism.* Boston, 1983.

Heldke, L. "John Dewey and Evelyn Fox Keller: A Shared Epistemological Tradition," in N. Tuana, ed., *Feminism and Science* (Bloomington, IN, 1989).

Lennon, K., and M. Whitford, eds. *Knowing the Difference: Feminist Perspectives in Epistemology.* London, 1994.

Lloyd, G. *The Man of Reason: "Male" and "Female" in Western Philosophy.* London, 1984.

Longino, H. *Science as Social Knowledge.* Princeton, 1990.

Lugones, M. "Playfulness, 'World'-Travelling, and Loving Perception," in A. Garry and M. Pearsall, eds., *Women, Knowledge, and Reality* (New York, 1988).

Nelson, L. H. *Who Knows: From Quine to a Feminist Empiricism.* Philadelphia, 1990.

Riley, D. *"Am I That Name?" Feminism and the Category of "Women" in History.* Minneapolis, 1988.

Scheman, N. *Engenderings: Constructions of Knowledge, Authority, and Privilege.* New York, 1993.

Scott, J. "Experience," in J. Butler and J. W. Scott, eds., *Feminists Theorize the Political* (New York, 1992).

Seigfried, C. H., ed. "Special Issue on Feminism and Pragmatism," *Hypatia,* Vol. 8, No 2 (1993).

Williams, P. *The Alchemy of Race and Rights: Diary of a Law Professor.* Cambridge, MA, 1991.

LORRAINE CODE

FEMINIST ETHICS. The umbrella of feminist ethics covers many approaches to ethics arising from overlapping motivations and histories. The motivations are feminist (many varieties); the histories are of women's oppression in what Iris Young calls its five faces: socially sanctioned exploitation, marginalization, powerlessness, cultural imperialism, and violence against women and girls. Despite the popularity of certain themes—opposition to hierarchies and dualisms, favoring circles and centers, deep suspicion of competition—feminist ethics is not a set of doctrines or positions, nor is it a single theory or world view, but it is a cluster of theorizings manifesting feminist perspectives on women's lives and motivated by commitments to resist further oppression, undo the damage of past oppression, and inspire better future alternatives. It has moved from an early approach emphasizing issues such as ABORTION and AFFIRMATIVE ACTION [S] to wide-ranging, pluralistic, and multileveled theorizing. Although inspired by women's lives, it is not only about women but about living well in the world. Its concerns range from domestic to environmental.

In 1957 African-American playwright Lorraine Hansberry (1930–65) wrote to *The Ladder,* a lesbian magazine, calling for women to analyze ethical questions produced by a male-dominated culture (Card, 1991). French philosopher Simone de BEAUVOIR (1908–86) [S] was already doing it long before it had a label. The Second Wave of feminist politics of the late 1960s and early 1970s became a major influence on the feminist ethics that followed. In 1978 Sarah Hoagland used the term "lesbian ethics" in a workshop at a Women's Learning Institute in Maidenrock, Wisconsin, and in Boston Mary Daly subtitled her treatise *Gyn/Ecology* "The Metaethics of Radical Feminism." The term "feminist ethics" was soon heard in feminist responses to Carol Gilligan's study of patterns in women's moral development.

From such beginnings feminist ethics has struggled with tensions between rebellion against damaging, patriarchally constructed femininities and insistence upon respect for women's voices wherever they are heard, between emphasis on what women have suffered and emphasis on what women have done. In its efforts to command a respect for women largely absent from centuries of philosophical writing, it aims also to avoid either glorifying women's experience or presenting women merely as victims.

Feminist ethics is theorized at many levels of abstraction and has many traditions. Many theorists define and critique issues in particular areas such as reproduction, education, work, government, sexuality, self-defense, friendship, spirituality, or food. Some, in the tradition of APPLIED ETHICS [S], draw upon classical texts and principles, extending their applications; others, such as Janice Raymond, take their findings as bases for new theorizing. Historically oriented traditions critically reexamine classical texts, as Elizabeth V. Spelman (1988) does with PLATO [6; S] and ARISTOTLE [1; S], exposing misogyny and stereotypes but also searching out unexamined assumptions or even explicitly defended ideals that support oppressive social structures, or as Annette Baier (1985) does with René DESCARTES [2; S] in arguing that we are, first of all, "second persons," addressed as "you" by caretakers who socialize us. Some reclaim past defenses of women, such as those of Mary WOLLSTONECRAFT [S] and John Stuart MILL [5; S], against sexist attitudes and practices or seek out positions and values supporting feminist ideals, as Annette Baier does with the ethics of David HUME [4; S] (Kittay & Meyers, 1987).

Yet others, wishing to begin anew, articulate new theories, explore new principles, reexamine everyday moral concepts, and analyze such concepts as bitterness and attentive love, that have not been central to influential theories of the past. A major tradition in this vein is feminist care ethics, the revaluing, analysis, and development of caring as a fundamental moral value, taking as paradigmatic relationships central to many women's lives—female friendships, mother–child relationships, nursing, lesbian bonding. Care ethics focuses on relationships with particular others, encounters with real individuals. It values emotional responses and respects material needs. Its focus on agency allies it with character ethics, in contrast with act-oriented duty and consequentialist theories of the modern era (*see* CONSEQUENTIALISM [S]). Responsibility in care ethics suggests responsiveness to needs rather than a duty or obligation correlated with the rights of others.

Yet care ethics is not always feminist. Patriarchally constructed femininity has included care ethics that requires service and emotional bonding of wives to husbands and children, as well as philanthropic community service where possible, and requires unmarried women to devote themselves to a masculine God or to their nearest earthly kin. Women's voices speaking out of such contexts without a feminist perspective may simply endorse these requirements. Because of the possibility that a care ethic may be traditionally feminine rather than critically feminist, major questions for any proposed feminist care ethic are whether it valorizes women's subordination as servants and whether it glorifies female martyrdom (or whether it can readily be used to do either). Care ethics based on women's past experiences as mothers or nurses is vulnerable to these pitfalls.

Nevertheless, mothering is a significant part of many women's histories, and, accordingly, feminists have mined that experience for the wisdom it can yield. Sensitive to the dangers of endorsing servitude or glorifying martyrdom, Sara Ruddick articulates a theory of "maternal thinking," arguing for its extension into the sphere of international relations, and Virginia Held proposes a feminist morality that would take as paradigmatic relationships that would characterize ideal postpatriarchal families. Sara Ruddick's maternal thinking embodies ideals, such as "attentive love" (following Simone WEIL [8] and Iris Murdoch), that she finds implicit in three tasks that together define mothering as an activity. They are the tasks of preserving the child's life, fostering its growth, and making it acceptable to a society wider than its family of origin. Her goal is a nonviolent world where peace is the enduring outcome of the virtues of maternal thinking rather than the precarious outcome of adversarially oriented conflict resolution through mutual concessions.

Virginia Held's feminist morality for a noncontractual society includes postpatriarchal mothering as one among many paradigms that she would have displace from dominance the contract paradigms of human relationship pervasive in modern European moral philosophy. Aspects of mothering and family living that she finds important for ethics are the affectional nature of family bonding, the intrinsic character of the value of these relationships in contrast with the instrumental character of contractual ones, and the degree to which such relationships are not voluntary, all of which are aspects of social relationships not well captured by contract models.

An alternative to the mother model is Sarah Hoagland's lesbian ethics, a feminist care ethic that takes as paradigmatic relationships between lesbians primarily bonded with each other and not with men. She rejects mother–child paradigms for the ethics of adult interaction, because such relationships exemplify nonreciprocal caring, a problem for women's relationships with other adults in sexist societies (Card, 1991). Although she addresses lesbians living in community with lesbians and her work is inspired by the need for conflict resolution that would strengthen lesbian bonds and preserve lesbian community, the sense of community she intends is not geographical, and she leaves for others to answer whether such an ethic might also be valuable for them. Like Sara Ruddick, she explores "attending" as a form of ethical caring, citing midwifery as an example, and offers it as an alternative to the social-control orientation predominant in modern moral philosophy. Like Virginia Held, she is concerned about contexts we have not chosen but within which we can still make choices that make a difference.

Proponents of feminist care ethics disagree over the value of JUSTICE [4; S], RIGHTS [7; S], IMPARTIALITY [S], and institutions, concepts that evoke what Seyla Benhabib has called the "generalized other" rather than the "concrete other" of particular caring relationships (Kittay & Meyers, 1987). Sarah Hoagland does not find justice and rights useful concepts for lesbian community. Nel Noddings finds justice a poor substitute for caring in any community. Virginia Held finds justice indispensable but needing supplementation by care. Janice Raymond, reflecting on histories of female friendships ("gyn/affection"), finds that supportive institutions facilitate female bonding. And Marilyn Friedman acknowledges as a limit of the social conception of the self its inability to ground an unmediated global concern (Card, 1991).

Justice is defined as being at least partly independent of agents' motivations. A common assumption of those who reject justice is that caring is a remedy or a prophylactic against VIOLENCE [S], hostility, and neglect. Some of the data of mothering, nursing, and friendship encourage this view; many data of heterosexual interactions, and even of women's interactions with women as lovers or primary caretakers, raise questions about it. If violence, hostility, and neglect are also partly definable as independent of motives, some such concept as justice may be required to address them adequately. Thus, some theorists, such as Iris Young and Patricia Williams, call for a feminist, antiracist theory of justice, articulated from the perspectives of those with legacies of oppression rather than from perspectives of privilege. Reflecting on a bill of sale for her great-great-grandmother, impregnated at age eleven by her white owner, Patricia Williams (1991) finds the sound of rights "deliciously empowering." Iris Young (1990) calls for a theory of justice centered, not on distributive issues, as modern theories have been, but on issues of decision making, division of labor, and culture, taking domination and oppression as paradigmatic injustices rather than as unfairness in the economies of power and rights.

María Lugones makes cultural PLURALISM [S] the center of her theorizing, introducing a concept, " 'world'-traveling," that helps mediate the concerns of care and justice. World-traveling, willful exercise of a flexibility acquired spontaneously by members of a minority in an oppressive society, is shifting perceptually and emotionally from a construction of life where one is at home although many others are outsiders to other constructions of life in which some former outsiders are now at home and in which one may figure as an outsider oneself. Finding it an antidote to arrogance, which blocks both love and justice, María Lugones advocates animating world travel with nonagonistic playfulness. She illustrates with a tale of traveling to her mother's world, explaining that she could not love her mother well until she could enter that world.

Feminist perspectives on justice permeate feminist bioethics (or BIOMEDICAL ETHICS [S]), as feminist conceptions of care permeate ecofeminism (ecological feminism). Susan Sherwin notes that prefeminist bioethics posed questions of justice regarding rights of access to traditional health-care systems but ignored the ill design of such systems for responding to health needs created for many groups of women by an oppressive social system, needs such as those of women battered by partners or at risk for developing addictions or lacking adequately nutritious food supplies. Jan Raymond challenges reproductive liberalism's focus on choice, arguing that supporters and promoters of technological and contractual reproduction undermine women's reproductive rights. Both critique so-called surrogacy (contractual pregnancy) and new reproductive technologies (NRTs), especially in vitro fertilization (IVF; "test tube babies") (*see* GENETICS AND REPRODUCTIVE TECHNOLOGIES [S]), and between them cover further issues ranging from premenstrual syndrome and medical constructions of homosexuality to the international traffic in fetal tissue and in women and children for organ transplants.

Ecofeminism joins to holistic ENVIRONMENTAL ETHICS [S] a feminist sensitivity to parallels between oppressions of women and of other animals and the natural environment. Vegetarianism, defended vigorously by Carol Adams, is the most concrete issue widely discussed (*see* SPECIESISM [S]). Otherwise, ecofeminism has been more abstract than feminist bioethics, exploring issues ranging from who (or what) counts as "morally considerable" to the viability of such traditional philosophical dualisms as reason and feeling (or emotion), mind and matter, culture and nature. Karen Warren exposes a "logic of domination" common to oppressions of women and nature. Val Plumwood critiques dominant forms of RATIONALITY [S], arguing that philosophical dualisms have protected against acknowledging human dependency on nature and men's dependency on women.

(SEE ALSO: *Feminist Philosophy* [S])

Bibliography

Adams, C. J. *The Sexual Politics of Meat.* New York, 1990.

Baier, A. "Cartesian Persons," in *Postures of the Mind* (Minneapolis, 1985).

Beauvoir, S. de. *Le Deuxième sexe,* 2 vols. Paris, 1949. Translated by H. M. Parshley as *The Second Sex.* New York, 1952.

Card, C., ed. *Feminist Ethics.* Lawrence, KS, 1991.

Gilligan, C. *In a Different Voice: Psychological Theory and Women's Development.* Cambridge, MA, 1982.

Held, V. *Feminist Morality.* Chicago, 1993.

Hoagland, S. *Lesbian Ethics.* Palo Alto, CA, 1988.

Kittay, E. F., and D. T. Meyers, eds. *Women and Moral Theory.* Totowa, NJ, 1987.

Lugones, M. "Playfulness, 'World'-Traveling, and Loving Perception," *Hypatia,* Vol. 2 (1987), 3–19.

Murdoch, I. *The Sovereignty of Good.* London, 1970.

Noddings, N. *Caring: A Feminine Approach to Ethics and Moral Education.* Berkeley, 1984.

Plumwood, V. *Feminism and the Mastery of Nature.* London, 1993.

Raymond, J. G. *A Passion for Friends.* Boston, 1986.

———. *Women as Wombs.* San Francisco, 1993.

Ruddick, S. *Maternal Thinking.* Boston, 1989.

Sherwin, S. *No Longer Patient: Feminist Ethics and Health Care.* Philadelphia, 1992.

Spelman, E. V. *Inessential Woman: Problems of Exclusion in Feminist Thought.* Boston, 1988.

Warren, K. "The Power and Promise of Ecological Feminism," *Environmental Ethics,* Vol. 12 (1990), 125–46.

Weil, S. *La Pesanteur et la grace.* Paris 1974. Translated by E. Craufurd as *Gravity and Grace.* London, 1952.

Williams, P. *The Alchemy of Race and Rights.* Cambridge, MA, 1991.

Young, I. *Justice and the Politics of Difference.* Princeton, NJ, 1990.

CLAUDIA CARD

FEMINIST LEGAL THEORY. Feminist legal theory is the study of the philosophical foundations of law and JUSTICE [4; S], informed by women's experiences and with the goal of transforming the legal system and our understanding of it to improve the quality of our jurisprudence and of women's lives. All feminists working in law share the convictions that the historical and ongoing exclusions of women from law's protective domain have injured women and that the exclusion of women from the study of law has stunted both our understanding of law and our ethical ideals for it. Feminists have accordingly sought to transform the rules and principles governing particular areas of law—torts, criminal law, constitutional law—so as to make them more responsive to women's needs and more reflective of women's perspectives. Feminist legal theorists, distinctively, examine the consequences—both for women and for jurisprudence—of the exclusion of women's input into our shared understanding of the law's philosophical foundations. Toward that end feminists have examined competing philosophical understandings of the nature of law, have attempted to show how they fail to reflect women's perspectives, and then have attempted in each case to reinvigorate them by centralizing, rather than marginalizing, women's experiences. The hope is that by correcting that historical exclusion, both the quality of our justice and the quality of women's lives will be enhanced.

Some feminist legal theorists—sometimes called liberal-feminist scholars—argue that women's lives will be most improved by simply extending to women what are widely regarded as two of the central promises of law in a liberal regime: first, the promise of "formal equality," by which is meant that the state's legal institutions will "treat like causes alike," and second, the promise to each individual of as wide a sphere as possible of individual autonomy. Women, liberal feminists argue, are "like men" in all the ways that should matter to the state, and accordingly should be treated, wherever possible, in precisely the same way as men by the law. Women and men are the same in their abilities: women, like men, can engage in the professions and trades, wage war, fairly serve on juries, administer estates, and vote responsibly, and the law must accordingly not discriminate between them on the basis of a false claim of difference and must also forbid discrimination against them in the private sector on the basis of such false claims (Williams, 1984). Similarly, women and men are the same in their needs: women, like men, need protection against violence, meaningful work and civic participation, and, most important, a wide range of freedom within which to develop their individual life plans. The law should therefore extend to women the same protection against private violence and the same sphere of autonomy it extends to men (McClain, 1992). By pursuing the logic of these applications of fundamental liberal principles to the law's treatment of women, liberal feminist legal theorists have contributed to a virtual revolution in the relations of women, men, and the state, ranging from the construction of bans on private and state discrimination on the basis of gender to the ongoing expansion of women's reproductive freedom and choices so as to maximize their social and political autonomy.

As critics of liberal feminism have pointed out, however, women are not "like men" in all ways, and as a consequence a rigid application of liberal premises to the sometimes distinctive situation of women will often backfire. Where women are unlike men, the blanket insistence on equal treatment will sometimes impoverish actual women, albeit toward the admirable end of a gender-blind utopian society (Becker, 1987). Equal distribution of property at the time of divorce, for example, will impoverish the majority of divorcing women who have less earning potential than their husbands. The equal refusal of an employer to grant maternity or parental leave upon the birth of a child will disproportionately hurt female workers, who, because of their greater biological role in the process of reproduction, will need more time out of the workplace than will men, if they are to enjoy the same "rights" as men to be both workers and parents (Littleton, 1987). The refusal of the state to extend the protection of social security to career homemakers treats women and men similarly but disproportionately harms women because women are disproportionately represented in the ranks of unpaid domestic labor. At the professional level tenure policies and partnership tracks, equally applied, hurt women more than men, because of the differing reproductive cycles of the two sexes. To take an extreme and only partly hypothetical example, a state that failed altogether to criminalize rape would on one level treat men and women similarly and thereby abide by the liberal mandate of equal treatment, but women would obviously be disproportionately harmed by such a regime. In all of these cases, the even-handed application of legal rules harms women because of the very real differences—whatever their cause—between women and men's economic, political, and social lives.

Partly in response to the perceived theoretical and practical inadequacies of liberal feminist legal theory, and partly as a response to work in other fields on the differences between men and women's psychological lives, a number of feminists in legal studies, sometimes called difference or cultural feminists, have sought to place at the center of inquiry, not the many ways in which women and men are the same or similar, but, rather, the ways in which women and men are arguably different. This focus on difference has in turn led to three promising areas of inquiry. First, difference feminists in legal studies have put forward a modified or quasi-liberal theory of equality sometimes called an acceptance theory (Littleton, 1987). According to this view, the state's moral (and constitutional) obligation to treat citizens equally entails that the state is obligated, not only to provide equal treatment of the sexes wherever the sexes are similarly situated, but also to provide different treatment wherever necessary to ensure an equal acceptance of differences, so that those differences, whatever their origin, do not cause women harm. Since women (but not men) get pregnant, bear children, and lactate, for example, the law must fashion rules of employment and civic engagement that will facilitate the acceptance of those differences in the public and economic spheres, whether or not that in turn requires different or similar treatment of the sexes in various legal regimes. Since women engage in more unpaid domestic labor, the liberal mandate of equality demands that family law, divorce law, and social security law should develop in ways that will render that difference harmless.

Second, difference feminists have tried to explicate the distinctive harms women suffer that have little or no correlate in men's lives, on the assumption that simply by virtue of their difference, among other things, the harms that women suffer often go unnoticed as well as unaddressed (West, 1987). Women suffer from sexual assault, sexual harassment, and sexual violence in greater numbers and in different ways than do men. Women suffer unwanted and nonconsensual pregnancies in ways men do not. Arguably, and again whatever the cause, women are more harmed than men by the loss of children in custody disputes and are more vulnerable than men to the threat of such loss, which significantly weakens their economic bargaining position both in the family and at the point of divorce. If women are to enjoy legal protection against harms, the laws governing the social interactions that occasion these harms must be responsive to the existence and the different nature of the harms that women differentially and distinctively experience.

Third, difference feminists have sought to delineate a feminist approach to judging that reflects women's arguably different approach to moral and ethical questions. If it is true, as a number of feminist educators and philosophers argue, that women's moral reasoning is more contextual, more caring, more rational, and less "principled" and rationalistic than men's, then women's reasoning about the virtue of justice, and hence women's approach to judging, should reflect those differences. Some difference feminists have looked to the reflections and writings of female judges, lawyers, and law students to try to determine whether or not there is such a difference. Others have assumed that there is such a difference and then attempted to work through the implications for our understanding of legal justice of such a moral perspective.

Radical feminist legal theory, sometimes called dominance feminism, is also an attempt to fashion a feminist theory of law that avoids the pitfalls of liberal feminist legal theory, but it does so in a different way. The central question for feminists working in law, according to radical feminist theorists, is not whether women and men are fundamentally alike or dissimilar but how the state might be employed toward the greater empowerment of women. Women are unlike men in one significant respect: women as a group lack power (MacKinnon, 1989). Liberal feminists are wrong to downplay or disregard that difference, and difference feminists are wrong to focus on any other differences. A focus on the differential treatment of women by the state, whether with the aim of eradicating those differences, as liberals wish to do, or expanding upon them, as difference feminists wish, will be at best distracting. Disempowerment, not difference, is the source of the problem, and patriarchy, not law, is the source of women's disempowerment. Law reflects patriarchal influences, but patriarchy also exists independent of law. Consequently, law can be and should be employed to end it.

Loosely reflecting the logic of critical legal scholars' Gramscian analysis of the relation of law and market capitalism (*see* GRAMSCI, ANTONIO [3], radical feminists have sought to highlight the nonlegal ways in which patriarchal power is created and reinforced in culture and then legitimated by legal rules and institutions. Women are disempowered, for example, by the violence done them through rape, sexual harassment, and street hassling as well as other forms of sexual assault. That disempowerment is then underscored through the distorting messages and the attacks on women's self-esteem occasioned by pornography, the culture of romance, and other societal influences, all of which aim to render that disempowerment in some sense voluntary, and all of which render problematic the liberal feminist insistence on expanding individual autonomy as a means for improving women's well-being. Absent feminist intervention, the law's role in this process of disempowerment and cooptation is largely to legitimate those harms: the constitutional doctrine of privacy, laws governing and only partially regulating rape and domestic violence, and the constitutional protection accorded to even extremely damaging assaultive speech all serve to trivialize or render invisible the harms women sustain and to protect or even celebrate the events that cause them. Law does not itself cause these harms, but it contributes to a culture that tolerates them.

There is, however, nothing necessary about the handmaidenlike role of law in sustaining patriarchy; it only reflects current distributions of sexual and gendered power. Arguably, all of these forms of patriarchal power, and certainly those employing violence, can and should be prohibited by law. The law currently legitimates a good bit of the disempowerment occasioned by rape by underregulating it, but that can be changed: rape laws can be expanded, and enforcement of those laws strengthened, and to do both would go a long way toward emasculating patriarchy. The goal of radical feminist theory is simply to employ the law in precisely this utterly conventional way toward the unconventional goal of first prohibiting and then eradicating the violence that sustains a patriarchal cultural regime.

Finally, a number of feminists engaged in legal theory have sought to appropriate the tools of postmodern analysis to free liberal, difference, and radical feminist legal theory from the presumed dangers of their essentialist premises. Two distinct projects have emerged from this effort, one critical and one reconstructive. First, postmodernists have joined with African-American, lesbian, and other arguably marginalized feminist legal scholars in an attempt to criticize the consciously or unconsciously racist or heterosexist assumptions in feminist legal theory, thus laying the groundwork for the emergence of a feminist jurisprudence strengthened by its recognition of women's racial, sexual, ethnic, and cultural differences (Harris, 1990). Second, postmodernists have joined with cultural critics from other disciplines in an attempt to highlight the ways in which perceived differences between the genders are themselves socially constructed rather than biologically mandated (J. Williams, 1989). Both projects resonate with long-standing feminist (as well as postmodernist) goals—the first in its insistence on respecting and honoring the voices of outsiders, including those women who find themselves "outside" mainstream feminist discourse, and the second in its insistence on locating within culture, rather than nature, the causes of women's oppression and the key to ending it.

(SEE ALSO: *Feminist Philosophy* [S], and *Philosophy of Law, Problems of* [6; S])

Bibliography

Becker, M. "Prince Charming: Abstract Equality," *Supreme Court Review,* Vol. 5 (1987), 201–47.

Harris, A. "Race and Essentialism in Feminist Legal Theory," *Stanford Law Review,* Vol. 42 (1990), 581–616.

Littleton, C. "Reconstructing Sexual Equality," *California Law Review,* Vol. 75 (1987), 1279–1337.

MacKinnon, C. *Toward a Feminist Theory of the State.* Cambridge, 1989.

McClain, L. "Atomistic Man Revisited: Liberalism, Connection, and Feminist Jurisprudence," *Southern California Law Review,* Vol. 65 (1992), 1171–1264.

West, R. "The Difference in Women's Hedonic Lives: A Phenomenological Critique of Feminist Legal Theory," *Wisconsin Women's Law Journal,* Vol. 3 (1987), 81–129.

Williams, J. "Deconstructing Gender," *Michigan Law Review* (1989), 797–845.

Williams, W. "Equality's Riddle: Pregnancy and the Equal Treatment/Special Treatment Debate," *Review of Law and Social Change,* Vol. 13 (1984–85), 325–80.

ROBIN WEST

FEMINIST PHILOSOPHY. Feminist uses and adaptations of Western philosophies can be found in almost all historical periods. In the early modern period theorists such as Mary WOLLSTONECRAFT [S] and Harriet Taylor adapted the democratic philosophies of ROUSSEAU [7; S] and the utilitarians to argue for the equality of women. Socialists such as Flora Tristan and Clara Zetkin used the theories of utopian socialists, socialist anarchists, and Marxists to argue for women's rights as workers (see MARXISM [S]). African abolitionists such as Sojourner Truth drew on black liberationist theology and Africanist social theory to argue against slavery (*see* AFRICAN PHILOSOPHY; LIBERATION THEOLOGY [S]). In the revolutions of the 1960s and 1970s racial feminists found inspiration in the philosophy of black power and black separatism. Much feminist theory developed along lines of nonfeminist social theory, moving from liberal democratic rights and equality, to socialist or Marxist claims to economic freedom and parity, to radical demands for reform in sexual, family, and social life.

Inherent in early modern classics of feminist democratic and socialist theory such as Harriet Taylor and John Stuart MILL's [5; S] *The Subjection of Women* (1869), Wollstonecraft's *Vindication of the Rights of Women* (1792), and Alexandra Kollantai's Marxist *The Social Basis of the Woman Question* (1909) were distinct approaches and problematics. In the last three decades of the twentieth century these approaches generated distinct lines of feminist philosophizing that have introduced sexuality and family life as questions of philosophical interest and also changed how the method, purpose, and origin of philosophy are conceived (Nye, 1995).

Prominent in feminist philosophy is the use of gender as an analytic category, a change not easily accommodated within the scope of the philosophical as it has been understood since ancient Greece. For Greek philosophers and subsequent philosophers man's essence, nature, rights, and proper life is the proper subject of philosophy, "man" understood as a general term for what is human with no specific reference to gender. Even as some philosophers overcame prejudice and admitted that women or nonwhite races and peoples were human and capable of philosophical thought, they typically continued to philosophize about morality, knowledge, and truth without reference to race or sex.

Feminist insistence on gender as a crucial determinant of meaning and reference has interjected the specificity and physicality of bodies and sexuality into philosophical inquiries traditionally framed in general and abstract terms. Attention to gender has also introduced questions elided in the public affairs of politics, the state, religious establishments, and centers of learning which were the matrix for establishment philosophizing. Because ideas of gender change from one culture and historical era to another, insistence on gender as an analytic category has introduced a controversial historical element. The distinction of philosophy had been taken to be its timelessness, its concern with the eternal, the universal, the nature of man beyond history, culture, ethnicity. Feminists focused on gender as a category with reference to a diversity of private lives as well as to generalized procedures of public life, turned away from essentialist accounts of man to the examination of complex and diverse interactions between social structures and individual subjects.

The antiphilosopher Karl MARX [5] compromised philosophical truth by claiming its dependence on "class consciousness" and inspired an independent line of social feminist philosophizing. But in much MARXIST PHILOSOPHY [5] "class" and "production" were universals in their own right, ultimate determinants of social experience and reality. Feminist theorists, concerned with large areas of family life left out of Marxist theory and communist agendas for social reform, were critical of material as well as conceptual forms of philosophical FOUNDATIONALISM [S]. Instead, they tended to find in the experiences, lives, and needs of diverse women interlocking determinants of class, race, gender, and culture that admitted of no abstracted or essentialist treatment.

Feminist theories in the 1970s and 1980s held out hope that "postmodern" nonfoundationalist and nonessentialist paradigms could be used to feminist advantage. In Britain and North America after World War II, a dominant positivist/analytic style of philosophy had mutated to less ambitious and more professionalized ordinary-language philosophy, NATURALIZED EPISTEMOLOGY [S], or cognitive psychology. English-speaking philosophers no longer saw themselves as dictating standards of truth and knowledge but as describing and clarifying in relatively minor ways the evolving logic of successful sciences. Analytic feminists such as Janet Radcliffe Richards and Jean Grimshaw promoted these humbler forms of linguistic and logical analysis as useful ways to clarify issues of interest to women. Others such as Louise Antony and Lynn Nelson found in the postpositivist logicist philosophy such as that of W. V. O. QUINE [7; S] an alternative to foundationalism that might further feminist attempts to change systems of beliefs. Jane Duran championed a new cognitivism in academic PHILOSOPHY OF MIND [S], arguing that the empirical study of thinking processes leaves open the possibility of diverse feminine thinking styles.

In France, HUSSERL's [4; S] phenomenology and the STRUCTURALISM [S] of the 1950s had given way to Michel FOUCAULT's [S] post-Nietzschean studies of the generation of forms of knowledge as modes of power and Jacques DERRIDA's DECONSTRUCTION [S] of any attempt to ground linguistic or logical structure in human presence, mind, or voice. Many feminists welcomed in these poststructuralist theories a radicalism missing from the increasingly solipsistic and academic turnings of English-speaking philosophy. In Germany the Frankfurt school of critical theorists attempted a less dogmatic version of Marxism to repair the practical and theoretical failures of orthodox Marxist theory, grafting onto materialism theories of consciousness and subjectivity (*see* CRITICAL THEORY [S]). Feminist social theorists such as Nancy Fraser, Seyla Benhabib, and Iris Young found critical theory in general, and HABERMAS's [S] theory of human needs and communicative truth in particular, useful in understanding and addressing the ideological and cultural roots of women's oppression.

A FEMINIST HISTORY OF PHILOSOPHY

One major feminist innovation was in the history of philosophy. In the 1970s and 1980s came revisionary feminist philosophical readings of virtually the entire established canon of major philosophers. A number of these rereadings were published in a groundbreaking 1983 collection of articles (*Discovering Reality*) edited by Merrill Hintikka and Sandra Harding.

In that volume and elsewhere ARISTOTLE [1; S], like PLATO [6; S] one of the canonical founders of philosophy, was a frequent subject of feminist critique. Feminists found misogyny and an oppressive gender and racial subtext in Aristotle's metaphysics, ethics, biology, and politics. Also given special attention was the entire body of liberal democratic theory: LOCKE [4; S], Rousseau, HOBBES [4; S], as well as John RAWLS [S]. Susan Okin, Carole Pateman, Lorenne Clark, Lynda Lange, and Jean Elshtain all uncovered in supposedly gender-neutral philosophical theories of democratic rights and freedoms—theories that had established much of the agenda for modern social theory—assumptions and implications concerning family life, reproduction, and male/female relations that were prejudicial to women.

There were accompanying attempts to find women philosophers to supplement a canon almost uniformly male. Work in this area has been conservative as well as revisionary. Radical critiques of the philosophical tradition, including standards of rationality and logic generated in philosophy, have been rejected by some women philosophers as extremist and even dangerous, playing into the hands of those who proclaim philosophy off limits to women. The hope was that, just as some male philosophers were relatively free of bias, so women philosophers could be found who had contributed to the mainstream history of philosophy. Margaret Atherton and others have researched historical figures such as Mary Astell and Damaris Masham, who took DESCARTES's [2; S] rationalism as support for a gender-neutral mental capacity. Attention was paid to contemporary analytic philosophers such as Iris Murdoch and Elizabeth ANSCOMBE [S], well known in university circles, as well as to important but marginalized twentieth-century thinkers such as Rosa Luxemburg, Simone WEIL [8], and Susanne Langer. Milestones were Mary Ellen Waithe's three-volume collection of women philosophers (*A History of Women Philosophers*) and the establishment of a Society for the Study of Women Philosophers affiliated with the American Philosophical Association.

More radical rereadings came from feminist philosophers interested in contemporary Continental styles of philosophy open to psychoanalytic and other interpretive perspectives in psychology. Susan Bordo (1987) used the structural psychology of Jean PIAGET [6] to argue that Cartesianism, usually taken as establishing the agenda for modern philosophy of knowledge, was in fact a "flight" from a "mother-world" of the Middle Ages to a masculine world of science. Using the post-Freudian object-relations theory of Nancy Chodorow, psychoanalyst Jane Flax argued that Descartes's RATIONALISM [7] was a form of pathology generated in masculine upbringing. Eva Kittay analyzed Plato's symptomatic use of the metaphor of philosophy as midwife. Perhaps most dazzling of all, the French analyst Luce Irigaray adapted Lacanian post-Freudian psychoanalysis to expose in philosophical texts a "phallomorphic" masculine imaginary.

Other radical critiques have drawn on the experiences of women of color. The Hispanic philosopher Maria Lugones used considerations of gender, class, and race in her interpretation of the uses and abuses of philosophical theory. The Indian-American critical theorist Gayatri Spivak called deconstruction to account for its own ethnocentricity. Gloria Anzaldua promoted a conceptual bilinguality that puts concepts into motion rather than establishes monolingual and rigid philosophical definitions.

Feminist philosophical readings of the history of philosophy have introduced new philosophical problematics. If the philosophical mind could not rise above its bodily, historical, social, or racial situation by way of reason or logic, then in what sense can there be a subject that has a sense of herself and can act free of social constraints and established meanings? To act effectively, knowledge is needed. The establishment of standards of rational justification and inference that define knowledge had been a mainstay of philosophical thought, but if standards of RATIONALITY [S] are gender or class specific, then how is any justification possible?

The question for feminists was not only academic but directly related to concerns about viable feminist practice. The energy with which it was discussed reflects feminist philosophy's characteristic mix of passionate practical concerns and abstract theory, of fact and normative judgment. Questions of the nature of mind, knowledge, or TRUTH [S] had been at the heart of PHILOSOPHY [6; S] since its inception, but much work of the canonical philosophers had been systematic, a striving for metaphysical grasps of ultimate determinants, ultimate structures of reality. Feminist philosophers, even as they looked for causes, conditions, or remedies, constantly returned to the concrete facts of women's lives and experience.

FEMINIST PHILOSOPHIES OF SUBJECTIVITY

A quiet explosion of feminist philosophy appeared in the 1980s and 1990s, scattered here and there in establishment journals and published in *Hypatia,* the flourishing journal of the new Society for Women in Philosophy. The self-identity and autonomy of those not in positions of power to form concepts and ideas was a frequent concern. On this question feminist philosophies of subjectivity tended to oscillate between two poles: promotion of an ideal of rational mental autonomy supposedly accessible to both men and women and the postmodern realization that our identities, beliefs, and desires are constructed in systems of thought and language beyond individual control. Much of feminist philosophy of mind and subjectivity between 1970 and 1990 was an attempt to negotiate a path between these two extreme positions. The first ruled out radical reforms in philosophical style, method, and content championed by many feminists; the second seemed to rule out autonomous understanding and action.

In her paper for *Discovering Reality,* Naomi Scheman expanded Wittgensteinian arguments against the possibility of a private language. Scheman gave a feminist interpretation of the tendency in modern philosophy to reify mental objects, citing men's interests in the privilege of science and the competitive capitalist free market, as well as child-rearing practices that leave parenting to women.

Drawing on phenomenological and existentialist approaches to the study of consciousness, Marilyn Frye in *The Politics of Reality* focused not on the private lives of subjects but on oppressive relations between subjects. Given that selves are always relationally defined, women and other inferiorized groups will have maimed identities. Frye brought the discussion of self and other, often highly abstract and illustrated with examples from a very limited range of experience, back to a fuller consideration of human identities and the reality of the actuality of unequal relations.

Similarly broadened were feminist treatments of the constitution of subjects in language and discourse popularized by French theorists such as Derrida and Foucault. Students of POSTMODERNISM [S] such as Linda Alcoff and Rosemary Hennessey problematized the apparent political stasis inherent in the view that subjects have no individual autonomy or capability of self-definition, making of the very position of being oppressively defined by others a possible progressive stance. Sandra Bartky and Judith Butler expanded Foucault's genealogical methods to describe the discipline exercised on the female body by the beauty industry as well as the construction of sexual identity in scientific discourse and literature.

These lines of thought led feminist philosophers to wider consideration of PERSONAL IDENTITY [6; S], especially the identity of those stigmatized by sex or sexual preference or because of race, class, or ethnicity. Major catalysts were lesbian philosophers and women of color. In the discursive structures of elitist and mass culture, in the very grammar of spoken language, sex is a primary positioning factor. Philosophers such as Judith Butler, Sarah Hoagland, Claudia Card, and Monique Wittig problematized sexual identity and the assumption of heterosexuality that holds it in place, going past questions of surface logical grammar to meanings that lay behind uses of words.

Persons of color had been virtually nonexistent in professional philosophy in North America and Europe and remained a small minority throughout the 1980s and 1990s. A few, such as Maria Lugones, taught philosophy and were active in the Society for Women in Philosophy; other women of color, not trained as professional philosophers—social theorist Bell Hooks, sociologist Patricia Hill Collins, critical theorist Gayatri Spivak—participated in feminist philosophical discussions that were increasingly interdisciplinary, introducing new ways of understanding the self and relations between selves and others not authorized in mainstream philosophy of exclusively European origin.

Mainstream philosophy in North America and Britain, as well as an important core of philosophy in France and Germany, tended to draw disciplinary boundaries around a specialty seen as threatened in an age of science. Feminist philosophers, concerned with existential problems of identity and human relation, forced those boundaries to draw back into philosophy insights from psychology, social theory, literary criticism, and other fields. As the French philosopher Michele LeDoeuff put it in her 1991 *Hipparchia's Choice,* feminist philosophy was modeled, not after Kant's "island of truth," but rather after a great seaport, trading ground for foreign goods and practices.

FEMINIST EPISTEMOLOGY

Women's exclusion from the production of knowledge in all fields had long been of concern to feminists. The limited success of equal-opportunity and fair-employment politics to enlist women in science, technology, economics, and other fields noted for the rigor and rationality of their methodologies posed for feminist philosophers a deeper question about the nature of, and access to, knowledge. Again, the masculinity of rationality was in question. Is knowledge as designed by men—currently exemplified by empirical physicalist science—unsuited to the feminine mind? More important, is knowledge as it has been designed by men knowledge at all?

The question of distinguishing what is knowledge from mere opinion was posed by Plato as a founding question of philosophy. Again, considerations of gender and interlocking considerations of economic and racial privilege has led to distinctive and destabilizing lines of feminist epistemological thought. Of foremost interest, as it was for most philosophers in the modern period, is the status of science. A number of nonfeminist studies of changing paradigms in the history of science, such as Thomas KUHN'S [S] *The Structure of Scientific Revolutions* (1970), had opened the door to "sociological" studies of the origins and genesis of science, which seemed to relativize science's claim to truth. Feminist studies in the history of science—for example, those by Carolyn Merchant (1980) and the theoretical biologist Evelyn Fox Keller

(1985)—further noted the important role gender metaphors played in the seventeenth century's reconceptualization of nature and science.

Although the logic of empiricist models for the decisive verifiability or falsifiability of empirical theories was already undergoing revision by establishment philosophers such as Quine who questioned the possibility of reference to scientific objects independent of theory, feminist studies constituted a more radical undermining of the positivistic attempt to establish scientific truth as objective and value free. If the constitutive methods of science could be linked to race or gender, then no adherence to a logic that reflected only those methods could ensure objectivity. Instead, there was, as Susan Bordo put it, a "flight to objectivity" motivated by subjective drives and intentions and specific personal and political interests.

This radical questioning of the possibility of objectivity in science was treated with skepticism by some feminist philosophers who defended "feminist empiricism" as a rigorous attempt to apply the standards of "good science" to eliminate bias and unwarranted conclusions in science. Feminist standpoint epistemology, as developed by Hilary Rose, Nancy Hartsock, and Sandra Harding, was another alternative, especially in the social sciences. Originally modeled on the Marxist claim that philosophy reflects the interest of a particular class, feminist standpoint theories claimed that a different view of reality is possible when science is done from the perspective of women's lives and not from the perspective of male generals and captains of industry. In the social sciences, Sandra Harding (1991) suggested the cognitive value of a "strong" objectivity and a "strong" reflexivity in feminist science that takes its own starting position and interests into consideration. Lorraine Code (1991) accepted a degree of relativism, emphasizing the moral choice that needs to be made between different forms of knowledge. Helen Longino (1990) mapped out ways in which scientific objects are constituted in research projects as social knowledge that underlies what is considered supporting evidence for theories. In all of these cases the distinction commonly made by philosophers between "a context of justification" and "a context of discovery," a distinction that validates the possibility of an "internal" logicist history of science without reference to social context or gender, was called into question.

Equally in question was the possibility of a purely logical and ahistorical philosophical knowledge. A central concern of twentieth-century philosophers, both in the United States and Europe, had been to define the specific nature of philosophical knowledge. On the Continent Husserl argued that the historical LIFEWORLD [S] could be bracketed, allowing a generalized study of phenomenological essences constitutive of objectivity; in England analytic philosophers defended the possibility of a study of logical or grammatical structures that would produce a nonempirical knowledge different from that of the scientist. Feminist epistemologists, many of them cognizant of new postmodern and poststructuralist questioning of essence and form, blurred boundaries between philosophy and linguistics, philosophy and psychology, philosophy and sociology. Perhaps most challenging was their questioning of the objectivity of philosophers' pretension to a "God's eye" view of the truth. (*See* FEMINIST EPISTOMOLOGY, AND ONTOLOGY [S])

FEMINIST SOCIAL PHILOSOPHY

Twentieth-century mainstream philosophy tended to focus on questions of knowledge and MEANING [5; S], sidelining considerations of politics and social justice as conceivable applications of first principles but peripheral to the core of philosophy. Feminist studies of the social nature of scientific knowledge reintroduced social theory as philosophically central. Instead of establishing self-evident truth and deducing a politics from it, a procedure that feminists argued may only constitute blindness to background assumptions that frame first principles, feminist epistemologists such as Sandra Harding and Helen Longino understood the social as epistemologically prior.

One of the most significant innovations of feminist social philosophy was attention to the family. In the mainstream philosophical tradition the political had been defined in opposition to private life. The family for many male philosophers was a "state of nature" assumed in political theory but subject to biological law rather than to normative political judgment. Feminist philosophers such as Susan Okin (1989) have argued that a necessary condition for justice in public life is justice in the family. Again, feminist concerns for shared parenting, equal responsibility for housework, support for working mothers, and childcare introduced a new concreteness into philosophical discussions of social justice.

If the liberal tradition had neglected the family, so had Marxists. Although many feminists approved Marxism's extension of philosophical scrutiny to the economic sphere, in which women were disadvantaged even more than men, they also noted the continued restricted scope of the social as understood by Marxist philosophers. Much of the essential work done by women—housework, service work, clerical work—was not considered productive and so outside the engine of transformative materialist dialectics; in addition, Marx and ENGELS [2] assumed a substratum of biological reproduction—birth, child rearing, sexuality—not subject to change or critical scrutiny. Feminist philosophers have been drawn to Marxism's critique of idealist ideology and to a materialist philosophy that takes the concrete facts of daily life as the primary reality, but they have done much conceptual work in adapting Marxist concepts and positions to feminist aims. Michelle Barrett, Anne Ferguson, Alison Jaggar, and Christine Delphy all developed versions of Marxism that reworked central Marxist concepts of production, alienation, and exploitation to accommodate the oppression of women.

Mainstream philosophers had also neglected sex. With a few exceptional treatments of love, since Plato sex had been the distraction from which the philosopher liberated his mind if not his body. One source for feminist critical work on sexuality was Foucault's historical studies of sexuality as a form of bodily discipline more intimately oppressive than laws or economic arrangements. With Foucault the very concept of the sexual as a natural fact of human life gave way to sexuality as constructed in variable discourses of power. In Foucault's account ultimate categories such as nature/society, public/private, body/mind shift in meaning with changes in institutional power. Jana Sawicki, Judith Butler, and others used Foucault as authority for a denaturalized sexuality subject to critical social judgment as well as to possible transformation.

Again, feminist philosophy was influenced by ideas and approaches outside philosophy. The poet Adrienne Rich's much-cited essay "Compulsory Heterosexuality and Lesbian Existence" introduced a socially enforced rather than "natural" heterosexuality. Nancy Chodorow's objectrelations psychology laid out a social origin for differing masculine and feminine approaches to intimacy. The cultural and ethnic variety of African-American sexual and family experience, as described by social theorists such as Angela Davis, Patricia Hill Collins, and Bell Hooks, inspired new social models.

Lines of thought developed within philosophy were used in original ways, as in Judith Butler's (1993) innovative use of speech-act theory to show the "performative" rather than biological nature of sexual identity or in Carole Pateman's (1988) re-formation of the social contract, backbone of much liberal philosophy, as a "sexual contract"—a contract prior to more superficial political agreements theorized by democratic philosophers. Unnoticed by male philosophers, the sexual contract, Pateman argued, is enforced in practices such as prostitution, forced marriage, dating and courting customs, rape, and pornography.

An independent line of feminist philosophy of law developed with critical attention to prejudice to women in legal theory and practice. Susan Brownmiller examined concepts underlying rape laws. Catharine MacKinnon, the feminist legal scholar, critiqued the legal language devised by men and called attention to painful experiences of women for which there was no legal language. In a direct application of feminist philosophy, MacKinnon and other feminists were successful in winning legal recognition of sexual harassment as a legal offense and launched a movement to have pornography, described alternatively as free speech or as obscenity, redescribed in feminine terms as a systematic depiction of the degradation of women (*see* FEMINIST LEGAL THEORY [S]).

Inherent in MacKinnon's and other feminists' work was a PHILOSOPHY OF LANGUAGE [S]. For MacKinnon language was not a structure to be mapped or the grammar of a form of life to be described but a shifting and changing instrument of understanding and response. Such a philosophy of language exemplifies visionary hope for a common language and a society that responds to men and women.

A further extension of that possibility came in the philosophies of women such as Gloria Anzaldua and Maria Lugones. Hispanic, Asian, and African-American feminist philosophers emphasized the importance of travel between social worlds, of a culturally literate philosophy that did not insist on one method, conceptual scheme, logic, or language but that negotiated incommensurate social forms and idioms. Here the vision was less of a common language than it was of a multilingual internationalist philosophy in constant motion as concepts and perceptions clash and mix. (*See* FEMINIST SOCIAL AND POLITICAL PHILOSOPHY [S])

FEMINIST VALUES

Plato identified philosophy as concern about what is of value rather than what exists as fact. Feminist studies in philosophical epistemology and psychology indicate that no knowledge is free of considerations of value. Intermingled even in the factual sciences are considerations of what is desirable in appearance, conduct, character, and social and economic arrangements. Feminist philosophers, however, showed little interest in developing an axiology or general theory of value that would underlie judgments in morals, aesthetics, and politics. Instead, what emerged were networks of interlocking, broadly based concerns about the quality of human life in ethics, art, relations with nature, and life-styles.

In moral philosophy the social psychologist Carol Gilligan's researches into an alternative feminine voice in ethics cleared the way for new paradigms such as Nel Nodding's ethics of care and Sara Ruddick's maternal ethics. Problems of living within as well as separated from discriminatory society were addressed in Sara Hoagland's *Lesbian Ethics*. Annette Baier reunited moral passion and critical judgment in a nonfoundational feminist Humean ethics. APPLIED ETHICS [S] was of particular interest to feminist philosophers, especially in medical practice, reproductive technologies, pedagogy, and animal rights. Feminist work in these areas did not simply apply established theories such as deontology (*see* DEONTOLOGICAL ETHICS [2]) or UTILITARIANISM [8] to new issues, as did much mainstream work in applied ethics, but, consistent with its mingling of the practical and theoretical, feminist philosophy tended to draw out from ethical situations new ways of conceiving value.

Feminists were also critical of mainstream aesthetics, with its historical beginnings in eighteenth-century elitist and Eurocentric definitions of fine art. Aestheticians such as Hilde Hein, Patricia Mills, Estella Lauter, and Heide

Gottner-Abendroth blurred the line between craft or folk art and fine art, critiqued the objectification of women's bodies in art, took popular culture seriously as a determinant of taste, and developed original concepts of creativity, beauty, and artistic intention (*see* FEMINIST AESTHETICS AND CRITICISM [S]).

Many feminist philosophical concerns—the historical constitution of knowledge, the justice of social arrangements, the ethics of conduct, the critique of patriarchal religions, and the experience of beauty in nature—were linked to work identified as ecofeminist. Susan Griffin's (1978) critical examination of concepts of femininity, science, nature, the body, and God in the context of a poetic descriptive account of women's and men's experience opened lines of questioning that both converged with and diverged from developing theoretical perspectives in environmental, animal rights, and peace movements. Collections of papers followed (Diamond, 1990) that integrated work in feminist philosophy of knowledge, ethics, aesthetics, and society.

Twentieth-century philosophy in both the United States and Europe had tended to become increasingly academic, professionalized, and concerned with defending its own identity. Feminist philosophy, in contrast, has defined itself as interdisciplinary, has insisted on historical understanding, and has mingled theory with the personal and political, reconceiving philosophy as a humane inquiry into issues of human concern common to all sexes, races, and cultures.

(SEE ALSO: *Feminism and Continental Philosophy; Feminism and Pragmatism; Feminist Ethics; Feminist Philosophy of Science* [S])

Bibliography

OVERVIEWS OF FEMINIST PHILOSOPHY

Nye, A. *Feminist Theory and the Philosophies of Man.* New York, 1989.

———. *Philosophy and Feminism: At the Border.* New York, 1995.

Tong, R. *Feminist Thought.* Boulder, CO, 1989.

REPRESENTATIVE COLLECTIONS OF PAPERS IN FEMINIST PHILOSOPHY

Antony, L., and L. Nelson, eds. *A Mind of One's Own: Feminist Essays on Reason and Objectivity.* Boulder, CO, 1993.

Garry, A., and M. Pearsall, eds. *Women, Knowledge, and Reality.* Boston, 1989.

Harding, S., and M. Hintikka. *Discovering Reality.* Dordrecht, 1983.

Nicholson, L., ed. *Feminism/Postmodernism.* New York, 1990.

FEMINIST PHILOSOPHY OF SUBJECTIVITY

Anzaldua, G. *Making Face Making Soul-Hacienda: Creative and Critical Perspectives by Women of Color.* San Francisco, 1990.

Bartky, S. *Femininity and Domination: Studies in the Phenomenology of Oppression.* New York, 1990.

Butler, J. *Bodies that Matter.* New York, 1993.

Fry, M. *The Politics of Reality.* Trumansburg, NY, 1983.

FEMINIST EPISTEMOLOGY

Bordo, S. *The Flight to Objectivity.* Albany, NY, 1987.

Code, L. *What Can She Know: Feminist Theory and the Construction of Knowledge.* Ithaca, NY, 1991.

Harding, S. *Whose Science? Whose Knowledge? Thinking from Women's Lives.* Ithaca, NY, 1991.

Keller, E. F. *Reflections on Gender and Science.* New Haven, 1985.

Longino, H. *Science as Social Knowledge: Values and Objectivity in Scientific Inquiry.* Princeton, NJ, 1990.

Merchant, C. *The Death of Nature: Women, Ecology, and the Scientific Revolution.* San Francisco, 1980.

SOCIAL PHILOSOPHY

Fraser, N. *Unruly Practices: Power, Discourse, and Gender in Contemporary Social Theory.* Minneapolis, 1989.

Jaggar, A. *Feminist Politics and Human Nature.* Totowa, NJ, 1983.

LeDoeuff, M. *Hipparchia's Choice.* Oxford, 1989.

Okin, S. *Justice, Gender, and the Family.* Princeton, NJ, 1989.

Pateman, C. *The Sexual Contract.* Stanford, 1988.

MacKinnon, C. *Feminism Unmodified.* Cambridge, 1987.

FEMINIST VALUES

Card, C., ed. *Feminist Ethics.* Lawrence, KS, 1991.

Diamond, I., and G. Orenstein, eds. *Reweaving the World.* San Francisco, 1990.

Ecker, G., ed. *Feminist Aesthetics.* Boston, 1986.

Griffin, S. *Women and Nature.* New York, 1978.

Held, V. *Feminist Morality: Transforming Culture, Society, and Politics.* Chicago, 1993.

Hoagland, S. *Lesbian Ethics: Towards a New Value.* Palo 1988.

Noddings, N. *Caring: A Feminist Approach to Ethics and Education.* Berkeley, 1984.

Ruddick, S. *Maternal Thinking.* Boston, 1989.

ANDREA NYE

FEMINIST PHILOSOPHY OF SCIENCE.

Feminist philosophy of science arises at the intersection of feminist interests in science and philosophical studies of science. Feminists have taken an active interest in the sciences both as a key resource in understanding and contesting sexist institutions and systems of belief (see SEXISM [S]), and as an important locus of gender inequality and source of legitimation for this inequality. Feminist practitioners in many sciences, especially in the life and social sciences, typically engage two lines of critique: they document inequalities in the training, representation, and recognition of women in the sciences, and they identify myriad ways in which, far from eliminating the contextual biases of a pervasively sexist society, standard scientific methodologies frequently reproduce them in the content of even the most credible and well-established scientific theories.

The work of feminist philosophers of science is continuous with these critiques. Some feminist philosophers contribute to the analysis of androcentrism in the content and practice of particular sciences, in some cases linking these to inequities in the role played by women in science. The form these analyses take necessarily varies with the type of science in question. Critiques of disciplines concerned with an overtly gendered subject matter—the social and behavioral sciences and some branches of the life sciences—draw attention to ways in which unexamined, often stereotypic, assumptions about gender roles, relations, and identities delimit the subject of inquiry, define categories of analysis and description, shape assessments of plausibility that define the range of hypotheses to be taken seriously (e.g., in comparative evaluation), and inform judgments about the bearing of evidence on these hypotheses. Women may be simply left out of account; behaviors, patterns of practice or development, and values and roles associated with men may be treated as normative for the population as a whole; where women diverge from male-defined norms they may be treated as deviant, immature, or anomalous; gender differences may be assumed irrelevant or, alternatively, taken as a given, a parameter for analysis rather than a variable; and the description and analysis of gendered subjects may be structured by conceptual categories that embody highly specific (enthnocentric) assumptions about the form that gender roles, identities, institutions, and values may take. In short, critiques in these domains call attention to ways in which the social and behavioral sciences (including ethology) are pervasively androcentric in content (see Bleier, 1988; Haraway, 1989; contributions to Harding & Hintikka, 1983; Longino & Doell 1983; Tuana, 1989; Wylie et al., 1990).

When the subject domain of a science is not overtly gendered, as in the case of most natural and life sciences, it may be projectively gendered, as when gendered categories are used to describe natural phenomena or when scientific categories have (gendered) social meanings (Potter, 1988). And even when the subject is not characterized in gendered terms, feminist critics find that the enterprise and practice of science may be conceptualized in gendered terms, metaphorically characterized as the domain of men or as exemplifying masculine qualities of intellect and disposition (see Keller, 1985). Whether or not these metaphors directly shape the content of science or, indeed, accurately characterize the practice of a majority of scientists, they do articulate and reinforce a conception of scientific inquiry that aligns it with attributes that are valorized as masculine (see Martin, 1988).

The philosophical significance of these discipline-specific critiques lies in the questions they raise for our understanding of science, specifically, its objectivity, the role of values and interests in science, the status of scientific evidence and of extant methodologies for developing and evaluating scientific theory. If androcentrism is pervasive in much that is accepted as "good," even exemplary, science—if it is by no means limited to examples of manifestly "bad" science (from Harding, 1986)—then feminist critiques of science challenge us to rethink the relationship between what Longino has described as "contextual" and "constitutive" values (these correspond roughly to standard distinctions between cognitive or epistemic considerations "internal" to science and the noncognitive, sociopolitical factors that many believe are properly "external" to science). In taking up these questions the interests of feminist philosophers of science intersect with themes central to postpositivist philosophy of science. Feminist critiques of specific sciences illustrate, and draw attention to the implications of, central antifoundationalist claims about the complexity and contingency of scientific practice. If scientific theories are routinely (indeed, perhaps, necessarily) underdetermined by all available evidence, and if hypotheses are never evaluated independently of one another and the evidence supporting (or refuting) them is always itself richly interpreted (the theses of holism and the theory-ladenness of evidence), then it seem unavoidable that nonevidential values and interests, features of the "external" context of science, must play a role not only in the formulation but also in the evaluation of hypotheses. The contribution of discipline-specific feminist critiques is the insight that these contextual factors may include gendered interest, values, and social structures.

Although feminist philosophers are sometimes charged with advocating an untenable, "cynical," and self-defeating relativism (Haack, 1993) because of their insistence that social factors such as gender shape the practice and results of science, in fact neither feminist critics within the sciences nor feminist philosophers of science show much sympathy for extreme forms of social constructivism or contextualism on which epistemic considerations are reduced to social, political factors. Harding's (1986) discussions of a "postmodern" epistemic stance and some of Haraway's (1989) reflections on hybrid constructions of nature may be seen to move in this direction. But Harding was explicitly "ambivalent" about postmodern options at the time she proposed them and has since elaborated a thesis of "strong objectivity" according to which an understanding of the standpoint (the social location, interests, values) of epistemic agents serves as a resource in producing and evaluating "less partial and less distorted" knowledge claims (1991). Haraway has likewise elaborated the concept of "situated knowledges" with the aim of capturing the sense in which it is reasonable to require "a no-nonsense commitment to faithful accounts of a 'real' world" while yet acknowledging the radical historical and social contingency of all knowledge production (1991). In a similar vein, while Keller reaffirms the value of psychodynamic analyses of the masculine orientation of science (e.g., as elaborated in Keller, 1985), she distances herself from strong sociological theses and argues the need for feminist analyses of science that attend to "logical and empirical constraints" and account for the "technological prowess" that makes scientific claims so compelling for scientists and for the world at large (1992, p. 3). The central preoccupation of feminist philosophers of science who elaborate a positive account of scientific inquiry is to understand the ways in which the (gendered) standpoint of epistemic agents and epistemic communities shapes inquiry while yet making sense of constraints imposed by constitutive values such as the standard requirements of epistemic adequacy, reliability, internal coherence, and consistency.

A number of positions have been explored in this connection. Feminist standpoint theory is one such approach. Harding's (1991) formulation draws on the earlier proposals of feminists, such as Hartsock (1983), who are influenced both by Marxist-derived epistemologies and by psychoanalytic theory, and on the work of black and minority feminist theorists who draw attention to the insights afforded by subdominant status (Collins, 1991; Narayan, 1988). The central thesis of standpoint theory, as developed by feminist theorists, is that the empirical evidence to which epistemic agents have access, their powers of discernment and breadth of understanding, may be both enhanced and limited by their social location and associated experience, values, and interests. For example, those who must understand a dominant world of privilege from which they are excluded as well as the subdominant world(s) of which they are members may well be better situated to understand both worlds, in empirical detail and with critical precision, than those who are beneficiaries of systemic privilege. The epistemic partiality and authority of knowledge claims, and therefore the effective assessment of their epistemic adequacy, is thus contingent on understanding the conditions under which they are produced and authorized, the standpoint of epistemic agents and communities.

A number of feminist philosophers of science have argued that the social dimensions of scientific practice (including but not limited to its gendered dimensions) can be understood in terms compatible with a modified empiricism. Longino's (1990) carefully worked distinction between contextual and constitutive values provides a framework for identifying the various points at which epistemic considerations leave room for the play of social factors, institutional context, political commitment, and personal interests in the formulation of descriptive categories, the interpretation of data as evidence, and the evaluation of hypotheses against evidence. At the same time she accords constitutive (epistemic) values a central role, arguing that standards of rational acceptability can be identified that are independent of individual interests and that the social nature of science (e.g., institutional structures that encourage rigorous critical scrutiny of knowledge claims) serves as much to protect scientific knowledge from idiosyncratic bias as to render it vulnerable to such bias. In a similar vein Hankinson-Nelson (1990) argues that an empiricist theory, which grounds knowledge in evidence and construes evidence in experiential terms, is compatible with a feminist reconceptualization of the agents of inquiry as communities, not abstract individuals, which are historically situated and of socially specified form. Sophisticated feminist empiricisms offer an account of epistemic virtues that transcend standpoint-specific interests—the virtues of empirical adequacy, reliability, scope of applicability, and explanatory power, which different standpoints help or inhibit us from realizing—without invoking an untenable (asocial) foundationalism.

Despite significant philosophical differences between proponents of these positions, feminist philosophers of science share an ambition to develop an account of science that resolves (or circumvents) the polarized debate between objectivists and rationalists on one hand and constructivists and relativists on the other. This is conceived both as a contribution to postpositivist philosophy of science, in which the terms of debate are most clearly articulated, and to feminist theory, where questions about the proper grounds for evaluating knowledge claims are a matter of immediate practical concern.

(SEE ALSO: *Feminist Philosophy* [S])

Bibliography

Bleier, R. *Feminist Approaches to Science*. Elmsford, NY, 1988.

Collins, P. H. "Learning from the Outsider Within," in Mary M. Fonow and J. A. Cook, eds., *Beyond Methodology: Feminist Scholarship as Lived Research* (Bloomington, IN, 1991).

Haack, S. "Knowledge and Propaganda: Reflections of an Old Feminist," *Partisan Review*, Vol. 60 (1993), 556–64.

Haraway, D. *Primate Visions: Gender, Race and Nature in the World of Modern Science*. London, 1989.

———. "Situated Knowledges: The Science Question in Feminism and the Privilege of Partial Perspective," in *Simians, Cyborgs, and Women: The Reinvention of Nature* (New York, 1991).

Harding, S. *The Science Question in Feminism*. New York, 1986.

———. *Whose Science? Whose Knowledge? Thinking from Women's Lives*. Ithaca, NY, 1991.

———, and M. B. Hintikka, eds. *Discovering Reality*. Boston, 1983.

Hartsock, N. "The Feminist Standpoint," in S. Harding and M. B. Hintikka, eds., *Discovering Reality* (Boston, 1983).

———. *Reflections on Gender and Science*. New Haven, 1985.

Keller, E. F. *Secrets of Life, Secrets of Death: Essays on Language, Gender, and Science*. New York, 1992.

Longino, H. E. *Science as Social Knowledge.* New Jersey, 1990.

———, and R. Doell. "Body, Bias, and Behavior: A Comparative Analysis of Reasoning in Two Areas of Biological Science," *Signs,* Vol. 9 (1983), 206–27.

Martin, J. "Science in a Different Style," *American Philosophical Quarterly,* Vol. 25 (1988), 129–40.

Narayan, U. "Working Together across Difference," *Hypatia,* Vol. 32 (1988), 31–48.

Nelson, L. H. *Who Knows: From Quine to a Feminist Empiricism.* Philadelphia, 1990.

Potter, E. "Modeling the Gender Politics in Science," *Hypatia,* Vol. 3 (1988), 19–35.

Tuana, N., ed. *Feminism and Science.* Bloomington, IN, 1989.

Wylie, A., K. Okruhlik, L. Thielen-Wilson, and S. Morton, "Philosophical Feminism: A Bibliographic Guide to Critiques of Science," *Resources for Feminist Research,* Vol. 19 (1990), 2–36.

ALISON WYLIE

FEMINIST SOCIAL AND POLITICAL PHILOSOPHY. Feminism recognizes gender structures as fundamental to virtually all societies; it is committed to the normative equality of women and rejects the view that the inferior position of women is inevitable. Feminism does not seek to replace domination by men with domination by women, but to overcome domination. Some feminists argue that gender is the most fundamental form of domination, underlying such other forms as racial, class, and ethnic domination.

To restructure something as fundamental and pervasive as the gender structure of society is usually seen by feminists as revolutionary. It is a revolution thought to be taking place in consciousness and culture as well as in the arenas of political power, legal decision, and economic activity. Most feminists hold that this revolution is well underway but is subject to much resistance and many reverses. Feminist social and political philosophy has developed feminist critiques of traditional social and political philosophy and is rethinking social and political theory and practice from a feminist point of view.

CATEGORIES OF FEMINIST SOCIAL AND POLITICAL PHILOSOPHY

The work of feminists dealing with society and politics is often described in terms of such categories as liberal feminism, socialist feminism, and radical feminism. The views expressed within these categories often overlap, but arguments for them tend to have developed out of different traditions and to address different problems. All three approaches have recognized the need to concern themselves with racial and class diversity and with global and environmental problems.

In the United States liberal feminism (*see* LIBERALISM [4; S]) developed in the late 1960s with the awareness that the liberal principles of freedom and equality proclaimed by democratic political theory and such foundational documents as the U.S. Declaration of Independence and the French Declaration of the Rights of Man were not being applied to women. Liberal feminists pressed for increased representation of women in government and elsewhere and an end to legal and other gender inequalities. They called for equal opportunities for women in occupations previously closed to or prejudiced against women. Liberal feminists demanded an end to sexual double standards and demanded that women have rights to control their own reproduction, hence that legal prohibitions against ABORTION [S] be ended. The implications of equality for family structures were thought to require that men share responsibility for childcare and housework, and women for obtaining income; some thought this would require a fundamental restructuring of capitalism.

Socialist feminism developed out of the Marxist tradition (*see* MARXISM [S]) and saw the need for women to overcome the oppressions of both class and gender. Socialist feminists saw capitalism as deeply implicated in the oppression of women. Equal opportunities alone would not liberate women unable to make use of such opportunities, and the disempowerment women suffered was often of a kind not addressed by the liberal agenda. Socialist feminists went far beyond Marxism in seeing women as oppressed, not only by economic dependence, but also by such factors as the division of labor within the household and in characteristic relations in which women provide more emotional support for men than men provide for women. Concepts such as alienation were adapted to analyze the ways in which women are alienated as women—for instance, from their bodies, constantly under male sexual scrutiny—not only as workers or nonworkers under capitalism. In general, whereas liberal feminism tends to take capitalism as a given economic system in need of reform, socialist feminism tends to think capitalism must be replaced.

Radical feminism has fewer roots in established traditions of political and social philosophy. Some radical feminists have been influenced by anarchist thought; others have asserted that feminism must build only on feminism itself, not on any of the male-dominated social or political theories of the past or present. Radical feminism has often seen sexuality, rather than political inequality or the economic system, as central to the oppression of women. Many radical feminists argue that male sexuality has been constructed in conjunction with the domination of women, and often with violence against women. They see pornography and domestic violence as highly important contributors to male domination and female disempowerment. Some radical feminists argue for separatism for women, advocating that women form cultural and other communities of their own. Many feminists argue that women should evaluate their work by the standards of other women rather than seek the approval of male elites. Lesbian separatism is a strand of radical feminism. Lesbian feminism has developed critiques of mainstream feminism on sexuality, family structure, ethics, strategies for liberation, and the concept of woman.

All branches of feminist social and political philosophy deplore discrimination against women of color, but work by black and Latina feminists has gone beyond countering discrimination. It offers distinctive perspectives and insights on such issues as domination, race and gender identity, and social knowledge.

Feminists in the non-Western world have argued for the construction of their own theories and interpretations of what feminism implies for their often very different cultures and circumstances. Western formulations of demands for equality are not always helpful. Non-Western feminists face the task of empowering women within their own cultures without accepting cultural nationalisms that see preserving non-Western cultures as requiring the maintenance of norms and practices that disempower women. Non-Western feminists often urge Western feminists to consider how Western economic and military policies and colonialist attitudes harm non-Western women. (*See* NATIONALISM AND INTERNATIONAL RELATIONS [S])

FEMINIST RECONCEPTUALIZATIONS

Attention has been paid by feminist theorists to many specific social and political issues such as AFFIRMATIVE ACTION (S) remedies for discrimination; strategies to achieve equal pay and advancement for women; reproductive choice, including abortion; contracted motherhood and its risks for the further exploitation of women; the double burdens of women of color; rape and domestic violence; pornography, prostitution, and the formation of male sexuality; compulsory heterosexuality and injustices toward lesbians; and sexual harassment, especially in the workplace.

In addition, feminists have recognized the need for thoroughgoing reconceptualizations of many of the fundamental concepts of social and political thought. These reconceptualizations have in turn deeply affected the development of feminist social and political philosophy. Among such reconceptualizations are the following.

The Distinction Between Public and Private. Feminists from all approaches and fields have questioned traditional distinctions between public and private, noting that personal relations between women and men are deeply affected by the greater social, economic, and political power of men in the public sphere. Public law and policy on everything from marriage regulations, to restrictions on abortion, to policies that fail to provide social support for childcare and fail to protect women from domestic violence and rape all structure women's private lives. From a feminist perspective what had been thought to belong to a private sphere beyond politics is seen instead to be deeply embedded in the power relationships of the political. The early feminist slogan "the personal is political" reflects this insight. But the implications are even deeper than at first realized. Not only should such considerations as equality and self-determination be applied to the personal realm and to women, but when the concerns of women are taken as seriously as the concerns of men, society and politics themselves may require almost total restructuring. For instance, concern for the upbringing and education of children, and protection of children and women from violence and abuse, would have to be accorded central rather than peripheral importance in how society would be structured.

The Concept of Person. In a wide range of areas from psychology and moral development to law and sociology feminists have recognized the need for a more satisfactory concept of the person than those previously dominant. Many feminists criticize the liberal political concept of the autonomous, atomic, individual as a construct reflective of a male point of view that artificially ignores human relatedness and interdependence. But many feminists are also critical of communitarian views of persons in which women are defined by their roles in the practices and traditions of their communities. Feminist views recognize that a person is partly constituted by her relations with others—for instance with her parents, her friends and lovers or spouse, her children; at the same time such a person has the capacity to restructure radically her relations with others and to her community. When persons are seen in this light, the social and political structures thought appropriate for such persons will be different from traditional ones. Instead of government and law being built to serve the self-interest of individuals, as advocated by liberal political theory, government may be evaluated in terms of the human relationships it reflects or affects. Relationships of trust and caring will be seen as relevant to political life as well as to personal life. But PERSONS [6] will not be the communal members of much communitarian and some conservative thought; they will be continually changing persons shaping their own development in relationships with others.

Requirements for Equality. An unresolved debate among feminists has centered on how to interpret what equality requires. It is recognized that gender-blind categories that ignore the ways women differ from men—for instance, that only women get pregnant—can put women at a serious disadvantage in provisions such as those for health care and family leave. On the other hand feminists often argue that traditional distinctions between women and men used in law and social norms to uphold the subordination of women must be ended. Thus, when the law specifies, as it has, that the husband has a right to decide where a couple will live, gender becomes, to feminists, a "suspect category," and a commitment to equality requires that it not be used. Some feminists see a solution in seeking equally advantageous outcomes for women and men. Then, recognizing gender when it contributes to such an outcome is appropriate, but when gender distinctions lead to disadvantages for women, they should not be made (*see* EQUALITY, MORAL AND SOCIAL [3].

Traditional social and political theory has been criticized as inadequate for dealing with issues of race and culture. Feminists have attended to inequalities among women and to differences of history, experience, and outlook among women of different racial or ethnic groups and different nations and regions of the world. Feminists have argued that differences between women and men and between members of different racial or cultural groups can be noted and appreciated without supposing that to see persons as different is to see some as superior to others. Difference need not imply hierarchy; equality need not require sameness. At the same time many feminists have argued that to reject the concept of "woman" entirely, on the grounds that there is no "essential" woman, only many different women, can undermine the feminist project itself. Arguments for the equality of women—whatever the differences between them—continually need to be reaffirmed. (*See* RACISM [7; S]; SEXISM [S])

Freedom and Oppression. Liberal political theory has seen freedom in negative terms, as freedom from hindrance or interference. It has recommended a scheme of rights in which individuals are as free as possible from interference by others and by government, consistent with similar freedom for all others. Marxists have criticized this conception of freedom as failing to consider the material resources needed for a human being to be a free agent: being free to starve or freeze is not really being free to act. Feminists usually share with Marxists a recognition that to be free one must have the capacity to act freely, as well as to be free from interference, but feminists are aware of a wide range of interferences and incapacitations to which neither liberals nor Marxists have attended.

The liberation of women requires an end to oppressive state interferences with women's reproductive choices and to oppressive domestic situations where women are subject to abuse; and it requires economic independence for women through employment or some equivalent such as family allowances. It also requires the psychological empowerment of women to overcome traditional practices of disregarding and trivializing women and their views and of seeing women as sexual objects and exploitable caregivers.

The Value of Care in Political Life. Much feminist work has been done in ethics and moral theory. Care and nurturing, empathy and compassion, and the cultivation of human relatedness have been recognized as important moral values and concerns. The emphasis on JUSTICE [4; S] and abstract rules in dominant moral theories such as Kantian ethics (*see* DEONTOLOGICAL ETHICS [2]) and UTILITARIANISM [8] have been thought by many feminists to provide a distorted view of morality as a whole. Though justice and rules may be necessary for political and legal theory and organization, many feminists have found such rationalistic and individualistic approaches deficient for much of morality. As feminists have developed alternative, more satisfactory views, the term 'ethics of care' has often been used to indicate what many take to be a central concern.

Some feminists think an adequate feminist ethic can be based on care rather than on justice. Others think these and other values must be integrated into a feminist ethic. With the questioning of the distinction between public and private has come a realization that traditional efforts to associate care with the household and the supposedly "natural" mothering done by women, and to associate justice with men and public life, are misguided. Women need justice and fairness in the household and in how the tasks of caring labor are divided; women and children need justice and protection against VIOLENCE [S] in the private sphere. At the same time public policies, law, and international affairs need to be much more influenced than they have been by feminist values of care and concern. For instance, the way children and old people are cared for should be a social concern, not something for which government takes no responsibility. The ways bureaucracies might deal with persons in caring ways that foster self-determination, rather than with insensitive disregard, is an important public issue. And how nations can come to trust one another so that more resources can be devoted to meeting people's needs and fewer wasted on armaments should be an important concern of international affairs. (*See* FEMINIST ETHICS [S])

Feminists often believe that feminist perspectives and values should influence how we deal with global and environmental problems: we should recognize the responsibilities of persons and nations to care about and for the victims of famine, genocide, armed conflict, and exploitation, to take needed measures to prevent these, and to take proper care of the environment to be inhabited by future generations.

(SEE ALSO: *Feminist Philosophy* [S])

Bibliography

Bartky, S. L. *Femininity and Domination: Studies in the Phenomenology of Oppression.* New York, 1990.

Bartlett, K. T., and R. Kennedy, eds. *Feminist Legal Theory: Readings in Law and Gender.* Boulder, CO, 1991.

Benhabib, S. *Situating the Self: Gender, Community, and Postmodernism in Contemporary Ethics.* New York, 1992.

Collins, P. H. *Black Feminist Thought: Knowledge, Consciousness, and the Politics of Empowerment.* Boston, 1990.

Eisenstein, Z. *The Radical Future of Liberal Feminism.* New York, 1981.

Ferguson, A. *Blood at the Root: Motherhood, Sexuality, and Male Domination.* London, 1989.

Fraser, N. *Unruly Practices: Power, Discourse, and Gender in Contemporary Social Theory.* Minneapolis, 1989.

Friedman, M. *What Are Friends For?: Feminist Perspectives on Personal Relations and Moral Theory.* Ithaca, NY, 1993.

Gould, C. C., ed. *Beyond Domination: New Perspectives on Women and Philosophy.* Totowa, NJ, 1984.

Hartsock, N. C. M. *Money, Sex, and Power: Toward a Feminist Historical Materialism.* New York, 1983.

Held, V. *Feminist Morality: Transforming Culture, Society, and Politics.* Chicago, 1993.

Jaggar, A. M. *Feminist Politics and Human Nature.* Totowa, NJ, 1983.

Lugones, M. C., and E. V. Spelman. "Have We Got a Theory for You! Feminist Theory, Cultural Imperialism, and the Demand for 'The Woman's Voice,'" *Women's Studies International Forum (Hypatia),* Vol. 6 (1983), 573–81.

MacKinnon, C. A. *Toward a Feminist Theory of the State.* Cambridge, MA, 1987.

Okin, S. M. *Justice, Gender, and the Family.* New York, 1989.

Ruddick, S. *Maternal Thinking: Toward a Politics of Peace.* Boston, 1989.

Shanley, M. L., and C. Pateman, eds. *Feminist Interpretation and Political Theory.* University Park, PA, 1991.

Tong, R. *Feminine and Feminist Ethics.* Belmont, CA, 1993.

Tronto, J. C. *Moral Boundaries: A Political Argument for an Ethic of Care.* New York, 1993.

Young, I. M. *Justice and the Politics of Difference.* Princeton, 1990.

VIRGINIA HELD

FICTIONALISM, MATHEMATICAL. Mathematical fictionalism is the view that mathematical theories are strictly speaking false but that it is often useful to pretend they are true. It thus combines a skeptical rejection of mathematical theories with the recommendation that we should embrace them as useful fictions.

Fictionalists argue that their view is preferable to both realist and reductionist philosophies of mathematics. Mathematical realists hold that mathematical objects such as numbers and sets really exist, though not in the world of space and time. The central problem facing mathematical realism is to explain how we can have knowledge of these mathematical objects, given that our normal senses give us no access to them. Fictionalists, however, simply sidestep this difficulty by denying that we have any knowledge of mathematical objects to start with.

Mathematical reductionists offer a different solution to the problem of mathematical knowledge. They argue that it is wrong to read mathematics as making claims about objects outside space and time in the first place. Versions of reductionism are that mathematics is about marks on paper, or that it consists of hypothetical claims about what follows from axions, or that it simply abbreviates logical truths. Fictionalists make the same objection to all these versions of reductionism. They argue that they misrepresent the real meaning of mathematical claims. Reductionist views may make mathematical claims knowable, but only by changing what mathematicians say. Fictionalists admit that they too recommend a change in normal mathematical practice, namely that we should stop believing mathematical claims. But they point out that it is far easier to change our attitude to mathematics than to change its content.

One obvious objection to fictionalism is that natural science as well as mathematics seem to commit us to mathematical objects. Does this mean that fictionalists have to disbelieve natural science, along with mathematics? Hartry Field addresses this and other objections to fictionalism in his influential *Science without Numbers* (1980). In Field's view natural science's commitment to mathematical objects is relatively superficial. He argues that most familiar scientific theories can be given "nominalistic" reformulations that are free of reference to mathematical objects and, moreover, yield superior explanations of the empirical data.

Field allows that it is convenient for scientific reasoning to be able to appeal to mathematical objects and associated mathematical theories. This is why he thinks mathematics is a useful fiction. But he insists that this usefulness is no reason to believe mathematics is true. This leaves him with a problem, however. If mathematics is not true, why should we trust the inferences it underpins? Field's answer is that it is nevertheless "conservative," in the sense that any inferential moves it allows between nominalist claims could in principle, though not in practice, be made by logic alone.

There are a number of technical objections to Field's views. Critics have complained that his nominalized science in effect still requires a continuum of space-time points and elements of higher-order logic. How far this reduces the attraction of fictionalism is a matter for debate. But in any case fictionalism poses a serious challenge to more traditional positions in the philosophy of mathematics.

(SEE ALSO: *Mathematical Logic;* and *Philosophy of Logic* [S])

Bibliography

Field, H. *Science without Numbers.* Oxford, 1980. The original statement of the fictionalist point of view.

———. *Realism, Mathematics, and Modality.* Oxford, 1989. Field develops his position and responds to criticisms.

Irvine, A., ed. *Physicalism in Mathematics.* Dordrecht, 1990. Contains a number of articles on fictionalism.

Papineau, D. "Mathematics and Other Non-natural Subjects," in *Philosophical Naturalism* (Oxford, 1993). Defends fictionalism against competing views.

DAVID PAPINEAU

FOLK PSYCHOLOGY. In everyday commerce with our fellows all of us attribute propositional attitudes—beliefs, desires, intentions, and the like—to aid in explaining and predicting behavior. These attitudes possess intentional mental content; we attribute the belief that *p* and the desire that *q*. When, for example, Achilles returns to battle, we may explain his action so: Achilles wants to avenge the death of Patroklos, and he believes that killing Hektor, and so reentering the fray, is the best way to accomplish this. This commonsense framework of intentional description, explanation, and prediction has come to be termed *folk psychology.* (Strictly speaking, *folk psychology* applies both to nonintentional qualitative as well as to intentional psychological phenomena. Philosophers have concentrated their attention upon folk intentional psychology.) The chief philosophical issues are engaged when we turn to various efforts to characterize the nature and status of folk psychological explanation.

The most influential view (in part, at least, the result of the dominance of functionalist accounts of the mental) is that folk psychology constitutes an empirical theory of mind and behavior (Churchland, 1981; Sellars, 1963). According to this "theory-theory" (Morton, 1980), we make use of an implicit theory when offering folk psychological explanations. *Belief, desire, intention,* and the like are theoretical terms whose meaning and reference are secured by their place in a network of implicit folk psychological laws. One such law might be stated as follows: If *A* desires or intends that *v* and believes that *k* is necessary for *v,* then, *ceteris paribus, A* tries to bring it about that *k.* The point is, however, quite general. Our ability to offer folk psychological explanations is a matter of our drawing upon a store of commonsense laws that connect behavior, internal states, and stimuli.

Much of the discussion of folk psychology has focused upon the consequences of the theory-theory. One immediate consequence is that folk psychology might be false in the way that any empirical theory might be false. Vindicationists argue that folk psychology is very likely a correct theory of mind and behavior. Eliminativists argue that folk psychology is very plausibly a false theory. In its role as a causal explanatory theory, folk psychology awaits replacement by a neurological—or, at least, a nonintentional—account of behavior (Stich, 1983).

The eliminativist–vindicationist debate hinges upon the anticipated relationship between folk psychological explanation and scientific psychological explanation. Since both folk psychology and a scientific psychology offer causal explanations of what is intuitively the same class of explananda, if we are to regard folk psychology as, by and large, a correct theory, we are presumably committed to thinking that the cognitive sciences will, in some way, serve to vindicate the explanations of folk psychology (Kim, 1989).

A notable advocate of this brand of vindicationism, Jerry Fodor, has argued that a scientific psychology will count as vindicating folk psychology just in case it postulates states that (1) are semantically evaluable; (2) have causal powers; and (3) are found to conform to the tacit laws of folk psychology (Fodor, 1987). Each of these has given rise to eliminativist complaint.

Insofar as intentional content figures essentially in folk psychological explanation, it may seem quick to demonstrate that such explanations are not respectable:

1. The causes of behavior supervene upon the current, internal, physical states of the organism.
2. Intentional mental content does not supervene upon such states.
3. The science of psychology is concerned to discover the causes of behavior.
4. Therefore, psychology will not trade in the intentional idiom.

If the argument is correct, folk psychological explanation would be deeply suspect because intentional mental content would be irrelevant to the causal explanation of behavior. The argument is, however, suspect on many fronts. First, one might dispute the sense of behavior in (1) and with it the notion that respectable explanation must be "individualistic" (Burge, 1986). Second, one might grant that while truth-evaluable content is "wide" and so fails to supervene upon states of the individual, there is a kind of content—"narrow" content—that respects individualist scruples.

Content-based objections such as the above focus upon the puzzling status of intentional properties in a physical universe; and many theorists point to the allegedly irreducible nature of intentional mental content as a way of undermining the integrity of folk psychology (Churchland, 1986). Another family of eliminativist worries focuses upon matters structural. It is claimed that if certain connectionist models of our cognitive architecture are correct, then there will literally be no states or events that play the causal role that intentional mental states play in folk psychology. Folk psychology appears committed to the view that intentional mental states are "functionally discrete" internal states possessed of a specific causal syndrome (Ramsey, Stich, & Garon, 1991). Yet on connectionist models there are no such discrete internal states with the causal roles that belief, desire, and so forth are presumed to play.

If these objections give some taste of the eliminativist assault, they serve as well to highlight an assumption held by many vindicationists and eliminativists alike: folk psychology possesses (in Fodor's terminology) theoretical "depth" (1987, p. 6). It posits unobservable states and events in aid of the explanation of observed phenomena. The explanations of folk psychology are, then, structurally informative insofar as they offer information about the structure of causal relations that hold between behavior, stimuli, and unobservable internal states. Only on such a supposition is it plausible to suggest that folk psychology will go the way of caloric and phlogiston. And this is why the vindicationist holds that the survival of folk psychology demands that there be a scientific level of description of our cognitive architecture that mirrors the folk psychological one.

Much hinges upon the resolution of this dispute. If the eliminativist is correct, there are no beliefs and desires and no actions. It is, for example, just false that human beings very often intend to do what they most desire. Nothing will remain of our conception of ourselves as deliberators and actors. This seems incredible, but of course the eliminativist will answer that this is but another case in which what has appeared patently obvious to folk turns out to be radically false.

Even so, it is argued that, more than incredible, ELIMINATIVISM [S] is self-refuting or pragmatically incoherent (Baker, 1987). The charge here is not that eliminativism is self-contradictory or internally inconsistent. Rather, the claim is that there is no perspective from which the doctrine can be coherently put forth. For if eliminativism is true, there are no actions. Yet the eliminativist asserts the truth of eliminativism, and assertion is certainly an action. Moreover, the eliminativist presumably asserts eliminativism because he takes it to be true, because he takes it to be well-supported by the available evidence. But what sense can be made of justification or even truth without the intentional framework of folk psychology? This argument is sometimes developed in concert with the suggestion that folk psychological principles are, not contingent regularities, but normative principles that are true a priori.

Whatever the merits of the foregoing line of argument, the prima facie oddity that attaches to radical eliminativism suggests that while it is one thing to assert that intentional mental states will not figure in the ontology of some ideal COGNITIVE SCIENCE [S], it is quite another to assert that there are, really, no intentional mental states. In hopes of saving the folk psychological phenomena, an alternative conception of the nature of folk psychology rejects the assumption that folk psychology does offer such informative causal explanations. Rather, folk psychological explanations are silent about the internal mechanisms and processes of cognition and behavior. Since its explanations are not informative enough to be in competition with the cognitive sciences, folk psychology can be understood to be insulated from scientific advances.

In an influential series of papers, Daniel Dennett (1987) advocates such a view. According to him, folk psychological explanation and prediction proceed on the assumption of RATIONALITY [S]. When we predict what an agent will do, we ask what it would be rational to do given the subject's beliefs and desires. And, to be an intentional system, to have beliefs truly attributable to one, is just to be a system whose behavior is so predictable. Folk psychological description, then, does not aim at the description of internal mental processes. And, while an empirically informative psychology will reject the intentional idiom, folk psychological explanation is adequate in its own preserve. Even so, it is not easy to see how this brand of instrumentalism about the intentional makes folk psychology anything more than a *façon de parler.*

Other philosophers who offer versions of this suggestion emphasize that many of the folk explanations we regard as true bear no easy relation to science (Chastain, 1988; Horgan & Graham, 1991; Horgan & Woodward, 1985). We may, for example, explain why Ajax slipped by pointing out that the ground was slimy. In such a case we are in command of a folk law to the effect that slimy surfaces are apt to produce slippings. But sliminess and slipperiness are certainly not scientific kinds—nothing like them will figure in the explanations of science. Still, it would be mad to suggest the explanation is false or that there are no slippery or slimy things; nor need we be instrumentalist about such things.

Such explanations can survive most any developments in the sciences. Moreover, we are likely to regard a more fundamental scientific account as a way of spelling out, and so vindicating, the folk slimy/slippery account. With such folk explanations all we demand is that there be some more basic scientific account of the processes we describe in terms of "slimy" and "slippery." The source of the robustness of such explanations is precisely their relative uninformativeness. Indeed, we folk recognize the fact that sliminess and slipperiness don't play any deep or informative role in the causal explanations in which they figure. Rather, their role would appear to be of the following nature: there is something about the substance picked out as "slimy" that causes events picked out as "slippings." And so, just by virtue of the fact that they offer scant information about the relevant causal processes, they are insulated from any threat of elimination posed by developments in the sciences.

Finally, it is urged that we adopt a similar view of the status of folk psychology. Thus, just as there are slimy things, there are beliefs and desires; and just as it is true that Ajax slipped because the ground was slimy, so it is true that Achilles behaved so because he believed and desired as he did. It should nonetheless be emphasized that this appealing conclusion has been secured at some considerable price: folk psychological explanations, though serviceable for everyday purposes, are about as uninformative and superficial as causal explanations can be. It is not at all clear that, for example, our conception of ourselves as reasoners—a conception that appears to demand a certain view of the nature of mental processes—can withstand so deflationary a reading. One might well conclude that this gives to the eliminativist everything but what she wants.

In broad terms, then, the theory-theory has one of two results. First, folk psychology is an informative account of mind and behavior but one that is gravely at risk of elimination; second, folk psychology is extraordinarily unlikely to be displaced, but this because it is an exceedingly uninformative theory.

Perhaps what demands reevaluation is the theory-theory itself. According to that view our mastery of the psychological vocabulary as well as our capacity to explain and to predict are grounded in a command of psychological laws. But, it is argued that no one has succeeded in stating such laws in an adequate fashion and that, in any case, the information necessary for the construction of such laws is far beyond the ken of folk (Goldman, 1993; Schiffer, 1991). After all, even very young children have an impressive grip upon the folk psychological framework. Moreover, the theory-theory seems to result in a particularly strange account of the self-attribution of the propositional attitudes. Indeed, it has been alleged that the theory-theory results in troubling asymmetries between first and third personal folk psychologizing (Blackburn, 1992; Moran, 1994).

If we wish to deny that folk psychological explanation is founded upon theorizing, we will need another account. Robert Gordon (1986) and Alvin Goldman (1989) have resuscitated the view that our comprehension of others proceeds via simulation. In the effort to understand others we make adjustments for their cognitive and affective conditions and then, using these as inputs, allow our own psychological processes to run "offline." In prediction, the resulting simulated belief or intention is attributed to the subject.

Advocates of this account claim that simulation is a far simpler and more psychologically plausible account of our folk psychologizing. The verdict of developmental psychologists is, however, mixed (Harris, 1993; Wellman, 1990). One benefit of simulation theoretic accounts is, nonetheless, clear: if folk psychology is not a theory it cannot be a false theory. On such a conception, the eliminativist worry cannot so much as be raised.

(SEE ALSO: *Philosophy of Mind* [S])

Bibliography

Baker, L. R. *Saving Belief.* Princeton, NJ, 1987.

Blackburn, S. "Theory, Observation, and Drama," *Mind and Language,* Vol. 7 (1992), 187–203.

Burge, T. "Individualism and Psychology," *Philosophical Review,* Vol. 45 (1986), 3–45.

Chastain, C. "Comments on Baker," in R. Grimm and D. Merrill, eds., *Contents of Thought* (Tucson, AZ, 1988).

Churchland, P. S. *Neurophilosophy.* Cambridge, MA, 1986.

Churchland, P. "Eliminative Materialism and the Propositional Attitudes," *Journal of Philosophy,* Vol. 78 (1981), 67–90.

Dennett, D. *The Intentional Stance.* Cambridge, MA, 1987.

Fodor, J. *Psychosemantics.* Cambridge, MA, 1987.

Goldman, A. "Interpretation Psychologized," *Mind and Language,* Vol. 4 (1989), 161–85.

———. "The Psychology of Folk Psychology," *Behavioral and Brain Sciences,* Vol. 16 (1993), 15–28.

Gordon, R. "Folk Psychology as Simulation," *Mind and Language,* Vol. 1 (1986), 158–71.

Harris, P. "From Simulation to Folk Psychology: The Case for Development," *Mind and Language,* Vol. 7 (1992), 120–44.

Horgan, T., and G. Graham. "In Defense of Southern Fundamentalism," *Philosophical Studies,* Vol. 62 (1991), 107–34.

Horgan, T., and J. Woodward. "Folk Psychology Is Here to Stay," *Philosophical Review,* Vol. 44 (1985), 197–226.

Kim, J. "Mechanism, Purpose, and Explanatory Exclusion," *Philosophical Perspectives,* Vol. 3 (1989), 77–108.

Morton, A. *Frames of Mind.* Oxford, 1980.

Ramsey, W., S. Stich, and J. Garon. "Connectionism, Eliminativism, and the Future of Folk Psychology," in J. Greenwood, ed., *The Future of Folk Psychology* (Cambridge, 1991).

Schiffer, S. "*Ceteris Paribus* Laws," *Mind,* Vol. 100 (1991), 1–17.

Sellars, W. "Empiricism and the Philosophy of Mind," in *Science, Perception, and Reality* (New York, 1963).

Stich, S. *From Folk Psychology to Cognitive Science.* Cambridge, MA, 1983.

Wellman, H. M. *The Child's Theory of Mind.* Cambridge, MA, 1990.

DION SCOTT-KAKURES

FORMAL INDICATION. The central methodological device for concept formation in the hermeneutics of the early Martin HEIDEGGER [3; S], draws its initial inspiration from the speculative grammar of DUNS SCOTUS [2], that "doctor subtilis" who sought to formalize *haecceitas* (thisness) into a nongeneric category analogizing BEING [1]. For what formal indication first indicates is the full immediacy of the individual human situation expressed in the indexical particularities 'I,' 'here,' 'now,' 'this' and captured in the singular experience of 'being here' *(Dasein).* But by way of the 'intentionality' of such an experience, it also indicates the nexus of relations that already traverse this immediacy: with-others, amidst-things, in-the-world, and so forth. Most important, INTENTIONALITY [4] as sheer "self-directedness toward" promises to develop that most elusive aspect of immediacy, its temporality. TIME [8], that underlying background that relentlessly orders experience, is ultimately what intentionality as formal indication seeks to formalize in its full structural dynamics, catching time, as it were, in the act of its individuating contextualizing (*see* TIME CONSCIOUSNESS [S]). The early Heidegger develops an intertwining series of guiding formal indications to schematize this intentional dynamics in an ever more complex and concrete vectorial web: a triple-sensed intentionality brought to focus in a generative "temporalizing" sense (1920–22), *Dasein* (1923), being-in-the-world (1923–24), to-be (1925), ex-sistence (1926), and transcendence (1927–29). Formal indication accordingly also guides the search for the appropriate nonsubstantifying syntax in the formal grammars of classical languages required to express the purportedly "ineffable" immediacy of experience. A nonobjective ontological logic or "grammaontology" of time's tenses is thereby developed from a reexamination of transitive-intransitive relations, exclamatory impersonals of indexical happenings, middle-voiced infinitives, reflexives, double genitives, prepositionals, adverbials, and so on.

(SEE ALSO: *Temporality and Time* [S])

Bibliography

Imdahl, G. " 'Formale Anzeige' bei Heidegger," *Archiv für Begriffsgeschichte,* vol. 37 (1994), 306–32.

Kisiel, T. *The Genesis of Heidegger's "Being and Time."* Berkeley, 1993.

Pöggeler, O. "Heideggers logische Untersuchungen," in *Forum für Philosophie Bad Homburg,* ed., *Martin Heidegger: Innen- und Außeansichten* (Frankfurt, 1989).

THEODORE KISIEL

FOUCAULT, MICHEL, French philosopher, historian, and social critic, was born in Poitiers in 1926. He studied at the Sorbonne, earning his licence de psychologie in 1950 and the diplôme de psycho-pathologie from the Université de Paris in 1952. He directed the Institut Français in Hamburg as well as the Institut de Philosophie at the Faculté des Lettres in the Université de Clermont-Ferrand. Foucault lectured widely at universities throughout the world, and he was awarded a chair at the Collège de France. He died in 1984.

Foucault's scholarly career is commonly divided into three fairly distinct periods. In his "early," archaeological writings Foucault investigated the internal relations that obtain between language and knowledge and the discursive practices within which both are produced. In the genealogical writings of his "middle" period he focused on the historical transformations and manifestations of power. In the ethical writings from his "late" period he turned his attention to the historical conditions that have collectively presided over the formation of the modern subject. By Foucault's own reckoning this periodization charts a shift, not in the guiding interest of his scholarly activity, but in his critical orientation to it. Throughout his career he sought to account for the emergence within modernity of the self-constituting subject, a being contingently endowed with a historically circumscribed complement of powers and potentialities.

The most significant development in Foucault's thinking occurred in the late 1960s, when he diverted his primary focus from discursive practices to the power relations that inform and sustain them. The defining characteristic of power is its capacity for "infinite displacement" within a complex network of discursive practices. All discourse is ultimately concerned with power, albeit in complicated, disguised ways. Because power can be effective only when it remains partially hidden, it always shelters itself within a discourse about something else. Power is both ubiquitous and capillary in its manifestations, and it announces its presence only as a diversion from its more central concerns.

In order to investigate hidden power relations, and to deliver a critique of concrete social practices, Foucault developed the method known as genealogy. By tracing the historical descent of authoritative discursive practices the genealogist is able to chart the shifting relationships between power and knowledge within the historical transformation of these practices. The genealogist can glimpse power only as it adjusts and reconfigures itself within the social and political relations it strategically inhabits, as it silently transforms institutions and discursive practices. Foucault was especially concerned to investigate the exclusionary power of discursive practices, including those responsible for the institutionalized definitions of madness, criminality, and sexual deviancy.

Foucault's turn to ethics comprised an extension of the development of his genealogical method. His contribution to ethics involved neither the articulation of a new moral theory nor the advocacy of an alternative to the signature techniques of bio-power. He was concerned rather to investigate the conditions under which particular subjects are formed and to expose the hidden power interests that are served by each type of subject. He consequently centered his ethical investigations on the process he called subjectivation, whereby human beings are gradually transformed into subjects invested with unique powers and limitations. Of specific concern to him, especially in his final writings, were the techniques of subjectivation deployed by bio-power, which organizes the resources of modern societies under the pretense of attending to the care of the species and the health of individual human beings.

Foucault's ethical period is marked by his rejection of the "repressive hypothesis," which maintains that power, in all of its manifestations, is strictly juridical and coercive. Foucault opposed this hypothesis with his own genealogy of the various transformations responsible for the emergence in the modern period of bio-power, which displaces its self-aggrandizing designs behind a numbing reverence for health and well-being. The success of the regimes devoted to the expansion of bio-power demonstrates that truth is, not the enemy of power, but its silent partner in a complex network of totalizing strategies.

Foucault's ethical investigations revealed that regimes of power can realize their ends only if human beings are transformed into productive subjects, invested with a limited capacity for self-legislation. Although he located in the dominant regimes of bio-power a masked impulse toward domination, he also acknowledged their productive, empowering roles in the formation of the modern subject. The subjects depicted in his later genealogies are not simply the unwitting products of clandestine discursive practices, for they are able to resist the totalization of power within its most ambitious and monolithic regimes. To expose the mobilization of power within mechanisms of transformation is to render it temporarily less effective and less dangerous. Power can neither be eradicated nor contained, but its inexorable tendency toward domination can often be neutralized within local regimes.

Foucault never completed the ambitious genealogical agenda he set for himself. The guarded optimism conveyed by his final writings has been taken up by successor genealogists, and the articulation of a Foucaultian political position remains, for some, an ongoing project.

(SEE ALSO: *Archaeology; Order of Things;* and *Subject* [S])

Bibliography

MAJOR WORKS BY FOUCAULT IN ENGLISH TRANSLATION

The Archaeology of Knowledge. Translated by Alan M. Sheridan Smith. New York, 1972.

The Order of Things: An Archaeology of the Human Sciences. Unidentified translation. New York, 1973.

Madness and Civilization: A History of Insanity in the Age of Reason. Translated by R. Howard. New York, 1973.

The Birth of the Clinic: An Archaeology of Medical Perception. Translated by A. M. Sheridan Smith. New York, 1975.

Language, Counter-Memory, Practice: Selected Essays and Interviews. Edited by D. Bouchard. Translated by D. Bouchard and S. Simon. Ithaca, NY, 1977.

Discipline and Punish: The Birth of the Prison. Translated by A. Sheridan. New York, 1979.

The History of Sexuality, Vol. 1, *An Introduction.* Translated by R. Hurley. New York, 1980.

Power/Knowledge: Selected Interviews and Other Writings 1972–1977. Edited by C. Gordon. Translated by C. Gordon, L. Marshall, J. Mepham, and K. Soper. New York, 1980.

The Foucault Reader. Edited by P. Rabinow. New York, 1984.

The History of Sexuality, Vol. 2, *The Use of Pleasure.* Translated by R. Hurley. New York, 1985.

The History of Sexuality, Vol. 3, *The Care of the Self.* Translated by R. Hurley. New York, 1986.

Politics, Philosophy, Culture: Interviews and Other Writings 1977–1984. Edited by L. D. Kritzman. Translated by A. Sheridan, et al. New York, 1988.

The Final Foucault. Edited by J. Bernauer and D. Rasmussen. Cambridge, MA, 1988.

WORKS ON FOUCAULT

Dreyfus, H. L., and P. Rabinow. *Michel Foucault: Beyond Structuralism and Hermeneutics,* 2d ed. Chicago, 1983.

Miller, J. *The Passion of Michel Foucault.* New York, 1993.

DANIEL CONWAY

FOUNDATIONALISM *See*: CLASSICAL FOUNDATIONALISM [S]

FOURFOLD, THE. Works of HEIDEGGER [3; S] composed around 1950 drew deeply on poetic and religious thought in contemplating our environment. "The Thing" is a meditation on an earthenware jug that can serve at table or in a liturgy; "Building Dwelling Thinking" evokes the old stone bridge of Heidelberg and other bridges. Meditation on them leads us to the earth that supports them and constitutes them, to the sky above that yields sunlight and rain, to ourselves, the mortals, whose life is stayed by these things, and finally to the divinities whom we invoke in travel and to whom we make our offerings. In their deepest currents these meditations show us how earth and sky, mortals and immortals, draw together to constitute a harmony, a fourfold (*Geviert*).

The fourfold developed out of the theme of the world in *Being and Time* with its assemblies of the "ready-to-hand" and out of the meeting of world and earth in the 1935 lectures on *The Origin of the Work of Art.* In the 1950s Heidegger contrasted the fourfold very sharply with the "frame" (*Gestell*), the deracinated universal dimension assumed by modern science and imposed upon the earth by technology. The fourfold appears in the poetry of HÖLDERLIN [4] and Trakl, and, in its still deeper background, it is the "world" of China's *Tao Te Ching,* India's *Bhagavad-Gita,* Israel's book of *Genesis,* and Greece's *Iliad,* and it is the immutable vista of the aboriginal peoples of America and all the continents of earth. It forms the background for philosophy (see Plato's *Gorgias* 508a).

Bibliography

Heidegger, M. *Vorträge und Aufsätze.* Pfullingen, 1954.

———. *Poetry, Language, Thought,* translated by A. Hofstadter. New York, 1971.

GRAEME NICHOLSON

FREEDOM. An important recent contribution to the philosophical discussion of FREEDOM [3] is Hannah ARENDT's [S] thoughts on the tragic (and dramatic) nature of free action as a political phenomenon. Arendt's views, which virtually summarize the entire Continental tradition's contribution to this problem, argue against that tradition's identification of freedom with inner freedom, be it the contemplative indifference to worldly events celebrated by Stoics (*see* STOICISM [8]) or the sovereign will over conflicting, good and evil volitions extolled by Christians. Inner freedom, she argued, is experientially and historically derivative of the political freedom that first made its appearance with the Greek polis. Indeed, it is opposed to political freedom; Stoic indifference implies resignation to nature's necessity, while Christian sovereignty—whose freedom really consists in a kind of suspension or paralysis caused by inner division—implies resolution through undivided will power or suppression of dissent.

Arendt argues that free action must also be distinguished from such worldly activities as the laborious production of consumer goods, which is necessitated by biological imperative, and the artful fabrication of culture, whose creative freedom remains hidden. Again, she insists that free action not be confused with freedom from want or with negative freedom from constraint, both of which constitute its necessary presuppositions. Although the ascertainment of ends (intellect) and the power to command their execution (will) also condition action, freedom as such consists, as KANT [4; S] taught, in acting on the basis of some universal principle. Acting in this manner implicates two stages of freedom: the spontaneous beginning of something undetermined and unpredictable—what Arendt, in reference to AUGUSTINE'S [S] comment on the miracle of birth, calls natality; and its historical continuation and augmentation in the founding of laws and constitutions, which have their ultimate warrant in acts of promise making. The performative nature of promises indicates the inherently communicative—public and plural—nature of freedom as a political phenomenon.

Arendt's discussion of the French and American revolutions underscores the tension between these two stages of freedom and between freedom and social EQUALITY [3]. For Arendt, the failure of these revolutionary traditions to distinguish the social question from the political question led to a devaluing of freedom in the name of biological and historical necessity or the efficient administration of social equality. In revolutionary movements modeled on the French example—itself a secular manifestation of Christian, theocentric absolutism—the privileging of the social question inevitably reduces freedom to a totalitarian will-to-power (*see* NIETZSCHE [5; S]) exercised in the name of a sovereign, general will (*see* ROUSSEAU [7; S]). Yet Arendt herself conceded that the full range (or plurality) of opinions requisite for political discussion, choice, and action could scarcely obtain without eliminating social domination.

Arendt's discussion of revolution also illuminates the tension between Kantian and republican conceptions of freedom. The sheer spontaneity associated with the private invocation of principle seems to render public action arbitrary and meaningless. Conversely, the public interpretation of political action as possessing an enduring sense beyond what the actors themselves originally intended—and one often legitimated by appeal to historical precedent—seems to render action heteronomous. Arendt hoped to mitigate this tension by appeal to Kant's account of aesthetic judgment, which finds universal—albeit exemplary rather than teleological—meaning in the irreducibly unique, undetermined, and otherwise inexplicable deeds that make up political life (*see* DETERMINISM AND FREEDOM, and JUDGMENT AND ACTION [S]).

Bibliography

Arendt, H. *On Revolution.* New York, 1963.

———. "What Is Freedom," in *Between Past and Future: Eight Exercises in Political Thought,* expanded ed. New York, 1968.

———. *The Life of the Mind,* 2 vols. Mary McCarthy, ed. New York, 1978.

———. *Lectures on Kant's Political Philosophy.* R. Beiner, ed. Chicago, 1982.

DAVID INGRAM

FREGE, GOTTLOB. By far the most important event for Frege scholarship that took place after 1967 was the publication of a volume containing all those of Frege's unpublished writings that had not been destroyed in the wartime bombing of Münster: the *Nachgelassene Schriften* (1969). This allowed a far clearer view of Frege's philosophical development than had been obtainable from his published writings alone. It was translated into English as *Posthumous Writings* (1979) and was followed by the publication of Frege's surviving correspondence in *Wissenschaftlicher Briefwechsel* (1976). The main items of this were translated in *Philosophical and Mathematical Correspondence* (1980).

In the Encyclopedia of 1967, the division of FREGE'S [3] career into five periods was misjudged. It is better to recognize only three: from his earliest writings up to 1886 (the early period); from 1891 to July 1906 (the middle or mature period); and from August 1906 until his death in 1925. He published nothing in the years 1887–90, during which, by his own account, he was rethinking his logical doctrines. The early period, which includes the two masterpieces *Begriffsschrift* and *Grundlagen,* was one of rapid development. The middle period was introduced by the lecture "Function und Begriff," in which he expounded his new views in concise form, and includes the famous essays "Über Sinn und Bedeutung" and "Über Begriff und Gegenstand" of 1892 and both volumes of *Grundgesetze* (1893 and 1903). Its termination was marked by Frege's realization that his attempted solution of the RUSSELL [7] contradiction would not work; thanks to the *Nachgelassene Schriften,* this can be precisely dated. During the middle period, no changes of mind can be detected, so that the writings of that period may be treated as presenting a single body of ideas. The acknowledgment that his attempt to solve the Russell contradiction was a failure affected Frege profoundly: it meant that his life's work had failed. Although it had led him into many side-turnings, he had, almost from the beginning, devoted himself to accomplishing a single large task: the construction of a definitive foundation for number theory and analysis; virtually everything he had written had been directed toward that end. Now it appeared that his attempt had been vitiated by a single huge error, which he came to see as the admission of classes, which he had characterized as the extensions of concepts. (In *Grundgesetze,* the notion of a class is generalized to that of a value-range, the extension of a function; both the more and the less general notions Frege now saw as chimerical.) At first he sought to isolate and expound systematically what remained intact, his logical doctrines purged of the extensions of concepts; but he fell for many years into a condition of discouragement and abandoned the project. He took it up again, with some vigor, in the years after World War I and, toward the very end of his life, began an attempt at constructing a geometrical foundation for arithmetic.

In the 1967 Encyclopedia article the change from the early to the middle period was presented as consisting principally in the addition of some important new doctrines, notably that of the distinction between SENSE [S] *(Sinn)* and REFERENCE *(Bedeutung)* [S]. It was much more than that. The distinction was not a mere systematization of what had been left unsystematic; it was the first acknowledgment of *any* distinction between the significance of a term and that which it signified. In the writings of the early period no such distinction is anywhere to be found. The attempt has been made, in particular by Baker and Hacker (1984), to present Frege's ideas of that period as together forming a coherent theory as systematic and as tenable as that of the middle period; but such an attempt must fail, because no coherent theory that altogether ignores that distinction can be devised. This is why Frege's dual use of "concept" *(Begriff)* is so puzzling to those who read *Grundlagen* for the first time: sometimes he speaks of attaining a concept, at others he says that a statement of number serves to say something about a concept. We cannot coherently run together what we talk about with the meaning of the term we use to talk about it.

The sense of a sentence—the thought it expresses—is what is *grasped* by one who understands it: it comprises what, in knowing the language, he knows about it that is relevant to its truth or falsity. It does not comprise anything that one need not know in order to know the language (extraneous information); nor does it comprise any aspect of the sentence's meaning that does not bear on its being true or otherwise (such aspects Frege classifies as its 'coloring'). The sense of a component expression is its contribution to the sense of the whole: what, in virtue of knowing the language, one must grasp concerning that expression in order to understand the sentence. The notion of *Bedeutung* is always presented by Frege as stemming from the relation of a name to its bearer; but its function in the philosophy of his middle period is essentially that of the semantic value of an expression. The theory concerns the mechanism whereby the truth-value of a sentence is determined: the *Bedeutungen* of its component expressions are what have to be determined in the process of determining the truth-value of the whole. This is why, if the truth-value of a sentence in which it occurs can be affected by the presence of an expression, the possession of a *Bedeutung* by that expression cannot be called in question; it is also why sentences must be accorded a *Bedeutung,* since they can be components of more complex sentences.

Sluga (1980) has shown that Georg W. F. HEGEL's [3; S] influence had waned in Germany when Frege was writing; it was therefore wrong to credit him with helping to overcome that influence. He was nevertheless unquestionably a realist. Jean van Heijenoort, followed by Hintikka, attributed to Frege a rejection of semantics as an impossible attempt to survey language as if from outside language. This is probably a correct account of his view in his early period. The context principle, as stated in *Grundlagen,* denies that the connection between a term and its content in reality can be apprehended by a mental association between them: all legitimate questions, in the formal mode, concerning the content of expressions, are equivalent to questions in the material mode, that is, framed *within* the language. This yields a view of content or reference analogous to the minimalist view of truth propounded by Frank Plumpton RAMSEY [7]: the principle exemplified by "The content of the name 'Chicago' " enshrines the *whole* explanation of the notion of content. But van Heijenoort's interpretation does not apply to the views of Frege's middle period. The theory of *Bedeutung* is, precisely, a semantic theory. It is not possible to view language, as such, from outside; but it is possible to speak in one language about another, as Frege stated in German the semantics of the formal language of *Grundgesetze.* The distinction between object-language and metalanguage is made explicitly in the late unpublished fragment "Logical Generality."

In *Grundlagen* the context principle serves, in practice, as a guide to finding a correct definition of number. So viewed, it requires one to find a means of specifying, without circularity, the truth-conditions of those sentences in which we normally employ the term to be defined: it is then a requirement on a correct definition of it that it yield those truth-conditions for such sentences. It will confer truth-conditions on other sentences, which we do not ordinarily use and are not interested in; their possible unnaturalness is no objection to the definition, which has done all that is required of it.

This left an unanswered question: how can we come to understand the primitive expressions of a formal theory and, in particular, the domain over which its variables range? Frege attempted to answer this question in *Grundgesetze,* as it applied to terms for value-ranges: it there took the form, "How can we secure *Bedeutungen* for such terms?" His answer was an appeal to the context principle. Admittedly, though he still allowed a salient role for sentences in the theory of sense, he no longer recognized them as categorically different from singular terms in the theory of *Bedeutung;* but in practice this made no difference. Without a distinction between significance and thing signified, it has some plausibility to maintain that, if all sentences containing certain terms have been assigned truth-conditions, all that is needed to give those terms a content has been done. But Frege continued to maintain this about *Bedeutung:* he supposed that the *Bedeutung* of a term could be fixed by laying down the *Bedeutungen* of more complex terms (and the truth-conditions of sentences) containing it. He thus attempted simultaneously to specify the *Bedeutungen* of value-range terms and the domain of the individual variables. The result was a grossly ill-founded set of inductive specifications, which, partially incorporated into the axioms, led to contradiction. The problem of how we attain a grasp of the intended range of the variables of a fundamental mathematical theory remains unsolved. Frege's attempt to solve it was indeed a failure; he deserves credit for formulating and for facing it.

Bibliography

WORKS BY FREGE

Collected Papers. Edited by B. McGuinness. Oxford, 1984.

Nachgelassene Schriften. Hamburg, 1969.

Philosophical and Mathematical Correspondence. Edited by B. McGuinness. Oxford, 1980.

Posthumous Writings [translation of *Nachgelassene Schriften*]. Translated by P. Long and R. White. Oxford, 1979.

Wissenschaftlicher Briefwechsel. Hamburg, 1976.

WORKS ON FREGE

Baker, G. P., and P. M. S. Hacker. *Frege: Logical Excavations.* Oxford, 1984.

Dummett, M. *Frege: Philosophy of Language,* 2d ed. London, 1981.

———. *Frege: Philosophy of Mathematics.* London, 1991.

———. *Frege and Other Philosophers.* Oxford, 1991.

———. *The Interpretation of Frege's Philosophy.* London, 1991.

Haaparanta, L., and J. Hintikka, eds. *Frege Synthesized.* Dordrecht, 1986.

Klemke, E. D., ed. *Essays on Frege.* Urbana, IL, 1968.

Resnick, M. *Frege and the Philosophy of Mathematics.* Ithaca, NY, 1986.

Schirn, M., ed. *Studien zu Frege.* Bad Canstatt, 1976.

Sluga, H. *Gottlob Frege.* London, 1980.

———, ed. *The Philosophy of Frege,* 4 vols. New York, 1993.

van Heijenoort, J. "Logic as Calculus and Logic as Language," *Synthese,* Vol. 17 (1967), 324–30.

von Kutschera, F. *Gottlob Frege.* Berlin, 1989.

Wright, C. *Frege's Conception of Numbers as Objects.* Aberdeen, 1983.

———, ed. *Frege: Tradition and Influence.* Oxford, 1984.

MICHAEL DUMMETT

FREUD, SIGMUND, has seen an explosion in historical scholarship, accelerated by the publication of Freud's correspondence with Wilhelm Fleiss and by the appearance of other original source materials. As a result, the sources of Freud's psychoanalytic work are now firmly placed in late-nineteenth-century biology, physiology, medicine, and neurology. Freud's philosophy of science and methodological views are understood as adaptations of standard opinions in those subjects at the time; much more is known about the outcomes of Freud's treatments and the backgrounds of his patients; and his changes of opinion have been thoroughly and repeatedly documented. Minor questions of interpretation and major questions of the motives for changes in Freud's doctrines remain. The picture of FREUD [3] that has emerged shows him to have been largely unsuccessful in the early years of psychoanalytic practice in curing patients, justifiably dubious in the late 1890s about the reliability of his methods of diagnosis and inference, and subsequently disingenuous, or at least very inaccurate, about the development of his views.

Freud's doctrine, his evidence, his arguments, and ahistorical reinterpretations of his work by Paul RICOEUR and by Jürgen HABERMAS [S] have been scathingly criticized by Adolf Grunbaum in a sustained series of essays and in two books. Grunbaum emphasized that Freud offered a "tally argument" for the correctness of psychoanalytic interpretation, based on the assumption that only correct interpretations of the source of a disorder will cause permanent removal of symptoms. Grunbaum argues that data on placebo effects and spontaneous remission provide overwhelming empirical evidence against this "necessary condition thesis." A substantial portion of the literature written on Freud by philosophers in the 1980s and 1990s consists of responses to Grunbaum, none disputing his empirical claims (see the contribution by Edward Erwin in Earman et al., 1993).

Perhaps because of these historical and critical developments, and almost certainly because the rise of cognitive psychology has offered better prospects, there are few positive projects in recent philosophy that are framed around Freud, Freudian theory, or Freudian themes. One such is accounts offered by Donald DAVIDSON [S], Herbert Fingarette, and others of paradoxes of rationality—weakness of will, self-deception, and others—in terms of a SELF [S] divided into parts with competing beliefs, desires, and resources. Weakness of will is then explained as a compromise result, or as the temporary dominance of one part over another; self-deception is explained by the existence of separate memory structures, each accessible only to one of two or more inner agents, and so forth.

Influenced by neo-Wittgensteinian literature, Marcia Cavell has propounded a view in which the truth or falsity of claims of meaning, as in dream interpretation, are determined socially, not by any history of private thoughts. The maneuver may be aimed at saving Freudian theory from charges of falsehood or at least unreliability, but if so whether it succeeds or fails depends largely on the community selected. The general scientific society has decided that Freud was wrong about a great deal and that Cavell is wrong about what makes for TRUTH [S] and falsehood. Cavell also raises interesting questions about what neonates and babies experience and how they subsequently come to be able to describe their own experiences. Similar questions that have recently been the subject of a large body of research in developmental psychology (see Alison Gopnik, 1996) seem remote from any Freudian theory.

Patricia Kitcher has offered a historical/philosophical reconstruction of Freud's enterprise as an attempt to construct a multidisciplinary science of the mind, drawing on psychology, anthropology, biology, physiology, and, of course, clinical phenomena. So read, Freud's effort is almost unique in the human sciences, which have more typically been formed by emulating developments in some particular influential science, most recently cognitive psychology.

The similarities between Freud's general theoretical views before the turn of the century and those of contemporary cognitive psychology, especially "connectionist" models of mental processing, has been noticed by several writers (see CONNECTIONISM [S]). The scientific ambition Freud embraced—to identify the structure and processes of mind chiefly from observational evidence—is not unlike the similar task contemporary cognitive psychologists undertake on the basis of experimental behavior. The methodological issues on which Freud took a stand confront contemporary cognitive psychologists almost exactly as they did Freud: the appropriate role for statistical reasoning as against reasoning from example and counterexample; the value of evidence from abnormal subjects in reasoning about normal mental structure; the proper reconstruction of causal hypotheses and the nature of sound inference to causal relations; how to separate universal features from individual idiosyncrasies; how to obtain any evidence about the mentation of the very young; the relation between theoretical descriptions of mental processes and those of everyday belief-desire psychology; the relation, if any, between behavioral evidence and physiological evidence; and, most generally, whether theoretical claims about normal mental processing are radically underdetermined by behavioral evidence, no matter whether clinical or experimental. These parallelisms suggest that many of those methodological criticisms of the Freudian enterprise that do not turn on Freud's idiosyncrasies might usefully be addressed to pieces of contemporary cognitive science. Thus far few philosophers have been inclined to turn the tables.

(SEE ALSO: *Psychoanalytic Theories, Logical Status of* [6])

Bibliography

Cavell, M. *The Psychoanalytic Mind.* Cambridge, MA, 1993.

Cohen, R., and L. Laudan, eds. *Physics, Philosophy, and Psychoanalysis.* Reidel, 1983.

Earman, J., et al., eds. *Philosophical Problems of the Internal and External Worlds: Essays on the Philosophy of Adolf Grunbaum.* Philadelphia, 1993.

Erwin, E. *A Final Accounting: Philosophical and Empirical Issues in Freudian Psychology.* Cambridge, MA, 1996.

Gopnik, A. *Words, Thoughts, and Things.* Cambridge, MA, 1996.

Grunbaum, A. *The Foundations of Psychoanalysis.* Berkeley, 1984.

———. *Validation in the Clinical Theory of Psychoanalysis.* Rome, 1993.

Kitcher, P. *Freud's Dream: A Complete Interdisciplinary Science of Mind.* Cambridge, MA, 1992.

Macmillan, M. *Freud Evaluated.* Cambridge, MA, 1996.

Masson, J. *The Complete Letters of Sigmund Freud to Wilhelm Fleiss.* Cambridge, MA, 1985.

Neu, J., ed. *The Cambridge Companion to Freud.* Cambridge, 1991.

Pribram, K., and M. Gill. *Freud's Project Reassessed.* New York, 1976.

Sulloway, F. *Freud: Biologist of the Mind.* New York, 1979.

Wollheim, R., ed. *Freud: A Collection of Critical Essays.* Garden City, NY, 1974.

CLARK GLYMOUR

FUNCTIONALISM. Functionalism is one of the major proposals that have been offered as solutions to the MIND–BODY PROBLEM [5]. Solutions to the mind–body problem usually try to answer questions such as: What is the ultimate nature of the mental? At the most general level, what makes a mental state mental? Or more specifically, what do thoughts have in common in virtue of which they are thoughts? That is, what makes a thought a thought? What makes a pain a pain? Cartesian dualism said the ultimate nature of the mental was to be found in a special mental substance. BEHAVIORISM [1] identified mental states with behavioral dispositions; physicalism, in its most influential version, identifies mental states with brain states (*see* PHYSICALISM, MATERIALISM [S]). Functionalism says that mental states are constituted by their causal relations to one another and to sensory inputs and behavioral outputs. Functionalism is one of the major theoretical developments of twentieth-century analytic philosophy, and provides the conceptual underpinnings of much work in COGNITIVE SCIENCE [S].

Functionalism has three distinct sources. First, PUTNAM [S] and Fodor saw mental states in terms of an empirical computational theory of the mind (*see* COMPUTATIONAL MODEL OF MIND, THE [S]). Second, SMART's [S] "topic neutral" analyses led ARMSTRONG [S] and Lewis to a functionalist analysis of mental concepts. Third, WITTGENSTEIN's [8; S] idea of meaning as use led to a version of functionalism as a theory of MEANING [5; S], further developed by SELLARS [S] and later Harman.

One motivation behind functionalism can be appreciated by attention to artifact concepts such as *carburetor,* and biological concepts such as *kidney.* What it is for something to be a carburetor is for it to mix fuel and air in an internal combustion engine—*carburetor* is a functional concept. In the case of the kidney, the *scientific* concept is functional—defined in terms of a role in filtering the blood and maintaining certain chemical balances.

The kind of function relevant to the mind can be introduced via the parity-detecting automaton illustrated in the figure below, which tells us whether it has seen an odd or even number of '1's. This automaton has two states, S_1 and S_2; one input, '1' (though its input can be nothing) and two outputs, it utters either the word "Odd" or "Even." The table describes two functions, one from input and state to output, and another from input and state to next state. Each square encodes two conditionals specifying the output and next state given both the current state and input. The left box says that if the machine is in S_1 and sees a '1', it says "odd" (indicating that it has seen an odd number of '1's) and goes to S_2. The right box says, similarly, that if the machine is in S_2 and sees a '1', it says "even" and goes back to S_1.

Now suppose we ask the question: "What is S_1?" The answer is that the nature of S_1 is entirely relational, and entirely captured by the table. We could give an explicit characterization of 'S_1' as follows:

> Being in S_1 = being in the first of two states that are related to one another and to inputs and outputs as follows: being in one of the states and getting a '1' input results in going into the second state and emitting "Odd"; and being in the second of the two states and getting a '1' input results in going into the first and emitting "Even."

Making the quantification over states more explicit:

> Being in S_1 = Being an x such that ∃P∃Q[If x is in P and gets a '1' input, then it goes into Q and emits "Odd"; if x is in Q and gets a '1' input it gets into P and emits "Even"& x is in P] (Note: read '∃P' as 'There is a property *P*'.)}

This illustration can be used to make a number of points. (1) According to functionalism, the nature of a mental state is just like the nature of an automaton state: constituted by its relations to other states and to inputs and outputs. All there is to S_1 is that being in it and getting a '1' input results in such and such, and so forth. According to functionalism, all there is to being in pain is that it disposes you to say 'ouch', wonder whether you are ill, it distracts you, and so forth. (2) Because mental states are like automaton states in this regard, the illustrated method for defining automaton states is supposed to work for mental states as well. Mental states can be totally characterized in terms that involve only logico-mathematical language and terms for input signals and behavioral outputs. Thus functionalism satisfies one of the desiderata of behaviorism, characterizing the mental in entirely nonmental language. (3) S_1 is a second order state in that it consists in having *other* properties, say mechanical or hydraulic or electronic properties, that have certain relations to one another. These other properties, the ones quantified over in the definitions just given, are said to be the *realizations* of the functional properties. So, although functionalism characterizes the mental in nonmental terms, it does so only by quantifying over realizations of mental states, which would not have delighted behaviorists. (4) One functional state can be realized in different ways. For example, an actual metal and plastic machine satisfying the machine table might be made of gears, wheels, pulleys and the like, in which case the realization of S_1 would be a mechanical state; or the realization of S_1 might be an electronic state, and so forth. (5) Just as one functional state can be realized in different ways, one physical state can realize different functional states in different machines. This could happen, for example, if a single type of transistor were used to do different things in different machines. (6) Since S_1 can be realized in many ways, a claim that S_1 *is* a mechanical state would be false (at least arguably), as would a claim that S_1 is an electronic state. For this reason, there is a strong case that functionalism shows physicalism is false: if a creature without a brain can think, thinking cannot be a brain state. (But see the section on functionalism and physicalism below.)

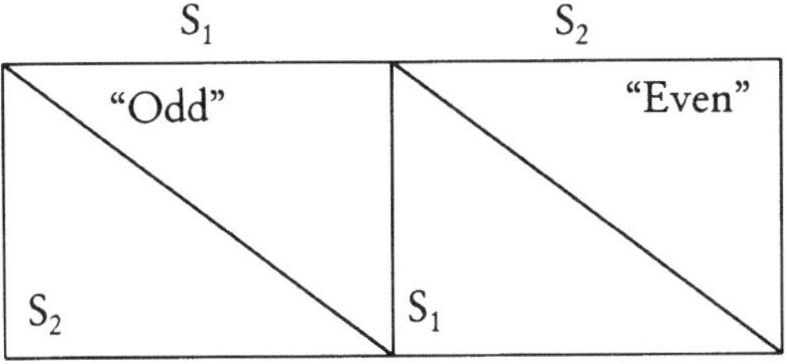

The notion of a realization deserves further discussion. In the early days of functionalism, a first-order property was often said to realize a functional property in virtue of a 1-1 correspondence between the two realms of properties. But such a definition of realization produces far too many realizations. Suppose, for example, that at t_1 we shout 'one' at a bucket of water, and then at t_2 we shout 'one' again. We can regard the bucket as a parity-detecting automaton by pairing the physical configuration of the bucket at t_1 with S_1 and the heat emitted or absorbed by the bucket at t_1 with "odd"; by pairing the physical configuration of the bucket at t_2 with S_2 and the heat exchanged with the environment at t_2 with "even"; and so on. What is left out by the post hoc correlation way of thinking of realization is that a true realization must satisfy the *counterfactuals* implicit in the table. To be a realization of S_1, it is not enough to lead to a certain output and state given that the input is a '1'; it is also required that had the input been a '0', the S_1 realization would have led to the other output and *state.* Satisfaction of the relevant counterfactuals is built into the notion of realization mentioned in (3) above (see Lycan, 1987).

Suppose we have a theory of mental states that specifies all the causal relations among the states, sensory inputs, and behavioral outputs. Focusing on pain as a sample mental state, it might say, among other things, that sitting on a tack causes pain, and that pain causes anxiety and saying 'ouch'. Agreeing for the sake of the example to go along with this moronic theory, functionalism would then say that we could define 'pain' as follows: being in pain = being in the first of two states, the first of which is caused by sitting on tacks, which in turn causes the other state and emitting 'ouch'. More symbolically

> Being in pain = Being an x such that ∃P∃Q[sitting on a tack causes P & P causes both Q and emitting 'ouch' & x is in P]

More generally, if T is a psychological theory with n mental terms of which the 17th is 'pain', we can define 'pain' relative to T as follows (the 'F_1' ... 'F_n' are variables that replace the n mental terms, and i_1, etc. And o_1, etc. indicates):

> Being in pain = Being an x such that $\exists F_1 \ldots \exists F_n$ $[T(F_1 \ldots F_n, i_1, \text{etc.}, o_1, \text{etc.})$ & x is in $F_{17}]$

In this way, functionalism characterizes the mental in nonmental terms, in terms that involve quantification over realizations of mental states but no explicit mention of them; thus functionalism characterizes the mental in terms of structures that are tacked down to reality only at the inputs and outputs.

The psychological theory T just mentioned can be either an empirical psychological theory or else a commonsense "folk" theory, and the resulting functionalisms are very different. In the latter case, conceptual functionalism, the functional definitions are aimed at capturing our ordinary mental concepts. In the former case, "psychofunctionalism," "the functional definitions are not supposed to capture ordinary concepts but are only supposed to fix the extensions of mental terms. The idea of psychofunctionalism is that the scientific nature of the mental consists not in anything biological, but in something "organizational," analogous to computational structure. Conceptual functionalism, by contrast, can be thought of as a development of logical behaviorism. Logical behaviorists thought that pain was a disposition to pain *behavior.* But as Geach and CHISHOLM [S] pointed out, what counts as pain behavior depends on the agent's beliefs and desires. Conceptual functionalists avoid this problem by defining each mental state in terms of its contribution to dispositions to behave—and have other mental states.

FUNCTIONALISM AND PHYSICALISM

Theories of the mind prior to functionalism have been concerned both with (1) what there *is,* and (2) what gives each type of mental state its own identity, for example what pains have in common in virtue of which they are pains. Stretching these terms a bit, we might say that (1) is a matter of ONTOLOGY [5; S] and (2) of METAPHYSICS [S]. Here are the ontological claims: dualism told us that there are both mental and physical substances, whereas behaviorism and physicalism are monistic, claiming that there are only physical substances. Here are the metaphysical claims: behaviorism tells us that what pains (for example) have in common in virtue of which they are pains is something behavioral; dualism gave a nonphysical answer to this question, and physicalism gives a physical answer to this question. Turning now to functionalism, it answers the metaphysical question without answering the ontological question. Functionalism tells us that what pains have in common—what makes them pains—is their function; but functionalism does not tell us whether the beings that have pains have any nonphysical parts. This point can be seen in terms of the automaton described above. In order to be an automaton of the type described, an actual concrete machine need only have states related to one another and to inputs and outputs in the way described. The machine description does not tell us how the machine works or what it is made of, and in particular it does not rule out a machine which is operated by an immaterial soul, so long as the soul is willing to operate in the deterministic manner specified in the table (see Putnam, 1988 and the paper by Fodor in Block, 1980).

In thinking about the relation between functionalism and physicalism, it is useful to distinguish two categories of physicalist theses: one version of physicalism competes with functionalism, making a metaphysical claim about the physical nature of mental state properties or types (and is thus often called "type" physicalism). As mentioned above, on one point of view, functionalism shows that type of physicalism is false.

However, there are more modest physicalisms whose thrusts are ontological rather than metaphysical. Such physicalistic claims are not at all incompatible with functionalism. Consider, for example, a physicalism that says that every actual thing is made up entirely of particles of the sort that compose inorganic matter. In this sense of physicalism, most functionalists have been physicalists. Further, functionalism can be modified in a physicalistic direction, for example, by requiring that all properties quantified over in a functional definition by physical properties. Type physicalism is often contrasted with *token* physicalism. (The word 'teeth' in this sentence has five letter tokens of three letter types.) Token physicalism says that each pain (for example) is a physical state, but token physicalism allows that there may be nothing physical that all pains share, nothing physical that makes a pain a pain.

It is a peculiarity of the literature on functionalism and physicalism that while some functionalists say functionalism shows physicalism is false (see the papers by Putnam, Fodor, and Block and Fodor in Block [1980], some of which are also in the other anthologies), others say functionalism shows physicalism is true. (See the papers by Lewis and Armstrong in Block [1980], and Rosenthal [1991].) In Lewis's case, the issue is partly terminological. Lewis is a conceptual functionalist about "having pain." Having pain on Lewis's regimentation could be said to be a rigid designator of a functional property. (A rigid designator names the same thing in each possible world. 'The color of the sky' is nonrigid, since it names red in worlds in which the sky is red. 'Blue' is rigid, since it names blue even in worlds in which the sky is red.) 'Pain', by contrast, is a nonrigid designator conceptually equivalent to a definite description of the form 'the state with such and such a causal role'. The referent of this phrase in us, Lewis holds, is a certain brain state, though the referent of this phrase in a robot might be a circuit state, and the referent in an angel would be a nonphysical state. Similarly, 'the winning number' picks out '17' in one lottery and '596' in another. So Lewis is a functionalist (indeed a conceptual functionalist) about having pain. In terms of the metaphysical issue described above—what do pains have in common in virtue of which they are pains—Lewis is a functionalist, not a physicalist. What a person's pains and the robot's pains share is a causal role, not anything physical. Just as there is no numerical similarity between 17 and 596 relevant to their being winning numbers, there is no physical similarity between human and Martian pain that makes them pains. And there is no physical similarity of any kind between human pains and angel pains. However, on the issue of the scientific nature of pain, Lewis is a physicalist. What is in common to human and Martian pain in his view is something conceptual, not something scientific.

FUNCTIONALISM AND PROPOSITIONAL ATTITUDES

The discussion of functional characterization given above assumes a psychological theory with a finite number of mental state terms. In the case of monadic states like pain, the sensation of red, and so forth, it does seem a theoretical option simply to list the states and their relations to other states, inputs and outputs. But for a number of reasons, this is not a sensible theoretical option for belief-states, desire-states, and other PROPOSITIONAL ATTITUDE [S] states. For one thing, the list would be too long to be represented without combinatorial methods. Indeed, there is arguably no upper bound on the number of propositions, any one of which could in principle be an object of thought. For another thing, there are systematic relations among beliefs: for example, the belief that John loves Mary and the belief that Mary loves John. These belief states represent the same objects as related to each other in converse ways. But a theory of the nature of beliefs can hardly just leave out such an important feature of them. We cannot treat 'believes-that-grass-is-green', 'believes-that-grass-is-blue', and so forth, as unrelated primitive predicates. So we will need a more sophisticated theory, one that involves some sort of combinatorial apparatus. The most promising candidates are those that treat belief as a relation. But a relation to what? There are two distinct issues here. One issue is how to state the functional theory in a detailed way. (See Loar [1981] and Schiffer [1987] for a suggestion in terms of a correspondence between the logical relations among sentences and the inferential relations among mental states.) A second issue is what types of states could possibly realize the relational propositional attitude states. Field (1978) and Fodor (in Block, 1980) argue that to explain the productivity of propositional attitude states, there is no alternative to postulating a LANGUAGE OF THOUGHT [S], a system of syntactically structured objects in the brain that express the propositions in propositional attitudes. (See Stalnaker, 1984, chapters 1–3, for a critique of Field's approach.) In later work, Fodor (1987) has stressed the systematicity of propositional attitudes mentioned above. Fodor points out that the beliefs whose contents are systematically related exhibit the following sort of empirical relation: if one is capable of believing that Mary loves John, one is also capable of believing that John loves Mary. Fodor argues that only a language of thought in the brain could explain this fact.

EXTERNALISM

The upshot of the famous "twin earth" arguments has been that meaning and content are in part in the world and in the language community. Functionalists have responded in a variety of ways. One reaction is to think of the inputs and outputs of a functional theory as *long-arm* as including the objects that one sees and manipulates. Another reaction is to stick with *short-arm* inputs and outputs that stop at the surfaces of the body, thinking of the intentional contents thereby characterized as *narrow*—supervening on the nonrelational physical properties of the body. There has been no widely recognized account of what narrow content is, nor is there any agreement as to whether there is any burden of proof on the advocates of narrow content to characterize it. (See the papers by Burge, Loar, and Stalnaker in Rosenthal, 1991; see also Goldman, 1993.)

MEANING

Functionalism says that understanding the meaning of the word 'momentum' is a functional state. On one version of the view, the functional state can be seen in terms of the role of the word 'momentum' itself in thinking, problem solving, planning, and so forth. But if understanding the meaning of 'momentum' is this word's having a certain function, then there is a very close relation between the meaning of a word and its function, and a natural proposal is to regard the close relation as simply identity, that is, the meaning of the word just *is* that function. (See Peacocke, 1992.) Thus functionalism about content leads to functionalism about meaning, a theory that purports to tell us the metaphysical nature of meaning. This theory is popular in cognitive science, where in one version it is often known as procedural semantics, as well as in philosophy where it is often known as conceptual role semantics. The theory has been criticized (along with other versions of functionalism) in Putnam (1988) and Fodor and LePore (1992).

HOLISM

Block and Fodor (in Block, 1980) noted the "damn/darn" problem. Functional theories must make reference to any difference in stimuli or responses that can be mentally significant. The difference between saying 'damn' and 'darn' when you stub your toe can, in some circumstances, be mentally significant. So the different functionalized theories appropriate to the two responses will affect the individuation of every state connected to those utterances, and for the same reason, every state connected to those states, and so on. His pains lead to 'darn', hers to 'damn', so their pains are functionally different, and likewise their desires to avoid pain, their beliefs that interact with those desires, and so on. Plausible assumptions lead to the conclusion that two individuals who differ in this way share almost nothing in the way of mental states. The upshot is that the functionalist needs a way of individuating mental states that is less fine-grained than appeal to the whole theory, a molecularist characterization. Even if one is optimistic about solving this problem in the case of pain by finding something functional in common to all pains, one cannot assume that success will transfer to beliefs or meanings, for success in the case of meaning and belief may involve an analytic/synthetic distinction (Fodor and LePore, 1992).

QUALIA

Recall the parity-detecting automaton described at the beginning of this article. It could be instantiated by two people, each of whom is in charge of the function specified by a single box. Similarly, the much more complex functional organization of a human mind could "in principle" be instantiated by a vast army of people. We would have to think of the army as connected to a robot body, acting as the brain of that body, and the body would be like a person in its reactions to inputs. But would such an army really instantiate a mind? More pointedly, could such an army have pain, or the experience of red? If functionalism ascribes minds to things that do not have them, it is too liberal. Lycan (1987) suggests that we include much of human physiology in our theory to be functionalized to avoid liberalism; that is, the theory T in the definition described earlier would be a psychological theory plus a physiological theory. But that makes the opposite problem, chauvinism, worse. The resulting functional description will not apply to intelligent Martians whose physiologies are different from ours. Further, it seems easy to imagine a simple pain-feeling organism that shares little in the way of functional organization with us. The functionalized physiological theory of this organism will be hopelessly different from the corresponding theory of us. Indeed, even if one does not adopt Lycan's tactic, it is not clear how pain could be characterized functionally so as to be common to us and the simple organism. (See Block, "Troubles with Functionalism," which appears in all the anthologies in the bibliography.)

Much of the force of the problems just mentioned derives from attention to phenomenal states like the look of red. Phenomenal properties would seem to be intrinsic to (nonrelational properties of) the states that have them, and thus phenomenal properties seem independent of the relations among states, inputs and outputs that define functional states. Consider, for example, the fact that lobotomy patients often say that they continue to have pains that feel the same as before, but that the pains do not bother them. If the concept of pain is a functional concept, what these patients say is contradictory or incoherent—but it seems to many of us that it is intelligible. All the anthologies have papers on this topic; see also Lycan (1987), chapters 8, 9, 14, and 15 of Shoemaker (1984), and Hill (1991).

The chauvinism/liberalism problem affects the characterization of inputs and outputs. If we characterize inputs and outputs in a way appropriate to our bodies, we chauvinistically exclude creatures whose interface with the world is very different from ours—for example, creatures whose limbs end in wheels or, turning to a bigger difference, gaseous creatures who can manipulate and sense gases but for whom all solids and liquids are alike. The obvious alternative of characterizing inputs and outputs themselves functionally would appear to yield an abstract structure that might be satisfied by, for example, the economy of Bolivia under manipulation by a wealthy eccentric, and would thus fall to the opposite problem of liberalism.

It is tempting to respond to the chauvinism problem by supposing that the same functional theory that applies to a person also applies to the creatures with wheels. If they thought they had feet, they would try to act like us, and if we thought we had wheels, we would try to act like them. But notice that the functional definitions have to have some specifications of output organs in them. To be neutral among all the types of bodies that sentient beings could have would just be to adopt the liberal alternative of specifying the inputs and outputs themselves functionally (*see* QUALIA [S]).

TELEOLOGY

Many philosophers (see the papers by Lycan and Sober in Lycan, 1990, and Lycan, 1987) propose that we avoid liberalism by characterizing functional roles teleologically. We exclude the armies and economies mentioned because their states are not for the right things. A major problem for this point of view is the lack of an acceptable teleological account. Accounts based on evolution smack up against the swamp-grandparents problem. Suppose you find out that your grandparents were formed from particles from the swamp that came together by chance. So, as it happens, you do not have any evolutionary history to speak of. If evolutionary accounts of the teleology underpinnings of content are right, your states do not have any content. A theory with such a consequence should be rejected.

CAUSATION

Functionalism dictates that mental properties are second-order properties, properties that consist in having other properties that have certain relations to one another. But there is at least a prima facie problem about how such second-order properties could be causal and explanatory in a way appropriate to the mental. Consider, for example, provocativeness, the second-order property that consists in having some first-order property (say redness) that causes bulls to be angry. The cape's redness provokes the bull, but does the cape's provocativeness provoke the bull? The cape's provocativeness might provoke an animal protection society, but is not the bull too stupid to be provoked by it? (See Block, 1990.)

Functionalism continues to be a lively and fluid point of view. Positive developments in recent years include enhanced prospects for conceptual functionalism and the articulation of the teleological point of view. Critical developments include problems with causality and holism, and continuing controversy over chauvinism and liberalism. (*See* CAUSATION [2; S]; PHILOSOPHY OF MIND [S])

Bibliography

Beakley, B., and P. Ludlow, eds. *Philosophy of Mind: Classical Problems, Contemporary Issues.* Cambridge, MA, 1992.

Block, N., ed. *Readings in Philosophy of Psychology,* 2 vols. Vol. 1. Cambridge, MA, 1980.

———. "Can the Mind Change the World?" in G. Boolos, ed., *Meaning and Method: Essays in Honor of Hilary Putnam,* (Cambridge, 1990).

Field, H. "Mental representation," *Erkentniss,* Vol. 13 (1978), 9–61.

Fodor, J. *Psychosemantics.* Cambridge, MA, 1987.

———, and E. LePore. *Holism.* New York, 1992.

Goldman, A. *Readings in Philosophy and Cognitive Science.* Cambridge, MA, 1993.

Hill, C. S. *Sensations.* Cambridge, 1991.

Loar, B. *Mind and Meaning.* Cambridge, 1981.

Lewis, D. "Reduction of Mind," in S. Guttenplan, ed., *A Companion to Philosophy of Mind* (Oxford, 1995).

Lycan, W. G. *Consciousness.* Cambridge, MA, 1987.

———, ed. *Mind and Cognition.* New York, 1990.

Peacocke, C. *A Study of Concepts.* Cambridge, MA, 1992.

Putnam, H. *Representation and Reality.* Cambridge, MA, 1988.

Rosenthal, D., ed. *The Nature of Mind.* Oxford, 1991.

Schiffer, S. *Remnants of Meaning.* Cambridge, MA, 1987.

Shoemaker, S. *Identity, Cause and Mind.* Cambridge, MA, 1984.

Stalnaker, R. C. *Inquiry.* Cambridge, MA, 1984.

NED BLOCK

FUSION OF HORIZONS. The fusion of horizons *(Horizontverschmelzung)* is GADAMER's [S] characterization of the event of understanding. It is the merging of the interpreter's horizon with the supposed horizon of the text or that of the other. The term 'horizon' indicates that there is a variable limit to what can be understood. Horizons may expand and contract. That one is limited to a particular horizon implies that an absolute viewpoint is unattainable. The fusion of horizons occurs within the hermeneutic circle of understanding.

The interpreter's horizon is constituted by the prejudices *(Vorurteile)*—whether legitimate, illegitimate, conscious, or unconscious—that have been inherited through one's acculturation and experience. (Here, 'prejudice' has a neutral rather than a negative meaning.) Prejudices would include one's current judgments concerning meaning, values, life, and reality. One's horizon forms one's world view or linguistic perspective. The horizon situates the interpreter in the temporal, linguistic continuum of EFFECTIVE HISTORY [S].

The other horizon is said to be the text's or the other's, but this horizon does not exist in itself and must be constituted during the process of understanding. Gadamer argues that neither the author's intention nor a determinate, objective meaning for linguistic signs can function as the criterion for the constitution of the text's horizon. Rather, the interpreter must project a meaning (a set of prejudices) for the text from his or her own perspective using the preconception of completion *(Vorgriff der Vollkommenheit)* and following the ideality and ontological valence of the word.

This preconception states that one must *initially* presuppose the text to be both coherent as well as truthful. If, following one's own prejudices, an incoherence or error is detected, then the interpreter must project another meaning to satisfy this preconception, thereby enabling the projection of a different horizon for that text. The ideality of the word is the possibly changing 'meaning' of a word that is carried by human memory through effective history. Eminent texts acquire ontological valence, a power to call readers into their own saying.

Within the hermeneutic circle the movement back and forth from the interpreter to the text constitutes and reconstitutes the text's horizon. The interpreter both actively considers possibilities using whatever text-critical methodologies are deemed appropriate (without, however, being able to attain an absolute meaning in itself) and passively attends to the saying power of the language contained in the ideality and ontological valence of the word. This latter prevents a nihilistic relativization of meaning.

The fusion of horizons occurs in the event of understanding when the differences between the two horizons are adjudicated with reference to the subject matter in question. Sometimes the intepreter's prejudice may be legitimated, at other times the text's. A new prejudice may also come forth in the process of understanding and both horizons be altered. The event of understanding concludes with the constitution of a new fused horizon.

Since the interpreter's horizon is inherited from the past and the horizon of the text or other is projected from the situation of the interpreter, it is more accurate to speak of one horizon in continual development. The methodological separation of the two horizons is meant to underline the importance of projecting the other's horizon. It also uncovers the tension between the familiar and the foreign in this developing horizon, which explains why the site of hermeneutics is in this between.

(SEE ALSO: *Language in Gadamer* [S])

Bibliography

Gadamer, H.-G. *Gesammelte Werke.* Tübingen, 1985ff.

———. *Truth and Method,* 2nd revised ed., translated by J. Weinsheimer and D. Marshall. New York, 1989.

Grondin, J. *Hermeneutische Wahrheit? Zum Wahrheitsbegriff Hans-Georg Gadamers.* Königstein, 1982.

Hoy, D. C. *The Critical Circle: Literature and History in Contemporary Hermeneutic.* Berkeley, 1978.

Matika, E. *Gadamer—Bibliographie.* Frankfurt a. M., 1995.

Schmidt, L. K. *The Epistemology of Hans-Georg Gadamer. An Analysis of the Legitimization of 'Vorurteile'.* Frankfurt a. M., 1987.

———, ed. *The Specter of Relativism: Truth, Dialogue, and 'Phronesis' in Philosophical Hermeneutics.* Evanston, IL, 1995.

Wachterhauser, B., ed. *Hermeneutics and Truth.* Evanston, IL, 1994.

Warnke, G. *Gadamer: Hermeneutics, Tradition and Reason.* Stanford, CA, 1987.

Weinsheimer, J. C. *Gadamer's Hermeneutics.* New Haven, 1985.

LAWRENCE K. SCHMIDT

FUZZY LOGIC. Fuzzy logics are multivalued logics intended to model human reasoning with certain types of imprecision. The field of fuzzy logic originated with a 1965 paper by Lotfi Zadeh, a professor of engineering at the University of California, Berkeley. It is significant that the inventor of fuzzy logic was neither a philosopher nor a linguist. Since 1965 research in fuzzy logic has always had an engineering and mathematical bent, while the philosophical foundations of fuzzy logic have always been under attack.

Many different formal systems have been proposed under the general name of fuzzy logic, but there is wide acceptance that the fundamental principles of fuzzy logic are

(1) $t(A \wedge B) = \min\{t(A),t(B)\}$

(2) $t(A \vee B) = \max\{t(A),t(B)\}$

(3) $t(\neg A) = 1 - t(A)$.

In these axioms A and B represent arbitrary propositions. The truth value of A, a real number between 0 and 1, is denoted $t(A)$. The first axiom above says that the truth value of $A \wedge B$ is the lesser of the truth value of A and the truth value of B. The second and third axioms concerning disjunction and negation are to be understood similarly.

At the same time that Zadeh introduced fuzzy logic, he also introduced fuzzy SET THEORY [7; S], a variant of naive set theory (i.e., everyday set theory as opposed to a foundational set theory such as the Zermelo-Fraenkel axioms) with the basic axioms

(1) $\mu(x \in P \cap Q) = \min\{\mu(x \in P),\mu(x \in Q)\}$

(2) $\mu(x \in P \cup Q) = \max\{\mu(x \in P),\mu(x \in Q)\}$

(3) $\mu(x \in P^c) = 1 - \mu(x \in P)$.

Here $\mu\,(x \in P)$ denotes the degree to which x is a member of the set P. Since 1965 many branches of mathematics have been generalized along fuzzy set theory lines.

There are two fundamental differences between fuzzy logics and conventional logics such as classical predicate calculus or modal logics (*see* MODAL LOGIC [S]). Although these differences are technical, they are of considerable philosophical significance. First, conventional logics (except intuitionistic logics) require for every proposition that either it or its negation be true, that is, that $t(A \vee \neg A) = 1$ in fuzzy logic notation. In fuzzy logics this "law of the excluded middle" does not hold. Second, there is no consensus about a semantics for fuzzy logic that is well-defined independently of its PROOF THEORY [S], that is, the inferential axioms given above. In contrast, conventional logics have well-accepted semantics, for example Tarskian MODEL THEORY [S] (*see* TARSKI, ALFRED [8]) for predicate calculus, and Kripkean (*see* KRIPKE, SAUL [S]) possible worlds semantics for modal logics.

Fuzzy logics are claimed to be capable of representing the meanings of intrinsically imprecise natural language sentences, such as "Many Texans are rich," for which the law of excluded middle fails. There is disagreement as to whether fuzzy methods successfully represent the complexities of concepts such as "many" and "rich." What is clear is that the rules of fuzzy logic cannot be used for reasoning about frequentist or subjective types of uncertainty, whose properties are captured by standard PROBABILITY [6; S] theory. The central issue here is that the probability of a compound proposition such as $A \wedge B$ is not a function just of the probabilities of the propositions A and B: the probability of $A \wedge B$ also depends on the relationship between the propositions A and B, in particular on their independence or correlation.

The tolerance for ambiguity found in fuzzy logic, and specifically the rejection of the law of the excluded middle, is a revolutionary idea in MATHEMATICAL LOGIC [S]. Some advocates of fuzzy logic claim that tolerance for ambiguity is also revolutionary philosophically, since Western philosophy, from PLATO [6; S] through DESCARTES [2; S], has supposedly been an intrinsically dualistic tradition. According to this argument, fuzzy logic has been better received in Japan and other Asian countries than in the West because of the holistic, subtle nature of the Eastern intellectual tradition. Apart from the dualistic oversimplification of the distinction between "Western" and "Eastern" thought, this claim also ignores the continuous holistic tradition in European philosophical thought, from ZENO [8] through PASCAL [6] to HEIDEGGER [3; S] and WITTGENSTEIN [8; S].

There has been much ARTIFICIAL INTELLIGENCE [S] research on using fuzzy logic for representing real-world knowledge, and there has been some recent convergence between this work and parallel work by a distinct research community on knowledge representation using classical logics, nonmonotonic logics, and probability theory. So far this research has remained almost exclusively theoretical. In contrast, engineering work on using fuzzy logic for controlling complex machines heuristically has been highly successful in practice.

A fuzzy controller is a device, usually implemented as software for an embedded microprocessor, that continually monitors readings from sensors, and makes decisions about actuator settings. For example, a controller for the automatic transmission of a car monitors road speed, the position of the accelerator pedal, and other factors, and decides whether to shift gears down or up, or not to shift. The knowledge possessed by a fuzzy controller is typically represented as rules such as

$$\mu(\textit{speed}, \text{MODERATE}) \wedge \mu(\textit{pedal}, \text{FULL-DOWN}) \rightarrow \mu(\textit{shift}, \text{DOWN})$$

Here *speed* and *pedal* are sensory readings, *shift* is a possible actuator setting, and MODERATE, FULL-DOWN, and DOWN are fuzzy sets. Through inference rules for the fuzzy connectives $\wedge$ and $\rightarrow$, the degree of membership of *speed* in MODERATE and of *pedal* in FULL-DOWN determines the desired degree of membership of *shift* in DOWN. Given a set of rules, a fuzzy controller continually computes the degree to which the antecedents of each rule are satisfied, and selects a conclusion that is the weighted average of the conclusion of each rule, where rules are weighted using these degrees.

Fuzzy controllers are widely used for two basic reasons. First, since the action chosen at each instant is typically the result of interpolating several rules, their behavior is smooth. Second, fuzzy controller rule sets are easy for humans to read and understand intuitively, hence easy to construct by trial and error.

(SEE ALSO: *Philosophical Logic* [S])

Bibliography

Elkan, C. "The Paradoxical Success of Fuzzy Logic," *IEEE Expert,* Vol. 6 (August 1994), 3–8.

Mamdani, E. H. "Application of Fuzzy Algorithms for Control of Simple Dynamic Plant," *Proceedings of the Institution of Electrical Engineers,* Vol. 121 (1974), 1585–88.

Zadeh, L. A. "Fuzzy Sets," *Information and Control,* Vol. 8 (1965), 338–53.

Zimmermann, H.-J. *Fuzzy Set Theory—And Its Applications.* Holland, 1991.

CHARLES ELKAN

G

GADAMER, HANS-GEORG, a Heidelberg philosopher and student of Martin HEIDEGGER [3; S], is best known for his HERMENEUTIC PHILOSOPHY [S] put forward in his *Wahrheit und Methode* (*Truth and Method,* 1960). Widely regarded as the most significant German philosopher after Heidegger, Gadamer wrote on PLATO [6; S], Georg Wilhelm Friedrich HEGEL [3; S], Heidegger, Aristotle's practical philosophy, reason in an age of science, aesthetics, poetics, Paul Celan, and other topics.

BIOGRAPHY

Gadamer was born in Marburg in 1900 and grew up in Breslau. His mother died when he was four. His father was a well-known university research scientist in pharmacological chemistry. In 1919 Gadamer's father was called from the University of Breslau to a research chair at the University of Marburg. Gadamer entered Marburg as a second-year student with interests in literature, art history, and classical philology. But he was soon drawn to the great neo-Kantian philosopher and Platonist, Paul NATORP [5], under whom he completed his doctoral dissertation in 1922 on pleasure in the Platonic dialogues. In 1923 Gadamer journeyed for the summer semester to Freiburg to hear Martin Heidegger, who was offering bold new interpretations of ARISTOTLE [1; S] and other philosophers. When Heidegger moved to Marburg in the fall of that year, Gadamer became his assistant and he remained so until 1928. During this time Gadamer also studied with Nicolai HARTMANN [3], took seminars in classical philology under Paul Friedländer and others, and in 1927 was certified in classical philology. In 1928 he completed his habilitation under Heidegger on "Plato's dialectical ethics," based on the *Philebus.*

Gadamer remained another ten years in Marburg waiting for a call to a full-time teaching appointment. After 1933 his chances for a call were practically blotted out by his not being in good standing with the Nazis. But he remained active in the academic life at Marburg, which boasted some of Germany's leading intellectuals—Rudolf BULTMANN [1] in theology; Nicolai Hartmann; Stefan George, the charismatic poet; Richard Hamann, the iconoclastic art historian; and finally, Friedländer and others, who represented the great philological tradition of Ulrich von Wilamowitz-Moellendorff.

In 1938 Gadamer was finally called to a chair in philosophy at Leipzig, where he was able to survive through the war years as a politically unthreatening classical humanist. Because of his political integrity he was elected rector at Leipzig after the war. In 1947 he managed to escape the stultifying atmosphere of the new communist regime by being called to a position at Frankfurt University. He was at Frankfurt but two years when in 1949 he was called to fill Karl JASPERS's [4] chair at the University of Heidelberg.

Gadamer remained in Heidelberg as chair in philosophy until his retirement in 1968. A gifted lecturer, he concentrated in the 1950s on topics that later became part of *Truth and Method.* At the same time, he worked to revive Hegel studies in Germany, and rebuilt a war-shattered department into one of the strongest in Germany. In 1952, along with Helmut Kuhn, he founded the *Philosophische Rundschau,* a journal dedicated to reviewing current books and discussing major issues in philosophy.

After 1968 Gadamer continued to lecture and offer seminars in Heidelberg as an honored emeritus professor, but now he allowed himself to accept invitations to speak in other countries and to serve as a guest professor at various universities, especially in the United States and Canada. This fed a growing interest in hermeneutics in the United States, an interest manifested in the number of dissertations and books being written on the subject. English translations of Gadamer's works began to appear: *Truth and Method* (1975), *Philosophical Hermeneutics* (1976), and *Hegel's Dialectic* (1976) being among the first.

In *Truth and Method* Gadamer's concepts can be logically divided into those within *Truth and Method* and those in the shorter writings after it. The latter category includes further writings defending and defining hermeneutics, writings in modern and ancient philosophy, and in aesthetics and poetics.

In *Truth and Method* Gadamer articulated the most detailed and nuanced account of the "event of understanding" in the history of philosophy. He based much of his thinking on Heidegger, Hegel, and Plato. From Heidegger's *Origin of a Work of Art* he drew strength for a powerful reassertion of the "truth" of art, and from Heidegger's *Being and Time* and later writings he drew concepts that called into question the goal of objectivity in interpretation. From Hegel and Plato he drew emphases on tradition, history, and dialogue. From Wilhelm DILTHEY [2] and Heidegger he drew an emphasis on the horizonal character of consciousness and the operativeness of history in all understanding. Understanding, he argues, takes place in a consciousness in which history—that is, tradition—is always already at work, shaping, predisposing, predefining what the process of understanding involves. His term for this is *wirkungsgeschichtliches Bewußtsein,* "effective historical consciousness" (*see* EFFECTIVE HISTORY [S]), and the encounter with the other, as person or as text, is a matter of *Horizontverschmelzung* (FUSION OF HORIZONS [S]).

In *Truth and Method* Gadamer shows the development after Kant of fateful conceptual turns in the course of eighteenth- and nineteenth-century philosophy, philology, and hermeneutics that have led to present presuppositions about understanding and the conditions for its possibility. He traces the dream of scientific objectivity in humanistic and social scientific knowledge in the nineteenth century, especially in Friedrich Daniel Ernst SCHLEIERMACHER [7] and Dilthey, and the promising philosophical transformation of this "problematic" of understanding through Heidegger's phenomenological analysis of existential temporality and the historical situatedness of and the participation of history in understanding. He accepts Heidegger's description of the "forestructure" of understanding, adding to it his concept of an "anticipation of completeness" in all understanding. He argues that the process of understanding has the structure of a dialogue and can be likened to a game in that it follows rules and operates in a language that transcends it; thus, he emphasizes the "linguisticality" *(Sprachlichkeit)* of understanding and even ultimately its ontological character: "Being that can be understood is language," he asserted (*Truth and Method,* p. 432). Finally, one of the most distinctive and important of the contributions of *Truth and Method* is its insistence on a moment of "application" in all understanding.

The book's overarching goal, however, was to cause the artwork to be seen in a new way. While the title might lead one to expect it to be concerned with methods in the *Geisteswissenschaften,* Gadamer's professed aim is to defend the claim of artworks to be "true." In Gadamer's view the experience of encountering truth in great works of art demonstrates the limits of a science-oriented concept of understanding; the meaning and power of such artworks elude scientific modes of understanding. Gadamer wrote a good deal in explanation and defense of *Truth and Method.* These writings are now collected in volume 2 of his collected works.

Gadamer's writings on modern philosophy range through the Continental tradition since Kant and are influenced principally by Plato, who casts a shadow even over his modern writings; by Heidegger, about whom he has written more than about any other modern philosopher; by Hegel, whose importance in modern philosophy Gadamer repeatedly defended; and by Edmund HUSSERL [4; S] whose phenomenology Gadamer used and treated as a major element in his thought. Most of his essays on ancient philosophy are directly or indirectly connected with Plato. From Plato he draws his model of dialogue, in which partners participate in quest of a truth that transcends the individual seeker. Gadamer's ethical thinking as well as his dialectical hermeneutics go back to Plato's "dialectical ethics" of respect for the other person, of openness, of seeking to strengthen the partner's case in order not merely to win a debate to one's own satisfaction but to move together toward truth, a result that benefits both sides and that both sides affirm.

Art and poetry are a major theme in Gadamer's writings throughout his career. In 1934 Gadamer wrote on "Plato and the Poets," and in the 1940s he was writing essays on HÖLDERLIN [4], GOETHE [3], Immerman, and RILKE [7]. His articles after *Truth and Method* tend to select more sober and difficult poets like Stefan George, Gottfried BENN [1], and Paul Celan. His essays on aesthetics and poetics continue to emphasize the truth of art, the need for dialogical openness, and the priority of the artwork's character of play. At the same time, another issue arises: What about basically nonrepresentational poetry? What about the "no longer beautiful" poetry of the modern (or postmodern) dark lyric? After a number of writings that struggle successfully with the dark lyric, such as *Wer bin ich und wer bist du?* ("Who Am I and Who Are You?", 1973), on poet Paul Celan, Gadamer poses the problem in somewhat different terms. For Gadamer it is a "task of philosophy" to develop a context within which one can still recognize and deal with—or "understand"—modern and postmodern art.

Gadamer's essay "The Relevance of the Beautiful" presents a twentieth-century defense of such art. In this essay experience becomes the reference point, even group experiences as one finds them in the historical record. Gadamer includes, not just experiences recorded in artworks or great poetry, which would create a circular argument, but in anthropological records of such things as (1) the role of play in human life, (2) the high experiences of festiveness in our own and other cultures, and (3) the power of participation in symbolic religious rites. In groping for an explanation of the power of art and a defense of its legitimacy, Gadamer offers an analysis of three categories—play, symbol, and festival.

In his essay "The Truth of the Artwork" (1960), Gadamer pointed to a threefold insufficiency of scientific thinking: (1) the insufficiency of scientific thinking, by itself and without recourse to standards outside itself, to grapple with ethical problems such as human rights, abortion, ecology, or planning the future; (2) its incapacity to account for the experience of beauty in art and poetry or to lay down principles for its creation; and (3) its insufficiency to meet, or even account for, the spiritual needs of human beings. All these suggest that a recourse to the absolute priority of scientific presuppositions cannot serve us well in dealing with the encounter with ethical problems, artworks, or the divine. Art, like ethics and the divine, seems to move beyond the competence of the categories of scientific thinking. And they can claim to be "true." This is a major theme both in *Truth and Method* and in later writings.

In "Wort und Bild" ("Word and Image," 1992) Gadamer takes the final step and attempts to articulate aesthetic categories that apply both to plastic/pictorial arts and arts of the word. Among the several concepts to which he turns are the Greek concept of the fine *(kalon)* and to our experience of the rightness and absoluteness of art.

(SEE ALSO: *Hermeneutic Philosophy; Language in Gadamer* [S])

Bibliography

MAJOR WORKS BY GADAMER

Platos dialektische Ethik: Phänomenologische Interpretationen zum "Philebos," 3d ed. Leipzig, 1931. Translated by R. M. Wallace as *Plato's Dialectical Ethics: Phenomenological Interpretations Relating to the "Philebus."* New Haven, 1991.

Wahrheit und Methode: Grundzüge einer philosophischen Hermeneutik. Tübingen, 1960. Translated as *Truth and Method,* edited by G. Barden and J. Cumming. New York, 1975; rev. ed., 1989.

Hegels Dialektik: Fünf hermeneutische Studien. Tübingen, 1971. Translated by P. C. Smith as *Hegel's Dialectic: Five Hermeneutical Studies.* New Haven, 1976.

Wer bin ich und wer bist du?: Ein Kommentar zu Paul Celans Gedichtfolge "Atemkristall." Frankfurt, 1973.

Vernunft im Zeitalter der Wissenschaft: Aufsätze. Frankfurt, 1976. Translated as *Reason in the Age of Science.* Cambridge, MA, 1981.

Die Aktualität des Schönen: Kunst als Spiel, Symbol, und Fest. Stuttgart, 1977. Translated by N. Walker as "The Relevance of the Beautiful." In R. Bernasconi, ed., *The Relevance of the Beautiful and Other Essays* (Cambridge, 1986).

Die Idee des Guten zwischen Plato und Aristoteles. Heidelberg, 1978. Translated as *The Idea of the Good in Platonic–Aristotelian Philosophy.* New Haven, 1986.

Heideggers Wege. Tübingen, 1983. Translated as *Heidegger's Ways.* Albany, NY, 1994.

Gessamelte Werke. 10 vols. Tübingen, 1985–. Contains all of the above works.

COLLECTIONS OF GADAMER'S WORKS IN ENGLISH

Philosophical Hermeneutics, edited and translated by D. E. Linge. Berkeley, 1976.

Dialogue and Dialectic: Eight Hermeneutical Studies on Plato, translated by P. C. Smith. New Haven, 1980.

The Relevance of the Beautiful and Other Essays, edited by R. Bernasconi. Cambridge, 1986.

Dialogue and Deconstruction: The Gadamer–Derrida Encounter, edited by D. Michelfelder and R. E. Palmer. Albany, NY, 1989. Includes five essays by Gadamer.

Hans-Georg Gadamer on Education, Poetry, and History, edited by Dieter Misgeld and G. Nicholson. Albany, NY, 1992.

Literature and Philosophy in Dialogue: Essays in German Literary Theory, translated by R. H. Paslick. Albany, NY, 1992.

WORKS ON GADAMER

Hoy, D. C. *The Critical Circle: Literature, History, and Philosophical Hermeneutics.* Berkeley, 1978.

Schmidt, L. K. *The Epistemology of Hans-Georg Gadamer.* New York, 1985.

Warnke, G. *Gadamer: Hermeneutics, Tradition, and Reason.* Stanford, CA, 1987.

Weinsheimer, J. C. *Gadamer's Hermeneutics: A Reading of "Truth and Method."* New Haven, 1985.

Wright, K., ed. *Festivals of Interpretation: Essays on Hans-Georg Gadamer's Work.* Albany, NY, 1990.

RICHARD E. PALMER

GENETICS AND REPRODUCTIVE TECHNOLOGIES. Modern genetics and technological aids to human reproduction, like other advances in science and technology, have created ethical problems heretofore unencountered. Biomedical developments have also posed new conceptual, epistemological, and metaphysical problems. This article addresses these philosophical concerns as well as the more widely discussed ethical implications of contemporary genetics and reproductive technologies. One conceptual and ethical link between these two fields is the prospect of "designing our descendents." This prospect has been viewed by some as a boon to humankind (Fletcher, 1974) and by others as a fearsome possibility to be avoided at all costs (Ramsey, 1970).

The Human Genome Initiative, a "big science" project launched by the U.S. government to map and sequence the entire human genome, has heightened concerns about the privacy and confidentiality of genetic information, the uses to which such information might be put, and the possibility of stigmatizing individuals or groups because of their genetic constitution. The knowledge the human genome project can yield is massive in contrast to previous efforts to acquire information about human genetics.

The contemporary science of genetics provides, not only an understanding of heritable traits, but also the capability to diagnose the probability or certainty of transmitting to offspring genetic conditions such as sickle-cell disease, Tay Sachs disease, or cystic fibrosis. The ability to identify and locate specific genes that render a person likely to manifest heritable conditions, such as Huntington's disease and certain forms of cancer, raises profound questions about the wisdom and desirability of learning about future contingencies when no cure exists and preventive measures are of uncertain efficacy.

A conceptual question is prompted by the rapid advances in genetics: What constitutes genetic disease? The traditional concept of disease relies on the ability of medical scientists to identify deviations from the normal physiological functioning of an organism. Asymptomatic diseases, such as hypertension, can be detected by diagnostic instruments even though the individual feels no symptoms of illness. With the discovery of genes that render an individual with a family history highly likely to develop a particular disease later in life, how should the individual who carries the gene be characterized? Does the person in whom the gene is found have a genetic disease or not? The individual has no symptoms and the disease may never express itself. Yet merely being susceptible opens the possibility of harm to the interests of such individuals, making them vulnerable to actions by others such as insurance companies who seek to deny insurance on grounds of a preexisting condition or employers who refuse to hire workers with a known propensity for illness.

Beyond the problems posed by diagnosis and prediction in genetics are those of intervention: Is gene therapy intrinsically different from traditional medical therapy? Even if gene therapy by means of manipulating somatic cells poses no special problem, what about altering germ-line cells, a procedure that would affect future generations? (*See* DISTANT PEOPLES AND FUTURE GENERATIONS [S]) If genetic manipulation to correct defects is ethically permissible, what, if anything, would be wrong with alterations intended to provide genetic enhancement? Are efforts to improve human intelligence, appearance, or other attributes by genetic means essentially different from the traditional methods of education, physical or mental training, or behavior modification (President's Commission for the Study of Ethical Problems, 1982)?

Attempts to improve the quality of the human gene pool, or "positive eugenics," have generally been viewed with disfavor, especially after the policies in Nazi Germany promoting racial hygiene (Proctor, 1988). Yet eugenic practices remain at the level of individual choice. The recipients of donated sperm are typically given information about physical and other personal characteristics of donors, allowing them to choose sperm from a donor whose traits they hope to replicate in the child. The prospect of genetic enhancement using the techniques of recombinant DNA manipulation can allow for more precision and wider applications than older approaches such as selective sperm banking.

Knowledge that one carries a gene for a heritable disease can pose a profound dilemma for the individual. An early form of this dilemma arose when carrier screening was the only way to determine whether a couple would pass on a genetic disease to their offspring. A couple then had to decide whether to take the chance that a child would be born with the heritable condition. With the advent of various forms of prenatal diagnosis (amniocentesis, chorionic villus sampling, blood tests), the presence of some genetic diseases in a fetus can be detected. The ethical question in such cases is whether to abort an afflicted fetus (*see* ABORTION [S]). In the case of both carrier screening and prenatal diagnosis, trained genetics counselors have uniformly taken a nondirective approach. The norm in genetics counseling has generally been to provide unbiased information to enable individuals or couples to make an informed decision (*see* INFORMED CONSENT [S]) whether to initiate a pregnancy or to abort a fetus found to have a genetic disease (Lappe, 1971; President's Commission for the Study of Ethical Problems, 1983).

As the science of genetics yields an increasing amount of information, individuals are faced with making decisions about prophylactic medical interventions. For example, a woman who learns that she carries a gene for an inherited form of breast cancer may contemplate bilateral mastectomy before any clinical signs appear. The epistemological problem posed by such scenarios is a familiar philosophical one: decision making under risk and uncertainty. If the woman decides to undergo a major, disfiguring operation, she does so with the knowledge that she might escape the disease entirely. But if she forgoes the preventive step, she runs the risk of developing a dread disease that may be curable if detected early but that also has a high mortality rate.

The knowledge by individuals or couples that they are at risk for transmitting a genetic disease to offspring is one indication for embarking on the use of reproductive technologies. The couple may elect to use donated sperm or ova. A far more common indication for the use of reproductive technologies, however, is infertility or subfertility on the part of one or both members of a couple. Methods include in vitro fertilization (IVF)—fertilizing a human ovum outside the womb; the use of sperm of ova contributed by third parties or the womb of a woman not intended to be the rearing parent (surrogacy); cryopreservation (freezing) of fertilized ova, which are termed 'preembryos'; and embryo splitting.

Frequently discussed ethical issues include concerns about destruction of the traditional family when third parties are used as gamete donors or surrogates (Macklin, 1991); worries about the effect on children who learn that they were born as a result of these techniques; and the opposite worry about harmful effects of struggling to maintain family secrets. Prior to the first IVF birth in 1978, fears were expressed that IVF would produce a higher than normal incidence of birth defects, but scientific evidence gathered over the years has shown this concern to be unwarranted. The objection that being created with the aid of gametes from a third party can harm the interests of children is countered by the metaphysical observation that these are children who would never have existed but for the use of these techniques.

Different religions are opposed to the use of some or all of these reproductive technologies. The Roman Catholic Church has urged prohibition of virtually all forms of assisted reproduction (Congregation for the Doctrine of the Faith, 1987). The church's opposition is based on the fact that these techniques separate the procreative and unitive functions of marriage. Some authorities in Orthodox Judaism allow insemination from non-Jewish sperm donors but prohibit donation from Jews, in order to prevent consanguinity; others oppose all third-party donations out of fear of consanguinity and also by analogy with adultery. Islamic law prohibits the use of sperm or eggs from anyone other than the married couple on grounds that the results are similar to adultery (Serour, 1992). Since the identity of gamete donors is normally kept confidential, a secular concern is that a brother and sister may unwittingly mate or marry, unaware that they have a genetic parent in common.

Possibly the most intriguing philosophical issues posed by reproductive technologies are those that arise from the newfound ability to separate the genetic from the gestational procreative functions. IVF permits an ovum from one woman to be fertilized and the resulting embryo implanted in a different woman. This creates the entirely novel situation of two different "mothers": the genetic mother, who supplies the egg; and the gestational mother, who undergoes pregnancy and childbirth. Apart from the emotional or other psychological consequences that may result from such arrangements, the separation of the woman's procreative role into two distinct biological functions requires a conceptual decision of whether the individual who performs each function properly deserves the appellation 'mother' (Macklin, 1991).

A variation on this conceptual theme stems from research that demonstrates the capability of transplanting ovaries from an aborted fetus into an adult woman who lacks ovaries of her own. The woman into whom the ovaries are transplanted is a mother in the traditional sense of one who is pregnant and gives birth to the child. Is it appropriate to construe the aborted fetus as the "genetic mother"? The conceptual oddity of this construal suggests that "mother" is a concept laden with connotations that do not permit its expansion to include aborted fetuses. Although the aborted fetus is without question the source of the genetic material from which the new life was created, it is semantically odd to conclude that the aborted fetus is the genetic mother.

A persistent quandary relates to the status of extracorporeal embryos. The product of IVF is termed a 'preembryo,' partly because of its early developmental stage but also because it is unimplanted. The ability to freeze embryos indefinitely and thaw them for use later poses both conceptual and ethical questions. When disputes arise concerning the ownership of embryos, should the embryos be construed as "people" or as "property" (Annas, 1989; Robertson, 1990)? Should anyone other than the couple who contributed the gametes have the authority to destroy frozen embryos? If it is permissible to destroy embryos that are not intended for implantation, is it permissible to do experiments on the embryos? Controversy exists over the splitting of embryos, a technique sometimes called cloning (Robertson, 1994). One objection holds that such deliberate duplication destroys genetic individuality and thus devalues the uniqueness of each individual.

Genetics and reproductive technologies pose new philosophical questions about the scope and limits of such familiar concepts as disease, individuality, parent, mother, and the family. The importance accorded to human reproduction and lineage throughout history is a reminder that such questions are not merely abstract concerns of philosophers but deeply rooted in the lives of individuals and communities.

(SEE ALSO: *Biomedical Ethics* [S])

Bibliography

Annas, G. J. "A French Homunculus in a Tennessee Court," *Hastings Center Report,* Vol. 19 (1989), 20–22.

Congregation for the Doctrine of the Faith. *Instruction on Respect for Human Life in Its Origin and on the Dignity of Procreation.* Vatican City, 1987.

Fletcher, J. *The Ethics of Genetic Control: Ending Reproductive Roulette.* Garden City, NY, 1974.

Lappe, M. "The Genetic Counselor: Responsible to Whom?" *Hastings Center Report,* Vol. 2 (1971), 6–8.

Macklin, R. "Artificial Means of Reproduction and Our Understanding of the Family," *Hastings Center Report,* Vol. 21 (1991), 5–11.

Milunsky, A., and G. J. Annas, eds. *Genetics and the Law III.* New York, 1985.

President's Commission for the Study of Ethical Problems in Medicine and Biomedical and Behavioral Research. *Splicing Life.* Washington, DC, 1982.

President's Commission for the Study of Ethical Problems in Medicine and Biomedical and Behavioral Research. *Screen-*

ing and Counseling for Genetic Conditions. Washington, DC, 1983.

Proctor, R. N. *Racial Hygiene: Medicine under the Nazis.* Cambridge, MA, 1988.

Ramsey, P. *Fabricated Man: The Ethics of Genetic Control.* New Haven, 1970.

Robertson, J. A. "In the Beginning: The Legal Status of Early Embryos," *Virginia Law Review,* Vol. 76 (1990), 437–517.

Robertson, J. A. "The Question of Human Cloning." *Hasting Center Report,* Vol. 24 (1994), 6–14.

Serour, G. I. "Medically Assisted Conception: Islamic Views," in G. I. Serour, ed., *Proceedings of the First International Conference on Bioethics in Human Reproduction Research in the Muslim World* (Cairo, 1992).

RUTH MACKLIN

GÖDEL, KURT (1906–78), logician, was born in Brno, Czech Republic, and educated at the University of Vienna, where he became Privatdozent in 1933. In 1940 he joined the Institute for Advanced Study in Princeton, New Jersey, where he remained for the rest of his career. Following HILBERT [3], Gödel was instrumental in establishing MATHEMATICAL LOGIC [S] as a fundamental branch of mathematics, achieving results such as the incompleteness theorems that have had a profound impact on twentieth-century thought. (*See* GÖDEL'S THEOREM [3]; LOGIC, HISTORY OF; MATHEMATICS, FOUNDATIONS OF [4]; RECURSIVE FUNCTION THEORY [7]; SYSTEMS, FORMAL [8].) In philosophy, by contrast, he represents the path not taken. His few publications in this area tend to focus on the more immediate ramifications of his own (and closely related) mathematical work. A fair amount of synthesis and reconstruction is needed if one is to consider him as a philosopher.

A close student of the history of philosophy, Gödel follows PLATO [6; S], LEIBNIZ, and HUSSERL [4; S] as opposed to the more fashionable ARISTOTLE [1; S], KANT [4; S], and WITTGENSTEIN [8; S]. (On Kant, however, see Gödel, 1946–49 and 1961.) Methodologically, two patterns in his thinking stand out. First, a tendency to move from the possible to the actual is revealed, via the notion of necessity, in his Leibnizian ONTOLOGICAL ARGUMENT FOR THE EXISTENCE OF GOD [5] (Gödel, 1970). He relies here on the S5 modal principle, (possibly necessarily P ⊃ necessarily P). It can also, arguably, be discerned in his mathematical Platonism (*see* PLATONISM, MATHEMATICAL [S])—since the distinction of the possible from the actual, relevant to material being, collapses in the formal realm of mathematics. (See Yourgrau, 1991.) Finally, in relativistic cosmology (Gödel, 1949, 1950) he concludes from the possible existence of rotating universes, where time is merely 'ideal', to its ideality in the actual world. Second, he is preoccupied with probing mathematically the limits of 'formal' methods in systematizing 'intuitive' concepts. In his first incompleteness theorem, for example, by applying an ingenious arithmetization of metamathematics to a formal system of arithmetic, he is able to construct a formula expressing its own unprovability and thus to prove (as he made explicit later) the indefinability within the system of the 'intuitive' concept of arithmetic truth. (See Feferman, 1983.) Along the same lines one might view his results in cosmology as demonstrating the limits of relativistic space-time in representing the 'intuitive' concept of time, although here, interestingly, Gödel's response is to abandon the 'intuitive' concept. (See Yourgrau, 1991, 1995.)

From a broader perspective Gödel isolates two basic philosophical worldviews: one with a "leftward" direction, toward SKEPTICISM [7; S], MATERIALISM [5], and POSITIVISM [6], the other inclined toward "the right," toward spiritualism, IDEALISM [4], and theology (or metaphysics; Gödel, 1961). He puts EMPIRICISM [2] on the left and a priorism on the right and points out that although mathematics, qua a priori science, belongs "by its nature" on the right, it too has followed the spirit of the times in moving toward the left—as witnessed by the rise of Hilbert's formalism. With FREGE [3; S] Gödel resists this trend, pointing to his incompleteness theorems as evidence that "the Hilbertian combination of materialism and aspects of classical mathematics . . . proves to be impossible" (1961, p. 381). But Frege's mathematical philosophy is held together by two strands that may appear to be in tension with one another: on one side his Platonism and conceptual realism, on the other his conception of arithmetic as analytic (that is, as resting on our definitions and on the laws of logic) and his "context principle" (which seems to put our sentences—hence language—at the center of his philosophy). (See Dummett, 1991.) This second aspect of Frege's thought, via RUSSELL [7; S] and Wittgenstein, helped persuade the positivists of the Vienna Circle (whose meetings Gödel attended) that mathematics is "without content," a mere matter of (more or less arbitrary) linguistic conventions concerning the syntax of (formal) language. This conclusion was, however, rejected by both Frege and Gödel (1944; 1951; 1953–59), Frege hoping, contra Kant, "to put an end to the widespread contempt for analytic judgments and to the legend of the sterility of pure logic" (1884, p. 24; see also 1879, p. 55). Gödel, for his part, insists that " 'analytic' does not mean 'true owing to our definitions', but rather 'true owing to the nature of the concepts occurring therein' " (1951, p. 321). (See Parsons, 1994.)

Frege and Gödel are in further agreement, "against the spirit of the times," that the fundamental axioms of mathematics should be not simply mutually consistent but (nonhypothetically) true. They also reject Hilbert's conception of axiom systems as 'implicit definitions', Gödel insisting that a formal axiomatic system only partially characterizes the concepts expressed therein. Indeed, his incompleteness theorem makes the point dramatically: "Continued appeals to mathematical intuition are necessary. . . for the solution of the problems of finitary number theory. . . . This follows from the fact that for every axiomatic system there are infinitely many undecidable propositions of this type" (1947 [1964], p. 269). And it is in our ability—if indeed we possess it—to 'intuit' new axioms in an open-ended way that Gödel sees a possible argument to the effect that minds are not (Turing) machines (Gödel, 1951; Wang, 1974). What kind of intuitions, however, are these? Gödel does, it is true, employ a Kantian term here, but he does not mean concrete immediate individual representations, and on just this point he faults Hilbert: "What Hilbert means by 'Anschauung' is substantially Kant's space-time intuition. . . . Note that it is Hilbert's insistence on *concrete* knowledge that makes finitary mathematics so surprisingly weak and excludes many things that are just as incontrovertibly evident to everybody as finitary number theory" (1958 [1972], p. 272, n. b). (See also 1947 [1964], p. 258.) Note, further, that mathematical intuition, though a form of a priori knowledge, does not ensure absolute certainty, which Gödel rejects (Wang, 1991); rather, as with its humbler cousin, sense perception, it too may attain various degrees of clarity and reliability. (See Gödel, 1951, his remarks on Husserl in 1961, and Parsons, 1995, 1995a.)

Frege and Hilbert, then, serve as useful coordinates in mapping Gödel's philosophy, in its tendency to "the right." What, then, if one chooses EINSTEIN [2] as a third coordinate? Note first that "idealistic" in the title of Gödel (1949) is not a gesture toward a mind-centered philosophy like that of BERKELEY [1; S]. Rather, Gödel is pointing to the classic Platonic distinction between APPEARANCE AND REALITY [1]. Though the world may appear (to the senses) as if temporal, this is in fact an illusion. Only 'reason'—here, mathematical physics—can provide a more adequate cognition of reality (i.e., of Einstein-Minkowski space-time). Gödel makes a sharp distinction between intuitive time, which 'lapses', and the 'temporal' component of space-time. By his lights, already in the special theory of relativity (STR) intuitive time has disappeared, since "the existence of an objective lapse of time means . . . that reality consists of an infinity of layers of 'now' which come into existence successively" (Gödel, 1949, pp. 202–3), whereas the relativity of simultaneity in the STR implies that "each observer has his own set of 'nows', and none of these various systems of layers can claim the prerogative of representing the objective lapse of time" (p. 203).

These observations, however, rely on the equivalence of all 'observers' or reference frames in the STR, whereas in the general theory of relativity (GTR), of which the STR is an idealized special case, the presence of matter and the consequent curvature of space-time permit the introduction of 'privileged observers', in relation to which one can define a 'world time' (which, one might say, objectively lapses). Gödel's discovery is that there exist models of the GTR—the rotating universes—where, probably, no such definition of a world time is possible. In particular, these worlds permit 'time travel', in the sense that, "for *every* possible definition of a world time one could travel into regions of the universe which are past according to that definition," and "this again shows that to assume an objective lapse of time would lose every justification in these worlds" (1949, p. 205). The idea, here, is clearly that if a time has 'objectively lapsed' it no longer exists and so is not *there* to be revisited (in the future). Hence, by contraposition, if it can be revisited, it never did 'objectively lapse' in the first place. To describe the Gödel universe as 'static', however, as opposed to our own, would be misleading. The time traveler's rocket ship, for example, would move at a speed of at least $1/\sqrt{2}$ of the velocity of light! It would seem to observers, just as in our world, to be moving at great speed, and in general the denizens of Gödel's universe would experience time much as we do. And, indeed, that is why Gödel moves from the mere possible existence of the Gödel universe to the ideality of time in the actual world, since "the experience of the lapse of time can exist without an objective lapse of time, no reason can be given why an objective lapse of time should be assumed at all" (p. 206; see Saritt, 1994; Stein, 1970, 1994; Wang, 1995; and Yourgrau, 1991, 1994.)

Here, then, is another example of the Janus-faced quality of Gödel's thinking (presaged already in his arithmetization of metamathematics)—contributing, mathematically, to "the left" while at the same time, as he sees it, pointing to "the right."

Bibliography

WORKS BY GÖDEL

The Foundations of Arithmetic [1884], translated by J. L. Austin. Evanston, IL, 1980.

"Russell's Mathematical Logic" [1944], in *Collected Works,* Vol. 2. New York, 1990.

"What Is Cantor's Continuum Problem?" [1947; 1964], in *Collected Works,* Vol. 2. New York, 1990.

"A Remark about the Relationship between Relativity Theory and Idealistic Philosophy" [1949], in *Collected Works,* Vol. 2. New York, 1990.

"Some Observations about the Relationship between Theory of Relativity and Kantian Philosophy" [1950], in *Collected Works,* Vol. 3. New York, 1994.

"Some Basic Theorems on the Foundations of Mathematics and Their Implications" [1951], in *Collected Works,* Vol. 3. New York, 1994.

"Is Mathematics Syntax of Language?" [1953–59], *Collected Works,* Vol. 3. New York, 1994.

"On an Extension of Finitary Mathematics Which Has Not Yet Been Used" [1958; 1972], translated by L. F. Boron, rev. K. Gödel, in *Collected Works,* Vol. 2. New York, 1990.

"The Modern Development of the Foundations of Mathematics in the Light of Philosophy" [1961], translated by E. Köhler and H. Wang, in *Collected Works,* Vol. 3. New York, 1994.

"Ontological Proof" [1970], in *Collected Works,* Vol. 3. New York, 1994.

WORKS ON GÖDEL AND RELATED TOPICS

Buldt, B., et al., eds. *Wahrheit und Beweisbarkeit: Leben und Werk Kurt Gödels.* Vienna, 1995.

Dawson, J. *Logical Dilemmas: The Life and Work of Kurt Gödel.* Wellesley, 1995.

Dummett, M. *Frege: Philosophy of Mathematics.* Cambridge, MA, 1991.

Feferman, S. "Kurt Gödel: Conviction and Caution," in S. G. Shanker, ed., *Gödel's Theorem in Focus* (London, 1988).

Frege, G. "Begriffsschrift: A Formula Language, Modeled upon That of Arithmetic, for Pure Thought" [1879], translated by S. Bauer-Mengelberg, in J. van Heijenoort, ed. *From Frege to Gödel: A Source Book in Mathematical Logic, 1879–1931* (Cambridge, MA, 1967).

Kreisel, G. "Kurt Gödel," *Biographical Memoirs of Fellows of the Royal Society,* Vol. 26 (1980), 149–224.

Parsons, C. "Quine and Gödel on Analyticity," in P. Leonardi, ed., *On Quine: New Essays* (San Marino, 1995).

———. "Platonism and Mathematical Intuition in Kurt Gödel's Thought," *The Bulletin of Symbolic Logic,* Vol. 1, No. 1 (1995a), 44–74.

Savitt, S. "The Replacement of Time," *Australian Journal of Philosophy,* Vol. 72, no 4 (1994), 463–74.

Shanker, S. G., ed. *Gödel's Theorem in Focus.* London, 1988.

Stein, H. "On the Paradoxical Time-Structures of Kurt Gödel," *Philosophy of Science,* Vol. 37 (1970), 589–601.

———. "Introductory Note to Gödel, 1946/9," in K. Gödel, *Collected Works,* Vol. 3 (New York, 1994).

Wang, H. *From Mathematics to Philosophy.* New York, 1974.

———. *Reflections on Kurt Gödel.* Cambridge, MA, 1987.

———. "Philosophy through Mathematics and Logic," in R. Haller and J. Brandl, eds., *Wittgenstein—towards a Re-Evaluation: Proceedings of the Fourteenth International Wittgenstein-Symposium* (Vienna, 1990).

———. "To and From Philosophy: Discussions with Gödel and Wittgenstein," *Synthese,* Vol. 88 (1991), 229–77.

———. "Time in Philosophy and in Physics: From Kant and Einstein to Gödel," *Synthese,* Vol. 102 (1995), 215–34.

Yourgrau, P. "Review Essay: Hao Wang, *Reflections on Kurt Gödel,*" *Philosophy and Phenomenological Research,* Vol. 1 (1989), 391–408.

———. *The Disappearance of Time: Kurt Gödel and the Idealistic Tradition in Philosophy.* Cambridge, 1991.

———. "Philosophical Reflections on Gödel's Cosmology," in B. Buldt et al., eds., *Wahrheit und Beweisbarkeit: Leben und Werk Kurt Gödels* (Vienna, 1995).

PALLE YOURGRAU

GOODMAN, NELSON, one of the foremost philosophers of the twentieth century, has produced works that have transformed EPISTEMOLOGY [3; S], METAPHYSICS [5; S], and the philosophy of art. *The Structure of Appearance,* which grew out of his Ph.D. dissertation, shows how to develop interpreted formal systems that solve or dissolve perennial epistemological problems. *Fact, Fiction, and Forecast* poses and solves the new riddle of induction, demonstrating that to block the inference to 'All emeralds are grue', we must consider the ways our terms have actually been used inductively in the past. *Languages of Art* reconceives aesthetics, arguing that the arts function cognitively, so aesthetics is a branch of epistemology.

GOODMAN [3] attended Harvard, both as an undergraduate and as a graduate student. During graduate school, he supported himself by running an art gallery. He spent most of his academic career as professor of philosophy at the University of Pennsylvania. During the final decade of his teaching career he was professor of philosophy at Harvard. He founded Project Zero, an ongoing research program in arts education at the Harvard Graduate School of Education, and the Harvard Summer Dance program. He is an avid, eclectic collector of art.

ART

Nelson Goodman's trailblazing *Languages of Art* reorients aesthetics. Active engagement, not passive contemplation, marks the AESTHETIC ATTITUDE [S]. Understanding rather than appreciation is its goal. Aesthetics, as Goodman construes it, belongs to epistemology.

Works of art are symbols that require interpretation (*see* ART, INTERPRETATION OF [S]). *Languages of Art* provides a taxonomy of syntactic and semantic systems deployed in the arts and elsewhere, detailing their strengths and limitations. Two modes of reference are basic. Denotation links names to bearers, predicates to instances, representations to the things they represent. 'George Washington', 'the first U. S. president', and the Gilbert Stuart portrait all denote Washington. In exemplification, a symbol points up, hence refers to properties it serves as a sample of. A fabric swatch exemplifies its pattern; a Mondrian painting, squareness. Ubiquitous in art, exemplification is also widespread in science, advertising, indeed anywhere we adduce samples and examples (Goodman, 1976).

REFERENCE [S] need not be literal. Metaphorical reference, Goodman maintains, is real reference; metaphorical truth, real truth. 'Bulldog' genuinely, albeit metaphorically, denotes Churchill. 'Churchill is a bulldog' is genuinely, although not literally, true. Michelangelo's *Moses* genuinely, albeit metaphorically, exemplifies rage. Expression is metaphorical exemplification by a work of art functioning as such. The *Moses* thus expresses the rage it exemplifies (Goodman, 1976; 1984).

Some reference is complex. In allusion, a referential chain composed of denotational and exemplificational links connects a symbol to its referent (Goodman, 1984). Two chains figure in variation, one exemplifying features that a variation shares with its theme, the other exemplifying features that contrast with the theme (Goodman and Elgin, 1988).

Scientific symbols, Goodman maintains, are relatively attenuated, aesthetic symbols relatively replete. A scientific symbol is normally univocal, its full import readily apparent. An aesthetic symbol may bear multiple correct interpretations and symbolize along several dimensions simultaneously. Exactly what it symbolizes may never be settled. The same item may qualify as a symbol of either kind, depending on how it functions. So 'When is art?' not 'What is art?' is the crucial question. When, how, and to what effect does a symbol function aesthetically (Goodman, 1978)?

Art advances understanding, not only because interpretation is a cognitive process. Encounters with art afford insights that extend beyond the aesthetic realm. Discoveries made, orientations adopted, and patterns discerned in aesthetic contexts transfer and make sense of other aspects of experience.

WORLDMAKING

In *Ways of Worldmaking* Goodman returns to constructionalist themes first explored in *The Structure of Appearance.* Worlds, he contends, are made, not found. Since the elements of any group are alike in some respects and different in others, mere examination will not reveal whether two manifestations are of the same thing or two things of the same kind. To settle such matters requires criteria of individuation and classification. Category schemes supply them. But category schemes are human constructs. In devising them we demarcate the individuals and kinds that make up a world. Different demarcations yield divergent but equally tenable world versions. One might characterize light as a stream of particles; another, as a sequence of waves. Each may be right relative to its own world version, wrong relative to its rival's. Neither is right or wrong absolutely.

If overlapping world versions all supervened on a single base, such differences would be ontologically innocuous. They do not. A physicalist version, for example, neither supervenes on nor underlies a phenomenalist version. Nor does any neutral version underlie them both. Since we can and do construct multiple, individually adequate, but irreconcilable world versions, there are, Goodman concludes, many worlds if any.

Worldmaking is not always deliberate. Also in *Ways of Worldmaking,* Goodman analyzes a series of psychological experiments and shows how, with only sparse cues, the visual system constructs the apparent motion it detects. Nor is worldmaking always discursive. Nonverbal schemes structure things in ways no description precisely captures. The arts as well as the sciences construct viable world versions.

Despite Goodman's recognition of multiple ways of worldmaking and multiple worlds made, he does not contend that every version makes a world. Only right versions do. Rightness does not reduce to truth, for some truths are wrong, some falsehoods right, and some symbols right though neither true nor false. Rightness involves fitting and working—fitting with past cognitive practice and working to promote cognitive ends. Consistency, cogency, projectibility, and fairness of sample figure in the rightness of tenable world versions (Goodman, 1978; Goodman and Elgin, 1988).

(SEE ALSO: *Aesthetics, History of; Aesthetics, Problems in* [1; S])

Bibliography

WORKS BY GOODMAN

Problems and Projects. Indianapolis, 1972.

Languages of Art, 2d ed. Indianapolis, 1976.

The Structure of Appearance, 3d ed. Dordrecht, 1977.

Ways of Worldmaking. Indianapolis, 1978.

Fact, Fiction, and Forecast, 4th ed. Cambridge, MA, 1983.

Of Mind and Other Matters. Cambridge, MA, 1984.

Reconceptions in Philosophy and Other Arts and Sciences, with C. Z. Elgin. Indianapolis, 1988.

Esthétique et connaissance: Pour changer de sujet, with C. Z. Elgin. Combas, 1990.

A Study of Qualities. New York, 1990. Goodman's Ph.D. dissertation.

WORKS ON GOODMAN

Elgin, C. Z. *With Reference to Reference.* Indianapolis, 1983.

Scheffler, I. "The Wonderful Worlds of Goodman," in *Inquiries* (Indianapolis, 1986).

Schwartz, R. "The Power of Pictures," *Journal of Philosophy,* Vol. 82 (1985), 711–20.

Stalker, D., ed. *Grue: The New Riddle of Induction.* La Salle, IL, 1994.

CATHERINE Z. ELGIN

GOURNAY, MARIE LE JARS DE (1565–1645), was the editor of the first complete text of Montaigne's *Essais,* author of feminist, moral, and religious tracts, and literary writer and theorist. Born into an aristocratic family in Paris, she mastered Latin and translated DIOGENES LAERTIUS' [2] *Life of Socrates* in her youth. At eighteen or nineteen, having read with enthusiasm Montaigne's *Essais,* books 1 and 2, she met with the author, which inspired her novel (*see* MONTAIGNE [5]). Their friendship led to her becoming his "adopted daughter," which, in the sixteenth century, implied a literary partnership. Thus, in 1594, Montaigne's widow sent her the final manuscript of his *Essais,* which Gournay edited, later annotated, and published, together with a long "Préface," in 1595.

The "Préface" attempts to defend Montaigne against the main criticisms advanced by his contemporaries: (1) Against the charge that his Latinisms and neologisms did harm to the French language, Gournay stressed the importance of Montaigne's usages. Gournay would later make a name for herself as the protectoress of ancient French words and would defend the innovative, metaphorical use of language against Malherbe and other moderns. (2) In response to Dominique Baudius's and Etienne Pasquier's claim that Montaigne's frank discussion of love was indecent, a point PASCAL [6] would later take up, Gournay argued that the ancients rightly took such discussion as a prerequisite for the self-knowledge needed for virtue. (3) The charge of philosophical obscurity was countered with a skeptical attack against the critics' capacity for judgment: "The gift of judgment is the thing in the world that men possess in more varied proportion." (4) Gournay defended Montaigne's digressive style against the objection that it precluded treating a topic thoroughly and evidenced a lack of method. Since Gournay and Montaigne were steeped in SKEPTICISM [7; S], Gournay could hardly imagine Montaigne producing rigorous, linear proofs. (5) The accusation of heresy, leveled especially at the "Apologie de Raymond Sebond," was the criticism Gournay was most anxious to refute. Her defense of Montaigne's religious orthodoxy is of particular interest, since it rests on one of the clearer statements that we have of his FIDEISM [3]—a doctrine that she shared: "Who, likewise, could tolerate these new Titans of our century, these scalers of the heavens, who think that they will manage to know God by their own means?" "Judgment alone puts us in direct possession of God: which is to know nothing of Him and to worship Him on the basis of faith." (6) Montaigne's focus on the self and use of confessional autobiography had been attacked as vain and pointless. Gournay argued that Montaigne was instructing us in the Platonic art of self-examination; she was one of the first to see the epistemic and moral significance of the first-person philosophical voice, which would play such an important role in the works of DESCARTES [2; S] and ROUSSEAU [7; S]. (7) Beginning with the 1625 edition, Gournay countered the charge that Montaigne was ignorant of the sciences by providing a skeptical, humanist understanding of a "true science": That which aids us in conducting ourselves as "honnêtes hommes" and in leading a good life. The subjects of which Montaigne might have been ignorant were "pure scholastic amusements."

After defending the Jesuits in a pamphlet, for which she was attacked in print, Gournay published a collection of classical translations, and a feminist tract, *Egalité des hommes et des femmes* (The Equality of Men and Women, 1622).

Egalité is arguably the first modern philosophical response to the *querelle des femmes,* or "woman question." Gournay's innovative contribution was to combine (1) skeptical attacks, including the use of *reductio* arguments, against traditional views on the intellectual and moral inferiority of women with (2) evidence on behalf of the thesis of equality based on the authority of holy scripture, the early church fathers, and the ancient philosophers whom the church has recognized. As a Christian skeptic and fideist, Gournay saw (1) and (2) as consistent.

Gournay's moral essays reflect not only Pyrrhonism and fideism but the Christian stoicism that made up part of her *morale provisoire.* They appear in her collected works: *L'Ombre de la Damoiselle de Gournay* (The Shadow of Mademoiselle de Gournay, 1626) and *Les Advis ou Les Presens de la Demoiselle de Gournay* (The Advice and Presents of Mademoiselle de Gournay, 1634; 1641).

She corresponded with Anna Maria van Schurman, Justus LIPSIUS [4], Saint Francis de Sales, La Mothe le Vayer, Abbé de Marolles, and Cardinal Richelieu. In her final years Gournay participated in the salons of the Duchesse de Longueville and the Comtesse de Soissons; her own salon was, arguably, the seed from which the French Academy grew.

Bibliography

WORKS BY GOURNAY

Le Proumenoir de Monsieur de Montaigne... [Paris, 1594]. Delmar, NY, 1985.

"Préface" in M. Montaigne, *Les Essais de Michel Seigneur de Montaigne* (Paris, 1595). Various editions of the preface appeared in subsequent editions of Montaigne's *Essais.*

Adieu de l'Ame du Roy de France... avec La Défence des Pères lésuites. Paris/Lyon, 1610.

Versions de quelques pièces de Virgile, Tacite et Saluste... Paris, 1619.

Eschantillons de Virgile (n.p., n.d.).

Egalité des hommes et des femmes [n.p., 1622]. first modern edition in Schiff (below). English translation by E. O'Neill in J. Sterba, ed., *Social and Political Philosophy in Perspective: Classical Western Texts in a Feminist and Multicultural Perspective* (Belmont, CA, 1994) and in Bijvoet (below).

Remerciment au Roy. Paris, 1624.

L'Ombre de la Damoiselle de Gournay. Paris, 1626. Included *Proumenoir,* essays on education, morals, feminist issues, religion, poetry and literary and philological topics, translations from the *Aeneid* and the works of Tacitus, Salust, Ovid, and Cicero.

Les Advis ou Les Presens de la Demoiselle de Gournay. Paris, 1634. Included the material in *L'Ombre,* an additional translation from the *Aeneid* and new moral essays; the 1641 edition included "La Vie de la demoiselle de Gournay."

Correspondence with Schurman is found in Anna Maria van Schurman, *Opuscula* (Leiden, 1648).

Correspondence with Lipsius is in J.-F. Payen, "Recherches sur Montaigne: Correspondance relative à sa mort," *Bulletin du Bibliophile* (1862).

The correspondence with Lipsius, Dupuy, and Richelieu, along with autobiographical, feminist, moral and literary essays, appears in *Fragments D'un Discours Féminin,* edited by E. Dezon-Jones (n.p., 1988).

WORKS ON GOURNAY

Albistur, M., and D. Armogathe. *Histoire du féminisme français,* Vol. 1. Paris, 1977.

Baillet, A. *Jugemens des Savans sur les principaux ouvrages des auteurs.* Paris, 1694.

Bayle, P. *Dictionnaire Historique et Critique.* Paris, 1697.

Bijvoet, M. "Editor of Montaigne: Marie de Gournay," in K. Wilson and F. Warnke, eds., *Women Writers of the Seventeenth Century* (Athens, GA, 1989).

Boase, A. *The Fortune of Montaigne: A History of the Essays in France.* London, 1935.

Bonnefon, P. *Montaigne et ses amis.* Paris, 1898.

Feugère, L. J. *Les Femmes poètes du XVIe siècle.* Paris, 1860.
Ilsley, M. H. *A Daughter of the Renaissance: Marie le Jars de Gournay, Her Life, and Works.* The Hague, 1963.
La Forge, J. de. *Le Cercle des femmes sçavantes.* Paris, 1663.
McDowell Richardson, L. *The Forerunners of Feminism in French Literature from Christine of Pisa to Marie de Gournay.* Baltimore, 1929.
Menagiana. Paris, 1754.
Richards, S. A. "Feminist Writers of the Seventeenth Century." M.A. thesis, 1914.
Sainte-Beuve, C.-A. *Tableau historique et critique de la Poésie Française et du Théâtre Français au XVIe siécle.* Paris, 1828.
Schiff, M. *La Fille d'Alliance de Montaigne, Marie de Gournay.* Paris, 1910.
Somaize, A. de. *Le Grand Dictionnaire des Précieuses.* Paris, 1660.
Zedler, B. "Marie le Jars de Gournay," in M. E. Waithe, ed., *A History of Women Philosophers,* Vol. 2 (Dordrecht, 1989).

EILEEN O'NEILL

GRICE, HERBERT PAUL (1913–1988), was born and educated in England. He taught at St. John's College, Oxford, until 1967, when he moved to the University of California at Berkeley. He taught there until his death. He published little until near the end of his life but had a great influence through students and the wide circulation of unpublished manuscripts. His earliest work dealt with perception, but he subsequently moved to problems in language, ethics, and metaphysics. Concern about REASON [7] and RATIONALITY [S] unites these investigations. His historical idols were ARISTOTLE [1; S] and KANT [4; S].

One early concern was a defense of the causal theory of PERCEPTION [6; S]. This defense required separating the scientific part of the task of analyzing perception from that of the philosopher. This distinction relies on an underlying notion of analysis closely related to the analytic/synthetic distinction for which Grice and STRAWSON [S] provided a brief spirited defense. Three subsequent papers represent intricate attempts to define meaning using only commonsense psychological concepts such as intention, belief, and desire. If this program had succeeded it would have provided a more elaborate defense of the analytic/synthetic distinction.

Grice's best-known contribution is that of a conversational implicature. A conversational implicature of an assertion is something that is conveyed to a thoughtful listener by the mode of expression rather than by the words themselves. Implicatures arise from the fact that conversation is normally governed by principles including cooperation, truthfulness, and informativeness and that both parties are aware of these. The two best-known applications of this concept are to perception and logic. Grice was concerned to provide an account of sense-data discourse in terms of how things seemed to the perceiver. An objection to this is that it is odd to say in a normal case of the perception of a table that it seems to the subject that a table is present. Grice's concept of conversational implicature can explain the oddity as a result of the fact that a stronger statement can be made, thus leaving room for the seems statement to be true.

Grice also scouts the possibility of defending the claim that the logician's material conditional is an adequate representation of the indicative conditional of English by explaining the apparent divergence as a matter of conversational implicatures. If one knows the truth values of P and Q, then one can make a more informative statement than $P \supset Q$, so the only conversationally appropriate use of $P \supset Q$ is when the speaker does not know the truth of either component but only that they are so connected that the truth of P guarantees the truth of Q. The conversational use of $P \supset Q$ requires a connection that is not part of the truth condition of the compound. Part of the definition of a conversational implicature requires that the hearer should be able to reason out the intentions of the speaker and, in conjunction with the conversational principles, discern the implicit message. This places an important role on reasoning, especially inasmuch as in typical cases the reasoning is not conscious in the hearer.

Grice devotes considerable energy to investigating rationality, reasoning, and reasons. He emphasizes that reasoning is typically directed to the goal of producing reasons relevant to some end in view. This intentional activity involves the ability to make reason-preserving transitions. Grice defines "reason preserving" as analogous to "truth preserving" in deductive logic. A transition is reason preserving just in case; if one has reasons for the initial set of thoughts, beliefs, actions, or intentions, then one does for the subsequent set as well.

Grice uses this general account of reasoning to investigate moral reasoning and moral reasons. He emphasizes the connections between reasons, actions, and FREEDOM [3]. Strong rational evaluation—which Grice sees as essential to freedom—involves the rational evaluation and selection of ends, including ultimate ends.

How are we to choose ultimate ends? Grice answers that we should choose ends that have unrelativized value. Grice grants that the concept of unrelativized value requires defense. Typically, things have value only relative to ends and beneficiaries. My concern for the focus of relativization gives the value concept a "bite" on me, it ensures that the value concept carries weight for me. So how are we to understand unrelativized value?

Grice turns to final causation for a special kind of value. A tiger is a good tiger to the degree it realizes the final end of tigers. Grice defines a good person as one who has as part of his or her essential nature an autonomous finality consisting in the exercise of rationality. Grice's philosophical psychology supports this conception of persons as end-setters. Freedom intimately involves the ability to adopt and eliminate ends. One does not (ideally) arbitrarily select and conform to ends; one does so for reasons. This makes being an end-setter an instance of unrelativized value; for to take a consideration as an ultimate justification of action is to see it as having value. Grice defines unrelativized value in Aristotelian style as whatever would seem to possess such value in the eyes of a duly accredited judge; and a duly accredited judge might be identifiable as a good person operating in conditions of freedom. Of course, we are still talking about what is of value for and to persons. But the point was not to avoid this "relativization"; the point was to avoid relativization to this or that kind of person.

Bibliography

WORKS BY GRICE

Studies in the Way of Words. Cambridge, MA, 1989. A collection including most of the important works published during his lifetime.

The Conception of Value. New York, 1991. A posthumous publication of the John Locke Lectures, delivered 1979.

"In Defence of a Dogma," with P. F. Strawson, *Philosophical Review,* Vol. 65 (1957), 141–58. A defense of the analytic/synthetic distinction, widely reprinted and discussed.

WORK ON GRICE

Grandy, R. E., and R. Warner. *Philosophical Grounds of Rationality: Intentions, Categories, Ends.* Oxford, 1986. A festschrift celebrating Grice's work, with an introduction and a response by Grice.

Richard E. Grandy
Richard Warner

H

HABERMAS, JÜRGEN, German philosopher and leading representative of the Frankfurt school of critical theory, was born in 1929 in Düsseldorf. After World War II he studied in Göttingen, Zürich, and Bonn, where he submitted a dissertation on Schelling in 1954. From 1955 to 1959 he was Theodor Adorno's assistant at the Institute for Social Research in Frankfurt. After habilitating at Marburg University in 1961, he taught philosophy and sociology at the universities of Heidelberg and Frankfurt before becoming co-director of the Max Planck Institute in Starnberg. In 1983 he returned to the University of Frankfurt, where he was professor of philosophy until his retirement in 1994.

Habermas's life and work have remained deeply influenced by the traumatic events of his youth under National Socialism (*see* GERMAN PHILOSOPHY AND NATIONAL SOCIALISM [3]). From the time of his involvement with the German student movement in the 1960s he has been one of Germany's most prominent public intellectuals, speaking out on a wide array of issues, from violations of civil liberties and the attempted "historicizing" of the Holocaust to immigration policy and the manner of German reunification.

Habermas's scholarly work, which aspires to a comprehensive CRITICAL THEORY [S] of contemporary society, ranges across many of the humanities and social sciences. His early and influential *Strukturwandel der Öffentlichkeit* (1962) was a historical, sociological, and philosophical account of the emergence and transformation of the liberal public sphere as a forum for critical public discussion of matters of general concern. While the historical structures of that sphere reflected the particular constellations of interests that gave rise to it, the idea it claimed to embody, the idea of legitimating political authority through rational discussion and reasoned agreement, remains central to democratic theory. Habermas returned to these themes three decades later in *Faktizität und Geltung* (1992), where he applied the idea of justification by appeal to generally acceptable reasons to the deliberations of free and equal citizens in a constitutional DEMOCRACY [2; S]. The primary function of the system of basic RIGHTS [7; S], he argued, is to secure personal and political autonomy; and the key to the latter is the institutionalization of the public use of REASON [7] in the legal-political domain.

One might read Habermas's extensive writings in the intervening decades as a protracted examination of the cultural, psychological, and social preconditions of and barriers to accomplishing this. The essays of the early 1960s, a number of which were collected in *Theorie und Praxis* (1963), introduced the idea of studying society as a historically developing whole for purposes of enlightening political consciousness and guiding political practice. The methodology and epistemology behind this approach were elaborated in the later 1960s in *Zur Logik der Sozialwissenschaften* (1967) and *Erkenntnis und Interesse* (1968). A principal target in both books was the neopositivist thesis of the unity of scientific method, particularly the claim that the logic of inquiry in the human sciences is basically the same as in the natural sciences. The former work started from an examination of the nature and role of *Verstehen* in social inquiry and argued that access to symbolically prestructured object domains calls for interpretive procedures designed to grasp the meanings on which social interactions turn. Intersubjective meanings constitutive of sociocultural lifeworlds can neither be wholly objectified, as POSITIVISM [6] supposes, nor simply reappropriated, as hermeneutics proposes. Psychoanalysis suggests an alternative approach, in which explanatory and interpretive procedures are combined with a critique of ideology in a historically oriented theory with practical intent.

In *Erkenntnis und Interesse* Habermas undertook a historical and systematic study of "the prehistory of modern positivism" in an attempt to free the ideas of reason and rationality from what he regarded as a "scientistic misunderstanding." Tracing the development of the critique of knowledge from KANT [4; S] through German idealism to MARX [5], and its transformation into the methodology of science in early positivism, he elaborated his own position in critical encounters with three classic but flawed attempts to overcome positivism from within methodology: PEIRCE's [6; S] reflections on natural science, DILTHEY's [2] on cultural inquiry, and FREUD's [3; S] on self-reflection. In each case he examined the roots of cognition in life and argued for an internal connection of knowledge with 'anthropologically deep-seated' human interests. A key feature of this 'quasi-transcendental' theory of cognitive interests was the basic distinction between the interest in prediction and control of objectified processes and the interests in mutual understanding and distortion-free communication with speaking and acting subjects.

There followed a series of studies of basic structures of communication, organized as a three-tiered research program. The ground level consisted of a general theory of communication in natural languages, a 'universal pragmatics', as Habermas called it. This served as the foundation for a general theory of socialization in the form of a developmental account of the acquisition of communicative competence. Building on both of these, Habermas sketched a theory of sociocultural evolution as the historical development of forms of communicative interaction and mutual understanding. These accounts of communication, socialization, and social evolution enabled him to anchor moral theory in the theory of social action (*see* COMMUNICATIVE ACTION [S]). Arguing that our basic moral intuitions spring from something deeper and more universal than contingent features of particular traditions, his DISCOURSE ETHICS [S] sought to reconstruct the intuitive grasp of the normative presuppositions of social interaction possessed by competent social actors generally.

The work of the 1960s and 1970s culminated in the monumental *Theorie des kommunikativen Handelns* (1981), in which Habermas developed a concept of communicative rationality freed from the subjectivistic and individualistic premises of modern social and political theory, together with a two-level concept of society that integrated the competing paradigms of 'LIFEWORLD' [S] and 'system'. On this basis he then sketched a critical theory of modern society that focused on 'the colonization of the lifeworld' by forces arising from the economy and the state: systemic mechanisms such as money and power drive processes of social integration and symbolic reproduction out of domains in which they cannot be replaced. The phenomena that Max WEBER [8] pointed to in his vision of an 'iron cage' and that Marxists have dealt with in terms of 'reification' arises from an ever-increasing 'monetarization' and 'bureaucratization' of lifeworld relations. This relentless attack on the communicative infrastructures of society can be contained, he argued, only by a countervailing expansion of the areas of life coordinated via communication, and in particular by the subordination of economic and administrative subsystems to decisions arrived at in open and critical public debate. Thus, the antidote to colonization is democratization, and the key to the latter is an effectively functioning cultural and political public sphere. What distinguishes this critique of modernity from the welter of counterenlightenment critiques during the last two centuries is Habermas's unflinching defense of ENLIGHTENMENT [2] rationality—a defense, to be sure, that is itself informed by the critique of RATIONALISM [7] and that emphasizes the ongoing, unfinished character of the project of enlightenment.

Bibliography

WORKS BY HABERMAS

Knowledge and Human Interests, translated by J. Shapiro. Boston, 1971.

Theory and Practice, translated by J. Viertel. Boston, 1973.

Communication and the Evolution of Society, translated by T. McCarthy. Boston, 1979.

Autonomy and Solidarity: Interviews with Jürgen Habermas, edited by Peter Dews. London, 1986.

The Theory of Communicative Action, 2 vols., translated by T. McCarthy. Boston, 1984, 1987.

The Structural Transformation of the Public Sphere, translated by T. Burger and F. Lawrence. Cambridge, MA, 1989.

Moral Consciousness and Communicative Action, translated by C. Lenhardt and S. Nicholsen. Cambridge, MA, 1990.

Between Facts and Norms: Contributions to a Discourse Theory of Law and Democracy, translated by W. Rehg. Cambridge, MA, 1995.

WORKS ON HABERMAS

Bernstein, R., ed. *Habermas and Modernity.* Cambridge, MA, 1985.

McCarthy, T. *The Critical Theory of Jürgen Habermas.* Cambridge, MA, 1978.

Rehg, W. *Insight and Solidarity: The Discourse Ethics of Jürgen Habermas.* Berkeley, 1994.

White, S., ed. *The Cambridge Companion to Habermas.* Cambridge, 1995.

THOMAS MCCARTHY

HAECCEITISM. *See*: MODALITY, PHILOSOPHY AND METAPHYSICS OF [S]

HARE, R. M. (Richard M.), sometime White's Professor of Moral Philosophy at Oxford University, is famous as the inventor of universal prescriptivism. This is a metaethical doctrine, a thesis about what moral words mean. But Hare uses his metaethic to generate an ethic. Anyone who employs the moral concepts consistently in full awareness of the facts must wind up a utilitarian. Hare claims that his UTILITARIANISM [8] is the product of conceptual analysis rather than of moral intuition. To rely on intuitions is a philosophical sin, since it leads to relativism (Hare, 1991). His theory is developed in three books, *The Language of Morals* (1952), *Freedom and Reason* (1963), and *Moral Thinking* (1981).

Prescriptivism is a variant of NONCOGNITIVISM [S]. Moral judgments are action guiding, and the explanation of this is that they are prescriptive: they are not primarily designed to state facts but to prescribe actions. They are more akin to orders than statements or propositions. Nevertheless, moral judgments do have descriptive content, though this will depend upon the moral opinions of the speaker (Hare, 1963). Thus, if Captain Bligh says that Burkitt is a scoundrel, we can assume he is disobedient. Indeed, even words such as ought have descriptive content, though this too will vary with the moral opinions of the speaker. Typically, the descriptive content of an ought judgment will consist in the factual considerations—the reasons—that can be advanced in its support. Thus, if Bligh asserts that Burkitt ought to be flogged, this will be because it would be an act of punishing disobedience. That the flogging would be such an act is the descriptive content of "Burkitt ought to be flogged." (Whence it follows that, if Burkitt has not been disobedient, the ought judgment will be factually false.) In Hare's view moral judgments are universalizable. Thus, if Bligh thinks that Burkitt ought to be flogged, he is committed to the view that anyone in relevantly similar circumstances—anyone who has been similarly disobedient to a king's officer—ought to be flogged likewise. He must assent to the imperative "Let me be flogged in the hypothetical case in which I am in Burkitt's position!"—which includes having committed Burkitt's heinous acts of disobedience (Hare, 1963). Finally, moral judgments are overriding. They take precedence over any other imperatives the subject may accept. Thus, if Bligh thinks himself morally obliged to have Burkitt flogged, this takes precedence over his aesthetic obligation not to sully the pure air of the Pacific with Burkitt's distasteful groans. Sincere moral commitment entails action. Weakness of the will as traditionally conceived is not a genuine possibility. Thus, Hare reinstates the Socratic paradox that we cannot willingly do wrong (Hare, 1952; 1963).

What about utilitarianism? Hare first points out that the metaethic generates a method for refuting moral "conjectures." Bligh considers the maxim "I ought to have Burkitt flogged." He universalizes this to derive the principle that anyone in relevantly similar circumstances ought to be flogged likewise. This in turn entails the imperative "Let me be flogged if I am in Burkitt's position!" But Bligh cannot assent to this unless he is a fanatic—someone who prefers flogging the disobedient to remaining unflogged himself. Thus, Bligh must rescind his original "ought" (Hare, 1963). But this is only a method for vetoing moral maxims and a method, moreover, that leads to moral paralysis. As Hare himself points out, a guilty prisoner could challenge the judge to universalize the maxim that the accused ought to be put away and derive the imperative "Let me be imprisoned if I am in the accused shoes!"—an imperative she could accept only if she had a fanatical preference for imprisoning the guilty rather than staying out of jail herself (Hare, 1963). Nonfanatical judges would have to give up sentencing and justice would founder! But Hare offers a utilitarian solution. The correct course is to go the rounds of the affected parties and opt for the action that is subject to the weakest veto[es]. Thus, the judge must take into account the likely depredations of the prisoner and ask herself whether she can accept such imperatives as "Let me be robbed if the prisoner is released and allowed to carry on with his course of crime and I am one of his victims!" If not, and if the vetoes of the prisoner's potential victims outweigh his preference not to go to jail, then to jail he must go. The criminal-justice system can survive without fanaticism, and Hare's method becomes utilitarian. But does Hare derive utilitarianism from his conceptual analysis or assume utilitarianism to rescue that analysis from disaster (Roxbee Cox, 1986)?

The fanatic remains a problem. She can consistently subscribe to a persecuting principle if she assents to the imperatives in which she is on the sharp end. In *Moral Thinking* Hare deprives her of this possibility. He claims it is a conceptual truth that if I fully represent to myself what an unpleasant experience is like for someone—an experience that they would prefer to stop—I now acquire an equally strong preference not to have that experience were I in their shoes. Hence, a fanatic who fully represents to herself the sufferings of her potential victims cannot assent to the imperative that she should suffer were she in their position. For she has a preference as strong as theirs that she should not. If, however, Hare's conceptual truth is neither conceptual nor a truth, then fanaticism remains an option (Seanor & Fotion, 1991).

(SEE ALSO: *Ethical Theory; Nondescriptivism* [S]

Bibliography

WORKS BY HARE

The Language of Morals. Oxford, 1952. Hare sets forth his metaethic.

Freedom and Reason. Oxford, 1963. Hare develops his metaethic and devises an engine of moral argument to enforce utilitarian conclusions. But he admits the fanatic is immune.

Moral Thinking: Its Levels, Methods, and Point. Oxford, 1981. Hare draws a distinction between intuitive and critical thinking and invents a conceptual truth to dispose of the fanatic. Only amoralists can avoid utilitarianism.

Essays in Ethical Theory. Oxford, 1989a. Hare develops and defends his ideas and attacks his philosophical rivals. Contains a memorably savage critique of John Rawls for relying on intuition, a reply to J. L. Mackie, his chief Oxford opponent, and a bibliography of his extensive writings.

Essays on Political Morality. Oxford, 1989b. A collection on applied ethics.

WORKS ON HARE

Roxbee Cox, J. W. "From Universal Prescriptivism to Utilitarianism," *Philosophical Quarterly,* Vol. 36 (1986), 1–15. Challenges Hare's derivation of utilitarianism.

Seanor, D., and N. Fotion, eds. *Hare and Critics: Essays on Moral Thinking with Comments by R. M. Hare.* Oxford, 1991. The best essays are by Brandt, Singer, Gibbard, and Vendler. Hudson's essay lists some of the important criticisms Hare has faced. Extensive bibliography.

Singer, P. *Practical Ethics,* 2d. ed. Oxford, 1993. Hare's method is applied to practical affairs by his most gifted disciple.

Taylor, C. C. W. "Critical Notice of R. M. Hare's *Freedom and Reason,*" *Mind,* Vol. 74 (1965), 280–90. Still perhaps the best critique of Hare.

CHARLES R. PIGDEN

HEGEL, GEORG W. F., changed his major philosophical views very little from the publication of his first major work, the *Phenomenology of Spirit,* in 1807 until his death in 1831. This stability and continuity have not made it any easier for commentators to agree on what those views were. Disagreement about Hegel's basic position and its implications is still widespread, even more so after a great resurgence of HEGEL [3] studies after World War II.

In the Anglophone philosophical world, Hegel's position is still often summarized as an objective IDEALISM [4], thanks largely to his influence on early twentieth-century British objective idealists such as BRADLEY [1]. He is said to have believed that only "mind" (the preferred translation of *Geist* until the A. V. Miller translation of *Phenomenology of Spirit* was first published in 1977) was "real"; or that no determinate individual object could be said to be real. Such an object was really a "moment" of the interrelated and temporally developing structure of the one true substance, the ABSOLUTE [1], or absolute mind. Such a substance was said to develop over time; the nature of that development was a process of greater self-consciousness, and this development was reflected in, or the underlying basis of, the great social and political changes of world history, as well as intellectual changes in philosophy, art, and religion. Since Hegel appeared to have claimed a full and final "absolute knowledge," an "encyclopedic" account of such a structure, or the relation between "logic," philosophy of nature, and philosophy of spirit could be given. (A compelling demonstration that such an objective-idealist or "internal relations" view could *not* have been Hegel's position was published by the German Hegel scholar Rolf-Peter Horstmann in 1984, *Ontologie und Relationen.*)

Some aspects of such views of what Hegel really meant persist in many postwar interpretations but have not provoked much serious discussion or the interpretive variants that once characterized the work of MCTAGGART [5], Mure, CAIRD [2], and STACE [8]. Other interpretations and emphases have predominated. Many commentators have become interested in Hegel less as an object of purely historical research and more as a possible contributor to perennial and current philosophical controversies.

Charles Taylor's 1975 study, *Hegel,* while offering a comprehensive commentary on all aspects of Hegel's work, emphasized Hegel's insights into the emerging problems of the modern social and political world—problems such as social fragmentation, ALIENATION [1], and the proper understanding of the modern goals of FREEDOM [3; S] and some sort of harmony with self. Taylor showed that many of Hegel's theoretical intentions could also best be understood against the backdrop of such concerns, and his approach became influential.

Hegel's understanding of the intellectual and social dimensions of modernization was also important in the work of many CRITICAL THEORY [S] or Frankfurt school neo-Marxist philosophers (a group sometimes even designated as "neo-Hegelian" Marxists because of their attention to the social function of ideas and culture without a reliance on traditional Marxist versions of economic materialism; *see* MARXIST PHILOSOPHY [5]; MARXISM [S]). In the work of the most important "second generation" critical theorist, Jürgen HABERMAS [S], Hegel also plays a large role in what Habermas calls, in a book title, *The Philosophical Discourse of Modernity.* Hegel is called "the first philosopher who made modernity a problem" (p. 4)—this by raising many questions about the sufficiency of the modern notions of SUBJECTIVITY [S] and RATIONALITY [S].

In other developments, Klaus Hartmann in several influential articles proposed what he called a "nonmetaphysical" reading of Hegel, one that emphasized Hegel's category theory and the unusual "logic" of categorial relations, all as more or less autonomous philosophical problems, not necessarily wedded to any metaphysics of absolute mind. A group of German philosophers who came to be known as the Heidelberg school began to work in a more contemporary way on the single greatest problem that preoccupied the German idealists as a whole, and Hegel especially: the problem of self-consciousness, or "reflection," how the mind could be said to be both the subject of its own consciousness and object to itself at the same time. (The most important and influential work on this aspect of the idealists and Hegel in particular has been Dieter Henrich's.) Since, for many post-Kantian idealists, any possible cognitive or practical relation to the world was an active comporting of oneself toward the world, or a "self-relation in relation to an other," the problem of self-relation was argued to be fundamental in any epistemology or account of human agency (*see* KANT [4; S]). These elements have also been emphasized by those who argue that Hegel should be read much more as a post-Kantian idealist, as much more decisively influenced by Kant's founding arguments about the possibility of any self-conscious experience than by, say, SPINOZA [7; S] or SCHELLING [7].

Hegel's contributions to all such problems—the nature and implications of modern social life, the possibility of self-consciousness and self-knowledge, the nature of the mind-world, and agency problems—reappear with great urgency in his ethical and social theory and in many interpretations. Debates about whether Hegel's 1821 *Elements of the Philosophy of Right* encouraged an accommodation of the conservative rulers of the Prussian state, or whether he was guilty of a kind of "organicist" anti-individualism, have been replaced by an emerging consensus that Hegel belongs within, if idiosyncratically, the modern liberal political tradition (*see* LIBERALISM [4; S]). This recognition has been somewhat complicated by "communitarian" writers (*see* COMMUNITARIANISM [S]) and "traditionalist" writers suspicious of the modern reliance on claims of rationality as decisive in ethical life. Many such writers have occasionally enlisted arguments in a case against the classical liberal tradition. Hegel's position on the importance and "priority" of the ethical community in ethical life (*Sittlichkeit*) has sometimes been understood such that anyone who believes in the priority of prevolitional attachments or commitments in ethical deliberation (e.g., such attachments are necessary for deliberation to get started or have direction but cannot themselves be products of such deliberation) is labeled a neo-Hegelian. But Hegel believes that modern ethical life (the institutions and practices of modern social existence, the modern family, civil society, and the legal, constitutional state) are not just "ours" and "prior." He believes they are rational, raising the still much-debated question of how he distinguishes rational from nonrational ethical communities.

A great deal of scholarly work has been done in the postwar period on Hegel's texts, especially on the dating and organization of his Jena-period lecture materials. Karl-Heinz Ilting has compiled, edited, and published an extensive collection of Hegel's lecture notes on political philosophy, and a new critical edition of Hegel's works has begun to appear. New English translations of the *Phenomenology,* the *Logic,* the *Philosophy of Right,* the *Aesthetics* lectures, Hegel's letters, and many other works have also appeared.

Bibliography

WORKS BY HEGEL

GERMAN

Gesammelte Werke, edited by Rheinisch-Westfälischen Akademie der Wissenschaften. Hamburg, 1968–. Of great value to serious students of Hegel in the original.

Philosophie des Rechts: Die Vorlesung von 1819/20, edited by D. Henrich. Frankfurt, 1983.

Vorlesungen über Rechtsphilosophie 1818–31, edited by K.-H. Ilting. Stuttgart, 1974. Contains an invaluable collection of student notes and additions.

Werke in zwanzig Bänden. Frankfurt, 1971. Useful paperback version of the 1832–45 Moldenhauer and Michel edition.

ENGLISH

The Difference between Fichte's and Schelling's System of Philosophy, translated by H. S. Harris and W. Cerf. Albany, NY, 1977.

Elements of the Philosophy of Right, edited by A. Wood, translated by H. B. Nisbet. Cambridge, 1991.

Faith and Knowledge, translated by W. Cerf and H. S. Harris. Albany, NY, 1977.

Hegel: The Letters, translated by C. Butler and C. Seiler. Bloomington, IN, 1984.

Hegel's Aesthetics: Lectures on Fine Art, translated by T. M. Knox. Oxford, 1965.

Lectures on the Philosophy of Religion: The Lectures of 1827, edited by P. Hodgson, translated by R. F. Brown, P. C. Hodgson, J. M. Stewart, and H. S. Harris. Berkeley, 1983.

Phenomenology of Spirit, translated by A. V. Miller. Oxford, 1977.

Science of Logic, translated by A. V. Miller. London, 1969.

WORKS ON HEGEL

HEGEL'S INTELLECTUAL DEVELOPMENT

Dickey, L. *Hegel: Religion, Economics, and the Politics of the Spirit.* Cambridge, 1977.

Görland, I. *Die Kantkritik des jungen Hegel.* Frankfurt, 1966.

Harris, H. S. *Hegel's Development.* 2 vols. Oxford, 1972–83.

Henrich, D., and K. Düsing, eds. *Hegel in Jena.* Bonn, 1980.

Kimmerle, H. *Das Problem der Abgeschlossenheit des Denkens: Hegels System der Philosophie in den Jahren 1800–1804.* Bonn, 1970.

Peperzak, A. *La jeune Hegel et la vision morale du monde.* The Hague, 1960.

HEGEL'S BASIC POSITION AND HIS SYSTEM

Adorno, T. *Hegel: Three Studies,* translated by S. W. Nicholsen. Cambridge, MA, 1993.

Beiser, F., ed. *The Cambridge Companion to Hegel.* Cambridge, 1993. Contains a comprehensive bibliography of recent work on Hegel.

Brockard, H. *Subjekt: Versuch zur Ontologie bei Hegel.* Munich, 1970.

DeVries, W. *Hegel's Theory of Mental Activity.* Ithaca, NY, 1988.

Fackenheim, E. *The Religious Dimension in Hegel's Thought.* Chicago, 1967.

Harlander, K. *Absolute Subjektivität und kategoriale Anschauung.* Meisenheim, 1969.

Hartmann, K. *Die ontologische Option.* Berlin, 1976.

Henrich, D. *Hegel im Kontext.* Frankfurt, 1971.

Hösle, V. *Hegels System.* 2 vols. Hamburg, 1987. Includes a comprehensive bibliography of recent work on Hegel.

Houlgate, S. *Freedom, Truth, and History: An Introduction to Hegel's Philosophy.* London, 1991.

Inwood, M. J. *Hegel.* London, 1983.

———, ed. *Hegel.* Oxford, 1985. Contains a comprehensive bibliography of recent work on Hegel.

MacIntrye, A., ed. *Hegel: A Collection of Critical Essays.* Notre Dame, IN, 1972.

McCumber, J. *The Company of Words: Hegel, Language, and Systematic Philosophy.* Evanston, IL, 1993.

O'Brien, G. D. *Hegel on Reason and History.* Chicago, 1975.

Peperzak, A. *Selbsterkenntnis des Absoluten: Grundlinien der Hegelsche Philosophie des Geistes.* Stuttgart, 1987.

Pinkard, T. *Hegel's Dialectic: The Explanation of Possibility.* Philadelphia, 1988.

Pippin, R. B. *Hegel's Idealism: The Satisfactions of Self-Consciousness.* Cambridge, 1989. Includes a comprehensive bibliography of recent works on Hegel.

Plant, R. *Hegel.* Bloomington, IN, 1973.

Rockmore, T. *Hegel's Circular Epistemology.* Bloomington, IN, 1986.

Rose, G. *Hegel Contra Sociology.* Atlantic Highlands, NJ, 1981.

Rosen, S. *G. W. F. Hegel: An Introduction to the Science of Wisdom.* New Haven, 1974.

Soll, I. *An Introduction to Hegel's Metaphysics.* Chicago, 1969.

Taylor, C. *Hegel.* Cambridge, 1977.

White, A. *Absolute Knowledge: Hegel and the Problem of Metaphysics.* Athens, OH, 1983.

Wohlfahrt, G. *Der spekulative Satz: Bemerkungen zum Begriff der Spekulation bei Hegel.* Berlin, 1981.

HEGEL'S PHENOMENOLOGY AND LOGIC

Baum, M. *Die Entstehung der Hegelschen Dialektik.* Bonn, 1986.

Bubner, R. *Dialektik und Wissenschaft.* Frankfurt, 1962.

Düsing, K. *Das Problem der Subjektivität in Hegels Logik.* Bonn, 1976.

Flay, J. *Hegel's Quest for Certainty.* Albany, NY, 1984. Includes a comprehensive bibliography of recent work on Hegel.

Forster, M. *Hegel and Scepticism.* Cambridge, MA, 1989.

Fulda, H. *Das Problem einer Einleitung in Hegels Wissenschaft der Logik.* Frankfurt, 1965.

———, ed. *Materialen zu Hegels Phänomenologie des Geistes.* Frankfurt, 1973.

———. *Hegels Wissenschaft der Logik: Formation und Rekonstruktion.* Stuttgart, 1986.

Henrich, D. *Die Wissenschaft der Logik und die Logik der Reflexion.* Bonn, 1987.

Horstmann, R.-P. *Ontologie und Relationen: Hegel, Bradley, Russell, und die Kontroverse über interne und externe Relationen.* Königstein, 1984.

Labarriere, P. *La Phénoménologie de l'esprit de Hegel.* Paris, 1979.

Marx, W. *Hegel's Phenomenology of Spirit: Its Point and Purpose—A Commentary on the Preface and Introduction.* New York, 1975.

Pinkard, T. *Hegel's Phenomenology: The Sociality of Reason.* Cambridge, 1994.

Pöggeler, O. *Hegels Idee einer Phänomenologie des Geistes.* Freiburg, 1973.

Puntel, B. *Darstellung, Methode, und Struktur: Untersuchungen zur Einheit der systematischen Philosophie G. W. F. Hegels.* Bonn, 1973.

Robinson, J. *Duty and Hypocrisy in Hegel's Phenomenology of Mind.* Toronto, 1977.

Rohs, P. *Form und Grund: Interpretation eines Kapital der Hegelschen Wissenschaft der Logik.* Bonn, 1969.

Rosen, M. *Hegel's Dialectic and Its Criticism.* Cambridge, 1982.

Shklar, J. *Freedom and Independence: A Study of the Political Ideas in Hegel's Phenomenology of Mind.* Cambridge, 1976.

Solomon, R. *In the Spirit of Hegel.* Oxford, 1983.

Theunissen, M. *Sein und Schein: Die kritische Funktion der Hegelschen Logik.* Frankfurt, 1978.

Westphal, M. *History and Truth in Hegel's Phenomenology.* Atlantic Highlands, NJ, 1978.

HEGEL'S PRACTICAL PHILOSOPHY

Avineri, S. *Hegel's Theory of the Modern State.* Cambridge, 1972.

Brod, H. *Hegel's Philosophy of Politics: Idealism, Identity, and Modernity.* Boulder, CO, 1992.

Cullen, B. *Hegel's Social and Political Thought: An Introduction.* Dublin, 1979.

D'Hondt, J. *Hegel in His Time: Berlin 1818–1831,* translated by J. Burbidge. Peterborough, NH, 1988.

Fessard, G. *Hegel, le Christianisme, et l'histoire.* Paris, 1990.

Fleischman, E. *La Philosophie politique de Hegel.* Paris, 1964.

Hardimon, M. *The Project of Reconciliation: Hegel's Social Philosophy.* Cambridge, 1993.

Henrich, D., and R.-P. Horstmann. *Hegels Philosophie des Rechts: Die Theorie der Rechstformen und ihre Logik.* Stuttgart, 1982.

Marcuse, H. *Reason and Revolution.* Boston, 1960.

Pelczynski, Z. A., ed. *Hegel's Political Philosophy: Problems and Perspectives.* Cambridge, 1971.

———. *Hegel and Civil Society.* Cambridge, 1984.

Peperzak, A. *Philosophy and Politics: A Commentary on the Preface to Hegel's Philosophy of Right.* The Hague, 1987.

———. *Hegel's praktische Philosophie: Ein Kommentar zur enzyklopädischen Dartstellung der menschlichen Freiheit und ihre objektive Verwirklichung.* Stuttgart, 1991.

Pinkard, T. *Democratic Liberalism and Social Union.* Philadelphia, 1987.

Riedel, M. *Theorie und Praxis im Denken Hegels.* Frankfurt, 1965.

———. *Materialen zu Hegels Rechtsphilosophie.* 2 vols. Frankfurt, 1975.

Ritter, J. *Hegel and the French Revolution,* translated by R. D. Winfield. Cambridge, MA, 1982.

Siep, L. *Hegels Fichtekritik und die Wissenschaftslehre von 1804.* Freiburg, 1970.

———. *Praktische Philosophie im Deutschen Idealismus.* Frankfurt, 1992.

Smith, S. *Hegel's Critique of Liberalism.* Chicago, 1989.

Stepelevich, L. S., and D. Lamb. *Hegel's Philosophy of Action.* Atlantic Highlands, NJ, 1983.

Taylor, C. *Hegel and Modern Society.* Cambridge, 1979.

Theunissen, M. *Hegels Lehre vom absoluten Geist als theologisch-politischer Traktat.* Berlin, 1970.

Tunick, M. *Hegel's Political Philosophy: Interpreting the Practice of Legal Punishment.* Princeton, NJ, 1992.

Walsh, W. H. *Hegelian Ethics.* London, 1969.

Wasczek, N. *The Scottish Enlightenment and Hegel's Account of Civil Society.* Dordrecht, 1988.

Wildt, A. *Autonomie und Anerkennung: Hegels Moralitätskritik in Lichte seiner Fichte Rezeption.* Stuttgart, 1982.

Wood, A. *Hegel's Ethical Thought.* Cambridge, 1990.

AESTHETICS

Bungay, S. *Beauty and Truth: A Study of Hegel's Aesthetics.* Oxford, 1986.

Desmond, W. *Art and the Absolute: A Study of Hegel's Aesthetics.* Albany, NY, 1986.

Fulda, H., ed. *Hegel und die Kritik der Urteilskraft.* Stuttgart, 1990.

ROBERT B. PIPPIN

HEIDEGGER, MARTIN (1889–1976), German philosopher, counts as one of the major forces of twentieth-century European thought. Once considered to be principally an "existentialist" thinker, HEIDEGGER [3] insisted to the end that his only concern was the question about the meaning of 'Being', and his later work justified the claim.

BEGINNING OF THE WAY

Asked in 1962 to describe the origins of his experience, Heidegger explained that his question was given to him by reading Franz BRENTANO's [1] doctoral dissertation, "On the Manifold Meaning of Being [*Seiendes*] in Aristotle" (1862). If a being (*Seiendes,* Aristotle's *on*) is understood as what-is, then "is" obviously has manifold meanings. "How can they be brought into comprehensible accord? This accord can not be grasped without first raising and settling the question: whence does Being as such (*Sein*) (not merely beings as beings) receive its determination?" (Preface to Richardson, 1974). Accordingly, Being (*Sein*), as different from beings (*Seiende*), would be the Is of what-is, the process of letting everything that is show itself as what it is. What is the meaning of such a BEING-PROCESS [S] as different from the beings it lets be manifest (the "ontological difference"), even if these be taken in their ensemble?

In private conversation Heidegger would expand this to say that his initial reading of ancient authors offered no answer to his question. Hence, equally original with the experience of the question was the experience of its inherent negativity, or finitude—that is, its forgottenness. Yet the word "is" was everywhere, and those who used it (especially the philosophers) had to have some understanding of what it meant, even if they remained oblivious of that meaning. The only way to get an answer to the question would be to interrogate this obscured understanding in the being (human) that was gifted with it.

Given the question, Heidegger relates that three factors were especially significant in his pursuit of an answer: (1) the discovery (through HUSSERL [4; S]) of phenomenology as a method, the term being derived from the Greek *logos* (to make manifest) and *phainesthai* (to show oneself)—a process eventually identified as the Greek sense of *hermeneuein,* hence a HERMENEUTIC PHENOMENOLOGY [S] of its very nature; (2) the experience of TRUTH [S] as essentially revelation (in Aristotle's *Metaphysics,* book 9, and *Nicomachean Ethics,* book 6); (3) the experience of BEING [1] (*ousia*) as a noun born of a participle suggesting presence (*Anwesenheit*) or the present (*Gegenwart*)—in any case something of a temporal nature. The being that says "is"—the "There" (or "Here": *Da*) among beings through which the Is (Being: *Sein*) becomes articulated—will be referred to as *Dasein,* a term that later became anglicized. But already a temporal structure in it could be discerned, at least in retrospect: its openness to the Being-process, its coming-to-be-itself, by reason of this openness, is a coming that may be called its future (*Zukunft*); but such a future comes to a Dasein that already is, with an alreadiness that may be called its past (*Gewesenheit*); finally, by reason of what it is already coming-to-be, Dasein can let every being (including itself) be present as showing itself as what it is, a structure that may be called its present (*Gegenwart*). Future, past, and present—these are the components (eventually "ecstases") of time. They would have to be justified by phenomenological analysis, of course, but with the advantage of hindsight one can appreciate the import of Heidegger's subtitle for part 1 of *Being and Time,* indisputably his major work (1927): "The Interpretation of Dasein in Terms of Temporality, and the Explication of Time as the Transcendental Horizon for the Question of Being."

Given this conception of what makes Dasein to be what it is (its "essence": *Wesen*), which Heidegger named "existence" (later elaborated as SELF and CARE [S]), it is understandable how the phenomenological/hermeneutic analysis, beginning with the everyday facticity of Dasein as simply being-in-the-world, could be taken to be an "existentialism." But Heidegger's own project was never lost sight of: to understand Dasein's temporality (*see* TEMPORALITY AND TIME [S]) and consequent HISTORICITY [S] as propaedeutic to questioning the meaning of Being itself in its relation to time.

THE TURN (*die Kehre*)

The philosophical public first heard Heidegger speak of a "turn" in his way with the publication of the *Letter on Humanism* (1947), but those close to his unpublished work (courses, lectures, etc.) could hardly be unaware of a shift of emphasis in his approach to the Being-question that could be dated from at least 1930. Precisely what the shift consists in and how it came about are issues of debate among specialists, but the simplest way to understand it may be within the context of the essay "On the Essence of Truth," a lecture first delivered in 1930 but not published until 1943.

After reviewing classical conceptions of truth as some kind of correspondence between knower and known, Heidegger analyzes the knowing process as involving an openness of Dasein to the Open that permits a being to come to presence as to-be-known. This Open he calls *Aletheia,* which he will henceforth understand in the radical Greek sense of non- (alpha privative) concealment (*-lethe*). But in part 6 of the essay, Aletheia is experienced as more than the horizon within which beings are encountered and reveal themselves as true. Rather, it is experienced as an active force, a process that assumes an initiative of its own by revealing itself to Dasein—but concealing itself as well. The concealing takes a double form: (1) concealing its own concealment so that its self-concealment is forgotten ("mystery": *das Geheimnis*); (2) compounding the forgottenness by seducing Dasein into wandering about in ever deeper forgetfulness of the mystery ("errancy": *die Irre*). This shift of focus from Dasein as disclosing Being to Being as revealing itself to, and concealing itself from, Dasein characterizes the entire later period of Heidegger's address to the Being-question. Whatever else is said about the celebrated "turn," it must take account of this fact.

One immediate consequence of this shift of focus was a new way of conceiving history, no longer in terms of Dasein, but now in terms of Being-as-Aletheia sending/withdrawing itself, always in finite fashion. This self-sending (*sich-schicken*) is received by Dasein, and the correlation of the two Heidegger calls "destiny" (*Geschick*), which, in turn, constitutes an "epoch" of history. Sometimes the self-sending of Being is taken in a limited sense as bestowed upon an individual thinker (e.g., PARMENIDES [6]); sometimes it is taken in a very broad sense as determining the entire history of metaphysics. In any case, the combination of these epochs constitutes the history of Being—that is, Being-as-history (*Seinsgeschichte*)—and, to think the Being-question, one must do so in terms of its history, through retrieval (*Wiederholung*) of its past.

THE "LATER" HEIDEGGER

This is a general term that refers to no identifiable date but designates Heidegger's effort to think the Being-question after the turn in his way. It is marked by certain differences of style and terminology (e.g., Dasein comes to be called the "clearing" [*Lichtung*] of Being) as well as by the shift of focus just mentioned, but Heidegger's basic preoccupation remains the same. The period is represented by no dominant published work comparable in stature to *Being and Time* but rather by published versions of lecture courses, interpretations of poetry, and sundry collections of essays. For heuristic purposes one may survey the drift of Heidegger's thought after the turn by polarizing remarks around three separate moments that may be considered as "early," "middle," and "late" with regard to this period itself: *Introduction to Metaphysics* (1935); *Letter on Humanism* (1947); *Time and Being* (1960).

Introduction to Metaphysics was not published until 1953 and, in retrospect, made unmistakably clear the import of the turn, though echoes of *Being and Time* remained. (After reformulating the Being-question, Heidegger examines the Greek grammar and syntax of Being and then reflects on the limitation of its meaning through its differentiation from modalities with which it is often associated—Being "and" Becoming/Seeming/Thinking/the Ought.) The spine of the course is the meditation on Being and thinking in terms of Parmenides' gnome: *to gar auto noein estin te kai einai* ("for thinking and Being are one"). Here Being (*einai*) is interpreted as emerging-abiding-presence (*physis*), or (by analogy with HERACLITUS's [3] *logos*) as a primordial gathering into presence, or (always by implication) Aletheia. Thinking (*noein*), the function of Dasein, is the effort to bring to containment the overpowering advance of Being or (less dramatically) to respond to (correspond with) its self-sending. To say that Being and thinking are *auto* does not mean that they are the same in the sense of identical but that they are "one" because they are necessarily correlative. If Dasein's only function is to be the There of Being, Being reciprocally has need of its There as the clearing through which it can reveal itself. It is this correlation that constitutes the destiny (*Geschick*) of Being in any given epoch.

Letter on Humanism is the published response to several questions posed by the French student of Jean-Paul SARTRE [7; S], Jean Beaufret, the first of which was: "How can we restore meaning to the word 'humanism'?" Heidegger, in substance, replies that HUMANISM [4] is a metaphysical notion: "Every humanism is either grounded in a metaphysics or is itself made to be the ground of one," with its standard conception of human being as a "rational animal." But this conception sells human being short, measures it by a zoological standard of sheer animality rather than in terms of its unique prerogative of access to Being. Accordingly, Heidegger's conception of human being is not at all a humanism in the metaphysical sense but, if the term must be retained, offers a humanism of a higher sort.

With this much said, the import of the letter derives in large degree from the fluid epistolary style that permits the author to discourse freely on a wide range of significant issues that receive more thorough treatment elsewhere. By way of summary, several of these are worth noting:

The Polemic Against Metaphysics. Heidegger's complaint about metaphysics is that it is oblivious of the very Being that makes its enterprise possible. In the early years he spoke about laying the groundwork for metaphysics through fundamental ontology (*see* ONTOLOGY AND FUNDAMENTAL ONTOLOGY [S]). Later the project was called the overcoming of metaphysics (*see* METAPHYSICS, OVERCOMING OF [S]). Defined by Aristotle as the interrogation of *on hei on,* of beings as beings, metaphysics became either the study of beings in their commonality (ontology) or of beings in their ultimate ground in a supreme being (theo-logy)—hence, it is onto-theo-logical in its very structure. Dealing exclusively with beings, metaphysics is utterly forgetful of Being (i.e., Aletheia-as-history), their ground.

The Critique of Technology. When NIETZSCHE [5; S], in the final paroxysm of the epoch of metaphysics (see "Nietzsche's Word 'God is dead' "), speaks of "mastery over the earth" (*Erdherrschaft*) as the proper task for human being under the sway of will-to-power, this for Heidegger is harbinger of another, more ominous, epoch, one marked by the destiny (*Geschick*) of Being in his own time whose effect he describes as *die Technik*, ambiguously translated as "technology" (see "The Question Concerning Technology"). The menace in this, as he sees it, is not scientific progress as such but the way an instrument is used in achieving this progress (e.g., a hydroelectric dam on the Rhine)—as no more than a "standby reserve" (*Bestand*) of power to be subjected increasingly to human control. To give a name to the self-disclosure of Being whose effect is this steady submission of beings to human manipulation, Heidegger invents the word *Gestell:* the collective prefix *Ge-* combining the various forms of *stellen* (*vor-/nach-/gegen-/zurück-*, etc.) that suggest such control. So far, English has had to settle for a more or less literal translation of the banal meaning of *Gestell* in German: "enframing." In any case, failure to recognize this destiny for what it is—this is the true "danger" (*Gefahr*) of the epoch. Is there any "salvation" (*Rettung*) from such a danger? Only by recognizing both danger and destiny as signs of Being's bestowal—and withdrawal—in/as an epoch of history.

Language: House of Being. This celebrated metaphor, introduced to the public in the letter to Beaufret, signals the importance that language (*see* LANGUAGE AND HEIDEGGER [4; S]) had assumed for Heidegger in his pursuit of the Being-question by the mid-1940s. In *Being and Time* the problem of language found a place in the phenomenological analysis only as one of the existential components of Dasein under the name of *Rede* ("discourse"), which translated the Greek *logos.* After the turn, logos in *Introduction to Metaphysics* is thought of homologously with physis, einai (and Aletheia) in Heraclitean terms. Thus interpreted, LOGOS [5] is understood as a gathering process that collects all beings unto themselves and lets them be manifest as what they are. It is precisely in this guise that logos comes to be thought of as aboriginal language—language in its origins. Heidegger elaborates this theme in a lecture course of 1944, entitled " 'Logos' (Heraclitus Fg. 50)" (see *Vorträge und Aufsätze*), adding that the task of humans is to respond to—rather, to correspond with (*homologein*)—Being as it reveals itself as logos, bringing it into words. To attend in this fashion to the address of Being is to "poetize" (*Dichten; see* POETIZING AND THINKING [S]), and in this respect thinker and poet share a common task. The problem is to understand how the two tasks differ.

Heidegger does not claim that Heraclitus thought the relation between Being and language in this fashion explicitly but rather that the relation is accessible to subsequent thinking through a retrieve of Heraclitus's experience. This conception of the origin of language, suggestive though it be, is limited, at best, to a specifically Greek phenomenon and, as such, takes no account of the Judaic experience of language (also a part of the Western tradition), still less of non-Western experiences of language and thought, with all of their untold wealth.

Time and Being brings Heidegger's endeavor full circle. The title of this lecture was especially provocative, for it was the same formula that announced the third section (which never appeared) of part 1 of *Being and Time.* For many readers, much of the work published after the turn performed the task that had been projected there. The themes discussed had been wide-ranging. Besides those already mentioned, there had been essays on various issues, for example, on the origin of a work of art, on building, on dwelling, and on "things" in their relation to the WORLD [5]—that is, to the FOURFOLD [S] of earth and sky, the gods and mortals. Finally, the task of thought that Heidegger sought to pursue and to urge, whether under the rubric of "thinking-as-thanking" (*Danken*) (see *What Is Called Thinking,* part 2) or "releasement" (*Gelassenheit*) (see *Conversation on a Country Path*), paralleled, after the turn, what *Being and Time* called "resoluteness," the gesture of acquiescence by which Dasein achieves authenticity.

What readers at the time were not aware of was a major manuscript, entitled *Beiträge zur Philosophie: Vom Ereignis,* that Heidegger drafted but did not edit (1936–38) and was published only posthumously (1989). The most decisive word in the essay, *Ereignis,* normally translated as "event," is here given the sense of an event that "gives" or "appropriates." Though this term occurs with increasing frequency and shifting significance after 1936, its sense as "appropriating event" did not receive full development for the reading public until *Time and Being.* In *Being and Time* the author declares that "there is" (*es gibt,* literally "it gives") Being only insofar as Dasein is. In *Letter on Humanism* he interprets the earlier formula to mean that the giver is Being itself. In *Time and Being,* Being does not do the giving; it is, itself, given.

In this essay Heidegger returns to the earliest form of the question that first set him on his way: what is the meaning of Being in terms of time? Clearly, Being is not a being but rather is given (*es gibt Sein*). Nor is time a being; it, too, is given (*es gibt Zeit*). Neither is prior to the other, yet each reciprocally determines the other, and in this reciprocity each is given unto its own (*Eigene*). Being is understood as coming-to-presence (*Answesen*) but includes a nonpresencing (*Abwesen*), a withdrawal, too. For the present (*Gegenwart*) that emerges out of the presencing process implies a nonpresent of a twofold kind: that of the past (*Gewesen*), which is no longer present; that of the future (*Sukunft*), which is still withheld from the present. Pres-absencing (*An-/Abwesen*), then, comes to this:

> Approaching (*Ankommen*), being not yet present, at the same time gives and brings about what is no longer present, the past, and, conversely, what has been offers future to itself. The reciprocal relation of both at the same time gives and brings about the present (*Time and Being,* 13).

The two modes of the nonpresent in the pres-absencing process constitute, then, the withdrawal that is ingredient to Being's self-donation. Where, for whom, does this take place? For human being!

> If man were not the constant receiver of the gift given by the "It gives presence," if that which is extended in the gift did not reach man, then not only would Being remain concealed in the absence of the gift, not only closed off, but man would remain excluded from the scope of: It gives Being. Man would not be man. (*Time and Being,* 12)

But what is "It" (*Es*) that does the giving of Being and time, each unto its own and to the other? The appropriating event (*Ereignis*)!

> What remains to be said? Only this: Appropriation appropriates. Saying this, we say the Same, in terms of the Same about the Same. . . . But what if we take what was said and adopt it unceasingly as the guide for our thinking, and consider that this Same is not even anything new, but the oldest of the old in Western thought: that ancient something which conceals itself in *A-letheia?* (*Time and Being,* 24)

The appropriating event, then, anticipated in the *Beiträge* (1936), here (1960) comes into its own as the final name for Aletheia, which is, for Heidegger, the first name of all.

CONCLUSION

No one (beginning with Heidegger himself) denies the density of *Time and Being,* with which his effort at thought comes, in effect, full circle. Here at last was one way to answer the question, Whence does Being as such (not merely beings as beings) receive its determination? Any attempt to assess Heidegger's contribution to the history of twentieth-century philosophical thought must begin with the single-mindedness of his enterprise. Everything turns on how one assesses his experience of Aletheia: on the one hand this term surely characterizes the uniqueness of Heidegger's own extraordinary philosophical gift; on the other, as in Greek tragedy, it may help to account for the singularity of the failure for which history will hold him responsible. Confronted by mystery and errancy, he, too, was subject to the finitude of Aletheia as it revealed itself in him. It is in this context that the question of Heidegger's political involvement must be raised: did the very nature of the enterprise lead to his transient tryst with Nazism (and if so, how?) or simply fail to prevent it? This leaves to Heidegger's readers the delicate task of trying to make for themselves a judicious assessment of the relationship between the content of his thought and the conduct of his life.

(SEE ALSO: *Art, Nature of in Heidegger; Artworks, Ontological Status of in Heidegger; Authenticity; Formal Indication; Philosophy of History; Truth in Heidegger* [S])

Bibliography

WORKS BY HEIDEGGER

GESAMTAUSGABE (1973–93, FRANKFURT)

PUBLISHED WORKS, 1910–76

Frühe Schriften [1912–16], ed. F.-W. von Herrmann. 1978.

Sein und Zeit [1927], ed. F.-W. von Herrmann. 1977.

Sein und Zeit, 17th ed., reprint of 15th rev. ed. Tübingen, 1993.

Kant und das Problem der Metaphysik [1929], ed. F.-W. von Herrmann. 1991.

Erläuterungen zu Hölderlins Dichtung [1936–68], ed. F.-W. von Herrmann. 1978.

Holzwege [1935–46], ed. F.-W. von Herrmann. 1978.

Wegmarken [1919–58], ed. F.-W. von Herrmann. 1976.

Unterwegs zur Sprache [1950–59], ed. F.-W. von Herrmann. 1985.

Aus der Erfahrung des Denkens [1910–76], ed. H. Heidegger. 1983.

Seminare [1951–73], ed. C. Ochwadt. 1986. (Heraklit: Freiburg 1966/1967, with E. Fink; Vier Seminare: Le Thor 1966, 1968, 1969; Zähringen 1973; Züricher Seminar: Aussprache mit Martin Heidegger am 6. 11. 1951.

LECTURE COURSES, 1919–44

MARBURG LECTURE COURSES, 1923–28

Einführung in die phänomenologische Forschung [Winter], ed. F.-W. von Hermann. 1994.

Platon: Sophistes [Winter 1924–25], ed. I. Schüssler. 1992.

Prolegomena zur Geschichte des Zeitbegriffs [Summer 1925], ed. P. Jaeger. 1979.

Logik: Die Frage nach der Wahrheit [Winter 1925–26], ed. W. Biemel. 1976.

Grundbegriffe der antiken Philosophie [Summer 1926], ed. F.-K. Blust. 1993.

Die Grundprobleme der Phänomenologie [Summer 1927], ed. F.-W. von Herrmann. 1975, 1989.

Phänomenologische Interpretation von Kants Kritik der reinen Vernunft [Winter 1927–28], ed. I. Görland. 1977, 1990.

Metaphysische Anfangsgründe der Logik im Ausgang von Leibniz [Summer 1928], ed. K. Held. 1978, 1990.

FREIBURG LECTURE COURSES, 1928–44

Die Grundbegriffe der Metaphysik: Welt–Endlichkeit–Einsamkeit [Winter 1929–30], ed. F.-W. von Herrmann. 1983, 1992.

See also: "Unbenutzte Vorarbeiten zur Vorlesung vom Wintersemester 1929/30: *Die Grundbegriffe der Metaphysik: Welt–Endlichkeit–Einsamkeit,*" Heidegger Studies, Vol. 7 (1991), 5–14.

Vom Wesen der menschlichen Freiheit: Einleitung in die Philosophie [Summer 1930], ed. H. Tietjen. 1982.

Hegels Phänomenologie des Geistes [Winter 1930–31], ed. I. Görland. 1980, 1988.

Aristoteles: Metaphysik θ 1–3 [Summer 1931], ed. H. Hüni. 1981, 1990.

Vom Wesen der Wahrheit: Zu Platons Höhlengleichnis und Theätet [Winter 1931–32], ed. H. Mörchen. 1988.

Hölderlins Hymnen "Germanien" und "Der Rhein" [Winter 1934–35], ed. S. Zeigler. 1980, 1989.

Einführung in die Metaphysik [Summer 1935], ed. P. Jaeger. 1983.

Die Frage nach dem Ding: Zu Kants Lehre von den transzendentalen Grundsätzen [Winter 1935–36], ed. P. Jaeger. 1984.

Schelling: Über das Wesen der menschlichen Freiheit [Summer 1936], ed. I. Schüssler. 1988.

Nietzsche: Der Wille zur Macht als Kunst [Winter 1936–37], ed. B. Heimbüchel. 1985.

Nietzsches metaphysische Grundstellung im abendländischen Denken: Die Lehre von der ewigen Wiederkehr des Gleichen [Summer 1937], ed. M. Heinz. 1986.

Grundfragen der Philosophie: Ausgewählte "Probleme" der "Logik" [Winter 1937–38], ed. F.-W. von Herrmann. 1984, 1992.

Nietzsches Lehre vom Willen zur Macht als Erkenntnis [Summer 1939], ed. E. Hanser. 1989.

Nietzsche: Der europäische Nihilismus [2nd trimester 1940], ed. P. Jaeger. 1986.

Die Metaphysik des deutschen Idealismus: Zur erneuten Auslegung von Schelling "Philosophische Untersuchungen über das Wesen der menschlichen Freiheit und die damit zusammenhängenden Gegenstände" (1809) [1st trimester 1941], ed. G. Seubold. 1991.

Nietzsches Metaphysik [for Winter 1941–42, not delivered] and *Einleitung in die Philosophie: Denken und Dichten* [Winter 1944–45], ed. P. Jaeger. 1990.

Grundbegriffe [Summer 1941], ed. P. Jaeger. 1981, 1991.

Hölderlins Hymne "Andenken" [Winter 1941–42], ed. C. Ochwadt. 1982, 1992.

Hölderlins Hymne "Der Ister" [Summer 1942], ed. W. Biemel. 1984.

Parmenides [Winter 1942–43], ed. M. Frings. 1982.

Heraklit 1: Der Anfang des abendländischen Denkens (Heraklit) [Summer 1943]; and *Heraklit 2: Logik—Heraklits Lehre vom Logos* [Summer 1944], ed. M. Frings. 1979, 1987.

EARLY FREIBURG LECTURE COURSES, 1919–23

Zur Bestimmung der Philosophie: 1. Die Idee der Philosophie und das Weltanschauungsproblem [War Emergency Semester 1919]; *2. Phänomenologie und transzendentale Wertphilosophie* [Summer 1919], ed. B. Heimbüchel. 1987.

Grundprobleme der Phänomenologie [Winter 1919–20], ed. H.-H. Gander. 1992.

Phänomenologie der Anschauung und des Ausdrucks: Theorie der philosophischen Begriffsbildung [Summer 1920], ed. C. Strube. 1993.

Phänomenologie des religiosen Lebens: 1. Einleitung in die Phänomenologie der Religion; 2. Augustinus und der Neuplatonismus; 3. Die philosophischen Grundlagen der mittelalterlichen Mystik, edited by M. Jung and T. Regehly. 1995.

Phänomenologische Interpretationen zu Aristoteles: Einführung in die phänomenologische Forschung [Winter 1921–22], ed. W. Bröcker and K. Bröcker-Oltmanns. 1985.

Ontologie: Hermeneutik der Faktizität [Summer 1923], ed. K. Bröcker-Oltmanns. 1988.

UNPUBLISHED MANUSCRIPTS

Beiträge zur Philosophie (Vom Ereignis), ed. F.-W. von Herrmann. 1989.

Hegel: 1. Die Negativität. Eine Auseinandersetzung mit Hegel aus dem Ansatz in der Negativität 1938–39, 1941; 2. Erläuterung der "Einleitung" zu Hegels Phänomenologie des Geistes 1942, ed. I. Schüssler. 1993.

Feldweg—Gespräche [1944–45], ed. I. Schüssler. 1995.

Bremer und Freiburger Vorträge: 1. Einblick in das Was ist [Bremen, 1949]; *2. Grundsätze des Denkens* [Freiburg, 1957], ed. P. Jaeger. 1994.

WORKS NOT IN GESAMTAUSGABE

Antwort: Martin Heidegger im Gespräch, ed. G. Neske and E. Kettering. Pfulligen, 1988. (Contains "Die Selbstbehauptung der deutschen Universität" [the rectoral address], "Das Rektorat, 1933/34: Tatsachen und Gedanken," "Nur noch ein Gott kann uns retten" [the *Spiegel* interview], and "Martin Heidegger im Gespräch: Mit Richard Wisser.")

"Aus einer Erörterung der Wahrheitsfrage," in *Zehn Jahre Neske Verlag* (Pfulligen, 1962).

Der Begriff der Zeit: Vortrag vor der Marburger Theologenschaft Juli 1924. Tübingen, 1989.

"Brief an Jean Beaufret," *Heidegger Studies,* Vol. 3/4 (1987/1988), 3–4.

"Brief an William J. Richardson" (April 1962), in W. J. Richardson, *Heidegger: Through Phenomenology to Thought,* 3d ed. (The Hague, 1974).

Der Feldweg [1949], 3d ed. Frankfurt, 1962.

Gelassenheit [1959], 9th ed. Pfulligen, 1988.

Hebel—der Hausfreund [1957], 5th ed. Pfulligen, 1985.

"Hegel und die Griechen" [1958], in *Die Gegenwart der Griechen im neueren Denken.* Festschrift für Hans-Georg Gadamer zum 60. Geburtstag (Tübingen, 1960).

"Hölderlins Himmel und Erde" [1959], in *Hölderlin Jahrbuch* (Tübingen, 1960).

"Die Idee der Phänomenologie und der Rückgang auf das Bewußtsein," Versuch einer zweiten Bearbeitung eines Artikels von E. Husserl. *Husserliana,* Vol. 9 (The Hague, 1962).

Identität und Differenz [1957], 8th ed. Pfulligen, 1986.

Die Kunst und er Raum. St. Gallen, 1969.

Martin Heidegger, zum 80. Geburtstag von seiner Heimstadt Messkirch. Frankfurt, 1969.

Nietzsche, Vols. 1 and 2 [1961], 4th ed. Pfulligen, 1982.

"Phänomenologische Interpretationen zu Aristoteles: Anzeige der Hermeneutische Situation," ed. H.-U. Lessing, in *Dilthey Jahrbuch für Philosophie und Geschichte der Gewissenschaften,* Vol. 6. Göttingen, 1989.

Phänomenologie und Theologie. Frankfurt, 1970. (Includes "Phänomenologie und Theologie" [1927]; "Einige Hinweise auf Hauptgesichtspunkte für das theologische Gespräch über 'Das Problem eines nichtobjektivierenden Denkens und Sprechens in der heutigen Theologie' " [1964].)

Der Satz vom Grund [1957], 6th ed. Pfulligen, 1986.

"Sprache und Heimat," in *Dauer und Wandel.* Festschrift zum 70. Geburtstag von Carl J. Burckhardt (München, 1961).

Die Technik und die Kehre [1962], 7th ed. Pfulligen, 1988.

Überlieferte Sprache und technische Sprache [1962], ed. H. Heidegger. St. Gallen, 1989.

"Die Unumgänglichkeit des Da-seins ('Die Not') und Die Kunst in ihrer Notwendigkeit (Die bewirkende Besinnung)," *Heidegger Studies,* Vol. 8 (1992), 6–13.

Vorträge und Aufsätze [1954], 5th ed. Pfulligen, 1985.

Vom Wesen des Grundes [1929?], 7th ed. Frankfurt, 1983.

"Vom Ursprung des Kunstwerkes: Erste Ausarbeitung," *Heidegger Studies,* Vol. 5 (1989), 5–22.

"Vorbemerkung des Herausgebers, zu: Edmund Husserls Vorlesungen zur Phänomenologie des inneren Zeitbewußtseins," *Jahrbuch für Philosophie und phänomenologische Forschung* [Halle], Vol. 9, 367–68.

Was heißt Denken? Tübingen, 1954.

Was ist das—die Philosophie? [1955], 9th ed. Pfulligen, 1988.

Zur Frage nach der Bestimmung der Sache des Denkens, ed. H. Heidegger. St. Gallen, 1984.

Zur Sache des Denkens [1963–66], 2d ed. Tübingen, 1976.

Zur Seinsfrage [1955], 4th ed. Frankfurt, 1977.

"Zu Überwindung der Aesthetik: Zu 'Ursprung des Kunstwerks,' " *Heidegger Studies,* Vol. 6 (1990), 5–10.

LETTERS

Martin Heidegger, Elizabeth Blochman: Briefwechsel, 1918–1969, ed. J. Storck. Marbach am Neckar, 1989.

Martin Heidegger, Karl Jaspers: Briefwechsel, 1920–1963, ed. W. Biemel and H. Saner. Frankfurt, 1990.

Martin Heidegger, Erhart Kastner: Briefwechsel, 1953–1974, ed. Heinrich Petzet. Frankfurt, 1986.

ENGLISH TRANSLATIONS

GESAMTAUSGABE

Sein und Zeit

Being and Time, trans. J. Macquarrie and E. Robinson. New York, 1962.

Kant und das Problem der Metaphysik

Kant and the Problem of Metaphysics, trans. R. Taft. Bloomington, IN, 1990.

Erläuterung zu Hölderlins Dichtung

"Remembrance of the Poet," trans. D. Scott, in Werner Brock, ed., *Existence and Being* (Chicago, 1949).

"Hölderlin and the Essence of Poetry," trans. D. Scott, in *Existence and Being.*

Holzwege

"The Origin of the Work of Art," trans. A. Hofstadter, in *Poetry, Language, Thought* (New York, 1971).

"The Age of the World Picture," trans. W. Lovitt, in *The Question Concerning Technology* (New York, 1977).

"The Word of Nietzsche: 'God Is Dead,' " in *The Question Concerning Technology.*

"What Are Poets For?" in *Poetry, Language, Thought.*

"The Anaxamander Fragment," trans. D. F. Krell and F. Capuzzi, in *Early Greek Thinking* (New York, 1975).

"Hegel's Concept of Experience," trans. K. R. Dove, in *Hegel's Concept of Experience* (New York, 1970).

Wegmarken

"What Is Metaphysics?" trans. D. F. Krell, in *Basic Writings* (New York, 1977).

"On the Essence of Truth," trans. J. Sallis, in *Basic Writings.*

"Postscript to 'What Is Metaphysics?' " trans. R. F. C. Hull and A. Crick, in *Existence and Being.*

"Plato's Doctrine of Truth," trans. J. Barlow, in *Philosophy in the Twentieth Century,* Vol. 3, *Contemporary European Thought,* ed. W. Barrett and H. D. Aiken (New York, 1971).

"Letter on Humanism," trans. F. A. Capuzzi, with J. G. Gray and D. F. Krell, in *Basic Writings.*

"The Way Back into the Ground of Metaphysics," trans. W. Kaufmann, in *Existentialism from Dostoevsky to Sartre* (Cleveland, 1956).

"Kant's Thesis about the Thing," trans. T. E. Klein and W. E. Pohl, *Southwestern Journal of Philosophy,* Vol. 4, No. 3 (Fall 1973), 7–33.

"On the Being and Conception of *Physis* in Aristotle's Physics, B,1," trans. T. J. Sheehan, *Man and World,* Vol. 9 (1976), 219–270.

Unterwegs zur Sprache

On the Way to Language, trans. P. D. Hertz. New York, 1971.

"Language," in *Poetry, Language, Thought.*

Aus der Erfahrung des Denkens

"Why Do I Stay in the Provinces?" trans. T. J. Sheehan, in T. J. Sheehan, ed., *Heidegger: The Man and the Thinker* (Chicago, 1981).

Seminare (1951–73) [Heraklit]

Heraclitus Seminar, 1966/1967, with Eugen Fink, trans. C. H. Seibert. University, AL, 1982.

Prolegomena zur Geschichte des Zeitbegriffs

History of the Concept of Time: Prolegomena, trans. T. Kisiel. Bloomington, IN, 1985.

Die Grundprobleme der Phänomenologie

The Basic Problems of Phenomenology, trans. A. Hofstadter. Bloomington, Ind. 1982.

Metaphysische Anfangsgründe der Logik im Ausgang von Leibniz

The Metaphysical Foundations of Logic, trans. M. Heim. Bloomington, IN, 1984.

Fundamental Concepts of Metaphysics: World, Finitude, Solitude, trans. W. McNeill and N. Walker. Bloomington, IN, 1995.

Hegels Phänomenologie des Geistes

Hegel's Phenomenology of Spirit, trans. P. Emad and K. Maly. 1988.

Aristotle's Metaphysics Theta, 1–3: On the Essence and Actuality of Force, trans. W. Brogan and P. Warnek. Bloomington, IN, 1995.

Einführung in die Metaphysik

Introduction to Metaphysics, trans. R. Manheim. New Haven, 1959.

Die Frage nach dem Ding

What Is a Thing?, trans. W. B. Barton and V. Deutsch. Chicago, 1967.

Grundfragen der Philosophie: Ausgewählte "Probleme" der "Logik"

Basic Questions of Philosophy: Selected "Problems" of "Logic," trans. R. Rojcewicz and A. Schuwer. Bloomington, IN, 1994.

Grundbegriffe

Basic Concepts, trans. G. E. Aylesworth. Bloomington, IN, 1993.

Parmenides

Parmenides, trans. A. Schuwer and R. Rojcewicz. Bloomington, IN, 1993.

WORKS NOT IN GESAMTAUSGABE

Antwort: Martin Heidegger im Gespräch

Martin Heidegger and National Socialism: Questions and Answers, trans. L. Harries. New York, 1990. (Contains "The Self-Assertion of the German University" [the rectoral address], "The Rectorate 1933/34: Facts and Thoughts," "Only a God

Can Save Us" [the *Spiegel* Interview], and "Martin Heidegger in Conversation, with Richard Wisser.")

Der Begriff der Zeit

The Concept of Time, trans. W. McNeill. Oxford, 1992.

Brief an William J. Richardson

"Letter to Father Richardson," in *Heidegger: Through Phenomenology to Thought,* 3d. ed. (The Hague, 1974).

Der Feldweg

The Pathway, trans. T. R. O'Meara, O. P. (Revisions: Thomas J. Sheehan), *Listening,* Vol. 8 (1973).

Gelassenheit

Discourse on Thinking, trans. J. M. Anderson and E. H. Freund. New York, 1966.

Identität und Differenz

Identity and Difference, trans. J. Stambaugh. New York, 1969. German text included in appendix.

Die Kunst und der Raum

"Art and Space," trans. C. H. Siebert, *Man and World,* Vol. 6, (1973).

Martin Heidegger, zum 80. Geburtstag von seiner Heimstadt Messkirch

"Homeland," trans. T. F. O'Meara, *Listening,* Vol. 6 (1971), 231–38.

Nietzsche, Volume One

Nietzsche, Vol. 1, *The Will to Power as Art,* ed. and trans. D. F. Krell. New York, 1979.

Nietzsche, Vol. 2, *The Eternal Recurrence of the Same,* ed. and trans. D. F. Krell. New York, 1984.

Nietzsche, Vol. 3, *The Will to Power as Knowledge and as Metaphysics,* ed. D. F. Krell, trans. J. Stambaugh, D. F. Krell, and F. A. Capuzzi. New York, 1987.

Nietszche, Volume Two

Nietzsche, Vol. 3, *The Will to Power as Knowledge and as Metaphysics,* "The Eternal Recurrence of the Same and the Will to Power."

Nietzsche, Vol. 4, *Nihilism,* "European Nihilism," ed. D. F. Krell, trans. F. A. Capuzzi. New York, 1982.

Nietzsche, Vol. 3, *The Will to Power as Knowledge and as Metaphysics,* "Nietzsche's Metaphysics."

Nietzsche, Vol. 4, *Nihilism,* "Nihilism as Determined by the History of Being."

"Metaphysics as the History of Being," trans. J. Stambaugh, in *The End of Philosophy* (New York, 1973).

"Sketches for a History of Being as Metaphysics," in *The End of Philosophy.*

"Recollection in Metaphysics," in *The End of Philosophy.*

Phänomenologische Interpretationen zu Aristotles

"Phenomenological Interpretations with respect to Aristotle: Indications of the Hermeneutic Situation," trans. M. Baur, *Man and World,* Vol. 25 (1992), 355–93.

Phänomenologie und Theologie

"The Problem of Non-Objectifying Thing and Speaking," in J. Gill, ed., *Philosophy and Religion* (Minneapolis, 1968).

Der Satz vom Grund

The Principle of Reason, trans. R. Lilly. Bloomington, IN, 1991.

Die Technik und die Kehre

"The Question Concerning Technology," trans. W. Lovitt, in *The Question Concerning Technology.*

"The Turning," trans. W. Lovitt, in *The Question Concerning Technology.*

Vorträge und Aufsätze, Volume One

"The Question Concerning Technology," in *The Question Concerning Technology.*

"Science and Reflection," in *The Question Concerning Technology.*

"Overcoming Metaphysics," in *The End of Philosophy.*

"Who Is Nietzsche's Zarathustra?" trans. B. Magnus, *Review of Metaphysics,* Vol. 20 (1967), 411–31.

Vorträge und Aufsätze, Volume Two

"Building, Dwelling, Thinking," in *Poetry, Language, Thought.*

"The Thing," in *Poetry, Language, Thought.*

". . . Poetically Man Dwells . . . ," in *Poetry, Language, Thought.*

Vorträge und Aufsätze, Volume Three

"Logos (Heraclitus, Fragment B 50)," in *Early Greek Thinking.*

"Moira (Parmenides VIII, 34–41)," in *Early Greek Thinking.*

"Aletheia (Heraclitus, Fragment B 16)," in *Early Greek Thinking.*

Vom Wesen des Grundes

The Essence of Reasons, trans. T. Malick. Evanston, IL, 1969.

Was heißt Denken?

What Is Called Thinking? trans. F. D. Wieck and J. G. Gray. New York, 1972.

Zur Sache des Denkens

On Time and Being, trans. J. Stambaugh. New York, 1972.

Zur Seinsfrage

The Question of Being, trans. J. T. Wilde and W. Kluback. New Haven, 1958.

OTHER TRANSLATIONS

Basic Writings, ed. D. F. Krell. New York, 1977.

Early Greek Thinking, trans. D. F. Krell and F. Capuzzi. New York, 1975.

The End of Philosophy, trans. J. Stambaugh. New York, 1973.

Existence and Being, ed. W. Brock. Chicago, 1949.

Hegel's Concept of Experience, trans. K. R. Dove. New York, 1970.

Identity and Difference, trans. J. Stambaugh. New York, 1969.

Kant and the Problem of Metaphysics, trans. R. Taft. Bloomington, IN, 1990.

The Piety of Thinking, trans. J. Hart and J. Maraldo. Bloomington, IN, 1976.

WORKS ON HEIDEGGER

BIBLIOGRAPHIES AND INDEXES

Franzen, W. *Martin Heidegger.* Stuttgart, 1976.

Index zu Heideggers "Sein und Zeit," ed. H. Feick, 4th ed., updated by S. Zeigler. Tübingen, 1991.

Martin Heidegger: A Bibliography, ed. J. Nordquist. Santa Cruz, CA, 1990.

Sass, H.-M. *Martin Heidegger: Bibliography and Glossary.* Bowling Green, OH, 1982.

The Cambridge Companion to Heidegger, ed. C. Guignon. Cambridge, 1993.

GENERAL

Antwort: Martin Heidegger im Gespräch. Hrsg. E. Kettering. Pfullingen, 1988.

Barash, J. *Martin Heidegger and the Problem of Historical Meaning.* The Hague, 1988.

Beaufret, J. *Dialogue avec Heidegger.* 4 vols. Paris, 1973–85.

Bernasconi, R. *The Question of Language in Heidegger's History of Being.* Atlantic Highlands, NJ, 1985.

Birault, H. *Heidegger et l'expérience de la pensée.* Paris, 1978.

Bourdieu, P. *The Political Ontology of Martin Heidegger,* trans. P. Collier. Stanford, CA, 1991.

Caputo, J. *Demythologizing Heidegger.* Bloomington, IN, 1993.

Dallmayer, F. *The Other Heidegger.* Ithaca, NY, 1993.

Derrida, J. *Of Spirit: Heidegger and the Question,* trans. G. Bennington and R. Bowlby. Chicago, 1989.

Dreyfus, H. *Being-in-the-World: A Commentary on Heidegger's "Being and Time," Division I.* Cambridge, MA, 1990.

Foti, V. *Heidegger and the Poets.* Atlantic Highlands, NJ, 1992.

Grondin, J. *Le Tournant dans la pensée de Martin Heidegger.* Paris, 1987.

Haar, M. *Heidegger and the Essence of Man,* trans. W. McNeill. Albany, NY, 1993.

Janicaud, D. *L'Ombre de cette pensée: Heidegger et la question politique.* Grenoble, 1990.

Kisiel, T. *The Genesis of Heidegger's "Being and Time."* Berkeley, 1993.

Kockelmans, J. *On the Truth of Being: Reflections on Heidegger's Later Philosophy.* Bloomington, IN, 1984.

Kolb, D. "Heidegger at 100, in America," *Journal of the History of Ideas,* Vol. 52 (1991), 140–51.

Krell, D. *Intimations of Mortality: Time, Truth, and Finitude in Heidegger's Thinking of Being.* University Park, PA, 1986.

Lacoue-Labarthe, P. *Heidegger, Art, and Politics: The Fiction of the Political,* trans. C. Turner. Oxford, 1990.

Marx, W. *Heidegger and the Tradition,* trans. T. Kisiel and M. Greene. Evanston, IL, 1971.

Mehta, J. *Martin Heidegger: The Way and the Vision.* Honolulu, 1976.

Okrent, M. *Heidegger's Pragmatism.* Ithaca, NY, 1988.

Ott, H. *Martin Heidegger: A Political Life,* trans. A. Blunden. New York, 1993.

Pöggeler, O. *Martin Heidegger's Path of Thinking,* trans. D. Magurshak and S. Barber. Atlantic Highlands, NJ, 1987.

Richardson, W. *Heidegger: Through Phenomenology to Thought.* Preface by M. Heidegger. 3d. ed. The Hague, 1974.

Petzet, H. *Encounters and Dialogues with Martin Heidegger, 1929–1976,* trans. P. Emad and K. Maly. Chicago, 1993.

Rosen, S. *The Question of Being: A Reversal of Heidegger.* New Haven, 1993.

Schürmann, R. *Heidegger on Being and Acting: From Principles to Anarchy,* trans. C.-M. Gros. Bloomington, IN, 1987.

Taminiaux, J. *Heidegger and the Project of Fundamental Ontology,* trans. M. Gendre. Albany, NY, 1991.

The Heidegger Case: On Philosophy and Politics, ed. T. Rockmore and J. Margolis. Philadelphia, 1992.

Von Herrmann, F.-W. *Subjekt und Dasein: Interpretationen zu "Sein und Zeit."* Frankfurt, 1974; 2d. ed., 1985.

Zarader, M. *Heidegger et les paroles de l'origine.* Préface de E. Levinas. Paris, 1990.

Zimmerman, M. *Heidegger's Confrontation with Modernity.* Bloomington, IN, 1990.

COLLECTIONS

Heidegger: A Critical Reader, ed. H. Dreyfus and H. Hall. Oxford, 1992.

Heidegger and Modern Philosophy: Critical Essays, ed. M. Murray. New Haven, 1978.

Heidegger et la question de Dieu, ed. R. Kearney and J. O'Leary. Paris, 1980.

Heidegger: Perspektiven zur Deutung seines Werkes, ed. O. Pöggeler. Köln, 1969.

Heidegger: The Man and the Thinker, ed. T. Sheehan. Chicago, 1981.

Martin Heidegger, ed. M. Haar. Paris, 1983.

Reading Heidegger: Commemorations, ed. J. Sallis. Bloomington, IN, 1993.

The Cambridge Companion to Heidegger, ed. C. Guignon. Cambridge, 1993.

WILLIAM J. RICHARDSON

HERMENEUTIC PHENOMENOLOGY.

DILTHEY [2] scholars such as Georg Misch and Eduard SPRANGER [8] already regarded Edmund HUSSERL's [4; S] phenomenology as hermeneutical, as a process of exposing hidden meaning and as a method of explicating the implicit structures of experience. But it was Martin HEIDEGGER [3; S] who expressly brought the two traditions together in what he in 1919 first called a phenomenological hermeneutics. More than a superficial grafting, the addition of "hermeneutic" to phenomenology is meant to explicate its essence more originally (*see* HERMENEUTIC PHILOSOPHY [S]). Instead of a spontaneous self-showing readily accessible to intuition, the primal phenomena are regarded as concealed and so in need of the labor of exposure. Heidegger therefore displaces Husserl's experiential structure of intentionality as intuitive fulfillment of initially empty signification with a more basic structural process of explication of implicit but already understood meaning (*see* INTENTIONALITY IN HUSSERL [S]). Interpretive exposition and not intuition becomes the basic mode of knowing, understanding and not signifying intending is the basic mode of human being.

The early Heidegger's "hermeneutics of facticity" of the contextually situated "historical I" (later *Dasein*) in fact draws its proximate inspiration, not only from the philosophical hermeneutics of SCHLEIERMACHER [7] and Dilthey, but also from the neo-Kantian tradition from FICHTE [3] (he coined the term facticity) to Emil Lask, which sought to found historical science in the factic categories of "value individuality" and "motivation." But Heidegger undermines this twofold tradition's hermeneutic distinction between the "understanding" historical-cultural sciences and the "explanatory" natural sciences by posing the more rudimentary phenomenological problem of the "genesis of the theoretical" as such from the background of protopractical understanding and interpretation, from that human experience that spontaneously articulates itself in "getting around" the world by "getting by" with things, "getting along" with others, and "getting with" oneself. Thus, the "hermeneutic 'as'" is first exemplified from human commerce with tools in a contextured world that already implicates us in a tradition of "usage," to which we comply in this interpretive instance of explicative appliance by "letting the implication apply." A life rooted in care already implicitly interprets itself, from circumspective concern to inspective or solicitous regard to the lucid perspicuity of distressed self-caring. Historically situated existence in its facticity is thoroughly hermeneutical, so that an overtly phenomenological hermeneutics *of* facticity, in its expository interpretation of care in its temporal and discursive structures, is but a repetition of an implicit panhermeneutic process already indigenous to life.

A radically hermeneutic ontology accordingly assumes the focal task of explicating the central interpretive tendency operative in the various basic movements of the life that "in its being goes about [*geht um* = is concerned with] this very being." This formula of the self-referential movement of Being itself in *Being and Time* (1927) becomes the formal indication of the understanding-of-Being that defines the very being of factic Dasein. This self-referential movement preceding any subject–object reflectivity, accordingly a temporal-historical circular movement of being to being circumscribing the understanding *of* Being that Dasein is, is the temporalized translation of the seemingly static reflective "*self*-directedness toward" of the phenomenological structure called intentionality, the source of the giving of meaning in human experience. Inescapably situated in the hermeneutic-ontological magnitudes of tradition and language, temporally driven by the erotic question of the sense of Being, the understanding-of-Being is the all-pervasive central core of all of Heidegger's thought. Thus, the later Heidegger (1959) still identifies the accustomed "usage" of the human being by Being itself, through the "hidden pull" of its tradition of language, as the "hermeneutic relation."

The dislocating circular dynamics of situated meaning-formation is first made manifest in the historically precedented structure indigenous to the "hermeneutic situation" of understanding. This prestructure of the understanding is tensed temporally by a prepossession, preview, and preconception that circularly structure meaning into a "toward-which-according-to-which" something becomes understandable as something. Meaning thus indicates the articulative direction for cultivating the prestructure of understanding into the as-structure of interpretation. Already inescapably finding itself in a hermeneutic situation, following the temporal promptings of dispositioning understanding in a discursive medium of self-mediating meaning, Dasein appropriates and explicates its most immediate conditions of access to itself and to its world. Through historical self-explication, by working out the presuppositional constellation already at work in interpreting anything whatsoever, self-referential understanding-*of*-Being becomes fully itself, comes full circle again and again "to its matter itself." Being itself is accordingly the "event" of situated *hermeneia,* of unconcealing concealing, of the original "clearing" of sense in human experience.

Repeated review and deepening re-vision of his hermeneutic situation is the strategy that Heidegger himself applies to his own ever more radical philosophical discourse, as it develops from the fundamental-ontological hermeneutics of human being to the destructive retrieve of the fundamental historicity of the thinking of Being itself. The merit of Hans-Georg GADAMER's [S] less radical "philosophical hermeneutics" is the reapplication of the situational dynamics of Heidegger's "hermeneutics of facticity" to its more customary loci in the humanities. Gadamer's masterwork, *Truth and Method,* based in the hermeneutic intentionality of our "thrown" belonging to the project of tradition, proposes no method but seeks simply to understand phenomenologically how the understanding (contextualized "truth") that is bound by tradition naturally "happens" by way of that tradition in our humanistic experiences of art, history, and language. Unique features of Gadamer's account of "hermeneutic experience" are the dialectical encounter between interpreter and transmitted text itself taken as interrogating dialogue partner, the productivity of the temporal distance between them that exposes precedented possibilities mediating present and past into a FUSION OF HORIZONS [S], the resulting translation of that tradition to a new (thus unprecedented) whole, how history itself is at work in restoring our understanding of an initially alien past, how the "speculative" play of language itself is the ultimate source of this healing productivity ("the medium mediates"), and insistence on the completion of the process of understanding interpretation in the moment of application (to our time, to our language, the two transcendental magnitudes of hermeneutics).

Bibliography

Gadamer, H.-G. *Gesammelte Werke.* Tübingen, 1986–.

Gadamer, H.-G. *Wahrheit und Methode: Grundzüge einer philosophischen Hermeneutik.* Tübingen, 1960. Published as Vols. 1–2 of *Gesammelte Werke.* Translated and newly revised by J. Weinsheimer and D. G. Marshall as *Truth and Method.* New York, 1989.

Heidegger, M. "A Dialogue on/from Language between a Japanese and an Inquirer," in *Unterwegs zur Sprache* (Pfullingen, 1959). Translated by P. D. Hertz as *On the Way to Language.* New York, 1971.

———. *Gesamtausgabe.* Frankfurt, 1975–.

———. *Sein und Zeit.* Halle, 1927. 16th ed., Tübingen, 1986. Translated by J. Macquarrie and E. S. Robinson as *Being and Time.* New York, 1962.

Kisiel, T. *The Genesis of Heidegger's "Being and Time."* Berkeley, 1993.

THEODORE KISIEL

HERMENEUTIC PHILOSOPHY. While hermeneutics, per se, is generally identified with the "art of understanding"—that is, with the methods and principles for understanding texts—in the twentieth century it was transformed into a philosophical position closely associated with Hans-Georg GADAMER [S] and Paul RICOEUR [S]. Two forerunners to Gadamer and Ricoeur are Wilhelm DILTHEY [2], who in 1990 saw hermeneutics as a methodological foundation for the human sciences, and Martin HEIDEGGER [3; S], who, as early as 1919 and later in *Being and Time* (1927), used the word *Hermeneutik* to indicate an alternative kind of interpretation embedded in existential understanding.

After the publication of *Truth and Method,* Gadamer encountered opposition from Emilio Betti and E. D. Hirsch, Jr., who objected that Gadamer offered no means of achieving objectively valid interpretations, and from the neo-Marxist Jürgen HABERMAS [S], who found in Gadamer's affirmation of tradition no room for the "moment of critique."

Paul Ricoeur spent World War II in a concentration camp writing a translation of HUSSERL's [4; S] *Ideas* between the lines. In early work on phenomenology of the will and the fallibility of man he turned to the interpretation of symbols and devoted a volume to the symbolism of stain and evil (1960). He then wrote on FREUD's [3; S] view of interpretation (1965), and in *The Conflict of Interpretations* (1968) he tried to mediate the conflict between Anglo-American and Continental philosophy. His book on the living metaphor (1974) and a three-volume work on time and narrative also contributed to hermeneutics (*see* METAPHOR IN RICOEUR [S]).

Beginning in 1967 Jacques DERRIDA [S] offered a continuation of Heideggerian thought that contrasts with that of both Gadamer and Ricoeur, yet since it deals heavily with the question of interpretation one may include it within the category of hermeneutic philosophy. In 1979 Richard Rorty's *Philosophy and the Mirror of Nature* made hermeneutics a new paradigm for philosophizing, a contrast with the philosophizing that invents systems and seeks to lay foundations for future thought.

Bibliography

Betti, E. "Hermeneutics as the General Methodology of the *Geisteswissenschaften,*" in J. Bleicher, ed., *Contemporary Hermeneutics* (London, 1980).

Bruns, G. *Hermeneutics Ancient and Modern.* New Haven, 1993.

Dilthey, W. "The Rise of Hermeneutics," *English Literary History,* Vol. 3 (1972), 230–44.

Gadamer, H.-G. *Wahrheit and Methode.* Tübingen, 1960. Translated as *Truth and Method,* edited by G. Barden and J. Cumming. New York, 1975; rev. trans., 1989.

Grondin, J. *An Introduction to Philosophical Hermeneutics.* New Haven, 1994.

Habermas, J., "The Hermeneutic Claim to Universality," in J. Bleicher, ed., *Contemporary Hermeneutics* (London, 1980).

Heidegger, M. *Sein und Zeit.* Tübingen, 1927. Translated by J. Macquarrie and E. Robinson as *Being and Time.* New York, 1962.

Hirsch, E. D., Jr. "Gadamer's Theory of Interpretation," Appendix 2 in *Validity in Interpretation* (New Haven, 1967).

Palmer, R. E. *Interpretation Theory: Schleiermacher, Dilthey, Heidegger, Gadamer.* Evanston, IL, 1969. An introduction to hermeneutic philosophy.

Ricoeur, P. *La symbolique du mal.* Paris, 1960. Translated by E. Buchanan as *Symbolism of Evil.* Boston, 1969.

———. *De l'interprétation. Essais sur Freud.* Paris, 1965. Translated by Denis Savage as *Freud and Philosophy: An Essay on Interpretation.* New Haven, 1970.

———. *Le conflit des interprétations.* Paris, 1969. English title: *Conflict of Interpretations,* edited by D. Ihde. Evanston, IL, 1974.

———. *Métaphore vive.* Paris, 1975. Translated by R. Czerny as *The Rule of Metaphor.* Toronto, 1977.

———. *Temps et récit.* Paris, 1983–85. Translated by K. McLaughlin and D. Pellauer as *Time and Narrative.* 3 Vols. Chicago, 1984–88.

Rorty, R., "From Epistemology to Hermeneutics," and "Philosophy without Mirrors," in *Philosophy and the Mirror of Nature* (Princeton, NJ, 1979).

RICHARD E. PALMER

HERMENEUTICS AND AESTHETICS *See:* HERMENEUTIC PHENOMENOLOGY, HERMENEUTIC PHILOSOPHY [S]

HILDEGARD OF BINGEN (1098–1179), was born in Bermersheim near Alzey in Rheinhessen and entered a Benedictine enclosure in 1106. She was elected abbess of her monastery in Disibodenberg in 1136 and founded a new monastery in Rupertsberg in 1150. Monasteries before the Council of Trent were not strictly enclosed, and between 1158 and 1171 Hildegard took four major public teaching tours along the Rhine. In addition to writing extensive correspondence with kings, popes, spiritual friends, and masters from Paris, she wrote six major books and several minor texts.

Hildegard made original contributions to prescholastic science, music, drama, linguistics, mystical theology, and philosophy. Drawing upon her experience in the Benedictine hospice as a physician-nurse, Hildegard systematized information about the medicinal powers of plants and minerals. The creativity of her musical compositions is evident in contemporary recordings. She wrote the first extant morality play, composed a secret language, and was the first Christian writer to elaborate an extensive feminine dimension of the divine.

Immersed in the common texts of medieval cosmology available through her monastic library, Hildegard described the human being as a unified soul-body microcosm in structural harmony with the universe or macrocosm. She developed a rationale for a complementarity between men and women by describing complex

interactions of elements and humors, bodily structures, diseases, and human character. Her writings contain relevance for philosophical issues in metaphysics, epistemology, psychology, anthropology, phenomenology, ethics, and mysticism.
(SEE ALSO: *Women in the History of Philosophy* [S])

Bibliography

WORKS BY HILDEGARD

Scivias [Know the Ways, 1141–51], edited by A. Fürkötter, in *Corpus christianorum: Continuatio medievalis* (Turnhout, 1978), Vols. 43–43a. Translated into English by Mother C. Hart and J. Bishop as *Know the Ways.* New York, 1990.

Liber simplicis medicinae [also known as *Physica* and *Subtilitatum diversarum naturarum creaturum livri novem*; Natural History or Book of Simple Medicine, 1151–58], edited by C. Daremberg and F. A. Reuss, in *Patrologiae cursus completus: Series latina,* edited by J.-P. Migne (Paris, 1841–64). Vol. 197:1125–1352. And *Causae et curae* [Causes and Cures or Book of Compound Medicine], edited by Paul Kaiser. Leipzig, 1903. Portions translated into English by W. Strelow and G. Hertzka in *Hildegard of Bingen's Medicine* (Santa Fe, NM, 1988).

Leider (Symphonia armonie celestium revelationum) [Symphony of the Harmony of Celestial Revelations, ca. 1158], edited by P. Barth, M.-I. Ritscher, and J. Schmidt-Görg. Salzburg, 1969. Translated by B. Newman in *Saint Hildegard of Bingen: Symphonia.* Ithaca, NY, 1988.

Ordo virtutum [Play of the Virtues, ca. 1158], edited by P. Dronke, in *Poetic Individuality in the Middle Ages* (Oxford, 1970).

Liber vitae meritorum, per simplicem hominem a vivente luce revelatorum [Book of Life's Merits, 1158–63], edited by J.-B. Pitra, in *Anelecta Sanctae Hildegardis* (Monte Cassino, 1882). Translated by B. Hozeski as *Hildegard of Bingen: The Book of Rewards of Life (Liber Vitae Meritorum).* New York, 1993.

De operatione Dei [On the Activity of God; also known as *Liber divinorum operum simplicis hominis* (Book of Divine Works)], edited by J. D. Mansi, in *Stephanus Balluzius: Miscellanea* (Lucca, 1761). Reprinted in *Patrologiae cursus completus: Series latina,* edited by J.-P. Migne. Vol. 197:741–1038. Edited by M. Fox in *Hildegard of Bingen's Book of Divine Works with Letters and Songs* (Sante Fe, NM, 1987).

Lingua ignota [Unknown Language] in *Patrologiae cursus completus: Series latina,* edited by J.-P. Migne, Vol. 197. Translated into German by F. W. E. Roth in *Die Lieder und die unbekannte Sporache der hl. Hildegardis* (Weisgaden, 1860).

WORKS ON HILDEGARD

Allen, P. "Hildegard of Bingen," in *The Concept of Woman: The Aristotelian Revolution (750 BC–1250 AD).* (Montreal, 1985).

———. "Hildegard of Bingen's Philosophy of Sex Identity," *Thought,* Vol. 64, No. 254 (Sept. 1989), 231–41.

Flanagan, S. *Hildegard of Bingen: A Visionary Life.* London, 1990.

Lauter, W. *Hildegard-Bibliographie.* 2 vols. Alzey, Germany, 1970–84.

Newman, B. *Sister of Wisdom: St. Hildegard's Theology of the Feminine.* Berkeley, 1989.

Qualibet: Newsletter of the International Society of Hildegard von Bingen Studies, Vols. 1–10 (1984–94).

Scholz, B. W. "Hildegard of Bingen on the Nature of Woman," *American Benedictine Review,* Vol. 31 (1980), 361–83.

Singer, C. *From Magic to Science: Essays on the Scientific Twilight.* New York, 1958.

PRUDENCE ALLEN

HISTORICITY. Martin HEIDEGGER [3; S] follows Wilhelm DILTHEY [2] in making historicity central to his hermeneutics of the facticity of the situated "historical I" (later *Dasein*). Its immanent historicity is the experience *of* experience spontaneously giving life a familiarity or "understanding" of itself. This original understanding of a historical life temporally explicating itself to itself becomes *the* lifelong topic for recapitulation by a hermeneutic ontology (later "thinking *of* being").

With the possibility of death, this return to the "history that we ourselves are" assumes a future term. Historicity thus receives its basic sense from the more comprehensive kairological temporality singling out the historical individual and its generation. Forerunning one's death is at once forerunning one's fate and the destiny of the individual's generation. The hav*ing*-been that still *is,* the very motion of historicity, comes to meet us from the future in a forerunning recapitulation of precedented possibilities transmitted from an owned heritage (inheritance, heredity). Recapitulation is the explicit self-transmission of tradition, delivering oneself over to one's unique moment of decision and leeway of opportunity called fate. Recapitulation also revokes, as critique of current interpretedness, as reversal of the oblivious absorption in the present characterizing disowned historicity, as destruction of its averaged presuppositions by cultivation of one's own total hermeneutic situation.

Owned historiography is likewise "temporalized" (generated, maturated) from the future. Philosophy's destruction of the history of ontology, genealogical reconstruction of its conceptions of originating experiences, accordingly expose the unthought now to be thought in what is already thought.

"Historicity" recedes in the later Heidegger and is replaced by commemorative thinking of the history *of* being, in the hermeneutical usage (custom, habitat's habit) of human being by being, destined to be thought.

Bibliography

Heidegger, M. *Sein und Zeit* [1927], 16th ed. Tübingen, 1986. Translated by J. Macquarrie and E. S. Robinson as *Being and Time.* New York, 1962. §§ 6, 74.

Kisiel, T. *The Genesis of Heidegger's "Being and Time".* Berkeley, 1993.

Pöggeler, O. "'Historicity' in Heidegger's Late Work," in R. W. Shahan and J. N. Mohanty, eds., *Thinking about Being: Aspects of Heidegger's Thought* (Norman, OK, 1984).

Ruin, H. *Enigmatic Origins: Tracing the Theme of Historicity Through Heidegger's Works.* Stockholm Studies in Philosophy, 15. Stockholm, 1994.

THEODORE KISIEL

HOBBES, THOMAS, became the subject of a great increase in the rate of publications after 1967, an increase that is largely attributable to the three hundredth anniversary of his death, marked in 1979, and the four hundredth anniversary of his birth, marked in 1988. The second of these saw the establishment of *Hobbes Studies,* a journal devoted to HOBBES [4], though the International Hobbes Association and its newsletter were established some years earlier. Interest in Hobbes's work—though more low-key—had existed beforehand.

The interest in Hobbes expressed itself not only in new writings about him but also in new editions of his work and the publication of some of his previously unpublished work. The major project of producing the Clarendon edition of Hobbes's works, begun by Howard Warrender, received a setback with his death in 1985 after only two volumes were completed, but an editorial board was set up to carry on the work. The first English translation of part of *De Homine* appeared in 1972, and Jones's translation of *Thomas White's De Mundo Examined* appeared in 1976.

Little has been added to our detailed knowledge of the events of Hobbes's life. Miriam M. Reik published *The Golden Lands of Thomas Hobbes,* an intellectual biography, and Arnold Rogow published *Thomas Hobbes: Radical in the Service of Reaction.* But the most interesting source to read on the subject remains Aubrey (1898).

Of the work done on Hobbes since 1967, most has been concerned with his moral and political philosophy. Other aspects of his work have not been completely ignored: Maurice Goldsmith's *Hobbes's Science of Politics* (1966) encouraged concern with Hobbes's ideas of science and scientific method, and J. W. N. Watkins's *Hobbes's System of Ideas* argued that Hobbes's argument was intended to move smoothly all the way from his philosophical ideas to his political theory. Thomas Spragens's *The Politics of Motion* concerned itself with the relationship between Hobbes's ideas about cosmology and his ideas about politics. Similar issues have been of interest to Richard Tuck in some of his papers. Very few publications dealt with Hobbes's views on scientific matters just for their own sake, though a notable exception was Shapin and Schaffer's *Leviathan and the Air Pump,* an account of the dispute between Hobbes and BOYLE [1] about the value of the experimental method.

The most influential book on Hobbes since 1967 has probably been David Gauthier's *The Logic of Leviathan* (1969). This book led the reaction to Warrender's interpretation of Hobbes, which was until then the most generally accepted interpretation. Gauthier introduced into discussion of Hobbes's moral theory the use of game theory, starting from the idea that "Hobbes takes seriously . . . the supposition that . . . all men are naturally selfish" (p. 90); then, working from the further claim that, on Hobbes's account, "both rights and obligations must have a prudential foundation" (p. 93), Gauthier constructed a Hobbesian argument that rational people must set up a sovereign if they are to achieve their own advantage and concludes that the Hobbesian "moral" system is nothing more than universal prudence (p. 98). Despite the work of Bernard Gert (in, for example, "Hobbes and Psychological Egosim," 1967) designed to show that Hobbes did not, in fact, regard people as naturally selfish, this general approach to Hobbes achieved great popularity and for some time was the received approach. Jean Hampton employed the games-theoretical approach to interpreting Hobbes in its finest detail in *Hobbes and the Social Contract Tradition* (1986). She did purport to be interpreting Hobbes, making the undefended claim that there is nothing anachronistic in using modern games theory to elucidate Hobbes and going on to say that "Euclid would feel himself vindicated rather than violated if his faulty proofs were corrected so that his conclusions could be derived from his axioms, and Hobbes would feel the same" (p. 137). But better arguments are not the same as the arguments they are better than; in fact, the games-theoretic versions of Hobbes's arguments cannot be what Hobbes actually intended.

Many people writing of Hobbes in the games-theoretic school do not claim to be arguing for an interpretation of Hobbes's text but simply use Hobbes as a starting point. This is true, for example, of Gregory Kavka's *Hobbesian Moral and Political Theory*, a very popular member of the games-theoretic set that makes the point explicit at the start. This is also true of many of the attempts to sort out a Hobbesian model for the study of international affairs, a move that has shared with the games-theoretic approach the assumption that the strong form of Hobbes's condition of mere nature is at least a coherent notion and can therefore constitute part of such a model.

Arguments against the prevailing games-theoretic interpretations of Hobbes came from Deborah Baumgold in *Hobbes's Political Theory* and R. E. Ewin in *Virtues and Rights* (1991), the latter arguing that the condition of mere nature is not a coherent notion and was intended by Hobbes as part of a *reductio* argument. Gert's work began a trend away from reading Hobbes as a psychological egoist (1967).

Work has been done, by Richard Tuck and others, on the historical Hobbes, most of it started off by Keith Thomas's "The Social Origins of Hobbes's Political Thought" and such writings of Quentin Skinner as "The Context of Hobbes's Theory of Political Obligation" (1966). More such work would be welcome. It has become common to distinguish between the "philosophers' Hobbes"—the Hobbes who saw himself as setting up a science of morality and of politics and as making a large part of his contribution to the debates by doing so—and "the historians' Hobbes"—the Hobbes who quite clearly saw himself as making a contribution to the debates about practical affairs of his time. Debates in the field of Hobbes scholarship will move further forward as these two strands come closer together again.

Bibliography

Aubrey, J. *Brief Lives,* edited by E. O. Dick. London, 1950.

Chappell, V., ed. *Essays on Early Modern Philosophers: Thomas Hobbes.* New York, 1992.

Curley, E. "Reflections on Hobbes: Recent Work on His Moral and Political Philosophy," *Journal of Philosophical Research,* Vol. 15 (1990), 169–250.

Ewin, R. E. *Virtues and Rights: The Moral Philosophy of Thomas Hobbes.* Boulder, CO, 1991.

Gauthier, D. *The Logic of Leviathan.* Oxford, 1969.

Gert, B. "Hobbes and Psychological Egoism," *Journal of the History of Ideas,* Vol. 27 (1967), 503–20.

Goldsmith, M. M. *Hobbes's Science of Politics.* London, 1966.

Hampton, J. *Hobbes and the Social Contract Tradition.* Cambridge, 1986.

Skinner, Q. "The Context of Hobbes's Theory of Political Obligation," *Historical Journal,* Vol. 9 (1966), 286–317.

Zagorin, P. "Hobbes on Our Mind," *Journal of the History of Ideas,* Vol. 51, No. 2 (1990), 317–35.

ROBERT E. EWIN

HUME, DAVID (1711–1776), has traditionally been viewed, in EPISTEMOLOGY [S] and ethics alike, as the exponent of a radical, destructive SKEPTICISM [7; S] that results when the empiricist premises of LOCKE [4; S] and BERKELEY [1; S] are pursued to their remotest consequences. Though this remains the view of the generality of philosophers, there is a growing consensus among specialists in HUME'S [4] thought that, far from being an innovator in the subjectivist theory of ideas, he merely exploited the skeptical arguments of his predecessors to clear the ground for a moderate, realist NATURALISM [5].

The subordination of skepticism to naturalism stems from the work of Norman Kemp Smith in the early twentieth century, and he remains the outstanding proponent of this view. He distinguished two components in Hume's naturalism: (1) the thesis that our beliefs and actions are founded not on reason but on sentiments rooted in human nature; and (2) the attempt to explain these beliefs and actions causally by means of quasi-mechanical associative propensities. Some commentators give pride of place to the second component, principally because it was in the course of elaborating and defending his explanations that Hume begat the notions that have influenced subsequent philosophy (Beauchamp & Rosenberg; Fogelin; Stroud; Wright). However, most historically focused naturalist interpretation emphasizes the first component, particularly in the guise of a "philosophy of common life" (Baier; Capaldi; Livingston). The central idea is that Hume's entire corpus, from the *Treatise* to the *Essays* and *History of England,* is set within the framework of historically grounded, continuously evolving social institutions and public language. Even Hume's talk of 'perceptions' and 'association of ideas' should be referred not to a solipsistically isolated, individual consciousness—a bundle of perceptions that is neither mind nor body—but to our ordinary, everyday selves. The theme of common life thus bestows a unity, a grand design, on the whole of Hume's intellectual achievement.

EPISTEMOLOGY

Psychology. Though the rise of the naturalist view has discouraged interpreters from examining in detail Hume's claims to be an innovator in the subjectivist theory of ideas, there are some exceptions. First, Hume's relation to Husserlian PHENOMENOLOGY [6; S] has been the object of considerable attention (Murphy), as has his relation to INTENTIONALITY [4; S] theory (Livingston). Second, the increasing tendency to regard Hume as a metaphysical realist (see examples below) has focused attention on relative ideas (relations with an imperceptible term) and inconceivable suppositions (realities posited in the absence of any impression or idea). Third, since Kemp Smith's case for naturalism is predicated on peculiar construals of such key notions of Hume's philosophy as vivacity, relation, and association, antinaturalist interpreters have offered alternatives and, in the process, illuminated Hume's accounts of sense certainty, memory, time consciousness, and aspect seeing (Waxman).

Induction, Causation, and Philosophy of Science. Hume's skepticism about INDUCTION [4] is a subject of considerable controversy, with some interpreters treating it as a restricted critique of a narrowly philosophical, Cartesian view of empirical rationality, while others relate it to a broader, more ordinary notion of probable reasoning. Either way, naturalist interpreters treat Hume's skepticism as epistemic rather than ontological or conceptual and tend to combine it with ontological realism about both CAUSATION [2; S] and bodies (Beauchamp & Rosenberg; Stroud); some contend that he was a realist about necessary connections as well as regularities and so classify him among Cartesian rationalists (Strawson; Wright). Methodologically, much attention has been paid to how the normative principles of science Hume derived from his naturalist account of causation (in *Treatise,* bk. 1, pt. 3, sec. 15) are self-consciously exemplified in his own philosophizing (Baier; Wilson).

Body and Mind. Hume's general account of identity in terms of fictions of imagination is generally regarded as the weakest point in his epistemology, though an exception tends to be made for his way of framing the problem of PERSONAL IDENTITY [6; S] and his critique of alternative accounts. The main focus of interpreters is whether Hume's subjectivist approach is compatible with belief in the ontological reality of bodies, minds, and substances and, if so, whether he adopted a commonsense ("vulgar") realism or a scientific ("double existence") REALISM [7; S]. Hume's assertion that "we may well ask, *What causes induce us to believe in the existence of body?* but 'tis in vain to ask, *Whether there be body or not?*" (*Treatise,* bk. 1, pt. 4, sec. 2) is widely taken to confirm that he accepted the mind-independent reality of the external world. Those belonging to the common-life school emphasize the continuum between vulgar and scientific belief, while dissenters attribute to Hume one or another form of indirect realism (skeptical in the case of Wright, scientific in that of Wilson). In general, naturalist interpreters suppose that Hume's account of personal identity, wittingly or not, premises the reality of the external world (Bricke, Pears) and perhaps human society and language as well (Baier; Livingston). The reverse, however, has also been maintained (Waxman) on the ground that there can be no standard for the externality and independence of objects other than relation to the mind (a corollary of Hume's espousal of Locke's account of temporal succession).

MORAL PHILOSOPHY

Hume's theory of the passions was long denigrated as evincing the worst features of the associationalist, "Newtonian" strand of his thought: blind mechanism substituted for contextualized understanding, theory riding roughshod over data, psychology smothering philosophy. Thanks to several fine historical and textual studies (Àrdal; Baier; Norton), a new appreciation of the subtlety and explanatory power of the theory has emerged and, with it, of how for Hume human nature is inherently a moral nature. For example, if we accept that Hume viewed moral reason as inherently social (Baier) and practical—a "we-do," not an "I-think," reason (Capaldi)—the traditional picture of him, as moral subjectivist and skeptic, becomes untenable (holdouts include Fogelin and, to a lesser extent, J. L. MACKIE [S]). Nor can it be taken for granted any longer that Hume's antirationalist sentimentalism is incompatible with moral realism or moral cognitivism (Norton).

SCHOLARSHIP

Under the ægis of the Hume Society and its journal, *Hume Studies* (1975–), Hume scholarship has burgeoned. Long-neglected aspects of his thought—religion, aesthetics, politics, philosophy of history—have begun to receive the scholarly attention they require and deserve. A new critical edition of Hume's philosophical, political, and literary writings under the editorship of Tom L. Beauchamp, David Fate Norton, and M. A. Stewart is planned by Oxford Clarendon Press and should further promote this process.

Bibliography

Àrdal, P. S. *Passion and Value in Hume's "Treatise."* Edinburgh, 1966. A detailed textual analysis of Hume's theory of the passions.

Baier, A. *A Progress of Sentiments.* Cambridge, MA, 1991. An authoritative, highly persuasive vision of the *Treatise* as reason's onerous progress toward self-comprehension, which it finds in society.

Beauchamp, T. L., and A. Rosenberg. *Hume and the Problem of Causation.* New York, 1981. An attempt to defend Hume's views on induction and causation against contemporary views.

Bricke, J. *Hume's Philosophy of Mind.* Edinburgh, 1980.

Capaldi, N. *Hume's Place in Moral Philosophy.* New York, 1989. Maintains that Hume wrought a Copernican revolution in philosophy by substituting a "we-do" orientation for the "I-think" of his predecessors. Contains an extended, if jaundiced, survey of Hume scholarship.

Chuo University. *David Hume and the Eighteenth Century British Thought: An Annotated Catalogue,* edited by S. Ikeda. Tokyo, 1986, 1988.

Fogelin, R. *Hume's Skepticism in the "Treatise of Human Nature."* London, 1985. Aspires to restore Hume's skepticism to a status equal, and complementary, to his naturalism, both in epistemology and in morals.

Gaskin, J. C. *Hume's Philosophy of Religion,* 2d ed. New York, 1988.

Hall, R. *50 Years of Hume Scholarship.* Edinburgh, 1978.

Harrison, J. *Hume's Moral Epistemology.* Oxford, 1976.

Levine, M. *Hume and the Problem of Miracles: A Solution.* Dordrecht, 1989.

Livingston, D. W. *Hume's Philosophy of Common Life.* Chicago, 1984. Maintains that Hume adopted the approach of the social historian even in epistemology.

Mackie, J. L. *Hume's Moral Theory.* London, 1980. A projectivist reading of Hume's sentimentalism, with a keen analysis of his account of virtue.

Murphy, R. *Hume and Husserl: Towards Radical Subjectivism.* Boston, 1980.

Norton, D. *David Hume: Common-Sense Moralist, Sceptical Metaphysician.* Princeton, 1984. Contains an excellent account of Hutcheson and examines other influences on Hume.

———, ed. *The Cambridge Companion to Hume.* Cambridge, 1993. Contains an excellent bibliography.

Pears, D. *Hume's System.* Oxford, 1990. Attempts to balance Hume's empiricism and naturalism by correlating the first to a theory of meaning and the second to a theory of truth.

Snare, F. *Morals Motivation and Convention: Hume's Influential Doctrines.* Cambridge, 1991.

Stove, D. C. *Probability and Hume's Inductive Scepticism.* Oxford, 1973.

Strawson, G. *The Secret Connexion: Causation, Realism, and David Hume.* Oxford, 1989.

Stroud, B. *Hume.* London, 1977. Presents Hume as advancing a theory of human nature in which the traditional conception of man as rational animal is overturned.

Waxman, W. *Hume's Theory of Consciousness.* Cambridge, 1994. A critique of the premises of the naturalist interpretation and a defense of the traditional view of Hume as a more extreme subjectivist, skeptical successor to Locke and Berkeley.

Whelan, F. G. *Order and Artifice in Hume's Political Philosophy.* Princeton, 1985.

Wilson, F. *Laws and Other Worlds.* Dordrecht, 1986.

Wright, J. *The Skeptical Realism of David Hume.* Manchester, 1983. Presents Hume as an epistemological skeptic but ontological realist about bodies and causes.

WAYNE WAXMAN

HUSSERL, EDMUND. Between 1970 and 1995 several of HUSSERL's [4] major works (including, most prominently, *Logische Untersuchungen, Krisis der europäischen Wissenschaften und die transzendentale Phänomenologie, Formale und transzendentale Logik, Phänomenologische Psychologie,* and *Ideen II*) were translated into English. Twenty additional volumes in the *Husserliana* series appeared, some making important works easily available again (such as Husserl's early writings on mathematics and formal logic), others making available for the first time Husserl's lectures and research manuscripts on intersubjectivity, ethics, the constitution of spatiality, and imagination and memory. Moreover, the scholarly reception of two volumes published shortly before 1970, one on passive synthesis and the other a critical edition of Husserl's lectures on time-consciousness, have strongly influenced the way that scholars view Husserl's work. These developments have not led to a whole-scale revision of the general view of Husserl's PHENOMENOLOGY [6; S] that had been based primarily upon the *Cartesianische Meditationen* and the *Ideen I.* Scholars continue to agree that for Husserl intentionality is the fundamental structure of consciousness (*see* INTENTIONALITY IN HUSSERL [S]), that the objects of human cognition are intentional objects, and hence that the analysis of consciousness and its correlative objects is the proper starting point for philosophy. The method of phenomenological reduction retains its central position in discussions of Husserlian phenomenology. The publications and translations between 1970 and 1995 have nonetheless influenced the discussion significantly.

First of all, they have allowed readers to come to a better understanding of the internal motives for the development of Husserl's thinking. Previously, it was common to attribute many of the changes in Husserl's positions between major works to outside influences. Shifts in Husserl's thinking between the *Philosophie der Arithmetik* and the *Logische Untersuchungen* were attributed to a critical review of the former work by FREGE [3; S], and the emphasis upon the lifeworld (*see* LIFE-WORLD IN HUSSERL [S]) in the *Krisis* was widely viewed as a response to HEIDEGGER'S [3; S] *Sein und Zeit.* The edition of Husserl's early essays on logic and the foundation of mathematics in *Aufsätze und Rezensionen (1890–1910),* however, establishes that Husserl himself had become dissatisfied with many of his earlier formulations and adopted positions similar to those of the *Logische Untersuchungen* before Frege's review was composed. Similarly, closer attention to Husserl's analyses of the personalistic world in *Ideen II* and to other manuscripts such as the lectures on passive synthesis and those published in *Erfahrung und Urteil* show that his analyses of the lifeworld emanate from phenomenological research conducted prior to the appearance of Heidegger's major work. At the same time, however, the publication of a critical edition of the *Sechste cartesianische Meditation* and of the intersubjectivity lectures demonstrate the collaborative aspects of Husserl's relationship to his assistants Eugen Fink and Edith Stein and their influence on his work. The publication of Husserl's correspondence also makes it possible to situate Husserl much better against the backdrop of his age and his intellectual and cultural milieu.

Second, these publications demonstrate that Husserl's painstaking phenomenological analyses extended to a much wider range of areas than logic and the theory of perception and thereby shifted much of the discussion from questions of methodology to specific topics. The focus of *Ideen I* and *Cartesianische Meditationen* is the proper methodology for phenomenology. For many years *Ideas I* was the only major work by Husserl available in English. It was joined by *Meditations* and two shorter works, *The Idea of Phenomenology* and "Philosophy as a Rigorous Science," both programmatic pieces, during the early 1960s. Thus, it was natural for questions of phenomenological method to dominate the discussion, especially since much of what Husserl himself published during his lifetime dealt more with the general outlines of the program of phenomenology than with concrete phenomenological analyses of specific domains. (Of course, in works that were long available in German, one finds concrete phenomenological analyses, but these are limited primarily to the foundations of logic, mathematics, and the natural sciences.) The *Husserliana* volumes completed since 1966 have not only provided much more detailed discussions of Husserl's analyses of perception and his work on the foundations of mathematics and logic, but have also made accessible for the first time extended discussions of intersubjectivity, the foundations of the human sciences, ethics, and religion. Phenomenology turns out to be more than just a method. It also involves the project of exploring the structures of an extremely wide range of regions and the foundational relationships that govern them. It also becomes apparent that the ultimate object of analysis is concrete human life as a culturally situated, practically involved, historical interaction with cultural objects, persons, and institutions—along with unique abstractive cultural formations such as modern natural science, logic, and mathematics. Husserl shows how such complex formations are constituted first on the basis of simpler operations beginning with the simplest acts of sense perceptions on the part of individuals, up through the formation of theoretical judgments, and how these are conjoined with acts of willing and valuing, to form practical and evaluative judgments. Moreover, after tracing out the simple elements involved in the constitution of intersubjectivity, all of this takes place within an intersubjective, cultural, and historical environment. Finally, Husserl tries to show how all of these developments are guided by the norm of rationality, of intentions and anticipations that each in its own way claims to have some basis in experience and may be justified or refuted through recourse to the simple or complex experiences that they implicitly aim at. Husserl tries to show how the guiding concept of evidence is not limited to the scientific or philosophical realm but is rather the expression of a fundamental structure of conscious life that ultimately issues in the norms of autonomy and self-responsibility that are exemplified explicitly in truly philosophical existence but also serve as the implicit norm for all human existence.

Finally, the new publications have made scholars careful about identifying Husserl's phenomenology with the Cartesian project of finding an absolute foundation for knowledge in truths that are eternal, completely certain, and irrefutable through reflection of a conscious ego that is completely and immediately self-transparent. The very confident and final tone of Husserl's early pronouncements concerning the possibility of constructing transcendental phenomenology as a science that can achieve results once and for all with absolute certainty has been called into question. Already in *Formale und transzendentale Logik,* Husserl points out that evidence with regard to ideal objects (which includes meanings or senses, the primary objects of phenomenological analysis) is not apodictic in the sense of being beyond doubt. Scholars have come to see that Husserl also recognized the important role of passive, prepredicative elements in valuing and knowing that are not easily and directly accessible to subjective reflection. Analysis of kinaesthesis in *Phänomenologische Psychologie, Ideen II,* and *Analysen zur passiven Synthesis* make clear that the subject of knowledge is not just a pure consciousness but an embodied agent. Much of the impetus for the reevaluation of Husserl has also come as a response to challenges from Emanuel LEVINAS [S], Maurice MERLEAU-PONTY [5; S], and Jacques DERRIDA [S], who have joined the previously well-known Martin Heidegger in claiming to be followers of Husserl in phenomenology while rejecting what each identifies as inappropriate Cartesian elements in Husserl's phenomenology. These figures have exhibited new directions in which Husserl's phenomenological project may be taken and have also prompted Husserl's defenders to emphasize those insights that anticipate many of his successors' positions and to reinterpret Husserl's work as a whole in a way that makes him less open to the charges of Cartesianism. (SEE ALSO: *Consciousness in Phenomenology: Husserl; Constitution in Husserl; Experience and Judgment; Intersubjectivity in Husserl; Intuitionism in Formal Science in Husserl; Passive Synthesis and Association; Phenomenological Psychology; Psychology and Logic; Space; Subjectivity in Husserl; Time Consciousness; Transcendental Logic* [S])

Bibliography

WORKS BY HUSSERL

Logische Untersuchungen. Husserliana, Vols. 18–19. The Hague, 1984. Translated by J. N. Findlay as *Logical Investigations.* New York, 1970.

Cartesianische Meditationen. Husserliana, Vol. 1. The Hague, 1950. Translated by D. Cairns as *Cartesian Meditations.* The Hague, 1960.

Ideen zu einer reinen Phänomenologie und phänomenologischen Philosophie: Erstes Buch (Ideen I). Husserliana, Vol. 3. The Hague, 1950. Translated by F. Kersten as *Ideas Pertaining to a Pure Phenomenology and to a Phenomenological Philosophy.* The Hague, 1982. The first translation by R. Gibson was available after 1931 and had a decisive influence on the understanding of Husserl.

Die Krisis der europäischen Wissenschaften und die transzendentale Phänomenologie. Husserliana, Vol. 6. The Hague, 1954. Translated by D. Carr as *The Crisis of European Sciences and Transcendental Phenomenology.* Evanston, IL, 1970. Husserl's extensive discussion of the lifeworld makes clear that the concrete world of pretheoretical experience is the basis for the abstract spheres that had often been taken as fundamental for Husserl.

Ideen zu einer reinen Phänomenologie und phänomenologischen Philosophie: Zweites Buch (Ideen II). Husserliana, Vol. 4. The Hague, 1952. Translated by A. Schuwer and R. Rojcewicz as *Ideas Pertaining to a Pure Phenomenology and Phenomenological Philosophy: Book Two.* Dordrecht, 1989.

Phänomenologischen Psychologie. Husserliana, Vol. 9. The Hague, 1962. Translated by J. Scanlon as *Phenomenological Psychology.* The Hague, 1977.

Zur Phänomenologie des inneren Zeitbewußtseins (1893/1917). Husserliana, Vol. 10. The Hague, 1966. Translated by J. Brough as *Concerning the Phenomenology of Inner Time Consciousness.* Dordrecht, 1991. Previous translation by J. Churchill in 1964. The new translation makes available supplementary texts from the critical edition in German that illuminate the history of the development of Husserl's thinking on the issue.

Analysen zur Passiven Synthesis. Husserliana, Vol. 11. The Hague, 1966. The most extended treatments (along with *Erfahrung und Urteil*) of the genesis of predicative thinking out of the realm of prepredicative experience.

Philosophie der Arithmetik: Mit ergänzenden Texten (1890–1901). Husserliana, Vol. 12. The Hague, 1970.

Zur Phänomenologie der Intersubjektivität. Husserliana, Vols. 13–15. Extensive excerpts from lectures and research manuscripts make available for the first time detailed analyses of Husserl's thinking on intersubjectivity. Prefaces by the editor, I. Kern, are especially helpful.

Formale und transzendentale Logik. Husserliana, Vol. 17. The Hague, 1974. Translated by D. Cairns as *Formal and Transcendental Logic.* Evanston, IL, 1969.

Aufsätze und Renzensionen (1890–1910). Husserliana, Vol. 22. The Hague, 1979. Husserl essays and reviews during this period concerned primarily logic and the foundation of mathematics. Makes available once again several important documents that make clear how Husserl's views in these areas evolved.

Phantasie, Bildbewuβtsein, Erinnerung: Zur Phänomenologie der anschaulichen Vergegenwärtigungen. Husserliana, Vol. 23.

Vorlesungen über Ethik und Wertlehre, 1908–1914. Husserliana, Vol. 18. First publication of lectures on the theory of values and the principles of rational practical choice.

Aufsätze und Vortrage (1922–37). Husserliana, Vol. 27. Dordrecht, 1989. The "Kaizo articles" locate Husserl's phenomenological philosophy within a broader project of cultural and ethical renewal and bring out clearly the ethical dimension of the notion of evidence.

Erfahrung und Urteil. Meiner, 1985. Translated by J. Churchill and K. Ameriks as *Experience and Judgment.* Evanston, IL, 1973.

"Philosophie als strenge Wissenschaft," in *Husserliana,* Vol. 25 (Dordrecht, 1987). Translated by Q. Lauer as "Philosophy as a Rigorous Science," in E. Husserl, *Phenomenology and the Crisis of Philosophy* (New York, 1965).

WORKS ON HUSSERL

Bernet, R., I. Kern, and E. Marbach. *An Introduction to Edmund Husserl's Phenomenology.* Evanston, IL, 1993. A good overview of the development of Husserl's thinking in terms of his attempts to come to grips with central issues that emerge in his early work.

Derrida, J. *Introduction à "L'Origine de la géométrie" de Husserl.* Paris, 1962. Translated by J. Leavey as *Edmund Husserl's Origin of Geometry: An Introduction.* Stony Brook, NY, 1978.

———. *La Voix et le phénomène.* Paris, 1967. Translated by D. Allison as *Speech and Phenomena.* Bloomington, IN, 1973.

Elliston, F., and P. McCormick, eds. *Husserl: Expositions and Appraisals.* Notre Dame, IN, 1977. Assembles classic essays on controversial questions concerning Husserl's phenomenology.

Heidegger, M. *Sein und Zeit.* Tübingen, 1972. Translated by J. Macquarrie and E. Robinson as *Being and Time.* San Francisco, 1972.

Levinas, E. *Totalité et infini.* The Hague, 1961. Translated by A. Lingis as *Totality and Infinity.* Pittsburgh, 1969.

Merleau-Ponty, M. *Phénoménologie de la perception.* Paris, 1946. Translated by C. Smith as *Phenomenology of Perception.* London, 1962.

Mohanty, J. N., and W. McKenna, eds. *Husserl's Phenomenology: A Textbook.* Lanham, MD, 1989. Helpful introductory essays.

Sepp, H. R. *Edmund Husserl und die phänomenologische Bewegung.* Freiburg, 1988. Documents in texts and photographs Husserl's life, intellectual development, and influences.

THOMAS NENON

HYPATIA, A.D. 370/75–415, was a philosopher, mathematician, and astronomer who, though female and pagan, achieved the honor of being named by the Christian Roman government to the position of philosopher at the museum of Alexandria. Students reading philosophy at the ALEXANDRIAN SCHOOL [1] would also study mathematics and astronomy as technical, applied disciplines of the more traditional studies of METAPHYSICS [S] and COSMOLOGY [2]. Hypatia's father, Theon of Alexandria, was the museum's most famous mathematician-astronomer, and it is largely through Theon that we have a reliable source of Ptolemy's *Syntaxis Mathematica (Almagest).* Hypatia likely assumed the directorship of the school of philosophy circa 400. The recently converted Christian, Synesius of Cyrene, later the Bishop of Ptolemais, became her student in 393. From Synesius's works we surmise that Hypatia's early philosophical teachings concentrated on Plato's metaphysical works, especially the *Timeaus.* Her later mathematical and astronomical writings can be understood primarily as applications of Neoplatonist metaphysical and cosmological theories (*see* NEOPLATIONISM [5]). Hypatia was an eclectic philosopher with a Cynic's literary and personal style that may have had as much to do with her risky status as both woman and pagan as with her philosophical affiliation. Accounts of outrageous tactics to counter sexist male student behavior may be apocryphal (Lewis, 1921; Toland, 1720). Nevertheless they provide insight into the personality of a defensive female professor in a brutally misogynist environment. A traditional middle platonist, Hypatia was sympathetic to Porphyryian metaphysics and to stoicism. In 415, she was savagely dismembered by a gang of monks. She appears to have been succeeded by Hierocles.

Bibliography

Bregman, J. *Synesius of Cyrene: Philosopher-Bishop.* Berkeley, 1982.

Evrard, E. "A Quel titre Hypatie enseigna-t-elle la philosophie?" *Revue des études grecques,* Vol. 90 (1977), 69–74.

Halma, N. B. *Theon et Hypatie, Commentaires de Theon d'Alexandrie sur le troisième livre de l'almageste de Ptolemee.* Paris, 1820.

———. *Almageste de Ptolémée, Commentaires de Théon D'Alexandrie sur le premier livre de la composition mathématique de Ptolémée.* Paris, 1821.

Heath, T. *A History of Greek Mathematics.* Oxford, 1921.

———. *Greek Astronomy.* Oxford, 1932.

———. *Diophantus of Alexandria.* New York, 1960.

Index Bibliothecae Medicae. Florence, 1882.

Knorr, W. *Textual Studies in Ancient and Medieval Geometry.* Boston, 1989.

Lampropoulou, S. "Hypatia philosophe Alexandrine," *Athenai, Bibliopholeion.* Athens, 1977.

Lewis, T. *The History of Hypatia, a Most Impudent Schoolmistress of Alexandria. . . .* London, 1921.

Ligier, H. *De Hypatia philosophà et eclectismi alexandrini fine.* 1879.

Meyer, W. A. *Hypatia von Alexandria.* Heidelberg, 1886.

Montulca, J. F. *Histoire des mathématiques.* Paris, 1960.

Rome, A. "Le Troisième livre des commentaires sur l'almageste par Théon et Hypatie," *Annales de la société scientifique de Bruxelles,* Vol. 46 (1926), 1–14.

———. "Observations d'équinoxes et de solstices dans le chapitre 1 du livre 3 du commentaire sur l'almageste par Théon d'Alexandrie," *Annales de la société scientifique de Bruxelles,* Vol. 57 (1937), 213–36 (première partie); Vol. 58 (1938), 6–26 (second partie).

———. *Commentaires de Pappus et de Théon d'Alexandrie sur l'almageste, tome III, Théon d'Alexandrie commentaire sur les livres 3 et 4 de l'almageste.* Studi e testi 106. Vatican City, 1943.

Suidae [*sic*] S. *Lexicon.* Stuttgart, 1967–71.

Tannery, P. *Diophanti Alexandrini Opera Omnia.* 2 vols. Lipsiae, 1893–95.

———. "L'Article de Suidas sur Hypatia," *Annales de la faculté des lettres de Bordeaux.* Bordeaux, 1880.

———. *Mémoires scientifiques.* Toulouse, 1912.

Toland, J. *Hypatia, or the History . . .* in *Tetradymus.* London, 1720.

Usener, H. "Fasti Theonis Alexandrini," in T. Mommsen, ed., *Chronica Minora Sasc. IV. V, VI, VII.* (Berlin, 1898).

Waithe, M. E. "Hypatia of Alexandria," in *A History of Women Philosophers,* Vol. 1, *Ancient Women Philosophers 60 BC–500 AD* (Dordrecht, 1987).

MARY ELLEN WAITHE

I

IDENTITY. The word 'is' is multiply ambiguous. When it can be expanded to read 'is the same thing as', or 'is identical with', or (in numerical contexts) 'is equal to', it expresses the relation of identity. The simplest identity statements contain the 'is' of identity flanked by singular terms, either names or definite descriptions: 'Samuel Clemens is Mark Twain'; 'The U.S. president in 1996 is Bill Clinton'; 'Four is the sum of two and two'. A more complex identity statement might, for example, combine the 'is' of identity with quantifiers: 'Every even number is the sum of two primes'.

IDENTITY [4], on its face, is simple and unproblematic: it is that relation that everything bears to itself and to nothing else. Yet discussions of identity in contemporary philosophical logic and metaphysics are brimming with controversy. From where does this controversy arise? Some of it is not genuine, being based on confusion; and some of it, though genuine, is not genuinely about identity. However, a residue of controversy survives, owing to the view, perpetrated by Peter Geach, that identity statements are meaningless unless relativized, that there is no absolute relation of identity.

SOURCES OF CONFUSION

One source of confusion is the ambiguity of 'identical' in English. We do sometimes say that two things are identical, as when we speak of identical twins, or say that some coat is identical with some other. This is qualitative identity: things are qualitatively identical if they resemble one another sufficiently in relevant qualitative respects. Numerical identity is different: two things, no matter how closely they resemble one another, are never numerically identical. Numerical identity is the topic of this article.

A second source of confusion is English grammar, which allows, for example, 'Clemens is identical with Twain' to be rewritten equivalently as 'Clemens and Twain are identical' or as 'they are identical'. But then it seems that two persons (or two *somethings*) are being said to be identical, which is absurd. A general response is familiar from other cases: surface grammar often misrepresents the underlying logic: one must beware inferring logical from grammatical form. More specifically, it can be verified that plural noun phrases in English do not, in all contexts, entail or presuppose reference to a plurality.

A third source of confusion is FREGE's [3; S] puzzle of informative identity statements, sometimes introduced by the following argument. To say of something that it is identical with itself is trivial, to say of something that it is identical with something else is false; therefore, identity statements are all either trivial or false, and there can be no point in asserting them. This conclusion is manifestly incorrect: identity statements are often both true and informative, as witness, 'the capital of Honduras is Tegucigalpa'. The puzzle is to say where the argument goes wrong.

One response rejects the second premise by taking identity to be a relation between names or descriptions rather than between the objects named or described: identity is then the relation of co-designation, the relation that holds between singular terms whenever those terms designate the same object. That would indeed allow identity statements to be both true and informative. But the response is not viable, for many reasons. For one, it fails to account for uses of identity that do not involve singular terms, such as: 'Everything is identical with itself'. For another, it fails to allow identity statements between different singular terms to be uninformative, as they are when the singular terms are synonymous. For another, it fails to provide a unified solution to analogous puzzles of informativeness, such as how 'the capital of Honduras is in Honduras' and 'Tegucigalpa is in Honduras' can differ in informativeness, even though both ascribe the same property to the same thing.

A better response is due to Frege. Identity is a relation between objects; a simple identity statement is true just in case the objects referred to by the singular terms stand in that relation. But singular terms have sense in addition to reference; a true identity statement is informative just in case its singular terms differ in sense. (Just what is included in the sense of a singular term varies from theory to theory; but note that senses must be rich enough to allow co-designative proper names—such as 'Mark Twain' and 'Samuel Clemens'—to differ in sense.) Now the puzzle may be solved by rejecting the argument's first premise: one can say informatively of an object that it is identical with itself by referring to the object twice over, using singular terms that differ in sense. That is how 'The capital of Honduras is Tegucigalpa' manages to be both true and informative. Identity statements are useful in ordinary language because we often refer to the same object from different points of view, using terms with different senses. (Frege's statement of the puzzle, and his solution, is in Frege, 1892; see also KRIPKE [S], 1980; Salmon, 1986.)

THE LOGIC OF IDENTITY: LEIBNIZ'S LAW

Relations may be classified according to their general, logical characteristics. The logical characteristics of the identity relation are easily enumerated. First, as already noted, identity is reflexive: every object is identical with itself. Second, identity is symmetric: if an object x is identical with an object y, then y is identical with x. Third, identity is transitive: if an object x is identical with an object y, and y is identical with an object z, then x is identical with z. A relation that is reflexive, symmetric, and transitive is called an equivalence relation. Finally, identity is the strongest equivalence relation, entailing all other equivalence relations: if an object x is identical with an object y, then x bears R to y, for every equivalence relation R. Since being the strongest equivalence relation (or, equivalently, being the strongest reflexive relation) uniquely characterizes identity in purely logical terms, identity may properly be classified as a logical relation and the theory of identity as a branch of logic.

All of the logical characteristics of identity can be derived from a single principle, sometimes called LEIBNIZ'S [4; S] law: An object x is identical with an object y if and only if every property of x is a property of y and vice versa. Leibniz's law is a biconditional and thus the conjunction of two conditionals, one giving a necessary, the other a sufficient, condition for identity to hold. Say that an object x is indiscernible from an object y just in case every property of x is a property of y and vice versa. The half of Leibniz's law that gives a necessary condition proclaims the indiscernibility of identicals: if x is identical with y, then x is indiscernible from y. This principle is useful for establishing nonidentity: to show that x is not identical with y, it suffices to find a property had by x but not by y or vice versa. Most famously, perhaps, the principle has been used to argue that persons are not identical with their bodies. The half of Leibniz's law that gives a sufficient condition proclaims the identity of indiscernibles: if x is indiscernible from y, then x is identical with y (more on this below).

(Note that Leibniz's law is stated within second-order logic: it involves quantification over properties. The first-order theory of identity substitutes for Leibniz's law an axiom schema containing, for each [monadic] predicate of the language, an axiom stating: if x is identical with y, then x satisfies the predicate if and only if y satisfies the predicate. This schema, together with an axiom of reflexivity, entails the entire first-order theory of identity. The first-order theory is weaker than the full second-order theory; in particular, no logically sufficient condition for identity is expressible within first-order logic.)

The indiscernibility of identicals is beyond dispute: if x and y are identical, then there is only one thing; how can that one thing both have and not have some property? Nonetheless, the principle has been disputed. Consider the following attempt at a counterexample (discussed in QUINE [7; S], 1953). It is true that Giorgione was so called because of his size, let us suppose, and that Giorgione is identical with Barbarelli; yet, apparently contrary to the principle, it is not true that Barbarelli was so called because of his size. But to see this as a violation of the indiscernibility of identicals, one would have to hold that the predicate 'is so called because of his size' expresses some genuine property of objects and expresses the same property when applied to 'Giorgione' as when applied to 'Barbarelli'. On the contrary, when considered in isolation the predicate expresses no property at all but rather a relation between objects and names. When applied to 'Giorgione' it expresses the property was-called-Giorgione-because-of-his-size; and that property is true of Barbarelli, in accord with the indiscernibility of identicals. Other attempts at counterexamples are more subtle than this; but all seem to involve naively reading subject-predicate sentences as simple property-to-object attributions. (For examples involving modality see Cartwright, 1971; Quine, 1953).

IDENTITY OF INDISCERNIBLES

The other half of Leibniz's law proclaims the identity of indiscernibles; but now one must be careful just what 'indiscernible' means. If indiscernibles have *all* of their properties in common, where properties are conceived abundantly, then the identity of indiscernibles is trivially true. For, on an abundant conception of property, for any object y there is the property is-identical-with-y. Now suppose that x is indiscernible from y. Then, since y has the property is-identical-with-y, x must have this property too; that is, x is identical with y, as was to be shown. (On abundant vs. sparse conceptions of properties, *see* PROPERTIES [S].)

If we interpret 'indiscernible' instead in terms of properties more sparsely conceived, for example, as 'indiscernible in all qualitative respects', then we arrive at a substantial metaphysical principle, the identity of qualitative indiscernibles; the trivial "proof" above is blocked because properties such as is-identical-with-a (where 'a' names some object) are not (or, at any rate, are not trivially) qualitative. There are different versions of the principle, however, corresponding to different interpretations of 'qualitatively indiscernible'; and for each version one might ask whether the principle is logically necessary, is contingently true, or neither. Let us consider three versions.

According to the strongest (and least plausible) version, objects that share all of their intrinsic qualitative properties—intrinsic duplicates—are identical. This principle seems to be false even at the actual world: according to current physics, distinct elementary particles of the same kind—for example, distinct electrons—have all of their intrinsic properties (charge, mass, etc.) in common.

According to the second (and most familiar) version, objects that share all of their intrinsic and extrinsic qualitative properties—absolute indiscernibles—are identical. Absolute indiscernibles must not only be intrinsic duplicates, they must be exactly similarly situated with respect to all of their surroundings. But, surely it is at least possible that there be distinct yet absolutely indiscernible objects; that is, the principle is not necessarily true. For, to take the standard counterexample (from Black, 1952), it is logically possible that the world contains nothing but two perfectly round globes, exactly similar down to their smallest parts and separated, say, by one meter. The globes share all of their intrinsic qualitative properties, having the same mass, shape, and so on. And the globes share all of their extrinsic qualitative properties—for example, each is one meter from a globe of a certain mass, shape, and so on. (Note that properties that would only be expressible using names for the globes, such as is-one-meter-from-globe$_1$, are not qualitative). In short, the globes are absolutely indiscernible; yet they are two, not one.

A defender of the identity of absolute indiscernibles might simply deny that there is any such possibility; but there is a substantial cost. The claim that it is logically possible that there be nothing but two absolutely indiscernible globes can be backed up by a subsidiary argument (Adams, 1979). Surely, there could be nothing but two almost indiscernible globes, differing, say, only in the placement of a single atom. To hold that that atom could not have been shifted in a certain way (because, if it had, there would have been two absolutely indiscernible globes), but that any other atom could have been shifted in that way, would amount to an implausibly inegalitarian approach to what is and is not possible.

Perhaps an even weaker version of the principle should be considered: objects that share all of their qualitative properties, and stand in the same qualitative relations to any given object—relative indiscernibles—are identical. (On absolute vs. relative indiscernibility, see Quine, 1960.) The possibility just considered of the two globes is not a counterexample to the necessity of this version: the globes are discerned by spatial relations; each globe is one meter from the other globe but not one meter from itself. A counterexample, however, is not far to seek. Consider the possibility that there be nothing but two absolutely indiscernible globes standing in no spatial relation (or other qualitative external relation) to one another, two absolutely indiscernible 'island universes'. (This possibility can be motivated, too, by first considering 'almost' island universes, connected, say, by a single 'wormhole'.) Such globes would be relatively, as well as absolutely, indiscernible; they stand in no relations that could serve to discern them. So even this weakest version of the identity of qualitative indiscernibles seems not to be a necessary truth. (Indeed, it may not be contingently true: so-called 'identical particles' in quantum mechanics are arguably distinct but absolutely and relatively indiscernible.)

IS IDENTITY DEFINABLE?

Identity has been characterized many times over. Do any of these characterizations provide a (noncircular) definition of the identity relation? Can identity be understood in terms not involving identity? Our initial characterization—that everything is identical with itself and with nothing else—clearly will not do as a definition: to be 'else' is to be other, that is, nonidentical. Moreover, the characterization of identity as the strongest equivalence relation fares no better: identity characterized by quantifying over all relations, identity included.

Leibniz's law gives a necessary and sufficient condition for identity by quantifying instead over properties. But among the quantified properties are haecceities, properties of being identical with some given object (*see* HAECCETISM [S]). The question whether an object x shares with an object y the property of being identical with y is just the question whether x is identical with y; the purported definition takes one around in a circle. Similarly defective is the oft-heard definition 'x is identical with y if and only if x and y belong to the same classes'. The question whether x, like y, belongs to the class whose only member is y is just the question whether x is identical with y.

What if some version of the identity of qualitative indiscernibles were necessarily true (contrary to what was argued above)? That would indeed provide a noncircular criterion for the identity of *objects*. But the identity or distinctness of qualitative properties (and relations) would remain undefined. Indeed, any purported definition of identity would have to quantify over some sort of entity; the definition could not be understood without a prior understanding of the identity and distinctness of the entities quantified over. We must conclude, then, that identity, at least as applied to the most basic entities, must be taken as primitive and unanalyzable; there is no fully general (noncircular) definition of identity.

Questions remain, some of which might seem to pose problems for the classical conception of identity. We shall see, however, that in each case replies exist that leave classical identity unscathed. (Each of the issues raised below is discussed in Lewis, 1993.)

PARTIAL IDENTITY

Classical identity is all or nothing; it never comes in degrees. Yet, when objects overlap, we may say they are 'partially identical, partially distinct'; and when objects extensively overlap, we may say they are 'almost identical'. Do we have here a challenge to classical identity? No, we have an ambiguity: identity, in the sense that admits of degrees, is simply overlap; identity, in the classical sense, is equivalent to the extreme case of total overlap. The two notions of identity are not in conflict; they fit together as well as you please.

VAGUE IDENTITY

Classical identity is determinate and admits of no borderline cases. That is not to say that identity statements cannot be vague or indeterminate in truth value (*see* VAGUENESS [8; S]). If I say 'that cloud in the sky is identical with A', where 'A' names some precisely specified aggregate of water molecules, what I say may be neither determinately true nor false. But such vagueness resides in the reference of singular terms—in this case, 'that cloud in the sky'—not in the identity relation itself.

Some philosophers, however, hold that there is vagueness, not only in our reference to objects, but in the objects themselves; not only in our language and thought, but in the world. Let us suppose, charitably, that such a view makes sense. Might not these vague objects be vaguely identical? That depends. If vague identity is understood so that vaguely identical objects are neither determinately identical nor determinately not identical, then the answer is no, as the following argument shows. (Versions are in Evans, 1978; Salmon, 1981). Suppose *a* and *b* are vaguely identical; then they differ in some property, namely, being vaguely identical with *b*. For although *a* has the property, *b* does not: nothing is vaguely identical with itself. By the indiscernibility of identicals, then, *a* is (determinately) not identical with *b*. So, vaguely identical objects are (determinately) not identical! That sounds odd; but there is no contradiction if vague identity is understood in some way that detaches it from indeterminacy of truth value. So understood, vague identity poses no challenge to classical identity.

TEMPORARY IDENTITY

The Greek philosopher HERACLITUS [3] argued that one cannot bathe in the same river twice, something as follows. Rivers flow. The stretch of water that comprises the river on Monday is not the same as the stretch of water that comprises the river on Tuesday. But a river is not something separate and distinct from the stretch of water that comprises it; be it on Monday or on Tuesday, the river and the stretch of water are one and the same. It follows, by a double application of the indiscernibility of identicals, that the river on Monday is not the same as the river on Tuesday. If one bathes in the river on Monday, and returns to bathe at the same place on Tuesday, one has not bathed in the same river twice.

One wants to say: on Monday, the river is identical with a certain stretch of water; on Tuesday, the same river is identical with a different stretch of water. More generally, identity can be temporary, holding at some times but not at others. Temporary identity, however, is disallowed by the above argument, not just for rivers, but for all entities whatsoever. Should we abandon the classical notion of identity that the argument presupposes?

There are at least two responses to Heraclitus's problem compatible with classical identity. According to the first response (inspired by ARISTOTLE [1; S]), when we say that a river *is* just a certain stretch of water, we are using not the 'is' of identity but the 'is' of constitution; and constitution is never identity (see Lowe, 1989). On this view there are two fundamentally different kinds of entities that occupy space and persist through time. There are ordinary material objects, such as rivers, trees, statues, and tables; and there are portions of matter that may temporarily constitute the ordinary objects. At any time an ordinary object is constituted by some portion of matter or other; but at no time is it identical with that portion of matter, either wholly or in part. In particular, the very same river is constituted by one stretch of water on Monday and by a different stretch of water on Tuesday. No conflict arises with the laws of classical identity, and Heraclitus's problem is solved.

This response, however, is not without problems. A dualism of ordinary objects and the portions of matter that constitute them is neither necessary nor sufficient to solve the general problem of temporary identity. It is not sufficient, because some cases of temporary identity have nothing to do with constitution. Consider a tree that, at some bleak stage of its career, consists of nothing but a trunk. Later, however, the tree sprouts new branches and leaves. Then we have another prima facie case of temporary identity: the tree is identical with the trunk at the bleak time but not identical with the trunk at the happier time. In this case, however, invoking constitution is of no avail: neither the trunk nor the tree constitutes the other, in the relevant sense. (This example is from Hirsch, 1982.)

Nor is such a dualism necessary to solve the problem of temporary identity, because another response is available, one (arguably) more economical in its ontological commitments (see Hirsch, 1982; Quine, 1950). On this second response objects that persist through time are composed of (more-or-less) momentary stages, of temporal parts. A persisting river is a sum of stages unified in a way appropriate for rivers; a persisting aggregate of water molecules is a sum of stages unified in a way appropriate for portions of matter. A persisting river and a persisting aggregate of water molecules may overlap by having a stage in common; in that case a stage of the river and a contemporaneous stage of the aggregate of water molecules are identical. But the persisting river is not identical with the persisting aggregate of water molecules: later stages of the river are in about the same place as earlier stages and are no less spatially continuous; later stages of the aggregate of water molecules are downstream of earlier stages and are spatially scattered. When we say that, at any time, a river is nothing separate and distinct from the water that comprises it, this must be understood as asserting not an identity between persisting objects but an identity between stages. Identity between stages, however, is all one needs to avoid the uneconomical dualism of the constitution view. All objects that occupy space and persist through time are composed of a single kind of entity: stages of portions of matter. (The stage view of persistence is argued for in Lewis, 1986.)

Heraclitus's problem is now easily solved. One cannot bathe in the same river stage twice; but one can bathe in the same river twice by bathing successively in two river stages belonging to a single persisting river. That these two stages are not stages of a single persisting aggregate of water molecules is irrelevant. There is no conflict with classical identity.

CONTINGENT IDENTITY

A change in example, however, makes trouble for the stage view of persistence. Consider a statue called *Goliath* that consists entirely of a lump of clay called Lumpl; and suppose that the statue and the lump came into being, and ceased to exist, at exactly the same times. Then, on the stage view, every stage of *Goliath* is identical with a stage of Lumpl and vice versa; *Goliath* and Lumpl are the same sum of stages and so are identical. But, surely, they are not necessarily identical. *Goliath* could have been destroyed without destroying Lumpl—say, by being squashed—in which case *Goliath* would have lacked Lumpl's final stages and would have been a distinct sum from Lumpl. So, *Goliath* and Lumpl are identical, but only contingently identical. (The example is from Gibbard, 1975.)

Trouble arises because contingent identity, no less than temporary identity, is incompatible with identity, classically conceived—or so the following argument seems to show. Consider the property is-necessarily-identical-with-*y*, for some object *y*. Surely *y* has it: everything is necessarily identical with itself. Now suppose an object *x* is identical with *y*. Then, by the indiscernibility of identicals, *x* has the property as well; that is, *x* is necessarily identical with *y*. Thus, objects are necessarily identical if identical at all; objects are never contingently identical.

Whether this argument is unassailable will depend upon one's interpretation of modal properties, of modality *de re*. If objects have their modal properties absolutely, in and of themselves, then the argument is sound. Since *Goliath* and Lumpl are not necessarily identical, they are not identical at all. *Goliath* and Lumpl are numerically distinct objects that occupy the same place at all times that they exist. *Goliath* is not identical with any sum of matter-stages, contradicting the stage view of persistence.

The stage view can be preserved, however, if one takes the view that modal predicates do not apply to objects absolutely, in and of themselves; their application is relative to how the objects are conceived, classified, or referred to. For example, could the lump of clay—that is, the statue—have survived a squashing? *Qua* lump of clay, it could; *qua* statue, it could not. There is no violation of the indiscernibility of identicals because the modal predicate 'could survive a squashing' expresses no property when considered out of context and expresses different properties when attached to 'the lump of clay' (or 'Lumpl') and to 'the statue' (or *Goliath*). In this way the stage view can accept the contingent identity of Lumpl and *Goliath,* without forfeiting classical identity. (For versions of this strategy, see Gibbard, 1975; Lewis, 1971.)

RELATIVE IDENTITY

Classical identity is absolute: whether identity holds between objects does not depend upon how those objects are conceived, classified, or referred to. In ordinary language we often say '*a* is the same *F* as *b*', for some general term '*F*'; but this is naturally analyzed as a restriction of absolute identity: *a* is *F*, and *b* is *F*, and *a* is (absolutely) identical with *b*.

Geach has argued, on the contrary, that all identity statements are relative: '*a* is the same *F* as *b*' cannot be analyzed as restricted absolute identity, because there is no absolute identity; when we say simply '*a* is the same as *b*', some general term '*F*' must be supplied by context, or what we say is meaningless (Geach, 1970). To support his claim, Geach has presented examples in which we would say: *a* and *b* are the same *F*, and *a* and *b* are *G*'s, but *a* and *b* are not the same *G*. Consider the word 'tot'. It contains three letter tokens, two letter types. The first letter token and the last letter token are not the same letter token, but they are the same letter type. That contradicts the claim that 'the same *F*' is to be analyzed as restricted absolute identity.

The defender of classical identity has a simple and natural reply: sometimes the relation is-the-same-*F*-as is not restricted identity but rather some weaker equivalence relation; that is, sometimes it is a species of qualitative, rather than numerical, identity (see Perry, 1970). For example: if I say that you are wearing the same coat as I am, I (probably) do not mean the numerically same coat. Similarly, letter tokens of the same type are qualitatively similar—equiform—not numerically identical. To the extent that Geach's point is just that 'the same *F*' cannot always be analyzed as restricted identity, it is a point no one should deny.

Any rejection of absolute identity, it seems, must be based upon arguments of a more abstract sort. Indeed, Geach explicitly rejects the standard characterization of identity through Leibniz's law on the grounds that second-order quantification over properties leads to paradox. And he rightly points out that, within first-order logic, characterizations of identity are inevitably relative to the predicates of the language. But how does this impugn the meaningfulness of absolute identity? Does Geach's argument simply amount to the demand, Define absolute identity, or count it as meaningless? That demand, certainly, is too strong. No fundamental notion of logic or metaphysics could meet it.

Bibliography

Adams. R. M. "Primitive Thisness and Primitive Identity," *Journal of Philosophy,* Vol. 76 (1979), 5–26.

Black, M. "The Identity of Indiscernibles," in *Problems of Analysis* (Ithaca, NY, 1954).

Cartwright, R. "Identity and Substitutivity," in M. Munitz, ed., *Identity and Individuation* (New York, 1971).

Evans, G. "Can There Be Vague Objects?" *Analysis,* Vol. 38 (1978), 208.

Frege, G. "Uber Sinn und Bedeutung," *Zeitschrift fur Philosophie und philosophische Kritik,* Vol. 100 (1892), 25–50. Translated by P. Geach and M. Black as "On Sense and Reference," in *Philosophical Writings of Gottlob Frege* (Oxford, 1952).

Geach, P. T. "Identity," *Review of Metaphysics,* Vol. 21 (1967), 3–12.

Gibbard, A. "Contingent Identity," *Journal of Philosophical Logic,* Vol. 4 (1975), 187–221.

Hirsch, E. *The Concept of Identity.* Oxford, 1982.

Kripke, S. *Naming and Necessity.* Cambridge, MA, 1980.

Lewis, D. "Counterparts of Persons and Their Bodies," *Journal of Philosophy,* Vol. 68 (1971), 203–11.

———. *On the Plurality of Worlds.* Oxford, 1986.

———. "Many, But Almost One," in K. Campbell, J. Bacon, and L. Reinhardt, eds., *Ontology, Causality, and Mind: Essays in Honour of D. M. Armstrong* (Cambridge, 1993).

Lowe, E. J. *Kinds of Being.* Oxford, 1989.

Perry, J. "The Same *F*," *Philosophical Review* (1970), 181–200.

Quine, W. V. O. "Identity, Ostension, and Hypostasis," *Journal of Philosophy,* (1950).

———. "Reference and Modality," in *From a Logical Point of View* (New York, 1953).

———. *Word and Object.* Cambridge, MA, 1960.

Salmon, N. *Reference and Essence.* Princeton, NJ, 1981.

———. *Frege's Puzzle.* Cambridge, MA, 1986.

PHILLIP BRICKER

IMPARTIALITY. A more complex concept than is generally recognized, impartiality does not require giving equal weight to the interests of all, as many philosophers assume, but at most involves giving equal weight to the interests of all those whose interests are being appropriately considered. Often, impartiality does not even involve considering the interests of people in any straightforward sense of interests. An impartial baseball umpire should call balls and strikes without being influenced by how his calls will affect any of the players on the competing teams.

The most common characterization of impartiality is that it requires that like cases be treated alike. This characterization is taken as trivially true by almost all philosophers, but it is mistaken. Consider an umpire who changes the strike zone every three innings, starting with a wide zone, going to a narrow one, and then returning to a wide one, because he is upset and believes that umpires are not appreciated. If he changes it without regard to which team benefits or is harmed by this change, then he is impartial with regard to the two teams in calling balls and strikes. Although his not treating like cases alike (i.e., calling balls and strikes differently in the first and fifth innings) makes him a bad umpire, it does not affect his impartiality.

Even if he changes the strike zone whenever he feels like it but is not influenced by which pitcher, batter, or team is benefited or harmed by this erratic change in the strike zone, he remains impartial with regard to the two teams. He is not consistent, but impartiality should not be confused with consistency. A good umpire is supposed to be consistent as well as impartial. An inconsistent umpire will be suspected of not being impartial, but if he is not influenced by who is benefited or harmed, he remains impartial with respect to calling balls and strikes with regard to the two teams.

Thus, understanding what it means to say that a person is impartial requires specifying the group with regard to which she is impartial and the respect in which she is impartial with regard to that group. A person is impartial in the most fundamental sense insofar as she acts impartially. The following is an analysis of the basic concept of impartiality: *A is impartial in respect R with regard to group G if and only if A's actions in respect R are not influenced at all by which member(s) of G are benefited or harmed by these actions.*

Acting impartially is not sufficient for acting morally, for one may be impartial in an unacceptable respect (e.g., a burglar who does not discriminate on the basis of race, sex, or any other irrelevant characteristic in choosing his victims) or with regard to an unacceptable group (e.g., a racist who hires impartially with regard to all members of the favored race when he should be impartial with regard to qualified people of all races who apply for the job). Making explicit the respect in which a person is impartial and the group with regard to which she is impartial enables one to examine whether or not the respect and group are acceptable. Impartiality is taken to be praiseworthy only because it is usually presupposed that a person is impartial with regard to an acceptable group in an acceptable respect. The person herself need not be included in the group with regard to which she is impartial. A mother can be impartial with regard to all of her children with respect to providing them with spending money; that she keeps more money for herself does not affect her impartiality with regard to her children.

One must include oneself in the group toward whom one acts impartially when the concern is with the impartiality required by morality, but that one is included in the group is not an adequate specification of that group. All agree that this group must include, at least, all currently existing actual moral agents, but people disagree about who else is included. Disputes about ABORTION [S] and the treatment of animals are disputes about whether or not fetuses or nonhuman animals are included in the group toward which morality requires impartiality (*see* ANIMAL RIGHTS AND WELFARE [S]).

The respect in which morality requires one to be impartial is only with regard to those moral rules prohibiting killing, causing pain, deceiving, breaking promises, and so on. For it is only with regard to these kinds of moral rules, those that can be formulated as prohibitions, that it is humanly possible to act impartially with regard to a group that contains all other moral agents. No one can act impartially with regard to all in this group with respect to relieving or preventing pain or acting on any other positive moral ideal. Thus, morality cannot require such impartiality.

(SEE ALSO: *Ethical Theory* [S])

Bibliography

Baier, K. *The Moral Point of View.* Ithaca, NY, 1958.

Firth, R. "Ethical Absolutism and the Ideal Observer," *Philosophy and Phenomenological Research,* Vol. 12 (1952), 317–45.

Gert, B. *Morality.* New York, 1988. See especially chapter 5, "Impartiality."

Hare, R. M. *Moral Thinking.* Oxford, 1981.

Kant, I. *Grounding for the Metaphysics of Morals.* 1785.

Singer, M. G. *Generalization in Ethics.* New York, 1961.

BERNARD GERT

INDEXICALS. Suppose that Natasha says "I am right and you are wrong" to Joey. Natasha's utterance of "I" designates Natasha and her utterance of "you" designates Joey. The truth-conditions of her statement are that Natasha is right and Joey is wrong.

Now suppose that Joey responds by uttering the exact same words back to Natasha: "I am right and you are wrong." He has said the same words, with the same meaning, but he has not said the same thing. Joey's utterance of "I" designates Joey and his utterance of "you" designates Natasha. The truth-conditions of his statement are that Joey is right and Natasha is wrong. Joey has directly disagreed with Natasha.

In this article, "meaning" refers to the rules or conventions that are associated by a language with the expressions in it, the rules that one learns when one learns the language. Given this, the meanings of Natasha's words and of Joey's are the same. What differs is the objects the particular expressions designate and the truth conditions of the statements. This aspect of utterances will be called "content."

The crucial differences between the first and second utterances were the speakers and the addressees. Such facts about an utterance can be called its "context." Differences in the contexts of the utterances account for the differences in their contents.

(The role of context in this case differs from that in a case of homonymity or ambiguity. With homonymity the context helps us determine which word is being used; with ambiguity, which meaning of a word or phrase is being used. But in this case context still has a role to play after questions of words and meanings have been settled. The meanings of "I" and "you" direct us to features of the context, to determine who is designated.)

The content of an utterance using "I" or "you" is determined by contextual facts about the utterance in accord with their meaning. Such expressions we call indexicals.

In addition to "I" and "you," the standard list of indexicals includes the personal pronouns "my," "he," "his," "she," "it," the demonstrative pronouns "that" and "this," the adverbs "here," "now," "today," "yesterday," and "tomorrow," and the adjectives "actual" and "present" (Kaplan, 1989). The words and aspects of words that indicate tense are also indexicals. And many other words—for instance, "local"—seem to have an indexical element.

According to David Kaplan's account, each indexical, and each sentence containing an indexical, has a meaning or character that is a function from contexts to content. The character of "I" is a function whose value, for each context, is the speaker or agent of that context. The character of "now" is a function whose value, for each context, is the time of that context. The character of "you" is a function whose value, for each context, is the person addressed by the speaker in that context. The character of the sentence spoken by Natasha and Joey is a function whose value, for a context with a speaker *x* and an addressee *y*, is the proposition that *x* is right and *y* is wrong. Natasha and Joey's words have the same characters, but their utterances have different contents.

In the formal development of his theory, Kaplan equates content with the intensions of intensional semantics. He criticizes earlier attempts to provide a formal theory within this framework for treating contexts on a par with "circumstances of evaluation" (Kaplan, 1989, pp. 507ff.). The context determines which proposition is expressed by Joey's utterance of "I am right and you are wrong"; the circumstance of evaluation determines whether or not the proposition is true. The necessity for such a distinction was seen by Hans Kamp (1971).

(Kaplan notes that at the level of character it makes sense to talk about the logic of indexicals. "I am here now" is a truth in the logic of indexicals, because, given its character, this sentence will have a true content at each context. The content will be contingent and can be expressed by a sentence that is not a logical truth.)

Kaplan's concept of content corresponds to "what is said" by an utterance (let us call this "official" content). This is what someone who knows the meaning and the context grasps. Other philosophers have thought it important also to bring in the concept of token-reflexive or diagonal content. This is what someone who knows the meaning but does not know the context grasps (Burks, 1949; Perry, 1993; Stalnaker, 1981).

Consider an utterance **u** of "Je ne comprends pas l'anglais" made by Erin during a cocktail party. Suppose that Natasha hears the words and understands French but does not see who said them. Joey hears the words, understands French, and also sees that Erin said them. Based on her knowledge of French, Natasha can assign utterance-reflexive truth conditions to **u:** Natasha knows that **u** is true iff (if and only if) (1) the speaker of **u** does not understand English. Joey, since he knows who is talking, can assign nonreflexive truth conditions to **u:** Joey knows that **u** is true iff (2) Erin does not understand English. Natasha knows what the world has to be like for **u** to be true, given the meaning of the words in **u.** Joey knows what the world has to be like, given the meaning of the words in **u** *and* the relevant facts about context. What Joey knows, (2), is the official content of Erin's remark. It is what we would ordinarily say Erin *said.* Erin did not *say* (1); she did not make a remark about her own utterance. Nevertheless, (1) corresponds to an important level of understanding that we must take account of to explain the cognitive significance of sentences containing indexicals. (When Erin said what she did, she probably wanted her listeners to grasp that the person in front of them, at whom they were looking and with whom perhaps trying to converse in English, did not understand that language. This would be an easy inference from the proposition expressed by (1)—that the person who was producing the utterance they were hearing did not understand English. To understand Erin's plan, we seem to need the reflexive content of Erin's remark, and not only its official content.)

(SEE ALSO: *Philosophy of Language* [S])

Bibliography

Burks, A. "Icon, Index, and Symbol," *Philosophical and Phenomenological Research,* Vol. 9 (1949), 673–89.

Castañeda, H.-N. " 'He': A Study in the Logic of Self-Consciousness," *Ratio,* Vol. 8 (1966), 130–57.

Evans, G. "Understanding Demonstratives," in H. Parret and J. Bouveresse, eds., *Meaning and Understanding* (Berlin, 1981).

Kamp, H. "Formal Properties of 'Now,' " *Theoria,* Vol. 37 (1971), 237–73.

Kaplan, D. "Demonstratives," in J. Almog, J. Perry, and H. Wettstein, eds., *Themes from Kaplan* (New York, 1989).

Nunberg, G. "Indexicality and Deixis," *Linguistics and Philosophy,* Vol. 16 (1993), 1–43.

Perry, J. *The Problem of the Essential Indexical and Other Essays.* New York, 1993.

Recanati, F. *Direct Reference: From Language to Thought.* Oxford, 1993.

Stalnaker, R. "Indexical Belief," *Synthese,* Vol. 49 (1981), 129–51.

Yourgrau, P., ed. *Demonstratives.* Oxford, 1990.

JOHN PERRY

INDISCERNIBLES. When artworks indiscernible from real counterparts became a historical possibility, accounting for the difference became philosophically urgent. These included Marcel Duchamp's 1917 "ready-made" *Fountain,* in fact an ordinary urinal; Constantin Brancusi's 1927 *Bird in Space,* which looked to customs officials more like a kitchen utensil than a sculpture; and Andy Warhol's 1964 *Brillo Box,* which looked like a soap-pad carton. The possibility of such works makes it plain that the art–reality difference cannot be regarded as perceptual, for though there are minor observable differences in all these cases, they are hardly of a kind to ground the distinction between art and reality. And since for any artwork an ordinary object can be imagined indiscernible from it, the meaning of "artwork" cannot be taught by means of examples. These works raise questions of whether aesthetic considerations belong to the definition of art. Moreover, since the possibility of artworks

indiscernible from real counterparts was not an artistic option before the twentieth century, these works raise the further question of how historical considerations relate to artistic understanding, for not even the artist's intention that they be regarded as artworks could have been formed in earlier historical periods.
(SEE ALSO: *Art, Definition of* [S])

Bibliography

Danto, A. C. *The Transfiguration of the Commonplace.* Cambridge, MA, 1981. Chapter 1.

———. *Connections to the World: The Basic Concepts of Philosophy.* New York, 1985. Chapter 2.

ARTHUR C. DANTO

INFERENCE TO THE BEST EXPLANATION.

In an inductive inference, we acquire a belief on the basis of evidence that is less than conclusive. The new belief is compatible with the evidence, but so are many competing hypotheses we are unwilling to infer. This raises a question of description and a question of justification. What are the principles that lead us to infer one hypothesis rather than another? Do we have any reason to believe that these principles are good ones, leading us to accept hypotheses that are true and to reject those that are false? Inference to the best explanation offers partial answers to both questions.

According to this model, explanatory considerations are a fundamental guide to inductive inference. We decide which of the competing hypotheses the evidence best supports by determining how well each of the competitors would explain that evidence. Seeing the ball next to the broken vase, I infer that my children have been playing catch in the house, because this is the best explanation of what I see. Having measured the red shift of a star's characteristic spectrum, the astronomer infers that the star is receding from the earth with a specified velocity because no other hypothesis would explain the evidence so well.

Although inference to the best explanation gives a natural account of many inferences in both science and ordinary life, the model needs further development before it can be properly assessed. What, for example, should be meant by *best*? It is sometimes taken to mean likeliest, but inference to the likeliest explanation is a disappointingly uninformative model since the main point of an account of inference is to say what leads one hypothesis to be judged likelier than another. A more promising approach construes *best* as loveliest. On this view, we infer the hypothesis that would, if correct, provide the greatest understanding.

This is a promising approach, but it raises questions that the literature has only begun to answer. An account is needed of the explanatory virtues, specifying what makes one explanation lovelier than another. Then it needs to be shown that loveliness is in fact our guide to judgments of likeliness. If this can be done, then the model may give an illuminating description of inductive practice.

Inference to the best explanation has also been used in attempts to justify our inductive practices, to show that those hypotheses we judge likely to be correct really are so. For example, it has been argued that we have good reason to believe that our best scientific theories are true since the truth of those theories is the best explanation of their wide-ranging predictive success. This argument has considerable plausibility, but it faces serious objections. If scientific theories are themselves accepted on the basis of inferences to the best explanation, then to argue in the same way that those inferences lead to the truth seems to beg the question. Moreover, it is not clear that the truth of a theory really is the best explanation of its predictive success since this seems no better an explanation than would be the truth of a competing theory that happens to share those particular predictions.
(SEE ALSO: *Epistemology* [S])

Bibliography

Harman, G. "The Inference to the Best Explanation," *Philosophical Review,* Vol. 74 (1965), 88–95.

Lipton, P. *Inference to the Best Explanation.* London, 1991.

Thagard, P. "The Best Explanation: Criteria for Theory Choice," *Journal of Philosophy,* Vol. 75 (1978), 76–92.

PETER LIPTON

INFINITE, THE.

Emmanuel LEVINAS [S] uses the expression *l'infini* to describe a reality that surpasses all that can be contained, grasped, perceived, or understood by human consciousness and yet determines the basic structure of human subjectivity. 'The infinite' does not indicate the *apeiron* (which is another name for Levinas's *il y a*) or the indefinite, and it is not primarily a name for God. Neither is it the opposite of the finite within one genus or encompassing universe. It transcends the dimension of all phenomena and oppositions.

Levinas introduces the infinite by referring to René DESCARTES's [2; S] *Meditations on the First Philosophy,* in which he points out that the idea of the infinite cannot be deduced or constructed by the human mind. As an originary and irreducible idea, it determines the mind as being related to something greater than what it can contain. Levinas accepts this formal analysis in stating that the cogito "thinks more than it can think" (*Collected Philosophical Papers,* 1987, p. 56). The human subject discovers itself affected by a primordial affection even before consciousness awakens to it. The passivity implied in this affection contradicts any attempt to define the human subject as absolutely free: prior to being free, human beings are marked by transcendence, a constitutive desire for the infinite.

The phenomenological concretization of the formal structure thus discovered is given by a description of the human other (*see* OTHER, THE [S]). The infinite is revealed in the appearance of another human who looks at or speaks to me. Although all human beings are finite, the encounter with the other confronts me with the infinite insofar as the incomprehensible fact of the other's reality coincides with, or rather is, the absolute command or claim that is the core of all morality. The confrontation with "the face" awakens me to the infinite (absolute and inexhaustible) responsibility of my being-for-the-other. The idea of the infinite is thus revealed as a primarily affective and practical relation. Since knowledge is a form of grasping and assimilation, the infinite is not primarily the object of a theoretical attitude; rather, transcendence is at the same time ethical and metaphysical.

Levinas does not reject the traditional use of 'the infinite' as one of the names for God but insists that there is no other way to get in touch with God than by being touched by the human other and taking one's ethical responsibility seriously. God's infinity is much more enigmatic than the human other's. God is the one who has passed into an immemorial past before all pasts, leaving the human other and me in his TRACE [S].

Bibliography

Levinas, E. *Totalité et infini; Essai sur l'extériorité.* The Hague, 1961.

———. "La philosophie et l'idée de l'infini," in *En découvrant l'existence avec Husserl et Heidegger,* 2d. ed. (Paris, 1967).

———. "Infini," in *Encyclopaedia Universalis,* Vol. 8 (Paris, 1968), 991–94.

———. "Sur l'idée de l'infini en nous," in *Entre nous: Essais sur le penser-à-l'autre* (Paris, 1991).

ADRIAAN PEPERZAK

INFINITESIMALS. The ubiquitous use of infinitely small quantities in mathematics dates back at least to the seventeenth century. Despite continuing qualms as to their legitimacy and their supposed elimination as a result of the thoroughgoing reform movement of the nineteenth century, infinitesimals have continued to be used, especially in applied mathematics. The logician Adolf Fraenkel gave what was no doubt the widely accepted view when he stated, "The infinitely small is only to be understood as a manner of speaking based on the limit concept, hence a *potential* infinite; it is a matter of variable . . . [positive] numbers or quantities that can ultimately decrease below any arbitrarily small positive value. A fixed [positive] number different from zero that can serve as a lower bound to all finite positive values is not possible" (1928, p. 114, my translation, emphasis in original). In 1960 Fraenkel's one-time student Abraham Robinson showed how to obtain just such a "fixed number" and thereby vindicated the discredited infinitesimal methods.

The benefits of the free use of infinitesimal methods were amply demonstrated by the success of LEIBNIZ's [4; S] version of the differential and integral calculus and the continued use of these methods by the Bernoulis and especially by Leonhard Euler. Working mathematicians had no difficulty in knowing just which properties of ordinary numbers infinitesimals could be assumed to possess and just when it was legitimate to equate such quantities to zero. But the lack of any clear justification for these methods provided an opening for scathing attacks such as that of George BERKELEY [1; S]. The need for rigorous methods was felt by mathematicians themselves and eventually supplied (Edwards, 1979; Robinson, 1974).

Robinson's key insight was that the methods of MODEL THEORY [S] could be used to construct a powerful rigorous theory of infinitesimals. Thus, for example, we may consider a first-order language in which a constant symbol is provided as a "name" for each real number, a function symbol is provided as a "name" for each real-valued function defined on the real numbers, and the only relation symbols are $=$ and $<$. Let T be the set of all true sentences of this language when each symbol is understood to have its intended interpretation. Let δ be a new constant symbol, and let W consist of the sentences of T together with the infinite set of sentences:

$$\delta > 0$$
$$\delta < 1, \delta < \frac{1}{2}, \delta < \frac{1}{3}, \delta < \frac{1}{4}, \ldots$$

Since any finite subset of W can be satisfied in the ordinary real numbers by interpreting δ as a sufficiently small positive number, the compactness theorem for first-order logic guarantees that W has a model. But in that model, the element serving to interpret δ must be positive and less than every positive real number (i.e., infinitesimal). The structure with which we began of real numbers and real-valued functions can readily be embedded in the new model. Thus if r is a real number and c_r is the constant of the language that names r, we may regard the element of the new model that serves to interpret c_r as simply r itself. Functions can be embedded in the same way. One speaks of the new model as an enlargement.

Moreover, because $T \subseteq W$, all true statements about the real numbers that can be expressed in our language are also true in this enlargement. A false statement about the real numbers is likewise false in the enlargement: if the statement S is false, then $\neg S$ is a true statement about the reals and hence is also true in the enlargement. It is this transfer principle, the fact that statements are true about the real numbers if and only if they are true in the new enlarged structure, that makes precise just when an assertion about ordinary numbers can be extended to apply to infinitesimals as well.

The enlargement will contain infinitely large as well as infinitesimal elements. This is readily seen by applying the transfer principle to the statement that every nonzero real number has a reciprocal. One may even speak of infinite integers; their existence follows on applying the transfer principle to the statement that for any given real number there is a positive integer that exceeds it.

The basic facts of real analysis can be established on this basis using modes of argument that would earlier have been quite correctly regarded as illegitimate. For example, the basic theorem that a continuous function on a closed interval assumes a maximum value can be proved by dividing the interval into infinitely many subintervals, each of infinitesimal length, and selecting an endpoint of such a subinterval at which the function's value is greatest (Davis, 1977; Robinson, 1974). By beginning with a more extensive language, it is possible to apply infinitesimal methods to branches of mathematics requiring a more substantial set-theoretic basis (e.g., topology, functional analysis, probability theory). It has even proved possible to use these "nonstandard" methods to settle certain open questions in mathematics.

For those with qualms concerning nonconstructive methods in mathematics, these infinitesimal methods are bound to seem unsatisfactory. Because the underlying language is built on an uncountable "alphabet," the use of the compactness theorem hides an application of some form of the axiom of choice. This in turn is reflected in a basic indeterminacy; we can establish the existence of enlargements but cannot specify any particular enlargement. Robinson himself has emphasized that although nonstandard analysis "appears to affirm the existence of all sorts of infinitary entities," one always has the option of taking the "formalist point of view" from which "we may consider that what we have done is to introduce *new deductive procedures* rather than new mathematical entities" (1974, p. 282, emphasis in original).

(SEE ALSO: *Mathematical Logic;* and *Philosophy of Logic* [S])

Bibliography

Davis, M. *Applied Nonstandard Analysis.* New York, 1977.

Edwards, C. H., Jr. *The Historical Development of the Calculus.* New York, 1979.

Fraenkel, A. *Einleitung in die Mengenlehre,* 3d ed. Berlin, 1928; reprint, New York, 1946.

Robinson, A. *Nonstandard Analysis,* 2d ed. Amsterdam, 1974.

MARTIN DAVIS

INFORMED CONSENT.

A fundamental requirement of both ethics and the law is that medical treatment cannot be given to competent patients without their informed consent. This represents a rejection of more traditional authoritarian or paternalistic accounts of the physician/patient relationship in which the physician had decision-making authority in favor of a process of shared decision making between physicians and patients. In this respect informed consent helps shape the nature of nearly all health-care treatment decision making. Informed consent also has special importance in a narrower class of cases in which patients and their physicians are unable to agree on a course of treatment. In these cases a competent patient is given the right to refuse any recommended treatment, even including life-sustaining treatment, no matter how strongly the physician or others believe that the treatment should be undertaken.

There are two principal moral values that are served by and justify the informed-consent requirement in health care. The first is patient well-being—arguably the fundamental goal of all health care. The concept of patient well-being, as opposed to the apparently more objective goals of protecting and promoting patients' health and lives, signals the important respect in which what will best serve a particular patient's well-being is often to a significant degree a subjective determination that depends on the particular aims and values of the patient in question. Increasingly, there are medically acceptable alternative treatments (including the alternative of no treatment), no one of which is best for all patients with a particular medical condition. The patient's participation in decision making is therefore necessary in order to select the treatment that best fits his or her aims and values. The other fundamental moral value that undergirds the informed-consent requirement is individual self-determination or autonomy. Self-determination in this context is the moral right of ordinary persons to make significant decisions about their lives for themselves and according to their own aims and values. Requiring that health care not be rendered without a competent patient's informed consent respects this right of self-determination. The informed-consent requirement reflects the fundamental moral point that it is the patient and the patient's body that undergo the treatment, and so it should be the patient who is morally entitled to authorize or refuse the treatment.

Three conditions are necessary for ethically valid informed consent—that the patient's decision be informed, voluntary, and competent. The requirement that the decision be informed places a responsibility on the patient's physician to provide the patient with information, in an understandable form, about the patient's condition or diagnosis and the prognosis if no treatment is provided, together with the alternative treatments that would improve that prognosis, along with their risks and benefits. This typically does not require that the physician provide, or that the patient understand, complex medical and scientific information, but rather information about how the various alternatives would likely affect the patient's pursuit of his or her plan of life. Legal requirements regarding how much and which information must be provided vary, but the ethical ideal is to provide the information that the particular patient would reasonably want to know in order to make his or her decision.

The requirement that the consent be voluntary means that treatment must not be rendered against the patient's will, either by force or by coercing the patient's choice. More important, it also forbids physicians from manipulating the patient's choice through selective provision of information, playing on the patient's fears, and other means. Ethically objectionable manipulation, as opposed to appropriate informing and persuasion, aims to produce a different choice from what a competent patient would have made if fully informed and freely choosing.

The third requirement of competence is the most complex. Usually, patients are either clearly competent, with their normal decision-making capacities intact, or clearly incompetent, unable to make any decision. In borderline cases in which there is significant, but not total, impairment of the patient's decision-making capacities, the competence determination is often controversial. The competence evaluation should address the process of the patient's decision making in order to determine whether there are significant impairments, limitations, or mistakes in that process that have resulted in a choice different from what the patient would have wanted in the absence of those impairments, limitations, or mistakes. The proper standard of competence in borderline cases is controversial but increasingly understood to be a variable standard, requiring a higher level of understanding and reasoning when the patient's well-being would be seriously affected by the decision in question and a lower level when there would be only limited impact on the patient's well-being. While treatment refusal may reasonably trigger an evaluation of the patient's competence, it should not serve as any evidence of the patient's incompetence—that evidence must come from impairments or limitations that cannot be remedied in the process of the patient's reasoning. When the requirements for ethically valid informed consent (that is, informed, voluntary, and competent) are met, the patient's choice should be reasonably in accord with his or her well-being, and his or her self-determination will have been respected.

When the patient has been determined to be incompetent to make his or her own treatment choices, a surrogate or proxy, typically a close family member, should substitute for the patient in the decision-making and consent process. The patient's informed consent is also not required in emergency conditions, when taking time to obtain consent would involve serious risks to the patient's well-being, or when the patient has waived his or her right to give consent and has authorized another to make the treatment decision.

(SEE ALSO: *Applied Ethics; Biomedical Ethics,* [S])

Bibliography

Appelbaum, P. S., C. W. Lidz, and A. Meisel. *Informed Consent: Legal Theory and Clinical Practice.* New York, 1987.

Faden, R., and T. L. Beauchamp. *A History and Theory of Informed Consent.* New York, 1986.

DAN W. BROCK

INNATISM. *See:* NATIVISM, INNATISM [S]

INTENSIONAL LOGIC. There are two central uses of the term 'intensional': (1) one semantic, and (2) one ontological.

1. A language (or its logic) is said to be extensional if, within it, equivalent formulas can be substituted for one another salva veritate: $(A \leftrightarrow B) \rightarrow (\ldots A \ldots) \leftrightarrow (\ldots B \ldots)$. A language is said to be intensional if it is not extensional, that is, if it violates this substitutivity principle. For example, "x is a creature with a heart" and "x is a creature with a kidney" are equivalent (they apply to the same things). But when we substitute the former for the latter in the true sentence, "It is necessary that, if x is a creature with a kidney, x has a kidney," we get a false sentence, "It is necessary that, if x is a creature with a heart, x has a kidney." Intensional language is used for such matters as modality, propositional attitudes, PROBABILITY [6; S], explanation, and counterfactuality. (*See* EXPLANATION, THEORIES OF; EXPLANATION, TYPES OF; MODALITY, PHILOSOPHY AND METAPHYSICS OF; and PROPOSITIONAL ATTITUDE [S])

2. An entity x is said to be extensional if it satisfies the following principle of extensionality: for every entity y in the same ontological category as x, if x and y are equivalent, they are identical. An entity x is said to be intensional if it is not extensional, that is, if this principle of extensionality does not hold for it (i.e., there is some equivalent entity y in the same ontological category that is not identical to x). Sets are paradigmatic extensional entities; properties, relations, concepts, and propositions are paradigmatic intensional entities. For example, even though being a creature with a kidney and being a creature with a heart are equivalent properties (the same things have them), they are not identical.

The leading view is that the underlying source of intensionality in natural language is a certain sort of complex abstract singular term known as an "intensional abstract." Examples are 'that' clauses, gerundive phrases, infinitive phrases, and so on. The connection between the two uses of 'intensional' is that intensional abstracts are terms for intensional entities. For example, 'that $5 + 7 = 12$' denotes the proposition that $5 + 7 = 12$; 'being red' denotes the property of being red; and so on.

There are two main projects in intensional logic, one for each of the two uses of the term. The first project is to formulate logical laws governing substitutivity conditions for intensional abstracts. The main challenge is to find techniques for representing systematically the subtle distinctions arising in intensional language. The second project is to formulate logical laws governing the fundamental logical relations relative to which the intensionality of an entity is characterized. In the case of properties, for example, this fundamental logical relation is the relation of having a property. In the case of a concept, it is the relation of falling under a concept. The main challenge in this area is to find systems of laws for such relations which are faithful to our intuitions and which, at the same time, avoid logical paradoxes (e.g., the intensional version of Russell's paradox—the property of being a property which does not have itself).

RUSSELL [7] and WHITEHEAD's [8] *Principia Mathematica* (1910) undertook both projects at once, as did Church's Frege-style "A Formulation of the Logic of Sense and Denotation" (1952). In connection with the second project mentioned above, these logicians avoided the logical paradoxes by imposing a rigid type theory. From about 1960 there has been a burst of activity in intensional logic. Throughout this period, until his death in 1995, Church continued to work on his own Frege-style approach (*see* FREGE, GOTTLOB [3; S]). In the 1960s and early 1970s, however, most of the new work on intensional logic was inspired by Carnap's *Meaning and Necessity* (1947), in which CARNAP [2; S] attempted to explicate the informed notion of a possible world. Montague, Kaplan, Bressan, Cocchiarella, T. Parsons, D. Lewis, Gallin, Partee, and a host of others applied Carnapian possible-worlds semantics—and enrichments of it (following Bayart, Kanger, Kripke [S], and Hintikka)—to various intensional languages. Most of the efforts were carried out in the setting of some form of type theory. In the case of Montague, this took the form of a categorial grammar, which led to a flurry of work on natural language syntax.

Two main difficulties, one for each use of 'intensional', confront all these approaches to intensional logic. The first has to do with the use of rigid type theories to resolve the paradoxes. There is overwhelming linguistic evidence that natural languages do not have the sort of rigid type structure posited by Russell and Church. Indeed, there are various ways in which natural language is type-free. For example, everything (regardless of category) is self-identical, even self-identity. Moreover, the sentence just used is not infinitely ambiguous along type lines, as Russell thought. Appreciation of such facts has led a number of logicians to develop type-free resolutions of the paradoxes. Contributions along these lines have been made by Fitch, Gilmore, Feferman, Aezel, Turner, and many others.

The second difficulty, associated with the logic for intensional abstracts, is the problem of fine-grained content. On the standard POSSIBLE-WORLDS [S] approach, intensional abstracts (e.g., 'that 5 + 7 = 12' and 'that 1 + 1 = 2') denote the same thing as long as they are necessarily equivalent. But this is clearly mistaken: for example, it is possible to be thinking that 1 + 1 = 2 and not to be thinking that 5 + 7 = 12.

Certain possible-worlds theorists working within a type-theoretic framework (e.g., Cresswell) have attempted a reductionist approach to fine-grained content; on this approach "complex" intensional entities (e.g., propositions) are identified with sequences or abstract trees whose elements are possible-worlds constructs. A reductionist approach (adopted by, e.g., Perry & Barwise, 1983) which is not wedded to type theory takes certain intensions as primitive and then reduces all remaining "complex" intensions to set-theoretical constructions out of these primitive intensions. There is also a nonreductionist algebraic approach (e.g., Bealer, Menzel, Parsons) which is type-free and which takes all intensional entities, "complex" and "noncomplex," at face value as *sui generis* entities.

A fine-grained intensional logic must accommodate, not only intensional distinctions of the above sort, but also those associated with the paradox of analysis (Langford & Moore, 1942), Mates's puzzle (1950), and Frege's original 1892 puzzle (how can 'that Hesperus = Phosphorous' and 'that Hesperus = Hesperus' denote different propositions?). Around 1970 Donnellan and Kripke mounted persuasive arguments undermining Frege's own solution to the latter puzzle (a solution upon which Church's approach to fine-grained content is based), according to which proper names express descriptive intensions (e.g., 'Aristotle' expresses the descriptive concept of being the most famous philosopher of antiquity). Evidently, the nonreductionist theory is the most promising approach to these further problems of fine-grained intensional logic.

Bibliography

Barwise, J., and J. Perry. *Situations and Attitudes.* Cambridge, MA, 1983.

Bealer, G. *Quality and Concept.* Oxford, 1982.

———. "A Solution to Frege's Puzzle," in J. Tomberlin, ed., *Philosophical Perspectives* 7 (Atascadero, CA, 1993), pp. 17–61.

Church, A. "Outline of a Revised Formulation of the Logic of Sense and Denotation," *Noûs,* Vol. 7 (1973), 23–33, and *Noûs* Vol. 8, (1974), 135–56.

Chierchia, G., B. Partee, R. Turner, eds. *Property Theories, Type Theories, and Semantics.* Dordrecht, 1988.

Cresswell, M. J. *Structured Meanings.* Cambridge, MA, 1985.

Feferman, S. "Toward Useful Type-free Theories," *The Journal of Symbolic Logic,* Vol. 49 (1984), 75–111.

Gallin, D. *Intensional and Higher-Order Modal Logic.* Amsterdam, 1975.

Gilmore, P. C. "The Consistency of Partial Set Theory Without Extensionality," *Proceedings of Symposia in Pure Mathematics* 8, Part II (1974), 147–53.

Kaplan, D. *Foundations of Intensional Logic,* doctoral dissertation, University of California in Los Angeles, 1964.

Kripke, S. *Naming and Necessity.* Cambridge, MA, 1980.

Thomason, R. *Formal Philosophy: Selected Papers of Richard Montague.* Hew Haven, 1974.

GEORGE BEALER

INTENTIONALITY IN HUSSERL. For HUSSERL [4; S] the doctrines of his teacher Franz BRENTANO [1] form the point of departure for his analyses of intentionality. Like Brentano, he thinks that intentionality is the distinguishing mark of mental states, that intentionality concerns the directedness of these states to objects, and that the object to which the intention is directed may or may not exist apart from its "mental inexistence." In Husserl's first extended discussion of intentionality in the fifth logical investigation, he analyzes intentionality in terms of subjective acts of meaning. Here he distinguishes between the material and the quality of an act. The material or content pertains to the object of the act, for instance, a person or a state of affairs; it is not to be confused with the "sense experiences" upon which the perception or representation of the object is based, since these are not intentions or even the object of an intention but exist only as nonindependent moments of the intention as a whole. The quality refers to the way in which the act is related to that material or content—for instance, perceiving, imagining, desiring, hating, or esteeming it. Together the matter and the quality make up the "intentional essence" of the act.

Husserl also follows Brentano in his thesis that complex forms of intentions, such as desiring or valuing, are based on simple representational acts that found them: one cannot desire or have an aversion to ice cream without some idea of ice cream. Particularly important for Husserl are the objectifying acts, those that establish a relationship to their object in such a way that they may be fulfilled or disappointed through intuitions. In the case of a complete fulfillment the identity of intention and object would be established, so that the object would be both intentional and being. In the case of disappointment the object turns out to be otherwise than intended or nonexistent except as intended. The object of the intention in the case of an object like a tree or a house is accordingly not a psychic but a transcendent physical object that may or may not exist and be as it is intended. The analyses of the sixth logical investigation turn on the intimate relationship between intention and fulfillment in the relationship to the intended object. "Meaning" then emerges as the particular way of being directed to the object or some aspect of it, which may or may not be fulfilled. The object itself is simply that which is given in an adequately fulfilled intention.

In *Ideen I* Husserl continues to place intentionality at the center of his analyses of consciousness, but he introduces a new terminology to explain the relationship between intention and object. The term "noesis" is employed to describe the subjective side of intending an object; "noema" is the name for the object as intended. Again, as in *Logische Untersuchungen,* experience in the form of intuition may or may not show that there is an actual object corresponding to the noema. However, there is necessarily a parallel between noesis and noema, so that an analysis of the essential noetic structures of consciousness can also reveal essential noematic or ontological structures as well. In this work Husserl not only differentiates between the quality of an intention and its matter (which he now calls its "noematic core"). He also introduces into the full notion of the noema the mode of attentiveness—that is, whether it is presented as background or foreground, as the focal point of consciousness or as part of the horizon for the current focal point. Furthermore, he introduces into the notion of the noema the doxic modality, the degree or kind of belief attached to the core that corresponds to the noetic believing. He asserts that the *Urdoxa,* of which all other modalities are modifications, is a sure belief in the actuality of the posited entity. Here he also introduces the controversial notion of "hyletic data." Husserl classifies together the strictly sensual components of an intention, using the Greek term *hyle,* "matter" or "stuff." He contrasts this with the intentional *morphé* or form that makes up the specifically intentional character of the intention, which is most closely associated with the noesis. In fact he even states: "The stream of phenomenological being has a material and a noetic stratum" (*Ideen I,* sec. 85). Most commentators agree that this presents a problem for the noetic-noematic parallel, since the noematic core clearly includes those elements of the object that correspond to our sense impressions. One's evaluation of Husserl's position here depends upon how strongly one reads the opposition between matter and form, passively received sense impressions, and the active operations of consciousness that organize the sensual elements in such a way as to establish an intentional relationship to a perceived object. In any case intentionality is associated more closely with the active, conscious, synthetic side of consciousness than with the passive, receptive elements. At the same time Husserl believes that the telos of intentionality, its rationality, is directed to evidence—that is, the confirmation of the intention through the appropriate intuition, which in the case of physical objects includes sense impressions but may take on other forms for other kinds of nonphysical objects that correspond to other kinds of intentions.

In much of his later work Husserl tried to correct an overemphasis upon the propositional, focused, clearly active elements of consciousness involved in intentionality and strike a balance between them and the passive, prepredicative syntheses that underlie them. Here the implicit intentionalities involved in habitualities of thinking, feeling, and acting become recognized as important elements in concrete intentionality. The emphasis upon the background horizon for theory and practice counterbalances the continued interest in questions of formal logic, mathematics, and science. In those analyses in which Husserl analyzes the intentionality involved in concrete human existence he also sets the stage for later phenomenologists such as MERLEAU-PONTY [5; S] to conceive of intentionality, not only as an activity of consciousness, but as bodily intentionality, as the fundamental characteristic of an organism as a whole. For Husserl, however, his emphasis upon PHENOMENOLOGY [6; S] as a pure science pursued in a reflective attitude led him to continue to think of intentionality above all as a feature of consciousness and as an activity that at least ideally should be evaluated in terms of its suitability for an autonomous, self-responsible, and self-aware agent.

Bibliography

Dreyfus, H., ed. *Husserl, Intentionality, and Cognitive Science.* Cambridge, MA, 1982. An anthology that includes several classic articles on the concept of intentionality in Husserl and discussions of its contemporary relevance.

Husserl, E. *Cartesianische Meditationen. Husserliana,* Vol. 1, edited by S. Strasser. The Hague, 1950. Translated by D. Cairns as *Cartesian Meditations.* The Hague, 1960. The fourth meditation indicates how intentionality is related to temporality and how intentionality involves passive as well as active genesis.

———. *Logische Untersuchungen.* Tübingen, 1968. Translated by J. N. Findlay as *Logical Investigations.* New York, 1970. Esp. the first investigation regarding meaning-bestowing acts, the fifth investigation regarding the structure of intentionality, and the sixth investigation regarding fulfillment and the relation to objects.

———. *Ideen zu einer reinen Phänomenologie und phänomenologischen Philosophie, Buch 1. Husserliana,* Vol. 3. The Hague, 1976. Translated by F. Kersten as *Ideas Pertaining to a Pure Phenomenology and Phenomenological Philosophy. First Book.* The Hague, 1982. Secs. 84ff. describe intentionality as the main theme of phenomenology and introduce the concepts of hyletic data, noesis, and noema. Sec. 128 deals with the relationship between noema and object and defines the concept of a "noematic core."

THOMAS NENON

INTERNALISM. *See:* INTERNALISM VERSUS EXTERNALISM [S]

INTERNALISM VERSUS EXTERNALISM.

Internalism and externalism are positions regarding the nature of positive epistemic status. The central claim of internalism is that the epistemic status of a belief depends importantly on factors internal to the believer's perspective or point of view, as opposed to factors such as the causal genesis of the belief or the reliability of the believer's cognitive faculties. Different versions of internalism spell out the internalist constraint in different ways, but all focus on the importance of *S*'s perspective where epistemic evaluation is concerned. Externalism is simply the denial that epistemic status so depends on the believer's perspective. An example of internalism is the position that the epistemic status of a belief depends only on what *S* knows to be the case. An externalist opposing such a view might think that the status of *S*'s belief depends on how the belief was caused, even if *S* does not know how the belief was caused.

Two important kinds of internalism are perspectival internalism and access internalism. Perspectival internalism claims that epistemic status depends entirely on what is internal to the actual perspective of the believer. Different versions of perspectival internalism define actual perspective in different ways, but usually it is in terms of what the believer believes, justifiably believes, or knows. Access internalism claims that epistemic status depends only on what is easily accessible to the believer's perspective. Access internalism also has many versions, depending on how one defines the believer's perspective and on what kind of accessibility is required.

The internalist constraints posited by access and perspectival internalism are very general. More restricted kinds of internalism place constraints only upon specific factors contributing to epistemic status. Thus grounds internalism is the position that the grounds or evidence for *S*'s belief must be appropriately internal to *S*'s perspective. Norm internalism is the position that the rules or norms governing *S*'s beliefs must be appropriately internal. For each of the versions of internalism specified we may define a version of externalism as the denial of that position.

Why would someone be an internalist? Historically, internalists have accepted a deontological conception of positive epistemic status, or a conception that closely associates epistemic status with the concepts of responsibility, praise, and blame. But since whether one's believings are responsible seems to depend more on one's perspective than on factors outside that perspective, internalists have argued for analogous constraints on epistemic status.

(SEE ALSO: *Epistemology* [S])

Bibliography

Alston, W. "Concepts of Epistemic Justification," *Monist,* Vol. 68 (1985), 57–89.

———. "Internalism and Externalism in Epistemology," *Philosophical Topics,* Vol. 14 (1986), 179–221.

BonJour, L. "Externalist Theories of Empirical Knowledge," in P. A. French, T. E. Uehling, and H. K. Wettstein, eds., *Studies in Epistemology,* Midwest Studies in Philosophy, Vol. 5 (Minneapolis, 1980).

Goldman, A. "The Internalist Conception of Justification," in P. A. French, T. E. Uehling, and H. K. Wettstein, eds., *Studies in Epistemology,* Midwest Studies in Philosophy, Vol. 5 (Minneapolis, 1980).

Greco, J. "Internalism and Epistemically Responsible Belief," *Synthese,* Vol. 85 (1990), 245–77.

Plantinga, A. *Warrant: The Current Debate.* Oxford, 1993.

Pollock, J. *Contemporary Theories of Knowledge.* Totowa, NJ, 1986.

JOHN GRECO

INTERSUBJECTIVITY IN HUSSERL. Intersubjectivity is a crucial problem for HUSSERL [4; S] because transcendental PHENOMENOLOGY [6; S] proceeds through subjective reflection and holds that all forms of objectivity may constitute themselves for consciousness. How then can one account for others as subjects and not merely as objects? Since direct access to transcendental subjectivity comes only through reflection, how can one have access to the subjectivity of another consciousness? This problem threatens the very conception of transcendental phenomenology as a science, since science involves the claim to objectivity as intersubjective validity. Thus, Husserl must show justification for our belief in the existence of other subjects. He outlines his solution in the fifth of his *Cartesianische Meditationen;* volumes 13–15 of the *Husserliana* fill in the details and document the development of these views.

The fifth Cartesian meditation intends to show that phenomenology is not a solipsistic enterprise. Husserl begins by attempting to abstract from any commitment to the existence of other subjects and any other elements of consciousness whose existence depends upon others; what remains he calls the sphere of ownness. Within this primordial sphere there is still a stratum of the world as the correlate of my isolated but continuing experience, a stratum he calls "nature within ownness" that must be distinguished from the full notion of intersubjectively constituted nature. Within this sphere there is also one unique object, namely one's own lived body (*Leib*), that is the organ of passively received sense impression and of movement and activity. Even as an isolated individual, one is thus capable of recognizing objects within the world, of constituting oneself as a unity of body and soul, and of organizing the world in terms of use and value predicates. However, a subject who has constituted the notion of a lived body as a unity of physical and psychic nature in one's own case is also capable of recognizing some other entities that resemble its own lived body in their appearance and behavior. The apprehension of these entities as lived bodies involves seeing them and their behavior as an expression (*Ausdruck*) of mental states. He calls this apprehension *Einfühlung* or "empathy"—although he admits that this term is easily misleading. He also describes it as an "appresentation," since the specifically subjective side of the other, his or her first-person awareness as such, is still never given to me directly. One can have genuine awareness of the other's mental states, but only on the basis of some externally observable deed or statement. The experience of the other is thus said to be founded on, but not reducible to, the physically observable states of his or her body as a material object in the world.

In imputing to the other a subjectivity like mine, I also constitute the idea of a world that is the same for all in spite of different perspectives, an intersubjective nature, and I can see myself as an object for others, as a part of that intersubjective world. Moreover, one can also constitute on this basis a world of shared values, a cultural world that ultimately could serve as the norm against which all individual beliefs and actions can be measured.

Bibliography

Gurwitsch, A. *Phenomenology and the Theory of Science.* Evanston, IL, 1975. Chap. 5.

Husserl, E. *Cartesianische Meditationen. Husserliana,* Vol. 1, edited by S. Strasser. The Hague, 1950. Translated by D. Cairns as *Cartesian Meditations.* The Hague, 1960. The fifth meditation is Husserl's best-known treatment of intersubjectivity.

———. *Ideen zu einer reinen Phänomenologie und phänomenologischen Philosophie, Zweites Buch. Husserliana,* Vol. 4, edited by M. Biemel. The Hague, 1952. Translated by R. Rojcewicz and A. Schuwer as *Ideas Pertaining to a Pure Phenomenology and to a Phenomenological Philosophy. Second Book.* Dordrecht, 1989. The third section, "The Constitution of the Spiritual World," is Husserl's most extensive treatment of the personalistic attitude within which we conduct our everyday lives surrounded by cultural objects and other persons.

———. *Zur Phänomenologie der Intersubjektivität. Husserliana,* Vols. 13–15, edited by I. Kern. The Hague, 1973. An extensive selection of excerpts from Husserl's research manuscripts. Kern's introductions to each volume provide helpful overviews of the issues that guided the development of Husserl's thinking on intersubjectivity.

Schutz, A. "The Problem of Transcendental Intersubjectivity in Husserl," in *Collected Papers,* Vol. 3 (The Hague, 1970). Schutz and Gurwitsch (see above), two close followers of Husserl, provide good summaries and some of the classic criticisms of Husserl's theory.

THOMAS NENON

INTROSPECTION. The term 'introspection' might be defined as the direct, conscious examination or observation by a subject of his or her own mental processes. The term is derived from two Latin words, *spicere* ("to look") and *intra* ("within").

From at least the time of René DESCARTES [2; S] up to the early twentieth century, it would have been considered unproblematic that the mind can reflect (or bend its attention back) upon itself. In the eighteenth and nineteenth centuries, if not earlier, self-reflection began to be interpreted, in the main, as introspection. In turn, to introspect one's own mental processes was explained in terms of the capacities (1) to focus the full glare of one's conscious attention upon the task of observing some particular, first-level, conscious process (or mental act), which was an item in one's stream of consciousness, and (2) to report in a privileged and incorrigible way upon the results of such observation. This introspective act was considered to be a form of inner, though nonsensuous, perception, and deliberate parallels were frequently drawn between it and ordinary outer perception by means of our senses, such as those of vision or hearing.

In the nineteenth century, Franz BRENTANO [1] and other philosophical psychologists were at pains to distinguish introspection (sometimes called inner observation) from its close relative, self-consciousness (sometimes called inner perception). Introspection was a deliberate act of focusing a subject's attention on some inhabitant in his stream of consciousness. Self-consciousness was an indeliberate but inescapable, though partial, concomitant awareness on the part of a subject of at least some features of some of his first-level conscious mental acts. To put it metaphorically, introspection was a deliberate ogling with the inner mental eye; self-consciousness was unavoidably catching sight of something out of the corner of one's mental eye.

However, even as this canonical version of introspection was being formulated, doubts were being voiced about the possibility of splitting consciousness into two processes that operated at two different levels at the same time. Pushing aside these doubts, the early psychological introspectionists—such as Wilhelm WUNDT [8], Edward B. Titchener, Narziss Ach, Karl Bühler, and William JAMES [4; S]—believed that either introspection proper or some version of self-consciousness was nevertheless the only possible method for inaugurating a truly empirical, that is, scientific, psychology. For only the subject of mental acts or processes can have "eye witness," knowledge by acquaintance of the denizens of his or her stream of consciousness. So, the very first psychological laboratories were devoted to introspection (for this term came to be used for both introspection proper and for scientific versions of self-consciousness). In carefully designed laboratories bristling with chronograph and tachistocope, subjects were asked to produce detailed introspective reports on various aspects of the inner conscious effects of carefully controlled stimuli applied to their senses.

These experiments resulted in some of the most tedious literature that psychology has ever produced. Also, there could be found little or no agreement about results across schools or from one laboratory to the next. Yet another consequence, which Wundt, for example, readily admitted, was that introspection experiments seemed confined to a study of comparatively trivial mental episodes.

Surprisingly, the failure of introspectionism did not lead many people to question the inherent model of introspection. As psychology and philosophy wound their way through BEHAVIORISM [1] and versions of the mind–brain identity theory to contemporary forms of PHYSICALISM [S], such as FUNCTIONALISM [S], both were faithful to the original, classical model of introspection. They abandoned the Cartesianism of the psychological introspectionists and questioned the privileged status of introspection reports, but they did not question the basic two-level picture—that introspection was a second-level monitoring, observing, registering, or tracking of some first-level process or processes.

Thus, classical psychological behaviorists such as John Broadus WATSON [8] or B. F. Skinner gave, as at least one account of one employment of introspection, that it was a literal monitoring by the subject of his thinking (which for a classical behaviorist was to be analyzed as inner truncated movements in the muscles of speech, or "stopped short" speech). Only the repeated failure of experiments seeking to verify this theory led to the abandonment of that particular, and now notorious, explanation.

The philosophers, or most of them, also championed some version of the two-level account of introspection, and still do. Even the most tough-minded of the physicalists, such as David M. ARMSTRONG [S] or Daniel Dennett, stick resolutely to a two-level monitoring account of introspection. Thus, in *A Materialist Theory of the Mind* Armstrong describes introspection as one part of the brain scanning another part of the brain such that the subject, whose brain it is, generates (in entirely causal fashion) a belief about the nature of the first-level, scanned, brain process. In *Content and Consciousness* and again in *Brainstorms* and *Consciousness Explained,* in an uncompromising functionalist account of mind, Dennett describes introspection in terms of one part of the brain "accessing" another (like one part of a computer accessing another) and then, via the speech center, "printing out" the results.

In philosophy and psychology since the 1950s, there has been a minority view that this two-level account of introspection is simply mistaken. Humans have no such second-level inspecting or scanning or monitoring capacity. Earlier, Gilbert RYLE (1949 [7]) argued convincingly that this two-level account did not make theoretical sense. Unfortunately, he substituted for it an unconvincing behaviorist account (in terms of the ordinary perceptual "retrospection" of ordinary behavior). More recently, psychologists and philosophers (such as Wilson and Nisbett, 1977, and Lyons, 1986) have suggested that, besides those theoretical grounds for rejecting the two-level account of introspection, there are also empirical grounds for rejection drawn from contemporary experimental psychology, anthropology, and the brain sciences. In contemporary introspective experiments subjects produced reports that were more like stereotyped and predictable "folk" interpretations than detailed eyewitness accounts of inner events. Besides, it seems that in cultures more or less uninfluenced by European culture people do not claim to have powers of introspection. More important, there does not seem to be any part of the brain that functions as a monitor of those neurophysiological states that maintain and control conscious states. Finally, it seems both possible and more plausible to give an account of what humans are doing, when they claim to be introspecting, in terms of the exercise of the internal but quite ordinary capacities of memory and imagination. This opposition of views has not yet been resolved, and, because of this, introspection (like consciousness itself) is likely to receive more direct and sustained treatment in the closing years of the century.

(SEE ALSO: *Philosophy of Mind* [S])

Bibliography

IN PHILOSOPHY

Armstrong, D. M. *A Materialist Theory of the Mind.* London, 1968.

Brentano, F. *Psychology from an Empirical Standpoint* (1874). Edited by O. Kraus and L. McAlister. Translated by A. C. Rancurello, D. B. Terrell, and L. McAlister. 1973.

Churchland, P. M. *Matter and Consciousness: A Contemporary Introduction to the Philosophy of Mind.* Cambridge, MA, 1984.

Dennett, D. *Content and Consciousness.* London, 1969.

———. *Brainstorms: Philosophical Essays on Mind and Psychology.* Brighton, 1979.

———. *Consciousness Explained.* Boston, 1991.

Dretske, F. "Introspection," *Proceedings of the Aristotelian Society,* Vol. 94 (1994), 263–78.

Hamlyn, D. W. "Self-Knowledge," in *Perception, Learning, and the Self: Essays on the Philosophy of Psychology* (London, 1983).

Lyons, W. *The Disappearance of Introspection.* Cambridge, MA, 1986.

Ryle, G. *The Concept of Mind.* London, 1949.

IN PSYCHOLOGY

Boring, E. G. "A History of Introspection," *Psychological Bulletin,* Vol. 50 (1953), 169–89.

Danziger, K. "The History of Introspection Reconsidered," *Journal of the History of the Behavioral Sciences,* Vol. 16 (1980), 241–62.

Hebb, D. O. "The Mind's Eye," *Psychology Today,* Vol. 2 (1969), 55–68.

Humphrey, N. *Consciousness Regained: Chapters in the Development of Mind.* Cambridge, 1983.

James, W. *The Principles of Psychology* (1890), 2 vols. 1950.

Miller, G. *Psychology: The Science of Mental Life.* Middlesex, 1966.

Titchener, E. B. *A Primer of Psychology.* London, 1899.

Nisbett, R. E., and T. D. Wilson. "Telling More than We Can Know: Verbal Reports on Mental Processes," *Psychological Review,* Vol. 84 (1977), 231–59.

Wundt, W. *An Introduction to Psychology.* Translated by R. Pintner. London, 1912.

WILLIAM LYONS

INTUITION. In the history of philosophy INTUITION [4] has been used primarily as a term for an intellectual, or rational, episode intimately tied to a priori knowledge. The term has sometimes been used in a broader way to include certain sensory episodes (appearances) and certain introspective episodes (e.g., inner awareness of the passage of time). In contemporary philosophy this broader use has fallen out of fashion (except among Kantians), and the narrower use prevails.

An intuition in this sense is simply a certain kind of seeming: for one to have an intuition that P is just for it to seem to one that P. This kind of seeming is intellectual, not sensory or introspective, in the following sense: typically, if it is possible for someone to have the intuition that P, then it is possible for someone to have the intuition that P in the absence of any particular sensory or introspective experiences relevant to the truth or falsity of the proposition that P. For this reason, intuitions are counted as "data of reason" not "data of experience." In this connection, intuitions are sometimes called "a priori intuitions" or "rational intuitions."

Intuition must be distinguished from belief: belief is not a seeming; intuition is. For example, I have an intuition—it still seems to me—that the naive set-abstraction axiom from set theory is true despite the fact that I do not believe that it is true (because I know of the set-theoretical paradoxes). There is a rather similar phenomenon in sense perception. In the Müller-Lyer illusion, it still seems to me that one of the two arrows is longer than the other, despite the fact that I do not believe that one of the two arrows is longer (because I have measured them). In each case, the seeming persists in spite of the countervailing belief. Similar considerations show that intuitions must likewise be distinguished from guesses, hunches, and common sense.

Many philosophers identify intuitions with linguistic intuitions. But this is mistaken if by "linguistic intuition" they mean intuitions about words, for most of our intuitions simply do not have any linguistic content. Other philosophers think of intuitions as conceptual intuitions. Nothing is wrong with this if "conceptual intuition" is understood broadly enough. But there is a common construal—originating in HUME'S [4; S] notion of relations of ideas and popular with logical positivists—according to which conceptual intuitions are all analytic. The problem is that countless intuitions are not analytic on the traditional construal of that term (convertibility into a logical truth by substitution of synonyms). For example, the intuition that, if region r_1 is part of region r_2 and r_2 is part of region r_3, then r_1 is part of r_3. Possibility intuitions are also not analytic (e.g., in epistemology the intuition that the Gettier situations are possible). In response, some philosophers have countered that possibility intuitions are just intuitions of consistency, but this view is mistaken on several counts. For example, it is consistent to hold that region r_1 is part of r_2, r_2 is part of r_3, but that r_1 is not part of r_3, despite the fact that such a thing is not possible.

Standard practice in logic, mathematics, linguistics, and philosophy is to use intuitions as evidence. (For example, in epistemology Roderick CHISHOLM [S] uses intuitions to show that traditional phenomenalism is mistaken, and Edmund Gettier uses intuitions to show that the traditional identification of knowledge with justified true belief is mistaken. In metaphysics Saul KRIPKE [S] uses intuitions to show that, if water is H_2O, then it is necessary that water is H_2O. In PHILOSOPHY OF MIND [S], Hilary PUTNAM [S] uses intuitions to show that logical behaviorism is mistaken, and so forth.) A great many philosophers believe that use of intuitions is essential to the indicated disciplines.

Radical empiricists, who doubt that intuitions have evidential weight, usually defend their view by pointing to the fact that intuitions can be unreliable. They cite, for example, the fact that our intuitions about naive set theory are in conflict with our intuitions about classical logic. But this shows only that traditional infallibilism is mistaken, not that intuitions lack evidential weight. After all, sense perceptions have evidential weight even though they can be unreliable. (Incidentally, although various cognitive psychologists—Wason, Johnson-Laird, Rosh, Nisbett, Kahneman, Tversky, and others—have examined human rationality with a critical eye, their studies have not attempted to test empirically the reliability of intuitions, and it will be quite difficult to do so.)

Why should intuitions have evidential weight? A plausible answer is that intuitions have an appropriate tie to the TRUTH [S]: as a noncontingent fact, if a subject's cognitive conditions (intelligence, attentiveness, and so forth) were suitably close to ideal, the subject's intuitions would be sufficiently reliable to permit the subject to arrive at a mostly true theory regarding the subject matter of those intuitions. This is a consequence of an analysis of what it is to possess concepts determinately: a necessary and sufficient condition for determinately possessing one's concepts is that one's intuitions have this kind of tie to the truth; if the subject's intuitions lacked this sort of tie to the truth, that would only show that the subject did not determinately possess those concepts (or that the subject's cognitive conditions were not sufficiently good). In contemporary philosophy, many have come to accept (some form of) this moderate rationalist theory of intuitions and concept possession.

Bibliography

Bealer, G. "A Priori Knowledge and the Scope of Philosophy," *Philosophical Studies* (1966), with replies by E. Sosa and W. Lycan in the same volume.

BonJour, L. "Against Naturalized Epistemology," *Midwest Studies in Philosophy,* Vol. 19 (1994).

Kahneman, D., and A. Tversky. "On the Study of Statistical Intuitions," in D. Kahneman, P. Slovic, and A. Tversky, eds., *Judgment Under Uncertainty* (Cambridge, 1982).

GEORGE BEALER

INTUITIONISM. Intuitionism is a form of constructivism about mathematics and logic that has its origins in the work of L. E. J. BROUWER [1] and A. Heyting. It should be distinguished both from other forms of constructivism (e.g., finitism, Bishop's constructive mathematics, recursive mathematics, predicativism) and from classical or platonistic viewpoints.

Philosophical research on intuitionism has been greatly stimulated by the work of Michael DUMMETT [S] (1976, 1977, 1978). Dummett has offered a meaning-theoretic argument in favor of intuitionism and against classical or platonistic viewpoints. On the classical truth-conditional view of MEANING [5; S], TRUTH [S] is understood in such a way that the principle of bivalence ($A \vee \neg A$) holds, and truth is divorced from the ability to recognize truth. This view is supported by a platonistic or realistic metaphysics, according to which all statements have definite truth values by virtue of some mind-independent reality. Dummett, however, wishes to proceed from general conditions about language use and the ability to learn and communicate meaning, rather than from metaphysical views about whether or not there is a mind-independent mathematical reality. He argues that we cannot justify a notion of truth on which the principle of bivalence holds.

The core of the argument is that the meaning of a statement must be construed in terms of what it is for a person to know the meaning. Knowledge of meaning must ultimately be implicit. That is, if we define the meaning of an expression by using other expressions then there must be knowledge of the meaning of these other expressions. To avoid an infinite regress, we must finally arrive at expressions for which meaning is implicit. Implicit knowledge can be ascribed to a person only if it is fully manifestable in our behavior or practice. This is Dummett's version of WITTGENSTEIN'S [8; S] idea that meaning is determined by use. Intuitionism satisfies the condition that the user of a language must be able fully to manifest his or her knowledge of meaning because it explains meaning in terms of constructions (= proofs). The knowledge of truth-conditions of undecidable statements (e.g., involving quantification over infinite domains), however, cannot be fully manifestable if truth is understood platonistically or according to the classical view of logic and mathematics.

Dummett has claimed that the conclusion of his argument depends upon the rejection of meaning holism, and he has provided a deep investigation into its other conditions. By linking knowledge of meaning with the full manifestability of that knowledge in linguistic practice, Dummett's view of intuitionism is quite different from Brouwer's solipsistic view. Brouwer held that not only could mental constructions not be adequately captured in formal systems, but they were fundamentally languageless.

Dummett's work has thus shown how intuitionism is related to many broader philosophical issues about semantics and the realism/antirealism debate. An extensive literature has developed on this basis, and various aspects of Dummett's views on intuitionism have been widely discussed and criticized. Some critics have claimed that the requirement of 'full' manifestability is too strong and should be weakened (see Prawitz, 1977). Another response is that a finitist could apply Dummett's argument to intuitionism itself to show that its idealizations, like those of the platonist, are unfounded (see Wright, 1993). Some critics think that manifestability is actually compatible with the existence of classical mathematics. It has been argued that mathematics does not seem to involve a molecular meaning theory, and that Dummett's approach is focused too narrowly on logic and arithmetic (see Troelstra & van Dalen, 1988). There has also been some concern about how intuition has disappeared from intuitionism as a consequence of the focus on meaning-theoretic issues. It has been argued that intuitionism needs a (nonsolipsistic) notion of intuition (see Parsons, 1986). Moreover, this concern about intuition does not have to preclude a theory of meaning (see Tieszen, 1994).

Many other significant conceptual advances in intuitionism are related to work that is more technical in nature (see Troelstra & van Dalen, 1988). There has been much interest in the metamathematics of intuitionism, and a good deal of research has been carried out on the proof theory of intuitionistic formal systems. Beth and KRIPKE [S] models for intuitionistic logic have been developed and used extensively. These models are now seen as special cases of categorical semantics, which also includes topos semantics and sheaf models. The intuitionistic type theories of Per Martin-Löf (1984) constitute an important new development and have been studied extensively. There has been further research on intuitionistic set theory. Theories of choice and lawless sequences have been greatly expanded, leading to further results in intuitionistic real analysis. This work will, it is hoped, lead to a deeper understanding of the nature of the continuum. There has also been some interesting work on the theory of the creative subject.

Continuing efforts to reconstruct other areas of mathematics in an intuitionistically acceptable fashion have met with some success, and there have been some especially interesting efforts to forge connections between intuitionism and computer science.

Bibliography

Brouwer, L. E. J. *Collected Works I,* edited by A. Heyting. Amsterdam, 1975.

Dummett, M. *Elements of Intuitionism.* Oxford, 1977.

———. "The Philosophical Basis of Intuitionistic Logic," in *Truth and Other Enigmas* (Cambridge, MA, 1978).

George, A. "How Not to Refute Realism," *Journal of Philosophy,* Vol. 40 (1993), 53–72.

Martin-Löf, P. *Intuitionistic Type Theory.* Naples, 1984.

McDowell, J. "Anti-Realism and the Epistemology of Understanding," in H. Parrett and J. Bouveresse, eds., *Meaning and Understanding* (Berlin, 1981).

McGinn, C. "Truth and Use," in M. Platts, ed., *Reference, Truth and Reality* (London, 1980).

Parsons, C. "Intuition in Constructive Mathematics," in J. Butterfield, ed., *Language, Mind and Logic* (Cambridge, 1986).

Prawitz, D. "Meaning and Proofs: On the Conflict Between Classical and Intuitionistic Logic," *Theoria,* Vol. 43 (1977), 1–40.

Sundholm, G. "Proof Theory and Meaning," in D. Gabbay and F. Guenther, eds., *Handbook of Philosophical Logic II* (Dordrecht, 1986).

Tieszen, R. "What Is the Philosophical Basis of Intuitionistic Mathematics?" in D. Prawitz, B. Skyrms, and D. Westerståhl, eds., *Logic, Methodology and Philosophy of Science IX* (Amsterdam, 1994).

Troelstra, A., and van Dalen, D. *Constructivism in Mathematics,* Vols. I and II. Amsterdam, 1988.

Wright, C. *Realism, Meaning and Truth,* 2d ed. Oxford, 1993.

RICHARD TIESZEN

INTUITIONISM IN FORMAL SCIENCES IN HUSSERL. For HUSSERL [4; S], intuition is the basis and the ultimate telos for all human cognition. In his investigations into the origin of logical operations and the validity of logical principles, Husserl attempts to show how all complex operations arise on the basis of simpler operations that ultimately rest upon simple activities of sense perception along with the operations of combination and abstraction performed upon them. More important, he asserts that claims to knowledge within logic must be legitimized by noninferential confirmation that is not a matter of linguistic or other social convention. Just as empirical claims about physical objects find their confirmation or refutation through intuition in the form of sense perceptions, more complex categorial claims aim at confirmation through more complex intuitions involving but not reducible to sense intuitions, and assertions concerning logical principles aim at confirmation through their own specific sort of intuition that Husserl refers to as eidetic. Logical truths share with mathematical truths the property of referring to ideal rather than physical or psychological states. In both cases the appropriate form of intuition involves grasping invariant and abstract relationships. Hence, Husserl's intuitionism in logic is intended as an alternative to conventional or linguistic theories of logical truth, on the one hand, and psychologistic, subjectivist theories on the other.

Bibliography

Husserl, E. *Logische Untersuchungen.* Tübingen, 1968. Translated by J. N. Findlay as *Logical Investigations.* New York, 1970. The "Prolegomena" in Vol. 1 contains Husserl's confrontation with psychologism; the sixth logical investigation introduces the notion of categorial intuition.

———. *Ideen zu einer reinen Phänomenologie und phänomenologischen Philosophie, Buch 1. Husserliana,* Vol. 3. The Hague, 1976. Translated by F. Kersten as *Ideas Pertaining to a Pure Phenomenology and Phenomenological Philosophy: First Book.* The Hague, 1982. The best-known passage on the difference between fact and essence is contained in part 1, chapter 1. Sections 69ff. and section 79 describe eidetic intuition in more detail.

———. *Formale und transzendentale Logik. Husserliana,* Vol. 17, edited by P. Jannsen. The Hague, 1974. Translated by D. Cairns as *Formal and Transcendental Logic.* The Hague, 1969. See esp. sections 55ff. and sections 101ff.

THOMAS NENON

J

JAMES, WILLIAM, is to classical American philosophy as PLATO [6; S] was to Greek and Roman philosophy, an originating and inspirational fountainhead. Thinkers as diverse as C. S. PEIRCE [6; S], Josiah ROYCE [7], John DEWEY [2; S] and the late work of A. N. WHITEHEAD [8] took their point of departure from William JAMES [4], especially his monumental *Principles of Psychology.* Influential philosophers elsewhere were also deeply influenced by James, for instance Henri BERGSON [1], Edmund HUSSERL [4; S], Miguel de UNAMUNO [8], and Ludwig WITTGENSTEIN [8; S].

With the completed publication of all of James's writings, including his manuscripts and notebooks, the full range and philosophical virtuosity of his work comes into focus. For too long the thought of William James was taken to be novel and intriguing but lacking in technical sophistication. In reading James the first response is one of elation at the apparent simplicity and obvious elegance of the literary style. After several careful and close readings, however, the philosophical depth and complexity emerge. The consequence of these more mature readings of James's thought are now found in many areas of contemporary philosophy, for example, the PHILOSOPHY OF MIND [S], ethics, and the PHILOSOPHY OF RELIGION [S]. More significant still is that James represents a very helpful philosophical stance, one that is chary of narrowness and rigid conceptual schematisms and affirms the messages of human experience no matter the source. William James believes that philosophy itself is "the habit of always seeing an alternative." He was convinced as well that no matter how recondite the issue in question—for example, the meaning of consciousness or his innovative doctrine of radically empirical relations—the kernel of the position taken could be articulated in prose accessible to the intelligent reader as well as to the philosopher.

The most salutary result of recent commentaries on the philosophy of William James has been the rescue of two of his most beleaguered positions, that of the pragmatic theory of truth and his doctrine of "The Will to Believe." In both areas James's thought was often subject to mocking dismissal and shallow interpretations. With the completion of James's *Works,* the girth and sophistication of his philosophy is now apparent. Witness, for example, the sterling introductory essays by H. Standish Thayer on James's theory of truth as found in "Pragmatism" (*Works,* 1975) and "The Meaning of Truth" (*Works,* 1975). Similarly, one finds an equivalently clarifying essay by Edward H. Madden in his introductory essay to "The Will to Believe" (*Works,* 1979).

The divide that has existed between mainstream analytic philosophy and pragmatism is no longer purposeful. Transformations of this conflict are now at hand. Hilary PUTNAM [S], for decades a major figure in contemporary philosophical thought, writes in his *Pragmatism* (1995) as follows:

> I believe that James was a powerful thinker, as powerful as any in the last century, and that his way of philosophizing contains possibilities which have been too long neglected, that it points to ways out of old philosophical "binds" that continue to afflict us. In short, I believe that it is high time we paid attention to Pragmatism, the movement of which James was arguably the greatest exponent.

Although in no way gainsaying the importance of specific philosophical contentions held by James, nonetheless it can be said that the most signal reason for paying serious attention to this work is found in his philosophical attitude, his approach to philosophical inquiry. William James was no stranger to philosophical debate or argument, as one finds in his brilliant and jousting correspondence with F. H. BRADLEY [1]. Yet James was uneasy about closure, answers, and finality of any kind. In a

"Notebook" entry of 1903 James writes of "bad taste," by which he means

> All neat schematisms with permanent and absolute distinctions, classifications with absolute pretensions, systems with pigeon-holes, etc., have this character. All 'classic,' clean, cut and dried, 'noble,' fixed, 'eternal,' *Weltanschauungen* seem to me to violate the character with which life concretely comes and the expression which it bears of being, or at least of involving, a muddle and a struggle, with an 'ever not quite' to all our formulas, and novelty and possibility forever leaking in.

For the thought and person of William James, the novel call of experience inevitably trumps categories of explanation. Consequently, possibility rather than solution becomes the philosophical watchword, especially in matters of profound human importance.

(SEE ALSO: *Pragmatism* [6; S]; *Pragmatic Theory of Truth* [6]; *Pragmatist Epistemology* [S])

Bibliography

Since the original publication of *The Encyclopedia of Philosophy,* virtually all of William James's writings have been published in a critical edition. Under the general editorship of Frederick Burkhardt, see *The Works of William James,* 19 volumes (Cambridge, MA, 1975–88). Williams James is widely admired for his brilliant style of writing, and nowhere is that more apparent than in his letters. To that end, with John J. McDermott as general editor, publication has begun on a critical edition of *The Correspondence of William James,* edited by Ignas Skrupskelis and Elizabeth Berkeley (Charlottesville, 1992–). Four of the twelve volumes have been published. Of recent commentaries the finest and most thorough is that of Gerald Myers, *William James: His Life and Thought* (New Haven, 1986). Other recent studies of note include: Charlene Haddock Seigfried, *William James's Radical Reconstruction of Philosophy* (Albany, NY, 1990); Eugene Fontinell, *Self, God, and Immortality: A Jamesian Investigation* (Philadelphia, 1986); George Cotkin, *William James: Public Philosopher* (Baltimore, 1990); Samuel Henry Levinson, *The Religious Investigations of William James* (Chapel Hill, 1981); and T. L. S. Sprigge, *James and Bradley: American Truth and British Reality* (Chicago, 1993). For an "Annotated Bibliography of the Writings of William James" and complete selections from his major works, see John J. McDermott, ed., *The Writings of William James* (Chicago, 1977). The entire family is chronicled by R. W. B. Lewis in *The Jameses: A Family Narrative* (New York, 1991).

JOHN J. MCDERMOTT

JUDGMENT AND ACTION. In the classical tradition of ARISTOTLE and AQUINAS [1; S], the judgment that guides action is intimately connected to a practical wisdom *(phronesis),* or prudential art, cultivated by experience and habituation in customary modes of behavior. In modern times, beginning with KANT [4; S], judgment acquires an altogether different sense, one based on an impartial consideration of possible points of view. These two senses of judgment—the former typically associated with the standpoint of the political or moral actor faced with practical decision, the latter with the historical or aesthetic spectator who understands, interprets, and narrates action retrospectively and disinterestedly—intersect in the political philosophy of Hannah ARENDT [S].

Arendt's reconsideration of the classical relationship between judgment and action acknowledges the basic facts of modern secularization: decline of transcendent religious authority and shared tradition, on one hand, and deterioration of public spaces requisite for spontaneous political action, on the other. Prior to *The Life of the Mind* (1978), Arendt still affirmed the intimate connection between "a judgment of the intellect" and knowledge of the rightness and wrongness of practical aims (1968, p. 152). Indeed, she insisted that moral and political agents living in modern conditions are especially obligated to judge the laws, opinions, and actions of their society from the common—if not universal—standpoint of "all those who happen to be present" (p. 221). What made Eichmann evil was precisely his failure to exercise independent judgment; conversely, what made the Founding Fathers of the American Revolution so distinguished was their original and unprecedented interpretation of the republican ideal as an inalienable right, requiring protection by a separate, impartial body of judges.

Arendt's late lectures on Kant's political philosophy revise this connection between action and judgment. With the deterioration of public spaces requisite for exercising practical judgment, judgment ceases to be linked with the two faculties of practical reasoning—knowing and willing—and instead takes on the function of retrospective interpretation. As a vicarious form of action, historical spectatorship preserves the memory of those all-too-rare and tragically ill-fated moments of political action—such as the Paris Commune of 1871, the resistance of the Warsaw Ghetto, and the Hungarian revolt of 1956—by judging their universal, exemplary validity. Rescuing these unprecedented displays of spontaneous self-determination from the oblivion of history, judgment dignifies what otherwise appears to be an unbearable, arbitrary, compulsive—in short, utterly contingent and irresponsible—act of freedom.

HABERMAS [S] and others have rightly criticized Arendt for dissociating the common sense guiding judgment from any relationship to truth or justice. Her earlier work, for example, links the cultivation of common sense to the agonal exchange of opinions. Since this communication is constrained by the very real effects of social domination, it remains prejudiced by ideological distortions. By contrast, her later work (following Kant) links historical judgment to an ideal *sensus communis,* or hypothetical community of taste (feeling). Here judgment achieves impartiality by imaginatively representing the standpoints of other persons as they might have been communicated, had these persons been free from domination and constraint. No doubt, an accurate account of responsible judging lies somewhere between these extremes of realism and idealism, as even Arendt herself suggests; for judging, it seems, bears witness to rationality only when tempered by the real—mutual and impartial—criticism that obtains between actors who aspire to ideal freedom and equality. (*See* FREEDOM [S].)

Bibliography

Arendt, H. "The Crisis in Culture: Its Social and Its Political Significance," in *Between Past and Future: Eight Exercises in Political Thought* (New York, 1968). Contains the fullest account of phronetic judgment.

Beiner, R., ed. *Hannah Arendt: Lectures on Kant's Political Philosophy*. Chicago, 1982. Posthumously published account of historical judgment.

Habermas, J. "Hannah Arendt's Communications Concept of Power," *Social Research,* Vol. 44 (1977), 22–3.

DAVID INGRAM

JUSTICE. The subject of JUSTICE [4]—and in particular distributive or social justice as distinguished from criminal or corrective justice—has received more philosophical attention during the last third of the twentieth century than during the entire rest of the century, and arguably the topic has been more central to recent ETHICAL THEORY [S] than to the ethical thought of any other historical period. The cause of these developments has in large measure been the work of John RAWLS [S] who, in a series of articles culminating in his book *A Theory of Justice,* reintroduced political philosophy in "the grand manner" after decades of less ambitious and more semantically oriented work in that area.

Rawls explicitly introduced his own theory of justice as a way of countering utilitarian ideas about social ethics that had never, even in the heyday of analysis and metaethics, entirely lacked for influence. His view is an idealized version of traditional social-contract theory, understood through the lens of Kantian views about autonomous choice (*see* SOCIAL CONTRACT [7]). According to Rawls, justice is best understood in terms of those principles that free and equal beings would agree to as defining the terms of their future social cooperation, given fair conditions for the making of such a choice. Rawls imagines the choice thus characterized as being made in an "original position" by rationally self-interested but nonenvious contractors who are behind a "veil of ignorance" that prevents them from tailoring principles to their own advantage because they are ignorant of what in fact would be to their advantage. Perhaps most notable in the conditions Rawls sets for social justice are his insistence that in contemporary societies civil liberties trump considerations of individual well-being or social welfare (rights of association and free speech cannot be abridged simply in order to promote the prosperity of any group) and his claim, known as "the difference principle," that inequalities in social benefits and burdens are justified only if they make the least advantaged group better off than they otherwise could be.

From the moment of its appearance, *A Theory of Justice* called forth a great number and variety of criticisms, as well as further developments, of Rawls's views. Early on, Robert Nozick, in *Anarchy, State, and Utopia,* argued that the whole idea of "distributive justice" mistakenly treats social rewards and goods as if they were part of a pie waiting to be distributed by some central social mechanism. On Nozick's libertarian view, social justice is not some sort of ideal social pattern that must be maintained by whatever mechanisms are required, as Rawls and others have thought, but consists, rather, in letting economic and social choices be made freely over time, even if considerable inequalities in welfare eventually result.

Others have criticized Rawls for the emphasis he places on individual liberties at the expense of community or communitarian values, and in a related criticism it has been argued by William Galston and Michael Sandel, among others, that, by keeping ideas about human and social flourishing out of sight in discussing the principles of justice, Rawls unnecessarily impoverishes and undermines the plausibility of his theory.

Others, like Norman Daniels, have discussed the difficulties for Rawls's difference principle of considerations about the just distribution of medical services and technology. If those needing the most medical attention are the worst off in society, then making them as well off as possible will likely cause an enormous drain on all other social resources and thus on the well-being of others in society, and it is far from clear what justice really requires in this familiar kind of situation. Recently, too, philosophers and others inspired by Carol Gilligan's *In a Different Voice* have held that interrelatedness is more basic to human social reality than atomistic contractarian views like Rawls's can allow for, and Susan Okin, in *Justice, Gender, and the Family,* has questioned Rawls's assumption that issues of justice do not arise within families.

Over the years, however, many philosophers influenced by Rawls have in a variety of ways departed from Rawls's specific views while seeking to retain some of the Kantian, social-contractarian, and/or egalitarian tendencies of the original. This has been true of Okin's work but also, for example, of the writings of Ronald Dworkin, Thomas Nagel, and Thomas Scanlon.

In *Taking Rights Seriously,* Dworkin argues that Rawls's theory of justice is based in the idea of RIGHTS [7; S], rather than being goal based or duty based, and goes on to offer a rights-based account of social justice (which he takes to be implicit in Rawls's views) centered on the idea that all men and women have a right to equality of concern and respect. Nagel, in *Equality and Partiality,* explores Rawls's view that just social arrangements must be acceptable to *all* parties (the unanimity condition) and delves into the practical and moral difficulties that result from the insistence on unanimity. Scanlon in various papers accepts Rawls's unanimity condition but has attempted to apply it more widely as a basis for morality in general, not just political or social justice, relying, to that end, on the idea of *reasonableness* in accepting or rejecting rules (in contrast with Rawls's idea of nonenvious self-interested rational contractors).

In the meantime, reawakened by Rawls's challenge, utilitarians and sympathizers of UTILITARIANISM [8] have sought to revitalize their approach to social morality and demonstrate its superiority to Rawls's proposal. Still others have been inspired in large measure by the way Rawls mines the history of philosophy for the means of large-scale political theorizing. Some of Rawls's own students have taken the cue more from KANT [4; S] himself than from Rawls's modified Kantian approach and have used that as the basis for ideas about social justice. In *Constructions of Reason,* for example, Onora O'Neill, using Kant's ethics of the individual as a basis for social criticism, criticizes certain capitalistic social arrangements as unjust because they involve treating workers or women or children as mere means.

Even VIRTUE ETHICS [S], which has long been thought to be hopelessly mired in antidemocratic political values (of the sort one finds in PLATO [6; S] and ARISTOTLE [1; S]), has found new sustenance in the rather more enlightened and democracy-friendly notions of human brotherhood [*sic*] and human dignity that are to be found in ancient STOICISM [8]. (Kant is thought to have gotten the idea that humans have a dignity beyond price from SENECA's *Epistles* [7].) Thus, as Martha Nussbaum points out, Aristotle defends a rather democratic and egalitarian notion of social cooperation except for the conditions he attaches to citizenship; so that, if, in the way suggested by Stoic ideals, one extends the rights of citizens to women and manual laborers and, indeed, to all adults, we get a conception of social justice that is rather "social democratic" and modern.

In a slightly different vein, Michael Slote has argued that egalitarian democratic values can be justified by reference to the Stoic ideal of *autarkeia* (self-sufficiency), expanded so that it includes, not only a certain independence from "worldly goods," but also a refusal to be parasitical upon others. On such a virtue-ethical conception, social justice depends on the extent to which a society's members possess and its institutions reflect motivations that accord with this ideal.

Although all these theories owe some sort of debt to Rawls, they differ in important ways, and the debate among them is likely to remain a central focus of ethical and political thought for the foreseeable future.

(SEE ALSO: *Social and Political Philosophy* [S])

Bibliography

Daniels, N. *Just Health Care.* New York, 1985.

———. *Reading Rawls: Critical Studies on Rawls's "A Theory of Justice."* Standford, CA, 1989.

Dworkin, R. *Taking Rights Seriously.* Cambridge, MA, 1978.

Galston, W. *Justice and the Human Good.* Chicago, 1980.

Gilligan, C. *In a Different Voice.* Cambridge, MA, 1982.

Nagel, T. *Equality and Partiality.* New York, 1991.

Nozick, R. *Anarchy, State, and Utopia.* New York, 1974.

Nussbaum, M. "Aristotelian Social Democracy," in R. B. Douglass, G. Mara, and H. Richardson, eds., *Liberalism and the Good* (London, 1990).

Okin, S. *Justice, Gender, and the Family.* New York, 1989.

O'Neill, O. *Constructions of Reason: Explorations of Kant's Practical Philosophy.* New York, 1990.

Parfit, D. *Reasons and Persons.* New York, 1984.

Rawls, J. *A Theory of Justice.* Cambridge, MA, 1971.

Sandel, M. *Liberalism and the Limits of Justice.* New York, 1982.

Scanlon, T. "Contractualism and Utilitarianism," in A. Sen and B. Williams, eds., *Utilitarianism and Beyond* (New York, 1982).

Slote, M. "Virtue Ethics and Democratic Values," *Journal of Social Philosophy,* Vol. 24 (1993), 5–37.

MICHAEL SLOTE

K

KANT, IMMANUEL, continues to exercise significant influence on philosophical developments, and his philosophy continues to generate an ever-growing body of scholarly literature. Work on KANT [4] has progressed in two main directions. Central doctrines of the *Critique of Pure Reason* have been reconstructed, examined, and revised in the light of current philosophical concerns and standards; and the focus of scholarship has widened to include aspects and parts of Kant's work hitherto neglected, especially in his practical philosophy and aesthetics. Both in style and substance there has been a considerable convergence between the Anglo-American ("analytic") and the German ("Continental") interpretation of Kant.

CRITIQUE OF PURE REASON

Further advances in interpreting the first *Critique* have occurred in three related areas: the nature and validity of Kant's overall argumentative procedure, with special emphasis on the deduction of the categories; the meaning and function of transcendental idealism and the associated distinction between things in themselves and appearances; and the role of mental activity in Kant's theory of experience.

The deduction of the categories, in which Kant sought to identify and justify the basic concepts underlying all our experience and its objects, has become the center of major interpretive efforts. Stimulated by the neo-Kantian analytic metaphysics of Peter F. STRAWSON [S], philosophers have attempted to distill a type of argument from Kant's text that refutes skeptical doubts about the reality of the external world and other minds by showing how the skeptical challenge tacitly and unavoidably assumes the truth of the very assumptions it sets out to deny—the reality of external objects and other minds (*see* SKEPTICISM [7; S]).

While the force of such "transcendental arguments" remains controversial, the analytic-reconstructive approach to the deduction of the categories has also resulted in more text-based interpretations that reflect the whole spectrum of Kant scholarship. Readings of the deduction start either from the assumption of experience and proceed from there analytically to the necessary conditions of experiences (the categories and the principles based on them) or take as their starting point some conception of self-consciousness or self-knowledge, either understood in Cartesian purity (a priori unity of apperception; *see* DESCARTES [2; S]) or in phenomenological embeddedness (empirical self-consciousness), and argue from there to the synthetic conditions for the very possibility of such self-awareness. A key insight shared by many interpreters is the mutual requirement of object knowledge and self-knowledge in Kant.

In interpretations of Kant's transcendental idealism a major alternative has opened up between those scholars that see things in themselves and appearances as different aspects of one and the same things ("two-aspect view") and those that regard the two as so many different sets of objects ("two-object view"). On the former view appearances are genuine objects. On the latter view they are representations. While the textual evidence is not conclusive for either view, the two-aspect theory has found many adherents because of its ontological economy and its avoidance of a phenomenalist reduction of things to representations.

The central role of human subjectivity in the deduction of the categories and in the defense of transcendental idealism has led to a renewed interest in Kant's philosophy of mind. Kant's philosophical psychology is more and more seen as an integral part of his theoretical philosophy. Special areas of interest are the essential role of imagination in perception and experience, the distinction between inner sense and apperception, and the relation between subjective or psychological and objective or logical grounds of knowledge. While no one advocates the derivation of the logical from the psychological in the manner of a reductive PSYCHOLOGISM [6], the exact function of specifically psychological considerations in transcendental philosophy remains controversial. There is a minimal consensus that the self involved in the grounding of experience is distinct from the transcendent, noumenal self of the metaphysics of the soul, so forcefully rejected by Kant in the transcendental dialectic of the first *Critique,* and equally to be distinguished from the empirical self known through inner experience. Interpreters typically stress the formal and functional rather than material and substantial sense of this "third," transcendental self in Kant.

OTHER WORKS

Important new work on other parts of Kant's philosophy has occurred in three main areas: practical philosophy, especially ethics; the *Critique of Judgment,* especially its aesthetics; and philosophy of science.

Scholarship on Kant's ethics has widened beyond the limited concern with the principle of morality (categorical imperative) to include other aspects of Kant's ethics as well as the position of Kant's moral theory within his practical philosophy as a whole and within the wider architectonic of the critical philosophy. A main inspiration of the work on Kant's ethics has been the neo-Kantian political philosophy of John RAWLS [S], who seeks to extract from Kant's formal approach to morality procedural guidelines for the ideal construction of the principles of social conduct. Increased attention has been paid to Kant's account of agency, the possible grounding of the categorical imperative in a generic conception of practical rationality, and the key features of Kant's moral psychology—including the theory of motivation, the role of moral judgment, and the function of subjective principles of action (maxims). The move beyond the traditional confines of Kant's foundational ethical writings extends to his philosophy of law and doctrine of virtues as contained in the *Metaphysics of Morals,* his philosophy of religion, and his political philosophy and philosophy of history contained in a number of smaller pieces written in a more popular vein. The picture of Kant's practical philosophy that emerges from these reconstructions, revisions, and rediscoveries is that of a highly complex theory that is well able to respond to the charges and challenges posed by UTILITARIANISM [8] and COMMUNITARIANISM [S].

In work on the *Critique of Judgment* the standard emphasis on Kant's theory of aesthetic judgments has been widened considerably in recognition of the role of the third *Critique* as a synthesis of theoretical and practical philosophy in a comprehensive philosophy of human cultural development. Much of the scholarship on Kant's philosophy of the natural sciences has focused on the *Opus Postumum* and its attempts to specify the transition from an a priori theory of material nature to physics proper.

Bibliography

WORKS BY KANT

The Cambridge Edition of the Works of Immanuel Kant, 14 vols., edited by P. Guyer and A. Wood. Cambridge, 1992–. Once completed, this edition will contain all of Kant's published works, plus substantial selections from his lectures on logic and metaphysics, his handwritten literary remains, and his correspondence—all in English translation. The following volumes have been published so far: *Theoretical Philosophy, 1755–1770,* edited by M. Walford with R. Meerbote; *Lectures on Logic,* edited by M. Young; *Opus Postumum,* edited by E. Förster.

WORKS ON KANT

Allison, H. E. *Kant's Transcendental Idealism.* New Haven, 1983.

———. *Kant's Theory of Freedom.* Cambridge, 1990. Allison's books are sympathetic accounts of the main doctrines of the first *Critique* and Kant's ethics, respectively.

Ameriks, K. *Kant's Theory of Mind.* Oxford, 1982. Emphasizes the metaphysical dimension of Kant's philosophical psychology.

Aquila, R. E. *Representational Mind.* Indianapolis, 1983.

———. *Matter in Mind.* Indianapolis, 1989. Aquila's books are phenomenological readings of the transcendental aesthetics and the deduction, respectively.

Friedman, M. *Kant and the Exact Sciences.* Cambridge, MA, 1992. Special emphasis on the *Opus Postumum.*

Guyer, P. *Kant and the Claims of Taste.* Cambridge, MA, 1979.

———. *Kant and the Claims of Knowledge.* Cambridge, MA, 1987.

———. *Kant and the Experience of Freedom.* Cambridge, MA, 1993. Guyer's three books are critical accounts of Kant's aesthetics, his epistemology, and his theory of culture, respectively.

———, ed. *The Cambridge Companion to Kant.* Cambridge, MA, 1992. Fourteen essays on the major aspects of Kant's work by the leading scholars in the field; includes extensive bibliography.

Henrich, D. *The Unity of Reason.* Cambridge, MA, 1994. Essays on Kant's theoretical and practical philosophy, including the influential study "Identity and Objectivity" (1976).

Herman, B. *The Practice of Moral Judgment.* Cambridge, MA, 1993. Argues for a complex conception of moral judgment and moral personality in Kant.

Kersting, W. *Wohlgeordnete Freiheit: Immanuel Kants Rechts- und Staatsphilosophie.* Frankfurt, 1993. A comprehensive account of Kant's legal and political philosophy.

Kitcher, P. *Kant's Transcendental Psychology.* Oxford, 1990. Reads Kant as a precursor to contemporary functionalist philosophy of mind.

Makkreel, R. A. *Imagination and Interpretation in Kant.* Chicago, 1990. Stresses the hermeneutical dimension of Kant's critical philosophy.

O'Neill, O. *Constructions of Reason.* Cambridge, 1989. Places Kant's ethics in the context of his theories of reason, agency, and freedom.

Prauss, G. *Erscheinung bei Kant.* Berlin, 1971.

———. *Kant und das Problem der Dinge an sich.* Bonn, 1974.

———. *Kant über Freiheit als Autonomie.* Frankfurt, 1983. Prauss's three books are critical studies on things in themselves, the constitution of experience, and the relation between moral autonomy and the spontaneity of the mind in Kant, respectively.

Strawson, P. F. *The Bounds of Sense: An Essay on Kant's Critique of Pure Reason.* London, 1966. The classic analytic commentary on the core doctrines of the first *Critique.*

Sullivan, R. *Immanuel Kant's Moral Theory.* Cambridge, 1989. A sympathetic account of Kant's ethics and other practical philosophy.

Walker, R., ed. *Kant on Pure Reason.* Oxford, 1982. Includes the two classic pieces: B. Stroud, "Transcendental Arguments" (1968), and D. Henrich, "The Proof-Structure of Kant's Transcendental Deduction" (1969).

Yovel, Y. *Kant and the Philosophy of History.* Princeton, NJ, 1980. Examines the relation among morality, history, and religion.

GÜNTER ZÖLLER

KIERKEGAARD, SØREN A., has been the subject of sharply rising scholarly interest in recent years. In addition to several important works devoted to reexamining KIERKEGAARD's [4] relation to HEGEL [3; S], and numerous specialized treatments of key themes and problems in the authorship, newer studies have explored the significance of Kierkegaard's thought from literary, political, and historical viewpoints.

Niels Thulstrup (1967) traces the development of Kierkegaard's critical engagement with Hegel from 1835 to the conclusion of the pseudonymous authorship in 1846. Thulstrup carefully delineates the main sources of Kierkegaard's knowledge of Hegelian philosophy. This is an invaluable service, considering that much of what Kierkegaard knew about the German philosopher was actually gleaned from secondary sources. Of special interest are the Danish Hegelians, Heiberg and Martensen, and the anti-Hegelians, Sibbern and Møller. Thulstrup also examines the influence of important German writers such as Erdmann, FICHTE [3], SCHELLING [7], Trendelenburg, Marheinecke, and Werder. The notable tendency in this work to read Hegel through a Kierkegaardian lens leads the author to conclude that the two "have nothing in common as thinkers." However, this conclusion has been challenged by other commentators who claim to find deeper parallels in their thought.

Several such parallels are noted by Mark C. Taylor (1980). Taylor points out, for instance, that both thinkers see the spiritlessness of modernity as the chief obstacle to selfhood and that both attempt to recover spirit through a process of "aesthetic education." For Hegel, however, spiritlessness represents a form of self-alienation that can be overcome only by a reconciliation of self and other, a mediation of the individual's personal and social life; while for Kierkegaard, the threat to spirit lies in the modern tendency to objectify and systematize, to dissolve the distinction between the individual and "the crowd." Taylor argues that Kierkegaard's exclusive emphasis on the individual is ultimately self-negating, since the self is never merely the self but bears a necessary and internal relation to the other. Hegel's relational conception of selfhood is thus shown to be more adequate and more comprehensive than Kierkegaard's, which "necessarily passes over into its opposite—Hegelian spirit" (p. 272). There remains a genuine question, however, about whether Kierkegaard's critique of "the crowd" precludes the possibility of a genuine human community in which individual responsibility is preserved.

Stephen N. Dunning (1985) goes even further than Taylor, suggesting that a relational conception of selfhood is implicit in the dialectical structure of Kierkegaard's writings. Dunning argues that the solitude of the self is "always a moment in a development that embraces interpersonal relations that can be contradictory (the aesthetic stage), reciprocal (the ethical stage), or paradoxically both incommunicable and reciprocal (the religious stage)" (pp. 248–49). According to this reading the *Postscript* describes a religious dialectic that culminates in a paradoxical unity of the self as both "other to itself (in sin) and restored to itself by God" (p. 249), and at the same time related to the entire community of Christians by a deep bond of sympathy. In this way, the theory of stages confirms the Hegelian insight that the solitary self is incomprehensible apart from the relational structures that give it meaning. It has been noted, however, that the formal similarities between Kierkegaardian and Hegelian dialectic may mask important conceptual differences noted by Thulstrup and Taylor.

Three studies of Kierkegaard's moral and religious philosophy deserve special mention. The first is Gregor Malantschuk's excellent study (1968). Working mainly from the journals, Malantschuk shows that the authorship is governed by a qualitative dialectic, which is aimed at illuminating the subjective dimensions of human existence, while the later polemical writings make use of a quantitative dialectic, which invokes the visible degradation of Christ as a judgment on Christendom. The dialectical method is thus seen to be the golden thread that runs through all of Kierkegaard's writings and places the individual works in the larger context of his avowed purpose as a religious author.

C. Stephen Evans's study of the *Fragments* and *Postscript* (1983) is widely recognized as one of the best general introductions to the Climacus writings available in any language. Though the book is written for the "ordinary" reader rather than the specialist—there is no critical engagement with the secondary literature—students and scholars alike have found it immensely useful for its coherent presentation of the main themes in Kierkegaard's religious philosophy, including his complex use of irony and humor in connection with the theory of indirect communication. The clarity of Evans's exposition is unsurpassed, even by his 1992 book, which returns to many of the issues addressed in the earlier work.

M. Jamie Ferreira (1991) explores one of the most difficult conceptual problems in the authorship: the nature of religious conversion. Challenging volitionalist and antivolitionalist accounts of the Kierkegaardian leap, Ferreira reconceptualizes the transition to faith as a "reorienting, transforming, shift in perspective" (p. 57). Central to this account is the concept of surrender, which is explicated in terms of the imaginative activities of suspension and engagement. Based on this analysis, Ferreira offers a compelling refutation of the popular but mistaken assumption that Kierkegaard viewed ethical and religious choice as criterionless and hence immune to critical appraisal. Her analysis suggests rather that the more wholeheartedly one chooses, the more likely one is to discover whether one has made the wrong choice. On this reading passionate engagement is not meant to guarantee that one will continue in a choice no matter what, but it does ensure that one will experience more fully what is implied by a choice. In this way passionate engagement is seen to facilitate the possibility of critical appraisal.

Louis Mackey (1971) uses the tools of literary criticism to explore the complex relation between the literary and philosophical dimensions of Kierkegaard's authorship. Mackey argues that even the most philosophical of Kierkegaard's books, the *Fragments* and *Postscript,* call into question the very nature of the philosophical enterprise. His use of literary devices, intended to create a poetic indirection, always leave the reader somewhere between assertion and irony. Mackey goes on to make a more general point about the relation between philosophy and poetry, observing that "all humane philosophy is a poetic and for that reason an indirect communication" (p. 295). Indeed, the philosophers of Western tradition have in this sense, he claims, "always been poetic philosophers" (p. 295). This theme is developed further in Mackey (1986), which attempts to situate Kierkegaard in relation to current trends in deconstructionist thought and literary practice.

Bruce Kirmmse (1990) traces the political, economic, and social history of Denmark from 1780 to 1850, giving us a detailed picture of the cultural milieu in which Kierkegaard lived and wrote. Focusing on the boundaries between the public and the private, between politics and religion, Kirmmse lays a foundation for understanding the connection between Kierkegaard's critique of society and his attack on the established church. The exposition is facilitated by a discussion of Kierkegaard's important religious writings, which are frequently overlooked in major surveys of his thought. Until recently Kierkegaard's social and political views had received scant attention in the secondary literature. Other notable discussions can be found in chapters 8 and 9 of Alastair Hannay (1982) and in Merold Westphal (1987).

Bibliography

Dunning, S. N. *Kierkegaard's Dialectic of Inwardness: A Structural Analysis of the Theory of Stages.* Princeton, NJ, 1985.

Evans, C. S. *Kierkegaard's "Fragments" and "Postscript": The Religious Philosophy of Johannes Climacus.* Atlantic Highlands, NJ, 1983.

———. *Passionate Reason: Making Sense of Kierkegaard's "Philosophical Fragments."* Bloomington, IN, 1992.

Ferreira, M. J. *Transforming Vision: Imagination and Will in Kierkegaardian Faith.* Oxford, 1991.

Hannay, A. *Kierkegaard.* London, 1982.

Kirmmse, B. H. *Kierkegaard in Golden Age Denmark.* Bloomington, IN, 1990. Contains an extensive scholarly bibliography.

Mackey, L. *Kierkegaard: A Kind of Poet.* Philadelphia, 1971.

———. *Points of View: Readings of Kierkegaard.* Tallahassee, FL, 1986.

Malantschuk, G. *Dialektik og Eksistens hos Søren Kierkegaard* [1968]. Translated by H. V. Hong and E. H. Hong as *Kierkegaard's Thought.* Princeton, NJ, 1971.

Taylor, M. C. *Journeys to Selfhood: Hegel and Kierkegaard.* Berkeley, 1980.

Thulstrup, N. *Kierkegaards forhold til Hegel.* Copenhagen, 1967. Translated by G. L. Stengren as *Kierkegaard's Relation to Hegel.* Princeton, NJ, 1980.

Westphal, M. *Kierkegaard's Critique of Reason and Society.* Macon, GA, 1987.

STEVEN M. EMMANUEL

KNOWLEDGE AND MODALITY. The modalities have played a central role in discussions of a priori knowledge (*see* A PRIORI AND A POSTERIORI [1]; and KNOWLEDGE, A PRIORI [S]) largely through the influence of Immanuel KANT ([1781] 1965; [4; S]), who maintained that

(1) all knowledge of necessary truths is a priori; and
(2) all a priori knowledge is of necessary truths.

Saul KRIPKE (1971, 1980; [S]) has challenged the Kantian account by arguing that some necessary truths are known a posteriori and some contingent truths are known a priori. A cogent assessment of the controversy requires some preliminary clarification.

The distinction between a priori and a posteriori knowledge is epistemic. *S* knows a priori that *p* just in case *S* knows that *p* and *S*'s justification for believing that *p* is independent of experience. The distinction between necessary and contingent propositions is metaphysical. A necessarily true (false) proposition is one that is true (false) but cannot be false (true). Anthony Quinton (1963–64), R. G. Swinburne (1975), and others have defended the Kantian account by defining the a priori in terms of the necessary. Such definitions beg the substantive philosophical issue in question.

When discussing knowledge of modality, one must take into account the following distinctions: (A) *S* knows the general modal status of *p* just in case *S* knows that *p* is necessary (necessarily true or necessarily false) or that *p* is contingent; (B) *S* knows the specific modal status of *p* just in case *S* knows that *p* is necessarily true or *S* knows that *p* is contingently true or *S* knows that *p* is necessarily false or *S* knows that *p* is contingently false; and (C) *S* knows the truth value of *p* just in case *S* knows that *p* is true or *S* knows that *p* is false.

Utilizing these distinctions, three different readings of (1) can be discerned:

(1A) If *p* is a necessary truth and *S* knows that *p* is necessary, then *S* knows a priori that *p* is necessary.
(1B) If *p* is a necessary truth and *S* knows that *p* is necessarily true, then *S* knows a priori that *p* is necessarily true.
(1C) If *p* is a necessary truth and *S* knows that *p* is true, then *S* knows a priori that *p* is true.

Kant's defense of (1) is based on the premise that experience teaches us what is the case but not what must be the case. This premise supports (1A) but not (1B) or (1C). For it does not rule out a posteriori knowledge of the truth value of necessary propositions. Yet Kant goes on to argue that knowledge of the truth value of mathematical propositions is a priori since such propositions are necessary. This argument presupposes (1C). But from the fact that *S* knows a priori that *p* is necessary, it does not follow that *S* knows a priori that *p* is true. Hence, Kant's argument overlooks the distinction between knowledge of general modal status and knowledge of truth value.

Kripke's argument against (1) involves a related oversight. He maintains that (a) if *P* is an identity statement involving rigid designators or a statement asserting that an object has an essential property, then one knows a priori that if *P* then necessarily *P*. Since (b) one knows that *P* by empirical investigation, Kripke concludes (c) one knows a posteriori that necessarily *P*. Kripke's argument, if sound, establishes that knowledge of the specific modal status of some necessary propositions is a posteriori. This result does not contravene (1A), which is the principle Kant defends. Kripke's claim to the contrary overlooks the distinction between knowledge of general modal status and knowledge of specific modal status. From the fact that *S* knows a posteriori that *p* is necessarily true, it does not follow that *S* knows a posteriori that *p* is necessary. Kripke's (b), however, does contravene (1C), which Kant does not defend but presupposes.

Reading (1A) has not gone unchallenged. Philip Kitcher (1980) argues that even if knowledge of the general modal status of propositions is not based on experiential evidence, it does not follow that such knowledge is a priori, since it might still depend on experience. Albert Casullo (1988) argues that the Kantian claim that a posteriori knowledge is limited to the actual world overlooks the fact that much of our practical and scientific knowledge goes beyond the actual world.

Kripke also argues that some contingent truths are known a priori. His examples are based on the observation that a definite description can be employed to fix the REFERENCE [S], as opposed to give the MEANING [5; S], of a term. Consider someone who employs the definition description 'the length of *S* at t_0' to fix the reference of the expression 'one meter'. Kripke maintains that this person knows, without further empirical investigation, that *S* is one meter long at t_0. Yet the statement is contingent, since 'one meter' rigidly designates the length that is in fact the length of *S* at t_0 but, under certain conditions, *S* would have had a different length at t_0. In reply, Alvin Plantinga (1974) and Keith Donnellan (1979) contend that, without empirical investigation, the reference fixer knows that the sentence '*S* is one meter long at t_0' expresses a truth but not the truth that it expresses.

(SEE ALSO: *Epistemology* [S])

Bibliography

Casullo, A. "Kripke on the A Priori and the Necessary," *Analysis,* Vol. 37 (1977), 152–59.

———. "Necessity, Certainty, and the A Priori," *Canadian Journal of Philosophy,* Vol. 18 (1988), 43–66.

Donnellan, K. "The Contingent A Priori and Rigid Designators," in P. French, T. Uehling, and H. Wettstein, eds., *Contemporary Perspectives in the Philosophy of Language* (Minneapolis, 1979), 45–60.

Kant, I. *Critique of Pure Reason [1781].* Translated by N. K. Smith. New York, 1965.

Kitcher, P. "Apriority and Necessity," *Australasian Journal of Philosophy,* Vol. 58 (1980), 89–101.

Kripke, S. "Identity and Necessity," in M. K. Munitz, ed., *Identity and Individuation* (New York, 1971), 135–64.

———. *Naming and Necessity.* Cambridge, 1980.

Plantinga, A. *The Nature of Necessity.* Oxford, 1974.

Quinton, A. "The A Priori and the Analytic," *Proceedings of the Aristotelian Society,* Vol. 64 (1963–64), 31–54.

Swinburne, R. G. "Analyticity, Necessity, and Apriority," *Mind,* Vol. 84 (1975), 225–43.

ALBERT CASULLO

KNOWLEDGE, A PRIORI. For as long as the concept of knowledge has been the subject of systematic theorizing, it has seemed obvious to most philosophers that there are at least two kinds: knowledge whose justification depends on outer, empirical experience, and knowledge whose justification does not. The former is referred to as "a posteriori" knowledge and the latter as "a priori."

Historically, the truths of logic (Not both p and not p), mathematics (7 + 5 = 12), and conceptual analysis (All bachelors are unmarried) have been regarded as the paradigm examples of a priori knowledge. One important feature that all these examples have in common is that they involve necessary truths. Saul KRIPKE [S] (1980) has suggested that we may have a priori knowledge even of some contingent propositions; however, this claim remains controversial (see Donellan, 1977).

The central question is: What does it mean for knowledge "not to depend on outer, empirical experience"? It is generally agreed that what is at issue here is the independence of the warrant or the justification for the belief, rather than any of its other features. In particular, it is consistent with a belief's constituting a priori knowledge that experience is required for the thinker to acquire the concepts ingredient in it.

So our central question becomes: What does it mean for the warrant for a belief not to depend on empirical experience? This being a philosophical term of art, it would be pointless to seek that single meaning which ordinary users of the phrase might be said to express by it. Rather, the correct procedure is to define various possible notions that could reasonably be said to fall under the concept of an "experience-independent warrant," and then investigate which of them, if any, best fits the paradigm examples.

The weakest relevant notion is this: S knows that p a priori if and only if (1) S possesses a justification for believing that p that's of a strength sufficient for knowledge; (2) this justification does not appeal to outer empirical experience; and (3) the other conditions on knowledge are satisfied. We may call this "weak a priori knowledge."

Weak a priori knowledge is by no means uninteresting. That there are propositions that can be justified with a strength sufficient for knowledge without recourse to empirical experience is a very significant claim in the theory of knowledge. Moreover, it does seem that, prima facie anyway, the three classes of proposition outlined above satisfy this definition. Hence, this concept can legitimately lay claim to constituting the minimal core of the notion of a priori knowledge.

Is there a conception of apriority that is stronger than weak and that equally well fits the paradigm examples? Historically, philosophers have insisted that the correct conception of apriority goes beyond that of weak apriority in incorporating the idea of immunity to rational revision.

What does it mean to say that a belief is "immune to rational revision"? And is it plausible to claim that the concept of apriority demands it?

Beginning with the first question, there are a number of different ways to understand immunity to rational revision between which philosophers have perhaps not always sufficiently distinguished. There are at least two independent dimensions along which disambiguation must be sought. First, does "rationally unrevisable" mean unrevisable in light of *any* future evidence, or only: unrevisable in light of any future *empirical* evidence? Second, does "rationally unrevisable" mean *known* not to be rationally revisable in light of the right sort of future evidence, or only: not in fact rationally revisable in light of that sort of evidence, whether or not that fact is known?

It is hard to see what motivation there could be for incorporating a notion of unrestricted unrevisability into the concept of a priori knowledge, as opposed merely to that of unrevisability in light of future empirical evidence. In general we do not insist that a source of justification be infallible as a condition of its being a source of justification: why should we insist on such a stringent condition in the case where the justification is a priori (see Albert Casullo, 1988)? Certainly, the paradigm examples do not support such a condition: it is easy to describe intuitively compelling cases of mathematical belief that are warranted a priori though false. We may, therefore, safely put to one side the idea of unrestricted unrevisability.

What about the more restricted idea of unrevisability in light of future empirical evidence? This idea is more compelling—not in the sense that the concept of weak a priori knowledge entails it, but in the sense that at least some of the paradigm examples support it.

Thus, it not only seems true of the logical principle of noncontradiction that it is justifiable without recourse to empirical evidence; it also seems true of it that it cannot be disconfirmed by any future empirical evidence. If this is right, then the theory of knowledge has reason to take seriously not merely the concept of weak a priori knowledge, but also a conception of such knowledge that incorporates a condition of rational unrevisability in light of future empirical evidence. We may call such a conception one of "strong" a priori knowledge.

Now, strictly speaking, to say that a proposition is not defeasible in light of future empirical evidence and to say that it is known not to be defeasible by such evidence, are two different things. It is one thing to say of a given proposition that no further empirical evidence could bear on it, and another to say of that proposition that it is known to have that property. Nevertheless, there has been a persistent tendency in the literature to run these two thoughts together.

This tendency has been most clearly manifest in writings that have wanted to promote a skepticism about the a priori. Willard van Orman QUINE [7; S] (1951), and following him Hilary PUTNAM [S] (1983), have pointed out that we have often been wrong in the past about which propositions are rationally immune to empirical disconfirmation. For example, Euclid's parallel postulate used to be regarded as strongly a priori, even when interpreted as a claim about physical space. However, later developments in mathematical and physical theory showed how such a claim could be false after all. From the existence of such cases of mistaken classification, these philosophers have wanted to conclude that there is no such thing as a priori knowledge in the first place.

But this sort of skepticism overshoots the arguments adduced in its favor by quite a margin. At most what those arguments show is that we do not always know when a proposition is strongly a priori. And that is very different from saying that there are not any strongly a priori propositions.

One will be tempted to suppose that any proposition that is strongly a priori must also be known to be strongly a priori only if one conflates the idea of the a priori with that of the certain. A certain belief is precisely a belief of which one can correctly claim that it will not be disconfirmed by any possible future evidence. Nothing, however, in the paradigm examples of the a priori suggests that we have certain beliefs in this sense.

Much recent writing has tended to be skeptical about the existence of a priori knowledge. As just mentioned, some of these skeptical arguments depend upon assuming an implausibly demanding conception of a priori knowledge. However, the best skeptical arguments proceed by pointing out that no one has satisfactorily explained how any proposition might be known a priori, even when this is construed as involving only weak apriority. There is a genuine puzzle here: How can we be warranted in believing a factual proposition without recourse to empirical evidence?

Historically, philosophers attempted to answer this question by appealing to a faculty of INTUITION [4; S]. However, no one has succeeded in giving a satisfactory account of this faculty and of how it is able to deliver warranted judgments.

More promising has been the project of attempting to explain a proposition's apriority by appeal to its epistemic analyticity. An epistemically analytic proposition is such that a thinker's grasp of it by itself suffices for his being justified in believing it to be true. If a significant range of a priori propositions were analytic in this sense, then their apriority would be explainable without recourse to a peculiar evidence-gathering faculty of intuition.

Quine (1951, 1976), and following him Gilbert Harman (1960), have attempted to establish that there are no analytic propositions in this sense. However, Paul Boghossian (1995) has argued that those arguments are far from conclusive. And both Boghossian (1995) and Peacocke (1993) have tried to provide a model for how the mere grasp of a proposition by a thinker could suffice for the thinker's being justified in believing that proposition to be true.

(SEE ALSO: *Epistemology* [S])

Bibliography

Boghossian, P. "Analyticity," in C. Wright and B. Hale, eds., *A Companion to the Philosophy of Language* (Cambridge, 1995).

Casullo, A. "Revisability, Reliabilism, and A priori Knowledge," *Philosophy and Phenomenological Research,* Vol. 49 (1988), 187–213.

Donellan, K. "The Contingent A priori and Rigid Designators," *Midwest Studies in Philosophy,* Vol. 2 (1977), 12–27.

Harman, G. "Quine on Meaning and Existence I," *Review of Metaphysics,* Vol. 21 (1960), 124–51.

Kripke, S. *Naming and Necessity.* Cambridge, MA, 1980.

Peacocke, C. "How are A Priori Truths Possible?" *European Journal of Philosophy,* Vol. 1 (1993), 175–99.

Putnam, H. " 'Two Dogmas' Revisited," in *Realism and Reason* (Cambridge, 1983).

Quine, W. V. O. "Two Dogmas of Empiricism," *Philosophical Review* (1951), reprinted in *From a Logical Point of View* (Cambridge, MA, 1953).

———. "Carnap and Logical Truth" [1954], reprinted in *The Ways of Paradox* (Cambridge, MA, 1976).

PAUL ARTIN BOGHOSSIAN

KNOWLEDGE, SPECIAL SORTS OF. *See:* KNOWLEDGE AND MODALITY; KNOWLEDGE, A PRIORI; and MORAL EPISTEMOLOGY [S]

KNOWLEDGE, SPECIAL SOURCES OF. *See:* DEDUCTION, INFERENCE TO THE BEST EXPLANATION, and INTROSPECTION [S]; INTUITION [4; S]; MEMORY [5; S]; PERCEPTION [6; S]; TESTIMONY [S]

KRIPKE, SAUL AARON, American philosopher and logician, was born in Bay Shore, New York, in 1940. He received his B. A. from Harvard in 1962, and subsequently held positions at Harvard, Rockefeller, and elsewhere. Since 1977 he has been McCosh Professor of Philosophy at Princeton.

PHILOSOPHY

Only a rough, brief treatment of the PHILOSOPHY OF LANGUAGE [S] and analytic metaphysics in Kripke's two books is possible here. Applications to PHILOSOPHY OF MIND [S], and puzzles about belief and other issues in lesser works, have also generated much discussion.

In *Naming and Necessity* Kripke supports, using intuitive counterexamples and other arguments, the following doctrines among others about naming. Proper names do not denote or refer through mediation of descriptive connotation or sense (as maintained by G. FREGE [3; S]) but "directly" (as maintained by J. S. MILL [5; S]); proper names (e.g., "Phosphorus") are not synonymous with definite descriptions (e.g., "brightest object in the eastern sky before sunrise"). Names, unlike descriptions, designate "rigidly," continuing to designate the same thing even when discussing counterfactual hypotheses (e.g., "If there had been a brighter object, Phosphorus would have been only second brightest"). It is usually contingent that the bearer of the name also satisfies the description but always necessary that the bearer of the name is itself (e.g., Phosphorus could have failed to be brightest but not to be Phosphorus).

Also defended are the following doctrines about necessity. Something may be necessary (e.g., Hesperus, alias Phosphorus, could not have failed to be identical to itself, Phosphorus, alias Hesperus), though it is neither linguistically analytic nor epistemologically a priori (e.g., it is synthetic a posteriori that planets seen morning and evening and named "Phosphorus" and "Hesperus" are the same). A thing has nontrivial "essential" properties, ones it could not have existed without, including being what it is (e.g., identical with Phosphorus) and being the sort of thing it is made of or from what it is (e.g., made of rock).

A mechanism for direct reference is suggested: the first user of the proper name or "initial baptist" may fix its reference by some description ("the bright object over there by the eastern horizon"), the second user may use the name with the intention of referring to whatever the first user was referring to, while perhaps being ignorant of the original description, and so on in a "historical" chain. (Some commentators say "causal" chain, but there need not be any causal connection between initial baptist and thing named, which may be a mathematical object.)

Kripke adapts his doctrines to other designating expressions, especially natural-kind terms. Kripke's work and the partly complementary, partly overlapping work of K. Donnellan (descriptions), D. Kaplan (demonstratives), and H. PUTNAM ([S] natural-kind terms) together constitute what in the 1970s was the "new," and has become the received, theory of reference.

In *Wittgenstein: On Rules and Private Language,* Kripke advances as noteworthy, though not as sound, an argument inspired by his reading of the *Philosophical Investigations,* though these are not unqualifiedly attributed to their author, the later WITTGENSTEIN [8; S]. On Kripke's reading the target of the argument is any theory (like the "picture theory" of the early Wittgenstein in the *Tractatus Logico-Philosphicus*) that conceives of meaning as given by conditions for truth, conceived as correspondence with facts. Kripke compares his reading of Wittgenstein to the reading of HUME [4; S] that takes seriously Hume's protestations that he is only a mitigated, not an extreme, skeptic. So read, Wittgenstein's attack on correspondence theories of meaning consists, like Hume's attack on rationalist theories of inference, of two phases.

First, a "skeptical paradox." Consider an ascription of meaning, say that according to which by "plus" I mean *plus*, so that 125 is the right answer to the question "what is 68 plus 57?" as I mean it. To what fact does this correspond? Not the record of how I have worked sums in the past. (Perhaps I have never worked this one before, and many rules are compatible with all the ones I have worked so far.) Not my ability to state general rules for doing sums, since this only raises the question what fact corresponds to my meaning what I do by the words in these rules. Not my behavioral dispositions (nor anything in my brain causally underlying them), since what answer I am disposed to give is one question and what answer would be the right one another question; and I am disposed to give wrong answers fairly often. Further considerations suggest it cannot be introspectable feelings accompanying calculation either. No candidates seem to remain, so if meaning consists in conditions for truth and truth of correspondence with facts, then ascriptions of meaning like "What I mean by 'plus' is *plus*," are neither true nor meaningful, and no one ever means anything by anything.

Second, a "skeptical solution." This suggests an alternative to the corresponding theory of meaning. The suggested alternative involves community usage but otherwise defies concise summary, as does the critical literature on Kripke on Wittgenstein, almost coextensive with Wittgenstein studies from the 1980s on.

One objection (actually anticipated by Kripke) is that Wittgenstein does, following F. P. RAMSEY [7], accept talk of "truth" and "facts" in a deflated sense, in which sense to say "It is true or a fact that by 'plus' I mean *plus*" amounts to no more than saying "By 'plus' I mean *plus*," which Wittgenstein would on Kripke's reading want to say, being no extreme skeptic. So a straightforward statement of Wittgenstein's view as the thesis that there are no "facts" corresponding to meaning ascriptions will not do. But as Kripke notes, one of the tasks of a reading of Wittgenstein is precisely to explain why he does not state his view in straightforward philosophical theses. One rival reading explains this by interpreting Wittgenstein as a "therapist" who aims not to answer philosophical questions but to dissuade us from asking them, and criticizes Kripke for overlooking this "therapeutic" aspect. But such a reading may be less utterly irreconcilable with the reading of Wittgenstein as skeptic than its proponents recognize, since historical skepticism was itself a form of psychotherapy, aiming to achieve philosophic *ataraxia.*

LOGIC

Kripke has worked on RECURSION THEORY [S] on ordinals, intuitionistic analysis, relevance logics, and other branches of logic. Perhaps best known to philosophers, and cited also in the literature on linguistics semantics, theoretical computer science, category theory, and other disciplines, is his work on relational models for modal logics, consisting of a set X (of "states of the world"), a binary relation R (of "relative possibility") thereon, plus an assignment to each atomic formula p of the set of those x in X at which p is true. The assignment extends to all formulas, taking $\Box A$ to be true at x if A is true at every y with xRy. Truth at all x in all models with R reflexive (and transitive) (and symmetric) coincides with provability in the modal system **T** (respectively **S4**) (respectively **S5**). For sentential MODAL LOGIC [S], such results follow on combining work from the 1940s on algebraic modelings by A. Lindenbaum and J. C. C. McKinsey with representations of algebraic by relational structures due to B. Jónsson and A. TARSKI ([8]; circa 1950), but this was noted only after Kripke's independent discovery (late 1950s). Despite this anticipation and others he cites, it was Kripke's papers of the early 1960s, presenting with full proofs modelings for predicate as well as sentential logic, and intuitionistic as well as modal logic, with applications to decision and other problems, that transformed the field—in recognition whereof relational models are customarily called Kripke models. While Kripke *qua* philosopher defends the thesis that things that are identical are necessarily so (as in the Hesperus example), Kripke *qua* logician provides a modeling method for modal predicate logic that is equally applicable to systems with and without this thesis and similarly for other controversial theses.

Also well known is Kripke's work on truth. A truth predicate in a language *L* permitting quotation (or other self-reference) would be a predicate *T* such that the following holds with any sentence of *L* in the blanks:

(1) '*T*(" ___________")' is true if and only if " ___________" is true.

The LIAR PARADOX [S] shows there cannot be a truth predicate in *L* if *L* has no truth-value gaps. There are several treatments of such gaps, including S. C. Kleene's trivalent and B. van Fraasen's supervaluational schemes. Each, given a partial interpretation *I* of a predicate *U* (under which *U* is declared true of some items, declared false of others, not declared either of the rest), dictates which sentences containing *U* are to be declared true, declared false, or not declared either. If *U* is being thought of as "is true," this amounts to dictating a new partial interpretation I^* of *U*. For a partial interpretation with $I = I^*$, or fixed point, (1) holds. Assuming a rather special treatment of gaps, R. M. Martin and P. Woodruff established the existence of a fixed point. Kripke's work, in addition to more purely philosophical contributions, shows how theorems on inductive definitions yield a minimal fixed point (contained in any other, and explicating an intuitive notion of "groundedness"), a maximal intrinsic fixed point (not declaring true anything declared false by any other fixed point), and many others, for any reasonable treatment of gaps.

Bibliography

"Semantic Considerations on Modal Logic," *Acta Philosophica Fennica,* Vol. 16 (1963), 83–94. A less technical member of the series of papers presenting Kripke models.

"Outline of a Theory of Truth," *Journal of Philosophy,* Vol. 72 (1975), 690–715.

Naming and Necessity. Cambridge, MA, 1980. Transcript of lectures given in 1970; this book version supersedes earlier publication in an anthology.

Wittgenstein: On Rules and Private Language. Cambridge, MA, 1982. This book version supersedes earlier partial publication in an anthology.

JOHN P. BURGESS

KUHN, THOMAS S. In the 1960s the PHILOSOPHY OF SCIENCE [S] saw some upheaval in its general orientation. In the earlier decades more or less steady progress seemed to have been achieved within the framework of LOGICAL POSITIVISM [5], at least in some of the key questions. But now some of these results were challenged—for instance, about explanation and reduction, together with some of their underlying presuppositions. As it turned out, the most important figure in this new movement was Thomas S. Kuhn, who was trained as a theoretical physicist, then turned to the history of science, and finally moved on to the philosophy of science. He became world famous with his 1962 book, *The Structure of Scientific Revolutions (SSR),* which is the most widely distributed book ever written in the history and philosophy of science. Why was the impact of this book so strong?

First, *SSR* challenged the existing tradition in the philosophy of science by exposing its discrepancies with the history of science. This was a controversial move, since in the decades before *SSR,* philosophy of science was mostly understood as normative, and criticizing it by the results of a descriptive discipline apparently meant to commit the naturalistic fallacy. But the discrepancies had to be understood anyway, and from the 1960s on this brought the history of science in closer contact with the philosophy of science.

Second, some of *SSR*'s central terms have had a tremendous career, not only in philosophy of science, but also in many other fields, especially the term 'paradigm', which meant "scientific achievements that some particular scientific community acknowledges for a time as supplying the foundation for its further practice" (*SSR,* p. 10). This specific practice of science in which there is a consensus about foundations was not seen in standard philosophy of science before Kuhn; he called it 'normal science', another of Kuhn's key terms. Furthermore, at this point a sociological element of Kuhn's philosophy became apparent, namely an explicit reference to scientific communities. Along with other factors this sort of reference made Kuhn very influential in many branches of the social sciences.

Third, Kuhn directed attention to what he called 'scientific revolutions'. These episodes of scientific development were seen to terminate one phase of normal science and commence a new one. Because of scientific revolutions, the development of science is not, as was often thought, a cumulative accretion of knowledge. Rather, revolutionary breaks bring about change in concepts, problems, legitimate solutions, and, in a sense, the world in which the community works. The relation between the two phases of normal science is thus of a special (and controversial) nature; Kuhn termed this relation 'incommensurability'. Incommensurability makes the comparison of competing theories more difficult and subtle than simply balancing the number of correct and incorrect predictions of the two theories, though comparison is not entirely impossible. Neither does it necessitate a conception of scientific change that is devoid of any progress. Rather, science is progressive, but not in the sense of approaching the truth. The sciences' progress is purely instrumental in the sense that the accuracy of predictions indeed becomes better and better, but not in the sense that we know more and more about the nature of things.

Finally, as a consequence of incommensurability, the commonly held view about reduction was seriously called into question. Whereas, under the image of cumulative scientific development, earlier theories seemed reducible to their successors, the meaning change usually accompanying revolutions prohibited such clear-cut reductions.

Bibliography

WORKS BY KUHN

The Copernican Revolution: Planetary Astronomy in the Development of Western Thought. Cambridge, 1957.

The Structure of Scientific Revolutions. Chicago, 1962. 2d ed., 1970.

The Essential Tension: Selected Studies in Scientific Tradition and Change. Chicago, 1977.

Black Body Theory and the Quantum Discontinuity, 1894–1912. Oxford, 1978.

With J. L. Heilbron, P. Forman, and L. Allen. *Sources for the History of Quantum Physics: An Inventory and Report.* Philadelphia, 1967.

WORKS ON KUHN

Barnes, B. *T. S. Kuhn and Social Science.* London, 1982.

Gutting, G., ed. *Paradigms and Revolutions: Applications and Appraisals of Thomas Kuhn's Philosophy of Science.* Notre Dame, IN, 1980.

Horwich, P., ed. *World Changes: Thomas Kuhn and the Nature of Science.* Cambridge, 1993.

Hoyningen-Huene, P. *Reconstructing Scientific Revolutions: Thomas S. Kuhn's Philosophy of Science,* translated by A. T. Levine. Chicago, 1993. Includes bibliographies of Kuhn's works and of the secondary literature.

Lakatos, I., and A. Musgrave, eds. *Criticism and the Growth of Knowledge.* London, 1970.

PAUL HOYNINGEN-HUENE

L

LANGUAGE. What is a LANGUAGE [4]? Is it an internal component of a speaker's mind, or is it wholly dependent on our external behavior? Is it a matter of social practice, or are languages to be viewed as independently existing abstract objects? Arguments have been offered in favor of each of these conceptions.

Adherents to these different positions can agree that linguistic theories provide the most precise way of characterizing particular languages. A theory, or grammar, supplies a set of rules describing the semantic properties of the basic expressions and their permissible syntactic combinations into meaningful wholes. The disagreements that arise concern the interpretation of linguistic theories and the nature of the linguistic objects and properties they describe.

Platonists, for instance, argue that languages are purely formal, or abstract entities, whose natures are fully specified by formal theories. For the platonist, linguistics is a branch of mathematics. In contrast, mentalists see linguistics as a branch of cognitive psychology and take linguistic theories to be about the psychological states or processes of linguistically competent speakers. For others, linguistic theories can be seen as systematizing a vast range of facts about the behavior of an individual or community of speakers, with the rules describing regularities in individual or social practice.

For platonists, such as Katz and Soames, languages with their properties of MEANING [5; S] and structure exist independently of speakers. A firm distinction is drawn between languages and linguistic competence: theories of the former are not to be confused with theories of the latter. The formal properties of a language, on which its identity depends, owes nothing to its users. Speakers of those languages may be blind to some of its properties of meaning or structure, although these may be deduced from the theory. Moreover, languages with just these formal properties exist whether anyone speaks them or not. They may be defined, according to Lewis, as sets of expression meaning-pairs, with the set of human (or natural) languages making up a very small portion of the set of all possible languages. The task for platonists is to explain what makes one rather than another of these abstract entities the language of a given individual or population. To explain this the platonist must define an *actual-language relation* between speakers, or populations, and particular abstract objects (see Schiffer for discussion). This may depend, as Lewis thinks, on facts about the conventions that exist among a population of speakers. Or it may be based upon psychological facts about speakers' competence such as the claim that speakers have internalized a grammar that somehow generates either the set, or a subset, of the sentences described by the formal theory.

Mentalists, such as CHOMSKY [S] and Fodor, insist to the contrary that the best account of speakers' actual languages should fit the facts about the meanings and structures individuals actually give to expressions: theories of language should be tailored to the contours of linguistic competence. Thus for Chomsky, a theory of language is a theory of a speaker's knowledge of language. The formal entities described by platonists are just projections of the linguistic properties that speakers give to the expressions they produce and respond to. For mentalists, language is not in the world. The world contains only marks and sounds. Language is in the mind of speakers and consists in the assignments of meaning and structure given to particular marks and sounds.

For Chomsky, a grammar is a theory of the speaker's linguistic competence: an internalized system of rules or principles a person uses to map sounds to meanings. This is a body of tacit knowledge that the speaker puts to use in the production and comprehension of speech. It contains a largely innate, and species-specific, component common to all human language users. The workings of this component are described by universal grammar. Linguistic competence is just one of the factors affecting linguistic performance. Memory, attention, and other cognitive factors contribute to the actual production of speech. For Fodor, by contrast, the rules of grammar describe the actual psycholinguistic mechanisms at work in our production and comprehension of language. Language is just one of the perceptual modules, or sensory input systems, that serve our central cognitive processing.

In contrast to the platonist and mentalist construals of language, behaviorists insist that grammars are merely theoretical representations of a speaker's practical abilities: the ability to use expressions in particular ways. For QUINE [7; S], a language is a set of dispositions to verbal behavior. Quine argues that the only evidence for linguistic theory is linguistic behavior, and that many grammars will serve equally well to generate the set of sentences a speaker is disposed to produce and respond to. Thus grammars and the sentence structures they describe are construed as artifacts of theory. Chomsky denies that behavior provides the only evidence for testing theories of grammar. Psycholinguistic evidence and language acquisition are also relevant. He also argues that we could not have learned to produce and respond to so many novel sentences just on the basis of observed behavior. The data are too impoverished to support such inductive inferences: sentences alike in surface structure differ in underlying levels of structure, and speakers respond to them differently. Chomsky concludes that speakers must bring their own internally generated representations of structure to bear on the evidence. Predictions of the sentences they find acceptable and unacceptable, and the interpretations they can and cannot allow, will be based on the fewest linguistic generalizations that fit the pattern of elicited data, and explain any gaps in the data. Claims about a speaker's grammar are thus based on INFERENCE TO THE BEST EXPLANATION [S] about the principles by which she generates structural descriptions (SDs) for the utterances she hears. A speaker's language is an internally generated set of structures.

DAVIDSON [S], like Quine, accepts that all facts about meaning must be exhibited in behavior. But unlike Quine, he holds that the assignments of meaning depend on facts about what the speaker believes and intends. Thus linguistic meaning cannot be reduced to behavior. The notions of belief and meaning are settled together by a total theory for interpreting what a speaker says and does.

Finally, is language an essentially social phenomenon? DUMMETT [S] argues that a language is a shared social practice upon which the possibility for communication among speakers depends. Lewis, although a platonist, also argues that facts about the conventional regularities maintained by populations relate them to particular languages. Chomsky and Davidson, on the other hand, conclude that the fundamental notion of language is that of an individual's language, or idiolect. Differences in grammar and vocabulary between speakers ensure that no two speakers have exactly the same language: they can still communicate because there is often overlap in idiolects, and they can work out what others are saying. Chomsky distinguishes between E-languages, which are ill-assorted, externally described, and extensionally characterized social practices, and I-languages, which are the intensionally characterized, internalized grammars of individuals that assign SDs to expressions. For Chomsky, the former notion is ill-defined, so only the latter is of use in the scientific study of language. He argues that a language L cannot be identified apart from its structure, and the structure of L is the structure assigned to it by its speaker(s). He thus casts doubt on BEHAVIORISM [1]. Many languages will share the same sounds: whether a string of sounds is a sentence depends on how different speakers perceive those sounds. Relative to one structural assignment, the sound string may be grammatical, relative to another it may not. Quine's and Lewis's idea of a set of well-formed strings, which can be generated by different grammars, becomes problematic; instead we have a set of structures that speakers assign to sounds and signs. We might reconstruct the notion as follows: an E-language is a set of grammatical strings, where a 'string' is grammatical if it has at least one structural description (SD), which is permitted by the I-language of some set of speakers in the sense that it conflicts with no principles of universal grammar (UG).

In the case of meaning, Tyler Burge has argued that word meaning depends on the social norms operating in the speaker's community; while PUTNAM [S] stresses that the meaning and REFERENCE [S] of natural terms are settled by a group of experts to whom ordinary speakers defer in their use of these terms. These social factors are compatible with the claim that the primary notion of language is that of an idiolect, as they concern vocabulary items only. Each of these different conceptions of language may coexist, all of them serving a different philosophical or scientific interest.

(SEE ALSO: *Language, Philosophy of* [4]; *Philosophy of Language* [S])

Bibliography

Burge, T. "Wherein Is Language Social," in A. George, ed., *Reflections on Chomsky* (Cambridge, MA, 1989).

Chomsky, N. *Knowledge of Language: Its Nature, Origin, and Use.* Westport, CT, 1986.

Davidson, D. "Radical Interpretation," in his *Inquiries into Truth and Interpretation* (Saffron Walden, Essex, Eng., 1984).

Dummett, M. "Language and Communication," in A. George, ed., *Reflections on Chomsky* (Cambridge, MA, 1989).

Fodor, J. "Some Notes on What Linguistics Is About," in J. Katz, ed., *The Philosophy of Linguistics* (Saffron Walden, Essex, Eng., 1983).

Katz, J., ed. *The Philosophy of Linguistics*. Saffron Walden, Essex, Eng., 1983.

Lewis, D. "Languages and Language," in his *Philosophical Papers*, Vol. 1 (Saffron Walden, Essex, Eng., 1983).

Putnam, H. "The Meaning of Meaning," in his *Philosophical Papers*, Vol. 2 (Saffron Walden, Essex, Eng., 1975).

Quine, W. V. O. "Methodological Reflections on Current Linguistic Theory," in D. Davidson and G. Harman, eds., *Semantics of Natural Language* (Norwell, MA, 1972).

Schiffer, S. "Actual-Language Relations," in J. Tomberlin, ed., *Philosophical Perspectives* (Atascadero, CA, 1973).

Soames, S. "Semantics and Psychology," in J. Katz, ed., *The Philosophy of Linguistics* (Saffron Walden, Essex, Eng., 1985).

BARRY C. SMITH

LANGUAGE IN DERRIDA. At the heart of Jacques DERRIDA's [S] analysis of LANGUAGE [4; S] is his identification of Western metaphysics with logocentrism (*see* METAPHYSICS [S]). Logocentrism has various forms, but it amounts to the claim that reason as the locus of truth maintains an ideal existence free from the materiality of language. Derrida's identification of Western philosophy as logocentric was a decisive development of Martin HEIDEGGER's [3; S] identification of metaphysics with the priority of presence. It provided a basis from which Derrida could show that logocentrism was not totally absent from Heidegger's thought, thereby challenging those among Heidegger's followers who claimed that he had overcome metaphysics (*see* METAPHYSICS, OVERCOMING OF [S]).

In discussions of Derrida the focus often falls on his challenge to the tendency within Western philosophy to treat writing as a supplement to speech, as, for example, when PLATO [6; S] presents it as an aid to memory. This has led to a widespread belief that Derrida champions writing at the expense of speech. It is true that the privileging of speech over writing is symptomatic of logocentrism's tendency to favor the alleged transparency of speech and the speaker's mastery over it. Nevertheless, Derrida's real interest is not in what is normally understood by writing but in what he calls arche-writing. Arche- or proto-writing is the condition of all forms of language, indeed of all organized systems. It is not an origin, but a problematization of the discourse about origins. Derrida's continued use of the word "writing" in this context is strategic and a consequence of his conviction that, so long as writing has been treated as a supplement to speech, it marks the place where the historical repression of arche-writing is most clearly marked. Arche-writing cannot be added to speech but dictates it.

Derrida develops this account in a number of places, but its basis is most clearly set out in *Of Grammatology*. Derrida does not advocate grammatology in the sense of a science of writing. However, engaging in his own form of grammatology, in the sense of a provisional science of textuality, Derrida finds that both linguistics and psychoanalysis, although seemingly well placed to challenge logocentrism, nevertheless fail to recognize the tension within the founding concepts of ontology. This tension is particularly acute in the case of a discussion of writing where the resistance of language to pure ideality is most marked. However, once made thematic, this tension need not be regarded negatively. By shifting the focus to textuality Derrida draws attention to the way that one can find within the language of Saussure and Sigmund FREUD [3; S], and not just what they say about language, both the symptoms of metaphysics and the trace of what it represses. Hence, the structures learned from reading them, such as *différance, supplément* (S), and *trace* (S), could be generalized and found throughout the texts of Western metaphysics.

Bibliography

Derrida, J. *De la grammatologie*. Paris, 1976. Translated by G. Spivak as *Of Grammatology*. Baltimore, 1976.

Johnson, C. *System and Writing in the Philosophy of Jacques Derrida*. Cambridge, MA, 1993.

ROBERT BERNASCONI

LANGUAGE IN GADAMER. Gadamer's primary philosophical goal in *Truth and Method* is to engage the question of truth through the elaboration of an ontology of LANGUAGE [4; S]. Following Martin HEIDEGGER [3; S], he originally locates the question at the level of existence itself in the experience of responsible concern for this "being-in-question" which we, as persons, are. GADAMER [S] asserts that this experience will be understood only in, through, and as language. This is his "hermeneutic universalism": that being, insofar as it can be understood, is language.

Thus, for Gadamer, language, reality, and understanding belong together (*Zugehörigkeit*) originally and universally; each is meaningless except in relation to the others. Language is the ontological center of MEANING [5; S]; linguisticality is therefore prior to any human language and to every act of understanding. Gadamer calls this ontological priority of language to its every human occurrence its virtuality (*Virtualität*), the superabundance of meaning that always invites further interpretation. Hence, language for Gadamer is fundamentally dialogical—it unfolds itself according to its own inner speculative dialectic that is everywhere governed by the logic of question and answer. This view represents his appropriation of Hegel's thought, transposed into the context of the absolute linguisticality of being, which, however, always remains finite and historical.

These Hegelian and Heideggerian elements of Gadamer's ontology of language are mediated in his hermeneutics, however, by his allegiance to Greek thought. From

ARISTOTLE [1; S] he adapts the notion of *phronesis* and concludes that all interpretation involves the application (*Anwendung*) of fundamental and universal human questions to the interpreter's concrete existence. With PLATO [6; S] he embraces the figure of SOCRATES [7; S] as embodying the first principle of philosophical existence: care of the soul through a discipline of dialogue that takes the logic of question and answer as its primary rule. This discipline constitutes the warrant of truth wherever it is to be found in human experience. Thus, Gadamer's theory of language enacts its own meaning: understanding occurs as engaged conversation with tradition in which there is "no progress, but only participation."

Bibliography

Gadamer, H.-G. *Wahrheit und Methode: Grundzüge einer philosophischen Hermeneutik.* Tübingen, 1965. Pp. 361–465.

Weinsheimer, J. C. *Gadamer's Hermeneutics: A Reading of "Truth and Method."* New Haven, 1985. Pp. 213–59.

FRANCIS J. AMBROSIO

LANGUAGE AND HEIDEGGER. The theme of language remained subordinate in HEIDEGGER'S [3; S] work all through the 1920s—*Being and Time,* sec. 34, was his main treatment of it. The theme began to loom larger after 1933, as he became increasingly occupied with the poetry of Friedrich HÖLDERLIN [4]. The 1934–35 lecture course "Hölderlin's *Germania* and *The Rhine*" was followed in 1935 by the programmatic address "Hölderlin and the Essence of Poetry." On the one hand, he drew upon the poetry to emphasize national and religious themes; on the other hand, he devoted extraordinary care to eliciting the way the poems spoke, the character of their singing and saying, their silences, and their hints. He began to see in lyric poetry the very essence of language itself, everyday speech being nothing more than "a forgotten and used-up poem" (1971, p. 208). In keeping with that view Heidegger did not merely interpret the poems; rather, he sought to allow the language of the poems to penetrate his own language. Increasingly, his texts were suffused with quotations and covert citations from the poems of Hölderlin, and, as the years went by, from the poems of Georg Trakl, Stefan George, and Rainer Maria RILKE [7]. This was particularly pronounced whenever Heidegger's thought turned to the topic of language itself: he drew upon poems for names that would serve to express the very power of words. In his poem "Homecoming," Hölderlin evokes a cloud hovering over the Alpine peaks, and Heidegger reads the cloud (*die Wolke*) as a reference to poetry and language. Later, in the *Letter on Humanism,* he would write that "language is the language of being as the clouds are the clouds of the sky." Reading Hölderlin's *Germania,* Heidegger hears the eagle of Zeus say that language is "the flower of the mouth." Language itself "comes to language," it is brought to utterance, when it is named by the words of the poet.

At the focus of Heidegger's thought on LANGUAGE [4; S], then, is the single word—"Das Wort" is one of his essays—not the linguistic system, the syntactic and lexical totality of structural linguistics or the diachronic totality of the philologist. Even within a single poem, it is usually a single word that interests Heidegger, not the poem's overall rhetorical and euphonic effect. It is as if the single word were itself a poem. The character of Heidegger's interest in the word, however, is certainly in keeping with his heritage as a philosopher rather than a rhetorician or a critic. The power of the word—to name—is a relationship to beings and to Being. Many different studies of the poetic word elaborate Heidegger's views of its power. The word allows a thing to come into presence as a thing, a power that Heidegger names *Bedingnis,* using a term from GOETHE [3] (*On the Way to Language*). The poet has submitted to *Bedingnis:* "where the word fails, no thing may be" (Stefan George). Yet its power is not a "ground of the possibility" for things, not a condition (*Bedingung*). The important study "Language" ("Die Sprache") says that the poem and the word speak, that is to say, they name the things, which is to say they call out to them, or invite them to approach, bid them come. Yet by preserving a silence as well, they shelter the things in absence, they still them. Putting a variation on the imagery of Georg Trakl's poetry, Heidegger thinks of language here as the "calling of silence," calling to things and to the world at once. In a lengthy published dialogue with a Japanese, Heidegger seeks to refashion the Japanese word for language, *koto ba,* into another poetic image, "flower petals, that thrive out of radiant tidings." These are for Heidegger hints (*Winke*) as to the nature and being of language, and indeed hinting is the very work of language and poetry.

Bibliography

Heidegger, M. *Unterwegs zur Sprache.* Pfullingen, 1959. Translated by P. Hertz and J. Stambaugh as *On the Way to Language.* New York, 1971.

———. *Poetry, Language, Thought,* translated by A. Hofstadter. New York, 1971.

———. *Erläuterungen zu Hölderlins Dichtung (1936–1968),* edited by F.-W. von Herrmann. Frankfurt, 1991.

———. *Existence and Being,* edited by W. Brock. Chicago, 1949. Contains two Hölderlin interpretations.

GRAEME NICHOLSON

LANGUAGE AND THOUGHT. Should questions about thought—about intentionality, beliefs, and concept possession, for example—be approached directly or, instead, indirectly via the PHILOSOPHY OF LANGUAGE

[S]? There are two slightly different ways in which questions about LANGUAGE [4; S] and MEANING [5; S] might seem to offer illumination of issues concerning thought. One way relates to language that is explicitly about thoughts, as when someone says, "Bruce believes that boomerangs seldom come back." The idea that a philosophical investigation of thought should proceed via a study of the logical properties of language that is about thoughts is a particular case of a more general view that philosophy of language enjoys a certain priority over metaphysics.

The other way relates to the use of language to *express* thoughts, and this provides the topic for the present entry. Suppose that Bruce believes that boomerangs seldom come back, and expresses this thought in the English sentence: "Boomerangs seldom come back." Which takes priority, the meaning of the English sentence or the content of Bruce's thought?

A claim of priority is the converse of a claim of one-way dependence: X enjoys priority over Y if Y depends on X but X does not depend on Y. Thus, a question of the relative priority of X and Y has four possible answers: X has priority; Y has priority; X and Y are mutually dependent; X and Y are independent. But the question of the relative priority of thought and language is still unclear, until the relevant kind of priority has been specified. It is useful to distinguish three kinds of priority question: ontological, epistemological, and analytical (see Avramides, 1989, for a similar distinction).

To say that thought enjoys *ontological priority* over language is to say that language is ontologically dependent on thought, while thought is not so dependent on language. That is, there can be thought without language, but there cannot be language without thought. To say that thought enjoys *epistemological priority* over language is to say that the route to knowledge about language (specifically, about linguistic meaning) goes via knowledge about thought (specifically, about the contents of thought), while knowledge about thought can be had without going via knowledge about language.

Donald DAVIDSON [S] denies both these priority claims. As for ontological priority, he argues (1975) that there cannot be thought without language: in order to have thoughts (specifically, beliefs), a creature must be a member of a language community, and an interpreter of the speech of others. As for epistemological priority, Davidson argues (1974) that it is not possible to find out in detail what a person believes without interpreting the person's speech.

Analytical priority is priority in the order of philosophical analysis or elucidation. To say that X is analytically prior to Y is to say that key notions in the study of Y can be analyzed or elucidated in terms of key notions in the study of X, while the analysis or elucidation of the X notions does not have to advert to the Y notions. On the question of the relative analytical priority of thought and language, there are, then, four positions to consider: two priority views, and two no-priority views.

PRIORITY FOR THOUGHT

A philosophical account of the content of thoughts—of INTENTIONALITY [4]—can be given without essential appeal to language, and the notion of linguistic meaning can then be analyzed or elucidated in terms of the thoughts that language is used to express. The analytical program of Paul GRICE [S] was aimed at an analysis of linguistic meaning in terms of the beliefs and intentions of language users, though Grice did not offer any account of the intentionality of mental states themselves (Grice, 1989; see also Schiffer, 1972). There are many proposals for explaining the intentionality of mental states without appeal to linguistic meaning, and these might be coupled with an elucidation of linguistic meaning in terms of mental notions. It is widely reckoned, however, that the Gricean analytical program cannot be carried through (Schiffer, 1987).

PRIORITY FOR LANGUAGE

An account of linguistic meaning can be given without bringing in the intentionality of thoughts, and what a person's thoughts are about can then be analyzed in terms of the use of language. This view can be found in Michael DUMMETT's [S] work (1973, 1991, 1993). If a theorist attempts to give a substantive account of linguistic meaning in accordance with this view, then the resources that can be invoked are seriously limited, since the account cannot presume upon everyday psychological notions such as belief and intention. Because of this, it would not be surprising to find hints of BEHAVIORISM [1] in work that is influenced by this view.

NO PRIORITY—INTERDEPENDENCE

There is no way of giving an account of either intentionality or linguistic meaning without bringing in the other member of the pair. The two notions have to be explained together. This is Davidson's view (Davidson, 1984). He thus maintains an ontological, epistemological, and analytical no-priority position. While the three no-priority claims go together quite naturally, it is important to note that they are separable claims and that the analytical no-priority claim is not entailed by the ontological and epistemological no-priority claims.

NO PRIORITY—INDEPENDENCE

The notions of intentionality for mental states and of linguistic meaning are unrelated. This view might be defended if a language is considered as an abstract entity, composed of a set of expressions together with a function that assigns a value to each expression (a proposition to each sentence, for example). On such a conception, meaning is a purely formal notion. But for the notion of linguistic meaning as it applies to a public language in use, this fourth view is implausible.

Bibliography

Avramides, A. *Meaning and Mind: An Examination of a Gricean Account of Language.* Cambridge, MA, 1989.

Davidson, D. "Belief and the Basis of Meaning," *Synthese,* Vol. 27 (1974), 309–23.

———. "Thought and Talk," in S. Guttenplan, ed., *Mind and Language.* (Oxford, 1975).

Dummett, M. *Frege: Philosophy of Language.* London, 1973.

———. *Truth and Other Enigmas.* London, 1978.

———. *Inquiries into Truth and Interpretation.* Oxford, 1984.

———. *The Logical Basis of Metaphysics.* Cambridge, MA, 1991.

———. *The Seas of Language.* Oxford, 1993.

Grice, H. P. *Studies in the Way of Words.* Cambridge, MA, 1989.

Schiffer, S. *Meaning* [1972]. Oxford, 1988.

———. *The Remnants of Meaning.* Cambridge, MA, 1987.

Sellars, W. S., and R. M. Chisholm. "Intentionality and the Mental," in H. Feigl, M. Scriven, and G. Maxwell, eds., *Minnesota Studies in the Philosophy of Science, Volume 2: Concepts, Theories, and the Mind–Body Problem* (Minneapolis, 1958).

MARTIN DAVIES

LANGUAGE OF THOUGHT. Simply stated, the language-of-thought thesis (LOT) holds that thinking (i.e., cognition) is carried out in a languagelike medium, where the thoughts that constitute thinking are themselves sentencelike states of the thinker. Since the demise of philosophical BEHAVIORISM [1] in the early 1960s the LOT thesis has enjoyed considerable support as a central tenet of a more encompassing representationalist theory of mind (RTM). Proponents of RTM, led by Jerry Fodor, have mounted a sustained defense of LOT.

RTM offers an account of PROPOSITIONAL ATTITUDES [S]—beliefs, desires, doubts, and so on—according to which propositional attitudes relate the possessor of the attitude to a MENTAL REPRESENTATION [S] (cf. Fodor, 1981). Mental representations have both semantic and physically realized formal properties: they are semantically evaluable (e.g., as being true or false, as being about or referring to certain entities or properties); they stand in inferential relations to other mental representations; and, like words, pictures, and other representations, they also have certain formal properties (e.g., shape, size, etc.) in virtue of being physical, presumably neural, entities. Mental representations, and hence propositional attitudes, have their causal roles in thinking and behavior in virtue of their formal properties. Propositional attitudes inherit semantic properties from the mental representations that are one of their relata. RTM is silent as to what kind or sort of representation these mental representations are (cf. Fodor, 1987, pp. 136–38).

LOT supplements RTM with a specific proposal or hypothesis about the character of mental representations: like sentences of a language, they are structured entities, and their structures provide the basis for the particular semantic and causal properties that propositional attitudes exhibit. More specifically, they are syntactically structured entities, composed of atomic constituents (concepts) that refer to or denote things and properties in the world. The semantic properties of a mental representation, including both truth conditions and inferential relations, are determined by the representation's syntactic structure together with the semantic properties of its atomic constituents. Mental representations, in other words, have a combinatorial semantics. The causal properties of a representation are similarly determined by the representation's syntactic structure together with the formal properties of its atomic constituents.

Three sorts of arguments have been advanced in support of LOT. The first makes much of the apparent semantic parallels between thoughts and sentences. Both beliefs and declarative sentences, for example, are typically meaningful, truth valued, and intentional (in the sense of being about something). Both stand in various inferential relations to other beliefs and assertions. One obvious explanation of these parallels is that thought has a languagelike character, individual thoughts a sentencelike structure. A second sort of argument focuses on the productivity and systematicity of thought. Thought, like language, is productive in the sense that there are indefinitely many, indefinitely complex thoughts. Whatever can be said can also be thought. Thought, like language, is also systematic in the sense that you can think one thought (e.g., that the child bit the monkey) if and only if one can also think certain other systematically related thoughts (that the monkey bit the child). Again, one obvious explanation is that thought has a languagelike character, individual thoughts a sentencelike structure. A third sort of argument claims that much cognitive scientific theorizing seems committed to LOT. Specifically, our best theories of rational choice, perception, and learning seem committed to the claim, not simply that cognition is a matter of the creation and manipulation of mental representations, but also that these representations are sentential in character. It is claimed, for example, that our best theories of learning are a species of hypothesis testing. But such a procedure, it is argued, presupposes the existence of a language, that is, a language of thought in which the hypothesis being tested is formulated.

Proponents of LOT readily concede that these arguments are not decisive. Each is an instance of INFERENCE

TO THE BEST EXPLANATION [S], and as such each is vulnerable to refutation by some alternative explanation that does not appeal to a language of thought.

Critics of LOT find the foregoing sorts of arguments unpersuasive for any of a number of reasons. Either they believe that there are equally good explanations that don't appeal to a language of thought, or they deny the phenomena that LOT is said to explain, or they hold that the proposed explanations either rest on false presuppositions or are so sketchy and incomplete as not to merit the name, or they believe that these explanations have entailments so implausible as to impugn the explanatory premise that there exists a language of thought. Thus, for example, the argument from learning discussed above apparently entails that to learn a language one must already know a language. Many critics find in this entailment a reductio of LOT. Proponents such as Fodor, by contrast, have courageously embraced this entailment, arguing that all concepts, including, for example, our concept of a Boeing 747, are innate. Whatever the specific merits and defects of the arguments and counterarguments, it seems fair to say that the existence of a language of thought remains an open empirical question.

(SEE ALSO: *Philosophy of Mind* [S])

Bibliography

DEFENDING LOT

Field, H. "Mental Representations," *Erkenntnis,* Vol. 13 (1978), 9–61.

———. *The Language of Thought.* New York, 1975.

———. *Representations.* Cambridge, MA, 1981.

———. "Why There Still Has to Be a Language of Thought," in *Psychosemantics* (Cambridge, MA, 1987).

CRITICIZING LOT

Churchland, P. M., and P. S. Churchland. "Stalking the Wild Epistemic Engine," *Noûs,* Vol. 17 (1983), 5–18.

Dennett, D. C. "Brain Writing and Mind Reading," in *Brainstorms* (Cambridge, MA, 1978).

Dennett, D. C. "A Cure for the Common Code," in *Brainstorms* (Cambridge, MA, 1978).

Loar, B. "Must Beliefs Be Sentences?" in P. Asquith and T. Nickles, eds., *Proceedings of the PSA, 1982* (East Lansing, MI, 1983).

Schiffer, S. *Remnants of Meaning.* Cambridge, MA, 1987.

ROBERT J. MATTHEWS

LAWS OF NATURE.

The laws of nature are the general ways of working of the physical and mental world. Many natural scientists have as one of their great aims the uncovering of these laws. The topic of laws of nature has been the subject of vigorous discussion in contemporary philosophy. Three broad tendencies have emerged, with a number of important variations within these tendencies.

THE REGULARITY OR HUMEAN VIEW

Since the work of David HUME [4; S], at least, there have been many philosophers, particularly those in the empiricist tradition, who have tried to analyze both causes and laws (which they tend not to distinguish very clearly) in terms of mere regular successions or other regularities in the behavior of things (*see* EMPIRICISM [2]). Laws tell us that, given a phenomenon of a certain sort, then a further phenomenon of a certain sort must occur in a certain relation to the first phenomenon. Particularly since the rise of quantum physics, this may be modified by saying that there must be a certain PROBABILITY [4; 6] that the further phenomenon will occur. Regularity theorists see this "must" as mere universality: this is what always happens.

A great many difficulties have been raised against this position (for a fairly full listing see Armstrong, 1983, pt. 1). The most important of these are as follows.

1. The intuitive difference between merely accidental uniformities and nomic (lawlike) uniformities. The traditional example is the contrast between the accidental uniformity that every sphere of gold has a diameter of less than one mile and the nomic uniformity that every sphere of uranium 235 has a diameter of less than one mile, because that diameter would ensure "critical mass" and the explosion of the sphere.

2. Laws of nature "sustain counterfactuals." If it is a law that arsenic is poisonous, then if, contrary to the facts, you had drunk arsenic, then you would have been very sick. But from the fact that no human being of Neanderthal race ever spoke English, it by no means follows that if, contrary to fact, some of them had lived in an English-speaking society, they would not have spoken English. The uniformity that Neanderthals spoke no English does not sustain counterfactuals.

3. A regularity theorist cannot give a satisfactory solution to the problem of INDUCTION [4]. If laws are mere regularities, what rational grounds have we for believing that observed uniformities will continue to hold in the future and for the unobserved generally?

4. A regularity theorist is likely to identify merely probabilistic laws with actually occurring frequencies. This identification is difficult, because such laws do not actually rule out distributions with the "wrong" frequencies. All that probabilistic laws do is to make such frequencies improbable; they do not make them nomically impossible.

5. Science admits certain laws that may well have no positive instances falling under them. The most famous example is NEWTON's [5] first law of motion. An unin-

stantiated law would have to be a vacuous uniformity, but there are far too many such uniformities all to be laws.

Those who continue to work in the regularity tradition try to meet these and other difficulties largely by distinguishing "good" uniformities that deserve to be called laws and "bad" ones that do not. There are two main approaches, the epistemic and the systematic.

Epistemic theorists emphasize the nature of the evidence that we have for claiming that certain uniformities obtain. References and criticism may be found in Suchting (1974), Molnar (1974), Dretske (1977), and ARMSTRONG [1] (1983). Brian Skyrms's (1980) resiliency account is a sophisticated epistemic approach. His basic idea is that we give assent to a generalization, and count it lawlike, only if we find it to hold under a wide variety of circumstances and conditions. For criticism of Skyrms, see Tooley (1987) and Carroll (1990).

The systematic approach has been championed by David Lewis, explicitly basing himself on a suggestion made by F. P. RAMSEY [7]. Lewis says that "contingent generalization is a *law of nature* if and only if it appears as a theorem (or axiom) in each of the true deductive systems that achieves the best combination of simplicity and strength" (1973, p. 73). Further discussion may be found in Lewis (1986). He himself finds that his greatest difficulties are associated with probabilistic laws. For criticism of Lewis see Armstrong (1983), Tooley (1987), Carroll (1990).

STRONG LAWS

One who judges that no regularity theory of laws can succeed may wish to argue that laws are something stronger than mere uniformities or statistical distributions. Laws may be called strong if their existence entails the existence of the corresponding uniformities and so on but the reverse entailment fails to hold.

Traditional theories of strong laws tended to see these laws as holding necessarily. Given all the antecedent conditions, the consequent is entailed. In the days when Euclidean geometry was unchallenged, geometrical models were attractive (see, among many, DESCARTES [2; S], HOBBES, LOCKE [4; S]). As with geometrical theorems, this necessity was thought to be discoverable, at least potentially, a priori. Granted that laws might in practice be discovered by experience, just as the Pythagorean theorem might be discovered by measuring and adding areas, it was still thought that a sufficiently powerful intellect might spell out the necessity involved without the aid of experience. This approach seems to have been abandoned by contemporary philosophers (though there are hints in Martin, 1993). It now seems agreed, in general, and in agreement with regularity theorists, that the laws of nature can be discovered only a posteriori.

Upholders of strong laws do, however, differ among themselves whether these laws are contingent or necessary. The contingency view (also held by regularity theorists) is represented by Fred Dretske (1977), Michael Tooley (1977, 1987) and D. M. Armstrong (1983). These three evolved their rather similar views independently and almost simultaneously. Laws are argued to be dyadic relations of necessitation holding contingently between universals, schematically N(F,G). Such a relation entails the regularity that all Fs are Gs, but the regularity does not entail N(F,G). Dretske presents the central idea with particular clarity; Tooley and Armstong develop the theory more fully. Tooley argues that the possibility of certain sorts of uninstantiated laws demands uninstantiated universals, leading him to what he calls a factual Platonism about universals. Armstrong, however, tries to get along with instantiated universals only.

The theory appears to be able to handle probabilistic laws (see Armstong, 1983, chap. 9; Tooley, 1987, chap. 4). The connection between universals envisaged by the theory may be thought of as involving connections of differing strength holding between antecedent and consequent universals. The greatest strength, one (exactly one, not one minus an infinitesimal), represents the probability involved in an old-style deterministic law. The consequent universal must be instantiated if the antecedent universal is. Numbers between nought and one give the lesser probability of the consequent being instantiated under these conditions. This probability is an objective one. The antecedent universal, if instantiated, bestows an objective propensity, as some say, for the instantiation of the consequent.

An obvious cost of this sort of theory is that it must postulate universals. This is a stumbling block to many. But by far the most important criticism of this account has been developed by Bas van Fraassen (1989, chap. 5; see also the discussion-review of this book by him, Earman, Cartwright, and Armstrong, 1993). He poses two difficulties: the identification problem and the inference problem. The first is the problem of identifying in a noncircular way the nature of the necessitation relation supposed to hold between the universals involved in the law. The second is the problem, given a concrete account of this relation, of understanding why it is legitimate to infer from the fact that the universals are so related to the existence of corresponding uniformities or frequencies in the world. Van Fraassen argues that solving the one problem makes it impossible to solve the other. A clear account of the relation makes the inference problematic; a clearly valid inference makes the relation no more than something that validates the inference.

The view that laws of nature are necessities discovered a posteriori is developed by Sydney Shoemaker (1980) and Chris Swoyer (1982). They build on Saul KRIPKE's [S] (1980) arguments for a posteriori knowledge of necessity, and Kripke hints that laws of nature may have this status. Their view depends upon taking a different view of properties from that found in Dretske, Tooley, and Armstrong. For the latter, properties are conceived of as 'categorical' or self-contained entities. But for Shoemaker and Swoyer, properties, either singly or in combination, are nothing apart from the laws they enter into. They might be described as pure powers or dispositions to produce law-governed consequences.

On this view, therefore, if it is a law that property F ensures possession of property G, then it is the very essence of F so to ensure G, and so the law is necessary. That there are things having property F is contingent, but that F ensures G is necessary. It seems, then, that the dispute between contingent strong laws and necessary ones depends on the true theory of properties. See Richard Swinburne's (1983) critical comments on Shoemaker.

The view of properties just discussed might be called dispositionalism as opposed to categoricalism. There are theorists who favor a view of properties that gives them both a categorical and a dispositional (or power) side; see Evan Fales (1990) and C. B. Martin (1993). It is to be noted that both in pure dispositionalism and this mixed theory there is a strong tendency to regard laws as not fundamental but rather analyzable in terms of causal relations holding between individual events and particulars (singular causation). These causal relations, and so their laws, are determined by the nature of the dispositions or powers that particulars have.

ELIMINATIVISM ABOUT LAWS

The regularity theory of laws is a deflationary theory. It holds that there is less to being a law than one might naturally think. It also faces a number of serious difficulties. One response, rather typical of our age, is to meet the difficulties, not by proposing a strengthened theory of laws, but by taking the deflation further and arguing that there are no such things as laws. This is the position taken by van Fraassen in *Laws and Symmetry* (1989). A natural comparison is with ELIMINATIVE MATERIALISM [S], which denies the existence of the mind in favor of the brain.

Van Fraassen begins with a systematic criticism, first of Lewis's version of the regularity theory, and then of various strong views. The rejection of laws he links to his "constructive empiricism," according to which the aim of science is not truth in general but only empirical adequacy, defined as truth with respect to what is observed. Beyond the observable, all that can usefully be done is the constructing of models that are in a deep way adequate to the phenomena and that may be true but about which we can have no special reason to think them true. In these constructions considerations of symmetry play an energizing role.

A certain skepticism about laws is also to be found in Nancy Cartwright's *How the Laws of Physics Lie* (1983). Her skepticism concerns the fundamental as opposed to more messy phenomenological laws. The former may explain better, but the latter are truer to the facts! The distinction she is concerned with is one made by physicists, and the "phenomenological" laws go far beyond van Fraassen's observables. Cartwright accepts these laws because the entities they deal with, though perhaps unobserved, appear to exist and to act as causes. In *Nature's Capacities and Their Measurement* (1989), she argues that the world is a world of singular causes, individual entities interacting with each other. The nature of these interactions is determined by the capacities of these entities. Her capacities seem close to the dispositions and powers that contemporary necessitarians identify with properties.

Bibliography

Armstrong, D. M. *What Is a Law of Nature?* Cambridge, 1983.

Carroll, J. "The Humean Tradition," *Philosophical Review,* Vol. 99 (1990), 261–76.

———. *Laws of Nature.* Cambridge, 1994. Contains a useful set of references.

Cartwright, N. *How the Laws of Physics Lie.* Oxford, 1983.

———. *Nature's Capacities and Their Measurement.* Oxford, 1989.

Dretske, F. "Laws of Nature," *Philosophy of Science,* Vol. 44 (1977), 248–68.

Fales, E. *Causation and Universals.* London, 1990.

Kripke, S. *Naming and Necessity.* Oxford, 1980.

Lewis, D. *Counterfactuals.* Cambridge, MA, 1973.

———. *Philosophical Papers,* Vol. 2. New York, 1986.

Martin, C. B. "Power for Realists," in J. Bacon, K. Campbell, and L. Reinhardt, eds., *Ontology, Causality, and Mind* (Cambridge, 1993).

Molnar, G. "Kneale's Argument Revisited," in T. Beauchamp, ed., *Philosophical Problems of Causation* (Belmont, CA, 1974).

Shoemaker, S. "Causality and Properties," in *Identity, Cause, and Mind* (Cambridge, 1984).

Skyrms, B. *Causal Necessity.* New Haven, 1980.

Suchting, W. A. "Regularity and Law," in R. S. Cohen and M. W. Wartofsky, eds., *Boston Studies in the Philosophy of Science* (Dordrecht, 1974).

Swinburne, R. "Reply to Shoemaker," in L. J. Cohen and M. Hesse, eds., *Aspects of Inductive Logic* (Oxford, 1983). See also Shoemaker's paper in the same volume.

Swoyer, C. "The Nature of Natural Laws," *Australasian Journal of Philosophy,* Vol. 60 (1982), 203–23.

Tooley, M. "The Nature of Laws," *Canadian Journal of Philosophy,* Vol. 7 (1977), 667–98.

———. *Causation: A Realist Approach.* Oxford, 1987.

van Fraassen, B. *Laws and Symmetry.* Oxford, 1989.

———, J. Earman, D. M. Armstrong, and N. Cartwright. "A Book Symposium on Laws and Symmetry," *Philosophy and Phenomenological Research,* Vol. 53 (1993), 411–44.

DAVID M. ARMSTRONG

LEIBNIZ, GOTTFRIED WILHELM, and the entire range of current scholarship concerning him have, since 1969, been the subjects of a single bibliographic source created by the Leibniz Archiv of the Niedersachsische Landesbibliothek in Hanover, namely, the periodical *Studia Leibnitiana.* Two other volumes should be noted in this regard: Albert Heinekamp's edition of *Leibniz Bibliographie: Die Literatur über Leibniz* (Frankfurt, 1984), which covers the secondary literature on Leibniz up to 1980; and Wilhelm Totok's *Leibniz Bibliographie,* vol. 14 of his *Handbuch der Geschichte der Philosophie* (Frankfurt, 1981).

The following aims to supplement L. J. Russell's 1967 bibliography in the original *Encyclopedia* [4], using the categories he employed, with some of the significant items that have appeared since then.

WORKS BY LEIBNIZ

Sämtliche Schriften und Briefe. Four volumes of Leibniz's philosophical works and one volume of his philosophical correspondence have appeared to date. The philosophical work is covered through 1676 and the correspondence through 1685. In addition, another volume contains the *Nouveaux essais sur l'entendement humain.* Volumes completing coverage of the philosophical work to 1690 are scheduled to appear.

Various relatively short pieces of Leibniz's philosophical work and correspondence have appeared; for details, consult the bibliographies published in *Studia Leibnitiana.* There have also been numerous revisions of texts, for which the same source is recommended.

COMMENTARIES AND INTERPRETATIONS

Adams, R. *Leibniz: Determinist, Theist, Idealist.* New York, 1994.

Becco, A. *Du simple selon G. W. Leibniz.* Paris, 1975.

Belaval, Y. *Études leibniziennes.* Paris, 1976.

Broad, C. D. *Leibniz: An Introduction.* Cambridge, 1975.

Brown, S. *Leibniz.* Minneapolis, 1984.

Burkhardt, H. *Logik und Semiotic in der Philosophie von Leibniz.* Munich, 1980.

Costabel, P. *Leibniz and Dynamics.* Ithaca, NY, 1973.

Dascal, M. *La Sémiologie de Leibniz.* Paris, 1978.

———. *Leibniz: Language, Signs, and Thought.* Amsterdam, 1987.

———, and E. Yakira, eds. *Leibniz and Adam.* Tel Aviv, 1993.

Duchesneau, F. *Leibniz et la méthode de la science.* Paris, 1993.

———. *La dynamique de Leibniz.* Paris, 1994.

Fichant, M., ed. *Gottfried Wilhelm Leibniz, la réforme de la dynamique.* Paris, 1994.

Frankfurt, H., ed. *Leibniz: A Collection of Critical Essays.* Garden City, 1972.

Heinekamp, A. *Das Problem des Guten bei Leibniz.* Bonn, 1969.

———, W. Lenzen, and M. Schneider, eds. *Mathesis rationis: Festschrift für Heinrich Schepers.* Munster, 1990.

Hooker, M., ed. *Leibniz: Critical and Interpretive Essays.* Minneapolis, 1982.

Ishiguro, H. *Leibniz's Philosophy of Logic and Language,* 2d ed. Cambridge, 1990.

Jolley, N. *Leibniz and Locke: A Study of the "New Essays Concerning Human Understanding."* Oxford, 1984.

———, ed. *The Cambridge Companion to Leibniz.* Cambridge, 1995.

Kauppi, R. *Uber die leibnizsche Logik.* New York, 1985.

Kulstad, M., ed. *Essays on the Philosophy of Leibniz.* Houston, 1977.

Kulstad, M., ed. *Leibniz on Apperception, Consciousness, and Reflection.* Munich, 1991.

Lamarra, A., ed. *L'infinito in Leibniz problemi e terminologia.* Rome, 1990.

Leclerc, I., ed. *The Philosophy of Leibniz and the Modern World.* Nashville, 1973.

Mates, B. *The Philosophy of Leibniz: Metaphysics and Language.* New York, 1986.

McRae, R. *Leibniz: Perception, Apperception, and Thought.* Toronto, 1976.

Mugnai, M. *Leibniz's Theory of Relations.* Stuttgart, 1992.

Okruhlik, K., and J. R. Brown, eds. *The Natural Philosophy of Leibniz.* Dordrecht, 1985.

Parkinson, G. H. R. *Logic and Reality in Leibniz's Metaphysics.* Oxford, 1965.

Rescher, N. *Leibniz: An Introduction to His Philosophy.* Totowa, NJ, 1979.

———. *Leibniz's Metaphysics of Nature.* Dordrecht, 1981.

———. *G. W. Leibniz's "Monadology." An Edition for Students.* Pittsburgh, 1991.

Robinet, A. *Architectonique disjonctive, automates systémiques, et idéalité dans l'oeuvre de G. W. Leibniz.* Paris, 1986.

MacDonald Ross, G. *Leibniz.* Oxford, 1984.

Rutherford, D. *Leibniz and the Rational Order of Nature.* Cambridge, 1995.

Sleigh, C. R., Jr. *Leibniz and Arnauld: A Commentary on Their Correspondence.* New Haven, 1990.

Wilson, C. *Leibniz's Metaphysics.* Princeton, NJ, 1989.

Wilson, M. *Leibniz' Doctrine of Necessary Truth.* New York, 1990.

Yost, R. M., Jr. *Leibniz and Philosophical Analysis.* New York, 1985.

Woolhouse, R. S., ed. *Leibniz: Metaphysics and Philosophy of Science.* New York, 1981.

ENGLISH TRANSLATIONS

De Summa Rerum: Metaphysical Papers, 1675–1676, trans. G. H. R. Parkinson. New Haven, 1992.

Discourse on Metaphysics, trans. P. Lucas and L. Grint. Manchester, 1953.

"Discourse on Metaphysics" and Related Writings, trans. R. Niall, D. Martin, and S. Brown. Manchester, 1988.

General Investigations Concerning the Analysis of Concepts and Truths, trans. W. H. O'Briant. Athens, GA, 1968.

The Leibniz–Arnauld Correspondence, trans. H. T. Mason. Manchester, 1967.

Logical Papers, trans. G. H. R. Parkinson. Oxford, 1966.

"Monadology" and Other Philosophical Essays, trans. P. Schrecker and A. M. Schrecker. New York, Macmillan, 1965.

New Essays on Human Understanding, trans. P. Remnant and J. Bennett. Cambridge, 1981.

Philosophical Essays, trans. R. Ariew and D. Garber. Indianapolis, 1989.

Philosophical Papers and Letters, trans. L. E. Loemker, 2d ed. Dordrecht, 1969.

Philosophical Writings, trans. M. Morris and G. H. R. Parkinson. London, 1973.

The Political Writings of Leibniz, trans. P. Riley. Cambridge, 1972.

BIOGRAPHICAL

Aiton, E. J. *Leibniz: A Biography.* Bristol, 1985.

Müller, K., and G. Krönert. *Leben und Werk von Gottfried Wilhelm Leibniz.* Frankfurt, 1969.

ROBERT SLEIGH

LEVINAS, EMMANUEL, was born in 1906 in Kaunas, Lithuania, of Jewish parents. His education familiarized him with the Hebrew Bible and the Russian novelists. After having studied at the gymnasiums in Kaunas and Charkow, Ukraine, he traveled to Strasbourg, where he studied philosophy from 1924 to 1929. He spent the academic year of 1928–29 in Freiburg, where he attended the last seminars given by Edmund HUSSERL [4; S] and the lectures and seminars of Martin HEIDEGGER [3; S]. His dissertation, *La théorie de l'intuition dans la phénoménologie de Husserl,* was published in 1930. In 1930 Levinas settled in Paris, where he worked for the Alliance Israélite Universelle and its schools located throughout the Mediterranean. In 1947 he became the director of the École Normale Israélite Orientale, the training facility for teachers of those schools. In 1961 he was appointed professor of philosophy at the University of Poitiers and in 1967 at the University of Nanterre. In 1973 he moved to the Sorbonne, where he became an honorary professor in 1976. Levinas died on December 25, 1995, a few days before his 90th birthday.

WORKS

Until World War II most of Levinas's writing focused on introducing the phenomenology of Husserl and Heidegger into France. His early commentaries on their work were collected in *En découvrant l'existence avec Husserl et Heidegger* (1949). His first personal essay was the article "De l'évasion" (1935), whose central question was whether it is possible to evade the totalizing tendency of being. The search for an answer coincided with the beginning of his criticism of Heidegger's ontology. Levinas's first personal book, with the anti-Heideggerian title *De l'existence à l'existant* (*From Existence to Existents* or *From Being to Beings*), was published in 1947. In the same year he gave a lecture series under the title *Le temps et l'autre* (*Time and the Other*), in which some central thoughts of his later work are anticipated. A part of *De l'existence à l'existant* to which Levinas later refers with approval is its phenomenology of *il y a* ('there is'), that is, being in its most general and indeterminate or empty sense, preceding all determination, order, and structure. Levinas describes it as a formless and obscure night and a silent murmur, an anonymous and chaotic atmosphere or field of forces from which no being can escape. It threatens the existing entities by engulfing and suffocating them. As such, being is horrible, not because it would kill—death is not an evasion from it—but because of its depersonalizing character. All beings are caught in the anonymity of this primordial materiality—much different from the giving essence of *es gibt* as described by Heidegger.

The work that made Levinas famous is *Totalité et infini. Essai sur l'extériorité* (1961). As an attack on the entirety of Western philosophy, including Heidegger's ontology, this work tries to show why philosophy has not been faithful to the most important facts of human existence and how its basic perspective should be replaced by another one. The "totality" of the title stands for the absolutization of a panoramic perspective from which reality is understood as an all-encompassing universe. All kinds of relation, separation, exteriority, and alterity are then reduced to internal moments of one totality. Borrowing from PLATO's [6; S] *Sophist,* Levinas affirms that Western philosophy reduces the other (*to heteron*) to 'the Same' *(tauton)* (*see* OTHER, THE [S]). The resulting tautology is an egology because the totalization is operated by the consciousness of an ego that does not recognize any irreducible heteronomy.

The relative truth of the ego's autonomy is shown in a phenomenology of the way in which human beings inhabit the world. Levinas characterizes this "economy" (from *oikos* = house, and *nomos* = law) as vitality and enjoyment of the elements. Implicitly polemicizing against Heidegger's description of *Dasein*'s being-in-the-world, he focuses on the dimension of human eating, drinking, walking, swimming, dwelling, and laboring, a dimension more primordial than the handling of tools and much closer to the natural elements than scientific or technological objectification.

The INFINITE ([S]; *l'infini*), which Levinas contrasts with the totality, is another name for "the Other" insofar as this does not fit into the totality. In order to determine the relation between consciousness, the totality, and the infinite, Levinas refers to René DESCARTES's [2; S] *Meditations on the First Philosophy,* in which Descartes insists on the fact that the idea of the infinite is original and cannot be deduced from any other idea. It surpasses the capacity of consciousness, which in it "thinks more than it can think" (see Levinas's *Collected Philosophical Papers,* p. 56). The relation between the ego and the infinite is one of transcendence: the infinite remains exterior to consciousness, although this is essentially related to its "height."

The concrete sense of the formal structure thus indicated is shown through a phenomenology of the human other, whose "epiphany" reveals an absolute command: as soon as I am confronted, I discover myself to be under an absolute obligation. The fact of the other's existence immediately reveals to me the basic ought of all ethics. On this level is and ought are inseparable. Instead of the other (*l'autre* or *autrui*), Levinas often uses the expressions "the face" *(le visage)* or "the speech" (*la parole,* also *le langage*) because the other's looking at me and speaking to me are the two most striking expressions of the other's infinity or "height." As the relation between an economically established ego and the infinite other, the intersubjective relation is asymmetrical: the other appears primarily not as equal to me but rather as "higher" and commanding me. I am responsible for the other's life, a responsibility that puts infinite demands on me, but I cannot order another to give his or her life for me.

In his second major work, *Autrement qu'être ou au-delà de l'essence* (1974), Levinas continues his analyses of the relationship between the ego and the other but now emphasizes the basic structure of the ego, or rather of the "me" in the accusative, as put into question, accused, and unseated by the other. The relationship is described as nonchosen responsibility, substitution, obsession, being hostage, persecution. Subjectivity (the "me" of *me voici*) is determined as a nonchosen being-for-the-other and, thus, as basically nonidentical with itself, a passivity more or otherwise passive than the passivity that is opposed to activity. Subjectivity is primarily sensibility, being touched and affected by the other, vulnerability.

In the course of his analyses Levinas discovered that the other, me, and the transcendence that relates and separates them do not fit into the framework of phenomenology: neither the other nor I (me) is phenomenon; transcendence does not have the structure of intentionality. Through phenomenology Levinas thus arrived at another level of thinking. He did not join Heidegger's call for a new ontology, however.

In *Autrement qu'être* Levinas gives a new description of the way being "is": *esse* is *interesse;* being is an active and transitive "interestingness" *(intéressement),* which permeates all beings and weaves them together in a network of mutual interest. If ontology is the study of (this) being, it is not able to express the other, transcendence, and subjectivity. Transcendence surpasses being. Appealing to Plato, who characterized the good as *epekeina tès ousias,* Levinas points at transcendence, infinity, and otherness as "otherwise" and "beyond" the realm of being (or essence).

The other, subjectivity, and transcendence—but then also morality, affectivity, death, suffering, freedom, love, history, and many other (quasi-)phenomena—resist, not only phenomenology and ontology, but all kinds of objectification and thematization. As soon as they are treated in a reflective discourse, they are converted into a said *(dit)*. The saying *(dire)*, in which the "otherwise than being" (that which is not a phenomenon, a being, or a theme) addresses itself to an addressee, is lost in the text of the said. However, thematization and objectification are inevitable, especially in philosophy and science, but also in the practical dimensions of law, economy, and politics. The organization of justice cannot do without generalization and grouping of individuals into totalities. The transition from the asymmetrical relation between the other and me to the generalities of justice is founded in the fact that the other human who, here and now, obligates me infinitely somehow represents all other humans.

How does the intersubjective and asymmetric transcendence differ from the relationship to God? "Otherness," "infinity," and "beyond" do not apply to God in the same way as to the human other. God is neither an object nor a you; no human being can meet with God directly, but God has left a TRACE [S]. The infinite responsibility of the one for the other refers to an election that precedes freedom. In coming from an immemorial, anachronical "past," responsibility indicates the "preoriginary" "illeity" of God. The *il* or *ille* of "the most high" is sharply distinguished from the chaotic anonymity of *il y a;* the dimensions of economy, morality, and justice separate the indeterminacy of being from the beyond-all-determinacy of God. However, as the practical and theoretical recognition of the relationship between God and humans, religion cannot be separated from ethics: the only way to venerate God is through devotion to human others.

Besides the two books summarized here, Levinas wrote many articles. Most of these were collected in *Humanisme de l'autre homme* (1972), *De Dieu qui vient à l'idée* (1982), *Hors sujet* (1987), and *Entre nous* (1991).

Like all other philosophers, Levinas has convictions that cannot be reduced to universally shared experiences, common sense, or purely rational principles. In addition to his philosophical work he wrote extensively on Jewish questions from an orthodox Jewish, and especially Talmudic, point of view. In his philosophical writings he quotes the Bible perhaps as often as Shakespeare or Dostoyevsky, but these quotations are not meant to replace philosophical justification of his assertions. Phenomenological rigor and emphasis are typical of his method, even where he points beyond the dimensions of phenomena and conceptuality.

Bibliography

A complete bibliography of primary and secondary texts published between 1929 and 1989 is given in Roger Burgraeve, *Emmanuel Levinas; une bibliographie primaire et secondaire (1929–1985) avec complément 1985–1989.* Leuven, 1990.

The most important philosophical books of Levinas are:

La théorie de l'intuition dans la phénoménologie de Husserl. Paris, 1930; 2d. ed. 1963. Translated by A. Orianne as *The*

Theory of Intuition in Husserl's Phenomenology. Evanston, IL, 1973.

De l'existence à l'existant. Paris, 1947; 2d. ed., 1978. Translated by A. Lingis as *Existence and Existents.* The Hague, 1978.

Le temps et l'autre. Montpellier, 1979 (2d. ed. of Levinas's contribution to *Le choix, le monde, l'existence* [Paris, 1948]). Translated by R. Cohen as *Time and the Other.* Pittsburgh, 1987.

En découvrant l'existence avec Husserl et Heidegger. Paris, 1949; 2d. ed., 1967. Partially translated by A. Lingis in *Collected Philosophical Papers (v. infra).*

Totalité et Infini. Essai sur l'extériorité. The Hague, 1961. Translated by A. Lingis as *Totality and Infinity: An Essay on Exteriority.* Pittsburgh, 1969.

Humanisme de l'autre homme. Montpellier, 1972.

Autrement qu'être ou au-delà de l'essence. The Hague, 1974. Translated by A. Lingis as *Otherwise than Being or Beyond Essence.* The Hague, 1981.

De Dieu qui vient à l'idée. Paris, 1982.

Collected Philosophical Papers, trans. A. Lingis. Boston, 1987. Contains the English translation of twelve thematic essays from several volumes and journals.

Hors sujet. Montpellier, 1987.

Entre nous: Essais sur le penser-à-l'autre. Paris, 1991.

SECONDARY LITERATURE

Bernasconi, R., and S. Critchley, eds. *Re-reading Levinas.* Bloomington, IN, 1991.

Bernasconi, R., and D. Wood, eds. *The Provocation of Levinas: Rethinking the Other.* London, 1988.

Chalier, C., and M. Abensour, eds. *Emmanuel Levinas.* Paris, 1991.

Cohen, R., ed. *Face to Face with Levinas.* Albany, NY, 1986.

Peperzak, A. *To the Other. An Introduction to the Philosophy of Emmanuel Levinas.* West Lafayette, IN, 1993.

———, ed. *Ethics as First Philosophy. The Significance of Emmanuel Levinas for Religion, Literature and Philosophy.* New York, 1995.

Greisch, J., and J. Rolland, eds. *Emmanuel Levinas. L'éthique comme philosophie première.* Paris, 1993.

Wyschogrod, E. *Emmanuel Levinas: The Problem of Ethical Metaphysics.* The Hague, 1974.

ADRIAAN PEPERZAK

LIAR PARADOX, THE.

Attributions of truth and falsehood under certain conditions generate the liar paradox. The most famous illustration of this comes from the Epistle to Titus, in which St. Paul quotes approvingly a remark attributed to Epimenides: "One of themselves, even a prophet of their own, said, The Cretans are always liars, evil beasts, slow bellies. This witness is true" (King James version). Let us suppose that Epimenides, the Cretan prophet, did say that the Cretans are always liars, and let us consider the status of his utterance—call it *E*—under the following two conditions. (1) A Cretan utterance counts as a lie if and only if it is untrue. (2) All Cretan utterances, except perhaps *E,* are untrue. Now, if *E* is true, then, since *E* is a Cretan utterance, not all Cretan utterances are untrue. Hence, Cretans are not always liars (by (1)), and so *E* must be untrue. On the other hand, if *E* is untrue, then indeed all Cretan utterances are untrue (by (2)). Hence, Cretans are always liars (by (1)), and so *E* is true after all. Both the hypotheses, that *E* is true and that *E* is not true, yield, therefore, a contradiction. Yet the steps in the argument are all apparently valid, and the initial setup is not impossible. This is the liar paradox.

The paradox was discovered by Eubulides of Miletus (fourth century B.C.E.) and has exercised logicians down the ages to the present time. (See Bocheński, 1961; Spade, 1988.) For principally two reasons, interest in the paradox has been especially great in this century. First, arguments similar to that found in the liar wreaked havoc in several prominent logical systems (e.g., those of Gottlob FREGE [3; S] and Alonzo Church). This prompted a search for systems that were immune from paradox. Second, the rise of semantical studies created a need for a better understanding of the notions of truth, reference, and the like. The notions are fundamental to semantical investigations, but the paradoxes reveal a profound gap in our understanding of them. (The notion of reference, like other semantical notions, exhibits, under certain conditions, paradoxical behavior. *See* LOGICAL PARADOXES [5].)

The liar and related paradoxes raise a number of difficult conceptual problems. One is the normative problem of designing paradox-free notions of truth, reference, and the like. Another is the descriptive problem of understanding the workings of our ordinary, paradox-laden notions. The work on the paradoxes in the first half of this century is, perhaps, best viewed as addressing the normative problem. (*See* RUSSELL, BERTRAND ARTHUR WILLIAM [7]; TYPES, THEORY OF [8].) The work in the second half is best viewed as addressing the descriptive problem. Some of this work is outlined below.

Let us sharpen the descriptive problem a little. For simplicity, let us restrict our attention to a fragment, *L,* of our language that contains no problematic terms other than 'true'. All other terms in *L* have, let us suppose, a classical interpretation. How should 'true' be interpreted? A natural demand is that the interpretation must validate the T-biconditionals, that is, all sentences of the form,

(T) *'B'* is true if and only if (iff) *B,*

where *B* is a sentence of *L.* The argument of the liar paradox shows, however, that every possible classical interpretation of 'true' is bound to make some T-biconditionals false. (This is a version of Alfred TARSKI's [8] indefinability theorem.) How, then, should we interpret 'true'? Should we abandon the natural demand? Or the classical framework? Or the naïve reading of the T-biconditionals? Essentially, the first course is followed in the contextual approach, the second in the fixed-point approach, and the third in the revision approach.

THE CONTEXTUAL APPROACH

This approach takes 'true' to be a context-sensitive term. Just as the interpretation of 'fish this long' varies with contextually supplied information about length, similarly, on the contextual approach, with 'true': its interpretation also depends upon contextual information. There is no consensus, however, on the specific information needed for interpretation. In the levels theory due to Tyler Burge and Charles Parsons, the context supplies the level at which 'true' is interpreted in a Tarskian hierarchy of truth predicates. In the Austinian theory of truth developed by Jon Barwise and John Etchemendy, the relevant contextual parameter is the "portion" of the world that a proposition is about. In the singularity theory of Keith Simmons, the relevant information includes certain of the speaker's intentions.

Contextual theories assign to each occurrence of 'true' a classical interpretation, though not the same one to all occurrences. This has several characteristic consequences: (1) Occurrences of 'true' do not express global truth for the entire language (by Tarski's indefinability theorem). They express instead restricted or "quasi" notions of truth; the former possibility is realized in the levels theory, the latter in the singularity theory. (2) Truth attributions, even paradoxical ones, have a classical truth value. Paradox is explained as arising from a subtle, unnoticed, shift in some contextual parameter. (3) Classical forms of reasoning are preserved. But caution is in order here: Whether an argument exemplifies a classically valid form turns out to be nontrivial. For example, the argument "a is true, $a = b$; therefore, b is true" exemplifies a classically valid form only if 'true' is interpreted uniformly, but this is nontrivial on the contextual approach.

THE FIXED-POINT APPROACH

This approach interprets 'true' nonclassically. It rests on an important observation of Saul KRIPKE [S], Robert Martin, and Peter Woodruff. Consider again the language L, and assign to 'true' an arbitrary partial interpretation $\langle U, V\rangle$, where U is the extension and V the anti-extension (i.e., the objects of which the predicate is false). We can use one of the partial-valued schemes (say, Strong Kleene) to determine the sentences of L that are true (U'), false (V'), and neither-true-nor-false. This semantical reflection defines a function, κ, on partial interpretations; $\kappa(\langle U, V\rangle) = \langle U', V'\rangle$. The important observation is that κ has a fixed point: There exist $\langle U, V\rangle$ such that $\kappa(\langle U, V\rangle) = \langle U, V\rangle$.

Certain partial-valued schemes have a least fixed point, which is a particularly attractive interpretation for 'true'. It is also the product of an appealing iterative construction: we begin by supposing that we are entirely ignorant of the extension and the anti-extension of 'true'; we set them both to be $\varnothing$ (the null set). Despite the ignorance, we can assert some sentences and deny others. The rule "Assert 'B is true' for all assertible B; assert 'B is not true' for all deniable B" entitles us to a new, richer, interpretation, $\kappa(\langle\varnothing, \varnothing\rangle)$, for 'true'. But now we can assert (deny) more sentences. The rule entitles us to a yet richer interpretation $\kappa(\kappa(\langle\varnothing, \varnothing\rangle))$. The process, if repeated sufficiently many times, saturates at the least fixed point.

Under fixed-point interpretations, the extension of 'true' consists precisely of the truths and the anti-extension of falsehoods. The T-biconditionals are, therefore, validated. They are not, however, expressible in L itself: fixed points exist only when certain three-valued functions, including the relevant 'iff', are inexpressible in L.

THE REVISION APPROACH

This approach holds truth to be a circular concept. It is motivated by the observation that truth behaves in a strikingly parallel way to concepts with circular definitions. Suppose we define G thus:

x is $G =_{\mathrm{Df}} x$ is a philosopher distinct from Plato *or*
x is Plato but not G.

The definition is circular, but it does impart some meaning to G. G has, like truth, unproblematic application on a large range of objects. It applies to all philosophers distinct from Plato and fails to apply to nonphilosophers. On one object, Plato, G behaves paradoxically. If we declare Plato is G, then the definition rules that he is not G; if we declare he is not G, the definition rules that he is G. This parallels exactly the behavior of truth in the liar paradox.

The revision account of truth rests on general theories of definitions, theories that make semantic sense of circular (and mutually interdependent) definitions. Central to these theories are the following ideas. (1) A circular definition does not, in general, determine a classical extension for the definiendum (the term defined). (2) It determines instead a rule of revision. Given a hypothesis about the extension of the definiendum G, the definition yields a revised extension for G, one consisting of objects that satisfy the definiens (the right side of the definition). (3) Repeated applications of the revision rule to arbitrary hypotheses reveal both the unproblematic and the pathological behavior of the definiendum. On the unproblematic the revision rule yields a definite and stable verdict, irrespective of the initial hypothesis. On the pathological this ideal state does not obtain.

The ingredient needed to construct a theory of truth once we have a general theory of definitions is minimal: it is just the T-biconditionals, with 'iff' read as '$=_{\mathrm{Df}}$'. This reading was suggested by Tarski, but, as it results in a circular definition, it can be implemented only within a general theory of definitions. Under the reading, the T-biconditionals yield a rule of revision. Repeated applications of this rule generate patterns that explain the ordinary and the pathological behavior of truth. The revision approach thus sees the liar paradox as arising from a circularity in truth. The approach has been developed by, among others, Anil Gupta, Hans Herzberger, and Nuel Belnap.

The three approaches, it should be stressed, do not exhaust the rich array of responses to the paradoxes in this century.

Bibliography

Antonelli, A. "Non-Well-Founded Sets via Revision Rules," *Journal of Philosophical Logic,* Vol. 23 (1994), 633–79.

Barwise, J., and J. Etchemendy. *The Liar: An Essay on Truth and Circularity.* New York, 1987.

Bocheński, I. M. *A History of Formal Logic.* Notre Dame, IN, 1961.

Chapuis, A. "Alternative Revision Theories of Truth," *Journal of Philosophical Logic,* Vol. 24 (1996).

Epstein, R. L. "A Theory of Truth Based on a Medieval Solution to the Liar Paradox," *History and Philosophy of Logic,* Vol. 13 (1992), 149–77.

Gaifman, H. "Pointers to Truth," *Journal of Philosophy,* Vol. 89 (1992), 223–61.

Gupta, A., and N. Belnap. *The Revision Theory of Truth.* Cambridge, MA, 1993.

Koons, R. C. *Paradoxes of Belief and Strategic Rationality.* Cambridge, 1992.

McGee, V. *Truth, Vagueness, and Paradox.* Indianapolis, 1991.

Martin, R. L., ed. *The Paradox of the Liar,* 2d ed. Reseda, CA, 1978. Contains a useful bibliography of material up to about 1975; for later material consult the bibliography in Gupta and Belnap, 1993.

Martin, R. L., ed. *Recent Essays on Truth and the Liar Paradox.* New York, 1984. Contains the classic papers of Parsons, Kripke, Herzberger, and others; a good place to begin the study of the three approaches.

Priest, G. *In Contradiction.* Dordrecht, 1987.

Russell, B. "Mathematical Logic as Based on the Theory of Types," in *Logic and Knowledge* (London, 1956).

Sainsbury, R. M. *Paradoxes.* Cambridge, 1988.

Simmons, K. *Universality and the Liar.* New York, 1993.

Spade, P. V. *Lies, Language, and the Logic in the Late Middle Ages.* London, 1988.

Tarski, A. "The Semantic Conception of Truth," *Philosophy and Phenomenological Research,* Vol. 4 (1944), 341–76.

Visser, A. "Semantics and the Liar Paradaox," in D. Gabbay and F. Guenthner, eds., *Handbook of Philosophical Logic,* Vol. 4 (Dordrecht, 1989).

Yablo, S. "Hop, Skip, and Jump: The Agonistic Conception of Truth," in J. Tomberlin, ed., *Philosophical Perspectives,* Vol. 7 (Atascadero, CA, 1993).

Yaqūb, A. M. *The Liar Speaks the Truth.* New York, 1993.

ANIL GUPTA

LIBERALISM. LIBERALISM [4] is commonly defined as a political philosophy that places a primary value on liberty, especially the liberty of individuals from interference by the state. Since the 1950s liberals have increasingly defined liberty as the neutrality of the state with regard to differing conceptions of the good life. Liberal thinkers have combined this commitment to "value neutrality" with a belief in the necessity of economic growth for providing the prosperity required for a just society.

The most important philosopher to reformulate liberalism in these terms is John RAWLS [S]. In his book *A Theory of Justice,* Rawls justifies a liberal welfare state that could provide a basis for the equal enjoyment of individual liberties. Rawls combined advocacy of a principle of "an equal right to the most extensive basic liberty" with his "difference principle," which justified only those inequalities that were "to the greatest benefit of the least advantaged" in society. Rawls hypothesized that individuals would derive these two principles through rational deliberation in an "original position" in which "knowledge of the circumstances of one's own case" was excluded. Rawls's theory revitalized social contract theory in Anglo-American philosophy, after its virtual eclipse by UTILITARIANISM [8].

The first major criticism of Rawls's work, by Robert Nozick, emphasized the distance that Rawls's welfare-state liberalism had gone from the classical liberal (now "libertarian") view that espoused the value of a minimal state. Nozick argued that redistributive schemes such as Rawls's were inherently unjust, since they imposed an "end-state" in violation of previous consensual exchanges between individuals.

Isaiah Berlin's distinction between negative and positive freedom—between a freedom from interference and a freedom to achieve certain ends—lay at the root of this divergence between libertarians and liberals. In response, Gerald MacCallum argued that all conceptions of freedom combined negative and positive elements; one implication of this argument was that there could not be a coherent liberalism that did not include a positive conception of the role of the state in furthering particular social goals.

Subsequently, Ronald Dworkin asserted that liberalism is primarily a philosophy of equality, not of liberty per se, since liberties were best secured through the achievement of an equal society in which all could pursue their own ends. Dworkin argued that a consequence of this egalitarianism was that liberalism should be based on a strong conception of human RIGHTS [S]. In his work *Taking Rights Seriously,* he argues that human rights generally were based not on a right to liberty as such but on a right to "treatment as an equal."

In the 1980s philosophers criticized the Rawls–Dworkin view of an egalitarian liberalism in two ways. First, Joseph Raz criticized Dworkin's emphasis on rights-based theories of morality and law. In particular, Raz maintained that the idea of liberty was best understood not as a right to treatment as an equal but as a collective good. Raz attacked both the concept of a "rights-based morality" and the notion of a liberal theory of equality as unable to account for moral reasons for action such as might be found in concepts of virtues, goods, or consequences.

Second, Michael Sandel and Charles Taylor criticized the Rawlsian conception of JUSTICE [4; S] on the basis of a philosophy of COMMUNITARIANISM [S] derived from rereadings of ARISTOTLE [1; S] and HEGEL [3; S]. The communitarian critique of liberalism was based on the idea that individuals come to have desires and ends only through socialization within a particular society; liberalism cannot therefore account for how individuals come to have an interest in liberty at all. Sandel and Taylor, as well as Michael Walzer, argued that Rawls simply assumed the existence of autonomous individuals without acknowledging the constitutive role of an already existing community in forming these individuals.

Rawls responded to this criticism by reformulating his theory as a "political liberalism" rather than as a general theory of justice. Rawls's "justice as fairness" was therefore a theory of the best distribution of goods within a particular political culture—that of the Anglo-American liberal democracies. As Walzer subsequently maintained, communitarianism could then be seen as a corrective to an overemphasis in liberal theory on the presumed autonomy of individuals in modern capitalist societies.

The devolution of most communist societies in the early 1990s encouraged a brief triumphalist mood within liberalism. In the most notable expression of this mood, Francis Fukuyama argued that modern liberal democracy should be universally acknowledged as the only legitimate form of government at the end of the twentieth century. The most important question about liberalism was therefore whether it could withstand assaults from antiliberal societies—now more frequently based on ethnic nationalism or religious fundamentalism than on Marxism-Leninism.

Two themes of liberalism in the 1990s were to some extent responses to this view. On the one hand, some liberal thinkers such as Rawls turned to a consideration of how liberal principles might be applied to relations between states and peoples on the global level. On the other hand, thinkers such as Benjamin Barber criticized liberalism for its advocacy of representative democracy to the exclusion of participatory institutions.

In response to these new problems, liberals increasingly reconceptualized liberal society as one that protects diverse ways of life through a political procedure guaranteeing agreement of all concerned. Both Rawls's political liberalism and the discourse ethics of the German philosopher Jürgen HABERMAS [S] are examples of this procedural approach. The dialogue between these two figures in the mid-1990s suggests that liberalism at the millennium may well be understood as a procedural theory of democracy that can serve to protect diverse cultures within which individuals can claim autonomy. Whether such a theory can withstand the developing criticisms by ecologists and feminists of the other assumption of liberalism—that of the value of a growth-oriented society—remains to be seen.

Bibliography

Barber, B. *Strong Democracy.* Berkeley, 1984.

Berlin, I. *Four Essays on Liberty.* Oxford, 1969.

Dworkin, R. *Taking Rights Seriously.* Cambridge, MA, 1977.

———. "Liberalism," in S. Hampshire, ed., *Public and Private Morality* (Cambridge, 1978).

Fukuyama, F. "The End of History?" *National Interest,* no. 16 (1989), 3–18.

Habermas, J. *Theorie des Kommunikativen Handelns.* Frankfurt, 1981.

———. "Reconciliation Through the Public Use of Reason: Remarks on John Rawls' *Political Liberalism," Journal of Philosophy,* Vol. 92 (1995), 109–31.

MacCallum, Jr., G. C. "Negative and Positive Freedom," *Philosophical Review,* Vol. 76 (1967), 312–34.

Nozick, R. *Anarchy, State, and Utopia.* New York, 1974.

Rawls, J. *A Theory of Justice.* Cambridge, MA, 1971.

———. "The Law of Peoples," in S. Shute and S. Hurley, eds., *On Human Rights: The Oxford Amnesty Lectures 1993* (New York, 1993).

———. *Political Liberalism.* New York, 1993.

———. "Reply to Habermas," *Journal of Philosophy,* Vol. 92 (1995), 132–80.

Raz, J. *The Morality of Freedom.* Oxford, 1986.

Sandel, M. J. *Liberalism and the Limits of Justice.* Cambridge, 1982.

Taylor, C. *Philosophical Papers,* Vol. 2: *Philosophy and the Human Sciences.* Cambridge, 1985.

Walzer, M. *Spheres of Justice.* New York, 1983.

———. "The Communitarian Critique of Liberalism," *Political Theory,* Vol. 18 (1990), 6–23.

OMAR DAHBOUR

LIBERATION THEOLOGY. Theology of liberation is the name of a movement that arose in the churches, both Catholic and Protestant, of Latin America during the last third of the twentieth century. It also describes a theological trend that is found, sometimes under different names and with somewhat different emphases, across the world.

The earliest and still definitive statement of the movement is *A Theology of Liberation* by Gustavo Gutierrez (1988). The basic principles he sets forth are as follows.

First, theology is critical reflection on Christian praxis. Faith, charity, and commitment to God and others in the struggle for humanity and justice are primary. Theology relates this praxis to the sources of REVELATION [7] and the history of the church.

Second, biblical revelation commits the church to God's "preferential option for the poor." The poor are, by their condition, involved in a struggle to realize their humanity, to become "subjects of their own history," against the political, economic, and social powers that marginalize and oppress them. This struggle is revolutionary, not reformist. The church belongs with the poor in the midst of it, doing theology in a revolutionary situation.

Third, the struggle of the poor for social JUSTICE [4; S] is a work of human self-creation that finds its source, meaning, and hope in God's work. Salvation history is at the heart of human history, in creation, covenant, Christ's incarnation, and the coming kingdom of God. Political liberation is a partial salvific event, a historical realization of the kingdom that looks forward to its ultimate fulfillment by divine grace operating in the human struggle, informing its character and directing it toward ever larger goals of human community.

Three developments of this theology, in response to both defenders and critics, are especially important.

First, How is the truth claim of liberation theology validated? Juan Luis Segundo (1976) describes it as a hermeneutical circle. Experience of reality from the perspective of the poor leads to ideological suspicion toward received structures of authority, morals, and dogma. This leads to a new awareness of God, which in turn creates a new hermeneutic for interpreting the biblical story. One does not escape ideology through this circle. But biblical revelation at one pole and the human condition of the poor on the other direct and correct it toward political and spiritual liberation. Paulo Freire develops the same line of thought as a teaching method in *The Pedagogy of the Oppressed,* with its emphasis on learning to be human in Christian base communities through defining and struggling against oppressive powers while being transformed by God's saving love in the struggle.

Second, How are the poor defined? The Latin American theologians have clearly a universal dependent economic class in mind, created by exploiting landlords, industrialists, and bankers with their political and military agents. Black theologians in the United States and South Africa, however, have maintained that the defining category is race. Dalit Christians in India find it in the religion-based caste system. A chorus of ethnic minorities throughout the world define it in terms of their own culture, language, or nation, seeking liberation from a dominant, oppressive majority. All these agree on God's preference for the poor and on divine promise in the human struggle. They differ in defining the poor and therefore on the universality versus the particularity of that promise.

Third, What does liberation theology owe to MARXISM [S], and is that debt theologically legitimate? The question arises on two levels. First, the hermeneutic of suspicion, which probes the roots of all truth claims in social experience and interest and defines theology as reflection on social praxis, owes much to MARX [5]. It contradicts the teaching of St. Thomas AQUINAS [1] about the universality of REASON [7] and NATURAL LAW [5] as perfected by revelation. It reflects, however, the REFORMATION'S [7] understanding of reason distorted by human sin and is rooted, liberation theologians would claim, in the way God is known in the biblical history of calling, covenant, and promise. The question remains how divine revelation corrects and redeems the self-understanding also of the poor.

Defining the social condition of the poor in terms of dehumanizing economic exploitation and class struggle clearly borrows from Marx. Miguez Bonino (1976) acknowledges this explicitly, as do many others. They claim, however, that this analysis is the secular expression in modern industrial society of a theme in Christian history that finds its source in the Hebrew prophets and the incarnation of Christ: the saving work of God liberating the people from the economic and political power of organized human sin. Regardless of the future of Marxism as an analytical tool, this struggle and this promise will continue. The question is how the power analysis it requires can become a more subtle and insightful guide to Christian understanding and action than Marxism was.

Bibliography

Freire, P. *Pedagogy of the Oppressed.* New York, 1971.

Gutierrez, G. *The Power of the Poor in History.* Maryknoll, NY, 1983.

———. *A Theology of Liberation,* rev. ed. Maryknoll, NY, 1988.

Miguez Bonino, J. *Doing Theology in a Revolutionary Situation.* Philadelphia, 1975.

———. *Christians and Marxists: The Mutual Challenge to Revolution.* Grand Rapids, MI, 1976.

Segundo, J. L. *The Liberation of Theology.* Maryknoll, NY, 1976.

CHARLES C. WEST

LIBERTARIANS. *See:* SOCIAL AND POLITICAL PHILOSOPHY [S]

LIBERTY. One of the central concerns of SOCIAL AND POLITICAL PHILOSOPHY [S] has been the issue of what limits, if any, there are to the right of the state to restrict the liberty of its citizens. Unless one is convinced of the truth of ANARCHISM [1], there are some actions with which the state may legitimately interfere, and unless one accords no value to personal liberty, there are some actions the state must leave to the discretion of the individual. One of the tasks of political philosophy is to develop and elaborate a theory to determine where these boundaries lie.

In his classical defense of LIBERALISM [4; S]—*On Liberty*—John Stuart MILL [5; S] gave one influential answer to this question. The only reason that could justify the use of coercion against a person is to prevent harm to other people. Such a reason might not be decisive—it might be that the use of coercion would be ineffective or too costly or would violate the rights of privacy—but it brings the action in question within the scope of legitimate state power.

Other reasons, according to Mill, do not justify legal coercion. One cannot restrict someone's actions because they are harmful to that person; PATERNALISM [S] is not legitimate. One cannot restrict someone's actions because they are wrong or immoral (but not harmful to others); legal moralism is not legitimate. One cannot restrict someone's actions because their character would be improved by doing so; moral paternalism is not legitimate.

Obviously, a theory that puts such heavy weight on the notion of harm gives rise to disputes about the nature and limits of that notion. If conduct is offensive to others, does that count as harming them? If not, do we need a separate principle to justify prohibiting offensive conduct such as public nudity or racist graffiti? If we are competing for a job and you get it, am I harmed by this? Does only physical damage count as harm or emotional damage as well? Am I harmed by simply knowing that behind the walls of your house you are engaged in activities that I would find repulsive or wicked? If someone defaces the flag, is anyone harmed by this? If I consent to some action that is otherwise damaging to me, am I still harmed? Can I be harmed after my death—for example, by attacks on my reputation?

One of the most fully developed views that seeks to provide answers to these and similar questions is that of Joel Feinberg. He argues that any notion of harm that is going to play a role in answering normative questions will itself be normative in character. He accordingly defines the notion of harm in terms of a wrongful setback to a person's interests. To some extent, naturally, this shifts philosophical attention to the concept of interests.

PATERNALISM

The normative issue raised by paternalism is when, if ever, the state or an individual is entitled to interfere with a person for that person's good. Examples of laws that have been justified in paternalistic terms include requiring motorcyclists to wear helmets, forcing patients to receive blood transfusions against their wishes, or requiring individuals to save for their retirement (Social Security).

The reasons that support paternalism are those that support any benevolent action—promoting the welfare of a person. The reasons against are those that militate against any interference with the autonomy of individuals—respect for their desire to lead their own lives. Normative debates about the legitimacy of paternalism involve disputes about many issues including the nature of welfare (can we produce good for a person against that individual's preferences and evaluations?), the correctness of various normative theories (CONSEQUENTIALISM [S] vs. autonomy or rights-based theories; *see* RIGHTS [7; S]), and the relevance of hypothetical consent (in Mill's famous example of the man walking across a bridge that, unknown to him, is about to collapse, we may stop him, since he would not want to cross the bridge if he knew its condition).

LEGAL MORALISM

The issue of whether the state may enforce morality—the subject that was brought to philosophical prominence by the debate between Lord Devlin and H. L. A. HART [3]—is present in discussions of the legalization of homosexuality, pornography, surrogate motherhood, and active EUTHANASIA [S]. The focus of such discussion is not the harm of such activities but their immorality and whether if they are immoral that is sufficient reason for the state to proscribe them. Since it is clearly the case that one of the grounds for proscribing murder is its immorality, the question arises as to what it might mean to deny that the state should take morality into account in limiting liberty. The best answer is that we may distinguish within the immoral different realms—for example, matters having to do with rights as opposed to matters having to do with ideals of conduct. Those who are opposed to the enforcement of morality are really opposed to enforcing certain areas of morality. Much of the discussion goes on under the heading of the "neutrality" of the liberal state.

Bibliography

Devlin, P. *The Enforcement of Morals.* London, 1965.

Dworkin, G. "Paternalism," *The Monist,* Vol. 56 (1972), 64–84.

Feinberg, J. *The Moral Limits of the Criminal Law,* 4 vols. New York, 1984–88.

Mill, J. S. *On Liberty.* London, 1959.

Hart, H. L. A. *Law, Liberty, and Morality.* Stanford, CA, 1963.

GERALD DWORKIN

LIFE-WORLD IN HUSSERL. HUSSERL [4; S] employs the term life-world in his later works to designate the ultimate foundation of mathematics, logic, and science. The life-world, as that which is concrete and immediate, is contrasted with the abstract and derivative character of the world of objects of the specialized disciplines such as the natural sciences. Most scholars agree that the positive description of the life-world is ambiguous, since it is introduced primarily by way of contrast to the limitations of a particular sphere or attitude it grounds. Because Husserl identifies several different ways in which these disciplines and attitudes are limited, the alternative characteristics of the life-world do not necessarily coincide and are in some cases hardly compatible with one another.

Three main characteristics of the life-world can be identified: (1) the life-world connotes the straightforward and simple experiential basis for logic and science; as such it is pregiven, prepredicative, and immediate; (2) it is concrete in the sense that it includes the full range of objects of human experience, including use and value traits (this is opposed to the abstractness of the strictly theoretical world of the natural sciences); (3) it is relative and perspectival with regard to space, time, and cultural situatedness. This again contrasts with the attempt of the objective sciences to abstract from all relativities in order to achieve universal validity. What is common to all three senses of the life-world is that, in each case, they identify an aspect or stratum of the world that is presupposed—but nonetheless overlooked or even denied—by the positive sciences.

The life-world, as the experiential basis for other sciences that presuppose it, figures prominently in *Formale und transzendentale Logik* and in Husserl's lectures on phenomenological psychology. In *FTL* Husserl emphasizes that logic's ability to serve as a source of truth rests ultimately upon a source outside logic, namely prepredicative experience as the direct intuitive access to individual objects and as the ultimate source of experiential judgments. Section 10 of *Erfahrung und Urteil* explicitly calls this world of experience the life-world. In his phenomenological psychology Husserl emphasizes a different aspect of the prepredicative experience—not as the source of our direct access to individual physical objects, but rather the way that our original experience precedes any clear distinction between body and soul, nature and spirit. In this sense the experiential basis precedes Cartesian dualisms and must be examined as the source for the legitimacy of any distinctions between the spheres of inanimate nature and personhood or spirit that arise through abstraction from this experiential basis.

In *Krisis* Husserl demonstrates how science as a practice emerges from a practical sphere of cultural life that looks at objects as useful, valuable, and socially significant. This world of life is historical, even if not usually explicitly so. Husserl's aim is to show how the practice of science is rooted in the life-world in which science is merely one practice among others, although it is a particularly significant one that arose at a historically late period for specific practical interests.

Finally, Husserl emphasizes how this practical everyday world is one that is relative to the experience of temporally, spatially, and communally situated individuals with specific sorts of sense organs and historical experiences. Although the logical abstractions of the objective sciences can transcend the subjective life-worlds, they are still tied to, and dependent upon, the life-world evidences of everyday experience. The guiding theme throughout these different senses is that the life-world, as the unified original ground of experience, takes precedence over the abstract and derivative worlds of science that arise from it.

Bibliography

Bernet, R., I. Kern, and E. Marbach. *Edmund Husserl: An Introduction to His Thought.* Evanston, IL, 1993, Chap. 9. Lays out clearly the tensions between the use of the concept in different works and stages of Husserl's development.

Carr, D. "Husserl's Problematic Concept of the Life World," in F. Ellison and P. McCormick, eds. *Husserl, Expositions and Appraisals* (Notre Dame, IN, 1977). A concise outline of some of the problems raised by the concept of life-world in the *Krisis.*

Husserl, E. *Die Krisis der europäischen Wissenschaften und die transzendentale Phänomenologie,* edited by W. Biemel. The Hague, 1954. Translated by D. Carr as *The Crisis of European Sciences and Transcendental Phenomenology.* Evanston, IL, 1970. The most extensive and well-known discussion of the life-world. See esp. secs. 33ff.

———. *Erfahrung und Urteil.* Hamburg, 1972. Translated by J. Churchill and K. Ameriks as *Experience and Judgment.* Evanston, IL, 1973. "Life-world" is mentioned in secs. 10ff. and sec. 38.

———. *Formale und transzendentale Logik. Husserliana,* Vol. 17, edited by P. Jannsen. The Hague, 1974. Translated by D. Cairns as *Formal and Transcendental Logic.* The Hague, 1969. Chapters 4 and 7 point to the necessity for a grounding of truth in an experiential realm that precedes the logic of judgments.

THOMAS NENON

LOCKE, JOHN (1632–1704), has been, for the last three decades, the subject of a rapid expansion of interest, stimulated by Oxford University Press's Clarendon edition of his works. The eight-volume edition of LOCKE'S [4] correspondence has opened new areas of information and exploration. So far in that series, we have definitive editions of the *Essay* (including editions of the drafts and other relevant writings), the work on education, his paraphrases of St. Paul's epistles, and the papers on money. The *Reasonableness of Christianity* is in press, the journals will soon appear (again, opening a vast and important insight into Locke's reading, book buying, travels, opinions), and other works will follow. These editions, and the research that went into their production, have provided new resources for work on almost all aspects of Locke's life and writings, as well as material relating to his intellectual environment.

Antedating the Clarendon series was another medium for interest in Locke: *The Locke Newsletter,* founded and edited by Roland Hall. Beginning in 1970, published once a year (more or less), the newsletter has published articles on all aspects of Locke's thought. Included in each number is a list of recent books and articles on Locke, in many languages. This is a valuable source for keeping up to date on the publications about Locke. Another source of information on publications about Locke is the *Reference Guide* by Yolton and Yolton. Two other bibliographic resources are Attig's listings of Locke editions, and the much fuller descriptive bibliography of all editions of Locke's publications by Jean S. Yolton. The latter, a work long overdue, describes many different copies of Locke editions, which were located and examined in many different libraries and countries.

Among the topics in Locke's *Essay,* three have received special attention: the representative theory of PERCEPTION, PERSONAL IDENTITY [6; S], and matter theory. The first of these in recent discussions has involved a debate over the nature of ideas: are they special entities (e.g., images) standing between perceivers and objects, or are they simply the means for our access to the physical world? On the second topic it is becoming increasingly recognized that memory is not the crux of Locke's concept of person; it is consciousness, a wider and richer process (one with clear moral overtones) that focuses our awareness of self. A person for Locke is a moral being composed of the thoughts, feelings, and actions performed throughout a life. Consciousness is not a property of some immaterial substance, at least not so far as we can discover. The third topic has been given detailed attention via Locke's use of the corpuscular theory (see Alexander, 1985). Some recognition has been given to Locke's movement toward the Newtonian concept of matter as force and power. Locke anticipated this development in his talk of the qualities of body being primarily powers. The substantiality of matter begins to fade under Locke's analysis of PRIMARY AND SECONDARY QUALITIES [6]. The chapter on POWER [6] in the *Essay,* the power of persons and the power of matter, is the longest and most complex chapter in that work (see J. W. Yolton, 1993).

Locke's social and political thought has received even more attention throughout the decades, especially over the last dozen or so years. Laslett's early dating of *Two Treatises,* and his locating that work in its historical context, have been developed by writers such as Dunn, Harris, and Marshall (and many others). The central role of property and the relation of that concept to the person is generally recognized (see Tully, 1980). His *Two Treatises* elaborates a concept of PROPERTY [6] that starts with each person's having property in his person. Acquisition of other possessions is a function of that original self-property. The tension between the interests and rights of the individual and those of society (or the community of mankind) is much discussed (see especially Gobetti, 1992). The focus on CONSCIOUSNESS [2] as defining the person in his *Essay* indicated the central place of the individual in Locke's civil society (*see* CONSCIOUSNESS IN ANGLO-AMERICAN PHILOSOPHY [S]). At the same time majority decisions were allowed to restrain individual actions. The power of the people is sanctioned by a SOCIAL CONTRACT [7] that obliges the ruler or legislative body to act for the good of the citizens, in conformity with the laws of nature. The interconnections between Locke's moral views and his social and political thought have been discussed by Marshall (1984). The issue of religious toleration has focused some of the recent treatments of Locke's political and religious writings, but all of the TOLERATION [8] writings by Locke await their inclusion in the Clarendon editions.

Locke's religious interests in the Bible and in what is required of a Christian have been clarified by recent studies (e.g., Wainwright's edition of the *Paraphrases,* 1987), but this area will be further illuminated when the Clarendon edition of *Reasonableness* appears. Locke's relation to the Latitudinarians and the role of original sin in his thinking have been explored by Spellman (1988). Coleman's (1983) systematic study of Locke's moral theory set the stage for some of the recent attention to this aspect of Locke's thought.

Another newly developing area of Locke studies concerns the reception of his doctrines in Europe, especially in France. The difficulties the French had with the term 'consciousness' when translating this English term have been interestingly analyzed by Davies (1990). Reactions to Locke's books in French-language journals and the impact of his doctrines (especially thinking matter) on Enlightenment thinkers have been presented by several writers (Hutchison, 1991; Schøsler, 1985, 1994; J. W. Yolton, 1991). The full story of the reception of Locke's doctrines in Europe (especially in Germany, Portugal, and Holland) in the eighteenth century has yet to be written. Fruitful research programs are waiting for scholars.

A number of collections of articles can be consulted to fill out this brief sketch of newer developments in Locke studies (Chappell, 1994; Harpham, 1992; Thompson, 1991).

Bibliography

RECENT EDITIONS OF LOCKE'S WORKS

De Beer, E. S., ed. *The Correspondence of John Locke.* 8 vols. Oxford, 1976–89.

Kelly, P., ed. *Several Papers relating to Money, Interest, and Trade.* Oxford, 1991.

Laslett, P., ed. *Two Treatises of Government,* 3d ed. Cambridge, 1989.

Nidditch, P. H., ed. *Essay concerning Human Understanding.* Oxford, 1975.

———, and G. A. J. Rogers, eds. *Drafts for the Essay concerning Human Understanding and other Philosophical Writings,* Vol. 1. Oxford, 1990. Includes drafts A and B; other volumes planned.

Wainwright, A. P., ed. *Paraphrases and Notes on the Epistles of St. Paul.* 2 vols. Oxford, 1987.

Yolton, J. W., and J. S. Yolton, eds. *Some Thoughts concerning Education.* Oxford, 1989.

WORKS ON LOCKE

Alexander, P. *Ideas, Qualities, and Corpuscles: Locke and Boyle on the External World.* Cambridge, 1985.

Ashcraft, R. *Revolutionary Politics and Locke's "Two Treatises of Government."* Princeton, 1986.

Attig, J. C., ed. *The Works of John Locke: A Comprehensive Bibliography from the Seventeenth Century to the Present.* Westport, CT, 1985.

Ayers, M. *Locke.* 2 vols. London, 1991.

Chappell, V., ed. *The Cambridge Companion to Locke.* Cambridge, 1994.

Colman, J. *John Locke's Moral Philosophy.* Edinburgh, 1983.

Davies, C. *"Conscience" as Consciousness: The Self of Self-Awareness in French Philosophical Writing from Descartes to Diderot.* Studies on Voltaire and the Eighteenth Century, 272. Oxford, 1990.

Dunn, J. *The Political Thought of John Locke: An Historical Account of the Argument of the "Two Treatises of Government."* Cambridge, 1969.

Franklin, J. H. *John Locke and the Theory of Sovereignty: Mixed Monarchy and the Right of Resistance in the Political Thought of the English Revolution.* Cambridge, 1978.

Gobetti, D. *Public and Private: Individuals, Households, and Body Politic in Locke and Hutcheson.* London, 1992.

Goyard-Fabre, S. *John Locke et la raison raisonnable.* Paris, 1986.

Harpham, E. J., ed. *John Locke's "Two Treatises of Government": New Interpretations.* Lawrence, KS, 1992.

Harris, I. *The Mind of John Locke: A Study of Political Theory in Its Intellectual Setting.* Cambridge, 1994.

Hutchison, R. *Locke in France, 1688–1734.* Studies on Voltaire and the Eighteenth Century, 290. Oxford, 1991.

Mackie, J. L. *Problems from Locke.* Oxford, 1976.

Marshall, J. *John Locke: Resistance, Religion, and Responsibility.* Cambridge Studies in Early Modern British History. Cambridge, 1994.

Passmore, J. "Locke and the Ethics of Belief," *Proceedings of the British Academy,* Vol. 64 (1978), 185–208.

Rogers, G. A. J. "Locke, Anthropology, and Models of the Mind," *History of the Human Sciences,* Vol. 6 (1993), 73–87.

———, ed. *Locke's Philosophy: Content and Context.* Oxford, 1994.

Schochet, G. J. "Toleration, Revolution, and Judgment in the Development of Locke's Political Thought," *Political Science,* Vol. 40 (1988), 84–96.

Schøsler, J. *La Bibliothèque raisonnée (1728–1753): Les Réactions d'un périodique français à la philosophie de Locke au XVIIIe siècle.* Odense, 1985.

———. "Le Christianisme raisonnable et le débat sur le 'Socinianisme' de John Locke dans la presse française de la première moitié du XVIIIe siècle," *Lias,* Vol. 21, no. 2 (1994), 295–319.

Schouls, P. A. *Reasoned Freedom: John Locke and Enlightenment.* Ithaca, NY, 1992.

Spellman, W. M. *John Locke and the Problem of Depravity.* Oxford, 1988.

Thiel, U. *Locke's Theorie der personalen Identität.* Bonn, 1983.

Thompson, M. P., ed. *John Locke und Immanuel Kant.* Berlin, 1991.

Tomida, Y. "Idea and Thing: The Deep Structure of Locke's Theory of Knowledge," *Analecta Husserliana,* Vol. 66 (1995), 3–143.

Tuck, R. *Natural Rights Theories: Their Origin and Development.* Cambridge, 1979.

Tully, J. *A Discourse on Property: John Locke and His Adversaries.* Cambridge, 1980.

Vaughn, K. I. *John Locke, Economist and Social Scientist.* Chicago, 1980.

Vienne, J.-M. *Expérience et raison: Les fondements de la morale selon Locke.* Paris, 1991.

Walmsley, P. "Locke's Cassowary and the Ethos of the Essay," *Studies in Eighteenth-Century Culture,* Vol. 22 (1992), 253–67.

Walmsley, P. "Dispute and Conversation: Probability and the Rhetoric of Natural Philosophy in Locke's *Essay,*" *Journal of the History of Ideas,* Vol. 54 (1993), 381–94.

Winkler, K. P. "Locke on Personal Identity," *Journal of the History of Philosophy,* Vol. 29 (1991), 201–26.

Wood, N. *The Politics of Locke's Philosophy: A Social Study of "An Essay concerning Human Understanding."* Berkeley, 1983.

Yolton, J. S. *John Locke: A Descriptive Bibliography.* Bristol, England, 1996.

———, and J. W. Yolton. *John Locke: A Reference Guide.* Boston, 1985.

Yolton, J. W. *Locke and the Compass of Human Understanding: A Selective Commentary on the Essay.* Cambridge, 1970.

———. *Locke and French Materialism.* Oxford, 1991.

——— . *A Locke Dictionary.* Oxford, 1993.

JOHN W. YOLTON

LOGIC. *See:* MATHEMATICAL LOGIC, and PHILOSOPHICAL LOGIC [S]

LOGIC, NONSTANDARD. Logic is that discipline that aims to give an account of what inferences are valid and why. Although it is common to distinguish between two sets of criteria for validity—inductive and deductive—most work in the history of logic has focused on deductive validity. Since the mathematization of logic around the turn of this century, accounts of deductive validity have been given for inferences couched in formal languages. A common practice is to specify validity in terms of some set of axioms or rules and justify it by way of some semantics. To obtain applications of the account, an understanding of the relationship between the formal language and the vernacular (often in the form of some imprecisely specified translation manual) has also to be provided.

The correct characterization of and justification for validity have historically been matters of philosophical contention. There is, however, an orthodoxy (if not unanimity) on the issue that dates back to around the 1920s. The account is essentially that of FREGE's [3; S] *Begriffschrift* and RUSSELL [7] and WHITEHEAD's [8] *Principia Mathematica,* as cleaned up and articulated by subsequent logicians such as HILBERT [3] and Gentzen. It is often known (rather inappropriately) as classical logic and is to be found in virtually any modern logic textbook (see LOGIC, MODERN [4]).

Despite the relative orthodoxy, classical logic faces a number of problems. These have bred dissatisfaction and attempts to articulate rival accounts of deductive validity. Such accounts are commonly referred to as nonstandard logics.

MODAL AND INTUITIONIST LOGICS

Criticisms of classical logic go back to the 1920s. One was given by C. I. Lewis, who objected to paradoxes of "material implication" such as $\alpha \rightarrow (\neg\alpha \rightarrow \beta)$. He constructed systems of logic that contained a notion of strict implication that avoided these paradoxes. This led to an investigation of the logic of modalities, such as necessity and possibility, and modal logic developed (see LOGIC, MODAL [4] and MODAL LOGIC [S]). Lewis's original critique of classical logic is now generally thought to be based on a confusion of the connective 'if' and the relation of entailment. Consequently, modal logic is now usually thought of as an augmentation of classical logic by modal functors rather than as a rival. This development was accentuated by the discovery of world semantics for modal logics in the 1960s by KRIPKE [S] and others. World semantics have, however, provided the basis for the semantics of many new logics. One of these, another augmentation of classical logic, tense logic, was invented by PRIOR [S]. In this, temporal operators—for example, F (it will be the case) and P (it was the case)—are added to the language and given suitable semantic conditions.

A second early critique was provided by Brouwer and other intuitionists (see LOGIC, HISTORY OF [4]). Arguing on the basis of a critique of a Platonist philosophy of mathematics, they rejected a number of principles of classical logic, such as $\neg\neg\alpha \rightarrow \alpha, \neg\forall x\alpha \rightarrow \exists x\neg\alpha$. For example, the second of these fails because the mere fact that you can show, for instance, that not all numbers have a certain property does not show how to construct a number that does not have it, which is what is required to ground an existence claim. In the light of these criticisms Heyting formulated an axiom system for intuitionist logic with an informal semantics in terms of provability. After a fairly quiet period the study of intuitionist logic took off again in the 1960s and 1970s. Kripke demonstrated that the logic has a world semantics; DUMMETT [S] introduced new arguments for INTUITIONISM [S] (not just in mathematics) based on the PHILOSOPHY OF LANGUAGE [S]; and applications of the logic in computer science were discovered.

MANY-VALUED AND QUANTUM LOGICS

A third critique dating back to the 1920s was provided by LUKASIEWICZ [5]. Arguing on the basis of the indeterminacy of future events, he introduced a system of logic where sentences can be neither true nor false, and so classical principles such as $\alpha \vee \neg\alpha$ fail. The system was quickly generalized to ones where sentences can have arbitrarily many semantic values, many-valued logics (see LOGIC, MANY-VALUED [4]). The study of many-valued logics accelerated in the 1960s and 1970s. Many logicians suggested that certain kinds of sentences might have no truth value: for example, they are "meaningless" ('It's 3 P.M. at the North Pole'); they are paradoxical ('This sentence is false'); they are vague ('Dry grass is green'). Consequently, we have seen the articulation of various three-valued logics (sometimes called partial logics). Consideration of VAGUENESS [8; S] also makes it tempting to suppose that truth comes by degrees. A natural way of handling this insight is by using a different sort of many-valued logic, where sentences can have as truth value any real number between 0 (wholly false) and 1 (wholly true). Under the influence of writers such as Zadeh, such logics, now usually called fuzzy logics, have found applications in ARTIFICIAL INTELLIGENCE [S]. (*See* FUZZY LOGIC [S])

In the 1930s REICHENBACH [7] and Destouches-Février suggested that various problems in quantum mechanics made it appropriate to use a three-valued logic there. These ideas were not very successful, but similar problems led Birkhoff and von NEUMANN [5] to suggest a more sophisticated approach around the same time. This is now usually called quantum logic (and has, again, received much further attention by logicians such as PUTNAM [S] since the 1960s). They argued that the classical principle of distribution, $\alpha \wedge (\beta \vee \gamma) \vdash (\alpha \wedge \beta) \vee (\alpha \wedge \gamma)$, fails in the microworld. For example, it may be true (verifiable) of a particle that it has a position and one of a range of momenta, but each disjunct attributing to it that position and a particular momentum is false (unverifiable). To construct a logic in which distribution fails, they proceeded essentially as follows. In standard world semantics, sentences can be thought of as taking subsets of the set of worlds as semantic values, and the logical constants can be interpreted as Boolean operations. In quantum mechanics the possible states of the system form a mathematical structure known as a Hilbert space, and it is natural to take the semantic values to be subspaces of this space. Logical constants are then interpreted as appropriate operations on subspaces. For example, disjunction in interpreted as the span of (the smallest space containing) two subspaces.

RELEVANT AND PARACONSISTENT LOGICS

The 1960s and 1970s saw not only the development of many older nonstandard logics but the production of many new kinds. One of these was relevant logic. This grew, like modal logic, from dissatisfaction with the paradoxes of material implication (and those of strict implication, such as $\alpha \wedge \neg\alpha \vdash \beta$). Building on early work of Church and Ackermann, Anderson, Belnap, and coworkers constructed axiom systems for three propositional (and later predicate) logics E, R, and T, which satisfied the criterion that if $\alpha \to \beta$ is provable, α and β share a propositional parameter. Semantics for the systems came a little later. In particular, world semantics were provided by Routley and Meyer. In the light of these it became clear that there are many more, and possibly more important, systems in the family. One of these is closely related to linear logic, proposed independently in the 1980s by Girard for its applications in computer science.

There are two features of world semantics for relevant logics that distinguish them from those of modal logic. The first is that a ternary relation (instead of a binary one) is used to give the truth conditions of the conditional: $\alpha \to \beta$ is true at world w if and only if (iff) for all worlds x, y such that $Rwxy$, if α is true at x, β is true at y. The second is that some technique is required to produce worlds that are inconsistent or incomplete. This can be done in two ways. The first is to have an operator on worlds, *, such that α is true at world w iff α is not true at world w^*. (For the worlds of ordinary modal logic, * can be thought of as just the identity function.) The second is to allow sentences to take one of four truth values: true only, false only, both, neither ({1}, {0}, {1, 0}, ϕ). These semantics therefore combine the techniques of both modal and many-valued logic. Standard relevant logics invalidate not only the paradoxes of material implication but also the disjunctive syllogism: $\neg\alpha \wedge (\alpha \vee \beta) \vdash \beta$. Much of the critique of relevant logic has focused on this fact.

A related contemporary nonstandard logic is paraconsistent logic. A logic is paraconsistent iff the inference $\alpha, \neg\alpha \vdash \beta$ fails. (A paraconsistent logic may or may not be relevant.) Paraconsistent logics were developed independently by Jaśkowski, da Costa, and others. Their principle concern was the use of such a logic to make inferences in a sensible way in situations where the information from which conclusions are drawn may be inconsistent—for example, from scientific theories whose principles conflict, or where the information is that in some computational data base. Semantics for paraconsistent logics use techniques such as those used in relevant logic to allow contradictions to be true in an interpretation. Some (though not all) paraconsistent logicians, such as Priest, have endorsed the view that some contradictions may actually be true (*simpliciter*): dialetheism. A major argument for this view is provided by the paradoxes of self-reference (see LOGICAL PARADOXES [5]). Consistent solutions to these are notoriously problematic.

CONDITIONAL AND FREE LOGICS

Dissatisfaction with the material conditional (at least as an account of English subjunctive conditionals) triggered another nonstandard logic around the 1970s: conditional logics. A number of counterexamples were provided by Stalnaker and others to classical principles such as transitivity ($\alpha \to \beta, \beta \to \gamma \vdash \alpha \to \gamma$) and antecedent strengthening ($\alpha \to \beta \vdash (\alpha \wedge \gamma) \to \beta$). For example, if you strike this match it will light; hence, if you strike this match and it is under water it will light. In conditional logics these inferences are invalid. The major technique used to achieve this end is a selection function, s, which, given a world, w, and a sentence, α, picks out a set of worlds $s(w, \alpha)$. Intuitively, this can be thought of as the set of worlds relevantly similar to w where α is true. The truth conditions are then as follows: $\alpha \to \beta$ is true at w iff β is true at every world in $s(w,\alpha)$. Standard conditional logics validate the paradoxes of strict implication, but relevant conditional logics may be obtained by combining the appropriate semantic techniques.

Another kind of nonstandard logic takes issue with the principle built into classical semantics that every name denotes (an existent object). (Consider, e.g., 'Sherlock Holmes'.) Logics that reject this are called free logics. One approach to free logics is to take all sentences containing nondenoting terms to be truth valueless. This idea gives rise to various three-valued logics, proposed in the 1960s by Smiley and others. A sophistication of this idea was proposed by van Fraassen. Given any evaluation of this kind, a supervaluation is any two-valued evaluation that agrees with it except where it makes a sentence neither true nor false. Logical validity is now defined in terms of supervaluations rather than evaluations. This construction allows all classical validities to be preserved.

A rather different approach was suggested by Leonard, Lambert, and others around the same time. This approach modifies the classical rule of existential generalization, $\exists x\alpha(x) \to \alpha(c)$ (and its dual, universal instantiation), by adding a conjunct to the antecedent to the effect that c exists. An appropriate semantics can be obtained by allowing constants to denote objects outside the domain of quantification. This is a form of Meinongianism (see MEINONG [5]), since it allows nonexistent objects to be named (but not quantified over). Some neo-Meinongians (e.g., Routley) allow them to be quantified over as well. This requires no change to the formal machinery of classical logic. All that has to be changed is the canonical interpretation of the quantifiers in English. Thus '$\exists x\alpha$' is now read, not as 'There exists an x such that α', but as 'For some x, α', where this expression is devoid of any existential commitment.

Whether or not any of the nonstandard logics discussed here are correct, their presence serves to remind that logic is not a set of received truths but a discipline where competing theories concerning validity vie with each other. The case for each theory—including a received theory—has to be investigated on its merits. This requires detailed philosophical investigations concerning existence, truth and contradiction, truth in quantum mechanics, or whatever is appropriate. Detailed discussions can hardly be attempted here. Some can be found in the items cited in the bibliography, which should also be consulted for further historical and technical details.

(SEE ALSO: *Mathematical Logic; Philosophical Logic* [S])

Bibliography

Anderson, A., N. Belnap and J. M. Dunn. *Entailment: The Logic of Relevance and Necessity*, 2 vols. Princeton, NJ, 1975–92. A reference book for the original systems of relevance logic.

Dummett, M. *Elements of Intuitionism.* Oxford, 1977. A discussion of the foundations of intuitionist logic.

Gabbay, D., and F. Guenthner. *Handbook of Philosophical Logic*, 4 vols. Dordrecht, 1983–89. For discussions of temporal logic, conditional logic, partial logic, many-valued logic, relevance logic, intuitionist logic, free logic, and quantum logic, see, respectively, Vol. 2, chaps. 2, 8; Vol. 3, chaps. 1, 2, 3, 4, 6, and 7.

Haack, S. *Deviant Logic.* Cambridge, 1974. An introduction to the general philosophical issues surrounding nonstandard logics and to some of the logics.

Harper, W. L., R. Stalnaker, and G. Pearce, eds. *Ifs.* Dordrecht, 1981. A collection of papers on aspects of conditional logic.

Lambert, J. K. *Philosophical Applications of Free Logic.* Oxford, 1991. A collection of essays on various aspect of free logic.

Mittelstaedt, P. *Quantum Logic.* Dordrecht, 1978. An exposition of quantum logic.

Priest, G. *In Contradiction: A Study of the Transconsistent.* The Hague, 1987. A defense of dialetheism and dialetheic logic.

Priest, G., R. Routley, and J. Norman. *Paraconsistent Logic: Essays on the Inconsistent.* Munich, 1989. A reference book for paraconsistent logic.

Prior, A. *Past, Present, and Future.* Oxford, 1967. A classic exposition of tense logic and its philosophical aspects.

Rescher, N. *Many-valued Logic.* New York, 1969. A modern survey of many-valued logics.

Routley, R., V. Plumwood, R. K. Meyer, and R. T. Brady. *Relevant Logics and Their Rivals.* Atascadero, CA, 1982. A reference for the newer systems of relevant logic.

Yager, R. R., and L. A. Zadeh. *An Introduction to Fuzzy Logic Applications in Intelligent Systems.* Dordrecht, 1992. An introduction to the applications of fuzzy logic in AI.

GRAHAM PRIEST

LOGICAL CONSEQUENCE. Logical consequence is a relation between a set of sentences and a sentence said to follow logically from it. Closely related notions are logical validity and logical truth: an argument is logically valid iff (if and only if) its conclusion is a logical consequence of the set of its premises; a sentence is logically true iff it is a logical consequence of any set of sentences. Other notions definable in terms of logical consequence are logical consistency, logical equivalence, theory, and so forth.

Modern logic offers two distinct concepts of logical consequence: a proof-theoretical concept, "derivability" or "provability," symbolized by $\vdash$, and a semantic concept, "logical consequence (proper)," "logical implication," or "logical entailment," symbolized by $\models$. Given a formal system $\mathscr{L}$ (a formal language together with a proof system and a system of models), the two concepts are defined as follows: if σ is a sentence and Σ is a set of sentences, then $\Sigma \vdash \sigma$ iff there is a proof of σ from Σ, and $\Sigma \models \sigma$ iff every model of Σ is a model of σ, i.e., iff there is no model in which all the sentences of Σ are true and σ is false. GÖDEL's [S] 1930 completeness theorem establishes the coextensionality of $\vdash$ and $\models$ in standard first-order logic, but in general the two notions are not coextensional (*see* GÖDEL'S THEOREM [3]). The term "logical consequence" is usually reserved for the semantic notion, a tradition followed in this article.

The semantic definition of logical consequence is due to Alfred TARSKI (1936; [8]). An informal version of this definition was implicit in earlier works by Gödel, HILBERT [3], and others, but it was Tarski's treatment of logical consequence and related semantic notions that allowed a rigorous mathematical study of these notions and led to the modern conception of logic as constituted by two equally fundamental disciplines: PROOF THEORY [S] (the theory of $\vdash$) and MODEL THEORY [S] (the theory of $\models$).

Tarski claimed his definition captured the intuitive, everyday notion of logical consequence. He characterized this notion by the following two traits: (i) if σ is a logical consequence of Σ, then "it can never happen" (1936, p. 414) that all the sentences of Σ are true and σ is false; (ii) logical consequences are formal, and as such they are dependent on the form of the sentences involved, not on the particular objects referred to in these sentences. Neither the proof-theoretical definition nor the substitutional definition of logical consequence, Tarski contended, accurately captures the intuitive notion. The proof-theoretical definition leaves some genuinely logical consequences unaccounted for, and it follows from Gödel's incompleteness theorem that no matter how many new (finite, structural), rules we add to the proof-theoretical apparatus, any reasonably rich (higher-order) deductive theory would have consequences which follow logically from it in the intuitive sense yet are not provable from its theorems. The substitutional definition fails in languages with an insufficient stock of nonlogical (substitutional) terms. This definition says that σ is a logical consequence of Σ iff there is no substitution under which all the sentences of Σ are true and σ is false (where substitutions preserve grammatical categories, are uniform, and are restricted to nonlogical constants), but if the language lacks in expressive resources, a failure to satisfy (i) may not be witnessed by an appropriate substitution. Tarski's own definition uses semantic tools (1933). Semantics, according to Tarski, deals with concepts relating language to the "world" (objects in a broad sense), the basic notion being satisfaction—a relation between a formula and a sequence of objects (in the universe of discourse). Model of σ (Σ) is defined in terms of satisfaction: Let σ (Σ) be a sentence (a set of sentences) of a formalized language L. By replacing all the nonlogical constants of σ (Σ) by variables in a proper manner, i.e., preserving syntactic categories as well as identities and differences, we obtain an open formula (a set of open formulas), σ^* (Σ^*). A sequence of objects is a model of σ (Σ) iff it satisfies σ^* (all the sentential functions in Σ^*).

Tarski ended his discussion of logical consequence with a qualifying note: the semantic definition of logical consequence is adequate given the standard division of terms to logical and nonlogical, but while this division is not arbitrary, an adequate criterion for logical terms might never be found. Tarski's semantic definition of logical consequence was likened (by Berg, 1962, and others) to an earlier substitutional definition due to Bolzano (1837). It is important, however, to keep in mind the differences between the semantic and the substitutional methods, in particular, the objectual nature of Tarskian semantics as opposed to the purely linguistic or conceptual nature of substitutional semantics. Another debated historical issue is the relation between Tarski's 1936 notion of model and the modern notion (see Etchemendy, 1988; Hodges, 1986; Sher, 1991.)

The intuitive adequacy of the semantic definition was questioned by several authors. Boolos (1985), Kreisel (1967), and McGee (1992) examined the limitations incurred by restricting logical models to structures whose universes are proper sets: the semantic definition reduces logical consequence to preservation of truth, or validity, in all set structures, but intuitively logical consequence is validity in all structures whatsoever, including structures whose constituents are proper classes. Kreisel concluded, based on Gödel's completeness theorem, that at least in the case of standard first-order languages, preservation of truth in all set models ensures preservation of truth in all class models. Boolos and McGee found the restriction of models to set-theoretical structures problematic in second-order languages.

Etchemendy (1990) investigated the semantic definition from a broader perspective, distinguishing between two basic types of semantic theories, so-called representational and interpretational theories. In representational semantics models represent possible worlds, and preservation of truth in all models is preservation of truth under all possible changes in the actual world relative to a fixed language. In interpretational semantics, models represent variations in language, and preservation of truth in all models is preservation of truth under all reinterpretations of the nonfixed (nonlogical) vocabulary relative to a fixed world (the actual world). Interpretational semantics is an upgraded, objectual version of substitutional semantics (the range of reinterpretation of terms is not restricted by the lexical resources of the given language), and Etchemendy regarded modern semantics as exemplifying this type of theory. The semantic definition of logical consequence, however, fails in interpretational semantics. The conceptual resources of interpretational semantics are rather restricted, and as a result: (i) interpretational semantics cannot establish an adequate distinction between logical and nonlogical terms; and (ii) interpretational semantics cannot distinguish between accidental and necessary generality (truth in all models is no more than accidental generality). It follows that the interpretational notion of logical consequence collapses to that of material consequence. Etchemendy's interpretational construal of Tarskian semantics and the underlying dichotomy of interpretational vs. representational semantics were criticized by García-Carpintero (1993) and Sher (1996). Alternative conceptions designed to vindicate the semantic definition were developed by the above two authors, and a more restricted defense was proposed by McGee (1992).

The notion of logical consequence is sensitive to choice of logical terms, order of variables, and compositional structure (e.g., linear vs. branching quantifier-prefixes). This means that a theory of the scope of logic (logical form) must take into account considerations pertaining to the resulting notion of logical consequence. QUINE (1970; [7; S]) regarded the "remarkable concurrence" of diverse definitions of logical consequence in standard first-order logic—in particular, the coextensionality of the semantic and proof-theoretical definitions (completeness)—as a reason for drawing the line there, ruling out second-order logic as well as branching quantification as part of logic proper, but other philosophers (e.g., Boolos, 1975) contested Quine's restrictions. Following Mostowski (1957), Lindström (1966) and Tarski (1966) proposed invariance under isomorphic structures or, more restrictedly, invariance under permutations of the universe, as a criterion for logical terms, leading to a generalized (abstract, model-theoretic) conception of first-order logic. McCarthy (1981), Peacocke (1976), Sher (1991), and Tharp (1975) examined this and other criteria for logical terms in light of the adequacy of the resulting notion of logical consequence, arriving at a wide array of views on the scope of LOGICAL TERMS [S] and logic.

(SEE ALSO: *Mathematical Logic* and *Philosophical Logic* [S])

Bibliography

Berg, J. *Bolzano's Logic.* Stockholm, 1962.

Bolzano, B. *Wissenschaftslehre.* Sulzbach, 1837. Translated by B. Terrell as *Theory of Science.* Dordrecht, 1973.

Boolos, G. "On Second-Order Logic," *Journal of Philosophy* 72 (1975), 509–27.

———. "Nominalist Platonism," *Philosophical Review,* Vol. 94 (1985), 327–44.

Etchemendy, J. "Tarski on Truth and Logical Consequence," *Journal of Symbolic Logic,* Vol. 53, (1988), 91–106.

Etchemendy, J. *The Concept of Logical Consequence.* Cambridge, MA, 1990.

García-Carpintero, M. "The Grounds for the Model-theoretic Account of the Logical Properties," *Notre Dame Journal of Formal Logic,* Vol. 34 (1993), 107–31.

Hodges, W. "Truth in a Structure," *Proceedings of the Aristotelian Society,* 1986, 135–51.

Kreisel, G. "Informal Rigour and Completeness Proofs," in I. Lakatos, ed., *Problems in the Philosophy of Mathematics* (Amsterdam, 1967), 138–71.

Lindström, P. "First Order Predicate Logic with Generalized Quantifiers," *Theoria,* Vol. 32 (1966), 186–95.

McCarthy, T. "The Idea of a Logical Constant," *Journal of Philosophy,* Vol. 78 (1981), 499–523.

McGee, V. "Two Problems with Tarski's Theory of Consequence," *Proceedings of the Aristotelian Society,* Vol. 92 (1992), 273–92.

Mostowski, A. "On a Generalization of Quantifiers," *Fundamenta Mathematicae,* Vol. 42 (1957), 12–36.

Peacocke, C. "What Is a Logical Constant?" *Journal of Philosophy,* Vol. 73 (1976), 221–40.

Quine, W. V. O. *Philosophy of Logic.* Englewood Cliffs, NJ, 1970.

Sher, G. *The Bounds of Logic: A Generalized Viewpoint.* Cambridge, MA, 1991.

———. "Did Tarski Commit 'Tarski's Fallacy'?", *Journal of Symbolic Logic,* Vol. 61 (1996).

Tarski, A. "Pojecie Prawdy w jezykach nauk dedukcyjnych," monograph. *Prace Towarzystwa Naukowego Warszawskiego, Wydzial III Nauk Matematyczno-fizycznych,* 34, Warsaw, 1933. Translated by J. H. Woodger as "The Concept of Truth in Formalized Languages." English translation and a postscript by the author appear in Tarski (1983), 152–278.

———. "O Pojciu Wynikania Logicznego," *Przeglad Filozoficzny,* Vol. 39 (1936), 55–68. Translated by J. H. Woodger as "On the Concept of Logical Consequence." English translation by J. H. Woodger appears in Tarski (1983), 409–20.

———. *Logic, Semantics, Metamathematics,* 2d. ed. Indianapolis, 1983.

———. "What Are Logical Notions?" (1966), *History and Philosophy of Logic,* Vol. 7 (1986), 143–54.

Tharp, L. H. "Which Logic Is the Right Logic?" *Synthese,* Vol. 31 (1975), 1–21.

GILA SHER

LOGICAL FORM. Consider the argument

> All amanitas are mycorrhizas;
> all mycorrhizas are symbionts;
> therefore all amanitas are symbionts.

You can discern its validity without fully grasping its content. How? One answer is that you recognize its form as one that guarantees that if its premises are true, so is its conclusion. Now consider

> Aaron was a father;
> Esau was a father;
> therefore Aaron and Esau were fathers.

This too is patently valid. But replace "father(s)" by "brother(s)" throughout and one gets an argument of the same apparent form, with true premises and a false conclusion. Such examples abound. So if logical validity depends on form, it cannot be apparent grammatical form. (Parallel considerations apply with consistency in place of validity—the two are interdefinable.) Usually, when one tries to spell out the logically relevant difference between corresponding arguments, it does seem to be a difference in form. Hence the hypothesis of logical form: statements (derivatively arguments) have a special kind of form responsible for their logical properties.

FORMALIZATION

More support for the hypothesis comes from the success of formalization, the translation of arguments from natural language into an interpreted formal language for which there are formal analogues of logical properties. For a formal language there must be a specification of sentences, of admissible interpretations, and of truth/falsehood of a sentence under an admissible interpretation. An argument in a formal language is formally valid just when there is no admissible interpretation in which the premises are true and the conclusion false. Any formal language is so designed that sentences with the same syntactic form have the same logical properties; hence, syntactically matching arguments are all formally valid if one of them is. Formalization of a part of one's natural language is validity preserving when all clearly logically (in)valid arguments in that part are translated into formally (in)valid arguments. Formalization is successful only if it is validity preserving, the more successful the more it translates.

A significant part of English is successfully formalizable in the language of first-order predicate calculus with identity (PC), and formalization of ever larger parts supports the idea of logical form as syntactic form in some validity-preserving comprehensive formalization.

DOUBTS

One source of doubt about the hypothesis of logical form is that certain practices of formalization are quite counterintuitive yet seem optimal. Consider

> Bill ran for office in 1993;
> so Bill ran for office.

To get a validity-preserving translation of such arguments in an interpreted version of PC, we construe the original sentences as existential:

> There is a running for office and it was by Bill and it was in 1993;
> so there is a running for office and it was by Bill.

If the original sentences were really existential, it would be self-contradictory to claim that, though Bill ran for office, there are no such things as runnings for office. But this is ontological thrift, not self-contradiction.

Such counterintuitive construals do not threaten the hypothesis of logical form, since they can be dispensed with by enriching the syntax of the language of PC with a category of predicate modifiers. Members of this category combine with a predicate to form another predicate, satisfied only by satisfiers of the first. Treating "in 1993" as a predicate modifier, satisfiers of "ran for office in 1993" are guaranteed to be satisfiers of "ran for office"; thus a validity-preserving formalization is available consonant with logical intuition.

A second source of doubt is the availability of seemingly acceptable nonequivalent formalizations of a statement. For example, "red is the color of blood" may be formalized in at least four nonequivalent ways, using "R" and "B" for predicates "is red" and "is blood," "r" and "b" as constants (names) for the color red and the substance blood, and "c" for the function expression "the color of": Rb; $(\forall x)(Bx \rightarrow Rx)$; $r=c(b)$; $(\forall x)(Bx \rightarrow r=c(x))$. Adding categories to PC only exacerbates the problem, but restriction to PC is not a complete escape, and some types of expression force us beyond PC—for example, binary quantifiers (Barwise & Cooper, 1981).

Considerations of uniformity will narrow down the class of validity-preserving comprehensive formalizations of a natural language; but there may remain more than one. If so, arguments may have more than one logical form (Sainsbury, 1991). However, if only one of these formalizations presents forms we actually respond to in making judgments of validity, the hypothesis of logical form would still be part of the explanation of our logical intuitions.

SEMANTIC STRUCTURE AND LOGICAL FORM

As logical form so often diverges from apparent syntactical form, yet seems to be a structural aspect of the way we understand statements, a natural speculation is that logical form is semantic structure.

The basic units of semantic structure are semantic categories of semantically simple expressions, two expressions belonging to the same category if they have the same type of value (e.g., individual, function from individuals to truth values, truth value). Assuming that an unambiguous statement is composed in a unique way from semantically simple constituents, its semantic structure is representable by its compositional tree, with constituents replaced by their categories. On this account, semantic structure is too gross to be logical form: statements of the form "P and Q" and "P or Q," though not logically equivalent, have the same semantic structure, since "and" and "or" both serve as functions from pairs of truth values to truth values, hence belong to the same semantic category (Evans, 1976).

Perhaps two statements have the same logical form when they have the same semantic structure and the same logical constants in the same positions. If so, choices of formalization may be guided by intuitions of semantic structure as well as by logical intuitions. This would favor, for example, the binary formalization of universal quantifiers, instead of the hidden-"if" version (Davies, 1981); and the number of acceptable formalizations may be reduced.

Against the view of logical form as semantic structure with positioned logical constants stands the difficulty of defining the class of logical constants. On one view there is no such class (Etchemendy, 1983). When defining admissible interpretations, we can choose to hold constant the interpretations of any expressions we like. In addition to the usual list we could also hold constant the interpretations of "knows that" and "believes that"; then the argument

> George knows that Bill has won;
> hence, George believes that Bill has won.

would be valid, since there would be no admissible interpretation under which the formalized premise is true and the formalized conclusion untrue. Such examples are sometimes treated as evidence that there is nothing intrinsic to an expression that makes it a logical constant. But this is a mistake. The semantic value of a logical constant must be a function from the semantic values of the expressions it combines with. "Knows that" fails this test: in the case above "knows that" takes the individual George and the proposition that Bill has won to a truth value, but which truth value depends on a contingent, hence variable, relation between George and that proposition; the same goes for "believes that." Although the hidden-"if" universal quantifier also fails this test, the binary universal quantifier does not. For example, in "all men are sinners" the binary "all" takes the extension of "men" and the extension of "sinners" (in that order) to truth if the first is included in the second, to falsehood if not.

Though passing this test is necessary for logical constanthood, it is not sufficient, as "and 7 is prime and" passes. Perhaps an expression is a logical constant just when it is semantically simple and passes the test, or is composed of such expressions. Until we have grounds for confidence in a definition of logical constanthood, the view of logical form as semantic structure with positioned logical constants remains uncertain.

SYNTACTIC STRUCTURE AND LOGICAL FORM

The divergence between logical form and apparent grammatical form does not entail that logical form is nonsyntactical. In some theories of syntax a sentence has more than one syntactical level; apparent grammatical form is only surface-level phrase structure, so logical form may be closely linked with (or even coincide with) syntax at another level. If some level of syntax is appropriate for semantic interpretation, the prospect of a unified account of syntax, semantics, and logical form emerges (Neale, 1994).

One of the major approaches to syntax, Government and Binding theory, associates three levels with each sentence. Structure at one of these levels, s-structure, represents apparent grammatical form; by a series of syntactically constrained moves (especially of quantifier noun phrases) from s-structure one reaches the level known as LF, at which quantifier scope is made explicit (May, 1985). LF appears to present structural representations to which a formal truth definition is applicable and would therefore be the level of syntax appropriate for semantic interpretation (Larson & Ludlow, 1993; Neale, 1994). Thus, logical form may be LF with positioned constants.

This approach brings two other benefits. First, by providing a systematic account of the derivation of LF from s-structure, it helps solve the problem of finding a comprehensive system of translation into an appropriate formal language. Second, the approach is formulated so as to distinguish those aspects of syntax common to all natural languages, thus promising to illuminate what in logical form the human mind is generally sensitive to. (*See also* SEMANTICS [7; S]; SYNTAX [S])

LOGICAL AND LINGUISTIC KNOWLEDGE

If logical form has a linguistic explication, knowledge of validity based on form would be partly linguistic knowledge. But this seems wrong, because the situation described by the conclusion of a valid argument must accompany the situation described by the premises, however those situations are described. Taking the comparative suffix "er" followed by "than" as a logical constant guaranteeing transitivity, the following is valid:

> Jack is older than Bob and Bob is older than Ted; therefore, Jack is older than Ted.

The premise of this argument describes exactly the same situation as "Jack was born before Bob and Ted was born after Bob." Had we used this sentence as the premise instead, the resulting argument would still have been recognizably valid, but not on the basis of logico-linguistic form.

This does not warrant skepticism about linguistic accounts of logical form. We must distinguish between what constitutes validity and ways of recognizing validity. An argument is logically valid when it is recognizably valid from its logical form. Validity is more comprehensive than logical validity, and the aim of explicating it in information-based terms (Barwise, 1989) is not in conflict with the aim of clarifying logical validity in terms of linguistic forms.

(SEE ALSO: *Language, Philosophy of* [4]; *Mathematical Logic, Philosophy of Language,* and *Philosophy of Logic* [S])

Bibliography

Barwise, J. *The Situation in Logic.* Stanford, 1989.

Barwise, J., and R. Cooper. "Generalized Quantifiers and Natural Language," *Linguistics and Philosophy,* Vol. 4 (1981), 159–219.

Davies, M. *Meaning, Quantification, Necessity.* London, 1981.

Etchemendy, J. "The Doctrine of Logic as Form," *Linguistics and Philosophy,* Vol. 6 (1983), 319–34. The case against.

———. *The Concept of Logical Consequence.* Cambridge, MA, 1990. Argues against the Tarskian view.

Evans, G. "Semantic Structure and Logical Form," in G. Evans and J. McDowell, eds., *Truth and Meaning* (Oxford, 1976).

Kamp, H., and U. Reyle. *From Discourse to Logic.* Dordrecht, 1993. Formal semantics with representations of discourse rather than sentences as the units for interpretation.

Larson, R., and P. Ludlow. "Interpreted Logical Forms," *Synthese,* Vol. 95 (1993), 305–55.

May, R. *Logical Form: Its Structure and Derivation.* Cambridge, MA, 1985. A study of the syntactical level LF.

Neale, S. "Logical Form and LF," in C. Otero, ed., *Noam Chomsky: Critical Assessments* (London, 1994).

Sainsbury, M. *Logical Forms.* Oxford, 1991. The best starting point. See especially chap. 6.

MARCUS GIAQUINTO

LOGICAL KNOWLEDGE. Logical knowledge can be understood in two ways: as knowledge of the laws of logic and as knowledge derived by means of deductive reasoning. Most of the following is concerned with the first of these interpretations; the second will be treated briefly at the end. Furthermore, only deductive logic will be treated: as yet, there is no set of laws of inductive logic enjoying the kind of consensus acceptance accorded to deductive logic.

To begin with, we must specify what is a law of logic—not an entirely straightforward task. There are three, not all mutually exclusive, conceptions of logic laws. First, one could take them to be valid schemata (of statements), such as the familiar law of excluded middle, ⌜*p* or not *p*⌝. A second conception is that they are valid rules of inference, such as the familiar *modus ponens*—that is, from ⌜$p \rightarrow q$⌝ and *p* infer *q*. The third conception of logic law, due to Gottlob FREGE [3; S] and Bertrand RUSSELL [7], takes them to be maximally general, true (not valid) second-order quantified statements (see Goldfarb, 1979). The following discussion is confined, by and large, to the second conception; but the philosophical problems canvased arise with respect to the other conceptions as well.

In order to appreciate the problems involved in the analysis of knowledge of logical laws, note first that, however these laws are conceived, knowledge of them appears to be propositional. That is, to know a law of logic is to know that a rule of inference (or a schema) is valid (or a statement true). But, given the classical analysis of knowledge as justified true belief, it follows that knowledge of the validity of a rule of inference requires justification. There are two uncontroversially entrenched forms of justification: inductive and deductive justification. By the nature of inductive reasoning an inductive justification of validity shows, at best, that a rule of inference usually leads from true premises to a true conclusion (or that it is sufficiently highly likely to do so). This is too weak; a valid rule of inference, as noted above, necessarily leads from true premises to true conclusions. So it appears that the justification of validity must be deductive.

On the basis of this conclusion it can be shown that the justification of the validity of any rule of inference either is circular or involves an infinite regress. The argument has two parts. To begin with, there certainly are deductive justifications of rules of inference that raise no serious philosophical questions. Take the justification of the rule "existential specification" in Benson Mates's widely used *Elementary Logic:* "To justify this rule, . . . we observe that . . . we may . . . obtain the inference it permits [using certain basic rules]. . . Assuming . . . that the basic rules . . . are [valid], . . . the above description of how any [existential specification] inference can be made using only [those] rules . . . shows that [existential specification] is [valid], too" (Mates, 1972, p. 123). The rule is justified by explicitly assuming the validity of other rules, so the justification here is only relative. If all logical laws are justified in this way, then, plausibly, the justification of any given rule will be either circular, by explicitly assuming its own validity, or will involve an infinite regress.

One might conclude from this that there must be some set of rules that are not justified on the basis of the assumed validity of other rules. Let us call these rules fundamental. Unfortunately, there is a simple argument that the justification of fundamental rules will involve a similar circularity or infinite regress.

What counts as a deductive justification of a proposition depends on what forms of inference are taken to be valid. For, if any rule of inference used in an argument is invalid, then the argument could not constitute a deductive justification of anything. Let us formulate this point as: a deductive argument presupposes the validity of the rules of inference it employs. Given this formulation, we can state an intuitive principle: if an argument for the validity of a rule of inference presupposes the validity of that very rule, then the argument is circular. To distinguish this notion of circularity from the one used above, let us call this pragmatic circularity, and the former, direct circularity.

Suppose a fundamental rule of ρ is justified by an argument π. Now either π employs nonfundamental rules, or it does not. Suppose π employs a nonfundamental rule σ. By the first part of the argument, σ is justified by assuming the validity of fundamental rules. Again, either the justification of σ assumes the validity of ρ or it does not. Now assume further that if an argument employs a rule whose justification assumes the validity of another, then it presupposes the validity of the second. Thus, in the first case, the justification of ρ is pragmatically circular. In the second case, the justification of ρ presupposes the validity of a set of other fundamental rules.

Now suppose that π does not employ nonfundamental rules. Then, either it employs ρ or it does not. In the first case the justification is pragmatically circular. In the second, again, the justification of ρ presupposes the validity of a set of other fundamental rules. Hence, the justification of any fundamental rule either is pragmatically circular or involves an infinite regress. (See Goodman, 1983, pp. 63–64; see also Bickenbach, 1978; Dummett, 1973; and Haack, 1976.)

One might object to the notion of circularity of argument used in the second part of the argument. Unlike the more familiar variant of circularity, the conclusion in this case is not actually assumed as a premise but is presupposed by the inferential transitions. Thus, it is unclear that this sort of circular argument suffers from the principal difficulty afflicting the more familiar sort of circular argument, namely, that every conclusion is justifiable by its means.

This, however, is not a very strong objection. One might reply, to begin with, that pragmatically circular arguments are just as objectionable as directly circular ones in that both assume that the conclusion is not in question, by assuming its truth in the one case and by acting as if it were true in the other. Moreover, while it is unclear that every rule of inference is justifiable by a pragmatically circular argument, it is clear that such an argument can justify both rules that we take to be valid and rules that we take to be fallacies of reasoning. For example, the following is an argument demonstrating the validity of the fallacy of affirming the consequent (see Haack, 1976):

1. Suppose $\ulcorner p \rightarrow q \urcorner$ is true.
2. Suppose q is true.
3. By the truth table for "$\rightarrow$," if p is true and $\ulcorner p \rightarrow q \urcorner$ is true, then q is true.
4. By (2) and (3), p is true and $\ulcorner p \rightarrow q \urcorner$ is true.
5. Hence, p is true.

Second, one might accept that deductive justification is not appropriate for fundamental logical laws but conclude that there is another kind of justification, neither deductive nor inductive, for these laws. There have been two proposals about a third kind of justification.

One proposal, due to Herbert Feigl (1963), claims that fundamental logical laws require pragmatic, instrumental justification. An immediate difficulty is, What counts as a pragmatic justification of a logical law? Surely, if there is anything that a rule of inference is supposed to do for us, it is to enable us to derive true conclusions from true premises. So, it looks as if to justify a logical law pragmatically is to show that it is suited for this purpose. And that seems to require showing that it is valid. Feigl is aware of this problem and argues that, in the context of a pragmatic justification, circularity is not a problem, since all that such a justification is required to do is provide a recommendation in favor of doing things in some particular way, not a proof that this way necessarily works. It is not clear, however, that this constitutes a compelling response to the philosophical problem of justifying deduction, since, far from needing a letter of reference before employing deductive reasoning, its use is inescapable.

Another proposal for a third kind of justification is due to J. E. Bickenbach (1978), who argues that rules of inference are justified because they "fit with" specific instances of arguments that we accept as valid; for this reason he calls this kind of justification "instantial." The problem with this approach is that, in the case of rules of inference having some claim to being fundamental, such as *modus ponens,* it is plausible that we take the validity of the rule to be conceptually prior to the validity of any instance of it. For example, in the case of *modus ponens,* where there appear to be counterinstances to the rule, such as the sorites paradox, we take the problem to lie not in *modus ponens* but in vague concepts. Hence, whatever force "instantial" justification has, it seems incapable of conferring on fundamental rules of inference the kind of conceptual status we take them to have.

One might simply accept the conclusion of the argument, that fundamental logical laws cannot be justified, as indicating the philosophical status of these laws: they are simply constitutive rules of our practice of deductive justification. That is, there is no such thing as deductive justification that fails to conform to these rules, just as there is no such thing as the game of chess in which the queen is allowed to move in the same way as the knight. This third response leads to at least two philosophical questions: (1) How do we identify the fundamental laws of logic? (2) Is there such a thing as criticism or justification, as opposed to mere acceptance of a deductive practice?

A natural way to answer the first question is to take the fundamental rules to be determined by the meanings of the logical constants. This answer has been developed in some detail by Dag Prawitz (1977) and Michael DUMMETT [S] (1991). Following Gerhard Gentzen (1969), they take the natural deduction introduction and elimination rules for a logical constant to be determined by the meaning of that constant. (More detail on the answer is provided in the final paragraph of this article.) Part of an answer to the second question has been provided by A. N. PRIOR [S] (1967) and Nuel Belnap (1961), who showed that there exist sets of rules of inference that we can recognize as internally incoherent.

This third response has the consequence that our relation to the fundamental laws of logic is not one of knowledge classically construed and, hence, is different from our relation to other laws, such as the laws of physics, or of a country.

We turn now to the notion of knowledge derived from deductive reasoning. The question this notion raises, first studied by J. S. MILL [5; S] (1950, bk. 2, chap. 3), is to explain how deductive reasoning could be simultaneously necessary and informative. It is undeniable that we can understand the premises and the conclusion of an argument without knowing that the former implies that latter; this is what makes it possible for us to gain information by means of deductive reasoning. This fact does not by itself conflict with the necessity of deductive implication, since there is no conflict between the existence of something and our lack of knowledge thereof. But, a problem can arise if the explanation of the necessity of deductive implication entails constraints on the notion of understanding. The following are two ways in which the problem of deduction arises.

First, consider Robert Stalnaker's (1987) analysis of the notions of proposition and of understanding. The proposition expressed by a statement is a set of the possible worlds, the set of those worlds in which the proposition is true. To understand a statement is to know the proposition it expresses; hence, to understand a statement is to know which possible worlds are those in which the proposition it expresses is true. These claims have two consequences: first, that all necessary statements, and hence all deductive valid statements, express the same proposition, namely, the set of all possible worlds; second, to understand any necessary statement is to know that the proposition it expresses is the set of all possible worlds. From these consequences it would seem to follow that in virtue of understanding any valid statement, one would know that it is necessarily true. It seems plausible that if one understands the premises and the conclusion of a valid argument, then one must also understand the conditional whose antecedent is the conjunction of the premises and whose consequent is the conclusion. But if the argument is valid, so is this conditional. Hence, if an argument is valid, then anyone who understood its premises and conclusion would know that this conditional expressed a necessary truth. It is now plausible to conclude that one can know whether an argument is valid merely on the basis of understanding its premises and conclusion by knowing whether the corresponding conditional expressed a necessary truth.

Next, consider Dummett's (1973, 1991) analysis of deductive implication. According to this analysis, deductive implication is based on the meanings of the logical constants. Thus, for example, the fact that p and q imply $\ulcorner p$ and $q\urcorner$ is explained by the fact that the meaning of "and" is such that the truth condition of $\ulcorner p$ and $q\urcorner$ is satisfied just in case those of p and of q are. Similarly, the meaning of the existential quantifier is such that if the truth condition of ⌜*a* is *F*⌝ is satisfied, then so must the truth condition of ⌜There is an *F*⌝. Thus, corresponding to each logical constant, there is an account of the truth conditions of logically complex statements in which that constant occurs as the principal connective, in terms of the truth conditions of its substatements. This account explains the validity of rules of inference to those statements from their substatements and hence determines the set of fundamental rules, rules whose validity must be acknowledged by anyone who understands the meanings of the logical constants. But there are, as we have seen, cases in which we can understand the premises and the conclusion of an argument without knowing that the former implies the latter. So, how is deductive implication to be explained in those cases? This question is easy to answer if all the inferential transitions in these arguments are instances of fundamental rules determined by the senses of the constants. But the fact is otherwise; we acknowledge a number of rules of inference that are not reducible to fundamental rules. The problem is thus not an epistemological one; it arises because our conception of deductive implication includes rules whose necessity is not explainable on the basis of our understanding of the logical constants.

(SEE ALSO: *Knowledge, A Priori* [S])

Bibliography

Belnap, N. "Tonk, Plonk, and Plink," in P. F. Strawson, ed., *Philosophical Logic* (Oxford, 1967).

Bickenbach, J. E. "Justifying Deduction," *Dialogue*, Vol. 17 (1979), 500–516.

Dummett, M. A. E. "The Justification of Deduction," in *Truth and Other Enigmas* (Cambridge, MA, 1973).

———. *The Logical Basis of Metaphysics.* Cambridge, MA, 1991.

Feigl, H. "De Principiis Non Disputandum . . . ?" in M. Black, ed., *Philosophical Analysis* (Englewood Cliffs, NJ, 1963).

Gentzen, G. "Investigations into Logical Deduction," in *Collected Papers,* edited by M. E. Szabo (Amsterdam, 1969).

Goldfarb, W. D. "Logic in the Twenties," *Journal of Symbolic Logic,* Vol. 79 (1979), 1237–52.

Goodman, N. *Fact, Fiction, and Forecast.* Cambridge, MA, 1983.

Haack, S. "The Justification of Deduction," *Mind,* Vol. 85 (1976), 112–19.

Mates, B. *Elementary Logic.* Oxford, 1972.

Mill, J. S. *A System of Logic,* in *Philosophy of Scientific Method,* edited by E. Nagel (New York, 1950).

Prawitz, D. "Meaning and Proof: On the Conflict between Classical and Intuitionistic Logic," *Theoria,* Vol. 48 (1977), 2–4.

Prior, A. N. "The Runabout Inference Ticket," in P. F. Strawson, ed., *Philosophical Logic* (Oxford, 1967).

Stalnaker, R. *Inquiry.* Cambridge, MA, 1987.

Strawson, P. F., ed. *Philosophical Logic.* Oxford, 1967.

SANFORD SHIEH

LOGICAL TERMS.

The two central problems concerning logical terms are demarcation and interpretation. The search for a demarcation of logical terms goes back to the founders of modern logic, and within the classical tradition a partial solution, restricted to logical connectives, was established early on. The characteristic feature of logical connectives, according to this solution, is truth-functionality, and the totality of truth functions (Boolean functions from n-tuples of truth values to a truth value) determines the totality of logical connectives. In his seminal 1936 paper, "On the Concept of Logical Consequence," TARSKI [8] demonstrated the need for a more comprehensive criterion by showing that his semantic definition of logical consequence—the sentence σ is a logical consequence of the set of sentences Σ iff (if and only if) every model of Σ is a model of σ—is dependent on such a demarcation. (Thus suppose the existential quantifier is not a logical term, then its interpretation will vary from model to model, and the intuitively logically valid consequence, "Rembrandt is a painter; therefore there is at least one painter," will fail to satisfy Tarski's definition. Suppose "Rembrandt" and "is a painter" are both logical terms, then the intuitively logically invalid consequence, "Frege is a logician; therefore Rembrandt is a painter," will satisfy Tarski's definition.) Tarski, however, left the general demarcation of logical terms an open question, and it was not until the late 1950s that the first steps toward developing a systematic criterion for logical predicates and quantifiers were taken.

In his 1957 paper, "On a Generalization of Quantifiers," A. Mostowski proposed a semantic criterion for first-order logical quantifiers that generalizes FREGE's [3; S] analysis of the standard quantifiers as second-level cardinality predicates. Technically, Mostowski interpreted a quantifier, Q, as a function from universes (sets of objects), A, to A–quantifiers, Q_A, where Q_A is a function assigning a truth value to each subset B of A. Thus, given a set A, the existential and universal quantifiers are defined by: for any $B \subseteq A, \exists_A(B) = T$ iff $B \neq \phi$ and $\forall_A(B) = T$ iff $A - B = \phi$. Intuitively, a quantifier is logical if it does "not allow us to distinguish between different elements" of the underlying universe. Formally, Q is logical iff it is invariant under isomorphic structures of the type $<A,B>$, where $B \subseteq A$; that is, Q is a logical quantifier iff for every structure $<A,B>$ and $<A',B'>$: if $<A, B> \cong <A',B'>$, then $Q_A(B) = Q_{A'}(B')$. Quantifiers satisfying Mostowski's criterion are commonly called *cardinality quantifiers,* and some examples of these are "$!\delta x$" ("There are exactly δ individuals in the universe such that . . ."), where δ is any cardinal, "Most x" ("There are more x's such that . . . than x's such that not . . ."), "There are finitely many x," "There are uncountably many x," and so forth. In 1966, P. Lindström extended Mostowski's criterion to terms in general: A term (of type n) is logical iff it is invariant under isomorphic structures (of type n). Thus, the well-ordering predicate, W, is logical since for any A,A′, $R \subseteq A^2$ and $R' \subseteq A'^2$: if $<A,R> \cong <A',R'>$, then $W_A(R) = W_{A'}(R')$. Intuitively, we can say that a term is logical iff it does not distinguish between isomorphic arguments. The terms satisfying Lindström's criterion include identity, n–place cardinality quantifiers (e.g., the 2-place "Most," as in "Most A's are B's"), relational or polyadic quantifiers like the well-ordering predicate above and "is an equivalence relation," and so forth. Among the terms not satisfying Lindström's criterion are individual constants, the first-level predicate "is red," the first-level membership relation, the second-level predicate "is a property of Napoleon," and so forth. Tarski (1966) proposed essentially the same division.

The Mostowski–Lindström–Tarski (MLT) approach to logical terms has had a considerable impact on the development of contemporary MODEL THEORY [S]. Among the central results are Lindström's characterizations of elementary logic, various completeness and incompleteness theorems for generalized (model-theoretic, abstract) logics, and so forth. (See Barwise & Feferman, 1985). But whereas the mathematical yield of MLT has been prodigious, philosophers, by and large, have continued to hold on to the traditional view according to which the collection of (primitive) logical terms is restricted to truth-functional connectives, the existential and/or universal quantifier and, possibly, identity. One of the main strongholds of the traditional approach has been QUINE [7; S], who (in his 1970 book) justified his approach on the grounds that (1) standard first-order logic (without identity) allows a remarkable concurrence of diverse definitions of logical consequence, and (2) standard first-order logic (with or without identity) is complete. Quine did not consider the logicality of nonstandard quantifiers such as "there are uncountably many," which allow a "complete" axiomatization. Tharp (1975), who did take into account the existence of complete first-order logics with nonstandard generalized quantifiers, nevertheless arrived at the same conclusion as Quine's.

During the 1960s and 1970s many philosophers were concerned with the interpretation rather than the identity of logical terms. Thus, MARCUS [S] (1962, 1972) and others developed a substitutional interpretation of the standard quantifiers; DUMMETT [S] (1973) advocated an intuitionistic interpretation of the standard logical terms based on considerations pertaining to the theory of meaning; many philosophers (e.g., van Fraassen) pursued "free" and "many-valued" interpretations of the logical connectives; Hintikka (1973, 1976) constructed a game theoretic semantics for logical terms. In a later development, Boolos (1984) proposed a primitive (non-set-theoretic) interpretation of "nonfirstorderizable" operators, which has the potential of overcoming ontological objections to higher-order logical operators (e.g., by Quine).

In the mid-1970s philosophers began to search for an explicit, general philosophical criterion for logical terms. The attempts vary considerably, but in all cases the criterion is motivated by an underlying notion of logical consequence. Inspired by Gentzen's proof-theoretic work, Hacking (1979) suggests that a logical constant is introduced by (operational) rules of inference that preserve the basic features of the traditional deducibility relation: the subformula property (compositionality), reflexivity, dilution (stability under additional premises and conclusions), transitivity (cut), cut elimination, and so forth. Hacking's criterion renders all and only the logical terms of the ramified theory of types genuinely logical. Koslow's (1992) also utilizes a Gentzen-like characterization of the deducibility relation. Abstracting from the syntactic nature of Gentzen's rules, he arrives at a "structural" characterization of the standard logical and modal constants. Both Koslow and Hacking incorporate lessons from an earlier exchange between PRIOR [S] (1960, 1964) and Belnap (1962) concerning the possibility of importing an inconsistency into a hitherto consistent system by using arbitrary rules of inference to introduce new logical operators.

Peacocke (1976) approaches the task of delineating the logical terms from a semantic perspective. The basic property of logical consequence is, according to Peacocke, a priori. α is a logical operator iff α is a noncomplex n-place operator such that given knowledge of which objects (sequences of objects) satisfy an n-tuple or arguments of α, $<\beta_1, \ldots, \beta_n>$, one can know a priori which objects satisfy $\alpha(\beta_1, \ldots, \beta_n)$. Based on this criterion Peacocke counts the truth-functional connectives, the standard quantifiers, and certain temporal operators ("In the past . . .") as logical, while identity (taken as a primitive term), the first-order membership relation, and "necessarily" are nonlogical. Peacocke's criterion is designed for classical logic, but it is possible to produce analogous criteria for nonclassical logics (e.g., intuitionistic logic). McCarthy (1981) regards the basic property of logical constants as topic neutrality. He considers Peacocke's condition as necessary but not sufficient, and his own criterion conjoins Peacocke's condition with Lindström's invariance condition (MLT). The standard first-order logical vocabulary as well as various nonstandard generalized quantifiers satisfy McCarthy's criterion, but cardinality quantifiers do not (intuitively, cardinality quantifiers are not topic-neutral). Sher (1991) considers necessity and formality as the two characteristic features of logical consequence. Treating formality as a semantic notion, Sher suggests that any formal operator incorporated into a Tarskian system according to certain rules yields consequences possessing the desired characteristics. Viewing Lindström's invariance criterion as capturing the intended notion of formal operator, Sher endorses the full-fledged MLT as delineating the scope of logical terms in classical logic.

The theory of logical terms satisfying Lindström's criterion has led, with various adjustments, to important developments in linguistic theory: a systematic account of determiners as generalized quantifiers (Barwise & Cooper, Higginbotham & May); numerous applications of "polyadic" quantifiers (van Benthem, Keenan); and an extension of Henkin's 1961 theory of standard branching quantifiers, applied to English by Hintikka (1973), to branching generalized quantifiers (Barwise and others).

(SEE ALSO: *Mathematical Logic; Philosophical Logic* [S])

Bibliography

Barwise, J. "On Branching Quantifiers in English," *Journal of Philosophical Logic,* Vol. 8 (1979), 47–80.

———, and R. Cooper. "Generalized Quantifiers and Natural Language," *Linguistics and Philosophy,* Vol. 4 (1981), 159–219.

———, and S. Feferman, eds. *Model-Theoretic Logics.* New York, 1985.

Belnap, N. "Tonk, Plonk, and Plink," *Analysis,* Vol. 22 (1962), 130–34.

Boolos, G. "To Be Is to Be a Value of a Variable (or to Be Some Values of Some Variables)," *Journal of Philosophy,* Vol. 81 (1984), 430–49.

Dummett, M. "The Philosophical Basis of Intuitionistic Logic," in *Truth and Other Enigmas.* Cambridge, MA, 1978.

Hacking, I. "What Is Logic?" *Journal of Philosophy,* Vol. 76 (1979), 285–319.

Henkin, L. "Some Remarks on Infinitely Long Formulas," in *Infinitistic Methods.* Warsaw, 1961.

Higginbotham, J., and R. May. "Questions, Quantifiers and Crossing," *Linguistic Review,* Vol. 1 (1981), 41–79.

Hintikka, J. "Quantifiers vs. Quantification Theory," *Dialectica,* Vol. 27 (1973), 329–58.

———. "Quantifiers in Logic and Quantifiers in Natural Languages," in S. Körner, ed., *Philosophy of Logic* (Oxford, 1976), 208–32.

Keenan, E. L. "Unreducible n-ary Quantifiers in Natural Language," in P. Gärdenfors, ed., *Generalized Quantifiers* (Dordrecht, 1987).

Koslow, A. *A Structuralist Theory of Logic.* Cambridge, 1992.

Lindström, P. "First Order Predicate Logic with Generalized Quantifiers," *Theoria,* Vol. 32 (1966), 186–95.

McCarthy, T. "The Idea of a Logical Constant," *Journal of Philosophy,* Vol. 78 (1981), 499–523.

Marcus, R. Barcan. "Interpreting Quantification," *Inquiry,* Vol. 5 (1962), 252–59.

———. "Quantification and Ontology," *Noûs,* Vol. 6 (1972), 240–50.

Mostowski, A. "On a Generalization of Quantifiers," *Fundamenta Mathematicae,* Vol. 42 (1957), 12–36.

Peacocke, C. "What Is a Logical Constant?" *Journal of Philosophy,* Vol. 73 (1976), 221–40.

Prior, A. N. "The Runabout Inference-Ticket," *Analysis,* Vol. 21 (1960), 38–9.

———. "Conjunction and Contonktion Revisited," *Analysis,* Vol. 24 (1964), 191–95.

Quine, W. V. O. *Philosophy of Logic.* Englewood Cliffs, NJ, 1970.

Sher, G. *The Bounds of Logic: A Generalized Viewpoint.* Cambridge, MA, 1991.

Tarski, A. "On the Concept of Logical Consequence" [1936], in *Logic, Semantics, Metamathematics,* 2d ed. (Indianapolis, 1983), 409–20.

———. *Logic, Semantics, Metamathematics,* 2d. ed. Indianapolis, 1983.

———. "What Are Logical Notions?" [1966], *History and Philosophy of Logic,* Vol. 7 (1986), 143–54.

Tharp, L. H. "Which Logic Is the Right Logic?" *Synthese,* Vol. 31 (1975), 1–21.

van Benthem, J. "Polyadic Quantifiers," *Linguistics and Philosophy,* Vol. 12 (1989), 437–64.

van Fraassen, B. C. "Singular Terms, Truth-Value Gaps, and Free Logic," *Journal of Philosophy,* Vol. 63 (1966), 481–95.

GILA SHER

M

MACKIE, JOHN LESLIE, was born in Sydney, Australia, in 1917, and educated under John ANDERSON [1] at the University of Sydney and at Oxford, where he graduated with a first in literae humaniores in 1940. After the war he returned to an academic position at the University of Sydney. In 1955 he took up the Chair in Philosophy at the University of Otago, then in 1959 he returned to the University of Sydney to replace Anderson in the Challis Chair. He left for Great Britain in 1964, going first to fill the foundation Chair of Philosophy at the new university in York. In 1967 he became Fellow of University College, Oxford, where he remained, becoming University Reader in 1978, until his death in 1981.

His work is characterized by an acute, unwearied, dispassionate analysis of alternative solutions to problems, striving for full and plain clarity, and by careful exploration and appraisal of alternative arguments in support of proposed solutions. Mackie applied this analytic reason across a very broad field. He made contributions to, among other topics, logic (particularly the understanding of paradoxes; CONDITIONALS [S] and the theory of causality; the interpretation of counterfactual conditionals; the theory of SPACE [7; S] and TIME [8; S]; the theological problem of EVIL [3; S]; the theory of ethics; the relations between reason, morality, and law; the PHILOSOPHY OF MIND [S]; the PHILOSOPHY OF BIOLOGY [S]; and the interpretation of LOCKE's [4; S] epistemology and metaphysics and of HUME's [4; S] ethics.

For many years he published a succession of important articles but no books. This pattern changed in 1973, with the appearance of *Truth, Probability, and Paradox,* a collection of essays on logical themes. It was followed in rapid succession by *The Cement of the Universe,* which presents his views on causation; *Problems from Locke,* which concerns characteristically Lockean themes, including primary and secondary qualities, perception, substance, universals, identity, and innate ideas; *Ethics: Inventing Right and Wrong,* a sustained argument for an error-projection account of human moral thinking; and *Hume's Moral Theory.* In 1982 appeared the posthumous *The Miracle of Theism,* whose subtitle—*For and Against the Existence of God*—sufficiently indicates its contents. This burst of productivity propelled Mackie to the forefront among British philosophers of his generation.

The distinctive theses for which he is principally celebrated are four: in philosophical theology the patiently argued insistence on the failure of all attempts to reconcile the existence of evil with the classical Christian conception of God as omnipotent, omniscient, and completely benevolent; in philosophical logic the theory that counterfactual conditionals, despite appearances, are not really propositions but, rather, condensed and elliptically expressed arguments from their antecedent as premise to their consequent as conclusion; in metaphysics the account of causal factors as INUS conditions—that is, Insufficient but Necessary parts of Unnecessary but Sufficient conditions for the occurrence of the effect; in ethics his thesis that there are no moral facts of the sort required by the semantics of moral discourse, which must therefore be expounded as arising from a widespread error.

The denial of objective moral facts is the aspect of his thought that most clearly shows the influence of his Andersonian education. When considering our behavior and its effects, our attitudes and feelings are what lead us to assume, falsely, the existence in human situations of objective features of right or wrong, good or bad, corresponding to and validating those attitudes and feelings. As there are no such validating properties, we must take on ourselves the responsibility for the judgments we make.

(SEE ALSO: *Causation,* and *Nondescriptivism* [S])

Bibliography

WORKS BY MACKIE

Truth, Probability, and Paradox: Studies in Philosophical Logic. Oxford, 1973.

The Cement of the Universe: A Study of Causation. Oxford, 1974.

Problems from Locke. Oxford, 1976.

Ethics: Inventing Right and Wrong. Harmondsworth, Middlesex, 1977.

Hume's Moral Theory. London, 1980.

The Miracle of Theism: Arguments for and against the Existence of God. Oxford, 1982.

Mackie, J., and P. Mackie, eds. *Selected Papers,* 2 vols. Oxford, 1985.

WORKS ON MACKIE

Honderich, T., ed., *Morality and Objectivity: A Tribute to J. L. Mackie.* London, 1985. Contains comprehensive Mackie bibliography.

KEITH CAMPBELL

MARCUS, RUTH BARCAN, though she has published in a number of areas, is best known for her groundbreaking papers in modal and philosophical logic. In 1946 she initiated the first systematic treatment of quantified MODAL LOGIC [S] (see Barcan, 1946), therein provoking W. V. O. QUINE's [7; S] decades-long attack upon the meaningfulness of quantification into alethic modal contexts. The ensuing dispute focused attention on the phenomenon of referential opacity and led to important developments in LOGIC [S], METAPHYSICS, and PHILOSOPHY OF LANGUAGE [S]. In subsequent papers Marcus extended the first-order formalization to second order with identity (Barcan, 1947) and to modalized set theory (Marcus, 1963, 1974). Particularly significant theses presented in these works were the axiom $\Diamond(\exists x)Fx \rightarrow (\exists x)\Diamond Fx$, known as the Barcan formula (Barcan, 1946), and the proof of the necessity of identity (Barcan, 1947; Marcus, 1961). It is of some historical interest that Marcus introduced the now standard "box" operator for necessity.

Marcus's response to criticisms of quantified modal logic took many forms and was a theme to which she returned repeatedly throughout her career. In her 1961 paper (and elsewhere) she sought to dispel certain puzzles about substitutivity of identity in modal contexts; she was an early advocate of a substitutional interpretation of the quantifiers for certain purposes (Marcus, 1961, 1962, 1972), as for example in modal and fictional discourse; she maintained that quantification into modal contexts involves no commitment to an objectionable essentialism (Marcus, 1961), and she later developed and defended a version of Aristotelian essentialism within a modal framework (Marcus, 1967, 1976). Finally, in the mid-1980s she offered an explicit defense of the metaphysical actualism that had informed her early papers in modal logic (Marcus, 1985/86). Here once again Marcus employed an objectual interpretation of the quantifiers, construing our core modal discourse as counterfactual discourse about actual objects.

Allied doctrines of enduring significance either originated or evolved in other writings by Marcus. For example, she introduced a flexible notion of extensionality whereby languages and theories are extensional to the extent that they identify relatively stronger equivalence relations with relatively weaker ones (Marcus, 1960, 1961). She also proposed that ordinary proper names are contentless directly referential tags (Marcus, 1961). In so doing, Marcus rejected earlier "descriptivist" accounts, often associated with Gottlob FREGE [3; S] and Bertrand RUSSELL [7], and laid the cornerstone of the so-called new theory of direct reference later elaborated by Saul KRIPKE [S], Keith Donnellan, David Kaplan, and others.

Writing in moral theory (*see* ETHICAL THEORY [S]), Marcus exposed defects in the structure of standard deontic logic (Marcus, 1966; *see* LOGIC, DEONTIC [4]). She also argued that moral dilemmas are real and, moreover, that their reality is compatible with the consistency of the moral principles from which they derive (Marcus, 1980). Reasoning from a straightforward analogue of semantic consistency, she called into question familiar arguments from the existence of moral dilemmas to ethical antirealism. The resulting account also yielded some second-order principles of conflict avoidance.

Finally, in a series of papers on the nature of belief (Marcus, 1981, 1983, 1990), Marcus rejected language-centered theories according to which beliefs are attitudes to linguistic or quasi-linguistic entities (sentences of English or "Mentalese," for instance). Her proposal was that an agent *X* believes that *S* if and only if *X* is disposed to respond as if *S* obtains, where *S* is a possible state of affairs and what is to count as such a response is a function of environmental factors and internal states such as *X*'s needs and desires. This object-centered theory, as opposed to the language-centered views of Donald DAVIDSON [S] and Jerry Fodor, for example, more naturally accommodates unconscious beliefs and beliefs of infralinguals and nonlinguals. It also accommodates a more robust notion of RATIONALITY [S] and explains, as its rivals cannot, why a fully rational agent would not believe a contradiction. In the wide sense of the term, a rational agent is one who, among other things, strives to maintain the global coherence of the behavioral—that is, verbal as well as nonverbal—indicators of his beliefs. Thus, although a rational agent might assent to a contradiction, his assent would not "go over" into a belief. Indeed, upon discovering the contradiction, he would retract his earlier (contradictory) belief claim. On Marcus's view, just as one cannot know what is false, one cannot believe what is impossible.

Ruth Barcan Marcus was professor of philosophy and chair of the department at the University of Illinois at

Chicago from 1964 to 1970, professor of philosophy at Northwestern University from 1970 to 1973, and the Reuben Post Halleck Professor of Philosophy at Yale, where she succeeded her mentor Frederick B. Fitch, from 1973 to the time of her retirement in 1992. In addition to her scholarly achievements Marcus changed the face of the philosophical profession by her efforts on behalf of women. Perhaps most noteworthy in this connection was the reform of hiring practices instituted by the American Philosophical Association during her tenure as an officer and subsequently as chairman of its National Board of Officers.

Bibliography

Barcan, R. C. "A Functional Calculus of First Order Based on Strict Implication," *Journal of Symbolic Logic,* Vol. 11 (1946), 1–16.

———. "The Identity of Individuals in a Strict Functional Calculus of First Order," *Journal of Symbolic Logic,* Vol. 12 (1947), 12–15.

Marcus, R. B. "Extensionality," *Mind,* Vol. 69, No. 273 (1960), 55–62.

———. "Modalities and Intensional Languages," *Synthese,* Vol. 13 (1961), 303–22.

———. "Interpreting Quantification," *Inquiry,* Vol. 5 (1962), 252–59.

———. "Classes and Attributes in Extended Modal Systems," *Proceedings of the Colloquium in Modal and Many Valued Logic, Acta philosophica fennica,* Vol. 16 (1963), 123–36.

———. "Iterated Deontic Modalities," *Mind,* Vol. 75, No. 300 (1966), 580–82.

———. "Essentialism in Modal Logic," *Noûs,* Vol. 1 (1967), 91–96.

———. "Essential Attribution," *Journal of Philosophy,* Vol. 67 (1971), 187–202.

———. "Quantification and Ontology," *Noûs,* Vol. 6 (1972), 240–50.

———. "Classes, Collections, and Individuals," *American Philosophical Quarterly,* Vol. 11 (1974), 227–32.

———. "Dispensing with Possibilia," Presidential Address, *Proceedings of the American Philosophical Association,* Vol. 49 (1976), 39–51.

———. "Moral Dilemmas and Consistency," *Journal of Philosophy,* Vol. 77, No. 3 (1980), 121–35.

———. "A Proposed Solution to a Puzzle about Belief," in P. French, T. Uehling, H. K. Wettstein, eds., *Foundations of Analytical Philosophy,* Midwest Studies in Philosophy, Vol. 6 (Minneapolis, 1981).

———. "Rationality and Believing the Impossible," *Journal of Philosophy,* Vol. 75 (1983), 321–37.

———. "Possibilia and Possible Worlds," in R. Haller, ed., *Grazer philosophische Studien,* Vols. 25 & 26 (1985/86), 107–32.

———. "Some Revisionary Proposals about Belief and Believing," *Philosophy and Phenomenological Research* (Supplement 1990), 133–54.

———. *Modalities.* Oxford, 1994.

DIANA RAFFMAN
G. SCHUMM

MARXISM. Post–World War II Marxist theory has been decisively shaped by social changes: the growing irrelevance of orthodox Marxist political movements and the moral and economic decline (and eventual collapse) of the Soviet empire; the emergence of politically radical social movements based in nationalism, gender, and race rather than economic class; changes in the world capitalist economy; and increasing environmental degradation. These developments are reflected in divergent formulations of HISTORICAL MATERIALISM [4]; the adaptation and transformation of Marxism by the new social movements; neo-Marxist theories of contemporary capitalism; and "eco-Marxism."

Western Marxists such as Herbert Marcuse, the early Jürgen HABERMAS [S], and Jean-Paul SARTRE [7; S] resisted the dogmatic and positivist versions of historical materialism found in MARX [5] and in the Second and Third Internationals. These writers denied that a theoretical analysis of capitalist society could provide laws of historical development. Rather, they believed that at best economic theory could describe certain continuing contradictions in the social order, the resolutions of which necessarily depended on the self-awareness and political organization of contending social groups. Given the rise of FASCISM [3] out of the depression and the triumph of capitalist hegemony over the industrial working classes after World War II, political revolution could no longer be thought of as a direct consequence of predictable economic collapse. It was necessary to investigate social forces that seemed to make the working class not only politically passive but also psychically attached to bourgeois authority. These forces included, not just conscious beliefs, but unconscious personality structures; not just the experience of work, but those of sexuality and family life as well. Consequently, Marxist theory had to encompass psychology and cultural theory as well as economics and politics. It was further claimed that any assimilation of Marxism into a natural-science model was itself an element in political totalitarianism. Habermas (1970) developed this position into a critique of "science and technology as ideology." When we identify social theory with natural science, he argued, we fail to distinguish between science's goal of controlling nature and social theory's goal of understanding and liberating human beings. As a result we end up treating people like things.

French Marxist Louis Althusser posed an influential counterview (1970), arguing that, while different aspects of society did possess a "relative autonomy" from the economy, it was class structure that always determined historical outcomes "in the last instance." Claiming to present the scientific view of Marxism, and in a move that anticipated later developments of postmodern thought, Althusser asserted that subjectivity was an effect of social structures and not a primary constituent of them (*see* MODERNISM AND POSTMODERNISM [S]).

Anglo-American philosophy has seen a sophisticated reformulation of some of Marx's original claims about the social primacy of technological development. Analytical Marxist G. A. Cohen developed a "functional" analysis in which a universal human drive to develop forces of production conditioned social relations to change to support such development. Other analytic Marxist philosophers attempted to articulate a distinct moral perspective in Marx to ground claims about the immorality of capitalist exploitation and to critique the individualism of the dominant liberal paradigms of writers such as John RAWLS [S].

With the rise of radical social movements of racial minorities and women, Marxist theory was challenged to integrate accounts of patriarchy and RACISM [7; S] with its traditional focus on class exploitation and technological development. Theorists argued that racism and sexism were not reducible to or simple consequences of class power. They were embedded in Western culture and conferred certain limited privileges on the white and/or male working class itself. Rather than depending solely on the concept of economic exploitation, or the traditional Marxist notion that the liberation of the working class would liberate all other subject groups, socialist or Marxist-feminist theorists and black liberationists analyzed the mutually supportive, conflicting, and at times disparate elements of class, racial, and gender domination (*see* FEMINIST SOCIAL AND POLITICAL PHILOSOPHY and LIBERATION THEOLOGY [S]).

From the 1960s to the 1990s the structural evolution of capitalism led to new versions of Marxist economic and sociological theory. Baran and Sweezy's analysis (1966) revealed how dominant sectors of the economy had become controlled by a small number of firms and that consequently the classic price competition and overproduction oscillations of the nineteenth and early twentieth centuries had given way to stagnation as a result of an unutilizable surplus. Other theorists (e.g., Wallerstein, 1974–80) redefined capitalism as a capitalist "world-system" constituted by exploitative trade relations between a developed Western core and an underdeveloped periphery. Both the monopoly capital and the world-system models were challenged by the "global capitalism" perspective (Ross & Trachte, 1990), which sees an international economy dominated by multinational firms, intranational competition rather than a dominant Western core, and increased power for capitalists as international mobility allows them to evade local labor movements, governments, and environmental regulations.

Many writers claimed that the increased role of the state in the national economy mitigated the business cycle and redirected class struggles to competition over state resources. James O'Connor (1973) foresaw that contradictions between state support of capitalist accumulation and democratic legitimation would eventually cause a "fiscal crisis of the state." Habermas (1975), writing under the shadow of the political uprisings of the 1960s and 1970s, described conflict between ideals of democracy and equality and state support of capitalist accumulation as causing a "legitimation crisis."

Responding to the continued dominance of capitalism and the failure of almost all state-controlled COMMUNISM [2], theorists of SOCIALISM [7] have also raised the possibility of alternative forms of a socialist economy, especially a socialism in which consumer demand is allocated by markets but is not at the same time controlled by private ownership of the forces of production.

Marxist theoreticians have responded to the worsening environmental crisis, not only by using familiar Marxist concepts to explain it, but by positing (O'Connor, 1988) an "eco-Marixst" analysis in which capitalist destruction of the environment becomes the "Second Contradiction of Capital." On this view capitalism's tendency to destroy its own physical basis of production (through ecological devastation) now coexists with the resistance it generates from the labor force as a major source of its own undoing.

In sum, Marxism continues to evolve and mutate, with many of its basic concepts (the critique of ideology, the analysis of capitalism) still essential to socially critical perspectives such as postmodernism and feminism. If it is now virtually impossible to delineate any simple Marxist orthodoxy, or to say where Marxism ends and other left perspectives begin, one can (as in other intellectual traditions) trace the historical roots of philosophical perspective and revolutionary social intent from Marx, through enormous historical change, to the Marxisms of the present.

Bibliography

Althusser, L. *For Marx.* New York, 1970.

Baran, P., and P. Sweezy. *Monopoly Capital.* New York, 1966.

Buchanan, A. E. *Marx and Justice: The Radical Critique of Liberalism.* Totowa, NJ, 1982.

Cohen, G. A. *Karl Marx's Theory of History: A Defence.* Princeton, NJ, 1978.

Eisenstein, Z., ed. *Capitalist Patriarchy and the Case for Socialist Feminism.* New York, 1979.

Gottlieb, R. S. *History and Subjectivity: The Transformation of Marxist Theory.* Atlantic Highlands, NJ, 1993.

Habermas, J. *Towards a Rational Society.* Boston, 1970.

———. *Legitimation Crisis.* Boston, 1975.

Kuhn, A., and A. Wolpe, eds. *Feminism and Materialism.* London, 1978.

Le Grand, J., and S. Estrin, eds. *Market Socialism.* Oxford, 1989.

Marcuse, H. *Eros and Civilization.* New York, 1962.

———. *One-Dimensional Man.* Boston, 1964.

O'Connor, J. *The Fiscal Crisis of the State.* New York, 1973.

———. "Capitalism, Nature, Socialism: A Theoretical Introduction," *Capitalism, Nature, Socialism,* Vol. 1 (1988).

Reich, M. *Racial Inequality: A Political-Economic Analysis.* Princeton, NJ, 1980.

Ross, R., and K. Trachte. *Global Capitalism: The New Leviathan.* Albany, NY, 1990.

Sargent, L., ed. *Women and Revolution.* Boston, 1981.
Sartre, J.-P. *Search for a Method.* New York, 1963.
Wallerstein, I. *The Modern World-System,* 2 vols. New York, 1974–80.

ROGER S. GOTTLIEB

MATHEMATICAL LOGIC. Mathematical logic is the study of logic by mathematical methods. The field has developed since the mid-twentieth century, like others in mathematics, dividing into branches whose mutual connections are often looser than the connections each has with outside fields. The volume of philosophically oriented work has decreased in relative terms but has still increased in absolute terms, owing to the overall growth of the field. The many subdivisions of mathematical logic are grouped into four main divisions: MODEL THEORY, PROOF THEORY, RECURSION THEORY, and SET THEORY [S].

SET THEORY

Axiomatic set theory provides the framework within which mainstream mathematics is developed, and so it is a major object of logical investigation. The mainstream axiom system for set theory (ZFC) consists of the Zermelo-Fraenkel axioms (ZF) plus the axiom of choice (AC). By the incompleteness theorem of K. GÖDEL [S], for this or any similar system (assuming it consistent), there is a hypothesis that is both consistent with the system (irrefutable) and independent of the system (unprovable). Gödel conjectured that for the system ZFC the old conjecture about sets of real numbers known as the continuum hypothesis (CH) is such a hypothesis. Besides thus conjecturing that CH is consistent with but independent of ZFC, he also conjectured that AC is consistent with but independent of ZF, and he proved consistency in both cases.

The most important development in set theory and arguably in all mathematical logic since the mid-twentieth century has been the proof in the early 1960s of independence for both cases by P. J. Cohen. His method of "forcing" has since been applied by R. M. Solovay and others to establish the consistency and independence of many hypotheses. Anticipating such developments, Gödel had urged that new axioms should be sought, axioms that might be justifiable intrinsically as further expressions of an intuitive conception of set only partially expressed by the axioms of ZFC, or extrinsically as having attractive or useful consequences in areas nearer mainstream practice in pure or applied mathematics. Two directions have especially been pursued in seeking new axioms.

So-called large cardinal axioms, for which some claim an intrinsic justification, assert the existence of sets far larger than any that can be proved to exist in ZFC, which already include sets far larger than any encountered in mainstream mathematical practice. The so-called determinacy axiom for a class of sets of real numbers pertains to infinite games in which a set from the class is dealt to two players, who then generate a real number by alternately choosing the digits of its decimal expansion, with the first or second player winning accordingly as the number thus generated does or does not belong to the set; the axiom states that, given any set from the class, for one or the other player there will be a winning strategy, a rule telling that player what to choose as a function of the opponent's previous choices, which if followed will result in a win for the player in question. An extrinsic justification has been claimed for such axioms, since they imply that simply definable sets of real numbers are also well behaved in various respects; for instance, there is no counterexample to CH among them.

Work of the self-styled "cabal" of A. Kechris, D. A. Martin, Y. N. Moschovakis, J. Steel, and H. Woodin culminated in the 1980s in a proof of a close connection between the two kinds of axioms: suitable large cardinal axioms imply enough determinacy axioms to settle most outstanding questions of interest about simply definable sets of real numbers. There is also a partial converse. But the question whether or not there is a counterexample to CH among arbitrary, as opposed to simply definable, sets of real numbers is not decided by large cardinal or any other widely accepted axioms: the status of CH (if regarded as having a definite truth value) remains open.

RECURSION THEORY

Recursion theory begins with a rigorous definition of decidability for sets of natural numbers (or of objects like logical formulas that can be indexed by natural numbers), in terms of the existence of an algorithm of a certain specified kind that will for any given number in finite time determine whether or not it is in the set. The core area of pure recursion theory as a subject in its own right is degree theory, the classification of undecidable sets of natural numbers (or in a subsequent generalization called α-recursion theory, of certain ordinal numbers) by their degree of undecidability. Work in this area displays immense technical sophistication but claims little philosophical relevance and so will be slighted here, as will be the many positive and negative results about the decidability or undecidability of various particular mathematically significant sets of formulas. But to mention at least the most famous of these, work of Y. Matijacevič in the early 1970s showed the undecidability of the set of polynomial equations in several variables for which there is a solution in integers. This implies that no reasonable axiom system will be able to settle the status of all such simple-seeming equations.

Recursion theory includes a general theory of definability applicable to undecidable sets of natural numbers and to sets of real numbers, which has played a large role in work in set theory. It also includes complexity theory, concerned with the subclassification of decidable sets by considering how fast the number of steps of computation needed to determine whether a given *n* belongs to the set grows as a function of *n*. For instance, if there is a polynomial function of *n* that bounds this number of steps for all *n*, then the set is said to be polynomial-time decidable. The distinction between sets that are and that are not polynomial-time decidable is an idealization of the philosophically interesting distinction between sets for which it is feasible in practice and sets for which it is only possible in principle to decide whether a given number belongs.

Complexity theory is an example of an area on the border between mathematical logic and theoretical computer science, which was historically an offshoot of recursion theory but has long since far outgrown its parent discipline. Today, computer science is the locus of many of the most important applications of all branches of mathematical logic. Areas of application range from the design of circuits to questions of more direct philosophical interest connected with ARTIFICIAL INTELLIGENCE [S]. (*See* COMPUTATION [S].)

MODEL THEORY

Model theory begins with a rigorous definition of logical consequence, in terms of the nonexistence of countermodels or interpretations of a certain specified kind in which the premise is true and the conclusion false. (*See* LOGICAL CONSEQUENCE [S].) Model-theoretic methods have played a large role in set theory. The core area of pure model theory is stability theory, the classification of theories by the number of their models of any given uncountable size (pursued especially by S. Shelah). This work is more technically sophisticated than philosophically relevant and will be passed over here, along with the many applications of model theory to abstract algebra and related areas of mathematics. One such application has, however, captured the imagination of philosophers, namely A. Robinson's nonstandard analysis. (*See* INFINITESIMALS [S].)

Another area of model theory that has generated philosophical interest is the study of extensions of classical or first-order logic. These are of two kinds. In logics with infinitary connectives of conjunction and disjunction, or generalized quantifiers such as "there exist uncountably many," the classical notion of model due to A. TARSKI ([S] essentially, a set with some distinguished relations on it) is retained. (*See* LOGICAL TERMS [S].) Closely related to the study of such logics is abstract or comparative model theory, inaugurated by a result of P. Lindström, according to which classical logic is in a sense that can be made precise the only logic for which both the compactness theorem of Tarski and the transfer theorem of L. Löwenheim and T. Skolem hold.

In logics with operators for necessity and possibility, or related notions of special philosophical interest, a different notion of model, elaborated by S. KRIPKE [S] and others in the years around 1960 (essentially an indexed family of Tarski models, the indices being called possible worlds), is used. For this, among other reasons, the study of such logics is sometimes considered to fall outside mathematical logic; but however classified, it is a philosophically significant area of applications of model-theoretic and other methods of mathematical logic. (*See* LOGIC, NONSTANDARD; MODAL LOGIC; PROVABILITY [S].) Several such logics have applications in theoretical computer science (though such applications often involve abandoning any literal adherence to their original philosophical interpretations and motivations).

PROOF THEORY

Proof theory begins with a rigorous definition of logical deducibility, in terms of the existence of proofs or sequences of steps leading by rules of a certain specified kind from premise to conclusion. The traditional core of proof theory has been the comparative study of classical mathematics on the one hand and nonclassical, restricted forms of mathematics on the other hand. Three of these latter, in order from most to least restrictive, are finitism, constructivism, and predicativism. (*See also* INTUITIONISM [S].) It had been the original goal of D. HILBERT [3] to prove (finitistically) that any finitistically meaningful and classically provable mathematical statement is finitistically provable: in jargon the goal was to prove that orthodox mathematics is conservative over finitist mathematics, with respect to the class of finitistically meaningful statements. Such a conservativeness result would have provided, from a finitist standpoint, an indirect justification of classical mathematical practice. However, it follows from Gödel's incompleteness theorem that classical mathematics as a whole is not thus conservative over finitist, constructive, or predicative mathematics.

A modified program has had the goal of proving the conservativeness of one or another significant fragment of classical mathematics with respect to one or another significant class of statements over one or another significantly restricted form of mathematics. An indispensable preliminary to this program was to find formal theories codifying finitist or constructive or predicative mathematics at least as well as ZFC codifies classical mathematics. This preliminary task was largely accomplished by the end of the 1950s, since which time there has been considerable progress on the program proper.

Noteworthy has been the work of the schools of S. Feferman (an important contributor to codifying predicativism) and H. Friedman. The former has steadily produced more and more flexible systems more and more comfortably accommodating more and more substantial fragments of classical mathematics, while remaining conservative (for an appropriate class of statements) over restrictive forms of mathematics. The latter, with its program of *reverse mathematics,* has produced increasingly stronger fragments WKL_0, ACA_0, ATR_0, Π^1_1-CA_0 of classical mathematics that are conservative over finitist, constructive, predicative, and a liberalized predicative mathematics respectively, and that are claimed to constitute natural stopping points within classical mathematics, in the sense that most often when a major classical theorem is not provable in one system in the series, it actually implies the characteristic axioms of the next stronger system. The same school has also continued the project, which began with the work of J. Paris and L. Harrington, of identifying simple and natural results of finite combinatorics that, in a sense that can be made precise, lie just beyond the power of finitist or constructive or predicative mathematics to prove.

In a sense proof-theoretic study of proposed restrictions of classical mathematics and set-theoretic study of proposed extensions (in both of which recursion-theoretic and model-theoretic methods are indispensable) are complementary activities, working at opposite ends of the same continuum. Between them they supply a picture that is steadily growing clearer of just how far ordinary practice in pure and applied mathematics does or does not exploit the irreducibly infinistic and nonconstructive and impredicative methods that classical axioms in principle supply.

Bibliography

Barwise, J., ed. *Handbook of Mathematical Logic.* Amsterdam, 1977. A comprehensive survey of all branches of the field.

Bulletin of Symbolic Logic. Established in 1995 as an official organ of the Association for Symbolic Logic. Contains in each issue survey/expository articles intended for a nonspecialist readership, which chronicle the progress of the field.

Gabbay, D., and F. Guenthner, eds. *Handbook of Philosophical Logic,* 4 vols. Dordrecht, 1983–89. A comprehensive survey of its field, covering classical logic as well as philosophically motivated nonclassical logics.

Mueller, G. H. et al., eds. *Ω-Bibliography of Mathematical Logic,* 6 vols. Berlin, 1987.

See also the bibliographies of the articles on the separate branches of mathematical logic.

JOHN P. BURGESS

MEANING. What is it for a sentence—or a substantial expression, such as a word or phrase—to have a particular meaning in a given language? While it is widely agreed that the meaning of a sentence, phrase, or word must have something to do with the way that the expression is used by speakers of the language, it is not at all obvious how to move from that vague idea to a precise answer to our question. One problem is that utterances of a given sentence might be used to convey all manner of messages, many of which would be far removed from what we intuitively regard as the literal linguistic meaning of the sentence. Any account of meaning in terms of use must find a way to avoid having every innovative or idiosyncratic feature of use registered as an aspect of meaning. There are two ideas about linguistic meaning that might help with this problem. One is the idea that linguistic meaning is a matter of convention. The other is the idea that linguistic meaning is compositional; that is, the linguistic meaning of a sentence depends in a systematic way on the meanings of the words and phrases from which the sentence is constructed.

Linguistic Meaning Is Conventional. To define the meaning of a sentence as the message or messages that the sentence is, or can be, used to convey is inadequate, because too inclusive. In order to exclude the innovative or idiosyncratic features of language use, we might reach for the notion of a rule of language: what it is for a sentence to mean that *p* is for there to be a rule saying that the sentence is to be used (or may be used) to convey the message that *p*. However, if a rule is something that is formulated explicitly (in language), then the proposal may just reintroduce the notion of linguistic meaning; and that would be unsatisfactory if the project is to define or analyze the notion of linguistic meaning in other terms. So, instead of the notion of an explicitly formulated rule we can make use of the notion of a convention, defined as a rationally self-perpetuating regularity (Lewis, 1969). The resulting proposal is that what it is for a sentence S to mean that *p* in the language of a given population is for there to be a convention in that population to use utterances of S to convey the message that *p*.

Linguistic Meaning Is Compositional. The term 'theory of meaning' can be applied to two very different kinds of theory. On the one hand, there are semantic theories that specify the meanings of the expressions of some particular language; on the other hand, there are metasemantic theories that analyze or explain the notion of meaning. We should expect the idea that meaning is compositional to be reflected in semantic theories. The way in which the meanings of sentences depend on the meanings of words and phrases should be revealed in a semantic theory by having the meaning specifications for whole sentences derived logically from more basic principles that specify the meanings of words and phrases.

Many features of the messages conveyed by the use of a sentence will not be seen simply as the results of contributions to meaning made by the words in the sentence—contributions that would be repeated in other sentences—but rather as the products of interaction between the meaning of the sentence and other background assumptions. (The study of this interaction is called PRAGMATICS [S]. See Davis, 1991.) It is true, for example, that a letter of reference that says only, "Mr. X's command of English is excellent, and his attendance at tutorials has been regular," is likely to convey the message that Mr. X is not a talented philosopher (GRICE [S], 1975). But this message is not the logical product of the meanings of the words and phrases used. Rather, the letter writer is able to convey that message by relying on shared assumptions about what information would be relevant in the circumstances. (See Grice's early [1961] proposals about pragmatics.)

Two Approaches to the Study of Meaning. These ideas, that meaning is conventional and compositional, can be seen at work in two important approaches to the study of linguistic meaning, on which this article focuses. One is Paul Grice's program for analyzing the concept of literal linguistic meaning in terms of psychological notions such as belief and INTENTION [4] (Grice, 1989). The other is Donald DAVIDSON'S [S] project of illuminating the notion of meaning by considering how to construct compositional semantic theories for natural languages (Davidson, 1984).

GRICE'S ANALYTICAL PROGRAM

The Gricean analytical program can be regarded as having two stages (for overviews, see Avramides, 1989; Neale, 1992). The first stage aims to characterize a concept of speaker's meaning that corresponds, roughly, to the idea of conveying, or attempting to convey, a particular message (Grice, 1957, and other papers, 1989). The second stage then aims to use the concept of speaker's meaning, along with the notion of a convention, to build an analysis of literal linguistic meaning. (In fact, Grice himself did not introduce the notion of convention, but used a slightly different idea. See Grice, 1989; Lewis, 1969, 1975; Schiffer, 1972.)

The basic idea of the first stage of the program is that an agent who is attempting to convey a message—perhaps the message that it is time for tea—makes an utterance (which might or might not be linguistic in nature) with the intention that the hearer should come to believe that it is time for tea and should believe it, at least in part, in virtue of recognizing that this is what the utterer intends him or her to believe. The analysis of speaker's meaning was refined and complicated in the face of counterexamples (Grice, 1989; STRAWSON [S], 1964; Schiffer, 1972), but it retained the crucial feature of not itself importing the notion of literal meaning. This feature is shared by the analysis of convention as a rationally self-perpetuating regularity, and so the prospects are good that the analysis of meaning resulting from Grice's program can meet the requirement of noncircularity.

Problems with Grice's Program. Grice's program does, however, face a number of serious objections. One problem concerns the application of the program to sentences that are never used at all—perhaps because they are too long or too implausible. Clearly, the Gricean analysis of literal meaning cannot be applied directly to these sentences. If we want to say that there is, nevertheless, a fact of the matter as to what un-used sentences mean, then we seem bound to appeal to the meanings of the words and phrases from which un-used sentences are built. But now we come to the most serious problem for the program, namely, how to analyze the notion of meaning as it applies to subsentential expressions.

Parties to a convention know what the relevant regularity is, and their belief that they and others have conformed to the regularity in the past gives them a reason to continue conforming to it. Thus, the Gricean program involves crediting speakers of a language with knowledge about regularities of use. While this is plausible in the case of the use of complete sentences, it is problematic when we move to subsentential expressions. Words and phrases are used in complete sentences, and they make a systematic contribution to the meanings of the sentences in which they occur. Regularities of use for words and phrases are regularities of contribution to the messages that sentences are used to convey. But spelling out in detail how words and phrases (and ways of putting them together) contribute to the meanings of complete sentences is a highly nontrivial project. So, it is not plausible that every speaker of a language knows what these regularities of contribution are.

The problem for the Gricean program is that it seems bound to attribute to ordinary language users knowledge that they do not really have. It may be that we can deal with this problem by invoking some notion of *tacit* (CHOMSKY [S], 1986) or *implicit* (DUMMETT [S], 1991, 1993) knowledge (Loar, 1981). But the dominant consensus—and the view of one of the most authoritative exponents of Grice's program (Schiffer, 1987)—is that the project of analyzing literal meaning in terms of intentions and beliefs cannot be completed.

DAVIDSON AND TRUTH-CONDITIONAL SEMANTICS

Any metasemantic theory can be used to provide conditions of adequacy on semantic theories. Thus, consider the Gricean metasemantic proposal:

> Sentence S means that *p* in the language of population G if and only if (iff) there is a convention in G to use utterances of S to convey the message that *p*.

And suppose that a semantic theory for a particular language L delivers as one of its meaning specifications:

> Sentence S1 means (in L) that wombats seldom sneeze.

Then, according to the metasemantic proposal, one necessary condition for the correctness of the semantic theory is that there should be a convention in the population of L-speakers to use utterances of S1 to convey the message that wombats seldom sneeze.

This kind of transposition can be carried out in the opposite direction too. Any condition of adequacy on semantic theories can be reconfigured as a partial elucidation of the concept of meaning—or of whatever other concept plays a key role in the semantic theory—and a great deal of philosophical work on the concept of meaning proceeds by considering constraints on semantic theories. Davidson's work (1984) provides an important example of this approach.

The Truth-Conditional Format. As we introduced the notion, a semantic theory is a theory that tells us what expressions mean. It is natural to suppose, then, that the key concept used in a semantic theory will be the concept of meaning, and that the format of the meaning specifications for sentences will be either:

The meaning of sentence S = *m*

or else:

Sentence S means that *p*

according as meanings are or are not regarded as entities. But Davidson (1967) rejects both these formats, and argues instead for the truth-conditional format:

Sentence S is true if and only if *p*.

His argument comes in two steps.

The first step is intended to rule out the idea that, to each word, each phrase, and each sentence, there should be assigned some entity as its meaning. This step proceeds by showing that, under certain assumptions about the assignment of entities, all true sentences would be assigned the same entity. (The argument that is used here is sometimes called the FREGE [3; S] argument.) Clearly, no such assignment of entities could be an assignment of meanings, since not all true sentences have the same meaning. However, it is possible to resist this first step by arguing that an assignment of meanings would not conform to the assumptions that are needed to make the Frege argument work.

Even though the first step is controversial, the second step in Davidson's argument remains important for anyone who begins by favoring the format:

Sentence S <u>means that</u> *p*.

We said that, given the compositionality of meaning, we should expect that, in a semantic theory, the meaning specifications for whole sentences will be derived from more basic principles that specify the meanings of words and phrases. But Davidson points out that the logical properties of the 'means that *p*' construction raise problems for the formal derivation of meaning specifications for sentences. In contrast, the truth-conditional format is logically well understood. And from the work of Alfred TARSKI [8] on certain formal languages (1944, 1956) we can carry over methods for deriving truth-condition specifications for sentences from axioms that assign semantic properties to words and phrases.

Conditions of Adequacy. If what a semantic theory tells us about each sentence of a language is to be cast in the truth conditional format:

Sentence S is true if and only if *p*

then what are the conditions of adequacy on semantic theories? We have already seen an adequacy condition on the internal structure of a semantic theory; namely, that it should reveal how the truth conditions of complete sentences depend on the semantic properties of words and phrases. But what conditions must the truth condition specifications themselves meet, in order to be correct?

Tarski imposed, in effect, the condition that the sentence that fills the '*p*' place should translate (or else be the very same sentence as) the sentence S. (This is Tarski's Convention T [1956].) This condition of adequacy can be transposed into a partial elucidation of the concept of truth in terms of the concept of translation. The concept of translation is sufficiently closely related to the concept of meaning that we can move from here to a partial elucidation of truth in terms of meaning:

If a sentence S means that *p* then S is true iff *p*.

But we cannot shed any light on the concept of meaning itself without bringing in extra resources.

The key notion that Davidson introduces is that of 'interpretation'. We imagine using the deliverances of a semantic theory to help interpret the linguistic behavior of speakers. For these purposes, we can abstract away from the details of the format, and use deliverances in the schematic form:

Sentence S ________ *p*

to license the redescription of utterances of a sentence S as linguistic acts of saying or asserting that *p*. Now, by providing a way of understanding speakers' specifically linguistic behavior, a semantic theory can play a part in the project of interpreting, or making sense of, them. So, any constraints on the project of overall interpretation of people can be reconfigured as partial elucidations of the key concepts used in semantic theories.

Two suggestions for overarching constraints on interpretation emerge from Davidson's work. One possible constraint is that speakers should be so interpreted that what they say and believe about the world turns out to be by and large correct. This is the "principle of charity" (Davidson, 1967, 1973). The other possible constraint—widely reckoned to be more plausible—is that speakers should be so interpreted that what they say and believe about the world turns out to be by and large reasonable or intelligible. This is sometimes called the "principle of humanity" (see Wiggins, 1980).

In the imagined project of interpretation, the deliverances of a semantic theory are used in schematic form. For these purposes, at least, it does not matter whether the semantic theory uses the 'means that *p*' format or the 'is true if and only if *p*' format. So we can, if we wish, say that the constraints on interpretation shed light on the concept of meaning and thence—by way of the connection between meaning and truth—on the concept of TRUTH [S].

MEANING AND USE

We began from the vague idea that meaning has something to do with use, and have focused on two approaches to the study of meaning, both of which lay stress upon such notions as conveying the message that *p*, saying that *p*, and asserting that *p*. Both approaches take the basic way of specifying the meaning of a sentence to involve a 'that *p*' clause, and both permit the straightforward connection between meaning and truth. However, there are other ways to develop the idea of a link between meaning and use. For example, we might regard knowing the meaning of a sentence as knowing how to use it appropriately. Or we might say that knowing the meaning of a sentence is knowing under what circumstances a speaker would be warranted in using the sentence to make an assertion. Many of these ways of linking meaning with use do not lead to specifications of meaning by way of a 'that *p*' clause, and so do not support the direct transfer of elucidation from the concept of meaning to the concept of truth. It is to metasemantic theories of this kind that the term 'use theory of meaning' is usually applied. Use theories of meaning are often coupled with the claim that there is nothing substantive to be said about the concept of truth (see Field, 1994; Horwich, 1990, 1995).

(SEE ALSO: *Meaning* [5]; *Philosophy of Language* [S]; and *Reference* [S])

Bibliography

Avramides, A. *Meaning and Mind: An Examination of a Gricean Account of Language.* Cambridge, MA, 1989.

Chomsky, N. *Knowledge of Language: Its Nature, Origin, and Use.* New York, 1986.

Davidson, D. *Inquiries into Truth and Interpretation.* Oxford, 1984.

Davis, S. *Pragmatics: A Reader.* Oxford, 1991.

Dummett, M. *The Logical Basis of Metaphysics.* Cambridge, MA, 1991.

———. *The Seas of Language.* Oxford, 1993.

Field, H. "Deflationist Views of Meaning and Content," *Mind,* Vol. 103 (1994), 249–85.

Grice, H. P. "Meaning," *Philosophical Review,* Vol. 66 (1957), 377–88. Reprinted in Grice, 1989.

———. "The Causal Theory of Perception," *Proceedings of the Aristotelian Society,* supplementary vol. 35 (1961), 121–52. Reprinted in Grice, 1989.

———. "Logic and Conversation," in P. Cole and J. Morgan, eds., *Syntax and Semantics, Volume 3: Speech Acts* (London, 1975). Pp. 41–58. Reprinted in Grice, 1989.

———. *Studies in the Way of Words.* Cambridge, MA, 1989.

Horwich, P. *Truth.* Oxford, 1990.

———. "Meaning, Use and Truth," *Mind,* Vol. 104 (1995), 355–68.

Lewis, D. *Convention.* Cambridge, MA, 1969.

———. "Languages and Language," in K. Gunderson, ed., *Language, Mind and Knowledge* (Minneapolis, 1975).

Loar, B. *Mind and Meaning.* Cambridge, 1981.

Neale, S. "Paul Grice and the Philosophy of Language," *Linguistics and Philosophy,* Vol. 15 (1992), 509–59.

Schiffer, S. *Meaning* [1972]. Oxford, 1988.

———. *The Remnants of Meaning.* Cambridge, MA, 1987.

Strawson, P. F. "Intention and Convention in Speech Acts," *Philosophical Review,* Vol. 73 (1964), 439–60.

Tarski, A. "The Concept of Truth in Formalized Languages," in A. Tarski, *Logic, Semantics, Metamathematics* (Oxford, 1956). Pp. 152–278.

Wiggins, D. "What Would Be a Substantial Theory of Truth?" in Z. van Straaten, ed., *Philosophical Subjects* (Oxford, 1980). Pp. 189–221.

MARTIN DAVIES

MEMORY. Philosophical work on MEMORY [5] continues to focus on the factive and epistemological notion of remembering that *p* for a given proposition *p*. It is widely agreed that if a subject *S* now remembers that *p* from some prior time *t*, then it is a fact that *p*, *S* knew at *t* that *p*, and *S* now knows that *p*.

Since 1960, discussions of memory knowledge have moved from the question of whether memory involves representations to the question of what memory involves over and above representations. One issue is the extent to which remembering that *p* entails a causal relation between the subject's current and past knowledge that *p*. Participants in this debate agree that remembering is not the mere retention of knowledge over time since one can remember that *p* after having for a time forgotten that *p*. Rather, remembering is the retaining or reacquiring of knowledge from internal sources (LOCKE, 1971 [S]). As Norman Malcolm puts it, *S* now remembers that *p* from a time *t* when *S* now knows that *p* because *S* knew that *p* at *t* (Malcolm, 1963). A key question is whether the "because" relation is a causal relation (Zemach, 1983) and, if so, what kind of causal relation *S* might know that *p* as a result of reading that *p* in his or her diary without thereby remembering that *p*. Remembering is accordingly taken by some to require a certain kind of causal chain between *S*'s current knowledge that *p* and *S*'s past knowledge that *p*—a chain that is psychologically internal to *S* in a way that a diary entry is not (Martin & Deutscher, 1966).

A second issue on which discussions of memory knowledge have focused is whether memory knowledge is justified at a temporal distance, so that memory knowledge is indebted to our past justification and thus susceptible to epistemic luck. Remembering that *p* is commonly taken to entail currently being justified in believing that *p*. On a traditional account of memory justification, one is currently justified in believing that *p* by memory in virtue of (or on the basis of) a current mental event (e.g., one's memory impression that *p* or one's beliefs that one remembers that *p*; Ginet, 1975; Pollock, 1974). On a nontraditional account, one is now justified by memory from a prior time *t* on the basis of one's original grounds for believing *p* at *t* (Naylor, 1983). The nontraditional account differs from the traditional one in entailing that there is memory justification at a temporal distance: one can be currently justified in believing that *p* by memory even if one has forgotten one's original grounds for believing that *p* and even if one lacks any other grounds deriving from a current mental event; indeed, one can remember without there being any memory impression and without its seeming to one that one remembers.

(SEE ALSO: *Epistemology* [S])

Bibliography

Ginet, C. *Knowledge, Perception, and Memory.* Dordrecht, 1975.

Locke, D. B. *Memory.* London, 1971.

Malcolm, N. "A Definition of Factual Memory," in *Knowledge and Certainty: Essays and Lectures* (Englewood Cliffs, NJ, 1963).

Martin, C. B., and M. Deutscher. "Remembering," *Philosophical Review,* Vol. 75 (1966), 161–96.

Naylor, A. "Justification in Memory Knowledge," *Synthese,* Vol. 55 (1983), 269–86.

Pollock, J. *Knowledge and Justification.* Princeton, NJ, 1974.

Zemach, E. M. "Memory: What It Is, and What It Cannot Possibly Be," *Philosophy and Phenomenological Research,* Vol. 44 (1983), 31–44.

FREDERICK F. SCHMITT

MENTAL CAUSATION. By 'mental causation' is meant cause and effect relationships in which mental phenomena act as causes. Mental phenomena—beliefs, desires, intentions, emotions, memories, experiences, bodily sensations, and the like—seem to have causal effects, both mental and physical. The very activity of conscious thinking seems to be a causal process involving thoughts and experiences; moreover, our sensory experiences work in conjunction with our prior beliefs to produce beliefs about our environment; and our bodily sensations can make us aware of bodily damage or irritation, and lead to our wincing, or moaning, or moving our bodies; when we act intentionally, our behavior is caused, in part, by our mental states; further, we can make decisions based on what we think, want, and value, and act on them so as to causally effect the course of events for better or worse through our behavior. Minds, it seems, have causal efficacy: they can change the world.

Philosophical issues arise when one begins to reflect on how mental causation is possible. Suppose that a mental state M (e.g., a desire) has a causal effect E. The question arises: how did M cause E? This question is intended here to ask not what other states M caused en route to bringing about E, but rather to ask what the underlying mechanism is by which M caused E. One possible answer is that there is no underlying mechanism: the causal transaction between M and E is basic, unmediated by any underlying mechanism. While this answer has not been conclusively refuted, it has seemed to many just too incredible to believe. Indeed, one reason many philosophers reject Cartesian interactionism—the doctrine that mental states are states of an immaterial, nonspatial substance that causally interact in the first instance with physical states of the brain and then, via such interactions, with other physical states—is that it appears to imply that there is basic mental causation. The assumption that mental causation is basic does not require the assumption of dualism, however. It could be claimed that while all substances are physical, certain mental properties are fundamental force-generating properties. On the evidence, however, this claim is false. Mechanics has no need of the hypothesis that individuals have mental properties (McLaughlin, 1992).

There is compelling evidence for the following physical determination thesis: for any physical occurrence P, there is (on any cross-section of the backward light-cone of P) some physical state that determines P (or, if causal determinism is false, that determines the objective chance of P). The claim that mental state M caused a physical effect P in a way unmediated by any underlying physical mechanism is logically compatible with physical determination. However, M would then cause P in a way that is independent of any physical causal chains leading to P. While this sort of causal overdetermination seems logically possible, many philosophers have found it too incredible to believe. Mental causes of physical effects, it is widely held, could not act independently of every physical cause of those effects. For a mental state M to have a physical effect P, the causal transaction between M and P would have to be implemented by some physical mechanism (Kim, 1993; McLaughlin, 1994).

Causal interactions between mental states themselves also seem to require implementation by a physical mechanism. On the evidence, every actual state (or event) that occurs in time, occurs in space-time. Given that, causal transactions between mental states are transactions between states occurring within space-time. The following principle of causation via physical effects seems plausible: if a state has an effect that occurs within a certain region of space-time, then it is has a physical effect that occurs within that region of space-time. (Notice that if two distinct states can occur within exactly the same region of space-time, then this principle does not imply that all causal effects are physical effects.) Since mental states occur within space-time, if this principle is correct, then every mental state that has any causal effects whatsoever, has physical effects. Given that a mental cause of a physical effect does not act independently of every physical cause of the effect, it is plausible that when a mental state M acts as a cause of an effect E, there is some physical state occurring within the same space-time region as M that acts as a cause of E. The physical state will be a stage of a physical causal process leading to E that implements the causal relationship between M and E. It should be apparent that essentially the same line of argument can be employed to argue that macrocausation—cause and effect relationships in which macrostates act as causes—is nonbasic causation: whenever a macrostate has an effect, there is always some underlying microphysical causal mechanism (of the sort postulated by microphysics) by which it has that effect (Kim, 1993; McLaughlin, 1994).

It is a received view today that to have a mind is not to possess an immaterial substance, or, for that matter, to possess any sort of substance at all. Rather, to have a mind is just to possess certain sorts of capacities, such as the capacity to think and the capacity to feel. On the evidence, properly functioning brains serve as the material seat of such capacities, though whether artifacts can serve as the seat of mental capacities is regarded as an open empirical question—this is the question of whether ARTIFICIAL INTELLIGENCE [S] is possible. In any case, we come to be in mental states at least partly through the exercise of mental capacities, and, on the evidence, the exercise of such capacities is somehow implemented by neurophysiological processes that are, in turn, implemented by chemical processes that are, themselves, implemented by quantum mechanical processes involving subatomic states and events.

On these assumptions, one natural suggestion, then, is that mental states are high-level macrostates of the brain, and that mental causation is thus a kind of macrocausation (Searle, 1991). This suggestion is, however, controversial: it is controversial whether mental states bear a macro/micro relationship to physical states. It is not understood how physical states could combine to constitute mental states. Indeed, we lack a well-supported theory of the nature of mental states.

It might be thought that if nonreductive materialism is true, the issue of the nature of mental states need not be addressed to explain how mental causation is possible. Nonreductive materialism combines the materialist thesis that every mental-state token is some physical-state token or other, and the nonreductive thesis that types of mental states do not reduce to types of physical states. The *relata* of causal relations are state tokens, not state types. Mental causation is just physical causation in which the physical cause happens to be a mental state as well (DAVIDSON [S], 1980).

While nonreductive materialism avoids token epiphenomenalism—the doctrine that no mental state has any causal effects—it faces the threat of another sort of epiphenomenalism. While the relata of causal relations are indeed state tokens, it is, nevertheless, fairly widely held that when two state tokens are causally related, they are so in virtue of something about them. The following principle of physical causal comprehensiveness seems true: whenever two physical states causally interact, they do so in virtue of falling under physical types. If every state is a physical state, then whenever any two states causally interact, they do so in virtue of falling under physical types. Since the nonreductive materialists deny that mental state types are physical state types, they face the problem of whether type epiphenomenalism is true: the thesis that no state has any causal effects in virtue of falling under a mental type (Kim, 1993; McLaughlin, 1989, 1994).

It has been widely argued that states can be causes in virtue of falling under macrostate types, even though such state types often fail to be identical to physical state types of the sort postulated by microphysics. Macrostate types seem to figure in counterfactual supporting causal patterns that can ground causal relations between particular state tokens. When macrocausation occurs, often the microphysical stages of the underlying mechanism will involve many elements that are irrelevant to the bringing about of an effect of the sort in question. Often a state's falling under a macrostate type will "screen-off" a state's falling under a microphysical state type for causal relevance vis-a-vis a certain sort of effect: that is, often, so long as an instance of the macrostate type occurred, the effect would have occurred even if the microphysical state type in question had not been instanced (albeit, then, some other microphysical state type would have been—see LePore & Loewer, 1987; PUTNAM [S], 1975; and Yablo, 1992). Everyday examples of this are in ample supply: the turning of a key with such-and-such macrofeatures may cause a lock with such-and-such macrofeatures to open; most of the microphysical details underlying this key turning will be irrelevant to whether the sort of lock in question will open when the sort of key in question is turned. If that sort of key turning had occurred, that sort of lock would have opened, even if the underlying microphysical states had been different. It has thus been argued that there are genuine causal patterns to be found at each level of organization of reality. These causal patterns are the business of the special sciences. Underlying mechanisms are nevertheless relevant: they are relevant to how the macrostates bring about their effects.

Macrostate types are typically not identical with any microphysical state types. Rather, it is claimed, macrostate types are realized by microphysical state types; and a given macrostate type may be multiply realizable, realizable by many distinct microstate types. It might be argued that mental state types are macrostate types that are realizable, perhaps multiply realizable, by microphysical state types. But for the causal relevance of mental types to be vindicated in this way, it must be the case that mental state types bear macro/micro relationships to physical state types. However, whether they do is, as we noted, a controversial issue.

It has been widely argued that state types can be realized by microphysical states without being related to them as macrostates to microstates, and realized in a way that renders the state types causally relevant. Functional states, for example, can be realized by physical states, even though they do not bear micro/macro relationships to them. According to the leading version of functionalism, functional states are second-order states: to be in a functional state is to be in some state that has a certain causal role. Dispositional states are arguably functional states. For something to be soluble, for instance, is (arguably) for it to be in some state such that, under appropriate conditions, it would begin to dissolve when immersed in a liquid. The states that have the causal roles in question are first-order states relative to the functional states, and are said to realize the functional states. Functional states, in worlds such as ours, the functionalist claims, are realized (perhaps multiply realized) by microphysical states.

The functionalist approach to the nature of mental states is today the leading approach (*see* FUNCTIONALISM [S]). Mental states, it is fairly widely claimed, are functional states that, like all functional states in worlds such as ours, are realized by microphysical states. However, a prima facie problem arises for mental causation on this functionalist view. It has been argued that such second states are not causally relevant; that, rather, it is their first-order realizations that are relevant to bringing about effects. Thus, it has been argued that it is not the solubility of an object that has causal effects, but rather the first-order structural state that realizes solubility that has effects. The view that functional states are causally irrelevant (though their first-order realizations are not) is, however, controversial; some philosophers argue that functional states do indeed have causal effects (for discussion see Jackson & Pettit, 1988; Block, 1990).

However this issue is resolved, problems of mental causation remain. Even if intentional mental states—PROPOSITIONAL ATTITUDE [S] states—are functional states, and such states have contents. The contents of intentional states play an essential role in explanations in which the states figure. For example, that the content of the belief that 'there is a snake in the room' figures essentially both in the rationalizing explanation, 'He decided not to enter the room because he believed there was a snake in the room', and in the nonrationalizing explanation, 'He began to quiver in fear because he believed there was a snake in the room'. According to externalist theories of content, however, the contents of intentional states are individuated, in part, by environmental factors. For this reason, it has been argued that an intentional state's having a certain content is a causally irrelevant feature of it. This issue is, however, also highly controversial. There are various theories that purport to explain how contents can be causally relevant, despite being individuated in part by environmental factors (Dretske, 1988).

A final problem should be noted. Even if intentional states such as beliefs, desires, and intentions are functional states, there is reason to think that certain mental states, phenomenal mental states, are not. Phenomenal mental states such as, for instance, states of pain seem to be essentially intrinsic states, not second-order states of being in states with certain causal roles. If this is right, then we lack an account of the nature of phenomenal states since functionalism is false for them. Yet phenomenal states seem paradigmatically causal: pains can make us wince, nagging headaches can put us in a bad mood, visual experiences can lead to beliefs about the scene before our eyes. That phenomenal states are epiphenomena seems quite implausible. Even if we could somehow know in our own case, without causal mediation, that we occupy them, how could we know that others are in phenomenal states if such states lack causal effects? However, philosophers who maintain that phenomenal states act as causes and that such causal action is implemented by physical mechanisms must either show how, despite appearances to the contrary, phenomenal states are functional states, or else explain in some other way how phenomenal states can be realized by physical states in such a way as to be causally efficacious.

The issues raised above are subjects of intensive philosophical investigation. Suffice it to note that philosophical problems concerning mental causation cannot be addressed independently of addressing the nature of mental states, and that the nature of mental states remains a topic of controversy.

(SEE ALSO: *Philosophy of Mind* [S])

Bibliography

Block, N. "Can the Mind Change the World?" in G. Boolos, ed., *Meaning and Method: Essays in Honor of Hilary Putnam* (Cambridge, 1990).

Davidson, D. *Actions and Events.* Oxford, 1980.

Dretske, F. *Explaining Behavior: Reasons in a World of Causes.* Cambridge, MA, 1988.

Heil, J., and A. Mele, eds. *Mental Causation.* Oxford, 1993.

Jackson, F., and P. Pettit. "Broad Contents and Functionalism," *Mind,* Vol. 47 (1988), 381–400.

Kim, J., ed. *Supervenience and Mind.* Cambridge, 1993.
LePore, E., and B. Loewer. "Mind Matters," *Journal of Philosophy,* Vol. 4 (1982), 630–42.
McLaughlin, B. P. "Type Dualism, Type Epiphenomenalism, and the Causal Priority of the Physical," *Philosophical Perspectives,* Vol. 3 (1989), 109–35.
———. "The Rise and Fall of British Emergentism," in A. Berckermann, H. Flohr, and J. Kim, eds., *Emergence or Reduction?* (Berlin, 1992).
———. "Epiphenomenalism," in S. Guttenplan, ed., *A Companion to the Philosophy of Mind* (Oxford, 1994).
Putnam, H. "Philosophy and Our Mental Life," in H. Putnam, ed., *Philosophical Papers,* Vol. 2 (Cambridge, 1975). Cambridge University Press.
Searle, J. *Rediscovering the Mind.* Cambridge, 1992.
Yablo, S. "Mental Causation," *Philosophical Review,* Vol. 101 (1992), 245–80.

BRIAN P. MCLAUGHLIN

MENTAL CONTENT. *See:* CONTENT, MENTAL [S]

MENTAL IMAGERY. Does Lincoln's nose point right or left on American pennies? If you drilled a hole through the floor of your upstairs bathroom, which room would the drill tip end up in? Does the tip of a racehorse's tail extend below its rear knees? Questions like these typically prompt people to form mental images. But just what are mental images?

According to the pictorial view, held by ARISTOTLE [1; S], DESCARTES [2; S], and the British Empiricists, for example, mental images—specifically visual images—are significantly like pictures in the way that they represent things in the world. Notwithstanding its widespread acceptance in the history of philosophy, the pictorial view is deeply puzzling. Mental images are not seen with real eyes; they cannot be hung on real walls; they have no objective weight or color. What, then, can it mean to say that images are pictorial? Mental images are also frequently indeterminate. For example, a mental image of a striped tiger need not represent any definite number of stripes. But, according to some philosophers, a picture of a striped tiger must be determinate with respect to the number of stripes. So, again, how can images be pictures? And what evidence is there for accepting a pictorial view of images?

Historically, the philosophical claim that images are picturelike rested primarily on an appeal to INTROSPECTION [S]. But it seems plausible to suppose that what introspection really shows about visual images is not that they are pictorial but only that what goes on in imagery is experientially much like what goes on in seeing (Block, 1983).

Perhaps the most influential alternative to the pictorial view has been what is now standardly labeled 'descriptionalism'. This approach has some similarity with the claim made by some behaviorists—that imaging is a matter of talking to oneself beneath one's breath—for the basic thesis of descriptionalism is that mental images represent in the manner of linguistic descriptions. This thesis, however, should not be taken to mean that during imagery there must be present inner tokens of the imager's spoken language in movements of the larynx. Rather, the hypothesis is that there is some languagelike neural code within which mental images are constructed.

Descriptionalism has its advocates in philosophy (e.g., Dennett, 1981) and has significant support in contemporary psychology. Nevertheless, since the early 1980s the pictorial view has made a comeback after having fallen out of favor. What has been responsible for this change more than anything else is the work of some cognitive psychologists, notably Stephen Kosslyn, who has developed an empirical version of the pictorial view that seems much more promising than any of its philosophical predecessors.

Kosslyn's view is complex, and only the barest sketch of its central idea can be provided in this entry. According to Kosslyn, mental images are to be conceived of on the model of displays on a cathode ray tube screen connected to a computer. Such displays are generated on the screen from information stored in the computer's memory. Now the screen may be thought of as the medium in which the picture is presented. This medium is spatial and is made up of a large number of basic cells, some of which are illuminated to form a picture. Analogously, according to Kosslyn, there is a functional spatial medium for mental imagery. In Kosslyn's view mental images are functional pictures in this medium.

It is not easy to see exactly what Kosslyn means by calling images functional pictures in a functional spatial medium. One important part of the position is that mental images function with respect to the representation of relative distance relations as if they were screen displays (even though, in reality, they need not be laid out in the brain with just the same spatial characteristics as real displays). Kosslyn hypothesizes that the imagery medium, which he calls the "visual buffer," is shared with visual perception. Each cell in the medium represents a tiny, just perceptible patch of object surface. The cells representing adjacent object parts need not themselves be physically adjacent (as in a real picture). Rather, like the cells in an array in a computer, they may be widely scattered.

This view is motivated by many intriguing experiments (see Tye, 1991, for a summary). Not all cognitive scientists agree with Kosslyn, however. Zenon Pylyshyn, for example, maintains that mental images are structural descriptions no different in kind from the representations involved in other areas of cognition. According to Pylyshyn, Kosslyn's experiments on imagery can be accounted for by reference to the task demands placed on subjects by the experimenter's instructions together with facts the subjects already tacitly know. No inner picturelike entity is needed.

It is far from clear that the appeal to tacit knowledge can explain all the imagery data (Kosslyn, 1980). But there are other descriptional theories of imagery that have no need of the doctrine of tacit knowledge (e.g., Hinton, 1979). The controversy between pictorialists and descriptionalists in psychology about imagistic representation has not been settled yet.

Another topic of interest to philosophers that also remains a source of considerable puzzlement is the phenomenal or subjective character of images. What is responsible for the technicolor phenomenology of a mental image of a striped tiger? Some philosophers maintain that the phenomenal aspects of imagery derive from images having special, intrinsic, introspectively accessible, nonintentional properties (or QUALIA [S]). But there is no general agreement.

(SEE ALSO: *Philosophy of Mind* [S])

Bibliography

Block N. "Mental Pictures and Cognitive Science," *Philosophical Review,* Vol. 92 (1983), 499–542.

Dennett, D. "The Nature of Images and the Introspective Trap," in *Content and Consciousness* (London, 1969).

Hinton, G. "Some Demonstrations of the Effects of Structural Descriptions in Mental Imagery," *Behavioral and Brain Sciences,* Vol. 3, (1979), 231–50.

Kosslyn, S. *Image and Mind.* Cambridge, MA, 1980.

———. *Image and Brain: The Resolution of the Imagery Debate.* Cambridge, MA, 1994.

Pylyshyn, Z. "The Imagery Debate: Analog Media versus Tacit Knowledge," *Psychological Review,* Vol. 88 (1981), 16–45.

Tye, M. *The Imagery Debate.* Cambridge, MA, 1991.

MICHAEL TYE

MENTAL REPRESENTATION. Mental representations are the coin of contemporary cognitive psychology, which proposes to explain the etiology of subjects' behavior in terms of the possession and use of such representations. "How does a subject manage to move through her darkened bedroom without stumbling over the furniture? She has an accurate mental representation of the room's layout, knows her initial position in the room, and is able to use this representation, in roughly the way a mariner uses a chart, to navigate through the room." "How does a sighted subject manage to recover information, available in the retinal image, about 'what's where' in her environment? She computes a series of representations, using information present in the retinal image, that eventuates in a three-dimensional representation of the distal objects present in the subject's visual field." "Why do native speakers of English have difficulty recognizing the grammaticality of so-called garden-path sentences such as 'The horse raced past the barn fell'? In recovering the meaning of a sentence, a speaker first constructs a representation of the syntactic structure of the sentence. In the case of garden-path sentences, the parsing processes that construct this representation mistakenly take the sentence's subject noun phrase to be a complete sentence, thus concluding that the entire sentence is ungrammatical." Cognitive ethologists offer similar explanations of many animal behaviors: foraging red ants are said to practice a form of dead reckoning to maintain a representation of their current location relative to their nest, which they use to find their way back; migratory birds are said to navigate using representations of various sorts (celestial, magnetometric, topographic, etc.) that are either innate or learned as juveniles.

If, as these explanations apparently assume, mental representations are real entities that play a causal role in the production of a subject's behavior, then presumably it makes sense to ask about the form in which the information contained in these representations is encoded. This question has been the focus of considerable debate, especially with respect to MENTAL IMAGERY [S]. Descriptionalists argue that, subjective impressions to the contrary notwithstanding, all mental representation, including mental imagery, is descriptional in form; mental representations are said to represent in a way similar to the ways linguistic descriptions represent. Descriptionalists subscribe to a LANGUAGE OF THOUGHT [S] hypothesis, according to which all human cognition is conducted in a quasi-linguistic medium. Pictorialists, by contrast, argue at least some mental representation, notably those involved in mental imagery, represent in ways similar to the ways pictures represent. The issues in dispute here are not straightforwardly empirical. Neither party believes that we literally have descriptions or pictures in our heads; rather, their claims are about similarities to the respective ways that pictures and descriptions represent. But it is precisely these similarity claims that render this debate obscure. What are the respective ways that pictures and descriptions represent, and what are the salient similarities such that if they hold they would justify characterizing mental representations as being of one form rather than the other? It is not obvious that there are definitive answers to either of these questions.

To describe the representations to which psychological and ethological explanations appeal as mental is not to imply that their possessors are conscious of them; typically the representations are nonconscious or subconscious. Nor is it to imply that these representations are nonphysical; there is no commitment here to dualism. Psychologists and ethologists presume that the representations to which their explanations appeal are neurologically realized, physical structures. The point of describing the representations as mental is simply to emphasize the particular explanatory role that these representations play in these explanations. The explanations undertake to explain a kind of purposive behavior on the part of a subject, in which the particular behavior exhibited by the subject is typically modulated in a characteristic fashion, not only by the goal or purpose of the behavior, but also by the environment in which the behavior is exhibited. Thus, for example, our subject's movement through her darkened bedroom is modulated by her knowledge of the current layout of the room. The mental representations that figure in these explanations serve two distinct explanatory roles: (1) they explain why a subject behaves in one way rather than another—she behaves as she does because she currently has this particular representation rather than another, and this representation is causally efficacious in the etiology of her behavior—and (2) they explain how the subject's behavior manages to be modulated (in characteristic ways) by her environment. Mental representations are able to play this dual explanatory role by virtue of possessing both physico-formal and semantic (intentional) properties that are linked in such a way as to ensure that a subject's environment can modulate her behavior. Basically, the cognitive processes that make use of mental representations are causally sensitive to the physico-formal properties of these representations that encode their semantic properties in much the way that sound-reproduction processes are sensitive to the physico-formal properties of records, tapes, and CDs.

Commonsense psychological explanations of behavior standardly appeal to beliefs, desires, intentions, and other so-called propositional attitudes (e.g., "Jones went to the refrigerator because he wanted a beer and believed there to be one there"). Behaviorists and eliminativists (*see* ELIMINATIVE MATERIALISM, ELIMINATIVISM [S]) have challenged the legitimacy of these explanations, arguing that propositional attitudes either do not exist or do not figure in the etiology of behavior. Impressed with the prominent explanatory role of mental representations in cognitive psychological and ethological explanations, many philosophers of mind, notably Jerry Fodor, have proposed establishing the materialistic respectability of these explanations by appeal to the notion of mental representation. Their strategy is to explicate propositional attitudes in terms of mental representations. They defend a doctrine called the "Representational Theory of Mind" (RTM, for short), which holds that possessing a propositional attitude (e.g., believing that it is sunny today) is a matter of having a mental representation that (1) expresses the propositional content of that attitude (viz., that it is sunny today) and (2) plays a causal-functional role in the subject's mental life and behavior characteristic of the attitude in question (viz., the characteristic role of beliefs in modulating goal-satisfying behavior). More formally, for any organism O, any attitude A toward the proposition P, there is a mental representation MR such that MR means that (expresses the proposition that) P and a relation R (which specifies the characteristic causal-functional role of the MRs that are associated with a given A); and O bears attitude A to P if and only if O stands in relation R to MR. So formulated, RTM is silent as to the form of the mental representations that express the propositional contents of attitudes; however, proponents of RTM invariably assume that these representations are syntactically structured entities, composed of atomic constituents (concepts) that refer to or denote things and properties in the world. More colorfully, these representations are sentences in the language of thought. The structure and meaning of these sentential representations purportedly explain the particular semantic and causal properties that propositional attitudes exhibit.

RTM is clearly realist in its construal of propositional attitudes: it purports to explain, not only what they are, but also how they could have both the causal and semantic properties that common sense attributes to them (viz., of being causally efficacious in the production of other thoughts and of behavior, and of being semantically evaluable, as, e.g., true or false). RTM is equally realist in its construal of mental processes, which, it holds, are causal sequences of the tokenings of mental representation. These sequences are said to be proof-theoretic in character, with the sequential states in a thought process functioning like premises in an argument. Thought processes are, like arguments, generally truth preserving (*see* MENTAL CAUSATION [S]).

Proponents of RTM claim to find strong empirical support for the doctrine in the apparent explanatory (and predictive) successes of COGNITIVE SCIENCE [S], whose theories are heavily committed to the existence of mental representations. Critics tend to dismiss this claimed support, arguing that what is at issue is not whether there are mental representations but whether there are mental representations with the particular properties demanded by RTM. Critics argue that propositional-attitude contents cannot always be paired with mental representations in the way that RTM requires: a subject may bear a certain attitude to a proposition but lack, among the many mental representations that cognitive scientific theories attribute to her, any mental representation of that particular proposition. Thus, for example, more than one critic has pointed out that, while David Marr's computational theory of early vision (see his *Vision* [1982]) attributes to the visual system the assumption that objects in the visual field are rigid in translation, the theory does not attribute to the visual system an explicit representation of that assumption; rather, the assumption is implicit in the operation of visual processes. Proponents, for their part, have tended to dismiss such counterexamples as "derivative" cases, arguing that RTM nonetheless holds for what they term the "core" cases of propositional attitudes. Such a response presumes that there is a non-question-begging characterization of the class of core cases. It also presumes that the class so characterized includes those propositional attitudes that figure in the commonsense psychological explanations that RTM is intended to vindicate. It remains an open question whether either of these presumptions can be met.

Other critics of RTM have challenged the doctrine's apparent commitment to "classical" cognitive architectures that presume a principled distinction between mental representations, on the one hand, and the computational processes that are defined over these representations, on the other. These critics point out that connectionist computational models of cognition do not preserve such a distinction, so that, if, as these critics presume, cognitive architecture is connectionist rather than classical, then RTM is untenable (*see* CONNECTIONISM [S]). Not surprisingly, proponents of RTM have been in the forefront of efforts to demonstrate that cognitive architecture is not connectionist.

Still other critics of RTM have focused on the semantics of the postulated mental representations, arguing that, if RTM is to provide a materialistic vindication of explanations that appeal to propositional attitudes, it must be possible to provide a "naturalistic" semantics, a theory of content, for these representations. By such a semantics these critics understand a materialistic account, invoking no intentional or semantic notions, of how it is possible for mental representations to have the semantic properties that they do (of being about things in the world, of being truth valued, etc.). There is general agreement among critics and proponents alike that none of the proposed naturalistic semantics is adequate, but, where critics see in these failures the symptoms of RTM's untenability, proponents see the beginnings of a difficult but eventually successful research project. There is disagreement among critics as to the import for cognitive science itself of there possibly being no naturalistic semantics for mental representations. Some argue that it would impugn the claimed explanatory role of mental representations; others argue that it would not. Whatever the upshot of these arguments, the untenability of RTM would not in and of itself impugn the explanatory role of mental representations in cognitive science, since that commitment to mental representations does not entail RTM. One can perfectly well be a representationalist in the way that most cognitive scientists are without also being a proponent of RTM.

(SEE ALSO: *Philosophy of Mind* [S])

Bibliography

Block, N., ed. *Imagery*. Cambridge, MA, 1981. A collection focusing on debate between descriptionalists and pictorialists regarding mental imagery.

Field, H. "Mental Representation," *Erkenntnis*, Vol. 13 (1978), 9–61.

Fodor, J. A. "Fodor's Guide to Mental Representation," *Mind*, Vol. 94 (1985), 55–97.

———. "The Persistence of the Attitudes," in *Psychosemantics* (Cambridge, MA, 1987).

Marr, D. *Vision*. Cambridge, MA, 1982.

Matthews, R. "Troubles with Representationalism," *Social Research*, Vol. 51 (1984), 1065–97.

———. "Is There Vindication through Representationalism?" in B. Loewer and G. Rey, eds., *Meaning in Mind: Fodor and His Critics* (Oxford, 1991).

Pylyshyn, Z. "The Explanatory Role of Representations," in *Computation and Cognition* (Cambridge, MA, 1984).

Sterelny, K. *The Representational Theory of Mind: An Introduction*. Oxford, 1990.

Stich, S., and T. Warfield, eds. *Mental Representation: A Reader*. Oxford, 1994. An excellent collection of papers on theories of content for mental representation; includes Field (1978) and Fodor (1985).

ROBERT J. MATTHEWS

MEREOLOGY. Mereology (from Greek *meros*, "part") is the theory (often formalized) of part, whole, and cognate concepts. The notion of part is almost ubiquitous in domain of application, and for this reason HUSSERL [4; S] assigned its investigation to formal ontology. ARISTOTLE [1; S] observed that the term part was used in various ways such as for a subquantity, a physical part (leg of an animal), a part in definition (animal is part of man), a part in extension (man is part of animal). Part concepts had obvious applications in geometry and were among Euclid's undefined terms. Several senses of "part" are expressible using the preposition "in," but not all uses of "in" express parthood.

Until the twentieth century it was generally assumed that the concept of part was sufficiently clear not to require elucidation, but gradually the need for a formal treatment became apparent. Euclid's maxim that the whole is greater than the part appeared to be contradicted by infinite classes, for example. In 1901 Husserl proposed a general theory of part and whole and distinguished several kinds of parts, notably dependent and independent parts. Explicit formal theories of part and whole were developed around 1914 to 1916 by WHITEHEAD [8] and LEŚNIEWSKI [4], who worked independently of each other. They had different motivations: Whitehead wanted an empirical basis for geometry, whereas Leśniewski wished to offer a paradox-free class theory. Mereology was later formulated within first-order predicate logic by Leonard and GOODMAN [3; S], who called it "the calculus of individuals." Mereology has often been employed by nominalists as a partial substitute for set theory, but it is not intrinsically a nominalistic theory: part relations are definable via endomorphisms in many mathematical domains.

The most natural basic concept of mereology is that of a (proper) part to its (larger) whole. A coincident of an object is the object itself or something that shares all parts with it. An ingredient of an object is a part or coincident of it. Two objects overlap if and only if they share an ingredient, and they are disjoint if and only if they do not. The relation of part to whole has some minimal formal properties: it is (1) existence entailing; (2) asymmetrical; (3) transitive; and (4) supplementative. That means (1) that if one thing is part of another, if either the part or the whole exists, so does the other; (2) that if one thing is part of another, the second is not part of the first; (3) that a part of a part of a whole is itself a part of the whole; and (4) that if an object has a part, it has another part disjoint from the first. Principles (3) and (4) have occasionally been doubted, (4) unconvincingly. Some meanings of "part" are not transitive; for example, a hand is said to be part of the body, but an arbitrary chunk of flesh is not, and for such concepts counterexamples to (3) may sound plausible, but only because they restrict the general (and transitive) concept, to mean, for example, organ, functional part, immediate part, assembly component.

Beyond such minimal properties mereologists often make further assumptions. Very often it is assumed that objects with the same ingredients are identical: such a mereology is extensional. Extensionality makes good sense for homogeneous domains such as regions of space or masses of matter, but some objects of distinct sorts seem to be able to coincide, at least temporarily, without identity. Another assumption often made is that any two objects make up a third, indeed that any nonempty collection of objects constitutes a single object, their mereological sum. The minimal properties together with extensionality and this general-sum principle constitute the classical mereology of Leśniewski and Leonard/Goodman: it is as rich in parts as an extensional theory can be, differing algebraically from Boolean algebra only in lacking a null element. It does, however, have an ontologically maximal object or universe, the sum of all there is, which by extensionality is unique. Whitehead denied that there was a universe: for him every object is part of something greater, so he rejected the sum principle. Whitehead also denied there are atoms, that is, objects without parts: for him, every object has a part. This antiatomism, together with supplementarity, ensures that every object has nondenumerably many parts. Whitehead thus denies geometrical points, and his method of extensive abstraction is directed to logically constructing substitutes for points out of classes of extended objects, an idea also carried through by TARSKI [8]. As the examples indicate, the issue whether atomism or antiatomism holds is independent of general mereology. Formally, the best worked-out forms of mereology are those of Leśniewski and his followers; they have shown that any of a wide range of mereological concepts may be taken as sole primitive of the classical theory.

Beyond extensional mereology attention has focused on the combination of mereological notions with those of space, time, and modality. Thus, Whitehead and a number of more recent authors combine mereological with topological concepts to define such notions as two regions' being connected, or their abutting (externally or internally), using mereology as its modern authors intended, as an alternative framework to set theory. When time is considered, matters become more complex. Some objects have temporal parts, including phases, and perhaps momentary temporal sections. States, processes, and events (occurrents) are uncontroversial cases of objects that are temporally extended, but many modern metaphysicians apply the same analysis to ordinary things such as bodies and organisms, giving them a fourth, temporal dimension, though this view is not uncontested. Whether or not continuants (spatially extended objects with a history but not themselves temporally extended) are thus reduced to occurrents, a number of chronomereological concepts may be defined and applied, such as temporary part, initial part, final part, permanent part, temporary overlapping, growth, diminution, and others, though their formulation will vary as applying to occurrents or continuants.

Embedding mereological notions within a modal framework likewise opens up a wider range of concepts such as essential part, accidental part, dependent part, accidental overlapping. Combining these in their turn with temporal notions allows the definition of concepts such as accidental permanent part, essential initial part, and so on. In general, where mereological notions are enriched with others, their interactions become multifarious and lose the algebraic elegance of the classical theory while gaining in applicability and usefulness.

In modal mereology much attention has been paid to R. M. CHISHOLM's [S] thesis of mereological essentialism, which states that every part of a continuant is both essential and permanent to that continuant (though, conversely, a part may outlast the whole and need not have it as whole). Chisholm's position is presaged in LEIBNIZ [4; S] and BRENTANO [1]. Since it appears to be contradicted by everyday experience of such things as rivers, mountains, organisms, and artifacts, it is natural for Chisholm to regard such mereologically fluctuating things as not "real" continuants but as *entia successiva,* supervenient upon successions of continuants for which mereological essentialism holds.

The ubiquity and importance of mereological concepts ensure them a growing place within COGNITIVE SCIENCE [S] and formal representations of commonsense knowledge, and there is no doubt that mereology is firmly established as a part of formal ontology.

(SEE ALSO: *Metaphysics* [S])

Bibliography

Chisholm, R. M. *Person and Object: A Metaphysical Study.* London, 1976.

Husserl, E. "On the Theory of Wholes and Parts," in *Logical Investigations,* 2 vols. (London, 1970).

Leonard, H. S., and N. Goodman. "The Calculus of Individuals and Its Uses," *Journal of Symbolic Logic,* Vol. 5 (1940), 45–55.

Leśniewski, S. "On the Foundations of Mathematics," in *Collected Works* (Dordrecht, 1992).

Simons, P. M. *Parts: A Study in Ontology.* Oxford, 1987.

Whitehead, A. N. "Principles of the Method of Extensive Abstraction," in *An Enquiry Concerning the Principles of Natural Knowledge* (Cambridge, 1919).

PETER SIMONS

MERLEAU-PONTY, MAURICE [*This entry consists of three articles. In his first essay, Martin C. Dillon presents an overview of the French philosopher's contributions to the field. In his second piece, Dillon discusses Merleau-Ponty's philosophy of psychology. The third article, contributed by Sonia Kruks, presents Merleau-Ponty's views on political theory.*]

MERLEAU-PONTY, MAURICE (1908–61), French philosopher associated with existential PHENOMENOLOGY [6; S], was the youngest philosopher ever to be appointed to the chair once occupied by Henri BERGSON [1] at the Collège de France. He is known primarily for developing an ontology that recognizes the philosophical significance of the human body. His early interest in the resonance between the emergent school of gestalt psychology and the phenomenology of Edmund HUSSERL [4; S] and Martin HEIDEGGER [3; S], coupled with lively participation in contemporary debates in politics, human sciences, and the arts, led to a radical reassessment of transcendental philosophy. He died abruptly at the age of fifty-three, leaving his last major work, *Le Visible et l'invisible,* unfinished. Claude Lefort has edited the extant text, four chapters and an appendix, and published it together with extensive working notes dated from January 1959 to March 1961.

THE LIVED BODY

Merleau-Ponty revolutionized Western thinking about the body, which since ancient Greece had taken it to be either insignificant or a detriment to knowledge, by demonstrating its constitutive role in the process of human understanding. He showed, for example, that it is through bodily motility that the various adumbrations or perspectival views of an object can be synthesized into a unitary whole. Our understanding of objective space, the three-dimensional Cartesian grid of length, breadth, and height, is an abstraction from lived space, space articulated by the body's capacity to move purposively, to grasp things, to maintain the equilibrium that allows for stable visual coordinates, to interrogate its environment. Furthermore, the body's ability to perceive the world is grounded in the body's double role as sensor and sensed, subject and object of experience: I could not touch an object were I not myself, as body, an object capable of being touched, nor could I see were my eyes not themselves objects located within the surroundings to which they are sensitive. The classical dualism, which views the body and otherworldly objects as disjunct from the mind as the subject or agency of disembodied thought, is replaced with Merleau-Ponty's model of corporeal intentionality, in which the body is revealed as having an intelligence of its own, manifest in reflex as in habitual activities, which allows it to interact with the world at a level prior to the reflexivity of deliberate conceptualization.

REVERSIBILITY THESIS

The transcendental role of the body, its ability to project its organizational schemas into the world, is inseparable from the body's own status as physical object subject to the worldly forces impinging upon it. These roles are inseparable, but not coincident. There is a divergence of the body as sensing from the body as sensed: the finger that touches the thumb or is touched by it does not form an identity with the thumb; rather, the two bodily parts co-exist in an ambiguous relationship of reversibility within the encompassing matrix of bodily being-in-the-world. Finger and thumb can reverse roles, the erstwhile sensor becoming the sensed, just as the hand that feels the table can sense itself being touched by the table, yet neither of these roles would be possible were it not for the other.

THE FLESH OF THE WORLD

Merleau-Ponty takes the reversibility of subject and object roles in the case of human flesh as emblematic of a global manner of being, which he designates as chiasm or intertwining. The term 'flesh' is generalized to encompass worldly being as such. The world is taken as an arena of interaction in which every entity is what it is in relation to every other. This is not a pananimism, but rather an attempt to rectify the post-Socratic reduction of nature to inert materiality in a movement of thought which is as consonant with the ancient concept of *physis* as it is with the contemporary notion of world as ecosystem. The figure of the chiasm, the intersection or intertwining marking the point at which things touch each other as they cross, refers to the dynamics of worldly unfolding or global temporality in which the interaction of things brings about change. The brute or savage being of the world, the factuality of its transcendence, is counterbalanced with the relatedness of its denizens apparent in the relatively abiding structures human intelligence organizes under the heading of science. We are that aspect of the flesh of the world that is capable of the reflective relationship of conceptualization or understanding, but other aspects of the world betray other forms of corporeal reflexivity in the complex of interaction that encompasses organic cycles, weather systems, geological formation, and so forth as each of these contributes and responds to all the others.

VISIBLE AND INVISIBLE

Merleau-Ponty's thesis of the primacy of perception evolves from the middle phase of his thinking, when he published *Phénoménologie de la perception* and set forth the view that "the perceived world is the always presupposed foundation of all RATIONALITY [S], all value and all existence," to later phases in which this thesis had to be expanded to accommodate the findings of extensive analyses of language based on his unique interpretation of the philosophical significance of Saussurean semiotics. There is controversy regarding his later thinking on the relative primacy of language and PERCEPTION [6; S], but general agreement that the relationship between the two is that of intertwining: language, conceived as sign system, might be conceived as an invisible nexus of relations that is apparent in the visible world and is itself perceptible in speech and writing. The controversy centers on two questions regarding origins or foundations. Does the invisible structure of language reflect organization perceived in the world or does it constitute that nexus of relations? The second question challenges the legitimacy of asking the first: is it possible to separate perception from language in such a way that one could even ask about the primacy of one with respect to the other? Merleau-Ponty regards language as flesh, akin to the flesh of the body in its reflexivity, its relatedness to itself and world, but "less heavy, more transparent." In general, the structure of the visible-invisible relation can be defined as asymmetrical reversibility: just as the object I touch can be seen (although its tactile aspect remains invisible as such), so can the hidden or horizonal aspects of a given theme be brought into focal vision, but only through the loss of their horizonality.

(SEE ALSO: *Merleau-Ponty, Maurice* [5])

Bibliography

WORKS BY MERLEAU-PONTY

Les Aventures de la dialectique. Paris, 1955. Translated by J. Bien as *Adventures of the Dialectic.* Evanston, IL, 1973.

Les Philosophes célèbres. Paris, 1956.

Le Visible et l'invisible. Edited by C. Lefort. Paris, 1964. Translated by A. Lingis as *The Visible and the Invisible.* Evanston, IL, 1968.

Résumés de cours, Collège de France, 1952–1960. Paris, 1968. Translated by J. O'Neill as *Themes from the Lectures at the Collège de France, 1952–1960.* Evanston, IL, 1970.

La Prose du monde. Paris, 1969. Translated by J. O'Neill as *The Prose of the World.* Evanston, IL, 1973.

Existence et dialectique. Paris, 1971.

Consciousness and the Acquisition of Language. Translated by H. J. Silverman. Evanston, IL, 1973.

Texts and Dialogues. Edited by H. J. Silverman and J. Barry, Jr. Atlantic Highlands, NJ, 1991.

WORKS ON MERLEAU-PONTY

Burke, P., and J. Van der Vecken, eds. *Merleau-Ponty in Contemporary Perspective.* Dordrecht, 1993.

Busch, T., and S. Gallagher, eds. *Merleau-Ponty, Hermeneutics, and Postmodernism.* Albany, NY, 1992.

Casey, E. S. "Habitual Body and Memory in Merleau-Ponty," *Man and World,* Vol. 1 (1984), 279–98.

Dillon, M. C. *Merleau-Ponty's Ontology.* Bloomington, IN, 1988.

———, ed. *Merleau-Ponty Vivant.* Albany, NY, 1991.

Johnson, G. *The Merleau-Ponty Aesthetics Reader.* Evanston, IL, 1993.

Johnson, G., and M. Smith, eds. *Ontology and Alterity in Merleau-Ponty.* Evanston, IL, 1990.

Langer, M. M. *Merleau-Ponty's Phenomenology of Perception: A Guide and Commentary.* Tallahassee, 1989.

Madison, G. B. *The Phenomenology of Merleau-Ponty.* Athens, OH, 1981.

Pietersma, H., ed. *Merleau-Ponty: Critical Essays.* Lanham, MD, 1989.

Silverman, H. J. *Inscriptions: Between Phenomenology and Structuralism.* New York, 1987.

Watson, S. "Language, Perception, and the Cogito in Merleau-Ponty's Thought," in John Sallis, ed., *Merleau-Ponty: Perception, Structure, Language* (Atlantic Highlands, NJ, 1981).

MARTIN C. DILLON

PHILOSOPHY OF PSYCHOLOGY. From the earliest of his writing until the last, Merleau-Ponty maintained the thesis of the irreducibility of the figure-ground or theme-horizon structure articulated by gestalt theory. This thesis holds that PERCEPTION [6; S] and cognition are fundamentally relational, hence stand in opposition to such standpoints as that of sense-data theory based on the notions of perceptual atoms, elemental simples, or discrete QUALIA [S].

In his *Phénoménologie de la perception,* Merleau-Ponty offers an extended case study of Schneider, a World War I soldier debilitated by a shrapnel wound in the occipital region of his brain. The point of the study is to demonstrate the inadequacy of the standpoints of EMPIRICISM [2] or PHYSICALISM [S], on the one hand, and intellectualism or transcendentalism, on the other, to provide an accurate description of Schneider's afflictions, which are neither purely physiological nor purely intentional but involve a degeneration of the lived body resulting in aberrent forms of substitution behavior in such domains as sexual responsiveness, existential spatiality, motility, expression, and memory.

Merleau-Ponty is unique among phenomenologists in reinterpreting Freudian notions regarding the UNCONSCIOUS [8] in a positive way and integrating them within his own body of theory. This appropriation involved some modification, to be sure, specifically that of asserting a continuity between conscious and unconscious aspects of human experience at the level of prereflective horizonality. Merleau-Ponty steers a middle course between FREUD's [3; S] relatively mechanistic account of such phenomena as repression, which attributes it to an autonomous function of censorship and dissemblance, and Jean-Paul SARTRE's [7; S] relatively voluntaristic account, which attributes repression to an act of self-deception on the part of a consciousness recoiling from the implications of its own FREEDOM [3]. Merleau-Ponty interprets behavior traditionally subsumed under the heading of repression in terms of a process of habituation operating at prepersonal or unreflective levels in which the body's response to worldly events becomes sedimented as a style of contending with a domain of existence permeated with negative significance. Thus, the aphonia and anorexia of a girl whose family has forbidden her to see her lover is understood, neither as a reversion to an infantile phase of oral sexuality, as Freud would have it, nor as a recoil from responsibility in the mode of magical transformation, as Sartre would have it, but as a refusal of coexistence, a withdrawal from the communal world of eating and talking, which acquires the autonomy of a habit exacerbated by former habitualities favoring oral modes of responding to the world.

In addition to his interests in gestalt psychology (*see* GESTALT THEORY [3]) and Freudian psychoanalysis, Merleau-Ponty was also well acquainted with the work done by his sometime colleague Jean PIAGET [6] in developmental psychology and the work of Jacques Lacan, a contemporary known for his reinterpretation of Freudian themes along semiological lines. There are frequent references to Piaget in *La Structure du comportement* and *Phénoménologie de la perception,* and an extended response to Lacan's seminal thinking on the mirror stage in a late essay entitled "Les Relations avec autrui chez l'enfant." Perhaps Merleau-Ponty's greatest contribution to psychological theory lies in his articulation of an ontological framework capable of consolidating the findings of thinkers across the full spectrum of ideologies from eidetic analysis to experimental and behavioral research: he unremittingly refused to endorse the radical distinctions between the a priori and the a posteriori (*see* A PRIORI AND A POSTERIORI [1]), between transcendental and empirical approaches, which have functioned to isolate the various schools through polarized opposition.

Bibliography

WORKS BY MERLEAU-PONTY

"Les Relations avec autrui chez l'enfant," in *Les Cours de Sorbonne* (Paris, 1960). Translated by W. Cobb as "The Child's Relations with Others," in J. M. Edie, ed., *The Primacy of Perception* (Evanston, IL, 1964).

"Phenomenology and Psychoanalysis: Preface to Hesnard's *L'Oeuvre de Freud,*" trans. A. L. Fisher, *Review of Existential Psychology and Psychiatry,* Vol. 18 (1982–83), 67–72.

WORKS ON MERLEAU-PONTY

Dillon, M. C. "Merleau-Ponty and the Psychogenesis of the Self," *Journal of Phenomenological Psychology,* Vol. 9 (1978), 84–98.

———. "The Implications of Merleau-Ponty's Thought for the Practice of Psychotherapy," in Kah Kyung Cho, ed., *Philosophy and Science in Phenomenological Perspective* (The Hague, 1984).

Giorgi, A. *Psychology as a Human Science.* New York, 1970.

Kockelmans, J. J. "Merleau-Ponty on Sexuality," *Journal of Existentialism,* Vol. 6 (1965), 9–30.

———. "The Function of Psychology in Merleau-Ponty's Early Works," *Review of Existential Psychology and Psychiatry,* Vol. 18 (1982–83), 119–42.

Krell, D. F. "M. Merleau-Ponty on 'Eros' and 'Logos,' " *Man and World,* Vol. 7 (1974), 37–51.

Levin, D. M. "Eros and Psyche: A Reading of Merleau-Ponty," *Review of Existential Psychology and Psychiatry,* Vol. 18 (1982–83), 219–39.

Lingis, A. *Libido: The French Existentialist Theories.* Bloomington, IN, 1985.

O'Connor, T. "Behaviour and Perception: A Discussion of Merleau-Ponty's Problem of Operative Intentionality," *Human Context,* Vol. 7 (1975), 32–48.

Olkowski, D. "Merleau-Ponty's Freudianism: From the Body of Consciousness to the Body of Flesh," *Review of Existential Psychology and Psychiatry,* Vol. 18 (1982–83), 97–116.

O'Neill, J. "The Specular Body: Merleau-Ponty and Lacan on Infant Self and Other," *Synthese,* Vol. 66 (1986), 201–17.

Pontalis, J. B. "The Problem of the Unconscious in Merleau-Ponty's Thought," trans. W. Ver Eecke and M. Greer, *Review of Existential Psychology and Psychiatry,* Vol. 18 (1982–83), 83–96.

MARTIN C. DILLON

POLITICAL THEORY. Merleau-Ponty engaged with both LIBERALISM [4; S] and MARXISM [S] as he sought a political theory that could support concrete human FREEDOM [3; S]. Because human beings are embodied and situated subjects, he argued that freedom can arise only in engagement with an already given world. This world includes residues of prior human action "sedimented" in such social institutions as language, class, and political organizations. Freedom is an ambiguous venture. For although rooted in the given world, it always outstrips our ability to know opening onto an unpredictable and contingent future. Particularly in the world of politics, where POWER [6] is at issue and multiple projects always intersect, good intentions may thus give rise to unintended, often violent, consequences. However, Merleau-Ponty insisted, political actors must always bear responsibility for such unintended consequences, otherwise all checks on VIOLENCE [S] would cease.

Such views led Merleau-Ponty to be critical of traditional normative political theory, which attempts to develop universal principles and erroneously posits the theorist as standing "nowhere," a surveying, disembodied consciousness. Worse, pursuing normative principles without regard for their actual consequences can function ideologically to legitimize violence. Immediately after World War II Merleau-Ponty was particularly critical of liberalism, which, he argued, used abstract principles of freedom to justify capitalist exploitation and the violence of colonial rule. Instead, Merleau-Ponty turned to MARX [5] for a theory of human "existence and coexistence" that resonated with his own commitment to a concrete HUMANISM [4].

In the late 1940s Merleau-Ponty offered "critical support" to communist movements. But at the same time he also argued that twentieth-century "orthodox" forms of Marxism (i.e., Soviet and Communist Party Marxism) were dangerously abstract. Their claims about the universal and indubitable logic of history, much like liberalism's abstract universal principles, served to justify a disregard for actual consequences and a willingness to sacrifice human lives and well-being for abstract truths—as evidenced in Stalinist terror.

By the mid-1950s Merleau-Ponty ceased privileging Marxism, arguing that the objective and subjective aspects of the Marxian dialectic had come asunder (*see* DIALECTICAL MATERIALISM [2]), with crude objectivism dominating in Soviet-style Communism and subjectivism in a theory such as Sartre's. Instead, he argued for a "heroic liberalism," one that would realize that its own principles were relative and that would permit their contestation by opposing forces.

Some commentators have suggested that Merleau-Ponty's critique of universal principles and historical logic anticipated the work of later poststructuralist critics of Western thought. However, unlike such later thinkers, Merleau-Ponty eschewed extreme relativism (*see* ETHICAL RELATIVISM [3]; and MORAL RELATIVISM [S]), arguing that certain general values do continuously emerge from human existence. Since we all share the experience of embodiment and since our subjectivities and freedom are intrinsically interconnected, our own freedom demands a politics of mutual respect for the freedom of others. Thus, in both his existential Marxism of the 1940s and his heroic liberalism of the 1950s, Merleau-Ponty called for a politics that would allow space for otherness and ambiguity and would facilitate plurality rather than oneness.

Bibliography

WORKS BY MERLEAU-PONTY

Les Aventures de la dialectique. Paris, 1955. Translated by J. Bien as *Adventures of the Dialectic.* Evanston, IL, 1973.

Humanisme et terreur. Paris, 1947. Translated by J. O'Neill as *Humanism and Terror.* Boston, 1969.

Sens et non-sens. Paris, 1948. Translated by H. L. Dreyfus and P. A. Dreyfus as *Sense and Non-Sense.* Evanston, IL, 1964.

Signes. Paris, 1960. Translated by R. McCleary as *Signs.* Evanston, IL, 1964.

WORKS ON MERLEAU-PONTY

Cooper, B. *Merleau-Ponty and Marxism: From Terror to Reform.* Toronto, 1979.

Kruks, S. *The Political Philosophy of Merleau-Ponty.* Atlantic Highlands, NJ, 1980.

Whiteside, K. H. *Merleau-Ponty and the Foundation of an Existential Politics.* Princeton, NJ, 1988.

SONIA KRUKS

METAPHOR. Metaphors have an emotive force and aesthetic dimension that have long been recognized. What has made metaphor so compelling to contemporary philosophers, however, has been its importance to cognition. AESTHETICS [S] and PHILOSOPHY OF RELIGION [S] are no longer the sole province of the study of metaphor. Instead, most of the research is located in PHILOSOPHY OF LANGUAGE, PHILOSOPHY OF SCIENCE, and COGNITIVE SCIENCE [S]. The ubiquity of metaphor and its contribution to all forms of discourse, the apparent anomaly of metaphor in light of standard accounts of language, and the increased interest by philosophers to provide theories for natural (rather than formal or artificial) languages have made an account of metaphor an important criterion of adequacy for theories of language. The limits of literality have similarly been felt in accounts of science and cognition. Max BLACK's [1] (1962) seminal work connecting the use of scientific models to metaphors opened an area of inquiry now pursued by psychologists and cognitive scientists as well as philosophers of science. Some philosophers join questions of the role of metaphor in science to debates concerning scientific realism (Boyd, 1979; Hesse, 1970). The work emanating from theories of language and theories of science and cognition converge in concerns about meaning change, computer modeling of discovery processes, linguistic competencies, creativity, and religious discourse (Soskice, 1985).

While many questions remain, a few issues have been settled. The view of metaphor as an isolated word or phrase that is an occasional, unsystematic, and deviant phenomenon in language valued for its rhetorical force but disdained for its ability to mislead or be used in place of proper argument has been challenged. Metaphors have come to be understood as syntactically complex (Black, 1962; Tirrell, 1991) attributions that may or may not be grammatically deviant (Stern, 1985). In the tradition of I. A. Richards (1936) and Black, metaphors are generally taken to implicate entire conceptual domains or semantic fields (Kittay, 1987) through which a metaphor is interpreted, extended, and even systematically integrated into the language (Lakoff & Johnson, 1980). They either exploit some similarity between the metaphorically used term (the vehicle or source) and the concept spoken of (the topic or target) or create or intimate a similarity. While the similarity appealed to in earlier discussions pertained to intrinsic properties or properties associated with vehicle and topic, similarity has increasingly come to mean a relational or structural similarity—akin to models and analogies—between the contexts or domains (Black, 1962; GOODMAN [3; S], 1968) implicated in the metaphor.

While earlier debates concerned metaphor's cognitive value, current debates accept its cognitive function and ask if this function is properly assigned to metaphoric meaning and whether it is a distinctive form of cognition not reducible to other forms such as the capacity to recognize similarity and make comparisons. The outcome of the debate is important to the nature of language, of thought, and of epistemic enterprises such as science. If metaphors have meaning, then a theory of language must explain how such meaning is determined, and any account of mind in which linguistic capacity plays a central role for cognition must similarly explain how cognitive faculties make use of, and make possible, metaphorical thought. Similarly, if the use of metaphorical language in knowledge domains such as science is not reducible to literal language, then we need metaphor in order to understand and explain what is knowable. Furthermore, if we need metaphor to access scientific knowledge, as well as for aesthetic or evocative purposes, then the domains such as art and religion may be more akin to science—or related in more interesting ways—than we have presumed (Fleischacker, 1994). But if metaphors perform their cognitive function without generating a distinctive meaning, then theories of language that are based on literal language suffice; metaphoric contributions to cognition are assimilable to other, already understood or accepted cognitive abilities; the cognitive role of metaphor would be valuable only as heuristic (although, in the case of combinatorially complex problems, the heuristic contribution of metaphor itself may be irreplaceable), and we maintain a clear delineation between the scientific and the poetic.

The position propounding metaphoric meaning and the cognitive irreducibility of metaphor was staked out by Black and has been buttressed by arguments and evidence gathered by philosophers of science, cognitive psychologists, philosophers of language, and linguists. However, the parsimony of the opposing position, and its elegant articulation by Donald DAVIDSON (1978; [S]), continues to make it attractive, despite the counterintuitive claim that metaphors have no meaning and the weighty evidence of metaphor's importance in all cognitive endeavors.

Philosophers claiming that metaphors have meaning generally begin by accepting some version of the interaction theory of metaphor (*see* METAPHOR [5], for a summary of theories of metaphor) but have utilized the resources of many different semantic theories (e.g., possible-world semantics [Bergman, 1982; Hintikka & Sandu, 1994], semantic-field theory [Kittay, 1987], cognitive semantics [Gibbs, 1994; Lakoff & Johnson, 1980; Sweetser, 1990], a componential semantics [Levin, 1977], a Wittgensteinian semantic, and David Kaplan's semantics for demonstratives [Stern, 1985]). Some use speech-act theory, claiming that metaphors are a feature of speaker meaning rather than sentence meaning (Searle, 1981) or that metaphors are, in the end, elliptical similes after all (Fogelin, 1988).

Newer comparison theories, versions of the theory that metaphors are elliptic similes or implicit comparisons and so do not have a distinctive meaning, explore the notion of figurative rather than literal similarity (Glucks & Keysar, 1990; Ortony, 1979). Some of these theories offer a causal theory, opposing it to a semantic theory, claiming that metaphors cause us to make comparison by "intimating similarities" and have a causal effect of creating intimacy among speaker and listener (Cohen, 1978; Cooper, 1986). Questions remain concerning the relation between metaphor and literal language (e.g., Can the distinction be drawn in a clear fashion? Is the interpretative process the same or different? Is language originally metaphorical or literal?) and other nonliteral languages (see Hintikka & Sandu, 1994; Jakobson, 1960).

The importance of metaphor in science was stressed by Mary Hesse (1970), who developed the understandings of metaphors as systematic analogies in which the "neutral"—that is, unexplored analogical relations—provide a distinctive source for predictive claims. Dedre Gentner (1982), a cognitive psychologist, along with her associates has identified features, such as systematicity and higher-order relations, that make some metaphors more productive for cognitive purposes than others.

Noting the affinity between metaphor and analogy has permitted a number of researchers in philosophy and psychology to make headway with computational approaches to metaphor—a promising tool for testing theories of metaphor and for understanding the extent to which accounts of metaphor are amenable to formal and precise accounts (Holyoak & Thagard, 1989; Steinhart & Kittay, 1994). Making use of advances in our understanding of metaphor, theorists have explored the role of metaphor in creativity, in language acquisition and concept formation, and in both the consolidation and the breakdown of habituated patterns of thought such as cultural prejudice. These latter developments (which have especially been taken up by feminist philosophers and other social critics) bring the question of the cognitive role of metaphor full circle, reconnecting it to its rhetorical force.

Bibliography

Bergman, M. "Metaphorical Assertions," *Philosophical Review*, Vol. 91 (1982), 229–45.

Black, M., ed. *Models and Metaphors*. Ithaca, NY, 1962.

Boyd, R. "Metaphor and Theory Change: What Is 'Metaphor' a Metaphor For?" in A. Ortomy, ed., *Metaphor and Thought* (Cambridge, 1979).

Cohen, T. "Metaphor and the Cultivation of Intimacy," *Critical Inquiry*, Vol. 5 (1978), 3–12.

Cooper, D. *Metaphor*. Oxford, 1986.

Davidson, D. "What Metaphors Mean," in S. Sacks, ed., *On Metaphor* (Chicago, 1978).

Fleischacker, S. "Frustrated Contracts, Poetry, and Truth," *Raritan,* Vol. 13, No. 4 (Spring 1994), 47–70.

Fogelin, R. *Figuratively Speaking.* New Haven, 1988.

Gentner, D. "Are Scientific Analogies Metaphors?" in D. S. Maill, ed., *Metaphor: Problems and Perspectives* (New York, 1982).

Gibbs, R. *The Poetics of Mind: Figurative Thought, Language, and Understanding.* Cambridge, 1994.

Goodman, N. *Languages of Art.* Indianapolis, 1968.

Glucksberg, S., and B. Keysar. "Understanding Metaphorical Comparisons: Beyond Similarity," *Psychological Review,* Vol. 97 (1990), 3–18.

Hesse, M. *Models and Analogies in Science.* Notre Dame, IN, 1970.

Hintikka, J., and G. Sandu. "Metaphor and Other Kinds of Nonliteral Language," in J. Hintikka, ed., *Aspects of Metaphor* (Dordrecht, 1994).

Holyoak, K. J., and P. Thagard. "Analogical Mapping by Constraint Satisfaction," *Cognitive Science,* Vol. 13 (1989), 295–355.

Jakobson, R. "Closing Statement: Linguistics and Poetry," in T. A. Sebeok, ed., *Style in Language* (Cambridge, MA, 1960).

Kittay, E. F. *Metaphor: Its Cognitive Force and Linguistic Structure.* Oxford, 1987.

Lakoff, G., and M. Johnson. *Metaphors We Live By.* Chicago, 1980.

Levin, S. R. *The Semantics of Metaphor.* Baltimore, 1977.

Ortony, A. "The Role of Similarity in Similes and Metaphors," in A. Ortony, ed., *Metaphor and Thought* (Cambridge, 1979).

Richards, I. A. *The Philosophy of Rhetoric.* Oxford, 1936.

Searle, J. "Metaphor," in M. Johnson, ed., *Philosophical Perspectives on Metaphor* (Minneapolis, 1981).

Soskice, J. M. *Metaphor and Religious Language.* Oxford, 1985.

Steinhart, E., and E. F. Kittay. "Generating Metaphors from Networks: A Formal Interpretation of the Semantic Field Theory of Metaphor," in J. Hintikka, ed., *Aspects of Metaphor* (Dordrecht, 1994).

Stern, J. "Metaphor as Demonstrative," *Journal of Philosophy,* Vol. 82 (1985), 677–710.

Sweetser, E. *From Etymology to Pragmatics: The Body-Mind Metaphor in Semantic Structure and Semantic.* Cambridge, 1990.

Tirrell, L. "Reductive and Nonreductive Simile Theories of Metaphor," *Journal of Philosophy,* Vol. 88 (1991), 337–58.

EVA F. KITTAY

METAPHOR IN RICOEUR. *See:* RICOEUR, PAUL [S]

METAPHYSICS. The period since 1960 has featured a great deal of work on issues in METAPHYSICS [5]. Much of this work is best considered under more specific headings such as PHILOSOPHY OF MIND, ACTION THEORY, PHILOSOPHY OF LANGUAGE, PHILOSOPHY OF MATHEMATICS, PHILOSOPHY OF SCIENCE [S], and metaethics. Hence, such vital topics as the MIND–BODY PROBLEM [5], PERSONAL IDENTITY [6; S], personal FREEDOM [3], the theory of TRUTH [S], the nature of mathematical truth and existence, DETERMINISM [2], CAUSATION [2; S], the nature of theoretical entities, and the existence and nature of moral facts will be set aside. Furthermore, limitations of space exclude consideration of several other important topics such as the debate between realists and antirealists (*see* REALISM/ANTIREALISM [S]).

The period under review has included a number of surprising developments in metaphysics. The most general and important is the restoration of metaphysics itself to its historically central position in philosophy. It is no exaggeration to say that 'metaphysics' was a term of derision for most of the first half of the century and that even in 1960 metaphysics was often either regarded as nonsense or viewed with great suspicion. By 1990 this legacy of POSITIVISM [6] had largely disappeared. One reason is that a number of philosophers produced work that undeniably was metaphysics but, just as undeniably, was meaningful, lucid, rigorous, and important. Three closely related and central topics arguably constitute the most significant development in metaphysics since 1960.

Perhaps the most striking of the three is the rehabilitation of Aristotelian essentialism, initiated prominently by Ruth Barcan MARCUS and Saul KRIPKE [S]. The doctrine of essentialism holds that some things have nontrivial essential (or necessary) properties—that they could not exist without having those properties. For example, an essentialist might hold that any specific dog is necessarily a mammal. It is important to distinguish this from the claim that it is necessary that all dogs are mammals. For that claim could still be true even if all the actual dogs had been ducks and hence not mammals. Since in that circumstance they would not be dogs, their nonmammality would not threaten the necessity of all dogs' being mammals. The existence of such nontrivial essential properties would apparently undercut the common assumption that knowledge of necessity cannot be empirical. The effort to rehabilitate essentialism was resisted by many, notably and influentially by Willard Van Orman QUINE [7; S].

The discussion of essentialism was part of a surge of interest in all aspects of modality, including purely logical and semantic topics as well as philosophical. Quine's suspicions about essentialism partly reflected a more general worry that the very concept of necessity was hopelessly obscure, and much effort was expended in trying to provide the concept with clear philosophical foundations. Many hoped to achieve this by appealing to the Leibnizian notion of POSSIBLE WORLDS [S]. Some sought to analyze necessity (roughly, as truth in all possible worlds). Others attempted no analysis but hoped nevertheless to illuminate the notion by appealing to worlds. Several ontologically different conceptions of possible worlds emerged.

These included: worlds as (at least partly) concrete entities, like our own universe: worlds as idealized linguistic or quasi-linguistic entities; worlds as special states of affairs or propositions; and worlds as mere metaphor. Key contributors to the foundational discussion included Robert Merrihew Adams, Roderick CHISHOLM [S], Kit Fine, David Kaplan, David Lewis, Alvin Plantinga, Arthur N. PRIOR [S], and Peter van Inwagen (in addition to Kripke, Marcus, and Quine).

Many philosophers, notably Jaakko Hintikka and Robert Stalnaker, used possible worlds in treating a variety of other topics. Examples include the semantics of counterfactual CONDITIONALS [S] and the analysis of dispositionality, theories of PROPOSITIONAL ATTITUDES [S], especially belief, and even the analysis of such notions as rationality and obligation. Although possible worlds became widely accepted, partly as a result of their seeming success in these sorts of projects, a fair amount of skepticism has persisted, even among those who do not find the notion of necessity obscure.

The surge of interest in MODALITY [S] may be seen as reflecting the decline of a certain metaphysical and methodological dogma that was another legacy of positivism. In its metaphysical aspect the dogma asserts the obscurity of intensional notions as compared with extensional. Methodologically, it counsels us to work as much as possible in strictly extensional terms. Modality was a prime target of the dogma because it did not seem clearly amenable to a fully extensional treatment. (For example, it has been claimed that the substitution of coreferential expressions in modal contexts does not always preserve truth value.)

But another main target of the dogma is intensional entities—for example, properties. They are intensional in the sense that distinct properties may have the same 'extension', that is, exactly the same instances. This is in sharp contrast with sets, no two of which may have just the same members. So, champions of the dogma of extensionalism, in particular Quine, urged that if abstract entities are to be tolerated at all, sets should be preferred over properties. The period witnessed a good deal of ingenious work in which various notions were held to be reducible to set-theoretic constructions. But the growing respectability of modality loosened the grip of extensionalism. This made the philosophical world safe for a revival of Platonism, especially concerning properties, relations, and propositions (*see* PLATO [6; S]). Of course, Platonism was never really dead. Many leading philosophers—for example, Chisholm—did not embrace nominalism or even extensionalism. The revival consisted in a new willingness of many nominalists to take a fresh look at Platonistic positions, and in the emergence of defenses of PROPERTIES [S] (PUTNAM, 1970 [S]) and theories of properties (Bealer, 1982). Property theories quickly found promising applications in such areas as natural-language semantics.

The decline of extensionalism has also had significant effects in other areas of metaphysics. (For example, it seems indirectly implicated in a revived interest in mind–body dualism.) But extensionalism still has able defenders—an obituary is premature.

(SEE ALSO: *Colors; Constructivism; Determinism and Freedom; Event Theory; Extrinsic and Intrinsic Properties; Identity; Mereology; Nonexistent Object; Persistence; Platonism, Mathematical; Projectivism;* and *Time, Being, and Becoming* [S])

Bibliography

Bealer, G. *Quality and Concept.* Oxford, 1982.

French, P. A., T. E. Uehling, Jr., and H. K. Wettstein, eds. *Studies in Essentialism,* Midwest Studies in Philosophy, Vol. 11. Minneapolis, 1986.

Kripke, S. A. *Naming and Necessity.* Cambridge, MA, 1972.

Lewis, D. *On the Plurality of Worlds.* Oxford, 1986.

Marcus, R. B. *Modalities.* Oxford, 1993.

Putnam, H. "On Properties," in N. Rescher, ed., *Essays in Honor of Carl G. Hempel* (Dordrecht, 1970).

Quine, W. V. O. *Word and Object.* Cambridge, MA, 1960.

MICHAEL JUBIEN

METAPHYSICS, OVERCOMING OF. *Überwindung der Metaphysik* is a phrase that begins to appear in HEIDEGGER'S [3; S] writing about 1936. Between his 1929 Freiburg inaugural address "What Is Metaphysics?" and his 1935 Freiburg lecture course published as *Introduction to Metaphysics,* Heidegger was ready to speak of his own work as metaphysical in character, and his courses from those years undertook many positive appropriations of classical metaphysical works from ARISTOTLE [1; S] to SCHELLING [7]. He began to refer to the overcoming of metaphysics (the very words that Rudolf CARNAP [2; S] had used to describe his logical-positive program) in connection with his new appraisal of the history of thought and the "history of being." The essay "Überwindung der Metaphysik," begun in 1936 and published in *Vorträge und Aufsätze* (1954), is deeply connected with the multivolume text of Heidegger's lectures on NIETZSCHE [5; S], begun in 1936, and with the more esoteric works of that period. Heidegger had come to see a unitary history of Western thought and life, determined profoundly by the Platonic definitions of the forms, the entities that were to constitute the truth of entities as a whole. All philosophy, up to German idealism, worked out all the possibilities for science and life that were given while we still remained under the aegis of ancient ontology. Metaphysics was that framework that posited the truth of entities as a whole, God as the creator, and man as the being whose life was to be guided by truth. HEGEL [3; S] brought metaphysics to its most complete form, and then with Nietzsche everything was turned upside down: God is dead, truth is error, and man is a thing that is to be overcome. Heidegger's lectures and esoteric treatises granted Nietzsche's point that traditional metaphysics was nihilistic in its denial of this world yet argued that Nietzsche's own reversal of metaphysics remained metaphysical, his indictment of NIHILISM [5] still nihilistic.

That metaphysics is "overcome" does not, for Heidegger, mean that it is finished as a force in history. Especially in the 1940s and 1950s he insisted that modern science and technology are the same as metaphysics—the truth about beings as a whole—and are now unfolding their power globally. "Overcoming" does not mean a historical surpassing of which we are now capable, the way we might flatter ourselves at having overcome superstition. Heidegger's point reflects the subtle view he always had of time and history: the past is never merely passed or surpassed, not even "sublated" (*aufgehoben*) in the sense of the Hegelian dialectic; it is present and even comes to us as an advent, a future. The insistent framework, from Plato to technology, will shape man in accord with truth. But this insistence is driven by the repression of nontruth, denying the darkness and mystery of man's being, for indeed we surpass beings both toward being and toward nonbeing. Overcoming metaphysics, then, can be nothing but an awakening to it, to the actual constitution of its insistence.

Bibliography

Heidegger, M. *Nietzsche.* 2 vols. Pfullingen, 1961. Translated by D. Krell and F. Capuzzi as *Nietzsche.* 4 vols. New York, 1979–87.

———. *Introduction to Metaphysics,* trans. R. Manheim. Garden City, NY, 1961.

———. *The End of Philosophy,* trans. J. Stambaugh. New York, 1973.

GRAEME NICHOLSON

METAPHYSICS, OVERCOMING OF, IN DERRIDA. Insofar as it makes sense to talk of overcoming metaphysics in relation to DERRIDA [S], one should think less of a transgressive gesture that the philosopher performs and more of thinkers in our epoch responding to the condition that Derrida calls the *clôture* (closure) of philosophy. Derrida employed this phrase to avoid the problems of Heidegger's discussion of the "end of philosophy," which allegedly conveys the sense that Western philosophy completes itself when its unity becomes apparent (*see* METAPHYSICS, OVERCOMING OF [S]). The idea of the closure of philosophy, by contrast, recognizes the fissures that break through the limits of philosophy while at the same time acknowledging philosophy's capacity to extend those limits.

From the perspective of DECONSTRUCTION [S] the idea of being outside metaphysics is contradictory because it remains committed to the metaphysical opposition between an inside and an outside. Deconstructive double reading avoids this dilemma by finding within metaphysical texts a rupture that transcends metaphysics while at the same time recognizing that texts that claim to surpass metaphysics are never entirely free of it. In a sense deconstruction's response to the overcoming of metaphysics is to say that there never was metaphysics in the sense imagined.

Bibliography

Critchley, S. "The Problem of Closure in Derrida," in *The Ethics of Deconstruction.* Oxford, 1992.

Derrida, J. *L'Écriture et la différence.* Paris, 1967. Translated by A. Bass as *Writing and Difference.* Chicago, 1978.

ROBERT BERNASCONI

MILL, JOHN STUART. The publication of the *Collected Works* of John Stuart Mill, in thirty-three volumes (1963–91), has provided a mine of information about Mill's life and thought and will do so for years to come. The six volumes of letters and many volumes of essays, speeches, and journals show that most of his writing was not on narrowly philosophical topics. Much of it was on concrete political issues of his day.

The Mill Newsletter began publication in 1965 under the editorship of John M. Robson. It carried long and short articles, news of new and forthcoming books and articles, and a continuing bibliography of works on Mill. In 1989 it merged with *The Bentham Newsletter* to become *Utilitas: A Journal of Utilitarian Studies.* It has provided a vehicle for Mill scholarship including but not limited to his philosophy.

The most widely read philosophical works of John Stuart MILL [5] continue to be his essays *Utilitarianism* and *On Liberty.* Debates concerning UTILITARIANISM [8] in the second half of the twentieth century, such as the distinction between act utilitarianism and rule utilitarianism and the plausibility of each, have included controversies on the interpretation and plausibility of Mill's position on these issues. Also, those attacking or defending LIBERALISM [4; S] have inevitably included references to Mill's essay as one of the most representative statements of the liberal position. With the development of FEMINIST PHILOSOPHY [S] his essay *The Subjection of Women* has also received renewed attention as an early feminist statement, sometimes dismissed as the "liberal feminist" position but sometimes defended against its critics.

Two controversial topics in Mill's utilitarianism continue to receive attention: his distinction between pleasures on grounds of superiority or inferiority of quality as well as quantity and his alleged "proof" of the principle of utility. In the early part of the twentieth century, the first of these was generally regarded as either inconsistent with his HEDONISM [3] or as nonsense, and the second was regarded as a classic case of fallacious reasoning. In the second half of the twentieth century, these have been defended, although not always in the same ways. Some "friends" of Mill have tried to reduce the distinction of qualities to a quantitative distinction; others have insisted that Mill is correct in recognizing the phenomenal diversity of pleasurable experiences; but even among the latter there is disagreement about whether Mill is correct in correlating the distinction to the distinctively human (as opposed to nonhuman animal) faculties and whether qualitatively distinct pleasures are consistently preferred by those who are qualified by experiences of both.

Mill's "proof" has been the subject of numerous interpretations and controversy. It is no longer dismissed as a collection of fallacies, but whether it is a sound argument with plausible assumptions is still a matter of great debate.

The consistency between Mill's apparently hedonistic utilitarianism and his essay *On Liberty* has been another topic of extensive discussion. Here again the discussion has been more friendly to Mill, but with differences in interpretation. Some commentators have claimed consistency for him by a reinterpretation of his utilitarianism to make it nonhedonistic, with a conception of happiness that essentially involves the free exercise of rational capacities. Others have seen in Mill's psychological assumptions, with a complex phenomenal account of pleasure including "higher" and "lower" and the necessity for self-development as a necessary condition for the higher pleasures, a basis for consistency which remains hedonistic.

Whether Mill was a rule utilitarian was one of the questions that generated the distinction between act utilitarianism and rule utilitarianism. The essay by J. O. Urmson (1953) interpreting Mill as a rule utilitarian has been challenged and supported by citations both pro and con from Mill texts. A middle position, argued by Fred R. Berger (1984) and others, is that Mill endorsed a "strategy" for achieving the greatest happiness that was ostensibly rule utilitarian but that he seemed to think that if all hidden utilities were taken into consideration there would be no conflict between the two positions. Acts that violate useful rules weaken the rules and undermine the rule-abiding character of the agent. Acts that form part of a collection of acts that have bad consequences can theoretically be assigned a fraction of those bad consequences. Whether these moves are adequate to remove the conflict is suspect.

In chapter 5 of *Utilitarianism* Mill has a theory of rights correlative to some but not all morally significant actions, and he restricts the morally obligatory to those actions for which punishment has utility; in *August Comte and Positivism* (in *Collected Works,* Vol. 10:337–39) he clearly states a theory of morally meritorious action that goes beyond what is morally required. These would indicate that Mill's moral theory has a structure that is more complicated than any simple act- or rule-formulation.

Mill's *On Liberty* attempts to distinguish between conduct that concerns others and conduct that concerns only oneself. Strictly construed, very little conduct concerns only oneself. Studies of *On Liberty* by C. L. Ten (1980), John Gray (1983), and J. C. Rees (1985) have reinterpreted the distinction in terms of concerning the "interests" of self or others. Mill is seen to be holding the view that there is a right to LIBERTY [S] that is a right to autonomy. There is controversy, however, over the substance of this right and also over the "harm principle" that limits it.

Mill's contribution to the development of psychological theory and the applications of his theory in classical economics and in moral philosophy is the subject of an important study by Fred Wilson (1990).

Bibliography

Berger, F. R. *Happiness, Justice, and Freedom: The Moral and Political Philosophy of John Stuart Mill.* Toronto, 1982.

Donner, W. *The Liberal Self: John Stuart Mill's Moral and Political Philosophy.* Ithaca, NY, 1991.

Edwards, R. B. *Pleasures and Pains: A Theory of Qualitative Hedonism.* Ithaca, NY, 1979.

Gray, J. *Mill on Liberty: A Defence.* London, 1983.

Laine, M. *Bibliography of Works on John Stuart Mill.* Toronto, 1982.

Lyons, D. "Mill's Theory of Morality," *Noûs,* Vol. 10 (1976), 101–20.

———. "Liberty and Harm to Others," in W. E. Cooper, K. Nielsen, and S. C. Patten, eds., *New Essays on John Stuart Mill and Utilitarianism* (Guelph, Ont., 1979).

McCloskey, H. J. *John Stuart Mill: A Critical Study.* London, 1971.

Mill, J. S. *Collected Works of John Stuart Mill,* 33 vols. Toronto, 1933–91.

The Mill Newsletter, Vols. 1–23 (1965–89).

Rees, J. C. *John Stuart Mill's "On Liberty."* Oxford, 1985.

Ryan, A. *John Stuart Mill.* New York, 1970.

———. *J. S. Mill.* London, 1974.

Skorupski, J. *John Stuart Mill.* London, 1989.

Ten, C. L. *Mill on Liberty.* Oxford, 1980.

Urmson, J. O. "The Interpretation of the Moral Philosophy of J. S. Mill," *Philosophical Quarterly,* Vol. 3 (1953), 33–39.

Utilitas, Vol. 1– (1989–).

West, H. R. "Mill's "Proof" of the Principle of Utility," in H. B. Miller and W. Williams, eds., *The Limits of Utilitarianism* (Minneapolis, 1982).

Wilson, F. *Psychological Analysis and the Philosophy of John Stuart Mill.* Toronto, 1990.

HENRY R. WEST

MODALITY, PHILOSOPHY AND METAPHYSICS OF. This has received considerable attention in METAPHYSICS [5; S] and other areas of philosophy since the 1950s. During this period the notion has flourished, despite some determined resistance. This entry will first treat the foundations of modality, including modal skepticism, and then two specific issues important to those who accept modal notions. The discussion will be confined to logical modality—that is, to necessity and possibility as (supposed) modes of truth and predication. There will be no specific discussion of MODAL LOGIC [S] or its semantics.

Consider the sentence

(1) Necessarily, nine is odd.

What does it mean? Clarence Irving LEWIS [4], a pioneer of modal logic, would likely have taken its meaning as captured by

(2) "Nine is odd" is analytically true.

where "analytically true" means true in virtue of the meanings of the terms it contains. Willard Van Orman QUINE [7; S], a persistent and important critic of modal notions, has at least two objections (Quine, 1960). First, (2), unlike (1), does not refer to the number nine but rather to the sentence "Nine is odd." So, it is an unlikely candidate for making clear sense of (1). Second, although Quine would not automatically object to necessity taken as a predicate of sentences (provided it expressed a coherent concept), he is famous for having questioned the coherence of the notion of ANALYTICITY [S].

In (1) "necessarily" apparently attaches to a complete sentence to form a new sentence. If so, it functions as what logicians call an operator, like the negation operator of first-order logic. But such operators may also attach to open formulas. So, a modal logic built on this model will contain analogues of sentences like

(3) Something is necessarily odd.

We will see below that Quine would find any such account obscure and unacceptable. But the modern development of quantified modal logic, initiated in the work of Ruth Barcan MARCUS [S], has favored precisely this approach. And the development of formal semantics for such systems, notably in the (independent) work of Stig Kanger, Saul KRIPKE [S], and Jaakko Hintikka, convincingly vitiates any charge of formal obscurity or incoherence. If modality is obscure or incoherent, it is so for philosophical reasons, perhaps of the sort Quine offered in attacking analyticity. But recent discussion of necessity, following Kripke, has sharply distinguished necessity from analyticity.

To say that a sentence expresses a necessary truth is to say that what it expresses could not have failed to be true. To say that a sentence is analytically true is to say that it is true solely in virtue of the meanings of the words it contains. These are clearly different notions. A common tendency to confuse them undoubtedly stemmed from the conviction that, even if they were different, they were still coextensive. But, having called attention to the confusion, Kripke (1972) argued that various sentences that are not analytically true nevertheless express necessary truths.

Saying that necessary truths are those that could not have failed to be true gives, not so much a helpful characterization of necessity, as a mere paraphrase of 'necessary'. We still want to know what the necessity of a truth consists in—that is, what insulates it from possible falsity. The need for a clear characterization intensified as more philosophers came to believe that some nontrivial truths really are necessary and as modal skeptics continued to press charges of obscurity or incoherence.

One approach to this foundational problem would be to provide an explicit analysis of the modal notions using more basic concepts that may independently be held to be clear and coherent. Another would be to claim that the notions of necessity and possibility are primitive—that there are no more fundamental concepts with which to analyze them. Certainly this approach would not convert many skeptics unless accompanied by some new and convincing illumination of the modal notions.

An important foundational first step is to distinguish logical, or what is sometimes called metaphysical, modality from that reflected in other modal idioms, especially epistemic and physical. Such modal concepts often concern what is necessary (or possible) given that certain conditions hold. In contrast, metaphysical necessity is the notion of what is necessary, period. If, say, physical necessity is conceived as what is necessary given the actual laws of physics, then physical necessity has been characterized in terms of metaphysical necessity, for questions of physical necessity are reduced to questions of the metaphysical necessity of conditional statements.

Discussion of modal foundations has almost always involved the notion of POSSIBLE WORLD(S) [S]. (In fact, a fascination with worlds has sometimes obscured the foundational problem, leaving it addressed only indirectly or not at all.) A proposition is held to be necessary if it is true at all (relevant) worlds; a proposition is possible if it is true at some world or other. These formulations may be taken variously: as genuine analyses of the modal notions; as important characterizations of the modal notions; or merely as providing a picturesque metaphor, helpful in thinking about modality. The recent interest in possible worlds is, of course, partly inspired by LEIBNIZ [4; S] but also by formal developments in the semantics of quantified modal systems.

Proponents of worlds have offered several different conceptions falling into two major kinds that may (somewhat misleadingly) be called concrete and abstract. Concrete worlds are entities like the actual physical world around us but causally isolated from the actual world and from each other. (There is room here for partly or entirely nonphysical worlds and perhaps also for an entirely empty world.) Concrete worlds are existing entities, and each is held to be actual with respect to itself. Because these worlds do not overlap, no entity existing in any world also exists in any other world. Hence, questions about what is possible or necessary for a given individual are answered by appeal to a counterpart relation that may hold between pairs of individuals in different worlds. Something is possible for a given individual if it is true at some world of a counterpart of that individual. Theories of modality along these lines are called counterpart theories. Such theories conform to possibilism—the view that there truly are merely possible objects. (Actualism is the denial of possibilism.) The originator and leading proponent of this conception of modality is David Lewis (1986). For Lewis modal operators are quantifiers over possible worlds. So, a noniterated assertion of necessity is simply an assertion that a certain nonmodal state of affairs holds at all possible worlds. Thus, it is natural to see counterpart theories as offering an analysis of modality. But it has been argued that, even if there are other isolated concrete worlds, it is difficult to see how goings on there can be relevant to modal questions here (Jubien, 1988).

There are several treatments of worlds as abstract entities. For example, they have been taken to be entities of their own special kind (Davies, 1981); certain propositions (Prior & Fine, 1976); certain states of affairs (Plantinga, 1974); and certain sets of propositions (Adams, 1974). Such treatments are often similar in structure and spirit and share certain virtues and (alleged) vices.

Robert Adams (1974) takes worlds to be maximal consistent sets of propositions. But consistency is explicitly understood in terms of the possible (joint) truth of propositions. So the treatment cannot support an analysis of possibility in terms of worlds. Its virtue lies in providing a precise concept for the often vaguely conceived notion of possible world and thereby enhancing whatever illumination worlds can provide for modality in general. It has, however, been argued that this and other maximality-driven accounts produce paradox (Jubien, 1988).

A crucial issue for those who accept modal notions is whether contingent entities like people or physical objects have nontrivial essential properties, properties that they could not have failed to have. The leading proponent of an affirmative answer has been Kripke, and many have been converted to his position.

Essentialism is often characterized as the acceptance of (nontrivial) *de re* necessities, in which a property is held to be necessarily instantiated by a thing (or a necessary property is held to be instantiated). In ordinary English,

(4) Necessarily, Cicero is human.

and

(5) Cicero is necessarily human.

are perhaps not normally taken as making distinct assertions. But if (5) is taken to entail

(6) Something is necessarily human.

then the modality is genuinely *de re* and goes beyond the merely *de dicto* sense in which (4) may be taken to entail "Necessarily, something is human" but not to entail (6).

Quine (1960) found the very notion of necessary properties nonsensical, arguing that any necessity or contingency in an attribution of a property to a thing must depend on how that thing is described, not on how the thing is, independent of any particular description. But Kripke (1972) insisted that this cannot be right. He urged, with respect to a variety of examples, that one simply cannot imagine the thing in question not having the property in question. Thus, one might ask whether we could imagine Cicero himself but without his being human. Whereas we find no difficulty imagining Cicero to fail of being an orator or being Roman, it seems much more difficult, if not impossible, to imagine him not being human.

It is vital that we assume for the sake of such thought experiments that the thing in question actually does have the property in question. The reason is that we are asking whether any of a thing's (actual) properties are essential. So, epistemic cases, in which we have been incorrect all along about the actual properties, are ruled out. (It is irrelevant that Cicero might prove to have been a robot or an extraterrestrial.) It is also vital that we take our inability to imagine something as good evidence of its impossibility.

Many who initially thought they could, for example, imagine Cicero not being human became persuaded that there is a better way to describe what they imagined, one that does not entail that Cicero is not necessarily human. It has been argued that, while such thought experiments do support nontrivial essentialism, they do not support necessity *de re,* and thus that there are really two doctrines where there is commonly thought to be one (Jubien, 1993).

A central question for essentialists is whether the essential properties of a thing include its 'haecceity' (or 'thisness'). Cicero's haecceity is the supposed property of being Cicero, a property that is normally taken to be primitive and nonqualitative. Such a property would also be an essence of Cicero. In possible-worlds terminology, an essence of a thing is an essential property that no other thing has in any world. But one may accept essences without accepting haecceities.

Defenders of haecceities, like Adams (1979), often make their case using an example borrowed from Max BLACK [1]. Here is one version. Imagine that the world consisted simply of two qualitatively indistinguishable globes. Then it seems that there must be another world that is qualitatively indistinguishable from the first but in which the positions of the globes are interchanged. It is hard to make sense of this intuitive possibility (or perhaps even of the initial idea that there are two globes rather than one) without thinking that there is some nonqualitative way in which the globes differ. So it has been held that they differ by having different haecceities, and haecceities have been held to provide the conceptual underpinning for all of the alternative possibilities for things.

One version of this view is that haecceities are needed to account for transworld identity and hence that any illuminating treatment of possibility in terms of possible worlds rests on the acceptance of haecceities. But Kripke (1972) emphatically denied that there is a problem of transworld identity in the first place. To think that there is would be to imagine that worlds are presented to us purely qualitatively and that we must somehow figure out whether a given individual exists in another world from the qualitative features displayed by individuals in that world. But Kripke would insist that we do not normally think of worlds in this way at all. We normally describe worlds partly in terms of specific individuals that they contain. Thus, we say, for example, "Consider a world in which Cicero is not an orator." Assuming we are right that there are such worlds, it is automatic that Cicero inhabits them, and there is no problem of checking the features of various individuals to determine which one is Cicero. For Kripke it is a matter of stipulation that Cicero inhabits these worlds, and this is quite independent of the matter of haecceities. Those who see a problem of transworld identification and invoke haecceities in order to solve it are very likely assuming that the role of worlds is to provide an analysis of the modal notions, an assumption that Kripke rejects.

Others have argued for different reasons that haecceities are not needed to make sense of genuine possibilities for things (CHISHOLM, 1986 [S]). It has also been argued that things have qualitative essences that, for example, support a distinction between the two-globe worlds but that no such property could serve as an essence of, say, Cicero (Jubien, 1993).

Obviously, there can be no problem of transworld identification in counterpart theories since it is impossible for an individual to inhabit different worlds. So the question of haecceitism must take a different form. For Lewis (1986) the key question is whether what an individual's otherwordly counterparts represent as possible for that individual depends strictly on qualitative features of those counterparts. He claims it does and considers himself an antihaecceitist on this basis.

Important contributors to the contemporary philosophical discussion of modality not mentioned above include David M. ARMSTRONG [S], Graeme Forbes, David Kaplan, Richard Montague, Hilary PUTNAM [S], Nathan Salmon, Brian Skyrms, Robert Stalnaker, and Peter van Inwagen.

Bibliography

Adams, R. M. "Theories of Actuality," *Noûs,* Vol. 8 (1974), 211–31.

———. "Primitive Thisness and Primitive Identity," *Journal of Philosophy,* Vol. 76 (1979), 5–26.

Chisholm, R. M. "Possibility without Haecceity," in P. A. French, T. E. Uehling, Jr., and H. K. Wettstein, eds., *Studies in Essentialism,* Midwest Studies in Philosophy, Vol. 11 (Minneapolis, 1986).

Davies, M. K. *Meaning, Quantification, Necessity: Themes in Philosophical Logic.* London, 1981.

Forbes, G. *The Metaphysics of Modality.* Oxford, 1985.

French, P. A., T. E. Uehling, Jr., and H. K. Wettstein, eds. *Studies in Essentialism,* Midwest Studies in Philosophy, Vol. 11. Minneapolis, 1986. A valuable collection.

Jubien, M. "Problems with Possible Worlds," in D. F. Austin, ed., *Philosophical Analysis* (Dordrecht, 1988).

———. *Ontology, Modality, and the Fallacy of Reference.* Cambridge, 1993.

Kripke, S. A. *Naming and Necessity.* Cambridge, MA, 1972.

Lewis, D. *On the Plurality of Worlds.* Oxford, 1986.

Marcus, R. B. *Modalities.* Oxford, 1993.

Plantinga, A. *The Nature of Necessity.* Oxford, 1974.

Prior, A. N., and K. Fine. *Worlds, Times, and Selves.* London, 1976.

Quine, W. V. O. *Word and Object.* Cambridge, MA, 1960.

MICHAEL JUBIEN

MODAL LOGIC. The main developments since 1960 fall mainly under four headings: (1) formal analysis of modal logic, (2) epistemic logic, (3) conditional logic, (4) dynamic logic, and (5) the PROVABILITY [S] interpretation of modal logic.

FORMAL DEVELOPMENTS

By 1960 a great many modal logics had been proposed. Thanks to the advent of possible worlds semantics a unified, systematic treatment became possible. The central concept was the normal modal logic, a logic in which all truth-functional tautologies and all instances of the so-called KRIPKE [S] schema $\Box(A \supset B) \supset (\Box A \supset \Box B)$ are valid and which respects the rules of modus ponens (if $A \supset B$ and A are valid, then so is B) and of necessitation (if A is valid, then so is $\Box A$). The 1970s saw a great number of formal results of an increasingly mathematical character. Particularly interesting from a philosophical point of view was the discovery, by Kit Fine and S. K. Thomason, independently, that the relational Kripke semantics has a certain limitation—there are normal modal logics incomplete with respect to that semantics.

EPISTEMIC LOGIC

In his book *Knowledge and Belief* (1962), Jaakko Hintikka proposed to give indexed modal operators epistemic or doxastic interpretations; that is, a box operator $\Box_i$ would be read as "the agent i knows that" or "the agent i believes that." One contentious topic was the status of this kind of logic: is it normative or descriptive or neither? Moreover, knowledge in Hintikka's sense implies various forms of omniscience. For example, is it reasonable that, as in Hintikka's system, agents should know all logically valid propositions or that they should know all logical consequences of their knowledge? Yet another topic was the so-called KK-thesis. Discussing the schemata $\Box_i A \supset \Box_i \Box_i A$ and $\neg\Box_i A \supset \Box_i \neg\Box_i A$, Hintikka felt the former ("positive introspection") should be regarded as valid, the latter ("negative introspection") not. In the theoretical computer science community, which became interested in epistemic logic in the 1980s, the general consensus, reached without much debate, is that both are valid.

In 1969 David Lewis introduced the concept of common knowledge, which has since become important not only in philosophical analysis but also in theoretical computer science and economics. A proposition A is common knowledge within a group of agents if and only if, for every number n and every choice $i_1, \ldots, i_n$ of agents in the group, $\Box_{i_1} \ldots \Box_{i_n}A$ obtains (that is, i_1 knows that ... i_n knows that A). It has been shown that common knowledge can make a crucial difference to problems concerning communication or other forms of rational action.

CONDITIONAL LOGIC

Toward the end of the 1960s, Robert C. Stalnaker and David Lewis, independently, presented logical analyses of conditional propositions, including counterfactuals ("if it were the case that A, then it would be the case that B" and "if it were the case that A, then it might be the case that B"). Both give a possible-worlds account according to which the truth of a conditional (of the kind in question) relative to a world depends on the truth of the consequent in one or several worlds selected from among those in which the antecedent is true (worlds in which the antecedent is true "under ideal circumstances," to use a phrase of Lennart Åqvist). Thus to determine, in a certain situation, the truth of the counterfactual proposition "If I had struck this match five seconds ago, it would have lighted" one has to consider, perhaps as a thought experiment, those situations which differ from the given situation *as little as possible except that* the match is struck; if it lights in those situations the counterfactual is true, otherwise it is not. The difficulty is to elucidate the expression "as little as possible except that."

Brian F. Chellas has shown that there is a close connection between Stalnaker's and Lewis's semantics and ordinary possible worlds semantics for modal logic; on Chellas's account "if it were the case that A, then it would be the case that B" can be read as "it is A-necessary that B"; and "if it were the case that A then it might be the case that B" can be read as "it is A-possible that B" (in symbols, $\Box_A B$ and $\Diamond_A B$, respectively). Chellas's reduction has the methodological advantage that it allows techniques of formal modal logic to bear on the formal problems of analyzing CONDITIONALS [S].

DYNAMIC LOGIC

In modal logic the only nonclassical operators are the box $\Box$ (the necessity operator), and the diamond $\Diamond$ (the possibility operator). Dynamic logic, created by Vaughan Pratt in the late 1970s, may be seen as a generalization over modal logic inasmuch as it postulates a set of terms such that for each term α there is one box operator and one diamond operator, for typographical reasons written as $[\alpha]$ and $<\alpha>$, respectively. Originally the intended interpretation of terms was as computer programs, but other interpretations are also possible, for example, as actions or events. If A is a formula then $[\alpha]A$ may be read as "after α it is always the case that A" and $<\alpha>A$ as "after α it is sometimes the case that A."

The interest of dynamic logic depends on the many operations on terms and formulas that are possible. For example, interpreting terms as actions, if α and β are actions, then $\alpha + \beta$ is the disjunctive action consisting in doing either α or β, and $\alpha;\beta$ is the composite action consisting in doing first α and then, without interruption, β. If α is an action, then α^* is the action consisting of doing α any finite number of times. If A is a proposition, then ?A is the action consisting in testing the truth of A; if A obtains, the answer is affirmative, if A is false there is no answer. It is worth noting that in Pratt's semantics $[\alpha + \beta]C \equiv ([\alpha]C \wedge [\beta]C)$ is generally valid but $[\alpha][\beta]C \equiv [\beta][\alpha]C$ is not.

The operations +, ; and * (sum, composition, and the Kleene star) are called the three regular operations. Much of the early interest in dynamic logic was due to the fact that important aspects of reasoning about actions could be formalized within the new language. For example, there is a sense in which commands like "if it is true that A then do α else do β" and "while it is true that A do α" can be rendered. From a philosophical point of view the importance lies in the fact that in dynamic logic and extensions of dynamic logic one is able to refer to and talk about actions directly.

OTHER DEVELOPMENTS

In a series of papers in the late 1960s and the early 1970s, Richard Montague undertook to apply the techniques achieved in the study of intensional logic to natural languages. Although this grandiose development falls outside this entry, it is worth noting that the Montague program may be seen as taking to an extreme but logical conclusion ideas originating at least in part in the analysis of modal logic.

(SEE ALSO: *Mathematical Logic,* and *Philosophical Logic* [S])

Bibliography

Guenthner, F., and D. M. Gabbay. *Handbook in Philosophical Logic,* Vol. 2. Dordrecht, 1984.

Fagin, R., J. Y. Halpern, Y. Moses, and M. Y. Vardi. *Reasoning about Knowledge.* Cambridge, MA, 1995.

Lenzen, W. *Recent Work in Epistemic Logic.* Amsterdam, 1978.

Lewis, D. *Counterfactuals.* Oxford, 1973.

Montague, R. *Formal Philosophy.* Edited by R. H. Thomason. New Haven, 1974.

KRISTER SEGERBERG

MODEL THEORY. Model theory began as a branch of mathematics, and its main advances between 1960 and 1995 lay in mathematics. But some aspects of model theory interested philosophers and linguists during this period, and by the 1990s it was also becoming an important tool in computer science.

Nonstandard analysis—invented by Abraham Robinson in 1960—is an application of model theory that uses the compactness theorem to add INFINITESIMALS [S] to the field of real numbers. One can then use these infinitesimals roughly as LEIBNIZ [4; S] intended; for example, one calculates a derivative as (almost) a ratio dy/dx of two infinitesimals dy and dx. In 1976 Jerome Keisler published an undergraduate textbook of calculus using nonstandard methods.

Though nonstandard analysis soon lost contact with the mainstream of model theory, it set a paradigm. Thus, one could apply model theory to branches of mathematics by identifying the first-order relations (i.e., those relations defined by first-order formulas) in certain structures, and then using the compactness theorem or other general theorems of model theory. Two remarkable successes along these lines were the proof by James Ax, Simon Kochen, and Yuri Ershov in 1965 of a number-theoretic conjecture of Emil Artin (so far as it is true), and Ehud Hrushovski's proof in 1993 of a diophantine conjecture of Serge Lang.

The 1960s saw an invasion of model theory by techniques from combinatorial and descriptive SET THEORY [S]. Set theorists realized that certain model-theoretic methods (ultraproducts and indiscernibles) yielded information about the set-theoretic universe and especially about the effects of large cardinals. In 1965 Michael Morley used indiscernibles to prove an old conjecture describing those first-order theories, which in some uncountable cardinality have only one model up to isomorphism.

Morley's work formed a new paradigm, in which model theorists classified first-order theories according to whether their models are chaotic or form a well-structured family. In 1982 Saharon Shelah proved that the class of all models of a complete theory in a countable first-order language is either highly structured, in the sense that one can catalogue the models by intuitively meaningful invariants, or hopelessly unstructured. This took Shelah some twelve years' work, during which he created stability theory. In the mid-1980s model theorists realized that stability theory is a model-theoretic analogue of algebraic geometry, and many links with algebraic geometry (particularly the theory of algebraic groups) came to light.

The period 1982–92 saw axiomatic descriptions of important classes of definable sets in algebraic geometry. One consequence was the creation (by Lou van den Dries, Anand Pillay, and Charles Steinhorn) of a new branch of function theory dealing with O-minimal fields, whose first-order relations resemble those of the field of real numbers.

Here we turn from mathematics to applications in philosophy and elsewhere.

Around 1990 several philosophers attacked what they took to be a consensus that logical truth means truth in all models, thinking of models as POSSIBLE WORLDS [S]. In fact there never was such a consensus. For first-order logic (though not in general) one can show by the completeness theorem that the logical truths are exactly the sentences true in all models; but as Georg Kreisel in 1969 and Willard Van Orman QUINE [7; S] in 1970 made clear, this argument does not involve possible worlds.

However, there are ways to represent possibility and other modalities in terms of models. During the 1950s several writers explored how one might axiomatize the notion that one structure is possible relative to another. Saul KRIPKE [S] gave in 1959 the formulation that came to be accepted: one considers a set of structures and a binary relation of possibility between them. In the model theory of MODAL LOGIC [5; S], a sentence 'Necessarily A' is true in a structure M if and only if A is true in all structures possible relative to M.

One can apply these notions to various kinds of possibility. An important example is TIME [8], where the structures possible relative to a structure M are those representing times later than M. During the 1970s Vaughan Pratt and others used similar ideas to represent the execution of computer programs through time. By the mid-1980s model-theoretic techniques appeared in the theory of processes in computer science. For example, the model-theoretic technique of back-and-forth, a device for comparing two structures by choosing elements alternately from the first and second structure, yielded the bisimulation test for comparing two processes.

In 1970 Richard Montague adapted the model theory of modal logic to formalize the SEMANTICS [7; S] of a fragment of English containing problematic expressions such as 'necessarily', 'believe that', 'wish to', and 'change'. This heroic effort created Montague semantics, a sophisticated application of models to the semantics of natural languages. In 1985 the generalized phrase structure grammar (GPSG) of Gerald Gazdar et al. used a modified form of Montague semantics as its semantic component. Nevertheless it became clear that language devices such as cross-reference between sentences need ideas that depart further from classical model theory. For example, the discourse representation theory of Irene Heim and Hans Kamp uses the notion of an element in a structure being accessible to an expression.

Another development was to stay with models in the classical sense, but to study properties definable in non-first-order languages. This work began within mathematics, but by 1990 it had moved completely to computer science. For example, one can represent a data base as a finite structure; then a query to the data base asks whether a certain formal sentence is true in the structure. Data-base queries often ask questions that have no first-order formalization, such as whether one element can be reached from another in a finite number of steps. The model-theoretic technique of back-and-forth has proved invaluable for measuring the expressive power of data-base query languages.

(SEE ALSO: *Mathematical Logic* [S])

Bibliography

Hodges, W. A. *Model Theory.* Cambridge, 1993.

van Benthem, J. *A Manual of Intensional Logic.* 2d ed. Stanford, CA, 1988.

WILFRID A. HODGES

MODERNISM AND POSTMODERNISM.

Modern philosophy is construed as beginning sometime in the Renaissance. A philosophy that seeks new foundations for knowledge was offered as an alternative to that provided by the ancient philosophers. Modern philosophy was presented as starting afresh from new beginnings—turning to nature directly (BACON [1]), turning to the mind directly (DESCARTES [2; S]), turning to experience directly (HOBBES [4; S]). The "quarrel between the ancients and the moderns" resulted from this basic disagreement as to the sources of philosophical knowledge.

Modern philosophy turned away from the past and toward the future, toward the advancement of knowledge, toward human understanding, and toward progress through method or through experience. With the break between the continental rationalists (Descartes, MALEBRANCHE [5], LEIBNIZ [4; S], and SPINOZA [7; S]) and the British empiricists (Hobbes, LOCKE [4; S], and HUME [4; S]) at the end of the eighteenth-century Enlightenment, a new formulation in modern philosophy was called for. KANT [4; S] brought together in his "critical" philosophy the commitments to the analytic exercise of the mind, on the one hand, and the empirical reception through the senses on the other. With Kant, modern philosophy combined the "transcendental unity of apperception" with the "manifold of experience." Modern philosophy was no longer based on a theory of representation—representation to the mind through reason or representation to the mind through experience—but on the linking of transcendental subjectivity and empirical objectivity. This "doublet," as FOUCAULT [S] came to name it, accounted for a whole new way of philosophizing.

Modernism is distinguished from modern philosophy in that it is linked to certain movements in art and literature that began sometime around the end of the nineteenth century. While drawing upon some similar characteristics of "modern philosophy," modernism in art, literature, and philosophy involved novelty, break with tradition, progress, continuous development, knowledge derived either from the position of the subject or from claims to objectivity, and concomitantly the crisis in knowledge produced by this very dichotomy. Hence in modernism, at the same time that certain theories based knowledge on a centered, transcendental, interpreting subjectivity, and others based knowledge on certain, atomistic, analytic, empirical objectivity, the crisis in knowledge created a sense of uncertainty, paradox, incompleteness, inadequacy, emptiness, and void. Modernism in art and literature involved a shift away from the dichotomies of ROMANTICISM [7] and REALISM [7; S] to the stream of consciousness, lived and internal time-consciousness, transcendental subjectivity, narrated remembrance and awareness, portrayed speed, mechanisms, objects, and abstractions. Latent content was allowed to penetrate through the surfaces of manifest content. Understanding would have to delve more deeply than surfaces and mere appearances. A phenomenology would be needed in order to inventory the contents of consciousness (HUSSERL [4; S]) or a psychoanalysis to delve the depths of what the mind was really thinking (FREUD [3; S]); or a LOGICAL POSITIVISM [S] would take the alternative tack by excluding all knowledge that cannot be verified logically and empirically (RUSSELL [7], early WITTGENSTEIN [8; S], AYER [1]). Modernism in philosophy involved at each stage the Kantian combination of the empirical and the transcendental, the objective and the subjective, the material and the intellectual—but each time measuring the doublet with weight on one side or the other.

The disintegration of modernism in philosophy was internal. The radical claims of logical positivism excluded all that was of value: metaphysics, aesthetics, axiology, and so forth. The rigorous science of transcendental PHENOMENOLOGY [6; S] excluded the very existence of what it was investigating. The dualism of creative evolutionism left an irreparable dichotomy between lived experience and objective knowledge. The pragmatism of radical empiricism failed to provide a way to interpret the meanings of experience. The center of modernism in philosophy could not hold because its very foundations were in question. But attempts to retrieve it from itself by the turn to language [4; S]—ordinary language, analytic philosophies of language, hermeneutics of language, semiologies of language—could not resolve the dilemmas of human existence. Modernism in philosophy faced the absurd, the ambiguous, and the dialectical. And it worked these theories to their limits.

In the mid-1960s philosophy came to look at its epistemological formations and to ask whether the humanisms and anthropologisms of modern philosophy had not circumscribed themselves. MERLEAU-PONTY's [5; S] interrogations were reformulated in Foucault's ARCHEOLOGY [S] of knowledge. The human sciences placed the optimisms and pessimisms of modern philosophy in question by circumventing the theory of "man." Knowledge formations were articulated in terms of multiple spaces of knowledge production and no longer according to a central source or position, or ego, or SELF [S], or subject, nor according to a multiplicity of sense-data, objective criteria, material evidence, or behaviors. Knowledge formations crossed disciplines and operated in multiple spaces where questions of structure, frame, margin, boundary, edge, limit, and so on, would mark any discursive practice. In other words, knowledge was no longer produced from a center, foundation, ground, basis, identity, authority, or transcendental competency. Knowledge was dispersed, multiple, fragmented, and theoretically varied. Knowledge was no longer based on continuity, unity, totality, comprehensiveness, and consistency. Knowledge began to be understood in terms of discontinuity, difference, dissemination, and differends.

By the early 1970s postmodernism—a term that Daniel Bell used in connection with postindustrial society in the 1950s, that architects appealed to in the 1960s, and that art and literary historians invoked in the 1970s—had still not been invoked in connection with philosophy. DERRIDA's [S] grammatology and theory of "difference" in 1967 (building upon HEIDEGGER's [3; S] account of "the end of philosophy and the task of thinking") turned into a full-fledged DECONSTRUCTION [S] in the 1970s. Deleuze and Guattari's notion of the rhizomal thinking (as opposed to hierarchical, authorizing arborescent thinking) marked a move against psychoanalytic theories based on Oedipal authority and paternal insistence. Their idea of nomadism placed emphasis on knowledge, experience, and relations that were not organized around a central concept. Kristeva's account of the revolution in poetic language marked the distinction between the semiotic and the symbolic. Where symbolic—scientific, theoretical, phallic, paternal—thinking had pervaded philosophy and science, Kristeva invoked the semiotic as the poetic, fluid, receptacle-like, maternal thinking that has been hidden in modern thought. Yet postmodern was hardly the term that was invoked to describe this kind of philosophizing. Correspondingly, the more restricted study of phenomenology and EXISTENTIALISM [3; S] in philosophy gave way to the more multiple and diverse theories implicit in continental philosophy: deconstruction, archeology of knowledge, semanalysis, schizoanalysis, feminist theory, and so forth. Yet, while poststructuralism (in connection with Foucault, Derrida, Deleuze, Kristeva, et al.) was hailed as the successor to structuralism (Lévi-Strauss, Barthes, Lacan, Althusser), and existential phenomenology (Heidegger, SARTRE [7; S], Merleau-Ponty, de BEAUVOIR [S]), postmodernism was still not a relevant category in philosophy until well into the 1980s. As time passed, postmodernism and postmodern thought came to take precedence over POSTSTRUCTURALISM [S] as the prevalent theoretical formulation.

Postmodern thought means the appeal to differences—differences in theories, differences in formulations, differences in identities. Postmodern thought rejects hierarchies and genealogies, continuities and progress, resolutions and overcomings *(Überwindungen).* Postmodern thought, in fact, cannot operate outside of the modern, for it is itself what can be called an "indecidable." The postmodern signals the end of modernity, but it operates at the same time necessarily within the modern. To claim that the postmodern is outside the modern is to identify it as other than the modern, but that which is outside or other reinscribes the identity of the modern and therefore the postmodern inscription within it. Hence the postmodern both marks places of difference within the modern and calls for an alternative to the modern. The postmodern in any case does not call for the destruction of the modern, not does it seek to deny the modern, since it is necessarily part of the modern.

The postmodern involves the question of the end or limit or margin of what is in question. History, man, knowledge, painting, writing, the modern—each is posed in terms of its end. The end is not as much a matter of termination or conclusion any more than a matter of goal and aspiration. The postmodern involves, as Vattimo notes, a *Verwindung* of modernity—a getting over, a convalescence, a recovering from modernity. This means that modernity is itself placed in question and no longer taken as an unquestioned given. The cracks and fissures in modernity, the places where modernity cannot be fully aware of itself, the moments of unpresentability in the modern—these are the concerns of postmodern thought. As Lyotard has noted in his famous *The Postmodern Condition* (1984), the postmodern involves the presentation of the unpresentable in presentation itself—that is, in modernity, the concern was to present something new, something unheard of, something unique, something shocking, something unpresentable. The postmodern involves the presentation of the unpresentable in presentation itself—the formulation of the moments of unpresentability as they mark what is presented. Lyotard calls attention to the role of the "differend" as the place of conflict between two alternative positions. The differend does not belong to either side. It belongs only to the place between, to the gap between the two presentations on either side. This is the postmodern moment—such moments or events with which the modern is distinctively scarred and animated.

Bibliography

Derrida, J. *Margins of Philosophy.* Translated by A. Bass. Chicago, 1982.

Foucault, M. *The Order of Things.* Translator anon. New York, 1970.

Kristeva, J. *Revolution in Poetic Language.* Translated by M. Waller. New York, 1984.

Lyotard, J.-F. *The Postmodern Condition.* Translated by G. Bennington and B. Massumi. Minneapolis, 1984.

———. *Toward the Postmodern.* Translated by R. Harvey and M. Roberts. Atlantic Highlands, NJ, 1993.

Natoli, J., and L. Hutcheon, eds. *A Postmodern Reader.* Albany, NY, 1993.

Silverman, H. J., ed. *Postmodernism—Philosophy and the Arts.* New York, 1990.

———. *Textualities: Between Hermeneutics and Deconstruction.* New York, 1994.

Vattimo, G. *The End of Modernity.* Translated by J. R. Snyder. Baltimore, 1988.

HUGH J. SILVERMAN

MORAL EPISTEMOLOGY. Moral epistemology is concerned with the epistemic evaluation of moral judgments and theories. It does not seek to determine whether specific moral judgments or theories are known, justified, warranted, rational, reasonable, or what have you. It is the business of moral theorists and the ordinary people who make and act upon moral judgments to make such determinations. The moral epistemologist's interest in the evaluation of moral judgments and theories is more general: her aim is to determine how, if at all, moral judgments or theories might be justified, rational, and so forth. Other areas of EPISTEMOLOGY [S] are similar: for example, epistemologists studying perception seek a general understanding of how visual perception justifies beliefs, not to determine whether specific perceptual beliefs are justified.

Questions about moral epistemology are fundamental, and attempts to answer them go back at least to PLATO [6; S] and SOCRATES [7; S]. Nonetheless, it can seem the field developed only in the last quarter of the twentieth century. Though moral epistemology has always been included in metaethics, which is defined as the study of the meaning and justification of moral statements, the inclusion of epistemological questions under this definition is misleading since twentieth-century metaethics has focused almost exclusively on questions of meaning. Moreover, after flirting with intuitionism (which either left moral knowledge mysterious or subsumed it under our knowledge of our concepts or language—see, e.g., MOORE [5], 1903, and ROSS [7], 1930), metaethics settled in for a long infatuation with NONDESCRIPTIVISM [S] (see, e.g., Gibbard, 1990, HARE [S], 1952, and STEVENSON [S], 1937). Because nondescriptivism holds that the point of moral language is not to state facts, and that moral claims are therefore neither true nor false, questions about the justification of moral statements drop out of nondescriptivist metaethics, at least if these questions are understood as epistemological. Intelligible questions about the justification, reasonableness, or RATIONALITY [S] of moral statements remain. But such questions are practical, not epistemological: they seek, for example, a reason for believing that it is in one's own interest to abide by the dictates of morality.

Normative ethics has emphasized questions of MEANING [5; S] as well, and this has also dampened the development of moral epistemology. If substantive moral questions are answered by analysis of moral language or concepts, there is nothing distinctive about moral knowledge. The epistemology of conceptual analysis should apply equally well whether the analysis produces ethical theories or theories in another area of philosophy.

Two developments in the 1970s focused attention on moral epistemology. One was the widespread self-conscious adoption of reflective equilibrium as a method of moral injury. (The method was [arguably] employed by philosophers long before it was explicitly described and self-consciously employed.) GOODMAN (1965) [3; S] first described reflective equilibrium and advocated it for justifying principles of induction. RAWLS (1971) [S] further developed the method and applied it to moral inquiry. Reflective equilibrium is a coherence method. One must begin the process of theory construction with one's considered moral judgments, which can be of any level of generality, and formulate a system of principles that yield these judgments. But then one must proceed via a process of mutual adjustment. When the emerging theory is found to conflict with central, very confidently made considered judgments, the inquirer must revise the theory. But if a well-confirmed element of the theory that is independently plausible is found to conflict with less firmly held considered judgments, then these judgments are revised. The decision regarding what to revise is made for each case on the basis of what seems most likely to be correct to the inquirer, all things considered. (This description fits Goodman's original approach, known as narrow reflective equilibrium. Rawls advocated a method of wide reflective equilibrium, which directs the inquirer to bring her moral judgments and theory into coherence with any background beliefs or theories that might be relevant, again via a process of mutual adjustment. [On wide versus narrow reflective equilibrium, see Daniels, 1979, or DePaul, 1993.].)

Since reflective equilibrium seems to grant first the inquirer's considered moral judgments and later her judgments of what is more likely to be correct crucial roles in inquiry, it has been widely criticized as a sophisticated version of intuitionism, which makes for an unreliable and extremely conservative method. (Brandt, 1979, is a representative critic of the use of reflective equilibrium in ethics. Stich, 1990, criticizes reflective equilibrium as a general philosophical method.) One response admits that an argument for the reliability of considered moral judgments is needed while stressing that the required argument cannot be produced prior to employing the equilibrium method. The fact that we cannot now produce the required argument therefore is no decisive objection since the argument can only emerge as part of the coherent system that reflective equilibrium will eventually produce. (See Daniels, 1979.) Although no one has done so in this context, one might also respond by appealing to a general coherentist epistemology (*see* co-

HERENTISM [S]) and rejecting the critic's apparent demand to have the foundations of moral knowledge established. (Brink develops this natural line of argument while defending MORAL REALISM [S]. See below.) Finally, one can respond by recognizing that there are a number of significant dimensions of epistemic evaluation. One might then grant that because reflective equilibrium relies on human intuition, it is likely unreliable and hence, if reliability is required for justification, unlikely to yield justified beliefs. One then defends the method by showing either that it, or that only it, yields other significant epistemic goods—for example, rational belief. (Using different terminology, and focusing on reflective equilibrium as a method for ethics or as a general philosophical method respectively, De Paul, 1993, and Sosa, 1991, have pursued this approach.)

The second development that prompted work in moral epistemology concerned metaphysical rather than methodological issues. The nondescriptivism of traditional analytic philosophy, which dominated metaethics through the middle of the twentieth century, left little room for substantive moral inquiry. But moral philosophers could not resist the lively debates about the pressing moral and political issues of the 1960s. They became involved in these debates, bringing argumentative strategies familiar in other areas of philosophy to bear upon substantive moral questions. These debates proceeded as though a question of truth were at stake, as though there were a fact of the matter to be determined, and as a consequence moral philosophy seemed tacitly to assume moral realism. It is, therefore, perhaps true to say that analytic nondescriptivism was abandoned more because philosophers simply became bored with the limits it imposed than because it was refuted. It is no surprise, then, that this tacitly accepted realism and descriptivism regarding moral language was challenged.

The new debate tended to focus more on the metaphysical issue regarding REALISM [7; S] rather than on descriptivism. One reason for this was that MACKIE (1977) [S], one of the most important critics of realism, was willing to grant that our ordinary moral language is in fact descriptive. But he went on to argue that the kind of realism about ethics to which our moral language commits us is metaphysically and epistemologically untenable. Moral facts are metaphysically "queer"; they cannot happily be fit into the natural world (a point also forcibly made by Harman, 1977), and our epistemic access to moral facts is at best problematic. On the metaphysical front, efforts to defend moral facts have for the most part attempted to assimilate them either to natural facts of the sort discovered by science (Boyd, 1988, and Brink, 1989) or to secondary qualities such as colors (McDowell, 1985, and Wiggins, 1987). (See also Goldman, 1988, who assimilates moral facts and inquiry to legal facts.)

Efforts to respond to the epistemological challenge to realism have followed suit. Those who see moral facts as akin to natural facts argue that something very much like reflective equilibrium is the method of scientific inquiry, that this is also the method of moral inquiry, and that in both cases the method is supported by a coherence account of epistemic justification. (Boyd, 1988, and Brink, 1989.) Those who assimilate moral properties to secondary qualities naturally take some sort of perceptual knowledge as a model for their moral epistemology. (McNaughton, 1988.) The model need not be something simple such as color perception. Moral epistemology is more plausibly modeled on more complicated types of PERCEPTION [6; S]—for example, perception of the tonal qualities of a complex musical composition, which requires special sensitivity acquired through extensive experience and perhaps a course of training.

Some philosophers are interested in modeling moral epistemology upon perception because of concerns about the way philosophical inquiry into morality is conducted rather than because of metaphysical worries about realism. They are dissatisfied with the rather dry, artificial nature of the traditional type of moral theorizing that is based on a scientific model and is so far removed from our ordinary experience of making moral judgments and decisions. One problem with such theorizing is that it tends to focus exclusively on abstract principles and thinly described, highly stylized examples. As a result, moral theorists tend to miss the very particular elements of real cases that can be morally crucial and have failed to notice what is involved in the kind of sensitivity required to notice and respond to such particulars (Nussbaum, 1990).

Although work in moral epistemology has flourished after the passing of traditional analytic nondescriptivism, such work tends to be done in the service of other interests and not because of the kind of pure interest that motivated, for example, much work on the epistemology of perception. In such circumstances there is more than the usual danger of distorting the object of inquiry to fit the theory.

Bibliography

Boyd, R. "How to Be a Moral Realist," in G. Sayre-McCord, ed., *Moral Realism* (Ithaca, NY, 1988).

Brandt, R. B. *A Theory of the Right and Good.* New York, 1979.

Brink, D. O. *Moral Realism and the Foundations of Ethics.* Cambridge, 1989.

Daniels, N. "Wide Reflective Equilibrium and Theory Acceptance in Ethics," *Journal of Philosophy,* Vol. 76 (1979), 256–82.

DePaul, M. R. *Balance and Refinement: Beyond Coherence Methods in Ethics.* London, 1993.

Gibbard, A. *Wise Choices, Apt Feelings.* Cambridge, MA, 1990.

Goldman, A. *Moral Knowledge.* London, 1988.

Goodman, N. *Fact, Fiction, and Forecast.* Indianapolis, 1965.

Hare, R. M. *The Language of Morals.* Oxford, 1952.

Harman, G. *The Nature of Morality.* New York, 1977.

Mackie, J. L. *Ethics: Inventing Right and Wrong.* New York, 1977.

McDowell, J. "Values and Secondary Properties," in T. Honderich, ed., *Morality and Objectivity* (London, 1985).

McNaughton, D. A. *Moral Vision.* Oxford, 1988.

Moore, G. E. *Principia Ethica.* Cambridge, 1903.

Nussbaum, M. *Love's Knowledge.* Oxford, 1990.

Rawls, J. *A Theory of Justice.* Cambridge, MA, 1971.

Ross, W. D. *The Right and the Good.* Oxford, 1930.

Sosa, E. "Equilibrium in Coherence?" in *Knowledge in Perspective: Selected Essays in Epistemology* (Cambridge, 1991).

Stevenson, C. L. "The Emotive Meaning of Ethical Terms," *Mind,* Vol. 46 (1937), 14–31.

Stich, S. *The Fragmentation of Reason.* Cambridge, MA, 1990.

Wiggins, D. *Needs, Values, and Truth: Essays in the Philosophy of Value.* Oxford, 1987.

MICHAEL R. DEPAUL

MORAL NATURALISM. Philosophical NATURALISM [5; S], considered in general, is not a unified doctrine but a broad label applied both to methodological stances (e.g., "The methods of philosophy are continuous with those of empirical science") and to substantive positions (e.g., "For a belief to be epistemically warranted is for it to be the product of a certain kind of causal process"). The two are often combined, as when a naturalistic interpretation of a given domain of discourse is justified as "the best explanation" of associated practices. However, the two are in principle independent. In the moral case, for example, it has been argued that a projectivist or noncognitivist interpretation gives a better explanation of moral practice than any substantive naturalism (Blackburn, 1984; Gibbard, 1990) (*see* PROJECTIVISM [S]).

But what makes a method or interpretation naturalistic? Attempts to give an explicit definition have largely been abandoned in favor of pointing. Roughly, naturalistic methods are those followed in actual scientific research (including—according to some but not all naturalists—mathematics and social sciences as well as natural sciences). And a naturalistic interpretation of a discourse is one based upon predicates or terms that play a role in the explanatory theories that research has generated.

This characterization of naturalism is informative but incomplete. There are vigorous debates within the PHILOSOPHY OF SCIENCE [S] over just what the methods, concepts, or posits of contemporary science are. Moreover, interpretation based upon naturalistic terms encompasses some quite different tasks. Some examples follow, but first we should ask, Why stay within naturalistic terms at all? Science is a theoretical, descriptive/explanatory enterprise while morality is held to be essentially practical and normative. One might think, no sooner did morality emerge from the shadow of religion than philosophers began trying to push it into the shadow of science. Is it never to be allowed to stand in its own right as a distinctive domain of inquiry?

An answer of sorts is possible. Morality by its nature cannot stand entirely on its own. Moral discourse is supervenient upon the nonmoral and, specifically, the natural—two actions or agents cannot differ in their moral qualities unless there is some underlying difference in their natural qualities (*see* SUPERVENIENCE [S]). This and other truisms about morality, such as 'Ought' implies 'can', tie moral evaluation to the natural world in ways that no ethical theory can altogether ignore. Moreover, morality presents us with various epistemic and metaphysical puzzles. We believe that we have come to possess at least some moral knowledge—but how? (See Harman, 1977.) We treat moral statements as if they stated genuine propositions—but can this idea be sustained in light of the normative role of moral judgment? We freely make moral judgments, but do they have presuppositions or make claims that are incompatible with our understanding of the natural world?

Hard determinists, for example, have challenged intuitive attributions of moral responsibility by arguing that the notion of free agency they presuppose is incompatible with the world revealed by physics (*see* DETERMINISM AND FREEDOM [S]). And J. L. MACKIE [S] is led to an "error theory" of morality by his diagnosis that moral evaluation attributes to states of the world an objective "to-be-pursuedness" that cannot be fit with any plausible empirical theory (Mackie, 1977).

KANT [4; S], for one, frankly accepted that he could see no way of reconciling the deliberative standpoint of morality with the causal perspective of science. Rational agents must, he held, postulate the compatibility of moral agency with the natural order, even though this remains inexplicable to them. But few philosophers have been willing to stop there. Empirical science affords the best-developed picture we have of ourselves and our world. Without the special authority of religion to back it up, morality inevitably becomes a focus of practical and theoretical concern.

Substantive moral naturalists in effect propose to overcome some of the mystery and potential conflict surrounding the relation of morality to our empirical self-understanding by showing just how much of morality might be found within the domain of the natural. This could be done by providing a naturalistic account of moral discourse that affords an analysis of moral terms (Lewis, 1989), or permits a worthwhile revision of moral language that nonetheless can serve virtually all the same functions (Brandt, 1979), or enables us to reduce moral properties to natural properties (Railton, 1993), or shows moral properties to be natural properties in their own right (e.g., thanks to their contribution to empirical explanation; see Boyd, 1988; Miller, 1985; Sturgeon, 1985). Substantive moral naturalism promises to explain such important features of moral discourse and practice as the applicability of notions of truth and falsity to moral claims, the supervenience of the moral upon the natural, the role of natural properties in justifying moral claims, and the possibility of semantic and epistemic access to moral notions through ordinary experience.

The first half of the twentieth century had not been kind to substantive moral naturalism (for a brief history, see Darwall et al., 1992). Condemned by G. E. MOORE (1903; [5]) for committing the "fallacy" of trying to close an "open question" by analytic means and rejected by nonfactualists (emotivists, prescriptivists, etc.) for failing to capture the special relation of moral evaluation to motivation and action, naturalism fell into disuse. But by mid-century naturalism had begun to win its way back. The initial steps were taken, independently, by Philippa Foot (1958–59) and Geoffrey Warnock (1967), who argued that one could not be competent in moral discourse unless one possessed some substantive, contentful moral concepts. Moral evaluation is distinguished from aesthetic or prudential, for example, in part because it has a certain descriptive, arguably natural content—namely, a concern with the effects of our actions on the well-being of others. If we came upon a society in whose behavioral code the key notion was *guleb,* a term applied in the paradigm case to warriors who have killed an enemy bare-handed, we would certainly mislead if we translated *guleb* as 'morally good' or 'just' rather than 'valiant' or 'courageous'.

Meanwhile, Peter Geach (1965) showed convincingly that existing nonfactualist views could not account for the full grammar of moral discourse, in particular, the logical behavior of unasserted moral claims in CONDITIONALS [S].

Foot (1972) took the next step as well, challenging the 'internalist' conception of the relation of moral evaluation to motivation that served as the basis for nonfactualism. She argued that ordinary moral agents are able to see themselves as motivated by a rationally optional concern for others. Those who lack such a concern might lack moral character, but they do not make a linguistic mistake in using the moral vocabulary.

This sort of moral 'externalism' offers an alternative explanation of why moral evaluation and motivation are so intimately related, at least in paradigm cases. Concern for others is a very basic part of normal human life. An Aristotelian would say that human nature itself is social; a Darwinian would emphasize the contribution of concern for others to inclusive fitness and to the possibility of benefiting from reciprocal altruism. Speculative biology apart, it is possible to see how social norms involving concern for others, keeping promises, and so forth might emerge and be sustained in virtue of their contribution to solving various serious coordination and collective-action problems. Such norms will function best only if well internalized by a major part of the population. It should therefore be unsurprising that moral judgment is usually accompanied by a positive attitude. Moreover, it should not be forgotten that moral judgment is a species of assertion and that assertion itself involves, not only signaling a cognitive attitude of belief, but also various forms of active endorsement or encouragement, as well as associated claims of authority. Moral externalism, by drawing upon these ingredients (and others) for an alternative explanation of the evidence—such as it is—offered on behalf of internalism, has attracted a number of defenders (see, for example, Boyd, 1988; Brink, 1989; Railton, 1986).

Another sort of naturalism, however, takes the opposite tack. It treats the purported relation to motivation as fundamental but interprets it in a subjectivist rather than nonfactualist manner. Subjectivist interpretations of moral discourse have historically faced difficulties in accommodating all the elements of an interconnected set of features of morality: the critical use of moral assessment, the nonrelativistic character of moral judgment and the possibility of genuine moral disagreement across social or cultural differences, the limits on empirical methods in resolving moral disputes, and the seemingly normative character of the relation between moral judgment and motivation. Can new forms of subjectivism succeed where others have failed?

Consider the simple subjectivist formula:

(1) Act A is morally good = A is such that one would approve of the performance of A.

Since approval is a positive attitude, (1) establishes a relationship with a source of motivational force. But is it the right relationship?

We do not typically regard our current tendencies to approve or disapprove as morally authoritative—they might, for example, be based upon hasty thinking or false beliefs. This has led naturalists to modify (1) to require that the approval be well informed and reflectively stable. (See, for example, Brandt, 1979, and Firth, 1952. For criticism, see Velleman, 1988.)

Moreover, not all species of approval have a moral flavor. I can approve of an act because of its aesthetic or pious qualities, for example. Some naturalists therefore amend (1) to restrict the object of approval (e.g., to the set of rules one would—reflectively, informedly, etc.—approve for a society in which one is going to live [cf. Brandt, 1979]). Others attempt to identify in naturalistic terms a specifically moral sort of attitude of approval or disapproval (e.g., an attitude of impartial praise or anger). Critics have argued that no noncircular characterization of this kind is possible (for a subjectivism without reductive ambitions, see Wiggins, 1987).

Formulas like (1) also threaten to yield relativism (*see* MORAL RELATIVISM [S]). Since they introduce a necessary link to facts about motivation, moral attribution becomes tied to contingencies of individual psychology. That seems wrong, since moral evaluation purports to abstract from individual interest and motive and to prescribe universality. If one is not correspondingly motivated, that is a deficiency in oneself rather than an excusing condition or a limit on the reach of moral judgment. Each of us recognizes that he or she can in this sense be motivationally defective from a moral point of view. (But see Harman, 1975, for a defense of a naturalistic moral relativism.) This has led naturalists to modify the formula away from the individualistic language of 'one' or 'I' and in the direction of a more inclusive 'we' or 'everyone' or even 'normal humans' (see, respectively, Lewis, 1989; Smith, 1994; and Firth, 1952). New problems arise. The notion of 'normal human' threatens to introduce a term that itself requires naturalization—since we believe that statistically "normal" humans might be motivationally defective from a moral point of view—for example, in lacking sympathy with those from other groups. (Of course, one could at this point also embrace circularity.) If we insist that everyone approve, there is again a risk that contingencies of motivational idiosyncrasies will receive authority—this time, in preventing us from attributing moral value to states of affairs virtually all (but still not quite all) of us approve heartily on reflection. A less ambitious alternative is to replace 'one' with 'us' and seek moral consensus where we may. This would help explain the "outreach" function of moral discourse without altogether removing the account's relativism.

An alternative approach avoids relativism by "rigidifying" the subjectivist formula (cf. Wiggins, 1987). One fixes the truth conditions of moral judgments by reference to the motivations *actually* prevalent in one's moral community (e.g., '*A* is such that we, with our actual motives and with full and informed reflection, would approve of it'). This secures the desirable result that changes in our motives will not in themselves change what is morally good. But it undermines some of the critical role of moral assessment in our own society (since, again, we can imagine that our actual motives are morally defective) and will have the result that those brought up in different social environments with different acquired motivations will lack a common subject matter even though they believe they are having a genuine moral disagreement (for discussion, see Johnston, 1989).

No moral naturalism has emerged that meets all the desiderata of an account of moral discourse and practice. Nonnaturalists and nonfactualists attribute this to a mistaken starting point. But no alternative account has met all the desiderata, either. Moral naturalists have often been accused of "changing the subject"—shifting the locus of attention from the position of the agent involved in practical deliberation to that of the scientist engaged in theoretical description. But this criticism begs the question. Naturalists seek to explain, not ignore, moral experience; if they are right, the phenomena they study are the very stuff of moral thought and action.

(SEE ALSO: *Ethical Theory* [S])

Bibliography

Blackburn, S. *Spreading the Word.* Oxford, 1984.

Boyd, R. "How to Be a Moral Realist," in G. Sayre-McCord, ed., *Essays on Moral Realism* (Ithaca, NY, 1988).

Brandt, R. *A Theory of the Good and the Right.* New York, 1979.

Brink, D. O. *Moral Realism and the Foundations of Ethics.* Cambridge, 1989.

Darwell, S., et al. "Toward *Fin de siècle* Ethics," *Philosophical Review,* Vol. 101 (1992), 317–45.

Firth, R. "Ethical Absolutism and the Ideal Observer," *Philosophy and Phenomenological Research,* Vol. 12 (1952), 317–45.

Foot, P. "Moral Beliefs," *Proceedings of the Aristotelian Society,* Vol. 59 (1958–59), 83–104.

———. "Morality as a System of Hypothetical Imperatives," *Philosophical Review,* Vol. 81 (1972), 305–16.

Geach, P. "Assertion," *Philosophical Review,* Vol. 74 (1965), 445–65.

Gibbard, A. *Wise Choices, Apt Feelings.* Cambridge, 1990.

Harman, G. "Moral Relativism Defended," *Philosophical Review,* Vol. 84 (1975), 3–22.

———. *The Nature of Morality.* New York, 1977.

Johnston, M. "Dispositional Theories of Value," *Proceedings of the Aristotelian Society,* Vol. 63 (1989), suppl., 139–74.

Lewis, D. "Dispositional Theories of Value," *Proceedings of the Aristotelian Society,* Vol. 63 (1989), suppl. 113–37.

Mackie, J. L. *Ethics: Inventing Right and Wrong.* New York, 1977.

Miller, R. "Ways of Moral Learning," *Philosophical Review,* Vol. 94 (1985), 507–56.

Moore, G. E. *Principia Ethica.* Cambridge, 1903.

Railton, P. "Moral Realism," *Philosophical Review,* Vol. 95 (1986), 163–207.

———. "Reply to David Wiggins," in J. Haldane and C. Wright, eds., *Reality, Representation, and Projection* (Oxford, 1993).

Smith, M. *The Moral Problem.* Oxford, 1994.

Sturgeon, N. "Moral Explanations," in D. Copp and D. Zimmerman, eds., *Morality, Reason, and Truth* (Totowa, NJ, 1985).

Velleman, D. "Brandt's Definition of 'Good,' " *Philosophical Review,* Vol. 97 (1988), 353–71.

Warnock, G. *Contemporary Moral Philosophy.* London, 1967.

Wiggins, D. "A Sensible Subjectivism?" In *Needs, Values, and Truth: Essays in the Philosophy of Value* (Oxford, 1987).

PETER RAILTON

MORAL PSYCHOLOGY. The intellectual division of labor makes a sharp distinction between moral philosophy and moral psychology. Moral philosophy is in the business of saying what ought to be, what is really right and wrong, good and evil; what the proper moral principles and rules are, what counts as genuine moral motivation, and what types of persons count as genuinely good. Most important, the job of moral philosophy is to provide philosophical justification for its shoulds, and oughts, for its principles and its rules.

Moral psychology, what KANT [4; S] called the "empirical side of morals," might tell us what people think ought to be done, what they believe is right or wrong, what they think makes a good person, and so on. But all the psychological facts taken together, including that they are widely and strongly believed, could never justify any of these views. Mottoes abound to express the basic idea: one cannot make inferences from 'is' to 'ought'; one cannot derive values from facts; the empirical tells us what is the case, the normative tells us what ought to be the case.

In the *Groundwork* (1785), Kant writes that a "worse service cannot be rendered morality than that an attempt be made to derive it from examples." Trying to derive ethical principles "from the disgusting mishmash" of psychological, sociological, or anthropological observation, from the insights about human nature that abound "in the chit-chat of daily life" and that delight "the multitude" and upon which "the empty headed regale themselves" is not the right way to do moral philosophy.

What is the right way to do moral philosophy? We need "a completely isolated metaphysics of morals, a pure ethics unmixed with the empirical study" of human nature (1785, pp. 408–10). Once moral philosophy has derived the principles that ought to govern the wills of all rational beings, then and only then should we seek "the extremely rare merit of a truly philosophical popularity" (p. 409). This is "Kant's dogma."

The sharp separation was not always the rule. Kant's target in the passages about the "disgusting mish mash" of observations that pervade "the chit-chat of ordinary life" includes not just ordinary people but the entire philosophical tradition, from PLATO [6; S] to HUME [4; S]. Indeed, until the eighteenth century moral philosophy was thought to involve close attention to human nature, character, motivation, the passions and emotions, the social bases of moral life, the virtues and vices of everyday life, moral education, the relation between being a decent person and living in a decent community, and individual and cultural difference.

Moral psychology has had a revival in the second half of the twentieth century. It involves work done both by empirical psychologists and philosophers and is devoted to reflection on how morals are acquired or developed, the role of emotions in moral life, how resistance to evil is inculcated, and so on. Of the many reasons for this revival, these are three of the most prominent: (1) How was the Holocaust possible? That is, how could seemingly decent people go off the moral deep end in the way they did during the Nazi era? (2) How can schools, especially schools in a secular society, teach moral values and encourage the development of decent character, moral sensitivity, and so on, without teaching a specific religious morality? (3) How does moral philosophy, especially the moral philosophical project of trying to find the right way to live, respond to the facts of pluralism and individual and cultural difference?

Immediately after the Second World War, a spate of literature appeared—*The Authoritarian Personality* (Adorno et al., 1993) being the most famous—which traced the roots of compliance to moral evil and moral conventionalism. Work by Stanley Milgram and Hannah ARENDT [S] and more recent work on the character of rescuers during the Holocaust reinforce the idea that in times of moral crisis individuals who believe in abiding conventional norms will do great moral harm.

With regard to issues of moral education and moral development, Lawrence Kohlberg's moral stage theory attempted to fill a vacuum. According to Kohlberg, there are universal stages of moral development (six in total). Most people reach only the middle conventional stages, but development to the postconventional stages (five and six), where one will resist evil such as the Holocaust, can be promoted by engaging children, adolescents, and adults in discussion of complex moral issues; this can be done without bringing religion into the discussions.

Carol Gilligan (1982), a colleague and collaborator of Kohlberg's, challenged the comprehensiveness of his stage theory. Distilled to its essence, the claim was that the theory was sexist. Gilligan describes a moral universe in which men, more often than women, conceive of morality as substantively constituted by obligations and rights and as procedurally constituted by the demands of fairness and impartiality, while women, more often than men, see moral requirements as emerging from the particular needs of others in the context of particular relationships. Gilligan dubs this latter orientation the "ethic of care," and insists that the former, the "ethic of justice," with its exclusive focus on justice reasoning, obscures both the care ethic's psychological reality and its normative significance.

Gilligan characterizes the two ethics as "different ways of viewing the world" that "organize both thinking and feeling," and that involve seeing things in different and competing ways. The JUSTICE [S] orientation organizes moral perception by highlighting issues of fairness, right, and obligation. Whereas the ethic of justice involves seeing others thinly, as worthy of respect purely by virtue of common humanity, morally good caring requires seeing others thickly, as constituted by their particular human face, their particular psychological and social self. Caring also involves taking seriously, or at least being moved by, one's particular connection to the other. Gilligan claims that once the dispositions that underlie such caring are acknowledged, the dominant conception of moral maturity among moral psychologists and moral philosophers will need to be reconceived.

At the same time the Kohlberg–Gilligan debate was getting hot, many philosophers were questioning impartial conceptions of moral life. The debate about IMPAR-

TIALITY [S], led by philosophers such as Lawrence Blum, quickly brought to the fore questions about the nature of love and friendship (are we supposed to be impartial to our friends and loved ones?), the role of emotions in moral life, questions about the legitimacy of different moral conceptions in a multicultural society, as well as general questions about how realistic our moral theories ought to be.

Bibliography

Adorno, T. W., et al. *The Authoritarian Personality.* New York, 1993.

Blum, L. *Impartiality and Particularity.* New York, 1994.

Flanagan, O. *Varieties of Moral Personality: Ethics and Psychological Realism.* Cambridge, MA, 1991.

Gilligan, C. *In a Different Voice: Psychological Theory and Women's Development.* Cambridge, MA, 1982.

Kohlberg, L. *Essays on Moral Development.* Vol. I., *The Philosophy of Moral Development: Moral Stages and the Idea of Justice.* San Francisco, 1981.

———. *Essays on Moral Development.* Vol. II., *The Psychology of Moral Development: The Nature and Validity of Moral Stages.* San Francisco, 1984.

OWEN FLANAGAN

MORAL REALISM. Moral realism holds that there exist moral facts and therefore properties (such as goodness, evil, rightness, wrongness, virtue, vice) that are not reducible to nonmoral facts or properties; these facts and properties, the theory holds, are independent of our awareness, the manner in which we think or speak, our beliefs and attitudes, and our feelings and desires. Moral properties may be exemplified by persons, actions, institutions, and so forth; their exemplifications are moral facts, correspondence to which constitutes the truth of moral judgments. Sophisticated moral antirealism need not reject all of these theses; it may accept some or all of them, but only after reinterpreting them, especially the conception of truth as correspondence to facts (Blackburn, 1984, 1993; Wright 1992) (*see* CORRESPONDENCE THEORY OF TRUTH [2]). Such reinterpretations are motivated by the plausibility of moral realism and would be needed only if it were found seriously deficient.

Moral realism is often called cognitivism, but properly speaking the latter is the view that moral beliefs and statements do or at least can express knowledge. And there may be moral facts of which we cannot have knowledge—for example, whether a certain action would ultimately produce more goodness than any of its alternatives would (Butchvarov, 1989; Fumerton, 1990). Cognitivism is opposed to MORAL SKEPTICISM [S], not to moral realism. On the other hand, if by cognitivism we mean merely that moral statements have truth value, then it might coincide with moral realism, but only if it also holds that some moral statements are true.

The issues moral realism raises are essentially metaphysical. First, What is it for something to be real? To be a part of the causal spatiotemporal network that science investigates? But we must add that we mean a real, not an imaginary, network, and then we would be guilty of circularity. Inattention to this metaphysical issue would vitiate any realism or antirealism (*see* REALISM, ANTIREALISM [S]), regardless of its subject matter. A second issue is whether there are such entities as properties at all and, if there are, what they are, especially whether they are UNIVERSALS [8] (i.e., capable of being exemplified by many particulars at the same time), as was held by PLATO [6; S] and George Edward MOORE (1903; [5]). A third issue concerns the relationship between moral properties and the nonmoral (whether natural or nonnatural) properties in virtue of which they can be attributed to particulars. Moral goodness can be attributed to a person only if the person has certain nonmoral properties such as kindness (Brink, 1989; Butchvarov, 1989; Moore, 1922; ROSS [7], 1930). How is this relationship between moral and nonmoral properties to be understood? If the moral properties are defined in terms of the nonmoral properties, then we have abandoned moral realism. If we claim that there is a law like connection between them (Brink, 1989), then we must ask what the nature of such "laws" might be; they are hardly scientific laws, and anyhow the nature of scientific laws is too obscure and controversial to support a helpful analogy. If we appeal to the formal SUPERVENIENCE [S] of moral on nonmoral properties (Post, 1987)—meaning by this that in particular cases the former could not be different unless the latter were different—but deny that the presupposed substantive relation of dependence of the moral on the nonmoral is causal, semantical, or logical, then we may be moral realists but we appeal to a relation at least as mysterious as Moore's nonnatural property of goodness (Moore, 1903, chap. 1), especially if we add that the nonmoral properties must be physical. Another view (Butchvarov, 1989, chap. 4) is that nonmoral properties exemplify moral properties in the distinctive way specific properties (e.g., red) exemplify their generic properties (e.g., color) and that particulars (such as persons and actions) exemplify moral properties only indirectly, by exemplifying nonmoral properties that exemplify moral properties directly. A person's kindness is a species, a kind, of goodness, not goodness itself, and the person exemplifies goodness indirectly, which is exemplified by kindness directly. But a genus such as goodness is not definable in terms of its species except as their disjunction, which is seldom possible and also violates the notion of definition. Even then it is the genus that guides us in the selection of the disjuncts. (Color cannot be defined as the disjunction of the specific shades of color, which are perhaps infinite in number. And while the species of goodness are probably not infinite in number, their disjunction can be arrived at only through a prior grasp of their genus.) But, although familiar, the genus–species relation requires extensive metaphysical elucidation. All three metaphysical issues can be properly resolved only by metaphysics, not by ethics.

The chief argument for moral realism is that it is the view implicit in common sense. We sometimes just "see" that something, say, an action or a person, is morally good, or bad, or right, or wrong. We regard moral judgments as true or false, disagree and argue about them, and sometimes attempt to live in accordance with them. We do not think that their meaning or use is to express attitudes or prescriptions of behavior or that they are about certain thoughts and feelings. Even a moral antirealist such as MACKIE [S] (1977) admits this but draws the conclusion that common sense is in error in its moral judgments, since there is nothing in reality to make them true. Could common sense be that wrong? There are philosophical arguments against moral realism. In ethics, as in all disciplines, one must begin with common sense, but one need not end with it.

One argument is phenomenological. HUME ([1739] 1888; [4; S]) claimed that when we perceive a case of murder we do not perceive the vice in it, nor can we infer it from what we do perceive by any legitimate principles of inference. A counterargument is that such a view rests on a rather primitive phenomenology, as contrasted, say, with that of Max SCHELER ([1913–16] 1973 [7]), probably also on the failure to recognize that moral properties are strictly speaking properties of properties and thus not discernible in the way properties directly exemplified by particulars are discernible. (You do not see color in the way you see a specific shade of red, but obviously you are, or on reflection can become, aware of it, in a quite nonmysterious way; nor are you tempted to identify color with red, since then you would also have to identify it with green, with blue, etc., thus implying that these are not different colors.) It has been argued that our awareness of moral properties is a mere "projection" of our attitudes (Blackburn, 1984; 1993, part 2; Hume, [1752] 1957). But this cinematographic metaphor requires detailed metaphysical unpacking, which is not provided.

A second argument is that moral properties have no place in the "scientific image" of the world, in particular that their existence is incompatible with PHYSICALISM [S], the view that everything is physical. They are not part of the subject matter of physics, they can enter in no causal relations, and appeal to them has no explanatory value, even with respect to our having the moral opinions we do have (Harman, 1977, chap. 1). But numbers and God are also not physical things, and it would be presumptuous and unphilosophical to deny their existence for just that reason. Nor has anyone shown that the reality of something requires it to have a causal or explanatory role. At any rate, it is not at all clear that moral properties do not have such a role. Much depends on what we understand by causality (*see* CAUSATION [2; S]) and EXPLANATION [S] (*see* EXPLANATION IN SCIENCE [3]), topics so obscure and controversial (as evident in the PHILOSOPHY OF SCIENCE [6; S], where they really belong) that a major position in ethics should not depend on opinions about them. (Scientific realism itself has been rejected by some on the grounds that it is insufficiently explanatory of our scientific observations and beliefs.) Why exactly may we not explain the Holocaust, as well as our belief that it was evil, in part by the evil of Hitler's character? And was not the evil of his character in part a cause of the Holocaust, as well as of our belief that it was evil? (See Sturgeon, 1984.)

A third argument draws attention to the existence of moral disagreement, especially among cultures (Mackie, 1977). There are three common responses. First, the extent and depth of the disagreement can be competently judged only outside ethics—by anthropologists. Second, disagreement may be due to ignorance of the moral facts, not to their nonexistence. Disagreement seems to be chiefly about the details of morality, for example those concerning sexual behavior. We know too little about these details, especially about their nonmoral properties. Disagreements about economic policies and effective child raising are also widespread, but is this a reason for rejecting realism in economics and child psychology? Third, moral disagreement is often due to misunderstanding (the concepts used, whether moral or nonmoral, are often too vague and unclear), to moral immaturity, and to clashes of self-interest (the rich and the poor may disagree on distributive JUSTICE [4; S]).

A fourth argument is that the relevance of moral facts to motivation and thus behavior is obscure, perhaps nonexistent (Mackie, 1977). A common response is that this too can be competently judged only outside ethics—this time, by psychology, since it concerns motivation (unless the issue is whether the recognition of moral facts logically entails the appropriate motivation, something moral realism need not and should not assert). But psychology is hardly advanced enough to provide an answer, and if we think that someday neuroscience will, we are just speculating.

(SEE ALSO: *Ethical Theory* [S])

Bibliography

Blackburn, S. *Spreading the Word.* Oxford, 1984.

———. *Essays in Quasi-Realism.* Oxford, 1993.

Brink, D. O. *Moral Realism and the Foundations of Ethics.* Cambridge, 1989.

Butchvarov, P. *Skepticism in Ethics.* Bloomington, IN, 1989.

Copp, D., and D. Zimmerman, eds. *Morality, Reason, and Truth.* Totowa, NJ, 1984.

Fumerton, R. A. *Reason and Morality.* Ithaca, NY, 1990.

Harman, G. *The Nature of Morality.* New York, 1977.

Hume, D. *A Treatise of Human Nature* [1739]. London, 1888.

———. *An Inquiry Concerning the Principles of Morals* [1752]. Indianapolis, 1957.

Mackie, J. L. *Ethics: Inventing Right and Wrong.* New York, 1977.

Moore, G. E. *Principia Ethica.* Cambridge, 1903.

———. "The Conception of Intrinsic Value," in *Philosophical Studies* (London, 1922).

Post, J. F. *The Faces of Existence: An Essay in Nonreductive Metaphysics.* Ithaca, NY, 1987.

Ross, W. D. *The Right and the Good.* Oxford, 1930.

Scheler, M. *Formalism in Ethics and Non-Formal Ethics of Values,* trans. M. S. Frings and R. L. Funk. Evanston, IL, 1973.

Sturgeon, N. "Moral Explanations," in D. Copp and D. Zimmerman, eds., *Morality, Reason, and Truth* (Totowa, NJ, 1984).

Wright, C. *Truth and Objectivity.* Cambridge, MA, 1992.

PANAYOT BUTCHVAROV

MORAL RELATIVISM. Moral relativism (e.g., Wong, 1984) involves two claims: (1) a moral judgment can be assigned objective truth conditions only relative to some moral framework; (2) there is no single objectively true morality; instead, there is a variety of moral frameworks, none of which can be objectively distinguished as the correct moral framework.

Moral relativism is opposed by moral absolutism on one side and moral nihilism on the other side. Moral absolutism insists that there is a single objectively true morality. Moral nihilism agrees with moral relativism in rejecting a single true morality but goes on to abandon morality and moral judgments, including relative moral judgments.

In arguing against moral absolutism, moral relativists point to the apparent impossibility of objectively resolving moral disagreements over ABORTION [S], vegetarianism, egoism (*see* EGOISM AND ALTRUISM [2]), and many other issues. Moral relativists argue (a) that we cannot settle by objective inquiry which moral framework is correct and (b) that this provides a strong reason to believe that there is no single correct moral framework. (Moral relativists take the latter reason to be analogous to the strong reason we have to believe there is no privileged spatiotemporal framework.)

Moral absolutists (e.g., Brink, 1989) reject either (a) or (b) or both. They observe that the mere existence of different opinions does not establish relativism and note that, even if there is no way objectively to demonstrate the correctness of any one moral framework, that may be more a limitation on our powers of demonstration than an argument that there is no single true morality.

On the other hand, nihilists, who agree with the conclusion that there is no single true morality, take this conclusion to provide a reason to reject morality altogether, just as those who believe that there is no single true religion tend to reject religion altogether rather than accepting "religious relativism." Moral relativists prefer an analogy with EINSTEIN'S [2] theory of relativity: talk of right and wrong, like talk of before and after, does make sense even though such talk has objective truth conditions only in relation to a choice of framework.

CONFLICT BETWEEN FRAMEWORKS

People who accept different moral frameworks typically have conflicting affective attitudes. One person may wish to end abortions, another may be indifferent to most abortions. In some sense they disagree with each other, but moral relativism does not appear to provide them with any way to express their disagreement. Each agrees that abortion is wrong relative to the first moral framework and that abortion is not wrong relative to the second.

Emotivists (Stevenson, 1944; 1963) argue against restricting moral terminology in the relativistic way and in favor of using moral terminology to express affective attitudes. In its crudest form emotivism offers a "Boo! Hurrah! Who cares!" account of the meaning of moral discourse. "Abortion is morally wrong" means something like "Boo to abortion!" and "Abortion is not wrong" means something like "Abortion, who cares?"

Somewhat more sophisticated versions of emotivism (HARE [S], 1952) treat moral judgments as imperatives: "Don't ever have an abortion!" versus "Have an abortion if you want to!" All these views differ from moral relativism in denying that moral judgments have a truth value. "Boo to abortion!" and "Don't have an abortion!" are neither true nor false.

Emotivism, unlike pure moral relativism, allows people with different moral frameworks to express moral disagreements. On the other hand the crudest forms of emotivism allow only the simplest forms of moral judgment and do not address more complex judgments such as (3) "Either contraception is morally wrong or abortion is not always morally wrong" (*see* EMOTIVE THEORY OF ETHICS [2]).

The most sophisticated form of emotivism, sometimes called PROJECTIVISM [S] (Blackburn, 1993), attempts to handle these more complex judgments as objective projections of subjective values. For example, a moral relativist might in this sense project his or her moral framework onto the world and then use moral terminology as if the projected morality was the single true morality, while at the same time admitting that this way of talking is only "as if." The supposed advantage of this projectivist usage is that it allows people with different moral frameworks to disagree with each other. Critics of the proposal might claim that it only allows such people to appear to disagree with each other!

TRUTH

If projectivism is intelligible, it may appear to threaten the relativist's principle (1). STEVENSON (1963 [S]) and Stoljar (1993) observe that projectivist moral judgments can be treated as having truth conditions, given a redundancy or disquotation theory of truth. Let us use all capital letters to indicate the projectivist usage, as in "MORALLY WRONG." Then, in this view of truth, the truth conditions of the nonrelative emotivist or projectivist judgment, "Abortion is MORALLY WRONG," are given disquotationally as follows: (4) "Abortion is MORALLY WRONG" is true if and only if abortion is MORALLY WRONG. Such a condition is not relative to a moral framework, which may appear to conflict with (1). However, the truth condition is also not an objective truth condition, since (in this view) it is not an objective matter whether abortion is MORALLY WRONG, so (4) does not in the end actually conflict with (1).

IS THERE A NEED FOR RELATIVE MORAL JUDGMENTS?

Let us return to the issue between moral relativism and NIHILISM [5]. Moral relativism denies that we should simply give up on morality in the way that a religious skeptic might give up on religion. There are practical reasons to want to retain morality and relative moral judgments.

Now projectivism claims to provide a nonrelativistic usage that may be more useful than a purely relativistic usage in allowing a way to express moral disagreements between people with different moral frameworks. If so, does that mean we can simply forget about relative moral judgments? Not necessarily, since projectivist moral judgments may be projections of relative moral judgments and unintelligible apart from an understanding of such relative judgments.

(SEE ALSO: *Ethical Theory* [S])

Bibliography

Blackburn, S. *Essays in Quasi-Realism.* Oxford, 1993.

Brink, D. *Moral Realism and the Foundations of Ethics.* Cambridge, 1989.

Hare, R. M. *The Language of Morals.* Oxford, 1952.

Harman, G. "Moral Diversity as an Argument for Moral Relativism," in D. Odegard and C. Stewart, eds., *Perspectives on Moral Relativism* (Millikan, Ont., 1991).

Mackie, J. *Ethics: Inventing Right and Wrong.* Harmondsworth, Middlesex, 1977.

Odegard, D., and C. Stewart. *Perspectives on Moral Relativism.* Millikan, Ont., 1991.

Stevenson, C. L. *Ethics and Language.* New Haven, 1944.

———. *Facts and Values.* New Haven, 1963.

Stoljar, D. "Emotivism and Truth Conditions," *Philosophical Studies,* Vol. 70 (1993), 81–102.

Wong, D. *Moral Relativity.* Berkeley, 1984.

GILBERT HARMAN

MORAL SKEPTICISM. The two main forms of SKEPTICISM [7] about morality are skepticism about moral truths and skepticism about reasons to comply with moral considerations. These doctrines challenge the cognitive significance or rational authority of morality.

Skepticism about moral truths denies that there are—or that we can know that there are—true moral propositions (or facts) that entail that something has a moral attribute. This form of skepticism seems to imply that rational and informed agents would give moral claims no credence. It has been supported by a variety of arguments, including arguments about moral disagreement. One deep motivation for it is the difficulty of explaining the normativity or action-guiding nature of moral claims.

Noncognitivists attempt to explain the normativity of moral judgments by supposing that their function is to express states of the speaker and to affect behavior rather than to express propositions. Noncognitivists would agree that there are no true moral propositions, since they hold that moral claims do not express propositions. Yet they do not view moral claims as defective. According to noncognitivists, one who makes a claim, such as "Truthfulness is morally required," expresses a moral attitude or acceptance of a moral norm (AYER [1], [1936] 1946; Gibbard, 1990; cf. HUME [4; S], [1739–40] 1978).

Cognitivists object that our moral thinking cannot be understood except on the assumption that moral claims express propositions. To avoid skepticism, cognitivists must believe that there are moral properties that are sometimes exemplified. For if no moral property exists, or if none is exemplified, it follows that there are no moral requirements, no moral goods or bads, no moral virtues or vices. It may follow that there are no *honest* persons, for example, although there may be truthful persons.

A skeptic might hold that moral properties exist but that none is exemplified. This position seems implausible, however, for if there is the property of wrongness, it would be astonishing if nothing were ever wrong. Alternatively, a skeptic might argue that there are no moral properties. According to widely accepted views about propositions, however, the proposition that lying is wrong, for example, would attribute the property wrongness to acts of lying. The property would be a constituent of the proposition. Hence, if there are no moral properties, these views about propositions may lead to the conclusion that no proposition is expressed by sentences such as "Lying is wrong."

J. L. MACKIE [S] argued that there are no moral properties (1977). We conceive of moral properties as intrinsic; if an action is wrong, it is wrong "as it is in itself." But we also conceive of moral properties as intrinsically action guiding; we can be motivated to act in an appropriate way simply by coming to know that an action would be wrong, regardless of any antecedent motivations. Yet, Mackie thought, it is not intelligible that it be intrinsic to an action's having an intrinsic property that the mere recognition that the action has the property could motivate a person. The idea of a moral property is not intelligible; moral properties would be metaphysically "queer."

Gilbert Harman (1977) argued for an epistemic version of skepticism about moral truths. He argued that there seems to be no good reason to affirm any moral proposition, for moral hypotheses are never part of the best explanation of any observation. There is always a better nonmoral explanation. The belief that there are true moral propositions is therefore unwarranted.

Skepticism about moral truth appears to have a life of its own in secular cultures, independent of skeptical arguments. Some people believe that moral truths are grounded in God's commands. A secular culture would tend to think, however, that all substantive facts are empirical and "natural." And natural facts do not seem to be normative in the way moral facts are normative. It is therefore difficult to see how a natural fact could be a moral fact.

The second skeptical doctrine is the thesis that there need be no reason to comply with moral considerations. According to this thesis, rational agents would not give attention to moral considerations, as such, in deciding how to live their lives. To be sure, we may desire to live morally, and this desire may give us a reason to live morally. Or we may find ourselves in a context in which living morally is in our interest. Yet these possibilities do not show that there is necessarily a reason to comply with moral considerations (Nielsen, 1974); they do not distinguish moral considerations from considerations of etiquette, for example.

Skepticism about compliance is typically motivated by the idea that morality can require actions that are not to the agent's advantage. Assuming that there are reasons for one to do something just in case it would be to one's advantage, this idea implies that there may be no reason to comply with morality.

The two main skeptical doctrines are closely linked, on certain ways of thinking. First, it may seem, we cannot be guaranteed to have reasons to comply with moral considerations unless there are moral truths of which we have knowledge. Second, a kind of "internalist" theory holds that moral facts are "constituted" by reasons. On this view there are no moral facts unless there are reasons of a relevant kind.

Internalist antiskeptical theories attempt to defeat both skeptical doctrines at once. Immanuel KANT [4; S] held, in effect, that if a moral imperative corresponds to a truth, it does so in virtue of the fact that it would be complied with by any fully rational agent (Kant, [1785] 1981). "Externalist" theories attempt to deal with skepticism about moral truths independently from skepticism about compliance (Sturgeon, 1985). Those who believe that moral truths are grounded in God's commands may suppose, for example, that God necessarily gives us reasons to comply.

Philosophers who accept one of the skeptical doctrines typically try to defuse it. Skeptics about rational compliance may argue that people with normal psychologies invariably have reasons to comply with morality. Skeptics about moral truth may argue that there nevertheless are reasons to engage in the practice of judging things morally.

(SEE ALSO: *Ethical Theory, Moral Realism,* and *Moral Skepticism* [S])

Bibliography

Ayer, A. J. *Language, Truth, and Logic* [1936]. London, 1946.

Copp, D. "Moral Skepticism," *Philosophical Studies,* Vol. 62 (1991), 203–33.

Gibbard, A. *Wise Choices, Apt Feelings: A Theory of Normative Judgment.* Cambridge, MA, 1990.

Harman, G. *The Nature of Morality: An Introduction to Ethics.* Oxford, 1977.

Hume, D. *A Treatise of Human Nature* [1739–40]. Edited by P. H. Nidditch. Oxford, 1978.

Kant, I. *Grounding of the Metaphysics of Morals* [1785]. Translated by James W. Ellington. Indianapolis, IN, 1981.

Mackie, J. L. *Ethics: Inventing Right and Wrong.* Harmondsworth, Middlesex, 1977.

Nielsen, K. "Why Should I Be Moral?" in W. K. Frankena and J. T. Granrose, eds., *Introductory Readings in Ethics* (Englewood Cliffs, NJ, 1974).

Nietzsche, F. *Basic Writings of Nietzsche.* Edited and translated by Walter Kaufmann. New York, 1968. See *The Genealogy of Morals* and *Beyond Good and Evil.*

Sturgeon, N. "Moral Explanations," in D. Copp and D. Zimmerman, eds., *Morality, Reason, and Truth* (Totowa, NJ, 1985).

DAVID COPP

MULTIPLE REALIZABILITY. Multiple realizability (MR) marks the pivotal point upon which a number of debates have turned. Most notably, Hilary PUTNAM [S] and Jerry Fodor reject the doctrine of reductive materialism (*see* REDUCTION, REDUCTIONISM [S]) on grounds that mental properties are "multiply realized" by the physical (Fodor, 1974; Putnam, 1967). At stake is the IDENTITY [4; S] of types or properties, the values of the abstract singular terms and predicates that factor crucially in the formulation of scientific laws. Briefly, property identity requires necessary coextension, with the aforementioned items always occurring together (cf. "water = H_2O"). Reductive materialism thus holds that all PROPERTIES [S] are necessarily coextensive with physical properties. Yet, by employing a functional analysis, Putnam and Fodor argue that mental properties fail to correlate with the physical in the requisite way, since the same function can be instantiated in (or subserved by) radically different physical structures (see FUNCTIONALISM [S]). Hence, any attempt at reducing psychology on the basis of such correlations must ultimately fail.

This suggests a general definition, where A and B are sets of properties, with A representing the realized properties and B serving as their realization base:

> A property F in A is subject to multiple realization in a set B if and only if there are distinct properties G and H in B such that (1) it is possible that an object realizes F by virtue of G but not H; (2) it is possible that an object realizes F by virtue of H but not G; and (3) there is no property K in the set B such that, necessarily, every object realizes F by virtue of K.

Clauses (1) and (2) jointly express the desired "variability," meaning that the base properties G and H are individually sufficient but not necessary to bring about F; while clause (3) expresses a form of "irreducibility," meaning that no other property in the set B is both necessary and sufficient for F, nothing coextensive in the way that would license identifying F with a property in the designated set B.

So defined, MR appears satisfied in a number of cases: the properties implicated in the classification of Aristotelian form to matter, various construals of function to substance, folk classifications of mental to physical, and their scientific progeny, a functionalist psychology vis-à-vis neuroscience. There is the much-heralded plasticity of psychological functions within the primate cerebral cortex (Johnson, 1993), and more so if these functions are distributed over physically diverse mechanical devices, as computer engineering will attest. For example, (1) an object can add by virtue of having a human cell assembly rather than, say, the Intel 80386 microprocessor, and (2) vice versa, with (3) no property in that set underlying every possible occurrence while serving to realize the adding function. This is the initial data to which Putnam and Fodor appeal, and this much goes virtually uncontested (but cf. Kim, 1972; Zangwill, 1992). Whether one may wield these facts against the doctrine of reductive materialism, however, depends upon the resolution of substantive philosophical issues. The debate is waged on three fronts.

First, there is a concern about reduction. For applying MR to a suitable range of psychofunctional and neuroscientific properties delivers nonreductivism in the proprietary sense that no identities exist between the specified types. Yet this is compatible with a different understanding of reduction that entails no identities or lawful coextensions. Alternative accounts are legion. One of the more interesting is Paul Churchland's (1979) suggestion that an explanatorily equipotent image of psychology might be derived from physical theory on the basis of a structural isomorphism (also Bickle, 1992). On the other hand, it remains a point of some consequence that MR forbids strict property identities, seeing that they underwrite claims about the ontology of reduction (Causey, 1977; Enc, 1983) and serve to distinguish reductive materialism from its eliminativist rival (*see* ELIMINATIVE MATERIALISM [S]). Moreover, the degree of variability exhibited by psychofunctional types might preclude the possibility envisaged, namely, a theory that is at once an image of psychology and roughly isomorphic to physical theory. For if psychology is radically incommensurate with physical theory, then so too is any approximate image (Endicott, 1993).

Second, there is a concern about the significance of MR. Specifically, many claim that the Putnam–Fodor-style argument is vitiated by the fact that mental and physical properties both enjoy this variability in their instances. Jaegwon Kim (1972) mentions the case of temperature (also Enc, 1983; Wilson, 1985). Others draw a parallel with Mendelian genetics (Richardson, 1979). The point is that a property can be undeniably physical and a paradigm of reduction in spite of its multiple realizability. So why, on account of that selfsame phenomenon, should one believe that psychological properties are nonphysical and irreducible? Still, critics of reductionism see important differences on this score. Some argue that only mental properties are initially excluded from the class of physical properties by any criterion of "physical" at play in the debate, and mental properties are consequently irreducible to the entire range of physical properties, given their realization base with respect to this class (Endicott, 1989). Others describe how mental types are conspicuously more diverse in their instances (Horgan, 1993; Pereboom & Kornblith, 1991).

Third, and finally, there is a concern about the correct interpretation of the properties. For one may reconstruct either the multiply realized types or their realization base so that MR no longer applies. Thus, the base properties might be extended by means of logico-mathematical operations, generating physical coextensions (e.g., Kim, 1978; cf. Owens, 1989; Teller, 1983). Or, a strategy more closely tied to scientific practice, Kim (1972, 1992) appeals to domain-specific properties and species-relative laws that promise local reductions of psychological phenomena (also Enc, 1983). So, whereas pain per se is realized in various ways across sentient creatures, the more restricted human pain is not. On the contrary, only human neurophysiology subserves human pain, and any physical diversity that underlies pain in other species is simply irrelevant. Nevertheless, critics respond that this reductive strategy misses important generalizations across domains (Block, 1978); ignores physical differences within the same species (Pereboom & Kornblith, 1991); and cannot overcome plasticity within the same individual over time without collapsing the distinction between type and token identities (Endicott, 1993). Such concerns illustrate the metaphysics and PHILOSOPHY OF SCIENCE [6; S] behind the debate over multiple realizability.

(SEE ALSO: *Philosophy of Mind* [S])

Bibliography

Bickle, J. "Multiple Realizability and Psychophysical Reduction," *Behavior and Philosophy*, Vol. 20 (1992), 47–58.

Block, N. "Troubles with Functionalism," *Minnesota Studies in the Philosophy of Science*, Vol. 9 (1978), 261–325.

Causey, R. *Unity of Science*. Dordrecht, 1977.

Churchland, P. *Scientific Realism and the Plasticity of Mind.* Cambridge, MA, 1979.

Enc, B. "In Defense of the Identity Theory," *Journal of Philosophy,* Vol. 80 (1983), 279–98.

Endicott, R. "On Physical Multiple Realization," *Pacific Philosophical Quarterly,* Vol. 70 (1989), 212–24.

———. "Species-Specific Properties and More Narrow Reductive Strategies," *Erkenntnis,* Vol. 38 (1993), 303–21.

Fodor, J. "Special Sciences, or the Disunity of Science as a Working Hypothesis," *Synthese,* Vol. 28 (1974), 77–115.

Horgan, T. "Nonreductive Materialism and the Explanatory Autonomy of Psychology," in S. Wagner and R. Warner, eds., *Naturalism: A Critical Appraisal* (Notre Dame, 1993).

Johnson, M. *Brain Development and Cognition: A Reader.* Oxford, 1993.

Kim, J. "Phenomenal Properties, Psychophysical Laws, and the Identity Theory," *Monist,* Vol. 56 (1972), 177–92.

———. "Supervenience and Nomological Incommensurables," *American Philosophical Quarterly,* Vol. 15 (1978), 149–56.

———. "Multiple Realization and the Metaphysics of Reduction," *Philosophy and Phenomenological Research,* Vol. 52 (1992), 1–26.

Owens, D. "Disjunctive Laws," *Analysis,* Vol. 49 (1989), 197–202.

Pereboom, D., and H. Kornblith. "The Metaphysics of Irreducibility," *Philosophical Studies,* Vol. 63 (1991), 125–45.

Putnam, H. "Psychological Predicates," in W. Capitan and D. Merrill, eds., *Art, Mind, and Religion* (Pittsburgh, 1967).

Richardson, R. "Functionalism and Reductionism," *Philosophy of Science,* Vol. 46 (1979), 533–58.

Teller, P. "Comments on Kim's Paper," *Southern Journal of Philosophy,* Vol. 22 (1983), suppl. 57–61.

Wilson, M. "What Is This Thing Called 'Pain'?: The Philosophy of Science behind the Contemporary Debate," *Pacific Philosophical Quarterly,* Vol. 66 (1985), 227–67.

Zangwill, N. "Variable Realization: Not Proved," *Philosophical Quarterly,* Vol. 42 (1992), 214–19.

RONALD ENDICOTT

N

NATIONALISM AND INTERNATIONAL RELATIONS. The publication of Elie Kedourie's *Nationalism* in 1960 marked the beginning of a renaissance of scholarship about NATIONALISM [5] and national identity. Kedourie saw nationalism as an unsuccessful attempt to solve the problem of political legitimacy in modern society by regarding the state as an expression of the will of a people. For Kedourie, who traced the ideology of nationalism to Enlightenment philosophies of the will (particularly those of KANT [4; S] and FICHTE [3]), the very idea of a self-determining political community was flawed; legitimacy should be solely a result of the ability of governments to manage conflicts.

In contrast to Kedourie, Ernest Gellner saw nationalism as an ideology of modern industrial society—promulgated by the educational institutions that train elites to manage modern bureaucracies. Both Kedourie and Gellner regarded nations as essentially modern phenomena. Anthony Smith, among others, held what has sometimes been characterized as a primordialist view of national identity. On this account nationalism constitutes the political response of traditional ethnic communities to the effects of modern market and state institutions. The modernist view of Walker Connor is more in accord with Kedourie and Gellner in regarding nations as groups who come to believe that they are ancestrally related. Thus, on this account, nations are a creation of nationalist ideology rather than a product of the interaction of already existent ethnic nationalities with modernization.

Discussions within international law concerning the consequences of decolonization in the 1960s paralleled the debate about the nature of national identity. For instance, Rupert Emerson argued that the concept of self-determination used by anticolonial movements did not necessarily apply to noncolonial settings. In earlier international law peoples who claimed a right to political independence were presumably non-self-governing. But once the concept of a people is given an ethnic or national meaning, there is no definite way to determine which nations ought to have rights to states. As Emerson pointed out, the definition of a nation as a culturally homogeneous people (or ethnic group) can be used to disrupt internationally recognized borders and self-governing political communities.

There has been much subsequent discussion about whether ethnically defined nations in the postcolonial world have distinct rights. A number of philosophers have argued recently that culturally homogeneous groups have rights to their own states, either as a result of the good of collective membership (Avishai Margalit & Joseph Raz), the desirability of consent to membership in a political community (Harry Beran), or the necessary presumption of communal membership for any theory of distributive justice (Michael Walzer). Critics of the principle of national self-determination have argued that group identity cannot justify rights to territorial takings (Lea Brilmayer) and that granting self-determination to nations undermines agreements that can safeguard environmental preservation and international peace (Jeremy Brecher).

Walzer, in his book *Just and Unjust Wars,* connected the issue of the rights of nations to theories of a just war. In his view nations could claim rights if they were able to conduct legitimate and successful secessions, even if these resulted in civil wars. However, Allen Buchanan argues that, while secessions may be justified as a means of avoiding systematic discrimination by a central government, they cannot be so justified simply as a result of the political assertion of a will to form a new state. With regard to international terrorism, Virginia Held has written that it is no different in principle from other forms of political violence and is therefore subject to the same considerations of justification as wars. Charles Beitz has similarly challenged the presumption against foreign interventions found not only in Walzer, but in international law generally, by arguing that its assumption of the autonomy of states is unwarranted. Finally, in response to Walzer, Robert Holmes has renovated a pacifist position regarding modern war in particular, since, he argues, modern war is so inherently destructive of innocent life that it can never be justified as a legitimate exercise in self-defense.

The renovation of concepts of national identity and just war put into question the idea that there were ever any universal entitlements or rights that could bridge the divisions between peoples and states. Two possible applications of universal ideas to international relations are the concepts of international distributive justice and human rights. Charles Beitz and Thomas Pogge have both written in defense of extending a conception of distributive justice based on John RAWLS's [S] theory to the global level, thus mandating a redistribution of wealth on a world scale. At the same time Jack Donnelly has attempted to give international human rights a philosophical foundation that avoids problems with both will- and interest-based notions of RIGHTS [7; S].

The attempts to justify national rights, along with arguments for universal human entitlements, raise the problem of which persons are entitled to membership in which states. Walzer has argued that citizenship cannot be determined in relation to prior considerations of JUSTICE [4; S], since it is only within a community in which some are members and others are not that a conception of justice has meaning. In response, Joseph Carens has presented the case for "open borders," arguing that there are no clear reasons in any contemporary theory of justice for restricting the freedom of movement of immigrants.

While the idea of the nation-state, which some regard as an unrealizable ideal at the end of the twentieth century, has been the most prevalent conception of a political community for some time, other ideas are being reconsidered. On the one hand Charles Taylor and Will Kymlicka advocate a multicultural community in which different cultural groups are explicitly recognized. On the other hand Jürgen HABERMAS [S], in discussing the viability of the European Community, has maintained the importance of keeping ascribed cultural identities separate from discursive political ones in the construction of political communities. It remains to be seen, however, whether concepts of cultural diversity or political discourse are sufficient for a new understanding of community.

(SEE ALSO: *Social and Political Philosophy* [S])

Bibliography

Beitz, C. R. *Political Theory and International Relations.* Princeton, NJ, 1979.

Beran, H. *The Consent Theory of Political Obligation.* London, 1987.

Brecher, J. " 'The National Question' Reconsidered from an Ecological Perspective," *New Politics,* Vol. 1 (1987), 95–112.

Brilmayer, L. "Secession and Self-Determination," *Yale Journal of International Law,* Vol. 16 (1991), 177–201.

Buchanan, A. E. *Secession.* Boulder, CO, 1991.

Carens, J. H. "Aliens and Citizens," *Review of Politics,* Vol. 49 (1987), 251–73.

Connor, W. *Ethnonationalism.* Princeton, NJ, 1994.

Donnelly, J. *The Concept of Human Rights.* New York, 1985.

Emerson, R. "Self-Determination," *American Journal of International Law,* Vol. 65 (1971), 459–75.

Gellner, E. *Nations and Nationalism.* Ithaca, NY, 1983.

Habermas, J. "Citizenship and National Identity," *Praxis International,* Vol. 12 (1992), 1–19.

Held, V. "Violence, Terrorism, and Moral Inquiry," *The Monist,* Vol. 67 (1984), 605–26.

Holmes, R. *On War and Morality.* Princeton, NJ, 1989.

Kedourie, E. *Nationalism.* London, 1960.

Kymlicka, W. *Liberalism, Community, and Culture.* Oxford, 1989.

Margalit, A., and J. Raz. "National Self-Determination," *Journal of Philosophy,* Vol. 87 (1990), 439–61.

Pogge, T. *Realizing Rawls.* Ithaca, NY, 1989.

Smith, A. D. *The Ethnic Origins of Nations.* Oxford, 1986.

Taylor, C. "The Politics of Recognition," in A. Gutmann, ed., *Multiculturalism and "The Politics of Recognition"* (Princeton, NJ, 1992).

Walzer, M. *Just and Unjust Wars.* New York, 1977.

OMAR DAHBOUR

NATIVISM, INNATISM. Although the thought that some human knowledge is innate (that is, not the product of learning) is an ancient one, it was revived with the 1957 publication of *Syntactic Structures,* Noam CHOMSKY's [S] short but ground-breaking treatise in linguistics. In that and much subsequent work, Chomsky argued for the intelligibility and desirability of an empirical study of LANGUAGE [4; S] that would take as its central goal the explicit and precise characterization of the linguistic knowledge of competent speakers. Not only must this characterization satisfy the obvious criterion of descriptive adequacy—namely, it must be faithful to the intricate range of facts regarding the nature of, and relations between, sound, structure, and meaning in human languages—but it must also make possible an account of language acquisition.

For Chomsky and many linguists, the most prominent features of first-language learning are that it proceeds without the benefit of explicit training; that all normal children display approximately the same patterns of acquisition; and that, relative to the wealth of knowledge the child acquires in just five or so years, language learning takes place rapidly and on the basis of little information. These features of language acquisition, Chomsky has contended, lead immediately to what he calls "Plato's Problem": how do humans manage to acquire such extensive linguistic knowledge so quickly and on the basis of such impoverished data?

A brief example from Chomsky (1980, pp. 160–61) may serve as an illustration. Consider the following four sentences of English:

(1) John betrayed the woman he loved.
(2) The woman he loved betrayed John.
(3) Everyone betrayed the woman he loved.
(4) The woman he loved betrayed everyone.

Any competent speaker of English will recognize certain facts about the interpretations of these sentences. In (1), "he" may refer to John. The same applies for (2), which can thus mean that the woman who he, John, loved betrayed John. Both (1) and (2) differ in this respect from a sentence such as "He betrayed the woman John loved," in which the pronoun cannot refer to John. If we replace the name "John" in (1) and (2) by the quantificational expression "everyone," we get (3) and (4), respectively. One might expect interpretations corresponding to those of (1) and (2). This is borne out for (3), which may indeed be understood to mean that every person *x* is such that *x* betrayed the woman whom *x* loved. But (4), surprisingly, cannot mean that every person *x* is such that the woman who *x* loved betrayed *x*; instead, we must take "he" to refer to some independently identified individual.

These as well as countless other subtle and superficially anomalous facts about their language are known to speakers without their having been taught them, and without their ever having observed any use of the relevant sentences. Indeed, it seems hard to see how such linguistic phenomena could have been explicitly conveyed to speakers, for the principles that organize them and reveal the deeper regularities they instance involve abstract concepts only recently articulated and of which speakers have no conscious grasp at all.

The only plausible hypothesis, according to Chomsky and others, is that the child is born already knowing much about his or her future language. But since children are not genetically predisposed to acquire a particular language (children of Hungarian parents would not find it any easier to learn Hungarian than they would Greek), it must be that they are born with considerable knowledge about any human language they might encounter. This could be, however, only if all possible natural languages share many underlying characteristics, that is, only if there are linguistic universals true for all languages despite their variegated surface appearance. In the face of the poverty of the stimulus to which the learning child is exposed and the richness of the linguistic knowledge that develops, it is natural to infer that the child is genetically endowed with innate knowledge of many universals that characterize fundamental properties of all learnable languages. (Some of these universals will, for instance, be involved in a deep explanation of such phenomena as the admissible interpretations of (1)–(4).) The process of language acquisition, on this view, consists in the child's determining which of all possible human languages—each one of which he innately knows a great deal about—is actually his own, that is, is the one spoken around him.

There is an interdependence between this conclusion about innate knowledge and the goal of descriptive adequacy mentioned above. The second informs the first, for as the characterization of human languages—what the child eventually comes to acquire, quickly, and on the basis of little evidence—reveals greater complexity, so the argument to innateness becomes the more plausible. And the first informs the second, for the assumption that there is innate knolwedge of linguistic universals encourages the search for a level of linguistic description that is deep enough to reveal the hidden kinship between superficially very different languages.

Linguistics, on this conception, becomes the branch of PSYCHOLOGY [7] that studies both the intricate knowledge speakers possess that enables their use of language, and the information available to them at birth that makes acquisition of this knowledge possible. In what came to be known as the cognitive revolution, other areas in psychology patterned themselves on linguistics: they sought to characterize the knowledge that underlay a particular range of abilities and they also strove to account for its acquisition, sometimes by appeal to knowledge or concepts innately given.

Chomsky and others have argued that the successes of this approach to linguistics, and to other areas in psychology, constitute a vindication of seventeenth-century rationalist thought over its empiricist opponents (*see* RATIONALISM [6]; EMPIRICISM [2]). Empirical research into language shows, it is claimed, that those who treat the human newborn as an empty vessel waiting to be filled by Nature are mistaken.

These claims have come in for considerable attack by philosophers, as have some of the methods and concepts of modern linguistics. It has been argued, for example, that it is unintelligible to attribute to the learning child propositional knowledge of the relevant kind (e.g., knowledge that a particular regularity holds for all human languages) on the grounds that such knowledge involves thoughts, and thoughts can be attributed only to creatures who already possess a language. We make no headway, this argument runs, in explaining how humans acquire language by attributing to them knowledge that they could intelligibly possess only if they had a language.

Even the contention that knowledge must be attributed to competent speakers in an explanation of their linguistic abilities (whether or not this knowledge is partly innate) has generated opposition. Worries have been expressed about a concept of knowledge that to some appears quite different from the standard one. Thus linguistic knowledge seems not to require justification, as do many familiar cases of knowledge. Furthermore, we are not conscious of our linguistic knowledge as we are of much other knowledge: we could not articulate the principles that constitute our knowledge of language—indeed, we very likely would not even be able to recognize them were they presented to us, involving as they do concepts of which we have no conscious understanding.

Such criticisms have led linguists and sympathetic philosophers to defend vigorously the coherence and importance of Chomsky's conception of linguistic knowledge. One of the most sustained and interesting debates has been between Chomsky and the philosopher W. V. O. QUINE [7; S]. Their fundamental disagreement is sometimes assumed to revolve around the issue of innateness, with Quine, the empiricist, portrayed as unwilling to countenance the appeal to innate knowledge. This way of putting the matter is only half right, however. It is correct that Quine finds Chomsky's notion of innate linguistic knowledge problematic, but that is not because Quine has objections to innateness; Quine himself believes that no learning is possible without something being given innately. Rather, what Quine finds troublesome is the notion of linguistic knowledge. For as conceived by Chomsky, it cannot be understood as a place holder for a collection of behavioral dispositions: someone may lack the ability to use language but still possess linguistic knowledge (this is what we might say, according to Chomsky, of one who, for whatever reason, temporarily loses her capacity to speak). This construal of knowledge of language, according to which it can be present but unmanifestable, is in tension with Quine's emphasis on the public nature of MEANING [5; S].

What this and other debates may ultimately indicate is less that there is disagreement about whether innate structures exist pertaining to the cognitive functioning of humans than that there is confusion and controversy over the precise nature of these structures.

(SEE ALSO: *Epistemology*)

Bibliography

Chomsky, N. *Syntactic Structures.* The Hague, 1957.

———. *Aspects of the Theory of Syntax.* Cambridge, 1965.

———. *Cartesian Lingusitics.* New York, 1966.

———. *Reflections on Language.* New York, 1975.

———. *Rules and Representations.* New York, 1980.

Otero, C., ed. *Noam Chomsky: Critical Assessments.* Vol. 2. New York, 1994.

Quine, W. V. O. "Methodological Reflections on Current Linguistic Theory," in D. Davidson and J. Hintikka, eds., *Semantics of Natural Language* (Boston, 1972).

———. "Linguistics and Philosophy," in *The Ways of Paradox and Other Essays* (Cambridge, 1976).

ALEXANDER GEORGE

NATURAL KINDS. *See:* PROPERTIES [S]

NATURALISM.

Philosophical NATURALISM [5] might be characterized in rough terms as the view that nature is all there is and all basic truths are truths of nature. But even those who can accept this description differ widely on three questions: (1) What is nature? (2) What kind of "is" expresses its identity with what there is? (3) What sorts of truths are basic, and in what way? Naturalism is more often presupposed than stated, and naturalists differ in their conceptions of the position. Thus, (1) may be answered ontologically, in terms of what kinds of entities count as natural, or methodologically, in terms of the methods of investigation that determine what counts as natural, or in other ways.

Naturalisms may be global, applying to everything, or domain specific, targeting one category of phenomenon, such as the mental. Any naturalism may be reductive or nonreductive. Reductive naturalisms may attempt either conceptual or nonconceptual REDUCTION [S]. Thus, in the PHILOSOPHY OF MIND [S] logical behaviorism seeks to reduce mental phenomena to behavioral (hence natural) phenomena by philosophical analysis; a mind–brain identity theory could claim that it is only an empirical fact that mental phenomena are physical (and thereby natural).

Nonreductive naturalism requires special comment. Its main division is perhaps between substantive and methodological versions. The former maintain that everything they apply to—e.g., mental phenomena, properties, numbers—is some specified kind of natural entity; the latter specify only a methodology, characteristically one deemed scientific, such that everything it applies to is thereby properly called natural. Thus, a substantive, nonreductive naturalism in the philosophy of mind might hold that mental properties are natural though not reducible to physical properties—the paradigmatically basic kind of natural properties. This claim might be defended by arguing that mental properties supervene on physical ones, where "supervene" implies that our mental properties, and thereby all psychological truths about us, are determined by physical properties and physical truths. It might also be held that any moral properties and truths there are depend similarly on physical properties and truths. By contrast, a methodological naturalist might hold that what counts as a natural property is determined, not by any specific ontological base of, say, physical properties, but rather by the success of scientific investigations, and scientific legitimation even of psychic properties not supervening on physical properties is not ruled out.

One way to avoid reduction of putative nonnatural entities is to eliminate them. Eliminative materialism, which claims that there are no mental phenomena, can be driven by naturalism (*see* ELIMINATIVE MATERIALISM, ELIMINATIVISM [S]). Elimination, even when motivated by naturalism, should be distinguished from *naturalization:* the latter brings the target phenomena into the natural domain; the former discountenances them. Thus, although eliminativism motivated by naturalism is not reductive regarding mental phenomena, it contrasts sharply with what is called nonreductive naturalism.

Naturalization can be attempted in any domain. Let us consider just three in which there has been much theorizing.

In METAPHYSICS [5; S], although a naturalist need not be a physicalist—holding that only physical phenomena are real, not even excepting such comparatively well-behaved abstract entities as sets—naturalism may be in some way derived from, or at least be motivated by, physicalism (*see* PHYSICALISM, MATERIALISM [S]). But how well do we understand the physical? It need not be, for example, the corporeal: consider the physical forces in action at a distance. If, however, we do not characterize the physical intrinsically in terms of some kind of property, we appear forced to define it by appeal to what physical scientists discover, or perhaps would ultimately discover. Then we cannot know a priori that, for example, irreducibly mentalistic explanations will not ultimately be part of what the people we call physicists consider their best overall account of reality. It could turn out, moreover, to be impossible to account adequately for science, not to mention philosophy, without positing some abstract entities such as numbers, propositions, and POSSIBLE WORLDS [S].

A further question concerns CAUSATION [2; S], which appears central for either substantive or methodological naturalisms. Suppose that mental properties in some sense must depend on physical properties, as nonreductive SUPERVENIENCE [S] requires. Robust naturalists tend to want more. Many naturalists seem committed to the causal closure of the physical world, roughly the view that all causes are, or depend exclusively on, physical causes, as opposed to the causal sufficiency of the physical: the existence of physical nomically sufficient conditions for every event. Causal sufficiency implies the possibility of a *comprehensive* physical science, but is not exclusive in the way closure is.

In EPISTEMOLOGY [3; S] consider just RELIABILISM [S]—roughly, the view that knowledge and justified beliefs are constituted by beliefs that are reliably produced (i.e., produced or sustained in a way that makes them likely to be true). Reliabilists may try to naturalize epistemology in at least two contrasting ways (*see* NATURALIZED EPISTEMOLOGY [S]). They may hold that epistemology, properly practiced, is a branch of psychology or that epistemology is committed to no irreducibly normative, and thereby nonnatural, properties. We might call the view that the truths of epistemology are empirical substantive epistemological naturalism, and the view that its only irreducible concepts are natural—with its apparent implication that all its truths are naturalistically expressible—conceptual epistemological naturalism. The latter view does not entail the former: an epistemologist could use only (naturalized) concepts and still countenance nonempirical epistemic principles.

In ethics reductive naturalism—the view that moral properties (e.g., obligatoriness) are natural properties remains controversial. We could, however, have conceptual naturalism here without substantive naturalism: even if moral concepts are reducible to natural ones, some moral truths could be a priori. A weaker view is normative naturalism, the nonreductive position that there are naturalistic, contingently necessary and sufficient conditions for applying moral terms. A position that leaves reductive naturalism open is explanationist naturalism—the view that moral properties are explanatory and ethical truths are confirmable by natural facts about individuals and society. As elsewhere, naturalists may proceed by elimination. An analogue of eliminativism in philosophy of mind is ethical NONCOGNITIVISM [S]: just as there are no mental properties, there are no moral ones. But whereas the former eliminativists commonly hold that we can have better ways to explain behavior than the mentalistic modes now employed, noncognitivists generally embrace moral discourse as invaluable—they simply decognitivize it: moral predicates are expressive or prescriptive, not descriptive or explanatory. Again we may have conceptual naturalism without substantive naturalism: even if moral concepts are reducible to natural ones, some moral truths could be a priori.

In any attempt to understand naturalism there is a danger of speaking as if it is clear when a view is reductive; but 'reduction' may be no clearer than when two predicates express the same property. Do they express the same property provided they are (1) synonymous, (2) analytically equivalent, (3) conceptually equivalent, (4) logically equivalent, (5) metaphysically equivalent, (6) synthetically a priori equivalent, (7) explanatorally equivalent, (8) nomically equivalent, (9) causally equivalent, or (10) something else again? The weaker the criteria for reduction, the more readily reductive naturalization can be achieved; the stronger these criteria, the more significant a nonreductive, substantive naturalization can be. As to methodological naturalism, if it takes SCIENTIFIC METHOD [7] as the only route to knowledge—and some such conviction also largely motivates substantive naturalisms—this leaves unclear just what is ruled out by a commitment to scientific method. And if we cannot characterize scientific method in quite definite terms and instead must conceive it as the investigative procedure the scientific community uses, where that community is understood—in the spirit of naturalism—historically and sociologically, then naturalism is functionally defined, in terms of how well the thesis or project in question fits whatever worldview has suitable scientific sanction. How clear, then, is our conception of naturalism if scientific method is essential to it? It may seem as clear—or contested—as our present understanding of scientific method. The question remains whether this understanding is firm enough to anchor a philosophical worldview.

Bibliography

Armstrong, D. M. *The Nature of Mind and Other Essays.* Ithaca, NY, 1981.

Kim, J. "The Myth of Nonreductive Materialism," *Proceedings of the American Philosophical Association* 63 (1989), 31–47.

Kitcher, P. "The Naturalists Return," *Philosophical Review,* Vol. 101 (1992), 53–114.

Kornblith, H., ed. *Naturalized Epistemology.* Cambridge, MA, 1985.

Nagel, E. *The Structure of Science.* New York, 1961.

Sellars, R. W. "Why Naturalism and Not Materialism," *Philosophical Review* 36 (1927), 216–25.

Post, J. *The Faces of Existence.* Ithaca, NY, 1987.

Quine, W. V. O. "Epistemology Naturalized," in *Ontological Relativity and Other Essays* (New York, 1969).

Wagner, S. J., and R. Warner, eds. *Naturalism: A Critical Appraisal.* Notre Dame, 1993.

ROBERT AUDI

NATURALIZED EPISTEMOLOGY. Movements to naturalize are influential in almost every area of philosophy, from PHILOSOPHY OF MIND to PHILOSOPHY OF LANGUAGE [S] to moral philosophy. The aim of these movements is to ensure that our philosophical theories are compatible with science—that is, make reference only to those properties and entities that science can countenance. Naturalized epistemologists share this aim, but they also argue that the practices and findings of science should play a more positive, active role in epistemological theorizing.

W. V. O. QUINE [7; S] coined the expression 'naturalized epistemology' and is the movement's most influential proponent. He rejects the analytic-synthetic distinction, and this in turn leads him to emphasize the holistic nature of our belief systems. Our beliefs cannot be neatly divided into those that purport to capture analytic truths, which are known a priori and as such are not subject to empirical disconfirmation, and those that capture synthetic truths, which are known a posteriori and are subject to empirical disconfirmation. Rather, our beliefs face the test of experience as a whole. When experiences fail to turn out as expected, we know that something in our belief system has gone wrong and is in need of revision, but no part of the system is in principle immune from revision. It is a short step from this conclusion to the view that there is no sharp separation between EPISTEMOLOGY [3; S] and science. Epistemology cannot be done without empirical input. It has to be naturalized.

Quine's most famous characterization of naturalized epistemology is that it turns epistemology into a chapter of psychology. This is accomplished by reformulating the traditional questions of epistemology to make them proper subjects of empirical studies. For example, the question, Do our sensory experiences justify our beliefs about the external world? is replaced with, How do sensory experiences cause us to believe what we do about the external world? The strategy is to make epistemology into a part of natural science and hence, in Quine's view, respectable.

Some other epistemologists who see themselves as doing naturalized epistemology reject many of Quine's positions, but they share his distaste for a priori theorizing in epistemology. Cartesian epistemology, in particular, is the common enemy. DESCARTES [2; S] thought of epistemology as first philosophy; the epistemologist's task is to tell us what intellectual methods and procedures we are justified in employing. Science can be of no help in this project, since a part of the project's motivation is to lay down rules for science itself.

In the eyes of naturalized epistemologists, this conception of epistemology forced Descartes and epistemologists influenced by him to resort to armchair speculation about what intellectual procedures, methods, and practices are to be trusted. Not surprisingly, they came to different conclusions. Descartes recommends the method of doubt; LOCKE [4; S] recommends the way of ideas; RUSSELL [7] insists that all knowledge ultimately depends on direct acquaintance with facts; and CHISHOLM [S] says that it is prima facie reasonable for us to trust INTROSPECTION [S], MEMORY [5; S], and PERCEPTION [6; S]. The problem common to all these recommendations, say naturalized epistemologists, is that they are the result of a priori reflections about what methods are to be trusted. The alternative is to abandon the Cartesian project and instead to make full use of science in thinking about epistemological questions.

Naturalized epistemologists appeal to science in a variety of ways. Some engage in detailed studies of the methods and practices of science. The assumption is that, insofar as we are interested in which intellectual procedures are trustworthy, we need to look carefully at how science works, since it is the most successful of all human intellectual enterprises.

Others have attempted to use the theory of evolution to address some of the central questions of epistemology, including, for example, the question of what reasons we have for trusting our cognitive faculties. For example, some evolutionary epistemologists argue that natural selection favors reliable cognitive faculties, since they are survival enhancing. So, it is to be expected that our cognitive faculties are reliable.

Still others apply the findings of COGNITIVE SCIENCE [S] to epistemology, citing studies that show recurrent patterns of errors in the way we reason. The errors arise, for example, from an insensitivity to sample size, an underutilization of known prior probabilities in making predictions, a tendency in certain kinds of situations to assign a higher probability to a conjunction than to one of its conjuncts, and so on. The assumption behind these projects is that epistemology has traditionally been interested in fashioning advice for the improvement of our intellectual lives, but for this we need to look at empirical studies that document the kinds of mistakes we have a tendency to make. We will then be in a position to guard against them.

Yet others follow Quine's advice more literally, focusing their attention on how our sense experiences lead to our beliefs, hypotheses, and theories. The emphasis is on how cognition actually functions, and the relevant sciences are psychology and neurobiology.

A recurrent objection to naturalized epistemology is that it is not normative and thus constitutes an abandonment of epistemology. If we turn epistemology into a chapter of psychology, in which its principal task is to describe how a relatively restricted sensory input produces a rich array of beliefs, then we are no longer interested in assessing which procedures, methods, and practices we are justified in believing. We are simply describing how we come to believe what we do.

In general, naturalized epistemologists have been eager to respond that they have no intention of abandoning the normative element within epistemology. Quine's view is that the normative is not jettisoned; it merely becomes a part of what he calls the "engineering" of truth seeking. If we assume that one of our goals is to believe truths and assume also that this goal is valuable, then the various sciences, from physics to psychology to mathematics, are in a position to give us advice about how to achieve this goal—advice that has normative implications. For example, physics advises us not to take soothsayers seriously, since their claims to reliability are incompatible with what physics tells us; psychology provides us with information about the conditions in which we are subject to perceptual illusions, wishful thinking, and other such cognitive problems; mathematics warns us against various kinds of statistical mistakes; and so on.

Alvin Goldman has a different response to the objection that naturalized epistemology is not normative. Unlike Quine, he does not altogether reject the analytic–synthetic distinction (*see* ANALYTIC AND SYNTHETIC STATEMENTS [1]), and as a result he is more comfortable than Quine in proposing a conceptual analysis of epistemic justification. The analysis he defends is a reliabilist one; epistemic justification is essentially a matter of having one's beliefs generated by reliable cognitive processes (see RELIABILISM [S]). Goldman points out that a naturalized approach to epistemology fits comfortably with this reliabilist account of epistemic justification, and it is this that allows epistemology to be both naturalized and normative. Reliabilism tells us that we are justified in employing an intellectual procedure, method, or practice insofar as the practice is reliable, and then science tells us which procedures, methods, and practices are in fact reliable.

Hilary Kornblith has yet another way of arguing that naturalized epistemology is normative. He claims that questions about how people ought to reason cannot be sharply separated from questions about how they actually reason, since any attempt to understand how people ought to reason has no choice but to begin with facts about how they do reason. This constraint, according to Kornblith, suggests that the two cannot radically come apart. But if so, studies of how we actually reason will always have important lessons for how we should reason.

A related problem for naturalized epistemology can be expressed in the form of a dilemma: the less closely a naturalized epistemology aligns itself with the methods and findings of science, the less distinct it will be from traditional approaches of epistemology; on the other hand, the more closely it aligns itself with the methods and findings of science, the less room there will be for radical challenges of those methods and findings.

Most naturalized epistemologists grasp the second horn of this dilemma, since they are not disposed to engage in radical critiques of science in any event. So, if it turns out to be impossible on their view to engage in such critiques, this is a small price to pay for an alternative to a priori epistemology. However, their opponents think that none of our intellectual endeavors, not even science, should be protected from radical challenges. They also point out that the tendency of naturalized epistemologists not to take seriously radical critiques of science is part of a larger refusal to take seriously any kind of radical skeptical worry.

Most naturalized epistemologists are more than willing to admit that they are unconcerned with refuting radical skeptical hypotheses such as Descartes's evil-demon hypothesis. In helping themselves to the conclusions of science at the beginning of their theorizing, they are presupposing the falsity of the radical skeptical hypotheses, and they see nothing wrong with this. On the contrary, they regard attempts to disprove radical skeptical hypotheses as examples of a failed epistemological tradition that sees it as the task of the epistemologist to vindicate simultaneously all of our intellectual capacities and methods. The alternative is to recognize that epistemological questions arise only at a relatively late stage of inquiry and that we have no choice but to use the results of previous inquiries to investigate these questions.

Bibliography

Goldman, A. *Epistemology and Cognition.* Cambridge, MA, 1986. A defense of a reliabilist theory of knowledge and epistemic justification.

Kornblith, H., ed. *Naturalizing Epistemology.* Cambridge, MA, 1994. The volume contains many of the most important articles on naturalized epistemology and a useful introduction.

Quine, W. V. O. "Epistemology Naturalized," in *Ontological Relativity and Other Essays* (New York, 1969). This is the article that has had the greatest influence on the naturalized epistemology movement.

———. *Pursuit of Truth.* Cambridge, MA, 1990. The first chapter contains a clear summary of Quine's epistemology as well as a discussion of why his naturalized epistemology is normative.

Stich, S. *The Fragmentation of Reason.* Cambridge, MA, 1990. The book explains the relevance of cognitive science to epistemology, criticizes the idea that the processes of natural selection ensure that our cognitive faculties are reliable, and defends a pragmatic account of cognitive evaluation.

RICHARD FOLEY

NEWCOMB'S PROBLEM. *See:* DECISION THEORY [S]

NIETZSCHE, FRIEDRICH, exerted much influence upon modern philosophy and literature, as Walter Kaufmann noted in his article on NIETZSCHE [5] in the 1967 edition of the *Encyclopedia of Philosophy.* Yet Kaufmann could scarcely have imagined the explosion of interest in Nietzsche's works, particularly in philosophical circles, that began in the mid-1960s and still continues unabated. Kaufmann's bibliography lists only two secondary works on Nietzsche written in English—his own *Nietzsche* and George A. Morgan's *What Nietzsche Means.* But since 1967 there have appeared almost two thousand volumes focused primarily on Nietzsche—more than half of them in English, the rest in French and German—and perhaps ten times that number of essays, articles, or book chapters have been published.

Charting the expanding horizons of Nietzsche's influence quickly becomes a sociological study of the dominant motifs of late twentieth-century culture, and charting the influence within philosophical inquiry is equally complex. There may in fact be no philosopher whose works admit less happily to a canonical or consensual interpretation, a claim supported by the staggering diversity of interpretations of Nietzsche's philosophy that have appeared since 1967. Nevertheless, some general observations can be made concerning the range of these new interpretations.

One can locate at least three primary factors in the increased philosophical attention to Nietzsche since 1967. First is the tremendous influence of Martin HEIDEGGER'S [3; S] reading of Nietzsche. Published in Germany in 1960, translated into French in 1962 and into English between 1979 and 1987, Heidegger's overarching interpretation of Nietzsche as the culminating figure in the history of metaphysics inspired an enormous range of exegetical and critical response while leading several generations of philosophers and philosophy students back to Nietzsche's texts.

A second reason can be located in the discovery of a "new Nietzsche" that emerged in conjunction with the rise of recent French philosophy. While perhaps most widely associated with Jacques DERRIDA [S] and the deconstructionist attention to questions of textuality and the styles of philosophical discourse, Nietzsche's inclusion, along with MARX [5] and FREUD [3; S], as one of the three "masters of suspicion," and his importance in the philosophical works of Michel FOUCAULT [S] and Gilles Deleuze have shown him to be an intellectual influence on much of what is called poststructuralist thought (*see* DECONSTRUCTION; POSTSTRUCTURALISM [S]). And, as in the case of Heidegger, the popularity of poststructuralist French thought brought with it a renewed interest—among literary critics and theorists, historians, political theorists, and philosophers—in Nietzsche's thinking.

The third reason for the increased attention to Nietzsche concerns the transformation of philosophy within the Anglo-American tradition. In the 1960s Kaufmann's and Arthur Danto's texts had first to justify Nietzsche as a philosopher whose ideas warranted serious philosophical consideration. As the scope of English-language philosophy has broadened there has appeared a distinctly Anglo-American tradition of Nietzsche interpretation informed by the ethical, metaphysical, and epistemological questions that occupy analytically trained philosophers.

To be sure, there is still much work offering interpretations of the "classical" Nietzschean themes: will to power, eternal recurrence, *Übermensch,* NIHILISM [5], perspectivism, and so forth. But other issues have appeared as well. For example, an attention to questions of texts and textuality has played a role in much of the recent literature. It has become increasingly common to distinguish between his published texts and his unpublished notes, especially as concerns themes whose primary expression is to be found in the "book" constructed by his literary executors after his death and titled *The Will to Power.* One also finds an increasing tendency to read Nietzsche's texts *as* texts, following their internal development as opposed to simply viewing them as collections of remarks from which one can pick and choose the comments relevant to one's own argument. A third theme emerging from the recent interest in textuality is an attention to the various styles of Nietzsche's philosophical prose—in other words, an attention to his use of metaphor, to the "literary" character of much of his writing (in particular, *Thus Spake Zarathustra*), to the different genres of writing (aphorism, essay, polemic, poem, etc.), and to other issues characterized collectively as the question of style.

A second range of topics within the recent literature addresses some of the classical philosophical questions. Does Nietzsche have a "theory of truth"? Does he have a "theory of knowledge"? An "ontology"? Is Nietzsche a metaphysician in the way that Heidegger defines metaphysics? Is Nietzsche an ethical naturalist? Within these questions a topic that continues to draw attention is the issue of self-reference: when Nietzsche makes claims (about truth, reality, being, subjectivity, etc.), do these claims refer or apply to or hold true for his own philosophical conclusions? The most obvious case where the question of self-reference arises concerns the question of truth and interpretation: if Nietzsche claims that "there is no Truth," or that "everything is an interpretation," are these claims put forward as "true"? If they are, then they appear to contradict themselves; but if they are not true, then why should we be interested in them? The issue has been extended beyond the confines of epistemology, however, and one finds discussions of the eternal recurrence or the *Übermensch* or the ascetic ideal in terms of the question of self-reference.

A third and final set of issues that warrants noting is the extension of Nietzschean themes into new areas not discussed, or only hinted at, in Kaufmann's initial entry. Among the most important topics producing much recent scholarship are Nietzsche's influence on postmodernism, his position on "woman" and his relevance for feminism, and his political philosophy and impact on twentieth-century political and social movements.

"Some are born posthumously," Nietzsche wrote in 1888. "One day my name will be associated with the memory of something tremendous," he claimed in *Ecce Homo,* at the beginning of a chapter entitled "Why I Am a Destiny." One hundred years later, these remarks appear prophetic, and at the end of the twentieth century it would be difficult to find a philosopher whose influence on matters philosophical and cultural exceeds that of Nietzsche.

Bibliography

WORKS BY NIETZSCHE

Nietzsche Briefwechsel: Kritische Gesamtausgabe, edited by G. Colli and M. Montinari. Berlin, 1975–. A complete edition of Nietzsche's correspondence.

Nietzsche Werke: Kritische Gesamtausgabe, edited by G. Colli and M. Montinari. Berlin, 1967–. Without question the most important publication since 1967.

WORKS ON NIETZSCHE

Abel, G. *Nietzsche: Die Dynamik der Willen zur Macht und die ewige Wiederkehr.* Berlin, 1984.

Allison, D. B., ed. *The New Nietzsche: Contemporary Styles of Interpretation.* New York, 1977.

Aschheim, S. E. *The Nietzsche Legacy in Germany, 1890–1990.* Berkeley, 1992.

Clark, M. *Nietzsche on Truth and Philosophy.* Cambridge, 1990.

Deleuze, G. *Nietzsche et la philosophie.* Paris, 1962. Translated by H. Tomlinson as *Nietzsche and Philosophy.* New York, 1983.

Derrida, J. *Spurs: Nietzsche's Styles,* translated by B. Harlow. Chicago, 1979.

Granier, J. *Le Problème de la vérité dans la philosophie de Nietzsche.* Paris, 1966.

Heidegger, M. *Nietzsche.* 2 vols. Pfullingen, 1961. Edited and translated by D. F. Krell et al. as *Nietzsche.* 4 vols. New York, 1979–87.

Janz, C. P. *Friedrich Nietzsche: Biographie.* 3 vols. Munich, 1978–79. The most definitive biography.

Klossowski, P. *Nietzsche et le cercle vicieux.* Paris, 1969.

Kofman, S. *Nietzsche et la métaphore.* Paris, 1972. Translated by D. Large as *Nietzsche and Metaphor.* Stanford, CA, 1994.

Krell, D. F., and D. Wood, eds. *Exceedingly Nietzsche: Aspects of Contemporary Nietzsche Interpretation.* London, 1988.

Lampert, L. *Nietzsche's Teaching: An Interpretation of "Thus Spake Zarathustra."* New Haven, 1987.

Magnus, B. *Nietzsche's Existential Imperative.* Bloomington, IN, 1978.

Müller-Lauter, W. *Nietzsche: Seine Philosophie der Gegensätze und die Gegensätze seiner Philosophie.* Berlin, 1971.

Nehemas, A. *Nietzsche: Life as Literature.* Cambridge, 1985.

Nietzsche-Studien: Internationales Jahrbuch für die Nietzsche-Forschung, Vols. 1– (1972–).

Schacht, R. *Nietzsche.* London, 1983.

Solomon, R. C., and K. Higgins, eds. *Reading Nietzsche.* New York, 1988.

Strong, T. B. *Friedrich Nietzsche and the Politics of Transfiguration.* Berkeley, 1975.

Warren, M. *Nietzsche and Political Thought.* Cambridge, MA, 1988.

ALAN D. SCHRIFT

NONCOGNITIVISM. *See:* NONDESCRIPTIVISM [S]

NONDESCRIPTIVISM. Nondescriptivists (or noncognitivists) hold that the function of normative judgments is not, or not primarily, to describe or state facts and that because of this, these judgments lack a truth value. A strong form of ethical nondescriptivism says that moral judgments have no descriptive function, but weaker forms say only that their nondescriptive function is primary or dominant.

Differing accounts of the nondescriptive function of moral language generate a variety of nondescriptivisms. Moral judgments have been said to express emotions, feelings, attitudes, or stances; and they have been characterized as tools for performing other nondescriptive tasks such as commanding, requesting, endorsing, or commending. A. J. AYER [1], whose position is called emotivism, said that "ethical terms" express emotions or feelings and that they "are calculated also to arouse feelings, and so to stimulate action" (1952, p. 108). C. L. STEVENSON [S], whose metaethical theory is called noncognitivism, argued that the major use of "ethical statements" is dynamic rather than fact stating. They are not, he said, primarily used to describe interests or attitudes but rather to change or intensify attitudes and to influence behavior. What Stevenson called the emotive meaning of ethical terms makes this dynamic use possible and also explains why ethical judgments, unlike factual ones, are capable of moving us to action.

From the thought that moral judgments are exclamations and disguised commands Ayer concluded that they "have no objective validity whatever" and that "it is impossible to dispute about questions of value" (1952, p. 110). Stevenson tried to show that there is a place for ethical arguments, but he did not go beyond the claim that a reason is "relevant" when it is likely to influence some attitude. This means, at least to the critics of Stevenson, that the relation between the premises and the conclusion of an ethical argument is psychological rather than logical and that there is no clear distinction between ethical argument and propaganda.

Both Ayer and Stevenson were in the positivist tradition, but by the 1950s an interest in ordinary language also led increasing numbers of analytic philosophers to nondescriptivism. These thinkers acknowledged that moral language can be used descriptively, but they insisted that its "primary" (basic, fundamental) use is to perform any of a number of nondescriptive speech acts. R. M. HARE [S] argued that the primary function of the word 'good' is to commend and that when we commend anything "it is always in order, at least indirectly, to guide choices, our own or other people's, now or in the future" (1952, p. 127). Words such as 'right' and 'ought' are used for giving advice or, as he said, for prescribing. According to Hare, the claim that something is good has both descriptive and prescriptive meaning. The descriptive meaning of the word 'good' changes as it is applied to different things, but the prescriptive meaning remains constant because 'good' is invariably used to commend. This is why the prescriptive meaning is primary.

Hare described his own position as nondescriptivism, but he was more positive than Ayer and Stevenson about the role and value of logic in ethical arguments. Moral judgments, he said, are a subclass of "prescriptive" rather than "descriptive" language—they are "universalizable prescriptions." Unlike attempts to persuade or to influence attitudes, a judgment that something is good or right is a prescription that is complete in itself, even if no change is brought about in the hearer's attitudes or behavior. Hare believed that there could be logical relations among prescriptive judgments, even commands; and he developed a logic of prescriptive discourse to account for those relations. In the end he concluded that while we can argue logically about what to do, a complete justification of a moral decision will always require the adoption, without justification, of some basic principle or principles as a part of a freely chosen "way of life."

P. H. Nowell-Smith offered a form of nondescriptivism he called multifunctionalism. He said that evaluative language is used "to express tastes and preferences, to express decisions and choices, to criticize, grade, and evaluate, to advise, admonish, warn, persuade and dissuade, to praise, encourage, and reprove, to promulgate and draw attention to rules; and doubtless for other purposes also" (1954, p. 98). Though his position is more complex than Hare's, he does agree that "the central activities for which moral language is used are choosing and advising others to choose" (p. 11).

After the contributions of Ayer, Stevenson, Hare, Nowell-Smith, and others, nondescriptivism was neglected as interest in APPLIED ETHICS [S] flourished and as those who did think about metaethics developed naturalistic forms of descriptivism. The new naturalists conceded that normative language has nondescriptive functions, but they then pointed out how those functions are compatible with simultaneous descriptive intent and therefore with the possibility of evaluating normative pronouncements in terms of truth and falsity. In the 1980s interest in metaethics was stimulated by new forms of nondescriptivism developed by Simon Blackburn and Allan Gibbard. The dominant issue at that time, however, was the dispute between moral (or ethical) realists and antirealists. Nondescriptivists are more likely to be antirealists, and descriptivists are more likely to be realists, but there are complications (*see* MORAL REALISM [S]).

Formerly, both intuitionists and naturalists were descriptivists. Intuitionists identified moral facts with nonnatural facts, and naturalists identified moral facts with natural facts. If one who believes that moral facts are natural facts can be said to be a moral realist, then both naturalists and intuitionists were moral realists and were in a position to say that moral judgments are true when they correctly describe some natural or nonnatural reality. But there is a way to combine descriptivism with antirealism and another way to combine nondescriptivism with at least the practices of the realist. J. L. MACKIE [S] develops a descriptivist account of much normative language, but he argues that judgments of moral obligation, which are thought to be both objective and prescriptive, and judgments of "intrinsic" value are always false. One who says that something is "good in itself" is always speaking falsely because nothing is good in itself.

Both Blackburn and Mackie begin with a Humean PROJECTIVISM [S] according to which the normativity we think we discover in nature is projected onto a value-free world by us. When we see and are moved by cruelty to the bull, we objectify our negative attitude, and promote it too, by saying that bullfighting is wrong. Projectivists are antirealists. Mackie combines his antirealism with descriptivism and takes this to result in an error theory. Blackburn begins with antirealism, adds his version of nondescriptivism or "expressivism," and emerges with what he calls quasi-realism, the idea that the linguistic practices of the realist—saying that bullfighting is really wrong, for example—are perfectly in order and that no error is made. One of his main concerns is to defend this quasi-realism by showing how we "earn the right" to "practice, think, worry, assert, and argue" as though moral commitments are true in some straightforward way (1984, p. 257).

Blackburn's view is that we do not describe reality correctly or incorrectly when we make moral claims—we express "stances." He characterizes a stance as a "conative state or pressure on choice and action" but admits that we could also call this an attitude. But whatever we call it, "its function is to mediate the move from features of a situation to a reaction, which in the appropriate circumstances will mean choice" (1993, p. 168).

Allan Gibbard also defends a nondescriptivist or "expressivist" account of normative judgments. Normative judgments, he says, take the form of saying that some act, belief, or feeling is "rational," or "makes sense." The point of making such a judgment is not to describe something, not to attribute a property to it, but "to express one's acceptance of norms that permit it" (1990, p. 7). A norm, according to Gibbard, is "a linguistically encoded precept," and the capacity to be motivated by norms "evolved because of the advantages of coordination and planning through language" (p. 57). There are norms of many kinds, but when we say that what someone did was morally wrong, we are expressing and endorsing norms that govern feelings of guilt by the agent and of anger by others.

Three arguments are traditionally deployed against nondescriptivists. According to the grammatical argument, since moral judgments are phrased in ordinary indicative sentences, there is a prima facie reason to treat them as statements and to treat those who make them as attempting to make statements. Nondescriptivists will reply that here the grammar is misleading, but they can then be asked to explain why this should be so. There is also a logical argument against nondescriptivism. If moral judgments lack a truth value, then it is impossible for them to play a role in truth-functional constructions (implication, conjunction, and negation, for example) and in arguments. It is also difficult to know how they are to be interpreted when they occur embedded in complex constructions such as statements of belief and doubt. According to what has been called the phenomenological argument, not only do moral claims look and behave like descriptive utterances, they "feel" like them too. When we claim that something is good or right, we do not seem, even to ourselves, to be merely expressing ourselves or ordering others to do things. Nondescriptivists will try to explain why these judgments have this distinctive feel, but descriptivists will insist that the feeling is important data that cannot easily be explained away.

Starting with Ayer, each nondescriptivist has been forced to develop some reply to these, as well as to other, difficulties. Blackburn, for example, responds to the logical argument by developing an expressivist account of truth. He wants to show how it makes sense to claim moral truth even if there are no moral facts and even if our moral claims are no more than expressions of stances or attitudes. Gibbard sketches a solution to the embedding problem that exploits the idea that when we make a normative statement we are expressing a state of mind that consists in "ruling out various combinations of normative systems with factual possibilities." He develops a formalism that allows him to use this idea to account for "the logical relations that hold among normative statements" (1990, p. 99).

Owing to the work of Blackburn and Gibbard, nondescriptivism is alive and well, but its prospects are uncertain because it is truly difficult to develop convincing and definitive answers to the objections from grammar, logic, and phenomenology. Furthermore, nondescriptivism needs a fact/value distinction, and this is something about which philosophers have become increasingly nervous. The early descriptivists tried to reduce values to facts, or they accepted the fact/value distinction and then relegated values to a philosophically insignificant pragmatic limbo. Since then there has been a tendency to argue that many statements that appear to be safely descriptive must be understood to have nondescriptive elements. Nondescriptivists now point out that even if the line between facts and values is blurred or moved, we can still draw an important distinction between assertions and expressions. This claim, however, will continue to be challenged by those who are impressed by the descriptive nature of norms or the normative nature of descriptions. (SEE ALSO: *Ethical Theory* [S])

Bibliography

Ayer, A. J. *Language, Truth, and Logic.* New York, 1952.

Blackburn, S. *Spreading the Word: Groundings in the Philosophy of Language.* Oxford, 1984.

———. "Wise Feelings, Apt Reading," *Ethics,* Vol. 102 (1992), 342–56.

———. "How to Be an Ethical Anti-realist," in *Essays in Quasi-Realism* (New York, 1993).

Darwall, S., A. Gibbard, and P. Railton. "Toward *Fin de Siècle* Ethics: Some Trends," *Philosophical Review,* Vol. 101 (1992), 115–89.

Gibbard, A. *Wise Choices, Apt Feelings: A Theory of Normative Judgment.* Cambridge, MA, 1990.

Hare, R. M. *The Language of Morals.* Oxford, 1952.

———. *Freedom and Reason.* Oxford, 1963.

Mackie, J. L. *Ethics: Inventing Right and Wrong.* Harmondsworth, Middlesex, 1977.

Nowell-Smith, P. *Ethics.* Harmondsworth, Middlesex, 1954.

Stevenson, C. L. *Ethics and Language.* New Haven, 1944.

———. "The Emotive Meaning of Ethical Terms," in *Facts and Values* (New Haven, 1963).

Urmson, J. O. *The Emotive Theory of Ethics.* New York, 1969.

RICHARD GARNER

NONEXISTENT OBJECT, NONBEING. We think and talk about things that do not exist—or so it seems. We say that Santa Claus lives at the North Pole and that unicorns are white. We admire Sherlock Holmes or judge him to be less or more clever than J. Edgar Hoover. People look for the Fountain of Youth. A childless couple may hope for a daughter. So, according to Alexius MEINONG [5] and others, there are things that do not exist. In order even to deny that Santa Claus or the Fountain of Youth exists, it seems, we must be able to identify what it is whose existence we are denying.

Bertrand RUSSELL's [7] rejection of this line of thought is well known. Expressions that appear to denote nonexistents are among those which, according to his theory of descriptions, lack denotation. (Russell shifted the emphasis from thoughts and other intentional attitudes, which appear to have nonexistents as objects, to the language in which they are expressed.) Many later analytic philosophers shared with Russell a distaste for what they saw as Meinong's bloated universe. Even those who rejected the theory of descriptions often assumed that apparent references to nonexistents can somehow be paraphrased away. But there have been few serious attempts since Russell's to show how this is to be done, and the task has proven to be much more difficult than it once seemed. Several sophisticated realist theories were developed after 1970 (Castañeda, 1979; Parsons, 1980; Routley, 1980; Van Inwagen, 1977; Wolterstorff, 1980; Woods, 1974). These have been countered by antirealist theories based on notions of pretense or make-believe (Evans, 1982; Walton, 1990; see also Currie, 1990).

Many recent discussions focus primarily or exclusively on fictional characters and other objects introduced by works of fiction. The issues concerning fictions may or may not differ significantly from those concerning other nonexistent objects of thought, but they are in some ways more compelling.

We speak easily and elaborately about fictional characters as though they are ordinary people, describing Sherlock Holmes as a detective who lives on Baker Street, and so on. Some take such descriptions at face value, understanding characters to possess the same kinds of ordinary properties that real people do and to differ only in being fictional rather than actual. Such literalists, as Fine (1982) calls them, usually accept that, unlike existing objects, most nonexistents are incomplete (Holmes neither has a mole on his back nor lacks one), and some are impossible (e.g., the round square).

Literalism threatens to get out of hand. We readily describe Holmes as a person and a detective, but we are also prepared to say, in much the same spirit (i.e., speaking "within the story"), that he and other characters exist. (Macbeth's dagger is a mere figment of his imagination, but Macbeth himself exists.) If Holmes and Macbeth are people, it is awkward to deny that they exist. How, in general, are we to treat propositions that are true-in-(the-world-of)-a-story, or fictional (Walton, 1990)? It is fictional both that Holmes is a person and that he exists. Other fictional propositions do not involve fictional particulars at all. It may be fictional in a story that Napoleon has magical powers or that there are such things as ghosts. "Napoleon has magical powers" and "There are such things as ghosts. "Napoleon has magical powers" and "There are such things as ghosts," understood literally and straightforwardly, are false. Why should "Holmes is a person and a detective" be treated differently?

The most obvious alternative to literalism is to treat fictional propositions as elliptical, to understand"Holmes is a detective," for instance, as short for "It is fictional (true-in-the-story) that Holmes is a detective." So Holmes is not, literally, a person or a detective; he is such that it is fictional that he possess these attributes. And although he exists-in-the-story, this does not mean that he exists. Some allow that Holmes actually (not fictionally) possesses other properties: he was created by Conan Doyle, he is a fictional character, he is admired by millions of readers.

Literalists about nonexistents generally take the golden mountain to be, literally, golden and a mountain, and a wished-for child to be, literally, a child. Those who reject literalism while allowing that nonexistents possess properties may understand the golden mountain merely to be thought to be golden and a mountain and regard the nonexistent child to be such that the couple wishes it to be a child.

Some take properties such as being a person and a detective to constitute (rather than characterize) fictions, identifying Holmes with the class of properties attributed to him in the stories or with an abstract particular corresponding to it (e.g., a "theoretical entity" or a "kind"). Variations on this strategy give different answers to questions about the identity and individuation of nonexistents. Are they platonic entities which are (some even say exist) necessarily and eternally, or are they created when, for example, the relevant story is written? If characters in different unrelated stories happen to have exactly the same characteristics attributed to them, are they identical? Can the same character appear in different stories if the characteristics attributed to it in them are not exactly the same?

Pretense or make-believe theories return to a more intuitive understanding of statements such as "Holmes is a detective" without embracing literalism. The speaker pretends to refer to an ordinary person and to attribute to him, in the ordinary way, the property of being a detective. Nothing is actually referred to, and what is said is not literally true. But this is pretense with a serious purpose. The speaker does actually assert something by engaging in the pretense, and the theory must explain what it is. Some statements are less easily construed as uttered in pretense than others. There are statements of propositions that are not fictional in a work of fiction (e.g., "Holmes is a fictional character"), ones that do not concern fiction at all (statements about wished-for children, Vulcan, etc.), and claims of existence and nonexistence. Pretense may figure in the explication of such statements even if they are not uttered in pretense.

(SEE ALSO: *Metaphysics,* and *Realism* [S])

Bibliography

Castañeda, H.-N. "Fiction and Reality—Their Fundamental Connections: An Essay on the Ontology of Total Experience," *Poetics,* Vol. 8 (1979), 31–62.

Chisholm, R. "Beyond Being and Nonbeing," *Philosophical Studies,* Vol. 24 (1973), 245–57.

Crittenden, C. *Unreality: The Metaphysics of Fictional Objects.* Ithaca, NY, 1991.

Currie, G. *The Nature of Fiction.* Cambridge, 1990.

Donnellan, K. "Speaking of Nothing," *Philosophical Review,* Vol. 83 (1974), 3–31.

Evans, G. *The Varieties of Reference,* edited by J. McDowell. Oxford, 1982.

Fine, K. "The Problem of Non-Existence: I. Internalism," *Topoi,* Vol. 1 (1982), 97–140.

Geach, P. "Intentional Identity," *Journal of Philosophy,* Vol. 20 (1967), 627–32.

Hintikka, J. "Are There Nonexistent Objects? Why Not? But Where Are They?" *Synthese,* Vol. 60 (1984), 451–58.

Howell, R. "Fictional Objects: How They Are and How They Aren't," *Poetics,* Vol. 8 (1979), 129–77.

Ingarden, R. *The Literary Work of Art: An Investigation on the Borderlines of Ontology, Logic, and Theory of Literature.* Translated by G. G. Grabowicz. Evanston, IL, 1973.

Katz, J. J., "Names without Bearers," *Philosophical Review,* Vol. 103, No. 1 (1994), 1–39.

Lewis, D. "Truth in Fiction," in *Philosophical Papers, Volume I* (New York, 1983). Pp. 261–80.

Meinong, A. "The Theory of Ojbects," in R. Chisholm, ed., *Realism and the Background of Phenomenology* (New York, 1960).

Parsons, T. *Non-Existent Objects.* New Haven, 1980.

Quine, W. V. O. "On What There Is," in *From a Logical Point of View* (New York, 1953).

Routley, R. *Exploring Meinong's Jungle and Beyond: An Investigation of Noneism and the Theory of Items.* Canberra, 1980.

Russell, B. "On Denoting," *Mind,* n.s. 14 (1905), 479–93.

Ryle, G. "Symposium: Imaginary Objects," *Proceedings of the Aristotelian Society,* Supp. Vol. 12 (1933).

Van Inwagen, P. "Creatures of Fiction," *American Philosophical Quarterly*, Vol. 14 (1977), 299–308.

Walton, K. L. *Mimesis as Make-Believe: On the Foundations of the Representational Arts.* Cambridge, MA, 1990.

Wolterstorff, N. *Works and Worlds of Art.* Oxford, 1980.

Woods, J. *The Logic of Fiction: A Philosophical Sounding of Deviant Logic.* The Hague, 1974.

KENDALL L. WALTON

NONVIOLENCE. *See:* VIOLENCE [S]

O

ONTOLOGY. For much of this century the discussion of ONTOLOGY [5] has been shaped by philosophical NATURALISM [5], according to which whatever exists is part of the natural world. Natural ontology is understood to exclude supernatural entities, Cartesian mental entities, and Platonic universals. From the naturalist perspective, any ontological question is, ultimately, a scientific question. The period since about 1960 has included significant work in ontology that, like typical earlier work in the century, falls under the aegis of naturalism. A prominent example is the development, within 'physicalism', of an array of different reductive, 'functional', and even 'eliminative' accounts of the mind and mental phenomena (*see* ELIMINATIVE MATERIALISM, ELIMINATIVISM [S]). But the period is perhaps more notable for the appearance of a variety of nonnatural ontological theories (even including versions of Cartesian dualism). This entry focuses on recent nonnatural ontology, along with naturalistic counterpoints.

Since 1960 much work in ontology has been influenced—in one way or another—by the prominent naturalist philosopher, Willard Van Orman QUINE [7; S]. Quine is well known for three contributions to the discussion. One is his 'criterion of ontic commitment' (Quine, 1960, section 49), often captured in the slogan, 'to be is to be a value of a bound variable'. Another is his doctrine of 'ontological relativity' (Quine, 1969, essay 2). The third is his influential insistence that the postulation of entities of any kind be accompanied by a statement of their 'identity conditions' (Quine, 1960, sections 42-3). It is ironic that Quine conceded the existence of sets—hardly occupants of the natural world—on the grounds that they are indispensable for physics and linguistics. Not only did this constitute a departure from strict naturalism, it also opened the floodgates for further 'indispensability' claims, often in favor of entities he would find much less acceptable than sets.

For Quine, the need for postulating nonnatural entities came most urgently from the effort to understand how human language works. But when we try to find specific linguistic pressure for sets, we fail. Instead, we find a need for 'intensional' entities like propositions (for example, to serve as 'meanings' of sentential utterances and as objects of 'attitudes' like belief), and properties and relations (to serve as meanings of predicates). Quine was fully aware of this (as were earlier contributors, notably FREGE [3; S], RUSSELL [7], CARNAP [2; S], and Church). But he thought the roles of these entities could be adequately played by (impure) sets, and that sets were more acceptable ontologically. Quine held that the principle of extensionality provided adequate identity conditions for sets, but that since no such conditions were available for intensional entities, they were (comparatively) obscure and therefore dubious.

But the strength of the direct pressure for intensional entities—from a variety of sources—became much more widely appreciated. Even naturalistically inclined philosophers found it hard to resist (PUTNAM [S], 1970). One important source was a growing interest in overtly intensional notions, especially alethic modality (MARCUS [S], 1993) and 'essentialism' (KRIPKE [S], 1972), which gave rise to the postulation of POSSIBLE WORLDS [S]. The acceptance of intensional entities was often accompanied by an effort to provide identity conditions (Putnam, 1970), but the demand for such conditions has also been questioned (Plantinga, 1974), and even rejected (Jubien, 1996).

The 1980s and 1990s not only witnessed an increased acceptance of intensional entities, it also featured them as objects of study in their own right. Notable here are theories of PROPERTIES [S] and theories of possible worlds, which sometimes draw heavily on MATHEMATICAL LOGIC [S], especially SET THEORY [7; S] and MODAL LOGIC [S]. A contemporary theory of properties that aspires to naturalism is D. M. ARMSTRONG's [S] (1978), which takes properties and relations to be constituents of 'states of affairs' in the spatiotemporal world. An important nonnaturalist theory is George Bealer's (1982), in which properties and relations are seen as independently existing entities of their own special kinds, and constituting part of the proper subject matter of logic.

The discussion of modality resulted in a variety of different theories of possible worlds (*see* MODALITY, PHILOSOPHY AND METAPHYSICS OF [S]). Several of these may be thought of as 'proposition-style' theories because their treatment of worlds crucially involves PROPOSITIONS [S] (or other proposition-like entities). (See Alvin Plantinga, 1974.) For example, one may take worlds to be 'maximal consistent' propositions. (A proposition is consistent if it is possibly true, and maximal if, for any proposition P, it either entails P or the negation of P.) Proposition-style theories are far from naturalistic since they take propositions to be irreducible, Platonic entities. But these theories are seen by their proponents as 'actualistic' in virtue of relying only on entities that actually exist.

A sharply contrasting view of worlds (and properties) is the 'counterpart' theory of David Lewis (1982). This theory is naturalistic, at least in spirit, but far from actualistic. According to Lewis, there exists a plenitude of 'possible worlds' in addition to the world we inhabit. These other worlds, however, are not abstract entities like propositions. They are concrete, spatiotemporal realms, more or less like our own world, but physically inaccessible from our world (and from each other). Each possible world is 'actual' from its own perspective and nonactual from the perspective of every other world. Because other worlds exist, but do not actually exist, they count (for us) as 'merely possible objects', and Lewis's theory is hence a version of ontological 'possibilism'. This strikingly lavish (though entirely naturalistic) ontology enables Lewis to give analyses of the modal notions, and reductive treatments of intensional entities like properties, relations, and propositions.

The period since 1960 has included a number of developments in ontology that we have not considered here. (One example is a renewed interest in MEREOLOGY [S] as it bears on the topic of physical objects; another is the discussion of the nature of events.) Important contributors to ontological discussions so far unmentioned include Robert M. Adams, Paul Benacerraf, Jonathan Bennett, John Bigelow, Hector-Neri Castañeda, Richard Cartwright, Roderick CHISHOLM [S], Donald DAVIDSON [S], Michael DUMMETT [S], Hartry Field, Graeme Forbes, Jerrold Katz, Jaegwon Kim, J. L. MACKIE [S], Terence Parsons, Richard Routley, Brian Skyrms, Robert Stalnaker, and Peter van Inwagen.

Bibliography

Armstrong, D. M. *Universals and Scientific Realism,* 2 vols. Cambridge, 1978.

Bealer, G. *Quality and Concept.* Oxford, 1982.

Jubien, M. "The Myth of Identity Conditions," *Philosophical Perspectives,* Vol. 10 (1996).

Kripke, S. A. *Naming and Necessity.* Cambridge, MA, 1972.

Lewis, D. *On the Plurality of Worlds.* Oxford, 1986.

Marcus, R. B. *Modalities.* Oxford, 1993.

Plantinga, A. *The Nature of Necessity.* Oxford, 1974.

Putnam, H. "On Properties," in N. Rescher, ed., *Essays in Honor of Carl G. Hempel* (Dordrecht, 1970).

Quine, W. V. O. *Word and Object.* Cambridge, MA, 1960.

———. *Ontological Relativity and Other Essays.* New York, 1969.

MICHAEL JUBIEN

ONTOLOGY AND FUNDAMENTAL ONTOLOGY. For the early HEIDEGGER [3; S], the one topic of philosophy, PHENOMENOLOGY [6; S], the pretheoretical original science of original experience, is variously called the preworldly "original something" (neo-Kantianism's term for "being"), "life in and for itself," "factic life," the "historical I," the "situation-I," later *Dasein,* literally "being here." This science of "being here" is thus ONTOLOGY [5; S], aiming to explicate the "original something" or "principle" out of which any being is how it is. It is therefore "fundamental" ontology ([1922] 1989, 1992) from which regional ontologies receive their ground and meaning. As theories of objects, traditional material and formal ontologies arise from the "objectless" *dynamis* of life itself. In explicating their fundamental concepts and the foundational crises of the sciences addressing their material and formal regions, ontology is a hermeneutical logic, concerned with the many ways in which being is said and interpreted in and from life itself. Fundamental research has the task of making the concrete interpretations already operative in factic life itself, from circumspective concern to inspective regard to the lucid perspicuity of distressed caring, categorically transparent in their preconception. Accordingly, philosophy is the explicit actualization of the interpretive tendency already operative in the life that "in its being goes about this very being." This self-referential movement of being itself now becomes the formal indication of the understanding-of-being, the single matter of a fundamental ontology.

Sein und Zeit (1927) relates fundamental ontology to an existential analytics of Dasein as end to means. The book's goal is not a complete ontology of Dasein or philosophical anthropology. Its circling aim is to elaborate the question of the sense of being from the understanding-of-being that Dasein itself is. This analytic of Dasein establishes that the very being of Dasein is TEMPORALITY [S] and that its understanding-of-being is accordingly made possible by the tensorality (*Temporalität*) of being itself. Fundamental ontology now becomes the more radical analytic of tensorality. The science of being, in distinction from the positive sciences, thus becomes a transcendental tensoral science, reflecting the ontological difference between beings and being itself. But just as the positive sciences project their particular beings onto the regional constitution of their being, so must transcendental ontology project being itself onto the tensorality that makes it possible, onto the "horizon of its understandability." To be a science, ontology must "objectify" being itself against the horizon of time.

Fundamental ontology's basic question of the sense of being itself, seen through four classical theses of being, articulates four basic problems of ontological phenomenology: the ontological difference, its distinction into what-being and way-to-be, the unity of the variety of ways-to-be, the truth of being. But to be open to new problems and its own inner transformation, fundamental ontology must revert back to its ontic origins in the factical existence of Dasein. Ontology is always already ontically founded, rooted in the original experiences of limit situations that make the question of being, not only the most fundamental, but also the most concrete of questions. Accordingly, fundamental ontology must be supplemented by the metaphysical ontic of beings as a whole, by a "metontology" (1928). Fundamental ontology and metontology together constitute the full concept of METAPHYSICS [5; S].

In the destructive retrieve of the history of ontology that also belongs to fundamental ontology, Heidegger discovers that KANT [4; S] also saw the possibility of founding ontology in tensorality, thus making it a critical science. But Heidegger's own quasi-Kantian effort to establish a critical tensoral science of being will shatter in the attempt to "schematize" the temporal ecstases of Dasein onto the horizons of the tensorality of being.

In 1928–29, after a decade of vacillation over this strange "pretheoretical original science" so unlike any positive science, Heidegger definitively abandons the project of making philosophy into a strict science. Superlatively a science from its abiding inner friendship (φιλεῖν; *philein*) with its subject matter, "scientific philosophy," like the formula "round circle," becomes a misleading and even dangerous superfluity. Instead of regarding it in its scientific results, as a "grounded totality of true propositions," we should allow philosophy its freedom to be simply "under way." Philosophy in this incessant transcending movement nevertheless continues to found the sciences and their respective regional ontologies, and moreover now accounts for their periodic revolutions.

The goal now is to grasp metaphysics as ontology more fundamentally, in a "step back" that overcomes its onto-theo-logical constitution. This hitherto unknown and ungrounded ground of metaphysics, beyond every effort to produce doctrinal systems called ontologies, is now the most worthy of questions. Heidegger nevertheless searches for clues to his one question in its three equiprimordial aspects—the time, truth, and language of being—by repeatedly examining their Greek counterparts, respectively the kinetic φύσις (phusis), the unconcealing ἀλήθεια (aletheia), and the prepredicatively structured λόγος (logos) of being itself. The relational locus for this language *of* being, variously indicated etymologically by the later Heidegger as the hold (*Verhältnis*), pull (*Bezug*), needy usage (*Brauch*), attentive bondage (*Zugehören*), and appropriation (*Ereignis* [S]) *of* being itself, *turns* out to be the "same" understanding-*of*-being that once was the topic of "fundamental ontology."

Bibliography

Heidegger, M. *Einleitung in die Philosophie* [1928–29]. Pittsburgh, Simon Silverman Phenomenology Center, Duquesne University, typescript. This first Freiburg course of Winter 1928–29, which signalizes the turn to the later Heidegger's thought, is dominated by the theme that philosophy is neither a science nor a doctrine of world views but something "more."

———. *Die Grundprobleme der Phänomenologie* [1927]. Gesamtausgabe Vol. 24, edited by W. F. von Herrmann. Frankfurt, 1975. Translated by A. Hofstadter as *The Basic Problems of Phenomenology*. Bloomington, IN, 1982. Heidegger's failure to schematize ecstatic temporality upon the horizon of the tensorality of beings.

———. *Kant und das Problem der Metaphysik* [1929]. Translated by R. Taft as *Kant and the Problem of Metaphysics*. Bloomington, IN, 1990. Kant's *Critique of Pure Reason* regarded as a fundamental ontology.

———. *Metaphysische Anfangsgründe der Logik im Ausgang von Leibniz* [1928]. Gesamtausgabe Vol. 26, edited by K. Held. Frankfurt, 1978. Translated by M. Heim as *The Metaphysical Foundations of Logic*. Bloomington, IN, 1984. Refers to the need for a "metontology" in order to supplement fundamental ontology.

———. "Phänomenologische Interpretationen zu Aristoteles (Anzeige der hermeneutischen Situation)" [1922], edited, with a postscript, by H.-U. Lessing, *Dilthey-Jahrbuch*, Vol. 6 (1989), 235–74. Translated by M. Baur as "Phenomenological Interpretations with Respect to Aristotle (Indication of the Hermeneutical Situation)," *Man and World*, Vol. 25 (1992), 355–93. This *Einleitung* to a planned book on Aristotle, written in October 1922, is the first reference to a *prinzipielle Ontologie*.

———. *Sein und Zeit* [1927]. 16th ed. Tübingen, 1986. Translated by J. Macquarrie and E. S. Robinson as *Being and Time*. New York, 1962. *Fundamentalontologie* by way of a *Daseinsanalytik*.

Kisiel, T. *The Genesis of Heidegger's "Being and Time."* Berkeley, 1993. The path to *Sein und Zeit* is traced especially in terms of the series of formal indications, from intentionality to transcendence, that guide the "logical" or linguistic explication of a fundamental ontology.

Krell, D. F. *Intimations of Mortality: Time, Truth, and Finitude in Heidegger's Thinking of Being*. University Park, PA, 1986. Part 1 contains essays relating fundamental ontology to metontology and a "frontal ontology" and discusses how fundamental ontology founders by seeking a fundamental temporal ecstasis.

Richardson, W. J. *Heidegger: Through Phenomenology to Thought*. The Hague, 1963. An exhaustive (for its time) tracking of the development from fundamental ontology in "Heidegger I" to foundational thought (*wesentliches Denken*) in "Heidegger II." Richardson in fact begins with Heidegger's sense of fundamental ontology from his 1929 book on Kant in order to introduce the sense of fundamental ontology in *Sein und Zeit* (1927).

THEODORE KISIEL

ORDER OF THINGS. *The Order of Things* is the standard English translation of Michel FOUCAULT's [S] *Les Mots et les choses* (1966). As its subtitle announces, *The Order of Things* undertakes "an archaeology of the human sciences," a project that involves an articulation of the epistemic principles that govern and integrate the human sciences in a certain historical period. Foucault developed his archaeological method of historical investigation in order to identify the unifying discourse shared and presupposed by the representative sciences of specific historical periods. ARCHEOLOGY [S] attends, not to the truth or meaning of the propositions circulating within scientific discourse, but to the common epistemic framework in which they are advanced and evaluated. By documenting the epistemic regularities exhibited by a cluster of sciences the archaeologist reveals the 'episteme', or structure of epistemic coherence, that integrates the historical period in question.

In *The Order of Things* Foucault attempts to identify the systems of epistemic coherence that inform, respectively, the Renaissance, the classical age, and modernity. Whereas the Renaissance was unified by the episteme of resemblance and similitude, the classical age was governed by the episteme of representation. Foucault refers to modernity as the "Age of Man," and he proposes as its unifying principle the attempt to appropriate human finitude as a new ground or foundation for the human sciences. Because he attempts to decipher the epistemic signature of modernity from within its evolving confines, his account of the "Age of Man" is somewhat more tentative than his accounts of preceding epochs.

Foucault is primarily concerned in *The Order of Things* to document the "profound upheaval" that occurred at the end of the eighteenth century, when the episteme of the classical age began to disintegrate. The project of representation, which had served to unify the episteme, proved itself incapable of accounting for the act and the agent of representing. "Man," the supposed focus of inquiry in the human sciences, had eluded the frame of representation.

Despite the systemic failure of the project of representation, and the disintegration of its corresponding episteme, "man" remains the object of scientific inquiry in the nineteenth and twentieth centuries. The "Age of Man," Foucault proposes, is defined by a series of ingenious (and failed) schemes to derive from human finitude itself the conditions of scientific knowledge. In the nineteenth century, for example, human beings were customarily treated as both knowing subjects and objects of their own knowledge; but this divided office only postponed the problem of accounting for "man" in his absence. Reflecting the fragmentation of their avowed subject matter, the human sciences now labor in the absence of the sort of epistemic convergence that presided over their birth and development. The very possibility of truth and knowledge is now in question, as the human sciences scramble to construct theories and propositions in the space vacated by their proper object of investigation.

Rather than bemoan the disappearance of "man," or attempt to restore epistemic coherence to the human sciences, Foucault presents the irrecuperable fragmentation of "man" as legislating new directions for scientific inquiry. *The Order of Things* proposes human finitude, not as a new certainty that might solve the epistemic riddles of the human sciences, but as a new possibility in its own right, within which fruitful experimental thinking might take place.

DANIEL CONWAY

OTHER, THE. The point of departure for LEVINAS's [S] use of the expression "the other" *(l'autre)* lies in PLATO's [6; S] *Sophist.* Levinas adopts the opposition between the identical, or the same *(tauton),* and the other *(to heteron)* as a formal schema for his attempt to overcome the philosophical tendency to reduce all plurality and alterity to the same of one encompassing totality.

Within the dimension of finite beings the same and the other seem to exclude one another—space, power, property, and so on must be divided—unless the other can be understood as a moment of the same. Does difference necessarily lead to violence and war? Or is an intrigue possible in which the other remains different from, and "exterior" to, the same without confusion and without violence?

The metaphysical tradition has answered these questions by stating that the One (or GOD [3]), as the INFINITE [S], can be neither opposed to nor located within the universe of the finite. Levinas shows that the finite subjectivity of the human ego is constituted by a relation to an infinite other, who, without oppressing the ego, provides it with an absolute significance. The emergence of a human other *(autrui)* liberates the ego from its spontaneous narcissism by revealing the ego's responsibility for the other. The "face-to-face" awakens me to the discovery of the fact that I am always already "for-the-other." The other and the same, as *autrui* and *me,* are separate and yet related. The other, as commanding me, appears infinite and higher than I, for my own consciousness, am. The relation is thus an asymmetrical one, but since the other's height does not depend on any act of free will, the relationship between the other and me is radically different from that between master and slave. The asymmetry of the "one-for-the-other" precedes the dimension of EQUALITY [3], human RIGHTS [7; S], universal JUSTICE [4; S], and fair politics.

Levinas sometimes uses "the other" to indicate God or "the most high." He rejects, however, the representation of God as a You or as a "face" that one could encounter directly. The only possibility of contact with God—and the quintessence of religion—lies in the practice of responsibility for other humans.

Bibliography

Levinas, E. *Totalité et infini. Essai sur l'extériorité.* The Hague, 1961.

ADRIAAN PEPERZAK

P

PACIFISM. Pacifism is moral opposition to war. The concept embraces a wide range of positions from an absolute prohibition of all use of force against persons to a selective and pragmatic rejection of particular forms of such force under varying circumstances. Pacifists vary on their moral grounds for rejecting war and on their commitments to varieties of NONVIOLENCE [S].

Etymologically, pacifism comes from the Latin *pax, pacis,* "peace" (originally "compact") + *facere,* "to make," and literally means "peacemaking." Often, pacifism is incorrectly identified as passivism, which derives from the Latin *passivus,* "suffering," and means being inert or inactive, suffering acceptance. Pacifists may be passivists but often are activists, choosing nonviolent means to resolve conflict and achieve personal and social goals.

Pacifism consists of two parts: the moral opposition to war and the commitment to cooperative social and national conduct based on agreement. Beyond the mere absence of war, peace is a condition of group order arising from within by cooperation among participants rather than order imposed from outside by domination by others. Pacifism's opposition to war is much more frequently reflected in philosophic literature than is its active creation of peace.

Moral opposition to war is discussed across the history of Western philosophy. While early considerations of the morality of war can be found in ancient Greek texts (e.g., PLATO [6; S], *Republic,* Book IV, 469c–471c), more thorough treatments are much later—notably from ERASMUS [3] in the sixteenth century and KANT [4; S] in the late eighteenth. Adin Ballou articulated pragmatic pacifism in the mid-nineteenth century, and William JAMES [4; S] explored pacifist philosophy in the early twentieth. Arguments for pacifism tend to focus on the evils of war, including human suffering—especially of innocents—and moral degradation of participants as well as the uncontrollability of modern warfare.

The case for pacifism varies with the form of pacifism being put forth. Absolute pacifism, the view that it is wrong under all circumstances to use force against persons, may rest on one interpretation of Kant's categorical imperative, on Gandhi's Satyagraha (truth force), on King's notion of Christian love, or on other moral bases. Weaker forms of pacifism may rest on interpretations of these same principles or on other grounds. Epistemological pacifists stress the impossibility of knowing sufficiently to warrant taking lives, while pragmatic pacifists trace the empirical history of war to emphasize failures in achieving the ends that were to justify carnage. Nuclear pacifists focus on the projected effects of thermonuclear exchange, and ecological pacifists consider the effects of modern war on ecosystems.

(SEE ALSO: *Social and Political Philosophy* [S])

Bibliography

Ballou, A. "Christian Non-Resistance," in S. Lynd, ed., *Nonviolence in America: A Documentary History* (Indianapolis, 1966).

Cady, D. L. *From Warism to Pacifism: A Moral Continuum.* Philadelphia, 1989.

Erasmus, D. *Complaint of Peace.* 1517.

Erasmus, D. *Praise of Folly.* 1512.

Gandhi, M. K. *Nonviolent Resistance,* ed. B. Kumarappa. New York, 1951.

Holmes, R. L. *On War and Morality.* Princeton, NJ, 1989.

James, W. "The Moral Equivalent of War" [1910], in R. Wasserstrom, ed., *War and Morality* (Belmont, CA, 1970).

Kant, I. *Perpetual Peace* [1795], ed. and trans. L. W. Beck. New York, 1957.

King, M. L., Jr. *A Testament of Hope: The Essential Writings of Martin Luther King, Jr.,* ed. J. M. Washington. New York, 1986.

Ruddick, S. *Maternal Thinking: Toward a Feminist Peace Politics.* Boston, 1989.

Sharp, G. *Power and Struggle,* part 1 of *The Power of Nonviolent Action.* Boston, 1973.

Teichman, J. *Pacifism and the Just War.* Oxford, 1986.

Tolstoy, L. *The Kingdom of God and Peace Essays* [1909], 2d ed. Oxford, 1951.

DUANE L. CADY

PASSIVE SYNTHESIS AND ASSOCIATION.

Husserl's own name for the sphere described in the lectures entitled *Analysen zur passiven Synthesis* is "transcendental aesthetics" (*see* HUSSERL [4; S]). This sphere encompasses the realm of "pure experience" that precedes determinate predicative thinking. Husserl describes the operations at work at the most basic levels of experience without voluntary or conscious effort on the part of the subject. These are synthetic operations that from the very outset organize the receptive elements of consciousness into unities that are directed at self-continuation. The level of passive synthesis establishes tendencies toward self-givenness that may be reinforced or revised in light of further experience, tendencies that, however, precede and escape propositional formulation. Even at the lowest levels, Husserl stresses, these operations are kinds of activities, but because they precede any voluntary or self-conscious actions on the part of the subject, they are referred to as passive rather than active. Husserl adopts the traditional term association to describe the way that the elements of sense perception are grouped together, but he rejects the mechanistic interpretation of that term, seeing association rather as the most basic form of unifying intentional activity based in the temporal structures of consciousness.

Bibliography

Holenstein, E. *Phänomenologie der Assoziation: Zu Struktur und Funktion eines Grundprinzips der passiven Genesis bei E. Husserl.* The Hague, 1972. A careful analysis of Husserl's writings on association and passive synthesis, it also compares Husserl to others in the psychology of perception.

Husserl, E. *Analysen zur passiven Synthesis (1918–1926). Husserliana,* Vol. 11, edited by M. Fleischer. The Hague, 1966.

———. *Erfahrung und Urteil.* Hamburg, 1972. Translated by J. Churchill and K. Ameriks as *Experience and Judgment.* Evanston, IL, 1973.

THOMAS NENON

PATERNALISM.

This term has long been in currency among moral and political philosophers, but its circulation became much wider, and its definitions much more precise, following the widely read debate over "the legal enforcement of morality" between Patrick Devlin (*The Enforcement of Morals,* 1965) and H. L. A. HART [3] (*Law, Liberty, and Morality,* 1963). Hart had endorsed the liberal doctrine of J. S. MILL [5; S], that the only legitimate reason for state interference with the LIBERTY [S] of one person is to prevent him from harming other persons. Mill was especially emphatic in denying that the actor's "own good, either physical or moral," is ever an adequate reason for interference or criminal prohibition ([1859], 1985, p. 9). What Mill denied in this passage is precisely what came to be called "legal paternalism" in the writings of his followers, including Hart nearly a century later. Thus, paternalism was regarded as a thoroughly unacceptable view by nineteenth-century liberals.

PHYSICAL AND MORAL

In his exchange with Devlin, however, Hart conceded that a certain amount of physical paternalism could be accepted by twentieth-century liberals, here departing from Mill who, he wrote, "carried his protests against paternalism to lengths that may now appear to us as fantastic" (Hart, 1963, p. 32). He cited, for example, Mill's criticism of restrictions on the sale of drugs. Devlin then responded by drawing a distinction between "physical paternalism," which protects people from physical harm that could be caused by their own voluntary conduct, and "moral paternalism," which offers similar protection against "moral harm" of the actor's own causing. Devlin could see no consistent way in which the physical paternalist like Hart could avoid commitment to moral paternalism, for if it is the prevention of harm that justifies prohibition in the one case, why not use state power to prevent an equal amount of harm, though of a different kind, in the other case? Similarly, Devlin concluded, there is no relevant difference between criminalization meant to prevent moral harm and criminal prohibitions meant to "enforce the moral law as such." The view that "enforcement of morality," quite apart from harm prevention, is a valid reason for criminal prohibitions is widely called "legal moralism." It is anathema to liberals.

One way in which liberals sometimes defend themselves from Devlin's argument is by maintaining that Devlin's moves from physical to moral harm and from preventing moral harm to "enforcing the moral law" do not follow logically. One liberal critic, Joel Feinberg (1986), even goes so far as to deny, in the teeth of the immense combined authority of PLATO [6; S] and ARISTOTLE [1; S] to the contrary, that "moral harm" is a coherent concept.

HARD AND SOFT

A distinction is commonly made between hard (or strong) paternalism and soft (or weak) paternalism. Hard paternalism justifies the forcible prevention of some dangerous but self-regarding activities even when those activities are done in a fully voluntary (i.e., free and informed) way. Soft paternalism, on the other hand, permits individuals or the state to prevent self-regarding dangerous behavior only when it is substantially nonvoluntary or when temporary intervention is necessary to establish whether it is voluntary or not.

Most soft paternalists are liberals strongly opposed to paternalism. Most of them, when they think of the paternalism they oppose, think of what is here called hard paternalism. Therefore they would prefer to go by the name of soft antipaternalists. The term hard antipaternalism could be reserved for the totally uncompromising liberal who would oppose interference even with some choices known to be involuntary, and with temporary compulsory intervention that is only for the purpose of determining whether the intended conduct truly is voluntary, and even with the imposition of compulsory education about risks or state-administered tests to assess the dangerous actor's understanding of the risks, with licenses required for self-regarding dangerous behavior, like mountain climbing. Clarity would be improved if philosophers would speak of paternalism only when what is meant is hard paternalism, justifying prohibition even of wholly voluntary self-regarding conduct, when dangerous. Then soft and hard antipaternalism would be the names of a moderate and extreme liberalism, respectively.

The controversy over paternalism in the criminal law is genuine and difficult. Those who are strongly opposed to paternalism find it not only mistaken but arrogant and demeaning. It is very difficult to reconcile it with even a minimal conception of personal autonomy (rightful self-government) when it proclaims that state officials may rightfully intervene even against my protests to "correct" my choices, and this on the ground that they know what is good for me better than I do myself. But if we reject paternalism altogether, we seem to fly in the face both of common sense and of long-established customs and laws. The state, for example, does not accept "consent" as a justification for mayhem or homicide. Similarly, the law of contracts will not validate certain agreements even though they are voluntary on both sides—when, for example, they are usurious or bigamous. One would be hard put to accept these traditional state-created disabilities without abandoning one's opposition to paternalism. But if we continue our adherence to paternalism, we may discover that in other areas paternalism justifies too much, the flat-out prohibition, for example, of whiskey, cigarettes, and fried foods, which tend to be bad for people too, whether they know it or not.

MEDICAL CONTEXTS

Writers on medical ethics confront paternalism at every turn, often in human contexts that are less familiar to those whose interest is primarily focused on criminal law (*see* BIOMEDICAL ETHICS). Those characteristic social situations have led to some forms of ethical analysis supplementary to those that prevail among the critics and defenders of "legal paternalism." For example, not all of the moral problems raised by paternalism in medical settings are problems for legislators drafting mandatory rules or other governmental officials such as judges or police officers. Moreover, paternalism is not exclusively a criterion for the legitimacy of coercion. Sometimes what is at issue is some other practice that normally has high moral costs, most notably deception rather than coercion, as in false but comforting statements to frightened patients or the unacknowledged or mendacious use of placebos. Sometimes a medical provider may have to decide whether to tell a "white lie" to his patient, not for the sake of her health, but rather as a way of preventing her from experiencing intense despair in her final hours about a matter having no direct connection with medical treatment. In a hypothetical case invented by Culver and Gert (1976, p. 46), a woman on her deathbed asks her physician how her son is doing, and the doctor replies that he is doing well even though he knows that "the son has just been killed trying to escape from jail after having been indicted [a fact unknown to his mother] for multiple rape and murder." An opponent of (hard) paternalism would probably consider the doctor's mendacity to be a violation of the patient's autonomy. A medical paternalist would probably argue that the truthful alternative in this case would be cruel to the point of indecency. They might both be right.

PROS AND CONS

Problems involving paternalism in medical contexts are quite diverse. They include not only truth-telling cases but also suicide attempts, requests for euthanasia, and the use of human volunteers in dangerous experiments. The paternalist position in these conflicts is that protecting volunteers or patients from harm and promoting their benefit should take precedence over respecting their autonomy by permitting them to act freely on their well-informed choices in matters that are almost exclusively self-regarding.

Beauchamp (1977) and Beauchamp and Childress (1979) in their influential works rejected hard paternalism nearly categorically, emphasizing that to overturn the deliberate choices of adult human beings that affect only them, or only them clearly and directly, is to deny that their lives really belong to them. The apparent exceptions—cases in which commonsense morality would seem to justify interference with the patient's voluntary choice—invariably turn out to be cases in which that choice is not fully voluntary after all; that is, the patient or volunteer subject had not been adequately informed about the risks he would be accepting, or he was not perfectly free of coercive influences, or some other condition, such as infancy, drug intoxication, high fever, rage, or depression, had diminished his capacity to act rationally. To restrict his liberties in such circumstances, or to motivate him by telling him a lie, would be to interfere with actions that are not fully voluntary in the first place. To interfere with dangerous self-regarding but less-than-voluntary behavior can be justified by soft paternalism (that is by soft *and* hard antipaternalism). Another example illustrates the point. "If we see a normally calm person who we know has been experimenting with hard drugs, go into a sudden frenzy, and seize a butcher knife with the clear intention of cutting his own throat, then [of course!] we have the right to interfere. In so doing we will not be interfering with his real self or blocking his real will. . . . His drug-deluded self is not his 'real self,' and his frenzied desire is not his 'real choice,' so we may defend him against these internal threats to his autonomous self, which is quite another thing than throttling that autonomous self with external coercion" (Feinberg, 1986, p. 14). Interference on this ground is no more paternalistic than interference designed to protect an individual from an attack by some berserk assailant. Paternalists have been quick to point out, however, that this example, and others like it, hardly fit the more usual examples of risky choice making.

Writing from the practical point of view, and a philosophical position more friendly to paternalism, Culver and Gert (1982), in response to Beauchamp, point out that many crucial questions remain for the soft antipaternalist analysis. Most of these stem from the vagueness of the distinction between voluntary and nonvoluntary. Culver and Gert remind us that voluntariness is usually a matter of degree with no conveniently placed bright lines to guide us. In this respect it resembles the concept of harm (which is also crucially involved in hard paternalists' calculations) and the degree of violation of a moral rule, like that forbidding telling lies, or that condemning coercion, and even the degree to which the overruled choices of, say, a patient, are purely self-regarding—another essential variable.

Culver and Gert, however, do not endorse the hard paternalistic position without limit. Rather, they hold that some (hard) paternalistic interventions are justified, and some are not, but reject the unqualified antipaternalism of Beauchamp and Childress, which denies that (hard) paternalistic prohibitions and interferences are ever justified, and the unqualified paternalism of many utilitarian writers, which holds that *all* paternalistic behavior is justified, except that which will be counterproductive in the long run.

Bibliography

Beauchamp, T. L. "Paternalism and Bio-behavioral Control," *The Monist,* Vol. 60 (1977), 62–80.

———, and J. F. Childress. *Principles of Biomedical Ethics.* New York, 1979.

Brock, D. "Paternalism and Promoting the Good," in R. Sartorius, ed., *Paternalism* (Minneapolis, 1983). This is one of the leading statements of a qualified utilitarian theory of paternalism.

Culver, C. M., and B. Gert. "Paternalistic Behavior," *Philosophy and Public Affairs,* Vol. 6 (1976), 45–7.

———. *Philosophy in Medicine.* New York, 1982.

Devlin, P. *The Enforcement of Ethics.* London, 1965.

Dworkin, G. "Paternalism," *The Monist,* Vol. 56 (1972), 64–84. An influential early article that helped shape twenty years of discussion.

———. "Paternalism: Some Second Thoughts," in R. Sartorius, ed., *Paternalism* (Minneapolis, 1983), 105–13.

Faden, R. R., and T. L. Beauchamp. *A History and Theory of Informed Consent.* New York, 1986. The definitive work on its subject.

Feinberg, J. *Harm to Self.* New York, 1986.

Hart, H. L. A. *Law, Liberty, and Morality.* Stanford, CA, 1963.

Kleinig, J. *Paternalism.* Totowa, NJ, 1983.

Mill, J. S. *On Liberty* [1859]. Indianapolis, 1985.

Sartorius, R., ed. *Paternalism.* Minneapolis, 1983. This excellent collection includes, in addition to the selections by Brock and Dworkin already cited, fifteen useful articles and a superb bibliography.

VanDeVeer, D. *Paternalistic Intervention: The Moral Bounds of Intervention.* Princeton, NJ, 1986.

JOEL FEINBERG

PEIRCE, CHARLES SANDERS (1839–1914), one of America's most original philosophers, produced a body of work remarkable for its scope and enduring relevance. For many years Peirce's principal contributions to mainstream philosophy were in LOGIC [4] and PHILOSOPHY OF SCIENCE [S], but changes in the philosophic terrain since 1967 have brought new areas of his thought to prominence. The resurgence of interest in pragmatism, due in large measure to its promotion by Richard Rorty, and the adoption of PEIRCE [6] by the Frankfurt School as the philosopher who may hold the key to the problem of modernity, have brought attention to Peirce's unique brand of PRAGMATISM [6; S] and to his philosophy of signs. Outside of philosophy, the active interdisciplinary field of semiotics that began in Chicago with Charles Morris acknowledges Peirce as the founder of modern sign theory.

Peirce was a late child of the ENLIGHTENMENT [2], a staunch believer in the universal applicability of mathematics and in the continuous growth of knowledge through sustained inquiry. He was a diligent student of the history of science and understood that the advancement of knowledge is crucially linked to nondeductive (inductive and abductive) reasoning and shared experimental methods. He was convinced that a prerequisite for successful experimentation is an external world resistant to actions arising from misconceptions of it. These views led Peirce to an anti-Cartesian epistemology rooted in perceptual experience and committed to fallibilism and the repudiation of deductive FOUNDATIONALISM [S]. Peirce generalized his view of the advancement of science to all forms of learning from experience, and he concluded that all meaningful conceptions are necessarily related to experiential expectations (conceived consequences). This is the epistemological motivation for his meaning-focused pragmatism (pragmaticism).

Sometimes Peirce is said to have equated TRUTH [S] with settled belief, but that applies only when belief is settled as the result of a steadfast application of scientific method. Other methods for overcoming doubt and settling belief, such as the a priori method or the methods of tenacity and authority, while not without some advantages, do not provide grounds for confidence that truth will be reached. Even the sustained application of scientific method can never issue in a guarantee that inquiry has "stormed the citadel of truth." Truth is always relative to propositions and is, therefore, grounded in the conventionality of symbolism (for propositions can only be expressed symbolically). The true represents the real precisely insofar as inquiry forces beliefs to yield to the dictates of an independent reality, but the "correspondence" of truth and reality that is hoped for at the end of inquiry is at best an ideal limit; we can never be certain that we have reached the truth. This is Peirce's fallibilism. It is typical of Peirce's philosophy that truth and reality are correlates in a triadic relation, where the mediating relate involves a community of inquirers (interpreters).

Peirce believed that the key to intelligence of any kind is sign action (which is always goal directed), and he formulated an elaborate semiotic theory to facilitate the analysis and classification of signs. Peirce's division of signs into icons, indexes, and symbols is his best-known semiotic bequest—although his distinction between tones, tokens, and types is also widely used—but these are only two of many triads that permeate his philosophy. Peirce held that minds are sign systems and thoughts are sign actions, and it is not too far-fetched to say that the mission of his semiotic is similar to that of modern-day COGNITIVE SCIENCE [S]. Peirce's epistemological shift from a focus on ideas to signs marks him as a forerunner, if not a founder, of philosophy's so-called linguistic turn and, also, of the modern—and postmodern—emphasis on textualism. Peirce's triadic theory of signs distinguishes semiotics from semiology, a generally dyadic theory of signs stemming from the work of Ferdinand de Saussure. Recently there have been attempts to reconcile these two approaches.

Current interest in Peirce's thought extends over most of philosophy. Peirce's graphical logic (his existential graphs) is used as a basis for computational linguistics. The recent move away from logicism has led to renewed interest in Peirce's philosophy of logic, according to which logic is not the epistemic foundation for mathematics. The rehabilitation of systematic and speculative thought has attracted attention to Peirce's evolutionary cosmology, which holds that the principal constituents of the universe are CHANCE [2], law, and habit formation. Peirce insisted that change is really operative in nature (his tychism), that continuity, in general, prevails (his synechism), and that love or sympathy has a real influence on the course of events (his agapism). He contributed America's most original and thoroughgoing phenomenology (his phaneroscopy), and he advanced unique views on religion and on the significance of sentiment and instinct. He stressed the importance of the existent and the individual while, at the same time, admiring the ideal and insisting that rationality is rooted in the social. Peirce's intellectual legacy is a rich system of thought that helps organize and unify a broad array of issues in modern philosophy.

Bibliography

WORKS BY PEIRCE

Writings of Charles S. Peirce: A Chronological Edition, edited by the Peirce Edition Project. Bloomington, IN, 1982–.

The New Elements of Mathematics by Charles S. Peirce, 4 vols., edited by C. Eisele. The Hague, 1976.

A History of Science: Historical Perspectives on Peirce's Logic of Science, 2 vols., edited by C. Eisele. The Hague, 1985.

Reasoning and the Logic of Things: The Cambridge Conferences Lectures of 1898, edited by K. L. Ketner. Cambridge, MA, 1992.

Complete Published Works Including Selected Secondary Material (microfiche edition), edited by K. L. Ketner et al. Greenwich, CT, 1977. A companion bibliography is also available: *A Comprehensive Bibliography of the Published Works of Charles Sanders Peirce with a Bibliography of Secondary Studies,* edited by K. L. Ketner. Greenwich, CT, 1977. Rev. ed., Bowling Green, OH, 1986.

The Essential Peirce: Selected Philosophical Writings, 2 vols., edited by N. Houser and C. Kloesel. Bloomington, IN, 1992–97.

WORKS ON PEIRCE

Apel, K.-O. *Charles S. Peirce: From Pragmatism to Pragmaticism,* trans. J. M. Krois. Amherst, MA, 1981.

Brent, J. *Charles Sanders Peirce: A Life.* Bloomington, IN, 1993.

Burch, R. W. *A Peircean Reduction Thesis.* Lubbock, TX, 1991.

Delaney, C. F. *Science, Knowledge, and Mind: A Study in the Philosophy of C. S. Peirce.* Notre Dame, IN, 1993.

Eisele, C. *Studies in the Scientific and Mathematical Philosophy of Charles S. Peirce,* edited by R. M. Martin. The Hague, 1979.

Esposito, J. L. *Evolutionary Metaphysics: The Development of Peirce's Theory of Categories.* Athens, OH, 1980.

Fisch, M. H. *Peirce, Semeiotic, and Pragmatism,* edited by K. L. Ketner and C. J. W. Kloesel. Bloomington, IN, 1986.

Freeman, E., ed. *The Relevance of Charles Peirce.* La Salle, IL, 1983.

Hausman, C. R. *Charles S. Peirce's Evolutionary Philosophy.* Cambridge, 1993.

Hookway, C. *Peirce.* London, 1985.

Houser, N., D. D. Roberts, and J. Van Evra, eds. *Studies in the Logic of Charles S. Peirce.* Bloomington, IN, 1996.

Ketner, K. L., ed. *Peirce and Contemporary Thought: Philosophical Inquiries.* New York, 1995.

Murphey, M. G. *The Development of Peirce's Philosophy.* Cambridge, MA, 1961.

Raposa, M. L. *Peirce's Philosophy of Religion.* Bloomington, IN, 1989.

Roberts, D. D. *The Existential Graphs of Charles S. Peirce.* The Hague, 1973.

NATHAN HOUSER

PERCEPTION. Broadly speaking, the Kantian tradition on the topic of PERCEPTION [6] is the view that perception is essentially a conceptual event or act. That is, each event or act of perception either is, or essentially includes, a conceptual component, usually regarded as a judging or the making of a judgment. And since judgments, when made, have propositional form, we can speak by extension of perception being or essentially including some propositional component. Of course, it is granted that there is more to perception than the conceptual element; there is also a sensory constituent, related in an important but variously specified way to the conceptual.

One familiar account of this relation is provided in causal theories of perception. On such a theory, as a result of a causal relation to the world a person experiences a sensation, which experience in turn occasions a judging or a taking something to be the case. On many versions of this theory, it is this latter element—the judging or taking—that, strictly speaking, is the perception. The experience of the sensation is causally necessary for, and so is a constant accompaniment of, a perception; but the sensory element is not strictly a constituent element in the event of perception.

The Kantian tradition is somewhat different from the causal theory, inasmuch as the conceptual factor and the sensory factor are both reckoned constituent elements in the perception. A perceptual event is an organic whole, a single event that has conceptual and sensory events as parts in something like the way that a complex event has simpler events as parts. An event of perception, then, is not to be identified with just the judging element, nor with the sensory element taken alone. Instead, perception is construed as the combined entity—sensing-and-judging.

The Kantian tradition has been well represented in philosophical work on perception over the past few decades. A case in point is the work of Wilfrid SELLARS [S]. On Sellars's view, sensations are theoretical entities we must postulate as occurring in perceptual experiences if we are adequately to explain perceptual propositional attitudes. These posits, what Sellars terms sense impressions, are not themselves objects of perceptual awareness, such as sensa. Instead, he construes sense impressions as events of sensing, along the lines of the adverbial account of sensations, so that a sense impression of red is the event of sensing red-ly. These sensing events, moreover, are wholly nonconceptual, not to be thought of as cognitive events.

The conceptual component included in every perception is a judging. Sellars typically represents a perception of an object as perceiving there to be something present before one. So, seeing a teacup on the table he takes as seeing there to be a teacup on the table. Sellars rejects the suggestion that the judging ingredient in this simple perception is to be expressed by "This is a teacup which is on a table" because he holds that the pure demonstrative "this" does not do justice to the complexity of the situation. Instead, he would express the judgment made as "This-teacup-before-me-now is on the table." This complex demonstrative is a fused expression, mental tokening of which Sellars treats as a taking *as* or a believing *in.* And, though the tokening is directed at the teacup on the table, in fact he tells us that the demonstrative refers to the sense impression. This is *mis-taking as,* which occurs even in veridical perception.

The judging proper Sellars takes to be a believing-*that.* It is believing, of what is in fact a sense impression, that it is on a table. The judging alone, however, is not itself the perception of the teacup. That event is the complex event consisting of the event of sensing, which is a cause of the events of tokening the relevant demonstrative and the judging.

Sellars' theory, here given just for what he terms the "manifest image," is a species of direct REALISM [7; S]. It does not countenance phenomenal entities as perceived intermediaries, as in the causal theory; and the mental tokening of the complex demonstrative is "directed at" the external physical object.

Another species of direct realism which stresses the importance of judgments is the theory of Romane Clark. Clark holds that the occurrence of a sense impression in a simple context of object perception literally is or contains demonstrative reference, typically to the cause of that occurrence. Sense impressions are not phenomenal individuals, and thus do not function as perceptual intermediaries, just as in Sellars's account. Their demonstrative reference will vary with context, just as the reference of linguistic demonstratives varies with change in context. However, unlike either Sellars or KANT [4; S], Clark takes the sense impressions themselves also to be conceptual entities: ". . . sense impressions are fully constitutive of sensuous judgments. They are not the contexts in which such judgments occur. They make up such judgments. They are, then, after all, conceptual entities" (Clark, 1973, p. 53).

Marginally related to the Kantian tradition are epistemic theories of perception. These theories, developed by David M. ARMSTRONG [S] and George Pitcher, may be characterized negatively as dispensing with sensations, at least for purposes of explicating perception; and positively as the thesis that perception is essentially an observer's acquisition of specific beliefs in certain ways, such as by the use of the sense organs. In the simplest case of veridical perception of a teacup, for example, the perception is just the acquisition of sundry teacup beliefs on that occasion and in that causal context. In cases where the perceived object appears differently from the way it is, as when a round pond appears elliptical, it is held that one acquires an inclination to believe that the pond is elliptical, where an inclination to believe is actually a belief (that the pond is elliptical) which is held in check or overridden by some stronger beliefs, perhaps by the background belief that this pond is actually round. And in a small number of cases, where it seems neither beliefs nor inclinations thereto are acquired, perception is identified with coming to be in a potential belief state (Armstrong), or with acquisition of a suppressed inclination to believe (Pitcher). Their ideas are similar: in these cases one comes to be in a state which would have been a belief state had certain inhibiting factors, most commonly other beliefs, not been present.

The beliefs or inclinations to belief one acquires will naturally be causally prompted by some object, in typical cases; and the beliefs or inclinations are held to be about this object, though of course they need not be in all cases correct. But in the normal case of veridical perception, this event just is the acquisition of true beliefs about the object.

Epistemic theories are marginally related to the Kantian tradition. They stress belief acquisition, and so require possession and utilization of various concepts as a constituent element in each perception. But these theories include no provision for demonstrative reference, do not reckon perception as having a judgmental ingredient, and dispense with the role of sensations, however construed, in perception.

Another theory, which has but a slight connection to the Kantian tradition, is Husserl's. HUSSERL [4; S] distinguishes between perception of objects and perception of facts. The latter he would take as including a judgment, but then so would everyone. There is no judging in the account Husserl gives of perception of objects, however, even though there is a role for concepts.

Husserl held that in every case of perception of objects there is some sensory input, what he calls "hyle" or "hyletic data." These are experiences that are not themselves conceptual events, and neither are they objects of perception. In these respects, Husserl's view of hyle is similar to Sellars's account of sense impressions.

Husserl takes perception to be a paradigm case of an intentional act, and so it is an act directed at an object—in the typical, veridical case, an external physical object or a quality of one. The directed nature of the act is not achieved by the fact that the hyle is caused by the external object, but rather by means of the hyle being "informed" or "filled." This filling or informing, any instance of which Husserl calls a *noesis,* is a bestowal of meaning to the hyle. The complex act, hyle-plus-meaning bestowal, constitutes perception of an object.

The example of the teacup can again be used. One looks at the teacup and, in the normal case, one is caused to have certain sensory experiences (hyle), which are interpreted as of a teacup. The latter interpreting is the meaning-bestowing phase or noesis; it supplies the directedness ingredient in the act. Semantically, the result of hyle thus informed by a noesis is best expressed by a complex demonstrative, perhaps, "This teacup now before me . . ." For this meaning-bestowal to occur, the agent must possess the relevant concept, and indeed this concept is used since it informs the hyle. But it is not used to make a judgment, or to predicate anything of the referent of the demonstrative. Instead, it is what gives sense to the demonstrative.

As a result of the meaning-bestowal phase acting on the hyle, one sees the teacup as a teacup. This event is strictly analogous, I believe, to Sellars's notion of "believing-in," and is connected in the same way to a complex demonstrative. But for neither of these philosophers is the seeing-as to be construed as a judging or as a predication, despite the fact that concepts are necessary if meaning-bestowing or interpretation is to occur.

Theories that seem to lie completely outside the Kantian framework have also been developed since the late 1960s. A nonepistemic account of seeing was proposed by Fred Dretske, where a nonepistemic theory is one in which a person's seeing an object does not logically require that the person thereby acquire any beliefs (nor, presumably, any knowledge) about that object. It requires, at most, that the agent visually discriminate the object from its background and from neighboring objects. Nor, for a nonepistemic theory, is perception to be explicated so as to include the making of a judgment.

A more general version of Dretske's view, applying to all of perception, has been worked out by James Cornman. For him, the sensory element of perception is explicated along adverbial lines; seeing something red, e.g., is taken to include sensing red-ly. More generally, perception of an object E is taken to include an event of E-sensing. What distinguishes Cornman's version of direct realism is that the event of E-sensing is held to be all there is to perception of an object or a quality of an object. He says that "Each event of a person having an experience of something, E, is identical with some event of the person E-sensing" (Cornman, 1975, p. 340). What is interesting is the manner in which Cornman construes E-sensing. Where Q is a minimal sensible quality of an object E (roughly, observable occurrent properties), then E-sensing is thought of as E-as-Q-sensing. In this way,

Cornman's view is akin to Husserl's, though Cornman makes no mention of the concepts necessary to perceive an object E as Q.
(SEE ALSO: *Epistemology* [S])

Bibliography

Armstrong, D. M. *A Materialist Theory of the Mind.* New York, 1968.

Clark, R. "Sensuous Judgments," *Noûs,* Vol. 7 (1973).

———. "Considerations for a Logic for Naive Realism," in P. Machamer and R. Turnbull, eds., *Studies in Perception* (Columbus, OH, 1978).

———. "Seeing and Inferring," *Philosophical Papers,* Vol. 22, 1993.

Cornman, J. *Perception, Common Sense and Science.* New Haven, 1975.

Dretske, F. *Seeing and Knowing.* New York, 1969.

Husserl, E. *Logical Investigations* [1901]. Translated by J. J. Findlay. New York, 1970.

———. *Ideas: General Introduction to Pure Phenomenology* [1913]. Translated by W. Boyce Gibson. London, 1931.

Pitcher, G. *A Theory of Perception.* Princeton, NJ, 1971.

Sellars, W. *Science, Perception and Reality.* New York, 1963.

———. "Givenness and Explanatory Coherence," a typescript widely circulated in 1973. A much shorter version of this paper, with no material on perception, was published in *Journal of Philosophy,* 1973.

———. "Reflections on Perceptual Consciousness," a typescript widely circulated in 1975 and presented as a lecture at Marquette University.

———. "Berkeley and Descartes: Reflections on the Theory of Ideas," in P. Machamer and R. Turnbull, eds., *Studies in Perception* (Columbus, OH, 1978).

———. "Sensa or Sensings: Reflections on the Ontology of Perception," *Philosophical Studies,* Vol. 41 (1982).

Soltis, J. *Seeing, Knowing and Believing.* London, 1966.

COMMENTARY

Follesdal, D. "Brentano and Husserl on Intentional Objects and Perception," and "Husserl's Theory of Perception," in H. Dreyfus, ed., *Husserl, Intentionality and Cognitive Science* (Cambridge, MA, 1982).

Maund, J. B. "The Non-Sensuous Epistemic Account of Perception," *American Philosophical Quarterly,* Vol. 13 (1976).

Mulligan, K. "Husserl on Perception," in D. Smith and B. Smith, eds., *The Cambridge Companion to Husserl* (New York, 1995).

Pappas, G. "Perception Without Belief," *Ratio,* Vol. 19 (1977).

Smith, D., and R. McIntyre. *Husserl and Intentionality.* Dordrecht, 1984.

GEORGE S. PAPPAS

PERSISTENCE. The data of theories of persistence—that is, of IDENTITY [4; S] across time—are cross-temporal identity sentences. For example:

> The huge elm in the garden is the sapling Grandfather planted on his tenth birthday.

Cross-temporal identity sentences (CTISs) seem to be equivalent to regimented cross-temporal identity sentences, sentences consisting of two time-involving definite descriptions (or terms) flanking the identity sign. Thus, the above CTIS seems to be equivalent to:

> The *x* such that *x* is now a huge elm in the garden = the *x* such that Grandfather planted *x* on his tenth birthday and *x* was then a sapling.

Theories of identity across time may be usefully categorized by reference to CTISs and regimented CTISs.

According to temporal-slice theories, the terms of a regimented CTIS refer—if they refer to anything—to instantaneous slices of temporally extended four-dimensional objects. For example, 'The *x* such that *x* is now a huge elm in the garden' refers to a huge, elm-shaped thing that exists only at the present moment.

There are two temporal-slice theories. According to revisionist temporal-slice theory, a CTIS is equivalent to the regimented CTIS it seems to be equivalent to. Since no regimented CTIS is true (its terms refer to objects that do not simultaneously exist and are therefore not identical), our everyday utterances of CTISs express falsehoods. According to reconciliationist temporal-slice theory, a CTIS is not equivalent to the regimented CTIS it seems to be equivalent to. The words, phrases, or grammatical constructions in CTISs that seem to express numerical identity instead express 'gen-identity', the relation that holds between two temporal slices just in the case that there is some extended four-dimensional whole of which they are both slices. (The question, In what cases is a certain region of space-time occupied by a "whole"? will not be addressed in this article.) A CTIS—a misnomer, because the class of sentences so designated are not identity sentences—can very well be true. It might be, for example, that 'the huge elm in the garden' and 'the sapling Grandfather planted on his tenth birthday' designate two instantaneous slices of one temporally extended four-dimensional object.

There are two theories of identity across time that are not temporal-slice theories. According to temporal-whole theory, the terms of a regimented CTIS denote four-dimensional wholes and could well denote the same whole. Regimented CTISs can therefore easily be true. CTISs are equivalent to the regimented CTISs they seem to be equivalent to and can easily be true. According to continuant theory the terms of regimented CTISs denote 'continuants', things that exist at more than one time and are capable of having different—in fact, logically incompatible—properties at different times. Continuants are not extended in time in any way that is analogous to spatial extension. Continuants have no proper temporal parts; there is no such thing as 'the temporal part of the elm that occupied the year 1952', for such a thing would have been spatially coextensive with the elm throughout

1952, and no other thing has ever been spatially coextensive with the elm. Regimented CTISs can well be true. It might well be that one could write the two phrases 'the x such that x is now a huge elm in the garden' and 'the x such that Grandfather planted x on his tenth birthday and x was then a sapling' on two slips of paper, paste both slips on a certain tree, and thus twice correctly label it. (And doing that would not be twice labeling either a four-dimensional tree or one of its slices but rather a thing that is in the garden now and was in the garden when *it* was younger and smaller.) CTISs are equivalent to the regimented CTISs they seem to be equivalent to and can easily be true.

Temporal-whole theory seems to be superior to both versions of temporal-slice theory. The three theories require more or less the same ontology, but temporal-whole theory seems to provide a more satisfying account of the way in which the objects contained in that ontology are related semantically to CTISs.

There are several well-known arguments for and against temporal-whole theory and continuant theory, and there are well-known "standard" replies to these arguments. (Only arguments directly related to the problem of identity across time will be considered here.)

First, it could be said that continuant theory implies that a persisting object must have incompatible properties. The sapling is not a full-grown elm; if, therefore, the sapling and the elm are numerically identical, there is an object that both is and is not a full-grown elm. To this objection continuant theory replies that there is one object that *is now* a full-grown elm and *was once* a sapling. Continuant theory, therefore, does not ascribe incompatible properties to this object. The "temporally relativized" properties being-a-full-grown-elm-now and being-a-sapling-on-Grandfather's-tenth-birthday do indeed belong ("timelessly") to the same continuant, but these two properties are compatible. (David Lewis, 1986, has posed a problem for continuant theory—"the problem of temporary intrinsics"—that is based on a more sophisticated version of this argument.)

Second, temporal-whole theory faces "counting" problems. Suppose there is now one elm in the garden. Temporal-whole theory implies that there are now in the garden (in the only sense in which any extended four-dimensional object can be 'now in the garden') a vast number of things—temporal parts of the 'whole tree'—that now have just the properties that the referent of 'the elm in the garden' is supposed to have. But only *one* thing now in the garden has those properties. To this, temporal-whole theory replies that there is nothing paradoxical about this, as a simple spatial analogy shows: the river that flows past this point has a vast number of parts that have *here* the same properties as the "whole river."

Third, temporal-whole theory implies that change is an illusion. A four-dimensional tree would be static; it could "grow" only in the sense of having a temporal part that comprised successively larger spatial "cross-sections." The reply to this is that a river may grow wider as it proceeds along its course; temporal change is precisely analogous to such "spatial change."

(SEE ALSO: *Metaphysics* [S])

Bibliography

Chisholm, R. M. *Person and Object: A Metaphysical Study.* La Salle, IL, 1976.

Heller, M. *The Ontology of Physical Objects.* Cambridge, 1990.

Jubien, M. *Ontology, Modality, and the Fallacy of Reference.* Cambridge, 1993.

Lewis, D. *On the Plurality of Worlds.* Oxford, 1986.

———. "Survival and Identity," in A. O. Rorty, ed., *The Identities of Persons* (Berkeley, 1976). Reprinted in D. Lewis, *Philosophical Papers,* Vol. 1 (New York, 1983), with postscripts. See particularly postscript B, "In Defense of Stages."

Thomson, J. J. "Parthood and Identity across Time," *Journal of Philosophy,* Vol. 80 (1983), 201–20.

van Inwagen, P. "Four-Dimensional Objects," *Noûs,* Vol. 24 (1990), 245–55.

PETER VAN INWAGEN

PERSONAL IDENTITY. At the center of the debate about PERSONAL IDENTITY [6] since the 1970s has been the work of Derek Parfit, whose ideas, first published in his article "Personal Identity" (1971) and then extended and elaborated in his monumental *Reasons and Persons* (1984, part 3) revitalized and to some extent transformed the topic. The following discussion explains how this has come about and relates Parfit's ideas to those of other influential writers on personal identity from the 1960s on, in particular Bernard Williams, Sydney Shoemaker, Robert Nozick, Roderick M. CHISHOLM [S], David Wiggins, and Richard Swinburne.

The starting point for the development of Parfit's ideas was provided by Bernard Williams in his article "Personal Identity and Individuation" (1956–57), in which he puts forward his famous reduplication argument, intended as an objection to any account of personal identity that entailed the possibility of reincarnation. No such account, he claimed, could rule out the possibility of a situation in which there were two equally good "candidates" for identity with an earlier person, and hence no such account could provide a sufficient condition of personal identity.

A consensus quickly emerged, however, among other writers on personal identity that the significance of Williams's argument was greater than he had seen. Though Williams himself remained recalcitrant, others saw that his argument consequently challenged, not just any account of personal identity that allowed for such possibilities as reincarnation, which involves a radical separation of personal identity from bodily identity, but any account of personal identity that proposed as a sufficient condition of personal identity a conceivably duplicable relation—that is, a relation that could conceivably take a one–many form. The result of this was to focus attention on the principle underlying Williams's argument, called "the only *x* and *y* rule" by David Wiggins in his discussion of the reduplication problem (1967, extensively revised and republished 1980), which emphasized the generality of the argument. The correct formulation of this principle is difficult, but roughly speaking it asserts that the question whether later *x* is the same person as earlier *y* can depend only on facts about *x* and *y* and the relationship between them, and no facts about any other individuals can be relevant to whether *x* is *y*.

One response to Williams, then, is simply to reject the only *x* and *y* rule and to elaborate an account of personal identity that explicitly packs into its sufficient condition the constraint that *x* is identical with *y* only if there is no third individual *z* who can be considered a better or equally good candidate for identity with *y*. Such an account of personal identity, in terms of psychological continuity, is elaborated by Sydney Shoemaker in his article "Persons and Their Pasts" (1970), in which he also fashions the important concept of quasi-memory as a way of responding to the objection that a vicious circle must necessarily be involved in explaining personal identity in terms of, possibly among other things, memory. Another sophisticated development of the best candidate approach is contained in Robert Nozick's book *Philosophical Explanations* (1981).

But the straightforward rejection of the only *x* and *y* rule is implausible, unless some account of its attractiveness is given. It is at this point that Parfit's ideas become relevant. In response to Williams's argument he proposes (1971, 1984) that identity does not matter in survival. What does matter is a relation of psychological connectedness-cum-continuity that does conform to the only *x* and *y* rule, but it seems plausible that identity obeys the only *x* and *y* rule only because we mistakenly identify this relation with identity.

The contention that identity does not matter in survival, which is Parfit's most discussed claim, is one component of the reductionist view of personal identity he recommends. Another component is that there need be no answer to a question of personal identity: personal identity may in some cases be indeterminate. In addition, Parfit holds that there are no facts about personal identity other than facts about mental states, their relations to one another, and their relations to physical bodies and the happenings therein. Persons are not "separately existing" entities, and a complete description of reality could be wholly impersonal.

Of these three components of the reductionist view the first is the most obscure. What Parfit means by it, however, is that we do not have among our basic concerns a desire for our own continued existence and well-being. Insofar as we are concerned about these our concern is derivative from a concern for those future people (in the actual world, contingently, ourselves) linked by certain relations of psychological continuity and connectedness to ourselves as we are now. The contention that personal identity may be indeterminate is a more straightforward claim. What Parfit has in mind is that in at least some of the puzzle cases described in the literature on personal identity our concepts, suited as they are in the first place to our actual circumstances, have no determinate application. Whether such indeterminacy is to be regarded as due merely to vagueness in language or to vagueness in the world is, however, a debatable point (see Evans, 1978, for the argument that it must be regarded as due merely to vagueness in language). Parfit's third contention, that facts about personal identity are nothing over and above facts about the relations of mental states, indicates the Humean influence on his views.

Opponents of the reductionist view are described by Parfit as nonreductionists, or as proponents of the simple view. One such nonreductionist is Roderick Chisholm, whose work (see Chisholm, 1976) is perhaps the most careful working out of such a view in the literature. Chisholm defends the simple view as the development of the views on personal identity of Bishop BUTLER [1] and Thomas REID [7; S] (Butler, 1897; Reid, 1941). Another philosopher who has defended the simple view, and has done so in conscious opposition to Parfit, is Richard Swinburne (see Swinburne, 1973–74). Swinburne emphasizes in particular the difficulty of making sense of the idea that one's own personal identity may be indeterminate and in doing so draws on arguments from Bernard Williams (1970).

These philosophers reject the whole Parfitian reductionist package. But the elements of the package are, arguably, separable. Or at least, so some philosophers have thought. Thus Sydney Shoemaker (1985) rejects the Parfitian claim that persons are reducible to their experiences in any sort of Humean way but accepts both that identity does not matter in survival and that personal identity can be indeterminate. Again David Lewis (1976) rejects Parfit's claim that identity does not matter in survival while accepting that personal identity can be indeterminate.

Parfit's reductionist thesis about personal identity is not easy to assess or respond to. But, just as no philosopher writing on personal identity can afford to ignore the work of LOCKE [4; S] or HUME [4; S], so, from now on, Parfit's work must be regarded similarly. Certainly, no other philosopher in this century has had such an impact on the debate about personal identity.

(SEE ALSO: *Philosophy of Mind* [S])

Bibliography

Chisholm, R. M. *Person and Object.* La Salle, IL, 1976.

Evans, G. "Vague Objects," *Analysis,* Vol. 38 (1978), 208.

Lewis, D. "Survival and Identity," in A. Rorty, ed., *The Identities of Persons* (Berkeley, 1976).

Nozick, R. *Philosophical Explanations.* Oxford, 1981.

Parfit, D. *Reasons and Persons.* Oxford, 1984.

———. "Personal Identity," *Philosophical Review,* Vol. 80 (1971), 3–27.

Reid, T. *Essays on the Intellectual Powers of Man,* ed. A. D. Woozley. London, 1941.

Shoemaker, S. "Critical Notice: Parfit's *Reasons and Persons,*" *Mind,* Vol. 44 (1985), 443–53.

———. "Persons and Their Pasts," *American Philosophical Quarterly,* Vol. 7 (1970), 269–85.

Swinburne, R. G. "Personal Identity," *Proceedings of the Aristotelian Society,* Vol. 74 (1973–74), 231–47.

Wiggins, D. *Sameness and Substance.* Oxford, 1980.

———. *Identity and Spatiotemporal Continuity.* Oxford, 1967.

Williams, B. A. O. "Personal Identity and Individuation," *Proceedings of the Aristotelian Society,* Vol. 57 (1956–57), 229–52. Reprinted in Williams, B. A. O., *Problems of the Self* (Cambridge, 1973).

HAROLD W. NOONAN

PHENOMENOLOGICAL PSYCHOLOGY. Phenomenological psychology departs from empirical psychology by suspending naturalistic assumptions about human consciousness and by adopting a unique method, namely the phenomenological reduction, as a means of access to consciousness. Furthermore, its aim as a science is to reveal essential features of consciousness, eidetic structures, that hold for consciousness in general. Within the reduction, the focus can either be mundane, that is, directed to the mental as a region within itself, or transcendental, that is, directed to consciousness as the unique region within which all other forms of objectivity are constituted. When phenomenological psychology proceeds as an eidetic science, any results it may obtain will hold for any possible existing consciousness, but it cannot make any assertions about which of the possibilities it identifies are instantiated factually, since it must suspend all judgments about empirical facts. Phenomenological psychology reveals that mental life is intentional and at bottom temporal, and that it constitutes itself as a complicated, yet unified web of intentional relationships. This has led it to be closely associated with Gestalt theories. The task of phenomenological psychology is to reveal the various strata of mental life including both its active and passive elements, to exhibit the essential relationships among them, and to show how the complex and abstract levels are constituted out of simpler and more basic simple elements of consciousness.

In his contribution on phenomenology composed for the *Encyclopaedia Britannica* in 1928, HUSSERL [4; S] introduced phenomenological psychology as a propaedeutic to transcendental phenomenology in general. Through the investigation of pure subjective consciousness, its forms and genesis, along with those of its correlative intentional objects, phenomenological psychology can provide the material for transcendental phenomenology. Phenomenological psychology makes clear that the starting point for phenomenology is consciousness as it presents itself to pure reflection (*see* CONSCIOUSNESS IN PHENOMENOLOGY: HUSSERL [S]). However, transcendental phenomenology proceeds one step further by bracketing out any necessary relationship to consciousness as a worldly phenomenon belonging to humans or any other animate beings, and by investigating the very nature of consciousness in general. Transcendental phenomenology is thus nothing other than a consequence of the universal epoché that belongs to the meaning of the transcendental question concerning the ultimate basis for cognition and its objects in general. From this perspective, the instantiation of consciousness in human and other animals is merely one example that can provide the point of departure for a change in attitude that leads to the notion of a pure transcendental consciousness in which all intentionalities, including the intention of oneself as an existing individual consciousness, are constituted.

Bibliography

Husserl, E. "Philosophie als strenge Wissenschaft," *Husserliana* Vol. XXV, edited by T. Nenon and H.-R. Sepp. Dordrecht, 1987. Translated by Q. Lauer as "Philosophy as a Rigorous Science" in *Phenomenology and the Crisis of Philosophy.* New York, 1965. Introduces his rejection of naturalistic approaches to the study of consciousness.

———. *Phänomenologische Psychologie, Husserliana* Vol. IX, edited by W. Biemel. The Hague, 1962. Translated by J. Scanlon as *Phenomenological Psychology.* The Hague, 1977. Provides detailed analyses illustrating Husserl's general methodology and many specific results. Contains all four drafts of Husserl's article for the *Encyclopaedia Britannica,* and the subsequent Amsterdam lecture, which was based upon that article.

Gurwitsch, A. "Husserl's Conception of Phenomenological Psychology," *Review of Metaphysics,* Vol. 19 (1965–66), 689–727.

Kockelmans, J. J. *Edmund Husserl's Phenomenology.* West Lafayette, IN, 1994. An introduction to Husserl's mature thinking through a careful and extensive commentary on the *Encyclopaedia* article.

THOMAS NENON

PHENOMENOLOGY. The development of PHENOMENOLOGY [6] is a consequence of the interpretation of the texts of the major figures, especially HUSSERL [4; S], and of independent phenomenological research. Quite often, the two projects have gone hand in hand. One major factor in the development of phenomenology during the period under review has been the ongoing publication of the Nachlass of the major figures (*Husserliana,* HEIDEGGER'S

[3; S] *Gesamtausgabe,* as well as MERLEAU-PONTY's [5; S] lectures). Another is the continuing conversation with analytic philosophy in the English-speaking countries, with structuralism and deconstructionism (*see* DECONSTRUCTION [S]) in France, and with hermeneutics (*see* HERMENEUTIC PHENOMENOLOGY, and HERMENEUTIC PHILOSOPHY [S]), CRITICAL THEORY [S], and the tradition of German idealism in Germany (*see* GERMAN PHILOSOPHY [3]).

One major starting point in the conversation with analytic philosophy has been Dagfinn Føllesdal's (1969) paper, which argues that Husserl's concept of Noema is a generalization of the Fregean notion of *Sinn* (see FREGE [3; S]). Both the Sinn and the Noema are abstract entities, to be distinguished from the object toward which an intentional act may be directed. While the historical claim underlying this thesis—namely, that Frege's was a major influence on the development of Husserl's thinking around the turn of the century—has been challenged (e.g., by Mohanty), the systematic thesis of Føllesdal (as opposed to Gurwitsch's thesis, that the Noema is the perceived object qua perceived and the object intended is but a system of noemata), has been influential. Jaakko Hintikka developed another aspect of Husserl's theory of INTENTIONALITY [S] by construing the Noema as a function from POSSIBLE WORLDS [S] to individuals in those worlds. The resources of the semantics of Frege and of possible worlds have been pulled together to interpret Husserl in the work of David Smith and Ronald McIntyre. Mohanty and Seebohm have cautioned against reducing the intentional thesis of Husserl to an extensional thesis of possible worlds and have emphasized the need for a theory of constitution of possible worlds, if the latter are not to be posited in a naively ontological thesis. Still others, notably Sokolowski and Bell, have questioned the validity of ascribing to Husserl a Fregean-type theory. Sokolowski takes the Husserlian Noema to be identical with the object (with the proviso "as intended"), and Bell reads Husserlian Gegenstand to be a component of the intentional act and so quite unlike the Fregean reference. From another perspective, Searle has found the Husserlian intentionality thesis useful for his own work but goes beyond Husserl by appropriating, from Heidegger via Dreyfus, the idea of Background of skills and practices, and more recently by developing a theory of we-intentionality that is irreducible to I-intentionalities (reminiscent of the Hegelian *Geist* as well as of a thesis advanced by David Carr). This last discussion connects with the way phenomenology has related itself to COGNITIVE SCIENCE [S]. Fodor's methodological SOLIPSISM [7] has been related by Dreyfus to Husserl's, while Searle's emphasis on Background clearly falls on the Heideggerean side of the divide.

The tension between Husserlian phenomenology and hermeneutics lies in that the former is concerned with consciousness, its contents and structures, the latter with the individual's ontological relatedness to his world and to others. This issue becomes, Is interpretation to be construed as the gift of a transcendental ego, or is it to be construed as an ontological feature of the mode of being of *Dasein?* Hans-Georg GADAMER's [S] theory of interpretation develops the latter alternative, while Paul RICOEUR [S] comes closest to mediating between Husserlian thinking, especially of the *Logical Investigations,* and an ontologically construed hermeneutics. We must also recall Ricoeur's work on metaphor (*see* METAPHOR IN RICOEUR [S]), in which, going beyond the traditional rhetorical and semantic theories of analytic philosophy, Ricoeur integrates them in such a manner as permits the poetic and disclosive dimension of language to emerge. Ricoeur's researches have also sought to mediate between time (the most radical subjectivity) and narrative (by which reality is redescribed, as by metaphors) and reestablish a certain reciprocity between them.

The most influential critique of classical phenomenology is offered by Jacques DERRIDA [S]. While it is more common to look upon Derrida's work as refuting Husserl's transcendental phenomenology, it is also possible to maintain that Derrida's work is a further radicalization of Husserl's genetic phenomenology, an alleged result of which is the demonstration that constitution involves a perpetual deferral and difference, also that a radicalization of Husserl's concept of horizonal character of intentionality would call into question all fixity and univocity of meanings, and that possibilities of nonfulfillment of intention are necessarily inherent in all intentionality. But those who ascribe to Husserl a metaphysics of presence fall into the opposite trap of reifying 'absence'. As Sokolowski has shown, Husserl's thinking rather exhibits a mutual involvement of presence and absence.

Of those from analytic philosophy who have pursued some kind of phenomenology, mention must be made of Castañeda's rich phenomenology of indexical reference (*see* INDEXICAL SIGNS [4], and INDEXICALS [S]) and of 'I' thought. In the latter context, he distinguishes between the ground floor of empirical I-guise and successive phases of transcendental I-guises, among all of which there is a sameness that is yet not strict identity.

In the United States there is a continuing tendency, inaugurated by Dreyfus and Rorty, to see in Heidegger a pragmatist philosopher, whereby clearly Heidegger's ontological concern with the meaning of BEING [1] (*see* BEING–PROCESS [S]) and the historical concern with the historicity of understanding of Being are either underplayed or sought to be altogether set aside. While it was at first usual to look upon Heidegger as an anti-science thinker, now—largely owing to the work of von Weizsäcker, Kockelmans, and Heelan—one has come to realize that Heidegger's thinking could form the basis for an understanding and appreciation of science and technology. In general, phenomenological thinking about science has exhibited three distinct features: First, following Husserl in the *Crisis,* some have attempted to reestablish the proper connection between science and LIFEWORLD [S]. The most important work on this front is due to Mittelstrass. Second, following also Husserl's work in the *Crisis,* but more inspired by Heideggerean thought about historicity of *Dasein* as also by KUHN's [S] work on history of science, some have looked upon science as a historical accomplishment marked by epochal changes, epistemological breaks, shifts of paradigm—thereby rejecting the prevailing obsession with the logical structure of scientific theories and also the reigning prejudice in favor of a naively realistic and positivist theory of science. But within phenomenology itself, this time following Husserl's original concern, there is also a continuing concern with the nature and structure of logic and mathematics as theories and with the origin of such theories, their relation to practice and also to the lifeworld, on the one hand, and the transcendental, thinking ego on the other.

Patrick Heelan has developed the view, using the conceptual resources of Husserl, Heidegger, and Merleau-Ponty, that scientific observation, like all perception, is hermeneutical. Hermeneutical phenomenology of science focuses, in his view, not so much on theory as on experimental phenomena. Heelan defends a sort of realism called by him hermeneutic or horizonal realism as opposed to the instrumentalism of some phenomenologists. Thus, according to Heelan, in particle physics many phenomena have actual existence only within the context of the measurement processes. Kockelmans emphasizes what he regards as the ontological aspect of science: he draws attention to the role of "objectifying thematization," which lies at the root of every scientific activity. In this latter concept he brings together Husserl's idea of "thematization" and Heidegger's idea that a certain fundamental understanding of being makes possible science, philosophy, and technology. Although Kockelmans accepts the Kuhnian thesis of epochs in the history of science, he nevertheless holds that history of science is guided by an ideal of reason and that each new paradigm is necessarily a historical synthesis.

From its inception phenomenology had a special relation of love and hate toward psychology; at a later phase, it developed a special interest in history. With regard to psychology, there has been a long tradition of original work in what is known as PHENOMENOLOGICAL PSYCHOLOGY [S]. To the period under review belong some works of Medard Boss, Aron Gurwitsch, Minkowski, and Ricoeur. Boss has applied his Heideggerean conception of *Daseinsanalytik* to such contexts as sexual perversion, dream, and psychosomatic illness. Drawing upon his work on lived space and lived time, Minkowski studies how these can undergo modifications in psychoses, schizophrenia, manic-depression and hallucinations. Gurwitsch's *Marginal Consciousness,* posthumously published, continues the work done in *The Field of Consciousness.* However, for research in descriptive psychology, possibly the most important results are to be found in Edward Casey's two books on imagining and remembering. This research has opened out new fields of investigation. For example, in his work on remembering, Casey explores a number of neglected, nonrepresentational forms of remembering, including body memory and place memory, reminiscing and commemorating.

In the phenomenology of history, a brief reference may be made to the important work done by Ricoeur, who seeks to mediate between lived time and cosmic time. The past is irrevocably gone, and our access to it across the historical distance is made possible by creative imagination. Here fiction, by its quasi-historical character, comes to our help. History is not a totality, an absolute mediation. Nevertheless, there is a search for meaning, which is open-ended without a Hegelian *Aufhebung.* The idea of one history is a Kantian-type regulative idea.

Bibliography

Bell, D. *Husserl.* London, 1990.

Castañeda, H.-N. *Thinking, Language, and Experience.* Minneapolis, MN, 1989.

Casey, E. S. *Imagining: A Phenomenological Study.* Bloomington, IN, 1976.

———. *Remembering: A Phenomenological Study.* Bloomington, IN, 1987.

Derrida, J. *Speech and Phenomena,* trans. D. Allison. Evanston, IL, 1973.

Dreyfus, H., ed. *Husserl, Intentionality, and Cognitive Science.* Cambridge, MA, 1982.

Føllesdal, D. "Husserl's Notion of Noema," *Journal of Philosophy,* Vol. 66 (1969), 680–87.

Gurwitsch, A. *Studies in Phenomenology and Psychology.* Evanston, IL, 1966.

———. *Marginal Consciousness,* ed. L. Embree. Athens, OH, 1985.

Heelan, P. *Space Perception and the Philosophy of Science.* Berkeley, CA, 1983.

Hintikka, J. *The Intentions of Intentionality and Other New Models for Modalities.* Dordrecht, 1975.

Kockelmans, J. *Ideas for a Hermeneutic Phenomenology of the Natural Sciences.* Dordrecht, 1993.

———, ed. *Phenomenological Psychology: The Dutch School.* Dordrecht, 1987.

Mittelstrasse, J. *Die Möglichkeit von Wissenschaft.* Frankfurt am Main, 1974.

Mohanty, J. N. *Husserl and Frege.* Bloomington, IN, 1982.

———. *The Possibility of Transcendental Philosophy.* Dordrecht, 1985.

Ricoeur, P. *Time and Narrative,* trans. K. Blamey and D. Pellauer. Chicago, 1988.

Searle, J. *Intentionality.* New York, 1983.

Smith, D., and R. McIntyre. *Husserl and Intentionality.* Dordrecht, 1982.

Sokolowski, R. "Husserl and Frege," *Journal of Philosophy,* Vol. 84 (1987), 523–28.

von Weizsäcker, C. F. *Zeit und Wissen.* Munich, 1992.

JITENDRA N. MOHANTY

PHENOMENOLOGY AND SCIENCE. In his later work, *Crisis of European Sciences,* Edmund HUSSERL [4; S] thematized the prescientific lifeworld as the foundation of the sense of the positive sciences (*see* LIFE-WORLD IN HUSSERL [S]). However, since the emergence of modern mathematical physics this prescientific world could be approached only from the fact that a stock of unquestionably obvious scientific knowledge was added to it. Hence, for any particular scientific theory (of any epoch) a reawakening of the formerly activated constitution of its sense is needed. To show, then, how entirely specific constitutions of scientific formations come about, all sedimentations must be reactivated down to the ultimate procedures that constitute science; these procedures were originally encountered in the world of plain intuitive givenness and everyday practical activity. Husserl himself attempted to articulate such a description for the paradigmatic case of geometry. The contemporary crisis of reason results from the shifts in the sense of what is given in the lifeworld, shifts that science itself does not question and cannot detect because they have become increasingly unintelligible.

Martin HEIDEGGER's [3; S] reflections on science are concerned with the function of modern science within the totality of meaning and being. He finds an unbridgeable gap between the mode of scientific EXPLANATION [S] and philosophical radicality because science cannot even account for the essence of its own field of study: it aims at technical domination (the capacity to control and predict results), but technique is not yet understanding. Therefore, any genuine reflection on the part of science must be extrascientific, in the sense that it must clarify the ontological status of its claims. Science is a mode of theoretical knowledge, which is itself a mode of being-in-the-world. The classical example for the ontological genesis of science is the rise of mathematical physics. What is decisive for its development consists neither in the emphasis on "facts" nor in its application of mathematics; it consists in the manner in which nature is mathematically projected. That is, modern science gives credit to the mathematical as that evident aspect of material things within which we are always moving (as original praxis) and according to which we experience them as things at all. Between us and the things the dialogue does not know of any limitation as long as we retain of nature what is calculable. The resulting harmony between the discovery of beings and the prior projection of their ontological structure is exemplified in the process of experimentation, which in modern science is always concomitant with mathematization. Elaboration precedes contemplation, whereas for the Greeks the passivity in the contemplative gaze was the decisive element of theory. To the rootlessness that has been a fruit of technical success, Heidegger ultimately opposes a return to the sources of our earthly lives.

Extending Husserl's reflections on the crisis of contemporary reason, Maurice MERLEAU-PONTY [5; S] points out that phenomenology has disavowed scientism, not science. The problem is that contemporary science has generated a cult of superstition and idolization, since it defies common science, and yet is capable of changing the world. In particular, physics abounds in paradoxes that contradict the classical representation of a world of things in themselves, and yet it has abandoned the search for ultimate foundations. Against this situation Merleau-Ponty argues that a rational basis of science actually lies in the prescientific reason implicated in our existence in a common world of perception. A broadened conception of reason should emerge from the investigation of the ambiguities of the perceptual field itself. Science and its paradoxes contribute to this investigation, even though the brute facticity of the world cannot be exhausted in terms of science's intelligible essences.

Bibliography

Bachelard, S. *La Conscience de Rationalité.* Paris, 1958.

Becker, O. "Beiträge zur phänomenologischen Begründung der Geometrie und ihrer physikalischen Anwendungen," *Jahrbuch für Philosophie und phänomenologische Forschung,* 6 (1923), 385–560.

Grieder, A. "Husserl on the Origin of Geometry," *Journal of the British Society for Phenomenology,* 20 (1983), 277–289.

Heelan, P. *Space Perception and the Philosophy of Science.* Berkeley, 1983.

Husserl, E. *The Crisis of European Sciences and Transcendental Phenomenology,* trans. D. Carr. Evanston, IL, 1970.

Kockelmans, J. *Phenomenology and the Physical Sciences.* Pittsburgh, 1966.

———. *Heidegger and Science.* Washington, DC, 1985.

Kockelmans, J., and T. Kisiel, eds. *Phenomenology and the Natural Sciences.* Evanston, IL, 1970.

Margenau, H. "Phenomenology and Physics," *Philosophy and Phenomenological Research,* 5 (1944), 269–80.

Ströker, E. *Philosophical Investigations of Space,* trans. A. Mickunas. Athens, OH, 1986.

PIERRE KERSZBERG

PHILOSOPHICAL LOGIC. While the years since 1960 have seen a number of significant developments in philosophical logic, it seems safe to say that the farthest reaching of these has been the advent of possible-world semantics. Taking at face value a slogan loosely attributed to LEIBNIZ [4; S]—"To be necessary is to be true in all possible worlds"—Saul KRIPKE [S] developed SEMANTICS [7; S] for MODAL LOGIC [S], according to which '$\Box P$' (read, 'Necessarily *P*') means that '*P*' is true in all POSSIBLE WORLDS [S], while '$\Diamond P$' (read, 'Possibly *P*') means that '*P*' is true in at least one possible world; or, more precisely, since, on some conceptions of modality, what is possible may depend on what is actual, for '□*P*' to be true in the actual world, '*P*' must be true in all worlds accessible from the actual world. (This development had a number of antecedents, going back to the work of J. C. C. McKinsey in the 1940s, but Kripke's contributions were unmistakably paramount.)

The metaphysical status of possible worlds is much disputed. David Lewis contends that other possible worlds are no less real than the actual world, though spatiotemporally disconnected from it. Others regard possible worlds as merely a mathematically useful fiction, with a wide variety of positions in between. Whatever their metaphysical inclinations, philosophers have found possible-world talk useful in understanding necessity and in a surprisingly wide variety of other applications.

The most striking effect of the new semantics on our understanding of necessity has been to facilitate a revival of essentialism, which had fallen into disrepute since the downfall of Aristotelian physics. Before the revival, philosophers had principally been interested in logical necessity, the sort of necessity that attaches to sentences whose truth is ensured by conventions of language. The new notion—not new to metaphysics, surely, but new to formal modal logic—is metaphysical necessity, according to which, even though 'Socrates was an alien from outer space' is conceptually possible, it is metaphysically necessary that Socrates, if he existed, was a human being, because humanity is part of Socrates' essence.

One impediment to the development of modal predicate calculus, stressed by W. V. O. QUINE [7; S], was this: the true premises '□ 9=9' and '9 = the number of planets' would appear logically to entail the absurd conclusion '□ 9 = the number of planets'. To understand why this inference fails required a deep analysis of the role of proper names, which, in turn, led to extensive and insightful investigations of the various ways we refer to things; notable here is David Kaplan's work on INDEXICALS [S] and demonstratives. A further consequence has been the general abandonment of the thesis that there are contingently true identity statements, in particular, of the thesis that the mind is contingently identical to the brain.

The formal logic is susceptible to many other interpretations, notably epistemic logic, developed by Jaakko Hintikka, which takes '□*P*' to mean 'It is known that *P*'. This has been extended to a general theory of PROPOSITIONS [S] that identifies a proposition with the set of possible worlds in which it is true. There are difficulties with the program—for example, according to it, all necessary truths express the same proposition, so that, in some sense, if we believe any necessary truth, we believe all of them—but it has nonetheless won many adherents.

Taking '□*P*' to mean that '*P*' is provable in, say, Peano arithmetic, we can use modal logic to investigate issues surrounding GÖDEL's [3; S] second incompleteness theorem. Robert Solovay has given a complete set of axioms; its surprising axiom is the formal version of Löb's theorem: '$(\Box(\Box P \rightarrow P) \rightarrow \Box P)$'.

Combining the possible world semantics for S4 (one of several modal deductive calculi invented by C. I. Lewis) with Gödel's 1931 result that questions about deducibility in intuitionistic logic could be reduced to questions about S4, Kripke got a semantics for intuitionistic logic, in which we can think of the "possible worlds" as representing the mathematician's epistemic state at various stages of inquiry. The importance of this result was increased by the revived interest in INTUITIONISM [S] inspired by the work of Michael DUMMETT [S], who advocated intuitionist logic on the basis of considerations from the PHILOSOPHY OF LANGUAGE [S] separate from the mathematical concerns that motivated BROUWER [1] and his followers.

Redeploying the machinery by identifying a possible world with an instant of time and letting the instants accessible from the present instant be those prior to it, we can read "◇Spot runs" as "Spot ran" and "□Spot runs" as "Spot has always run." Adopting analogous operators for future times, one gets an elegant theory of tense.

There are other applications of possible-world semantics besides the many applications we get by varying the interpretation of '□'. The most important of these is Robert Stalnaker's theory of CONDITIONALS [S], according to which, to say that if Sonia had struck the match, it would have ignited, is to say that, among the worlds in which Sonia struck the match, the world most similar to the actual world is a world in which the match ignited. The notion of similarity of worlds requires a great deal of clarification, of course, and attempts to clarify it have contributed a great deal to our understanding of conditionals. (While the acceptance of Stalnaker's account has been widespread, a rival theory deserves mention here. Ernest Adams developed a probabilistic account, according to which the probability of a simple conditional is the conditional probability of the consequent given the antecedent. David Lewis showed that this thesis cannot be directly extended to compound conditionals.)

As a final application of possible worlds, mention should be made of SUPERVENIENCE [S]. To say that the mental supervenes upon the physical will be to say that, for any worlds *W* and *V*, if there is a one-one correspondence between the individuals existing in the two worlds such that individuals in W have the same physical properties and stand in the same physical relations as the corresponding individuals in *V*, then individuals in *W* have the same mental properties and stand in the same mental relations as the corresponding individuals in *V*. Numerous variations in detail are possible. For many purposes, supervenience provides an attractively priced substitute for reducibility, since it enables us to express the idea that the physical facts determine the mental facts without being embarrassed by the fact that no one has any idea how to reduce the mental to the physical.

The development of modal, epistemic, and conditional logics was part of a broader pattern of going beyond the confines of the first-order predicate calculus in trying to give formal models of natural languages. Second-order logic has figured prominently, for example, in Boolos's result that plural quantification, as found in such locutions as 'There are some critics who only admire one another', is intertranslatable with second-order quantification. There are many other forms of quantification in English, a number of which have been investigated by Jon Barwise and Robin Cooper. Another departure from classical logic is 'free logic' (short for 'presupposition-free logic'), which eschews the classical presumption that proper names always denote.

Apart from the many applications of possible worlds, the busiest area of research has been the logic of TRUTH [S], looking for ways to circumvent the LIAR PARADOX [S]. All contemporary work on the liar paradox takes as its starting point TARSKI's [8] 1935 paper, "The Concept of Truth in Formalized Languages," and nearly all of it accepts Tarski's fundamental conclusion: in formulating a theory of truth, the language we talk about (the object language) must be essentially poorer in expressive power than the language we speak (the metalanguage). In particular, having no essentially richer metalanguage, we cannot hope to formulate an account of what it is for a sentence of English to be true. All we can hope for is to describe various useful fragments of English.

Again Kripke has been at the forefront, developing an account of truth-value gaps, according to which the paradoxical sentences fall into the gap between truth and falsity. We know from Tarski's formalization of the liar paradox that, in a language with classical logic that can describe its own syntax, it is not possible to assign an extension to the word 'true' in such a way that "*P*' is true" comes out true or false according as '*P*' is true or false. Yet Kripke has shown that, in a language with truth-value gaps, it is possible to arrange things so that "*P*' is true' is true, false, or undecided according as '*P*' is true, false, or undecided.

An alternative treatment is the 'revision theory' of Hans Herzberger, Anil Gupta, and Nuel Belnap, which provides a strategy, within classical, two-valued logic, for devising better and better candidates for the extension of 'true'. One starts out by making a blind guess what the extension of 'true' might be. Having a candidate for the extension of 'true' and assuming we already know the meanings of all the other terms, we get a model for the language, and we can say what sentences are true in the model. Our second candidate for the extension of 'true' will be the set of sentences true in the model in which the extension of 'true' is taken to be the first candidate. The process continues into the transfinite, giving us candidates for the extension of 'true' which better and better accord with our intuitions. This story has been extended by Gupta and Belnap to a general theory of circular definitions.

The third prominent approach, developed by Charles Parsons, Tyler Burge, and others, starts with Tarski's suggestions that we can construct a metalanguage for a given object language merely by adding a new predicate 'true in the object language', and that this process can be iterated, getting a metalanguage, a metametalanguage, and so on. To apply this construction to English, treat the English world 'true' as ambiguous, taking a given use of 'true' to mean 'true in the *n*th level metalanguage', for some contextually determined number *n*.

A rather different discussion about truth has contrasted disquotational theories of truth—which take sentences that follow the paradigm "'Snow is white' is true if and only if snow is white" as true by definition, being constitutive of the meaning of 'true'—with correspondence theories—which take it that the thoughts and practices of speakers fix a connection between expressions and the objects those expressions are about, and this connection, together with the nonlinguistic facts, makes true sentences true and false ones false. This discussion originates out of work by W. V. O. Quine and others that has seemed to show that the connections between words and their referents are much less direct than we would have hoped.

The 'sorites' paradox starts with the seemingly harmless observation that giving a single penny to a poor man still leaves him poor and leads, by a billion iterations, to the seemingly preposterous conclusion that giving ten million dollars to a poor man still leaves him poor. An especially prominent response has been Kit Fine's, which employs a technique of Bas van Fraassen's called 'supervaluations': say an ordinary, classical model of the language is acceptable if the extension it assigns to 'poor' includes all people who are definitely poor, excludes all the people who are definitely not poor, and, in adjudicating borderline cases, respects the principle that, if x is better off financially than y and x is poor, then y is poor. A sentence containing the word 'poor' is true if and only if it is assigned the truth value 'true' in all acceptable models. Under this proposal, we get to say that, if Nell is a borderline case of 'poor', then the sentence 'Nell is poor' is neither true nor false, and yet we get to maintain classical logic. (An analogous application of supervaluations enabled Kripke to get a version of his theory of truth that upholds classical logic in spite of truth-value gaps.) Other approaches require giving up classical logic in favor of either 3-valued, intuitionist, or FUZZY LOGIC [S]. Fuzzy logic, invented by Lofti Zadeh, assigns sentences numerical values between 0 (falsity) and 1 (truth). Yet other approaches involve denying that there are borderline cases, either by denying that anyone is either genuinely rich or genuinely poor (Peter Unger and Samuel Wheeler), or by insisting that the border between poor and nonpoor is, in fact, sharp, appearances to the contrary arising from our epistemic inability to determine who the richest poor person is (Timothy Williamson and Roy Sorensen).

A great deal must be left out of such a survey as this. Two more items need mention: (1) LOGICAL CONSEQUENCE [S], which contrasts Tarski's model-theoretic approach—taking a sentence to be a logical consequence of a set of premises just in case it is true in every model of the premises—with Gentzen's proof-theoretic approach, according to which the meaning of the logical operators is given by the rules of inference. (2) Relevant logic, which, taking offense at the classical doctrine that everything follows from a contradiction, insists that one's conclusions be connected to one's premises.

In all the sciences, contemporary research has been characterized by the increasing use of mathematical methods; for philosophy, this has principally meant the use of logical methods. We may expect this trend to continue.

(SEE ALSO: *Mathematical Logic* [S])

Bibliography

Adams, E. W. *The Logic of Conditionals.* Dordrecht, 1975.

Barwise, J., and R. Cooper. "Generalized Quantifiers and Natural Language," *Linguistics and Philosophy,* Vol. 4 (1981), 159–219.

———, and J. Etchemendy. *The Liar.* New York, 1987. Uses non-well-founded set theory to give a highly sophisticated contextualist solution to the liar paradox.

Belnap, N., and A. Anderson. *Entailment.* Princeton, NJ, 1975. Relevant logic.

Boolos, G. "To Be Is to Be the Value of a Variable (or to Be Some Values of Some Variables)," *Journal of Philosophy,* Vol. 81 (1984), 430–49. Connects second-order and plural quantification.

———. *The Logic of Provability.* New York, 1993. Includes Solovay's results.

Cresswell, M. J. *Logic and Languages.* London, 1973. Propositions as sets of possible worlds.

David, M. *Correspondence and Disquotation.* New York, 1994.

Dummett, M. *Elements of Intuitionism.* Oxford, 1971.

Etchemendy, J. *The Concept of Logical Consequence.* Cambridge, MA, 1990. A relentless attack on Tarski's theory.

Field, H. "The Deflationary Conception of Truth," in G. MacDonald and C. Wright, eds., *Fact, Science, and Morality* (Oxford, 1986). Disquotational vs. correspondence theories of truth.

Fine, K. "Vagueness, Truth, and Logic," *Synthese,* Vol. 30 (1975), 265–300. Uses supervaluations to solve the 'sorites' paradox.

Gabbay, D., ed. *Handbook of Philosophical Logic.* 3 vols. Boston, 1983. A useful guide to all areas of philosophical logic.

Gentzen, G. *Collected Papers.* Amsterdam, 1969. Classics of proof theory.

Gupta, A., and N. Belnap, Jr. *The Revision Theory of Truth.* Cambridge, MA, 1993. Embeds the revision theory of truth into a general account of circular definitions.

Harper, W., R. Stalnaker, and G. Pearce, eds. *Ifs.* Dordrecht, 1981. Fundamental papers on conditionals, including those of Stalnaker and Lewis.

Hintikka, J. *Models for Modalities.* Dordrecht, 1969. Important papers on modal and epistemic logic.

Horwich, P. *Truth.* Oxford, 1990. Defends a disquotational theory.

Hughes, R. I. G. *Philosophical Companion to First-Order Logic.* Indianapolis, 1993. A useful anthology.

Kaplan, D. "Demonstratives," in J. Almog, J. Perry, and H. Wettstein, eds., *Themes on Kaplan* (New York, 1976).

Kim, J. *Supervenience and Mind.* New York, 1993. Seminal papers on supervenience.

Kripke, S. "Semantical Analysis of Intuitionistic Logic I," in J. N. Crossley and M. A. E. Dummett, eds., *Formal Systems and Recursive Functions* (Amsterdam, 1965).

———. *Naming and Necessity.* Oxford, 1980. Fundamentally changed philosophical thinking about reference and modality.

Lambert, K. *Philosophical Applications of Free Logic.* New York, 1991.

Lewis, D. *On the Plurality of Worlds.* New York, 1986. Defends possible-world realism: other worlds are every bit as real as this one.

Linsky, L., ed. *Reference and Modality.* London, 1971. Fundamental papers by Kripke, Quine, and others. Arthur Smullyan's response to Quine's '□ 9 = the number of planets' argument is noteworthy.

Loux, M., ed. *The Possible and the Actual.* Ithaca, NY, 1979. Papers explore the status of possible worlds.

Martin, R., ed. *Recent Essays on Truth and the Liar Paradox.* New York, 1984. Includes the papers by Belnap, Burge, Gupta, Herzberger, Kripke, and Parsons.

McGee, V. *Truth, Vagueness, and Paradox.* Indianapolis, 1991. Attempts a self-contained theory of truth, without recourse to a richer metalanguage.

Montague, R. *Formal Philosophy.* New Haven, 1974. Important papers on modal logic and on the semantics of English.

Prior, A., and K. Fine. *Worlds, Times, and Selves.* Amherst, MA, 1977. Modal logic and tense logic.

Quine, W. V. O. *Philosophy of Logic,* 2d ed. Cambridge, MA, 1986.

———. *Ontological Relativity.* New York, 1990. Inscrutability of reference, among other topics.

Sorensen, R. *Blindspots.* Oxford, 1988. Vagueness as ignorance.

Tarski, A. *Logic, Semantics, Metamathematics,* 2d ed. Indianapolis, 1983. Includes the papers on truth and consequence.

Unger, P. "There Are No Ordinary Things," *Synthese,* Vol. 41 (1979), 117–54. Denies that vague terms refer.

Wheeler, S. "On That Which Is Not," *Synthese,* Vol. 41 (1979), 155–74. Denies that vague terms refer.

van Benthem, J. *A Manual of Intensional Logic,* 2d ed. Stanford, CA, 1988. Applications of possible world semantics.

van Fraassen, B. "Singular Terms, Truth Value Gaps, and Free Logic," *Journal of Philosophy,* Vol. 63 (1966), 464–95. Introduces supervaluations as a technique for free logic.

Williamson, T. *Vagueness.* London, 1994. Vagueness as ignorance.

Zadeh, L. "Fuzzy Logic and Approximate Reasoning," *Synthese,* Vol. 30 (1975), 407–28.

VANN MCGEE

PHILOSOPHY. Conceptions of philosophy have varied dramatically throughout its history. Western philosophy originated in ancient Greece, mainly in the writings of PLATO [6; S] and ARISTOTLE [1; S]. Such questions as the following occupied Plato and Aristotle: What is being? What is knowledge? What is justice? These questions take the form "What is *X*?", a form common to philosophical inquiry. What exactly do such questions seek? In particular, what, if anything, constitutes the correctness or incorrectness of an answer to a philosophical question of the form "What is *X*?" The latter two questions have attracted various answers from philosophers engaged in metaphysics, epistemology, and ethics. Still, those questions lead naturally to inquiry about the objectivity or subjectivity of answers to philosophical questions having the form "What is *X*?"

Plato and Aristotle regarded philosophical "What is *X*?" questions as inquiring about the essences of things. Plato's question "What is knowledge?" in the *Theaetetus,* for example, seeks to identify what knowledge itself is, what is essential to (or definitive of) all instances of knowledge. In general, Plato's "What is *X*?" questioning aims for a statement of the essence of *X* (*Meno* 72b; cf. *Euthyphro* 11a). Such a statement, according to Plato, would provide a definition *(logos)* of the essence of *X* (*Republic* 534b). Similarly, Aristotle regards philosophy as knowledge of essences, which on his view amounts to knowledge of definitions (*Metaphysics* 983a27f). The relevant definitions are neither stipulative nor conventional but real—that is, essence specifying in virtue of their signifying the properties that locate something in its proper genus or species. Aristotle was explicit about this approach to real definitions (*Categories* 2b28–3a5).

Plato and Aristotle were essence realists; they denied that essences depend on someone's conceiving of them as essential. They held, accordingly, that the correctness of answers to philosophical "What is *X*?" questions is conceiving independent and, in that respect, objective. Philosophical truths, according to Plato and Aristotle, are correspondingly objective. In addition, Plato and Aristotle distinguished philosophical truths from the empirical sciences. Aristotle regarded the subject of metaphysics, for instance, as "first philosophy": that is, the science that investigates things apart from the classifications peculiar to the special sciences. Metaphysics, according to Aristotle, is the science of being as such: being qua being. The views of Plato and Aristotle gave rise to a tradition holding that philosophy is autonomous—in both its methods and its truths—with respect to the empirical sciences. This tradition holds that philosophical truths are (1) necessary rather than contingent, (2) knowable a priori, and (3) substantive rather than merely prescriptive, stipulative, or conventional.

Another long-standing tradition, inspired by HUME [4; S] and various other empiricists, endorses the methodological and doctrinal autonomy of philosophy but denies that philosophical truths are substantive. This tradition regards philosophical truths as analytic, resulting from stipulative or conventional definitions, and as knowable a priori. In contrast, substantive truths, according to this tradition, are contingent and knowable a posteriori. Such twentieth-century positivists as A. J. AYER [1] and Rudolf CARNAP [2; S] represented this tradition; they opposed the rationalist view that philosophical truths are synthetic a priori. As philosophical truths are logically necessary, according to such philosophers, they are a priori, but they are not substantive or synthetic. In general, this empiricist tradition characterizes philosophy as offering conceptual truths that define general categories fundamental to the empirical sciences.

A more recent tradition, stemming from the views of W. V. O. QUINE [7; S], proposes that philosophy be "naturalized," that it be regarded as continuous with the natural sciences. Quine himself rejects the analytic–synthetic distinction as philosophically irrelevant and contends that there is no first philosophy, no philosophy prior to the natural sciences. Philosophy, Quine holds, is methodologically and doctrinally continuous with the natural sciences. Epistemology, for instance, is a branch of psychology; it is not a discipline that offers independent standards of assessment for the natural sciences. Quine denies, then, that philosophy is autonomous with respect to the natural sciences. He denies, accordingly, that philosophical truths are necessary or knowable a priori. Some other philosophers have offered less austere ways to naturalize philosophy, but Quine's approach attracts the most attention in contemporary philosophy.

A pressing issue for Quine's approach is, In the absence of any first philosophy, how are we to discern which of the various so-called sciences are genuinely reliable and thus regulative for purposes of theory formation? Our list of genuine sciences will perhaps include the dominant physics and chemistry but exclude astrology and parapsychology. Such a list, regardless of its exact components, seemingly depends on some first philosophy, some philosophical commitments prior to the natural sciences in question. It is an open question, however, whether such philosophical commitments are analytic or synthetic.

A very recent approach to philosophy emerges from the writings of Richard Rorty, who has acknowledged the influence of Thomas KUHN's [S] social-political approach to the sciences. If Quine's approach exalts the natural sciences, Rorty's elevates the social sciences. Rorty proposes, in particular, that we replace first philosophy with philosophy as the comparing and contrasting of cultural traditions. He offers a kind of PRAGMATISM [6; S] that aims to change the subject from Platonic and positivistic questions about the nature of truth and goodness to intellectual history of a certain sort. Rorty endorses the Hegelian view that philosophy is "its own time apprehended in thoughts," and he understands talk of "our own time" as including the notion of "our view of previous times." Rorty's pragmatism apparently merges philosophy with intellectual history and literary criticism, leaving no special subject matter for the discipline of philosophy.

Even if pragmatists wish to change the subject, we can still ask whether one approach to our intellectual history is more reliable—closer to the truth—than another. Indeed, we shall naturally raise such an issue when faced with incompatible lessons from alternative approaches to intellectual history. In raising such an issue, however, we shall also open questions about the nature of TRUTH [S], questions that appear to be philosophical and not merely historical or literary. Rorty's pragmatism owes us, at the least, an explanation of how philosophical issues about the nature of truth can actually be set aside. Such issues, contrary to Rorty's pragmatism, may be unavoidable in the end.

The original *Encyclopedia of Philosophy* article on PHILOSOPHY [5] identified the distinctive feature of philosophy as its being a critical discussion of critical discussion. It proposed that philosophy is distinctively metaphilosophy, or metainquiry: an inquiry about the character of inquiry. "The philosopher," according to the original article, "interests himself in such topics as the good, the beautiful, and the public interest, just because the mechanism for discussing differences of opinion about them strikes him as being inadequate" (p. 223). This is, it seems, an empirical claim to be assessed on the basis of evidence concerning what actually motivates philosophers. If this is so, the claim seems doubtful, at least given the ordinary significance of the term philosopher. Many philosophers investigate the nature of the good, the beautiful, the public interest, and so on without any particular interest in the adequacy of the mechanism for discussing difference of opinion. Special interest in the latter mechanism typically characterizes epistemologists, decision theorists, and students of methodology, but not philosophers in general. Perhaps philosophers should always be interested in the mechanism for discussing difference of opinion, but this normative proposal may fail to characterize all actual philosophers. It would be useful to have a characterization of philosophy that captures all those thinkers commonly called philosophers.

The later WITTGENSTEIN [8; S] is famous for characterizing philosophy as a kind of therapeutic metaphilosophy: philosophy dissolves philosophical problems by removing conceptual muddles. Even if philosophy can serve such a therapeutic purpose on occasion, it is debatable whether philosophy serves only that purpose. One controversial issue is whether every long-standing philosophical problem can be dissolved by the removal of conceptual confusion. Another relevant issue is whether philosophy might offer conceptual clarification for explanatory problem-solving purposes without thereby dissolving problems. Perhaps philosophy has a constructive explanatory role apart from the therapeutic dissolution of problems. In any case we must be especially careful not to identify one feature of philosophy as the distinctive trait of philosophy. Philosophy as commonly characterized is, for better or worse, a multifaceted discipline that resists simple characterization. Philosophy now includes, for instance, applied philosophy of various sorts, such as APPLIED ETHICS [S] involving business and health care (*see* BIOMEDICAL ETHICS, BUSINESS ETHICS [S]).

One might say that philosophy is what philosophers characteristically do. Given this theme, the discipline of philosophy will be as diverse as the works of its practitioners. This theme may capture what philosophy is, at least as commonly characterized. The explanatory burden would then fall to the notion of a philosopher, and the latter notion may be as contested as the notion of philosophy itself. Still, some inquirers may make progress by beginning with their notion of a philosopher, a notion that is perhaps less abstract for them than is the notion of philosophy itself. The concluding lesson is that the characterization of philosophy is, in its own right, a philosophical problem, and as such it resists any quick and simple treatment. The wages of philosophy are, more often than not, difficulty and complexity, even when philosophical progress ensues.

Bibliography

Baynes, K., J. Bohman, and T. McCarthy, eds. *After Philosophy: End or Transformation?* Cambridge, MA, 1987.

Cohen, A., and M. Dascal, eds. *The Institution of Philosophy: A Discipline in Crisis?* LaSalle, IL, 1989.

Mays, W., and S. C. Brown, eds. *Linguistic Analysis and Phenomenology.* London, 1972.

Moser, P. *Philosophy after Objectivity.* New York, 1993.

Moser, P., and D. H. Mulder, eds. *Contemporary Approaches to Philosophy.* New York, 1994.

Rajchman, J., and C. West, eds. *Post-Analytic Philosophy.* New York, 1985.

Rescher, N. *The Strife of Systems: An Essay on the Grounds and Implications of Philosophical Diversity.* Pittsburgh, 1985.

Rorty, R., ed. *The Linguistic Turn: Recent Essays on Philosophical Method.* Chicago, 1967.

Russell, B. *The Problems of Philosophy.* New York, 1912.

Unger, P. *Philosophical Relativity.* Minneapolis, 1984.

PAUL K. MOSER

PHILOSOPHY OF BIOLOGY. Revolutionary changes in molecular and evolutionary biology over the last half of the twentieth century have brought biology to the center of attention in the PHILOSOPHY OF SCIENCE [S]. The result has been significant advance in the traditional problems of teleology and functional analysis, reductionism and physicalism (*see* PHYSICALISM, MATERIALISM, and REDUCTION, REDUCTIONISM [S]), the nature of biological laws, theories and explanations, as well as new philosophical interest in biological questions about taxonomy and sociobiology.

EVOLUTIONARY THEORY

After a period of midcentury eclipse, Charles DARWIN'S [2] account of the appearance of design as the result of natural selection over blind but heritable variation regained its philosophical influence in the 1980s. It has been exploited to analyze intentionality, function, moral goodness, reliable belief production, and science's progress as the results of purely mechanical, purposeless processes. But this application required a vindication of the theory's status as cognitively significant. A traditional objection charges the theory of natural selection with being an empty tautology on the ground that its key explanatory term, fitness, is defined in the theory by appeal to what it explains—reproductive success. The result is that fitness differences simply redescribe reproductive-rate differences and cannot explain them. No evidence about differential rates of reproduction could falsify the claim that they reflect fitness differences. Even after the eclipse of strict falsification as a criterion for a theory's being scientific, opponents of Darwinism, creationists, and other antiphysicalists laid the charge of vacuousness against the theory.

That the theory of natural selection is not an empty tautology is a matter of agreement among philosophers of biology, in spite of the fact that many biology textbooks inadvertently trivialize the theory by defining fitness as reproductive rate. It is widely held that the source of this mistake in the textbooks is a failure to make a simple distinction. The theory is saved from vacuity because fitness is not to be defined in terms of reproductive rates. Rather fitness must be defined as the probabilistically expected rate of reproduction, which is distinct from the actual rate of reproduction, and provides a probabilistic explanation for the actual rate. Thus, the theory of natural selection asserts a causal chain between environmental forces of selection, a probabilistic propensity to reproduce in that environment, and an actual level of reproduction, which leads to differential perpetuation of traits. Biologists inadvertently trivialize the theory when they fail to distinguish the probabilistic propensity to reproduce from the actual level of reproduction.

One difficulty with the probabilistic propensity definition of fitness is that it identifies fitness with the units in which it is measured, rather like defining heat in terms of degrees on a thermometer. But heat is mean kinetic energy, not the units in which it is measured. Mutatis mutandis, one is tempted to ask, what is fitness, over and above the units in which it may be measured? Answers to this question reveal one of the most important features of biological phenomena and biological theory.

SUPERVENIENCE

Fitness is a relational term: an organism or trait has a level of fitness only in relation to an environment. A white coat in the Arctic is fitter than the same color in a rain forest. Two different traits in the same environment, say camouflage and running speed, may accord the same level of fitness. Similarly, different traits in different environments may accord the same level of fitness, as measured by the level of reproductive success they cause. If a large number of different packages of traits-in-environments can give rise to the same level of fitness, then fitness differences cannot be exhaustively defined in terms of their causes; the full definition will be an indefinitely long disjunction of different combinations of traits and environments. Fitness is supervenient on these packages: for any organism with a given fitness level, any other organism with the same traits in the same environment will have the same level of fitness. An organism's fitness is completely fixed by the relation between its traits and the environment, even though the reverse does not hold. Supervenience allows us to express the claim that fitness is nothing over and above the relation between traits and environments even though it is not reducible to this relation. Accordingly, we cannot define fitness in terms of its causes. When fitness is defined in terms of its effects—reproduction—the theory of natural selection is trivialized. When philosophers define it in terms of an intermediate probabilistic disposition, the result is foreign to the biologist's conception of fitness.

However, the relationship of supervenience turns out to characterize intertheoretical relations throughout biology and to enable the philosophy of science to explain the autonomy of biology from physical science consistent with physicalism. For when properties such as fitness are supervenient, but not reducible, then the regularities, generalizations, and laws expressed in these terms will not be reducible either (*see* SUPERVENIENCE [S]). (See the discussion of the reduction of genetics below.)

BIOLOGICAL THEORIES, LAWS, AND MODELS

Many philosophers have long denied the existence of biological laws, either because they argue for the distinctiveness of biology as a historical discipline or because they deny its status as a separate science. Beyond evolutionary theory's laws, generalizations in biology do not have features traditionally required of scientific laws: they are never exceptionless, their *ceteris paribus*—other things equal—clauses cannot be made precise, they advert to species and environments restricted to the Earth. For example, Mendel's "laws" of the segregation and assortment of genes have been disconfirmed by crossover, linkage, meiotic drive, and other genetic effects. But the result has not been replacement of Mendel's principles by more precise ones. Instead, biological theorizing has resorted to the development of models with local applicability. This has led philosophers to hold that biological theory does not proceed by the identification of explanatory laws of increasing generality. Instead, biological theory is a sequence of models that vary in the domains of phenomena to which they apply and are similar only in mathematical formalization, or underlying mechanism, or domain of application. Thus, the structure of biological theory differs significantly from theory structure elsewhere in natural science.

The puzzle remains why there are few strict laws in biology. One answer brings together supervenience and biological teleology.

FUNCTIONAL ANALYSIS AND EXPLANATION

Branches of biology, and especially anatomy, have always been organized around the search for the functions of organelles, cells, tissues, and organs. Before Darwin the best explanation for functions, (co-)adaptations, and biological purposiveness was the existence of a designer. Darwin recognized that by substituting for global design a succession of local environmental filters through which pass only the fitter among heritable variations he could explain apparent purposiveness as the result of long-term adaptation. Since Darwin biologists have employed the hypothesis that most traits and capacities have resulted from selection among randomly produced variants to provide powerful explanations for the adaptations biologists uncover. But it took philosophers over a century after the publication of *On the Origin of Species* to reach something approaching consensus on the role of Darwin's theory in the analysis of biological function.

"The function of the heart beat is to pump the blood." This truth discovered in the seventeenth century by William HARVEY [3] explains why hearts beat. But the explanation is problematical in two ways: first, the explainer—pumping the blood—is an effect of what it explains. This reverses the causal order that scientific explanation elsewhere honors. Second, the function of a heart is to pump the blood even when through deformity, injury, or disease it does not do so. Under these circumstances the explanatory power of a functional claim is mysterious. Philosophers long sought an analysis of functional systems that cashed them in for sets of causal claims about these systems as complexes of subsystems causally connected by feedback and feed-forward loops. Functional claims thus understood are abbreviations for complex causal claims (Nagel, 1977). Feedback/feed-forward analyses of function were, however, prone to counterexamples, and they made unwarranted distinctions between natural and artifact function. Such analyses also failed to exploit the biological foundation of functions in natural selection. It was Larry Wright (1976) who provided such an account: an event has many effects. The heart's beating has the effect of displacing a certain volume of air in the chest, of pushing the stomach down, stretching the tissue of the aorta, changing the color of the blood in the extremities, moving plaques of cholesterol along blood vessels, of making sounds a stethoscope detects. None of these effects are its functions. Another one of the heart beat's effects is pumping the blood, and this indeed is a function. Functions are effects, but not just any effects. They are effects that have been historically selected for their contributions to evolutionary fitness. In vertebrates the function of the heart's beating is to circulate blood, because the beating of every vertebrate heart has a certain *etiology:* over the course of evolutionary history vertebrate hearts and their predecessors were selected for their properties of efficient blood circulation; or the genes that code for hearts were selected for their phenotypic effects in efficient blood circulation. Wright's "etiological" analysis of function enables us to see how Darwinian theory underwrites functional claims in biology while preserving their continuity with artifact functions: for example, a bust functions as a door stop because of its etiology in literal, not natural, selection.

Above the level of the macromolecule, almost all biological concepts are functional ones, because they describe traits, dispositions, behaviors, and systems in terms of the effects that make them adaptations. But different structures can all have the same type of effect and thus fulfill the same function. Consider all the different mechanisms that keep time and therefore function as clocks. For this reason functional classifications that reflect selection for effects are blind to structural differences. Together with supervenience, the blindness to structure of selection or function explains much about biological theorizing. To see this consider the concept of 'gene'.

REDUCTION, EMERGENTISM, AND AUTONOMY

Until Francis Crick and James D. Watson uncovered the molecular mechanism of the Mendelian gene in the nucleic acids, the claim that biological processes were nothing but physical processes lacked concrete detailed evidence. Since their work biologists and philosophers have wrestled with the problem of how molecular biology and the rest of the sciences are related to one another. The problem is to reconcile the claim that the biological processes are nothing but physical ones, as Watson and Crick seemed to show for heredity, with the difficulty of actually effecting the reduction of Mendelian genetics or biological processes to purely physical ones.

Classical criteria for successful reduction require that the terms of the reduced theory be linked in definitions or general laws to the terms of the reducing theory and that the laws of the former be explained by the laws of the latter through deductive derivation. Meeting the first test requires a characterization of gene in terms of nucleic acids molecules. However, no satisfactory molecular characterization of the Mendelian gene is possible. "Mendelian gene" is a functional term; like most biological entities, genes are individuated by their functions: the phenotypes they help produce. Any number of physically quite different stretches of nucleic acid can in principle produce the same phenotypic effect, thus share a function, and so be classified as realizing the same Mendelian gene. In short, the Mendelian gene is supervenient on an indefinitely long disjunction of packages of molecular material, each of which will have the same phenotypic effect. Accordingly, no Mendelian gene is reducible to any single or small number of nucleic acid sequences, even though each Mendelian gene is nothing but a complex macromolecule. Without a connection between Mendelian genes and molecular ones, no Mendelian laws can be reductively explained by derivation from molecular ones.

But there are no strict Mendelian laws to be derived in any case. On the etiological analysis of function it is easy to see why. A biological generalization would link a functionally characterized kind either to another functional kind or to a structural kind: since the generalization's antecedent names a functional kind, its instances will differ from one another in physical properties because of the supervenience of functional kinds on a motley of structural properties. Thus, there will be no general structural kind common to this motley to figure in the consequent of the law we seek. If instead we seek a generalization linking the functional antecedent to a functional consequent, the diversity of physical structures on which the antecedent supervenes will almost certainly have no other common property that selection can turn into a function and so make the consequent of a law about functions linked to functions.

The supervenience of biological properties on physical ones, together with the absence of laws of the sort to be expected in physical sciences, leaves biology's relation to these disciplines problematical. The argument that biological explanations are somehow basic and autonomous from lower-level explanations that advert only to the physical constituents of biological systems is greatly strengthened by the impossibility of reduction. By the same token modern biology's physicalist commitments seem to be undermined by this conclusion.

Consider a concrete case: a Mendelian gene is nothing but a nucleic acid molecule. Thus, its causal properties are identical to those of the molecule. Consequently, if a Mendelian explanation of inheritance is autonomous from a molecular one, the autonomy cannot be grounded in differences between the causal processes they report. One alternative is that the autonomy is explanatory. Biological theories meet our explanatory needs and interests even when the processes they report are physical. An alternative strategy bases biology's autonomy on a denial of supervenience, asserting that biology discovers emergent nonphysical properties—ones that cannot be fully explained in terms of more basic underlying physical properties and relations. This approach has become unattractive in the light of advances in molecular biology.

LEVELS AND UNITS OF SELECTION

Controversy over reductionism has spread from the molecular/Mendelian interface to sociobiology and behavioral biology. Because of its attempts to explain human and infrahuman social and cultural traits genetically, sociobiology is often accused of reductionism in a different sense: of unwarranted reduction of the number of causal determinants of a trait or behavior by excluding environmental causes. This is a mistake sociobiologists rarely make, for the theory of natural selection clearly teaches that the environment works with the gene to create phenotypes and selects for those that confer heritable fitness. Conflicts among biologists and philosophers about the bearers of these traits have become a new arena of debate about reductionism.

Individual organisms are presumably the bearers of heritable traits selected for environmental fitness. However, some biologists long held that there can be selection for traits of groups of individuals, in particular social groups. Such group selection was held to best explain the emergence of cooperation among otherwise self-interested fitness maximizers. Groups of organisms might be selected for adaptive traits that were not adaptive for their members taken individually. Groups would thus constitute units of selection with traits not reducible to individuals' traits. A number of biologists, including G. C. Williams (1966) and Richard Dawkins (1976), rejected this argument for a mixture of biological and philosophical arguments. They held the reductionist view that the unit of selection is neither the group, nor the individual, but the gene. All evolution of species, populations, families, and individuals was to be understood as selection for traits of individual genes. Their arguments included appeals to parsimony in theory construction, the unlikelihood that the specialized conditions required for group selection would ever materialize, and the claim that the apparent adaptation of a group or individual trait could be explained by the actual adaptation of one or more traits of genes. The debate surrounding this thesis of 'genic' selection has focused on the question of whether there are significant generalizations about selection at higher levels of organization—the genotype, the individual, or a group of individuals—that genic selection cannot explain. Or can selection of "selfish" fitness-maximizing genes explain the cooperative fitness-reducing behavior and individual organisms that contain the "selfish" genes? Solving this problem requires clarity on a number of broad issues in the philosophy of science: what counts as a significant generalization and a reductive explanation, what counts as a group, as a reproducing individual, and as a trait to be acted on by selection?

ISSUES IN TAXONOMY

Since ARISTOTLE [1; S] species names have been held to characterize "natural kinds." But the absence of any set of conditions necessary and sufficient—essential—for membership in any species makes taxonomy problematical. This absence of "essentialism" in classification distinguishes biology from the physical sciences, which seek the essence of kinds on the model of the atomic structure of the chemical elements. Some biologists and philosophers have sought to account for "nonessentialism" about species by arguing that species, such as *cygnis olor,* the swan, or *Didus ineptus,* the dodo, are not kinds with instances but (spatiotemporally distributed) historical individuals—the lineage—with parts—the individual swans or dodos. This thesis may explain why no unique biological taxonomy seems forthcoming, why species concepts constitute more fundamental categories than higher taxa such as genus, order, or phylum. If species are individuals, it will be no surprise that there are no laws about them, nor a single mechanism of speciation.

Beyond these questions in the philosophy of science biology is widely held to have direct relevance to philosophers' concerns about the nature of life, thought, action, meaning, and value. Thus, its recent revolutionary developments have been applied to illuminate areas of BIOMEDICAL ETHICS, ANIMAL RIGHTS AND WELFARE [S], ecological protection, as well as traditional topics in moral philosophy. Whether descriptive biology can have normative or prescriptive implications for individual and social policy hinges on questions that have vexed moral philosophers since David HUME [4; S] first objected to inferences from what happens to be the case to what ought to be the case.

Bibliography

Brandon, R., and R. Burian. *Genes, Organisms, and Populations.* Cambridge, 1984.

Darwin, C. *On the Origin of Species.* London, 1859.

Dawkins, R. *The Selfish Gene,* 2d ed. Oxford, 1989.

Ereshefsky, M. *The Units of Evolution: Essays on the Nature of Species.* Cambridge, MA, 1992.

Hull, D. *Science as a Process.* Chicago, 1989.

Kitcher, P. *Vaulting Ambition: Sociobiology and the Quest for Human Nature.* Cambridge, MA, 1985.

Maynard Smith, J. *Evolution and the Theory of Games.* Cambridge, 1982.

Mayr, E. *Towards a New Philosophy of Biology.* Cambridge, MA, 1988.

Nagel, E. *Teleology Revisited.* New York, 1977.

Rosenberg, A. *The Structure of Biological Science.* Cambridge, 1985.

Ruse, M. *The Philosophy of Biology Today.* Albany, NY, 1988.

Sober, E. *Conceptual Issues in Evolutionary Biology,* 2d ed. Cambridge, 1994.

———. *The Nature of Selection,* 2d ed. Chicago, 1994.

Wilson, E. O. *On Human Nature.* Cambridge, MA, 1978.

Wright, L. *Teleological Explanation.* Berkeley, 1976.

ALEXANDER ROSENBERG

PHILOSOPHY OF HISTORY. Martin HEIDEGGER [3; S] is critical of two prevalent, "orthodox" treatments of the PHILOSOPHY OF HISTORY [6]: historiography *(Historie)* and Georg W. F. HEGEL's [3; S]. In contrast to Georg SIMMEL's [7; S] epistemological clarification of historiographical conceptualization or Heinrich RICKERT's [7; S] logic of the conceptualization of historiographical presentation, Heidegger wishes to illumine history *(Geschichte)* by following the guideline of authentic temporality from which it derives. History, in a genuine and primordial sense, cannot be an object of science. It does not deal with the past *(Vergangenheit)* since only something objectively present *(vorhanden)* can be past. Rather, history, since its prime concern is with human existence, is concerned with what has been *(Gewesenheit),* which is together with present and future.

Although Heidegger considers Hegel's treatment of history far more philosophical than that of the historiographers, he nevertheless states that Hegel, like ARISTOTLE [1; S], treats time in the context of a philosophy of nature. Thus, Hegel remains stuck in the "vulgar" interpretation of time and of history as something elapsing in that time. Hegel is unable to clarify the relation between Spirit as the negation of negation and time, and is thus forced to assert that Spirit first falls into time, an assertion he is then unable to clarify.

In a later essay, "The Onto-theo-logical Constitution of Metaphysics" (1969), Heidegger distances his own position from that of Hegel on three counts: (1) the matter of thinking; (2) the criterion for the conversation with the history of thinking; and (3) the character of this conversation. For Hegel the matter of thinking is being thought in absolute thinking with respect to beings; for Heidegger, being with respect to its difference from beings. For Hegel thinkers are incorporated into the dialectic of absolute thinking as elements of its stages; Heidegger seeks what has not been thought. For Hegel this conversation has the character of supersession *(Aufhebung)*; for Heidegger, the step back.

History for Heidegger is restricted to philosophy and constitutes the history of the forgottenness of being. Beginning with PLATO [6; S], being has increasingly withdrawn and concealed itself, usurped by philosophy's ever-growing preoccupation with beings. This history culminates in what Heidegger calls the end of philosophy,

which means the end of metaphysics. The phrase "the end of philosophy" does not mean that philosophy is "over"; the end could last for a very long time. The most crucial question is whether we remain stuck in representational, calculative, and manipulative thinking that perpetrates the activity of framing *(das Gestell)* or whether we become receptive to a nonobjectifying, nonmanipulative kind of thinking (*Andenken,* thinking toward, and *Besinnung,* sensing) that is open to belonging to being and appropriation *(Ereignis).*
(SEE ALSO: *Metaphysics, Overcoming of* [S])

Bibliography

Heidegger, M. *Identität und Differenz.* Pfullingen, 1957. Translated by J. Stambaugh as *Identity and Difference.* New York, 1969.

———. *Zur Sache des Denkens.* Tübingen, 1969. Translated by J. Stambaugh as *On Time and Being.* New York, 1972.

JOAN STAMBAUGH

PHILOSOPHY OF LANGUAGE. A number of influences contrived to keep the philosophy of language at the center of analytical philosophy in the years following 1960. One was the continued influence of the *Philosophical Investigations* of WITTGENSTEIN [8; S]. A second fertile source of interest was the theory of speech acts, as it was developed in the work of J. L. AUSTIN [1], whose untimely death in 1960 was closely followed by influential collections of his lectures and papers. A further influence was the emergence of linguistics as a full-fledged theoretical discipline, in the work of Noam CHOMSKY [S] and his followers. Paul GRICE's [S] seminal paper "Meaning" (1957) was becoming the primary focus of discussion of the relationship between a speaker's intentions in making an utterance and the meaning of the words occurring in it. Finally, W. V. O. QUINE's [7; S] *Word and Object* appeared in 1960; perhaps more than any other single work it dictated the subsequent directions in which the philosophy of language traveled.

Although Wittgenstein's work had alerted philosophers to a certain flexibility in our concept of what is meant by any human utterance, particularly by emphasizing concepts such as that of a family resemblance, or that of the open texture of terms, it was Quine who defended the wholesale skepticism about determinate meaning known as the thesis of the 'indeterminacy of radical translation'. In chapter 2 of *Word and Object* he presented the scenario of the radical translator, confined to the use of observation and scientific method in attempting to form hypotheses about the meanings of the sentences and words of a foreign people. Quine's thesis was that such hypotheses are underdetermined by the data: there will always be an indefinite number of ways of translating the foreign speech, no one of which can claim to be the single correct way. Quine was not merely pointing out the kind of choices that translators in practice make. His thesis was the more radical one that the rival translations need stand to each other in "no kind of equivalence, however loose," yet still nothing in the peoples' reactions or dispositions would determine one to be right and the others wrong. Nor is his point intended to be only one about learning a second language or a foreign language, for he immediately applied it to the "home" case, arguing that even in familiar interactions expressed in our first native language, the same massive indeterminacies arise. Finally, his point is not simply an instance of the familiar underdetermination of scientific theory by data, for in the general case of theoretical science we may believe that further facts exist to make true one theory or another, even if our empirical evidence leaves those further facts undetermined, whereas in the case of meaning there exists nothing—no mysterious mental fact—except the peoples' perceptions, actions, and behavior. There is here no further determining fact making it true that they mean one thing rather than another.

It might well be noticed that Quine and Wittgenstein are here surprisingly representative of cultural movements and philosophical traditions that at first blush seem quite alien to them. It was not only in the philosophical academies but in the wider culture that confidence in determinate meanings began to slip at this time. The loss of confidence, the fragmentations of authority, and the denial of uniquely correct "voices" or "versions" of history, experience, or even science were not only skeptical fantasies from the philosophical study, but also becoming matters of urgent concern in the humanities and in the culture in general. So, although Quine's thesis seemed incredible and even self-refuting to many philosophers (for we appear to have to understand, determinately, the rival interpretations suggested by different translation schemes), it focused attention in ways that were immediately recognized on the actual practices of translation, interpretation, and understanding that determine social relationships outside the study. In this way what might seem to be a domestic problem for abstract philosophical study became also an emblem of the 'postmodernist' climate, with many authors celebrating in different ways the denial of the 'given' or of any authoritative pivot on which practices of understanding would hinge. (*See* MODERNISM AND POSTMODERNISM [S])

In the following years Quine's austere conception of scientific method was enriched with other suggestions for the epistemology of interpretation. In particular DAVIDSON [S] influentially emphasized two aspects that had perhaps been underplayed by Quine. One was the importance of systematic semantic structure: to understand a language involves knowing how words and other subsentential elements contribute to the indefinite number of sentences in which they can occur. This knowledge, Davidson argued, can best be described by a fully formalized semantic theory of the kind that TARSKI [8] had developed for the rather different project of defining truth in a formal language. It would take as axioms whatever can properly be regarded as semanticaly primitive in the language studied (the object language) and deliver as theorems T-sentences, which are sentences saying of each sentence S of the language that S is true if and only if *p*. Such a theory therefore associates a truth condition with each sentence of the object language. Formally, Davidson's suggestion inaugurated the project of actually developing such a description of actual languages (a project about which Tarski had always been skeptical) and led to work on recalcitrant elements such as intensional contexts and descriptions of actions and events. Philosophically, it sparked a prolonged debate over the relationship between such a formal description of a language and the competence actually possessed by native speakers. Obviously, normal speakers do not explicitly know such theories, for even inadequate and simplified ones are extremely complex. The suggestion must be that they implicitly or tacitly know such theories, or at least that they have a competence that is modeled by such a theory even if there is no sense at all in which they know it. Problems of indeterminacy arise here also, since there will typically be an indefinite variety of formal theories capable of delivering the same theorems, so the question of which, if any, represents any truth about the speakers' actual psychologies is not easy to solve. Michael DUMMETT's [S] work dominated this discussion and allied troubles about whether the notion of a truth condition is one that should be regarded as foundational.

The second feature of Davidson's position has been the emphasis on a principle of charity as a key element in the interpretation of others. We learn what people mean by their sayings, it seems, only by supposing them to be rational. We must suppose them to be, by and large, believers in what is true (and, perhaps, lovers of what is good). If their motives and delusions were sufficiently bizarre and widespread, practices of translation would grind to a halt. Again, there is a question of the status of this imputation of rationality and what it teaches us about our own propensities to truth. And there is the urgent question of what else, apart from system and charity, is involved in interpretation. For if these were all that is involved, once more indeterminacy would threaten, since a speaker may be interpreted as speaking truly but about subject matter that may on other grounds seem foreign to their interests and concerns. The problem becomes one of deciding which perceptual and causal links to the world also constrain interpretation.

This is, in effect, the problem of REFERENCE [S], and the same period saw a resurgence of concern with the particular links to the world afforded by our practices of naming and using demonstratives to refer to things in our immediate environment. Since FREGE [3; S] it has been customary to think of reference as mediated by SENSE [S]: we refer to things by words that present their references in a certain way, as, for example, "Homer" presents the man only indirectly, as the apparently blind ninth-century B.C.E. Greek poet who wrote the *Iliad* and the *Odyssey,* and this way—the sense of the referring expression—mediates between it and the thing referred to. This model, essentially similar to that of RUSSELL's [7] theory of definite descriptions, was attacked by Ruth MARCUS [S], David Kaplan, and Saul KRIPKE [S], and their work gave rise to a new paradigm of 'direct reference' in which names are thought to function very much as Russell believed logically proper names to behave but in which the restriction of their references to Russell's items of immediate experience is dropped.

This approach to SEMANTICS [7; S] coincided with a new interest in theories of the mind that see it in computational terms, making transformations on elements thought of as elements in basic programming languages. This kind of functionalist model of the mind threatens the notion of reference, since to the computer the reference of elements is immaterial (it does not affect the software or hardware that '$' refers to a certain amount of money, for example). The principal lifeline for a genuine semantic notion of reference in the face of this challenge has usually been thought to be a causal theory, capable of selecting the "right" causal linkage to the external world to connect signs to objects. It is widely agreed that something must be added to causation to give a genuinely cognitive element, the relation that exists when we fix attention on a thing and form belief about that thing, but there exists no consensus on the right way to enrich the account. Many suggestions involve what Quine would call switching muses, already attributing cognitive grasp of a determinate kind to the subject whose reference to objects is being analyzed. Apart from these problems in the PHILOSOPHY OF MIND [S], the main purely semantic problems faced by the direct theory of reference have been Russell and Frege's old reasons for avoiding it: the possibility of understanding differently two names for the same thing and of understanding a name that in fact has no bearer. Direct theories try in various ways to avoid or deny these phenomena.

The indeterminacy Quine explored includes indeterminacy of reference, or the possibility of multiple interpretations of the objects about which a speaker is concerned. Further indeterminacy emerged in Kripke's interpretation of Wittgenstein's "rule-following considerations." In *Wittgenstein on Rules and Private Language* Kripke interpreted the central texts of the *Philosophical Investigations* as a response to a skeptical paradox similar to Quine's. The paradox suggests that no fact either in a subject's behavior or in occurrences in their mind can be sufficient to identify a single rule governing the application of functions and predicates that they use. Wittgenstein held that this would be true of the private language he describes, which is the reason why the hypothesis of such a language is a delusion, but Kripke's discussion suggests that the threat encompasses any language. Kripke offers a solution that involves both social elements, whereby persons manage to deem one another to be following specific rules, and an "anti-realist" element, whereby rule following is seen not as a real fact but rather as a kind of fiction or compliment we pay each other. Both elements of this position have excited fierce controversy, particularly among rival commentators wishing to show that they are untrue to Wittgenstein.

We have very little access to mind, apart from language. But we have very little access to language apart from mind. That is, the philosophies of mind and language are inextricably intertwined. Probably in 1960 it was easier to believe that authority flowed one way only, from the study of language to that of mind. By the late twentieth century this was no longer so. It was by then widely recognized that computational approaches to mind (*see* COMPUTATIONAL MODEL OF MIND [S]) are unlikely to welcome sharp division between the mental lives of language-using creatures (or computers) and those who live their lives or conduct their programs nonlinguistically. The lowly creature that perceives and responds, focuses attention on aspects of the environment, or is adapted for fleeing or feeding on some of its elements, may be a better starting point for a philosophy of reference or even predication and truth than the full-fledged competent user of a language. Not only did this change in the flow of authority affect writings of the late twentieth century, but it was abetted by developments within the philosophy of language itself. Certainly since CARNAP [2; S], but prominently in Wittgenstein, there have surfaced doubts about the very possibility of a substantive philosophy of language, a 'semantics' that would represent in some scientific way the function of parts of language and the epistemological status of the whole. Pursuing such a project might seem to be attempting to step outside our own skins, attempting to occupy a standpoint available only to some fantasized being that could theorize about language and the world without itself standing inside a particular linguistic clothing. A characteristic reaction to this problem became the adoption of varieties of "minimalisms," or philosophies counseling that in the end there is little substantive that we can say about the centrally contested concepts of semantics: TRUTH [S], reference, and MEANING [S].

(SEE ALSO: *Analyticity; Anaphora; Conditionals; Indexicals; Language; Logical Form; Metaphor; Phonology; Pragmatics; Propositions; Rule Following; Sense; Syntax;* and *Vagueness* [S])

Bibliography

Austin, J. L. *How to Do Things with Words.* Oxford, 1962.

Barrett, R., and R. Gibson. *Perspectives on Quine.* Oxford, 1990. A good entry to the debates that have centered on Quine's work.

Blackburn, S. *Spreading the Word.* Oxford, 1984. An introductory overview of the field.

Dummett, M. *The Seas of Language.* Oxford, 1993.

Evans, G., and J. McDowell, eds. *Truth and Meaning.* Oxford, 1976. A useful collection of essays largely representing a Davidsonian outlook.

Grice, P. *Studies in the Way of Words.* Cambridge, MA, 1989.

Horwich, P. *Truth.* Oxford, 1992. The best statement of modern minimalism, especially about the concept of truth.

Kripke, S. *Naming and Necessity.* Oxford, 1980.

———. *Wittgenstein on Rules and Private Language.* Oxford, 1982.

Martinich, A. P., ed. *The Philosophy of Language.* New York, 1985. The standard collection of important papers on the subject.

Quine, W. V. O. *Word and Object.* Cambridge, MA, 1960.

SIMON BLACKBURN

PHILOSOPHY OF LAW, PROBLEMS OF.

The philosophy of law has come a long way since 1967. At that time, the field was dominated by the LEGAL POSITIVISM [4] of H. L. A. HART [3], who wrote the original essay on PHILOSOPHY OF LAW, PROBLEMS OF, in *The Encyclopedia of Philosophy.* There were critics, of course, including Lon Fuller, a NATURAL LAW [5] theorist; but a much wider variety of approaches sprang up in the 1970s and 1980s.

Probably the most prominent individual has been Ronald Dworkin (1978, 1986), who began by distinguishing rules, such as "Don't drive over 65 MPH," from principles that specify requirements of morality, such as "People should not profit from their own wrongs," and from policies that set out goals, such as "Automobile accidents are to be decreased." According to Dworkin, Hart's legal positivism captured rules but not principles or policies, so it failed to include all parts of law. As a result, Hart ascribed discretion to judges whenever they are not bound by rules, but Dworkin argued that judges do not have discretion if they are still bound by principles. Dworkin also denied that the distinction between morality and law is as clear as Hart assumed.

Dworkin's alternative approach invoked an ideal judge named Hercules who develops a theory of political morality to justify all of the substantive and procedural precedents and statutes in the jurisdiction. Hercules' "soundest theory of law" then determined which rules and principles are valid and which legal obligations exist. Dworkin argued that Hercules would and judges should base their decision only on rules or principles rather than on policies (the RIGHTS [7; S] thesis), but there are enough principles to determine one right answer in every legal case, at least in the United States and Britain.

In his later work Dworkin has emphasized interpretation and analogized strings of judicial decisions to a chain novel game in which each successive player writes a new chapter and tries to make the whole novel as good as it can be. Just as previous chapters constrain chain novelists, so previous decisions constrain judges: and just as chain novelists rely on their views about what makes a novel good, so judges cannot make decisions without appealing to some moral values. More specifically, Dworkin argued that judges should ultimately base their decisions on a substantive moral theory whose fundamental principle requires the government to show equal concern and respect for all citizens but not necessarily to treat them all equally.

Although Dworkin's views attracted many followers, he was also criticized from many sides. Some conservative critics (e.g., Bork, 1990) objected that Dworkin's theory gives too much power to judges. These critics claimed instead that the original intentions of lawmakers and the original meanings of the words in laws determine what the law is and what judges should decide, so judges should not use their own moral beliefs to make legal decisions. Such judicial restraint was supposed to be the only way to maintain a legitimate separation of powers.

At the opposite extreme, pragmatists (e.g., Posner, 1990) have argued that Dworkin is too restrictive in his claim that judges should base their legal decisions only on rules and principles rather than on policies. According to pragmatists, court decisions are and should be based on the practical consequences of those decisions. One version of this claim has been espoused by members of the law and economics movement, who use the methods of economics to understand the content and evolution of law and claim that laws and judicial decisions do and should seek to maximize society's wealth. This focus on consequences would force judges to look at particular situations and thereby would take judges far from the traditional view of legal reasoning in terms of rules and rights.

Pragmatists' skepticism about rules has been shared by members of the critical legal studies movement (e.g., Unger, 1986). This group is diverse, but it is often associated with leftist political views and with strong claims about the indeterminacy of law. According to critical legal studies, there are usually or always enough precedents on both sides and enough vagueness in statutes for a judge to support any decision that she or he wants to make. In this respect, critical legal studies is often seen as a descendant of American LEGAL REALISM [4].

Another movement that gained prominence during the 1970s and 1980s is feminist jurisprudence (*see* FEMINIST LEGAL THEORY [S]). Many feminists have espoused a new methodology that pays more attention to the particular context of acts, laws, and judicial decisions. For example, the common construct of a genderless legal subject has been criticized as a myth, both because it overlooks important aspects of the context in which a person acts (namely, that person's gender and social stereotypes about that gender) and because of the context in which this construct itself arose. In their more substantive work feminist jurisprudes exposed the ways in which laws favor males or represent male perspectives in many areas including ABORTION [S], reproductive technology (*see* GENETICS AND REPRODUCTIVE TECHNOLOGIES [S]), sexual harassment, rape, battering, pornography, sex discrimination, and pregnancy leaves. Of course, feminists have disagreed in their approaches to these issues. Some have emphasized similarities between men and women, such as in mental capacity; others have emphasized differences between men and women, such as regarding pregnancy (Minow, 1990); and still others have emphasized the subtle ways in which law supports the dominance of men over women, such as by making it difficult to convict rapists and batterers (MacKinnon, 1987). Despite these and other disagreements, all feminists share the goal of improving the legal and social status of women.

Critical race theory has also questioned both the method and the substance of traditional jurisprudence (Bell, 1987, 1992). Its advocates have often employed fiction and first-person narratives (also used by some feminists) to show what law looks like from the perspective of a member of an underprivileged minority. Critical race theorists have focused on the law of discrimination and AFFIRMATIVE ACTION [S] and have shown how and why racial problems persist (*see* RACISM [7; S]). An important debate within critical race theory has concerned whether the rhetoric of rights aids or impedes the progress of racial minorities.

These movements mainly concern the nature of law and how judges ought to reason. There have also been developments regarding the substance of law and its evaluation. Some of these substantive developments were stimulated by new kinds of government programs and laws. For example, since the 1970s affirmative action programs have created great controversy. Some philosophers of law argued that affirmative action was justified as retribution or compensation for past injustices or that it served important social goals without violating any rights. Critics saw affirmative action as a form of discrimination, because it treated individuals according to their race, gender, or ethnic group. Then, in the 1980s new kinds of laws against pornography and against hate speech were proposed by some as necessary to achieve sexual and racial equality and criticized by others as vague and thus dangerous to speech that should be protected against censorship. Such substantive debates have occupied many philosophers of law, who have used their general theories of law to illuminate these particular issues and to argue for or against proposed laws.

Philosophers of law have also developed new theories for evaluating laws in several particular areas. One prominent example is punishment, where several philosophers have defended new versions of retributivism, some of which proportion punishment, not only to the harm done by the criminal, but also to the degree of responsibility of the criminal or instead to the unfair advantages gained by the criminal. There have also been advances in the theory of JUSTICE [4; S]. John RAWLS (1971; [S]) raised LIBERALISM [4; S] to new levels of sophistication, Robert Nozick (1974) countered with a forceful argument for libertarianism, and communitarians (*see* COMMUNITARIANISM [S]) criticized both theories for oversimplifying the nature of persons (e.g., Sandel, 1982). Such theories of justice might belong to political theory rather than to the philosophy of law itself, but they are discussed by philosophers of law, because these theories have very different implications about what kinds of laws should be passed or overturned. This interest in theories of justice is one instance of a general tendency of philosophers of law to use theories from related fields—a tendency that grew during the decades after 1967.

Bibliography

Bell, D. *And We Are Not Saved.* New York, 1987.

———. *Faces at the Bottom of the Well.* New York, 1992.

Bork, R. *The Tempting of America.* New York, 1990.

Dworkin, R. *Taking Rights Seriously.* Cambridge, 1978.

———. *Law's Empire.* Cambridge, 1986.

MacKinnon, C. *Feminism Unmodified.* Cambridge, 1987.

Minow, M. *Making All the Difference.* Ithaca, NY, 1990.

Nozick, R. *Anarchy, State, and Utopia.* New York, 1974.

Posner, R. *Problems of Jurisprudence.* Cambridge, 1990.

Rawls, J. *A Theory of Justice.* Cambridge, 1971.

Sandel, M. *Liberalism and the Limits of Justice.* Cambridge, 1982.

WALTER SINNOTT-ARMSTRONG

PHILOSOPHY OF MEDICINE. The subject matter unique to philosophy of medicine—as opposed to those issues that are best seen under the heading of PHILOSOPHY OF BIOLOGY [S]—is clinical medicine and its underlying methodology and assumptions. Crucial to philosophy of medicine is the family of terms disease, malady, health, normal, abnormal, condition, syndrome, all of which have evaluative aspects to their definitions. For all its scientific base, medicine must be a value-laden practice guided by the values of its practitioners and its public. It is in this regard, but not only in this regard, that the claim "Medicine is an art and a science" should be understood.

DISEASE, HEALTH, AND NORMALITY

A stable departure from physiological normality that causes death, disability, pain, loss of pleasure, or inability to achieve pleasure is the sort of entity that is called disease (Clouser, Culver, & Gert, 1981). The departure has to be stable enough so that it causes similar problems in similar people and so that it is recognizable by different medical practitioners as the same disease entity. When the departure is less clearly individuatable than a disease, the entity is referred to as a syndrome.

Normality and health are relative terms. They are relative to species, age, gender, (perhaps) social status, race, and ultimately to one's own physiology. A healthy (normal) eighty-five-year-old is quite different from a healthy (normal) twenty-year-old; and a healthy (normal) professional athlete is quite different from a healthy (normal) philosophy professor. Normal health is also relative to one's values. Unless a person feels comfortable doing what she wants to do, she can claim to be unhealthy by saying things like: "I just don't feel up to par." In this sense health is a theoretical state of a person.

The concept of biological variability derives its useful sense from the relativity of "normal." Biological variability makes generalization problematic in a way that generalizing from one billiard ball to any such object is not. Biological variability, meaning that no two organisms are exactly alike, is trivially true. It is unhelpful, except as a reminder that generalization is problematic.

Diseases are real to the extent that they are stable departures from normality (sometimes called "baseline") as defined above. Obviously, diseases are not like traditional physical objects. They can overlap and be in two places at the same time. (Mental diseases present their sorts of problems, which parallel issues in PHILOSOPHY OF MIND [S] and philosophy of psychology.) Diseases are real in that they cause real pain, disability, or both. Diseases are real in the sense that they can be reduced to physiological occurrences. Diseases are theoretical in the sense that they are not traditional physical objects, *and* they are identified only relative to a value structure that then becomes part of the medical theory. For example, given the current medical theory of Western scientific medicine, chronic fatigue syndrome is a disease. But against the backdrop of eighteenth-century medicine, it would have been seen primarily as a characteristic of some women and lazy men. Chiropractic medicine sees disease only in terms of misalignment of vertebrae. The reality of disease, a sense for reduction, and the theory-ladenness of disease exemplify traditional questions in PHILOSOPHY OF SCIENCE [6; S].

What is classifiable as a disease is also a function of what physicians are willing to do, what they are interested in, and what will be reimbursed. Thus, infertility is treated as a disease in large part because it is a terrible burden to some, it is interesting to deal with medically, and people are willing to pay for treatment. Being short is also treated as a condition worth reversing (in children) for the same sorts of reasons. This makes disease relative to culture and economic conditions.

Treating a condition as if it were a disease makes it a disease in a stipulative sense but not in the physiological sense. Baldness and bad breath would be conditions that might be very troublesome, most effectively treated medically, and yet still not classified as diseases. However, if they are caused by a disease, they may be considered signs of an underlying medical condition. Psychiatry periodically redecides whether certain psychological conditions should be considered diseases.

THE LOGIC OF DIAGNOSIS

Diagnosis and scientific EXPLANATION [3; S] present similar philosophical problems, especially with respect to explanation, causality, and laws (*see* CAUSATION [2; S]; LAWS OF SCIENCE [4]; and LAWS OF NATURE [S]). Diagnosis begins with history taking and moves on to the physical examination. The standard history questions assume that disease entities have a typical natural history to them.

Signs are objective characteristics such as blood pressure and broken bones. Symptoms are the subjective characteristics reported by the patient—for example, pain and lightheadedness. The signs and symptoms of disease vary with the stage of the disease. Thus, an early stage of any disease may be confused for the later stage of another. Physicians look for the best overall explanation for the condition, given the patient's individuating factors such as age, gender, occupation, stress factors, and so forth. The best explanation is assumed to be the most probable explanation, where the disease is considered to be the cause of the condition being investigated.

A standard procedure in diagnosis is the rule-out test. A physician limits the diagnosis to a few conditions and then does a test, which, if negative, will rule out one of the possible causes. This procedure is repeated until only one likely answer is left. This is in keeping with a simplistic version of falsification.

Doctors also use a simple confirmation strategy in diagnosis. Usually, more than one confirmatory test result is required before the diagnosis is accepted. Other predictions will have to be borne out by test results as well as physical findings and consistent history. Laboratory tests are crucial to modern-day diagnoses, although they present problems. Results are subject to false positives (disease reported when absent) and false negatives (disease not reported when present). The best test has a high true positive ratio and a low false positive ratio. Bayes's theorem (*see* BAYESIANISM [S]) can be used to calculate the probability that a person with a positive test actually does have the disease in question.

Since test results are continuous, cutoff points must be chosen. The cutoff points are chosen based on how serious an error would be. If a disease is fatal and can be treated safely, then a high false positive rate would be acceptable. For less worrisome conditions, compromise between the two figures is possible. Again, values are part of what looks like a very objective aspect of medicine. In this sense, medical diagnosis may be different from the usual picture of the scientific method. There are other differences as well.

Some of the crucial aspects of physical diagnosis—for example, interpreting heart sounds and kinds of rashes—are subjective and cannot be taught so much as they must be learned by practice. The apprenticeship of medical students and physicians (residents) is, in this sense, different from the time graduate students in science spend learning bench laboratory skills. Also, anecdotes play a role in diagnosis in a way that they would not in physics or most other sciences. Related to the reliance on anecdotes is that the best physicians just seem to "sense" that, no matter where the facts are pointing, something else is going on. Subjectivity, anecdotes, and intuition seem not, in general, to be good scientific methodology, and yet it seems to be precisely what separates the great clinicians from the ordinary ones. The key to understanding these great diagnosticians is probably pattern recognition.

Physicians often wait in order to let a disease show itself more clearly, sometimes confirming their diagnoses by followup: did the condition follow its predicted course; did the treatment have the expected effect and in the expected manner? If not, the diagnosis may well have been incorrect. Even if the followup is consistent with the diagnosis, the actual condition may have been different and may have remitted on its own or have been similar enough to the disease suspected so that it responded to the treatment. In these sorts of cases, physicians do not know that they were wrong. They will count these cases as successes and so use them to support a similar diagnosis the next time. There is no practical defense against this failing.

HOLISM AND REDUCTIONISM

Holistic medicine assumes that diseases are primarily a function of life-style and life events of the patient. A holistic approach to diagnosis will focus as much on psychosocial history as it will on traditional signs and symptoms. Stress as a factor in disease is very important in holistic accounts. Reductionistic medicine focuses more on physiology as the key to diagnosis, treatment, and taxonomy of disease. The reductionistic approach is the legacy of scientific medicine begun in the midnineteenth century (*see* REDUCTION, REDUCTIONISM [S]).

Bibliography

Bursztajn, H., R. Feinbloom, R. Hamm, and A. Brodsky. *Medical Choices, Medical Chances.* New York, 1990. Parts 1 and 2.

Clouser, K. D., C. M. Culver, and B. Gert. "Malady: A New Treatment of Disease," *Hastings Center Report* (June 1981), 11, 29–37.

Kelley, W., ed. *Textbook of Internal Medicine.* Philadelphia, 1992. Chaps. 6–8.

Margolis, J. "Thoughts on Definitions of Disease," *Journal of Medicine and Philosophy,* Vol. 11, No. 3 (Aug. 1986), 233–36.
Maull, N. "The Practical Science of Medicine," *Journal of Medicine and Philosophy,* Vol. 6, No. 2 (May 1981), 165–82.
McNeil, B., et al. "Primer on Certain Elements of Medical Decision Making," *New England Journal of Medicine,* Vol. 293, No. 5 (July 31, 1975), 211–15.
Merskey, H. "Variable Meanings for the Definition of Disease," *Journal of Medicine and Philosophy,* Vol. 11, No. 3 (Aug. 1986), 215–32.
Munson, R. "Why Medicine Cannot Be a Science," *Journal of Medicine and Philosophy,* Vol. 6, No. 2 (May 1981), 183–208.
Murphy, A. E. *The Logic of Medicine.* Baltimore, 1976.
Passmore, R., ed. *A Companion to Medical Studies,* vol. 3. Oxford, 1974.
Schaffner, K. "Philosophy of Medicine," in M. Salmon et al., eds. *Philosophy of Science* (Englewood Cliffs, NJ, 1992).
Wulff, H. *Rational Diagnosis and Treatment.* Oxford, 1976.

ARTHUR ZUCKER

PHILOSOPHY OF MIND. During the 1960s the philosophy of mind was shaking off its Cartesian and behaviorist past and entering a hopeful new phase. In Australia, J. J. C. SMART [S] and U. T. Place, prodded by C. B. Martin, had advanced an identity theory, according to which mental kinds (visual experiences of red, for instance) were held to be identical with physical (neurological) kinds (Smart, 1959). Identities of this sort, like the identification of water with H_2O, do not imply interdefinability: water is H_2O, even though the terms *water* and H_2O are not interdefinable.

The identity theory afforded a way of seeing how dualism could be avoided and the traditional MIND–BODY PROBLEM [5] solved without a commitment to BEHAVIORISM [1]. Even so, the theory came under attack from a variety of sources. Donald DAVIDSON (1970 [S]) pointed out that it was one thing to suppose that every mental token or particular is identical with some physical token or particular and quite another matter to imagine a one–one pairing of mental and physical types. My thinking of Vienna is identical, perhaps, with some neural event of type N_1; your thinking of Vienna could be identical with some neural event of type N_2. Mental particulars might be physical particulars, then, even though the relation between mental and physical kinds is not principled or reductive.

Why then should we suppose that every mental particular, every instance of a mental property or kind, is identical with some physical particular? How could such identities be anything more than fortuitous? To answer this question, Davidson appealed to SUPERVENIENCE [S], long a staple of ethical theorists. If the mental supervenes on the physical, two agents could not differ mentally without differing in some physical respect. Davidson regarded supervenience as nonreductive: if mental properties supervene on physical properties, this implies neither that mental properties are physical properties nor that there are strict laws relating the mental and the physical. Davidson dubbed the resulting view ANOMALOUS MONISM [S]: mental events are physical events, though there are no strict psychophysical laws.

Subsequent refinements of the notion of supervenience, notably those proposed by Jaegwon Kim (1984), have cast doubt on its anomalousness. One way of characterizing mental–physical supervenience is as follows: necessarily, if anything, x, has a mental property, M, there is some physical property, P, such that x has P, and necessarily, if anything, y, has P, y has M. Such a characterization allows for principled relations between mental properties and physical properties, or at any rate between mental properties and disjunctions of physical properties.

FUNCTIONALISM [S] represents another line of response to the identity theory: mental properties are identified with second-order, functional properties (Fodor, 1968). My thinking of Vienna is a matter of my being in a state with particular sorts of causal or dispositional relations to other states. If I am thinking of Vienna, then I am disposed to act in certain ways (to respond, perhaps, to your query, "A penny for your thoughts," with "Vienna") and to entertain other, related thoughts. What I actually do or think will depend on my other states of mind. I will not say that I am thinking of Vienna if I believe that I might be punished for having such a thought or if I want to deceive you. In this respect functionalism differs from old-fashioned behaviorism, which identified the having of particular kinds of thoughts with tendencies to behave in specific ways. Still, functionalism can be seen as a refinement rather than a rejection of behaviorism.

One sort of functionalism, computationalism (*see* COMPUTATIONAL MODEL OF MIND, THE [S]), depicts states of mind as relations between agents and syntactically defined internal symbols (Fodor, 1975). These symbols—sentences in a LANGUAGE OF THOUGHT [S]—owe their meaning to relations they bear to one another and to inputs and outputs. Mental operations, however, are fully characterizable syntactically—that is, without reference to the semantic features of mental items.

This picture, which underlies research in cognitive psychology and ARTIFICIAL INTELLIGENCE (AI) [S], has been challenged by connectionist (or neural network) models of mind (*see* CONNECTIONISM [S]). Connectionists regard minds, not as syntactic engines serially manipulating well-defined symbols, but as interconnected arrays of nodes whose relations yield outputs resembling the "fuzzy" categories of ordinary human cognition.

The computationalist model has been attacked as well by John Searle in a much-discussed thought experiment. Imagine that Wanda is placed in a room and Chinese characters are passed to her through a slot. When she receives these characters Wanda consults a code book that instructs her to pass other characters out through the slot. Wanda may be computationally equivalent to a Chinese speaker, yet she does not understand Chinese. So, Searle contends, computationalism (and functionalism generally) cannot account for a central component of our mental lives.

The identity theory purported to demystify the mind by showing how it might be possible to understand mental episodes as nothing more than physical occurrences. Inspired by W. V. O. QUINE [7; S] and Wilfrid SELLARS [S], Richard Rorty (1965) argued that we might see ascriptions of states of mind on the model of a scientific theory: mental terms resemble theoretical terms deployed in the sciences. Mental items are "posited" to explain behavior just as electrons are introduced to explain chemical phenomena. We "eliminate" entities postulated by a theory when we abandon the theory, however. We once explained the transfer of heat by positing a fluid, caloric, that flowed between material bodies. With the emergence of thermodynamics we eliminated caloric from our ontology. A similar fate might await beliefs, desires, and pains if neurobiology has its way (Churchland, 1981) (*see* ELIMINATIVE MATERIALISM; PHYSICALISM, MATERIALISM; and REDUCTION, REDUCTIONISM [S]).

EXTERNALISM AND THE REEMERGENCE OF THE MIND–BODY PROBLEM

Consider the so-called propositional attitudes: belief, desire, INTENTION [4], and the like. In believing (or desiring, or intending) we take up an attitude toward some proposition. I can believe, or hope, or fear, or (if I am a rainmaker) intend that it will rain. Could such states of mind supervene on our physical features? The question is pressing owing to the widely held supposition that the propositional content of agents' states of mind depends, not merely on agents' intrinsic physical features, but on relations that agents bear to their circumstances.

Contextual accounts of MENTAL CONTENT [S] are motivated by appeals to "Twin Earth" cases of a sort pioneered by Hilary PUTNAM [S] and extended by Tyler Burge (Burge, 1979; Putnam, 1975). What makes my thoughts about water concern water? Imagine a twin me existing on a planet indiscernible from Earth in all but one respect: on Twin Earth oceans and rivers contain, not water, not H_2O, but XYZ. When my Twin Earth counterpart has thoughts he would express by saying "there's water," his thoughts concern, not water, but XYZ, twin water. Mental differences between my twin and me are due, not to our intrinsic physical makeup, but to our circumstances. My thoughts concern water, and my twin's concern twin water, because my environment includes water, and his contains XYZ.

Such externalist or anti-individualist conceptions of mind might be thought to be incompatible with supervenience. We can, however, suppose that contextually fixed mental features of agents supervene on their physical features, provided we include among those physical features relations agents bear to their surroundings. Impressed by such considerations, Putnam, Jerry Fodor, and others have promoted a distinction between broad and narrow mental content: broad content is exhibited by states of mind whose supervenience base includes agents' contexts; narrow content supervenes on agents' intrinsic features. Agents, identical with respect to their intrinsic physical features but distinct with respect to their circumstances, have the same narrow states of mind even if they differ with respect to their broad mental states.

Fodor has argued that a properly scientific psychology can appeal only to agents' narrow features in explaining behavior: how I behave, including how I respond to incoming stimuli, depends on my intrinsic features (Fodor, 1981). To the extent that some states of mind are determined by relations I bear to my surroundings, these cannot be relevant to what I do. Fodor has cited such considerations as evidence for narrow content; others, skeptical of the notion, have concluded either that the explanation of behavior in terms of content is a nonstarter (Stich, 1983) or that psychological explanation is inherently anti-individualistic (Burge, 1979).

The rise of externalism has reinvigorated the mind–body problem. In identifying mental and physical properties, classical identity theories showed how mental and physical events could be causally related. Token identity and supervenience, however, reintroduce the problem. Suppose every mental particular is a physical particular. Suppose further that my thinking of Vienna is identical with some neurological event in my brain and that this event leads me to utter the sentence "Vienna is congested." The neurological event is a thinking of Vienna, and this event causes my utterance, but in what sense does the event's being a thinking of Vienna make any difference at all to what it causes? If we assume that the physical world is causally closed, it would apparently be possible in principle to offer a complete explanation of my behavior without reference to any mental properties I might happen to instantiate. Mental properties appear in this light to be epiphenomenal.

The problem is not merely that my thinking of Vienna might depend on my circumstances, although this makes the difficulty particularly acute. Assuming closure, two agents, indistinguishable with respect to their intrinsic physical characteristics, must behave identically given identical stimuli. If such agents differ mentally, these differences apparently lack causal relevance. Even if we reject externalism, however, so long as we suppose that the mental supervenes on the physical, it is hard to see how agents' mental properties could matter causally. Supervenience establishes property correlations. But the presence of a correlation, even a principled correlation, between the mental and the physical does not support the conclusion that the mental makes a causal difference if the physical does.

OTHER DEVELOPMENTS

Since the 1960s philosophers of mind have tended to repress the question of how CONSCIOUSNESS [2] fits into the physical world, focusing instead on INTENTIONALITY [4], the "ofness" or "aboutness" of thought. As a result, it remains unclear how best to understand the place of conscious phenomena. A functionalist account would seem unpromising (though see Dennett, 1991, and Shoemaker, 1975). Some philosophers, following Thomas Nagel (1974), have elected to home in on the "what-it's-likeness" of ordinary conscious experiences, arguing that attempts to accommodate consciousness to the physical world as we now understand it are bound to fail (*see* CONSCIOUSNESS IN ANGLO-AMERICAN PHILOSOPHY; CONSCIOUSNESS IN PHENOMENOLOGY [S]).

Since Smart's defense of materialism in 1959 the philosophy of mind has grown and diversified. At times solutions to long-standing philosophical problems seemed imminent. At other times the prospects have appeared less hopeful. Progress in philosophy is measured, not by the discovery of settled solutions to such problems, however, but by an improved and deepened understanding of the domain. So measured, progress in the philosophy of mind has been remarkable.

(SEE ALSO: *Action Theory; Folk Psychology; Mental Causation; Mental Imagery; Mental Representation; Multiple Realizability; Personal Identity; Qualia; Self;* and *Subjectivity* [S])

Bibliography

Burge, T. "Individualism and the Mental," *Midwest Studies in Philosophy,* Vol. 4 (1979), 73–121.

Churchland, P. M. "Eliminative Materialism and the Propositional Attitudes," *Journal of Philosophy,* Vol. 78 (1981), 67–90.

Davidson, D. "Mental Events," in L. Foster and J. Swanson, eds., *Experience and Theory* (Amherst, MA, 1970). Reprinted in *Essays on Actions and Events* (Oxford, 1980).

Dennett, D. C. *Consciousness Explained.* Boston, 1991.

Fodor, J. "Methodological Solipsism Considered as a Research Strategy in Cognitive Psychology," *Behavioral and Brain Sciences,* Vol. 3 (1981), 63–73.

———. *The Language of Thought.* New York, 1975.

———. *Psychological Explanation.* New York, 1968.

Kim, J. "Concepts of Supervenience," *Philosophical and Phenomenological Research,* Vol. 45 (1984), 153–76.

Nagel, T. "What Is It Like to Be a Bat?" *Philosophical Review,* Vol. 83 (1974), 435–50.

Putnam, H. "The Meaning of 'Meaning,' " in *Mind, Language, and Reality* (Cambridge, 1975).

Rorty, R. "Mind–Body Identity, Privacy, and Categories," *Review of Metaphysics,* Vol. 19 (1965), 24–54.

Searle, J. "Minds, Brains, and Programs," *Behavioral and Brain Sciences,* Vol. 3 (1980), 417–24.

Shoemaker, S. "Functionalism and Qualia," *Synthese,* Vol. 27 (1975), 291–315.

Smart, J. J. C. "Sensations and Brain Processes," *Philosophical Review,* Vol. 68 (1959), 141–56.

Stich, S. P. *From Folk Psychology to Cognitive Science.* Cambridge, MA, 1983.

JOHN HEIL

PHILOSOPHY OF PHYSICS. Of all the special sciences to which philosophy has given birth, physics is perhaps the oldest and most successful, as its archaic name, natural philosophy, attests. But despite its venerable status as an independent discipline, the more recent history of physics has highlighted its intimate interconnections—both epistemological and metaphysical—with philosophy. Radical developments in twentieth-century physics have prompted reflection on the character and reliability of scientific knowledge while at the same time challenging some of our most basic assumptions concerning the nature of the world and our relation to it. Moreover, physicists have sometimes appealed to characteristically philosophical arguments in the course of developing or defending their views. Most important to philosophy, perhaps, are the conceptual issues raised by fundamental physics itself.

RELATIVITY

EINSTEIN [2] created two theories of relativity, known as the special and the general theory. Each in turn involved radically new conceptions of space and time. Einstein (1905) based the special theory on two principles. The principle of relativity states that all states of uniform motion are physically equivalent. The principle of the constancy of the speed of light states that light travels at a definite speed in a vacuum, independent of the motion of its source. For Einstein the principle of relativity derived support from both experiment and symmetry considerations. The constancy of the speed of light was a consequence of the then accepted wave theory of light, for which there was much experimental support. Einstein was able to construct a theory from these principles only by modifying certain intuitive assumptions about time incorporated into physics since NEWTON [5]. He took these modifications to follow from a definition of simultaneity for events at different places, in accordance with which light travels at the same speed (in a vacuum) in both directions between these places.

Einstein's teacher Minkowski (1908) presented this special theory of relativity as explicitly postulating a radically new four-dimensional structure incorporating time as well as space. Minkowski spacetime is a generalization of Euclidean geometry. The analogues of points of Euclidean space are points of Minkowski spacetime, at each of which an instantaneous, spatially unextended, event may occur. A point in Euclidean space can be labeled by three numbers (x,y,z), which specify how far away it is from a fixed point o, as measured along each of three fixed, mutually perpendicular, directions. These numbers are called the point's coordinates, and o and the three directions define the corresponding Cartesian coordinate system with o as origin. Pythagoras's theorem implies that the square of the distance Δs between the points p and q is equal to the sum of the squares of the differences between p's coordinates and q's coordinates, as follows.

$$(1) \quad \Delta s^2(p,q) = (x_p - x_q)^2 + (y_p - y_q)^2 + (z_p - z_q)^2$$

The distance between two points does not depend on the choice of the Cartesian coordinate system. This invariance of distance characterizes the intrinsic geometric structure of Euclidean space. Analogously, each point in Minkowski spacetime may be labeled by four numbers (x,y,z,t): the first three numbers are Cartesian coordinates of the point's spatial location, and the fourth specifies the time an event may have occurred at the point. The fundamental invariant quantity defining the structure of Minkowski spacetime is the spacetime interval $\Delta I(p,q)$ defined by

$$(2) \quad \Delta I(p,q) = c^2\, \Delta t^2(p,q) - \Delta s^2(p,q)$$

(where $\Delta t(p,q)$ is the elapsed time, and $\Delta s(p,q)$ is the spatial distance, between the points p,q of Minkowski spacetime, and c is a number equal to the speed of light in a vacuum). Now let K,K' be two states of uniform, unaccelerated motion: suppose that (x,y,z,t) is a system of coordinates for Minkowski spacetime such that the (spatial) origin o of the Cartesian coordinate system (x,y,z) remains at rest in K, and (x',y',z',t') is a similar system whose spatial origin o' remains at rest in K'. Then the invariance of the Minkowski spacetime interval means that

$$(3) \quad c^2\Delta t'^2(p,q) - \Delta s'^2(p,q) = c^2\Delta t^2(p,q) - \Delta s^2(p,q)$$

Newton maintained that both the spatial distance and the temporal interval between every pair of spatiotemporally localized events constituted intrinsic relations between them. In such a Newtonian spacetime the interval given by equation (2) is consequently also invariant, provided that $\Delta t(p,q)$ represents the intrinsic temporal interval and $\Delta s(p,q)$ represents the intrinsic spatial distance between p and q. But if $\Delta s(p,q)$ is calculated according to equation (1) in the (x,y,z,t) system, and $\Delta s'(p,q)$ is given by an analogous equation in the (x',y',z',t') system, then equation (3) cannot hold in Newtonian spacetime if K,K' represent different states of motion. For in that case $\Delta t(p,q) = \Delta t'(p,q)$, but $\Delta s(p,q) \neq \Delta s'(p,q)$.

Equation (3) can hold in Minkowski spacetime because neither the spatial distance nor the temporal interval between any pair of noncoincident spatiotemporally localized events is an intrinsic quantity. In Minkowski spacetime not only the spatial distance but also the temporal interval between a pair of nonincident spatiotemporally localized events depends on the state of motion to which one chooses to relativize these quantities: it is only the Minkowski spacetime interval that remains an absolute quantity, independent of state of motion. Note that, relative to a state of motion, there is still an absolute distinction between spatial and temporal intervals, as the minus sign in equation (2) indicates.

Points p,q are said to be respectively timelike, spacelike, or null separated, depending on whether the spacetime interval $\Delta I(p,q)$ is positive, negative, or zero. Events at p,q are spacelike (timelike) separated just in case they occur at different places (times) with respect to all states of uniform motion. $\Delta I(p,q)$ may be zero even if $p \neq q$. Fixing any point o as the origin of a system of spatiotemporal coordinates (x,y,z,t), the locus of points q that are null separated from o forms the three-dimensional "surface" of a four-dimensional generalization of a cone in Minkowski spacetime with vertex at o—an important part of the intrinsic structure of Minkowski spacetime that is not relative to any state of motion. A light pulse emitted from o in a vacuum would form a spherical shell expanding about the place it was emitted. This expanding shell traces out what is called the forward null cone or light cone at o, consisting of all points of Minkowski spacetime at null separation from and invariantly later than o: points at null separation from and invariantly earlier than o are said to form the backward null cone at o.

The null-cone structure of Minkowski spacetime allows for processes (including light traveling in a vacuum) that propagate with invariant speed c. Requiring all other physical processes also to conform to the principle of relativity ensures that the laws of physics do not single out any privileged state of absolute rest. This is one way in which the special theory of relativity goes beyond the claim that spacetime is Minkowski.

The natural modifications required to make Newton's laws of motion conform to the principle of relativity imply that no massive body can be accelerated to or beyond the speed of light in a vacuum. But tachyons—hypothetical particles that always travel faster than light—are not thereby excluded. The special theory of relativity alone does not imply that the (invariant) speed of light in a vacuum forms an upper limit to the speed of signaling and information transmission. Nor does the theory itself imply that an event may be influenced only by events in or on its past null cone and may influence only events in or on its future null cone. But these conclusions do indeed follow, given plausible but not unquestioned substantive assumptions about causation and information transmission.

The special theory of relativity abandons previously unquestioned assumptions about time. The temporal interval between a pair of events is no longer an absolute quantity but a relation between these events and a state of motion. If the events are timelike separated, then any spacetime path joining them that represents a possible history of a point mass defines such a state of motion, and the length of this path corresponds to the elapsed time according to an ideal clock whose history coincides with that path. If the events are spacelike separated, then it is not only their temporal separation but also their temporal order that is relative to an arbitrarily chosen state of uniform motion. Hence, there is no absolute simultaneity: any pair of spacelike separated events are simultaneous relative to one state of uniform motion but occur at different times relative to other states of uniform motion. While this relativity of simultaneity is a basic consequence of relativity theory, REICHENBACH'S [7] (1928) further claim, that it is conventional which pairs of spacelike separated events we take to be simultaneous relative to a given state of uniform motion, sparked extensive philosophical debate. Against Reichenbach's claim one may note that the null-cone structure of Minkowski spacetime singles out a unique notion of simultaneity for distant events that implies the constancy of the one-way speed of light in a vacuum. Insofar as special relativity postulates Minkowski spacetime, it seems inappropriate to regard either Einstein's "definition" of distant simultaneity, or the constancy of the one-way speed of light, as true by convention. The revised assumptions about space and time imply a number of surprising, but well-confirmed, empirical predictions, while a number of alleged paradoxes are readily resolved by their consistent application.

Einstein realized that, despite its unprecedented empirical success, Newton's law of universal gravitation was incompatible with his special theory of relativity. He developed a radically new theory that came to be called the general theory of relativity, largely because Einstein (1916) took it to incorporate a generalization of his earlier principle of relativity to cover all states of motion, accelerated as well as uniform. According to the general theory of relativity, while spacetime approximates to the structure of Minkowski spacetime in any sufficiently small region, its large-scale structure may be quite different. For both the global four-dimensional structure of spacetime and the three-dimensional spatial geometry that derives from it depend on how matter and energy are distributed. When an apple falls to the earth, rather than being forced by gravity to execute a nonuniform motion in a fixed, background Minkowski spacetime, its trajectory is actually a spacetime geodesic, or "straightest path," in a spacetime whose structure deviates systematically from that of Minkowski spacetime, largely because of the nearby presence of the massive Earth. There is no force of gravity: there are just matter-induced deviations from Minkowski spacetime.

Since the structure of spacetime depends on the distribution of matter, many different spacetime structures are equally compatible with the general theory of relativity. An empty spacetime may (but need not!) have the global structure of Minkowski spacetime. Observations indicate that our universe is expanding. While the global structure of the observable universe conforms closely to one of a class of expanding, isotropic general relativistic spacetimes, it remains an open question which member of that class best represents it.

Other general relativistic spacetimes represent very different states of matter. According to the general theory, a sufficiently massive star will collapse irreversibly, and the spacetime structure around this collapse will be so distorted that not even light can escape from a spatial region surrounding the star, which is consequently called a black hole. Black holes contain spacetime singularities. A singularity is not a region of spacetime but rather constitutes an edge or boundary of spacetime. According to the theory, an object falling into a black hole will reach the singularity in a finite time, as recorded by an ideal clock carried with it: it will then no longer exist. But according to an ideal clock located far from the black hole, the object will never enter the black hole, and its clock will slow down indefinitely as it nears the black hole.

Spacetimes describing black holes have been widely applied as descriptions of distant objects in the observable universe. Other general relativistic spacetimes that do not appear to describe anything in our universe nevertheless pose intriguing philosophical problems. The famous logician Kurt GÖDEL [3; S] (1949) discovered one such general relativistic spacetime that appears to allow for the possibility of time travel into one's own past, even though its structure in fact rules out any global distinction between past and future. This discovery has prompted philosophical debate concerning whether this is indeed a possibility, and if so in what sense.

Other philosophical debates have been transformed by the development of relativity theory. LEIBNIZ [4; S] denied the substantial reality of space and time, arguing that spatial and temporal facts were reducible to relations between material objects and events: he further claimed that temporal relations were themselves reducible to causal relations. While Reichenbach took Leibniz's relationism to be vindicated by relativity, this verdict proved to be premature. Although spatial and temporal relations are relativized to states of motion, Minkowski spacetime itself is no more and no less substantial than Newtonian space and time. The dynamic nature of spacetime in general relativity appears to render it even more substantial, but on further analysis general relativity so transforms the substantivalist/relationist debate that it is difficult to award victory to any traditional view.

Robb (1914) developed Minkowski spacetime on the basis of a primitive relation of absolute (temporal/causal) precedence. Some interpret this as supporting a causal theory of time. But all general relativistic spacetimes are not so readily developed, and the epistemic and/or metaphysical credentials of the allegedly causal primitive have been questioned.

Following seminal work of POINCARÉ [6] (1902), Reichenbach (1928), and Grünbaum (1973) argued that equality of spatial distance and temporal interval, or in relativity the spacetime interval, is conventional. But realists such as Friedman (1983) have countered their arguments. (*See* RELATIVITY THEORY, PHILOSOPHICAL SIGNIFICANCE OF [7])

QUANTUM MECHANICS

Serious difficulties arose when physicists attempted to apply the physics of Newton and MAXWELL [5] to atomic-sized objects. By the 1920s a theory called quantum mechanics emerged that seemed capable of replacing classical physics here and, in principle, in all other domains. Quantum mechanics quickly proved its empirical success. But this was purchased at a high conceptual cost: there is still no consensus on how to understand the theory.

In Newton's mechanics the state of a system at a time is fixed by the precise position and momentum of each of its constituent particles. Their values determine the precise values of its energy and all other dynamical quantities. The state typically changes under the influence of forces, in accordance with Newton's laws of motion. At least in the case of simple isolated systems these laws imply that the initial state of a system determines its state at all later times, given the forces acting on it. In this sense the theory is deterministic.

While any particular method of observing a system may disturb its state, there is no theoretical reason why such disturbances cannot be made arbitrarily small. An ideal observation of a system's state would then not only reveal the precise position and momentum of each of its constituent particles at one time but also permit prediction of its exact future state, given the forces that will act on it and setting aside computational difficulties. (Though in certain so-called chaotic systems the future state may depend so sensitively on the exact initial state that practical limitations on measurement accuracy effectively preclude such predictions.)

Although it uses almost the same dynamical quantities, quantum mechanics does not describe a system to which it applies (such as an electron) by a state in which these all have precise values. Instead, the state of an isolated system is represented by an abstract mathematical object (i.e., a wave function or, more generally, a state vector). If it is left alone, a system's state vector evolves in such a way that the vector representing the system's state at later times is uniquely determined by its initial value. But this vector specifies only the probability that a measurement of any given dynamical quantity on the system would yield a particular result; and not all such probabilities can equal zero or one. Moreover, no attempt to establish a system's initial state by measuring dynamical quantities can provide more information than can be represented by a state vector. It follows that no measurement, or even theoretical specification, of the present state of a system suffices within the theory to fix the value that would be revealed in a later measurement of an arbitrary dynamical quantity. This is the sense in which the theory is indeterministic.

The famous two-slit experiment illustrates these features of quantum mechanics. If a suitable source of electrons is separated from a detection screen by a barrier in which two closely spaced parallel slits have been cut, then impacts of individual electrons on different regions of the screen may be detected. Quantum mechanics is able to predict the probability that an electron will be observed in a given region of the screen. The resulting probability distribution is experimentally verified by noting the relative frequency of detection in different regions, among a large collection of electrons. The resulting statistical pattern of hits is characteristic of phenomena involving interference between different parts of a wave, one part passing through the top slit and the other part through the bottom slit.

Now, according to quantum mechanics, the electrons have a wave function at all times between emission and detection. But the theory does not predict, and experiment does not allow, that any electron itself splits up, with part passing through each slit. The electrons' wave function specifies no path by which any particular electron travels from source to screen: it specifies only the probability that an electron will be detected in a given region of the screen. The theory neither predicts just where any electron will be detected on the screen nor has anything to say about how individual electrons get through the slits.

After heated discussions at Bohr's institute in Copenhagen in the 1920s, there emerged among many physicists a consensus that became known as the Copenhagen interpretation. A central tenet of this interpretation is that the quantum-mechanical description provided by the state vector is both predictably and descriptively complete. The most complete description of a system at a given time permits only probabilistic predictions of its future behavior. Moreover, this description, though complete, fails to assign a precise value to each dynamical quantity.

As an example, if a system's wave function makes it practically certain to be located within a tiny region of space, then the system's momentum must be very imprecise. A quantitative measure of the reciprocal precision with which quantities such as position and momentum are simultaneously defined is provided by the HEISENBERG [3] indeterminacy relations. According to the Copenhagen interpretation, rather than restricting our knowledge of an electron's precise simultaneous position and momentum, these relations specify how precise their simultaneous values can be.

Some, including Einstein, have objected to the Copenhagen interpretation of quantum mechanics because of its rejection of determinism in physics. But Einstein's main objections to the Copenhagen interpretation sprang from his conviction that it was incompatible with REALISM [S]. In its most general form realism is the thesis that there is an objective, observer-independent reality that science attempts (with considerable success) to describe and understand. To see how the Copenhagen interpretation seems to conflict with this thesis, consider once more the two-slit experiment.

If one performs an observation capable of telling through which slit each individual electron passes, then one will indeed observe each electron passing through one slit or the other. But performing this observation will alter the nature of the experiment itself, so that the pattern of detections on the screen will now look quite different. The characteristic interference pattern will no longer be observed: in its place will be a pattern that, ideally, corresponds to a simple sum of the patterns resulting from closing first one slit, then opening it and closing the other.

Observation of the electrons passing through the slits therefore affects their subsequent behavior. The Copenhagen interpretation further implies that it is only when this observation is made that each electron passes through one slit or the other! The observed phenomenon then so depends on its being observed that its objective reality is threatened. Moreover, the quantum-mechanical probabilities explicitly concern results of just such observations. Quantum mechanics, on the Copenhagen interpretation, then appears to be a theory not of an objective world but merely of our observations. If there is an objective world somehow lying behind these observations, then quantum mechanics seems notably unsuccessful in describing and understanding it!

A proponent of instrumentalism could rest easy with this conclusion: according to instrumentalism, the task of a scientific theory is simply to order previous observations and predict new ones, and quantum mechanics succeeds admirably at this task. But if the Copenhagen interpretation is correct, then the theory does so without even permitting a description of what lies behind these observations. Realists such as Einstein and POPPER [6] have therefore rejected the Copenhagen interpretation while attempting to accommodate the great success of quantum mechanics itself by offering an alternative interpretation of that theory.

According to the simplest realist alternative, a quantum system always has a precise value of every dynamical quantity such as position and momentum. The state vector incompletely describes a large number of similarly prepared systems by specifying the fraction that may be expected to have each value of any given quantity. On this view each electron follows its own definite path through one slit or the other in the two-slit experiment, and the wave function simply specifies the relative fractions that may be expected to take paths ending in each particular region of the screen.

Unfortunately, there are strong objections to this simple variety of realistic interpretation of quantum mechanics (see, e.g., Redhead, 1987). A technical objection is that this interpretation is inconsistent with features of the mathematical representation of quantities in the theory. More fundamentally, it turns out to conflict with Einstein's own assumption that the state of a system cannot be immediately affected by anything that is done far away from where it is located.

Einstein had two main arguments against the Copenhagen thesis that quantum mechanics is complete. He developed a version of the first argument in consultation with his colleagues Podolsky and Rosen, and their joint paper (Einstein, Podolsky, & Rosen, 1935; hereafter EPR) became a classic. The paper described a thought experiment in which quantum mechanics implies the possibility of establishing, with arbitrary accuracy, either the position or the momentum of one particle solely by means of a measurement of the corresponding quantity performed on a second particle. They argued that such a measurement would not affect the state of the first particle, given that the two particles are physically separated. They concluded that the first particle has both a precise position and a precise momentum, despite the fact that no quantum-mechanical wave function describes these quantities as having such simultaneous precise values.

Bohr (1935) rejected the conclusion of the EPR argument. His reply may be interpreted as maintaining the completeness of quantum mechanics by rejecting some of the argument's assumptions. Later work by Bell (1964) showed how one crucial assumption could be experimentally tested. This locality assumption is that the total state of two physically separated systems is given by the states of those two systems, in such a way that the state of one cannot be immediately affected by anything that is done to the other. In an experimental setup very similar to the one EPR had themselves described this assumption turns out to imply predictions that conflict with those of quantum mechanics itself! Subsequent verification of the quantum-mechanical predictions has provided strong evidence against this locality assumption (see, e.g., Redhead, 1987).

The failure of such unorthodox alternatives does not imply that the Copenhagen interpretation is correct, and several rival interpretations have been proposed by physicists, philosophers, and mathematicians. An examination of Einstein's second main argument against the Copenhagen interpretation may help explain why people have made such proposals.

If quantum mechanics is a universal theory, then it must apply not only to atoms and subatomic particles but also to ordinary objects like beds, cats, and laboratory apparatus. Now, while it may seem unobjectionable for an electron to have no definite position, it is surely ridiculous to suppose that my bed is nowhere in particular in my bedroom. The Copenhagen interpretation seems committed to just such ridiculous suppositions. For it is possible to transfer the alleged indeterminateness of a microscopic object's state to that of a macroscopic object by means of an appropriate interaction between them. Indeed, this is exactly what happens when a macroscopic object is used to observe some property of a microscopic object.

In SCHRÖDINGER'S [7] (1935) famous example, a cat is used as an unconventional apparatus to observe whether or not an atom of a radioactive substance has decayed. The cat is sealed in a box containing a sample of radioactive material. A Geiger counter is connected to a lethal device in such a way that if it detects a radioactive decay product, then the device is triggered and the cat dies. Otherwise, the cat lives. The size of the sample is chosen so that there is a 50 percent chance of detecting a decay within an hour. After one hour the box is opened.

The quantum-mechanical description couples the wave function describing the radioactive atoms to the wave function describing the cat. The coupled wave function after one hour implies neither that an atom has decayed nor that no atom has decayed: but it also implies neither that the cat is alive nor that it is dead. If this wave function completely describes the state of the cat, it follows that the cat is then neither alive nor dead! This is hard to accept, since cats are never observed in such bizarre states. Indeed, when an observer opens the box she will observe either a dead cat or a live cat. But if she finds a corpse, she is no mere innocent witness: rather her curiosity killed the cat.

Most proponents of the Copenhagen interpretation would reject this conclusion. They would claim that an observation had already taken place as soon as the decay of a radioactive atom produced an irreversible change in a macroscopic object (such as the Geiger counter), thus removing any further indeterminateness and causing the death of the cat. But this response is satisfactory only if it can be backed up by a precise account of the circumstances in which an observation occurs, thereby leading to a determinate result.

The problem of explaining just why and when a measurement of a quantum-mechanical quantity yields some one determinate result has come to be known as the measurement problem. The problem arises because if quantum mechanics is a universal theory, it must apply also to the physical interactions involved in performing quantum measurements. But if the Copenhagen interpretation is correct, then a quantum-mechanical treatment of the measurement interaction is either excluded in principle or else leads to absurd or at least ambiguous results.

One radical response to the measurement problem is due originally to Everett (1957). It is to deny that a quantum measurement has a single result: rather, every possible result occurs in some actual world! This implies that every quantum measurement produces a splitting, or branching, of worlds. A measurement is just a physical interaction between the measured system and another quantum system (the observer apparatus) that, in each world, correlates the result with the observer apparatus's record of it. One can show that the records built up by an observer apparatus in a world will display just that pattern that would have been expected if each measurement had actually had a single result.

Since every possible result actually occurs in every quantum measurement, the evolution of the physical universe is deterministic on this interpretation. Not only indeterminism but also nonlocality turns out to be a kind of illusion resulting from the inevitably restricted perspective presented by the world of each observer apparatus.

Though embraced by a number of prominent physicists, Everett's interpretation faces severe conceptual difficulties. It must distinguish between the physical universe and the "worlds" corresponding to each observer apparatus. But the status of these "worlds" is quite problematic. Moreover, it is unclear what can be meant by probability when every measurement outcome is certain to occur in some "world."

After writing a classic textbook exposition of the Copenhagen interpretation, Bohm (1952) rejected its claims of completeness and proposed an influential alternative that sought to restore determinism. On this alternative the state of a particle is always completely specified by its position. Changes in this position are produced by a physical force generated by a field described by the wave function of the entire system of which the particle is a component. Measurements of quantities such as energy and momentum are analyzed into observations of some system's position. Quantum mechanics is understood as offering probabilities for the results of these observations. Since each result is actually determined, in part by the initial positions of measured system and apparatus (which are not described by the wave function), quantum indeterminism is just a consequence of the incompleteness of the quantum description.

Bohm's interpretation clearly involves interactions that violate the locality assumption. A measurement on one particle can immediately affect the state of a distant particle by altering the force acting on it—a theoretical violation of the principle of relativity. But if the interpretation is correct, it turns out that this instantaneous action as a distance cannot be exploited to transmit signals instantaneously. The violation of locality and the principle of relativity is unobservable. (*See* QUANTUM MECHANICS, PHILOSOPHICAL IMPLICATIONS OF [7])

COSMOLOGY

In 1929 Hubble concluded from observations that distant galaxies are receding from one another, with velocities proportional to their distances apart. Subsequent observations confirmed and refined this picture of an expanding universe, which is well modeled by a symmetric general relativistic spacetime with an initial singularity, on the order of ten billion years ago. Theoretical investigations showed that this singularity is not merely an artifact of the symmetry of these models. If classical general relativity is true, then the initial singularity corresponds to an origin of the universe. This would imply that the universe did not come into existence at some moment in time—rather, time is coeval with the universe.

But there are grounds for doubting the applicability of general relativity to the extreme conditions of the hot, dense early universe: in these conditions qauntum effects are expected to be of crucial importance. Now despite its empirical success in less extreme conditions, the general theory of relativity does not mesh well with quantum theory: a fully satisfactory quantum theory of gravity has proven elusive. However, this has not prevented theoretical astrophysicists from speculating on how such a theory might prompt revisions in our understanding of the origin of the universe.

Linde has speculated that the vast observable universe originated as a tiny random quantum fluctuation within a "mother" universe, then briefly "inflated" at an enormous rate before settling down to its present stately rate of expansion. Such "baby universes" have continually formed in this random fashion from within preexisting universes in a potentially infinite sequence.

Hawking has suggested that the approximately classical general relativistic spacetime of our present universe may have emerged from a quantum spacetime whose temporal aspect cannot be distinguished from its spatial aspect. It would follow that as we trace the universe back in time we find no singularity: rather, what we call time merges gradually into a structure that does not possess a recognizably temporal aspect (*see* COSMOLOGY [2]).

STATISTICAL MECHANICS

Philosophical debates on the atomic theory began with the pre-Socratics (*see* ATOMISM [1]). In the nineteenth century these debates were continued within physical science as the atomic hypothesis came to play an increasingly important role in physics as well as chemistry. At issue was not merely the ontological status of unobservables, but also difficulties that arose in reconciling the putative microscopic constitution of matter with its irreversible macroscopic behavior, given the reversibility of the underlying mechanical laws. BOLTZMANN's [1] struggles to understand the thermodynamic behavior of gases introduced probability into physical theory and thereby gave rise to statistical mechanics, a theory whose conceptual foundations remain controversial. Boltzmann's thesis—that the basis of our distinction between past and future is ultimately just those statistical asymmetries that underlie thermodynamic irreversibility—was taken up and defended by Reichenbach and others against objections of some philosophers and physicists.

Replacement of classical mechanics by quantum mechanics as a fundamental microtheory has changed the context of such debates without resolving them. Indeed, quantum statistical mechanics raises fascinating philosophical issues of its own concerning the identity and individuality of different kinds of fundamental particles—issues that also arise in attempts to understand the empirically successful relativistic quantum field theories that, by formulating quantum mechanics in a relativistic spacetime, yielded physicists' deepest level of understanding of the world at the turn of the twenty-first century.

Bibliography

Bell, J. S. "On the Einstein-Podolsky-Rosen Paradox," *Physics,* Vol. 1 (1964), 195–200.

Bohm, D. "A Suggested Interpretation of the Quantum Theory in Terms of 'Hidden Variables,' " Parts 1–2, *Physical Review,* Vol. 85 (1952), 166–93.

Bohr, N. "Can Quantum-Mechanical Description of Physical Reality Be Considered Complete?," *Physical Review,* Vol. 48 (1935), 696–702.

———. *The Physical Writings of Niels Bohr,* Vols. 1–3. Woodbridge, CT, 1987. These essays develop Bohr's distinctive and influential philosophy of physics.

Cartwright, N. *How the Laws of Physics Lie.* Oxford, 1983. Argues that while physics reveals true causes, its fundamental laws explain only by distorting the truth.

Earman, J. *World Enough and Space-Time.* Cambridge, MA, 1989. A thorough treatment of the absolutist/relationist debate in historical context.

Earman, J., C. Glymour, and J. Stachel. *Foundations of Space-Time Theories.* Minneapolis, 1977. Contains a number of papers on the causal theory of time.

Einstein, A. "Zur Elektrodynamik bewegter Körper," *Annalen der Physik,* Vol. 17 (1905). Translated as "On the Electrodynamics of Moving Bodies" in H. A. Lorentz, A. Einstein, H. Minkowski, and H. Weyl, eds., *The Principle of Relativity* (London, 1923).

———. "Die Grundlage der allegemeinen Relativitätstheorie," *Annalen der Physik,* Vol. 49 (1916). Translated as "The Foundation of the General Theory of Relativity" in H. A. Lorentz, A. Einstein, H. Minkowski, and H. Weyl, *The Principle of Relativity* (London, 1923).

———, B. Podolsky, and N. Rosen. "Can Quantum-Mechanical Description of Physical Reality Be Considered Complete?" *Physical Review,* Vol. 47 (1935), 777–80.

Everrett, H., III. " 'Relative State' Formulation of Quantum Mechanics," *Reviews of Modern Physics,* Vol. 29 (1957), 454–62.

Friedman, M. *Foundations of Spacetime Theories.* Princeton, NJ, 1983.

Gödel, K. "A Remark about the Relationship between Relativity Theory and Idealistic Philosophy," in P. Schilpp, ed., *Albert Einstein: Philosopher-Scientist* (Evanston, IL, 1949).

Grünbaum, A. *Philosophical Problems of Space and Time,* 2d ed. Dordrecht, 1973.

Hawking, S. *A Brief History of Time*. New York, 1988. A provocative and superficially nontechnical book in which an influential mathematical physicist attempts to bring contemporary physics to bear on basic cosmological questions.

Horwich, P. *Asymmetries in Time*. Cambridge, MA, 1987. Contains a provocative defense of Gödel's analysis of the sense in which his model of general relativity would permit time travel to one's past.

Linde, A. *Inflation and Quantum Cosmology*. Boston, 1990.

Lorentz, H. A., A. Einstein, H. Minkowski, and H. Weyl, eds., *The Principle of Relativity*. London, 1923. Reprinted, New York, 1952.

Minkowski, H. "Space and Time," address delivered in Cologne, Germany (1908), in H. A. Lorentz, A. Einstein, H. Minkowski, and H. Weyl, *The Principle of Relativity* (London, 1923).

Poincaré, H. *La Science et l'hypothèse*. Paris, 1902. Translated by W. J. Greenstreet as *Science and Hypothesis*. New York, 1952.

Popper, K. R. *Quantum Theory and the Schism in Physics*. London, 1982.

Redhead, M. L. G. *Incompleteness, Nonlocality, and Realism: A Prolegomenon to the Philosophy of Quantum Mechanics*. Oxford, 1987.

Reichenbach, H. *Philosophie der Raum-Zeit-Lehre*. Berlin, 1928. Translated by M. Reichenbach and J. Freund as *The Philosophy of Space and Time*. New York, 1958.

Robb, A. A. *A Theory of Time and Space*. Cambridge, 1914.

Schilpp, P. *Albert Einstein: Philosopher-Scientist*. Evanston, IL, 1949. Contains Einstein's thoughtful intellectual autobiography as well as a number of philosophically rich exchanges between Einstein and his commentators.

Schrödinger, E. "Die gegenwärtige Situation in der Quantenmechanik," *Naturwissenschaften*, Vol. 23 (1935), 807–12; 823–28; 844–49. Translated by J. D. Trimmer as "The Present Situation in Quantum Mechanics: A Translation of Schrödinger's 'Cat Paradox' paper," in J. A. Wheeler and W. H. Zurek, eds., *Quantum Theory and Measurement* (Princeton, NJ, 1983).

Sklar, L., *Space, Time, and Spacetime*. Berkeley, 1974. An introduction to some main topics of philosophical reflection on the nature of space and time stimulated by developments in physics.

———. *Philosophy of Physics*. Boulder, CO, 1992. A useful nontechnical introduction to the field.

———. *Physics and Chance*. Cambridge, 1993. A wide-ranging introduction to philosophical issues raised by statistical mechanics.

Teller, P. *An Interpretive Introduction to Quantum Field Theory*. Princeton, NJ, 1995. A ground-breaking attempt by a philosopher to come to grips with the concepts of quantum field theory.

van Fraassen, B. *The Scientific Image*. Oxford, 1980. Develops an influential but controversial account of the structure and role of scientific theories focused especially on examples from physics.

Wheeler, J. A., and W. H. Zurek, eds. *Quantum Theory and Measurement*. Princeton, NJ, 1983. Contains reprints of Bell (1964), Bohm (1952), Bohr (1935), EPR (1935), and Everett (1957).

RICHARD HEALEY

PHILOSOPHY OF RELIGION. Analytical philosophy of religion, still in its infancy in 1967, has developed markedly since then. Other approaches have certainly continued to play a part in philosophy of religion written in English, even more so in other languages. Process philosophy, for example, inspired by the thought of Alfred North WHITEHEAD [8] and exemplified in the ongoing work of Charles Hartshorne and others, has retained influence in philosophy of religion and in theology, probably more than in other areas of philosophy. PHENOMENOLOGY [6; S], POSTMODERNISM [S], and other approaches characteristic of the European continent inspire important contributions to the subject. Indeed, there is often not a sharp line between different approaches. Continental writers such as KIERKEGAARD [4; S] figure extensively in undoubtedly analytical writing about religion, and analytical philosophy of religion makes such extensive use of medieval material as to be more or less continuous with neoscholastic treatments of the subject.

Although there had been a few earlier analytical essays about various religious issues, the main development of analytical philosophy of religion may be said to have begun in the 1950s with discussion of the "logical positivist" challenge to the cognitive significance of religious language. Most analytical philosophers then held, or were strongly tempted to hold, as an empiricist principle, that every (logically contingent) assertion, in order to have any cognitive meaning, must be verifiable or, more broadly, testable, in principle, by experience. It was charged, by Alfred Jules AYER [1], Antony Flew, and others, that the affirmations of religious belief typically do not satisfy this criterion of meaning (A. Flew, R. M. HARE [S], and B. Mitchell in Brody, 1974).

How, then, were the apparent truth claims of religions to be understood? Some were prepared, with Ayer, to treat major religious assertions as mere expressions of emotion, without any cognitive significance. Others sought ways of understanding such assertions as empirically verifiable in principle. John Hick (in Brody, 1974) argued, for instance, that "eschatological verifiability," in a life after death, provides at least a partial solution to the problem. Still others, while granting that empirical testability is decisive for the meaning of typical factual assertions, sought to establish a different, and not merely emotive, type of meaning that could be ascribed to religious assertions. The most influential attempts of this type were inspired by the later writings of Ludwig WITTGENSTEIN [8; S], particularly by his account of "language games" and their relation to forms of life.

The Wittgensteinian approach, as developed, for example, by Norman Malcolm (in Brody, 1992) and D. Z. Phillips (1970), has generated very interesting studies of the relation of religious language to religious life. It is widely criticized, by some as giving inadequate weight to the apparent straightforwardly realistic intent of typical religious assertions, and by some as improperly shielding religious claims from rational criticism by relativizing them to religious language games. It remains, nevertheless, an important strand in contemporary discussion. Of all that has been done in analytical philosophy of religion, it is probably the discussion of religious language in general, and Wittgensteinian themes in particular, that have most interested professional theologians, perhaps because these themes have seemed more relevant than more metaphysical discussions to the work of interpretation and reinterpretation of traditions in which theologians are so much engaged.

Within analytical philosophy during the 1950s the verifiability criterion of meaning was already undergoing severe criticism and has since been virtually abandoned in anything like its original form. Many analytical philosophers continue to consider themselves empiricists and seek alternative ways of excluding claims that they regard as objectionably metaphysical. Many others, however, see the permanent contribution of analytical philosophy, not in a form of EMPIRICISM [2], or in any set of doctrines, but in a method, style, or discipline that can be applied to virtually all the historic issues of metaphyics and ethics and can be used in developing and espousing almost any of the classic philosophical doctrines.

The majority of work done in analytical philosophy of religion since 1967 has been inspired by the later conception of analytical philosophy and has not focused on issues about religious language. It is characterized by metaphysical realism, taking the religious claims under discussion to be straightforwardly true or false. (For defense of this stance, see, e.g., Swinburne, 1977, chaps. 2–6.) Some have suggested calling it philosophical theology rather than philosophy of religion, because the principal subject of most of it is God rather than human religious phenomena, though atheists as well as theists have certainly been important participants in the discussion. On this basis, mainly since 1960, a very substantial body of literature, dealing with most of the traditional issues of philosophical theology and some new ones too, has been created.

Among the traditional topics the attributes of God received rather early analytical attention. (For general treatments see Swinburne, 1977, chaps. 7–15; Kenny, 1979; Wierenga, 1989.) Analysis of the concept of God was easily seen as an appropriate subject for analytical philosophy, and issues about the attributes had been connected, since the Middle Ages, with problems about predication, an appealing point of entry into philosophical theology for those interested in the philosophy of language. According to some of the most influential medieval theologians, God is so different from creatures that positive attributes of creatures cannot in general be predicated of God univocally, that is, in the same sense in which they are predicated of creatures. How then can we predicate anything of God? Various Scholastic theologians developed various solutions, the best known being the theory of analogical predication of Thomas AQUINAS [8; S]. Analytical philosophers of religion have taken up the problem and some of the medieval views, along with more contemporary concerns—for instance, about the ascription of psychological predicates to a being who is supposed not to have a body (*see* GOD, CONCEPTS OF [3]). (Cf. Maimonides, Aquinas, and Alston in Brody, 1992).

The two divine attributes that have received the most extensive analytical discussion are omniscience and eternity. The central issue about eternity is whether to understand it (as medieval and early modern theology generally did) as involving existence outside of time or rather as involving existence without beginning or end in time, as many contemporary thinkers have proposed. Critics of divine timelessness, such as Nelson Pike (1970) and Nicholas Wolterstorff (in Brody, 1992), have questioned the compatibility of timelessness with God's consciousness or action or interaction with creatures. Eleanor Stump and Norman Kretzmann, however, have presented an influential defense of the traditional timeless conception (in Brody, 1992), and the issue remains vigorously debated.

Omniscience and eternity are related topics, for one of the most discussed issues about God's knowledge concerns God's relation to time: does God have complete knowledge of the future? In particular, does God know, infallibly and in every detail, how free creatures will use their freedom? Traditional theologies generally gave an emphatically affirmative answer to this question; but some modern philosophers and theologians have disagreed, arguing that the doctrine of total, infallible foreknowledge compromises the freedom of the creatures. The extensive analytical literature on this issue (e.g., in Fischer, 1989) is continuous with older discussions, and opinion remains divided.

A related old debate, recently revived, concerns what has been called "middle knowledge": does God know, completely and infallibly, what every actual and even merely possible free creature would freely do (or would have freely done) in every possible situation in which that creature could act freely? In the late sixteenth century, Luis de Molina, a Jesuit, proposed an ingenious theory of divine providence according to which God uses such subjunctive (and largely counterfactual) conditional knowledge to control the course of history without having to interfere metaphysically with the freedom of creatures. This theory of middle knowledge was widely embraced by Jesuits, but opposed by Dominicans, who argued that there cannot be such determinate conditional facts about everything that would be freely done by particular creatures in all possible circumstances. This historic controversy was introduced into current analytical discussion by Anthony Kenny (1979) and Robert Adams (1987), who have both defended the Dominican objection to middle knowledge; but the opposite position has been argued by a vigorous school of contemporary Molinists, including Alvin Plantinga (1974) and Alfred Freddoso (1988).

Regarding the relation of God to ethics, it was almost universally held in the 1960s that fundamental ethical principles must be independent of theology and that an acceptable theological account of the nature of ethical facts is impossible. Since then, however, it has come to be widely held by theists, and granted by many nontheists, that facts about God, if God exists, could play a central role in explaining the nature of ethics and that theistic philosophers should be expected to avail themselves of this possibility. The most discussed type of theological theory in this area is the divine-command theory of the nature of ethical obligation, or of right and wrong (Helm, 1981). Several thinkers, such as Philip Quinn (1978), have tried to reformulate and explain the theory in such a way as to defend it against the traditional objections to it. Robert Adams (1987) has proposed a form of the theory that rests on semantical assumptions very similar to those of some of the most influential contemporary exponents of metaethical naturalism but employs different (theistic) metaphysical assumptions.

The grounds proposed for belief or disbelief in the existence of God have naturally claimed at least as much analytical attention as the attributes of God. This is a subject so intensively discussed for centuries that one might have expected little novelty in the treatment of it. But in fact investigations have been rather innovative, and the state of debate has changed significantly since 1960. One striking change is that the traditional arguments for the existence of God, then widely dismissed, even by theologians, as hopelessly discredited, have many defenders now.

This is connected with a more general phenomenon, which is that analytical philosophers, especially those inclined to construct and defend constructive metaphysical theories, demand less of arguments than has commonly been demanded in the past. Virtually no one thinks any one "theistic proof" conclusive; but if arguments must be either conclusive or worthless, there would be little useful reasoning about any of the most important philosophical issues. Theistic apologists are accordingly less apt to seek a single "knockdown" proof than to try to show that several traditional (and perhaps also novel) arguments have something of value to contribute to a "cumulative case" for theism, an approach exemplified by Richard Swinburne (1979). Extensive work has been done interpreting, developing, and criticizing all the main types of theistic arguments. Those that have probably received the most attention and development are the "ontological" and the "teleological" (to give them their Kantian names).

The fallaciousness of any ontological argument and the contingency of all real existence had become such commonplaces, especially among empiricists, that it had a certain "shock value" when Norman Malcolm in 1960 published a defense of an ontological argument (reprinted in Brody, 1992). Malcolm claimed to find in Anselm's *Proslogion,* besides the famous argument of its second chapter, a second ontological argument in which it is not existence but necessary existence that figures as a perfection. Malcolm also held that necessary existence cannot be excluded from theology on general philosophical grounds. Whether a statement expresses a necessary truth, he argued, depends on the language game in which it figures; and a religious language game can treat the existence of God as a necessary truth. These two features of Malcolm's article foreshadow the main tendencies in the development of ontological arguments since then: (1) attention to more modal versions of the argument and (2) the attempt to rehabilitate the idea of necessary existence. (*See* ONTOLOGICAL ARGUMENT FOR THE EXISTENCE OF GOD [5])

Ontological argument studies have been greatly influenced by the dramatic development of modal logic, which was gathering momentum in the 1960s and burst into the center of American philosophical consciousness in the 1970s. In 1962 Charles Hartshorne published a modal proof of the existence of God relying only on the premises that God's existence must be necessary if it is actual and that God's existence is at least possible. Subsequent discussion has established that this proof, and related proofs from slightly slenderer assumptions, are valid in the system of MODAL LOGIC [S] (S5) most widely thought to be appropriate for the context. David Lewis (in Brody, 1974) and Alvin Plantinga (1974) have given the argument a form that takes account of developments in modal predicate logic as well as modal propositional logic (or in *de re* as well as *de dicto* modality). The argument is still of limited value for proving the existence of God, because those who would otherwise doubt the conclusion are likely to doubt the possibility premise, given the rest of the argument. But the modal development of the argument is helpful in structuring discussion of questions about necessary existence.

In the 1950s it was the opinion of almost all analytical philosophers that the existence of a real being, such as God (as distinct from merely abstract objects, such as numbers), cannot be necessary in the strongest, "logical" sense. This opinion has come to be widely doubted, however, and the traditional view that God should be conceived as an absolutely necessary being has regained a following. (For contrasting views see Adams, 1987, chaps. 13–14, and Swinburne, 1977, chaps. 13–14.) Several factors have contributed to this change. The identification of necessity with analyticity, on which the rejection of necessary existence was commonly based, is under attack. W. V. O. QUINE's [7; S] influential doubts about the adequacy of the notion of analyticity led Quine himself to skepticism about necessity. But others, influenced in some cases by an interest in necessity *de re,* have been inspired to seek a more robustly metaphysical conception of necessity. Since a conception of the latter sort was generally held by the great philosophers of the Middle Ages and the seventeenth century, a growing and more sympathetic understanding of those periods of the history of philosophy has also tended to undermine the most dismissive attitudes toward the idea of necessary existence.

The most popular argument for the existence of God in the eighteenth century was the teleological or design argument, usually in a pre-Darwinian form drawing its evidence largely from biological adaptations (*see* TELEOLOGICAL ARGUMENT FOR THE EXISTENCE OF GOD [8]). This type of argument was discredited both by the devastating critique it received in David HUME's [4; S] *Dialogues Concerning Natural Religion* and by the development of an alternative explanation of the biological phenomena in terms of natural selection. A major rehabilitation of the design argument has been undertaken by Richard Swinburne (1979). Instead of the biological evidence, he takes as his principal evidence the most pervasive, highest-level regularities in the universe. Since they constitute the most fundamental laws of nature, to which all scientific explanations appeal, he argues, there cannot be any scientific explanation of them. There may therefore be no viable alternative to a theological explanation for them, if they are to be explained at all. Deploying the apparatus of Bayesian probability theory (*see* BAYESIANISM [S]), and responding to Hume's objections, Swinburne tries to establish that a theological explanation is indeed more plausible than no explanation at all. Swinburne's argument depends at some points on controversial metaphysical theses and has inspired an extended atheistic response by J. L. MACKIE [S] (1982); but the teleological argument has at least been shown to have much more philosophical life in it than had been thought.

The leading argument for ATHEISM [1], aside from the various critiques of theistic arguments, has long been the argument from evil (*see* EVIL, PROBLEM OF [3; S]). The evils that occur in the world are incompatible, it is argued, with the existence of an omnipotent, omniscient, perfectly good God. In the earlier years of analytical philosophy of religion this was usually a charge of demonstrable, logical incompatibility; and attempts to provide theists with a "solution" to the "problem of evil" concentrated accordingly on trying to show the possibility of a perfect deity having permitted the evils. Borrowing a Leibnizian idea, for instance, Nelson Pike argued that for all we know, this might be the best of all possible worlds (in Adams & Adams, 1990). Alvin Plantinga (1974) developed a much-discussed version of the traditional "free will defense," arguing that even if there are possible worlds containing less evil, and as much moral good, as the actual world, an omnipotent God may have been unable to create them because it may be that creatures (whether humans or angels) would not have freely done what they would have to do freely in order for one of those worlds to be actual. The adequacy of such theistic responses to the "logical" form of the argument from evil has been keenly debated, but it has probably become the predominant view that the argument does not afford much hope of a tight, demonstrative proof of atheism.

There has therefore been increasing interest in probabilistic arguments from evil, as presented, for example, by William Rowe (in Adams & Adams, 1990), whose thesis is that evils show theism to be implausible, or at least constitute evidence against theism, which might contribute to a cumulative case for atheism. Theistic responses to this type of argument must address issues of plausibility and not merely of possibility. Some have been methodological, attempting to show that the relevant probabilities cannot be determined, or that the explanatory structure of the situation keeps the evils from being even relevant evidence (e.g., Stephen Wykstra in Adams & Adams, 1990). Others have tried to give plausible accounts of why evils might have been necessary for greater goods. One widely debated hypothesis, developed in different ways by John Hick (in Adams & Adams, 1990) and Richard Swinburne (1979), for instance, is that evils, and possibilities of evil, play an essential part in making the world a context for the moral and spiritual development of free creatures.

All such explanations of why God would permit great evils have seemed to some morally or religiously objectionable. Among theists who take this view, Marilyn Adams has argued that we should accept that we simply do not know why God has permitted horrendous evils but that within a religion that affirms, as Christianity does, God's love for individuals who suffer them, it is important to have a coherent account of how God may be seen as redeeming them (Adams & Adams, 1990). She points to traditional religious ideas of suffering shared with God or with Christ as suggesting how horrendous evils might be "defeated" by forming an organic whole with incommensurably great religious goods.

One of the more dramatic developments of the period under review is the development of a defense of the rationality of theism that professes not to be based on arguments or evidence. Alvin Plantinga maintains that belief in the existence of God can be "properly basic," a basic belief being one that is not inferentially based on any other belief (in Plantinga & Wolterstorff, 1983). It has been held by many that some beliefs (formed, perhaps, in sensation or memory) do not need inferential support from other beliefs for their justification. Plantinga argues that more beliefs than some have supposed are reasonably held without being based on the evidence of other beliefs and that there is no compelling reason to deny that some religious beliefs have this basic status. He suggests that religious beliefs not based on "evidence" constituted by other beliefs may nonetheless be based on other sorts of "grounds," which might be found, for example, in religious experience. Plantinga's view (which he has dubbed "Reformed epistemology") has been keenly debated. One of the most discussed issues is whether it allows an adequate basis for distinguishing between rational and irrational religious beliefs. (For a moderately critical view see R. Audi in Audi & Wainwright, 1986).

A related but importantly different view has been developed by William Alston (1991). Religious experience has been a major subject of discussion in philosophy of religion (e.g., W. JAMES [4], W. T. STACE [8], and C. B. Martin in Brody, 1974; Wainwright, 1981), as it has been in modern theology. Not all of the discussion has been epistemological or focused on the justification of belief. Nelson Pike (1992), for instance, has written about the phenomenology of mysticism, arguing, against the older theory of Walter Stace, that there are mystical experiences of theistic as well as nontheistic content. Alston's approach is thoroughly epistemological, however, and he focuses on the experience of more ordinary religious believers rather than of those adepts typically singled out as "mystics." (*See* RELIGIOUS EXPERIENCE, ARGUMENT FOR THE EXISTENCE OF GOD [7]; and MYSTICISM, NATURE AND ASSESSMENT OF [5])

Relying on carefully discussed analogies with sense perception, Alston argues that in some circumstances experiences as of God addressing, or being present to, a person can reasonably be regarded as perceptions of God. His argument is placed in the context of a "doxastic practice" conception of the justification of beliefs. He argues that we are able to form and justify beliefs only in socially established practices in which we have learned to be responsive to such factors as experiential cues and communal traditions as well as to beliefs that we hold. In Alston's view we have no choice but to rely on socially established doxastic practices, and it is presumptively rational to do so, even though we typically have little or no independent evidence of the reliability of the practice. He argues that this presumption of rationality applies also to religious doxastic practices that are socially established, and in particular to practices in which participants have learned to form beliefs of having perceived God in various ways. Alston offers vigorous rebuttals of several major objections to basing religious beliefs on religious experience. In his opinion the most serious problem for his view, which he treats at some length, is that posed by the existence of diverse religious traditions whose well-established doxastic practices lead them to form apparently conflicting beliefs on the basis of their religious experience.

For philosophy of religion as for contemporary theology, the problem of conflicting truth claims of different religions is, if not a new issue, one that is coming into increasing prominence. John Hick (1989) has done much to draw attention to it. He argues that it is not plausible to suppose that one traditional form of religious experience is veridical while others are not, and he tries to articulate a way in which many apparently conflicting forms could all be at bottom veridical, proposing to regard them as apprehending different "phenomenal" manifestations of a single "noumenal" transcendent "reality." Not that Hick thinks all religious beliefs equally acceptable; the main criterion he proposes for the value of religious traditions and belief systems is their fruitfulness in producing morally and spiritually recognizable saints, people notably advanced in a transformation from self-centeredness to Reality-centeredness. Among the issues in the vigorous debate about Hick's view are the adequacy of the conceptual apparatus he borrows from KANT [4; S] and whether it is compatible (as he means it to be) with a fundamentally realist and cognitivist conception of religious belief.

(SEE ALSO: *Epistemology, Religious; Religious Experience; Religious Pluralism;* and *Theism, Arguments for and Against* [S])

Bibliography

Adams, M. M., and R. M. Adams, eds. *The Problem of Evil.* Oxford, 1990.

Adams, R. M. *The Virtue of Faith and Other Essays in Philosophical Theology.* New York, 1987.

Alston, W. P. *Perceiving God.* Ithaca, NY, 1991.

Audi, R., and W. J. Wainwright, eds. *Rationality, Religious Belief, and Moral Commitment: New Essays in the Philosophy of Religion.* Ithaca, NY, 1986.

Brody, B. A., ed. *Readings in the Philosophy of Religion: An Analytic Approach.* Englewood Cliffs, NJ, 1974; 2d ed., 1992. Somewhat different selections, both comprehensive and both excellent, in the two editions.

Freddoso, A. J., intro. and trans., L. de Molina. *On Divine Foreknowledge* (Part IV of the *Concordia*). Ithaca, NY, 1988.

Fischer, J. M., ed. *God, Foreknowledge, and Freedom.* Stanford, 1989.

Hartshorne, C. *The Logic of Perfection and Other Essays in Neoclassical Metaphysics.* Lasalle, IL, 1962.

Helm, P., ed. *Divine Commands and Morality.* Oxford, 1981.

Hick, J. *An Interpretation of Religion.* London, 1989.

Kenny, A. *The God of the Philosophers.* Oxford, 1979.

Mackie, J. L. *The Miracle of Theism.* Oxford, 1982.

Phillips, D. Z. *Faith and Philosophical Enquiry.* New York, 1970.

Pike, N. *God and Timelessness.* New York, 1970.

———. *Mystic Union.* Ithaca, NY, 1992.

Plantinga, A. *The Nature of Necessity.* Oxford, 1974.

———, and N. Wolterstorff, eds. *Faith and Rationality.* Notre Dame, IN, 1983.

Quinn, P. L. *Divine Commands and Moral Requirements.* Oxford, 1978.

Swinburne, R. *The Coherence of Theism.* Oxford, 1977.

———. *The Existence of God.* Oxford, 1979; 2d ed. 1991.

Wainwright, W. J. *Mysticism.* Madison, WI, 1981.

Wierenga, E. R. *The Nature of God.* Ithaca, NY, 1989.

ROBERT M. ADAMS

PHILOSOPHY OF SCIENCE. From 1960 to 1995 the philosophy of science experienced explosive growth, despite the often alleged death of LOGICAL POSITIVISM [5], which had served as the dominant school of thought for the preceding twenty-five years. Quantitative measures of this explosion can be provided through an examination of the number of new journals (at least ten such as *Economics and Philosophy, Biology and Philosophy,* and *Perspectives on Science*) that appeared in that time period, the number of Ph.D. programs specializing in or offering a specialty area in philosophy of science, the appearance of research centers dedicated to the philosophy of science (such as the University of Pittsburgh's Center for Philosophy of Science and Boston University's Center), and new departments or programs concentrating in this general area. More impressive than these numbers is the change in focus, best seen against the background of logical positivism.

At its core logical positivism can best be understood as metascience. Its subject matter was science, as the subject matter of science is the world. It was concerned with articulating the logic of concepts constitutive of science. Partially in response to what they considered the excesses of nineteenth-century German metaphysics, the early positivists viewed philosophical problems as problems of language. Their solution was to take the linguistic turn and focus on the construction and/or analysis of formal languages, using highly controlled mechanisms for introducing definitions and a clear logical structure. Since positivism held science to be the premier knowledge-producing activity, such an analysis guaranteed value both for understanding what knowledge is and for the reform of nonscientific knowledge. As a consequence, this attention to the logic of such general concepts as explanation, confirmation, and evidence, approached as linguistic phenomena, kept work in the philosophy of science at some remove from the worries of particular sciences. The argument in defense of this approach resembled an abstract solution to the problem of demarcating science from nonscience. Before biology, geology, or psychology could qualify as sciences the abstract conditions for being a science had to be established through the explication of these central concepts, understood as necessary and sufficient conditions of scientific status. A number of other assumptions were at work as well. For example, the positivist program was heavily reductionist, with physics understood as both foundational and the best justified of sciences. While not appreciated as such, for most of the years from the beginning of the positivist movement until deep into the 1970s, positivist philosophy of science was PHILOSOPHY OF PHYSICS [S], concentrating on specific problems within physics often under the guise of clarifying the more general conceptual problems of science at large (*see* REDUCTION, REDUCTIONISM [S]).

It is fashionable to speak of the death of positivism and to associate its decline with the appearance of Thomas Kuhn's *The Structure of Scientific Revolutions* in 1962 (*see* KUHN [S]). But positivism is not dead, and most of the severest blows were dealt to its viability as a successful philosophy of science before the publication of Kuhn's book. To recognize that positivism is not dead but flourishing is not to deny that it has undergone significant transformations. Some of its older characteristics, such as the attempt to display the structure of concepts using first-order predicate calculus, are no longer universally employed. Nor is it fashionable to attempt explications of universal concepts that apply across the sciences without modification. But a great deal of important work in philosophy of science still aims to uncover the strong logical relations between theory and evidence, with the primary goal of understanding the logical structure of science and scientific knowledge. In this context the development of the semantic view of theories (see the work of Bas van Fraassen and Fred Suppe) can easily be seen as an extension of the positivist agenda in the light of the knowledge gained concerning the limits of a strictly linguistic framework exploited using only basic logical techniques.

While it would be historically inaccurate to deny the importance of Kuhn's contribution to the transformation of the philosophy of science from a positivistic philosophy of physics to its current state, it is also important to note that positivism was under serious fire before his work appeared. Attacks on the justifiability of central assumptions, such as W. V. O. QUINE'S [7; S] rejection of the analytic–synthetic distinction and Wilfrid SELLARS'S [S] attack on epistemological foundationalism, appeared in the 1950s. Likewise, what has come to be called the historical turn, incorrectly credited to Kuhn, was well under way at the same time in the work of Norwood Russell Hanson (1961). Further, positivistically trained philosophers such as Carl HEMPEL [3] were highly sensitive to the limits of the approaches they employed and were undertaking continual modifications of key assumptions in attempts to meet the most severe objections, some of which were of their own making.

To be fair to positivism, despite the unjustifiable claims of hegemony, it was a vibrant and exciting research program that insisted on intellectual rigor and logical consistency, which is one reason why it continues to exercise a profound influence on the contemporary scene. Positivism gave us a standard for the philosophy of science that philosophers are largely unwilling to relinquish. This explains in part why contemporary critics of the philosophy of science refer to it as being in a state of crisis. But such criticism is misguided: in contrast, the philosophy of science is far more exciting than ever before, precisely because of its positivistic heritage, in two distinct ways. First, that heritage anchors philosophers of science either as they respond to current challenges to the role of philosophy in the analysis and understanding of science or as they work their way toward a new and better understanding of science. Second, because of positivism's goal of universal criteria there now exists a healthy dynamic tension between efforts to remain true to that objective and the need to deal with the particulars that form the focus of newer developments, such as those discussed below.

As noted above, during the heyday of positivism, there was an illusion of hegemony in the philosophy of science. Today there is no such illusion. Further, with the loss of hegemony comes the problem of explaining what is going on in the field. It is complicated, but four central features stand out on the contemporary landscape: (1) increasing attention to the problems of the individual sciences; (2) the historical turn; (3) new challenges to standard methodologies from feminists and from sociologists; and (4) the rise of the new experimentalism.

First, increasing amounts of work are now devoted to philosophical problems of individual sciences. This is not to say that the attempt to provide a characterization of science *tout court* has been abandoned. That ideal remains. But directing attention to the problems of the individual sciences—for example, explanation in biology—forces us to deal with the actual practice of science. In so doing we necessarily fall short of achieving an account—of explanation, for example—that meets a general ideal. This new focus on the particular drives a kind of dialectic between the general ideals for science and the needs generated by remaining true to the practices of actual scientists. As we focus on the practices of scientists we see a proliferation of philosophies of. . . . For example, the PHILOSOPHY OF BIOLOGY [S] is now a firmly established field of its own with a substantial cadre of researchers and its own journal. Philosophical problems of biology are sufficiently distinct from the old standard problems in the philosophy of physics that entrée into its discussion requires substantial background. The same is true for the philosophy of economics and the philosophy of psychology. Further, as philosophical work concerning science moves closer into specific sciences it becomes increasingly necessary to know something about the science and, perhaps more important, something about the literature on the philosophical topic at hand. Thus, when considering the problem of what constitutes a species in biology, it would be easy to consider this as merely an instance of a type–token problem and as a simple instance of the perennial philosophical problem of universals. But the interesting part of the problem comes from the biology itself, considering not only the functional role of species in biological theory but the peculiarities of the many–one problem in the context of an intrinsically changing "one." In addition, as we move toward the specific sciences, philosophical problems become increasingly tied to methodological problems within those sciences. For example, referring again to the problem of species, the difficulty of devising an adequate definition is exacerbated by the real-world difficulty of delimiting the individuals who are members of a species, not just in space, but also in time.

A second notable feature of contemporary philosophy of science is, of course, the turn to history. But in the context of contemporary developments, it is not too strong to claim that the turn to history alone is passé. On the one hand, like species, scientific methods and our understanding of evidential relations and the like have been shown to be evolving. Hence, analyses that go into any detail of the alleged timeless and universal concepts of evidence and explanation will fail. Yet, the still viable positivist ideal calls for just such universal accounts of the logic of the concepts involved in order to understand the sense of "science" at work. Further, from a methodological point of view, much recent philosophy of science has been enhanced and challenged by work in both history and sociology of science, not to mention CRITICAL THEORY [S], economics, and political science. To appreciate fully the force of the dynamic tension between the pull of general ideals and the push for detail, interdisciplinarity is increasingly demanded.

In *Structure,* Kuhn alerted the positivists to the fact that a detailed look at the history of science rendered a number of positivistic methodological and substantive assumptions nonoperative. Thus, Kuhn argued that a single instance of falsification was rarely, if ever, sufficient to justify rejection of a theory. Likewise, given the structure of the development of science that Kuhn proposed and defended, the very question of the rationality of scientific change was brought into doubt. Although subsequent historical work left many of Kuhn's own claims in question, this challenge motivated philosophers to test their ideas against history. What remained unclear was the methodology appropriate to meeting this challenge. Philosophers first began to use history to substantiate and illuminate philosophical theses without much awareness or acknowledgment of the canons of historiography. More often than not it appeared that one simply went out and found a historical case study that substantiated the philosophical assumptions being asserted. Philosophers of science became well versed in their individual favorite historical episode or two, but rarely was the history taken on its own ground. Historians of science naturally objected to this usurpation of history. And despite the turn to history, a genuine rift was developing in the 1970s between historians and philosophers of science.

In addition to the attacks of historians of science, the late 1970s saw the rise of the ironically named Strong Programme in the sociology of science. Advocates of the Strong Programme defended an extreme position regarding the claims of scientific knowledge—that they are merely the results of negotiations among the practitioners of science and that the world, as such, has nothing to do with scientific claims. Science, on this view, is social all the way down. This particular form of severe relativism arose at the same time as the newest version of the battle over scientific realism developed. The old debate was between scientific REALISM [S] and instrumentalism, and it concentrated on what can be called theory realism because of the positivistic turn to language and the characterization of theories as languages. Defenders of the new scientific realism—for example, Richard Burian and Ian Hacking—endorse the view that entities named in scientific theories and discovered through experimentation are real and that knowledge of them and their behavior is possible and in some cases actual. Philosophers in this camp found that, under this attack from the sociologists, they needed secure knowledge of the science and of its history to mount a reasonable counterattack. The problem was to find a way to reinsert the world into our account of science. On this point historians and philosophers of science kept common ground: science is about the world, and the activities of scientists are worth studying because they reveal important things about how we come to know what the world is like. For some philosophers it looked as if the philosophical arguments over the reality of nonobservable scientific entities paled in the face of the dogmatic assertions of the Strong Programme regarding the irrelevance of the nonsocial factors (i.e., the world) in understanding both the activities of scientists and the epistemic authority of scientific claims.

Another problem arose out of the turn to history and the reaction to the relativism of the sociology of science: as philosophers of science became more and more embroiled in arguments over the accuracy of historical details or immersed in the sophistication of their understanding of the subtleties of the science in question, the traditional normative role of philosophy appeared to disappear. That is, the strategy philosophers undertook was to become more like historians or scientists. In doing so the philosophical issues seemed to slip between the cracks. Here again we can see the effect of the dynamic tension between the goals of normative universal account and the need for accurate description.

Further, for some on the contemporary scene, the normative role of philosophy should be usurped and transformed into a political role. This attack comes on two fronts. The first is the result of the move to interdisciplinarity. The second comes from a different direction and leads us to the third major aspect of the contemporary landscape. First, the attack from interdisciplinarity.

Philosophy of science has always been under attack. The positivists were often misunderstood and withstood such charges as aiming to tell scientists how to do science—this despite the fact that they saw their normative role in the construction of criteria for adequate explanations, laws, theories, and evidence, satisfaction of which would guarantee that the claims under analysis were in fact scientific. They were concerned with showing that a science, reconstructed after the fact, met these criteria. But they were often charged with trying to reform the practice of science. Now the new interdisciplinarity has a name: science studies. It is not yet clear whether the mix of disciplines will produce a new discipline with its own methodology and domain of inquiry or whether it will result in an uneasy alliance of interests, methods, and criteria of adequacy. Nevertheless, there are subgroups within science studies with their own explicit normative agendas that range over a continuum. At one end, unlike the positivists, is a group that does want to tell scientists what to do. This goal is announced under the rubric of the democratization of science and represents an interesting blend of ideologies—primarily Marxists looking for a last venue but also extreme democrats who believe that if the people are going to pay for scientific research, they ought to have a significant say in where it goes. At the other end there are the scientists who reject any normative intrusions from outside.

Political agendas are not the exclusive property of sociologists of science, Marxists, and scientists. A new and refreshing voice has entered the discussion, sometimes with a political agenda, sometimes not. This is the voice of feminist philosophers of science (*see* FEMINIST PHILOSOPHY OF SCIENCE [S]). Their challenges to more standard philosophy of science, which sometimes amount to recirculated positivism, usually incorporate a healthy appreciation of the social domain of scientific inquiry. In some cases this amounts to a significant challenge to key epistemological assumptions ranging over yet another continuum. At one end of this continuum, seen in the work of Sandra Harding, is a set of issues concerning the impact of what is perceived to be a patriarchal social structure within the scientific community on both the role of women within science and, subsequently, on the range of acceptable points of view in the formulation and evaluation of scientific claims. At the other of the spectrum, found most prominently in the work of Helen Longino, is the acknowledgment of the problems created by the social environment but a strong defense of nongender-rendered epistemological criteria and standards.

The introduction of political and feminist agendas, however, has not answered the question concerning the normative dimensions of the philosophy of science, even within interdisciplinary science studies. This question requires an answer that focuses on the criteria for being scientific. One attempt to deal with this demand has been to take yet another turn, one that relies on history and sociology in part but that takes science to be the foremost player. This is the turn to naturalize the philosophy of science. Naturalized philosophy of science, the most recent incarnation of Quine's NATURALIZED EPISTEMOLOGY [S], is defended by Ronald Giere, Philip Kitcher, Larry Laudan, and a number of philosophers who took the turn to an examination of the problems of individual sciences. The move here is simple: biology, for example, is what biologists do. Who is a biologist is determined by appeal to historical and sociological criteria. The answer to the question of what constitutes good biology must come from the biologist or the practices of biology. It is then the philosopher's role to subject the criteria proposed by the scientist to rigorous analysis to see if they meet the standards of consistency and logical rigor common to all discourse. And there is one further job for the philosopher of science—that is, to see whether the criteria meet the goals and objects of the scientists working in the area under discussion.

There are at least two problems stemming from this approach that need solutions. First, what is the normative philosophical role here? Second, can whatever results philosophical analysis produces be taken beyond the boundaries of the particular scientific domain under discussion? The first problem resembles a similar problem confronting Quine's attempt to naturalize epistemology. Simply put, if we give up epistemology for, say, psychology, we are still left with questions such as, How does this account of how the human brain works explain what knowledge is? That is, a fully descriptive account of what, from a sociohistorical point of view, scientists do still leaves us with the question of whether or not it is good science. This question remains even if we answer positively the questions concerning logical rigor and whether or not the results of philosophical analyses show that the scientific results meet the scientists' objectives. The second problem speaks directly to the role and objectives of philosophy itself. If, as SELLARS [S] proposed, philosophy aims at a full-blown understanding of how the world in all its peculiarities hangs together, thus enabling us to make our way around in it successfully, the fragmentation represented by the historical and naturalistic turns, as well as the rise of philosophies of various sciences, seems to render this goal unobtainable. Philosophy as a synthesizing activity would appear to be increasingly out of fashion and difficult, if not impossible, to do.

Paradoxically, to accept this perspective would be to take an unphilosophical and at the same time characteristically philosophical point of view. This view is unphilosophical in the sense that it assumes that the current state of philosophical work is in some sense a final state. But there is no reason to assume that the current state of affairs will dominate in the future, and a few reasons why are suggested below when we turn to the fourth and final major feature of the contemporary landscape. This pessimistic point of view is, however, characteristically philosophical in the sense that announcements of the death of philosophy are a persistent feature of its history. One of its most vocal advocates in the period under discussion is Richard Rorty. But saying so does not make it so.

One way to revitalize some of the more praiseworthy aspects of the philosophy of science in the face of the apparent fragmentation occurring as a result of challenges from the history of science, the sociology of science, feminist critiques, and the naturalistic turn is to look at yet one more new feature of the landscape, the New Experimentalism. It is both possible and reasonable to understand these various challenges to the traditional philosophy of science as a reaction to the philosophy of science as history of ideas (i.e., ideas about science). Each of the new dimensions discussed above can be seen as an attempt to put some content into the philosophy of science, to give the philosophy of science some point of contact with the world of science as it actually works. This feature is characteristic of the New Experimentalism as well. Further, the analysis and appreciation of the role of experiments and the problems they both solve and present can be legitimate aspects of each of the other new features of the philosophy of science landscape. In short, philosophical issues surround experimentation, and experiments are or can be a common thread in discussions of science, irrespective of whether the main approach is historical, sociological, feminist, or naturalistic. And, obviously enough, this is because experiments are a common feature of science. There is also traditional philosophical content in the turn to experiments, overlooked by many positivists, since experiment is the heart of science's means of obtaining and evaluating evidence. There are many levels on which the role of experiments can be addressed. There are epistemological problems presented by the creation and use of experimental devices. After constructing a device for measuring certain features of a field, the first problem is to calibrate the device (see Hacking, 1983; Hanson, 1961). This involves a variety of aspects, certain assumptions about standard conditions, questions about the reliability of calibration devices and readouts, and a theory of calibration itself. Then there is the question of accurately reporting what is revealed. Here we have the basic question of working out how the results bear on the hypothesis under investigation and the theory being tested or developed. It is a problem of framing the results in the proper terms to make their precise relevance perspicuous. In addition, we have problems of separating the signal from the noise and detecting the object presented as an object and not a creation of the experimental device. And while work on experiments is fairly recent, incorporating sociological perspectives (Andy Pickering), historical/sociological perspectives (Steven Shapin and Simon Schaffer), historical perspectives (Jed Buchwald, Peter Galison), and philosophical perspectives (Robert Ackermann, Nancy Cartwright, Allan Franklin, Ian Hacking), the importance of experiments and experimental apparatuses for the epistemological authority of science already was well appreciated by Gaston BACHELARD [1] in the 1930s.

The recent emergence of the importance of understanding experiments for understanding science, and for an appreciation of the philosophical problems experiments present, has also made it possible to see how the philosophy of science, enriched by its new developments, can work through its recent fragmentation to a new and deeper holistic appreciation of the scientific enterprise. As work on experiments progresses, two things are increasingly evident: (1) experiments do not occur in a vacuum and (2) the broader context in which we need to see experiments provides the platform for the reemergence of a more traditional, normative, and synthetic role for the philosophy of science. To take these points in order, first consider the fact that experiments are not merely theory dependent. That is, we do not start with a theory and then construct an experiment to document some aspect of that theory. There is an important and overlooked interactive symbiosis between theories and instruments that generates highly creative and inventive experimental environments that are constantly being readjusted in the light of changes in any and all of its components (see the work of Hans-Joerg Rheinberger). There is a certain sense in which the instruments and techniques of experimentation, on the one hand, and theories, on the other hand, come to the experimental environment as equal partners. If we identify the science exclusively with the theories, we do an injustice to history. Nevertheless, we cannot discuss the design and significance of experiments without appreciating the theories. And yet, it is the experimental platform that increasingly seems to mold the theories as the science matures, and that platform increases in complexity (e.g., as instruments are embedded in computer arrays and stacked programs).

The New Experimentalism therefore provides us with the basis for reconceptualizing the development and character of science in the context of its technological infrastructure. The infrastructure also provides the vehicle for the incorporation of all of the various new facets of the philosophical landscape in the philosophy of science and also provides the philosophy of science with a new framework. Instead of seeing science as merely a collection of theories that meet certain logical criteria of adequacy, these recent developments give us science as a thoroughly human activity generating knowledge about the world through a technologically interactive framework.

If the New Experimentalism, fleshed out with detailed historical, social studies of the sciences, offers a promising new framework for the new philosophy of science, where does that leave the positivistic foundation, which, it was argued above, is still functioning? To begin with, that positivism is the foundation for contemporary work is a historical fact. From that fact it does not follow that for positivism to be an influence on the contemporary scene its original program must still be intact. We have noted throughout the dynamic tension between the universalistic goals of positivism and the fragmentation brought about by the increased attention to the details of the sciences. The proposal here is that the still-functioning search for universal criteria is the motivation to turn to the technological infrastructure of science. Mature sciences are increasingly characterized, if not captured, by their technological bases. This is yet another fact on the contemporary scientific landscape. The universal features and, perhaps, problems of contemporary science are increasingly a direct function of the supporting and interacting technological systems in which the science is embedded. It can be argued that the technological side provides the more encompassing framework in which to consider the scientific.

The shift from the universal criteria of positivism to the pervasive technological infrastructure is not perfectly smooth. The positivists' linguistic framework is not being exchanged for the technological. The manner in which we phrase our theories, our hypotheses, and our evidential claims remains crucial to the scientific process. Nor does the appeal to the technological deal well with the emergence of new sciences, since the claim is that the technological infrastructure is most evident in mature sciences. Nevertheless, the search for some universal feature(s) remains a deeply rooted feature of contemporary philosophy of science.

(SEE ALSO: *Philosophy of Science, History of,* and *Philosophy of Science, Problems of* [6]. *Explanation, Theories of; Explanation, Types of; Laws of Nature; Philosophy of Social Sciences;* and *Scientific Theories* [S])

Bibliography

Ackermann, R. J. *Data, Instruments, and Theory: A Dialectic Approach to Understanding Science.* Princeton, NJ, 1985.

Buchwald, J. Z. *The Creation of Scientific Effects: Heinrich Hertz and Electric Waves.* Chicago, 1994.

Burian, R. M. "Realist Methodology in Contemporary Genetics," in N. Nersessian, ed., *The Process of Science,* Vol. 3 of *Science and Philosophy* (Dordrecht, 1987).

Cartwright, N. *How the Laws of Physics Lie.* Oxford, 1983.

Franklin, A. *The Neglect of Experiment.* Cambridge, 1986.

Galison, P. L. *How Experiments End.* Chicago, 1987.

Giere, R. N. *Exploring Science: A Cognitive Approach.* Chicago, 1988.

Hacking, I. *Representing and Intervening: Introductory Topics in the Philosophy of Natural Science.* Cambridge, 1983.

Hanson, N. R. *Patterns of Discovery: An Inquiry into the Conceptual Foundations of Science.* Cambridge, 1961.

Harding, S. G. *Whose Science? Whose Knowledge? Thinking from Women's Lives.* Ithaca, NY, 1991.

Hempel, C. G. *Aspects of Scientific Explanation and Other Essays in the Philosophy of Science.* New York, 1965.

Kitcher, P. *The Advancement of Science: Science without Legend, Objectivity without Illusions.* New York, 1993.

Kuhn, T. S. *The Structure of Scientific Revolutions.* Chicago, 1962.

Laudan, L. *Progress and Its Problems: Towards a Theory of Scientific Growth.* Berkeley, 1977.

Longino, H. E. *Science as Social Knowledge: Values and Objectivity in Scientific Inquiry.* Princeton, NJ, 1990.

Pickering, A. *Constructing Quarks: A Sociological History of Particle Physics.* Chicago, 1984.

Quine, W. V. O. "Two Dogmas of Empiricism," *Philosophical Review,* Vol. 60 (1951), reprinted in *From a Logical Point of View.* Cambridge, MA, 1953.

Rheinberger, H. J. "Experiment, Difference, and Writing I: Tracing Protein Synthesis," *Studies in History and Philosophy of Science,* Vol. 23 (1994), 305–31.

———. "Experiment, Difference, and Writing II: The Laboratory Production of Transfer RNA," *Studies in History and Philosophy of Science,* Vol. 23 (1994), 389–422.

Rorty, R. *Philosophy and the Mirror of Nature.* Princeton, NJ, 1979.

Sellars, W. "Empiricism and the Philosophy of Mind," *Minnesota Studies in the Philosophy of Science,* Vol. 1 (1956), 253–329.

Shapin, S., and S. Schaffer. *Leviathan and the Air Pump: Hobbes, Boyle, and the Experimental Life.* Princeton, NJ, 1985.

Suppe, F. *The Semantic Conception of Theories and Scientific Realism.* Urbana, IL, 1988.

van Fraassen, B. C. *The Scientific Image.* Oxford, 1980.

JOSEPH C. PITT

PHILOSOPHY OF SOCIAL SCIENCES. The philosophy of social sciences comes in three varieties, as the metaideology, the metaphysics, and the methodology of the disciplines involved. The metaideology looks at how far different, traditional legitimations of social sciences succeed. The metaphysics looks at questions having to do with what social science posits—what things it says there are—and at how far those posits are consistent with more or less commonplace beliefs. And the methodology looks at questions regarding the nature of observations, laws, and theories in social science, the logic of INDUCTION [4] and confirmation, the requirements of understanding and explanation, and so on.

METAIDEOLOGY

The social sciences were conceived and pursued, from the very beginning, under the influence of ideals (particularly of scientific objectivity and progress) deriving from the eighteenth-century ENLIGHTENMENT [2] (Hawthorn, 1976). The first social scientists were economists and sociologists, as we would call them today, and they were self-consciously concerned about producing something that would count, not as philosophy, not as literature, not as common sense, but as science: as a project faithful to the image forged by natural science.

The scientific intention—the intention to make science—has remained characteristic of work in the social sciences. It puts social scientists, paradoxically, under an obligation of an ideological kind: the obligation to show that the sort of analysis they pursue is of a properly scientific kind. The metaideology of social science interrogates and assesses the ideologies whereby the social sciences try to legitimate what they do, to show that what they do is genuinely scientific in character.

Broadly speaking, there are three main ideologies that have been invoked—individually or in various combinations—by social scientists in the scientific legitimation of their enterprise. Each of these marks a feature that putatively distinguishes social science from mere common sense, mere social lore. The first ideology hails social science as an explanatory enterprise of culturally universal validity; the second as an enterprise that is interpretatively neutral, not being warped by people's self-understanding; and the third as an enterprise that enjoys evaluative independence: value-freedom. The universality, neutrality, and independence claimed are each meant to establish social science as objective, and therefore scientifically respectable, in a way in which common sense is not; each notion offers an explication of what scientific objectivity involves. Some approaches in the metaideology of social science, particularly those of a postmodern cast (Rosenau, 1992), reject all three ideologies out of hand: they reject any notion of objectivity in the area (*see* POSTMODERNISM [5]); others consider them one by one, under the assumption that they may come apart.

Social lore is always lore about a particular social milieu and culture, and an aspiration to cultural universality, if it can be vindicated, would certainly give social science a distinctive status. Such an aspiration is supported in a variety of traditions: among anthropologists and sociologists of a Durkheimian cast (*see* DURKHEIM [2]), among many Marxist scholars (*see* MARXIST PHILOSOPHY [5]), and among those economists who think that all human behavior, and the patterns to which it gives rise, can be explained by reference to *homo economicus* (*see* ECONOMICS AND RATIONAL CHOICE [2]).

But the metaideologists of social science have claimed many reasons to question the possibility of any universalist, or at least any straightforwardly universalist, theory. HERMENEUTIC PHILOSOPHY [S], which has long been dominant in Germany, and the analytical tradition sponsored by the work of the later WITTGENSTEIN [8; S] both suggest that any explanation of human behavior has to start with the culturally specific concepts in which people understand their environment and cannot aspire, therefore, to a substantive universality (McCarthy, 1978; Winch, 1958). The debate on these questions ranges widely, encompassing issues of cultural and other forms of relativism (Hollis & Lukes, 1982).

Social lore is not only particularistic, it is also designed to represent people as subjectively understandable or interpretable. We, the local consumers of such lore, know what it is like to be creatures of the kind represented and know how we would go about communicating with them. The second, and perhaps least persuasive, ideology of social science suggests that this disposition to represent people as subjectively understandable comes of a limited perspective that social science transcends. It suggests that social science can aspire to an objective explanation of people's behavior without worrying about whether the explanation fits with their self-understanding: without being anxious to ensure that it makes native sense of them and facilitates interpersonal communication. The ideology suggests that social science, in the received phrases, can aspire to a form of *Erklären,* or explanation, that need not service the needs of interpersonal *Verstehen,* or understanding.

Metaideologists of social science have claimed many reasons to question this aspiration to *Verstehen*-free explanation. Hermeneutic and Wittgensteinian thinkers both reject the idea that people can be properly understood without facilitating communication (Winch, 1958). And the many philosophers who follow the lead of Donald DAVIDSON [S] on interpretation argue that there is no interpreting human subjects without representing them as more or less rational and more or less interpersonally scrutable (Macdonald & Pettit, 1981).

Social lore is often evaluatively committed as well as particularistic and oriented to subjective understanding. It takes a form premised on an evaluative characterization of the status quo. Thus, it may characterize the beliefs and explain the behavior of rulers on the assumption that the regime they sustain is unjust. The third and most common legitimating ideology of social science, one associated in particular with the German sociologist Max WEBER [8], holds that in this respect—and perhaps in this respect only—social science can do scientifically better than social lore. It can acknowledge that the agents in the society have evaluative beliefs, and it can take account of these in its explanation of what they do, without itself endorsing any such beliefs; it can be objective, in the familiar sense of remaining uncommitted on evaluative questions.

Metaideologists of social science have also sought reasons to doubt this claim, but the debate has been confused by differences over what sorts of evaluative commitments would really be damaging to the pretensions of social science. The critique of social science on the grounds of not escaping a commitment to value has been nurtured by the appearance, in the later part of the century, of a variety of realist positions on the nature of value. If values are taken to be objective features of the world, then a social scientist's beliefs as to what those features are may well affect their interpretation of how certain subjects think and act; interpretation, after all, is bound to be influenced by the interpreter's view of the subject's environment (Hurley, 1989, chap. 5; Macdonald & Pettit, 1981, chap. 4; Taylor, 1981).

The metaideology of social science may concern itself with other issues: for example, whether the models used in social science, in particular within economics, are really empirical, scientific models and not just pieces of mathematics or exercises in a conversational rhetoric (Hausman, 1991; McCloskey, 1985; Rosenberg, 1992). These issues are not discussed here.

METAPHYSICS

The metaphysics of social science usually takes it as granted that there is no society without individual intentional agents: without subjects who apparently act, other things being equal, on the basis of their beliefs and desires (Pettit, 1993, pt. 1). The question that metaphysics raises bears on what more we should include in our metaphysical stock-taking of society; and on how the more we should include, if there is any, relates to individual intentional subjects.

There are two aspects of social life that are particularly relevant to this question. There is the social interaction between individuals in virtue of which various relationships get formed: relationships involving communication, affection, collaboration, exchange, recognition, esteem, or whatever. And there is the social aggregation of individual attitudes and actions in virtue of which various institutions get established: these institutions will include common instrumentalities such as languages, cultures, and markets; groups such as the club, union, or party, whose essence it is to have a mode of collective behavior; groups that may have only a nonbehavioral collective identity such as genders, races, and classes; and shared resources of the kind illustrated by museums, libraries, and states.

The metaphysics of social science concerns itself both with issues raised by interaction and with questions associated with aggregation, specifically with social interaction and aggregation. (On the definition of "social," see Ruben, 1985).

On the side of interaction the main issue in social philosophy is that which divides so-called atomists from nonatomists (Taylor, 1985). The atomist holds that individual human beings do not depend—that is, noncausally or constitutively depend—on social relationships for the appearance of any distinctive, human capacities. The nonatomist holds that they do. The atomist defends an image of human beings under which they come to society with all the characteristic properties that they will ever display; social life does not transform them in any essential manner. The nonatomist denies this, believing that it is only in the experience of social relationships that human beings come properly into their own.

The debate between atomists and nonatomists has centered on the connection between thought and language. Atomists have taken their lead from HOBBES [4; S], who argues that, however useful language is for mnemonic, taxonomic, and communicative purposes, thinking is possible without speech, even without any inchoate form of speech. Nonatomists have tended to follow ROUSSEAU [7; S] and the Romantic tradition with which he is associated—a tradition also encompassing HERDER [3] and HEGEL [3; S]—in arguing, first, that language is social and, second, that thought requires language.

The atomist tradition has been dominant in English-speaking philosophy, while the nonatomist has had a considerable presence in France and Germany. One source of nonatomism in the English-speaking world has been the work of the later Wittgenstein, in which it is suggested that following a rule—and, therefore, thinking—is possible only in the context of social practices and relationships (Wittgenstein, 1968). This very strong nonatomist thesis may also be weakened, so that the claim is that following a rule of a characteristic kind—say, a suitably scrutable kind—requires such a social context (Pettit, 1993, chap. 4). Another source of nonatomism in recent English-speaking philosophy has been the argument that the content of a person's thoughts is fixed, not just by what goes on in his head, but by the linguistic community to which he belongs and to which he aspires to remain faithful (Burge, 1979; Hurley, 1989).

What now of the issues generated by the aggregative aspect of society? There are a number of interesting questions raised by the aggregative structure of society, some having to do with the reducibility of aggregative theory to theory of a more psychological cast, others having to do with the status of aggregative individuals and the standing of the causal relevance we ascribe to such entities (Gilbert, 1992; James, 1984; Ruben, 1985; Tuomela, 1996). Perhaps the most pressing question, however, is whether the entities that appear with the social aggregation of individual attitudes and actions give the lie to our ordinary sense of intentional agency: whether it means that, contrary to appearances, we are in some way the dupes of higher-level patterns or forces (Pettit, 1993, chap. 3). The individualist, to use a name that also bears further connotations—see under "Methodology"—denies that aggregate entities have this effect; the nonindividualist insists that they do.

One extreme sort of individualism would say that intentional agency is not compromised by any aggregate, social entities, because in strict truth no such entities exist. A more plausible form of the doctrine would say that while there are indeed a variety of aggregate entities, there is nothing about those entities that suggests that our received, commonplace psychology is mistaken. No doubt, there are aggregate regularities associated with such entities: for example, a rise in unemployment tends to be followed by a rise in crime; the fact that something is in an organization's interest generally means that agents of the organization will pursue it; and so on. But the individualist will argue that those regularities do not signal the presence of forces unrecognized in commonplace psychology or the operation of any mechanism—say, any selection mechanism—that belies the assumptions of that psychology. That the regularities obtain can be explained within that psychology, given the context in which the relevant agents find themselves and given their understanding—perhaps involving relevant aggregate-level concepts—of that context.

METHODOLOGY

There are two sorts of methodological questions raised in the philosophy of social science: first, questions imported from the methodology of natural science having to do with such matters as observations and laws and theories, REALISM [S] and nonrealism in theory interpretation, statistical inference, confirmation, and explanation; second, questions that arise only, or arise distinctively, within the social sciences. Perhaps the two major questions of the latter kind bear on whether it is good explanatory practice to follow the individualistic and economistic assumptions, respectively, that characterize much social science. Here the emphasis will be on the issues of individualism and economism.

The methodological individualist, as characterized in the literature, is associated with a number of more or less outlandish doctrines: for example, that individuals each play indispensable roles, so that things would always have been significantly different if the actual individuals had not been around or if they had not done the things they actually did; that individuals are unaffected by their circumstances, or their relationships with one another, in the things they come to think and want; or that all social facts can be expressed in terms of a nonsocial psychology and that all social laws can be derived from the laws of such a psychology.

Methodological individualism is better understood, however, as a doctrine that has more clearly had respectable defenders as well as opponents: specifically, as the doctrine that it is always good explanatory practice to try to explain social events in terms of finer-grain, individualistic factors rather than by reference to aggregative antecedents. Such an explanatory individualism has been defended by Jon Elster (1985). He argues that aggregative antecedents are causally relevant in virtue of the causal relevance of individual factors and that staying at the aggregative level means leaving the productive mechanism in a black box; it amounts to a willful neglect of relevant facts.

Suppose that we have found a good aggregative explanation of some social phenomenon: say we find that secularization is explained adequately by urbanization or a rise in crime by a rise in unemployment. We gain further information about the causal history of such a phenomenon as we are informed about the individual-level factors at work in producing secularization or crime. But it may still be that the aggregative story gives us equally important causal information. It may be, for example, that while we learn more about the detail of the actual causal process in going individualistic we learn more about what would be enough to ensure an increase in secularization or crime—that there should be urbanization or unemployment—in spotting the aggregative connections. After all, we might have known the individual-level explanations without having come to recognize the aggregative connections. Perhaps the right line is neither explanatory individualism nor explanatory nonindividualism but explanatory ecumenism (Jackson & Pettit, 1992).

The second question bears on whether it is a good explanatory strategy in social science to make economistic assumptions about individual agents: to assume, as economists tend to do, that agents are rational in the way they form and reform their preferences and that their preferences are generally egoistic in character. There are lots of persuasive arguments for following an economistic strategy: arguments that point to the precision in model building and prediction that economistic assumptions allow (Becker, 1976). But it seems manifest, on the other hand, that the economistic story is not the whole truth about human beings (Hollis, 1977). For example, it is surely obvious that most of us do not make our decisions on the self-concerned, calculative basis that that story would seem to suggest.

But this consideration may not be decisive against economism. For what is possible is that while agents often do not calculate economistically, they tend sooner or later to give up on patterns of behavior that are not at least comparatively satisfactory in economistic terms (Pettit, 1993, chap. 5). Perhaps the fact that a pattern of behavior satisfies such economistic constraints is necessary to explain the resilience, if not the actual production and reproduction, of the behavior.

(SEE ALSO: *Confirmation Theory; Explanation, Theories of; Explanation, Types of; Philosophy of Sciences;* and *Scientific Theories* [S])

Bibliography

Becker, G. *The Economic Approach to Human Behavior.* Chicago, 1976.

Burge, T. "Individualism and the Mental," *Midwest Studies in Philosophy,* Vol. 4 (1979), 73–121.

Elster, J. *Making Sense of Marx.* Cambridge, 1985.

Gilbert, M. *On Social Facts.* Princeton, NJ, 1992.

Hausman, D. *The Separate and Inexact Science of Economics.* Cambridge, 1991.

Hawthorn, G. *Enlightenment and Despair: A History of Sociology.* Cambridge, 1976.

Hollis, M. *Models of Man: Philosophical Thoughts on Social Action.* Cambridge, 1977.

———, and S. Lukes, eds. *Rationality and Relativism.* Oxford, 1982.

Hurley, S. *Natural Reasons: Personality and Polity.* New York, 1989.

Jackson, F., and P. Pettit. "In Defence of Explanatory Ecumenism," *Economics and Philosophy,* Vol. 8 (1992), 1–21.

James, S. *The Content of Social Explanation.* Cambridge, 1984.

Macdonald, G., and P. Pettit. *Semantics and Social Science.* London, 1981.

McCarthy, T. *The Critical Theory of Jürgen Habermas.* Cambridge, MA, 1978.

McCloskey, D. *The Rhetoric of Economics.* Madison, WI, 1985.

Papineau, D. *For Science in Social Science.* London, 1978.

Pettit, P. *The Common Mind: An Essay on Psychology, Society, and Politics.* New York, 1993.

Rosenau, P. M. *Post-Modernism and the Social Sciences: Insights, Inroads, and Intrusions.* Princeton, NJ, 1992.

Rosenberg, A. *Economics: Mathematical Politics or Science of Diminishing Returns?* Chicago, 1992.

Ruben, D.-H. *The Metaphysics of the Social World.* London, 1985.

Ryan, A. *The Philosophy of the Social Sciences.* London, 1970.

Taylor, C. "Understanding and Explanation in the *Geisteswissenschaften,*" in S. H. Holtzman and C. M. Leich, eds., *Wittgenstein: To Follow a Rule* (London, 1981).

———. *Philosophy and the Human Sciences.* Cambridge, 1985.

Tuomela, R. *The Importance of Us.* Stanford, CA, 1996.

Winch, P. *The Idea of a Social Science and Its Relation to Philosophy.* London, 1958.

Wittgenstein, L. *Philosophical Investigations,* 2d ed., trans. G. E. M. Anscombe. Oxford, 1968.

PHILIP PETTIT

PHILOSOPHY OF TECHNOLOGY. To the three traditional sets of philosophical questions concerning being (metaphysics), knowledge (epistemology), and human action (ethics) modern philosophy added a fourth concerning history: What is the structure of history? What is the character of the modern (or any other) historical epoch? (*See* EPISTEMOLOGY, HISTORY OF and ETHICS, HISTORY OF [3]; EPISTEMOLOGY and ETHICAL THEORY [S]; METAPHYSICS, HISTORY OF [5]; and METAPHYSICS [S].) From the beginning, response to the fourth kind of question has involved reference to technology. For Francis BACON [1], for instance, the modern period is defined by the inventions of printing, gunpowder, and the compass (*Novum organum,* book 1, aphorism 129). Historical anthropologies commonly periodized human history on the basis of material artifacts: the stone age, the bronze age, the iron age, and so forth. And the substructure of "postmodernity" is constituted by advances in electronic communication from TV to computers.

TWO TRADITIONS IN THE PHILOSOPHY OF TECHNOLOGY

In the late nineteenth and early twentieth centuries the characterization of human history in terms of technology gave way to the first explicit theories about technology itself. For example, Franz Reuleaux's *Theoretische Kinematik* (1875) was the founding text in mechanical engineering. From a more general perspective Ernst Kapp's *Grundlinien einer Philosophie der Technik* (1877) outlined a theory of culture grounded in technics understood as the extension and differentiation of human anatomy, physiology, and behavior. The hammer, for instance, can function as an extension of the fist, the train as an extension of legs and feet, the camera as an extension of the eye; and vice versa the fist is a kind of hammer, the train a kind of foot, the eye a kind of camera. Elaborations of this view of technology as "organ projection" are at the foundation of a tradition of what Carl Mitcham (1994) has termed "engineering philosophy of technology" and can be seen reflected in the work of philosophers such as the Russian Peter Englemeier, the German Friedrich Dessauer, the Frenchman Gilbert Simondon, and the Spaniard Juan David García Bacca (all of whom have been largely ignored by Anglo-American philosophy).

Research engineer Dessauer, for instance, developed a neo-Kantian critique of the transcendental possibility of technological invention that sees technology as bringing noumenal power into the world. Simondon explores relations between parts, artifacts, and technical systems and the evolutionary manifestation of what he terms "technicity." Englemeier and García Bacca both see technological change as engendering world-historical transformations that are at once humanizing and transcending of the merely organically human. Additional contributions to this perspective can be found in the work of CYBERNETICS [2] and ARTIFICIAL INTELLIGENCE [S] theorists from Norbert Wiener (1948) to Kevin Kelly (1994). (The collections edited by Alan Ross Anderson [1964] and John Haugeland [1981] constitute good overviews of philosophical debates in this particular field.) Philosophical anthropologist Arnold GEHLEN [3], media theorist Marshall McLuhan, as well as contemporary engineers Samuel Florman and Henry Petroski provide other takes on engineering philosophy of technology. But for two of the most sophisticated alternative presentations of aspects of this philosophy see scientific philosopher Mario Bunge's (1985) metaphysics, epistemology, and ethics of technology, and David Rothenberg's (1993) comprehensive reduction of nature and the nontechnical to technology.

Philosophy of technology is more commonly identified, however, with what could be termed a counterphilosophy of technology that interprets technology, not as extending, but as encroaching on or narrowing the categories of human experience. Following KANT's [4; S] attempt "to deny [scientific] *knowledge,* in order to make room for *faith*" (*Critique of Pure Reason,* B), this "humanities philosophy of technology" seeks to limit technological action in order to make room for human culture in all its diversity. This tradition has been elaborated especially by the Continental philosophical tradition in the work of José ORTEGA Y GASSET [6], Martin HEIDEGGER [3; S], and Jacques Ellul.

Until quite recently, however, the problematic character of the phenomenon of technology remained in the background of philosophy. Technology constitutes what can be called a new philosophical issue, one that entered mainstream philosophical discourse only in the latter half of the twentieth century.

TECHNOLOGY AS A SOCIAL PROBLEM

The recognition of technology as a philosophical issue is based upon its parallel emergence as a social problem. A general name for this problem is that of technocracy—that is, the control of society by technical experts or by technical ways of thinking and acting. However, the precise understanding of the challenge of technocracy has varied from engineer apologists who see technocracy as a necessary good to humanities critics who reject it as an unnecessary evil. Indeed, one of the first requirements in the philosophy of technology is to clarify the problematic of technocracy.

Speaking generally, one can identify at least five competing and overlapping interpretations of technology as a social problem. First, there is a problem of the just distribution of technological products and powers—that is, technology as a political issue. Since the Industrial Revolution the social-justice question has found a variety of expressions in authoritarian and democratic regimes, in developed and developing countries (*see* JUSTICE [4; S]). Second is the problem of the alienation of workers from their labor under conditions constituted by the industrial means of production, which has been presented especially by Marxists as an economic and by some non-Marxist social scientists as a psychological issue (*see* MARXISM [S]; and MARXIST PHILOSOPHY [5]). Third is the problem of the destruction or transformation of culture by modern science and the technological development of new means of transportation and communication. Fourth is the problem of democratic participation. How are those who are not scientists or engineers to participate in technoscientific decision making or even decision making about science and technology? Indeed, the apparent need to rely on technical experts in many of the social institutions of high-tech democracies constitutes the challenge of technocracy in its restricted form (*see* DEMOCRACY [2; S]). Fifth is the industrial pollution of the natural environment, which is often seen as an ecological issue (*see* ENVIRONMENTAL ETHICS [S]). Competing proposals for "sustainable development" highlight this issue. Contemporary discussions of a range of APPLIED ETHICS [S] issues—from BIOMEDICAL ETHICS [S] to nuclear, environmental, and COMPUTER ETHICS [S]—prolong these interpretations of technology as a social problem and are often taken to constitute the substance of the philosophy of technology.

Again, speaking generally, one can note two broad approaches to such problems. One attempts to explain modern technology as rooted in human nature and culture (engineering philosophy of technology), the other interprets modern technical methods and effects as unwarranted constraints on action (humanities philosophy of technology). The engineering philosophical approach calls in one way or another for more technology, the humanities philosophical approach for some delimitation of technology.

In its most extreme form, then, the foreground of philosophical reflection on technology centers on questions of whether technology is good or bad—on arguments between utopian and dystopian views of technology (Ihde, 1986). This pro/con, positive/negative approach is inadequate for two reasons. It treats technology as a unified whole when in truth it is a complex amalgam of artifacts, knowledge, activities, and volition, each with diverse structural features scattered across historical epochs and social contexts. Second, it assumes clarifications of the meaning of good and bad, right and wrong, just and unjust as these have developed in the traditions of philosophy largely independent of any sustained reflection on technology. Reflection on ethics in technology or technologies may, however, demand a reevaluation of traditional ethical concepts and principles.

Underlying competing interpretations of technology as a social problem are variations of the three traditional philosophical questions. One concerns the epistemological question of the structure of technological (as related to or contrasted with scientific and aesthetic) knowing. Another is the metaphysical question of the relation between nature and artifice. Still a third is the ethical question of the proper creation and utilization of technoscientific powers, both within technoscientific institutions and in society at large. Philosophy of technology constitutes a progressive deepening and clarification of these questions by both engineering and humanities philosophers of technology.

TECHNOLOGY, TECHNICITY, TECHNICISM: EUROPEAN PHILOSOPHY OF TECHNOLOGY

The attempt to speak of "technology" rather than "technologies" rests on an ability to clarify some inner or essential feature of all technologies. Call this hypothetical essential feature "technicity." We can then immediately note that, prior to the modern period, technicity was at a minimum scattered throughout and heavily embedded within a diversity of human engagements, and indeed that philosophy took a stand against any separating of technicity from its embedding in particulars. PLATO's [6; S] argument in the *Gorgias,* for example, is precisely an argument against disembedding *techne* from social or cultural contexts and traditions, not to mention ideas of the good. What is distinctive about modern philosophy, by contrast, is the attempt, beginning with Galileo GALILEI [3] and René DESCARTES [2; S], to disembed technics from particular human activities, to study them in systematic ways, and thus to create technology.

John Stuart MILL [5; S] in his *Logic* (1843) already assumes the success of this disembedding project when he explains the practical value of science. For Mill the rationality of any art is grounded in a corresponding science.

> The art proposes to itself an end to be attained, defines the end, and hands it over to the science. The science receives it, considers it as a phenomenon or effect to be studied, and having investigated its causes and conditions, sends it back to art with a theorem of the combinations of circumstances by which it could be produced. Art then examines these combinations or circumstances, and according as any of them are or are not in human power, pronounces the end attainable or not. (*Logic,* book 6, chapter 12, section 2)

The pattern of technicity thus outlined is of the form $C \rightarrow E$, where E is an end or effect to be attained and C is the cause or condition of E. The remarkable thing about Mill's analysis is that art (or traditional technics) is not thought of as including any knowledge of means. Art is concerned only with determining the end and then putting into operation a means derived from science. It is the scientific study of means that constitutes what even during Mill's lifetime is coming to be called technology. Modern technicity can thus be defined as a systematic or scientific study of means that suspends examination of ends.

Among the first philosophers to analyze such a disembedding of means from ends was Ortega y Gasset. In the English translation of his *La rebelión de las masas* (1929), Ortega writes that "Three principles have made possible [the] new world: liberal democracy, scientific experiment, and industrialism. The two latter may be summed up in one word: technicism" (1932, p. 56). Ortega himself uses the more straightforward "técnica," but the term technicism is significant, and this in fact constitutes one of its first English occurrences with this sense. Prior to the 1930s "technicism" simply meant excessive reliance on technical terminology, whereas now it designates a unification of science and technics.

As part of a further "Meditación de la técnica" (1939) Ortega outlines a historical movement from the chance inventions that characterize archaic societies, through the trial-and-error techniques of the artisan, to the scientific technologies of the engineer. According to Ortega, the difference between these three forms of making lies in the way one creates the means to realize a human project—that is, in the kind of technicity involved in each case. In the first epoch technical discoveries are accidental; in the second, techniques emerge from intuitive skill. In both instances they are preserved and elaborated within the confines of myth and tradition. In the third, however, the engineer has undertaken scientific studies of technics and, as a result, "prior to the possession of any [particular] technics, already possesses technics [itself]" (*Obras completas,* 5:369). It is this third type of technicity that constitutes "modern technicism" (and here Ortega himself uses the term "tecnicismo").

But technicism, understood here as the science of how to generate all possible technical means, disembedded from any lived making and using, creates a unique historical problem. Prior to the modern period human beings were commonly limited by circumstances within which they at once were given a way of life and the technical means to realize it. Now, however, they are given in advance many possible ways to live and a plethora of technical means but no well-defined life. "To be an engineer and only an engineer is to be everything possibly and nothing actually," all form and no content (*Obras completas,* 5:366). There is in the midst of modern technicism what Ortega calls a crisis of imagination and choice. Insofar as people can be anything, why should they be any one thing at all?

According to Heidegger, as well, technicism covers over its own foundations. For Heidegger (1954) scientific technics or technology constitutes a new kind of truth: truth not as correspondence, not as coherence, and not as functional knowledge, but as revelation. Technology reveals Being in a way that it has never previously been revealed in history: as *Bestand,* or resource. A castle constructed with traditional technics on a cliff overlooking the Rhine River makes more fully present than before the stone that invests the landscape with its particular contours while it sets off the curve of the river against the backdrop of its walls and towers. A poured-concrete, hydroelectric power station, by contrast, compels the river to become an energy resource and converts the landscape into, not a place of human habitation, but a machine for the generation of electricity. The modern technicity that manifests itself in the disclosure of nature as resource Heidegger names *Gestell* or enframing.

Gestell at first sight appears to be a human work, something human beings in the course of history have chosen to do for their own benefit. It gives them power over nature. But as it digitalizes nature physically (dimensioned vectors), geographically (longitude and latitude), chemically (molecules, atoms, subatomic particles), and biologically (genetic mapping), it also transforms language (computer signal processing) and art (pixel imaging) so that impact outstrips original intentions. Hidden in the midst of *Gestell* is Being as event, that which lets this dominating transformation come to pass. *Gestell* is at once destiny and, precisely because it appears so clearly to be the result of a human activity, an obscuring of the transhuman destining that is its ground.

In the same year that Heidegger's *Die Frage nach der Technik* appeared Ellul published *La Technique,* later translated into English as *The Technological Society* (1964). For Ellul too what is happening is something transhuman, or at least transindividual, the emergence of a new social order in which people give themselves up to the systematic analysis of actions into constituent $C \rightarrow E$ elements, which are then evaluated in terms of output/input metrics. The scientific analysis of techniques extends technoscientific methods into economics, politics, education, leisure, and elsewhere and creates what he calls the technical milieu.

But in contrast to Heidegger Ellul's phenomenological characterization of this new reality—its rationality, artificiality, self-directedness, self-augmentation, indivisibility, universality, and autonomy—reveals the technical milieu as something opposed to the human. The human experience of the technical milieu is not as something human—although, insofar as one is able to look through it, all one is able to see is either the human of certain inexorable laws of artifice (such as those of supply and demand). Just as the natural milieu once provided a framework for human life, a differentiated but overriding order to which human beings adapted in a variety of ways, so now a much more homogeneous technical milieu presents itself, not as a realm of freedom that human beings have constructed, but as that which constructs them. In the words of social psychologist Kenneth Keniston, the problem is that "in our highly developed technological society we have adopted, usually without knowing it, the implicit ideology called 'technism,' which places central value on what can be measured with numbers, assigns numbers to what cannot be measured, and redefines everything else as self-expression or entertainment" ("The Eleven-Year-Olds of Today Are the Computer Terminals of Tomorrow," *New York Times,* Feb. 19, 1976, p. 35). Manfred Stanley (1978), in the single most extended critique of technicism, likewise sees it as an ethos of collective mentality in which "the entire world is symbolically reconstituted as one interlocking problem-solving system according to the . . . technological language of control" (p. 10).

TOWARD A NEW PHILOSOPHY OF TECHNOLOGY

The humanities philosophies of technology of Ortega, Heidegger, and Ellul constitute nodal points in Continental philosophy of technology, although the extent to which what such critiques define as modern technicity sufficiently reflects engineering and technological practice remains problematic. At least some philosophers (such as Friedrich Rapp, 1981) and engineers (such as David Billington, 1983, and Walter Vincenti, 1990) argue that the engineer is as much concerned with socially determined priorities and aesthetics as with efficiency, thus going beyond the $C \rightarrow E$ relationship. Nevertheless, by analogy with scientism, which refers to the unwarranted extension of science or the scientific method beyond its legitimate boundaries (which Kant attempted to determine), technicism can be described as the overextension of technicity. And it is unclear whether engineering philosophy of technology, imbued with the achievements of modern technicity whatever its form, ever adequately addresses the challenge of technicism. Against this background there has emerged a new philosophy of technology that, while continuing attempts to define the theoretical and practical limits of technology, has promoted more socially, technically, and historically detailed epistemological, metaphysical, and ethical studies.

One inspiration for a more technoscientifically sensitive approach is the work of John DEWEY [2; S]. In his *Theory of Valuation* (1939), for example, when Dewey turns from analysis of the valuation of ends to the valuation of means, he begins by citing Charles Lamb's satiric essay "A Dissertation upon Roast Pig" (1822). According to the story, which Lamb in typically modern fashion uses to poke fun at the nonscientific determination of means, roast pork was first accidentally discovered when a building burned down with some piglets in it. The owner, after singeing his fingers on the carcass and putting them to his lips for relief of the pain, then set about building houses, confining pigs in them, and burning them down in order to enjoy such a delicious taste again and again.

For Dewey, this is to pursue the $C \rightarrow E$ relation with a rational vengeance that artificially isolates E (the taste of roast pork) from other experiences and relates it only to a narrowly defined C (burning houses). It fails to appreciate the ways in which C itself is embedded in a network of human experiences that include other ends (shelter), which it destroys at the same time that it produces roast pork. The problem with the $C \rightarrow E$ model lifted from its social context is at least twofold: it fails to note how C is itself the E_P of a prior C_P and how the original C produces not only E but also supplementary or side effects E^{S1}, E^{S2}, ... E_{Sn} as well as secondary and tertiary effects E^2, E^3, ... E^n that can in fact be negative and undermine or counter the original value of E. Traditional technics, because of its limited rational analysis, kept means embedded in networks of custom and culture; modern technology, because of its more extensive rationality, transcends tradition. But according to Dewey, rational disembedding from traditional culture must be complemented by the conscious re-embedding in a rationally reconstructed social life and aesthetic experience.

Lewis Mumford's well-known criticism of what he calls monotechnics, the technics of power, which he contrasts to poly- or biotechnics, can be interpreted in similar terms. The problem with monotechnics is that it disembeds the $C \rightarrow E$ relation from the larger contexts of life and the biological world. For Mumford the "myth of the machine" is that the $C \rightarrow E$ relation is the source of all human benefit. In fact, it constitutes an unrealistic narrowing of technical action itself in a way that inevitably leads to the production of negative side effects and second-order consequences. Indeed, once these negative side effects became widely recognized during the late 1960s, a number of attempts at the rational re-embedding of technology emerged in the development of social institutions such as the Environmental Protection Agency (established 1970) and the U.S. Congress Office of Technology Assessment (1972).

Parallel to the public philosophical discussions from which these institutions emerged, Hans Jonas undertook fundamental inquiries into the phenomenon of life and the inherently practical character of modern science, an expression of life that can appear to deny its relationships to the organic. Further grounded in his studies of the metaphysics and epistemology of the scientific and technological revolutions of the seventeenth century and after, studies which in their own way re-embedded technoscience in modern history, Jonas (1979) undertook an extended philosophical scrutiny of the technicist projects of nuclear weapons and biomedical health care. In the presence of technical powers to end or alter human life Jonas reformulates the Kantian categorical imperative as "Act so that the effects of your action are compatible with the permanence of genuine human life" (1984, p. 11). Such a reformulation of the fundamental deontological principle again constitutes an attempt at the re-embedding of technology in moral philosophy.

Langdon Winner's (1986) conception of "technologies as forms of life" and call for the abandonment of "technological somnambulism" in favor of the comprehensive public design of technological projects constitute another attempt to re-embed technology in human practice. Winner's call is not unrelated to Ihde's (1990) phenomenology of the techno-lifeworld, which discloses two fundamental human-technology-world relations: instrumental relations, in which the technology is integrated into the human sensorium as its extension (the blindman's cane), and hermeneutic relations, in which the technology becomes part of the world to be interpreted (a thermometer). Both relations manifest an invariant structure that amplifies some aspect of the world (exact metric of temperature) while simultaneously reducing others (general sense of climate). Such an analysis reveals the strengths and weaknesses of both engineering and humanities philosophies of technology: the one stresses amplification, the other reduction. But amplification-reduction is in invariant pattern that, once appreciated, can serve as a foundational recognition for the reintegration of technology into human experience transformed into what Ihde calls techno-pluriculture. Paradoxically enough, Michel FOUCAULT's (1988; [S]) idea of "technologies of the self" may constitute an *extendo ad transformandum* of the idea of technicism.

Two related contributions to the re-embedding of technology can be found in the work of Albert Borgmann and Kristin Shrader-Frechette. Borgmann (1984) explains technicism as a political economy of the manufacture and consumption of products partaking of what he terms the device paradigm (the ideal of an artifact disengaged from bodily engagements). Against such patterns of techno-economic behavior he appeals to the ideal of a way of life lived with what he calls focal things and practices. Shrader-Frechette (1991), by contrast, explains technicism as a restricted conception of risk analysis that must be broadened in ways pointed to by Dewey. What unites both Borgmann and Shrader-Frechette is an attempt to throw bridges between philosophy of technology, economics, and public policy.

Among all these approaches to a new philosophy of technology is an attempt to recognize technology as a social construction that nevertheless exhibits tendencies to escape conscious human direction. The dangers and challenges of such a technicism are to be met, however, by the disciplined pursuit of philosophical reflection that merges with practical and public citizen participation in the transformation no longer simply of nature but of technology itself.

Bibliography

Anderson, A. R., ed. *Minds and Machines.* Englewood Cliffs, NJ, 1964.

Billington, D. P. *The Toward and the Bridge: The New Art of Structural Engineering.* New York, 1983.

Borgmann, A. *Technology of the Character of Contemporary Life: A Philosophical Inquiry.* Chicago, 1984.

Bunge, M. "Technology: From Engineering to Decision Theory," in *Treatise on Basic Philosophy,* vol. 7, *Philosophy of Science and Technology,* part 2, *Life Science, Social Science, and Technology* (Boston, 1985).

Ellul, J. *La Technique ou l'enjeu du siècle.* Paris, 1954. Rev. ed., Paris, 1990. Translated as *The Technological Society.* New York, 1964. See also two supplements: *Le Système technicien.* Paris, 1977. Translated as *The Technological System.* New York, 1980. *Le Bluff technologique.* Paris, 1988. Translated as *The Technological Bluff.* Grand Rapids, MI, 1990.

Foucault, M. *Technologies of the Self: A Seminar with Michel Foucault.* Edited by L. H. Martin, H. Gutman, and P. H. Hutton. Amherst, MA, 1988.

Haugeland, J., ed. *Mind Design: Philosophy, Psychology, Artificial Intelligence.* Cambridge, MA, 1981.

Heidegger, M. "Die Frage nach der Technik," in *Vorträge und Aufsätze* (Pfullingen, 1954). Translated as "The Question concerning Technology," in *The Question concerning Technology and Other Essays* (San Francisco, 1954).

Ihde, D. *Philosophy of Technology: An Introduction.* New York, 1986.

———. *Technology and the Lifeworld: From Garden to Earth.* Bloomington, IN, 1990.

Jonas, H. *Das Prinzip Verantwortung: Versuch einer Ethik für die technologische Zivilisation.* Frankfurt, 1979. Translated as *The Imperative of Responsibility: In Search of an Ethics for the Technological Age.* Chicago, 1984.

Kelley, K. *Out of Control: The Rise of Neo-Biological Civilization.* Reading, MA, 1994.

Mitcham, C. *Thinking through Technology: The Path between Engineering and Philosophy.* Chicago, 1994.

Mitcham, C., and R. Mackey. *Bibliography of the Philosophy of Technology.* Chicago, 1973.

Mitcham, C., and R. Mackey, eds. *Philosophy and Technology: Readings in the Philosophical Problems of Technology.* New York, 1972.

Mumford, L. *The Myth of the Machine,* Vol. 1: *Technics and Human Development.* New York, 1967.

Ortega y Gasset, J. *La rebelión de las masas.* Madrid, 1929. Translated as *The Revolt of the Masses.* New York, 1932.

———. "Meditación de la técnica," in *Ensimismamiento y alteración* (Buenos Aires, 1939).

Rapp, F. *Analytische Technikphilosophie.* Freiburg, 1978. Translated by R. Carpenter and T. Langenbruch as *Analytical Philosophy of Technology.* Boston, 1981.

Rothenberg, D. *Hand's End: Technology and the Limits of Nature.* Berkeley, 1993.

Shrader-Frechette, K. S. *Risk and Rationality: Philosophical Foundations for Populist Reforms.* Berkeley, 1991.

Stanley, M. *The Technological Conscience: Survival and Dignity in an Age of Expertise.* New York, 1978.

Vincenti, W. G. *What Engineers Know and How They Know It: Analytical Studies from Aeronautical History.* Baltimore, 1990.

Wiener, N. *Cybernetics of Control and Communication in the Animal and the Machine.* Cambridge, MA, 1948.

Winner, L. *The Whale and the Reactor: A Search for Limits in an Age of High Technology.* Chicago, 1986.

CARL MITCHAM
LEONARD WAKS

PHONOLOGY. Phonology is the branch of linguistics concerned with the articulatory and auditory domain of grammar—that is, with the theory of what AUSTIN (1962 [1]) called phonetic acts. Its subject matter links with but is distinct from that of SYNTAX [S], SEMANTICS [7; S], and PRAGMATICS [S]. It covers the forms in which the sounds of words are kept in memory and the manner in which the motions of speech organs are shaped by grammar.

Unlike syntax, semantics, and pragmatics (but like closely related morphology), phonology has been largely ignored by philosophers. On the whole, philosophers consider the fact that natural languages are primarily spoken rather than written as of little interest for what DUMMETT (1986 [S]) calls a "philosophical explanation" of language. This attitude stems largely from the mistaken but widely held view that spoken signs are arbitrary sounds whose individuating traits are those of noises. On that view, utterances contemplated apart from their semantic and syntactic features are merely tokens of acoustical types, bereft of grammatical properties, fully described by the physics of noises, and available for human communication simply because humans can perceive and produce them; there is nothing intrinsically linguistic about them. Nor is this attitude an accident. Historically, philosophers have had little incentive to reflect on the sound of language. Most belong to traditions that admit no crucial differences (except perhaps those that pertain to pragmatics) between natural languages and notational systems developed by scientists, mathematicians, or philosophers for the elaboration of their theories. Such notational systems have a syntax and a semantics of sorts, but they have no phonology. Their constituent elements are typically spatial ideographs that share little with the phonological structures of natural languages. Studying language with such a bias offers few reasons, if any, to focus on what is spoken rather than written. It can, however, entrap one in a false conception of linguistic signs, so false, in fact, as seriously to weaken philosophic doctrines built on it.

Phonology rests on a series of presumptions—each supported by a vast body of observations—that together entail that the sounds of natural languages are not arbitrary human noises, on a par with grunts or snorts, whose individuating attributes lie entirely outside the domain of grammar.

The first such presumption is that when people acquire a word they memorize the underlying phonological representation of that word, a representation that defines—but often only partially—how the word is pronounced. These representations have the structure of linearly arrayed discrete timing positions that are assigned pointers to articulatory organs (lips, blade of tongue, dorsum of tongue, root of tongue, velum, vocal cords) implicated in the pronunciation of the word, and pointers to actions these organs execute during speech. The first timing position for the English 'pin', for instance, points to the lips, the vocal cords, the velum, full closure of the first, stiffening of the second, and nonlowering of the third.

A second presumption is that these pointers (called phonological features) on timing positions are drawn from a finite repertoire, common to all languages, and that they are combined within and across timing positions in rule-governed ways. Some rules are common to all languages and reflect innate linguistic endowments, others are language specific and reflect the influence of linguistic exposure. No language, for instance, avails itself of nasal snorts. French admits rounding of the lips in combinations of features that English excludes (thus the sound *ü* in French but not in English). Korean, unlike English (except for *h*), admits aspiration in underlying phonological representations. German, unlike English, admits initial sequences corresponding to sounded *k* followed by sounded *n*. All languages assemble features in similar (three-dimensional-like) structures.

A third presumption is that underlying phonological representations, in isolation or when compounded in complex words, are subject to rule-governed processes that add, subtract, or modify phonological features, which group them into syllables, feet, and prosodic words, which assign stresses and (in some languages) tones, and which ultimately yield final articulatory instructions, so-called surface phonological representations related to, but often very different from, the underlying representations in memory. Processes of this sort account for the fact that, for example, 'leaf' occurs as 'leavz' (with *v* instead of *f*) in the plural, or that 'serene' is pronounced differently when alone than when a constituent of 'serenity', or that 'p' gets aspirated in 'pin' though not in 'spin'. The details of these rules, the manner of their application, the universality of their formats, and the options fixed by different languages are all objects of intense research and controversies. But the evidence in behalf of their reality seems irrefutable.

Phonology is of philosophic interest, not only because it brings into question analogies between contrived notational systems and natural languages, but also because it raises conceptual issues of its own. Two can be mentioned here.

First, individual spoken utterances are analyzable in both acoustical and phonological terms. No generalizable exact correspondences between these two analyses are known. None may be forthcoming. For instance, nothing acoustical corresponds to word division. How can this dualism be reconciled? Is there a cogent sense in which the objects of speech production are the same (or belong to the same types) as those of speech perception? Offhand, the problem resembles that raised by other events amenable to multiple descriptions. But in this case solutions must be attuned to much that is already understood about both phonology and acoustics. It is not a simple task.

Second, phonological theory associates multiple representations with each utterance—including an underlying representation and a surface one—and it describes them all in the same notation. Surface representations can be conceptualized as instructions (or intentions) to move articulators in certain ways; their ontological status, though unclear, is at least comparable to that of other familiar cases. Not so the other phonological representations. They do not have familiar analogues. The semantic domain of phonological notation therefore cannot be ontologically homogeneous. Furthermore, part of that domain is deeply perplexing.

(SEE ALSO: *Philosophy of Language* [S])

Bibliography

Anderson, S. R. *Phonology in the Twentieth Century.* Chicago, 1985.

Austin, J. L. *How to Do Things with Words.* Cambridge, MA, 1962.

Bromberger, S., and M. Halle. "The Ontology of Phonology," in S. Bromberger, ed., *On What We Know We Don't Know* (Chicago, 1992).

Dummett, M. In E. LePore, ed., *Truth and Interpretation: Perspectives on the Philosophy of Donald Davidson* (Oxford and New York, 1986).

Kenstowicz, M. *Phonology in Generative Grammar.* Cambridge, MA, 1994. An introduction to the field and a complete bibliography.

Quine, W. V. O. *Word and Object,* chap. 3. Cambridge, MA, and New York, 1960.

SYLVAIN BROMBERGER

MORRIS HALLE

PHYSICALISM, MATERIALISM. Physicalism, of which MATERIALISM [5] is a historical antecedent, is primarily an ontological doctrine concerning the nature of reality and, specifically, mental reality. It is the view that reality is ultimately constituted or determined by entities—objects, events, properties, and so on—that are physical. This thesis is often combined with a claim about the explanatory supremacy of physical theory (physics).

Any formulation of physicalism raises the question, What is meant by 'physical'? It is difficult to formulate a conception of the physical that is neither too strong, making physicalism obviously false, nor too weak, making physicalism trivially true. For example, what is physical may be simply identified through the language of physics. However, a problem arises over the conception of physics appealed to. Current physics seems too narrow since future extensions of physics would not count as physical; but the idea of a completed physics is too indeterminate since we have no clear idea of what that physics might include. One could attempt to characterize the physical in more general terms such as having spatial location or being spatiotemporal. However, this threatens to make physicalism trivially true since mental phenomena seem clearly to have spatial location in virtue of having subjects—persons—who have bodies. It may be preferable to appeal to the idea of a completed physics. Although at any particular time we may not know exactly what is physical and what is not (since we may not know whether we have completed physics), nevertheless what is physical is all and only what a completed physics countenances.

There are two main types of physicalist theses. First, there is ELIMINATIVE MATERIALISM [S], or physicalism. According to this there are not, and never have been, any mental entities, events, properties, and so forth. Strictly speaking, this is not a view about the nature of mental reality. Second, there is a group of doctrines that fall under the general heading of identity theories, some of which are stronger than others. These can be divided into two main categories. The stronger doctrines may be called type–type identity theories, or type physicalist theories, and the weaker doctrines may be called token identity theories, or token physicalist theories.

TYPE PHYSICALISM

Consider any mental phenomenon, such as my being in pain now. We can talk about this phenomenon as an individual occurrence of a certain kind in the mental life of a person and discuss its properties. We can also talk about the kind of phenomenon—pain—of which this event is an individual instance. Physical phenomena can be discussed in both of these ways. Type physicalism is the view that the mental types, properties, or kinds under which mental phenomena fall are identical with physical types, properties, or kinds. Pain—that type of phenomenon, occurrences of which are individual pains—is identical with some single type of physical phenomenon such as C-fiber stimulation.

Type physicalism has its origins in the doctrines espoused by the logical positivists and central-state materialists. It is a strong form of physicalism because it is reductionist. Many who endorse it believe that nothing short of it counts as a proper physicalism. They argue that even if it is in practice impossible for sentences containing mental terminology to be translated into or replaced by sentences containing physical and topic-neutral terminology, any view that holds that all mental phenomena are physical phenomena, but mental properties or kinds are not physical properties or kinds, is not worthy of the name 'physicalism'.

However, type physicalism suffers from two serious objections. The first, from phenomenal properties, specifically concerns sensations such as pain, afterimages, and the like. It is that phenomena of these kinds or types have "felt" properties, such as being dull, or stabbing, whereas phenomena of physical types do not. Given this, and given LEIBNIZ's [4; S] principle of the indiscernibility of identicals, it follows that sensation types are not identical with physical types since the phenomena that fall under them do not share all the same properties. A variant of this objection focuses on the distinctive point of view a subject has on its own experiences: a subject knows what it is like to have experiences in a way that others do not, and this subjective mode of access reveals the phenomenal aspect of the experience, whereas an "other" oriented point of view does not.

The second objection to type physicalism is that from MULTIPLE REALIZABILITY [S]. This claims that mental kinds or properties may be realized in physically diverse types of ways, hence that there is no single physical type with which a given mental type may be identified. The point is that even if each mental type were in fact to be realized by a single physical type, it is possible for pain to be realized by physically diverse types of states. The reason is that the introspective and behavioral basis upon which attributions of mental properties are typically made is silent on the potential internal physical realizers of mental properties. Given the claim that identical things are necessarily identical, the mere possibility that a given mental type should be realized by a physical type of state other than that which in fact realizes it is sufficient to refute the claim that that mental type is identical with any physical type that may realize it. This objection is not independent of a modal argument that trades on the thesis that identical things are necessarily identical. This argument concludes that, since it is possible that pain should exist in the absence of any type of physical phenomenon, pain is not identical with any type of physical phenomenon.

One response is to argue that mental types are identical with disjunctions of physical types. For example, pain may not be identical with C-fibre stimulation, but it may be identical with the disjunctive property, C-fibre stimulation, or A-fibre stimulation, or . . . , and so on. However, it is unclear whether these are bona fide properties. They do not have a unity of their own, viewed from a physical perspective; and it is arguable that we need a reason, apart from the fact that they all realize a given mental property, to think that they are properties in their own right.

TOKEN PHYSICALISM

Many consider one or the other of the above objections to be decisive against type physicalism and have opted instead for a weaker view, token physicalism. According to this, each individual mental event or phenomenon is identical with some physical event. One influential version of this is the view known as ANOMALOUS MONISM [S]. Token physicalism is compatible with the multiple realizability of mental properties by physical ones since it is not committed to the view that each individual occurrence of a given mental kind is identical with an occurrence of the same type of physical phenomenon. It also appears to avoid the objection from phenomenal properties in its original form since it can concede that mental kinds have associated with them felt aspects with which no physical kinds are associated. To the objection that mental events are not identical with physical events because it is no part of the nature of any physical event that it have a felt aspect, the following reply can be made. If token physicalism is true, no physical event is essentially of a mental type; but given that it is of a given mental type, it has what is essential to being of that type. Thus, if this pain is identical with this C-fibre stimulation, then it is not essentially a pain. However, given that it is, as it happens, a pain, it has (though not essentially) what is essential to being of that type, namely being felt.

Without an explanation of how mental types relate to physical ones, token physicalism threatens to succumb to the charge that it is dualist because it countenances the existence of nonphysical properties or types. A common strategy is to advance a SUPERVENIENCE [S] doctrine concerning the relation between mental and physical properties, according to which physical properties, although distinct from mental ones, in some sense determine them. There are many varieties of supervenience theses. The main difficulty is in finding one strong enough to do justice to the claim that physical properties determine mental ones without being so strong as to entail identities between mental and physical properties or types, and with these, reducibility.

(SEE ALSO: *Philosophy of Mind,* and *Reduction, Reductionism* [S])

Bibliography

Armstrong, D. M. *A Materialist Theory of Mind.* London, 1968. Defense of a type–type identity theory of the mental and physical.

Block, N., ed. *Readings in the Philosophy of Psychology,* Vol. 1. Cambridge, MA, 1980. Articles on type–type identity theories, token identity theories, reductionism, and functionalism.

Davidson, D. "Mental Events," in Lawrence Foster and J. W. Swanson, eds., *Experience and Theory* (Amherst, MA, 1970). Highly influential argument for a token identity of the mental and physical.

Hellman, G., and F. W. Thompson. "Physicalism: Ontology, Determination, Reduction," *Journal of Philosophy,* Vol. 72 (1975), 551–64. Defense of a supervenience doctrine.

Jackson, F., R. Pargetter, and E. Prior. "Functionalism and Type–Type Identity Theories," *Philosophical Studies,* Vol. 42 (1982), 209–25. Discussion of the relation between functionalism and type–type identity theories.

Kim, J. "Supervenience as a Philosophical Concept," *Metaphilosophy,* Vol. 12 (1990), 1–27. Discusses supervenience as a covariance relation and its relation to reduction.

Kripke, S. *Naming and Necessity.* Cambridge, MA, 1980. A modal argument against type–type and token identity theories.

Lewis, D. "An Argument for the Identity Theory," *Journal of Philosophy,* Vol. 63 (1966), 17–25. An argument for a type–type identity theory.

Macdonald, C. *Mind–Body Identity Theories.* London, 1989. A survey of type–type and token identity theories, and a defense of a token identity theory.

Nagel, T. "What Is It Like to Be a Bat?," *Philosophical Review,* Vol. 83 (1974), 435–50. Argues against identity theories of the mental and the physical.

Place, U. T. "Is Consciousness a Brain Process?," *British Journal of Psychology,* Vol. 47 (1956), 44–50. A defense of central-state materialism for sensations.

Smart, J. J. C. "Sensations and Brain Processes," *Philosophical Review,* Vol. 68 (1959), 141–56. A defense of central state materialism for sensations.

CYNTHIA MACDONALD

PLATO. *The following annotated bibliography prepared by Richard Kraut provides a review of some of the major scholarly works on Plato since the publication of the* Encyclopedia of Philosophy. *For an extended essay on Plato please refer to Gilbert Ryle's entry in volume 6. For a review of recent scholarly work on Socrates, please note the entry on Socrates in this* Supplement.

For general overviews of Plato's thought, see G. Vlastos, ed., *Plato,* 2 vols., (Garden City, NY, 1971), J. Gosling, *Plato* (London, 1973), and R. Kraut, *The Cambridge Companion to Plato* (Cambridge, 1992).

For treatments of some of the central themes of Plato's metaphysics, see N. White, *Plato on Knowledge and Reality* (Indianapolis, 1976), R. Patterson, *Image and Reality in Plato's Metaphysics* (Indianapolis, 1985), T. Penner, *The Ascent From Nominalism* (Dordrecht, 1987), J. Moravesik, *Plato and Platonism* (Oxford, 1992), G. Fine, *On Ideas* (Oxford, 1993), and M. McCabe, *Plato's Individuals* (Princeton, NJ, 1994). His later metaphysical development is treated by K. Sayre, *Plato's Late Ontology* (Princeton, NJ, 1983) and K. Dorter, *Form and Good in Plato's Eleatic Dialogues* (Berkeley, 1994).

For general treatments of Plato's moral philosophy, see T. Irwin, *Plato's Moral Theory* (Oxford, 1977), M. Nussbaum, *The Fragility of Goodness* (Cambridge, 1986),

T. Irwin, *Plato's Ethics* (Oxford, 1995). His political philosophy is surveyed in G. Klosko, *The Development of Plato's Political Theory* (New York, 1986). His attack on the artists is the subject of I. Murdoch, *The Fire and the Sun* (Oxford, 1977). His conception of love is discussed by G. Santas, *Plato and Freud* (Oxford, 1988) and A. Price, *Love and Friendship in Plato and Aristotle* (Oxford, 1989).

The two most influential scholars of recent decades who wrote in English about Plato were G. Vlastos and G. Owen. The former's essays about Plato can be found in *Platonic Studies* (Princeton, NJ, 1981) and *Studies in Greek Philosophy,* vol 2, edited by D. Graham (Princeton, NJ, 1995). The latter's essays on Plato are collected together in *Logic, Science and Dialectic,* edited by M. Nussbaum (Ithaca, NY, 1986).

For treatments of individual dialogues, see:

Laws: R. Stalley, *An Introduction to Plato's Laws* (Oxford, 1983), T. Saunders, *Plato's Penal Code* (Oxford, 1991);

Parmenides: R. Allen, *Plato's Parmenides* (Minneapolis, 1983), Mitchell Miller, *Plato's Parmenides* (Princeton, NJ, 1986), C. Meinwald, *Plato's Parmenides* (Oxford, 1991);

Phaedo: D. Gallop, *Plato, Phaedo* (Oxford, 1975), D. Bostock, *Plato's Phaedo* (Oxford, 1986);

Phaedrus: C. Griswold, *Self-Knowledge in Plato's Phaedrus* (New Haven, 1986), G. Ferrari, *Listening to the Cicadas (Cambridge, 1987);*

Philebus: G. Striker, *Peras und Apeiron* (Göttingen, 1970), G. Gosling, *Plato: Philebus* (Oxford, 1975);

Republic: N. White, *A Companion to Plato's Rebublic* (Indianapolis, 1979), J. Annas, *An Introduction to Plato's Republic* (Oxford, 1981), C. Reeve, *Philosopher-Kings* (Princeton, NJ, 1988);

Symposium: S. Rosen, *Plato's Symposium* (New Haven, 1987);

Timaeus: G. Vlastos, *Plato's Universe* (Seattle, 1975);

Theaetetus: J. McDowell, *Plato: Theaetetus* (Oxford, 1973), D. Bostock, *Plato's Theaetetus* (Oxford, 1988), M. Burnyeat, *The Theaetetus of Plato* (Indianapolis, 1990).

Chronological and stylometric issues are treated by L. Brandwood, *The Chronology of Plato's Dialogues* (Cambridge, 1990) and G. Ledger *Re-counting Plato* (Oxford, 1989).

Different methods of interpreting the dialogues are discussed in E. Tigerstedt, *Interpreting Plato* (Uppsala, 1977), C. Griswold, ed., *Platonic Writings, Platonic Readings* (London, 1988), and J. Klagge and N. Smith, eds., *Methods of Interpreting Plato and his Dialogues* (Oxford, 1992).

RICHARD KRAUT

PLATONISM, MATHEMATICAL. At least with reference to mathematics, "Platonism" in its most general meaning affirms the objective existence of abstract mathematical entities and the objectivity of truth about them (*see* PLATONISM AND THE PLATONIC TRADITION [6]). The terms can be specified in various ways. The most interesting is to understand objectivity in terms of philosophical REALISM [7; S]. This gives rise to a contrast of Platonism and CONSTRUCTIVISM [S], where different degrees of the one and the other influence what mathematics is acceptable. (*See* MATHEMATICS, FOUNDATIONS OF [5].) Michael DUMMETT (1973; [S]) has given a new version of the intuitionist critique of Platonism, with its rejection of the logical law of excluded middle, using meaning-theoretic arguments. Dummett's arguments help to make clear that acceptance of nonconstructive classical mathematics, at least where impredicative set-theoretic devices (*see* MATHEMATICS, FOUNDATIONS OF [5]) are involved, is bound up with realistic conceptions.

We should distinguish, however, between Platonism with regard to mathematical objects (Platonism$_1$), as opposed to regarding them as in some way constructions of our own, and Platonism with regard to truth (Platonism$_2$), which would hold that any properly formulated mathematical question has a true or false answer, whether or not it is possible to discover it. INTUITIONISM [S] rejects both. Some classic Platonist arguments, such as those given in defense of impredicative concept formations by RAMSEY [7], Bernays, and GÖDEL [S], are primarily defenses of Platonism$_1$. Dummett's primary target is Platonism$_2$. Many of Gödel's arguments, particularly in his discussion of the continuum problem (1964), are in defense of Platonism$_2$. Gödel's position has become much better understood in recent years, in particular as more documentation has become available (cf. Gödel, 1995).

It is possible to hold Platonism$_1$ and embrace classical logic and SET THEORY [7; S] without accepting Platonism$_2$. W. V. O. QUINE [7; S] holds such a position in the context of a view of meaning that has much in common with Dummett's but includes a holism that Dummett rejects. Other recent writers (Tait, 1986, and Maddy, 1992) seem also to hold a view of this kind, for quite different reasons (Maddy, 1989 and 1990 defend Platonism$_2$).

Recent research in MATHEMATICAL LOGIC [S] has some bearing on these issues. Platonism$_2$ hangs in the air if we have no hope of finding principles to decide questions in set theory that are undecidable by currently standard axioms. The continuum hypothesis (CH; see CONTINUUM PROBLEM [2]) was shown to be thus undecidable by Gödel and Paul Cohen; Gödel nonetheless hoped that new axioms would be found to decide it. Classical problems of descriptive set theory, also shown undecidable, are decided in a satisfying way by strong axioms of infinity. But these axioms leave CH undecided. It is still not known whether persuasive principles that decide CH will be found.

Other research has shown that much more of ordinary mathematics than had previously been thought can be developed in quite weak theories that can be understood in a non-Platonist way. Although mathematically straightforward statements that can be proved only by impredicative means can be given, they are not easy to come by without using such concepts in their formulation.

"Platonism" is also used in a weaker sense, to contrast with nominalism, that is (in this context) the rejection of abstract objects, at least abstract mathematical objects. Nominalism faces the difficulty that the language of mathematics speaks of objects, and it is hard to imagine how it could be so understood that these objects are not abstract. In this sense Platonism amounts to no more than accepting mathematical language at face value and accepting at least a substantial part of what is affirmed in mathematics as true. This would appear to make it a truism, as some writers (e.g., Tait, 1986) in fact say, but some nominalist strategies work by not accepting mathematical language at face value, and the most influential attempt of recent years (Field, 1980) denies that central parts of mathematics (arithmetic, analysis, set theory) are true and that truth is what the mathematician aims at.

Is there some difficulty with Platonism, even in this weak sense, that motivates the nominalist strategy? Two difficulties have had currency in recent years, both most dramatically presented by Benacerraf. The first (Benacerraf, 1965) is that mathematical objects do not have a well-defined identity, as is shown by the fact that, in foundational work, different constructions of number systems in terms of other objects (e.g., sets or numbers of other, perhaps more basic, systems) "identify" given numbers with different objects, and there seems to be no objective ground on which to choose between them. This fact is a reflection of the general fact that what matters in mathematics is structure, so that, for mathematical purposes, a system of numbers can be any system of objects with relations on them satisfying purely formal conditions. This observation has been used as the basis for programs to eliminate reference to mathematical objects, which are thus in the direction of nominalism even if not strictly nominalistic. But one can also reply that this is simply how mathematical objects are; they can at least metaphorically be described as positions in patterns (Resnik, 1981); the phenomenon pointed to is an instance of Quine's (1968) inscrutability of reference.

The second difficulty is that of giving an adequate epistemology for knowledge of abstract objects, particularly if what is demanded is a naturalistic theory (cf. Benacerraf, 1973). It is not obvious that reference to abstract objects is what is decisive for this difficulty; for example, one might discern it for logical truths that do not involve an abstract ontology or for statements involving some of the devices that have been proposed to eliminate reference to mathematical objects, such as MODALITY [S]. Moreover, it arises with more force (as Benacerraf admits) for stronger mathematical theories, embodying Platonism in the stronger sense considered above.

(SEE ALSO: *Metaphysics* [S])

Bibliography

Benacerraf, P. "What Numbers Could Not Be," *Philosophical Review,* Vol. 74 (1965), 47–73. Rept. in P. Benacerraf and H. Putnam, eds., *Philosophy of Mathematics: Selected Readings,* 2d ed. (Cambridge, 1983).

———. "Mathematical Truth," *Journal of Philosophy,* Vol. 70 (1973), 661–79. Rept. in P. Benacerraf and H. Putnam, eds., *Philosophy of Mathematics: Selected Readings,* 2d ed. (Cambridge, 1983).

———, and H. Putnam, eds. *Philosophy of Mathematics: Selected Readings,* 2d ed. Cambridge, 1983.

Bernays, P. "Sur le platonisme dans les mathématiques," *L'Enseignement mathématique,* Vol. 34 (1935), 52–69. Translated by C. Parsons in P. Benacerraf and H. Putnam, eds., *Philosophy of Mathematics: Selected Readings,* 2d ed. (Cambridge, 1983).

Dummett, M. "The Philosophical Basis of Intuitionistic Logic," in *Truth and Other Enigmas* (London, 1978).

Field, H. *Science without Numbers: A Defense of Nominalism.* Princeton, NJ, 1980.

Gödel, K. "Russell's Mathematical Logic," In P. A. Schilpp, ed., *The Philosophy of Bertrand Russell* (Evanston, IL, 1994). Rept. in *Collected Works,* Vol. 2.

———. "What Is Cantor's Continuum Problem?," rev. ed., in P. Benacerraf and H. Putnam, eds., *Philosophy of Mathematics: Selected Readings* (Englewood Cliffs, NJ, 1964; 2d ed., Cambridge, 1983). Rept. in *Collected Works,* Vol. 2.

———. *Collected Works,* S. Feferman et al., eds. Oxford, Vol. 1, 1986; Vol. 2, 1990; Vol. 3, 1995.

Maddy, P. "The Roots of Contemporary Platonism," *Journal of Symbolic Logic,* Vol. 54 (1989), 1, 121–44.

———. *Realism in Mathematics.* Oxford, 1990.

———. "Indispensability and Practice," *Journal of Philosophy,* Vol. 89 (1992), 275–89.

Quine, W. V. O. *Ontological Relativity and Other Essays.* New York, 1968.

Resnik, M. "Mathematics as a Science of Patterns: Ontology and Reference," *Noûs,* Vol. 15 (1981), 529–50.

Tait, W. W. "Truth and Proof: The Platonism of Mathematics," *Synthese,* Vol. 69 (1986), 341–70.

CHARLES PARSONS

PLURALISM. PRAGMATISM [6; S] and Continental hermeneutics have combined to produce a decided turn toward forms of pluralism in twentieth-century philosophy (Geyer; B. Singer). This has led to the rejection of any one favored epistemological method (e.g., the scientific method, scriptural exegesis, introspection) and any one favored basis for the reconstruction of reality (e.g., mind, matter). Neopragmatists propose to replace the notion of truth with notions such as 'fitting', 'useful', and 'warranted'. Given that what is 'fitting' is relative to the problem being faced and the means at one's disposal, we are left with the possibility of a plurality of ways of conceiving the world and of achieving our aims within it.

Moral pluralism opposes the monistic view that there is any one method of determining what is morally right (e.g., the utilitarian calculus or Kantian universalizability), and it also opposes the relativistic view that all things have value only with respect to a particular cultural context. Pluralists insist that a good life typically involves the desire, not for one, but for many kinds of 'goods', often of incommensurable value; moreover, the realization of certain 'goods' may conflict with and even preclude the realization of others. As such, pluralists believe that moral conflicts are inevitable and that there are not one but many alternative ways of resolving such conflicts (Kekes). The trend toward pluralism has also been influenced by our growing awareness of different cultures with nonequivalent conceptions of reality and 'the good life'.

The modern nation-state has evolved beyond the belief that it manifests the cultural orientation of a single 'race', usually its majority. The reality is that every nation is composed of numerous groups with different cultural orientations. And the state is considered the primary guarantor that minority views will be presented, respected, and given a voice in determining policy (Guttman). The rejection of the view that a Eurocentric male-dominated culture is the norm to be achieved universally has led to the demand that the cultures of non-Europeans, women, and minorities be recognized and granted equal voice (Taylor). In this way pluralism is considered by many to be an essential part of the liberal democratic state, and this has manifested itself in terms of educational policy as the rejection of monoculturalism and the demand for a multicultural orientation.

One form of multiculturalism has focused on the need of suppressed groups to have their cultures recognized. Such a demand for recognition may motivate certain proposals—for example, to replace a Eurocentric focus with an Afrocentric focus or a male-centered orientation with a feminist-centered orientation. Some argue that because of the past harms inflicted upon such groups, ostensibly because they were different, they are justified in embracing those differences in order to cleanse them of the negative valuations imposed by the hegemonic culture. It is right for such groups to adopt a separatist posture if this is the best means of achieving a redefinition of themselves that is positive and self-affirming (Young). Where members of the hegemonic culture have inflicted unjust harms on members of an oppressed group, some argue that the oppressed group has the right to cultural restitution. The domination of culture A by culture B may not be the result of culture A's not offering viable options; rather, it may be the result of unjust injuries and harms visited on culture A by culture B. In such cases groups sharing culture A have a right to 'moral deference', AFFIRMATIVE ACTION [S], and the preservation of their culture (Mosley, Nickel, Thomas).

Many have been concerned that multiculturalism might degenerate into a bedlam of different groups, each espousing its own brand of cultural authenticity. Critics argue that this would amount to merely replacing one culture's hegemony with another culture's hegemony. Multiculturalism in this sense would fail to reflect the pluralist maxim that no orientation is 'fitting' for every situation and that for a given end there may be several equally 'fitting' means (West, Yates).

An alternative form of multiculturalism, closer to pluralism, emphasizes the importance of diversity and cross-cultural communication. On this view the more cultural orientations there are for consideration, the better the likelihood of finding or constructing a 'fitting' adaptation to some current problem (Rorty). For this reason every culture should be allowed the opportunity of articulating itself to the public at large and of thereby influencing the manner in which individuals construct their character.

Pluralism does not end with the insistence on an equal voice for every culture but extends itself to the view that different biological species often have interests that may conflict with the interests of human beings. Some have argued that, just as RACISM [7; S] and SEXISM [S] accord special preference to white males and victimize women and non-Europeans, so SPECIESISM [S] accords special preference to the interests of human beings and unjustly victimizes nonhuman species (P. Singer). The insistence on a plurality of interests and capacities has been extended to include the interests of other animal species, as well as trees, rivers, and ecological systems (Wenz). (SEE ALSO: *Animal Rights and Welfare* [S], *Social and Political Philosophy* [S].)

Bibliography

Geyer, M. "Multiculturalism and the Politics of General Education," *Critical Inquiry,* Vol. 19 (1993), 499–533.

Guttman, A. "The Challenge of Multiculturalism in Political Ethics," *Philosophy and Public Affairs,* Vol. 22, No. 3 (Summer 1993), 171–206.

Kekes, J. *The Morality of Pluralism.* Princeton, NJ, 1993.

Mosley, A. "Preferential Treatment and Social Justice," in C. Peden and Y. Hudson, eds., *Terrorism, Justice, and Social Values* (Lewiston, NY, 1990).

Nickel, J. W. "Ethnocide and Indigenous Peoples," *Journal of Social Philosophy,* Vol. 25 (1994), 84–98.

Rorty, A. "The Advantages of Moral Diversity," *Social Philosophy and Policy,* Vol. 9, No. 2 (Summer 1992), 38–62.

Singer, B. "Pragmatism and Pluralism," *The Monist,* Vol. 75, No. 4 (October 1992), 477–91.

Singer, P. *Animal Liberation.* New York, 1990.

Taylor, C. *Multiculturalism and the Politics of Recognition.* Princeton, NJ, 1992.

Thomas, L. "Moral Deference," *Philosophical Forum,* Vol. 24, Nos. 1–3 (Spring 1992–93), 233–50.

Wenz, P. "Minimal, Moderate, and Extreme Moral Pluralism," *Environmental Ethics,* Vol. 15 (1993), 61–74.

West, C. *Beyond Eurocentricism and Multiculturalism.* Monroe, MA, 1993.

Yates, S. A. "Multiculturalism and Epistemology," *Public Affairs Quarterly,* Vol. 6 (1992), 435–56.

Young, M. Y. *Justice and the Politics of Difference.* Princeton, NJ, 1990.

ALBERT MOSLEY

POETIZING AND THINKING. It is hardly possible to overestimate the influence of poetry on Martin HEIDEGGER'S [3; S] thought. The relation of poetry to thinking also constituted a major theme of his philosophy. Heidegger's kind of "thinking" can be so close to poetry because it is not calculation *(ratio)*. Both poetry and thinking are engaged in a thoughtful questioning *(andenkendes Fragen)*. The thinker utters being; the poet names what is holy. Thus, the poet has access to something that the thinker lacks: names. Heidegger drew many of the "names" that appear in his later thought precisely from poets: RILKE [7], Stefan George, Georg Trakl, and, above all, HÖLDERLIN [4]. As Hans-Georg GADAMER [S] remarked, Hölderlin loosened Heidegger's tongue.

For Heidegger, the very core of language is poetry. Poetry is the source of language and makes it possible. Everyday language is a used-up poem. Thinkers and poets dwell on mountaintops that are distant from each other. Each fulfills his destiny of approaching the same (Being, the godhead, the holy) only by preserving his distinctness. The thinker is at home in the uncanny *(das Unheimische)*; the poet poetizes the homelike. Poetizing and thinking need each other when they touch upon what is ultimate. They then share the same neighborhood *(Nachbarschaft)*, which is saying.

(SEE ALSO: *Being-Process; Beiträge zur Philosophie; Fourfold, the;* and *Language and Heidegger* [S])

Bibliography

Heidegger, M. *Poetry, Language, Thought*, trans. A. Hofstadter. New York, 1971.

———. *Basic Writings*, ed. D. F. Krell. New York, 1977.

JOAN STAMBAUGH

POSSIBLE WORLDS. *See:* MODALITY, PHILOSOPHY AND METAPHYSICS OF [S]

POSTMODERNISM. *See:* MODERNISM AND POSTMODERNISM [S]

POSTSTRUCTURALISM. Poststructuralism is the name bestowed in the English-speaking philosophical and literary communities upon the ideas of several French philosophers whose work arose as a distinctly philosophical response to the privileging of the human sciences that characterized the structuralism of, among others, Claude Lévi-Strauss (anthropology), Louis Althusser (Marxism), Jacques Lacan (psychoanalysis), and Roland Barthes (literature). One can locate the emergence of poststructuralism in Paris in the late 1960s: Michel FOUCAULT [S] published *Les Mots et les choses* in 1966; Jacques DERRIDA [S] published *De la grammatologie, L'écriture et la différence,* and *La voix et le phénomène* in 1967; Gilles Deleuze published *Différence et répétition* in 1968 and *Logique du sens* in 1969.

Like their structuralist predecessors,the poststructuralists draw heavily from the ideas of Karl MARX [S] and Sigmund FREUD [3; S]. But unlike the structuralists, they draw at least as much from the third so-called master of suspicion—Friedrich NIETZSCHE [5; S]. Nietzsche's critique of truth, his emphasis upon interpretation and differential relations of power, and his attention to questions of style in philosophical discourse became central motifs for the poststructuralists as they turned away from the human sciences and toward philosophical-critical analyses of: writing and textuality (Derrida); relations of power, discourse, and the construction of the subject (Foucault); desire and language (Deleuze); questions of aesthetic and political judgment (Jean-François Lyotard); and questions of sexual difference and gender construction (Luce Irigaray, Julia Kristeva, Hélène Cixous).

Most of the poststructuralist philosophers began working in an intellectual environment dominated by Jean-Paul SARTRE'S [7; S] EXISTENTIALISM [3; S], and they all studied and were profoundly influenced by MAURICE MERLEAU-PONTY'S [5; S] thinking on language and corporeality, Martin HEIDEGGER'S [3; S] critique of the history of metaphysics, and Lacanian psychoanalysis. Like existentialism, a philosophical "movement" with which poststructuralism has a complicated relationship, it is impossible to locate any set of themes that unite all poststructuralist philosophers. That said, one can note certain motifs appearing frequently in their works: an attention to questions of language, power, and desire that emphasizes the context in which meaning is produced and makes problematic all universal truth and meaning claims; a suspicion of binary, oppositional thinking, often opting to affirm that which occupies a position of subordination within a differential network; a suspicion of the figure of the humanistic human subject, challenging the assumptions of autonomy and transparent self-consciousness while situating the subject as a complex intersection of discursive, libidinal, and social forces and practices; a resistance to claims of universality and unity, preferring instead to acknowledge difference and fragmentation (*see* DECONSTRUCTION [S]).

The impact of poststructuralism upon philosophy, literary studies, and social theory has been extensive. Twenty-five years ago, Continental philosophy was dominated by issues related to PHENOMENOLOGY [6; S], existentialism, and the works of Edmund HUSSERL [4; S], Heidegger, and Sartre; today the scope of Continental philosophy is focused increasingly on issues that originate in the works of post-1960 French thinkers. Derrida and deconstruction have been major forces in literary theory and criticism since the early 1970s. Since then Derrida has become a major influence in philosophical studies, and, together with Foucault, they have had the widest influence on English-language theorists.

Since 1980 other significant poststructuralist texts have begun attracting philosophical readers: Deleuze's important and innovative readings of major philosophical figures (HUME [4; S], SPINOZA [7; S], LEIBNIZ [4; S], KANT [4; S], Nietzsche, BERGSON [1]) and his analyses, alone and in collaboration with Félix Guattari, of psychoanalysis, cinema, art, literature, and contemporary culture; Lyotard's essays on postmodernism, politics, aesthetics, and art history, plus his important reflections on Kant's *Critique of Judgment;* Luce Irigaray's critical rereadings of Freud, the philosophical canon, and her reflections on language and sexual difference; Hélène Cixous's engendering writing and thinking its relations to the body, particularly the feminine body; Julia Kristeva's thinking on semiotics, abjection, and desire in language (see FEMINISM AND CONTINENTAL PHILOSOPHY [S]). Less influential but nevertheless significant poststructuralist work also is found in Pierre Bourdieu's reflexive sociology; Jean-Luc Nancy and Philippe Lacoue-Labarthe's work on aesthetics, politics, and questions of community; and Jean Baudrillard's sociological reflections on contemporary cultural practices.

Bibliography

Gilles Deleuze's most important works include *Différence et répétition,* Paris, 1968 (translated by P. Patton as *Difference and Repetition,* New York, 1994); *Logique du sens,* Paris, 1968 (translated by M. Lester as *The Logic of Sense,* New York, 1990); and, with Félix Guattari, *L'Anti-Oedipe,* Paris, 1972 (translated by R. Hurley, M. Seem, and H. R. Lane as *Anti-Oedipus,* Minneapolis, 1983); *Mille plateaux,* Paris, 1980 (translated by B. Massumi as *A Thousand Plateaus,* Minneapolis, 1987); and *Qu'est-ce que la philosophie?* Paris, 1991 (translated by H. Tomlinson and G. Burchell as *What Is Philosophy?* New York, 1994). Jean-François Lyotard's best-known works include *La condition postmoderne,* Paris, 1979 (translated by G. Bennington and B. Massumi as *The Postmodern Condition,* Minneapolis, 1983) and *Le différend,* Paris, 1983 (translated by G. Van Den Abbeele as *The Differend: Phrases in Dispute,* Minneapolis, 1988).

Among the better secondary works are G. Bennington, *Lyotard: Writing the Event,* Manchester, 1988; R. Bogue, *Deleuze and Guattari,* New York, 1989; V. Descombes, *Le Même et l'autre: Quarante-cinq ans de philosophie française (1933–1978),* Paris, 1979 (translated by L. Scott-Fox and J. M. Harding as *Modern French Philosophy,* Cambridge, 1980); P. Dews, *Logics of Disintegration: Post-Structuralist Thought and the Claims of Critical Theory,* London, 1987; M. Frank, *Was ist Neostrukturalismus?* Frankfurt, 1983 (translated by S. Wilke and R. Gray as *What Is Neostructuralism?* Minneapolis, 1989); and A. Schrift, *Nietzsche's French Legacy: A Genealogy of Poststructuralism,* New York, 1995.

ALAN D. SCHRIFT

PRACTICAL REASON APPROACHES.

Practical-reasoning theory is a kind of metaethical view—alongside NONCOGNITIVISM [S] and other cognitivisms such as NATURALISM [5; S] and rational intuitionism—that aims to understand ethics as rooted in practical reason.

Tradition divides the faculty of REASON [7] into two parts: theoretical and practical. Theoretical reason concerns what we should believe, practical reason what we should do. Beliefs aim to represent reality and are mistaken or in error when they do not. Theoretical reason's task, therefore, is to discover what is true of the independent order of fact to which belief is answerable. But what about practical reason? What could make it the case that an action is something a person ought to do?

Plainly, ethical convictions also aim at a kind of objectivity. If Jones thinks he should devote all his resources to conspicuous consumption but Smith thinks that he (Jones) should donate some to help the poor, their convictions conflict. Only one, at most, can be true.

Practical-reasoning theories aim to explain the objective purport of ethical conviction, but in a way that respects a fundamental distinction between theoretical and practical reason. Like noncognitivism, these theories sharply distinguish between ethics and those theoretical disciplines that aim to represent some independent reality, whether the order of nature or some supersensible metaphysical realm. They therefore reject both naturalism and rational intuitionism. But they also deny noncognitivism, since they hold that ethical propositions can be true or false.

According to practical-reasoning theories, objectivity consists not in accurate representation of an independent order, but in demands that are universally imposed within an agent's own practical reasoning. What marks ethics off from science is its intrinsically practical character, its hold on us as agents. It is because there is such a thing as practical reason, a form rational agents' deliberations must take, that there is such a thing as ethics.

But what form does rational deliberation take? Uncontroversially, practical reasoning includes reasoning from ends to means. The interesting debates concern what else it involves, if anything, and how instrumental reasoning is itself to be understood. Humeans maintain that means–end reasoning exhausts practical reason and that instrumental reason can be reduced to the use of theoretical reason in discovering means to ends. They tend not to be practical-reasoning theorists, however, since they argue that ethics fundamentally concerns what engages human sympathy or moral sentiment rather than what it is rational for a person to do. By contrast, practical-reasoning theorists deny that practical reason can be reduced to theoretical reason. As Christine Korsgaard has argued, even instrumental practical reason directs an agent who has already used theoretical reason in determining that *B* is the only means to his end *A* to undertake *B* (or to give up A as an end). In this way instrumental practical reasoning parallels the structure of *modus ponens* in theoretical reasoning (the move from "p" and "if p, then q" to "q").

Pursuing the analogy with theoretical reasoning (while insisting on irreducibility) further suggests that instrumental reasoning cannot exhaust practical reason. When we reason from our beliefs—for example, with *modus ponens*—we reason from their contents, not from the fact of our believing them. We reason from p and if p, then q, not from the facts that we believe that p and that we believe that if p, then q. Similarly, when we adopt an end, we do not simply select it by sheer fiat. Rather, we choose it as something (we think) there is some reason to do. Thus, when we reason from our ends, we do not reason from the fact that they are our ends but from our commitments to them as things it makes sense to do. That is why instrumental RATIONALITY [S] is so uncontroversial. As R. M. HARE [S] argued, it is questionable at best that it follows from the facts that a person's end is to kill someone in the most grisly possible way and that using a cleaver is such a way that the person ought, or has some normative reason, to use a cleaver. What is uncontroversial is simply that the support of reasons transfers from end to means, other things being equal, and from not taking the (only available) means to renouncing the end, other things being equal. It follows only that a person ought to use a cleaver or give up my end.

On grounds such as these, practical-reasoning theorists tend to hold that instrumental rationality cannot exhaust practical reason. But how are we to deliberate about ends? What makes something a reason for adopting an end? Since they hold that reasons for action are necessarily connected to the agent's deliberative perspective, practical-reasoning theorists generally adopt what Korsgaard has called the internalism requirement, according to which a reason must be something the agent could, in principle, be moved by in deliberation and act on. This makes it a necessary condition of something's being a reason for an agent that she would be moved by it insofar as she deliberated rationally.

But what then is rational deliberation? Practical-reason theorists are loath to derive a deliberative ideal by independently specifying paradigm reasons for acting and holding that deliberation is rational when it responds appropriately to them. That would theorize practical reason too much on the model of theoretical reason. Rather, they maintain that rational deliberation must be understood formally, so that reason for acting is a status consideration inherit when it is such that it would move an agent who formed her will in accordance with that deliberative ideal.

The aspects that have been considered so far are relatively common among practical-reasoning theories, although not, perhaps, universal. Within these theories, however, there is a major division between neo-Hobbesians and neo-Kantians. Although nothing on the surface of practical-reasoning theory might suggest this result, it is notable that both camps attempt to vindicate the commonsense idea that moral obligations are supremely authoritative. Both argue that (at least some central) moral demands are demands of practical reason.

NEO-HOBBESIANISM

Recent versions of this view have their roots in ideas advanced by Kurt Baier in the late 1950s and attempt to address a significant problem faced by Baier's early view. Baier argued that reasons for acting must ultimately connect with the agent's interests. This does not reduce all practical reasoning to prudential reasoning, since other forms may advance agents' interests also. Specifically, Baier argued that morality may be viewed as a system of practical reasoning that is in the interest of everyone alike. Since it is mutually advantageous for everyone to regard moral obligations as supremely authoritative, Baier concluded that they actually do create overriding reasons for acting.

David Gauthier objected to Baier's theory that, while it is in the interest of each that all regard interest-trumping moral reasons as supreme, it is unclear how this can show that an individual agent should so regard them, since it will still most advance her interest to act prudentially when morality conflicts with self-interest. Why, then, might it not be true that instrumental and prudential reasoning exhaust practical reason, even if a person should hope to live in a world in which other people view things differently and (mistakenly) treat moral reasons as authoritative?

Gauthier is himself responsible for the major recent neo-Hobbesian practical-reasoning theory. Like Baier, Gauthier begins from the premise that practical reasoning must work to advance the agent's interests, although here his account is more nearly "internalist," since he understands a person's interests to consist in what she would herself prefer were she to be fully informed. Also like Baier, Gauthier argues that the fact that mutual advantage may require individuals to constrain their pursuit of self-interest can be used to show that practical reason counsels this constraint. However, it is not enough that it be true that everyone would do better if everyone so constrained their prudential reasoning. The crucial point for Gauthier is that individuals can do better if they constrain self-interest by a willingness to abide by mutually advantageous agreements.

Two agents who appear to each other to be unconstrained pursuers of self-interest simply cannot make agreements, however mutually advantageous the agreements might be, if these agreements would require the agents to act contrary to their own interests. In what have come to be known as PRISONER'S DILEMMA [S] situations, therefore, mutually advantageous rational agreement between such persons is impossible. If each believes the other will rationally defect from the agreement on the condition that doing so is in her interest, then neither can rationally make the agreement.

Personal advantage therefore counsels presenting oneself to others as someone who is not an unconstrained maximizer of self-interest. Of course, it is possible, theoretically, for someone to do this while still deliberating as an unconstrained prudential reasoner. But it may not be practically possible, Gauthier argues, at least not for normal human beings. Human motivation may be sufficiently translucent—through involuntary response, for example—so that the least costly way of appearing to others as someone who can be relied upon to keep mutually advantageous, interest-constraining agreements is actually to be such a person. If that is so, then instrumental and prudential reason will not support themselves as principles to guide rational deliberation. On the contrary, they will recommend that agents deliberate in terms of an alternative conception of practical reason that counsels keeping mutually advantageous agreements, even when this is contrary to self-interest.

As a practical-reasoning theorist, Gauthier believes that reasons for acting cannot be understood except in relation to what should guide a rational agent in deliberation. And he believes that a rational agent is someone whose dispositions of choice and deliberation serve her best and most advance her interest. But just as indirect forms of ethical CONSEQUENTIALISM [S], such as character- and rule-consequentialism, face the objection that they are unstable and threaten to collapse either into act-consequentialism or deontology, Gauthier's indirect consequentialist theory of rationality may face the same objection. What motivates the move away from unconstrained prudence, on the grounds that it cannot support itself in the agent's practical thinking, is a view about the role a principle of rational conduct must be able to play in the deliberations of an autonomous rational agent that may be more Kantian than Hobbesian in inspiration.

NEO-KANTIANISM

This contemporary tradition may be held to date from Thomas Nagel's *The Possibility of Altruism* (1970) and John RAWLS's [S] reinvigoration of Kantian moral and political philosophy in *A Theory of Justice* (1971) and "Kantian Constructivism in Moral Theory" (1980). Nagel's book was read as having both a modest and a more ambitious agenda. His more modest goal, suggested by his title, was to show how such "objective" (or, as he later termed them, "agent-neutral") considerations as "that acting would be relative *someone's* pain" can be genuine reasons for acting. A consideration can be rationally motivating, he argued, even if the agent lacks any relevant desire for acting on it other than one that is motivated by the awareness of that very consideration. A person may be moved, for instance, by considering long-term interests. And if motivation at a distance is possible with prudence, it can happen with altruism as well. Altruistic and other agent-neutral considerations can be rationally motivating.

Nagel's more ambitious agenda was to argue that practical reasoning is subject to a formal constraint that effectively requires that any genuine reason for acting be agent neutral. Stressing the "motivational content" of genuine practical judgments, Nagel argued that avoiding a kind of solipsism is possible only if an agent is able to make the same practical judgment of himself from an impersonal standpoint as he does from an egocentric point of view. Since accepting practical judgments from one's own point of view normally motivates, Nagel maintained, making the same judgment of oneself from an impersonal standpoint should normally motivate also. But this will be so only if the reasons for acting that ground practical judgments are agent neutral. So it is a necessary condition for avoiding practical solipsism that agents take considerations such as that something will advance their own ends or interests as reasons only if they regard them as instantiating more general, agent-neutral reasons, such as that acting will advance someone's ends or interests. Nagel later retreated from this strong claim in a direction that is arguably even more Kantian. Autonomous agency, he later argued, involves an agent's acting on reasons she can endorse from an objective standpoint, and such a set of reasons will include both agent-relative and agent-neutral ones.

Neo-Kantian practical-reasoning theories have been put forward by a number of philosophers, including Alan Gewirth, Stephen Darwall, and Christine Korsgaard. Korsgaard's sympathetic reconstruction of KANT's [4] own arguments in a series of papers has been especially influential. Common to all these neo-Kantian approaches has been the idea that the practical reasoning of an autonomous agent has a formal structure, with its own internal standards and constraints, and that these provide the fundamental truth and objectivity conditions for ethical thought and discourse. Thus, Gewirth maintains that fundamental moral principles are derivable from propositions to which a rational agent is committed from within the deliberative standpoint in acting. And Korsgaard argues that even instrumental theorists are committed to the "hypothetical imperative" as a practical norm. Since, however, we regard ourselves to be free as agents to adopt and renounce ends, practical reason cannot possibly be exhausted by any mere consistency constraint, such as the hypothetical imperative. It follows, the neo-Kantians argue, that practical reason requires norms to regulate the choice of ends no less than to guide the choice of means. In choosing ends for reasons we commit ourselves implicitly to principles of choice as valid for all. But such a commitment is not, they claim, a hypothesis about some independently existing order of normative fact to which we might have cognitive access. That, after all, is precisely the difference between theoretical and practical reason. So the standards to which deliberation is subject must ultimately be based on some formal principle of impartial endorsement that is internal to free practical reasoning itself. And this will be so, they conclude, only if practical reasoning is regulated by some such principle as the categorical imperative, which requires that one act only on principles that one can will to regulate the deliberation and choices of all. If moral demands are ultimately grounded in the categorical imperative also, it will follow that moral demands are demands of practical reason. (SEE ALSO: *Ethical Theory* [S])

Bibliography

Baier, K. *The Moral Point of View.* Ithaca, NY, 1958.

Darwall, S. *Impartial Reason.* Ithaca, NY, 1983.

Falk, W. D. *Ought, Reasons, and Morality.* Ithaca, NY, 1986.

Gauthier, D. "Morality and Advantage," *Philosophical Review,* Vol. 76 (1967), 460–75.

———. *Morals by Agreement.* Oxford, 1986.

Gewirth, A. *Reasons and Morality.* Chicago, 1978.

Korsgaard, C. "The Source of Normativity," in G. Peterson, ed., *The Tanner Lectures on Human Values.* Salt Lake City, 1994.

Nagel, T. *The Possibility of Altruism.* Oxford, 1970.

———. *The View from Nowhere.* New York, 1986.

Rawls, J. *A Theory of Justice.* Cambridge, MA, 1971.

———. "Kantian Constructivism in Moral Theory," *Journal of Philosophy,* Vol. 77 (1980), 515–72.

STEPHEN DARWALL

PRAGMATICS. Pragmatics was defined by Morris (1938) as the branch of semiotics which studies the relation of signs to interpreters, in contrast with SEMANTICS [7; S], which studies the relation of signs to designata. In practice, it has often been treated as a repository for any aspect of utterance meaning beyond the scope of existing semantic machinery, as in the slogan 'Pragmatics=meaning minus truth conditions' (Gazdar, 1979). There has been some doubt about whether it is a homogeneous domain (Searle, Kiefer, & Bierwisch, 1980).

A more positive view emerges from the work of GRICE [S], whose *William James Lectures* (1967) are fundamental. Grice showed that many aspects of utterance meaning traditionally regarded as conventional, or semantic, could be more explanatorily treated as conversational, or pragmatic. For Gricean pragmatists, the crucial feature of pragmatic interpretation is its inferential nature: the hearer is seen as constructing and evaluating a hypothesis about the communicator's intentions, based, on the one hand, on the meaning of the sentence uttered, and on the other, on contextual information and general communicative principles that speakers are normally expected to observe. (For definition and surveys see Levinson, 1983.)

THE SEMANTICS-PRAGMATICS DISTINCTION

In early work, the semantics–pragmatics distinction was often seen as coextensive with the distinction between truth-conditional and non-truth-conditional meaning (Gazdar, 1979). On this approach, pragmatics would deal with a range of disparate phenomena, including (a) Gricean conversational inference, (b) the inferential recognition of illocutionary-force, and (c) the conventional meanings of illocutionary-force indicators and other non-truth-conditional expressions such as 'but', 'please', 'unfortunately' (Recanati, 1987). From the cognitive point of view, these phenomena have little in common.

Within the cognitive science literature in particular, the semantics–pragmatics distinction is now more generally seen as coextensive with the distinction between decoding and inference (or conventional and conversational meaning). On this approach, all conventional meaning, both truth-conditional and non-truth-conditional, is left to linguistic semantics, and the aim of pragmatic theory is to explain how the gap between sentence meaning and utterance interpretation is inferentially bridged. A pragmatic theory of this type is developed in Sperber and Wilson (1986).

IMPLICATURE

Grice's distinction between saying and implicating cross-cuts the semantics–pragmatics distinction as defined above. For Grice, 'what is said' corresponds to the truth-conditional content of an utterance, and 'what is implicated' is everything communicated that is not part of what is said. Grice saw the truth-conditional content of an utterance as determined partly by the conventional (semantic) meaning of the sentence uttered, and partly by contextual (pragmatic) factors governing disambiguation and REFERENCE [S] assignment. He saw conventional (semantic) implicatures as determined by the meaning of discourse connectives such as 'but', 'moreover' and 'so', and analyzed them as signaling the performance of higher-order speech acts such as contrasting, adding and explaining (Grice, 1989). An alternative analysis is developed in Blakemore (1987).

Among nonconventional (pragmatic) implicatures, the best known are the conversational ones: these are beliefs that have to be attributed to the speaker in order to preserve the assumption that she was obeying the 'cooperative principle' (with associated maxims of truthfulness, informativeness, relevance, and clarity), in saying what she said. In Grice's framework, generalized conversational implicatures are 'normally' carried by use of a certain expression, and are easily confused with conventional lexical meaning (Grice, 1989). In Grice's view, many earlier philosophical analyses were guilty of such confusion.

Grice's account of conversational implicatures has been questioned on several grounds:

(1) The status and content of the cooperative principle and maxims have been debated, and attempts to reduce the maxims or provide alternative sources for implicatures have been undertaken (Davis, 1991; Horn, 1984; Levinson, 1987; Sperber & Wilson, 1986).

(2) Grice claimed that deliberate, blatant maxim-violation could result in implicatures, in the case of METAPHOR [5; S] and irony in particular. This claim has been challenged, and alternative accounts of metaphor and irony developed, in which no maxim-violation takes place (Blakemore, 1992; Hugly & Sayward, 1979; Sperber & Wilson, 1986).

(3) Pragmatic principles have been found to make a substantial contribution to explicit communication, not only in disambiguation and reference assignment, but in enriching the linguistically encoded meaning in various ways. This raises the question of where the borderline between explicit and implicit communication should be drawn (Sperber & Wilson, 1986, 1995). It has even been argued that many of Grice's best-known cases of generalized conversational implicature might be better analyzed as pragmatically determined aspects of what is said (Carston, 1988; Recanati, 1989).

(4) The idea that the context for utterance interpretation is determined in advance of the utterance has been questioned, and the identification of an appropriate set of contextual assumptions is now seen as an integral part of the utterance-interpretation process (Blakemore, 1992; Sperber & Wilson, 1986).

PROSPECTS

Within the COGNITIVE SCIENCE [S] literature, several approaches to pragmatics are currently being pursued. There are computational attempts to implement the Gricean program via rules for the recognition of coherence relations among discourse segments (Asher & Lascarides, 1995; Hobbs, 1985). Relations between the Gricean program and speech-act theory are being reassessed (Tsohatzidis, 1994). The cognitive foundations of pragmatics and the relations of pragmatics to neighboring disciplines are still being explored (Sperber & Wilson, 1995; Sperber, 1994). Despite this diversity of approaches, pragmatics now seems to be established as a relatively homogenous domain.

(SEE ALSO: *Philosophy of Language* [S])

Bibliography

Asher, N., and A. Lascarides. "Lexical Disambiguation in a Discourse Context," *Journal of Semantics,* Vol. 12 (1995), 69–108.

Blakemore, D. *Semantic Constraints on Relevance.* Oxford, 1987.

———. *Understanding Utterances.* Oxford, 1992.

Carston, R. "Explicature, Implicature and Truth-Theoretic Semantics," in R. Kempson, ed., *Mental Representation: The Interface Between Language and Reality* (Cambridge, 1988).

Davis, S., ed. *Pragmatics: A Reader.* Oxford, 1991.

Gazdar, G. *Pragmatics: Implicature, Presupposition and Logical Form.* New York, 1979.

Grice, H. P. "Logic and Conversation," *William James Lectures* (Cambridge, MA, 1967).

———. *Studies in the Way of Words.* Cambridge, MA, 1989.

Hobbs, J. "On the Coherence and Structure of Discourse," Center for the Study of Language and Information (October, 1985).

Horn, L. "A New Taxonomy for Pragmatic Inference: Q-based and R-based Implicature," in D. Schiffrin, ed., *Meaning, Form and Use in Context* (Washington, DC, 1984).

Hugly, P., and C. Sayward. "A Problem About Conversational Implicature," *Linguistics and Philosophy,* Vol. 3 (1979), 19–25.

Levinson, S. *Pragmatics.* Cambridge, 1983.

———. "Minimization and Conversational Inference," in J. Verschueren and M. Bertuccelli-Papi, eds., *The Pragmatic Perspective* (Amsterdam, 1987).

Morris, C. "Foundations of the Theory of Signs," in O. Neurath, R. Carnap, and C. Morris, eds., *International Encyclopedia of Unified Science* (Chicago, 1938).

Recanati, F. *Meaning and Force.* Cambridge, 1987.

———. "The Pragmatics of What Is Said," *Mind and Language,* Vol. 4 (1989), 295–329.

Searle, J., F. Kiefer, and M. Bierwisch, eds. *Speech-Act Theory and Pragmatics.* Dordrecht, 1980.

Sperber, D. "Understanding Verbal Understanding," in J. Khalfa, ed., *What Is Intelligence?* (Cambridge, 1994).

Sperber, D., and D. Wilson. *Relevance: Communication and Cognition.* Oxford, 1986.

———. "Postface" to the second edition of *Relevance.* Oxford, 1995.

Tsohatzidis, S., ed. *Foundations of Speech-Act Theory: Philosophical and Linguistic Perspectives.* London, 1994.

DEIRDRE WILSON

PRAGMATISM. Not unexpectedly, given that PRAGMATISM [6] is not a doctrine but a method (as Charles PEIRCE [6; S] put it), the tradition of classical pragmatism is formidably diverse. Even the method—the pragmatic maxim—is differently interpreted by different pragmatists; and this diversity is compounded by the different doctrines and interests of the various pragmatists. But there is a pattern discernible within the diversity: a shift from Peirce's reformist, scientific philosophy, anchored by his realism about natural kinds and laws and about the objects of perception, through William JAMES's [4; S] more nominalist pragmatism, his insistence that "the trail of the human serpent is over everything" (1907, p. 37), through John DEWEY's [3; S] proposal that the concept of warranted assertibility replace the concept of truth, to the radicalism of F. C. S. SCHILLER's [7] avowedly Protagorean relativization of truth to human interests.

Contemporary pragmatisms are no less diverse, but the spectrum has shifted to the left. The more conservative neopragmatists are as akin to James as to Peirce, and the most radical go beyond Schiller's relativism to an anti-philosophical, sometimes anti-scientific, even anti-intellectual, stance—a stance so much at odds with the aspirations of the founders of pragmatism as to put one in mind of Peirce's complaints about writers who persisted in "twisting [the pragmatists'] purpose and purport all awry" (*Collected Papers,* 5.464).

Nicholas Rescher describes his philosophy as pragmatic idealism: IDEALISM [4], because it holds that "reality . . . as humans deal with it is *our* reality—our thought-world as we conceive and model it" (1994, p. 377); pragmatic, because it holds that, though our picture of reality is a mental construction, it is not a free construction but is objectively constrained by success or failure in practice, in prediction and attainment of purpose.

In some ways—not least in philosophizing unapologetically in the grand systematic manner—Rescher is much like Peirce; indeed, his conception of the interlocking cognitive, evaluative, and practical aspects of RATIONALITY [S] takes him further than Peirce into some of the territory of value theory. In other ways Rescher's pragmatism is more reminiscent of James: *inter alia,* for its stress on practical consequences and on a pluralism of perspectival truth-claims. So, too, is his idealism. *Qua* pragmatist Peirce denies the intelligibility of the in-principle-incognizable; *qua* "objective idealist" he maintains that "matter is just effete mind" (*Collected Papers,* 6.25). Rescher's idealism sounds more like the Jamesian serpent—or Deweyan interactionism.

In repudiating metaphysical REALISM [7; S] and endorsing internal realism, Hilary PUTNAM [S] evinced some sympathy with Peircean conceptions of truth and reality. But his conceptual relativism—"Our language cannot be divided into two parts, a part that describes the world 'as it is anyway' and a part that describes our conceptual contribution" (1992, p. 123)—sounded more like James. However, his argument against the irrealism of Nelson GOODMAN [3; S] (himself classifiable as a left-wing Jamesian of the boldest nominalist stripe) stressed the distinction between wholly conventional names such as "Sirius" and only partially conventional general terms such as "star." Putnam thus recalled Peirce's realism of natural kinds, and perhaps divided our language after all. It is not surprising, then, to find that most recently, in his Dewey lectures, he tends to a more realist stance.

Sympathetic in the 1950s and 1960s to the positivists' aspiration to a scientific single theory that explains everything" (Putnam, 1992, p. 2), Putnam is since then inclined to a pluralistic, problem-centered approach to philosophy. Here, as in his defense of DEMOCRACY [2] as a precondition for the application of intelligence to the solution of social problems, he acknowledges Dewey.

A year before the publication of W. V. O. QUINE's [7; S] "Two Dogmas," Morton G. White had invoked Dewey in describing the analytic–synthetic distinction as "an untenable dualism." Rejecting that distinction, adopting a holism of verification, insisting on the underdetermination of theory by data, Quine describes himself as going beyond C. I. LEWIS's [4] pragmatic a priori to a "more thorough pragmatism" that emphasizes pragmatic considerations in theory-choice generally. "Pragmatic" here suggests the relatively unconstrained rather than, as in Rescher, a kind of constraint. Quine refers approvingly to Schiller's view of truth as man-made as one of pragmatism's main contributions to EMPIRICISM [2]. But he hopes to avoid Schiller's relativism by means of a NATURALISM [5] that views philosophy as internal to science. This differs significantly from Peirce's and Dewey's aspiration to make philosophy scientific by applying the method of science to philosophical questions.

As another of pragmatism's main contributions Quine mentions Peirce's and Dewey's connecting belief and meaning to behavior. But Quine's BEHAVIORISM [1] is more stringent, in part because of the influence of B. F. Skinner, and in part because Quine's extensionalism leaves him uneasy, as Peirce was not, with any irreducibly dispositional talk.

As Putnam's allusions to the existentialist character of James's ethics indicate, some hope a neopragmatism might heal the analytic–Continental rift. One example is Karl-Otto Apel's grafting of pragmatic elements from Peirce and Jürgen HABERMAS [S] onto Alfred TARSKI's [8] semantic conception of truth. Another is Joseph Margolis's attempt, emphasizing both the biological roots and the "deep historicity" of human injury, and proposing a reconciliation of a modest realism with a weak relativism, to marry themes from Peirce with themes from Martin HEIDEGGER [3; S].

Richard Rorty describes himself as accommodating themes from Dewey with themes from Heidegger. Maintaining that "revolutionary movements within an intellectual discipline require a revisionist history of that discipline" (1983, p. xvii), Rorty dismisses Peirce as having merely given pragmatism its name. And he urges in the name of pragmatism that the project of a philosophical theory of knowledge should be abandoned; that science is exemplary only as a model of human solidarity; that philosophy is more akin to literature than to science; that it should be in the service of democratic politics; that truth is "not the kind of thing one should expect to have a philosophically interesting theory about" (1983, p. xiv) and that to call a statement true is just to give it "a rhetorical pat on the back" (1983, p. xvii); that pragmatism is antirepresentationalism.

There is some affinity between Rorty and Schiller. But Peirce, who was a pioneer of the theory of signs, of representation, and who desired "to rescue the good ship Philosophy for the service of Science from the hands of the lawless rovers of the sea of literature" (*Collected Papers,* 5.449), would disagree with Rorty's pragmatism in every particular. So too, except perhaps for his description of the best ethical writing as akin to "novels and dramas of the deeper sort" (1891, p. 316), would James. And so, most to the point, would Dewey, who hoped to renew the philosophical theory of knowledge by making it more scientific, and whose political philosophy is infused by the hope that the application of scientific methods would enable intelligent social reform, and by the conviction that a free society is a prerequisite of a flourishing science.

Bibliography

Apel, K.-O. "C. S. Peirce and the Post-Tarskian Problem of an Adequate Explication of the Meaning of Truth: Towards a Transcendental-Pragmatic Theory of Truth," in E. Freeman, ed., *The Relevance of Charles Peirce* (La Salle, IL, 1983).

Bernstein, R. "The Resurgence of Pragmatism," *Social Research,* Vol. 59 (1992), 813–40.

Goodman, N. *Ways of Worldmaking.* Hassocks, Sussex, 1978.

James, W. *Pragmatism,* edited by F. Burkhardt and F. Bowers. Cambridge, MA, and London, 1975.

———. "The Moral Philosopher and the Moral Life," *International Journal of Ethics,* Vol. 1 (1891); in G. Bird, ed., *William James: Selected Writings* (1994).

Margolis, J. *Pragmatism without Foundations.* Oxford, 1986.

Peirce, C. S. *Collected Papers,* edited by C. Hawthorne, P. Weiss, and A. Burks. Cambridge, MA, 1931–1958.

Putnam, H. *Renewing Philosophy.* Cambridge, MA, 1992.

———. *Words and Life.* Cambridge, MA, 1994. Sec 3, "The Inheritance of Pragmatism."

———. "Sense, Nonsense and the Senses: An Inquiry into the Powers of the Human Mind," *Journal of Philosophy,* Vol. XC1.9 (1994), 447–517.

Quine, W. V. O. "Two Dogmas of Empiricism," *Philosophical Review,* Vol. 60 (1951), 20–43.

———. "The Pragmatists' Place in Empiricism," in R. J. Mulvaney and P. M. Zeltner, eds., *Pragmatism: Its Sources and Prospects* (Columbia, SC, 1981).

Rescher, N. *A System of Pragmatic Idealism,* 3 vols. Princeton, NJ, 1992–94.

Rescher, N., et al. *Philosophy and Phenomenological Research,* Vol. 54 (1994), 377–457.

Rorty, R. *The Consequences of Pragmatism.* Hassocks, Sussex, 1983.

Thayer, H. S. *Meaning and Action: A Critical History of Pragmatism.* Indianapolis, 1968.

White, M. G. "The Analytic and the Synthetic: An Untenable Dualism," in Sidney Hook, ed., *John Dewey, Philosopher of Science and Freedom* (New York, 1950).

SUSAN HAACK

PRAGMATIST EPISTEMOLOGY. William JAMES's [4; S] observation that "when . . . we give up the doctrine of objective certitude, we do not thereby give up the quest or hope of truth itself" (1956, p. 17) succinctly expresses one important epistemological theme of traditional pragmatism: accommodation of a thoroughgoing fallibilism with a modest optimism about the possibility of successful truth seeking. Also characteristic of that tradition is its NATURALISM [5; S], its acknowledgment of the biological, and the social as well as the logical elements in the theory of knowledge, and its respect for science as, in Charles PEIRCE's [6; S] words, "the epitome of man's intellectual development" (*Collected Papers,* 7.49). Since 1968 these ideas have been variously worked out by some who are fully aware of their roots in pragmatism and have also entered the thinking of many who are not. More surprising, some self-styled neopragmatists defend epistemological positions (or anti-epistemological positions) quite unlike these classically pragmatist themes.

Both fallibilism and naturalism are prominent themes in W. V. O. QUINE's [7; S] epistemology, themes of which he acknowledges the pragmatist ancestry; his fallibilism, furthermore, like Peirce's, extends to mathematics and logic, and his naturalism, like Peirce's, has an evolutionary character. And he shares the pragmatists' regard for science. However, he seems drawn beyond a view of epistemology as resting in part on empirical assumptions about human cognitive capacities to conceiving of it as internal to the sciences of cognition; and thence, under pressure of the implausibility of supposing that psychology or biology could answer the questions about evidence, justification, and so forth, with which epistemology has traditionally been concerned, he seems drawn to a revolutionary scientism that would abandon the traditional questions in favor of questions the sciences can be expected to answer. Unlike his fallibilism and his modest, reformist naturalism, neither his scientism nor his revolutionary displacement of epistemology falls within the tradition of pragmatism.

Nicholas Rescher's approach, from its insistence that we humans "cannot function, let alone thrive, without knowledge of what goes on around us" (1994, p. 380) to its stress on the provisional, tentative character of all our estimates of truth, is unambivalently within the pragmatist tradition. But Rescher takes issue with Peirce's definition of truth, and therefore conceives of progress in terms of improvement over earlier stages rather than closeness to a supposed final stage.

Focusing on criteria of evidence and justification rather than on guidelines for the conduct of inquiry, Susan Haack adapts from the pragmatist tradition: her fallibilism, expressed in the thesis that justification comes in degrees; her weak, reformist naturalism, expressed in the thesis that our criteria of evidence have built into them empirical presuppositions about human cognitive capacities; her account of perception; and her strategy for the metajustification of criteria of justification.

In stark contrast to Rescher or Haack, Richard Rorty urges in the name of pragmatism that the philosophical theory of knowledge is misconceived; and, in contrast to Quine, that epistemology should be, not replaced by the psychology of cognition, but simply abandoned. Rorty likens his repudiation of epistemology to DEWEY's [3; S] critique of the "spectator theory." What Dewey intended, however, was to reform epistemology, to replace the quest for certain knowledge of eternal, unchanging objects with a realistic account of fallible, experimental, empirical inquiry. Rorty's revolutionary attitude derives from his conception of justification as a matter exclusively of our practices of defending and criticizing beliefs, not grounded in any connection of evidence and truth. This "conversationalist" conception of justification is motivated by his rejection of any conception of truth as meaning more than "what you can defend against all comers."

Often accused of relativism, Rorty denies the charge. He escapes it, however, only by shifting from contextualism ("*A* is justified in believing that *p* iff (if and only if) he can defend *p* by the standards of *his* community") to tribalism (" . . . iff he can defend *p* by the standards of *our* community" [1979, p. 308]). But tribalism is arbitrary if our practices of criticizing and defending beliefs are, as Rorty holds, not grounded in any connection of evidence and truth.

In not-so-stark contrast to Rorty, Stephen Stich urges in the name of pragmatism that it is mere epistemic chauvinism to care whether one's beliefs are true, and that justified beliefs are those that conduce to whatever the subject values. True, Stich cheerfully embraces relativism (and rejects tribalism since he thinks our epistemic practices too preoccupied with truth); and he looks to the sciences of cognition to help us "improve" our cognitive processing so as better to achieve what we really value. But, as more overtly in Rorty, the effect is profoundly anti-epistemological and "pragmatist" in quite another sense than the traditional one.

(SEE ALSO: *Epistemology* [S])

Bibliography

Haack, S. *Evidence and Inquiry*. Oxford, 1993.

James, W. *The Will to Believe* [1897]. New York, 1956.

Peirce, C. S. *Collected Papers,* edited by C. Hawthorne, P. Weiss, and A. Burks. Cambridge, MA, 1931–1958.

Quine, W. V. O. "Epistemology Naturalized," in *Ontological Relativity and Other Essays* (New York, 1967).

———. "Natural Kinds," in *Ontological Relativity and Other Essays* (New York, 1969).

———. "The Pragmatists' Place in Empiricism," in R. J. Mulvaney and P. M. Zeltner, eds., *Pragmatism: Its Sources and Prospects* (Columbia, SC, 1981), 21–40.

Rescher, N. *A System of Pragmatic Idealism,* Vol. 1, *Human Knowledge in Idealistic Perspective* (Princeton, NJ, 1992).

———. "Précis of *A System of Pragmatic Idealism,*" *Philosophy and Phenomenological Research,* Vol. 54, (1994) 377–90.

Rorty, R. *Philosophy and the Mirror of Nature*. Princeton, NJ, 1979.

Stich, S. P. *The Fragmentation of Reason*. Cambridge, MA, 1990.

SUSAN HAACK

PRECOGNITION.

See: ESP PHENOMENA, PHILOSOPHICAL IMPLICATION OF [S]

PREFERENTIAL TREATMENT.

See: AFFIRMATIVE ACTION [S]

PRESUPPOSITION.

Consider the following famous example from Bertrand RUSSELL [7].

(1) The present king of France is bald.

According to Russell, (1) is false because it asserts the existence of the present king of France. However, following STRAWSON (1952 [8; S]), a number of philosophers and linguists have maintained that, if there is no present king of France, an utterance of (1) fails to have a determinate truth value—in Strawson's words, the question of whether (1) is true or false "does not arise." On this view, (1) therefore does not assert or even entail the existence of the present king of France but rather "presupposes" his existence.

THE RANGE OF PHENOMENA

Sentences like (1) are argued to presuppose the existence of a particular individual, but there are many other presupposition effects. It has been argued, for example, that factive verbs such as "know" and "regret" presuppose the truth of their complement clauses and that "certain aspectuals"—a class of verbs such as "quit" and "continue"—also presuppose certain actions having taken place (this class covers the example "Have you stopped beating your dog?"). It also appears that a number of modifiers introduce presupposition effects, for example "again," "too," "even," and so forth. Karttunen (1973) argued that in propositional-attitude environments such as "Fred wants to sell his unicorn" it is presupposed that Fred believes he has a unicorn. A number of additional constructions that invoke presupposition effects have been explored, including those triggered by phonological stress. So, for example, if I say "I didn't go to the BASEBALL game," it arguably presupposes that I went to some other kind of game.

PRESUPPOSITION VERSUS ENTAILMENT

The philosophical controversy surrounding presupposition comes in at the very beginning—determining whether these are genuine cases of presupposition or are merely cases of entailment. To illustrate, consider (2)–(4):

(2) Fred stopped washing the dishes.
(3) Fred didn't stop washing the dishes.
(4) Fred had been washing the dishes.

According to the presupposition thesis, both (2) and (3) presuppose (4). Hence, if (4) is false, then (2) and (3) must lack determinate truth values. Alternatively, according to the entailment analysis, (2) entails (4). Should (4) be false, then according to the entailment analysis (2) will be false and (3) will be true. This dispute has all the makings of a stalemate, since it turns on speakers' intuitions about whether sentences lack genuine truth values under the relevant conditions or are merely false. Indeed, Strawson (1964) came to doubt whether the matter could in fact be settled by "brisk little formal argument[s]" and offered that each view could be reasonable, depending on one's interests. Others have put more stock in brisk little formal arguments, notably Wilson (1975), who offered an extensive critique of the presuppositional analysis.

THE PROJECTION PROBLEM

One of the most interesting questions to surface is the so-called projection problem for presupposition, first observed by Langendoen and Savin (1971). This problem involves the question of what happens when a construction with a presupposition is embedded in more complex constructions (e.g., in propositional-attitude constructions or in the scope of negation). To illustrate, when (2) is negated, yielding (3), it continues to presuppose (4)—the presupposition is said to be projected. Other constructions, such as "doubts that," do not always project presuppositions, and still others (such as the "wants" case from Karttunen, discussed above) project something weaker than the original presupposition. The question is therefore whether projection presupposition is arbitrary or whether it obeys certain specific rules. Much subsequent work has attempted to articulate those "projection rules" (see Gazdar, 1979; Heim, 1991; Karttunen, 1973; and Soames, 1979, 1982, for important examples).

SEMANTIC VERSUS PRAGMATIC PRESUPPOSITION

If one accepts that there are genuine instances of presupposition, there remains the question of whether presupposition is a reflex of semantics or pragmatics—that is, whether the presupposition follows from the meaning of the sentence or is merely part of the conversational background. Stalnaker (1974) gave several arguments in favor of the pragmatic alternative, including the interesting observation that, in a case like (5),

> (5) If Eagleton hadn't been dropped from the Democratic ticket, Nixon would have won the election

there seems to be a presupposition that Nixon lost, although the effect is weak, and, in the right context or given appropriate information, that presupposition can be overruled. This graded effect suggests that pragmatic phenomena are in play. Stalnaker also observed that the pragmatic alternative is useful in separating the question of entailment relations from the question of presupposition and in working out solutions to the projection problem. (But see Wilson, 1975, for criticism of pragmatic accounts of presupposition.)

APPLICATIONS

The doctrine of presupposition remains somewhat controversial, but at the same time it has found interesting applications. For example, van Fraassen (1968, 1970) argued that presupposition might be employed in the treatment of the "LIAR PARADOX" [S] and proposed that liar sentences are neither true nor false owing to a presupposition failure. Presupposition has also played an important role in work on the semantics of propositional attitudes, much of it extending from the work of Karttunen (1973). Heim (1992), for example, has updated the initial Karttunen analysis with features of Stalnaker's presuppositional analysis. Still other research (including unpublished work by Saul KRIPKE [S]) has investigated the interplay of presupposition and the analysis of discourse ANAPHORA [S]. (SEE ALSO: *Philosophy of Language* [S])

Bibliography

Gazdar, G. *Pragmatics.* New York, 1979.

Grice, P. "Presupposition and Conversational Implicature, in P. Cole, ed., *Radical Pragmatics* (New York, 1981).

Heim, I. "On the Projection Problem for Presuppositions," in S. Davis, ed., *Pragmatics* (Oxford, 1991).

———. "Presupposition Projection and the Semantics of Attitude Verbs," *Journal of Semantics,* Vol. 9 (1992), 183–221.

Karttunen, L. "Presuppositions of Compound Sentences," *Linguistic Inquiry,* Vol. 4 (1973), 169–93.

Langendoen, D. T., and H. Savin. "The Projection Problem for Presupposition," in C. Filmore and D. T. Langendoen, eds., *Studies in Linguistic Semantics* (New York, 1971).

Soames, S. "A Projection Problem for Speaker Presuppositions," *Linguistic Inquiry,* Vol. 10 (1979), 623–66.

———. "How Presuppositions Are Inherited: A Solution to the Projection Problem," *Linguistic Inquiry,* Vol. 13 (1982), 483–545.

Stalnaker, R. "Pragmatic Presuppositions," in M. Munitz and D. Unger, eds., *Semantics and Philosophy* (New York, 1974).

Strawson, P. *Introduction to Logical Theory.* New York, 1952.

———. "Identifying Reference and Truth-Values," *Theoria,* Vol. 3 (1964), 96–118.

van Fraassen, B. "Presupposition, Implication, and Self-Reference," *Journal of Philosophy,* Vol. 65 (1968), 136–52.

———. "Truth and Paradoxical Consequences," in R. L. Martin, ed., *The Paradox of the Liar* (New Haven, 1970).

Wilson, D. *Presuppositions and Non-Truth-Conditional Semantics.* London, 1975.

PETER LUDLOW

PRIOR, ARTHUR NORMAN, was born on December 4, 1914, at Masterton, near Wellington, New Zealand. He acknowledged an early philosophical debt to John Findlay. But his first academic post was at Canterbury University College, where he succeeded Karl POPPER [6]. He was the visiting John Locke Lecturer at Oxford in 1956, and in 1958 he was appointed a professor of philosophy at the University of Manchester. After short periods as a visiting professor at the University of Chicago and at the University of California at Los Angeles, he moved in 1966 to a tutorial fellowship at Balliol College, Oxford, and Oxford University appointed him to a concurrent readership. He died in 1969.

Prior's early intellectual interests were very much religious in character. He was influenced for several years by the theologian Arthur Miller, who combined a strict adherence to Presbyterian doctrine with an equally strong support for SOCIALISM [7] and opposition to NATIONALISM [5; S]. But Prior's PACIFISM [S] weakened, and he served from 1942 to 1945 in the New Zealand air force. And the central focus of his interests gradually shifted—helped by an occasional bout of ATHEISM [1]—from theology to ethics and logic. He exchanged ideas with a wide circle of friends and acquaintances, and his hospitality to students was legendary.

Prior's first book, *Logic and the Basis of Ethics* (1946) traced seventeenth-, eighteenth-, and nineteenth-century anticipations of G. E. MOORE'S [5] criticism of the so-called naturalistic fallacy. But his main claim to fame lies in his pioneering work on the formal logic of temporal relationships. His most important investigations in this field were published in *Time and Modality* (1957), *Past, Present, and Future* (1967), and *Papers on Time and Tense* (1968). But he also wrote on several logical topics in this Encyclopedia; he published a substantial survey of the current state of logical inquiry under the title of *Formal Logic* (1955; 2d ed., 1962); and a posthumous volume of papers, *Objects of Thought* (1971), was edited by P. T. Geach and A. J. P. Kenny.

Prior almost always used the Polish style of notation in the discussion of logical proofs and principles and was a convinced, though largely unsuccessful, champion of its virtues. The major inadequacy in his tense logic, however, was a failure to discuss or accommodate aspectual differences—roughly, differences between the meanings expressed by verbs in a perfect tense and those expressed by verbs in an imperfect tense (see Galton, 1984). Other criticisms may be found in L. J. Cohen's (1958) review of *Time and Modality* and in his subsequent controversy with Prior (*Philosophy,* Vol. 34 [1959]). In his *Formal Logic* Prior displayed an impressively wide acquaintance with logical systems outside the field of tense logic, and this book remains a useful text for anyone interested in comparisons between different axiomatizations of the propositional calculus, between different kinds of logical quantification, between different MODAL LOGICS [S], or between different three-valued or institutionist logics. But the treatment of metalogical issues in the book is occasionally rather selective: for example, in its discussion of completeness proofs for the predicate calculus as against its treatment of completeness proofs for the propositional calculus.

Outside the brilliant originality of his work on tense logic, perhaps Prior's most striking idea was expressed in "The Runabout Inference-Ticket" (1960), where he argued that, if the meaning of a logical connective consisted just in the logical uses to which it can be put (as many seemed to hold), then it would be easy to invent a connective with a meaning that would enable one to infer any conclusion from any premises.

Bibliography

WORKS BY PRIOR

Logic and the Basis of Ethics; Oxford, 1946.

Formal Logic. Oxford, 1955; 2d ed., 1962.

Time and Modality. Oxford, 1957.

"The Runabout Inference Ticket," *Analysis,* Vol. 21 (1960), 38–9.

Past, Present, and Future. Oxford, 1967.

Papers on Time and Tense. Oxford, 1968.

Objects of Thought, ed. P. T. Geach and A. J. P. Kenny. Oxford, 1971.

WORKS ON PRIOR

Cohen, L. J. Review of *Time and Modality, Philosophical Quarterly,* Vol. 8 (1958), 266–71.

Galton, A. *The Logic of Aspect.* Oxford, 1984.

L. J. COHEN

PRISONER'S DILEMMA. *See:* DECISION THEORY [S]

PRIVATE LANGUAGE PROBLEM. *See:* RULE FOLLOWING [S]; WITTGENSTEIN, LUDWIG J. J. [8; S]

PROBABILITY. The word probability is used in a wide variety of contexts in science, ordinary language, and philosophy. We say that the evidence for a scientific hypothesis or law cannot render it certain but can only confer a certain probability on it. We agree that the probability of heads on the toss of an ordinary coin is a half. PROBABILITY [6] is fundamental to quantum mechanics; does that mean that the universe is fundamentally probabilistic? A moral agent is not responsible for predicting the future, but he is responsible for taking into account the probable consequences of his actions. The ideas of probability and uncertainty thus enter into philosophy in a number of areas: epistemology, metaphysics, philosophy of science, ethics, and others.

But what is probability? Philosophers and mathematicians have offered a number of ways of understanding the term. None has been accepted universally, and thus a review of the current diversity of interpretations of probability is offered here, with the understanding that more than one interpretation may be useful to our understanding. This entry emphasizes the (few) changes that have occurred since the early 1970s.

There are three main kinds of interpretation of probability. The first construes probability as objective and empirical; these interpretations include but are not limited to the interpretation of probability as a relative frequency. The second construes probability as objective and logical: as measuring the force of an inconclusive argument. The third construes probability as subjective: as reflecting the propensity of an agent to act or to gamble on alternatives.

Objective empirical interpretations of probability construe it as an empirical property of the world: whether a statement of probability is true or false is a matter for empirical investigation. The view is inspired by the use of probability in connection with ideal gambling apparatus, the study of stochastic processes found in nature (for example, statistical mechanics), the theory of errors of measurement, and such special studies as meteorology and epidemiology.

Richard von Mises (1957) was perhaps the staunchest defender of this view. The details of his view are controversial, but it is a controversy that has not aroused much heat in recent years. Some writers (Cramér, 1951) found the conditions of randomness and the existence of limits unnecessary, given that we are dealing with models of natural phenomena. These writers (they include many philosophers and the majority of statisticians) adopt the view that all we have to know about probability is that it has the mathematical properties it is generally assumed to have and that for all practical purposes it can be measured by empirical relative frequencies.

Probability, on these interpretations, is essentially a property of infinite (or 'long') sequences. Yet we often talk of the probabilities of unique events, for example, the probability of heads on the next toss of this coin, or the probability of error in the measurement just made. A somewhat different empirical interpretation of probability was offered by POPPER [6] (1959) to accommodate these uses. This is the propensity interpretation of probability. On this view probability is relativized not to a sequence of trials but to a chance setup (Hacking, 1965), for example, tossing a U.S. quarter in a certain apparatus. This setup has a certain propensity to produce heads. Probability is an abstract (objective, empirical) property of the setup that is reflected in frequencies.

On any of these objective interpretations of probability, probability is relative. Thus, an event ('heads') has a probability relative only to a sequence of tosses, a chance setup, a model of tossed coin behavior. The same event may, therefore, have different probabilities relative to different sequences or setups. This is no embarrassment for the theory but presents a difficulty, recognized and discussed by REICHENBACH [7] (1949): the practical problem of which sequence or setup to take into account when using probabilities as a guide to action and choice. This has come to be known as the problem of the reference class. Relatively little has been written on this problem in recent years from the point of view under discussion.

Objective logical interpretations such as that put forward by John Maynard KEYNES [5] (1921) construe probability as measuring the logical force of an inconclusive argument based on all the available evidence. This approach focuses on another usage for emphasis: given what we know, there is little probability of rain tomorrow; the evidence indicates with high probability that the vector of this disease is a flying insect; the evidence renders this scientific hypothesis more probable than not.

Keynes did not offer a definition of probability. Rudolf CARNAP [2; S] (1950) launched a program to define probability by means of a measure on the sentences of a formal first-order language. Carnap hoped to find a unique additive, normalized measure m for the 'language of science' that would embody all rational constraints on probabilities. For m to be additive is for $m(s \vee t) = m(s) + m(t)$, when $s \wedge t$ is logically false, and for it to be normalized is for $0 \leq m(s) \leq 1$, for all s in the language.

Among the problems facing this view are those of finding an appropriate first-order language of science, showing that it is possible to define a function m on such a rich language, finding rational criteria that will dictate the choice of a single function. Considerable thought has been devoted to the second problem, though mainly in computer science (see Bacchus, 1992). The first and third proved daunting, and even Carnap became doubtful that the project was feasible, turning instead toward a partly subjective interpretation of probability. Little effort has been devoted since the 1960s to finding answers to the first and third problems.

An alternative objective logical approach, pursued by Kyburg (1961), took for granted (as Carnap did) the existence of objective knowledge of relative frequencies and focused on applying that knowledge in particular cases. Probabilities are construed as intervals, reflecting the logical force of argument, and are based on the knowledge of relevant statistics. The interpretation depends on a solution to Reichenbach's problem of the reference class (see Kyburg, 1983).

In response to Keynes, Frank RAMSEY [7] (1931) argued for a subjective approach to probability: while logic can determine relations among the agent's degrees of belief, it is no part of logic to measure the force of an inconclusive argument. Ramsey offered a dutch book argument in support of this position: if my degrees of belief represent the odds at which I am willing to bet on either side of a proposition, then a clever bettor can make a set of bets that I will be willing to take under which I am bound to lose no matter what happens, unless my degrees of belief conform to the probability calculus.

Probability, on this view, becomes a subjective matter: an agent may assign any probability he likes to a proposition. It is required only that the set of probabilities the agent assigns to a set of related propositions be coherent—satisfy the probability calculus.

The subjective view became important in statistics and philosophy when de Finetti (1937) showed that under certain conditions the probabilities that two agents assign to a proposition will converge as they get more evidence. This appears to mitigate the subjective aspect of this interpretation of probability, though it does require that the agents stick to their original probability assessments and update their degrees of belief in accord with Bayes's theorem, as discussed below. A modern exposition of the subjective point of view can be found in Howson and Urbach (1989).

Bayes's theorem is an uncontroversial theorem of the probability calculus. It says that the probability of a hypothesis *h,* given evidence *e,* is the initial or prior probability of the hypothesis *h,* multiplied by the probability of *e* given *h,* divided by the prior probability of the evidence *e.* BAYESIANISM [S] is ambiguous. The term is used to characterize at least those who take Bayes's theorem to be the most important way of updating probabilities in the light of new evidence. For this to make sense, it is not required that probabilities be assigned to sentences or propositions rather than to sequences or chance setups. The problem of assigning a probability to having urn *A* on the basis of a sample drawn from the urn, given that you know the composition of balls in both urn *A* and urn *B,* and that you know the chance of having been given urn *A* is a perfectly classical problem to which the frequency interpretation can give a perfectly classical answer. What excludes those who adopt an objective empirical view of probability from being called Bayesians is the fact that they reject the idea of assigning probabilities to sentences or to particular determinate facts.

An interesting (partial) defense of the subjective Bayesian position is provided by Earman (1992). Earman believes that subjective Bayesianism is the only game in town; but half the time he believes it will not work. He offers careful arguments on both sides.

The subjective Bayesian position is defended—as much as any position is—by philosophers who write on these subjects. This includes many philosophers who have given up hope of finding objective standards for inductive or scientific inference and who have embraced a general relativistic view of inference. For some such thinkers even the standards of subjective probability are too rigid; but for many others subjective probability represents the right mix between subjectivity and objectivity. Yet others find the arguments purporting to support the probability axioms as rational standards for belief (the dutch book arguments) lacking in cogency.

Little new work is being done in philosophy on probability. What is written tends to concern the subjective interpretation, pro or con, and for the most part to sound familiar. The empirical interpretation attracts little attention, in part, perhaps, because it is in reasonably coherent shape. Philosophers seem to have abandoned the goal of providing a compelling logical measure for all first-order languages. Kyburg's logical view has not caught on (see Kyburg, 1994).

The most active research in this area is being pursued by computer scientists interested in ARTIFICIAL INTELLIGENCE [S] (AI; see Bacchus, 1992; Cheeseman, 1988; Fagin & Halpern, 1989; Nilsson, 1986; Paris, 1995). Some of what is done there simply recapitulates the history of philosophical research in the area, but there is one new slant that may appear to help the subjectivist view to appear plausible. The focus of work in AI is largely practical, and that motivates a concentration on the relations among probabilities: If X's degrees of belief are probabilities, and we know that they are subject to such and such constraints, then what might (or should) his belief in proposition S be? We can consider this problem quite independently, according to this view, from the problem of the source of the original degrees of belief.

This is not philosophically satisfying without some view as to the source of these original degrees of belief. A weak account takes them simply to be assumptions (Cheeseman) and so not to need justification. A more common approach is simply to leave their source unspecified. It is indeed perfectly proper to separate the two problems of accounting for the original beliefs of the agent and of providing an account of the relations among degrees of belief in related statements.

(SEE ALSO: *Philosophy of Science* [S])

Bibliography

Bacchus, F. *Representing and Reasoning with Probabilistic Knowledge.* Cambridge, MA, 1992.

Carnap, R. *The Logical Foundations of Probability.* Chicago, 1950.

Cheeseman, P. "Inquiry into Computer Understanding," *Computational Intelligence,* Vol. 4 (1988), 58–66.

Cramér, H. *Mathematical Methods of Statistics.* Princeton, NJ, 1951.

Earman, J. *Bayes or Bust.* Cambridge, MA, 1992.

Fagin, R., and J. Y. Halpern. "Uncertainty, Belief, and Probability," in *Proceedings of IJCAI 1989* (Detroit, 1989).

Finetti, B. de. "Foresight: Its Logical Laws, Its Subjective Sources," in H. E. Kyburg and H. Smokler, eds., *Studies in Subjective Probability,* 2d ed. (New York, 1980). First appeared in French as "La Prévision: Ses lois logiques, ses sources subjectives," *Annales de l'Institut Henri Poincaré,* Vol. 7 (1937), 1–68.

Hacking, I. *Logic of Statistical Inference.* Cambridge, 1965.

Halpern, J. Y. "An Analysis of First Order Probability," *Artificial Intelligence,* Vol. 46 (1990), 311–50.

Howson, C., and P. Urbach. *Scientific Reasoning.* LaSalle, IL, 1989.

Keynes, J. M. *A Treatise on Probability.* London, 1921.

Kyburg, H. E. *Probability and the Logic of Rational Belief.* Middletown, CT, 1961.

———. "The Reference Class," *Philosophy of Science,* Vol. 50 (1983), 374–97.

———. "Believing on the Basis of Evidence," *Computational Intelligence,* Vol. 10 (1994), 3–20.

Mises, R. von. *Probability, Statistics, and Truth.* London, 1957.

Nilsson, N. "Probabilistic Logic," *Artificial Intelligence,* Vol. 28 (1986), 71–88.

Paris, J. B. *The Uncertain Reasoner's Companion: A Mathematical Perspective.* Cambridge, 1995.

Popper, K. "The Propensity Interpretation of Probability," *British Journal for the Philosophy of Science,* Vol. 10 (1959), 25–42.

Ramsey, F. P. *The Foundations of Mathematics and Other Essays.* New York, 1931.

Reichenbach, H. *Theory of Probability.* Berkeley, 1949.

HENRY E. KYBURG

PROJECTIVISM. Projectivism has its roots in David HUME'S [4; S] remark in the *Treatise* about the mind's "propensity to spread itself over external objects." We sometimes speak of properties of objects where in fact the features we notice are "projections" of our internal sentiments (or other qualities of our experience). The family of metaethical views claiming that value is a projection of our conative and affective physiological states is called projectivism by Simon Blackburn (1984), and the name has stuck. Blackburn proposes that "we say that [we] *project* an attitude or habit or other commitment which is not descriptive onto the world, when we speak and think as though there were a property of things which our sayings describe, which we can reason about, know about, be wrong about, and so on" (1984, pp. 170–71). In ethics projectivism is popular because it provides an explanation of how it is that moral judgment can have the logical role that it seems to have in deciding what to do. Believing that something has some property typically provides me with a reason to act only in conjunction with the desire to promote (or oppose) the realization of that property. But believing that something is good is (or has been taken historically to be) sufficient by itself to provide a person with a reason to act. Nor is this a coincidence; it is not that we humans happen to like good things, as we happen to like to eat sugary things. Rather, it is part of the logic of judgments of goodness that they provide reasons. How can this be? Projectivists explain: the judgment that something is good is the projection of our affinity toward it, our "appetite," as HOBBES [4; S] puts it.

There are three varieties of projectivism to distinguish. The most straightforward is the ERROR THEORY [S], advanced by J. L. MACKIE (1977 [S]; see also Robinson, 1948), according to which our projection of value into the world is an illusion. Ordinary moral judgments presuppose an objectivity or independence of moral properties that is simply not to be had, and so they are in error. Mackie sees moral thought and language much as an atheist sees religious talk and language. The believers are not conceptually confused, but they are ontologically mistaken. The second sort of projectivism regards moral properties as Lockean "secondary qualities," not illusions, but real properties that consist in dispositions to affect human perceivers in certain ways. According to John MacDowell (1987), a leading exponent, just as we do not understand what the blueness of an object is except as the disposition to look blue to us, so we do not understand what goodness is except as the disposition to seem good to us. The projection involved in attribution of secondary qualities, including values, involves no error at all.

A third sort of projectivism is NONCOGNITIVISM [S], or as it is more commonly called in discussions of projectivism, expressivism. The expressivist holds that moral judgments do not state propositions at all but rather serve to express some noncognitive mental state of the judge. Like secondary-quality theorists, expressivists deny that there is any mistake involved in moral judgment; true, there are no moral properties, and we speak as though there are, but this "speaking as though" is just a misleading feature of the surface grammar. In fact, according to expressivists, moral judgments do not serve the same semantic function as most declarative sentences, even though they look the same.

Blackburn's projectivist position (the most influential one of the 1980s) develops an expressivist analysis of moral language with enough logical richness and complexity to model real moral deliberation and argument. His idea is easier to make out against the background of common criticisms of expressivism. Richard Brandt (1959), among others, noted that people's ordinary thinking about moral judgments runs contrary to expressivism. We have generally believed that normative judgments are used to state facts, that they are true or false, and when we change our moral views we come to regard our earlier views as mistaken, not merely as different. (By contrast, when one's taste in dessert changes, one generally regards the old preference as merely different or, at worst, childish.) Brandt complained that expressivists had given no explanation of why we are so confused. Blackburn's theory is designed to meet such objections. While maintaining an underlying expressivist semantics, he tries to show why we speak and think as though moral judgments state facts, can be true or false, and so on.

Imagine that people initially spoke about ethics in a language like English but having a quite explicitly expressivist structure. Rather than saying, "Voting for this health-care bill is morally wrong," they said, "Boo, voting for this health care bill!" Now imagine that these speakers valued a kind of consistency of sentiment, so that it was regarded as a confusion if someone said, "Boo, eating mammals, and hooray, eating cows!" And suppose they also believed that some moral sensibilities could never survive reflection by a rational person, so that expressing one of those sensibilities would be conclusive evidence that the speaker simply had not thought carefully about the subject. The expressivist community might "invent a predicate answering to that attitude, and treat commitments as if they were judgments, and then use all the natural devices for debating truth" (Blackburn 1984, p. 195). Since Blackburn's theory seeks to defend realist-style reasoning without realist metaphysics, he calls it 'quasi-realism'.

An important objection to Blackburn's quasi-realism is made by Crispin Wright (1988) and Bob Hale (1990). Our moral language has a realist surface structure, and quasi-realism seeks to vindicate this structure without giving in to realist metaphysics. But if quasi-realism is successful—if every realist-sounding thing we say can be endorsed in good faith by the quasi-realist—then how will a quasi-realist be distinguishable from a full-blooded realist? As Wright puts it, Blackburn's program confronts a dilemma: either it does not account for all the realist logical features of moral language, in which case it fails, or it succeeds in accounting for all of them, "in which case it makes good all the things which the projectivist started out wanting to deny: that the discourse in question is genuinely assertoric, aimed at truth, and so on" (1988, p. 35).

Despite these difficulties, projectivism deserves to be taken seriously, not just in the metaphysics of value, but in other metaphysical domains as well. For example, there have been projectivists about mental states (Dennett, 1987—judging that someone has intentional states is taking "the intentional stance" toward the person), causes (saying that one event caused another is projecting one's psychological propensity to associate events of the first kind with events of the second in temporal sequence), probability (Finetti, 1972—judgments of probability project one's degree of credence into the world), and logical impossibility (Blackburn, 1984—projecting a certain kind of inconceivability). With the exception of the first, all of these sorts of projectivism are plausibly attributed to Hume, who should be regarded as the prototype projectivist.

(SEE ALSO: *Ethical Theory,* and *Realism* [S])

Bibliography

Ayer, A. J. *Language, Truth, and Logic.* Harmondsworth, Middlesex, 1971.

Blackburn, S. *Spreading the Word.* Oxford, 1984.

———. *Essays in Quasi-Realism.* New York, 1993.

Brandt, R. *Ethical Theory.* Englewood Cliffs, NJ, 1959.

de Finetti, B. *Probability, Induction, and Statistics.* London, 1972.

Dennett, D. *The Intentional Stance.* Cambridge, MA, 1987.

Geach, P. T. "Ascriptivism," Philosophical Review, Vol. 69 (1960), 221–25.

Gibbard, A. *Wise Choices, Apt Feelings.* Cambridge, MA, 1990.

Hale, B. "Can There Be a Logic of Attitudes?" in J. Haldane, ed., *Reality, Representation, and Projection* (London, 1990).

Harman, G. *The Nature of Morality.* New York, 1977.

MacDowell, J. *Projection and Truth in Ethics.* Lawrence, KS, 1987.

Mackie, J. L. *Ethics: Inventing Right and Wrong.* Harmondsworth, 1977.

Robinson, R. "The Emotivist Theory of Ethics," *Proceedings of the Aristotelian Society,* Vol. 22 (1948), supplement, 79–106.

Smart, J. J. C. *Ethics, Persuasion, and Truth.* London, 1984.

Stevenson, C. L. *Facts and Values.* New Haven, 1963.

Wright, C. "Realism, Anti-Realism, Irrealism, Quasi-Realism," in P. French, T. Uehling, and H. Wettstein, eds., *Realism and Antirealism,* Midwest Studies in Philosophy, Vol. 12 (Minneapolis, 1988).

JAMES DREIER

PROOF THEORY. The background to the development of proof theory since 1960 is contained in the article MATHEMATICS, FOUNDATIONS OF [5]. Briefly, Hilbert's program (HP), inaugurated in the 1920s, aimed to secure the foundations of mathematics by giving finitary consistency proofs of formal systems such as for number theory, analysis, and set theory, in which informal mathematics can be represented directly. These systems are based on classical logic and implicitly or explicitly depend on the assumption of "completed infinite" totalities. Consistency of a system S (containing a modicum of elementary number theory) is sufficient to ensure that any finitarily meaningful statement about the natural numbers that is provable in S is correct under the intended interpretation. Thus, in HILBERT'S [3] view, consistency of S would serve to eliminate the "completed infinite" in favor of the "potential infinite" and thus secure the body of mathematics represented in S. Hilbert established the subject of proof theory as a technical part of mathematical logic by means of which his program was to be carried out; its methods are described below.

In 1931 GÖDEL'S [S] second incompleteness theorem raised a prima facie obstacle to HP for the system Z of elementary number theory (also called Peano arithmetic—PA) since all previously recognized forms of finitary reasoning could be formalized within it. In any case Hilbert's program could not possibly succeed for any system such as set theory in which *all* finitary notions and reasoning could unquestionably be formalized. These obstacles led workers in proof theory to modify HP in two ways. The first was to seek reductions of various formal systems S to more constructive systems S′. The second was to shift the aims from foundational ones to more mathematical ones. Examples of the first modification are the reductions of PA to intuitionistic arithmetic HA and Gentzen's consistency proof of PA by finitary reasoning coupled with quantifier-free transfinite induction up to the ordinal ε_0, TI(ε_0), both obtained in the 1930s. The second modification of proof theory was promoted especially by Georg Kreisel starting in the early 1950s; he showed how constructive mathematical information could be extracted from nonconstructive proofs in number theory. The pursuit of proof theory along the first of these lines has come to be called relativized Hilbert program or reductive proof theory, while that along the second line is sometimes called the program of unwinding proofs or, perhaps better, extractive proof theory. In recent years there have been a number of applications of the latter both in mathematics and in theoretical computer science. Keeping the philosophical relevance and limitations of space in mind, the following account is devoted entirely to developments in reductive proof theory, though the two sides of the subject often go hand in hand.

METHODS OF FINITARY PROOF THEORY

Hilbert introduced a special formalism called the epsilon calculus to carry out his program (the nomenclature is related neither to the ordinal ε_0 nor to the membership symbol in set theory), and he proposed a particular substitution method for that calculus. Following Hilbert's suggestions, Wilhelm Ackermann and John von NEUMANN [5] obtained the first significant results in finitary proof theory in the 1920s. Then, in 1930, another result of the same character for more usual logical formalisms was obtained by Jacques Herbrand, but there were troublesome aspects of his work. In 1934 Gerhard Gentzen introduced new systems, the so-called sequent calculi, to provide a very clear and technically manageable vehicle for proof theory, and reobtained Herbrand's fundamental theorem via his cut-elimination theorem. Roughly speaking, the latter tells us that every proof of a statement in quantificational logic can be normalized to a direct proof in which there are no detours ("cuts") at any stage via formulas of a complexity higher than what appears at later stages. Sequents have the form $\Gamma\rightarrow\Delta$, where Γ and Δ are finite sequences of formulas (possibly empty). $\Gamma\rightarrow\Delta$ is derivable in Gentzen's calculus LK just in case the formula $A\supset B$ is derivable in one of the usual calculi for classical predicate logic, where A is the conjunction of formulas in Γ and B is the disjunction of those in Δ.

INTRODUCTION OF INFINITARY METHODS TO PROOF THEORY

Gentzen's theorem as it stood could not be used to establish the consistency of PA, where the scheme of induction resists a purely logical treatment, and for this reason he was forced to employ a partial cut-elimination argument whose termination was guaranteed by the principle TI(ε_0). Beginning in the 1950s, Paul Lorenzen and then, much more extensively, Kurt Schütte began to employ certain infinitary extensions of Gentzen's calculi (cf. Schütte, 1960, 1977). This was done first of all for elementary number theory by replacing the usual rule of universal generalization by the so-called ω-rule, in the form: from $\Gamma\rightarrow\Delta$,A(**n**) for each n = 0,1,2,..., infer $\Gamma\rightarrow\Delta$,(x)A(x). Now derivations are well-founded trees (whose tips are the axioms $A\rightarrow A$), and each such is assigned an ordinal as length in a natural way. For this calculus LK_ω, one has a full cut-elimination theorem, and every derivation of a statement in PA can be transformed into a cut-free derivation of the same in LK_ω whose length is less than ε_0. Though infinite, the derivation trees involved are recursive and can be described finitarily, to yield another consistency proof of PA by TI(ε_0). Schütte extended these methods to systems RA_α of ramified analysis (α an ordinal) in which existence of sets is posited at finite and transfinite levels up to α, referring at each stage only to sets introduced at lower levels. Using a suitable extension of LK_ω to RA_α, Schütte obtained cut-elimination theorems giving natural ordinal bounds for cut-free derivations in terms of the so-called Veblen hierarchy of ordinal functions. In 1963 he and Feferman independently used this to characterize (in that hierarchy) the ordinal of predicative analysis, defined as the first α for which TI(α) cannot be justified in a system RA_β for $\beta<\alpha$. William Tait (1968) obtained a uniform treatment of arithmetic, ramified analysis, and related unramified systems by means of the cut-elimination theorem for LK extended to a language with formulas built by countably infinite conjunctions (with the other connectives as usual). Here the appropriate new rule of inference is: from $\Gamma\rightarrow\Delta,A_n$, for each n = 0,1,2, ..., infer $\Gamma\rightarrow\Delta$,A, where A is the conjunction of all the A_n's.

Brief mention should also be made of the extensions of the other methods of proof theory mentioned above, concentrating on elimination of quantifiers rather than cut elimination. In the 1960s Burton Dreben and his students corrected and extended the Herbrand approach (cf. Dreben & Denton, 1970). Tait (1965) made useful conceptual reformulations of Hilbert's substitution method; a number of applications of this method to subsystems of analysis have been obtained in the 1990s by Grigori Mints (1994). Another approach stems from Gödel's functional interpretation, first presented in a lecture in 1941 but not published until 1958 in the journal *Dialectica;* besides the advances with this made by Clifford Spector in 1962, more recently there have been a number of further applications both to subsystems of arithmetic and to subsystems of analysis (cf. Feferman 1993). Finally, mention should be made of the work of Prawitz (1965) on systems of natural deduction, which had also been introduced by Gentzen in 1934 but not further pursued by him; for these a process of normalization takes the place of cut elimination. While each of these other methods has its distinctive merits and advantages, it is the methods of sequent calculi in various finitary and infinitary forms that have received the most widespread use.

PROOF THEORY OF IMPREDICATIVE SYSTEMS

The proof theory of impredicative systems of analysis was initiated by Gaisi Takeuti in the 1960s. He used partial cut-elimination results and established termination by reference to certain well-founded systems of ordinal diagrams (cf. Takeuti, 1987). In 1972 William Howard determined the ordinal of a system ID_1 of one arithmetical inductive definition, in the so-called Bachmann hierarchy of ordinal functions; the novel aspect of this was that it makes use of a name for the first uncountable ordinal in order to produce the countable (and in fact recursive) ordinal of ID_1. In a series of contributions by Harvey Friedman, Tait, Feferman, Wolfram Pohlers, Wilfried Buchholz, and Wilfried Sieg stretching from 1967 into the 1980s, the proof theory of systems of iterated inductive definitions ID_α and related impredicative subsystems of analysis was advanced substantially. The proof-theoretic ordinals of the ID_α were established by Pohlers in terms of higher Bachmann ordinal function systems (cf. Buchholz et al., 1981). The methods here use cut-elimination arguments for extensions of LK involving formulas built by countably and uncountably long conjunctions. In addition, novel "collapsing" arguments are employed to show how to collapse suitable uncountably long derivations to countable ones in order to obtain the countable (again recursive) ordinal bounds for these systems. An alternative functorial approach to the treatment of iterated inductive definitions was pioneered by Jean-Yves Girard (1985).

In 1982 Gerhard Jäger initiated the use of the so-called admissible fragments of Zermelo-Fraenkel set theory as an illuminating tool in the proof theory of predicatively reducible systems (cf. Jäger, 1986). This was extended by Jäger and Pohlers (1982) to yield the proof-theoretical ordinal of a strong impredicative system of analysis; that makes prima facie use of the name of the first (recursively) inaccessible ordinal. Michael Rathjen (1994) has gone beyond this to measure the ordinals of much stronger systems of analysis and SET THEORY [7; S] in terms of systems of recursive ordinal notations involving the names of very large (recursively) inaccessible ordinals, analogous to the so-called large cardinals in set theory.

SIGNIFICANCE OF THE WORK FOR HP AND REDUCTIVE PROOF THEORY

Ironically for the starting point with Hilbert's aims to eliminate the "completed infinite" from the foundations of mathematics, these developments have required the use of highly infinitary concepts and objects to explain the proof-theoretical transformations involved in an understandable way. It is true that in the end these can be explained away in terms of transfinite induction applied to suitable recursive ordinal notation systems. Even so, one finds few who believe that one's confidence in the consistency of the systems of analysis and set theory that have been dealt with so far has been increased as a result of this body of work. However, while the intrinsic significance of the determination of the proof-theoretic ordinals of such systems has not been established, that work can still serve behind the scenes as a tool in reductive proof theory. It is argued in Feferman (1988) that one has obtained thereby foundationally significant reductions, for example of various (prima facie) infinitary systems to finitary ones, impredicative to predicative ones, and nonconstructive to constructive ones. With a field that is still evolving at the time of writing, it is premature to try to arrive at more lasting judgments of its permanent value.

(SEE ALSO: *Mathematical Logic* [S])

Bibliography

Buchholz, W., S. Feferman, W. Pohlers, and W. Sieg. *Iterated Inductive Definitions and Subsystems of Analysis: Recent Proof-theoretical Studies.* Lecture Notes in Mathematics 897. New York, 1981.

———, and K. Schütte. *Proof Theory of Impredicative Systems.* Naples, 1988.

Dreben, B., and J. Denton. "Herbrand-style Consistency Proofs," in J. Myhill, A. Kino, and R. E. Vesley, eds., *Intuitionism and Proof Theory* (Amsterdam, 1970), 419–33.

Feferman, S. "Hilbert's Program Relativized: Proof-theoretical and Foundational Reductions," *Journal of Symbolic Logic,* Vol. 53 (1988), 364–84.

———. "Gödel's *Dialectica* Interpretation and Its Two-way Stretch," in G. Gottlob et al., eds., *Computational Logic and Proof Theory,* Lecture Notes in Computer Science 713 (New York, 1993).

Gentzen, G. *The Collected Papers of Gerhard Gentzen,* ed. M. Szabo. Amsterdam, 1969.

Girard, J.-Y. "Introduction to Π^1_2 Logic," *Synthese,* Vol. 62 (1985).

———. *Proof Theory and Logical Complexity.* Naples, 1987.

Hilbert, D., and P. Bernays. *Grundlagen der Mathematik.* Vols. 1–2, 2d ed. Berlin, 1968–70.

Howard, W. "A System of Abstract Constructive Ordinals," *Journal of Symbolic Logic,* Vol. 37 (1972), 355–74.

Jäger, G. *Theories for Admissible Sets: A Unifying Approach to Proof Theory.* Naples, 1986.

———, and W. Pohlers. "Eine beweistheoretische Untersuchung von $(\Delta^1_2\text{-CA})+(\text{BI})$ und verwandter Systeme," *Sitzungsber. Bayerische Akad. Wissenschaft Math. Nat. Klasse* (1982), 1–28.

Kreisel, G. "A Survey of Proof Theory," *Journal of Symbolic Logic,* Vol. 33 (1965), 321–88.

Mints, G. E. *Selected Papers in Proof Theory.* Naples, 1992.

———. "Gentzen-type Systems and Hilbert's Epsilon Substitution Method. I," in D. Prawitz et al., eds., *Logic, Methodology, and Philosophy of Science IX* (1994).

Myhill, J., A. Kino, and R. E. Vesley, eds., *Intuitionism and Proof Theory.* Amsterdam, 1970.

Pohlers, W. "Contributions of the Schütte School in Munich to Proof Theory," in G. Takeuti, *Proof Theory* (Amsterdam, 1987).

———. *Proof Theory: An Introduction.* Lecture Notes in Mathematics 1407. [New York], 1989.

Prawitz, D. *Natural Deduction.* Stockholm, 1965.

Rathjen, M. "Admissible Proof Theory and Beyond," in D. Prawitz et al., eds., *Logic, Methodology and Philosophy of Science IX* (1994).

Schütte, K. *Beweistheorie.* Berlin, 1960.

———. *Proof Theory.* Berlin, 1977.

Sieg, W. "Hilbert's Program Sixty Years Later," *Journal of Symbolic Logic,* Vol. 53 (1988), 338–48.

Simpson, S. G. "Partial Realizations of Hilbert's Program," *Journal of Symbolic Logic,* Vol. 53 (1988), 349–63.

Tait, W. "The Substitution Method," *Journal of Symbolic Logic,* Vol. 30 (1965), 175–92.

———. "Normal Derivability in Classical Logic," in J. Barwise, ed., *The Syntax and Semantics of Infinitary Languages,* Lecture Notes in Mathematics 72 (New York, 1968).

Takeuti, G. *Proof Theory,* 2d ed. Amsterdam, 1987.

SOLOMON FEFERMAN

PROPER NAMES AND DESCRIPTIONS.

See: REFERENCE [S]

PROPERTIES.

Our every assertion or thought involves properties or relations. Most simply, we predicate some property of some thing: the earth is round. Sometimes we refer to properties by name or by description: red is the color of blood. Sometimes our quantifiers range over properties: galaxies come in many shapes and sizes.

This familiarity with properties, however, does not reveal what properties are. Indeed, the question is equivocal, both in ordinary and in philosophical discourse. There are different conceptions of properties, equally legitimate, corresponding to the different roles that properties have been called upon to play (Bealer, 1982; Lewis, 1983, 1986). And for each conception there are different theories as to what sort of entity, if any, is best suited to play the role. The most fundamental division is between abundant and sparse conceptions of properties. On an abundant conception every meaningful predicate expresses some property or relation, including 'is blue or round', 'is on top of a turtle', 'is identical with the planet Mars'; a property's instances need not resemble one another in any intrinsic respect. Abundant properties are needed to serve as "meanings," or components of "meanings," in a compositional semantics for language. On a sparse conception of properties a predicate expresses a property only if the objects satisfying the predicate resemble one another in some specific intrinsic respect; perhaps 'has unit positive charge' and 'is ten kilograms in mass' are examples. Sparse properties are needed to provide an objective basis for the scientist's project of discovering the fundamental classifications of things and the laws that govern them. Properties, whether abundantly or sparsely conceived, are neither language- nor mind-dependent: they existed before there were beings to talk and think about them; they would have existed even had there never been such beings.

In this article only conceptions of properties are explicitly distinguished and discussed, although much of what is said applies also to relations and to propositions. Other philosophers' terms for 'property' in the abundant sense include 'attribute' (QUINE [7; S], 1970), 'propositional function' (RUSSELL [7], 1919), and 'concept' (Bealer, 1982; FREGE [3; S], 1884); 'universal' and 'quality' have for the most part been interpreted sparsely. Ordinary language allows abundant or sparse readings of 'characteristic', 'feature', 'trait', and more.

ABUNDANT CONCEPTIONS OF PROPERTIES

How abundant are the properties on the abundant conception? Whenever there are some things, no matter how scattered or dissimilar from one another, there is the abundant property of being one of those things. Thus, for any class of things, there is at least one abundant property had by all and only the members of that class. It follows that there are at least as many abundant properties as classes of things and that the abundant properties outrun the predicates of any ordinary language. (There are nondenumerably many classes of things—assuming an infinity of things—but at most denumerably many predicates in any ordinary language.) Abundant properties, owing to their very abundance, must be transcendent, rather than immanent: they are not present in their instances as constituents or parts. It is not plausible to suppose that an object has a distinct constituent for each and every class to which it belongs.

If we say that whenever there are some things, there is exactly one property had by all and only those things, then a property may be identified with the class of its instances. For example, the property of being human may be identified with the class of human beings. But there is a well-known objection to this identification (Quine, 1970). Consider the property expressed by 'is a creature with a heart' and the property expressed by 'is a creature with kidneys'. If properties are "meanings," or semantic values, of predicates, then the properties expressed by these two predicates are distinct. Yet, these predicates, we may suppose, are coextensive: as a matter of fact, any creature with a heart has kidneys, and vice versa; the class of creatures with a heart is identical with the class of creatures with kidneys. Thus, distinct properties correspond to the same class and cannot be identified with that class.

Different responses to the objection invoke different criteria of individuation for properties, that is, different criteria for deciding when properties, introduced, say, via predicates that express them, are one and the same. One response simply denies that 'is a creature with a heart' and 'is a creature with kidneys' express distinct properties. More generally, properties expressed by coextensive predicates are identical. Call this an extensional conception of properties. A property so conceived may be identified with the class of its instances. Extensional conceptions of properties are adequate to the semantic analysis of mathematical language and extensional languages generally (TARSKI [8], 1946).

A second response holds that 'is a creature with a heart' and 'is a creature with kidneys' express distinct properties, because it is logically possible for something to satisfy one predicate without satisfying the other. On this response properties expressed by necessarily coextensive predicates are identical; properties expressed by accidentally coextensive predicates are distinct. Call this an intensional conception of properties. If one accepts the standard analyses of logical possibility and necessity in terms of possibilia, then a property, on the intensional conception, may be identified with the function that assigns to each possible world the set of possible objects that has the property at the world. If one holds that each object exists at, and has properties at, only one world, then a property may more simply be identified with the class of (actual and) possible objects that has the property (Lewis, 1986). Properties, on the intensional conception, are appropriate semantic values for predicates of (standard) modal languages and intensional languages generally (CARNAP [2; S], 1947; KRIPKE [S], 1963).

A third response holds that the properties expressed by 'is a creature with a heart' and 'is a creature with kidneys' are distinct because they are structured entities with different constituents: the property expressed by 'is a creature with a heart' has the property expressed by 'is a heart' as a constituent; the property expressed by 'is a creature with kidneys' does not. On this response properties have a quasi-syntactic structure that parallels the structure of predicates that express them. Call two predicates isomorphic if they have the same syntactic structure and corresponding syntactic components are assigned the same semantic values. On a structured conception of properties, properties expressed by isomorphic predicates are identical; properties expressed by nonisomorphic predicates are distinct. (Structured conceptions are sometimes called hyperintensional because they allow necessarily coextensive predicates to express distinct properties.) Structured conceptions subdivide according to whether the unstructured semantic values are intensional or extensional and according to whether the relevant structure is surface grammatical structure, or some hypothetical deep structure, or structure after analysis in terms of some chosen primitive vocabulary. Structured properties may be identified with sequences of unstructured properties and other unstructured semantic values. Structured properties, on one version or another, have a role to play in the semantic analysis of propositional attitudes and of hyperintensional languages generally (Carnap, 1947; Cresswell, 1985).

Thus far, this article has assumed that predicates of ordinary language are satisfied by objects once and for all. In fact, most ordinary language predicates are tensed; they may be satisfied by objects at some times but not at others. For example, 'is sitting' is true of me now, but was false of me ten minutes ago. On a tensed conception of properties, whether or not a property holds of an object may also be relative to times. Most simply, tensed properties may be identified with functions from times to untensed properties. Tensed properties may be taken as semantic values for tensed predicates.

We have, then, a plurality of abundant conceptions of properties. Which is correct? One need not and should not choose. A plurality of conceptions is needed to account for the multiple ambiguity in our ordinary talk of properties. And it seems that both structured and intensional conceptions are needed for compositional semantics: structured properties are needed to provide distinct semantic values for predicates, such as 'is a polygon with three sides' and 'is a polygon with three angles', that are necessarily coextensive without being synonymous; intensional properties are needed to provide distinct semantic values for unstructured predicates that are accidentally coextensive. To accept a plurality of conceptions, it suffices to find, for each conception, entities that satisfy that conception's criteria of individuation.

Realists with respect to some conception of properties hold that entities satisfying the individuation criteria for the conception exist (*see* REALISM [S]). Realists divide into reductionists and antireductionists. Reductionists identify properties, under the various conceptions, with various set-theoretic constructions (in ways already noted): class, functions, or sequences of actual or possible objects (Lewis, 1986; *see* REDUCTION, REDUCTIONISM [S]). Antireductionists reject some or all of these identifications. For some antireductionists, classes are suspect or esoteric entities; classes are to be explained, if at all, in terms of properties, not vice versa (Bealer, 1982; Russell, 1919). For other antireductionists the problem is not with classes, but with the possibilia that comprise them (on intensional conceptions). Possible but nonactual entities are to be explained, if at all, in terms of uninstantiated properties, not vice versa (Plantinga, 1976). According to the antireductionist, properties are basic or primitive; it is merely posited that there are entities satisfying the appropriate individuation criteria. Some entities, after all, must be taken as basic; according to the antireductionist, properties are an acceptable choice.

Eliminativists hold that, strictly speaking, there are no properties (*see* ELIMINATIVE MATERIALISM, ELIMINATIVISM [S]). They take aim, typically, at intensional conceptions, at conceptions with modal criteria of individuation. They claim that modal notions, such as logical possibility and necessity (whether taken as primitive or analyzed in terms of possibilia), incorrigibly lack the clarity and precision required of a rigorous scientific semantics or philosophy (Quine, 1970). Eliminativists have the burden of showing how ordinary and philosophical discourse ostensibly referring to properties can be paraphrased so as to avoid such reference; or, failing that, of showing that such discourse is dispensible, merely a *façon de parler.*

SPARSE CONCEPTIONS OF PROPERTIES

On an abundant conception any two objects share infinitely many properties and fail to share infinitely many others, whether the objects are utterly dissimilar or exact duplicates. On a sparse conception the sharing of properties always makes for genuine similarity; exact duplicates have all of their properties in common. Whatever the sparse properties turn out to be, there must be enough of them (together with sparse relations) to provide the basis for a complete qualitative description of the world, including its laws and causal features. The sparse properties correspond one-to-one with a select minority of the abundant properties, on some intensional conception. ('Intensional', because distinct sparse properties may accidentally be instantiated by the same objects.) Those abundant properties that correspond to sparse properties are called natural (or perfectly natural, since naturalness presumably comes in degrees; Lewis, 1983, 1986). The naturalness of properties is determined not by our psychological makeup, or our conventions, but by nature itself.

How sparse are the properties, on a sparse conception? First, there is the question of uninstantiated properties. If sparse properties are transcendent, there is no difficulty making room for uninstantiated sparse properties; perhaps uninstantiated sparse properties are needed to ground laws that come into play only if certain contingent conditions are satisfied (Tooley, 1987). If, on the other hand, sparse properties are immanent, are present in their instances, then uninstantiated sparse properties must be rejected, because they have nowhere to be (ARMSTRONG [S], 1978, 1989). Of course, uninstantiated sparse properties may nonetheless possibly exist, where this is understood according to one's favored interpretation of modality.

Second, there is the question of the compounding of sparse properties (and relations). Disjunctions and negations of natural properties are not themselves natural: their instances need not resemble one another in any intrinsic respect. For example, instances of the property having-unit-positive-charge-or-being-ten-kilograms-in-mass need not resemble one another in either their charge or their mass. It follows that there are no disjunctive or negative sparse properties (Armstrong, 1978).

The case of conjunctive sparse properties is less clear. There are two views. According to the first, since instances of a conjunction of natural properties, such as having-unit-positive-charge-and-being-ten-kilograms-in-mass, resemble one another in some—indeed, at least two—intrinsic respects, there exists a sparse property corresponding to the conjunction. According to the second view, the sparse properties must be nonredundant; they must be not only sufficient for describing the world but minimally sufficient. On this view conjunctive sparse properties are excluded on grounds of redundancy: a putative conjunctive sparse property would hold of an object just in case both conjuncts hold.

Similarly, structural sparse properties, such as being-a-molecule-of-H_2O, may be admitted on the grounds that they make for similarity among their instances. Or they may be excluded on grounds of redundancy: a putative structural sparse property would hold of an object just in case certain other sparse properties and relations hold among the object and its parts. But the exclusion of structural (and conjunctive) sparse properties faces a problem. It rules out a priori the possibility that some properties are irresolvably infinitely complex: they are structures of structures of structures, and so on, without ever reaching simple, fundamental properties or relations (Armstrong, 1978). A sparse conception that allowed for this possibility would have to allow some redundancy; and if some redundancy, why not more? This suggests that conjunctive and structural sparse properties should generally be admitted. (An alternative treatment makes use of degrees of naturalness and has it that conjunctive and structural properties are natural to some lesser degree than the properties in terms of which they are defined; a world with endless structure has no perfectly natural properties.)

If structural sparse properties are admitted, the sparse properties will not be confined to fundamental physical properties; there will be sparse properties of macroscopic, as well as microscopic, objects. For example, the sparse properties will include specific shape-and-size properties, such as being-a sphere-ten-meters-in-diameter (which are arguably structural properties definable in terms of sparse distance relations). However, the vast majority of ordinary-language predicates—'is red', 'is human', 'is a chair', to name a few—fail to express natural properties to which sparse properties correspond; rather, these predicates express properties that, when analyzed in fundamental physical terms, are disjunctive (perhaps infinitely so) and probably extrinsic. (This judgment could be overturned, however, if there are irreducible natural properties applying to macroscopic objects—most notably, irreducible phenomenological properties of color, sound, and such.)

What are the properties on a sparse conception? There are three principal theories (or clusters of theories, since they each subdivide). According to the first, the properties sparsely conceived are just some of the properties abundantly conceived: the properties that are perfectly natural. What makes some properties natural and others unnatural? One version of the theory simply takes naturalness to be a primitive, unanalyzable distinction among abundant properties (Quinton, 1957; see also Armstrong, 1989; Lewis, 1986). But since a property is natural in virtue of the resemblances among its instances, it might seem more appropriate to take instead some relation of partial resemblance as primitive and to define naturalness in terms of resemblance. The resulting version, called resemblance nominalism, can be worked out in different ways with different primitive resemblance relation (Price, 1953; see also Armstrong, 1989; GOODMAN [3; S], 1951; Lewis, 1983). The chief objection to the view is that partial resemblance between ordinary objects, no less than naturalness of properties, cries out for analysis. When two objects partially resemble one another, the objection goes, they must have constituents that exactly resemble one another, perhaps constituents that are literally identical. More generally, it is argued, properties must be constituents of objects if properties are to play a role in the explanation of the natures and causal powers of objects; one cannot explain an object's nature or causal powers by invoking a class to which it belongs. Sparse properties, then, must be immanent, not transcendent, entities.

What are these constituents of ordinary things? Not ordinary spatial or temporal constituents—or, at least, not always. For even an object with no spatial or temporal extension might have a complex nature and stand in relations of partial resemblance. If sparse properties are immanent, then they must be nonspatiotemporal constituents of things. There are two prominent theories as to the nature of these constituents. The first theory takes them to be universals (Armstrong, 1978, 1989.) They are repeatable: each of them is, or could be, multiply instantiated. And they are wholly present in their instances: an immanent universal is located—all of it—wherever each of its instances is located. When objects resemble one another by having a sparse property in common, there is something literally identical between the objects. It follows that universals fail to obey commonsense principles of location, such as that nothing can be (wholly) in two places at the same time. But that is no objection. Such principles were framed with particulars in mind; it would beg the question against universals to require them to meet standards set for particulars.

On the other theory of sparse properties as immanent, the nonspatiotemporal constituents of ordinary particulars are themselves particulars, called tropes (Armstrong, 1989; Lewis, 1986; Williams, 1966) or abstract particulars (Campbell, 1981). When ordinary particulars partially resemble one another by having some sparse property—say, their mass—in common, then there are distinct, exactly resembling, mass tropes as constituents of each. On a trope theory sparse properties can be identified with maximal classes of exactly resembling tropes (perhaps including merely possible tropes). Exact resemblance between tropes is taken as primitive by trope theory; but it is a simple and natural primitive compared to the partial resemblance relation taken as primitive by an adequate resemblance nominalism.

A possible disadvantage of a universals theory is that it requires two fundamentally distinct kinds of entities: universal and particulars. An ordinary particular cannot simply be identified with a bundle of coinstantiated universals, lest numerically distinct but qualitatively identical particulars be identified with one another. On a universals theory there must be some nonqualitative, nonrepeatable constituent of ordinary particulars to ground their numerical identity. A trope theory, on the other hand, needs only tropes to make a world. Ordinary particulars can be identified with bundles of coinstantiated tropes; numerically distinct but qualitatively identical particulars are then bundles of numerically distinct but exactly resembling tropes.

The great advantage of a universals theory is that it promises to analyze all resemblance in terms of identity: exact resemblance is identity of all qualitative constituents; partial resemblance is partial identity, identity of at least one qualitative constituent. But it is unclear whether the promise can be kept. Objects instantiating different determinates of a determinable—such as unit-positive and unit-negative charge—seem to partially resemble one another by both being charged without there being any analysis of this resemblance in terms of the identity of constituent universals or, for that matter, the exact resemblance of constituent tropes. A universals theory and a trope theory would then have to fall back upon primitive partial resemblance between universals, or tropes. Some of the advantages of these theories over resemblance nominalism would be forfeited.

Of the three basic theories of sparse properties—resemblance nominalism, a theory of immanent universals, and a theory of tropes—only one can be true; the theories posit incompatible constituent structure to the world. However, assuming each theory is internally coherent, and adequate to the needs of science, the question arises, What sort of evidence could decide between them? It seems that a choice between the theories will have to be made, if at all, on the basis of pragmatic criteria such as simplicity, economy, and explanatory power. There is as yet no philosophical consensus as to what that choice should be.

(SEE ALSO: *Metaphysics* [S])

Bibliography

Armstrong, D. M. *Universals and Scientific Realism.* 2 vols. Cambridge, 1978.

———. *Universals: An Opinionated Introduction.* Boulder, CO, 1989.

Bealer, G. *Quality and Concept.* Oxford, 1982.

Campbell, K. "The Metaphysic of Abstract Particulars," in *Midwest Studies in Philosophy,* Vol. 6 (Minneapolis, 1981).

Carnap, R. *Meaning and Necessity.* Chicago, 1947.

Cresswell, M. *Structured Meanings.* Cambridge, MA, 1985.

Frege, G. *Die Grundlagen der Arithmetik* [1884]. Translated by J. L. Austin as *The Foundations of Arithmetic.* Oxford, 1950.

Goodman, N. *The Structure of Appearance.* Cambridge, MA, 1951.

Kripke, S. "Semantical Considerations on Modal Logic," *Acta Philosophica Fennica,* Vol. 16 (1963), 83–94.

Lewis, D. "New Work for a Theory of Universals," *Australasian Journal of Philosophy,* Vol. 61 (1983), 343–77.

———. *On the Plurality of Worlds.* Oxford, 1986.

Plantinga, A. "Actualism and Possible Worlds," *Theoria,* Vol. 42 (1976), 139–60.

Price, H. H. *Thinking and Experience.* London, 1953.

Quine, W. V. O. *Philosophy of Logic.* Englewood Cliffs, NJ, 1970.

Quinton, A. "Properties and Classes," *Proceedings of the Aristotelian Society,* Vol. 58 (1957), 33–58.

Russell, B. *Introduction to Mathematical Philosophy.* London, 1919.

Tarski, A. *Introduction to Logic,* 2d ed. Oxford, 1946.

Tooley, M. *Causation.* Oxford, 1987.

Williams, D. C. "The Elements of Being," in *The Principles of Empirical Realism* (Springfield, IL, 1966).

PHILLIP BRICKER

PROPOSITIONAL ATTITUDE. *See:* BELIEF ATTRIBUTION, and CONTENT, MENTAL [S]

PROPOSITIONAL KNOWLEDGE, DEFINITION OF. The traditional definition of propositional knowledge, emerging from Plato's *Meno* and *Theaetetus,* proposes that such knowledge—knowledge that something is the case—has three essential components (*see* PLATO [6; S]). These components are identified by the view that knowledge is justified true belief. Knowledge, according to the traditional definition, is belief of a special kind, belief that satisfies two necessary conditions: (1) the TRUTH [S] of what is believed and (2) the justification of what is believed. While offering various accounts of the belief condition, the truth condition, and the justification condition for knowledge, many philosophers have held that those three conditions are individually necessary and jointly sufficient for propositional knowledge.

The belief condition requires that one accept, in some manner, any proposition one genuinely knows. This condition thus relates one psychologically to what one knows. It precludes that one knows a proposition while failing to accept that proposition. Some contemporary philosophers reject the belief condition for knowledge, contending that it requires a kind of mentalistic representation absent from many cases of genuine knowledge. Some other contemporary philosophers endorse the belief condition but deny that it requires actual assent to a proposition. They propose that, given the belief condition, a knower need only be disposed to assent to a proposition. Still other philosophers hold that the kind of belief essential to propositional knowledge requires assent to a known proposition, even if the assent need not be current or ongoing. The traditional belief condition is neutral on the exact conditions for belief and for the objects of belief.

The truth condition requires that genuine propositional knowledge be factual, that it represent what is actually the case. This condition precludes, for example, that astronomers before Copernicus knew that the Earth is flat. Those astronomers may have believed—even justifiably believed—that the Earth is flat, as neither belief nor justifiable belief requires truth. Given the truth condition, however, propositional knowledge without truth is impossible. Some contemporary philosophers reject the truth condition for knowledge, but they are a small minority. Proponents of the truth condition fail to agree on the exact conditions for the kind of truth essential to knowledge. Competing approaches to truth include correspondence, coherence, semantic, and redundancy theories, where the latter theories individually admit of variations. The truth condition for knowledge, generally formulated, does not aim to offer an exact account of truth.

The justification condition for propositional knowledge guarantees that such knowledge is not simply true belief. A true belief may stem just from lucky guesswork; in that case it will not qualify as knowledge. Propositional knowledge requires that the satisfaction of its belief condition be suitably related to the satisfaction of its truth condition. In other words, a knower must have adequate indication that a belief qualifying as knowledge is actually true. This adequate indication, on a traditional view of justification suggested by Plato and KANT [4; S], is suitable evidence indicating that a proposition is true. True beliefs qualifying as knowledge, on this traditional view, must be based on justifying evidence.

Contemporary philosophers acknowledge that justified contingent beliefs can be false; this is fallibilism about epistemic justification, the kind of justification appropriate to propositional knowledge. Given fallibilism, the truth condition for knowledge is not supplied by the justification condition; justification does not entail truth. Similarly, truth does not entail justification; one can lack evidence for a proposition that is true.

Proponents of the justification condition for knowledge do not share an account of the exact conditions for epistemic justification. Competing accounts include epistemic COHERENTISM [S], which implies that the justification of any belief depends on that belief's coherence relations to other beliefs, and epistemic foundationalism, which implies that some beliefs are justified independently of any other beliefs. Recently, some philosophers have proposed that knowledge requires not evidence but reliable (or truth-conducive) belief formation and belief sustenance. This is RELIABILISM [S] about the justification condition for knowledge. Whatever the exact conditions for epistemic justification are, proponents of the justification condition maintain that knowledge is not merely true belief.

Although philosophers have not agreed widely on what specifically the defining components of propositional knowledge are, there has been considerable agreement that knowledge requires, in general, justified true belief. Traditionally, many philosophers have assumed that justified true belief is sufficient as well as necessary for knowledge. This is a minority position now, owing mainly to Gettier counterexamples to this view. In 1963 Edmund Gettier challenged the view that if one has a justified true belief that *p*, then one knows that *p*. Gettier's counterexamples are:

> (I) Smith and Jones have applied for the same job. Smith is justified in believing that (i) Jones will get the job, and that (ii) Jones has ten coins in his pocket. On the basis of (i) and (ii), Smith infers, and thus is justified in believing, that (iii) the person who will get the job has ten coins in his pocket. As it turns out, Smith himself will actually get the job, and he also happens to have ten coins in his pocket. So, although Smith is justified in believing the true proposition (iii), Smith does not know (iii).
>
> (II) Smith is justified in believing the false proposition that (i) Jones owns a Ford. On the basis of (i), Smith infers, and thus is justified in believing, that (ii) either Jones owns a Ford or Brown is in Barcelona. As it turns out, Brown is in Barcelona, and so (ii) is true. So although Smith is justified in believing the true proposition (ii), Smith does not know (ii).

Gettier counterexamples are cases where one has a justified true belief that *p* but lacks knowledge that *p*. The Gettier problem is the difficulty of finding a modification of, or an alternative to, the traditional justified-true-belief analysis that avoids difficulties from Gettier counterexamples.

Contemporary philosophers have not reached a widely accepted solution to the Gettier problem. Many philosophers take the main lesson of Gettier counter-examples to be that propositional knowledge requires a fourth condition, beyond the justification, belief, and truth conditions. Some philosophers have claimed, in opposition, that Gettier counterexamples are defective because they rely on the false principle that false evidence can justify one's beliefs. There are, however, examples similar to Gettier's that do not rely on any such principle. Here is one such example inspired by Keith Lehrer and Richard Feldman:

> (III) Suppose that Smith knows the following proposition, *m*: Jones, whom Smith has always found to be reliable and whom Smith has no reason to distrust now, has told Smith, his officemate, that *p*: He, Jones, owns a Ford. Suppose also that Jones has told Smith that *p* only because of a state of hypnosis Jones is in and that *p* is true only because, unknown to himself, Jones has won a Ford in a lottery since entering the state of hypnosis. Suppose further that Smith deduces from *m* its existential generalization, *o*: There is someone, whom Smith has always found to be reliable and whom Smith has no reason to distrust now, who has told Smith, his officemate, that he owns a Ford. Smith, then, knows that *o*, since he has correctly deduced *o* from *m*, which he also knows. Suppose, however, that on the basis of his knowledge that *o*, Smith believes that *r*: Someone in the office owns a Ford. Under these conditions, Smith has justified true belief that *r*, knows his evidence for *r*, but does not know that *r*.

Gettier counterexamples of this sort are especially difficult for attempts to analyze the concept of propositional knowledge.

One noteworthy fourth condition consists of a "defeasibility condition" requiring that the justification appropriate to knowledge be "undefeated" in that an appropriate subjunctive conditional concerning defeaters of justification be true of that justification. A simple defeasibility condition requires of our knowing that *p* that there be no true proposition, *o*, such that if *q* became justified for us, *p* would no longer be justified for us. If Smith genuinely knows that Laura removed books from the office, then Smith's coming to believe with justification that Laura's identical twin removed books from the office would not defeat the justification for Smith's belief regarding Laura herself. A different approach claims that propositional knowledge requires justified true belief sustained by the collective totality of actual truths. This approach requires a precise, rather complex account of when justification is defeated and restored.

The importance of the Gettier problem arises from the importance of a precise understanding of the nature, or the essential components, of propositional knowledge. A precise understanding of the nature of propositional knowledge, according to many philosophers, requires a Gettier-resistant account of knowledge.

(SEE ALSO: *Epistemology* [S])

Bibliography

BonJour, L. *The Structure of Empirical Knowledge.* Cambridge, MA, 1985.

Carruthers, P. *Human Knowledge and Human Nature.* New York, 1992.

Chisholm, R. *Theory of Knowledge,* 3d ed. Englewood Cliffs, NJ, 1989.

Goldman, A. *Epistemology and Cognition.* Cambridge, MA, 1986.

Lehrer, K. *Theory of Knowledge.* Boulder, CO, 1990.

Lewis, C. I. *An Analysis of Knowledge and Valuation.* La-Salle, IL, 1946.

Moser, P. *Knowledge and Evidence.* New York, 1989.

———, and A. vander Nat, eds. *Human Knowledge: Classical and Contemporary Approaches,* 2d ed. New York, 1995.

Pollock, J. *Contemporary Theories of Knowledge.* Lanham, MD, 1986.

Shope, R. *The Analysis of Knowing.* Princeton, NJ, 1983.
Sosa, E. *Knowledge in Perspective.* New York, 1991.

PAUL K. MOSER

PROPOSITIONS. On one use of the term, propositions are objects of assertion, what successful uses of declarative sentences say. As such, they determine truth values and truth conditions. On a second, they are the objects of certain psychological states (such as belief and wonder) ascribed with verbs that take sentential complements (such as 'believe' and 'wonder'). On a third use, they are what are (or could be) named by the complements of such verbs. Many assume that propositions in one sense are propositions in the others.

After some decades of skepticism about the worth of positing propositions, the last quarter of the twentieth century saw renewed interest in and vigorous debate over their nature. This can be traced in good part to three factors: the development in INTENSIONAL LOGIC [S] of formal models of propositions; (not altogether unrelated) attacks on broadly Fregean accounts of propositions (*see* FREGE [3; S]); and a spate of work on the nature of belief and its ascription.

"Possible-worlds semantics" is a collection of methods for describing the semantical and logical properties of expressions such as 'necessarily'; these methods developed out of work done by Saul KRIPKE [S], Richard Montague, and others in the 1960s. It illuminated the logic and semantics of modal terms such as 'necessarily', of conditionals and tenses, and other constructions as well. In such semantics one assigns a sentence a rule that determines a truth value relative to various "circumstances of evaluation" (POSSIBLE WORLDS [S], times, whatever); a sentence like *it is necessary that S* has its truth value determined by the rule so associated with S. The success of such accounts made it natural to hypothesize that propositions, *qua* what's named by expressions of the form *that S,* could be identified with such rules—equivalently, with sets of circumstances such rules pick out.

Such a conception of proposition provides too crude an account of objects of belief or assertion: it implausibly makes all logically equivalent sentences express the same belief and say the same thing. A partial solution to this problem supposes that propositional identity is partially reflected in sentential structure, taking propositions themselves to be structured. Given the working hypothesis that a proposition's structure is that of sentences expressing it, critical to determining the proposition a sentence (use) expresses are the contributions made by sentence parts (on that use).

Frege suggested that associated with names and other meaningful expressions are "ways of thinking" or *senses* of what the expressions pick out; one might suppose that sense and sentence structure jointly determine proposition expressed. Sense, in the case of names and other singular terms, has standardly been taken to be given by describing how one thinks of the referent. For example, the sense of 'Aristotle' for me might be given by 'the author of the *Metaphysics*'; if so, my uses of 'Aristotle taught Alexander' and 'the author of the *Metaphysics* taught Alexander' would, on a Fregean view, express the same proposition.

During the 1970s Kripke, David Kaplan, and others argued convincingly that this view is untenable: it is obvious, on reflection, that the truth conditions of the assertion or belief that Aristotle was *F* depend on Aristotle in a way in which the truth conditions of the assertion or belief that the author of the *Metaphysics* was *F* do not. So either ways of thinking are somehow tied to the objects they present (so that the way I think of Aristotle could not present anything but Aristotle), or the contributions of expressions to propositions must be something other than senses.

The success of accounts of intensional language that ignored sense in favor of constructions from references, along with the apparent failure of Fregean accounts, led in the 1980s to debate over the merits of what is variously called direct-reference theory, Millianism, and (neo-) Russellianism (*see* RUSSELL [7]), espoused at various times by a wide variety of theorists including Kaplan, Mark Richard, Nathan Salmon, and Scott Soames. On such views sense is irrelevant to individuating a proposition; indeed, it is irrelevant to semantics. In particular, what a name contributes to a proposition is its referent: the proposition that Twain is dead is the same singular proposition as the proposition that Clemens is.

Neo-Russellians identify the object of assertion and the referent of a 'that' clause with a Russellian proposition. They allow that there is such a thing as a "way of grasping" a proposition and that belief in a singular proposition is mediated by such. Against the intuition that, for example, A: Mo believes that Twain is dead, and B: Mo believes that Clemens is dead, might differ in truth value, direct-reference accounts typically suggest that a pragmatic explanation is appropriate. Just as an ironic use of a sentence can convey a claim without literally expressing it, so a sentence about Mo's beliefs might convey information about Mo's way of grasping a singular proposition, without that information being part of what the sentence literally says. If this is so, intuitions about A and B are explained pragmatically.

Those unhappy with this account of propositions have looked elsewhere. Many accounts of propositions identify the proposition determined by S with some construction from linguistic items associated with S and the semantic values of S's parts. James Higginbotham has identified the referents of 'that' clauses with phrase markers that may be annotated with referents; Richard has suggested that the referent of a 'that' clause be identified with something like the singular proposition it determines paired off with the sentence itself. In making linguistic items constitutive of propositions, these views run counter to ones, like Frege's and Russell's, that closely tie meaning and synonymity to propositional determination. On linguistic views of propositions the synonymity of 'groundhog' and 'woodchuck' does not assure the identity of the proposition that groundhogs are pests with the proposition that woodchucks are. Other theorists (Gareth Evans, for example) have attempted to revive a version of Frege's views of propositions.

Many philosophers continue to doubt the utility of positing propositions. Quineans (*see* QUINE [7; S]) argue that meaning and reference must be determined by behaviorally manifest facts but that such facts woefully underdetermine assignments of MEANING [5; S] and REFERENCE [S]; they conclude that there is nothing about language that need or could be explained by positing propositions. Stephen Schiffer has argued that propositions are a sort of "linguistic posit": that we accept nominalizations of the form *that S* as referring to singular terms and have coherent criteria for using sentences in which those terms occur is itself sufficient for its being true that there are propositions. Such a deflationist view implies neither the possibility of a substantive account of propositions (on which, for example, the proposition expressed by a sentence is compositionally determined), nor that propositions play a substantive role in explaining semantic phenomena.

(SEE ALSO: *Philosophy of Language* [S])

Bibliography

Evans, G. *The Varieties of Reference.* Oxford, 1982.

Frege, G. "Uber Sinn und Bedeutung," *Zeitschrift fur Philosophie and Philosophische Kritik,* Vol. 100 (1892), 25–50. Translated by P. Geach and M. Black as "On Sense and Reference," in P. Geach and M. Black, eds., *Translations from the Philosophical Writings of Gottlob Frege* (Cambridge, 1952).

Horwich, P. *Truth.* Cambridge, MA, 1990.

Kaplan, D. "Demonstratives," in J. Perry et al., eds., *Themes from Kaplan* (Oxford, 1989).

Kripke, S. *Naming and Necessity.* Cambridge, MA, 1980.

Lewis, D. "Attitudes *de dicto* and *de se,*" *Philosophical Review,* Vol. 88 (1979), 513–43.

Montague, R. *Formal Philosophy,* edited by R. Thomason. New Haven, 1974.

Quine, W. V. O. *Word and Object.* Cambridge, MA, 1960.

Richard, M. *Propositional Attitudes.* Cambridge, 1990.

Salmon, N., and S. Soames, eds. *Propositions and Attitudes.* Oxford, 1988.

Schiffer S. "A Paradox of Meaning," *Noûs,* Vol. 28, 279–324.

Stalnaker, R. *Inquiry.* Cambridge, MA, 1984.

MARK E. RICHARD

PROVABILITY. Even though provability logic did not come into its own until the early seventies, it has its roots in two older fields: metamathematics and MODAL LOGIC [S]. In metamathematics, we study what theories can say about themselves. The first—and most outstanding—results are GÖDEL'S [S] two incompleteness theorems. (*See* GÖDEL'S THEOREM [3].)

If we take a sufficiently strong formal theory T—say, Peano arithmetic—we can use Gödel numbering to construct in a natural way a predicate $Prov(x)$ in the language of T that expresses "x is the Gödel number of a sentence which is provable in T." About T we already know that it satisfies modus ponens:

> If it is provable that A implies B, then, if A is provable, B is provable as well.

Now it turns out that, using Gödel numbering and the predicate *Prov,* we can express modus ponens in the language of T, and show that in T we can actually prove this formalized version of modus ponens:

$$Prov(\ulcorner A \rightarrow B\urcorner) \rightarrow (Prov(\ulcorner A\urcorner) \rightarrow Prov(\ulcorner B\urcorner)).$$

When we rephrase both the normal and the formalized version of modus ponens using the modal operator $\Box$, reading $\Box A$ as "A is provable in T," we get the modal rule

$$\frac{A \rightarrow B \qquad A}{B} \tag{1}$$

and the modal axiom

$$\Box(A \rightarrow B) \rightarrow (\Box A \rightarrow \Box B). \tag{2}$$

Indeed both the rule and the axiom are well known from the basic modal logic K.

Similarly, we can show that if there is a proof of the sentence A in T, then T itself can check this proof, so T proves $Prov(\ulcorner A\urcorner)$—we shall call this principle *Prov*-completeness. Again, though in a less straightforward way than in the case of modus ponens, we can formalize the principle itself and see that T actually proves:

$$Prov(\ulcorner A\urcorner) \rightarrow Prov(\ulcorner Prov(\ulcorner A\urcorner)\urcorner).$$

When we rephrase the principle of *Prov*-completeness and its formalization in modal logical terms, we get the modal rule that is usually called necessitation:

$$\frac{A}{\Box A}, \tag{3}$$

and the modal axiom

$$\Box A \rightarrow \Box\Box A, \tag{4}$$

which is the transitivity axiom 4 well known from modal systems such as K4 and S4.

Finally, one might wonder whether T proves the intuitively valid principle that "all provable sentences are true," i.e., whether T proves $Prov(\ulcorner A\urcorner) \rightarrow A$. Unexpectedly, this turns out not to be the case at all. Löb proved in 1953, using Gödel's technique of diagonalization, that T proves $Prov(\ulcorner A\urcorner) \rightarrow A$ only in the trivial case that T already proves A itself!

Löb's Theorem has a formalization that can also be proved in T. Writing both the theorem and its formalization in modal terms, we get the modal rule

$$\frac{\Box A \rightarrow A}{A}, \tag{5}$$

and the modal axiom

$$\Box(\Box A \rightarrow A) \rightarrow \Box A, \tag{6}$$

usually called W (for well-founded) by modal logicians.

Now we can define provability logic, which goes by various names in the literature—*PRL*, *GL* (for Gödel/Löb), L (for Löb), and, in modal logic texts, *KW*4. It is generated by all the modal formulas that have the form of a tautology of propositional logic, plus the rules (1),(3),(5) and axioms (2),(4),(6) given above. One can prove that rule (5) and axiom (4) already follow from the rest, so that *PRL* is equivalently given by the well-known system K plus the axiom $\Box(\Box A \rightarrow A) \rightarrow \Box A$.

The main "modal" theorem about *PRL*—but one with great arithmetical significance—is the "fixed point theorem," which D. de Jongh and G. Sambin independently proved in 1975. The theorem says essentially that "self-reference is not really necessary." Suppose that all occurrences of the propositional variable p in a given formula A are under the scope of $\Box$-es, for example, $A(p) = \neg\Box p$ or $A(p) = \Box(p \rightarrow q)$. Then there is a formula B in which p does not appear, such that all propositional variables that occur in B already appear in $A(p)$, and such that $PRL \vdash B \leftrightarrow A(B)$. This B is called a fixed point of $A(p)$. Moreover, the fixed point is unique, or more accurately, if there is another formula B' such that $PRL \vdash B' \leftrightarrow A(B')$, then we must have $PRL \vdash B \leftrightarrow B'$. Most proofs of the fixed point theorem in the literature give an algorithm by which one can compute the fixed point.

For example, suppose that $A(p) = \neg\Box p$. Then the fixed point produced by the algorithm is $\neg\Box\bot$, and indeed we have $PRL \vdash -\Box\bot \leftrightarrow -\Box(-\Box\bot)$. If we read this arithmetically, the direction from left to right is just the formalized version of Gödel's second incompleteness theorem. Thus, if T does not prove a contradiction, then it is *not* provable in T that T does not prove a contradiction.

The landmark result in provability logic is Solovay's "arithmetical completeness theorem" of 1976. This theorem says essentially that the modal logic *PRL* captures *everything* that PEANO [6] arithmetic can say in modal terms about its own provability predicate. Before formulating Solovay's theorem more precisely, we turn to the semantics of *PRL*.

Provability logic has a suitable Kripke semantics, just like many other modal logics (*see* KRIPKE, SAUL [S]). Unaware of the arithmetical relevance of *PRL*, Krister Segerberg proved in 1971 that it is sound and complete with respect to finite irreflexive transitive frames, and even with respect to finite trees. This completeness theorem immediately gives a decision procedure to decide for any modal formula A whether A follows from *PRL* or not. Looking at the procedure a bit more precisely, it can be shown that *PRL* is "very decidable": like the well-known modal logics K, T, and $S4$, it is decidable in PSPACE. This means that there is a Turing machine that, given a formula A as input, answers whether A follows from *PRL*; the size of the memory that the Turing machine needs for its computations is only polynomial in the length of A.

The modal completeness theorem was an important first step in Solovay's proof of the arithmetical completeness of *PRL*. Suppose that *PRL* does not prove the modal formula A. Then there is a finite tree such that A is false at the root of that tree. Now Solovay devised an ingenious way to describe the tree in the language of Peano arithmetic. Thus he found a translation f from modal formulas to sentences of arithmetic, such that Peano arithmetic does not prove $f(A)$. Such a *translation* f respects the logical connectives (so, e.g., $f(B \wedge C) = f(B) \wedge f(C)$), and $\Box$ is translated as *Prov* (so $f(\Box B) = Prov(\ulcorner f(B) \urcorner)$). Thus Solovay's arithmetical completeness theorem gives an alternative way to construct many nonprovable sentences. For example, we know that *PRL* does not prove $\Box p \vee \Box\neg p$, so by the theorem, there is an arithmetical sentence $f(p)$ such that Peano arithmetic does not prove $Prov(\ulcorner f(p) \urcorner) \vee Prov(\ulcorner \neg f(p) \urcorner)$. In particular, if we suppose that Peano arithmetic does not prove any false sentences, this implies that neither $f(p)$ nor $\neg f(p)$ is provable in Peano arithmetic.

In recent years, logicians have investigated many other systems of arithmetic that are weaker than Peano arithmetic. They have given a partial answer to the question: "For which theories of arithmetic does Solovay's arithmetical completeness theorem still hold?" It certainly holds for theories T that satisfy the following two conditions:

1. T proves induction for formulas in which all quantifiers are bounded (like the quantifier $\forall x \leq y + z$) and T proves that for all x, its power 2^x exists. In more technical terms: T extends $I\Delta_0 + EXP$.
2. T does not prove any false Σ_1 sentences.

For such theories, it is also clear that *PRL* is sound if we read $\Box$ as $Prov_T$ (where $Prov_T$ is a natural provability predicate with respect to a sufficiently simple axiomatization of T). To sum up, we have the following theorem: If T satisfies 1 and 2, and A is a modal sentence, then

$$PRL \vdash A \Leftrightarrow \text{for all translations } f, T \vdash f(A).$$

This result shows a strength of provability logic: for many different theories, *PRL* captures exactly what those theories say about their own provability predicates. At the same time this is of course a weakness: for example, provability logic does not point to any differences between those theories that are finitely axiomatizable and those that are not.

In order to be able to speak in a modal language about such distinctions between theories, researchers have extended provability logic in many different ways, only a few of which are mentioned here. One way is to add a binary modality, $\rhd$, where for a given theory T, the modal sentence $A \rhd B$ stands for "$T + B$ is interpretable in $T + A$." It appears that the interpretability logic of $I\Delta_0 + superexp$ is different from the interpretability logic of Peano arithmetic.

Another way to extend the framework of *PRL* is to add propositional quantifiers, so that one can express principles like Goldfarb's:

$$\forall p \forall q \exists r \Box((\Box p \vee \Box q) \leftrightarrow \Box r).$$

Finally, one can of course study predicate provability logic. Vardanyan proved that the set of always provable sentences of predicate provability logic is not even recursively enumerable, so it has no reasonable axiomatization. (SEE ALSO: *Mathematical Logic* and *Philosophical Logic* [S])

Bibliography

Artemov, S. N., and L. D. Beklemishev. "On Propositional Quantifiers in Provability Logic," *Notre Dame Journal of Formal Logic*, Vol. 34 (1993), 401–19.

Boolos, G. *The Logic of Provability*. New York, 1993.

de Jongh, D. H. J., M. Jumelet, and F. Montagna. "On the Proof of Solovay's Theorem," *Studia Logica*, Vol. 50 (1991), 51–70.

Smoryński, C. *Self-reference and Modal Logic*. New York, 1985.

Solovay, R. M. "Provability Interpretations of Modal Logic," *Israel Journal of Mathematics*, Vol. 25 (1976), 287–304.

Visser, A. "Interpretability Logic," in P. P. Petkov, ed., *Mathematical Logic (Proceedings, Chaika, Bulgaria, 1988)* (New York, 1990).

RINEKE VERBRUGGE

PSYCHOLOGY AND LOGIC. The phenomenology of Edmund HUSSERL [4; S] grew from his reflections on the status of the laws of logic. His *Logical Investigations* lay down an allegedly ultimate foundation for logic through the refutation of any attempt to ground it in psychology. What is the nature of the subjectivity that formulates the laws of logic? Logical statements and truths are undoubtedly about and applicable to the particular events taking place in the consciousness of human individuals, yet they do not draw their evidence from the examination of such events. If they did, psychological science would provide an account of how such evidence is arrived at. But this procedure involves the fallacy of PSYCHOLOGISM [6]. Psychology is an empirical science: its propositions are vague (even if valuable) generalizations from experience, they are statements about approximate regularities, which necessarily fall short of the a priori validity contained in logical laws. Logic is neither a technology of right thinking nor a normative discipline. Since the laws of logic must be justified by apodictic inner evidence, subjectivity must therefore be defined in the very terms of how the idealities themselves make sense or "constitute" themselves independent of their applications and normative functions (*see* FREGE, GOTTLOB [3; S]). *Pure* logic avoids the relativization of reason involved in the line of proof adopted by psychologistic thinkers. It forms the indispensable theoretical foundation for all its applications, referring to nothing in the real processes of thought. How, then, will logical objectivity and truth be represented in CONSCIOUSNESS [2; S]? Answering this question implies the discovery and description of the grounds that are not already contained within formal logic itself and yet provide a grounding of this logic. Ideation (nonsensuous intuiting) is needed in order to accomplish this process: the grasping of something general is such that, in relation to a multiplicity of particular moments of the same kind, it can come into view as precisely this one and the same kind. In his later work Husserl acknowledged the existence of transcendental psychologism: the transcendental ego cannot be different from the intramundane, human ego.
(SEE ALSO: *Judgment and Experience,* and *Transcendental Logic* [S])

Bibliography

Gurwitsch, A. *Studies in Phenomenology and Psychology*. Evanston, IL, 1966.

Seebohm, T. "Psychologism Revisited," in T. Seebohm et al., eds., *Phenomenology and the Formal Sciences* (Dordrecht and Boston, 1991).

Tragesser, R. *Husserl and Realism in Logic and Mathematics*. Cambridge, MA, 1984.

Willard, D. A. "The Paradox of Husserl's Psychologism: Husserl's Way out," in J. Mohanty, ed., *Readings on E. Husserl's Logical Investigations* (The Hague, 1977).

PIERRE KERSZBERG

PUTNAM, HILARY (b. 1926), after receiving a B.A. from Pennsylvania (1948) and a year spent at Harvard (1948–1949), studied at UCLA, taking his doctorate in 1951 with a dissertation titled "The Concept of Probability: An Application to Finite Sequences." He taught at Northwestern (1952–1953), Princeton (1953–1961) and MIT (1961–1965), becoming Walter Beverly Pearson professor at Harvard in 1965. Since 1995 he has been Cogan University Professor there. He has been influential in most areas of philosophy, particularly in the philosophy of language, of logic, of mathematics, and of science.

Putnam is sometimes thought of as often changing his mind. (See, for example, the *Dictionary of Philosophers' Names.*) Sometimes he has. But in central respects he has held a single, though developing, position since the mid-1950s, a position that in some aspects resembles the later WITTGENSTEIN's [8; S]. This article sets out some constant central themes.

Putnam was among those American philosophers to benefit directly from the intellectual exodus from Europe caused by Nazism. He was a student of Rudolf CARNAP [2; S] and of Hans REICHENBACH [7]. Though his approach to issues is quite different from theirs, Reichenbach in particular had a lasting and often acknowledged influence on Putnam's thought. Putnam's innovations stand out when it is noted. In *Realism with a Human Face* (1990; p. 289), Putnam remarks,

> In *Theory of Relativity and A Priori Knowledge* (1922) Reichenbach listed a number of statements . . . each of which Kant would have regarded as synthetic *a priori,* and each of which can be held immune from revision . . . , but which *collectively imply statements that are empirically testable,* and that Kant would, therefore, have to regard as *a posteriori.*

Certain principles had, in KANT's [4; S] time, as good a claim as any to fix how particular spatial, temporal, and other concepts are to be applied, and thereby which concepts those were; to be intrinsic to the concepts involved, thus 'conceptual truths', thus a priori. Relativity theory allows us to see how they are at least jointly testable, so that some may turn out false. Such, it seems, is a fate to which a priori truths are liable.

Putnam reports Reichenbach as making a related point to his classes. Considering questions such as 'How can we show that that blackboard is wider than this ashtray?', he argued that any system of measurement, or of observation, treats some propositions that seem empirical (such as 'mere translation does not make things grow or shrink') as axiomatic. One cannot sensibly apply the system while doubting these propositions; they are not subject to confirmation or refutation within the system. But it could prove reasonable to replace the system with another in which these propositions are testable, so possibly false. In that sense they are empirical.

There are two contrasting reactions to these points. One is: what this shows is that every concept commits itself to a particular empirical theory. If the theory proves false, then the concept is incoherent, so without application and to be discarded. This was Paul Feyerabend's reaction, and it is also Paul Churchland's.

The other reaction is: if we are confronted with situations that force giving up what seemed conceptual truths, it may appear that the concepts whose applications seemed to be governed by those principles are, in fact, otherwise governed. Perhaps the application of the concept 'straight line' to items in the world is not governed by the Euclidean parallel postulate, but rather in such and such other way. That reaction grants face value to Reichenbach's point that the same proposition that is axiomatic in one system may be testable and false in another. This was Putnam's reaction. He developed the position and drew its implications in a powerful series of papers in the 1950s and 1960s (see Putnam, 1962a–d). Part of the idea is that what principles govern the application of a concept depends in part on how the world in fact is. Putnam defined that role for the world in "The Meaning of 'Meaning' " (1975). This last article, though not published until 1975, was completed by 1968.

By the early seventies, Putnam had begun to emphasize some new themes. For one thing, he became increasingly impressed with what he calls the 'interest relativity' of such notions as explanation and cause. The general point is: what a concept counts as applying to—the correct way of applying it—varies with the circumstances in which it is to be applied. A concept may count, on one occasion, as fitting what it does not count as fitting on another. That is continuous with Putnam's earlier reaction to Reichenbach. The point then was: what it is reasonable to judge as to how a concept operates depends on the conditions in which such judgments are made. The point now is: what those conditions are depends not just on how the world is, but may vary from occasion to occasion, given the world as it is. Not coincidentally, this point went along with other developments in Putnam's thought.

The first of these developments is what he calls 'internal realism', first presented in 1976, and amplified in his writings of 1981, 1983, 1987a, 1987b, and elsewhere (*see* REALISM [S]). The position includes four points. First, there are mundane, true things to say about what our words and thoughts are about: "the word 'gold' means (refers to) gold; this is gold"; "This is a chair; this is what 'chair' refers to," and so forth. Second, there are philosophical dicta that sound much like such mundanities, or their denials, or generalizations of these, but that say, or try to say, something quite different. They are bad answers to the following pseudo-problem. On the one hand, there are thoughts and words—items that purport to represent the world as being thus and so; on the other hand, the items the world in fact contains, which are what and how they are independent of what we think, or do not think, about them. How are our words and thoughts related to these items? How, if at all, does their truth depend on how those items are? And how could they be so related? Internal realism holds that the problem rests on a mistake; hence so do any 'solutions', which take it at face value.

Third, the mundane remarks (point one) are correct because they are a feature of how these words are (or are to be) used. But that formulation depersonalizes things misleadingly. The standard for the correctness of a statement cannot be fixed independently of what users of the relevant words and concepts—that is, human beings—are prepared to recognize as correct: what Putnam identifies as our (human) perceptions of rationality and reasonableness. What it is for a statement to be correct depends on the sorts of beings we are, and is not reducible to some set of principles that would have to hold anyway. Fourth, it is part of what we are prepared to recognize as rational that any concept might be applied correctly in different ways in different circumstances. What sometimes counts as the cause of the explosion may not at other times. It is because human RATIONALITY [S] is occasion-sensitive that the problem mentioned in point two is a pseudo-problem. We cannot sensibly take a 'God's-eye view' of how we relate to the world, trying to say how our concepts would apply without us.

The occasion-sensitivity of rationality does not mean that truth is relative, or that there are no objective facts—given a framework, or setting, in which concepts are to be applied. Nor does giving up on a God's-eye view mean a deflationist account of truth. Putnam insists that we cannot comprehend what truth is without understanding the role of truth in our lives, notably in our activities of asserting, and of treating assertions in the ways we do; and that deflationism does not help us understand the role of truth in human life.

In arguing against the possibility of a God's-eye view, Putnam has produced what are probably his most discussed arguments. In one he identifies the God's-eye view (what John McDowell has called 'the view of the cosmic alien') as one from which we may consider our own language as an uninterpreted calculus with a range of possible interpretations, and then ask which interpretation is the right one. In what he first saw as a generalization of the Skolem paradox, he argues that, in that case, *nothing* could make one interpretation the right one, so we could not ever be talking about anything (or about one thing rather than others). But we cannot pose serious problems without talking about definite things. This is a reductio of the idea of a God's-eye view (see "Models and Reality," Philosophical Papers, Volume 3).

In another argument Putnam considers the (apparent) question whether we might be brains in a vat: that we are, and always have been, nothing but brains, kept alive by a bath of nutrients, fed computer-generated stimuli through electrodes. He argues that if the God's-eye view is possible, then that we are, and that we are not such brains should both be possibilities. But for the words of the question to mean what a God's-eye view requires them to means we must be using them in ways that entail that we are not brains in vats. For, as argued in "The Meaning of 'Meaning'," what our words mean depends, *inter alia,* on how we are in fact connected to the world, and not just on what we may anyway be aware of. For our 'brain' to mean *brain,* and our 'vat' to mean *vat,* we must be connected to the world as brains in ways vats could not be. So we cannot formulate what, from a God's-eye view, ought to be a possibility, in a way that makes it possible. That is another reductio of the idea of a God's-eye view (see Putnam, 1981).

Equally important to internal realism are Putnam's arguments against a causal theory of REFERENCE [S]: arguments, based on the interest-relativity of causation, that our being causally linked to the world as we, in fact, are is not enough in itself to make some one interpretation of our language correct—once it is granted that the language we speak may coherently be viewed by us as less than fully interpreted, so open to interpretation. These arguments appear in many replies to critics, and notably in "Realism with a Human Face" (1990).

At about the time Putnam began to develop internal realism, he also began to change his way of thinking about human psychology, rejecting a picture of it, and with that, a view he once espoused—FUNCTIONALISM [S]. Viewed one way, a human being is an organism constructed in a particular way, a particular battery of mechanisms arranged to interact with each other and the environment in given ways. If, while taking that view, we ask what it is for someone to believe that Mars is a planet, or to have *any* propositional or other attitude—to be in a mood, experience an emotion, and so on—it is tempting to look for an answer by trying to identify some state(s) of some mechanism(s) such that for someone to believe that is for him to be structured like that. In that frame of mind, for example, one might speak seriously of someone having a "token of a mentalese sentence" in his "belief box." This is the picture Putnam rejects.

Against it Putnam notes that to ascribe belief to someone is to relate that person to the world as we view it, and to ourselves, as on the same side as ours, or a different one, with respect to such and such question as to how the world is, and so on. Given internal realism, this means that there will be different truths to tell on different occasions as to what a given person, as he is at a given time, then believes. So for someone to be as said to be when we say him to believe thus and so, cannot be for him to have some particular mechanism, otherwise identifiable, in some particular state. And so on for other mental states (see Putnam, 1989).

Putnam has been refining the ideas discussed above, notably the idea of a distinction between ordinary and philosophic statements, and applying them in new areas, such as philosophy of mathematics. The above indicates a few main themes, omitting Putnam's striking arguments for them.

Bibliography

WORKS BY PUTNAM

"The Analytic and the Synthetic" [1962a], reprinted in *Mind, Language and Reality, Philosophical Papers, Volume 2* (Cambridge, 1975).

"It Ain't Necessarily So" [1962b], reprinted in *Mathematics, Matter and Method, Philosophical Papers, Volume 1* (Cambridge, 1975).

"Dreaming and 'Depth Grammar'" [1962c], in *Philosophical Papers, Volume 2* (Cambridge, 1975).

"What Theories Are Not" [1962d], in *Philosophical Papers, Volume 1* (Cambridge, 1975).

"The Meaning of 'Meaning,'" in *Philosophical Papers, Volume 2* (Cambridge, 1975).

"Realism and Reason" [1976], reprinted in *Meaning and the Moral Sciences* (London, 1978).

Reason, Truth and History. Cambridge, 1981.

"Models and Reality," reprinted in *Realism and Reason, Philosophical Papers, Volume 3* (Cambridge, 1983).

The Many Faces of Realism. LaSalle, IL, 1987.

"Realism with a Human Face," in *Realism with a Human Face, Philosophical Papers, Volume 4* (Cambridge, MA, 1990).

Renewing Philosophy. Cambridge, MA, 1992.

Words and Life. Cambridge, MA, 1994.

WORKS ON PUTNAM

Clark, P., and B. Hale, eds. *Reading Putnam.* Oxford, 1994.

Ebbs, G. *Rule-Following and Realism.* Cambridge, MA, 1996.

Rorty, R. "Solidarity or Objectivity," in J. Rajchman and C. West, eds., *Post-analytical Philosophy* (New York, 1985).

CHARLES TRAVIS

Q

QUALIA. The word quale (or qualia) derives from the Latin for "quality." As used by Clarence Irving LEWIS [4] and those following him, it refers to qualities such as color patches, tastes, and sounds of phenomenal individuals. In this sense the term means what BERKELEY [1; S] meant by sensible qualities or later philosophers meant by 'sensa', or 'sense data'. Since the demise of sense-data theories, the term qualia has come to refer to the qualitative, or phenomenal, character of conscious, sensory states, so mental states, not phenomenal individuals, are the subjects of predication. Another expression for this aspect of mental life is the "raw feel" of experience, or "what it's like" to have certain sensory experiences. Qualia are part of the phenomenon of the subjectivity of consciousness, and they pose one of the most difficult problems for a materialist solution to the MIND–BODY PROBLEM (5).

In contemporary PHILOSOPHY OF MIND [S], the problem of qualia has confronted both of the principal versions of materialism: the central-state identity theory and FUNCTIONALISM [S]. Regarding the former, J. J. C. SMART (1959; [S]) posed the problem this way: even if one admits that sensations are identical to brain states, the qualitative character of a sensation seems itself to be a nonphysical property of the sensation and therefore an obstacle to a materialist REDUCTION [S]. In response Smart developed a "topic-neutral" analysis of qualia—the idea that our very notion of a quale is of a property of sensation that has a tendency to be caused by certain stimuli and cause certain judgments of similarity on our part. Functionalism is largely an outgrowth of this sort of analysis.

Another sort of argument against materialist reductions of qualia has its roots in René DESCARTES [2; S] and was revived by Saul KRIPKE (1980; [S]). If we consider any proposed reduction of the sort "Pain is the firing of C-fibers," it seems quite conceivable that it is false: there could be pain without C-fibers and C-fibers without pain. Yet since it is widely accepted that true identity statements are necessarily true, what seems conceivable with respect to pain and C-fibers shouldn't be. Hence, they must not be identical. Again, one sort of response has been to argue that a proper analysis of our notion of pain (or any other quale) would reveal that it was a functional notion, and this explains the conceivability of pain without C-fibers since pains could be realized in a variety of physical structures. With the right functional identity statement the felt contingency wouldn't arise.

For these reasons, among others, functionalism replaced the central-state identity theory as the dominant materialist doctrine in the philosophy of mind. With respect to qualia functionalism is the thesis that what it's like to have a certain sensory experience is analyzable in terms of the causal relations that hold among that experience, other mental states (e.g., beliefs, desires, and other sensory experiences), and stimuli and behavior. However, both the inverted qualia and absent qualia hypotheses pose serious problems for a functionalist theory of qualia.

The inverted qualia hypothesis is the idea that two creatures could be functionally identical and yet differ in their qualia. The most popular version of this hypothesis is the possibility of an inverted spectrum. Suppose Jack and Jill react exactly the same ways, both behaviorally and functionally, to light of every wavelength. However, it turns out that the way red looks to Jack is qualitatively similar to the way green looks to Jill, and similarly for yellow and blue. All the similarity relations among color experiences would be the same for the two, so there is no reason to think there need be a functional difference between them. Yet their qualia would differ. Hence, qualia can't be identified with functional states or properties.

The absent qualia hypothesis goes a step further. On this scenario, there is a creature that is functionally identical to a normal human being, and yet it has no conscious, qualitative experience at all; there is nothing it is like to be it. Ned Block (1980) proposed one way of making this possibility compelling. He has us imagine the entire nation of China organized—say by telephone connections—so as to realize the functional description of a human being. It seems ludicrous, he argues, to suppose the nation as a whole is experiencing anything.

Finally, another sort of argument (due to Jackson, 1982) against a materialist reduction of qualia is the knowledge argument: if any version of PHYSICALISM [S] is true, then someone in possession of all the physical facts should be able to determine what the qualitative character of a state is like. Yet it seems obvious that someone who knew all the neurophysiology and psychology there was to know, but who had never seen red, wouldn't know what it was like to see red. Hence, the qualitative character of sensations of red must not be a physical property.

Some philosophers have taken these and similar arguments to show that qualia are not physical properties (where functional counts as a form of physical for these purposes). One of the biggest problems with adopting this position is that it seems to lead to epiphenomenalism, the position that qualia do not causally interact with physical events. Yet it seems clear that when we cry out from pain it's the pain, the phenomenal experience, that is causing the crying. Though some are willing to abide epiphenomenalism (e.g., Jackson, 1982), most philosophers have sought other solutions.

Another sort of response in the spirit of nonmaterialism is to maintain that what these qualia-related arguments show is that we don't understand how physical processes give rise to qualitative experience. The mind–body problem is essentially an epistemological problem, and what we need are new conceptual tools to establish an explanatory connection between physical descriptions of what's going on in our brains and phenomenal descriptions. Philosophers taking this line (e.g., Levine, 1983, McGinn, 1991, and Nagel, 1974) differ as to how much of a problem it is that we seem unable to explain qualia in physical terms.

There are a number of materialist responses to the problem of qualia. Some philosophers argue that absent and inverted qualia are not possible, after all, and that functionalism provides the best theory of the nature of qualitative character (e.g., Lycan, 1987). Other philosophers, impressed by the inverted and absent qualia hypotheses, argue that a return to the central-state identity theory for sensory qualia is warranted. Sydney Shoemaker (1984), arguing that inverted qualia, but not absent qualia, are possible, adopts an in-between position: having qualia at all is a matter of functional organization, but which qualia one has is determined by how the functional states are physically realized.

Finally, some philosophers argue for eliminativism (*see* ELIMINATIVE MATERIALISM, ELIMINATIVISM [S]) with respect to qualia (e.g., Dennett, 1991, Rey, 1983). That is, they argue that our intuitive conception of qualitative character is so primitive, contradictory, or incoherent that it is unlikely that any real property of our mental states satisfies it.

Bibliography

Block, N. "Are Absent Qualia Impossible?" *Philosophical Review,* Vol. 89 (1980), 257–74.

———. "Troubles with Functionalism," in N. Block, ed., *Readings in Philosophy of Psychology,* Vol. 1 (Cambridge, MA, 1980).

Block, N., and J. A. Fodor. "What Psychological States Are Not," *Philosophical Review,* Vol. 81 (1972), 159–81.

Churchland, P. "Reduction, Qualia, and the Direct Introspection of Brain States," *Journal of Philosophy,* Vol. 82 (1985), 8–28.

Clark, A. *Sensory Qualities.* Oxford, 1993.

Davies, M., and G. W. Humphreys, eds. *Consciousness: Psychological and Philosophical Essays.* Oxford, 1993.

Dennett, D. C. "Quining Qualia," in A. J. Marcel and E. Bisiach, eds., *Consciousness in Contemporary Science* (Oxford, 1988).

———. *Consciousness Explained.* Boston, 1991.

Flanagan, O. *Consciousness Reconsidered.* Cambridge, MA, 1992.

Hardin, C. L. *Color for Philosophers: Unweaving the Rainbow.* Indianapolis, 1988.

Jackson, F. "Epiphenomenal Qualia," *Philosophical Quarterly,* Vol. 32, (1982), 127–36.

Kripke, S. *Naming and Necessity.* Cambridge, MA, 1980.

Levine, J. "Materialism and Qualia: The Explanatory Gap," *Pacific Philosophical Quarterly,* Vol. 64 (1983), 354–61.

Lycan, W. G. *Consciousness.* Cambridge, MA, 1987.

McGinn, C. *The Problem of Consciousness.* Oxford, 1991.

Nagel, T. "What Is It Like to Be a Bat?" *Philosophical Review,* Vol. 82 (1974), 435–50.

———. *The View from Nowhere.* New York, 1986.

Rey, G. "A Reason for Doubting the Existence of Consciousness," in R. Davidson, G. E. Schwartz, and D. Shapiro, eds., *Consciousness and Self-Regulation,* Vol. 3 (New York, 1983).

Smart, J. J. C. "Sensations and Brain Processes," *Philosophical Review,* Vol. 68 (1959), 109–30.

Shoemaker, S. *Identity, Cause, and Mind.* Cambridge, 1984. Specifically, chapters 9, 14, and 15.

JOSEPH LEVINE

QUINE, WILLARD VAN ORMAN, Edgar Pierce Professor of Philosophy Emeritus, at Harvard, author of twenty-one books and scores of journal articles and reviews, has made many significant contributions to METAPHYSICS [5; S], EPISTEMOLOGY [3; S], PHILOSOPHY OF

LANGUAGE [4; S], PHILOSOPHY OF SCIENCE [6; S], PHILOSOPHY OF MIND [S], LOGIC [4], philosophy of logic, and SET THEORY [S], and ETHICS ([3]; and ETHICAL THEORY [S]). These contributions are of a stature that firmly places QUINE [7] among the titans of twentieth-century Anglo-American philosophy.

In most of his publications following *Word and Object* (1960), Quine has sought to sum up, clarify, and expand on various themes found in that book. Quine can occasionally be seen changing his mind regarding some detail of his prior thought, but by and large he remains remarkably consistent.

NATURALISM

The keystone of Quine's systematic philosophy is NATURALISM [5; S]. Roughly, naturalism is the view that there is no suprascientific justification for science *and* that it is up to science to determine both what there is (ONTOLOGY [5]) and how we know what there is (epistemology). Moreover, Quine maintains that the best current science tentatively and fallibly plumps for a physicalist ontology and an empiricist epistemology.

Ontology: Physicalism. Since he maintains that what a (formalized) theory says there is is determined by the range of values of the bound variables of that theory, and since the bound variables of the best current scientific theory of the world (viz., physics) range over both physical objects and numbers, then, given his naturalism, Quine's physicalism embraces both concrete objects and abstract objects (*see* PHYSICALISM [S]). He is a scientific realist regarding (observable and unobservable) physical objects and a Platonic realist regarding numbers (or sets). However, in *Pursuit of Truth* (1980) Quine downgrades the philosophical importance of ontology, including physicalism. He does so because of ontological relativity (i.e., indeterminacy of REFERENCE [S]). The thesis is that a theory's ontology can be supplanted *salva veritate* by any one-to-one mapping of it. Ontological relativity thus engenders an attitude of indifference toward various equally apt ontologies for a given theory, including physical theory so called. At the same time it highlights the importance of a theory's ideology, that is, its lexicon of predicates. The philosophical point of Quine's thesis is, then, that what a theory says there is is less important to our understanding of the world than what a theory says about what there is.

There are two further senses in which Quine may be said to be a physicalist. First, as expected, he rejects Cartesian dualism of mind and body in favor of materialism. In this regard, he endorses Donald DAVIDSON'S [S] ANOMALOUS MONISM [S]: token identity, type diversity. Second, he is a physicalist in the sense in which physicalism is opposed to PHENOMENALISM [6] in epistemology (see below).

Epistemology: Empiricism. If the best current scientific theory (tentatively and fallibly) proffers a physicalist answer to the question of what there is, then what does it proffer in response to the question of how we know what there is? The answer is, in a word, EMPIRICISM [2]. Quine maintains that it is a finding of science that all that we come to know about the world begins with the activation of our nerve endings.

So, Quine endorses the naturalization of both ontology and epistemology. And although he downgrades the philosophical importance of ontology, he maintains the philosophical importance of epistemology. The central question of epistemology, according to Quine, is How do we acquire our theory of the world and why does it work so well? Any answer to this question must explain the relation between one's empirical data (the "meager input") and one's theory of the world (the "torrential output"). Much of what Quine wrote after *Word and Object* is, ultimately, devoted to answering this question. His own distinctive answer may be called externalized empiricism in order to differentiate it from approaches of other naturalized epistemologists (e.g., Donald Davidson; *see* NATURALIZED EPISTEMOLOGY [S]). Quine's empiricism is externalized in the sense that he takes sets of activated nerve endings as his data and sets of sentences as his theory of the world (as opposed, say, to impressions and ideas, respectively).

In Quine's hands, the general relation, R_1, holding between sets of activated nerve endings and sets of sentences gets analyzed into two relations. There is the causal relation, R_2, holding between holophrastically construed observation sentences and their respective patterns of activated nerve endings, and there is the logical relation, R_3, holding between those same observation sentences, now analytically construed, and standing sentences. Quine schematizes how the child or the race, beginning with verbal responses conditioned to their respective patterns of nerve endings (R_2), could have gone on to achieve verbal reference to bodies, substances, unobservables, and abstract objects (R_3). Moreover, his account of R_3 explains how observation sentences are logically related to theoretical sentences in such a way that no bridge principles are needed for linking observation and theoretic sentences. His account also highlights the hypothetico-deductive method of prediction and falsification and the moderately holistic character of theory revision.

Reciprocal Containment. Externalized empiricism is Quine's contribution to answering the central epistemological question of how we acquire our theory of the world and why it works so well. As such, his epistemology (empiricism) "contains" his ontology (physicalism): *nihil in mente quod non prius in sensu.* However, Quine's epistemologizing always takes place within some accepted theory of the world (the best one he can muster at the time), so his epistemology (empiricism) is itself contained within his ontology (physicalism). This latter containment is the central lesson of naturalism: there is no first philosophy. It is this latter containment that also makes Quine's epistemology such a radical departure from the tradition.

CHANGES OF MIND

Even though Quine's thought has been remarkably consistent since his first works appeared in the 1930s, he changed his mind on a few important matters. First, he downgraded the importance of ontology, discussed above. Second, in the context of radical translation, Quine dropped the idea that the linguist can translate the native's "Gavagai" as her own "Lo, a rabbit" just in case the native's stimulus meaning for "Gavagai" is approximately the same as the linguist's for "Lo, a rabbit." The problem is with making scientific sense of this "implicit homology assumption" regarding different people's nerve endings. Quine changed to the position that the linguist can translate the native's "Gavagai" as her own "Lo, a rabbit" just in case the linguist can empathize with the native to the extent that she can confidently conjecture that, were she in the native's position when he uttered (or assented to) "Gavagai," then she would have done likewise for "Lo, a rabbit." In this way the linguist is (tentatively) equating the native's "Gavagai" with her own "Lo, a rabbit" without relying on an implicit homology assumption. Third, since, according to Quine's externalized empiricism, the meager input underdetermines the torrential output, then it is conceivable that there could be two (or more) global theories of the world that are empirically equivalent, logically compatible, equally simple, and so forth. Would both be true? Quine's empiricism encourages an ecumenical response: both would be true. His naturalism encourages a sectarian response: only one would be true. Quine himself vacillated on the issue but eventually endorsed the sectarian response. This suggests that his commitment to naturalism runs deeper than his commitment to empiricism.

Bibliography

Among Quine's post–*Word and Object* books that bear directly on the topics discussed here are:

The Ways of Paradox and Other Essays. New York, 1966; enlarged ed., Cambridge, MA, 1976.

Ontological Relativity and Other Essays. New York, 1969.

Roots of Reference. La Salle, IL, 1974.

Theories and Things. Cambridge, MA, 1981.

Other of Quine's later books of interest are:

Set Theory and Its Logic. Cambridge, MA, 1963; rev. ed., 1969.

Philosophy of Logic. Englewood Cliffs, NJ, 1970; Cambridge, MA, 1986.

With J. S. Ullian, *The Web of Belief.* New York, 1970; rev. ed., 1978.

The Time of My Life. Cambridge, MA, 1985.

Quiddities. Cambridge, MA, 1987.

The secondary literature on Quine is immense and still growing. It includes:

Barrett, R., and R. Gibson, eds. *Perspectives on Quine.* Oxford, 1990.

Davidson, D., and J. Hintikka, eds. *Words and Objections.* Dordrecht, 1969.

Gibson, R. F., Jr. *The Philosophy of W. V. Quine: An Expository Essay.* Tampa, FL, 1982.

Hahn, L. E., and P. A. Schilpp, eds. *The Philosophy of W. V. Quine.* La Salle, IL, 1986.

Hookway, C. *Quine: Language, Experience, and Reality.* Stanford, CA, 1988.

Romanos, G. D. *Quine and Analytic Philosophy.* Cambridge, MA, 1983.

R. F. GIBSON

R

RACISM. RACISM [7] is the view that the human species is composed of different racial groups that can be arranged hierarchically from least to most superior. Before Charles DARWIN [2] racist theories were typically formulated in terms of lineage and type: current groups were claimed to be the progeny of certain original types, each of which exemplified a distinctive form of behavior. The current achievements of any existing group or nation were then explained by reference to the admixture of racial types from which it had descended. Darwin introduced the notion of race as a subspecies—a group within a particular species that has been isolated genetically from other members of that species and has as a result developed distinct morphological and/or behavioral attributes (Banton). Social DARWINISM [2] made the survival of a particular race the mark of its fitness. Eugenicists went further to argue that we should use our knowledge to create a superior class of human beings for the future. Recent attempts to provide justification for racist orientations include a resuscitation of the claim that Africans and African Americans have lower IQs than do Europeans and European Americans (Levin). In response some argue that research that could produce harm by furthering racist views should not be carried out; others argue that we have a moral obligation to pursue the truth no matter how uncomfortable it might be (Block & Dworkin). Clearly, however, the results of such research could be used equally to harm or help. If, for instance, it were found that people with high melanin content in their skin responded to a particular chemical compound that affected mental functioning, then it might be possible to manipulate that compound to either boost or retard intellectual performance.

Some philosophers have argued that the very concept of a race is an artifact of European expansionism, that races exist only as a grouping convenient to the classifier. Rejecting Europe's cultural imperialism thus requires that we reject classification by races (Appiah). In a similar vein certain biologists have argued that the concept of race has no biological validity (Alland). Other biologists insist there is compelling evidence for the existence of races (Dobzansky, Nei & Roychoudhury). However, even if races were sociohistorical creations, that would be no argument against their current existence (Goldberg).

Marxists argue that racism—belief in the superiority of one race over other races—is an ideological ploy to divide the lower classes so that the European and non-European proletariat fight one another instead of fighting capitalism. Others argue that racial differences are often independent of class differences and cannot be reduced to them. Many of the latter link race to nationalist sentiments and to the demand of reparation for past harms perpetuated into the present (Outlaw).

Racism may be independent of individual intent, as is often the case with institutional racism, where implementation of certain procedures causes unnecessary harm to groups historically considered inferior, without the implementer's intentionally willing such harm. Practices such as requiring training and experience that is irrelevant for a particular employment or educational opportunity, or recruiting through personal networks, often serve to perpetuate the effects of overt racist acts of the past and so are examples of institutional racism (Ezorsky, West). (SEE ALSO: *Social and Political Philosophy* [S])

Bibliography

Alland, A., Jr. *Human Diversity*. New York, 1973.

Appiah, K. A. *In My Father's House: Africa in the Philosophy of Culture*. New York, 1992.

Banton, M. *Racial Theories*. New York, 1987.

Block, N. J., and G. Dworkin. *The IQ Controversy*. New York, 1976.

Dobzansky, T. *Mankind Evolving.* New York, 1962.
Ezorsky, G. *Racism and Justice: The Case for Affirmative Action.* Ithaca, NY, 1991.
Goldberg, D. T. "Racist Discourse and the Language of Class," in A. Zegeye, L. Harris, and J. Maxted, eds., *Exploitation and Exclusion: Race and Class in Contemporary US Society* (New York, 1991).
———. *Racist Culture-Philosophy and the Politics of Meaning.* Cambridge, 1993.
Levin, M. "Race, Biology, and Justice," *Public Affairs Quarterly,* Vol. 8 (1994), 267–85.
Mayr, E. *The Growth of Biological Thought: Diversity, Evolution, and Inheritance.* Cambridge, MA, 1982.
Nei, M., and A. K. Roychoudhury. "Genetic Relationship and Evolution of Human Races," *Evolutionary Biology,* Vol. 14 (1983), 1–59.
Outlaw, L. "Race and Class in the Theory and Practice of Emancipatory Social Transformation," in L. Harris, ed., *Philosophy Born of Struggle* (Dubuque, IA, 1983).
West, C. *Race Matters.* Boston, 1993.

ALBERT MOSLEY

RATIONAL INTUITION. *See:* INTUITION [4; S]

RATIONALITY.

Philosophers have, at least characteristically, aspired to possess rationality but have not thereby sought exactly the same thing. Portrayed vaguely, rationality is reasonableness, but not all philosophers take rationality as dependent on reasons; nor do all philosophers have a common understanding of reasons or of reasonableness. Some theorists consider rationality to obtain in cases that lack countervailing reasons against what has rationality; they thus countenance rationality as, in effect, a default status. In ordinary parlance, persons can have rationality; so, too, can beliefs, desires, intentions, and actions, among other things. The rationality appropriate to action is practical, whereas that characteristic of beliefs is, in the language of some philosophers, theoretical.

Many philosophers deem rationality as instrumental, as goal oriented. You have rationality, according to some of these philosophers, in virtue of doing your best, or at least doing what you appropriately think adequate, to achieve your goals. If ultimate goals are not themselves subject to assessments of rationality, then rationality is purely instrumental, in a manner associated with David HUME's [4; S] position. Rationality, according to this view, is a minister without portfolio; it does not require any particular substantive goals of its own but consists rather in the proper pursuit of one's ultimate goals, whatever those goals happen to be. Many decision-theoretic and economic approaches to rationality are purely instrumentalist. If, however, ultimate goals are susceptible to rational assessment, as an Aristotelian tradition and a Kantian tradition maintain, then rationality is not purely instrumental. The latter two traditions regard certain rather specific (kinds of) goals, such as human well-being, as essential to rationality (*see* ARISTOTLE [1; S]; KANT [4; S]). Their substantialist approach to rationality lost considerable influence, however, with the rise of modern DECISION THEORY [2; S].

When relevant goals concern the acquisition of truth and the avoidance of falsehood, so-called epistemic rationality is at issue. Otherwise, some species of nonepistemic rationality is under consideration. One might individuate species of nonepistemic rationality by the kind of goal at hand: moral, prudential, political, economic, aesthetic, or some other. Some philosophers have invoked rationality "all things considered" to resolve conflicts arising from competing desires or species of rationality; even so, there are various approaches to rationality "all things considered" in circulation. The standards of rationality are not uniformly epistemic, then, but epistemic rationality can play a role even in what some call nonepistemic rationality. Regarding economic rationality, for instance, a person seeking such rationality will, at least under ordinary conditions, aspire to epistemically rational beliefs concerning what will achieve the relevant economic goals. Similar points apply to other species of nonepistemic rationality. A comprehensive account of rationality will characterize epistemic and nonepistemic rationality, as well as corresponding kinds of irrationality (e.g., weakness of will).

Taking rationality as deontological, some philosophers characterize rationality in terms of what is rationally obligatory and what is merely rationally permissible. If an action, for instance, is rationally obligatory, then one's failing to perform it will be irrational. Other philosophers opt for a nondeontological evaluative conception of rationality that concerns what is good (but not necessarily obligatory) from a certain evaluative standpoint. Some of the latter philosophers worry that, if beliefs and intentions are not voluntary, then they cannot be obligatory. Still other philosophers understand rationality in terms of what is praiseworthy, rather than blameworthy, from a certain evaluative standpoint. The familiar distinction between obligation, goodness, and praiseworthiness thus underlies three very general approaches to rationality.

Following Henry SIDGWICK [7; S], William Frankena has distinguished four conceptions of rationality: (1) an egoistic conception implying that it is rational for one to be or do something if and only if this is conducive to one's own greatest happiness (e.g., one's own greatest pleasure or desire satisfaction); (2) a perfectionist conception entailing that it is rational for one to be or do something if and only if this is a means to or a part of one's moral or nonmoral perfection; (3) a utilitarian conception implying that it is rational for one to be or do something if and only if this is conducive to the greatest general good or welfare (*see* UTILITARIANISM [8]); and (4) an intuitionist conception implying that it is rational for one to be or do something if and only if this conforms to self-evident truths, intuited by reason, concerning what is appropriate. The history of philosophy represents, not only these conceptions of rationality, but also modified conceptions adding further necessary or sufficient conditions to one of (1)–(4).

Given an egoistic conception of rationality, one's being rational will allow for one's being immoral, if morality requires that one not give primacy to oneself over other people. Rationality and morality can then conflict. Such conflict is less obvious on a utilitarian conception of rationality. In fact, if morality is itself utilitarian in the way specified (as many philosophers hold), a utilitarian conception of rationality will disallow rational immorality. A perfectionist conception of rationality will preclude rational immorality only if the relevant perfection must be moral rather than nonmoral; achieving nonmoral perfection will, of course, not guarantee morality. As for an intuitionist conception of rationality, if the relevant self-evident truths do not concern what is morally appropriate, then rational immorality will be possible. An intuitionist conception will bar conflict between rationality and morality only if it requires conformity to all the self-evident truths about what is morally appropriate that are relevant to a situation or person. So, whether rationality and morality can conflict will depend, naturally enough, on the exact requirements of the conception of rationality at issue.

Richard Brandt has suggested that talk of what it would be rational to do functions to guide action by both recommending action and by making a normative claim that evaluates the available action relative to a standard. An important issue concerns what kind of strategy of using information to choose actions will enable one to achieve relevant goals as effectively as any other available strategy. Brandt has offered a distinctive constraint on such a strategy: a rational decision maker's preferences must be able to survive their being subjected to repeated vivid reflection on all relevant facts, including facts of logic. This constraint suggests what may be called (5) a relevant-information conception of rationality: rationality is a matter of what would survive scrutiny by all relevant information.

A relevant-information conception of rationality depends, first, on a clear account of precisely when information is relevant and, second, on an account of why obviously irrational desires cannot survive scrutiny by all relevant information. Evidently, one could have a desire caused by obviously false beliefs arising just from wishful thinking, and this desire could survive a process of scrutiny by all relevant information where the underlying false beliefs are corrected. In any case, a relevant-information conception of rationality will preclude rational immorality only if it demands conformity to all relevant moral information.

The egoistic, perfectionist, utilitarian, and relevant-information conceptions of rationality are nonevidential in that they do not require one's having evidence that something is conducive to self-satisfaction, perfection, general welfare, or support from all relevant information. Many philosophers would thus fault those conceptions as insufficiently sensitive to the role of relevant evidence in rationality. If relevant evidence concerns epistemic rationality, we again see the apparent bearing of epistemic rationality on rationality in general. The latter bearing deserves more attention in contemporary work on nonepistemic rationality.

Philosophers currently divide over internalism and externalism about rationality. If rationality demands reasons of some sort or other, the dispute concerns two senses of talk of a person's having a reason to perform an action. An internalist construal of this talk implies that the person has some motive that will be advanced by the action. An externalist construal, in contrast, does not require that the person have a motive to be advanced by the action. Bernard Williams, among others, has suggested that any genuine reason for one's action must contribute to an explanation of one's action and that such a contribution to explanation must be a motivation for the action. He concludes that externalism about rationality is false, on the ground that external reasons do not contribute to explanation of action in the required manner. Externalism about rationality does allow that reasons fail to motivate, but this, according to externalists, is no defect whatever. Externalists distinguish between merely motivating reasons and justifying reasons, contending that only the latter are appropriate to rationality understood normatively; what is merely motivating in one's psychological set, in any case, need not be justifying. Perhaps, then, disputes between internalists and externalists will benefit from attention to the distinction between justifying and merely motivating reasons.

Modern DECISION THEORY [2; S] assumes that, in satisfying certain consistency and completeness requirements, a person's preferences toward the possible outcomes of available actions will determine, at least in part, what actions are rational for that person by determining the personal utility of outcomes of those actions. In rational decision making under certainty one definitely knows the outcomes of available actions. In decision making under risk one can assign only various definite probabilities less than 1 to the outcomes of available actions. (Bayesians assume that the relevant probabilities are subjective in that they are determined by a decision maker's beliefs—*see* BAYESIANISM [S].) In decision making under uncertainty one lacks information about relevant states of the world and hence cannot assign even definite probabilities to the outcomes of available actions. Acknowledging that rationality is purely instrumental (and thus that even Hitler's Nazi objectives are not necessarily rationally flawed), Herbert Simon has faulted modern decision theory on the ground that humans rarely have available the facts, consistent preferences, and reasoning power required by standard decision theory. He contends that human rationality is "bounded" in that it does not require utility maximization or even consistency. Rather, it requires the application of a certain range of personal values (or preferences) to resolve fairly specific problems one faces, in a way that is satisfactory, rather than optimal, for one. Simon thus relies on actual human limitations to constrain his account of rationality.

Contemporary theorists divide over the significance of human psychological limitations for an account of rationality. The controversy turns on how idealized principles for rationality should be. This raises the important issue of what exactly makes some principles of rationality true and others false. If principles of rationality are not just stipulative definitions, this issue merits more attention from philosophers than it has received. Neglect of this metaphilosophical issue leaves the theory of rationality as a subject of ongoing philosophical controversy.

Bibliography

Audi, R. *Intention and Reason.* Ithaca, NY, 1993.

Benn, S. I., and G. W. Mortimore, eds. *Rationality and the Social Sciences.* London, 1976.

Brandt, R. *A Theory of the Good and the Right.* Oxford, 1979.

Elster, J., ed. *Rational Choice.* New York, 1986.

Frankena, W. "Concepts of Rational Action in the History of Ethics," *Social Theory and Practice,* Vol. 9 (1983), 165–97.

Gauthier, D. *Morals by Agreement.* Oxford, 1986.

Hollis, M., and S. Lukes, eds. *Rationality and Relativism.* Oxford, 1982.

Mele, A. *Irrationality.* New York, 1987.

Moser, P., ed. *Rationality in Action.* Cambridge, 1990.

Nozick, R. *The Nature of Rationality.* Princeton, NJ, 1993.

Rescher, N. *Rationality.* Oxford, 1988.

Sidgwick, H. *The Methods of Ethics,* 7th ed. London, 1907.

Simon, H. *Reason in Human Affairs.* Stanford, CA, 1983.

Slote, M. *Beyond Optimizing: A Study of Rational Choice.* Cambridge, MA, 1988.

Williams, B. "Internal and External Reasons," in R. Harrison, ed., *Rational Action* (Cambridge, 1979).

PAUL K. MOSER

RAWLS, JOHN, is widely regarded as one of the most significant political philosophers of the twentieth century. He was born in Baltimore, Maryland, in 1921. Educated at Princeton, he taught at Cornell and the Massachusetts Institute of Technology before joining the faculty of Harvard University in 1962. Rawls's *A Theory of Justice,* published in 1971, revitalized political theory as an academic discipline and rejuvenated interest in the substantive social issues that had long been neglected by academic philosophers. Rawls continued to refine and defend his theory in a series of articles and lectures, the most important of which he revised and collected in his 1993 work, *Political Liberalism.*

JUSTICE AS FAIRNESS

The primary objective of Rawls's political theory is to articulate and defend a conception of JUSTICE [3; S] for a modern democratic regime. The theory begins with the idea of society as a "fair system of cooperation between free and equal persons." The principles of justice for such a society characterize its fair terms of cooperation by specifying its citizens' basic rights and duties and by regulating the distribution of its economic benefits. To formulate his particular conception of justice, Rawls invokes the familiar theory of the SOCIAL CONTRACT [7], according to which the legitimate rules for a society are arrived at by the autonomous agreement of its members. Rawls's version of the contract theory is distinctive, however, in its insistence upon the essential fairness of the point of view from which the agreement itself is conceived. This enables Rawls to appeal to the justificatory force of "pure procedural justice," the idea that the fundamental fairness of a procedure can ensure the justice of its outcome, provided that there is no independent criterion for the justice of that result. Fairness thus characterizes both the terms of the contractual agreement and the conditions in which that agreement is made. Rawls appropriately names the resulting theory "justice as fairness."

Rawls's contractarian or "constructivist" theory represents this fundamental ideal of fairness by situating the contracting parties in a hypothetical "original position." The most important feature of this theoretical model is the "veil of ignorance," which denies to the parties any knowledge of their actual natural endowments, their social position, or even their conception of what makes for a good life. The parties consequently cannot determine how proposed principles would affect their interests personally. The veil of ignorance thereby reflects our conviction that it would be patently unreasonable to allow principles that favored any individuals or groups merely in virtue of their possession of morally arbitrary attributes such as their race or sex or because they happened to affirm a particular religious or philosophical doctrine.

THE PRINCIPLES OF JUSTICE

Though deprived of knowledge of their particular ends, attachments, and aspirations, the parties in the original position are still rationally motivated to further their conception of the GOOD [3], whatever it is. They also have "higher-order interests" in developing and exercising the two "moral powers" that they share as free and equal beings: (1) the capacity to understand and act from a sense of justice and (2) the capacity to form, revise, and rationally pursue a conception of the good. The parties will therefore seek for themselves the best possible package of "primary goods," those all-purpose, socially regulable opportunities and resources needed to advance those interests. Rawls's enumeration of these primary goods includes basic RIGHTS [7; S] and liberties, the powers and prerogatives of offices and positions, income and wealth, and the social bases of self-respect. Assuming that a society has reached a minimal level of economic development, Rawls argues that the following two principles for allocating the primary goods would be selected:

> a- Each person has an equal right to a fully adequate scheme of equal basic liberties which is compatible with a similar scheme of liberties for all.
>
> b- Social and economic inequalities are to satisfy two conditions. First, they must be attached to offices and positions open to all under conditions of fair equality of opportunity; and second, they must be to the greatest benefit of the least advantaged members of society. (Rawls, 1993, p. 291)

Since the first principle is given absolute priority over the second, Rawls argues that the basic liberties guaranteed by it, such as freedom of religion or the right to run for political office, cannot be sacrificed for any amount of personal or collective economic benefit. Such liberties can be limited only to protect the central range of application of other conflicting liberties, as when the right to a fair trial necessitates some restrictions on the freedom of the press. Specific rights are included in the protection of the first principle if agents in the original position would rationally require them. Freedom of religion, for example, would be insisted upon by the parties, for they could not risk the possibility that their religion, should they have one, would be a minority faith subject to repression by a dogmatic majority.

The second principle deals with economic and social primary goods such as income and wealth. Its second condition, the so-called "difference principle," stipulates that any departures from equality of resources can be justified only if the resulting inequality benefits the least advantaged members of society. Thus, positions that require the development of talents and the expenditure of extraordinary effort might deserve greater economic rewards, but only if the increased productivity generated by such a differential would improve the condition of the least well off. Rawls argues that this requirement would be the reasonable and rational choice of individuals who, owing to the fairness conditions imposed in the original position, did not know their natural and social endowments and therefore could not determine their actual position in the social order.

The first part (of the second principle) stipulates that even the limited inequalities that would satisfy the difference principle are permissible only if the positions that give rise to them are open to all under conditions of "fair equality of opportunity." This strong requirement goes beyond mere prohibition of discrimination based on arbitrary features such as gender or race. It demands that all individuals of like natural ability and similar motivation should have the same opportunities throughout their entire lives, a requirement that obviously necessitates equal access to education, health care, and other social resources.

STABILITY

A viable political theory, Rawls insists, must be practical. The well-ordered society that it mandates must be feasible and stable given realistic economic, cultural, and psychological assumptions. In *A Theory of Justice* Rawls argued that a society regulated by justice as fairness would be stable, since the laws of MORAL PSYCHOLOGY [S] show that its members would tend to acquire and maintain a common comprehensive moral doctrine that would sustain it. In *Political Liberalism,* however, he admits that a liberal, nonauthoritarian regime will be characterized by a plurality of reasonable though incompatible comprehensive religious and moral doctrines. Nonetheless, he believes that the requirement of stability can be met by justice as fairness if we understand it as a political theory. As such, it regulates only the "basic structure" of society: the background institutions that specify political and civil rights and determine entitlements to other socially regulated goods. Members of a well-ordered society may therefore hold deeply conflicting comprehensive religious and moral views yet still endorse a common *political* conception of justice as the focus of an "overlapping consensus." Rawls stresses, moreover, that this consensus can be more than a mere modus vivendi, a practical compromise based on a tenuous balance of power. Rather, it can express a genuine moral commitment that reflects ideas and values implicit in the society's political culture, such as its conception of the citizen as a free and equal person and its willingness to rely on reasonable standards of public discourse in the conduct of its political affairs.

REFLECTIVE EQUILIBRIUM

Rawls's methodology has been as influential and as controversial as his substantive views. Declining to ground his views on any deep metaphysical or other philosophical truths, Rawls maintains that political theory should formulate a coherent set of principles that account for the considered convictions that we actually hold. The process goes beyond mere summarization of particular considered judgments, however, for it also postulates theoretical models, mediating ideas, and principles at all levels of generality. All judgments and principles are held open to revision in light of other aspects of the theory, until no further changes are needed to develop a compelling and coherent view. The resulting theory is then said to be in "reflective equilibrium." It is also "objective," Rawls contends, because it would gain the assent of all reasonable individuals on due reflection.

Bibliography

WORKS BY RAWLS

"Outline of a Decision Procedure for Ethics," *Philosophical Review,* Vol. 60 (1951), 177–97.

"Two Concepts of Rules," *Philosophical Review,* Vol. 64 (1955), 3–32.

A Theory of Justice. Cambridge, MA, 1971. A somewhat revised 1975 version has been translated into several languages.

"Kantian Constructivism in Moral Theory: The Dewey Lectures 1980," *Journal of Philosophy,* Vol. 77 (1980), 515–72.

"Themes in Kant's Moral Philosophy," in E. Förster, ed., *Kant's Transcendental Deductions* (Stanford, CA, 1989).

Political Liberalism. New York, 1993. Contains revised versions of several important papers published between 1974 and 1993.

"The Law of Peoples," in S. Shute and S. Hurley, eds., *On Human Rights: The Oxford Amnesty Lectures 1993* (New York, 1993).

WORKS ON RAWLS

Arneson, R., et al. "Symposium on Rawlsian Theory of Justice: Recent Developments," *Ethics,* Vol. 99 (1989).

Barry, B. *The Liberal Theory of Justice: A Critical Examination of the Principal Doctrines in "A Theory of Justice," by John Rawls.* Oxford, 1973.

Blocker, H. G., and E. Smith, eds. *John Rawls' Theory of Social Justice: An Introduction.* Athens, OH, 1980.

Daniels, N., ed. *Reading Rawls: Critical Studies of "A Theory of Justice."* New York, 1975.

Kukathas, C., and P. Pettit. *Rawls: "A Theory of Justice" and Its Critics.* Stanford, CA, 1990.

Martin, R. *Rawls and Rights.* Lawrence, KA, 1985.

Nozick, R. *Anarchy, State, and Utopia.* New York, 1974. Chap. 7.

Pogge, T. W. *Realizing Rawls.* Ithaca, NY, 1989.

Sandel, M. *Liberalism and the Limits of Justice.* Cambridge, 1982.

Wellbank, J. H., D. Snook, and D. T. Mason. *John Rawls and His Critics: An Annotated Bibliography.* New York, 1982.

ALAN E. FUCHS

REALISM. Contemporary philosophical REALISM [7] is not a single thesis but rather a diverse family of positions, unified chiefly by their invocation of certain characteristic images and metaphors. The realist about a region of discourse typically holds, for example, that our central commitments in the area describe a world that exists anyway, independently of us; that cognition in the area is a matter of detection rather than projection or constitution; and that the objects of the discourse are real things and not just linguistic or social constructions. Debates over realism defined in terms such as these persist in nearly every philosophical subdiscipline: from ethics and the PHILOSOPHY OF MIND [S] to the PHILOSOPHY OF SCIENCE [S] and the philosophy of mathematics. (Although it is common to describe a philosopher as a realist or nonrealist *tout court,* realism in one area is generally independent of realism in another, and advocates of global realism and its opposite number, global nonrealism, are comparatively rare.) Contemporary discussion is concerned in part with the evaluation of these discipline-specific realist theses. But it is also concerned (and increasingly so) with the more basic question of how exactly the realist's distinctive imagery is to be understood.

We may epitomize the realist's stance by saying that to be a realist about a region of discourse is to regard it as describing a genuine domain of objective fact. But what is it for a discourse to describe a "domain of fact"? And what is it for a domain of fact to be "objective"? These questions are usefully approached by attempting a taxonomy of the alternatives to realism. The nonrealist rejects the realist's rhetoric of objectivity. But this rejection can take a number of more determinate forms, and their variety sheds considerable light on what realism requires.

The realist's most basic commitment is to the view that statements in the target area purport to describe a world—to say how things stand with some distinctive range of objects or facts. This claim is often glossed as the minimal requirement that statements in the area be capable of truth or falsity. Realism is thus opposed at this most basic level to nonfactualism (also called irrealism or NONCOGNITIVISM [S]): the view that declarative statements in the target area cannot be evaluated as true or false and so cannot serve a descriptive function. Nonfactualist theses have been advanced mainly in moral philosophy, where it has been suggested that moral utterances serve to express emotional attitudes (emotivism; Blackburn, 1984; Gibbard, 1990) or to endorse or proscribe certain courses of action (prescriptivism; Hare, 1963; cf. Geach, 1963). But they have occasionally been proposed in other areas. Formalism in the philosophy of mathematics (the view that mathematics is a game with meaningless marks, manipulated according to formal rules) and instrumentalism in the philosophy of science (according to which theoretical statements function as uninterpreted tools for deriving predictions about future experience) are further examples of this kind of nonrealism.

To say that a region of discourse purports to describe a world is to say more than that its central commitments are apt for truth. It is to say, in addition, that they are aimed at TRUTH [S]—that they are typically put forward as genuine assertions about how things stand with their ostensible subject matter. Realism is thus opposed at this second level to fictionalism, the view that seeming assertions in the target area, though capable of truth, are in fact designed only to provide representations that are somehow "good" or "interesting" or "useful" for certain purposes. Fictionalist approaches have been developed mainly in the philosophy of science, where Bas van Fraassen's constructive empiricism provides a useful example (van Fraassen, 1980; cf. Churchland & Hooker, 1985). Van Fraassen agrees with the scientific realist, against the instrumentalist, that theoretical statements possess definite truth conditions and so constitute genuine representations of unobservable structures. However, he further maintains, this time against the realist, that the truth value of a theory is irrelevant to its acceptability from the standpoint of science. The aim of science on van Fraassen's view is empirical adequacy: the correct description of the observable world. Theories may posit unobservable things. But a good scientific theory—one that satisfies to some high degree all of the aspirations implicit in the scientific enterprise—may be largely false in its account of such matters, so long as it is a reliable guide to the observable world. In advancing a theory in what seems to be the assertoric mode, the scientist shows only that he accepts it as empirically adequate. Van Fraassen's fictionalism thus consists centrally in his contention that the endorsement of a scientific theory does not involve the belief that it is true or that the unobservables it posits exist. Generalizing, we may say that realism involves, in addition to the semantic thesis of truth aptitude, the pragmatic thesis of truth directedness, according to which the target discourse aims at truth, and the endorsement of a claim is normally an expression of one's belief that it is true. (See Field, 1980, for a fictionalist approach to the philosophy of mathematics.)

Before we have a position that is recognizable as realist we must add one further ingredient. It is not enough that our central commitments aspire to truth. They must also be true, or at least not wildly mistaken. Realism is thus opposed at this third level to a conception of the target area as involving a fundamental mistake about what the world contains. This "error-theoretic" alternative to realism is typified by J. L. MACKIE'S [S] view of morality (Mackie, 1977). According to Mackie, ethical discourse purports to describe a range of objective prescriptions: constraints on action that are somehow built into the fabric of nature. But since it can be shown (Mackie held) that there are no such items, it follows that morality is based on a mistake—the entities it purports to describe do not exist; the properties it trades in are not instantiated—and hence that moral discourse demands reconstrual, if not outright rejection. A more familiar instance of the error-theoretic approach is ATHEISM [1], the view that theological discourse is vitiated by the mistaken supposition that God exists. Agnostic versions are also possible, though in fact they have played no significant role outside the philosophy of religion.

A philosopher who holds that our core commitments in an area succeed in providing a true account of their intended subject matter may be called a minimal realist about that area. It is sometimes suggested that there is nothing more to realism than this minimal view and hence that once the questions of truth aptitude, truth directedness, and truth have been settled, there is no further space for debate about whether the discourse is to be understood "in a realistic fashion." There are, however, at least two reasons to resist this claim.

The first concerns the classification of reductionist positions. The behaviorist thesis that psychological statements can be reduced without remainder to claims about overt bodily movements and the like is clearly compatible with minimal realism about the mind. And yet the view that there is nothing more to being in pain than exhibiting "pain behavior" has generally been regarded as a clear alternative to a robust realism about mental states. It has thus become customary to insist that the realist's commitment to the truth of our views in the target area be a commitment to their truth on a literal or face-value construal (Blackburn, 1984, chap. 5; cf. Wright, 1983). The behaviorist translation of a simple psychological statement such as "Nadja is dreaming of Paris" will typically be a long conjunction of conditional claims describing the outward behavior Nadja would exhibit if prompted by various stimuli. But this paraphrase has a very different "surface form" from the psychological claim whose meaning it is meant to capture. And this suggests that on the behaviorist's account, the correct interpretation of psychological statements is not a face-value interpretation and hence that while he may endorse a version of minimal realism about the mental, the behaviorist should not be classed as a realist without qualification.

The second and more serious reason to resist the identification of realism with minimal realism is that minimal realism by itself involves no commitment to the mind independence or objectivity of the disputed subject matter. KANT'S [4; S] transcendental idealism has generally been regarded as a paradigmatic alternative to full-blown realism about the external world; and yet it is fully compatible with minimal realism as defined above. Objects in space and time are real, for Kant, in the sense that much of what common sense and science have to say about them is literally true. And yet there is another sense in which they are not fully real. The structure of the spatiotemporal world is "conditioned" for Kant by the structure of the mind that experiences it. Empirical investigation is therefore not addressed to a domain of fact that is altogether "independent of us." Clearly, Kant's position should not be described as a species of realism without qualification, its consistency with minimal realism notwithstanding.

Much of the most important work on realism has been devoted to explicating the commitment to objectivity that seems a necessary component of any fully realist position. The most natural thought is to identify objectivity directly with a straightforward sort of mind independence. A state of affairs will then count as objective if it would have obtained (or could have obtained) even if there were no minds or mental activity. But this precludes realism about the mind itself and also about any discourse in the social sciences that concerns itself with the products of human thought and action. And this is implausible. It should be possible to be a realist about psychology, for example, while conceding that the facts it describes are obviously mind dependent in the sense that they would not have obtained if there were no minds.

One influential approach to this problem is due to Michael DUMMETT [S], whose work is largely responsible for the current prominence of realism as a theme in Anglophone philosophy (Dummett, 1978; cf. Wright, 1992). On Dummett's view the dispute over realism, though ultimately an issue in METAPHYSICS [S], is best approached by recasting it as a dispute within the PHILOSOPHY OF LANGUAGE [S] about how to construct a theory of MEANING [5; S] for the target discourse. A theory of meaning in Dummett's sense is a representation in propositional form of what a competent speaker knows in virtue of which he understands his language. Dummett identifies realism with the view that a meaning theory must take the form of a classical two-valued semantic theory: an assignment of truth conditions to sentences that respects the principle of bivalence, according to which every sentence is determinately either true or false. Realism's slogan is: to understand a sentence is to know its truth condition. The leading alternative—sometimes called semantic antirealism—holds instead that to understand a sentence is to know the conditions under which it is correctly asserted. A view of this sort assigns each declarative sentence a class of "verification conditions," each of which must be the sort of condition a competent human being can in principle recognize as obtaining. A semantic theory constructed upon such a basis will generally fail to respect bivalence. The only notion of truth it makes available will be epistemically constrained: truth will be identified with knowable truth, and falsity with knowable falsity. On a view of this sort we shall not be entitled to say in advance that every well-formed question must have an answer, or that every statement of the form "*p* or not-*p*" must be true. This rejection of bivalence (and the closely related law of excluded middle) is the hallmark of semantic antirealism. To suppose that the only notion of truth we possess for a region of discourse is an epistemically constrained one is to suppose that the facts in the area are (as it were) cut to fit our intellectual capacities. Conversely, to insist that bivalence must hold regardless of our cognitive limitations is to conceive of the facts at which our thought is directed as obtaining (in one sense) independently of us.

A closely related proposal has been advanced by Hilary PUTNAM [S], (1978, 1987). Putnam identifies full-blown "metaphysical" realism directly with the view that truth is epistemically unconstrained. As Putnam frames the issue, the metaphysical realist's characteristic thought is that an ideal theory might be false, where an ideal theory is one that satisfies perfectly every criterion we normally employ in deciding what to believe in the target area. In the scientific case, for example, an ideal theory would be one that supplies accurate predictions of experimental outcomes while simultaneously displaying every internal theoretical virtue that scientists consider in the context of theory choice: simplicity, elegance, explanatory power, "intrinsic plausibility," and the like. It is natural to suppose that such a theory could be false. After all, the theoretical virtues that provide our only grounds for choice among empirically equivalent hypotheses seem importantly subjective. A theory that strikes us as particularly powerful because it provides informative answers to interesting questions might strike creatures with different interests as unacceptably silent on important matters; a theory that strikes us as "intrinsically plausible" might strike creatures with different histories or cultures as strange and unlikely. The thought that an ideal theory can be false thus seems a natural expression of an appropriate human modesty, according to which we can have no guarantee in advance that our contingent, biologically, and historically conditioned sense of theoretical virtue must be a reliable guide to the facts about the physical world.

Putnam rejects this natural thought. Metaphysical realism presupposes a concept of truth that is radically divorced from our notion of correct assertion. But according to Putnam such a concept is unattainable. Putnam's case for his view, like Dummett's, defies simple summary; but in rough outline it proceeds as follows. The only serious effort to explain an epistemically unconstrained notion of truth is a version of the correspondence theory of truth. This approach proceeds in two stages. First, subsentential expressions such as names and predicates are associated with objects and properties as their referents. Then truth as a feature of sentences is defined recursively according to a scheme well known to logicians (*see* TARSKI [8]). Putnam's central contention is that there is no credible account of the first stage. Every attempt to explain in realist terms how a word manages to refer to one object rather than another—that is, every attempt to explain how language "hooks on" to the world—is either plainly unsatisfactory or implies a radical indeterminacy of REFERENCE [S].

Putnam's alternative is to identify truth directly with "ideal acceptability," a position he calls internal realism. The position is realist, not simply because it is compatible with what has here been called minimal realism, but also because it eschews reductionism while remaining compatible with all of the ordinary denials of mind dependence that are part of our scientifically informed world view. Since it is plainly correct by ordinary standards to assert that mountains exist even when no one is aware of them, the internal realist will agree that mountains do not depend in this literal sense on our thought and are therefore in that sense objective. Still, the view does imply an internal connection at the global level between the way the world is and the way we are disposed to conceive of the world in what PEIRCE [6; S] called "the ideal limit of inquiry." According to the internal realist, we should not say (as the idealist would) that the mind somehow constructs the world but rather that "the mind and the world together make up the mind and the world" (Putnam, 1978).

It remains uncertain whether the efforts of Dummett, Putnam, and others to describe a plausible alternative to realism on the matter of objectivity can succeed. It is to be noted that the arguments they provide indict any epistemically unconstrained notion of truth whatsoever, and hence that if they succeed at all they imply a global antirealism according to which every region of human thought that satisfies the condition of minimal realism is directed at a region of fact that is somehow constituted in part by our thought about it. But this can be rather hard to believe. The difficulty emerges most dramatically when we consider discourse about the past. Most of us are inclined to believe that every (nonvague) question about the past must have an answer. There is a fact of the matter, we suppose, as to whether Genghis Khan was right-handed, even if we cannot in principle obtain any pertinent evidence. But it is likely that neither "Genghis Khan was right-handed" nor its denial is assertible. Any view according to which this implies that the statement is neither true nor false is therefore bound to strike us as initially incredible. Perhaps more important, there is reason to doubt whether a commitment to an epistemically constrained notion of truth always implies a rejection of the realist's rhetoric of objectivity and independence. It is conceivable, for example, that a moral realist for whom the demands of morality are entirely independent of our passions and interests might nonetheless insist that the moral facts—because they represent rationally compelling demands on human action—must be accessible in principle to human beings. Moral truth would then be epistemically constrained; and yet the realist's rhetoric of objectivity and independence would not be undermined.

To be a realist about a region of discourse is to hold at a minimum that our core commitments in the area are largely true when interpreted "at face value." However, this minimal characterization fails to capture the realist's commitment to the objectivity or mind independence of his subject matter. In some cases this further commitment can be understood as the requirement that the concept of truth appropriate to the target area be epistemically unconstrained. It remains unclear, however, whether this characterization is adequate to every case. The search for a fully general account of the realist's commitment to objectivity is perhaps the central open question in this part of philosophy.

Bibliography

Blackburn, S. *Spreading the Word.* Oxford, 1984.

———. "How to Be an Ethical Anti-Realist," in *Essays in Quasi-Realism* (New York, 1993).

Churchland, P., and C. Hooker, eds. *Images of Science.* Chicago, 1985.

Devitt, M. *Realism and Truth.* Cambridge, MA, 1991.

Dummett, M. *Truth and Other Enigmas.* Cambridge, MA, 1978. Especially the essays "Realism," "Truth," and "The Philosophical Basis of Intuitionistic Logic."

———. *The Seas of Language.* Oxford, 1994. Especially the essays "What Is a Theory of Meaning II" and "Realism."

Field, H. *Science without Numbers.* Princeton, NJ, 1980.

Geach, P. "Ascriptivism," *Philosophical Review,* Vol. 69 (1960), 221–25.

Gibbard, A. *Wise Choices, Apt Feelings.* Cambridge, MA, 1990.

Hare, R. M. *Freedom and Reason.* Oxford, 1963.

Honderich, T., ed. *Morality and Objectivity: A Tribute to J. L. Mackie.* London, 1985.

Mackie, J. L. *Ethics: Inventing Right and Wrong.* New York, 1977.

Putnam, H. *Meaning and the Moral Sciences.* Boston, 1978.

———. *The Many Faces of Realism.* La Salle, IL, 1987.

van Fraassen, B. *The Scientific Image.* Oxford, 1980.

Wright, C. *Frege's Conception of Numbers as Objects.* Aberdeen, 1983.

———. *Truth and Objectivity.* Cambridge, MA, 1992.

GIDEON ROSEN

RECURSION THEORY. Since 1960 RECURSIVE FUNCTION THEORY [7] (or recursion theory, as it is often called) has seen both new results on existing problems, particularly on degrees of unsolvability, and growth into new areas, particularly—under the influence of computer science—studies of the complexity of computations.

Recall that a set R of natural numbers is said to be Turing reducible to another set S if membership in R can be effectively decided by using an oracle for S. We further say that R and S are Turing equivalent if each is Turing reducible to the other. This equivalence relation partitions the collection of sets into so-called degrees of unsolvability. And Turing reducibility induces a partial ordering of these degrees.

The 1983 book by Manuel Lerman surveys known results on the structure of the degrees of unsolvability. Since publication of that book, Barry Cooper has shown that the jump operation, which is the operation of forming the recursively enumerable nonrecursive set K but relative to an oracle S, is definable from the partial ordering. Questions about automorphisms of the degrees continue to be worked on.

Classically, recursion theory dealt with functions defined on the set N of natural numbers, or—equivalently—on the set of words over some finite alphabet. This can be generalized in two directions. First, the theory extends very naturally to functions taking as arguments both members of N and total functions from N into N. This extended theory is included in the book by Hartley Rogers (1987). Beginning with work by Stephen Kleene in 1959, this sort of extension has been iterated to produce "higher type" recursion theory. We get a type hierarchy by taking the objects of type 0 to be the natural numbers, and the objects of type $k + 1$ to be the functions mapping objects of type k to the natural numbers. And the theory of recursive partial functions extends to functions taking as arguments these objects of higher type.

And there is a second direction in which recursion theory has been generalized. Identifying N with the first infinite ordinal ω, one might ask what other ordinals can usefully serve as the base set for a recursion theory. The answer turns out to be the so-called admissible ordinals. For example, the next admissible ordinal after ω is the "Church-Kleene" ordinal ω_1^{CK}, the least ordinal that is not the order type of a recursive well-ordering of N. The 1957 work of Friedberg and Muenik answering Post's problem was carried over, in the 1970s, to the context of an arbitrary admissible ordinal.

The growing field of computer science has greatly influenced work in recursion theory, with each field contributing to the other. At the heart of recursion theory is the concept of an "effective procedure": a mechanical procedure specified by explicit instructions for calculating the values of a function. In the context of computer science, those explicit instructions are a "program." And an effective procedure is one for which, in principle, a computer program could be written.

In another direction, Yiannis Moschovakis, in his 1993 paper, attempts to see how the concept of "an algorithm" might be made into a mathematically precise notion. He further relates this concept to FREGE's [3; S] notion of SENSE [S].

The concept of an effective procedure bears on the philosophy of mathematics, in particular on the notion of a "proof." A proof of a sentence σ (in some formal system) must be something that whose correctness we can verify. A proof of σ is not the same thing as σ itself; a proof must convincingly establish that σ is indeed a theorem of the system. But to accomplish that, it must be possible to go over the proof, line by line, and mechanically verify its correctness. That is, there must be an effective procedure that, given σ and a putative proof of σ (as its input), will eventually halt and announce (as its output) the acceptability of the proof if and only if the proof is indeed correct (*see* PROOF THEORY [S]).

Church's thesis identifies the informal notion of a function computable by an effective procedure with the mathematically precise notion of a recursive function. Alan Turing's original paper on what we now call Turing machines was guided by a desire to capture formally the notion of an effective procedure. Emil Post's work was similarly motivated. The equivalence of the Turing computability and Post computability to Alonzo Church's notion of λ-calculability has in no small measure contributed to the universal acceptance of Church's thesis as the correct formalization of an informal notion.

In particular, under Church's thesis we can conclude that what is provable in a given formal system must be *recursively enumerable.* A sentence σ is provable if and only if there exists a string π of symbols that is its proof. And the predicate "π is a proof of σ" must be recursive, or at least recursively enumerable. (It matters not at all whether we encode here strings of symbols by means of a GÖDEL [S] numbering or whether we develop directly the theory of recursive functions that operate on strings of symbols.) It follows from this fact that the set of provable sentences must be recursively enumerable.

Gödel's incompleteness theorem stems from the fact that what is provable in a formal system, be it first-order PEANO [6] arithmetic or the system in WHITEHEAD [8] and RUSSELL's [7] *Principia Mathematica* (1910–1913), is recursively enumerable, while what is true, say, in arithmetic, is not recursively enumerable. And hence a gap must remain.

But the recursive functions are the functions that are effectively computable in an ideal sense: no restrictions are imposed on the length of time the mechanical procedure might consume before producing its output, only that its output—if any—must appear in some finite length of time. Similarly, no restrictions are imposed on the amount of scratch paper that might be consumed while executing the procedure. And this idealized concept is exactly what is required for theoretical analysis of what, in principle, can be calculated.

If, however, one seeks to apply recursion theory to computer science, one finds the theory to be if anything too ideal. Even a simple computer can do everything a Turing machine can do in terms of reading a symbol, replacing it by a different symbol, and turning to the next (or to the preceding) symbol. But the Turing machine, an idealized device, never runs out of tape, and never breaks down, regardless of how long a time it runs. To an actual computer, memory space and running time are vitally important.

There are recursive functions f such that for large integers n, the number of steps required to calculate $f(n)$ is astronomically large. To be more precise, Michael Rabin proved that for any total recursive function g, we can find another total recursive function f taking only the values 0 and 1, such that for any choice of instructions I to compute f, the number of steps I uses to find $f(n)$ exceeds $g(n)$ for all but finitely many values of n. Taking $g(m) = 2^m$ and observing that 2^{100} microseconds is many times the age of the universe, one sees that some recursive functions, although computable in an idealized sense, are not "feasible" to compute in practice, at least for large inputs.

But this raises the question whether this informal notion of a computation that is feasible to execute in some practical sense admits any useful formalization at all. In recent years, as computers have become faster and their memory space has become larger, any quantitative estimates of what is feasible might seem foolhardy, to say the least.

In the early 1970s, through work of Stephen Cook, Richard Karp, and others, the proposal emerged that "polynomial time computability" might to be a useful formal notion to approximate the idea of feasible computability. Suppose that f is a recursive function defined on words (strings of symbols) over a finite alphabet. (For numerical computations, that finite alphabet might be the digits for base-10 notation.) One says that f is polynomial time computable if there are instructions I for f and a polynomial p such that for each input w, we obtain $f(w)$, following I, in no more than $p(|w|)$ steps, where $|w|$ is the length of the word w. And, as with recursive sets, one says that a set of words is polynomial time decidable (or belongs to P, for short) if its characteristic function is polynomial time computable.

While this description leaves many details open, such as the choice of formalization of recursiveness, it turns out that those details do not matter: they may affect the degree of the polynomial, but they do not affect the issue of whether or not such a bounding polynomial exists. And thus we obtain a stable notion.

The polynomial time computable functions form a subclass of the primitive recursive functions. And decidable problems can be examined anew. Take for example the satisfiability problem for propositional logic: given a formula φ of propositional logic, is there a truth assignment under which φ comes out true? This problem is well known to be decidable, that is, the set of satisfiable formulas is recursive. But is it in P? It is strongly conjectured by workers in the field that the answer is negative.

In fact, the satisfiability problem is typical of a broader class of decision problems that go under the name of "NP" (for nondeterministic polynomial time). That is, when the formula φ is indeed satisfiable, then a Turing machine, operating nondeterministically (when more than one instruction is applicable, the machine can "guess" which to use) can verify satisfiability in polynomial time. There is a rough (and imperfect) analogy here; the relation of NP to P is like the relation of recursive enumerability to recursiveness. But at least we can prove that some recursively enumerable sets are not recursive. The question whether $P = NP$ remains the most important open problem in theoretical computer science.

(SEE ALSO: *Mathematical Logic* and *Philosophical Logic* [S])

Bibliography

Barwise, J., ed. *Handbook of Mathematical Logic*. Amsterdam, 1978.

Cooper, S. B. "The Jump is Definable in the Structure of the Degrees of Unsolvability," *Bulletin of the American Mathematical Society*, Vol. 23 (1990), 151–58.

Lerman, M. *Degrees of Unsolvability*. Berlin, 1983.

Moschovakis, Y. N. "Sense and Denotation as Algorithm and Value," in J. Oikkonen and J. Väänänen, eds., *Logic Colloquium '90* (1993), 210–49.

Rogers, H. *Theory of Recursive Functions and Effective Computability*. New York, 1967.

Odifreddi, P. *Classical Recursion Theory*. Amsterdam, 1989.

Shoenfield, J. R. *Recursion Theory*. Berlin, 1993.

HERBERT B. ENDERTON

REDUCTION, REDUCTIONISM. Reduction is the absorption or subsumption of one theory, conceptual scheme, or mode of discourse by another. The notion of reduction is employed in a number of family-resemblance related ways relevant to METAPHYSICS [S], and it involves three interrelated dimensions or axes: ontological, semantic, and scientific. Ontologically reductionist positions typically assert that there are systematic identities between entities, kinds, properties, and facts posited respectively in a "higher-level" discourse and in a "lower-level," reducing, discourse. Semantically reductionist positions typically assert that there are systematic semantic equivalences between statements in a higher-level and in a lower-level discourse. Scientific reductionist positions typically assert that the laws and phenomena described in some scientific theory or theories are systematically explainable by those described in some other scientific theory, explainable in a way that absorbs the reduced theory into the reducing one.

Semantically reductionist projects have often been viewed as a major means of implementing ontological reductions. An example is logicism in philosophy of mathematics. Semantically, the logicist maintains that all the key concepts and terms of classical mathematics are definable via the terms and concepts of LOGIC [S] and SET THEORY [7; S], in such a way that all of pure mathematics is derivable (under these definitions) from logic plus fundamental assumptions about classes. (Logicists such as FREGE [3; S] and RUSSELL [7] considered set theory part of logic.) This definitional reduction, says the logicist, effects an ontological reduction of all the entities posited in pure mathematics to classes.

Another semantically reductionist position often linked to ontological reductionism is PHENOMENALISM [6]. Semantically, the phenomenalist maintains that every meaningful statement about empirical fact is equivalent to some statement about immediate experience, actual or possible. Ontologically, this position sometimes has been regarded as undergirding metaphysical idealism—as effecting an ontological reduction of everything real to something mental.

Scientifically reductionist projects, too, often have been viewed as a way to implement ontological reductions—although normally not by means of semantic-equivalence relations. In PHILOSOPHY OF SCIENCE [S] the received view is that reduction involves empirical, a posteriori, hypotheses asserting systematic identities between items in the ontologies of the reduced theory and the reducing theory: the reduced theory gets explained by being shown derivable from the reducing theory together with these identity hypotheses. Thus, scientific reduction is standardly regarded as a species of ontological reduction.

Paradigm examples of scientific reduction have a part/whole aspect: laws and phenomena involving complex wholes are explained in terms of laws and phenomena involving the parts of which those wholes are composed. (This is called microreduction.) A frequently cited example is the microreduction of classical thermodynamics to statistical molecular mechanics. The key empirical hypothesis is that a gas's temperature is identical to its mean molecular kinetic energy. From this identity statement, together with the principles of molecular mechanics, the principles of thermodynamics can be derived—for example, the Boyle/Charles law, asserting that a gas's temperature is directly proportional to its pressure and inversely proportional to its volume.

Some philosophers, however, deny that scientific reduction requires intertheoretic identity hypotheses. They maintain that genuine microreduction can be underwritten by universally quantified biconditional "bridge laws," even if these bridge laws express nomic correlations between distinct properties. On this alternative view the key empirical hypothesis in the reduction just mentioned is that temperature in gases is nomically coextensive with mean molecular kinetic energy—not that the two properties are identical.

A variety of reductionist positions have been advocated in recent metaphysics. Often these are regarded as articulating a materialist metaphysical stance toward their subject matter. In PHILOSOPHY OF MIND [7], for instance, it has been claimed that human psychology is microreducible to neurobiology—and that this reductionist thesis articulates a materialist conception of the mental. More generally, it has been claimed that each of the "special sciences" is microreducible to some other science, and hence (since microreduction is transitive) that all the special sciences are ultimately microreducible to fundamental microphysics. (This unity of science hypothesis is often regarded as articulating a general materialist metaphysics.) And in metaethics, it has been claimed (1) that there are genuine, objective, moral properties and facts (so-called MORAL REALISM [S]) and (2) that these are reducible to PROPERTIES [S] and facts describable in the nonmoral language of science.

Reductionism is often contrasted with the "emergentism" of philosophical thinkers such as Samuel ALEXANDER [1], Lloyd MORGAN [5], and C. D. BROAD [1]. These emergentists were not substance-dualists; they held that all concrete particulars are, or are wholly composed out of, physical entities. But they were not full-fledged physicalists either, because they denied that physics is a causally complete science. They maintained that at various junctures in the course of evolution, complex physical entities came into existence (living beings, for example, and conscious beings) that had certain nonphysical, "emergent," properties. These properties, they claimed, are fundamental force-generating properties, over and above the force-generating properties of physics; when such a property is instantiated by an individual, the total causal forces operative within the individual are a combination of physical and nonphysical forces, and the resulting behavior of the individual is different from what it would have been had the emergent force(s) not been operative alongside the lower-level forces. Furthermore, although emergent properties are supervenient upon lower-level properties, there is no explanation for why any given emergent property always gets instantiated when certain specific lower-order properties are instantiated; nor is there any explanation for why emergent properties generate the specific nonphysical forces they do. These facts are metaphysically and scientifically basic, in much the same way that the fundamental laws of physics are basic. They are unexplained explainers (*see* EMERGENT EVOLUTIONISM [2]).

Although emergentism is not widely espoused in metaphysics or the philosophy of mind, reduction is a widely debated issue. In philosophy of mind three broad camps can be distinguished among philosophers who espouse some version of materialism. First are the reductive materialists, who typically maintain both (1) that scientific reduction of psychology is a prerequisite for the reality of human mentality and (2) that psychology is indeed reducible to natural science, and ultimately to physics. Second are the eliminative materialists, who typically embrace thesis (1) of reductive materialism but then argue that thesis (2) is probably false (*see* ELIMINATIVE MATERIALISM, ELIMINATIVISM [S]). On their view humans do not really have beliefs, desires, hopes, fears, or the other mental states of commonsense psychology at all; these are posits of a radically false, prescientific, theory. Third are the nonreductive materialists, who deny thesis (1) of reductive materialism and who typically agree with eliminative materialists that thesis (2) of reductive materialism is probably false.

Although there are various versions of nonreductive materialism in philosophy of mind, four core tenets are commonly embraced. First, mental properties and facts are determined by, or supervenient upon, physical properties and facts. Second (and contrary to emergentism), physics is a causally complete science; the only fundamental force-generating properties are physical properties. More specifically, the human body does not instantiate any fundamental force-generating properties other than physical ones. Third, mental properties nonetheless have genuine causal/explanatory efficacy, via the physical properties that "realize" mental properties on particular occasions of instantiation. Thus, even though physics is a causally complete science, human behavior and human mental occurrences are causally explainable at both mental and physical levels of description; these different explanatory levels do not exclude one another but instead are compatible and complementary. Fourth (and again contrary to emergentism), psychophysical SUPERVENIENCE [S] relations are in principle explainable rather than being fundamental and *sui generis;* so the laws and causal generalizations of psychology are explainable too. These four tenets of nonreductive materialism can be generalized beyond philosophy of mind, for instance by extending them to the whole hierarchy of intertheoretic relations among the various sciences.

One influential nonreductive materialist position is the ANOMALOUS MONISM [S] of Donald DAVIDSON [S]. He holds that although concrete, spatiotemporally located, mental events and states are identical to concrete physical events and states (a form of ontological monism), nevertheless mental types—that is, kinds and/or properties—are neither identical to, nor lawfully coextensive with, physical types. (The monism is "anomalous" because it rejects bridge laws expressing either nomological coextensions or identities between mental and physical kinds or properties.) His argument for this position relies largely on the contention that the correct assignment of mental and actional properties to a person is always a holistic matter, involving a global, diachronic, "intentional interpretation" of the person.

Nonreductive materialists frequently argue that psychophysical reductionism runs afoul of the evident physical possibility that mental properties might be multiply realizable physicochemically, either across creatures with radically different physical constitutions or even within single creatures: realizable in humans by certain physicochemical properties instantiable only in organic matter and in silicon-based Martians by quite different physicochemical properties instantiable only in silicon; or realizable in humans, say, by a variety of distinct physicochemical properties. MULTIPLE REALIZABILITY [S] would block the coextensiveness of mental and physical predicates (in certain physically possible worlds, at least, if not in the actual world) and hence would block reduction via bridge laws or property identities. Likewise, in philosophy of science it is sometimes argued that the properties posited in higher-level sciences are in general multiply realizable by various distinct lower-level properties—and thus that physics and the various special sciences are interrelated, not via a hierarchy of microreduction (as the unity of science hypothesis asserts), but rather in accordance with the core tenets of nonreductive materialism.

Bibliography

Alexander, S. *Space, Time and Diety.* London, 1920.

Beckermann, A., H. Flohr, and J. Kim, eds. *Emergence or Reduction? Essays on the Prospects of Nonreductive Physicalism.* Berlin, 1992.

Broad, C. D. *The Mind and Its Place in Nature.* London, 1925.

Causey, R. "Attribute-identities in Microreductions," *Journal of Philosophy,* Vol. 69 (1972), 407–22.

Churchland, P. M. "Eliminative Materialism and Propositional Attitudes," *Journal of Philosophy,* Vol. 78 (1981), 67–90.

Davidson, D. "Mental Events," in L. Foster and J. W. Swanson, eds., *Experience and Theory* (Amherst, 1970).

Fodor, J. "Special Sciences (Or: The Disunity of Science as a Working Hypothesis)," *Synthese,* Vol. 28 (1974), 97–115.

Hellman, G., and F. Thompson. "Physicalism: Ontology, Determination, and Reduction," *Journal of Philosophy,* Vol. 72 (1975), 551–64.

Horgan, T. "Nonreductive Materialism and the Explanatory Autonomy of Psychology," in S. J. Wagner and R. Warner, eds., *Naturalism: A Critical Appraisal* (Notre Dame, IN, 1993).

Kemeny, J. G., and P. Oppenheim. "On Reduction," *Philosophical Studies,* Vol. 7 (1956), 6–19.

Kim, J. "The Myth of Nonreductive Materialism," *Proceedings and Addresses of the American Philosophical Association,* Vol. 63 (1989), 31–47.

McLaughlin, B. "The Rise and Fall of British Emergentism," in A. Beckermann, H. Flohr, and J. Kim, eds., *Emergence or Reduction? Essays on the Prospects of Nonreductive Physicalism* (Berlin, 1992).

Morgan, C. L. *Emergent Evolution.* London, 1923.

Nagel, E. *The Structure of Science.* New York, 1961.

Oppenheim, P., and H. Putnam. "Unity of Science as a Working Hypothesis," in H. Feigl, M. Scriven, and G. Maxwell, eds., *Minnesota Studies in the Philosophy of Science,* Vol. 2 (Minneapolis, 1958).

Putnam, H. "On Properties," in N. Rescher, ed., *Essays in Honor of Carl G. Hempel* (Dordrecht, 1969).

Quine, W. V. O. "Ontological Reduction and the World of Numbers," *Journal of Philosophy,* Vol. 61 (1964), 209–16.

Shaffner, K. "Approaches to Reduction," *Philosophy of Science,* Vol. 34 (1967), 137–47.

Sklar, L. "Types of Inter-theoretic Reduction," *British Journal for the Philosophy of Science,* Vol. 17 (1967), 109–24.

TERENCE E. HORGAN

REFERENCE. Reference is usually conceived as the central relation between language or thought and the world. To talk or think about something is to refer to it. Twentieth-century philosophy has found such relations particularly problematic. One paradigm of reference is the relation between a proper name and its bearer. On a more theoretical conception all the constituents of an utterance or thought that contribute to determining whether it is true refer to their contributions (e.g., a predicate refers to a property). In analytic philosophy discussion of reference was dominated until the 1960s by the views of FREGE [3; S] and RUSSELL [7] and modifications of them (e.g., by STRAWSON [S]). Criticisms of assumptions common to those views then provoked a revolution in the theory of reference. The alternatives include causal and minimalist theories.

OBJECTIONS TO DESCRIPTIVISM

One model of reference is that of descriptive fit. The paradigm is a definite description (e.g., "the tallest tree") that refers to whatever it accurately describes. Frege and Russell assimilated the reference of ordinary proper names to this case by supposing that speakers associate them with descriptions. Similar accounts were later given of mass terms (e.g., "blood"), natural-kind terms (e.g., "gorilla"), and theoretical terms in science (e.g., "inertia"). It was conceded that most terms are associated with vague and context-dependent clusters of descriptions and that reference might be to whatever they least inaccurately described, but such liberalizations did not challenge the underlying idea that descriptive fit determines reference. However, Keith Donnellan, Saul KRIPKE [S], and Hilary PUTNAM [S] proposed counterexamples to that idea. Suppose, for instance, that speakers associate the name "Jonah" with the Bible story. Traditional descriptivism concludes that the sentence "Although Jonah existed, those things happened only to someone else" is untrue. For if one person satisfied the relevant descriptions, "Jonah" would refer to him. But then descriptivism proves too much, for philosophical reflection cannot show that the Bible story is not a mere legend that grew up about a real person; if those things really happened to someone else, of whom no word reached the biblical writer, the name "Jonah" would still refer to the former, not the latter. Similarly, traditional descriptivism permits someone who thinks of gorillas primarily as ferocious monkeys to conclude falsely that the sentence "Gorillas exist, but they are not ferocious monkeys" is untrue.

A second criticism was this. Say that a term *t* rigidly designates an object *x* if and only if *t* designates (refers to) *x* with respect to all possible circumstances (except perhaps for circumstances in which *x* does not exist). Most descriptions designate nonrigidly: "the tallest tree" designates one tree with respect to present circumstances, another with respect to possible circumstances in which the former is outgrown. The descriptions that traditional descriptivists associated with names were nonrigid. However, names designate rigidly: although we can envisage circumstances in which the Danube would have been called something else instead, we are still using our name "Danube" to hypothesize circumstances involving the very same river. Thus, most descriptions do not behave like names.

The second criticism was met by a modification of descriptivism. The descriptions associated with a name were rigidified by a qualifying phrase such as "in present circumstances". "The tallest tree in present circumstances" rigidly designates what "the tallest tree" nonrigidly designates. The first criticism is less easily met. Some descriptivists used deferential descriptions such as "the person referred to in the Bible as 'Jonah' ". A more general strategy is to exploit the success of any rival theory of reference by building that theory into the associated descriptions. However, such moves jeopardize the connection between reference and speakers' understanding (a connection that descriptivism was intended to secure) as the descriptions that speakers supposedly associate with names become less and less accessible to the speakers themselves.

It is in any case clear that, as Russell recognized, not all reference is purely descriptive. If the sentence "It is hot now" is uttered at different times in exactly similar circumstances, associated with exactly the same descriptions, those descriptions are not what determines that it changes its reference from one time to the other. The reference of a token of "now" is determined by the time of its production and the invariant linguistic meaning of "now", the rule that any such token refers to the time of its production. Similarly, the presence of an object to the speaker or thinker plays an ineliminably nondescriptive role in the reference of demonstratives such as "this".

NONDESCRIPTIVISM

The Kripke–Putnam Picture. Kripke and Putnam proposed an alternative picture. Something *x* is singled out, usually demonstratively ("this river," "this kind of animal"). A name *n,* proper or common, is conferred on *x* ("Danube," "gorilla"). The name is passed on from one speaker to another, the latter intending to preserve the former's reference. Such intentions are self-fulfilling: *n* continues to refer to *x*. The beliefs that speakers would express in sentences containing *n* play no role in making *n* refer to *x,* so it can turn out that most of them are false. The picture involves two kinds of deference. Synchronically, there is division of linguistic labor: ordinary speakers defer to experts (e.g., in deciding which animals "gorilla" refers to). Diachronically, later speakers defer to earlier ones in a historical chain. Thus, reference typically depends on both the natural environment of the initial baptism (to fix the demonstrative reference) and the social environment of the later use. An individual speaker's understanding plays only a minor role. The account may be generalized (e.g., to many adjectives and verbs).

The picture needs qualification. Gareth Evans pointed out that a name can change its reference as a result of misidentification, even if each speaker intends to preserve reference. What matters is not just the initial baptism but subsequent interaction between word and object. Such concessions do not constitute a return to descriptivism.

Causal Theories. The Kripke–Putnam picture is often developed into a causal theory of reference, on which for *n* to refer to *x* is for a causal chain of a special kind to connect *n* to *x*. Such a theory goes beyond the original picture in at least two ways. First, although that picture required later uses of *n* to depend causally on the initial baptism, it did not require the initial baptism to depend causally on *x*. Kripke allowed reference to be fixed descriptively (not just demonstratively), as in "I name the tallest tree 'Albie' "; he merely insisted that the description did not give the meaning of the name. There is no causal connection between the name "Albie" and the tree Albie. Second, Kripke and Putnam did not attempt to define the notions they used in causal terms; the notion of an intention to preserve reference is not obviously causal.

Causal theories are often motivated by a desire to naturalize linguistic and mentalistic phenomena by reducing them to the terms of physical science. Such theories are therefore not restricted to proper names. Causal theorists will postulate that our use of the words "tall" and "tree" is causally sensitive to tallness and trees respectively, hoping thereby to explain the reference of "Albie". One problem for causal theories is that any word is at the end of many intertwined causal chains with different beginnings. It is extremely difficult to specify in causal terms which causal chains carry reference. For this reason, causal theories of reference remain programmatic.

Direct Reference. Consonant with the Kripke–Putnam picture, but independent of causal theories of reference, is the theory of direct reference developed by David Kaplan. A term *t* directly refers to an object *x* in a given context if and only if the use of *t* in that context contributes nothing to what is said but *x* itself. For Kaplan, proper names, demonstratives, and INDEXICALS [S] such as "now" refer directly. Ruth Barcan MARCUS [S] had earlier made the similar suggestion that proper names are mere tags. The reference of a directly referential term may be determined relative to context by its context-independent linguistic meaning, as for "now"; the claim is that what "now" contributes to the proposition expressed by an utterance of "It is hot now" is not its invariant linguistic meaning but the time itself.

Although all direct reference is rigid designation, not all rigid designation is direct reference: "the square of 7" rigidly designates 49, but the reference is not direct, for the structure of the description figures in the proposition expressed by "The square of 7 is 49". On one view all genuine reference is direct, sentences of the form "The *F* is *G*" being quantified on the pattern of "Every *F* is *G*" (as Russell held); "the *F*" is neither a constituent nor a referring term.

If "Constantinople" and "Istanbul" have the same direct reference, the proposition (C) expressed by "Constantinople is crowded" is the proposition (I) expressed by "Istanbul is crowded", so believing (C) is believing (I), even if one would not express it in those words. Similarly, when a term of a directly referential type fails to refer, sentences in which it is used express no proposition. The view is anti-Fregean. In suitable contexts Frege would attribute different senses but the same reference to "Constantinople" and "Istanbul" and a sense but no reference to an empty name; for him the sense, not the reference, is part of what is said or thought (*see* SENSE [S]). Russell held that logically proper names are directly referential but concluded that ordinary names are not logically proper. The challenge to defenders of the direct-reference view is to explain away the appearance of sameness of reference without sameness of thought and absence of reference without absence of thought, perhaps by postulating senselike entities in the act rather than the content of thought. The theory of direct reference concerns content, not the mechanisms of reference.

Minimalism. Traditional theorizing about reference is ambitious; the possibility of a broad and deep theory such as it seeks has been questioned by Richard Rorty, Robert Brandom, Paul Horwich, and others. The following schema constitutes a minimal account of reference ("*a*" is replaceable by singular terms):

(R) For any *x*, "*a*" refers to *x* if and only if $x = a$.

"London" refers to London and nothing else. A minimalist account adds to (R) the claim that (R) exhausts the nature of reference.

Some qualifications are necessary. First, if anything but a singular term replaces "*a*" in (R), the result is ill formed, for only singular terms should flank the identity sign. If expressions of other syntactic categories refer, those categories will require their own schemas. The schema for predicates might be:

(R′) For any *x*, "*F*" refers to *x* if and only if $x =$ *F*ness.

Second, the notion of a singular term must be explained (can "my sake" replace "*a*"?). Third, (R) does not say which singular terms refer. When "*a*" does not refer, (R) may not express a proposition. Fourth, (R) cannot be generalized by the prefix "In all contexts": "today" used tomorrow does not refer to today. Rather, (R) should be understood as instantiated by sentences in different contexts (e.g., uttered tomorrow with "today" for "*a*"). Fifth, when one cannot understand the term "*a*", one cannot understand (R). Thus, one will find many instances of (R) unintelligible.

One's grasp of the minimal theory is not a grasp of each of many propositions; it is more like one's grasp of a general pattern of inference. For (R) the pattern is in the sentences that express the propositions, not in the propositions themselves (it is not preserved when a synonym replaces the unquoted occurrence of "*a*"). This generality does not satisfy all philosophers. Many accept the minimal theory but reject minimalism, because they postulate a deeper (e.g., causal) theory of reference that explains (R) and (R′). Although the reductionist demand for strictly necessary and sufficient conditions for reference in more fundamental terms may be overambitious, a good picture of reference might still reveal more than (R) and (R′) without meeting that demand (*see* PHILOSOPHY OF LANGUAGE [S]).

Bibliography

Almog, J., J. Perry, and H. Wettstein, eds. *Themes from Kaplan.* New York, 1989.

Brandom, R. "Reference Explained Away: Anaphoric Reference and Indirect Description," *Journal of Philosophy,* Vol. 81 (1984), 469–92.

Devitt, M. *Designation.* New York, 1981.

Evans, G. *The Varieties of Reference.* Oxford, 1982.
Fodor, J. *Psychosemantics: The Problem of Meaning in the Philosophy of Mind.* Cambridge, MA, 1987.
French, P., T. Uehling, and H. Wettstein, eds. *Contemporary Perspectives in the Philosophy of Language,* Midwest Studies in Philosophy, Vol. 5 (Minneapolis, 1979).
Horwich, P. *Truth.* Oxford, 1990.
Kripke, S. *Naming and Necessity.* Oxford, 1980.
Lewis, D. "Putnam's Paradox," *Australasian Journal of Philosophy,* Vol. 62 (1984), 221–36.
Neale, S., *Descriptions.* Cambridge, MA, 1990.
Putnam, H. *Philosophical Papers,* Vol. 2, *Mind, Language, and Reality* (Cambridge, 1975).
Récanati, F. *Direct Reference: From Language to Thought.* Oxford, 1993.
Rorty, R. *Philosophy and the Mirror of Nature.* Princeton, NJ, 1980.
Schwartz, S., ed. *Naming, Necessity, and Natural Kinds.* Ithaca, NY, 1977.

TIMOTHY WILLIAMSON

REID, THOMAS (1710–1796). The significance of Reid lies in his criticism of the empiricist doctrines of his day (*see* EMPIRICISM [2]) and in the great influence he had on subsequent English-language and European philosophy. He became a minister of the Church of Scotland in 1737 and a regent at King's College, Aberdeen, in 1751. He was appointed to the Chair of Moral Philosophy at Glasgow University in 1764, succeeding Adam SMITH [7]. He displayed his greatest originality in the debate with his fellow Scotsman and near contemporary David HUME [4; S]. Reid's first published work, the *Inquiry* of 1764, dealt with sense perception, a central area of Hume's many-sided SKEPTICISM [7; S].

SENSE PERCEPTION AND SKEPTICISM

In sense PERCEPTION [6] a perceiver sees or touches external objects and makes judgments about them. In considering Reid's dispute with Hume we need to distinguish psychological and epistemological aspects. According to Hume's psychological account the perceiver has an impression and, insofar as she makes a judgment and forms a belief, she has an idea that is copied from the impression. The judgment itself is an idea whose particular vividness is due to the fact that it is embedded in impressions. This psychological model raises epistemological issues such as the following: if the idea is simply copied from the impression, and the impression is the only connection we have with the external world, then the judgment that we build on the idea copied from the impression will be warranted only within narrow limits. Insofar as ordinary judgments drawn from sense perception involve claims concerning objects that are distinct from us and have a permanent existence, those claims must remain illegitimate.

REID'S PSYCHOLOGICAL ACCOUNT

Reid holds that this skeptical model misrepresents the psychological facts. Sense perception, he argues, involves sensations, but that does not mean that judgments are copied from sensations. Instead, the sensation naturally suggests the presence of the external object by triggering in the perceiver a conception and a judgment. The latter, however, have no similitude to the sensation. In emphasizing that our conceptions and judgments are original acts related to objects, Reid offers an early statement of the intentionality of mental acts. When a conception or judgment is occasioned by the sensation, the corresponding perception is of the external object itself. Reid never deals extensively with thoughts about what does not exist, although at some points, especially in connection with universals, he is ready to embrace a view, akin to A. MEINONG'S [5], that there are acts with NONEXISTENT OBJECTS [S]. Now, if our conceptions are not copied from sensations, how do we get them? Reid adopts an innatist view: in the appropriate circumstances we get our conceptions "by our constitution" (*see* NATIVISM, INNATISM [S]).

EPISTEMOLOGICAL ASPECTS

Reid outlines his epistemological position at two levels. At the more superficial level he insists that judgments involved in sense perception are irresistible and that our assent is not left to us. But even if one takes Reid's theologically inspired naturalism into account, this approach seems unable to answer critical questions: are not many false judgments irresistible for those who make them? But Reid's epistemology also operates at a more sophisticated level. He notes that, according to the empiricist philosophers who follow DESCARTES [2; S], we have complete authority in judging what our own mental states are. But, Reid remarks, although CONSCIOUSNESS [2; S] may have been particularly favored by philosophers, it is only one of the various faculties that are given to us originally, in just the same way as consciousness is. He shows that it is inconsistent to rely on consciousness alone and to deny a similar authority to our other faculties. The very detection of errors of judgment stands or falls with our ability to make reliable use of our faculties most of the time. Here the epistemological and psychological aspects of Reid's work overlap. Because our psychological faculties are relevant for his epistemology, Reid draws up a list of the "first principles of common sense," a summary of what we can usually derive from our faculties.

Although his vocabulary is psychological, Reid is taking a line adopted by a number of contemporary philosophers critical of skepticism. These philosophers have argued that, if doubt is to be intelligible, it must be local. The skeptic who believes that she can generalize doubt must be reminded that a background of certainty is required if doubt is to be effective.

The American philosopher Keith Lehrer has sought an anticipation of his own coherentist epistemology in Reid. Lehrer observes that knowledge requires not only sources of information, but also the metamental evaluation of those sources, including the elimination of claims undermining the value of our information. Reid, by making explicit the veracity of our faculties among his first principles, has provided the main element of metamental evaluation. This elegant approach goes beyond anything that Reid himself wrote, but it correctly captures one aspect of his epistemology: the shift from the evaluation of judgments, which may be considered singularly by way of clear-cut criteria, to a second-order evaluation of our faculties themselves (*see* COHERENTISM [S]).

Bibliography

WORKS BY REID

Inquiry into the Human Mind. 1764.

Essays on the Intellectual Powers of Man. 1785.

Essays on the Active Powers of Man. 1788.

Philosophical Works, 8th ed. Edinburgh, 1895.

Philosophical Orations, trans. S. D. Sullivan, ed. D. D. Todd. Carbondale, IL, 1989. Includes bibliography.

Practical Ethics, ed. K. Haakonssen. Princeton, NJ, 1990. Includes a substantial introduction.

WORKS ON REID

Alston, W. P. "Thomas Reid on Epistemic Principles," *History of Philosophy Quarterly,* Vol. 2 (1985), 435–52.

Barker, S. F., and T. L. Beauchamp, eds. *Thomas Reid: Critical Interpretations.* Philadelphia, 1976.

Brentano, F. "Was an Reid zu loben," *Grazer philosophische Studien,* Vol. 1 (1975), 1–18.

Dalgarno, M., and E. Matthews, eds. *The Philosophy of Thomas Reid.* Dordrecht, 1989.

Daniels, N. *Thomas Reid's "Inquiry": The Geometry of Visibles and the Case for Realism,* 2d ed. Stanford, CA, 1989.

Ferreira, M. J. *Scepticism and Reasonable Doubt.* Oxford, 1986.

Gallie, R. D. *Thomas Reid and the "Way of Ideas."* Dordrecht, 1989.

Lacoste, L. M. *Claude Buffier and Thomas Reid.* Kingston, 1982.

Rowe, W. L. *Thomas Reid on Freedom and Morality.* Ithaca, NY, 1991.

Schulthess, D. "Reid and Lehrer: Metamind in History," *Grazer philosophische Studien,* Vol. 40 (1991), 135–47.

Wood, P. B. "Thomas Reid, Natural Philosopher." Ph.D. diss., University of Leeds, 1984.

DANIEL SCHULTHESS

RELATIVISM. *See:* AESTHETIC RELATIVISM, MORAL RELATIVISM, and PHILOSOPHY OF SCIENCE [S]

RELATIVITY. *See:* PHILOSOPHY OF PHYSICS [S]

RELEVANT ALTERNATIVES. On the relevant alternatives theory the main ingredient that must be added to true belief to make knowledge is that one be in a position to rule out all the relevant alternatives to what one believes. The important implication here is that some alternatives to what one believes are not relevant, so one can know in the face of some uneliminated possibilities of error.

This approach is largely motivated by its ability to handle cases similar to the following (adapted from Dretske, 1970). In all of our cases Wilma is now describing the epistemic state Fred was in earlier today when he had a good, clear look at what he confidently took to be—and what, in fact, were—some zebras at the local zoo. In ordinary case O nothing unusual was going on during Fred's trip to the zoo, and nothing funny is transpiring in Wilma's conversational setting as she says, "Fred knew that the animals he was seeing were zebras." By contrast, in case F the zoo was displaying convincing fake zebras—cleverly painted mules—in nine of its ten zebra exhibits. We may suppose that Fred was fooled by all nine sets of fakes before he finally encountered the real zebras. But it is that final episode that Wilma is currently talking about (and thus she is discussing a true belief of Fred's) when, unaware that there were any fakes at the zoo, she says, "Fred knew that the animals he was seeing were zebras." It seems that, since Fred did in fact know that the animals were zebras in case O, but did not know it in case F, Wilma is speaking the truth in O but is saying something false in F.

What accounts for this difference? In each case Fred believed—we may suppose with equal confidence—that the animals he was seeing were zebras. In each case this belief of Fred's was true. And we may suppose that Fred was equally justified in holding this belief in the two cases. What seems to block Fred from having knowledge in case F is that he could not rule out the possibility that he was seeing fake zebras. But Fred seems equally incapable of ruling out that alternative to what he believes in case O.

On the relevant alternatives approach the alternative that Fred was seeing fakes is, like other remote, fanciful alternatives, an irrelevant alternative in case O. But, because of the abundance of fake zebras that inhabited his surroundings in case F, that he was seeing fakes is a relevant alternative in that example. Thus, while Fred was incapable of ruling out that alternative in either case, this inability prevents him from knowing only in case F, where that alternative is relevant.

That believers need not be in a position to rule out all the alternatives to what they believe in order to be knowers seems to promise some relief from SKEPTICISM [7; S]. For many of the most powerful skeptical arguments reach the conclusion that we do not know what we ordinarily take ourselves to know by means of intuitively plausible claims to the effect that we are in no position to rule out various skeptical hypotheses (e.g., that one is a bodiless brain in a vat, that one is the victim of a powerful deceiving demon, etc.). But if these skeptical hypotheses are not relevant alternatives to what we believe, then our inability to rule them out does not preclude our having knowledge.

Several problems plague this antiskeptical strategy. One is that, absent some fairly clear criteria for when an alternative is relevant together with a non-question-begging argument to the effect that skeptical hypotheses do not meet these criteria, the bald claim that these hypotheses are irrelevant packs little punch against the skeptic. Another is that this strategy does not explain the persuasiveness of the skeptical arguments in question. If our concept of knowledge were such that alternatives such as the skeptical hypotheses are just irrelevant, then it seems the skeptic's inference (from our inability to rule out her hypothesis to our not knowing we think we know) would not have the intuitive pull it has for many of us. This second problem can perhaps be avoided by a different relevant alternatives strategy that allows the speaker's conversational context to affect which alternatives are relevant and does not simply declare the skeptic's hypotheses irrelevant.

In case F the presence and proximity of fakes in Fred's surroundings account for why the alternative that he is seeing fakes is relevant there. But consider another case exactly like case O with respect to the features pertaining to Fred and his surroundings. In this new case S, however, something funny *is* going on in Wilma's conversational context: she is discussing philosophical skepticism with her friend Betty, and, because Fred was in no position to rule out various skeptical hypotheses they have been discussing, she agrees with the skeptically inclined Betty that "Fred didn't know that the animals he was seeing were zebras." Here it can be maintained that because various skeptical alternatives have been brought up and taken seriously, those alternatives are relevant in case S, though they are irrelevant in O, and Wilma is therefore speaking a truth when in S she says that Fred did not know.

This approach seems to explain the power of the skeptical arguments: we find the skeptic's attack persuasive because she *makes* her alternatives relevant and thereby creates a context in which her skeptical assertions are true. That the skeptic speaks the truth here is a significant concession to the skeptic. But this approach protects the truth values of the claims to knowledge that we make in more ordinary contexts, where no skeptics are muddying the conversational waters with ordinarily irrelevant alternatives to what we believe. And it does so while, at the same time, explaining the persuasiveness of the skeptic's attack.

Bibliography

DeRose, K. "Contextualism and Knowledge Attributions," *Philosophy and Phenomenological Research,* Vol. 52 (1992), 913–29.

Dretske, F. "Epistemic Operators," *Journal of Philosophy,* Vol. 67 (1970), 1007–23.

Goldman, A. I. "Discrimination and Perceptual Knowledge," *Journal of Philosophy,* Vol. 73 (1976), 771–91.

Stine, G. "Skepticism, Relevant Alternatives, and Deductive Closure," *Philosophical Studies,* Vol. 29 (1976), 249–61.

Yourgrau, P. "Knowledge and Relevant Alternatives," *Synthese,* Vol. 55 (1983), 175–90.

KEITH DEROSE

RELEVANT LOGIC AND DIALETHIC LOGIC. *See:* LOGIC, NONSTANDARD [S]

RELIABILISM. Reliabilism is a type of externalist theory concerning the nature of epistemically justified belief. According to theories of the reliabilist type, a belief held by an individual is epistemically justified just in case that belief is reliably connected to the TRUTH [S]. According to "process reliabilism," developed and defended in detail by Alvin Goldman (1979, 1986, 1988, 1991), an individual's belief is justified provided the process that produces the belief is a reliable one. A belief-producing process is reliable just in case it is of a type that results in true beliefs more often than false ones. According to the "reliable indicator theory," a belief is justified just in case the individual's having that belief is a reliable indication that the belief is true, where reliable indication is defined in terms of objective probability. Versions of this kind of theory have been defended by ARMSTRONG [S] (1973), Alston (1989), Plantinga (1993a, 1993b), and Swain (1979), among others. In what follows, Goldman's reliable process theory will be the primary example of reliabilism under discussion.

In an early presentation of the process reliability theory, Goldman says: "The justificational status of a belief is a function of the reliability of the process or processes that cause it, where (as a first approximation) reliability consists in the tendency of a process to produce beliefs that are true rather than false" (1979, p. 9). It is not enough, however, to define justification merely in terms of having been caused by a reliable process. Suppose Mary has excellent memory but has been led to believe otherwise by a normally reliable authority. On a given occasion, she seems to remember a childhood event and comes to believe that this event occurred, despite the contrary evidence. Then, even though the belief is produced by a reliable process (memory), justification is lacking. The contrary evidence should have led Mary to be suspicious of the deliverances of her memory, and to resist believing. To cover this kind of scenario, Goldman adds to the quoted suggestion a further stipulation to rule out defeaters:

(PR) S's belief in p at t is justified =def. S's belief in p at t results from a reliable cognitive process, and

> there is no reliable or conditionally reliable process available to S which, had it been used by S in addition to the process actually used, would have resulted in S's not believing p at t. (Goldman, 1979, p. 13)

For purposes of illustration, we may take the definition (PR) to represent the core idea behind process reliabilism.

There are three primary kinds of problems that face process reliabilism as exemplified in (PR). First, there are possible scenarios involving systematic deception by a Cartesian evil demon which suggest that an individual's belief can be epistemically justified but not produced by a reliable process. Imagine two kinds of worlds, one in which things are as we believe them to be in our world, and another in which we have the same phenomenal experiences but are systematically deceived by an evil demon. If our beliefs are epistemically justified in the "normal" world, then they should also be justified in the "demon" world, according to this line of objection. But, in demon worlds, our beliefs would not be produced by reliable processes. This kind of objection is inspired, in part, by the internalist conviction that only those properties of a person's beliefs that are internally accessible to that person are relevant to justification. In a demon world, beliefs may fully satisfy such internal conditions, just as they do in "normal" worlds, while being mostly false.

The reliabilist can respond to this first problem in several ways. The most direct response is simply to deny the legitimacy of the examples. Since the environment, in a demon world, conspires against reliable belief production, individuals in such a world have few, if any, justified beliefs. While bold, such a response will seem highly counterintuitive to many. A related reply grants that there is a legitimate, internalistic, subjective notion of justification that holds even in demon worlds. There is, however, a stronger, objective notion of justification, captured by the reliabilist approach, which correctly distinguishes between demon worlds and more hospitable epistemic environments (see Goldman, 1988). It might be argued that this stronger notion is more suitable for larger theoretical purposes, such as the provision of a definition of knowledge and the provision of an account of the social influences on individual knowledge. Yet a third possible reply is to grant the examples, continue to maintain that there is only one significant kind of epistemic justification, and modify the reliabilist account so that subjects in demon worlds have epistemically justified beliefs after all (Goldman, 1986).

A second problem for reliabilism is illustrated by examples in which individuals arrive at true beliefs in a highly reliable manner, but are not aware that the process is a reliable one. Such examples cast doubt on the sufficiency of process reliabilism. Laurence Bonjour (1985) suggests an example in which an individual, Norman, has a rare but highly reliable clairvoyant ability. Norman is unaware that he has this ability. On certain occasions, Norman's clairvoyant ability causes him to have beliefs, for no apparent reason, concerning the whereabouts of the President of the United States. When this happens, the beliefs are invariably correct, and are irresistibly held by Norman, even when he has evidence suggesting that the President is elsewhere. Such beliefs, although reliably produced in Norman, are not epistemically justified, so it is argued.

There are, again, several responses that the reliabilist can make. The boldest, and perhaps most counterintuitive, is simply to deny the example. Although a subject like Norman violates internalist requirements that one must be aware of one's evidence, or at least of one's reliability, the reliabilist might argue that such requirements are unacceptable on independent grounds and should not determine the results in this kind of example. A less counterintuitive reply takes note of the fact that Goldman's initial insight into the reliabilist nature of epistemic justification requires that a subject has not forsaken available processes that might have resulted in a different belief, even when coupled with the original, reliable process. Norman, for example, has failed to take into account the fact that he has no evidence for the whereabouts of the President or, even worse, has failed to take into account some contrary evidence. Taking such things into account, it might be argued, is a process that Norman could and should have used. Had he done so, he would not have believed what he does, despite his clairvoyant promptings.

The third, and perhaps most troubling problem facing the process reliabilist's program is a technical one having to do with the exact specification, in a given case, of the process that will be taken to have produced a subject's belief. This is known as the "generality problem." It was noted by Goldman himself (1979) and developed in detail by Richard Feldman (1985). Suppose that Laura sees a sheep in the field, but the sheep is at some distance and could fairly easily be confused with a large dog. Although not quite sure what she is seeing, Laura comes to believe that there is a sheep in the field. Is her belief justified? For the reliable process theory, the answer depends on the type of process that led to the belief, for it is only types of processes that can have the statistical features required for reliability. It seems, however, that Laura's coming to believe that there is a sheep in the field is the "result" of a variety of types of processes, including: perceiving something, perceiving something at a distance of two hundred yards, perceiving something that is a sheep in broad daylight on Saturday, March 9, 1996, and so forth. Some of these process types are highly reliable (the last one, for example, is perfectly reliable, since it can only be exemplified once, and it results on that occasion in a true belief), while some are considerably less reliable. Laura's belief is either justified or not, depending upon which of these process types is chosen to instantiate the definition (PR). And, so the objection goes, there is no nonarbitrary way to make such a choice. Hence, process reliabilism is hopelessly indeterminant and arbitrary.

The reliabilist might respond to the generality problem by trying to find a way of specifying the belief-forming processes whose reliability will determine epistemic justification (see, for example, Goldman, 1986). It has also been suggested, by Goldman himself (1986), that justification might be construed as permissibility in accordance with rules, where the rules specify those basic reliable processes that one may follow in forming beliefs. Goldman has also proposed that specific kinds of reliable processes might be identified as "epistemically virtuous," with beliefs being justified provided they are formed in accordance with virtuous processes (1991).

Other versions of reliabilism may be able to avoid the generality problem by defining justification in terms of reliability related features of an individual's epistemic situation other than the process that results in the belief. One example is Plantinga's theory, which says that a belief is warranted provided that it has been reliably produced by a properly functioning faculty in an environment of the type for which it was designed (1993b). On a view of this kind, reliability becomes a feature of faculties, rather than processes.

(SEE ALSO: *Epistemology* [S])

Bibliography

Alston, W. "An Internalistic Externalism," in *Epistemic Justification: Essays in the Theory of Knowledge* (Ithaca, NY, 1989). Presents and defends a reliable indication version of reliabilism.

Armstrong, D. *Belief, Truth, and Knowledge.* Cambridge, 1973. An early presentation of a reliable indication theory.

Bonjour, L. *The Structure of Empirical Knowledge.* Cambridge, MA, 1985. See particularly Chapter 3, where important criticisms of externalist theories are developed.

Feldman, R. "Reliability and Justification," *Monist,* Vol. 68 (1985), 159–74. Presentation of the generality problem.

Goldman, A. "What is Justified Belief?" in George S. Pappas, *Justification and Knowledge* (Dordrecht, 1979). Early statement of the reliable process theory.

———. *Epistemology and Cognition.* Cambridge, MA, 1986. See particularly Part 1, in which the reliable process theory is defended, and in which the "rules" version is introduced.

———. "Strong and Weak Justification," *Philosophical Perspectives,* Vol. 2 (1988), 51–69. Suggestion that there are two forms of justification.

———. "Epistemic Folkways and Scientific Epistemology," in *Liaisons: Philosophy Meets the Cognitive and Social Sciences* (Cambridge, MA, 1991). Suggestion that reliability and epistemic virtue are connected.

Plantinga, A. *Warrant: The Current Debate.* Oxford, 1993a. See especially Chapter 9, in which detailed criticisms of process and other forms of reliabilism are presented.

———. *Warrant and Proper Function.* Oxford, 1993b. Presentation of the properly functioning faculties view.

Swain, M. *Reasons and Knowledge.* Ithaca, NY, 1979. See especially Chapter 4, which develops the reliable indication theory.

MARSHALL SWAIN

RELIGIOUS EXPERIENCE. Most of the philosophical work on religious experience that has appeared since 1960 has been devoted to its phenomenology and epistemic status. Two widely shared assumptions help account for this—that religious beliefs and practices are rooted in religious feelings and that whatever justification they have largely derives from them.

The majority of the discussions of the nature of religious experience are a reaction to Walter STACE [8], who believed that MYSTICISM [5] appears in two forms. Extrovertive mysticism is an experience of nature's unity and of one's identity with it. Introvertive mysticism is an experience of undifferentiated unity that is devoid of concepts and images; it appears to be identical with what others have called "pure consciousness"—a state in which one is conscious but conscious of nothing.

R. C. Zaehner argued that Stace's typology ignores love mysticism in India and the West. There are two types of introvertive mysticism—monistic (pure consciousness) and theistic. The latter is a form of mutual love that unites God and the mystic in an experience without images and with very little, if any, conceptual content. The most effective defense of a position of this sort is Nelson Pike's. Pike argues that the principal forms of mystical prayer in Christianity (quiet, rapture, and full union) are phenomenologically theistic. He defends his analysis against William Forgie, who denies that the identification of the experience's object with God can be part of its phenomenological content.

Phenomenological analyses of religious consciousness presuppose that we can distinguish descriptions of religious experience from interpretations. Ninian Smart proposed two tests for distinguishing descriptions—that the accounts be autobiographical and that they be relatively free from doctrinal concepts. The question of criteria remains vexed, however (see Wainwright, 1981, chap. 1).

Others have argued that, because religious experience is significantly constituted by the concepts, beliefs, expectations, and attitudes that the mystic brings to it, attempts to distinguish interpretation from description are misguided. For example, an influential article by Steven Katz contends that a mystic's experiences are largely shaped by his or her tradition. This has two consequences. First, there are no "pure" or "unmediated" mystical experiences and, second, there are as many types of mystical experiences as there are traditions.

Katz's "constructivism" has been attacked by Robert Forman and Anthony Perovitch among others. Since pure consciousness is devoid of content, it is difficult to see how it could be constituted by contents that the mystic brings to it. To argue that it must be mediated because all experience is mediated begs the question; on the face of it, pure consciousness is a counterexample to the thesis in question. Forman also argues that constructivism cannot adequately account for novelty—the fact that the mystic's experiences are often unlike what he or she expected (*see* CONSTRUCTIVISM, MORAL, and CONSTRUCTIVISM, CONVENTIONALISM [S]).

Defenses of religious experience's cognitive validity have taken several forms. William Wainwright argues that mystical experiences are presumptively valid because they are significantly similar to sense experiences. Both experiences have what George BERKELEY [1; S] called "outness"—the subject has the impression of being immediately presented with something transcending his or her own consciousness. Corrigible and independently checkable claims about objective reality are spontaneously made on the basis of both types of experience. There are tests in each case both for determining the reality of the experience's apparent object and for determining the genuineness of apparent perceptions of it. The nature of the tests, however, is determined by the nature of the experiences' alleged objects. Since the apparent objects of religious experience and ordinary perceptual experience differ, so too will the tests for veridical experiences of those objects.

Richard Swinburne's defense of religious experience's cognitive validity is based on the principle of credulity, which roughly states that apparent cognitions are innocent until proven guilty. This is a basic principle of RATIONALITY [S]; without it we would be unable to justify our reliance on MEMORY [5; S], sense PERCEPTION [6; S], and rational INTUITION [4; S]. The principle implies that there is an initial presumption in favor of how things seem to us, although this presumption can be overriden. What is true of apparent cognitions in general is true of religious experiences. They too should be accepted in the absence of good reasons for thinking them deceptive. Swinburne argues that there are none.

The most sustained defense of religious experience's epistemic credentials is William Alston's. Whereas Wainwright and Swinburne concentrate on perceptual (or perception-like) experiences, Alston focuses on perceptual practices. Doxastic (belief-forming) practices are basic when they provide our primary access to their subject matter. The reliability of a basic doxastic practice like memory cannot be established without circularity; any attempt to justify it relies on its own outputs. Alston argues that sense-perceptual practice and "Christian mystical practice" are epistemically on a par. Since both doxastic practices are basic, neither's reliability can be established without circularity. Both practices are socially established, internally consistent, and consistent with the outputs of other well-established practices. They are also self-supporting in the sense that they have the outputs we would expect them to have if they were reliable (successful predictions in the first case, for example, and moral and spiritual improvement in the second). Alston concludes that it is unreasonable to engage in sense-perceptual practice while rejecting the rationality of engaging in Christian mystical practice. The rationality at issue, however, is not epistemic. Neither practice can be shown to be epistemically rational, since it is impossible to establish their reliability without circularity. Alston intends to show only that it is practically or pragmatically rational to engage in them, although it should be noted that engaging in them involves accepting their outputs as true and therefore *believing* that they are reliable. Alston concedes that the existence of competing mystical practices weakens his case but denies that it destroys it. Critiques of Alston's work have tended to focus on this point (see, for example, Hasker, 1986).

The most significant attacks on religious experience's cognitive validity to have appeared since 1960 are Wayne Proudfoot's and Richard Gale's. Proudfoot argues that an experience's noetic quality should be identified with its embedded causal judgment (that the experience is caused by a tree, for example, or by God) and this judgment's affective resonance. The incorporated causal judgment has no intrinsic authority; it is merely one hypothesis among others and should be accepted only if it provides a better overall explanation of the experience than its competitors'. While the causal hypotheses embedded in religious experiences could be correct, they are in fact suspect; they appear to be artifacts of the subject's religious or cultural tradition and not products of nonnatural causes.

Proudfoot's identification of an experience's noetic quality with an incorporated causal judgment and its affective resonance is more plausible in some cases than others. Given my background knowledge, I believe that a certain sort of pain in one's tooth is caused by cavities. Believing this, and having a pain of that sort, I spontaneously form the belief that my pain is caused by a cavity. While my pain is not noetic, the experience as a whole is, since it incorporates a causal judgment. But the experience lacks "outness." It thus differs from sense perception, which (because of this quality) seems to have an intrinsic authority that noetic experiences like my toothache lack. Religious experiences are also diverse. Some, like my toothache, involve spontaneous causal attributions and nothing more. Others, however, are perception-like and have the same claim to intrinsic authority that sense perceptions do.

Richard Gale, on the other hand, argues that religious experience lacks the authority of sense experience. The only way of establishing religious experience's cognitivity is by showing that the tests for it are similar to those for sense experience. Arguments for religious experience's cognitive validity fail because the dissimilarities are too great. Alston and Wainwright contend that these dissimilarities can be explained by differences in the experiences' apparent objects. Gale objects that explaining the disanalogies does not explain them away and that there is a "tension" or "inconsistency" in claiming that the tests are similar (as they must be if the defense of religious experience's cognitivity is to be successful) and yet different in nature. The first point is dubious. Only relevant disanalogies count. The point of Wainwright's and Alston's explanations is to show that the disanalogies are not relevant—that is, that the features that tests for sense experiences have and tests for religious experiences lack are not ones we would expect the latter to have if religious experiences were veridical perceptions of their apparent objects.

Gale's most original (and controversial) contribution is his contention that veridical experiences of God are conceptually impossible. The argument is roughly this. Talk of veridical experiences is in place only where it makes sense to speak of their objects as existing "when not actually perceived" and as being "the common object of different" experiences of that type. Sense experiences exhibit this feature because their objects are "housed in a space and time that includes both the object and the perceiver." Religious experiences do not exhibit this feature because there are no "analogous dimensions to space and time" that house both God and the perceiver. Gale attempts to establish this by refuting P. F. STRAWSON's [7; S] claim that a "no space world . . . of objective sounds" is conceptually possible. We could neither reidentify sounds in such a world nor distinguish between numerically distinct but qualitatively identical ones. It would make no sense, therefore, to speak of sounds as the common objects of distinct auditory experiences or as existing when unperceived. Talk of veridical experiences of objective sounds would thus be out of place. A fortiori, talk of veridical experiences would be out of place in a nonspatial and nontemporal world. Therefore, since no common space (and, on some accounts, no common time) houses God and the mystic, talk of veridical perceptions of God is inappropriate.

A few general observations about discussions of religious experience since 1960 are in order. First, most defenses of religious experience's cognitive validity have been offered by theists. Stace is one of the few who has attempted to establish the veridicality of pure consiousness and other nontheistic experiences that lack intentional structure. Second, philosophical discussions of religious experiences tend to abstract them from the way of life in which they occur and thereby impoverish our understanding of them. Whether this penchant for abstraction adversely affects the discussion of phenomenological and epistemological issues, however, is more doubtful. Finally, a philosopher's assessment of the cognitive value of religious experience is affected by his or her metaphysical predilections. For example, those who assign a low antecedent probability to THEISM [8; S] will demand stronger arguments for theistic experiences' cognitive validity than those who do not. One's assessment of religious experience cannot be separated from one's general assessment of the relevant religious hypotheses. (SEE ALSO: *Philosophy of Religion* [6; S])

Bibliography

Alston, W. P. *Perceiving God.* Ithaca, NY, 1991.

Davis, C. F. *The Evidential Force of Religious Experience.* Oxford, 1989.

Forgie, W. J. "Theistic Experience and the Doctrine of Unanimity," *International Journal for Philosophy of Religion,* Vol. 15 (1984), 13–30.

———. "Pike's Mystic Union and the Possibility of Theistic Experience," *Religious Studies,* Vol. 30 (1994), 231–42.

Forman, R. K. C. "Introduction: Mysticism, Constructivism, and Forgetting," in R. K. C. Forman, ed., *The Problem of Pure Consciousness* (New York, 1990).

Gale, R. *On the Nature and Existence of God.* Cambridge, 1991. Chap. 8.

Gutting, G. *Religions Belief and Religious Skepticism.* Notre Dame, IN, 1982. Chap. 5.

Hasker, W. "On Justifying the Christian Practice," *New Scholasticism,* Vol. 60 (1986), 144–29.

Katz, S. T. "Language, Epistemology, and Mysticism," in S. T. Katz, ed., *Mysticism and Philosophical Analysis* (London, 1978).

Perovitch, A. N., Jr. "Does the Philosophy of Mysticism Rest on a Mistake?" in R. K. C. Forman, ed., *The Problem of Pure Consciousness* (New York, 1990).

Pike, N. *Mystic Union: An Essay in the Phenomenology of Mysticism.* Ithaca, NY, 1992.

Proudfoot, W. *Religious Experience.* Berkeley, 1985.

Smart, N. "Interpretation and Mystical Experience," *Religious Studies,* Vol. 1 (1965), 75–87.

Stace, W. T. *Mysticism and Philosophy.* Philadelphia, 1960.

Swinburne, R. *The Existence of God.* Oxford, 1979. Chap. 13.

Wainwright, W. J. *Mysticism: A Study of Its Nature, Cognitive Value, and Moral Implications.* Brighton, England, 1981.

Yandell, K. E. *The Epistemology of Religious Experience.* Cambridge, 1992.

Zaehner, R. C. *Concordant Discord.* Oxford, 1970.

WILLIAM J. WAINWRIGHT

RELIGIOUS PLURALISM. The fact that there is a plurality of religions is significant in different ways from different points of view. From a skeptical point of view their different and often incompatible beliefs confirm the understanding of religion as delusion. Thus, Bertrand RUSSELL [7] wrote that "It is evident as a matter of logic that, since [the great religions of the world] disagree, not more than one of them can be true" (1957, xi). From the point of view of an exclusive and unqualified commitment to any one religion the fact of religious plurality is readily coped with by holding that all religions other than one's own are false, or false insofar as their belief systems differ from one's own. But from a point of view that sees religion as a worldwide phenomenon that is not to be dismissed in toto as delusion but as the human response to a divine/transcendent/ultimate reality, the fact of plurality poses a major philosophical problem. On the one hand, the "great world religions" seem—to many impartial observers, at any rate—to affect human life for both good and ill to more or less the same extent. But on the other hand their respective belief systems, although having important similarities, also include starkly incompatible elements. According to some the Real (a term at home in the Judeo-Christian tradition and corresponding to the Sanskrit *sat* and the Arabic *al-Haqq*) is personal but according to others not personal. And within each group of religions there are wide differences. Is the ultimate Person the Christian Trinity or the Qur'anic Allah, or the Adonai of Judaism, or Vishnu, or Shiva? Is the nonpersonal Ultimate the Brahman of advaitic Hinduism, or the Tao, or the Dharmakaya or Void or Nirvana of the Buddhist traditions? And how could the Real be all of these at once? The logic of religious difference here is in fact very complex, as is shown by William Christian's analysis (1987).

The problem is particularly acute for a major form of religious apologetic that has become prominent in the 1980s and 1990s. This holds that the basic empiricist principle that it is rational, in the absence of specific overriding considerations, to base beliefs on experience should be applied impartially to all forms of putatively cognitive experience, including religious experience—unless, again, there are specific overriding considerations to the contrary. This has been argued directly by William Alston (1991) and others and indirectly by Alvin Plantinga (in Plantinga & Wolterstorff, 1983), whose defense of the rationality of holding "properly basic" religious beliefs presupposes RELIGIOUS EXPERIENCE [S] as their ground.

Most of the philosophers who employ this kind of apologetic have applied it only to specifically Christian beliefs. But it is evident that precisely the same argument is available for the belief systems of other religions. If Christian religious experience renders it epistemically justifiable (subject to the possibility of specific reasons to the contrary) to hold Christian beliefs, then Buddhist religious experience renders it epistemically justifiable, with the same qualification, to hold Buddhist beliefs, Muslim religious experience to hold Muslim beliefs, and so on. Thus, anyone who maintains that the Christian belief system is true, but that the belief systems of Buddhists, Muslims, and so on are false insofar as they differ from it, has implicitly reversed the original apologetic and is presenting Christian religious experience as the sole exception to the general rule that religious experience gives rise to false beliefs!

Alston, recognizing the challenge posed by the fact of religious diversity to the experiential apologetic, has responded by saying that in this situation it is proper for the Christian to continue within her own belief system, despite the existence of other equally well-justified alternatives, while, however, she seeks "a way to show in a non-circular way which of the contenders is correct' (1991, p. 278).

An alternative use of the experiential apologetic rejects the assumption that only one of the different religious belief systems can be true. This approach (Hick, 1989) distinguishes between, on the one hand, the ultimate religious reality, the Real, beyond the scope of our (other than purely formal) human conceptualities, and, on the other hand, the range of ways in which that reality is humanly conceived, and therefore humanly experienced, and therefore humanly responded to within the different religiocultural ways of being human. The epistemology operating here is one that, in the Kantian tradition, recognizes an important contribution by the perceiver to the form a reality is perceived to have. As THOMAS AQUINAS [8] wrote, "Things known are in the knower according to the mode of the knower" (*Summa Theologica,* II/II, 1, 2). And in religious knowing the mode of the knower differs from religion to religion. From this point of view the fact of religious diversity does not constitute a challenge to the experiential apologetic but rather a series of examples of its valid application.

Other philosophical responses to the fact of religious plurality, not specifically related to the experiential apologetic, include the "perennial philosophy" (e.g., Schuon, 1975; Smith, 1976), which distinguishes between the essence (or esoteric core) of religion and its accidental (or exoteric) historical forms. In their esoteric essence all the great traditions converge in a transcendental unity, the Absolute Unity that is called God. Experientially, this sees the mystics of the different religions as participating in an identical experience, although they articulate it in the different ways provided by their traditions. This view is opposed by those (e.g., Katz, 1978) who hold that all experience is concept laden and that mystical experience accordingly takes different forms within the different traditions.

There is also the view of John Cobb (in Kellenberger, 1993) that the religions are directed toward different ultimates, particularly the personal reality worshiped in the theistic religions and the nonpersonal process of the universe experienced in Buddhism. Yet other constructive suggestions include those of Joseph Runzo (1986), James Kellenberger (1989), and the authors included in the symposium *Inter-Religious Models and Criteria* (Kellenberger, 1993).

(SEE ALSO: *Philosophy of Religion, History of,* and *Philosophy of Religion, Problems of* [6]; and *Philosophy of Religion* [S])

Bibliography

Alston, W. P. *Perceiving God.* Ithaca, NY, 1991.

Christian, W. A. *Doctrines of Religious Communities.* New Haven, 1987.

Godlove, T. F. *Religion, Interpretation, and Diversity of Belief.* Cambridge, 1989.

Hick, J. *An Interpretation of Religion.* London, 1989.
Katz, S. T., ed. *Mysticism and Philosophical Analysis.* Oxford, 1978.
Kellenberger, J. *God: Relationships with and without God.* London, 1989.
———, ed. *Inter-Religious Models and Criteria.* London, 1993.
Krieger, D. J. *The New Universalism.* Maryknoll, NY, 1991.
Plantinga, A., and N. Wolterstorff, eds. *Faith and Rationality.* Notre Dame, IN, 1983.
Runzo, J. *Reason, Relativism, and God.* London, 1986.
Russell, B. *Why I Am Not a Christian.* London, 1957.
Schuon, F. *The Transcendent Unity of Religions.* Rev. ed. New York, 1975.
Smith, H. *Forgotten Truth.* Philadelphia, 1976.
Vroom, H. M. *Religions and the Truth.* Amsterdam, 1988.

JOHN HICK

RICOEUR, PAUL [*This entry consists of five articles written by Don Ihde. In the first, Ihde presents an overview of the French philosopher's contributions to the field. In the second, he discusses Ricoeur's ethical theory. The third presents the philosopher's views on evil. In the fourth article, Ihde discusses Paul Ricoeur's contribution to the study of metaphor. The last article describes Ricoeur's "philosophy of the will."*]

PAUL RICOEUR is one of France's most prominent and prolific contemporary philosophers. As of 1995 his bibliography ran to 120 pages of entries, including twenty-one books (in French). Ricoeur's earliest original works reflect the influence of phenomenology, in particular the phenomenology of Edmund HUSSERL [4; S]. The earliest systematic project was a massive "philosophy of the will" that was to deal with the concepts of freedom, will, evil, finitude, and the notion of humanity. Three books, *Freedom and Nature: The Voluntary and the Involuntary* (1950), *Fallible Man* (1960), and *The Symbolism of Evil* (1960) formed the core of this early work. The first of these was the most thoroughly phenomenological, dealing with the experience of human FREEDOM [3; S]. Its tone is existential in its focus on the human subject acting within an experiential field of decision (*see* EXISTENTIALISM [3; S]). This work is contemporaneous with works of Jean-Paul SARTRE [7; S] and Maurice MERLEAU-PONTY [5; S] and structurally similar to the existential phenomenology of both in that they interpret human action within situations or contexts. But already in this work the dialectical notion of a "diagnostics" was employed; this dialectic sought to deal with and integrate other methodologies into a much broadened notion of Husserlian phenomenology. Non-phenomenological sciences could provide clues or "indices" for hard-to-detect experiential phenomena. *Fallible Man* began the more religious turn often taken by Ricoeur's work, and in this work the notions of limit-concepts, largely Kantian in style, situate the notion of humanity as dialectically finite and infinite: humanity is "between" the finite and the infinite. Humanity, however, is marked by a fault line between these dimensions, and this occasions the experience of evil. *The Symbolism of Evil* explores this "fault" and introduces a much more hermeneutic approach and explores the concepts and experience of evil through the hermeneutic analysis of a cycle of religio-cultural myths (*see* HERMENEUTIC PHILOSOPHY [S]).

The incorporation of these increasingly hermeneutic concerns also marks *Freud and Philosophy* (1965) and *The Conflict of Interpretations* (1969), which immediately follow the first project. Increasingly dialectical, with a careful interrogation of some other bodies of theory, these works attempt to enrich hermeneutic theory by carefully undertaking critical studies of STRUCTURALISM [S], psychoanalysis, and the "hermeneutics of suspicion" that may be found in FREUD [3; S], MARX [5], and NIETZSCHE [5; S]. These thinkers are suspicious of simple rationalities and find various self-deceptive forces at work. Ricoeur terms this attitude the hermeneutics of doubt, which contrasts with the hermeneutics of belief arising both from classical hermeneutics (such as those associated with biblical hermeneutics), which implicitly holds to a belief that interpretation may uncover some original meaning-state, as well as HERMENEUTIC PHENOMENOLOGY [S] (including the work of both Hans-Georg GADAMER [S] and Martin HEIDEGGER [3; S]). A hermeneutics of belief must be chastened by a hermeneutics of suspicion.

Hermeneutics necessarily entails concerns with language. Ricoeur's habits of work are irenic and eclectic, and for much of his mid-period of work he also finds the notions of symbol, metaphor, and narrative to be central to hermeneutic techniques. Ricoeur often enters into dialogues and debates with ordinary-language philosophies, and he develops a major theory of METAPHOR [S] in *The Rule of Metaphor* (1975).

Ricoeur also has extended his hermeneutic concerns to more historical topics, and another trilogy, the three-volume *Time and Narrative,* marks yet another extension of his philosophy. Here concerns with both literary and historical concepts come into play. Narrative, the largest of the meaning units analyzed by Ricoeur, follows the progression from the symbol, his smallest unit, through myth and metaphorical structure, to the culmination in grander narrative. Not only is this a movement from smaller to larger units, but it is also a movement to the fields of literature and history, beyond the earlier fields of MYTH [5] and religion.

There is also to be found a continuity of thematic concerns throughout Ricoeur's career. If the earlier concentration upon a philosophy of the will necessarily must deal with the individual, that concern marks his very recent work as well. This can be seen in *Oneself as Another* (1992), in which Ricoeur traces out the internal dialectic of a complex notion of self, one in which one's self is also developed in relation to other selves, within oneself. In each thematic area one can find the examination of some region that is other, external, or exterior, balanced and reflected back upon that which is the same, internal or experienceable.

Ricoeur is a philosopher of complexity. He reads carefully in a field, deals respectfully with alternative approaches, and relates these dialectically to the core continuities of his own work, which retains a hermeneutic-phenomenological perspective. His work contains balanced, pluralistic, and nonsimplistic theories of a wide range of phenomena. He is deeply informed in a wide range of religious, cultural, historical, and social sciences, and his work is marked by ongoing discussion and argumentation.

Bibliography

WORKS BY RICOEUR

Fallible Man, translated by C. A. Kelbley. Chicago, 1965.

History and Truth, translated by C. A. Kelbley. Evanston, IL, 1966.

Freedom and Nature: The Voluntary and the Involuntary, translated by E. V. Kohak. Evanston, IL, 1966.

Husserl: An Analysis of His Phenomenology, translated by E. G. Ballard and L. E. Embree. Evanston, IL, 1967.

The Symbolism of Evil, translated by E. Buchanan. New York, 1967.

Freud and Philosophy: An Essay on Interpretation, translated by D. Savage. New Haven, 1970.

The Conflict of Interpretations: Essays in Hermeneutics, edited by D. Ihde. Evanston, IL, 1974.

The Rule of Metaphor: Multidisciplinary Studies of the Creation of Meaning in Language, translated by R. Czerny and K. McLaughlin. Toronto, 1978.

Hermeneutics and the Human Sciences: Essays on Language, Action, and Interpretation, edited and translated by J. B. Thompson. Cambridge, MA, 1980.

Time and Narrative, Vols. I, II, and III, translated by K. McLaughlin and D. Pellauer. Chicago, 1984, 1985, 1988.

From Text to Action: Essays in Hermeneutics, translated by K. Blamey and J. B. Thompson. London, 1991.

Oneself as Another, translated by K. Blamey. Chicago, 1992.

DON IHDE

ETHICAL THEORY. Paul Ricoeur does not develop a systematic or traditional ethical system, yet his works are rich in ethical insights. The three-volume *Time and Narrative* series is probably the richest in ethical suggestivity. Ricoeur argues that humans learn and locate ethical sensibilities through imagination, not simply the open imagination of sheer possibility, but a narrative-structured imagination that prefigures ethical possibilities. This he locates in fictive strategies developed primarily in literary types of narratives. Here possibility becomes concretely projective, but as fictive it is not yet historical.

Historical narrative, however, is relevant in that histories show consequences and provide a basis for ethical learning as well. Here the field of human actions is concretely traced out. Literary narrative prefigures, but historical narrative reconfigures. In Ricoeur's thought ethics is always developmental and is based upon a philosophical anthropology of human action. But human action takes its place within a meaning structure that is elucidated in narrative form. One can detect, even in this later development, links to the very earliest concerns of Ricoeur. The phenomenology of deciding within the context of the VOLUNTARY [S] is Ricoeur's earliest examination of human structured possibility. The later development, both actional and hermeneutic, sees the mediation of ethical development in terms of the concrete, productive imagination that results in poetic, fictive, and historical narratives.

Bibliography

WORKS BY RICOEUR

Fallible Man, translated by C. A. Kelbley. Chicago, 1965.

"Guilt, Ethics, and Religion," in *Talk of God* (New York, 1969).

"The Antinomy of Human Reality and the Problem of Philosophical Anthropology," in *Readings in Existential Phenomenology* (Englewood Cliffs, NJ, 1976).

"The Problem of the Foundations of Moral Philosophy," *Philosophy Today,* Vol. 22, no. 3/4 (1978), 175–92.

DON IHDE

EVIL, PROBLEM OF. Paul Ricoeur's theory of evil is complex and intercultural. It appears primarily in his *The Symbolism of Evil* (1960). Beginning with a phenomenology of symbolism, Ricoeur locates the foundational level of the experience of evil within symbolic "confessions" or expressions of evil experienced in defilement, sin, and guilt. All experience is open to primitive expressions. But expressions also always take place within already given contexts. These contexts are mythical and take a narrative shape. Primitive expressions thus reverberate with the higher-level myths.

Defilement presumes evil as exterior, coming upon one through some kind of quasi-physical touch or stain. This is the most primitive stage. Here, notions of "touch not" found in many cultures predominate. Next, the notion of sin is taken up in contexts of relationships such as the contractual relationship between God and his people. Sin is a breach of relationships and thus occurs between a self and an other. Finally, guilt, the most developed notion, interiorizes evil and makes it a phenomenon of one's action and responsibility. Here some type of willing initiates evil. Ricoeur suggests these are three stages in the experience of evil, but they are stages that never totally exclude the earlier and more primitive aspects.

At the level of religio-cultural myths the experience of evil is placed in mythic narratives that give shape to the phenomenon. In this larger field Ricoeur locates—primarily out of the ancient sources of the Western traditions—four strands of mythic narrative. The first is the cycle of creation stories that describe the original disorder and chaos of the cosmos, which, through often violent acts of the deities, gradually attains order and authority. Here, evil is identified with the disorderly and chaotic, and the repetition of founding acts both founds and preserves the good as order. A second strand is the tragic group of myths in which the gods, implicitly amoral or even evil, often act against the needs of humans. The gods set boundaries and conditions in which to become fully humane often leads to tragic results. These limits often preclude moral action. This strand is associated with ancient Greek culture. To act heroically, humanely, or nobly often entails doom; the catharsis found through tragedy is its redemption. The "Adamic" cycle (the third strand) is biblical in origin and presumes a good God and his creation, but then it is by human action that evil enters the world. Evil is moral or ethical in that it results from acts of will and freedom. But its instigation is also associated with human action. The fourth strand is that of an evolution of a captured soul that gradually becomes enlightened and "returns" to a previously unified state with the divine. Here, the human is "fallen" into a material body, from which the soul must be liberated through a return to a presumed original unity with the divine. Ricoeur associates this strand with the origins of Greek philosophical thought.

While each of these myths of evil is unique, the elements of each interact in a "cycle of myths," with no one myth ever attaining clear ascendancy. The higher experience of evil, then, is a dialectical one in which the extreme poles of evil brought on by free will interact with and find an evil "already there." The cycle of myths keeps the experience of evil from any simple, rationalistic solution, but it also retains the sense of complexity and mystery through the multiple strands of this experience. (SEE ALSO: *Evil, Problem of* [3; S]; and *Myth* [5])

Bibliography

Ricoeur, P. *The Symbolism of Evil,* translated by E. Buchanan. New York, 1967.

———. "Structure, Word, Event," *Philosophy Today,* Vol. 12, no. 2/4 (1968), 114–29.

———. "The Problem of the Double Sense as Hermeneutic Problem and as Semantic Problem," in *Myths and Symbols* (New York, 1969).

DON IHDE

METAPHOR. Paul Ricoeur's contribution to the study of METAPHOR [5; S] occurs most obviously in *The Rule of Metaphor* (1975), but the subject is a concern that runs through many of his works.

Ricoeur's theory of language is one that sees at its foundation a juncture of the experiential and the expressive, of experience and language. Symbols, the smallest meaning units in Ricoeur's repertoire, are expressions that describe primary experiences. Word and experience form a unity at this level. But even such primitives take their place in larger units, the largest being a narrative structure. But metaphors—and Ricoeur always stresses "living" or new metaphors as opposed to sedimented or "dead" metaphors—are medium-sized units that relate the various linguistic fields and roles in figurable ways. Although there can be "word metaphors," metaphor occurs primarily within a sentential context. Creative metaphor is a *deviance* from nonmetaphorical language that produces certain creative tensions. Arising from a primitive presemantic feature (such as found in symbols), metaphor may become predicative of new gestalts. Living, predicative metaphors are productive of possible creative imaginations. Ultimately, metaphors allow or stimulate redescriptions, which open new trajectories for human understanding. Rhetoric and hermeneutics are also skilled interpretive actions, and metaphor plays roles within them.

Metaphors are, in this sense, the poetic inventions that simultaneously celebrate the sheer possibility of language and prefigure imaginative trajectories; they may eventuate in redescriptions, including those by which humans conceive of themselves. Metaphors have complex structures that include iconographic, imagistic, and referential capacities. They are projectively imaginative and provide the material for much of human self-interpretation and for the reconfiguration of human possibilities. Ricoeur rejects the traditional analysis of metaphor as analogy but also rejects the Heideggerian "direct" meaning of metaphor. He argues that metaphors have a linguistic structure that is complex and suggestive, thus placing metaphor in a central role for productive imagination.

Bibliography

Ricoeur, P. "Creativity in Language: Word, Polysemy, Metaphor," *Philosophy Today,* Vol. 17 (1973), 97–111.

———. "Metaphor and the Central Problem of Hermeneutics," *Graduate Faculty Philosophy Journal* (New York), Vol. 3 (1973–1974), 42–58.

———. *The Rule of Metaphor: Multidisciplinary Studies of the Creation of Meaning in Language,* translated by R. Czerny and K. McLaughlin. Toronto, 1978.

DON IHDE

VOLUNTARY. Paul Ricoeur's "philosophy of the will" begins with *Freedom and Nature: The Voluntary and the Involuntary* (1950). Centrally influenced by a phenomenological method, Ricoeur locates the voluntary in the phenomenon of "deciding" (*see* PHENOMENOLOGY [6; S]). Not distant from similar concepts of existentialist philosophers of the time, particularly Jean-Paul SARTRE [7; S] and Maurice MERLEAU-PONTY [5; S], decision is related to a *project* that is intended and must be decided. In the process one "decides oneself." Ricoeur undertakes a phenomenology of such decision making and attempts analyses of intentionality, motivation, need, and other related issues.

Whatever is voluntary, Ricoeur contends, always finds itself located within a context or field, which is involuntary. Moreover, even within human action there are limits that are associated with one's embodiment. In a careful depiction of the history of decision Ricoeur takes account of the moments of hesitation, the process of attention, and the interaction of determination and indetermination. Beginning from the most clearly voluntary experiences, the analysis moves outward to more and more difficult to enact decisional processes. These entail skills, habits, and other forms of patterned bodily activities.

Eventually, however, there are also limits to what can be voluntary, and at the horizons of decidability lie the phenomena of necessity, limits, and consent to inevitability. Growth and genesis, and a particularly interesting discussion of *birth*—which in Ricoeur's sense is not experienced directly but is indirectly mediated through the narratives of others—responds to the other authors of the era (in having an existential-phenomenological base) who also address these issues, such as HEIDEGGER [4; S], Sartre, and others. It locates human freedom as a contextual freedom within, and in relation to, the involuntary. Ricoeur concludes that ours is an only or limited human freedom.

Bibliography

Ricoeur, P. *Freedom and Nature: The Voluntary and the Involuntary,* translated by E. V. Kohak. Evanston, IL, 1966.

———. "Phenomenology of Freedom," in *Phenomenology and Philosophical Understanding* (London, 1975).

DON IHDE

RIGHTS.

RIGHTS. The philosophical discussion of RIGHTS [7] has tended to focus on foundational issues, such as whether talk about rights can be dispensed with entirely, and on the resolution of conflicts, for example between rights and the general welfare.

RIGHTS AND DUTIES

If a statement about one person's rights tells us no more than that some other person has certain duties or obligations, then in theory rights would simply be duties from another point of view. A number of reasons have been suggested for believing that this elimination is not possible. For one thing, it would require a mutual entailment between rights statements and duty statements. But (it is argued) the entailment does not hold in either direction. It is true that a claim right (i.e., a claim on someone else) might entail a DUTY [2]; but, as Hohfeld long ago made us aware, since rights other than claim rights—liberty rights, powers, immunities—need not entail duties, not all rights have a corresponding and correlative duty. (Hohfeld was concerned only with legal relations, but Carl Wellman has argued that these distinctions pertain to moral rights as well as to legal rights.) Furthermore, it would seem that not every duty has a correlative right: It is sometimes said that though I may have a duty to give alms to the poor, no poor person has a right to receive alms from me.

We might overcome the first objection by arbitrarily limiting the use of "rights" to talk about claim rights. But it may also be that even if liberties, powers, and immunities do not have duties as simple correlatives, there is nevertheless some other more complex relationship between statements about these kinds of rights and statements about duties; Wellman has defended such a view. A liberty, for example, might be the *absence* of a duty to do otherwise.

The other side of the argument—there are duties to which no rights correspond—is, strictly speaking, irrelevant to the question whether rights are superfluous. It may be that all rights are duties, permissions, or prohibitions without all duties, permissions, and prohibitions being rights. Nevertheless, the attempt to determine which duties, permissions, or prohibitions correlate with rights raises another objection to the attempt to dispense with rights. For if, as some suppose, having a duty toward Y will translate into Y's having a right only if it is up to Y to decide whether the duty must be fulfilled, then it can be argued that rights, even claim rights, do not simply reduce to duties—an essentially normative element would seem to be left over. That is, Y's authority over the duty cannot itself be translated into some claim about the duties of others.

This distinction between rights holders as mere beneficiaries of duties and rights holders as authorities over duties has consequences for the issue of the distribution of rights. Who is capable of holding a right? If holding a right carries with it the authority to determine whether the corresponding duty must be fulfilled, then certain entities cannot have rights: animals cannot and fetuses cannot have rights, to mention two hotly debated issues (*see* ABORTION; ANIMAL RIGHTS AND WELFARE; and BIOMEDICAL ETHICS [S]). Of course, to say that a certain sort of animal cannot have rights is not to say that there is no duty to treat the animal in certain ways.

A second sort of objection to the elimination of rights is based on a different sort of asymmetry. Rights, it is said, are grounds for duties and therefore cannot simply be duties under another name. Thus, Joseph Raz has argued that an individual capable of having rights will have a right if the fact that something is in her interest is a sufficient reason for holding some other person to be under a duty toward her. There will therefore be a duty when there is a right, but they are not just different names for the same thing. This position does not seem to be necessitated by Raz's desire to make well-being the basis for duty; it may be that well-being is the basis for both the right and the duty and that the two are nevertheless the same thing under different names.

RIGHTS AND UTILITY

Rights function to protect the individual against depredations on behalf of the general welfare. Each person has a right, for example, not to be killed, even if her killing would lead to a marginal gain in utility. While some writers see this need for rights as a refutation of straightforward UTILITARIANISM [8], others have argued that there are versions of utilitarianism that can account for the existence of rights as limits to the public good. For example, L. W. Sumner argues that in the present state of our knowledge we simply cannot trust ourselves to make the right calculation of utility in certain types of circumstances, so that respect for rights in such circumstances may serve the function of keeping us headed for our consequentialist goal, in spite of ourselves.

Others have argued, however, that the ability to withstand utilitarian concerns is the very mark of a right. The interests protected by a right cannot simply be traded off either for greater future protection for those interests (Robert Nozick) or for any other collective goal whatever (Ronald Dworkin). This is the notion of rights as "trumps," and there are several different things it could mean. It could mean that rights are absolute, in the sense that the infringement of a right is never permissible, or it could mean that rights may be infringed only in the most extreme circumstances. The obvious possibility that rights themselves may come into conflict, so that one or the other must give way, makes both these interpretations implausible. Finally, it could mean that, while rights may vary as to the weight that they carry against other sorts of considerations, no right will yield to mere marginal improvements in utility. While this last reading is plausible, no one has yet been able to make clear precisely how rights are to be weighed against collective goals.
(SEE ALSO: *Social and Political Philosophy* [S])

Bibliography

Dworkin, R. *Taking Rights Seriously.* Cambridge, MA, 1977.

Feinberg, J. *Social Philosophy.* Englewood Cliffs, NJ, 1973.

———. *Rights, Justice, and the Bounds of Liberty.* Princeton, NJ, 1980.

Gewirth, A. "Why Rights Are Indispensable," *Mind,* Vol. 95 (1986), 329–44.

Golding, M. "The Concept of Rights: A Historical Sketch," in E. Bandman and B. Bandman, eds., *Bioethics and Human Rights* (Boston, 1978).

Martin, R. *A System of Rights.* Oxford, 1993.

Martin, R., and J. Nickel. "Recent Work on the Concept of Rights," *American Philosophical Quarterly,* Vol. 17 (1980), 165–80.

Nozick, R. *Anarchy, State, and Utopia.* New York, 1974.

Raz, J. *The Morality of Freedom.* Oxford, 1986.

Sumner, L. W. *The Moral Foundation of Rights.* Oxford, 1987.

Thompson, J. J. *The Realm of Rights.* Cambridge, 1990.

Wellman, C. *A Theory of Rights.* Totowa, NJ, 1985.

MICHAEL CORRADO

ROUSSEAU, JEAN-JACQUES. The writings of Jean-Jacques ROUSSEAU [7] continue to attract a wide range of readers throughout the world. Persistent questions concerning NATIONALISM [5], political legitimacy, and the social costs of technological progress sustain an ongoing interest in Rousseau's major political writings (*The Social Contract, Considerations on the Government of Poland,* the first and second discourses). Controversies over childrearing, the nature of language, and the role of the media in public life keep alive his educational and cultural writings (*Emile, Essay on the Origin of Languages, Letter to d'Alembert on the Theater*). Speculations about psychology and the arts of autobiography draw readers to Rousseau's personal writings (*The Confessions, Reveries of a Solitary Walker, Rousseau Judge of Jean-Jacques*). And new attitudes regarding LOVE [5], marriage, and eroticism provoke reconsideration of his romantic novel (*La Nouvelle Héloïse*). As the editors of a 1978 issue of *Daedalus* commemorating the bicentennial of Rousseau's death observed, Rousseau anticipated many of the moral, political, social, and aesthetic concerns that continue to preoccupy us today.

Three intellectual currents have contributed significantly to a growing body of scholarship on Rousseau. Feminist studies have offered fresh interpretations of his notoriously controversial writings about the nature, education, and status of women (see esp. *Emile,* book 5). Some feminist theorists (e.g., Okin, 1979) argue that Rousseau's advocacy of sexually differentiated social and political roles contradicts his egalitarian principles and undermines the logic and validity of his political theory. Others (e.g., Weiss, 1994) maintain that sexual differentiation constitutes a necessary social construct undergirding the unity of his entire system. At issue in many of these debates are fundamental questions about the usefulness for modern feminism of any theory that posits a close connection between a woman's essential "nature" and her moral role in society.

DECONSTRUCTION [S] has also affected the content and direction of Rousseau criticism, especially among scholars in language and literature departments. The French philosophers and literary critics who originated this movement in the 1960s and 1970s gave prime place to

Rousseau in the development of their ideas (see, e.g., DERRIDA [S], 1976). In seeking to expose the indeterminacy of the meaning of Rousseau's texts by examining details that are commonly overlooked (e.g., footnotes, metaphors, his choice of particular terms), deconstructionist critiques illuminate the multilayered quality of his prose and show that even an author committed to the truth may produce writings fraught with artifice.

A third important source of Rousseau criticism has been the legacy of Leo Strauss—a mid-twentieth-century political philosopher who is as well known for the habits of close textual analysis he passed on to his students as for the ideas put forth in his own writings (see, e.g., Strauss, 1953). Straussian interpretations take seriously Rousseau's claims that his political thought forms a single coherent system; they also emphasize his debt to classical sources. Most important, perhaps, the Straussian legacy includes a substantial number of English translations of Rousseau's work (e.g., by Allan Bloom, Victor Gourevitch, Christopher Kelly, Judith R. Bush, and Roger D. Masters)—thus making him more accessible to the general reader in North America.

Rousseau specialists have benefited from the publication of Rousseau's *Oeuvres complètes* and *Correspondance complète,* from the appearance of scholarly journals and associations devoted to Rousseau studies (*Annales de la Société Jean-Jacques Rousseau, Études Jean-Jacques Rousseau,* and the *Proceedings* of the North American Association for the Study of Rousseau), and from the publication of papers delivered at various conferences held in 1978 to commemorate his death and in 1989 to mark his relationship to the French Revolution.

Bibliography

WORKS BY ROUSSEAU

Oeuvres complètes. Ed. B. Gagnebin and M. Raymond. 5 vols. Paris, 1959–.

The Collected Writings of Jean-Jacques Rousseau. Ed. R. D. Masters and C. Kelly; trans. J. R. Bush, C. Kelly, and R. D. Masters. Hanover, NH, 1990–.

Correspondance complète de Jean-Jacques Rousseau. Ed. R. A. Leigh. 43 vols. Geneva, 1965–89.

Emile or On Education. Trans. A. Bloom. New York, 1979.

WORKS ON ROUSSEAU

Cranston, M. *Jean-Jacques: The Early Life and Work of Jean-Jacques Rousseau, 1712–1754.* New York, 1983.

———. *The Noble Savage: Jean-Jacques Rousseau, 1954–62.* Chicago, 1991.

Daedalus, "Rousseau for Our Time," special issue (Summer 1978).

de Man, P. *Allegories of Reading: Figural Language in Rousseau, Nietzsche, Rilke, and Proust.* New Haven, 1979.

Derrida, J. *Of Grammatology,* trans. G. Chakravorty Spivak. Baltimore, 1976.

Kelly, C. *Rousseau's Exemplary Life: The "Confessions" as Political Philosophy.* Ithaca, NY, 1987.

Launay, M. *Jean-Jacques Rousseau: Écrivain politique (1712–1762),* 2d ed. Geneva, 1989.

Masters, R. D. *The Political Philosophy of Rousseau.* Princeton, NJ, 1968.

Melzer, A. M. *The Natural Goodness of Man: On the System of Rousseau's Thought.* Chicago, 1990.

Miller, J. *Rousseau, Dreamer of Democracy.* New Haven, 1984.

Okin, S. M. *Women in Western Political Thought.* Princeton, NJ, 1979.

Roosevelt, G. G. *Reading Rousseau in the Nuclear Age.* Philadelphia, 1990.

Schwartz, J. *The Sexual Politics of Jean-Jacques Rousseau.* Chicago, 1984.

Shklar, J. N. *Men and Citizens: A Study of Rousseau's Social Theory.* Cambridge, 1969.

Starobinski, J. *J.-J. Rousseau: La transparence et l'obstacle.* Paris, 1971. Translated by A. Goldhammer as *Jean-Jacques Rousseau: Transparency and Obstruction.* Chicago, 1988.

Strauss, L. *Natural Right and History.* Chicago, 1953.

Weiss, P. A. *Gendered Community: Rousseau, Sex, and Politics.* New York, 1993.

GRACE G. ROOSEVELT

RULE FOLLOWING. In 1982 Saul KRIPKE [S] published *Wittgenstein on Rules and Private Language* and ushered in a new era of WITTGENSTEIN [8; S] interpretation. Although elements of Kripke's view of Wittgenstein could be found in the preceding literature (notably in Robert Fogelin's *Wittgenstein*), nothing had captured attention like his presentation of the 'rule-following considerations'.

Kripke presented his essay as a reconstruction of the problems Wittgenstein is addressing between around §140 and §203 of the *Philosophical Investigations.* These issue in the form of a paradox—that there can be no such thing as the meaning of a word; no fact of the matter that entails that a word is used according to a rule, whereby some applications of it are determined to be correct and other applications incorrect. In §201 Wittgenstein wrote "This [is] our paradox: no course of action could be determined by a rule, because every course of action can be made out to accord with the rule. The answer [is] if everything can be made out to accord with the rule, then it can also be made out to conflict with it. And so there would be neither accord nor conflict here."

The paradox is developed by Kripke through the figure of a "bizarre skeptic." The defender of common sense, here the view that words do indeed have meanings and obey rules, is challenged to show what this meaning consists in. The facts he or she can adduce typically include past applications and present dispositions to apply words in new cases. They may also include flashes of consciousness—for instance, if we associate a particular image with a term. But, Kripke's skeptic argues, these are not the kinds of facts that can determine the actual rule that governs the meaning of a word. The skeptic adduces three kinds of problems. First, our dispositions are finite, whereas a rule can cover a potential infinity of new cases. Second, our dispositions sometimes fail to match the relevant rules: this is precisely what happens when we mistakenly apply words to things to which they do not in fact apply. Third, the existence of a rule has normative implications. It determines correctness and incorrectness of application of the term it governs. Our dispositions, by contrast, have no such implication. There is nothing intrinsically wrong about bending our dispositions from moment to moment, in the way that there is about applying a term in a way that fails to accord with its meaning. Finally, the addition of flashes of consciousness is unlikely to help, for, as Wittgenstein himself said, any such fact itself stands in need of interpretation. A flash of consciousness cannot comprehend all the possible applications of a term and sort them into those that are correct and those that are not.

Kripke illustrates these points with the case of a strange arithmetical operator, 'quus'. For two numbers *n* and *m*, *n* quus *m* is identical with *n* plus *m* for sufficiently small or common numbers, but the two results (or calculations) diverge when *n* and *m* are greater than a certain value (the function is therefore reminiscent of GOODMAN's [3; S] predicate, 'grue'). We do not mean *n* quus *m* when we talk of *n* plus *m*. But our dispositions with 'plus' might match those of people who in fact use the term to mean quus; we might give the answer *n* quus *m* when we attempt to add *n* and *m*, since we make mistakes; and finally there is nothing right or wrong about having one disposition or another.

The conclusion is paradoxical, since nothing seems more certain than that we do succeed in attaching reasonably determinate meanings to terms. It may be true that the 'open texture' of terms suggests that meanings are never fully precise, capable of determining their application in any circumstances, however outlandish. Nevertheless, over an indefinite normal range of cases, there is no doubt that some applications are correct and others not, and any interpretation of us according to which we mean something along the lines of the 'quus' function is incorrect. Yet so long as the skeptic wins, we have no conception of our right to say such things. Kripke's own solution to the paradox is that the skeptic wins on his chosen ground. There is indeed no fact of the matter whether one rule rather than another governs the use of a term. But we can advance a 'skeptical solution' (HUME's [4; S] phrase from a different context) to the doubts. What there is instead is a practice of regarding ourselves and others in certain lights. We dignify each other as meaning one thing or another by our terms, and this ongoing practice is all that there is.

Kripke's work generated enormous interest and a variety of responses in the literature. Some outraged students of Wittgenstein argued that it was not at all his intention to produce a paradox but to lay bare the oversimplifications, or desire for a simple theory, that trap people into finding rule following problematic (Baker & Hacker, 1984). Many writers queried whether Wittgenstein could consistently have been content with a 'non-truth-conditional' account of rule following, which is what Kripke offers him, since Wittgenstein's abhorrence of theory and his belief that philosophy leaves everything as it is would make it impossible for him to say that it is not strictly speaking true that the application of words is correct or incorrect. Some (McDowell, 1981) detected a mischievous dislike of soft, humanly oriented facts in the setting up of the paradox and argued that a proper appreciation of the human constitution of rule following had wide implications for the notion of objectivity, as it occurs in domains such as aesthetics or ethics. Some (McGinn, 1984) found that Kripke had not looked hard enough for natural facts with which to identify the obtaining of a rule; others (Blackburn, 1985) embraced the thought that since the loss of a normative element in meaning was the main problem underlying the paradox, and since naturalistic theories of normativity have been proposed in many guises, a more generous sense of how to talk about facts solves the paradox. Paul Boghossian (1989) provided a summary of the state of the debate and a controversial contribution to it.

(SEE ALSO: *Philosophy of Language* [S])

Bibliography

Baker, G. P., and P. M. S. Hacker. *Scepticism, Rules, and Language.* Oxford, 1984.

Blackburn, S. "The Individual Strikes Back," *Synthese,* Vol. XX (1985).

Boghossian, P. "The Rule-Following Considerations," *Mind,* Vol. 98 (1989).

McDowell, J. "Non-Cognitivism and Rule-Following," in S. Holtzman and C. Leich, *Wittgenstein: To Follow a Rule* (London, 1981).

McGinn, C. *Wittgenstein on Meaning.* Oxford, 1984.

Wittgenstein, L. *Philosophical Investigations.* Oxford, 1953.

SIMON BLACKBURN

S

SARTRE, JEAN-PAUL (1905–80), wrote several major works after this Encyclopedia's first edition appeared, most notably the second volume of his *Critique of Dialectical Reason* and his multivolume study of Flaubert, *The Family Idiot.* A large amount of material has been published posthumously, including diaries and letters, essays, the scenario for a biographical film on FREUD [3; S], and the very important *Notebooks for an Ethics,* which he had promised at the end of *Being and Nothingness.* This subsequent work expands and modifies, but does not essentially change, his previous philosophical achievements, especially in philosophical psychology, social ontology, the philosophy of history, and ethics.

PHILOSOPHICAL PSYCHOLOGY

SARTRE's [7] concept of freedom expanded beyond the meaning-giving noetic freedom of *Being and Nothingness.* Not only did it come to include the "positive" freedom that overcomes socioeconomic scarcity, but it recognized the limits placed on an agent by class, peers, and especially early childhood experience. This last is particularly evident in his study of Flaubert's life and work. The family emerges as the major vehicle mediating social norms and values. So Sartrean freedom became less individualistic or omnipotent than his earlier work seemed to imply. Still, the maxim of Sartrean humanism remained the conviction that "you can always make something out of what you have been made into." If his vintage existentialist writings stressed the first part of this claim, his later work underscored the second (*see* EXISTENTIALISM [3; S]; FREEDOM [3]).

His relation to Freud, accordingly, became more nuanced. Though he continued to reject the Freudian UNCONSCIOUS [8], the concept of comprehension (the translucency of praxis to itself) began to serve as a functional equivalent, especially in *The Family Idiot.* Thus, Flaubert is supposed to have comprehended more than he knew, and the reader of *The Family Idiot* is enabled to know Flaubert better than he knew, but not better than he comprehended, himself. Sartre's quarrel with the unconscious continued to be its supposed denial of human freedom and RESPONSIBILITY [7], features that comprehension preserves.

SOCIAL ONTOLOGY

If the vintage existentialist Sartre is a philosopher of consciousness (*see* CONSCIOUSNESS IN PHENOMENOLOGY: SARTRE [S]), the later Sartre is a philosopher of praxis, defined as purposive human action in its material environment and sociohistorical context. The shift to praxis breaks the logjam in social ontology created by Sartre's looking/looked-at paradigm of interpersonal relations. Collective action (group praxis) and positive reciprocity are now possible in a way that was unthinkable in *Being and Nothingness.* Free organic praxis, the model of which is the Marxist notion of labor, is dialectical, totalizing, and translucent (it comprehends what it is about). In his later work Sartre accords a threefold primacy—namely, epistemic, ontological, and moral—to individual praxis.

Sartre speaks of the "translucency of individual praxis" as opposed to the opacity of the practico-inert, which he implies is the "intelligible limit of intelligibility." He distinguishes two forms of reason: the analytic, roughly Aristotelian logic, which is structural, abstract, and proper to the practico-inert, and the dialectical, which incorporates temporality in its comprehension and thus is processive and concrete. He respects the explanatory power of each but finds that dialectical reason, as totalizing, is closer to the lived reality of individual praxis. The intelligibility of social and historical causes is an enrichment of constitutive individual praxis.

The ontological primacy of praxis stems from Sartre's claim that "there are only individuals and real relations among them." Individual praxis alone is constitutive of whatever concrete reality obtains. So, abstract and impersonal processes such as colonialism or ideas such as racism, for example, are sustained by innumerable organic praxes that the practico-inert absorbs and transforms. The basic motive for forming groups is to liberate serialized (socially impotent) praxes from the alienating mediation of the practico-inert, supplanting the latter by the practical mediation of the praxes themselves.

Such "dialectical nominalism" avoids methodological and ontological holism and individualism (*see* HOLISM AND INDIVIDUALISM IN HISTORY AND SOCIAL SCIENCE [4]). Its vehicle is the "mediating third," the organic individual acting *as* group member, wherein each organic praxis makes itself "the same" "here" as the other member's praxes "there" in terms of action and practical concern. The model is the combat group or team where each participant becomes a member by acting with the others-as-same in a common project against the others-as-other. There is no collective subject, except organic praxes-in-practical relation. Yet group praxis is a qualitative enrichment of individual praxes, supporting new predicates such as "power" and "right/duty," and not a mere psychological attitude.

Sartre is fundamentally a moralist. His project of "existentializing" Marxist philosophy is an attempt to underscore those factors, abstract but especially concrete, that mediate historical change and individual action, since "it is men whom we judge and not physical forces" (*Search for a Method,* p. 47). The epistemic and ontological primacy culminates in the ethical primacy of individual praxis. Even the most impersonal and "necessary" social processes such as the rise of industrial capitalism or the spread of racist ideologies find their originating and sustaining power in free organic praxis to which moral judgments can be ascribed.

PHILOSOPHY OF HISTORY

Though HISTORICITY [S] has been a basic existentialist concept since Martin HEIDEGGER [3; S], Sartre gave history short shrift in *Being and Nothingness.* But his *War Diaries* reveal him to have been occupied with the theory of history in response to the successes in that field of his erstwhile friend Raymond Aron, as well as in reaction to the events of the Phony War in which he was then engaged. Only after the war did he resume these reflections, first in the posthumously published *Notebooks for an Ethics* under the rubric of morality and history, and then *ex professo* in the two volumes of his *Critique of Dialectical Reason.* In the latter the challenge is to discover whether history has only one meaning/direction *(sens)* and, if so, what the ontological and socioeconomic conditions for such might be. His hypothesis, and the claims it is only that (though frequent reference to "dialectical necessity" suggests otherwise), is that the fact of material *scarcity* (there are not enough of the world's goods to go around) has turned practico-inert mediation into the vehicle of VIOLENCE [S] and rendered history as we know it an unrelenting war of all against all.

What one might call his principle of totalization ("a man totalizes his era to the precise extent that he is totalized by it," *The Family Idiot,* 5:394)—a notion anticipated in G. Wright Mills's *The Sociological Imagination*—guides Sartre's approach to History with a Hegelian "H." Thus, Stalin's dialectical, totalizing relation to the Soviet Union in the 1930s (the subject of volume 2 of the *Critique*), or Flaubert's relation to the bourgeois literary world of Second Empire France (especially as analyzed in volume 5 of *The Family Idiot*), enables us to comprehend the agent and the age in spiraling interaction. Facts of individual biography illuminate historical phenomena, and vice versa, by a synthesis of HISTORICAL MATERIALISM [4] and EXISTENTIAL PSYCHOANALYSIS [3; S] that Sartre calls the "progressive-regressive" method. By this method the investigator uncovers the social conditions—for example, the nature of provincial bourgeois families and of Flaubert's intrafamilial relationships in French society at the time—by a regressive movement in order to chart progressively the agent's interiorization and exteriorization of these conditions in the project of living in this world historically. Rather than merely appealing to examples of historical movements or ideal types, this method aims to comprehend the concrete reality that is the organic individual as a "singular universal" interiorizing and exteriorizing these conditions.

ETHICS

With the availability of several manuscripts from the 1960s as well as the *Notebooks for an Ethics* and interviews given by Sartre toward the end of his life it is common to speak of Sartre's three attempts to formulate an ethics. The first is his well-known ethics of AUTHENTICITY [S], elaborated during the 1940s. The *Notebooks* corrects many misunderstandings of this ethics and of Sartre's image as a moral relativist and nihilist. A series of unpublished notes for lectures in the 1960s, the second, "dialectical" ethics uses the language of the *Critique* to promote the value of "integral humanity." His so-called ethics of the "We" is a tape dialogue with Benny Lévy cut short by Sartre's death. Still unpublished in its entirety, this third attempt appears to be of mainly biographical interest.

Bibliography

For a complete annotated bibliography of Sartre's works see M. Contat and M. Rybalka, eds., *The Writings of Jean-Paul Sartre* (Evanston, IL, 1973), updated in *Magazine littéraire* 103–4 (1975), 9–49, and by Michel Sicard in *Obliques* 18–19 (May 1979), 331–47. Rybalka and Contat have compiled an additional bibliography of primary and secondary sources published since Sartre's death in *Sartre: Bibliography, 1980–1992* (Bowling Green, OH: CNRS Editions, 1993).

WORKS BY SARTRE

Critique de la Raison Dialectique, précédée de questions de méthode, Vol. 1, *Théorie des ensembles pratiques.* Paris, 1960. Reprinted in new annotated edition, 1985. Prefatory essay translated by H. E. Barnes as *Problem of Method* (London, 1964) and *Search for a Method* (New York, 1963). Vol. 1 translated by A. Sheridan-Smith as *Critique of Dialectical Reason,* Vol. 1, *Theory of Practical Ensembles.* London, 1976.

L'Idiot de la famille, 3 vols. Paris, 1971–72. Vol. 3 rev. ed., 1988. Translated by C. Cosman as *The Family Idiot,* 5 vols. Chicago, 1981–93.

Between Existentialism and Marxism, translated by J. Mathews. London, 1974.

Oeuvres Romanesques. Paris, 1981.

Cahiers pour une morale, composed 1947–48. Paris, 1983. Translated by D. Pellauer as *Notebook for an Ethics.* Chicago, 1992.

Le Scénario Freud. Paris, 1984. Translated by Q. Hoare as *The Freud Scenario.* Chicago, 1985.

Critique de la raison dialectique, Vol. 2 (*inachevé*), *L'Intelligibilité de l'histoire,* edited by A. Elkhaim-Sartre. Paris, 1985. Translated by Q. Hoare as *Critique of Dialectical Reason,* Vol. 2 (unfinished), *The Intelligibility of History.* London, 1991.

Ecrits de jeunesse, edited by M. Contat and M. Rybalka. Paris, 1990.

WORKS ON SARTRE

Anderson, T. C. *Sartre's Two Ethics. From Authenticity to Integral Humanity.* Chicago, 1993.

Aronson, R. *Sartre's Second Critique.* Chicago, 1987.

Barnes, H. E. *Sartre and Flaubert.* Chicago, 1981.

Busch, T. *The Power of Consciousness and the Force of Circumstances in Sartre's Philosophy.* Bloomington, IN, 1990.

Catalano, J. *A Commentary on Sartre's Critique of Dialectical Reason,* Vol. 1. Chicago, 1986.

Cumming, R. *Phenomenology and Deconstruction,* Vol. 2, *Method and Imagination.* Chicago, 1992.

Detmer, D. *Freedom as Value: A Critique of the Ethical Theory of Jean-Paul Sartre.* La Salle, IL, 1988.

Flynn, T. R. *Sartre and Marxist Existentialism: The Test Case of Collective Responsibility.* Chicago, 1984.

Hollier, D. *Politique de la prose: Jean-Paul Sartre et l'an quarante.* Paris, 1982. Translated by J. Mehlman as *The Politics of Prose: Essay on Sartre.* Minneapolis, 1986.

Howells, C., ed. *The Cambridge Companion to Sartre.* Cambridge, 1992.

Lévy, B. *Le Nom de l'homme: Dialogue avec Sartre.* Lagrasse, 1984.

McBride, W. *Sartre's Political Theory.* Bloomington, IN, 1991.

Schilpp, P. *The Philosophy of Jean-Paul Sartre.* LaSalle, IL, 1981.

THOMAS R. FLYNN

SCIENCE, RESEARCH ETHICS OF. Sustained work on the ethics of scientific research by journalists, scholars, practitioners, and government officials began in the early 1980s, in the aftermath of scandals featuring researchers. One such researcher was Dr. John Long, a respected investigator of Hodgkin's disease at Massachusetts General Hospital. He had to resign and relinquish a large government grant after his collaborator discovered from a data logbook that Long had falsified results in response to a journal referee's criticism that their reported data were scanty (Kohn, 1986).

In an atmosphere of accountability the term that first gained currency was "fraud in science." This language clearly signaled that the self-correction processes of science were not protections against deception and cheating. In time the broader notion of misconduct took hold, especially in regulations of federal funding agencies. Eventually, emphasis on proper conduct came to the fore with the currency of the terms "research ethics," "responsible conduct in science," and especially "integrity" (Davis, 1990).

An important philosophical task is to delineate the subject matter of this part of ethics. The terms 'science', 'research', and 'ethics' require explication in light of their ultimate connection with institutions and of growing, but still partial, understanding of what scientists do (Galison, 1987; Latour and Woolgar, 1986).

The 1992 National Academy of Sciences report, *Responsible Science,* emphasizes "the research process," which includes "proposing, performing, evaluating, and reporting research activities" (p. 4). A broader view includes the social interactions of individuals and institutions; these interactions are governed by conventions and practices of research groups and peer communities (Zwolinek, 1992). Because the policies and procedures of universities, laboratories, funding agencies, scientific journals and societies, and peer review systems exert powerful influence on research processes, these components should, it seems, be encompassed as well. More external but also influential are pressures from journalists in the popular and scientific press.

What fields are included within the sciences? It seems that certain contextual features and research methods rather than the content or aims of investigation are determinative. Discussion concentrates on empirical research in fields that rely on substantial external funding (Davis, 1990).

The starting point for unpacking 'ethics' in the context of scientific research is the notion of misconduct. The definitions issued by U.S. government funding agencies in the late 1980s helped to clarify this notion, characterizing it as "serious deviation from accepted practices in proposing, carrying out, or reporting results from research" (NIH, 1988, p. 36347; NSF, 1991, p. 2228690). "Serious deviation" included fabrication, falsification, and plagiarism. Some scientists contest the "deviation from accepted practice" conception, holding that it is vague and threatens to curtail creativity because it leaves innovation indistinguishable from unethical conduct (Buzzelli, 1994).

This objection ignores context, especially the role of peer assessments, which serve to distinguish the innovative from the routine. If peers are expected to separate the innovative from the routine, they can also be expected to distinguish innovative research from conduct ethically unacceptable according to established standards for conducting research (Buzzelli, 1994; Zwolenik, 1992).

This response points to the central position of standards of practice and care in research communities. Many count on these standards as a guide to conduct and a basis for identifying misconduct (Buzzelli, 1994). This foundation of consensus places the burden for special ethical standards where it seems to belong and allows standards to be tailored to the character and circumstances of research and to evolve. The community-standards orientation, however, faces difficulties, notably from differences and conflicts between research programs about methodology. Rules of method carry normative force and are themselves subject to scientific debate (Schmaus, 1990). Furthermore, evidence indicates that research communities need to clarify their standards for conducting research (identifying underlying ethical considerations) and to delineate practices that serve the standards, while remaining ready to reassess as circumstances change (Swayze, 1993).

In view of the considerable differences in standards and conventions across research communities, the question arises whether there are shared core principles or ethical commitments that underlie specific standards. Some scientists favor the notion of integrity, which at root is the idea of moral wholeness or freedom from corruption, especially in relation to truth and fair dealing. Ascribed to persons, the notion of integrity implies constancy in meeting demands of morality. "Integrity of the research process" is understood as "adherence by scientists and their institutions to honest and verifiable methods" in research (NAS, p. 4). For the broader view of the research process (see above), this notion is inadequate.

Avoidance of deception, a key ethical commitment in science, seems to some philosophers the undergirding principle (Gert, 1993). However, it does not encompass (apparently) uncontroversial instances of ethical concern, such as violations of confidentiality in peer review. This principle is not well suited to addressing structures of science (e.g., peer review) or the relations of scientists and scientific research to the wider society. These latter dimensions are too integral to the doing of science and too salient in public discussion to be excluded.

What may serve to identify specific ethical concerns is the notion of answerability. For what are scientists answerable? Bench level practices include treatment of human and animal research subjects, advising and mentoring graduate students and postdoctoral fellows, gathering, recording, storing, and sharing data, preparing research reports, authorial practices, and practices related to intellectual property (Weil, 1993a). With closer ties between scientists and commerce threatening reliable judgment, conflict of interest must be included. In the structures of science, peer review is salient. Debate about the primary obligation to society pits a narrow interpretation, the obligation to pursue knowledge, against a broader conception, including, for example, a duty to avoid harmful consequences of research. Whether the broader conception can be derived from inherent features of science or must derive from conventions scientists have reasons to adopt is also debated (Davis, 1993; Kaiser, 1993). Favoring the latter position is its consonance with the foundation of consensus.

(SEE ALSO: *Applied Ethics* [S])

Bibliography

Buzzelli, D. E. "NSF's Definition of Misconduct in Science," *Centennial Review,* Vol. 38 (1994), 1–19.

Davis, M. "The New World of Research Ethics: A Preliminary Map," *International Journal of Applied Philosophy,* Vol. 5 (1990), 1–10.

———. "Science: After Such Knowledge, What Responsibility?" Center for the Study of Ethics in the Professions, Illinois Institute of Technology, Chicago, 1992.

Galison, P. L. *How Experiments End.* Chicago, 1987.

Gert, B. "Morality and Scientific Research," in *Ethics, Values, and the Promise of Science* (Research Triangle Park, NC, 1993).

Hackett, E. J. "A Social Control Perspective on Scientific Misconduct," *Journal of Higher Education* (May/June 1994), 242–60.

Kaiser, M. "Some Thoughts on the Responsibility of Scientists in Relation to the Growth of Fish-farming in Norway," *Studies in Research Ethics* [Göteborg, Sweden], No. 2 (1993), 19–32.

Kohn, A. *False Prophets: Fraud and Error in Science and Medicine.* Oxford, 1986.

Latour, B. *Science in Action: How to Follow Scientists and Engineers through Society.* Philadelphia, 1987.

———, and S. Woolgar. *Laboratory Life: The Construction of Scientific Facts.* Princeton, NJ, 1986.

National Academy of Sciences (NAS). *Responsible Science: Ensuring the Integrity of the Research Process,* Vol. 1. Washington, DC, 1992.

National Institutes of Health (NIH). "Responsibilities of PHS Awardee and Applicant Institution for Dealing with and Reporting Possible Misconduct in Science," *Federal Register,* Vol. 53 (1988), p. 36347.

National Science Foundation (NSF). "Misconduct in Science and Engineering: Final Rule," *Federal Register,* Vol. 56 (1991), p. 2228690.

Schmaus, W. "Honesty and Methods," *Accountability in Research: Policies and Quality Assurance,* Vol. 1 (1990), 147–53.

Swayze, J., M. Anderson, and K. S. Louis. "Ethical Problems in Academic Research," *American Scientist,* Vol. 81 (Nov.–Dec., 1993), 542–53.

Weil, V. "Ethics in Scientific Research and Graduate Education," *Studies in Research Ethics* [Göteborg, Sweden], No. 2 (1993a), 1–58.

———. "Teaching Ethics in Science," in *Ethics, Values, and the Promise of Science* (Research Triangle Park, NC, 1993b).

Zwolenik, J. J. "New Definitions of Misconduct: Priorities for the 1990s," *Knowledge,* Vol. 14, No. 2 (December 1992), 168–173.

VIVIAN WEIL

SCIENTIFIC THEORIES. Theories and models are two main artifacts produced by science. Divergent analyses of their functions, structures, and interpretations have been advanced that constrain interpreting other aspects of science.

FUNCTIONS OF THEORIES

Theories use theoretical laws to provide generalized descriptions that go beyond what is directly observable unaided by apparatus or contrived experimental circumstances. Theoretical REALISM [S] maintains that the function of theories is systematic description and explanation and that, to be adequate, all aspects of a theory's descriptions must be correct. Reductionism further requires that nonobservable content be reduced to the observable or some other empirical basis (see REDUCTION, REDUCTIONISM [S]). Instrumentalism construes the function of theories to be prediction of directly observable phenomena and requires only adequate description of directly observable aspects.

STRUCTURE OF THEORIES

Theories utilize specialized concepts, are expressed in technical language, and often invoke mathematical structures. Different philosophical analyses give each feature priority.

Operationalism. For Percy W. BRIDGMAN [1] theories link concepts that are operationally defined via mixes of basic measurement procedures constituting the concepts' entire meaning. The subject matter of science is operations, not absolute physical matter. Behaviorist S. S. Stevens operationally defined concepts as referring to mixes of objective gross physical behaviors. E. C. Tolman extended the notion to include stimulus-response overt behaviors mediated by intervening variables (*see* OPERATIONALISM [5]).

Syntactic Analyses. LOGICAL POSITIVISM [5] sought a theoretically adequate language for science where every sentence was true or false and contingent ones were empirically testable, hence meaningful. The syntax was symbolic logic. Descriptive vocabulary was trifurcated into mathematical and logical expressions, terms V_O descriptive of directly observable conditions, and the remainder V_T. Empirical testability was problematic only for "theoretical" expressions containing V_T terms. Restricting admissible V_T terms to those defined by correspondence rules C guaranteeing reference to something real ensured testability and meaningfulness.

Initially, V_T terms were shorthand abbreviations for complex directly observable conditions, hence eliminable explicit definitions. Technical difficulties handling dispositional concepts and the inadvisability of identifying theoretical entities with specific measurement procedures led Rudolf CARNAP [2; S] to introduce reduction sentences providing separate partial definitions of V_T terms for different experimental circumstances. Later, Carl G. HEMPEL [3] allowed interpretative systems that enabled testing observable consequences of entire theories without requiring each V_T term be tied contextually to specific directly observable consequences.

Embedded into this reformed language is the received view on theories (RV): a theory TC is set T of theoretical laws containing V_T terms conjoined with correspondence rules C as the axioms for a symbolic logic theory, where V_O terms refer to directly observables and referents of V_T terms are determined by C and V_O. Meaningfulness of terms and semantic reference are thus identified with ontological commitment, which means that positivistic-insistence theoretical terms referring to fictitious theoretical entities such as the luminiferous ether should be disallowed. The RV embodies theoretical realism, but the describable range of phenomena varies with allowed C. If only explicit definitions are allowed, the descriptive scope and range of ontological commitment are that of instrumentalism and many reductionisms. However, only instrumentalism would allow V_T terms not made referential by C.

Critics branded the RV untenable: Peter Achinstein, Hilary PUTNAM [S], and Frederick Suppe argued its V_T/V_O-term distinction could not coherently be drawn in any epistemologically significant manner. Norwood Russell Hanson argued that all observation is theory laden. Kenneth Schaffner and Wilfrid SELLARS [S] argued that correspondence rules were a heterogeneous confusion of meaning relationships, experimental design, measurement, and causal relationships. Patrick Suppes and Suppe argued that they did not accurately reflect how theories are connected to observational data. Achinstein and Putnam mistakenly charged that partial interpretation notions associated with more liberal C were incoherent. Suppes, Stephen Toulmin, and others questioned the appropriateness of first-order predicate logic formalism. Alternative views rooted in history of science by Thomas KUHN [S], Paul Feyerabend, Hanson, and Toulmin offered portraits conflicting with the RV. By the early 1970s few philosophers of science subscribed to the RV.

Another fundamental defect was that the RV improperly individuated theories. Linguistic entities contain language forms as constitutive parts, so changes in linguistic form create new entities. Since symbolic logic axiomatizations are proper parts of theories on the RV, theories are linguistic entities. Real scientific theories admit of alternative linguistic formulations (e.g., difference equation, partial differential equation, and Hamiltonian formulations of classical mechanics) and so are not linguistic entities. Furthermore, correspondence rules C are individuating parts, so development of new observational techniques yields replacement C'. Contrary to actual scientific practice, on the RV such formulation changes are changes in theory.

Semantic Conceptions (SC). Evert Beth, Suppe, Suppes, and Bas C. van Fraassen developed analyses construing theories as mathematical structures describing state-transition behavior mapped onto real-world systems. These theory structures were identified with configurated state spaces (van Fraassen), relational systems (Suppe), or set-theoretic predicates (Suppes) that represent states of systems as simultaneous values of variables and behaviors as state sequences allowed by theoretical laws. Linguistic formulations referred variously to theory structures or real-world systems and are not proper individuating theory parts. Alternative linguistic formulations are allowed. That no particular logic is imposed enables the SC to incorporate quantum logics.

The SC does not embrace any particular epistemology. Suppes, Suppe, and van Fraassen incorporate it into quite different views about testing, confirmation, and scientific knowledge. An observational–theoretical distinction is not essential to the SC, and only van Fraassen imposes one.

Since theories are not linguistic entities, empirical-content issues are not conflated with questions of meaningfulness of terms or linguistic ontological commitment. One propounds a theory with a theory hypothesis: theory structure T stands in mapping relationship M to class P of actual or possible real-world systems wherein T represents state-change behaviors in P. The M are unlike correspondence rules, concerning just representation of P by T, not meaning relations, experimental design, or causal interactions. Observational or experimental testing practices are included in neither T nor M and so are not individuating theory parts. However, Suppes and Suppe used the SC to analyze how date and experiment mediate connections between theory and world. Van Fraassen and Suppe analyzed linguistic relations between formulations, theory structures, and real-world systems.

Structuralist Approach. Closely related to SCs is the structuralist approach of Joseph Sneed, Wolfgang Stegmüller, and C. U. Moulines, which began with Sneed's application of Suppes's version of the SC to the problem of theoretical terms. Sneed argued that theoretical terms are those that in some contexts can be measured only by utilizing the theory. Sneed claims that circular testing is avoided, since a theory's empirical content varies with application and theory portions used to measure a theoretical term are not parts of the theory's empirical content in that application. A theory structure's inner core and a set of intended core-augmenting applications individuate theories. Theoretical cores and their extensions were exploited to investigate dynamics of theorizing—displaying how theories can develop and be extended while remaining the same theory and explicating Kuhn's normal science where paradigm theories undergo progressive development via puzzle solving.

Other Approaches. Despite lingering disputes over the relative superiority of syntactical versus semantic approaches, there has been no prominent development of syntactical theory analyses since the RV's demise. Maria Dalla Chiara, Giuliano Toraldo di Francia, M. Przełecki and Ryzard Wójcicki produced neopositivistic semantic structural analyses reminiscent of the RV but using SET THEORY [S], not symbolic logic.

THEORIES AND MODELS

The term model encompasses metamathematical models (mathematical structures satisfying formulae under some referential interpretation), scientific theories, and scientific models including iconic scale models. Suppes proposed analyzing models in science via metamathematical models. Under SC and structuralist approaches theory structures and physical systems are metamathematical models of theory formulations. Since V_O terms refer to directly observable conditions, and correspondence rules impose meaning relations between V_O and V_T terms, the RV interpretation of TC can be represented using metamathematical models.

Scientific models can be metamathematical models for equations or sentences. Some scientific models are simplified, often physical, analogues or icons of more complex structures or systems. Philosophers typically construe such models as having only heuristic or explanatory roles and incapable of providing new knowledge. Nevertheless, Norman Campbell claimed they were essential components of RV theories, claiming the choice of C would be irrational unless the V_T laws were given meaning by reference to familiar iconic models. Mary Hesse and Rom Harré argued that such models are essential for RV theories to be explanatory and indispensable for hypothesis discovery.

Experimental scientific results often are presented as models of data that are structural enhancements of embedded observational data. Science increasingly regards simulation models as just another form of experiment. Such models are not mere heuristics or explanatory analogues but yield new knowledge. Work by Suppes and Suppe shows that both sorts of models can be analyzed as mathematical structures similar to SC theory structures but where mapping relations to the world differ from the M of adequate theories.

REALISM, QUASI-REALISM, AND ANTIREALISM

Philosophers worry about ontological commitments of scientific theories. Theoretical realism, instrumentalism, and reductionism were the classic responses, asserting respectively that recourse to theoretical terms did or did not carry ontological commitments to hypothesized entities or that such commitments were reducible to observational or prior ontological commitments. As Dudley Shapere noted, such polarized philosophical options are artificial, since scientists often selectively make ontological commitments to some but not all theoretical terms.

Modern instrumentalism–realism–reductionism debates are closely tied to the RV. Defense of instrumentalism by Ramsey sentences (which eliminate theoretical terms by existentially quantifying them so as to enable the same V_O predictions) or Craig's theorem (for a theory TC with V_T there is theory T' without any of the V_T having the same V_O consequences) makes sense only in the context of RV construal of theories as axiomatic symbolic logic systems, assumption of an observational–theoretical term division, and conflation of meaning and reference issues with ontological commitment. Post-RV ontological commitment debates tend to ignore instrumentalism. David Lewis used modified Ramsey sentences to give a realist reductionistic account in terms of old or prior terms rather than observables.

On semantic approaches meaning and ontology issues get separated. When linguistic theory formulations L refer to theory structures, the only ontological commitments are mathematical. When propounding a theory as adequate, one asserts that a theory structure T stands in mapping M to possible real-world systems P. Choice of M determines ontological commitments.

Requirements on M for adequate theories are controversial. Realism asserts that scientific theories must be literally true to be adequate: each state variable in T is characteristic of P systems and the state transitions of P systems are exactly those allowed by T. Citing potentially unlimited factors not reflected in T affecting state variables, Suppe claims that literal truth is unattainable. Rather, the epistemologically attainable adequacy standard is a quasi-realism where M counterfactually asserts that the systems in P would behave in accordance with T were they isolated from outside influences. Ian Hacking and Nancy Cartwright advance entity realisms where theoretical terms refer but theories do not provide literally true descriptions of phenomena.

Antirealisms deny that adequate theories must be literally true, because not all state variables or other features of T need correspond to features in P. M determines which do. Let T^* be the T portion corresponding to P under M. T is empirically adequate when T^* provides a literally true characterization of P. Antirealism thus is realism with restricted scope. Van Fraassen's antirealism identifies T^* with actual observable portions of P. Empirical adequacy notions are applications of his theory of semi-interpreted languages where full semantic interpretations are given to theoretical assertions, including probabilistic and modal ones, using abstract semantic spaces. Freely chosen *loc* functions map world features into these semantic spaces, but not all features correspond to anything in the world. *Loc* functions specify range of ontological commitment. For scientific theories the T are embedded into semantic spaces, and empirical adequacy consists in P corresponding to the T^* portion.

Since empirical adequacy is literal-truth realism restricted to T^*, antirealism seems liable to the objections raised above against realisms. However, semi-interpreted languages are compatible with quasi-realism. Quasi-realisms with quite restricted ontological commitments are possible, but empirical adequacy would be replaced by counterfactual truth conditions.

Arthur Fine proposed the natural ontological attitude (NOA) as neutral common ground between realism and antirealisms: scientific statements are referential and true in some unanalyzed sense of truth; commitment to entities is only as strong as our belief assertions about them are true. Semantic and structuralist approaches augment NOA with metamathematical or semi-interpreted-language truth analyses.

(SEE ALSO: *Philosophy of Science* [S])

Bibliography

Beth, E. "Towards an Up-to-Date Philosophy of the Natural Sciences," *Methodos,* Vol. 1 (1949), 178–85.

Bridgman, P. W. *The Nature of Physical Theory.* Princeton, NJ, 1936.

Carnap, R. "Testability and Meaning," Parts 1 and 2, *Philosophy of Science,* Vol. 3 (1936), 420–66, Vol. 4 (1937), 1–40.

Cartwright, N. *How the Laws of Physics Lie.* New York, 1983.

Fine, A. *The Shaky Game: Einstein, Realism, and the Quantum Theory.* Chicago, 1986.

Hacking, I. *Representing and Intervening.* Cambridge, 1983.

Hempel, C. G. *Fundamentals of Concept Formation in Empirical Science.* Chicago, 1952.

Hesse, M. *Models and Analogies in Science.* Notre Dame, IN, 1966.

Lewis, D. "How to Define Theoretical Terms," in *Philosophical Papers,* Vol. 1. New York, 1983.

Przełecki, M., K. Szaniawski, and R. Wójcicki, eds. *Formal Methods in the Methodology of Science.* Wrocław, Poland, 1976. Contains a number of semantic approaches, most of them resembling the received view.

Sneed, J. *The Logical Structure of Mathematical Physics.* Dordrecht, 1971.

Stegmüller, W. *The Structure and Dynamics of Theories.* New York, 1976.

Stevens, S. S. "The Operational Definition of Psychological Concepts," *Psychological Review,* Vol. 42 (1935), 517–26.

Suppe, F. *The Structure of Scientific Theories,* 2d ed. Urbana, IL, 1977. Introduction and afterword provide a comprehensive account of the development of the positivistic received view, criticisms of it that led to its eventual demise, and postpositivistic attempts to understand scientific theorizing, including the semantic conception. Comprehensive bibliography.

———. *The Semantic Conception of Theories and Scientific Realism.* Urbana, IL, 1989. Extensive bibliography.

———. *Facts, Theories, and Scientific Observation.* Urbana, IL, 1996. Extensive bibliography.

Suppes, P. "A Comparison of the Meaning and Use of Models in Mathematics and the Empirical Sciences," in H. Freudenthal, ed., *The Concept and the Role of the Model in Mathematics and Natural and Social Sciences* (Dordrecht, 1961).

———. "Models of Data," in E. Nagel, P. Suppes, and A. Tarski, eds., *Logic, Methodology, and Philosophy of Science: Proceedings of the 1960 International Congress* (Stanford, CA, 1962).

———. "What Is a Scientific Theory?" in S. Morgenbesser, ed., *Philosophy of Science Today* (New York, 1967).

Tolman, E. C. *Purposive Behavior in Animals and Men.* New York, 1932.

van Fraassen, B. C. "Meaning Relations and Modalities," *Noûs,* Vol. 3 (1969), 155–68. Extends theory of semi-interpreted languages to include modal operators.

———. "On the Extension of Beth's Semantics of Physical Theories," *Philosophy of Science,* Vol. 37 (1970), 325–39. Develops a semantic conception of theories based upon his theory of semi-interpreted languages.

———. *The Scientific Image.* New York, 1980.

FREDERICK SUPPE

SELF. In its normal use the English expression "self" is not even quite a word, but something that makes an ordinary object pronoun into a reflexive one (e.g., "her" into "herself"). The reflexive pronoun is used when the object of an action or attitude is the same as the subject of that action or attitude. If I say Mark Twain shot *himself* in the foot, I describe Mark Twain not only as the shooter but as the person shot. In this sense "the self" is just the person doing the action or holding the attitude that is somehow in question. "Self" is also used as a prefix for names of activities and attitudes, identifying the special case where the object is the same as the agent: self-love, self-hatred, self-abuse, self-promotion, self-knowledge.

"The self" often means more than this, however. In psychology it is often used for that set of attributes that a person attaches to himself or herself most firmly, the attributes that the person finds it difficult or impossible to imagine himself or herself without. The term identity is also used in this sense. Typically, one's sex is a part of one's self or one's identity; one's profession or nationality may or may not be.

In philosophy the self is the agent, the knower and the ultimate locus of PERSONAL IDENTITY [6; S]. If the thought of future reward or punishment is to encourage or deter me from some course of action, I must be thinking of the person rewarded as me, as myself, as the same person who is now going to endure the hardship of righteousness or pass up the enjoyments of sin in favor of this ultimate reward. But this same self comes up in much more mundane transactions. If I pick up the cake and shove it in this mouth rather than that one, is it not because I think it will be me, the very same person who picks up the cake, that will have the pleasure of tasting it?

A straightforward view of the self would be that the self is just the person and that a person is a physical system. This view has been challenged on two fronts. First, the nature of FREEDOM [3] and CONSCIOUSNESS [2; S] has convinced many philosophers that there is a fundamentally nonphysical aspect of persons (*see* REDUCTION, REDUCTIONISM [S]). The second challenge stems from puzzling aspects of self-knowledge. The knowledge we have of ourselves seems very unlike the knowledge we have of other objects in several ways, and this has led some philosophers to rather startling conclusions about the self. In his *Tractatus,* Ludwig WITTGENSTEIN [8; S] tells us that "I am my world" and that "'the world is my world'" (1961, 5.63, 5.641). This should lead us to the rather surprising conclusion that I am the world, or that at least Wittgenstein was. He draws at least one conclusion that would follow from this: "at death the world does not alter, but comes to an end."

The contemporary philosopher Thomas Nagel has been led to a possibly less radical but still quite dramatic view. According to Nagel, when he says "I am Tom Nagel," at least in certain philosophical moods, the "I" refers to the "objective self," which is not identical with but merely contingently related to the person Tom Nagel. This self could just as well view the world from the perspective of someone other than him (Nagel, 1983). We need to discuss the puzzling features of self-knowledge that give rise to such views.

SELF-KNOWLEDGE

"Self-knowledge" seems to have a straightforward meaning: cases of knowledge in which the knower and the known are identical. But this does not seem sufficient. The philosopher MACH [5] once got on the end of a bus and saw a scruffy, unkempt, bookish-looking sort of person at the other end. He thought to himself,

(1) That man is a shabby pedagogue.

In fact, Mach was seeing himself in a large mirror at the far end of the bus. He eventually realized this and thought to himself:

(2) I am that man.

(3) I am a shabby pedagogue.

Now consider Mach at the earlier time. Did Mach have self-knowledge? In our straightforward sense it seems that he did. He knew that a certain person was a shabby pedagogue and, furthermore, that person was him. The knower and the known were the same. But this is not what we mean by self-knowledge. Self-knowledge is something Mach really had only when he got to step (3), when he would have used the word "I" to express what he knew.

Self-knowledge seems peculiar. First, it seems "essentially indexical." Statement (3) expresses self-knowledge because of the word "I"; it is hard to see how Mach could have expressed self-knowledge without using the first person. If he said "Mach is a shabby pedagogue," he would be claiming to know only what everyone else may have known. It does not seem that there is any objective characterization *D* of Mach, such that knowing that *he* is a shabby pedagogue amounts to knowing that *D* is a shabby pedagogue (Castañeda, 1966, 1968; Perry, 1990, 1993). (*See* INDEXICALS [S])

Secondly, we seem immune to certain sorts of misidentification with respect to self-knowledge. If we learn, in certain ways, that someone is in pain, then we cannot miss the fact that it is we who are in pain. That is, if Mach discovers that he has a headache in the ordinary way that a person discovers she has a headache, he can scarcely be wrong about *who* has the headache, if the range of choices is "I/you/that man," and so forth. Of course he can be wrong if the range of choices is "Mach/Freud/Wittgenstein," and so on, for he might not realize which of those people he is (Shoemaker, 1984).

Third, self-knowledge seems to play a unique cognitive role. If Mach desires that *he* do so and so, and believes that *he* can do so and so by executing such and such a movement, then he will execute that movement without further ado (Perry, 1990).

AGENT-RELATIVE KNOWLEDGE

At least some of these peculiarities of self-knowledge can be explained by taking self-knowledge to be a species of agent-relative knowledge. There are two quite different ways of cognizing objects (people, things, places, and times). We can think of them via their relationship to us, the role they are playing in our lives at the moment of thought: the object I see; the present moment; the place I'm at; the person I'm talking to. We need to think about things in the first way, when we are picking up information about them perceptually or interacting with them, since ways of knowing and acting are tied to these agent-relative roles. I can learn about the here and now by looking; I can learn about the person I am talking to by asking questions, and so forth.

But these agent-relative roles cannot be our only ways of thinking about objects of more than passing interest to us. Different objects play the same agent-relative roles at different times, and at any given time many of the objects we wish to retain information about will not be playing any agent-relative role for us. And we cannot accumulate information along such roles. Suppose I am in Tokyo on Tuesday but return to Palo Alto on Friday. From the facts that on Tuesday I truly thought "Japanese is the official language *here*" and on Friday I truly thought "Senator Stanford used to live near *here*" it does not follow that there is some place where Japanese is the official language and near which Senator Stanford used to live.

In order to retain and accumulate information about objects, to construct and maintain a coherent picture of the world, we need to have a way of conceiving of objects as existing independently of us, as occupying and then ceasing to occupy various agent-relative roles. That is, we need objective ways of thinking about objects. We keep track of them by names or descriptions that do not depend on their relationship to us: Cordura Hall, 4 P.M., June 23, 1995, the southernmost town in Santa Clara County, Aurora Fischer. These serve as our fundamental ways of thinking about those objects. Recognition consists in connecting our objective ways of thinking of objects with the roles those objects play at a given moment. Consider the knowledge I might express with "Today is July 4." This is knowledge that a certain day, objectively conceived ("July 4"), is playing a certain role in my life; it is the present day, the day on which the thinking and speaking take place. This kind of knowledge, "knowing what day it is," is quite crucial to successful application of other, more objective knowledge. If I know that the party is on July 4 and know that today is July 4, then I will form the right expectations about what the day will be like.

Similarly, I may be in Kansas City and know that Kansas City is a good place for a steak dinner. But if I do not know that I am in Kansas City, if I do not realize that Kansas City is playing the "here" or "this city" role in my life at this moment, I will not be able to apply the knowledge that Kansas City is a good place for a steak dinner.

And again, I may know that Aurora Fischer has important information about my schedule, but unless I realize that the person I am talking to is Aurora Fischer, I will not apply this information and say, "Can *you* tell me where this afternoon's meeting is?"

These kinds of knowledge are, like self-knowledge, "essentially indexical." We use "now" and "today" to express our knowledge of what time it is and "here" to express our knowledge of where we are. These locutions are not reducible to names or objective descriptions, just as "I" was not. I cannot express what I say when I say, "The meeting starts right now" by saying "the meeting starts at *D*" for any description *D* of the present moment.

We are also immune to certain sorts of misidentification when we use certain methods of knowing. There is a way of finding out what is going on around one, namely opening one's eyes and looking (Evans, 1985). Now when one learns what is going on in this way, one can hardly fail to identify the time at which this is happening as now and the place as here. And finally, the forms of thought we express with "now" and "here" seem to have a unique motivational role. If I want to do something here and now, I will simply do it.

SELF-KNOWLEDGE AS AGENT-RELATIVE KNOWLEDGE

"Self" is really the name of such an agent-relative role, that of IDENTITY [4; S]. As with other agent-relative roles, there are special ways of knowing and acting that are associated with identity. If Mach had wished to know, during the interval while he was confused, if the shabby pedagogue he was seeing had lint on his vest, he would have had to walk over to him and look. If Mach had wanted to know if he himself had lint on his vest, he could have simply lowered his head and looked. Had he done this, he would have had no doubt about whom the lint was on. If Mach found lint and wanted to brush it off, he would engage in self-brushing, a quick movement of the hand across one's front that each of us can use to remove lint from our own vest and no one else's.

Unlike the other agent-relative roles, identity is permanent. I will talk to many people, be in many places, live through many times in the course of my life. But there is only one person I will ever be identical with, myself. Hence, accumulation along "I" is valid, unlike accumulation along "here" or "now" or "that man."

Earlier we rejected the straightforward account of self-knowledge, as knowledge about a person by that very person. Now we can put forward an alternative. Self-knowledge is knowledge about a person by that very person, with the additional requirement that the person be cognized via the agent-relative role of identity. This agent-relative role is tied to normally self-informative methods of knowing and normally self-effecting ways of acting. When these methods are employed, there will be immunity of misidentification as to who is known about, or who is acted upon.

This role can serve as a person's fundamental concept of himself or herself. In this way our self-conceptions have structures that are different from our conceptions of other individuals of importance to us. If we understand the special way in which a person's self-knowledge is structured, we do not need to postulate anything but the person himself or herself for the knowledge to be about. (SEE ALSO: *Philosophy of Mind* [S])

Bibliography

Castañeda, H.-N. " 'He': A Study in the Logic of Self-Consciousness," *Ration,* Vol. 8 (1966), 130–57.

———. "On the Logic of Attributions of Self-Knowledge to Others," *Journal of Philosophy,* Vol. 65 (1968), 439–56.

Evans, G. "Understanding Demonstratives," in *Collected Papers* (Oxford, 1985).

———. *The Varieties of Reference.* Oxford, 1982.

Nagel, T. "The Objective Self," in C. Ginet and S. Shoemaker, eds., *Knowledge and Mind* (Oxford, 1983).

Perry, J. *The Problem of the Essential Indexical.* New York, 1993.

———. "Self-Notions," *Logos,* Vol. 11 (1990), 17–31.

Shoemaker, S. *Identity, Cause, and Mind.* Cambridge, 1984.

Wittgenstein, L. *Tractatus Logico-Philosophicus,* translated by D. F. Pears and B. F. McGuinness. London, 1961.

JOHN PERRY

SELF IN HEIDEGGER. Contrary to the ontological assumptions of the modern criterial problem of PERSONAL IDENTITY [S], the self for HEIDEGGER [3; S] is neither a substance nor a subject but the intentional movement of "existence" and its surrogate, "transcendence." The "*self*-directedness toward" of intentionality involves the middle-voiced paradox of a reflexive "self" that is at once "being directed toward" and "directing itself toward." Ex-sistence formally indicates a conatus of "having to be" without any final having, suggesting a self ever "under way," permanently expropriated and incomplete. The self thus becomes, not a goal to be realized, but a "being toward the end," whose finish is never to be actualized: (1) The end of death understood as the extreme possibility of impossibility of being-in-the-world by definition cannot in fact be had without destroying the self thus being defined. (2) There is an analogous paradox of expropriation at the other end (birth) for the "under way" self: to the extent that I already find myself in existence, it is not mine; yet, it is now all mine, as a possibility to own up to or to disown. (3) And disownership is itself a fact as well as ever-present possibility because of our initial ignorance of the terms of the existence first given to us, and because the dispersion of ordinary daily life conspires to maintain this inertial lag between a unique life and its comprehensive examination.

This oblivion of common anonymity must in some way be interrupted for proper self-discovery to occur. Heidegger formalizes this crisis-transition singling each of us out of anonymity through "the call of conscience": how it demands a response that first acknowledges the above triple "shortfall" (deficit, debit, lag) between me and my overall situation, and presents the challenge to orient myself toward the unique horizonal whole that is at once mine and not mine. This response of resolution unifies the self proper, owned and whole.

What then is self-identity or self-constancy in this circle of challenge-response that defines the self? (1) It is in the steadfastness of anticipatory resolution that transcends toward the holistic horizons of death, birth, and the world that define our possibilities. (2) It is the steadiness of persistent stretch across the tensed time between birth and death, ever exposed to time's expropriation. The "constant" self is not an already underlying substance to be possessed ("Become what you are"), but a persistent standing toward itself in its potential integrity, the dynamically tensed stasis of an ecstatic time oriented to the future ("Become what you are to be"). I am what I have to be. Who am I? I am what I care for: my possibilities, projects, tasks, choices—an I with futurally personal criteria of identity.

Bibliography

Görland, I. *Transzendenz und Selbst: Eine Phase in Heideggers Denken.* Frankfurt, 1981.

Heidegger, M. *Sein und Zeit* [1927]. 16th ed., Tübingen, 1986. Translated by J. Macquarrie and E. S. Robinson as *Being and Time.* New York, 1962. §§58, 64.

———. *Kant und das Problem der Metaphysik.* Frankfurt, 1929.

Zimmerman, M. E. *Eclipse of the Self: The Development of Heidegger's Concept of Authenticity,* 2d ed. Athens, OH, 1981.

THEODORE KISIEL

SELLARS, WILFRID STALKER (1912–1989), American philosopher and teacher, was born in Ann Arbor, Michigan, the son of Roy Wood SELLARS [7], the American critical realist, who taught at the University of Michigan. His early education took place in the United States and in France, where he attended the lycées Montaigne and Louis le Grand; it was continued at the University of Michigan (B.A., 1933), the University of Buffalo (M.A., 1934), and Oxford University, where he was a Rhodes scholar and received a B.A. With first-class honors in philosophy, politics, and economics. He received an M.A. from Oxford in 1940. After a year at Harvard University he began his career as a teacher of philosophy in 1938 at the University of Iowa. During the war he spent several years as an officer in the Naval Reserve, and in 1946 he went to the University of Minnesota, where he eventually became professor of philosophy, chairman of the philosophy department, founding coeditor of the journal *Philosophical Studies,* and a member of Herbert Feigl's Minnesota Center for the Philosophy of Science. In 1959 he joined the faculty of Yale University, and in 1963 he moved to the University of Pittsburgh, where he became University Professor of Philosophy and Research Professor of the Philosophy of Science. Apart from numerous interludes as visiting professor at other institutions, he remained at Pittsburgh until his death.

Although Sellars became an extremely prolific writer, in the early years of his career he had great difficulty putting his ideas on paper. His first scholarly essay, third in his list of publications, was "Realism and the New Way of Words"; it underwent seventeen major revisions, Sellars said in his "Autobiographical Reflections," before it finally appeared in print. In spite of its striking originality, his early work was strongly influenced by the logical empiricist movement, particularly by the work of Rudolf CARNAP [2; S]; in one essay, "Epistemology and the New Way of Words," he declared that philosophy "is properly conceived as the pure theory of empirically meaningful languages." From today's vantage point the most significant of his early essays would appear to be "Concepts as Involving Laws and Inconceivable without Them" (1948) and "A Semantical Solution of the Mind–Body Problem" (1953). Both show him to have been well ahead of his time in analytic philosophy. In the former he offered a clarification of necessity and natural law that anticipated the treatment of these notions in recent possible-world semantics, and in the latter he developed a distinctly functionalist view of intentional states (*see* FUNCTIONALISM [S]).

Sellars's best-known philosophical work is the lengthy essay "Empiricism and the Philosophy of Mind." This essay originated in lectures that Sellars gave in 1956 attacking what he called "the myth of the given." The cluster of ideas making up this doctrine was, he thought, the source of important errors in both the theory of knowledge and the PHILOSOPHY OF MIND [S]; and by exposing it for what it is, he hoped to lay the groundwork for an acceptable form of EMPIRICISM [2] and for a proper understanding of mental and sensory phenomena. The basic epistemic error prompted by the myth was the idea that empirical knowledge rests on a foundation of certain truth which is "given"—that is, knowable without inference—and provides the ultimate evidence for anything knowable by inference. The root error in the philosophy of mind prompted by the myth was the claim that, merely by having sensory experiences and conscious thoughts, we gain theoretically satisfactory conceptions of those experiences and thoughts. These corresponding errors are related by the belief, commonly held by those who accept the myth, that foundational empirical knowledge concerns the sensory and psychological items, the mere having of which supposedly results in their being adequately conceived of or understood.

In attacking the errors he saw in the myth Sellars defended the view that empirical knowledge cannot have a foundation—that the supposedly basic knowledge of psychological fact presumed by the myth cannot exist independently of general knowledge relating psychological experience to linguistic and other behavior—and that theoretically adequate conceptions of anything can be obtained only by a process of learning and can be known to be adequate only by reference to scientific theorizing about the sensory and cognitive capabilities of human beings. He argued that "empirical knowledge . . . is rational not because it has a *foundation* but because it is a self-correcting enterprise which can put *any* claim in jeopardy, though not *all* at once" (1991, pp. 127–196). As for commonsense sensory and psychological concepts, he argued that it is illuminating to think of them as resulting from an attempt to explain intelligent, nonhabitual human behavior by postulating appropriate "inner episodes" in substantially the way that theoretical scientists explain facts about observable objects by postulating unobservable micro-causes. In arguing this point he added that, when concepts of such inner episodes are developed, people can learn to use them in making first-person reports of what they are experiencing. Seen this way, psychological concepts are fundamentally intersubjective rather than private, and they are as subject to revision as any concept of theoretical science.

In "Philosophy and the Scientific Image of Man" (1960), Sellars developed the thesis that, although theoretical science is a natural development of commonsense thought about the world, it is not evidentially dependent upon it. Like David HUME [4; S], Sellars thought that scientific thinking yields a theoretical picture of humans in the world that is incompatible with the commonsense, or, as he called it, the "manifest," image of the same reality. These clashing images are not on a par, he thought; in purely descriptive respects, the scientific image is an improvement upon the manifest image, containing "successor concepts" to commonsense counterparts. (Water, on this view, is not identical with H_2O; the technical concept of H_2O applies to a common ingredient in most puddles, wells, clouds, and seas—one that is not accurately singled out by any commonsense concept.) A philosophically adequate picture of humans in the world is not fully descriptive, however; it is partly normative. Working out such a picture is an important philosophical task that has yet to be accomplished: the scientific image is not yet complete, and serious problems exist about how some normative matters can be incorporated into a significantly different image.

In later writings Sellars worked out highly original ideas on most central fields of philosophy. He produced, as Johanna Seibt observed, a unique scheme of "full scope nominalism," which purports to demonstrate the expendability of abstract entities for all their supposed explanatory functions; he worked out (he was the first to do so) a sophisticated "conceptual role" semantics; he developed a neo-Kantian view of moral obligation and the moral point of view; and he had original things to say about central figures and issues in the history of philosophy. At a time when systematic philosophy was decidedly out of fashion, he pursued the synoptic vision of humans in the world that PLATO [6; S] spoke of in the *Republic.* In parody of KANT [4; S] he liked to tell his students that, in philosophy, analysis without synthesis must be blind.

Bibliography

WORKS BY SELLARS

"Autobiographical Reflections," in H.-N. Castañeda, ed., *Action, Knowledge, and Reality: Critical Studies in Honor of Wilfrid Sellars* (Indianapolis, 1975).

Philosophical Perspectives: History of Philosophy. Atascadero, CA, 1977.

Philosophical Perspectives: Metaphysics and Epistemology. Atascadero, CA, 1977.

Pure Pragmatics and Possible Worlds: The Early Essays of Wilfrid Sellars, edited by J. F. Sicha. Atascadero, CA, 1980. Sellars's most significant early writings.

Science, Perception, and Reality. Atascadero, CA, 1991.

Naturalism and Ontology. Atascadero, CA, 1992.

Science and Metaphysics. Atascadero, CA, 1992.

WORK ON SELLARS

Seibt, J. *Properties as Processes: A Synoptic Study of Sellars' Nominalism.* Atascadero, CA, 1990.

BRUCE AUNE

SEMANTICS. The entry SEMANTICS [7] by Donald Kalish in the 1967 edition of the *Encyclopedia of Philosophy* remains an excellent overview of the approach to the field that developed out of PHILOSOPHICAL LOGIC [S]. Since the mid-1960s major advances in the application of the kinds of logical and philosophical techniques described there as pure semantics to the (descriptive) semantic analysis of natural languages have given rise to the formal semantics of natural language, which in turn has stimulated the development of new formal tools and techniques. Here we review the rapid growth of formal semantics, influenced especially by the work of Richard Montague. We outline central theoretical issues and note that formal semantics has become increasingly "naturalized" as a branch of linguistics. We will mention some controversies and critiques as well as some recent developments, and briefly describe some of the alternative stances concerning central issues.

By the 1960s the rigorous study of the SYNTAX [S] of natural language by Noam CHOMSKY [S] and his followers (Chomsky, 1957, 1965; Newmeyer, 1980) had made it more plausible that natural languages might be describable as complex but not "unruly" formal languages. Montague claimed further that natural languages could be treated as interpreted formal languages using the same techniques of formal semantics and PRAGMATICS [S] that he and others were successfully developing and applying to the description of artificial languages of logic. The title of his 1970 paper, "English as a Formal Language," embodied his claim, and in a relatively small number of papers written before his untimely death in 1971 (especially Montague, 1970a, 1970b, 1973, reprinted in the collection Montague, 1974), he set forth an explicit theoretical framework for formal semantics and pragmatics applicable to both artificial and natural languages, and illustrated its workings with explicit syntactic and semantic rules for "fragments" of both English and INTENSIONAL LOGIC [S]. (See also Lewis, 1970; Cresswell, 1973; Dowty et al [eds.], 1981; Gamut, 1991.)

Central to Montague's theory of "universal grammar" (Montague, 1970b) is an algebraic interpretation of the "compositionality principle," the principle that the meaning of an expression is a function of the meanings of its parts and of their mode of syntactic combination. According to Montague, both the syntax and the semantics of a language should be expressed as algebras, and the compositionality principle becomes the requirement of a homomorphism from the syntactic algebra to the semantic algebra.

In Montague's conception of syntax, following the logical tradition, syntactic rules recursively form well-formed expressions from other well-formed expressions, starting from basic ("lexical") expressions, and semantic rules then specify how the interpretation of the resulting expression is obtained from the interpretation of the (syntactic) parts. Syntactic and semantic rules thus come in pairs of the following sort, where A, B, and C are syntactic categories, F_i is a syntactic operation on expressions, and G_j is some semantic operation on interpretations, yielding an interpretation as result.

Syntactic rule n: if $\alpha \in A$ and $\beta \in B$, then $F_i(\alpha, \beta) \in C$.

Semantic rule n: If α is interpreted as α' and β is interpreted as β', then $F_i(\alpha, \beta)$ is interpreted as $G_j(\alpha', \beta')$.

For an artificial language, the elements of the syntactic algebra might be the well-formed expressions of various categories; but for a natural language, the ambiguity of surface strings conflicts with the homomorphism requirement. Montague's fragments illustrate two different means for the required "disambiguation": by adding elements such as brackets to the generated strings, or by taking the "derivation tree" or "analysis tree" of the expression as the relevant syntactic structure. Some linguists (such as Chomsky, 1975) have expressed skepticism about whether a disambiguated syntactic structure can be independently motivated for natural languages, suspecting that compositionality is a requirement that is not met for natural languages. Some linguists working at the interface between Chomskyan syntax and formal semantics use a level of LOGICAL FORM [S], a disambiguated syntactic representation that serves as the input to semantic interpretation.

It is still customary to distinguish theory of REFERENCE [S] from theory of MEANING [5; S], a distinction often analyzed in terms of *extensions* and *intensions,* whose history traces from FREGE [3; S] (1892), through CARNAP [2; S] (1956), to Montague. Montague's general framework makes only structural constraints on the nature of the semantic algebras, but typically the extensions are set-theoretic constructs built from two truth-values and a domain of entities. Montague analyzed intensions as functions from POSSIBLE WORLDS [S] to extensions: PROPOSITIONS [S] as functions from possible worlds to truth values, PROPERTIES [S] as functions from possible worlds to sets of individuals, and so forth, using a typed intensional logic.

Many critics of possible-worlds semantics argue that the possible-world reconstruction of intensions is "not intensional enough." When propositions are analyzed as sets of possible worlds, all necessarily equivalent sentences are treated as expressing the same proposition, and necessary equivalence is predicted to license substitution *salva veritate* in intensional contexts such as "Jones believes that____". One response is to treat the problematic contexts as "hyperintensional" (a term coined by M. J. Cresswell, 1985), and construct semantic values more fine-grained than Montagovian intensions, for example, "structured meanings" (Lewis, 1970; Cresswell, 1985). Another response is to argue about the nature of the problematic data and defend the adequacy of possible worlds semantics (as in Stalnaker, 1984.) A third approach is to blame the set-theoretic metatheory, in which possible-worlds semantics is formulated, and replace it with a (much more intensional) property theory (Turner, 1986, 1987; Chierchia & Turner, 1987). Some semanticists advocate working with possible situations, where situations are taken as parts of worlds (Kratzer, 1989; see also Barwise, 1981), as a means of achieving more fine-grained semantic values and simultaneously making possible a more straightforward account of other phenomena such as tense, aspect, nominalizations, and the semantics of event sentences. The semantics of PROPOSITIONAL ATTITUDES [S] remains one of the most difficult problems in semantics.

What is more basic than the use of possible worlds is the principle that truth conditions and entailment relations are among the crucial data for a semantic theory, and the working hypothesis that a semantics that is model-theoretic is better able to capture such data than an axiomatic or proof-theoretic approach.

An algebraic approach to semantic structure is implicit in Montague's work and explicit in Link (1983, 1987). On the algebraic perspective, the actual semantic values are not directly significant; what is important for the explanation of semantic properties of expressions is the algebraic structures on the space of semantic values. Link's analysis of the semantics of mass and count expressions employs a nonatomic semilattice structure underlying the semantics of the mass nouns, and an atomic-semilattice for the semantics of the count nouns (Link, 1983).

Other areas of formal semantics in which there has been productive work by philosophers and linguists (with linguists increasingly playing the major role in the United States) include the treatment of indefinite and definite articles, the semantics of quantification and ANAPHORA [S], the semantics of nominalizations, of event sentences, and of tense and aspect. Linguists commonly devote greater attention to the syntax-semantics interface and to issues of UNIVERSALS [8] and typology across natural languages, and philosophers and logicians commonly devote greater attention to the logical, metaphysical, and epistemological underpinnings of semantic theories; but the division of labor is not sharp.

Important extensions and revisions of Montague's theory include the development of approaches that more closely integrate formal pragmatics, the study of the interaction of language and aspects of the context in which language is used, with formal semantics. Such approaches include 'file change semantics' (Heim, 1982), 'discourse representation theory' (Kamp, 1981; Kamp & Reyle, 1993), and 'dynamic semantics' (Groenendijk & Stokhof, 1990, 1991; Chierchia, 1995). The dynamic perspective, viewing the semantic values of sentences not as ("static") truth conditions but as "context-change potentials" (Heim's term), appears to offer a better and more integrated account of anaphora, quantification, presupposition, and the semantics of a variety of context-dependent expressions.

The development of formal semantics opens up new tools for investigating questions concerning the universality vs. language-particularity of semantics (see Bach, 1986, on "natural language metaphysics").

There continue to be a wide range of approaches to semantics within philosophy, linguistics, psychology, anthropology, and other fields. Given the nonpsychologism of most formal semantics, inherited from its Fregean roots, its principal competitors are theories with a greater emphasis on mental representations or on the cognitive role of natural language expressions. Some, like Fodor (1975, 1987), posit a universal LANGUAGE OF THOUGHT [S] and see semantics as translation into the language of thought. Others, who can have versions compatible with formal semantics, seek to anchor the semantic interpretation of expressions to their conceptual role, emphasizing the logical space of distinctions we are able and disposed to draw. Continuing philosophical problems include the classic problems of INTENTIONALITY [4] and knowledge raised by BRENTANO [1] and WITTGENSTEIN [8; S] and the integration of the PHILOSOPHY OF MIND [S] with semantics and the PHILOSOPHY OF LANGUAGE [S].

Bibliography

Bach, E. "Natural Language Metaphysics," in R. Barcan Marcus, G. J. W. Dorn, P. Weingartner, eds., *Logic, Methodology and Philosophy of Science,* Vol. 7 (1986), 573–95.

Barwise, J. "Scenes and Other Situations," *Journal of Philosophy,* Vol. 78 (1981), 369–97.

Carnap, R. *Meaning and Necessity,* 2d ed. with supplements. Chicago, 1956.

Chierchia, G. *Dynamics of Meaning: Anaphora, Presupposition and the Theory of Grammar.* Chicago, 1995.

———, and R. Turner. "Semantics and Property Theory," *Linguistics and Philosophy,* Vol. 11 (1987).

Chomsky, N. *Syntactic Structures.* The Hague, 1957.

———. *Aspects of the Theory of Syntax.* Cambridge, MA, 1965.

———. "Questions of Form and Interpretation," *Linguistic Analysis,* Vol. 1 (1975), 75–109; also in R. Austerlitz, ed., *The Scope of American Linguistics* (Philadelphia, 1975).

Cresswell, M. J. *Logics and Languages.* London, 1973.

———. *Structured Meanings.* Cambridge, MA, 1985.

Dowty, D., R. Wall, and S. Peters, eds. *Introduction to Montague Semantics.* Dordrecht, 1981.

Fodor, J. A. *The Language of Thought.* New York, 1975.

———. *Psychosemantics: The Problem of Meaning in the Philosophy of Mind.* Cambridge, MA, 1987.

Frege, G. "Über Sinn und Bedeutung," *Zeitschrift für Philosophie und philosophische Kritik,* Vol. 100 (1892), 25–50. Translated as "On Sense and Reference," in P. T. Geach and M. Black, eds., *Translations from the Philosophical Writings of Gottlob Frege* (Oxford, 1952).

Gamut, L. T. F. *Logic, Language, and Meaning, Vol. II: Intensional Logic and Logical Grammar.* Chicago, 1991.

Groenendijk, J., and M. Stokhof. "Dynamic Montague Grammar," in L. Kalman and L. Polos, eds., *Papers from the Second Symposium on Logic and Language* (Budapest, 1990).

———. "Dynamic Predicate Logic," *Linguistics and Philosophy,* Vol. 14 (1991).

Heim, I. *The Semantics of Definite and Indefinite NP's,* Ph.D. dissertation, Amherst, MA, 1982.

Kamp, H. "A Theory of Truth and Semantic Representation," in J. Groenendijk, T. Janssen, and M. Stokhof, eds., *Formal Methods in the Study of Language; Proceedings of the Third Amsterdam Colloquium* (Amsterdam, 1981). Reprinted in J. Groenendijk, T. M. V. Janssen, and M. Stokhof, eds., *Truth, Interpretation and Information* (Dordrecht, 1984).

Kamp, H., and U. Reyle. *From Discourse to Logic.* Dordrecht, 1993.

Kratzer, A. "An Investigation of the Lumps of Thought," *Linguistics and Philosophy,* Vol. 12 (1989), 607–53.

Lewis, D. "General Semantics," *Synthese,* Vol. 22 (1970), 18–67; reprinted in D. Davidson and G. Harman, eds., *Semantics of Natural Language* (Dordrecht, 1972).

Link, G. "The Logical Analysis of Plurals and Mass Terms: A Lattice-Theoretic Approach," in R. Bauerle et al., eds., *Meaning, Use and Interpretation of Language* (Berlin, 1983).

———. "Algebraic Semantics of Event Structures," in J. Groenendijk, M. Stokhof, and C. Veltman, eds., *Proceedings of the Sixth Amsterdam Colloquium* (Amsterdam, 1987).

Montague, R. "English as a Formal Language," in B. Visentini et al., eds., *Linguaggi nella Societa e nella Tecnica* (Milan, 1970a).

———. "Universal Grammar," *Theoria,* Vol. 36 (1970b), 373–98; reprinted in Montague (1974).

———. "The Proper Treatment of Quantification in Ordinary English," in K. J. J. Hintikka, J. M. E. Moravcsik, and P. Suppes, eds., *Approaches to Natural Language* (Dordrecht, 1973).

———. *Formal Philosophy: Selected Papers of Richard Montague,* edited and with an introduction by R. Thomason (New Haven, 1974).

Newmeyer, F. J. *Linguistic Theory in America.* New York, 1980.

Stalnaker, R. C. *Inquiry.* Cambridge, MA, 1984.

Turner, R. "Formal Semantics and Type-Free Theories," in J. Groenendijk, D. de Jongh, and M. Stokhof, eds., *Studies in Discourse Representation Theory and the Theory of Generalized Quantifiers* (Dordrecht, 1986).

———. "A Theory of Properties," *Journal of Symbolic Logic,* Vol. 52 (1987), 455–72.

BARBARA H. PARTEE

SENSE. Sense is the distinctive central notion in theories of thought and language inspired by the later work of Gottlob FREGE ([3; S]; "sense" translates Frege's *Sinn*). For Frege what we think (not the act of thinking it) is a thought, an abstract object. Thoughts have quasi-syntactic structure. Any simple or complex constituent of a thought, even the thought itself, is a sense; thus, senses are abstract. Frege assumes that it is irrational to assent to a thought and simultaneously dissent from it. Since someone misled about astronomy may rationally combine assent to the thought that Hesperus is Hesperus with dissent from the thought that Hesperus is Phosphorus, the thoughts are distinct. Although the names "Hesperus" and "Phosphorus" have the same REFERENCE [S], they express different sense, two modes of presentation of one planet. The role of a sense is to present the thinker with a reference—that is, something on which the truth value (truth or falsity) of the thought depends; if the sense fails to present a reference, the thought lacks a truth value. For Frege the truth value of a thought is independent of where, when, and by whom it is thought. Thus, what reference a constituent sense presents is independent of when, where, and by whom it is thought. Sense determines reference, not vice versa.

Frege used his notion of sense to analyze the SEMANTICS [7; S] of thought attributions in natural language, as in the sentence "Someone doubts that Hesperus is Phosphorus". On Frege's account expression within such "that" clauses refer to their customary senses. This explains the presumed failure of the inference from that sentence and "Hesperus is Phosphorus" to "Someone doubts that Hesperus is Hesperus": the two names have different references within "that" clauses, for their customary senses are different. If sense determines reference, then the sense of "Hesperus" in "Someone doubts that Hesperus is Phosphorus" defers from its sense in "Hesperus is Phosphorus", since the reference differs. By appeal to iterated attributions such as "He doubts that she doubts that Hesperus is Phosphorus", it can be argued that Frege is committed to an infinite hierarchy of senses. His account involves the assignment of senses to natural-language expressions. However, in order to understand many words (e.g., proper names and natural kind terms), there is arguably no particular way in which one must think of their reference; they do not express senses common to all competent speakers. Fregeans therefore distinguish sense from linguistic meaning but in doing so sacrifice Frege's original account of thought attributions.

Sense must also be distinguished from linguistic meaning for context-dependent expressions such as "I". Two people may think "I am falling" and each refer to themselves, not the other. Since the references are distinct and sense determines reference, the senses are distinct, even though the mode of presentation is the same. Others cannot think the sense that one expresses with "I"; they can only think about it. Communication here does not amount to the sharing of thoughts, and "You think that I am falling" does not attribute to the hearer the thought that the speaker expresses with "I am falling". In contrast, the linguistic meaning of "I" is the same for everyone; it consists in the rule that each token of "I" refers to its producer. Unlike a sense, the rule determines reference only relative to context. Such cases reveal tensions within Frege's conception of sense. Sense cannot be both what determines reference and how it is determined. Since senses can be qualitatively identical but numerically distinct, they are not purely abstract objects, if qualitatively identical purely abstract objects must be numerically identical.

Although Fregeans distinguish sense from linguistic meaning, they still treat a given speaker on a given occasion as expressing senses in words. Frege gave the impression that the sense expressed by a word was a bundle of descriptions that the speaker associated with it: the word refers to whatever best fits the descriptions. However, this descriptive model of reference has fared badly for proper names and natural-kind terms. Nondescriptive models may also allow different routes to the same reference, but that is a difference in sense only if it is a difference in presentation to the thinker.

In spite of these problems a role for something like sense remains. An account is needed of the deductions that thinkers are in a position to make. When, for example, is one in a position to deduce "Something is black and noisy" from "That is black" and "That is noisy"? It is necessary but not sufficient that the two tokens of "that" refer to the same thing, for, even if they do, the thinker may lack evidence to that effect: perhaps one refers through sight, the other through hearing. What is needed is more like identity of sense than identity of reference. Thus, the theory of rational inference may still require a notion of sense. It does not follow that thinkers are always in a position to know whether given senses are identical, for it is not obvious that they are always in a position to know what deductions they are in a position to make.

Bibliography

Burge, T. "Sinning against Frege," *Philosophical Review,* Vol. 88 (1979), 398–432.

Campbell, J. "Is Sense Transparent?" *Aristotelian Society Proceedings,* Vol. 88 (1987–88), 273–92.

Dummett, M. *Frege: Philosophy of Language,* 2d ed. London, 1981.

Forbes, G. "The Indispensability of *Sinn,*" *Philosophical Review,* Vol. 99 (1990), 535–63.

Kripke, S. *Naming and Necessity.* Oxford, 1980.

McDowell, J. "On the Sense and Reference of a Proper Name," *Mind,* Vol. 86 (1977), 159–85.

Peacocke, C. "Sense and Justification," *Mind,* Vol. 101 (1992), 793–816.

Perry, J. *The Problem of the Essential Indexical and Other Essays.* Oxford, 1993.

Salmon, N. *Frege's Puzzle.* Atascadero, CA, 1986.

TIMOTHY WILLIAMSON

SENSIBILITY THEORIES. Sensibility theories concern MORAL REALISM [S] and its rivals MORAL RELATIVISM [S] and NONCOGNITIVISM [S]. Misunderstandings have tended to prevent any consensus here (e.g., Sturgeon, 1986, p. 139 n.34, in analyzing Hare and Blackburn unintentionally but seriously misquotes HARE [S]). Realism claims there are moral truths and properties to discover and know, and these truths and properties are objective in that they exist independently of beliefs and practices per se. Relativism claims moral truths are subjective in that they are relative to and dependent on endorsement by a relevant group's or individual's beliefs or practices. Noncognitivism claims there are no moral truths to know. This entry discusses the views of Blackburn (combining elements of realism and relativism into a view called PROJECTIVISM [S]); Harman (relativism); McDowell (realism); and so-called Cornell realists, Boyd, Brink, and Sturgeon. Our abilities to perceive moral properties and be motivated by them constitute our moral sensibility, which is the focus of this debate on whether objective moral knowledge exists.

On motivation the key issue concerns the prescriptive nature of morality. How can morality objectively and universally prescribe grounds for action that constrain and motivate us if, as David HUME [4; S] suggests, belief alone is inert and motivation always depends on the contingent presence of desire in the subject? Must there be a mysterious moral sense that detects queer moral properties? McDowell rejects Hume's belief/desire model and accepts internalism, which claims that knowledge that an act is moral implies some motivation to do that act. Externalism denies this. Harman and some noncognitivists such as MACKIE [S] are also internalists. But, though some standard accounts of moral realism omit Brink, his externalist moral realism seems the most defensible version of realism. Completely apathetic people who know they should give to famine relief are counterexamples to internalism. Dancy's alleged counterexample to externalism is looking before crossing the street without any desire to look. But this seems a habitual reflex rather than voluntary action relevant for morality. Externalism dodges Mackie's noncognitivist arguments by avoiding the necessity of postulating a mysterious moral sense or queer moral properties to sense, since externalism denies that morality has a strange and necessary motivational power over us. Rather, externalists think morality gives us intellectual grounds to be moral, which we might not care to be. But the desire to be moral is so common it is taken for granted and too often forgotten by the internalists.

Far from thinking morality is threatened by its dependence on our desires to move us, Blackburn claims, "We cannot become corrupt overnight" (1985, p. 14). But this seems somewhat naive, since we can easily imagine a corrupting evening.

The issue of perception concerns whether moral properties are like secondary qualities such as color and what explanatory role morality can play analogous to explanation in empirical science. Sturgeon (relying on Boyd) argues against Harman on moral explanations. McDowell would agree with Sturgeon that values can have causal relations, suggesting values can form moral explanations. The force of the abolitionists' moral arguments, for example, can help explain the end of slavery. Harman thinks no moral explanations can avoid reduction to nonmoral explanations. But this seems irrelevant, since biological explanations, for example, would still be significant even if one can reduce them to chemical explanations. Harman is led to relativism because he thinks morality, unlike science, is closed to discovery by observation. But we seem to observe moral values, or their absence, when we see, for example, courage, cowardice, honesty, and so forth.

Harris summarizes three serious flaws in Harman's relativism, which states that inner judgments (judgments of people rather than outer judgments, judgments of acts) are relative to culture. First, consider "Hitler showed himself to be evil by ordering the extermination of Jews." Harris claims, "if Harman is right, this should sound odd because it is an inner judgment and Hitler and the Nazi[s] . . . did not share our moral sensibilities. But surely there is a perfectly straightforward sense in which it is not odd" (1992, p. 31). Second, sometimes the impropriety of blaming people when they could not have been expected to act differently seems to be based on moral considerations rather than Harman's distinction between inner and outer judgments (e.g., Hitler was exposed to more moral views than some cannibals were and so it is more reasonable to criticize Hitler). Third, outer judgments may be more important for morality than the inner judgments Harman emphasizes.

Returning to science and morality, Blackburn claims, "that moral properties supervene upon natural ones is not a scientific fact, and it *is* criterial of incompetence in moralizing to fail to realize that they must do so" (1985, p. 14). But Brink denies this, since he insists "ethical supernaturalism can be defended" (1989, p. 211). Cornell realists, however, try to reduce moral properties to natural ones (e.g., utility). Brink's realism has other problems concerning self-evidence as perception. First, Brink seems to argue invalidly that there are no "self-evidently true" beliefs because no belief is "self-justifying" (1988, p. 117); for he admits: "Truth and justification appear to be distinct properties of beliefs" (p. 31). Second, Brink goes too far to conclude that "justification . . . should not guarantee truth" merely from his premise that justification need not guarantee truth (p. 31). A second argument is a justification that guarantees the truth of its conclusion. Third, Brink claims, "no belief about the world can also be the reason for thinking that that belief is true" (p. 117). Brink claims "neither moral nor non-moral beliefs can be self-evident" (p. 211). But what of counterexamples such as "Some belief exists," "Something exists," and "The world exists"? Further, any denial of a clear contradiction (e.g., "Ra did not create everything in the world including Ra") is self-justifying and self-evident.

Blackburn's view also has problems concerning PERCEPTION [6; S]. Blackburn thinks we project values onto the world rather than have causal relations with them. But McDowell thinks values are secondary qualities in the world. Blackburn claims, "Colours really exist, although the reality which contains them is not independent of the fact that there also exist human modes of perception" (1985, p. 13). But many nonhuman animals perceive color, and the wavelengths making up the spectrum of white light would still exist after human extinction. McDowell claims, "No doubt it is true that a given thing is red in virtue of some microscopic textural property of its surface; but a predication understood only in such terms—not in terms of how the object would look—would not be an ascription of the secondary quality of redness" (1985, p. 112). But he gives no argument for this key claim. Further, to say a thing reflects the red part of the spectrum is to say something about how it would look to an observer of that wavelength.

McDowell thinks pain, which is observable, gives us moral reason to avoid a painful act. Cornell realists would agree. But a masochist or extreme skeptic can still deny that we directly observe the evil in all pain. Further, Blackburn (1985, pp. 13–15) and Sinnott-Armstrong (1980, pp. 90 and 95) present several differences between values and secondary qualities that collectively help undermine McDowell's view.

In conclusion, Cornell realists rebut many of the attacks on realism, but they fail to provide any affirmative case for realism. They seem content to defend moral realism as no more objectionable than scientific realism, which has many controversies of its own.

(SEE ALSO: *Ethical Theory* [S])

Bibliography

Blackburn, S. "Errors and the Phenomenology of Value," in T. Honderich, ed., *Morality and Objectivity* (London, 1985).

Boyd, R. N. "How to Be a Moral Realist," in G. Sayre-McCord, ed., *Essay on Moral Realism* (Ithaca, NY, 1988).

Brink, D. O. *Moral Realism and the Foundations of Ethics.* Cambridge, 1989.

Dancy, J. "Intuitionism," in P. Singer, ed., *A Companion to Ethics* (Oxford, 1991).

Harman, G. *The Nature of Morality: An Introduction to Ethics.* Oxford, 1977.

Harris, C. E., Jr. *Applying Moral Theories,* 2d ed. Belmont, CA, 1992.

McDowell, J. "Values and Secondary Qualities," in T. Honderich, ed., *Morality and Objectivity* (London, 1985).

Mackie, J. L. *Ethics: Inventing Right and Wrong.* Harmondsworth, Middlesex, 1977.

Sinnott-Armstrong, W. "Moral Experience and Justification," *Southern Journal of Philosophy,* Vol. 29, Supplement (1990), 89–96.

Sturgeon, N. L. "Moral Explanations," in D. Copp and D. Zimmerman, eds., *Morality, Reason, and Truth: New Essays on the Foundations of Ethics* (Totowa, NJ, 1984).

———. "What Difference Does it Make Whether Moral Realism Is True?" *Southern Journal of Philosophy,* Vol. 24, Supplement (1986), 115–41.

STERLING HARWOOD

SET THEORY. Modern SET THEORY [7] began with a single discovery in 1963—the proof by Paul Cohen of Stanford University that CANTOR's [2] CONTINUUM PROBLEM [2] is undecidable on the basis of the accepted axioms of set theory.

The continuum problem asks for the cardinality of the real number continuum in terms of Cantor's system of infinite cardinal numbers, $\aleph_0$, $\aleph_1$, $\aleph_2$, . . . The 'continuum hypothesis', proposed by Cantor, is that the continuum has cardinality equal to the first uncountable cardinal, $\aleph_1$. In a classic monograph published in 1940, GÖDEL [S] had proved that the continuum hypothesis could not be disproved—it is consistent with the Zermelo-Fraenkel axioms of set theory. Cohen's 1963 result showed that the continuum hypothesis could not be proved in Zermelo-Fraenkel set theory, and hence is undecidable.

Important though the resolution of the continuum problem was in its own right—the problem was the first of the twenty-three "most significant open problems of mathematics" listed by David HILBERT [3] in his famous address of 1900—by far the greatest significance of Cohen's result lay in the method he used. Cohen invented a new technique, known as 'forcing', that can be used to construct models of set theory having particular properties. Using this method, one starts with a countable transitive model M of (Zermelo-Fraenkel) set theory and constructs a second transitive model N of set theory called a 'generic extension' of M, such that (1) $M \subseteq N$, and (2) M and N have the same set of ordinals. The method of forcing enables this to be done in such a way that certain properties of N can be controlled within M. In particular, Cohen was able to control within the initial model M certain aspects of the cardinal arithmetic of N—specifically that M and N have the same set of cardinals and, in N, the continuum has cardinality unequal to $\aleph_1$.

Following Cohen's breakthrough, Robert Solovay showed that the method of forcing had wide applicability. In particular, he developed a general theory of forcing and applied it to establish the undecidability of a number of open problems of set theory. Soon afterward, Dana Scott and Robert Solovay independently developed an alternative treatment of the method of forcing, the method of 'Boolean-valued models'. In this approach, one starts with a given universe of set theory—the universe one is working in—and constructs a class of 'Boolean-valued sets' in which the characteristic function of each 'set' has values ranging over a given (complete) Boolean algebra B. In the Boolean-valued universe, any set-theoretic proposition has a Boolean truth-value in the Boolean algebra B. The axioms of set theory and all the axioms of predicate logic have Boolean value 1. The value of other propositions can depend on the choice of B. By choosing the algebra B appropriately, a Boolean universe can be obtained in which the truth value of a particular proposition Φ can be made to be less than 1, which demonstrates that Φ cannot be a theorem of set theory.

Many undecidability results were obtained by constructing a particular Boolean algebra using a technique called 'iterated forcing', developed initially by Solovay and Tony Martin. Iterated forcing enables the construction of a generic extension N of a model M that has the properties one could obtain in principle by an increasing transfinite sequence $N_1, N_2, N_3, \ldots N_\alpha, \ldots$ of generic extensions. In the 1980s, Saharon Shelah developed a refinement of iterated forcing known as 'proper forcing'.

The method of forcing led to several developments in the theory of large cardinals. A 'large cardinal axiom' arises from the postulation of a certain set-theoretic property P when it is demonstrated that any set X for which P(X) holds must have 'large' cardinality. One of the criteria for an uncountable cardinal κ being called a 'large cardinal' is that κ is regular (i.e., equal to its own cofinality) and such that $2^\lambda < \kappa$ for all cardinals $\lambda < \kappa$. Such cardinals are said to be 'inaccessible' and are fixed points in the sequence of alephs, i.e., $\aleph_\kappa = \kappa$. Moreover, if κ is an inaccessible cardinal, then V_κ, the set of all sets of rank less than κ, is a model of set theory. By virtue of Gödel's incompleteness theorem, it follows that the existence of a cardinal having any particular 'large cardinal property' cannot be proved.

An example of a large cardinal property is the property P that says a set X of uncountable cardinality κ supports a κ-additive, two-valued measure defined on all subsets of X that vanishes on all singletons and is unity on X. The cardinality of such a set is said to be a 'measurable cardinal'. Measurable cardinals are fixed points for the function that enumerates the inaccessible cardinals. Despite a number of attempts to prove that measurable cardinals do not exist, it remains a possibility that the existence of such a cardinal is consistent with the Zermelo-Fraenkel axioms, and their present status is thus controversial.

The technique used by Gödel to prove that the continuum hypothesis is consistent with Zermelo-Fraenkel set theory involved his notion of 'constructibility'. The class of all constructible sets, L, is obtained by mimicking the recursive construction of the set-theoretic hierarchy by iteration of the power set operation, but instead of taking $V_{\alpha+1}$ to be the set of all subsets of V_α, one takes $L_{\alpha+1}$ to be the set of all subsets of L_α that are definable by means of a first-order formula interpreted over L_α (with constant symbols referring to fixed elements of L_α). In the case of limit ordinals γ, L_γ is defined to be the union of all L_α for $\alpha < \gamma$, just as the V_α-hierarchy. Gödel proved that L is a model of the Zermelo-Fraenkel axioms in which the continuum hypothesis is true. Scott proved that in the universe L there can be no measurable cardinals. In the early 1970s, Ronald Jensen developed a powerful analysis of the constructible hierarchy called the 'fine structure theory', which led to a number of major results both in set theory and in other areas of mathematics. In the 1980s generalizations of Jensen's techniques to structures other than the constructible hierarchy led to further advances in the theory of large cardinals.

(SEE ALSO: *Mathematical Logic* [S])

Bibliography

Barwise, J. ed. *Handbook of Mathematical Logic.* Amsterdam, 1977. Provides considerable coverage of the various advances made in the 1960s and the 1970s.

Devlin, K. *Constructibility.* New York, 1983. This is the standard reference for work on constructibility.

Jech, T. *Set Theory.* San Diego, CA, 1978. This is a comprehensive information source for the earlier work on forcing and large cardinals.

Shelah, S. "Around Classification Theory of Models," in *Lectures Notes on Mathematics Series,* Vol. 1182 (New York, 1986).

———. "Classification Theory and the Number of Non-Isomorphic Models," 2d rev. ed., *Studies in Logic and the Foundations of Mathematics,* Vol. 92 (1991).

KEITH DEVLIN

SEXISM. While the term 'RACISM' [7; S] has been in use among English speakers since the middle of the nineteenth century, it took one hundred more years for the term 'sexism' to make its way into English dictionaries. The earliest conceptual and political philosophical analyses of the term began appearing in the late 1960s.

This does not mean, however, that the concept was unknown. Liberal feminist philosophers such as Mary WOLLSTONECRAFT [S], Harriet Taylor, John Stuart MILL [5; S], and the authors of the Seneca Falls Declaration argued against unjustifiable appeals to nature as a reason to deny RIGHTS [7; S], privileges, and opportunities to girls and women. In the nineteenth century, Elizabeth Cady Stanton caused a furor when she published *The Women's Bible.* Marxists, anarchists, and socialists such as ENGELS [2], Emma Goldman, and Bebel analyzed the exploitation and alienation of women. In 1911 the socialist theorist/writer Charlotte Perkins Gilman entitled one of her major works *The Man-Made World of Our Androcentric*

Culture. After World War II, Simone de BEAUVOIR's [S] *The Second Sex* spelled out the manifold ways in which

> man represents both the positive and the neutral, as is indicated by the common use of *man* to designate human beings in general . . . there is an absolute human type, the masculine . . . humanity is male and man defines woman not in herself but as relative to him . . . She is the incidental, the inessential as opposed to the essential. He is the Subject, he is the Absolute—she is the Other. (1952, pp. 15–16)

Thus, it is fair to say that while the specific term sexism may not have been in the language, its coinage was preceded by at least 200 years of philosophical theorizing about practices of social injustice based on sex.

'Sexism' and 'sexist' can be defined as:

(1) morally and politically pejorative terms, which refer to

(2) both intentional and nonintentional particular and systemic personal, cultural, institutional, and ideological beliefs; attitudes, acts, and patterns of discrimination; of exploitation, oppression, stereotyping, marginalization, cultural domination, and violent social control

(3) directed primarily at girls and women on the basis of sex and gender, and

(4) are usually justified on the assumption of the natural superiority of males (when boys and men are primarily affected, it is called "reverse sexism").

PHILOSOPHICALLY MAPPING SEXISM

Sexism is conceptually and dynamically linked to other important terms and must be understood in relation to them. (See Figure 1.)

Gender Essentialism. This principle affirms that being gendered is essential to human subjectivity and that one's gender either does (the factual, naturalized claim) or should (the normative claim) permeate all the major dimensions of human subjectivity. Particular gender is usually ascribed on the basis of some allegedly sex-differentiated biological factor(s)—such as reproductive morphology or function, hormones, musculature, or brain structure—that is regarded as determinative of gender.

Genderism. This is a principle of social and cultural structure that maintains that having institutionalized genders is a central and necessary and/or normatively desirable principle of human organization and community, and that sanctions the construction, enforcement, and social control over gender.

Sex/Gender Dimorphism. This is a normative principle of social/cultural/political organization that creates, valorizes, and permits two and only two sex/gender patterns in public and in private. It requires all human beings to feel and express gender-coded dimensions of personality, cognition, behavior, and bodily makeup that are appropriate to one and only one of two possibilities. Under sexism these genders are viewed as opposites, as mutually exclusive, and as usually involving the full realization of humanity only by men, which leads to androcentrism. Theories, cultures, and practices that assume and preserve male-female, masculine-feminine, man-woman as mutually exclusive, total partitions of humanity can be said to be sex/gender dimorphic. Normative ideological commitments to sex/gender dimorphism often entail the prevention, metamorphosis, or eradication of behavior, individuals, and institutions that function as deviants, anomalies, and sex/gender transgressors.

Androcentrism. Captured in the slogan, "Males are the measure of all things," androcentrism refers to the assumption that men function as the universalizable paradigm of full personhood, that males represent the most mature, most fully realized exemplars of being human. From this central notion follow theories, public institutions, domestic households, policies, and practices that are centered on men's ideas, men's priorities, boys' and men's developmental patterns, men's needs, and men's norms (however variable these are across time and culture). "Androcentric solipsism," the extreme form of sexism, involves the factual or normative assumption that the conceptual, moral, social, political, and life-worlds of men as defined and constructed by men constitute all that exists or all that is worthy about being human. In an erotic context, androcentric sexuality is often referred to

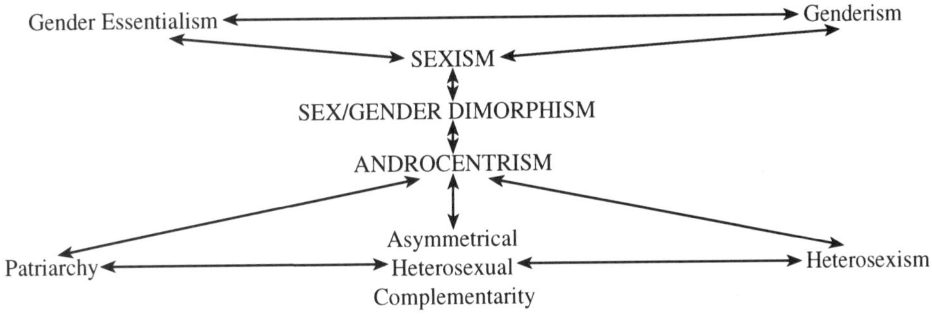

Figure 1

as phallocentrism. In the late twentieth century, under circumstances of transnational, postcolonial capitalism, absolute maximum androcentric privilege is largely reserved for wealthy, white men of European and North American heritage, although androcentric privilege is shared by all males relative to females when other factors are held constant.

Patriarchy. This principle of human organization views males and only males as legitimate authorities who are entitled to define and control the status of children and women in whatever domain in which they are actually or potentially present.

Asymmetrical Heterosexual Complementarity. This principle defines "normal or real women" in sexist contexts as dependent complements to men who, as adults, are independent subjects. Whatever is valuable about women derives from women's affiliation with men, their instrumental value for men, the relation of their creative and productive work to projects defined by men, and from their erotic, nurturant, and reproductive value in relation to bearing and rearing the offspring of men.

Heterosexism. This theoretical and political principle maintains that only heterosexual affiliations (erotic, reproductive, domestic, social)—consisting, preferably, of normal dominant masculine men with submissive feminine women—are natural (hence, normal) and should be made compulsory, enforced by law and other social control mechanisms, and be granted privileged status. Desires and choices of affiliations that are not heterosexual are to be regarded with fear and aversion (homophobia) and should be suppressed, punished, or eradicated either prenatally or therapeutically when they manifest themselves.

APPROACHES TO PHILOSOPHICAL ANALYSIS

Four distinct, mutually compatible philosophical approaches can be identified in the current philosophical scholarship:

Naming and Identifying Sexism. Philosophical attention is directed primarily at particular policies, institutions, concepts, definitions, linguistic practices, and behaviors usually in the public domain (e.g., education, judicial practice, health care, employment) to examine their sexist dimensions. This approach attends primarily to consequences and to outcomes and introduces the important notion of nonintentional sexism. It also introduces the notion that being a sexist can be an important multifaceted structure of a particular person's personality, temperament, and way of viewing and acting in the world.

Systemic Analyses of Sexism. Influenced by important texts such as Beauvoir's *The Second Sex* and Kate Millett's *Sexual Politics* and adopting the sustained critique of the public/private distinction by radical feminists, philosophical analyses of sexism build on particular social and political analysis of sexism to construct systemic theory. These theories also analyze the a priori role played by the assumed association of maleness, masculinity, activity, rationality, fully realized humanity, and consequent entitlement to dominate and by the correlative association of femaleness, femininity, passivity, irrationality, natural inferiority, and dependent status as inferior person or as chattel. Systemic philosophical theory examines the implications of these associations as principles for the conceptualization of the world at the level of theory and research, institutional and cultural structure, and for the normative, therapeutic, aesthetic, erotic, and corporeal production and reproduction of gender and sexual politics that sustain these associations and that prevent, silence, and/or eliminate critiques, challenges, and human beings who do not exemplify these associations.

Contextualizing Theory–Interdependence. This philosophical approach argues against the isolated separability of analyses of sexism. It maintains that any adequate critique of sexism must situate itself both theoretically and contextually in an interdependent relation to other major oppressive structural systems such as racism, classism, ableism, heterosexism, ageism, religious bias, and ethnocentrism. Rejecting any abstract model of human agency or individual identity, this approach privileges critical phenomenological narratives of lived subjectivity as an important starting point for any adequate philosophical understanding of sexism. It necessarily and invariably situates sexism as one facet of interlocking and variable systems, frames, dispositions, and behaviors involving privilege, domination, subordination, and oppression.

Constitutive Nonsexist and Antisexist Philosophizing. This approach emphasizes the decentering of androcentrism by engaging in philosophical theory and critique that create nonsexist and antisexist alternatives. In philosophy, this approach is most often found in the writings of lesbian and heterosexual feminist ethicists, epistemologists, metaphysicians, and social and political philosophers.

(SEE ALSO: *Feminist Philosophy and Social Philosophy* [S])

Bibliography

Addelson, K. P. "Love and Anger," in *Impure Thoughts: Essays on Philosophy, Feminism, and Ethics* (Philadelphia, 1991).

Ayim, M., and B. Houston. "A Conceptual Analysis of Sexism and Sexist Education," in *The Gender Question in Education* (Boulder, CO, 1996).

Baier, A. "What Do Women Want in a Moral Theory?" in *Moral Prejudices: Essays on Ethics* (Cambridge, MA, 1994). Originally published in *Noûs,* Vol. 19 (1985).

Baker, R. "'Pricks' and 'Chicks': A Plea for 'Persons'," in R. Baker and F. Elliston, eds., *Philosophy and Sex* (Buffalo, NY, 1975).

Beauvoir, Simone de. *The Second Sex.* Trans. H. M. Parshley (New York, 1952).

Bem, S. L. *The Lenses of Gender.* New Haven, 1993.

Bordo, S. R. "The Cartesian Masculinization of Thought," *Signs,* Vol. 11 (1986), 619–29.

Collins, P. H. *Black Feminist Thought: Knowledge, Consciousness, and the Politics of Empowerment.* New York, 1990.

Easlea, B. "Male Sexism and the Seventeenth-Century Scientific Revolution," in *Science and Sexual Oppression: Patriarchy's Confrontation with Women and Nature* (London, 1981).

Eichler, M. *Non-Sexist Research Methods.* New York, 1988.

Fausto-Sterling, A. *Myths of Gender: Biological Theories About Women and Men.* Revised edition. New York, 1992.

Frye, M. "Male Chauvinism—A Conceptual Analysis," in R. Baker and F. Elliston, eds., *Philosophy and Sex* (Buffalo, NY, 1975).

———. "Sexism," in *The Politics of Reality: Essays in Feminist Theory* (Trumansburg, NY, 1983).

Gould, C. C. "The Woman Question: Philosophy of Liberation and the Liberation of Philosophy," in C. C. Gould and W. Wartofsky, eds., *Women and Philosophy: Toward a Theory of Liberation* (New York, 1976).

Grimshaw, J. "The 'Maleness' of Philosophy," in *Feminist Philosophers: Women's Perspectives on Philosophical Traditions* (Brighton, Eng., 1986).

Harding, S. *Whose Science? Whose Knowledge?: Thinking from Women's Lives.* Ithaca, NY, 1991.

Hooks, B. *Ain't I a Woman: Black Women and Feminism.* Boston, 1981.

———. *From Margin to Center.* Boston, 1984.

Hubbard, R., M. S. Henifin, and B. Fried, eds. *Biological Woman—The Convenient Myth.* Cambridge, MA, 1982.

Jaggar, A. *Feminist Politics and Human Nature.* Totowa, NJ, 1983.

Keller, E. F. *Reflections on Gender and Science.* New Haven, 1985.

Lange, L., and L. Clark, eds. *The Sexism of Social and Political Theory.* Toronto, 1979.

Lloyd, G. *The Man of Reason: 'Male' and 'Female' in Western Philosophy.* Minneapolis, 1984.

Lugones, M., and E. V. Spelman. "Have We Got a Theory for You! Feminist Theory, Cultural Imperialism, and the Demand for 'the Woman's Voice'," *Hypatia,* Vol. 1 (1984), 578–81. Reprinted in A. al-Hibri and M. Simons, eds., *Hypatia, Reborn* (Bloomington, IN, 1990).

Maart, R. "Consciousness, Knowledge and Morality: The Absence of the Knowledge of White Consciousness in Contemporary Feminist Theory," in D. Shogan, ed., *A Reader in Feminist Ethics* (Toronto, 1993).

Martin, J. R. "The Ideal of the Educated Person," *Educational Theory,* Vol. 31, No. 2 (1981), 97–109.

———. "Methodological Essentialism, False Difference, and Other Dangerous Traps," *Signs,* Vol. 19 (1994), 619–29.

———. "One Woman's Odyssey: To Philosophy and Back Again," in *Changing the Educational Landscape: Philosophy, Women, and Curriculum* (New York, 1994).

McIntosh, "White Privilege and Male Privilege," in A. Minas, ed., *Gender Basics: Feminist Perspectives on Women and Men* (Belmont, CA, 1993).

Morgan, K. P. "Comprehensive Bibliography of Recent Feminist Philosophy and Theory, 1965–1988," in M. Ford, B. Houston, K. P. Morgan, and K. Pepper-Smith, eds., *Resources for Feminist Research: Documentation sur la Recherche Féministe,* Special Issue: Feminist Philosophy, Vol. 16, No. 3 (1987), 89–103.

Narayan, U. "The Project of Feminist Epistemology: Perspectives from a Nonwestern Feminist," in A. M. Jaggar and S. R. Bordo, eds., *Gender/Body/Knowledge: Feminist Reconstructions of Being and Knowing* (New Brunswick, NJ, 1989).

Nye, A. *Feminist Theory and the Philosophies of Man.* New York, 1988.

Rich, A. "Disloyal to Civilization: Feminism, Racism, Gynephobia," in *Lies, Secrets, and Silence* (New York, 1979).

———. "Compulsory Heterosexuality and Lesbian Existence," *Signs,* Vol. 5, No. 4 (1980), 631–60.

Ruth, S. "Methodocracy, Misogyny and Bad Faith: the Response of Philosophy," in D. Spender, ed., *Men's Studies Modified: The Impact of Feminism on the Academic Disciplines* (New York, 1981).

Scheman, N. "The Wizard of Oz, the Grand Canonical Synthesizer, and Me," in *Engenderings: Constructions of Knowledge, Authority, and Privilege* (New York, 1993).

Spelman, E. V. "Gender and Race: The Ampersand Problem in Feminist Thought," in *Inessential Woman: Problems of Exclusion in Feminist Thought* (Boston, 1988).

Thiele, B. "Vanishing Acts in Social and Political Thought: Tricks of the Trade," in C. Pateman and E. Gross, eds., *Feminist Challenges: Social and Political Theory* (Boston, 1986).

Vetterling-Braggin, M., ed. *Sexist Language: A Modern Philosophical Discussion.* Totowa, NJ, 1981.

Wasserstrom, R. A. "Racism and Sexism," in S. Bishop and M. Weinzweig, eds., *Philosophy and Women* (Belmont, CA, 1979).

Wylie, A., K. Okruhlik, S. Morton, and L. Thielen-Wilson. "Philosophical Feminism: A Bibliographic Guide to Critiques of Science," *Resources for Feminist Research: Documentation sur la Recherche Féministe,* Vol. 19, No. 2 (Toronto, 1990).

Young, I. M. "Five Faces of Oppression," in *Justice and the Politics of Difference* (Princeton, NJ, 1990).

KATHRYN PAULY MORGAN

SIDGWICK, HENRY (1838-1900), is renowned for giving classical UTILITARIANISM [8] its most sophisticated dress and greatly advancing substantive moral theory. Celebrated for his clarity and cool impartiality, SIDGWICK [7] was actually haunted by the specter of SKEPTICISM [7; S] in RELIGION [7] and morality. If he turned utilitarianism into a respectable academic philosophy, patiently distinguishing total from average utility, utilitarian from egoistic reasons, he also reluctantly brought it into the crisis of the ENLIGHTENMENT [2].

Educated in classics and mathematics at Trinity College, Cambridge, Sidgwick spent his entire adult life at Cambridge, becoming Knightbridge Professor in 1883. His extensive interests also covered theology, biblical criticism, poetry, ethics, political economy, jurisprudence, political theory, sociology, epistemology, metaphysics, and parapsychology (he was a founder and president of the Society for Psychical Research). He vastly influenced the Cambridge moral sciences curriculum and was a guiding force in the cause of women's higher education and the founding of Newnham College. In 1876 he married Eleanor Mildred Balfour, a force in her own right in psychical research and educational reform.

Sidgwick's masterpiece, *The Methods of Ethics* (1874), was a sustained effort at independent, secular moral theory resulting from his decade of "storm and stress" over the defense and reform of Christianity. It also reveals that, however indebted Sidgwick was to his chief mentor, J. S. MILL [5; S], his HEDONISM [3] was more consistently Benthamite, while his overall position was more eclectic, reconciling utilitarianism with arguments from ARISTOTLE [1; S], KANT [4; S], Joseph BUTLER [1], CLARKE [2], WHEWELL [8], John GROTE [3], and T. H. GREEN [3]. It rejects the empiricism and reductionism of earlier utilitarianism, and adheres to a sophisticated fallibilist intuitionism involving various tests for reducing the risk of error with respect to basic noninferentially known propositions: (1) clarity and precision, (2) ability to withstand careful reflection, (3) mutual consistency, and (4) consensus of experts.

The Methods is largely a systematic critical comparison of the 'methods' of ETHICAL EGOISM [S], commonsense or intuitional morality, and utilitarianism—for Sidgwick, the going procedures for determining, on principle, what one ought to do (though he would later devote as much attention to idealism and evolutionism). He takes the notion of 'ought' or 'right' as fundamental and irreducible and gives an internalist account of moral approbation. But he also holds that it is a plausible and significant (not tautological) proposition that ultimate good is pleasure or desirable consciousness; egoism and utilitarianism hence reduce to egoistic and universalistic hedonism. He then shows that earlier utilitarians exaggerated the conflict with common sense, confused the utilitarian and egoist positions, and failed to give their view rational foundations. His exhaustive examination of commonsense morality, after the manner of Aristotle, reveals time and again that such principles as veracity, fidelity, JUSTICE [S], and benevolence are either too vague and indeterminate or too conflicting and variably interpreted to form a system of rational intuitions. Indeed, common sense is even unconsciously utilitarian, since it is apt to resort to that view to complete its own system—for example, to settle conflicts between the duty to speak the truth and the duty to keep one's promises.

Thus, commonsense morality thought through ends in utilitarianism, though utilitarianism grounded on 'philosophical intuitionism', and utilitarianism can in turn rationalize much of commonsense morality as the (indirect) means to the greatest happiness. But no such reconciliation of utilitarianism and egoism is forthcoming, each being, on reflection, equally defensible. Kantian universalizability, the essence of justice, comports with either egoism or utilitarianism and cannot decide between them, though it is another self-evident principle. Sidgwick dismally concludes that there is a dualism of practical reason rendering it incoherent. Without help from epistemology or theology, he has no rational way to settle conflicts between individual self-interest and universal good.

Sidgwick's other intellectual and reformist interests often radiated from his fears about the implications of the dualism of practical reason. Although *The Principles of Political Economy* (1883) and *The Elements of Politics* (1891) tend rather to assume the utilitarian standpoint, they bespeak his concern that human emotions be shaped in a more deeply utilitarian direction, encouraging sympathetic, benevolent sentiments and reigning in egoistic ones. Both his reformism and his philosophical and scientific pursuits were brought to bear on the potential for such societal evolution and the perhaps limited place of reason and religion within it. Never as sanguine as COMTE [2], Mill, or SPENCER [7], his concern for reform was tempered by fear that skepticism and egoism would lead to social deterioration. If Sidgwick was as good at defending an agent-relative egoism as an agent-neutral utilitarianism, this was scarcely the result he sought.

Only by reading *The Methods* in the context of Sidgwick's other work and activities is there some hope of determining whether he was a true government house utilitarian, advocating that the publicity of moral principles be subject to felicific calculations congenial to paternalistic governments, or a defender of the plain person's capacity for genuine moral self-direction, as his focus on 'method' might suggest. At least, a sense of his view as a truly comprehensive moral and political one deeply informed by Kantianism and idealism makes it harder to view him as a naive 'encyclopedist' with no grasp of social theory or the historicity of his own philosophy. But whether he began, in his last decades, to doubt the quest for certainty enough to approximate the pragmatist *via media* is a very difficult question that has put Sidgwick back in the middle of debates over the shape and origins of contemporary LIBERALISM [S].

Bibliography

WORKS BY SIDGWICK

The Ethics of Conformity and Subscription. London, 1870.

The Methods of Ethics. London, 1874, 1877, 1884, 1890, 1893, 1901, 1907.

The Principles of Political Economy. London, 1883, 1887, 1901.

The Scope and Method of Economic Science. London, 1885.

Outlines of the History of Ethics for English Readers. London, 1886, 1888, 1892, 1896, 1902.

The Elements of Politics. London, 1891, 1897, 1908, 1919.

Practical Ethics: A Collection of Addresses and Essays. London, 1898, 1909.

Philosophy, Its Scope and Relations. Edited by J. Ward. London, 1902.

Lectures on the Ethics of T. H. Green, H. Spencer, and J. Martineau. Edited by E. E. Constance Jones. London, 1902.

The Development of European Polity. Edited by E. M. Sidgwick. London, 1903.

Miscellaneous Essays and Addresses. Edited by E. M. Sidgwick and A. Sidgwick. London, 1904.

Lectures on the Philosophy of Kant and Other Philosophical Lectures and Essays. Edited by J. Ward. London, 1905.

The Complete Works of Henry Sidgwick. Edited by B. Schultz. Charlottesville, VA, 1995. Contains, as a data base, all of Sidgwick's published works and a selection of his correspondence. Includes a comprehensive Sidgwick bibliography.

WORKS ON SIDGWICK

Kloppenberg, J. *Uncertain Victory: Social Democracy and Progressivism in European and American Thought, 1870-1920.* Oxford, 1986. The most extensive effort to link Sidgwick to pragmatism and progressivism in general.

MacIntyre, A. *Three Rival Versions of Moral Enquiry.* Notre Dame, IN, 1990. Presents Sidgwick as the arch-representative of the encyclopedist version, as opposed to genealogy and tradition.

Schneewind, J. B. *Sidgwick's Ethics and Victorian Moral Philosophy.* Oxford, 1977. The single most significant philosophical treatment of Sidgwick's ethics, providing the basis for the interpretation of him as a defender of the ordinary person's capacity for moral self-direction.

Schultz, B., ed. *Essays on Henry Sidgwick.* New York, 1992. Covers both Sidgwick's work in its historical context and the current philosophical interest in Sidgwick.

Williams, B. "The Point of View of the Universe: Sidgwick and the Ambitions of Ethics," *Cambridge Review,* 7 May 1982, pp. 183–91. Nicely surveys Sidgwick's ethics and points up why he could be considered a government house utilitarian.

BART SCHULTZ

SKEPTICISM. Skepticism regarding a subject matter is the view that knowledge about the subject matter is not possible. Many subject matters have come under skeptical attack. It has been argued, for example, that it is not possible to obtain knowledge about the external world, about as-yet-unobserved states of affairs, and about minds other than one's own. This entry will focus upon SKEPTICISM [7] about knowledge of the external world.

THE CARTESIAN SKEPTICAL ARGUMENT

The following skeptical argument is suggested by DESCARTES's [2; S] first meditation. Consider the skeptical hypothesis SK: There are no physical objects; all that exists is my mind and that of an evil genius, who causes me to have sense experience just like that which I actually have (sense experience representing a world of physical objects). This hypothesis, says the skeptic, is logically possible and incompatible with propositions implying the existence of the external world, such as that I have hands. The skeptic then claims that (1) if I know that I have hands, then I know that not-SK. To justify premise (1), the skeptic points out that the proposition that I have hands entails not-SK, and he asserts this closure principle: if S knows that ϕ and S knows that ϕ entails ψ, then S knows that ψ. The skeptical argument's other premise is that (2) I do not know that not-SK. To justify this premise, the skeptic points out that, if SK were true, then I would have sense experience exactly similar to that which I actually have. Since my sensory evidence does not discriminate between the hypothesis that SK and the hypothesis that not-SK, this evidence does not justify me in believing not-SK rather than SK. Lacking justification for my belief that not-SK, I do not know that not-SK. From (1) and (2) it follows that I do not know that I have hands. A similar argument can be given for each external-world proposition that I claim to know.

Those who think that minds are physical in nature might well balk at the skeptic's claim that the evil-genius hypothesis is logically possible. Accordingly, the skeptic will replace that hypothesis with this updated version of SK: I am a brain in a vat connected to a computer which is the ultimate cause of my (thoroughly unveridical) sense experience.

To see how the foregoing pattern of skeptical reasoning can be extended to other subject matters, let the target knowledge claim be that there are minds other than my own, and let the skeptical hypothesis be that the complex patterns of bodily behavior that I observe are not accompanied by any states of consciousness. The analogue to premise (2) will in this case be supported by the claim that, if the skeptical hypothesis were true, then I would have behavioral evidence exactly similar to that which I actually have.

DENYING THE LOGICAL POSSIBILITY OF SK

Let us consider two radical responses to the Cartesian skeptical argument. The evil-genius and vat hypotheses both depend on the assumption that the external world is mind-independent in such a way that it is logically possible for sense experience to represent there to be a physical world of a certain character even though there is no physical world, or at least no physical world of that character. An idealist will deny this assumption of independence. He will maintain that facts about physical objects hold simply in virtue of the holding of the right facts about sense experience. The idealist will then deny that the skeptical hypotheses are logically possible: any world in which the facts of sense experience are as they actually are is a world in which there is an external reality of roughly the sort we take there to be. Thus premise (2) is false: I know that not-SK in virtue of knowing the necessary falsity of SK.

The second radical response to the skeptical argument rests on a verificationist constraint on the meaningfulness of sentences (*see* VERIFIABILITY PRINCIPLE, VERIFICATIONISM [8; S]). Like the idealist, the verificationist holds that the sentence "I am a victim of thoroughgoing sensory deception" fails to express a logically possible hypothesis.

Given that the sentence fails to express a proposition for which sense experience could in principle provide confirming or disconfirming evidence, the verificationist counts the sentence as meaningless. Since the sentence expresses no proposition at all, it does not express a proposition that is possibly true.

The antirealist puts forward a similar view. He maintains that one's understanding of a sentence's meaning consists in a recognitional capacity that is manifestable in one's use of the sentence. Suppose that the conditions under which a sentence X is true transcend our powers of recognition. Then one's understanding of X's meaning could not be identified with one's grasping of X's recognition-transcendent truth conditions (since such a grasping could not, in turn, be identified with a manifestable recognitional capacity). This conception can be applied to sentences that allegedly express skeptical hypotheses. If we cannot detect the obtaining of their truth conditions, then what we understand when we understand skeptical sentences' meanings must be something other than their truth conditions. Grasping such sentences' meanings instead consists in grasping the detectable conditions under which they are warrantedly assertible. Thus, it would turn out that an allegedly problematic "skeptical" hypothesis fails to make any coherent claims about putative conditions in the world that outstrip our capacity for knowledge.

ATTACKING PREMISE (1)

Premise (1) has come under attack by those who think that the skeptic has succeeded in stating a hypothesis that is genuinely logically possible and not known to be false. On this strategy the closure principle is denied. This opens up the possibility that I know that I have hands even though I do not know that not-SK. For example, one might deny closure by maintaining that knowing that ϕ requires knowing only that the *relevant* alternative hypotheses to ϕ do not obtain. Skeptical hypotheses, it is then said, are not relevant alternatives to the propositions involved in ordinary knowledge claims.

ATTACKING PREMISE (2)

Let us turn to antiskeptical strategies that do not challenge premise (1) and that accept that SK is indeed logically possible. On these strategies premise (2) is attacked. For example, KANT [4; S] tried to show via a transcendental argument that, in allowing knowledge of certain key features of one's own mind, the Cartesian is already committed to the possibility of knowledge of the external world. Kant argued (in "Refutation of Idealism" in *Critique of Pure Reason*) that, in order to have knowledge of one's own temporally ordered inner states, one must also have knowledge of spatial objects outside one's mind, whose temporal ordering is related to that of one's inner states. A prima facie difficulty for the Kantian strategy is that arguing for a connection between knowledge of one's mind and knowledge of the external world seems to require the assumption of verificationism or IDEALISM [4], which would render superfluous the rest of the transcendental argument.

The INFERENCE TO THE BEST EXPLANATION [S] strategy relies on the idea that, even if two incompatible explanatory hypotheses are equally supported by the available evidence, I am still justified in rejecting one hypothesis if the other offers a better explanation of the evidence. It might be maintained that the ordinary hypothesis that the world is roughly as I take it to be offers a better explanation of my sensory evidence than does SK, in virtue of its greater simplicity. Thus, I can justifiably reject SK. The proponent of this strategy needs to specify the respect in which SK is more complex than the ordinary hypothesis and to make it plausible that hypotheses that are complex in the specified way are less likely to be true than simpler ones.

Another way to attack premise (2) is to deny that knowledge that not-SK requires possession of sensory evidence that figures in the justification of a belief that not-SK. This denial could be based on a reliabilist theory of knowledge, according to which knowing that ϕ is a matter of having a reliably produced true belief that ϕ (*see* RELIABILISM [S]). If reliabilism is correct, then in arguing that I do not know that not-SK the skeptic would have the difficult burden of showing that there is in fact some flaw in the belief-producing mechanism that yields my belief that not-SK (thereby rendering that belief unjustified).

Finally, one can use considerations from the PHILOSOPHY OF LANGUAGE [S] and the PHILOSOPHY OF MIND [S] to argue that SK is in fact false. According to semantic externalism, the Cartesian commits an error in attempting to construct thought experiments involving massive deception. He naively assumes that, starting with a subject S of thought and experience who is ensconced in a normal external environment, we can hold fixed the contents of S's thoughts and the meanings of his sentences while varying (in thought) S's external environment in such a way that S's thoughts come out predominantly false of his environment. According to the semantic externalist, the Cartesian fails to realize that the contents of one's thoughts and the meanings of one's sentences depend in certain ways on one's external environment. For example, Donald DAVIDSON [S] argues that, when we interpret a speaker's sentences as expressing various beliefs that he holds, we are constrained to attribute beliefs to him that are by and large true of the causal environment with which he interacts. This is because there is no rational basis for preferring one interpretation that finds him to be massively mistaken in his beliefs over another such interpretation. It is constitutive of beliefs and of sentential meanings that they are what are correctly attributed in correct interpretation, on Davidson's view. Thus, it follows from the very nature of belief and meaning that, contrary to what SK states, one is not massively mistaken.

To see another manifestation of this anti-Cartesian line of thought, consider Hilary PUTNAM's [S] Twin Earth, a planet just like Earth but for the circumstances that the clear, thirst-quenching liquid that the Twin Earthians call "water" is composed of XYZ molecules rather than H_2O molecules. The Twin Earthians' term "water" does not refer to water but rather to the liquid on Twin Earth with which they interact. Hence, my Twin Earth counterpart's word "water" does not have the same meaning as my word, and when he says "water is wet" he does not thereby express the thought that water is wet. Similarly, the semantic externalist maintains that, when my envatted twin in a treeless world uses the word "tree" in thought he does not refer to trees. Instead, he refers to the entities in his external environment that play a causal role with respect to his uses of "tree," a causal role that is analogous to that played by trees with respect to normal uses of "tree" in a tree-filled world. These entities might be states of the computer that systematically cause the brain in a vat to have "tree-like" sense experience. When he thinks the sentence "A tree has fallen," he does not thereby express the mistaken thought that a tree has fallen. Instead, he expresses a thought about computer states, which thought may well be true of his environment. In general, the brain in a vat is not massively mistaken about his world, contrary to what the Cartesian maintains.

We can use these considerations, together with the assumption that I have knowledge of the contents of my own thoughts, against premise (2) in the following way: I am now thinking that a tree has fallen; if SK is true, then I am not now thinking that a tree has fallen; thus, SK is false. This argument, however, is powerless against versions of the skeptical hypothesis on which the brain in a vat is indirectly causally linked to ordinary objects. If, for example, there are programmers of the computer who refer to trees, then it becomes plausible to suppose that the brain does so as well. Further, there is a prima facie problem as to whether I can claim knowledge of the contents of my own thoughts, given semantic externalism. Such knowledge seems to require independent knowledge of the content-determining causal environment in which I am located, knowledge the antiskeptical argument was meant to provide.

(SEE ALSO: *Epistemology* [S])

Bibliography

Ayer, A. J. *Language, Truth, and Logic.* New York, 1952. Verificationism.

Berkeley, G. *Three Dialogues between Hylas and Philonous.* Indianapolis, 1984. Idealism.

Brueckner, A. "Semantic Answers to Skepticism," *Pacific Philosophical Quarterly,* Vol. 72 (1992), 200–1. Semantic externalism.

Davidson, D. "A Coherence Theory of Truth and Knowledge," in E. LePore, ed., *Truth and Interpretation* (Oxford, 1986). Semantic externalism.

Descartes, R. *Meditations on First Philosophy,* in *The Philosophical Works of Descartes,* vol. 1, translated by Haldane and Ross. New York, 1955. The Cartesian skeptical argument.

Dretske, F. "Epistemic Operators," *Journal of Philosophy,* Vol. 67 (1970), 1007–1023. Denying the closure principle.

Dummett, M. "What Is a Theory of Meaning? (II)," in G. Evans and J. McDowell, eds., *Truth and Meaning* (Oxford, 1976). Antirealism.

Goldman, A. "What Is Justified Belief?" in G. Pappas, ed., *Justification and Knowledge* (Dordrecht, 1979). Reliabilism.

Kant, I. *Critique of Pure Reason,* translated by N. K. Smith. New York, 1965. Transcendental arguments.

Nozick, R. *Philosophical Explanations,* Chap. 3. Cambridge, MA, 1981. Denying the closure principle.

Putnam, H. "Meaning and Reference," *Journal of Philosophy,* Vol. 70 (1973), 699–711. Semantic externalism.

———. *Reason, Truth, and History,* Chap. 1. Cambridge, 1981. Semantic externalism.

Stroud, B., "Transcendental Arguments," *Journal of Philosophy,* Vol. 65 (1968), 241–56. Transcendental arguments.

Vogel, J. "Cartesian Skepticism and Inference to the Best Explanation," *Journal of Philosophy,* Vol. 87 (1990), 658–66.

ANTHONY BRUECKNER

SMART, JOHN JAMIESON CARSWELL, was born in Scotland in 1920. Working for almost all his career in Australia, he has been a leading figure in the development of the naturalistic and science-oriented approach to philosophy characteristic of the period following the mid-century dominance of conceptual analysis.

Educated at Glasgow (M.A. 1946, with honors in philosophy, mathematics, and natural philosophy) and Oxford, he came under the influence of Gilbert RYLE [7] and the linguistic analytic movement of that time. After a short period as a junior research fellow at Corpus Christi College, he accepted, at the age of twenty-nine, the chair of philosophy at the University of Adelaide. Smart moved to a readership at La Trobe University in Melbourne in 1972 and filled a chair in the Research School of Social Sciences of the Australian National University from 1976 until his retirement in 1985, following which he continued to be active in philosophy.

Soon after his arrival in Australia, Smart came to see philosophy as best pursued through reflection on the methods and successes of natural science. Showing the influence of David HUME [4; S] and of the contemporary American philosopher Willard Van Orman QUINE [7; S], Smart's metaphysics and epistemology have been consistently empiricist. He is extensionalist in logic, is nominalist in metaphysics, holds a regularity view of natural law, and is realist in the interpretation of scientific theories. In ethics he has defended an act utilitarian CONSEQUENTIALISM [S], not flinching from some of its more controversial implications.

Most of Smart's mature work has centered on three major themes—physical realism, materialism (*see* PHYSICALISM, MATERIALISM [S]), and UTILITARIANISM [8].

In a series of papers beginning with "The River of Time" (1949) and continuing through to *Our Place in the Universe* (1989), Smart argues for the four-dimensional space–time conception of the cosmos, which implies the equal reality of past, present, and future and the unreality of any flow of time. *Philosophy and Scientific Realism* (1963) saw the first appearance of another continuing theme: a realist stance toward unobservable theoretical entities in the natural sciences that appeals to INFERENCE TO THE BEST EXPLANATION [S]. The complex, interlocking set of experimental results that we have now obtained and validated about electrons, for instance, would constitute an incredible set of coincidences, for which there could be no intelligible accounting, unless the electron theory were close to the literal truth concerning those levels that transcend our direct observation.

Smart is a materialist: there are no spiritual or nonphysical mental realities. Our minds are our brains; our states of mind are states or processes occurring in the nervous system. Smart's "Sensations and Brain Processes" (1959) was an early expression of this central-state materialism. He expanded and defended its claims in subsequent discussions, both of the general issue and of its implications for secondary qualities, particularly color (*see* PHILOSOPHY OF MIND [S]).

From *An Outline of a System of Utilitarian Ethics* (1961) on, Smart has presented the utilitarian view that the actual consequences of our behavior determine its moral value. The consequences to consider concern the happiness of all sentient beings, judged from a natural, secular point of view. He recognizes the difficulties that questions of justice generate for an unbending utilitarian theory and has not been able to reach a definitive resolution of this conflict in his ethical thought. In *Ethics, Persuasion, and Truth* (1984) Smart presents a sophisticated subjectivist theory of the meaning and logical status of moral judgments.

Our Place in the Universe is his philosophic testament. Recapitulating many of the central themes of his writings, it draws them together in a naturalistic vision—of spatiotemporal physical reality and of the living, conscious systems to be found on earth—that is suffused with an attractive natural piety.

Bibliography

WORKS BY SMART

An Outline of a System of Utilitarian Ethics. Melbourne, 1961. Rev. ed., J. J. C. Smart and B. Williams, *Utilitarianism, For and Against.* London, 1973.

Philosophy and Scientific Realism. London, 1963.

Between Science and Philosophy: An Introduction to the Philosophy of Science. New York, 1968.

Ethics, Persuasion, and Truth. London, 1984.

Essays, Metaphysical and Moral. Oxford, 1987. This collects the more important of over 120 journal articles and book chapters.

Our Place in the Universe. Oxford, 1989.

WORK ON SMART

Pettit, P., R. Sylvan, and J. Norman, eds. *Metaphysics and Morality: Essays in Honour of J. J. C. Smart.* Oxford, 1987.

KEITH CAMPBELL

SOCIAL AND POLITICAL PHILOSOPHY.

It is generally agreed that the central task of social and political philosophy is to provide a justification for coercive institutions. Coercive institutions range in size from the family to the nation-state and world organizations, such as the United Nations, with their narrower and broader agendas for action. Yet essentially they are institutions that at least sometimes employ force or the threat of force to control the behavior of their members to achieve either minimal or wide-ranging goals. To justify such coercive institutions, we need to show that the authorities within these institutions have a right to be obeyed and that their members have a corresponding duty to obey them. In other words, we need to show that these institutions have legitimate authority over their members.

In philosophical debate at the end of the twentieth century, a number of competing justifications for coercive institutions have been defended: (1) a libertarian justification, which appeals to an ideal of LIBERTY [S]; (2) a socialist justification, which appeals to an ideal of equality; (3) a welfare liberal justification, which appeals to an ideal of contractual fairness; (4) a communitarian justification, which appeals to an ideal of the common good; and (5) a feminist justification, which appeals to an ideal of a gender-free society. Each of these justifications must be examined so as to determine which, if any, are morally defensible.

LIBERTARIANISM

Libertarians frequently cite the work of F. A. Hayek, particularly his *Constitution of Liberty* (1960), as an intellectual source of their view. Hayek argues that the libertarian ideal of liberty requires "equality before the law" and "reward according to market value," but not "substantial equality" or "reward according to merit." Hayek further argues that the inequalities due to upbringing, inheritance, and education that are permitted by an ideal of liberty actually tend to benefit society as a whole.

In basic accord with Hayek, contemporary libertarians such as John Hospers, Robert Nozick, and Jan Narveson define liberty negatively as "the state of being unconstrained by other persons from doing what one wants" rather than positively as "the state of being assisted by other persons in doing what one wants." Libertarians go on to characterize their social and political ideal as requiring that each person have the greatest amount of liberty commensurate with the same liberty for all. From this ideal libertarians claim that a number of more specific requirements, in particular a right to life, a right to freedom of speech, press, and assembly, and a right to property, can be derived.

The libertarian's right to life is not a right to receive from others the goods and resources necessary for preserving one's life; it is simply a right not to be killed. So understood, the right to life is not a right to receive welfare. In fact, there are no welfare rights in the libertarian view. Accordingly, the libertarian's understanding of the right to property is not a right to receive from others the goods and resources necessary for one's welfare, but rather a right to acquire goods and resources either by initial acquisition or by voluntary agreement.

By defending RIGHTS [7; S] such as these, libertarians can support only a limited role for coercive institutions. That role is simply to prevent and punish initial acts of coercion—the only wrongful actions for libertarians. Thus, libertarians are opposed to all forms of CENSORSHIP [S] and PATERNALISM [S], unless they can be supported by their ideal of liberty.

Libertarians do not deny that it is a good thing for people to have sufficient goods and resources to meet their basic nutritional needs, but they do deny that coercive institutions can be used to provide for such needs. Such good things as the provision of welfare to the needy are requirements of charity rather than JUSTICE [4; S], libertarians claim. Accordingly, failure to make such provisions is neither blameworthy nor punishable.

SOCIALISM

In contrast with libertarians, socialists take equality to be the ultimate social and political ideal (*see* EQUALITY, MORAL AND SOCIAL [3], and SOCIALISM [7]). In the *Communist Manifesto,* Karl MARX [5] and Friedrich ENGELS [2] maintain that the abolition of bourgeois property and bourgeois family structure is a necessary first requirement for building a society that accords with the political ideal of equality. In the *Critique of the Gotha Program,* Marx provides a much more positive account of what is required to build such a society: the distribution of social goods must conform, at least initially, to the principle from each according to his ability, to each according to his contribution. But when the highest stage of communist society has been reached, Marx adds, distribution will conform to the principle "from each according to his ability, to each according to his need." Contemporary socialists such as Kai Nielson and Carol Gould continue to endorse these tenets of MARXISM [S].

At first hearing, these tenets of Marxism might sound ridiculous to someone brought up in a capitalist society. The obvious objection is, How can you get persons to contribute according to their ability if income is distributed on the basis of their needs and not on the basis of their contributions?

The answer, according to socialists, is to make the work that must be done in a society as enjoyable in itself as possible. As a result, people will want to do the work they are capable of doing because they find it intrinsically rewarding. For a start socialists might try to get people to accept presently existing, intrinsically rewarding jobs at lower salaries—top executives, for example, would work for $300,000, rather than $900,000, a year. Yet ultimately, socialists hope to make all jobs as intrinsically rewarding as possible, so that once people are no longer working primarily for external rewards and are making their best contributions to society, distribution can proceed on the basis of need.

Socialists propose to implement their egalitarian ideal by giving workers democratic control over the workplace. They believe that if workers have more to say about how they do their work, they will find their work intrinsically more rewarding. As a consequence, they will be more motivated to work, because their work itself will be meeting their needs. Socialists believe that extending democracy to the workplace will necessarily lead to socialization of the means of production and the end of private property. By making jobs intrinsically as rewarding as possible, in part through democratic control of the workplace and an equitable assignment of unrewarding tasks, socialists believe people will contribute according to their ability even when distribution proceeds according to need. LIBERATION THEOLOGY [S] has also provided an interpretation of Christianity that is sympathetic to this socialist ideal.

Nor are contemporary socialists disillusioned by the collapse of the Soviet Union and the transformation of the countries in Eastern Europe. Judging the acceptability of the socialist ideal of equality by what took place in these countries would be as unfair as judging the acceptability of the libertarian ideal of liberty by what takes place in countries such as Guatemala or South Korea, where citizens are arrested and imprisoned without cause. Actually, a fairer comparison would be to judge the socialist ideal of equality by what takes place in countries such as Sweden and to judge the libertarian ideal of liberty by what takes place in the United States. Even these comparisons, however, are not wholly appropriate, because none of these countries fully conforms to those ideals.

WELFARE LIBERALISM

Finding merit in both the libertarian's ideal of liberty and the socialist's ideal of equality, welfare liberals attempt to combine both liberty and equality into one political ideal that can be characterized by contractual fairness (*see* LIBERALISM [4; S]).

A classic example of this contractual approach is found in the political works of Immanuel KANT [4; S]. Kant claims that a civil state ought to be founded on an original contract satisfying the requirements of freedom, equality, and independence. According to Kant, it suffices that the laws of a civil state are such that people would agree to them under conditions in which the requirements of freedom, equality, and independence obtain.

The Kantian ideal of a hypothetical contract as the moral foundation for coercive institutions has been further developed by John RAWLS [S] in *A Theory of Justice* (1971). Rawls, like Kant, argues that principles of justice are those principles that free and rational persons who are concerned to advance their own interests would accept in an initial position of equality. Yet Rawls goes beyond Kant by interpreting the conditions of his "original position" to explicitly require a "veil of ignorance." This veil of ignorance, Rawls claims, has the effect of depriving persons in the original position of the knowledge they would need to advance their own interests in ways that are morally arbitrary.

According to Rawls, the principles of justice that would be derived in the original position are (1) a principle of equal political liberty; (2) a principle of equal opportunity; (3) a principle requiring that the distribution of economic goods work to the greatest advantage of the least advantaged. Rawls holds that these principles would be chosen in the original position because persons so situated would find it reasonable to follow the conservative dictates of the "maximin strategy" and maximize the minimum, thereby securing for themselves the highest minimum payoff. In *Political Liberalism* (1993) Rawls explains how these principles could be supported by an overlapping consensus and thus would be compatible with a pluralistic society whose members endorse diverse comprehensive conceptions of the good.

COMMUNITARIANISM

Another prominent social and political ideal defended by contemporary philosophers is the communitarian ideal of the common good (*see* COMMUNITARIANISM [S]). As one might expect, many contemporary defenders of a communitarian social and political ideal regard their conception as rooted in Aristotelian moral theory (*see* ARISTOTLE [1; S]). Alasdair MacIntyre in *After Virtue* (1981) sees his social and political theory as rooted in Aristotelian moral theory, but one that has been refurbished in certain respects. Specifically, MacIntyre claims that Aristotelian moral theory must, first of all, reject any reliance on a metaphysical biology. Instead, MacIntyre proposes to ground Aristotelian moral theory on a conception of a practice. A practice, for MacIntyre, is "any coherent and complex form of socially established cooperative human activity through which goods internal to that form of activity are realized in the course of trying to achieve those standards of excellence which are appropriate to and partially definitive of that form of activity, with the result that human powers to achieve excellence, and human conceptions of the ends and goods involved are systematically extended." As examples of practices, MacIntyre cites arts, sciences, games, and the making and sustaining of family life.

MacIntyre then partially defines the virtues in terms of practices. A virtue, such as courage, justice, or honesty is "an acquired human quality the possession and exercise of which tends to enable us to achieve those goods which are internal to practices and the lack of which prevents us from achieving any such goods." However, MacIntyre admits that the virtues that sustain practices can conflict (e.g., courage can conflict with justice), and that practices so defined are not themselves above moral criticism.

Accordingly, to further ground his account, MacIntyre introduces the conception of a telos or good of a whole human life conceived as a unity. It is by means of this conception that MacIntyre proposes morally to evaluate practices and resolve conflicts between virtues. For MacIntyre, the telos of a whole human life is a life spent in seeking that telos; it is a quest for the good human life, and it proceeds with only partial knowledge of what is sought. Nevertheless, this quest is never undertaken in isolation but always within some shared tradition. Moreover, such a tradition provides additional resources for evaluating practices and for resolving conflicts while remaining open to moral criticism itself.

MacIntyre's characterization of the human telos in terms of a quest undertaken within a tradition marks a second respect in which he wants to depart from Aristotle's view. This historical dimension to the human telos, which MacIntyre contends is essential for a rationally acceptable communitarian account, is absent from Aristotle's view.

A third respect in which MacIntyre's account departs from Aristotle's concerns the possibility of tragic moral conflicts. As MacIntyre points out, Aristotle recognized only those moral conflicts that are the outcome of wrongful or mistaken action. Yet MacIntyre, following Sophocles, wants to recognize the possibility of additional conflicts between rival moral goods that are rooted in the very nature of things.

Rather than draw out the particular requirements of his own social and political theory, MacIntyre usually defends his theory by attacking rival theories; by and large, he has focused his attacks on liberal social and political theories and in this respect shares common ground with contemporary deconstructionists (*see* DECONSTRUCTION [S]). Thus, MacIntyre argues in his *Privatization of the Good* that virtually all forms of liberalism attempt to separate rules defining right action from conceptions of the human good. MacIntyre contends that these forms of liberalism not only fail but have to fail because the rules defining right action cannot be adequately grounded apart from a conception of the good. For this reason, MacIntyre claims, only some refurbished Aristotelian theory that grounds rules supporting right action in a complete conception of the good can ever hope to be adequate.

FEMINISM

Defenders of a feminist social and political ideal present a distinctive challenging critique to defenders of other social and political ideals (*see* FEMINIST SOCIAL AND POLITICAL PHILOSOPHY [S]). In his *The Subjection of Women,* John Stuart MILL [5; S], one of the earliest male defenders of women's liberation, argues that the subjection of women was never justified but was imposed upon women because they were physically weaker than men; later this subjection was confirmed by law. Mill argues that society must remove the legal restrictions that deny women the same opportunities enjoyed by men. However, Mill does not consider whether because of past discrimination against women it may be necessary to do more than simply removing legal restrictions: he does not consider whether positive assistance may also be required.

Usually it is not enough simply to remove unequal restrictions to make a competition fair among those who have been participating. Positive assistance to those who have been disadvantaged in the past may also be required, as would be the case in a race where some were unfairly impeded by having to carry ten-pound weights for part of the race. To render the outcome of such a race fair, we might want to transfer the ten-pound weights to the other runners in the race and thereby advantage the previously disadvantaged runners for an equal period of time. Similarly, positive assistance, such as AFFIRMATIVE ACTION [S] or preferential treatment programs, may be necessary if women who have been disadvantaged in the past by SEXISM [S] are now going to be able to compete fairly with men. According to feminists, the argument for using affirmative action or preferential treatment to overcome sexism in society is perfectly analogous to the argument for using affirmative action or preferential treatment to overcome RACISM [7; S] in society.

In *Justice, Gender, and the Family* (1989), Susan Okin argues for the feminist ideal of a gender-free society, in which basic rights and duties are not assigned on the basis of a person's biological sex. Since a conception of justice is usually thought to provide the ultimate grounds for the assignment of rights and duties, we can refer to this ideal of a gender-free society as "feminist justice."

Okin goes on to consider whether John Rawls's welfare liberal conception of justice can support the ideal of a gender-free society. Noting Rawls's failure to apply his original position-type thinking to family structures, Okin is skeptical about the possibility of using a welfare liberal ideal to support feminist justice. She contends that in a gender-structured society like our own, male philosophers cannot achieve the sympathetic imagination required to see things from the standpoint of women; nor can they do the original position-type thinking required by the welfare liberal ideal, because they lack the ability to put themselves in the position of women. According to Okin, original position-type thinking can really be achieved only in a gender-free society.

Yet at the same time that Okin despairs of doing original position-type thinking in a gender-structured society like our own, she herself purportedly does a considerable amount of just that type of thinking. For example, she claims that Rawls's principles of justice "would seem to require a radical rethinking not only of the division of labor within families but also of all the nonfamily institutions that assume it." She also claims that "the abolition of gender seems essential for the fulfillment of Rawls's criterion of political justice."

APPLICATIONS

Assuming that either libertarianism, socialism, welfare liberalism, communitarianism, feminism, or some combination of these ideals can be shown to be the most morally defensible, questions of application will still arise. For example, would the most morally defensible social and political ideal apply only within a nation-state, or would it apply more broadly to DISTANT PEOPLES AND FUTURE GENERATIONS [S] as well? Would it justify war or VIOLENCE [S], or would it require some form of PACIFISM [S] in international relations? Would it apply only to human beings or would it apply more broadly to animals and other living beings? These are important questions of application that must be answered.

Until recently, there was very little discussion of this last question. It was just widely assumed, without much argument, that social and political ideals apply only to humans. However, this lack of argument has recently been challenged by defenders of animal rights (*see* ANIMAL RIGHTS AND WELFARE [S]) on grounds of SPECIESISM [S]. Speciesism, they claim, is the prejudicial favoring of the interests of members of one's own species over the interests of other species. Determining whether this charge of speciesism can be sustained is vital to providing a justification of coercive institutions, particularly those of animal experimentation and factory farming, and thus is vital to fulfilling the central task of social and political philosophy as well.

(SEE ALSO: *Democracy, Nationalism and International Relations,* and *Pluralism* [S])

Bibliography

Gould, C. *Rethinking Democracy.* Cambridge, 1988.
Hayek, F. A. *The Constitution of Liberty.* Chicago, 1960.
Hospers, J. *Libertarianism.* Los Angeles, 1971.
MacIntyre, A. *After Virtue.* Notre Dame, IN, 1981.

———. *Three Rival Versions of Moral Enquiry*. Notre Dame, IN, 1990.

———. "The Privatization of the Good," *Review of Politics*, Vol. 52 (1990), 1–20.

Marx, K., and F. Engels. *The Communist Manifesto*. 1888.

Mill, J. S. *The Subjection of Women* [1869]. Indianapolis, 1988.

Narveson, J. *The Libertarian Idea*. Philadelphia, 1988.

Nielson, K. *Liberty and Equality*. Totowa, NJ, 1985.

Nozick, R. *Anarchy, State, and Utopia*. New York, 1974.

Okin, S. *Justice, Gender, and the Family*. New York, 1988.

Rawls, J. *A Theory of Justice*. Cambridge, MA, 1971.

———. *Political Liberalism*. New York, 1993.

Sterba, J. P. *How to Make People Just*. Totowa, NJ, 1988.

JAMES P. STERBA

SOCIAL EPISTEMOLOGY. Social epistemology has been an important field in philosophy since the early 1980s. It encompasses a wide variety of approaches that regard investigation of social aspects of inquiry to be relevant to discussions of justification and knowledge. The approaches range from the acknowledgment that individual thinkers can be aided by others in their pursuits of truth to the view that both the goals of inquiry and the manner in which those goals are attained are profoundly social.

Individualistic, rather than social, epistemologies have dominated philosophy since at least the time of DESCARTES [2; S] and throughout the history of analytic philosophy. The writings of PEIRCE [6; S] and WITTGENSTEIN [7; S], which present social epistemologies, are among the few exceptions, and they had little effect on epistemological work when they were published. Even the move to NATURALIZED EPISTEMOLOGY [S], taken by many epistemologists after QUINE'S [7; S] polemics in its favor, retained individualistic assumptions about knowledge and justification. Quine argued that epistemologists should attend to actual, rather than ideal, conditions of production of knowledge, but he concluded that "epistemology . . . falls into place as a chapter of psychology" (1969, p. 82), ignoring sociology of knowledge altogether.

Movements outside of epistemology motivated and cleared the way for social epistemology. First, and most important, the proliferation of interdisciplinary research on social aspects of scientific change following the publication of KUHN'S [S] *The Structure of Scientific Revolutions* pressured naturalistic epistemologists to take sociology of knowledge seriously. In particular the skeptical and relativistic conclusions of sociologists and anthropologists of science such as Barry Barnes, David Bloor, Steven Shapin, Simon Schaffer, Bruno Latour, Steve Woolgar, Harry Collins, Karin Knorr-Cetina, and Andy Pickering moved naturalistic epistemologists of science to take social accounts of scientific change seriously yet draw their own epistemic conclusions. Second, influential work during the late 1970s in PHILOSOPHY OF LANGUAGE [S] and PHILOSOPHY OF MIND [S]—core fields of philosophy—by PUTNAM [S], Burge, and others eschewed individualism and began producing social accounts. A more general openness to social approaches in philosophy followed.

Social epistemologies vary along two dimensions. First, there is a range of views about goals of inquiry. This range is the result of a more general, and older, debate in epistemology: goals range from correspondence truth (*see* CORRESPONDENCE THEORY OF TRUTH [2]) to pragmatic success to socially constituted truths. Second, attempts to attain epistemic goals are evaluated for different subjects of inquiry. Some social epistemologists evaluate the attempts of individual human beings, assessing the influence of social processes on individual reasoning and decision making. Others evaluate the aggregate efforts of groups of people, who may work together or separately. Such disagreements about the unit of inquiring subject for epistemic assessments are the defining debate for social epistemology. Therefore, examples are given of the twofold range of views with more attention on the second.

Goldman, Kitcher, and Kornblith take TRUTH [S] (or significant truth) to be a central goal of all kinds of inquiry. They assess various social processes and practices, such as communication control (Goldman, 1992), intellectual rivalry and credit seeking (Goldman, 1992; Kitcher, 1993), and reliance on experts (Kornblith, 1994) for their conduciveness to attaining truths. Some hold that, although truth is the ultimate epistemic goal, it is mediated by coherence of belief; they examine social processes for their conduciveness to coherence. For example, Lehrer (1990) argues that individual reasoning yields more coherent belief if it makes use of all the information residing in a community, and Thagard (1993) argues that delays in the transmission of information across a community can be conducive to finding a theory with maximal explanatory coherence.

Although the majority of social epistemologists regard truth as the most important epistemic goal, there are a range of other, less traditional, positions. Giere (1988), for example, claims that the goal of scientific inquiry is the attainment of theories that model the world through similarity relations rather than state truths about it and that social practices such as credit seeking should be assessed for their conduciveness to producing good models. More radically, Longino (1990) claims that the goal of scientific inquiry is to produce theories that are "empirically adequate" within a scientific community that satisfies particular criteria of objectivity; differences in values between members of the scientific community increase objectivity. Solomon (1994) claims that scientific goals are composed of empirical and pragmatic goals. Fuller (1993) writes of a range of epistemic goals espoused by scientific communities.

The most radical position is one that claims that our social epistemic practices construct truths rather than discover them and, furthermore, negotiate the goals of inquiry rather than set them in some nonarbitrary manner. Work in the "strong program" in sociology of science—notably by Latour, Shapin, and Woolgar—is frequently guided by such social constructivism (*see* CONSTRUCTIVISM, CONVENTIONALISM [S]). Rorty (1979) has similar views. Most contemporary epistemologists and philosophers of science are motivated by their disagreement with social constructivism, and they argue for the less radical positions described above.

The second dimension along which social epistemologies vary is the unit of inquiry that they assess. The most conservative social epistemology looks only at the effects of social processes on individual reasoning: Goldman's work on the effects of communication control (1992) and rhetoric (1994), Kornblith's work on suggestibility (1987) and reliance on experts (1994), and Coady's work on the role of trust in knowledge (1992) fall into this category. The claim is that individual human beings reason better when placed in a social situation where there is, for example, control of information that could mislead, criticism that employs rhetorical strategies, influence of others' beliefs, consultation with experts, and acceptance on trust of others' beliefs. Epistemic terms such as 'knows' and 'is justified' are, in practice, applied to individual human beings.

Many social epistemologists go further and regard division of cognitive labor as the most important component of the social nature of inquiry. It is wasteful to duplicate the efforts of others, beyond the minimum required to check robustness of results. Different individuals or research groups should, for the sake of efficiency, pursue different avenues of inquiry, especially when there is more than one promising direction to follow. Here it is the distribution of cognitive labor across a community, rather than the decisions of any particular individual, that is epistemically valuable. Kitcher (1993), Goldman (1992), and Shaked have argued that the desire for credit leads to effective division of cognitive labor; Thagard (1993) has argued that the same result is achieved by delays in dissemination of information; Giere (1988) thinks that interests and variation in cognitive resources distribute research effort; Solomon (1992) has argued that cognitive biases such as salience, availability, and representativeness can result in effective distribution of belief and thereby research effort.

Cognitive labor can be divided, not only for discovery and development of new ideas, but also for storage of facts, theories, and techniques that are widely accepted. Just as books contain information that no individual could retain, information is also stored in communities in ways that are accessible to most or all members of those communities, but not duplicated within each head. This is achieved when experts on different subjects, or with different experiences or techniques, comprise a useful variety of resources within a community. Campbell (1979) Kitcher (1993), and Lehrer (1990), among many others, hold that knowledge is social in this way.

Cognitive labor can also be divided for epistemic work in the process of coming to consensus. In traditional philosophies of science, consensus is presented as the outcome of the *same* decision of each member of a scientific community: a good consensus is the result of each scientist's choosing the best theory. Sarkar (1983) and Solomon (1994) each offer normative accounts of coming to consensus in which the epistemic work of selecting the best theory is distributed across the scientific community and no individual scientist need make a fair overall assessment of the merits of each theory.

More radically, social groups can be understood as having emergent epistemic qualities that are due to something other than the sum of the activities, memories, and abilities of their members. Gilbert (1987) argues that group knowledge need have no coincidences with the knowledge ascribed to members of a group. Hacking (1990) identifies conceptual change with linguistic change in a social group. Longino (1990) presents four conditions for objective knowledge: these are social conditions of openness, responsiveness to criticism, standards of inquiry, and equality of intellectual authority in a community of inquirers. Fuller (1993) argues that the goals of a science become apparent only through examining the activities and products of the relevant scientific community. Schmitt (1994) argues that group justificatory processes can achieve, through interactions, more than the sum of individual justifications. Solomon (1994) has argued that good distribution of biasing factors across a community is conducive to scientific progress.

It is not surprising to find that this variety of social epistemologies goes together with many different connections to other disciplines. Economics, ARTIFICIAL INTELLIGENCE [S] (especially distributed computation), COGNITIVE SCIENCE [S], race and gender studies, sociology of science, anthropology, and European philosophers (e.g., FOUCAULT [S], HABERMAS [S]) get frequent mention, either for the data or for the methodologies that they supply. It is likely that epistemological theories are not completely general (applying to all disciplines) but that they are at least in part relative to particular domains of application.

When epistemologies are deeply social, recommendations for inquiry will often be applicable to communities, or institutions, rather than to individuals. A future task for social epistemologists is to spell out the details of such recommendations. The traditional focus on individual epistemic responsibility may disappear or be transformed by the addition of new, socially relevant, recommendations.

(SEE ALSO: *Epistemology* [S])

Bibliography

Barnes, B., and D. Bloor. "Relativism, Rationalism, and the Sociology of Knowledge," in M. Hollis and S. Lukes, eds., *Rationality and Relativism* (Cambridge, MA, 1982).

Campbell, D. "A Tribal Model of the Social System Vehicle Carrying Scientific Knowledge," *Knowledge: Creation, Diffusion, Utilization,* Vol. 1. No. 2 (1979), 181–200.

Coady, C. A. J. *Testimony: A Philosophical Study.* Oxford, 1992.

Fuller, S. *Philosophy of Science and Its Discontents,* 2d ed. New York, 1993.

Giere, R. *Explaining Science: A Cognitive Approach.* Chicago, 1988.

Gilbert, M. "Modelling Collective Belief," in F. Schmitt, ed., *Synthese,* Vol. 73, No. 1 (1987), 185–204.

Goldman, A. *Liaisons: Philosophy Meets the Cognitive and Social Sciences.* Cambridge, MA, 1992.

Hacking, I. *The Taming of Chance.* Cambridge, 1990.

Kitcher, P. *The Advancement of Science.* Oxford, 1993.

Kornblith, H. "Some Social Features of Cognition," in F. Schmitt, ed., *Synthese,* Vol. 73, No. 1 (1987), 27–41.

———. "A Conservative Approach to Social Epistemology," in F. Schmitt, ed., *Socializing Epistemology* (Lanham, MD, 1994).

Kuhn, T. *The Structure of Scientific Revolutions,* 2d ed. Chicago, 1970.

Latour, E., and S. Woolgar. *Laboratory Life: The Construction of Scientific Facts,* 2d ed. Princeton, NJ, 1986.

Lehrer, K. *Theory of Knowledge.* Boulder, CO, 1990.

Longino, H. *Science as Social Knowledge.* Princeton, NJ, 1990.

McMullin, E., ed. *The Social Dimensions of Science.* Notre Dame, IN, 1992.

Quine, W. V. O. "Epistemology Naturalized," in *Ontological Relativity and Other Essays.* New York, 1969.

Rorty, R. *Philosophy and the Mirror of Nature.* Princeton, NJ, 1979.

Sarkar, H. *A Theory of Method.* Berkeley, 1983.

Schmitt, F., ed. *Synthese,* Vol. 73, No. 1 (1987). Special issue on social epistemology.

———, ed. *Socializing Epistemology.* Lanham, MD, 1994.

Shapin, S., and S. Schaffer. *Leviathan and the Air Pump: Hobbes, Boyle, and the Experimental Life.* Princeton, NJ, 1985.

Solomon, M. "Scientific Rationality and Human Reasoning," *Philosophy of Science,* Vol. 59 (1992), 439–55.

———. "A More Social Epistemology," in F. Schmitt, ed., *Socializing Epistemology* (Lanham, MD, 1994).

Thagard, P. "Societies of Minds: Science as Distributed Computing," *Studies in the History and Philosophy of Science,* Vol. 24 (1993), 49–67.

MIRIAM SOLOMON

SOCRATES. Scholars continue to find themselves unable to agree about the historicity of any of the extant portraits of SOCRATES [7]. One recent discussion, however, stands out for its painstaking review of the evidence: Gregory Vlastos's three chapters (2–4) on the historical Socrates in *Socrates: Ironist and Moral Philosopher.* Vlastos lists two groups of dialogues as falling within the early period: (1) what he calls the "elenctic dialogues" (*Apology, Charmides, Crito, Euthyphro, Gorgias, Hippias Minor, Ion, Laches, Protagoras,* and *Republic* I) and (2) what Vlastos calls "transitional dialogues" (*Euthydemus, Hippias Major, Lysis, Menexenus,* and *Meno*). From careful study of characterizations of Socrates and his philosophical views Vlastos identifies ten theses by which the Socrates of the early dialogues can be distinguished from the Socrates of the middle period and later dialogues. Vlastos concludes that the Socrates of the early dialogues is the historical Socrates; the Socrates of the later dialogues is only a character who speaks for PLATO [6; S] himself. Vlastos goes on to contrast the Socrates of Plato's early period with the Xenophontic Socrates and then to speculate about what it was that led Plato to modify his philosophical views, in the middle period, away from those of Socrates.

Most work on Socrates since the late 1970s shares Vlastos's view that a coherent picture of Socrates and Socratic philosophy can be found in the early dialogues of Plato. Whether this coherence is indicative of an authentically historical Socratic philosophy—as opposed to a coherent philosophy attributable only to a character named Socrates in Plato's early works—will no doubt remain the focus of intense scholarly controversy.

THE TRIAL

Until the early 1980s scholars had assumed that the motivation for the trial of Socrates was essentially some political prejudice against him. A prima facie problem for this view has always been that Socrates was charged with a religious crime, impiety. This problem was typically overcome by an appeal to the amnesty decree of 403, which forbade prosecution for crimes committed prior to the amnesty itself. Thomas C. Brickhouse and Nicholas D. Smith have disputed this account, arguing that the amnesty would not have made a political charge impossible and would not have prevented Socrates' prosecutors from appealing to the evidence traditionally supposed to have provided the real motives for the prosecution. Other studies have also questioned whether Socrates' political views would have merited a legal attack. Given no legal impediment to an explicitly political charge, and only ambiguous evidence of serious political motives for the trial, Brickhouse and Smith conclude that the religious charge accurately reflects the ground for the prosecution. This new interpretation allows a more straightforward understanding of Plato's account of the trial: we need not assume that Socrates is evading the "real" issues or making a defense that is largely irrelevant to the jurors' most serious concerns simply because he does not plainly address the political concerns scholars have cited.

PHILOSOPHICAL METHOD AND EPISTEMOLOGY

One major dispute among scholars has been about whether or not the *elenchos,* Socrates' method of asking questions and generating contradictions from his interlocutors' answers, can be used to construct and justify positive philosophical doctrines. One reason for doubting the "constructivist" understanding of Socrates' philosophizing is Socrates' own notorious profession of ignorance. If Socrates thought his elenchos could be used to generate and secure positive philosophical doctrine, why was he so persistent in his own disclaimers of knowledge?

Constructivists have attempted to answer this question by noting that Socrates does not always proclaim his own or other's ignorance; in fact, he occasionally makes and grants to others a variety of knowledge claims. Those inclined to the "constructivist" position have seen one sort of knowledge in Socrates' disclaimers of knowledge and at least another sort in the knowledge claims he makes and grants to others. The sort of knowledge he disclaims is constitutive of wisdom of the "greatest things" (see *Ap.* 22d7), and the reason Socrates is the "wisest of men" is that he alone recognizes just how deficient he is in *this* sort of knowledge (see *Ap.* 23b2–4). When Socrates claims to have knowledge or grants it to others, it is not this sort of knowledge, but some other sort.

ETHICS

Other interesting work has been done on Socratic ethics, in particular the relationships between goodness, virtue, and happiness (*eudaimonia*). No one doubts that Socrates is a eudaimonist—one who believes that eudaimonia is the final end or goal. But a number of different views have been published about exactly how Socrates saw the way the goodness of something was linked to its value in the pursuit of happiness, especially in the role virtue or excellence (*arete*) played in this pursuit. Is virtue merely instrumental to the pursuit of happiness, or is it in some way constitutive of the happy life? Also, is the possession of virtue necessary or even sufficient for happiness, or can one be virtuous, but not happy, or happy, but not virtuous? Scholars have offered different answers to these questions. No one has doubted, however, that Plato depicts Socrates himself as an exemplar of whatever goodness or virtue—and happiness—a human being can achieve. But because Socrates appears to equate virtue with the sort of knowledge he claims to lack, it would appear to follow that Socrates cannot be wholly virtuous. And yet he will regard himself as enjoying "inconceivable happiness," he claims, if only he will be allowed to pursue his elenctic mission in the afterlife unmolested (see *Ap.* 41c3–4). This can be true only if Socrates supposes either that virtue is not necessary for happiness or that he will be given in death the knowledge that he lacked in life.

Socrates' account of the "unity of the virtues," one of the salient features of Socratic ethics, has been the topic of a number of important studies. Many commentators now accept the view that the "unity thesis" defended in the *Protagoras* asserts that the different virtue names refer to one and the same cognitive state. Nevertheless, commentators remain divided over whether Socrates' belief that the virtues are really identical is consistent with all of his statements, made elsewhere in the early dialogues, that some virtues are proper parts of other virtues or of virtue as a whole. Commentators who seek to show how Socrates' various remarks form a coherent theory of virtue have generally tried to show how each of the virtues other than wisdom are all in some way parts of wisdom. No consensus has emerged, however, regarding exactly how these relationships must be understood.

Bibliography

Benson, H. H. "The Problem of the Elenchus Reconsidered," *Ancient Philosophy,* Vol. 7 (1987), 67–85.

———. "The Priority of Definition and the Socratic Elenchos," *Oxford Studies in Ancient Philosophy,* Vol. 8 (1990), 19–65.

———, ed. *Essays on the Philosophy of Socrates.* New York, 1992.

Brickhouse, T. C., and N. D. Smith. *Socrates on Trial.* Princeton, NJ, 1989.

———. *Plato's Socrates.* New York, 1994.

Irwin, T. H. *Plato's Moral Theory.* Oxford, 1977.

Kraut, R. *Socrates and the State.* Princeton, NJ, 1983.

Stokes, M. *Plato's Socrates Conversations: Drama and Dialectic in Three Dialogues.* Baltimore, 1986.

Vlastos, G. *Socrates: Ironist and Moral Philosopher.* Ithaca, NY, 1991.

———. *Socratic Studies,* edited by M. Burnyeat. Cambridge, 1994.

Woodruff, P. "Plato's Early Theory of Knowledge," in S. Everson, ed., *Companions to Ancient Thought,* Vol. 1, *Epistemology* (Cambridge, 1990).

NICHOLAS D. SMITH
THOMAS C. BRICKHOUSE

SPACE. Spatiality is an essential trait of all physical objects for HUSSERL [4; S]. He distinguishes the idea of objective space as conceived in modern natural science from our everyday experience of space and analyzes the constitutions of our different experiences of SPACE [7]. At the lowest level he describes the correlation between the sense of our own bodily awareness and mobility—our kinesthetic awareness—and our sense of a three-dimensional orientational space involving relationships such as beside, behind, near, and far, within which we perceive physical objects. Here spatial relationships do not refer to objective location but rather orient an individual subject's perceptual field, which is also organized around the null-point of a "here" as the subject's own bodily location. At the next level Husserl shows how the constitution of intersubjectivity involves the recognition of the possibility of a different "here" for another subject, from which my "here" can be seen as "there." This points to the idea of an intersubjectively objective space within which no "here" enjoys priority. Finally, Husserl shows how the idea of space as a mathematically measurable system of coordinates without any privileged center or reference to individual subjective perspectives emerges out of the attempt to achieve universally valid science.

Bibliography

Husserl, E. *Cartesianische Meditationen. Husserliana,* Vol. 1, edited by S. Strasser. The Hague, 1950. Translated by D. Cairns as *Cartesian Meditations.* The Hague, 1960. See especially secs. 53ff. on the constitution of intersubjective space.

———. *Die Krisis der europäischen Wissenschaften und die transzendentale Phänomenologie,* edited by W. Biemel. The Hague, 1954. Translated by D. Carr as *The Crisis of European Sciences and Transcendental Phenomenology.* Evanston, IL, 1970. See part 2 on mathematically conceived space and the emergence of modern science.

———. *Ding und Raum, Vorlesungen 1907. Husserliana,* Vol. 16, edited by U. Klaesges. The Hague, 1973. See especially secs. 44ff. concerning kinesthesis and the constitution of space as a field of perception. See the *Ergänzende Texte* for condensed summaries of these analyses.

THOMAS NENON

SPECIESISM. This is the name of a form of bias or discrimination that is much discussed in the contemporary debates over the moral status of animals. It amounts to discriminating on the basis of species; that is, it takes the fact that, say, baboons and humans belong to different species as a reason in itself to draw moral differences between them and on several counts.

First, speciesism sometimes manifests itself in consideration of who or what may be members of the moral community, of who or what is morally considerable (see Clark, Frey, Regan, Singer). For example, it is sometimes said that creatures who have experiences or are sentient count morally; to go on to affirm that (some) animals have experiences and are sentient but to deny that they count morally solely because they are not of the right species is a form of speciesism. If it really is the fact that creatures have experiences and are sentient that matters, then animals count; what has to be shown is why the fact that it is a baboon and not a human who has these characteristics matters morally.

Second, speciesism sometimes manifests itself in claims about pain and suffering. For instance, we usually take pain and suffering to be evils, to be things that blight a life and lower its quality, and animals can feel pain and suffer. Thus, suppose one pours scalding water on a child and on a cat: it seems odd to say that it would be wrong to scald the child but not wrong to scald the cat, since both feel pain and suffer, both have the quality of their lives diminished, and both instinctively reveal pain-avoidance behavior. To claim that scalding the child is wrong, but that scalding the cat is not wrong solely on the basis of the species to which each belongs is not in itself to give a reason why or how species-membership is morally relevant, let alone morally decisive (see Rachels, Sapontzis).

Third, speciesism sometimes manifests itself in claims about the value of life. Most of us think human life is more valuable than animal life; yet to think this solely on the basis of species exposes one to an obvious problem. If it is true that normal adult human life is more valuable than animal life, it by no means follows that all human life is more valuable than animal life, since it is by no means the case that all human lives are even remotely approximate in their quality. Thus, some human lives have a quality so low that those who are presently living those lives seek to end them; this, of course, is what the contemporary concern with EUTHANASIA [S] and physician-assisted suicide is all about. Indeed, some humans live in permanently vegetative states, where, as best we can judge, all talk of the quality of life seems beside the point. Are even these human lives more valuable than the lives of perfectly healthy baboons? To say that they are solely because they are human lives, lives lived by members of the species *homo sapiens,* even though it is true that healthy baboons can do all manner of things, can have all manner of experiences, is in effect to say that species-membership makes the crucial difference in value. It is not apparent exactly how it does this (see Frey). Of course, certain religions and cultural traditions may hold that humans have greater value than do animals, no matter what the quality or kind of lives lived; but these very same religions have put forward moral views that many today do not endorse, and these very same cultural traditions have held that, for example, whites are superior to blacks.

(SEE ALSO: *Animal Rights and Welfare* [S])

Bibliography

Clark, S. R. L. *The Moral Status of Animals.* Oxford, 1977.

———. *The Nature of the Beast.* Oxford, 1982.

Frey, R. G. *Interests and Rights: The Case Against Animals.* Oxford, 1980.

———. *Rights, Killing, and Suffering: Moral Vegetarianism and Applied Ethics.* Oxford, 1984.

———. "Moral Standing, The Value of Lives, and Speciesism," *Between the Species.* Vol. 4 (1988): 191–201.

Rachels, J. *Created from Animals: The Moral Implications of Darwinism.* New York, 1990.

Regan, T. *The Case for Animal Rights.* Berkeley, 1983.
Regan, T., and P. Singer, eds. *Animal Rights and Human Obligations,* 2nd ed. Englewood Cliffs, NJ, 1989.
Sapontzis, S. F. *Morals, Reason, and Animals.* Philadelphia, 1987.
Singer, P. *Animal Liberation,* 2nd ed. New York, 1990.
———. *Practical Ethics,* 2nd ed. Cambridge, 1993.

R. G. FREY

SPINOZA, BENEDICT (BARUCH) (1632–1677). The years following 1967 witnessed a major renewal of interest in SPINOZA's [7] philosophy. One factor facilitating this renewal was the decline—or at least moderation—of a linguistically oriented mode of philosophizing that had typically regarded Spinoza's metaphysical aims with deep suspicion and had frequently sought to locate the grounds of his doctrines in alleged linguistic or logical confusions. More positively, interest was stimulated by the publication, within a two-year period, of three groundbreaking interpretive studies (Curley, 1969; Gueroult, 1968; and Matheron, 1969). Increasingly, philosophers have interpreted Spinoza's metaphysical, ethical, political, and religious thought in ways that emphasize its relations to a modern scientific and naturalistic understanding of the universe.

METAPHYSICS

One important example of this trend concerns the interpretation of the relations holding among substance, attributes, and modes. Spinoza asserts that nothing exists except substance and modes and that all modes (including all individual things) are "in" and "conceived through" a single substance (God or Nature). Traditionally, this assertion has been understood to mean that all things inhere in God as qualities in a subject or substratum, so that the ontological status of ordinary individual things is reduced to that of mere qualities. Curley (1969), however, denied that the relation of inherence was central to Spinoza's conception of being "in and conceived through," emphasizing instead the causal character of these relations. Since attributes constitute (by definition, *Ethics,* pt. 1, def. 4) the essence of substance, this causal conception of the substance/mode relation led Curley to an interpretation of the divine attributes as fundamental pervasive facts about the universe, corresponding to the most basic laws of nature. He then interpreted the infinite modes (which, according to Spinoza [*Ethics,* pt. 1, prop. 21], follow from the "absolute nature" of the attributes) as facts corresponding to less basic nomological generalizations, which are logically entailed by the most basic laws of nature. Finally, he construed finite modes as particular facts about the universe, following from other particular facts in concert with the laws of nature associated with the attributes and infinite modes, though not from the laws of nature alone. Spinoza's doctrine that all modes are in and conceived through a single substance becomes, on this interpretation, not a doctrine about the relation of qualities to a single substratum, but rather a version of determinism about the relation of individual things to a naturalized conception of "God" as the single basic nomic structure of the universe.

While not denying the significance of the causal aspect of the substance/mode relation, and without ascribing to Spinoza acceptance of a Lockean substratum, Bennett (1984) nevertheless sought to reinstate an aspect of subject/quality inherence as part of the meaning of "in and conceived through." His way of doing so, while contrasting with Curley's interpretation, provides another example of the trend toward reading Spinoza in ways congenial to modern scientific naturalism. On Bennett's reading Spinoza's substance monism primarily expresses "the field metaphysic," according to which (1) the ultimate substantial independent reality (at least insofar as that reality is considered as extended) is space itself and (2) individual extended things are, at the deepest level, simply strings of spatiotemporally continuous place-times, strings whose elements are associated with one another by the changing distributions, through spatial regions, of physical qualities of space itself. This interpretation, if correct, provides a sense in which individual extended things would be "adjectival" upon the one extended substance. (It would then be necessary to apply a similar account to the attribute of thought.)

One well-known problem facing any interpretation of the substance/mode relation is the question of how merely temporary and local finite modes can "follow from" the nature of the eternal and infinite substance. One solution would begin by interpreting the attributes as essential natures of substance that are expressible (as Curley suggested) in the most basic laws of nature. These laws, when taken in connection with the plausibly Spinozistic requirement that the one substance (because infinite and unlimited) must manifest or express itself with the greatest amount of reality/perfection possible, would then logically and causally determine the entire infinite series of finite modes as the uniquely most perfect set of temporary and local self-manifestations or self-expressions (considered as distributions of qualities, in something like the way Bennett described) of the one substance. This infinite series would itself be an infinite mode, composed of finite, spatiotemporally limited parts. Such an interpretation could hope to explain how a substance both causes and is qualified by its modes and to do so in a way that is compatible with the absolute necessitarianism that Spinoza seems to enunciate in *Ethics,* pt. 1, props. 29, 33, and elsewhere. Absolute necessitarianism also seems to be required by what Gueroult (1968) identifies as Spinoza's most fundamental assumption: the doctrine that all things are intelligible or conceivable. For, when combined with Spinoza's doctrines that things must be understood or conceived through their causes (*Ethics,* pt. 1, ax. 4) and that causes necessitate (*Ethics,* pt. 1, ax. 3), this assumption of universal conceivability (arguably embodied in *Ethics,* pt. 1, ax. 2) requires that everything be necessary.

It is worth emphasizing that Spinoza would not distinguish between "logical" and "causal" necessitarianism, since for him logical consequence is not primarily a formal matter (as it was for Leibniz), but rather an expression of the laws of thought, a causal power both isomorphic to and identical with the dynamic causal power manifested in extension. Spinoza is often criticized for conflating the logical and the psychological, but his apparent failure to distinguish them sharply is intentional: logical consequence is best understood, on his view, as an aspect of divine psychology (i.e., the psychology of Nature itself).

ETHICS, POLITICS, AND RELIGION

Since 1967 there has also been increased interest in the naturalistic aspects of Spinoza's ethics, politics, and religion. Spinoza uses four fundamental terms of positive moral evaluation: 'good', 'virtue', 'free man', and 'in accordance with reason'. Each of these terms is definable naturalistically: 'good' as "what we certainly known to be useful to us" (*Ethics,* pt. 4, def. 1), where 'useful' is itself defined in terms of self-preservation; 'virtue' as "power" (*Ethics,* pt. 4, def. 8); 'free man' in terms of causal self-sufficiency (*Ethics,* pt. 1, def. 8) or of action in accordance with reason (*Ethics,* pt. 4, prop. 67); and 'in accordance with reason' itself in terms of self-preserving action produced by a specific natural, adequate cognitive faculty (*Ethics,* pt. 4, prop. 18 scholium). (Because every individual necessarily endeavors to preserve itself, certain cognitions of the world are also desires; when these cognitions are adequate, they are rational desires. Hence, reason is intrinsically practical.) His moral theory is also a species of VIRTUE ETHICS [S], inasmuch as the ultimate aim is neither the production of an end nor the performance of actions in accordance with duty or law, but rather the achievement and maintenance of a virtuous ("free," "blessed") state of being. Spinoza (seeking to avoid what he regards as the subjectivity of the common usage of 'good') defines a "good" action as one that certainly enables us to come closer to this state rather than as what someone who has already achieved this state would do; hence, there may be circumstances for Spinozistic ethics in which it would be "good" to do something other than what a "free" or "virtuous" person would do.

Like his ethical theory, Spinoza's political theory is naturalistic, treating "right" as coextensive with power and identifying the permissible with the actual, just as his metaphysics identifies the possible with the actual. There is, for Spinoza, a particularly close relationship between personal freedom and political freedom. Just as the human being is an individual whose freedom lies in his or her ability to achieve self-preservation through his or her own power and activity, so a political state is an individual whose freedom lies in its ability to preserve itself through its own power and activity (Matheron, 1969). One underlying purpose of Spinoza's political theorizing is to show that a political state that is free in the sense of allowing free thought and expression and thereby fostering the existence of citizens who are personally free is also the most free in the sense of being best able to maintain and enhance its own existence. In Spinoza's view one central political problem for a free state is the role of religion. While retaining scripture for the nonphilosophical masses, he seeks to derive from its own text the inessentiality to true religion of any particular dogmas or practices beyond the practice of justice and charity toward others (*Theological-Political Treatise,* chap. 13). Whereas the vulgar perceive God as a personal and supernatural lawgiver, the more philosophical understand God as Nature and His laws as the immutable laws of nature. Thus, natural science itself proves to be the best expression of the religious impulse—that is, the impulse to love God and to find one's blessedness in doing so.

Bibliography

WORKS BY SPINOZA

The Collected Works of Spinoza. Vol. 1, trans. E. Curley. Princeton, NJ, 1985. Upon its publication this became the standard English translation of the works it contains: *Ethics; Treatise on the Emendation of the Intellect; Short Treatise on God, Man, and His Well-Being; Principles of Descartes' Philosophy;* and the *Correspondence* (through 1665). The remainder of his philosophical works will appear in Vol. 2. (The 1967 article on Spinoza erroneously describes Spinoza's *Treatise of the Emendation of the Intellect [Tractatus de Intellectus Emendatione]* as having been discovered only in the nineteenth century. In fact, it was included [along with the *Ethics, Political Treatise, Correspondence,* and a *Hebrew Grammar*] in the *Opera posthuma* published shortly after Spinoza's death; it is the *Short Treatise on God, Man, and His Well-Being* that was discovered [in a Dutch transcription] in the nineteenth century.)

Ethics; Treatise on the Emendation of the Intellect; Selected Letters, trans. S. Shirley. 2d ed. Indianapolis, 1992.

Tractatus Theologico-Politicus, trans. S. Shirley. Leiden, 1989.

WORKS ON SPINOZA

Bennett, J. *A Study of Spinoza's "Ethics."* Indianapolis, 1984.

Curley, E. *Spinoza's Metaphysics: An Essay in Interpretation.* Cambridge, MA, 1969.

———. *Behind the Geometrical Method: A Reading of Spinoza's "Ethics."* Princeton, NJ, 1988.

———, and P.-F. Moreau. *Spinoza: Issues and Directions.* Leiden, 1990.

Donagan, A. *Spinoza.* Chicago, 1988.

Garrett, D., ed. *The Cambridge Companion to Spinoza.* Cambridge, 1996.

Gueroult, M. *Spinoza.* 2 vols. Paris, 1968–74.

Matheron, A. *Individu et communauté chez Spinoza.* Paris, 1969.

Yovel, Y., ed. *God and Nature: Spinoza's Metaphysics.* Leiden, 1991.

DON GARRETT

STEVENSON, CHARLES L. (1908–1979), constructed the first thorough account of the emotivist or expressivist theory of moral language (*see* EMOTIVE THEORY OF ETHICS [2]). His position is called NONCOGNITIVISM [S] because it emphasizes the conative side of ethical practice rather than the search for ethical knowledge and truth. In a series of articles and in his widely discussed 1944 book *Ethics and Language,* Stevenson argued that, since evaluative utterances are not, or not primarily, fact stating, they are not subject to assessment in terms of truth and falsity. Ethical disagreements, he said, often involve disagreement in belief, but they always involve disagreement in attitude. Disagreement in attitude can be resolved by argument if it is rooted in disagreement in belief; but we recognize that some disagreement in attitude may be fundamental, in which case we will be unable to reach agreement by rational methods.

By the time *Ethics and Language* appeared, emotivism had been sketched by A. J. AYER [1], who claimed that ethical utterances are disguised commands and exclamations. Others had introduced behavioral accounts of meaning, emphasized attention to the use of moral language, and questioned the RATIONALITY [S] of morality. Stevenson's contribution was to integrate these new ideas into a coherent theory, to distinguish the "theoretical" nature of his approach from normative ethics, or moralizing, and to emphasize the distinction between descriptive meaning and emotive meaning.

Stevenson argued that we can explain the meaning of an utterance such as "X is good" only if we can find a similar expression that is free from ambiguity and confusion and allows us to do and say everything we can do and say with the original expression. A "subjectivist" definition such as "This is good = I approve of this" at best accounts for the descriptive meaning of "This is good," but it completely neglects the emotive meaning. Stevenson characterized the emotive meaning of a word as its tendency, "arising through the history of its usage, to produce (result from) *affective* responses in people" (1963, p. 21). By leaving out any mention of emotive meaning the subjectivist definition makes it impossible to understand the nature of ethical disagreement, which is fundamentally a clash of attitudes. Stevenson's suggestion is that a proper analysis of "This is good" will satisfy the following pattern: "This is good = I approve of this; do so as well." The first element of the *definiens* (I approve of this) gives a subjectivist "descriptive meaning," and the second element of the *definiens* (Do so as well) gives the emotive meaning.

In a "second pattern of analysis," Stevenson dealt with cases in which the descriptive and emotive meanings are more closely related. In this connection he introduced the idea of a "persuasive definition." When we give such a definition we are trying to attach a new descriptive meaning to terms such as 'courage' or 'justice' while keeping the emotive meaning unchanged. The point of doing this is to change the direction of interests and attitudes, which is also the point of making a straightforward ethical judgment.

Stevenson earned degrees at Yale and Cambridge before receiving his Ph.D. from Harvard in 1935. He than taught at Harvard and at Yale, where his views about ethics were not popular. In 1946 he joined the philosophy department at the University of Michigan and remained there until his retirement. In addition to his landmark writings on ETHICAL THEORY [S], he wrote about aesthetics and the arts, especially music and poetry. He was a talented amateur musician and frequently performed on the piano or the cello with his friends and family.

Bibliography

Ayer, A. J. *Language, Truth and Logic.* New York, 1952.

Goldman, A. I., and J. Kim, eds. *Values and Morals: Essays in Honor of William Frankena, Charles Stevenson, and Richard Brandt.* London, 1978.

Stevenson, C. L. *Ethics and Language.* New Haven, 1944.

———. *Facts and Values.* New Haven, 1963.

Urmson, J. O. *The Emotive Theory of Ethics.* New York, 1969.

RICHARD GARNER

STRAWSON, P. F., succeeded Gilbert RYLE [7] as Waynflete Professor of Metaphysical Philosophy at the University of Oxford in 1968, retiring in 1987. He was knighted in 1977. Since 1966 he has published seven books, including *The Bounds of Sense* (1966) and *Skepticism and Naturalism* (1985). In these and other writings he has continued to explore a wide-ranging set of problems in METAPHYSICS [S], EPISTEMOLOGY [S], the PHILOSOPHY OF LANGUAGE [S], and the history of philosophy, including their interrelations, displaying the same profundity and abstractness of argument as in his earlier works, notably *Individuals.*

The Bounds of Sense, a book with links to part 1 of *Individuals,* is a critical and constructive study of KANT's [4; S] *Critique of Pure Reason,* in which Strawson attempts to determine what insights can be extracted from Kant's arguments when certain Kantian errors are eliminated. The chief error is transcendental idealism, which Strawson argues is both hard to interpret and incoherent, especially when applied to the SELF [S]. Another error is

Kant's conception of the necessities for which he argues, as corresponding to features we impose on experience and as classifiable as synthetic a prioris. Rather, Strawson suggests, the "necessities represent limits to what we can conceive of . . . as possible general structures of experience" (1966, p. 15).

Strawson, drawing on the transcendental deduction, claims that a self-conscious subject must acknowledge that some of his experiences are of an objective realm. The argument is that there can be a concept of oneself, the possessor of the experiences, only if there is the complexity of thought that is brought by regarding some experiences as being of objects independent of oneself. Further, drawing on the analogies, Strawson suggests that thinking of such objects itself requires that there be a "background of persistences and alterations" that are regular and that objects must fall under causal concepts. It follows that there is no genuine problem corresponding to the traditional one associated with EMPIRICISM [2]: of how to construct, and defend, a conception of the external world starting from self-consciously ascribed inner (sense-datum) experiences. Strawson also analyzes and adds to Kant's more critical arguments, for example, the attack on rational psychology in the paralogisms.

Strawson's study of Kant has inspired a debate as to whether Strawson himself has adequately defended the necessities. It has also inspired attempts to interpret transcendental idealism in a more sympathetic way.

In *Subject and Predicate in Logic and Grammar,* a book with clear links to part 2 of *Individuals,* Strawson returned to what distinguishes subject terms from predicate terms. Strawson's main thesis is that a variety of semantico-logical marks of the distinction can be viewed as consequences of a more fundamental contrast. In certain basic sentences the role of subject terms is to pick out spatio-temporal particulars, and the fundamental (though not only) role of predicate terms is to pick out a principle of classification (or a concept), according to which such particulars can be grouped. The subject–predicate distinction applies to sentences outside this basic class because of analogies with the basic case. In the second part of the book Strawson specifies a progressively rich range of functions a language must perform and speculates about different ways, in relation to the grammar of languages, they might be performed. Although displaying a brilliant sense of the role of elements in natural language, this style of speculative grammar has not attracted many other philosophers.

Skepticism and Naturalism: Some Varieties considers various traditional philosophical debates, which take the form of a choice between endorsing or being skeptical of certain natural beliefs or attitudes. In the case of SKEPTICISM [7; S] about the external world, Strawson argues—inspired by HUME [4; S] and WITTGENSTEIN [8; S]—that our nature makes it impossible to entertain skepticism seriously, and so the skeptic's arguments lapse. Strawson thereby recommends us not to rely on the type of transcendental argument he himself extracted from Kant. It has been extensively debated whether the psychological claims yield a proper reply. Strawson proposes different strategies to avoid revision of other fundamental beliefs, concerning, for example, secondary qualities, mentality, and MEANING [5; S]. In this book Strawson displays an interest in the abstract dynamics of philosophical disputes, a theme developed in *Analysis and Metaphysics: An Introduction to Philosophy.* In it Strawson outlines his conception of philosophy as analytical, rather than revisionary, and as displaying connections between our fundamental categories rather than reducing concepts to a limited range of simple categories. A theme of this book, as well as many of Strawson's articles—for example, those dealing with PERCEPTION [6; S] and the theory of language—is that philosophy should offer realistic descriptions of its subject matter, not oversimplifying in the interests of neatness of theory, nor springing from a mistaken desire to make philosophy like science. Given this stance, Strawson has criticized the programs of other leading philosophers such as QUINE [7; S], DAVIDSON [S], and DUMMETT [S].

Strawson's writings, with their goal of providing a realistically rich description—innocent of the pretensions of reduction and revision—of our basic thought about and contact with the world, have inspired many other recent philosophers, notably Gareth Evans and John McDowell.

Bibliography

WORKS BY STRAWSON

The Bounds of Sense. London, 1966.

Logico Linguistic Papers. London, 1971. Includes "Meaning and Truth," in which Strawson discusses Davidson.

Freedom and Resentment. London, 1974. Includes the very famous title paper, which attempts, along characteristically Strawsonian lines, to dissolve the conflict between responsibility and determinism, and other influential papers on perception.

Subject and Predicate in Logic and Grammar. London, 1974.

Skepticism and Naturalism: Some Varieties. New York, 1985.

Analysis and Metaphysics: An Introduction to Philosophy. Oxford, 1992.

WORKS ON STRAWSON

Philosophia, Vol. 10 (1981), 141–328. A collection of articles about many aspects of Strawson's work and a reply by Strawson.

Sen, P. B., and R. R. Verma. *The Philosophy of P. F. Strawson.* New Delhi, 1995. Contains important discussions by Putnam, Dummett, and Cassam and replies by Strawson.

Philosophical Subjects van Straaten, Z., ed. Oxford, 1980. Contains discussions of Strawson by Evans, McDowell, and Ishiguro and replies by Strawson.

PAUL F. SNOWDON

STRUCTURALISM. *See:* POSTSTRUCTURALISM [S]

SUBJECT. Throughout his career Michel FOUCAULT [S] challenged the traditional model of the subject as a metaphysical agency permanently endowed with ahistorical capabilities and powers. Rejecting the notion of an unchanging human essence or nature, he defined the subject as the contingent product of a confluence of historical forces. The constitution of SUBJECTIVITY [S] differs significantly from one historical period to the next, as evidenced by the wide range of capacities and limitations that have been attributed to subjects throughout history.

Foucault not only historicizes subjectivity but also divests individual subjects of the agency and causal efficacy that have traditionally been accorded them. In the writings from his archaeological period he interpreted subjectivity as the product of a more basic network of "autonomous" discursive practices. The governing discourse of any historical period not only produces the objects about which it speaks but also presides over the formation of the subjects who participate in its constituent practices. It is the discourse, Foucault believed, rather than the subjects who speak for it, that ultimately determines what is to count for knowledge in any historical period.

In the works of his genealogical period Foucault conceived of the subject as an unsuspecting pawn in clandestine games of power and truth. Subjects are produced historically through an intricate network of protracted disciplinary practices, all of which contribute to the satisfaction of hidden power interests. By virtue of their involuntary participation in discursive practices, human beings are transformed into specific types of subjects, uniquely abled and disabled to serve particular regimes of POWER [6]. Foucault consequently identified relations and regimes of power as the sources of the agency that is popularly attributed to individual human subjects.

In his writings on ethics Foucault began to carve out for the subject a modest domain of agency and causal efficacy. His investigations of ethics centered on the process of subjectivation (*assujettissement*): the fashioning of human beings into specific types of subjects who unwittingly serve hidden power interests by virtue of their unique complement of capabilities and limitations. His genealogies of the modern sexual subject revealed that the process of subjectivation is not strictly coercive and disabling. Power relations also manifest themselves in productive discursive practices, including those that distribute goods and information, satisfy limited desires, manage resources, and secure the material conditions of social harmony. Modern subjects are rendered docile through a battery of normalizing disciplines, but they also can turn the productive power invested in them against regimes of power that threaten to accede to domination.

Toward the end of his life Foucault gestured toward a partial recuperation of the agency of the subject, outlining the conditions under which subjects might constitute themselves in opposition to dangerous techniques of subjectivation. Under certain conditions modern subjects can—and do—resist the totalization of power within specific structures and local regimes.

(SEE ALSO: *Archaeology,* and *Order of Things* [S])

DANIEL W. CONWAY

SUBJECTIVIST EPISTEMOLOGY. A subjectivist epistemology is one that implies the standards of rational belief are those of the individual believer or those of the believer's community. Thus, subjectivism can come in either an individualistic form or a social form. A key negative test of subjectivism is whether an account implies that by being rational one is assured of having beliefs that are more reliable than they would be otherwise—that is, more reliable than they would be if one were not rational. Thus, reliabilist accounts of rational beliefs are paradigmatically objective (*see* RELIABILISM [S]). So are traditional foundationalist accounts (*see* CLASSICAL FOUNDATIONALISM [S]). By contrast, if an account implies that the standards one must meet if one's beliefs are to be rational are those that one would regard as intellectually defensible were one to be ideally reflective (Foley, 1987, 1993), then the account is subjective. Similarly, an account is subjective if it implies that one's beliefs are rational if they meet the standards of one's community (Rorty, 1979) or the standards of the recognized experts in one's community (Stich, 1985). Likewise, an account is subjective if it implies that one's beliefs are rational if they meet the standards of the human community at large, provided nothing else in the account implies that adhering to such standards will reliably produce true beliefs (*see* SOCIAL EPISTEMOLOGY [S]).

One of the considerations favoring a subjectivist epistemology is that it provides an attractive way of describing what is going on in skeptical scenarios—for example, one in which everything appears normal from my subjective point of view even though my brain has been removed from my body and placed in a vat, where it is being fed sensory experiences by a deceiving scientist. In such a scenario, almost everything I believe about my immediate surroundings would be false. Hence, I would have little knowledge about these surroundings, but what I believe about them might nonetheless be rational. Indeed, my beliefs would be as rational as my current beliefs about my surroundings. The most plausible explanation as to why this is so is that there is at least one important sense of rational belief according to which having rational beliefs is essentially a matter of meeting subjectively generated standards. Thus, by being envatted I may be deprived of the opportunity of having knowledge about my surroundings, but I am not necessarily also deprived of an opportunity of having rational beliefs.

(SEE ALSO: *Epistemology* [S])

Bibliography

Foley, R. *The Theory of Epistemic Rationality.* Cambridge, MA, 1987.

———. *Working without a Net.* New York, 1993.

Rorty, R. *Philosophy and the Mirror of Nature.* Princeton, NJ, 1979.

Stich, S. "Could Man Be an Irrational Animal?" *Synthese,* Vol. 64 (1985), 115–35.

RICHARD FOLEY

SUBJECTIVITY. Subjectivity is, primarily, an aspect of CONSCIOUSNESS [2; S]. In a sense, conscious experience can be described as the way the world appears from a particular mental subject's point of view. The very idea that there is a distinction between APPEARANCE AND REALITY [1] seems to presuppose the distinction between subjective and objective points of view.

There are two principal controversies surrounding subjectivity: first, whether subjectivity, as it is manifested in consciousness, is an essential component of mentality; and, second, whether subjectivity presents an obstacle to naturalistic theories of the mind.

Most philosophers agree that INTENTIONALITY [4]—the ability to represent—is characteristic of mentality. However, there is strong disagreement over whether subjectivity is also necessary. Those philosophers who think it is (e.g., Searle, 1992) argue that true (or what they call "original") intentionality can be attributed only to a conscious subject. On this view representational properties can be ascribed only to unconscious states, or to states of unconscious machines, in a derivative, or metaphorical, sense. The basic argument for this position is that, without a conscious subject interpreting a representation, there is nothing to determine its content, and therefore there is no representation at all.

Other philosophers reject this assimilation of intentionality and subjectivity, arguing that a theory of intentionality—one that applies equally to conscious and unconscious states—can be developed independently of a theory of subjectivity (e.g., Dretske, 1981, and Fodor, 1987). In particular they argue that conditions for the determination of representational content can be given in objective, even physicalistic, terms.

With respect to the second question—whether or not subjectivity presents a problem—one might argue as follows. A complete inventory of the world should, if it is truly complete, capture everything there is and everything going on. It seems natural to suppose that such a complete description is in principle possible and is in fact the ideal aim of natural science. But how could facts that are essentially accessible only from a particular subject's point of view be included; and, if they can't, doesn't this undermine the idea that the natural world constitutes a coherent, lawful, and objective whole?

For example, take the very fact of one's own existence. You could read through this hypothetical exhaustive description of the world, and it would include a description of a body at a particular spatiotemporal location, with particular physiological (or even nonphysical) processes going on inside it. However, what would be missing is the fact that this is your body—this is you. No collection of facts statable in objective terms seem to add up to the fact that this body is yours.

Or take the problem of PERSONAL IDENTITY [6; S]. From a point of view outside the subject, what it is that makes one the same person across time, whether it be a matter of bodily or psychological continuity, seems to admit of borderline cases, or matters of degree, or other sorts of indeterminacy. Yet from the point of view of the subject, what it is to be oneself seems to be a clear-cut, all-or-nothing matter. Either one continues to exist or one doesn't. It is hard to reconcile the objective and subjective perspectives on this question.

One particularly difficult manifestation of the problem of subjectivity is how to account for the fact that there is "something it is like" to be certain objects (say a human being), or occupy certain states (say, visual experiences), but not others (say, a rock, and its states). This is also known as the problem of QUALIA [S]. From an objective point of view there would seem to be nothing special about the neurological activity responsible for conscious experience that would explain what it's like for the subject.

Many philosophers argue that subjectivity does not present a special puzzle. For some (e.g., Searle, 1992) it is just a fact that the world contains both objective facts and irreducibly subjective facts; their relation requires no explanation and produces no mystery. For most, though, the demystification of the subjective is accomplished by some sort of reductionist strategy (e.g., Lycan, 1987, 1990, and Rosenthal, 1986). One influential model of subjectivity is the internal monitoring, or higher-order thought model. On this view, which fits well with a functionalist approach to the MIND–BODY PROBLEM [5] in general, subjectivity is principally a matter of some mental states representing other mental states. If this is what subjectivity amounts to, then any model of the mind that builds in the requisite architectural features will explain subjectivity. We already have a model of this sort of internal scanning with computers.

Advocates for the view that subjectivity presents no special mystery sometimes point to the perspectival character of indexical expressions such as "I" and "here" for support (*see* INDEXICAL SIGNS [4], and INDEXICALS [S]).

The idea is that it is generally acknowledged that the meaning of such expressions cannot be captured in nonindexical terms (see Perry, 1979), yet this doesn't give rise to any special philosophical problem or mystery. There are theories that take into account the special behavior of such terms consistent with a general theory that applies to nonindexical terms as well. Similarly, goes the argument, subjective phenomena can be incorporated into a more general theory of the world that applies to nonsubjective phenomena as well.

Yet another approach to the problem of subjectivity is eliminativism (e.g., Churchland, 1985, and Dennett, 1991) (*see* ELIMINATIVE MATERIALISM, ELIMINATIVISM [S]). Proponents of this view will grant that none of the models proposed to account for subjectivity really explains it, but, they argue, that is due to the fact that our intuitive conception of subjectivity—indeed of consciousness in general—is too confused or incoherent to be susceptible of scientific explanation. Subjectivity just isn't a real phenomenon, so there's nothing in the end to explain.

(SEE ALSO: *Self,* and *Philosophy of Mind* [S])

Bibliography

Churchland, P. "Reduction, Qualia, and the Direct Introspection of Brain States," *Journal of Philosophy,* Vol. 82 (1985).

Dennett, D. C. *Consciousness Explained.* Boston, 1991.

Dretske, F. *Knowledge and the Flow of Information.* Cambridge, MA, 1981.

Fodor, J. A. *Psychosemantics: The Problem of Meaning in the Philosophy of Mind.* Cambridge, MA, 1987.

Levine, J. "Could Love Be Like a Heatwave?: Physicalism and the Subjective Character of Experience," *Philosophical Studies,* Vol. 49 (1986).

Lycan, W. G. *Consciousness.* Cambridge, MA, 1987.

———. "What Is the 'Subjectivity' of the Mental?" *Philosophical Perspectives,* Vol. 4 (1990), 109–30.

McGinn, C., *The Subjective View.* New York, 1983.

———. *The Problem of Consciousness.* Oxford, 1991.

Nagel, T. "What Is It Like to Be a Bat?" *Philosophical Review,* Vol. 83 (1974), 435–50.

———. *The View from Nowhere.* New York, 1986.

Perry, J. "The Problem of the Essential Indexical," *Noûs,* Vol. 13 (1979), 3–21.

Rosenthal, D. "Two Concepts of Consciousness," *Philosophical Studies,* Vol. 49 (1986), 329–59.

Searle, J. *The Rediscovery of the Mind.* Cambridge, MA, 1992.

van Gulick, R. "Physicalism and the Subjectivity of the Mental," *Philosophical Topics,* Vol. 16 (1985), 51–70.

JOSEPH LEVINE

SUBJECTIVITY IN HUSSERL. For Edmund HUSSERL [4], subjectivity describes the capability of consciousness to be directly aware of its own states through reflection without recourse to sense perception. To the extent that this awareness involves no commitment to the spatial or temporal existence of the subject, nor any commitment to any empirically known facts about the subject other than those given through reflection, Husserl calls it "transcendental subjectivity." The transcendental subject is identified with an empirical subject through the identification of the subject of transcendental reflection with other characteristics known to the subject about him- or herself through empirical means. Since consciousness for Husserl is intentional, and all objectivity constitutes itself through and for transcendental subjectivity, the study of phenomenology may also be characterized as an analysis of transcendental subjectivity. In this perspective, phenomenology can become an eidetic science interested not in the particularity of an individual reflecting subject, but in the invariant structures of transcendental subjectivity and the object constituted for it. The method for achieving this Husserl terms "eidetic variation." The scope of the analysis is thereby extended beyond the actual consciousness of an existing subject to any imaginable consciousness whatsoever and any conceivable object for such consciousness.

Discussions of Husserl have focused on the notion of the subject as a self-transparent ego and the problems associated with many of the most basic synthetic activities involved in the genesis of objectivity that Husserl himself identifies, since not all of them are directly accessible to subjective reflection. Thus the focus on the subject in Husserl. Its identification with potential or actual self-consciousness has been criticized by some, and passages have been emphasized in which Husserl himself calls into question the traditional connotation of subjectivity as a substrate. In fact, in one manuscript Husserl himself argues that transcendental subjectivity is nothing at all except a form of activity that surpasses the notion of either subject or object, and instead is a kind of "Urstand" or originary stance that is the source of both subjectivity and objectivity as they are traditionally conceived.

Bibliography

Gurwitsch, A. *Studies in Phenomenology and Psychology.* Evanston, IL, 1966. A series of essays in which questions of the nature of the ego, subjectivity, and consciousness figure centrally. See especially chaps. 10 and 11 for his discussion of Husserl's position.

Husserl, E. *Cartesianische Meditationen, Husserliana,* Vol. I (1950). Edited by S. Strasser, and translated by D. Cairns as *Cartesian Meditations.* The Hague, 1960. See especially paras. 8–11 regarding the ego cogito as transcendental subjectivity, and the fourth Cartesian meditation concerning the nature of the transcendental ego and the idea of an ego in general. The fourth Cartesian meditation also indicates how the idea of a personal ego involves the ego as the bearer of habitualities.

———. *Ideen zu einer reinen Phänemonologie und phänomenologischen Philosophie, Buch I, Husserliana,* Vol. III (1976). Translated by F. Kersten as *Ideas Pertaining to a Pure Phenome-*

nology and Phenomenological Philosophy, First Book. The Hague, 1982. See especially paras. 27 ff. regarding the difference between transcendental and psychological reflection, and chaps. 34–62 on the intentionality of consciousness and its accessibility to pure reflection.

Marbach, E. *Das Problem des Ich in der Phänomenologie Husserls.* The Hague, 1974. Careful study of the tensions involved in Husserl's conception of the ego. Source of the citation from Husserl's *Nachla* concerning the ego as "Urstand" (p. 216).

Sartre, J.-P. "La transcendence de l'ego," *Recherches Philosophiques,* 6 (1936–37), 85–123. Translated by F. Williams and R. Kirkpatrick as *The Transcendence of the Ego* (New York, 1957). A classic discussion of Husserl's phenomenological conception of consciousness.

THOMAS NENON

SUPERVENIENCE. The core idea of the leading notion of supervenience is that there is an instance of supervenience when, but only when there cannot be a difference of some one sort without a difference of another sort (Lewis, 1986). According to this idea, if there can be no *A*-difference without a *B*-difference, then, and only then *A*-respects supervene on *B*-respects. Thus, for example, mental respects supervene on physical respects if and only if (iff) there can be no mental difference without a physical difference; and moral respects supervene on nonmoral respects iff there can be no moral difference without a nonmoral difference. This notion of supervenience is the notion of dependent-variation: variations in supervenient *A*-respects depend on variations in subvenient *B*-respects in that the former require the latter. Exact similarity in subvenient respects thus excludes the possibility of variation in supervenient respects. So, if mental respects supervene on physical respects, then exact similarity in physical respects excludes the possibility of difference in mental respects. Let us say that any *x* and *y* are *A*-duplicates just in case they are exactly alike in every *A*-respect; and likewise for *B*-duplicates. Then, *A*-respects supervene on *B*-respects, when, but only when *B*-duplicates cannot fail to be *A*-duplicates.

Various technical definitions have been proposed that formulate different types of dependent-variation (Kim, 1993). Quantifying over possible worlds (i.e., ways the world might be or counterfactual situations), the following characterize two types:

World-Weak Supervenience. In any world *w*, *B*-duplicates in *w* are *A*-duplicates in *w*.
World-Strong Supervenience. For any worlds *w* and *w**, and any individuals *x* and *y*, if *x* in *w* is a *B*-duplicate of *y* in *w**, then *x* in *w* is an *A*-duplicate of *y* in *w**.

Thus, according to world-weak supervenience, intraworld *B*-duplicates are invariably intraworld *A*-duplicates; while according to world-strong supervenience, both intraworld and cross-world *B*-duplicates are invariably *A*-duplicates. Strong implies weak, but not conversely; hence the names "strong" and 'weak." Subversions of each can be formulated by restricting the range of worlds, for example, to the nomologically possible worlds.

There is another intuitive notion of supervenience that is related to the notion of dependent-variation. It is the notion of a purely modal dependence-determination relationship. The dependence idea is that possessing a supervenient property requires possessing some subvenient property; the determination idea is that possession of that subvenient property will suffice for possession of the supervenient property. Thus, on this conception of supervenience, possessing a supervenient property requires possessing some subvenient property whose possession suffices for the possession of that supervenient property. A pair of technical definitions of property-supervenience have been proposed that distinguish strong and weak versions (Kim, 1993):

Operator-Weak Supervenience. Necessarily, for any *A*-property *F*, if something has *F*, then there is at least one *B*-property *G* such that it has *G*, and whatever has *G* has *F*.
Operator-Strong Supervenience. Necessarily, for any *A*-property *F*, if something has *F*, then there is at least one *B*-property *G* such that it has *G*, and necessarily whatever has *G* has *F*.

Of course, strong implies weak, but not conversely. Subversions of each can be formulated by restricting the kind of necessity in question.

On trivial assumptions, if necessity can be understood as universal quantification over POSSIBLE WORLDS [S], then operator-weak implies world-weak supervenience, and operator-strong implies world-strong. However, the converse implications fail. The reason is that both operator-weak and operator-strong imply that if something has an *A*-property, then it has some *B*-property (Haugeland, 1982; McLaughlin, 1995). But neither world-weak nor world-strong has that implication. The operator definitions are, however, arguably equivalent to the corresponding world-definitions in a special case of property-supervenience—understood as a relationship between nonempty sets of properties—namely, when the sets of properties in question are closed under Boolean operations of complementation and either conjunction or disjunction.

A third determinate of the relation of dependent-variation has been formulated (Haugeland, 1982; Hellman & Thomson, 1975; Horgan, 1982; Kim, 1993; Paull & Sider, 1992; Post, 1987):

Global Supervenience (1). Worlds that are *B*-duplicates (i.e., that are exactly alike in respect of the pattern of distribution of *B*-respects over individuals within them) are *A*-duplicates (i.e., exactly alike in respect of the pattern of distribution of *A*-respects over individuals within them).

Consider global property-supervenience. We are typically interested in the pattern of distribution of PROPERTIES [S] irrespective of the particular individuals they are distributed over. Thus, sameness of distributional pattern is typically understood not to require that the properties be distributed over numerically the same individuals. (On some theories of possible worlds, individuals are world-bound, and so properties could not possibly be distributed over numerically the same individuals in different worlds.) Nor is it typically required that properties be distributed over individuals that share some other sort of property. For, then, that other sort of property, whatever it is, will trivially globally supervene on any property whatsoever. To see this, suppose it was required for worlds to have the same distribution of *B*-properties, that *B*-properties in the worlds be distributed over individuals with the same spatial-temporal locations (or with counterpart spatial-temporal locations, if locations are world-bound). Then, properties such has having such-and-such a spatial-temporal location will trivially global-supervene on any property whatsoever. For, then, to be property duplicates of any sort, worlds would have to be spatial-temporal property duplicates (McLaughlin, 1995). Given such considerations, the notion of global supervenience is arguably best formulated as follows:

Global Supervenience (2). For any isomorphism, *I*, worlds that are *B*-duplicates under *I* are *A*-duplicates under *I*.

Thus, for example, mental respects globally supervene on physical respects just in case for any isomorphism, *I*, worlds that are physical-duplicates under *I* are mental-duplicates under *I*.

World-strong supervenience implies global, but there has been controversy over whether global implies world-strong, and even over whether it implies weak-weak. Global implies neither in virtue of LOGICAL FORM [S]; but the question is whether a global supervenience thesis will metaphysically necessitate the truth of corresponding world-strong and world-weak supervenience theses (Paull & Sider, 1992). It can be seen, however, that global fails to metaphysically necessitate world-weak, and thus that it fails also to so necessitate world-strong. It is incompatible with the world-weak supervenience of *A*-properties on *B*-properties for two individuals within a world to be *B*-duplicates yet fail to be *A*-duplicates. But that is compatible with the global supervenience of *A*-respects on *B*-respects. To see this, suppose, for the sake of argument, that states have unique constitutive properties, that mental properties are constitutive of mental states, physical properties of physical states, and that no such constitutive mental property is a physical property. Then, since such states will have distinct unique constitutive properties, no mental state is a physical states. Consider, then, properties such as having such-and-such a mental property as a constitutive property; call these mental-event-constituting properties; and call properties such as having such-and-such a physical property as a constitutive property, physical-event-constituting properties. Any two mental events will be exactly alike in respect of physical-event-constituting properties since they will lack any such property. However, since two mental events can differ in respect of their mental-event-constituting properties, world-weak supervenience fails. Nevertheless, global supervenience may very well hold in this case. If the assumptions are coherent, then global supervenience fails to imply world-weak, and thus fails as well to imply world-strong (McLaughlin, 1995).

Definitions of "multiple domain supervenience" have been formulated, which characterize notions of world-weak and world-strong supervenience that do not require that *B*-duplicates be *A*-duplicates, but only that there be some appropriate relationship (e.g., constitution) between the bearers of *B*-properties and the bearers of *A*-properties relative to which if two individuals are *B*-duplicates, individuals to which they bear the appropriate relationship, respectively, are *A*-duplicates. We lack sufficient space to formulate those definitions here. Suffice it to note that global supervenience is arguably equivalent to multiple domain world-strong supervenience (Kim, 1993).

Supervenience has been employed for a wide variety of philosophical purposes: to help characterize the relationship of mereological determination, the relationship of realization, the notion of emergence, the relationship between macrocausal relationships and the microcausal mechanisms that implement them, the relationship between special science laws and initial physical conditions and physical laws, and the notion of reduction, just to name some purposes (see Horgan, 1984; Kim, 1993; Post, 1987; Savellos & Yalcin, 1995).

Every variety of supervenience considered here seems required for reducibility. One source of interest in supervenience, however, is that it seems compatible with irreducibility. Neither world-weak, world-strong, nor global supervenience implies reducibility. Notice, for example, that if complementation is a property-forming operator, then the property not-*P*, world-weakly, world-strongly, and globally supervenes on property *P*. Moreover, operator-strong supervenience with merely nomological necessity fails to imply reducibility as well. If reducibility does not require an explanatory connection, however, then it is an open question whether the operator-strong supervenience with metaphysical necessity—and even whether the world-strong and the global supervenience across metaphysically possible worlds of one natural family of properties (e.g., mental properties) on another (e.g., physical properties)—suffices for reduction. Indeed, this is a topic of dispute. In any event, nonreductionists have in many cases conceded various varieties of supervenience, but denied reducibility is possible. Thus, it has been claimed, for instance, that while mental respects supervene on physical respects, mental respects fail to reduce to physical respects (DAVIDSON [S], 1980).

Since supervenience of every variety is required for reducibility, supervenience theses serve another purpose: they yield tests for whether reductive programs can succeed. Any would-be program of reduction according to which *A*-respects reduce to *B*-respects will imply some world-strong (indeed, some operator-strong) supervenience thesis to the effect that *A*-respects supervene on *B*-respects. A single counterexample can show that a strong supervenience thesis is false, and thus show that the program cannot succeed. Thus, suppose, for instance, that there is a program of attempting to reduce thinking that *P* to a kind of neurophysiological process. For the program to succeed, it will have to be that there can be no difference between individuals in respect to thinking that *P* without a difference in respect to their neurophysiological processes. If there is a single counterexample to this, then the reductive program is doomed to failure. (Twin-Earth thought-experiments might be invoked to try to provide such a counterexample.) Arguments that appeal to such counterexamples to reject reductive programs are arguments by appeal to false implied supervenience theses (FISTs) (McLaughlin, 1995).

(SEE ALSO: *Metaphysics,* and *Philosophy of Mind* [S])

Bibliography

Davidson, D. *Actions and Events.* Oxford, 1980.

Haugeland, J. "Weak Supervenience," *American Philosophical Quarterly,* Vol. 19 (1982), 93–103.

Hellman, G., and F. Thomson. "Physicalism: Ontology, Determination, and Reduction," *Journal of Philosophy,* Vol. 72 (1975), 551–64.

Horgan, T. "Supervenience and Microphysics," *Pacific Philosophical Quarterly,* Vol. 63 (1982), 29–43.

———, ed. *Southern Journal of Philosophy 22: The Spindel Conference on Supervenience Supplement.* Memphis, TN, 1984.

Kim, J. *Supervenience and Mind.* Cambridge, 1993.

Lewis, D. *On the Plurality of Worlds.* Oxford, 1986.

McLaughlin, B. P. "Varieties of Supervenience," in E. Savellos and U. Yalcin, eds., *Supervenience: New Essays* (Cambridge, 1995).

Paull, R. C., and T. R. Sider. "In Defense of Global Supervenience," *Philosophy and Phenomenological Research,* Vol. 52 (1992), 833–54.

Post, J. *The Faces of Existence.* Ithaca, NY, 1987.

Savellos, E., and U. Yalcin. *Supervenience: New Essays.* Cambridge, 1995.

BRIAN P. MCLAUGHLIN

SUPPLEMENT. *Supplement* is one of the key terms of DECONSTRUCTION's [S] challenge to Western metaphysics, understood as a unified body of thought that privileges presence. Jacques DERRIDA [S] used this term, much as he used *différance* and TRACE [S], to problematize the philosophical quest for a simple origin as a self-sufficient source. He articulated a "logic of supplementarity," which is said to be "inconceivable to reason," according to which the supplement, by delayed reaction, produces that onto which it is said to be added. The force of Derrida's analysis relies heavily on the close readings of philosophical texts in which he uncovered this logic, most notably his reading of Jean-Jacques ROUSSEAU [7; S] in *Of Grammatology.*

The logic of supplementarity uncovers the rules that structure some of the apparent contradictions found in the texts of metaphysics. In the case of an author who courts paradox as readily as Rousseau the task is particularly demanding, but for Derrida what constitutes consistency in any text can never be assumed. Derrida's diagnosis is that Rousseau wants to resist the conclusions he nevertheless cannot avoid: Rousseau's descriptions do not jibe with the declarations that reveal what he wants those descriptions to say. For example, Rousseau wants to identify the origin of language with speech and thereby make writing a "mere" supplement, but speech is itself a substitute for gesture, which is thereby, in a phrase whose apparent incoherence Derrida underlines, the "primordial" supplement. Derrida argued that instead of distinguishing Rousseau's use of "supplement" as "addition" from its use as "substitute," one should see the two senses as operating together. So, to continue with the example, much of what appeared contradictory in Rousseau's account of the origin of languages is found to arise from the fact that Rousseau wanted to locate the origin of language in the languages of the south but found himself having to draw constantly on the supplementary principles that he had associated with the languages of the north. The languages of the north were, therefore, not simply an external addition, but an alterity that must have been lodged within the system from the outset.

Derrida has exhibited the logic of supplementarity in other metaphysical texts. For example, in *Speech and Phenomena,* Derrida located this operation in Edmund HUSSERL's [4; S] account of language. Derrida identified a double tendency in Husserl, like that found in Rousseau. On the one hand Husserl wants to separate indication from solitary life, the strata of expression. On the other hand there are suggestions in Husserl's text that indication is constitutive of expression. The deconstruction of Husserl performed by this double reading is not a critique any more than the reading of Rousseau is. Neither thinker is criticized for failing to recognize the logic of supplementarity as such, not least because this logic has to be understood in terms of what metaphysics represses. The effacement of the primordial supplement is the condition of metaphysics, which itself can no longer be seen as constituting the unity it is sometimes held to be.

(SEE ALSO: *Language in Derrida* [S])

Bibliography

Derrida, J. *De la grammatologie.* Paris, 1967. Translated by G. Spivak as *Of Grammatology.* Baltimore, 1976.

———. *La Voix et le phénomène.* Paris, 1967. Translated by D. Allison as *Speech and Phenomena.* Evanston, IL, 1973.

ROBERT BERNASCONI

SYNTAX. Syntax is the theory of the construction of sentences out of words. In linguistics, syntax is distinguished from morphology, or the theory of the construction of words out of minimal units of significance, only some of which are words. According to this division, it is a matter of morphology that the word "solubility" decomposes into "dissolve" + "able" + "ity"; but it is a matter of syntax to analyze the construction of the sentence, "That substance is able to dissolve."

Although syntax is a traditional grammatical topic, it was only with the rise of formal methods growing out of the study of MATHEMATICAL LOGIC [S] that the subject attained sufficient explicitness to be studied in depth, in works by Harris (1957) and CHOMSKY [S] (1957). Since then a flourishing field has been created; for it was rapidly discovered that the syntax of human languages was far more complex than at first appeared. In this respect, the development of syntax is comparable to other fields of cognitive science such as human vision, problem-solving capacities, and the organization of commonsense knowledge, all of which gave rise to difficult problems once the goal of fully explicit representation was put in place.

The dawn of syntax is marked by the realization that the structure of sentences is hierarchical; that is, that behind the linear order of words and morphemes that is visible in natural languages there is another organization in terms of larger or smaller constituents nested one within another. Description of sentences at this level is said to give their phrase structure. Moreover, phrases of a given kind can occur within others of the same kind: it is this recursive feature of LANGUAGE [4; S] that enables sentences of arbitrary complexity to be constructed. The realization that phrase structure is recursive is very old. Assuming the categories of a complete noun phrase (NP) and sentence (S), ARNAULD [1] (1662) gives the examples (rendered here in English):

(1) ($_S$The divine law commands that [$_S$kings are to be honored])
(2) ($_S$[$_{NP}$Men [$_S$who are pious]] are charitable)

remarking that in (1) the embedded element "kings are to be honored" is a sentence occurring within a sentence, and that in (2) the relative clause has all the structure of a sentence, except that the relative pronoun "who" has replaced the subject.

In linguistic theory the recursive structure of syntax is expressed by principles of combination modeled after the clauses of an inductive definition. However, far more complex devices seem to be required for a compact description that helps to reveal the basis of the native speaker's ability. Chomsky's introduction of grammatical transformations opened the way to a variety of formalisms and developments (see Atkinson, Kilby, & Roca, 1988, for a useful overview). Chomsky also initiated the conception of linguistic theory as a study of the acquisition of a system of linguistic knowledge, or competence. Any human language is acquirable under ordinary experiential conditions by any normal child. The space between empirical evidence and the resulting linguistic competence is sufficiently great that a kind of readiness for language, universal grammar in Chomsky's terminology, is presupposed. Contemporary theory seeks to probe the basis for this readiness in terms of innate rules and principles of grammar. For a recent statement, see Chomsky and Lasnik (in Jacobs et al., 1993).

Within PHILOSOPHY [S] too the theory of syntax came to play an important role in the systematization of mathematics, and assumed central importance in CARNAP [2; S] (1934). Carnap distinguished between grammatical syntax, of the sort that a linguist might give in a description of a language, and logical syntax, whose aim was not only to specify the class of sentences (or well-formed formulae of a calculus) but also to use formal methods in constructing a theory of LOGICAL CONSEQUENCE and logical truth. Carnap employed the distinction between grammatical form and LOGICAL FORM [S], which plays a crucial part in WITTGENSTEIN's [8; S] views both in the *Tractatus* and in the *Philosophical Investigations,* and has become part of the lore of analytic philosophy. The scope of logical syntax in Carnap's terms took on much of the role of SEMANTICS [7; S] in later philosophical discussion. Even with the later distinction between syntax and model-theoretic semantics, syntactic properties of formalized languages are still crucial for properties of systems of logic (soundness and completeness), and PROOF THEORY [S] is established as a part of the syntax of mathematics.

In linguistic theory syntax and semantics have become increasingly intertwined disciplines, as it was realized that there are explanatory issues in relating linguistic forms to the specific meanings, or range of meanings, associated with them. Lappin (ed., 1995) contains a number of useful expositions on this theme; see also Larson and Segal (1995). The current research climate is in practice very different from conceptions associated with "ordinary language" philosophy: the contemorary view is not that ordinary speech lacks an exact logic, but rather that a diligent, collaborative effort is required to find out what the logic is. The concentration on logic implies that syntactic investigations have a metaphysical dimension. The patterns of inference of ordinary language call for formalization as part of a general account of the structure of individual human languages, or human language in general, and this formalization may in turn lead to proposals for reification, as in DAVIDSON'S [S] (1967) hypothesis that references to events are pervasive in ordinary action sentences.

On the side of linguistics proper, the problems of morphology have been treated in a progressively more syntactic manner as, for instance, our example "solubility" can be seen as built up by rules of a sort familiar from syntax. The result is the area now called morphosyntax, where the question whether morphology is a distinct level of linguistic organization is under active debate; see Hendrick (1995) for recent discussion.

(SEE ALSO: *Philosophy of Language* [S])

Bibliography

Arnauld, A. *La Logique, ou l'art de penser* [1662]. Translated by J. Dickoff and P. James as *The Art of Thinking* (Indianapolis, 1964).

Atkinson, M., D. Kilby, and I. Roca. *Foundations of General Linguistics,* 2d ed. London, 1988.

Carnap, R. *The Logical Syntax of Language.* London, 1937.

Chomsky, N. *Syntactic Structures.* The Hague, 1957.

———, and H. Lasnik. "The Theory of Principles and Parameters," in J. Jacobs, A. von Stechow, W. Sternfeld, and T. Vennemann, eds., *Syntax: An International Handbook of Contemporary Research* (Berlin and New York, 1993).

Davidson, D. "The Logical Form of Action Sentences," in N. Rescher, ed., *The Logic of Decision and Action* (Pittsburgh, 1967).

Harris, Z. "Co-Occurrence and Transformations in Linguistic Structure," *Language 33,* Vol. 3 (1957).

Hendrick, R. "Morphosyntax," in G. Webelhuth, ed., *Government and Binding Theory and the Minimalist Program* (Oxford, 1995).

Lappin, S., ed. *The Handbook of Contemporary Semantic Theory.* Oxford, 1995.

Larson, R., and G. Segal. *Knowledge of Meaning.* Cambridge, MA, 1995.

JAMES HIGGINBOTHAM

T

TEMPORALITY AND TIME. Acknowledging HUSSERL's [4; S] 'original phenomenological time' and BERGSON's [1] distinction of 'concrete duration' from objective 'cosmic' time as proximate sources, HEIDEGGER [3; S] in 1919–20 first broaches an original temporality as the ultimate sense and order (thus the 'a priori') of the motivated tendencies and rhythms of experienced experience (the nucleus of history, memory, and self-understanding) that articulate the immediacy of the individual human situation (later *Dasein*). Access to this underlying ordering immediacy of time is to be methodologically achieved by way of the FORMAL INDICATION [S] of intentionality, the sheer 'self-directedness toward' of experience articulated according to its relational, containing, and fulfilling senses. A sense of "temporalizing" (generating, ripening) unifies these three experiential vectors. A countersense of entropy soon follows in the inertial drag of "falling," lapsing. Countermovement and life's productive temporal movement belong together in an oppositional immediacy. Christianity provides the drama of the καιρός (kairos, critical moment) to focus oppositional temporality in the moment of critical juncture at the fullness of time, which decides between owned and disowned temporality, with original temporality being the source from which all other levels of time derive.

Kairological time is thus developed (1927) from a Dasein in radical transition (e.g., questioning, deciding, self-discovering), formally indicated as ex-sistence (dynamically beyond itself, ever 'toward') to articulate the situated intentionality of a CARE [S] not just of the self "being" directed but *of* this being itself in its entirety, by transcending to the horizons of the total situation, those of birth, death, and the world. The original (now "ex-static") temporality that comprehends these horizons displays its stasis in the self-constancy of responsive resolution anticipating its unique whole in a steady stretch between birth and death, drawing both "ends" into the fulfilling moment of integrity. This original temporality formalizing the dynamism of self-experience in its world is the ontological sense of care, the condition of possibility of its productive unity and finite wholeness. Its structure is ecstatic toward the unique lifetime of a self, horizonal in its wholeness, "temporalizing" originally out of the future. The derivative "handy" time of utilitarian concern focusing on the everyday is by contrast datable, spanned, public time expressing significance through the priorities of daily appointments. Ordinary time is an even more dispersive power of presence, manifesting itself as a uniform series of nows leveled of particular significance, lending itself to the punctilious division of scientific measurement, yet in its irreversible transitionality still displaying its origin in finite temporality.

The ecstatic temporality of Dasein projects the horizonal *Temporalität* of Being itself, opening the meaningful expanse that "worlds" and so "times" its beings. Heidegger, however, never succeeds in elaborating time, as the formal *logos* of phenomena, into an ontological "principle" discriminating the entire field of beings modally into their respective tensors from the unified interplay of horizonal schemata. But unifying temporality, already in 1927 called the "clear*ing*" empowering possibility and disclosing truth, reappears in the later Heidegger as the "time-play-space" of Being, and the unique "event" of endowment remains its final word.

Bibliography

Heidegger, M. *Die Grundprobleme der Phänomenologie* (1919/20), ed. H.-H. Gander. Gesamtausgabe Vol. 58. Frankfurt, 1993. Early Freiburg course of Winter 1919–20. Esp. pp. 258–63.

———. *Phänomenologie der Anschauung und des Ausdrucks,* ed. C. Strube. Gesamtausgabe Vol. 59. Frankfurt, 1993. Early Freiburg course of Summer 1920. Esp. pp. 150f.

———. *Sein und Zeit* [1927], 16th ed. Tübingen, 1986. Translated by J. Macquarrie and E. S. Robinson as *Being and Time.* New York, 1962. Esp. §§ 65, 69, 78–81.

———. *Die Grundprobleme der Phänomenologie,* ed. W.-F. von Herrmann. Gesamtausgabe Vol. 24. Frankfurt, 1975. Marburg course of Summer 1927. Translated by A. Hofstadter as *The Basic Problems of Phenomenology.* Bloomington, IN, 1982. Esp. §§ 19–22.

Kisiel, T. *The Genesis of Heidegger's "Being and Time."* Berkeley, 1993.

THEODORE KISIEL

TESTIMONY. An important, and relatively neglected, topic within EPISTEMOLOGY [S] is that of how the users of a common language may come to know things at second hand, by learning from what others tell them—either in person, or through the written word. Knowledge gained in this way is, within analytic philosophy, said to be gained through 'testimony'. Tellings of all kinds—serious assertoric utterances intended to inform their audiences—are instances of testimony. The information (or misinformation) recorded in train timetables, birth registers, minutes of meetings, official records, diaries, letters, historical works, textbooks, and all kinds of purported factual published and unpublished writings is also 'testimony' in an extended sense.

Philosophical concern with testimony is about whether (and if so, how) knowledge, or justified belief, may be acquired by means of it. PLATO ([6; S] in the *Theaetetus*) and AUGUSTINE ([1; S] in *De Magistro*), despising its second-hand character, denied that knowledge, as opposed to mere belief, can ever be acquired through it. Supporting their claim, one might argue that knowledge requires true understanding, which comes only with thinking through for oneself, not from relying another's report. But while this may hold for some very special subject matters such as religious or moral belief, it is absurd to deny that I can understand the proposition that the sun is an enormous and very distant ball of burning gases when I read this in a book, or that this afternoon's meeting is postponed when I am so told by a colleague. And it seems undeniable that we learn things, come to know them, in this way.

But how exactly does testimony effect the spreading of knowledge from one person to another within a linguistic community? The testifier asserts something to be so, and her audience, trusting her, comes to believe it. But what a person asserts is true, flukes apart, only if she is sincere and her belief about her subject matter is correct. Thus, one central issue in the epistemology of testimony is whether a hearer is epistemically entitled to take the sincerity and competence of her informant on trust, or if she should believe what she is told only when she has evidence of this. David HUME [4; S] famously took a reductionist position on this question, while Thomas REID [7; S] opposed this, asserting the naturalness and justifiedness of the complementary human dispositions to truthfulness and trustfulness.

The place of testimony within our system of empirical knowledge as a whole may also be investigated. Do we have a core of empirically based knowledge, gained through perception and retained in memory, which is independent of any reliance on testimony; or is all of our knowledge infected by dependence on testimony? Since any social creature's learning of language depends on teaching of word meanings by initiates, and all she knows is expressed by her in that language, it will require difficult argument to establish that we have any testimony-free knowledge.

Bibliography

Chakrabarti, A., and B. K. Matilal, eds. *Knowing from Words.* Synthese Library, Vol. 230. Dordrecht, 1994.

Coady, C. A. J. *Testimony: A Philosophical Study.* Oxford, 1992.

Fricker, E. "Telling and Trusting: Reductionism and Anti-reductionism in the Epistemology of Testimony," *Mind,* Vol. 104 (1995), 393–411.

Hume, D. *An Enquiry Concerning Human Understanding,* in P. H. Nidditch, ed., *Hume's Enquiries* (Oxford, 1975). Sec. 10, "Of Miracles."

Reid, T. *An Enquiry into the Human Mind,* ed. T. Duggan. Chicago, 1970. Chap. 6, sec. 24.

ELIZABETH FRICKER

THEISM, ARGUMENTS FOR/AGAINST. PHILOSOPHY OF RELIGION [S] enjoyed a renaissance in the final third of the twentieth century. Its fruits include important contributions to both natural theology, the enterprise of arguing for THEISM [8], and natural atheology, the enterprise of arguing against it. In natural theology philosophers produced new versions of ontological, cosmological, and teleological arguments for the existence of God (*see* COSMOLOGICAL ARGUMENT FOR THE EXISTENCE OF GOD [2]; ONTOLOGICAL ARGUMENT FOR THE EXISTENCE OF GOD [5]; and TELEOLOGICAL ARGUMENT FOR THE EXISTENCE OF GOD [8]). In natural atheology problems of evil, which have always been the chief arguments against theism, were much discussed, and philosophers debated proposed solutions to both the logical problem of evil and the evidential problem of evil (*see* EVIL, PROBLEM OF [3; S]).

NATURAL THEOLOGY

Building on work by Charles Hartshorne and Norman MALCOLM [5], Alvin Plantinga (1974) formulated a model ontological argument for the existence of God that employs the metaphysics of POSSIBLE WORLDS [S]. Let it be stipulated that being unsurpassably great is logically equivalent to being maximally excellent in every possible world and that being maximally excellent entails being omnipotent, omniscient, and morally perfect. The main premise of Plantinga's argument is that there is a possible world in which unsurpassable greatness is exemplified. From these stipulations and this premise he concludes, first, that unsurpassable greatness is exemplified in every possible world and hence in the actual world and, second, that there actually exists a being who is omnipotent, omniscient, and morally perfect and who exists and has these properties in every possible world. The argument is valid in a system of MODAL LOGIC [S] that can plausibly be claimed to apply correctly to possible worlds. Plantinga reports that he thinks its main premise is true and so considers it a sound argument.

However, he acknowledges that it is not a successful proof of the existence of God. A successful proof would have to draw all its premises from the stock of propositions accepted by almost all sane or rational persons. The main premise of this argument is not of that sort; a rational person could understand it and yet not accept it. In other words, not accepting the argument's main premise is rationally permissible. But Plantinga maintains that accepting that premise is also rationally permissible. Since he regards it as rational to accept the argument's main premise, he holds that the argument shows it to be rational to accept its conclusion. As he sees it, even though his ontological argument does not establish the truth of theism, it does establish the rational permissibility of theistic belief.

According to William L. Rowe (1975), Samuel CLARKE [2] has given us the most cogent presentation of the cosmological argument we possess. It has two parts. The first argues for the existence of a necessary being, and the second argues that this being has other divine attributes such as omniscience, omnipotence, and infinite goodness. As Rowe reconstructs it in contemporary terms, the first part of the argument has as its main premise a version of the principle of sufficient reason, according to which every existing thing has a reason for its existence either in the necessity of its own nature or in the causal efficacy of some other beings. It is then argued that not every existing thing has a reason for its existence in the causal efficacy of some other beings. It follows that there exists a being that has a reason for its existence in the necessity of its own nature. Next it is argued that a being that has a reason for its existence in the necessity of its own nature is a logically necessary being. It may then be concluded that there exists a necessary being.

Rowe takes care to ensure that his version of Clarke's argument is deductively valid. What is more, he maintains that the principle of sufficient reason that is its main premise is not known to be false because no one has set forth any convincing argument for its falsity. However, he claims that the argument is not a proof of the existence of a necessary being. As Rowe sees it, an argument is a proof of its conclusion only if its premises are known to be true, and no human knows that the principle of sufficient reason is true. Hence, even if the argument is sound, it is not a proof of its conclusion. Rowe leaves open the possibility that it is reasonable for some people to believe that the argument's premises are true, in which case the argument would show the reasonableness of believing that a necessary being exists. If the second part of the argument made it reasonable to believe that such a necessary being has other divine attributes, then the theist might be entitled to claim that the argument shows the reasonableness of theistic belief. So Rowe invites the theist to explore the possibility that his cosmological argument shows that it is reasonable to believe in God, even though it perhaps fails to show that theism is true.

Richard Swinburne's teleological argument is part of a cumulative case he builds for theism (Swinburne, 1979). Other parts of the case involve arguments from consciousness and morality, from providence, from history and miracles, and from RELIGIOUS EXPERIENCE [S]. Each part of the case is supposed to increase the probability of theism; the case as a whole is supposed to yield the conclusion that, on our total evidence, theism is more probable than not. The existence of order in the universe is supposed to increase significantly the probability of theism, even if it does not by itself render theism more probable than not.

In constructing his teleological argument, Swinburne appeals to general physical considerations rather than specifically biological order. There is a vast uniformity in the powers and liabilities of material objects that underlies the regularities of temporal succession described by the laws of nature. In addition, material objects are made of components of very few fundamental kinds. Either this order is an inexplicable brute fact or it has some explanation. Explanatory alternatives to theism such as the committee of minor deities suggested by HUME [4; S] seem to Swinburne less probable than theism, because theism leads us to expect one pattern of order throughout nature, while we would expect different patterns in different parts of the universe if its order were the product of a committee. So the alternatives are that the temporal order of the world has no explanation and that it is produced by God.

It is a consequence of Bayes theorem (*see* BAYESIANISM [S]) that this order increases the probability of theism if and only if it is more probable if God exists than if God does not exist. Swinburne offers two reasons for thinking that the order of the universe is more probable on theism than on its negation. The first is that the order seems improbable in the absence of an explanation and so cries out for explanation in terms of a common source. The second is that there are reasons for God to make an orderly universe: one is that order is a necessary condition of beauty, and there is good reason for God to prefer beauty to ugliness in creating; another is that order is a necessary condition of finite rational agents growing in knowledge and power, and there is some reason for God to make finite creatures with the opportunity to grow in knowledge and power.

The teleological argument plays a limited role in Swinburne's natural theology. Since it is an inductive argument, it does not prove the existence of God. Swinburne does not claim that by itself it shows that theism is more probable than not; nor does he claim that by itself it establishes the rational permissibility of belief in God.

Hence, only modest claims should be made on behalf of these three arguments for theism. Their authors are well aware that they do not prove the existence of God. However, they may show that belief in God is reasonable or contributes to a cumulative case for the rationality of theistic belief.

PROBLEMS OF EVIL

According to J. L. MACKIE [S] (1955), the existence of a God who is omniscient, omnipotent, and perfectly good is inconsistent with the existence of evil. If this is correct, we may infer that God does not exist from our knowledge that evil does exist. A solution to this logical problem of evil would be a proof that the existence of God is, after all, consistent with the existence of evil. One way to prove consistency would be to find a proposition that is consistent with the proposition that God exists and that, when conjoined with the proposition that God exists, entails that evil exists. This is the strategy employed in Alvin Plantinga's free-will defense against the logical problem of evil (Plantinga, 1974).

The intuitive idea on which the free-will defense rests is simple. Only genuinely free creatures are capable of producing moral good and moral evil. Of course, God could create a world without free creatures in it, but such a world would lack both moral good and moral evil. If God does create a world with free creatures in it, then it is partly up to them and not wholly up to God what balance of moral good and evil the world contains. The gift of creaturely freedom limits the power of an omnipotent God. According to Plantinga, it is possible that every free creature God could have created would produce at least some moral evil. Hence, it is possible that God could not have created a world containing moral good but no moral evil.

Consider the proposition that God could not have created a world containing moral good but no moral evil and yet creates a world containing moral good. The free-will defense claims that this proposition is consistent with the proposition that God is omniscient, omnipotent, and perfectly good. But these two propositions entail that moral evil exists and thus that evil exists. Hence, if the defense's consistency claim is true, the existence of a God who is omniscient, omnipotent, and perfectly good is consistent with the existence of evil. Therefore, the free-will defense is a successful solution of the logical problem of evil if its consistency claim is true. That claim certainly appears to be plausible.

Most philosophers who have studied the matter are prepared to grant that the existence of God is consistent with the existence of evil. The focus of discussion has shifted from the logical to the evidential problem of evil. The evils within our ken are evidence against the existence of God. The question is whether they make theism improbable or render theistic belief unwarranted or irrational.

William L. Rowe (1988) presents the evidential problem of evil in terms of two vivid examples of evil. Bambi is a fawn who is trapped in a forest fire and horribly burned; she dies after several days of intense agony. Sue is a young girl who is raped and beaten by her mother's boyfriend; he then strangles her to death. According to Rowe, no good state of affairs we know of is such that an omnipotent, omniscient being's obtaining it would morally justify that being's permitting the suffering and death of Bambi or Sue. From this premise he infers that no good state of affairs is such that an omnipotent, omniscient being's obtaining it would morally justify that being in permitting the suffering and death of Bambi or Sue. If there were an omnipotent, omniscient, and morally perfect being, there would be some good state of affairs such that the being's obtaining it would morally justify the being's permitting the suffering and death of Bambi or Sue. Hence, it may be concluded that no omnipotent, omniscient, and morally perfect being exists.

The first step in this argument is an inductive inference from a sample, good states of affairs known to us, to a larger population, good states of affairs without qualification. So it is possible that no good state of affairs known to us morally justifies such evils but some good state of affairs unknown to us morally justifies them. But Rowe argues that the inference's premise gives him a reason to accept its conclusion. We are often justified in inferring from the known to the unknown. If I have encountered many pit bulls and all of them are vicious, I have a reason to believe all pit bulls are vicious.

William P. Alston (1991) challenges Rowe's inference. As he sees it, when we justifiably infer from the known to the unknown, we typically have background knowledge to assure us that the known sample is likely to be representative of the wider population. We know, for example, that character traits are often breed-specific in dogs. According to Alston, we have no such knowledge of the population of good states of affairs because we have no way of anticipating what is in the class of good states of affairs unknown to us. He likens Rowe's reasoning to inferring, in 1850, from the fact that no one has yet voyaged to the moon that no one will ever do so.

The disagreement between Rowe and Alston illustrates the lack of a philosophical consensus on a solution to the evidential problem of evil. It is safe to predict continued debate about whether horrible evils such as the suffering and death of Bambi or Sue provide sufficient evidence to show that theistic belief is unjustified or unreasonable.

Bibliography

Alston, W. P. "The Inductive Argument from Evil and the Human Cognitive Condition," in James E. Tomberlin, ed., *Phil-*

osophical Perspectives, Vol. 5, *Philosophy of Religion* (Atascadero, CA, 1991).

Mackie, J. L. "Evil and Omnipotence," *Mind,* Vol. 64 (1955), 200–12.

Plantinga, A. *The Nature of Necessity.* Oxford, 1974.

Rowe, W. L. *The Cosmological Argument.* Princeton, NJ, 1975.

———. "Evil and Theodicy," *Philosophical Topics,* Vol. 16, no. 2 (1988), 119–32.

Swinburne, R. *The Existence of God.* Oxford, 1979.

PHILLIP L. QUINN

TIME, BEING, AND BECOMING. The major debate in the philosophy of time, being, and becoming is between defenders of the tenseless theory of time and defenders of the tensed theory of time. The tenseless theory implies that temporal features of events consist only of relations of simultaneity, earlier, and later and that all events are ontologically equal, regardless of when they occur. The tensed theory implies that the basic temporal concepts are of the future, present, and past and that present events have a superior ontological status to past or future events; present events exist, but past events no longer exist, and future events do not yet exist. For most of the twentieth century the debate between tenseless theorists and tensed theorists concerned whether tensed sentences (types or tokens) can be translated by tenseless sentences. If a noon, July 1, 1994, utterance of "the event E is no longer present" is translated by "the event E is earlier than noon, July 1, 1994," this would show that the tensed utterance conveys the same temporal information as the tenseless sentence—namely, that the event E is earlier than noon, July 1, 1994, and is equally as real as the events on noon, July 1, 1994. If the tensed utterance cannot be translated, then it arguably conveys a different sort of temporal information—namely, that event E no longer has presentness or no longer "exists" in the present tensed sense.

The major development in the 1980s and 1990s is the development of the so-called new tenseless theory of time and responses to this theory by defenders of the tensed theory. The new tenseless theory is that tensed sentences cannot be translated by tenseless sentences but that it is nonetheless true that tensed sentences convey only the temporal information conveyed by tenseless sentences. The new theory implies that tensed sentences have only tenseless truth conditions. For example, it may be argued that a noon, July 1, 1994, utterance of "the event E is no longer present" is true if and only if the event E occurs earlier than noon, July 1, 1994. Since facts involving the relations of earlier, later, and simultaneous are both necessary and sufficient to make tensed sentences true, there is no need to suppose that tensed sentences commit us to facts about what is present, past, or future.

The new tenseless theory of time appears to be correct insofar as it implies that tensed sentences cannot be translated by tenseless ones; however, its further implication that tensed sentences have only tenseless truth conditions may be challenged. It appears to be false, for example, that "Jane is running" as uttered at noon, July 1, 1994, is true if and only if Jane runs at noon, July 1, 1994. There are possible worlds in which the mentioned sentence-utterance, call it U, is true and yet it is false that Jane is running at noon, July 1, 1994. Suppose that times are sets of simultaneous events and that "noon, July 1, 1994" refers to the set of simultaneous events that is actually 1,993 years, six months and twelve hours after the conventionally assigned birthdate of Jesus. There is a possible world exactly similar to the actual world except for the fact that the utterance U belongs to a different set of simultaneous events, a set that includes every event included in noon, July 1, 1994 (which means it includes Jane's running), except for some minor difference; say, the set does not include the decision actually made by David to have lunch. Since U occurs simultaneously with Jane's running in this world, U is true; nonetheless, it does not occur at noon, July 1, 1994. Thus, a necessary condition of the truth of the utterance of "Jane is running" is not that it occur at noon, July 1, 1994.

How might a defender of the new tenseless theory respond to this argument? The defender might modify the tenseless theory so that it implies that the tenseless truth conditions are world indexed. It would imply that "Jane is running" as uttered at noon, July 1, 1994, in world W is true if and only if Jane runs at noon, July 1, 1994, in world W. Since the possible world is mentioned in the truth-condition sentence, the objection based on what occurs in a different possible world is avoided. However, this response does not seem satisfactory, since by mentioning the world the truth-condition sentence is no longer relevant to the meaning or semantic content of the utterance U. The reason for this is that the criterion for the truth of a world-indexed truth-condition sentence implies that any sentence with the same truth value as U in world W may be placed after the biconditional and we will have a true truth-condition sentence. For example, if Jane runs at the mentioned time and snow is white in world W, then "Jane is running" as uttered at noon, July 1, 1994, in world W is true if and only if snow is white in world W. But this sentence fails to give us any idea about the meaning of "Jane is running" and thus cannot be said to capture the temporal ontology implied by the sentence-utterance. In order for a truth-condition sentence to explain the meaning of a sentence-utterance, it must state the necessary and sufficient conditions of the utterance's truth in each world in which the utterance occurs, not simply in one world.

The above-mentioned problems with the new tenseless theory of time may be avoided by tenseless theorists if they reject the idea that the truth conditions of tensed sentence-utterances involve dates; they may argue instead that the truth conditions are facts about the temporal relation of the event described by the utterance to the utterance itself. But this version of the new theory faces a distinct set of problems. Suppose there are two simultaneous utterances U and S of the sentence type "Jane is running." These two utterances, or what is stated by these two utterances, are logically equivalent. But they are not logically equivalent if their truth conditions are facts about the temporal relation of the event reported by U and S. The tenseless truth condition of U would be "U occurs simultaneously with Jane's running," and the truth condition of S would be "S occurs simultaneously with Jane's running," but "U occurs simultaneously with Jane's running" neither entails nor is entailed by "S occurs simultaneously with Jane's running." The utterance U could have occurred even if S did not occur, and vice versa. Thus, this version of the new tenseless theory also does not appear to succeed.

If the new tenseless theory of time cannot succeed in supplying the requisite truth conditions, then it is reasonable to conclude that tensed utterances have tensed truth conditions. But different proponents of the tensed theory offer different accounts of the nature of these truth conditions. Some argue the conditions require that events possess transient properties of futurity, presentness, or pastness, but other defenders of the tensed theory argue that there are logical difficulties in the way of admitting such properties and claim that tenses do not commit us to any sort of properties, relations, or individuals. One problem with the latter version of the tensed theory is that its proponents have not explained what sort of item the tenses refer to or ascribe. If the "is" in "Jane is running" does not ascribe a property or relation and does not refer to an individual, then what is the ontological category of the item to which the "is" has a semantic relation?

The version of the tensed theory that implies that tenses ascribe properties of futurity, presentness, or pastness has an answer to this question, but it implies an infinite regress of property ascriptions. For example, if "Jane is running" is true just in case Jane's running exemplifies presentness, then the "exemplifies" must be present tensed, implying that the exemplification of presentness by Jane's running itself exemplifies presentness. But since the last occurrence of "exemplifies" is also present tensed, it implies a further exemplification of presentness, and so on infinitely. This regress is benign, but the fact nonetheless remains that this version of the tensed theory commits us to a complicated ontology. It is safe to say that no consensus has been reached as to the correct version of the tensed theory or whether it is better justified than the tenseless theory.

(SEE ALSO: *Time* [8])

Bibliography

Le Poidevin, R. *Change, Cause, and Contradiction: A Defense of the Tenseless Theory of Time.* Cambridge, 1992.

Mellor, D. H. *Real Time.* Cambridge, 1981.

Oaklander, L. N. *Temporal Relations and Temporal Becoming.* Lanham, MD, 1984.

Oaklander, L. N., and Q. Smith, eds. *The New Theory of Time.* New Haven, 1994. This book contains essays by M. Beer, B. Garrett, H. S. Hestevold, D. Kaplan, D. Kiernan-Lewis, M. MacBeath, D. H. Mellor, L. N. Oaklander, G. Schlesinger, Q. Smith, C. Williams, and D. Zeilicovici.

Priest, G. "Tense, *Tense,* and TENSE," *Analysis,* Vol. 46 (1987), 184–87.

Smart, J. J. C. "Time and Becoming," in P. van Inwagen, ed., *Time and Cause* (Boston, 1981).

Smith, Q. *Language and Time.* New York, 1993.

Smith, Q., and L. N. Oaklander. *Time, Change, and Freedom.* New York, 1995.

Sośa, E. "The Status of Becoming: What Is Happening Now," *Journal of Philosophy,* Vol. 77 (1979), 26–42.

QUENTIN SMITH

TIME, DIRECTION OF. Our experience of the temporality of things seems to be an experience of a radically asymmetric structure of the world. We have an access to knowledge of past events that is not given us to events in the future. That is, we have records and memories of past events but not of future events. Our concerns with the past (regret, for example) are radically unlike our concerns for the future (anxious anticipation, for example). Intuitively we take it that the direction of causation or determination among events is always from past to future. Some also have metaphysical intuitions about the asymmetry. The past, they say, is "fixed" and has "determinate reality," whereas the future remains ontologically merely a realm of open possibilities.

One might take these asymmetric features of TIME [8] as irreducible primitives and our awareness of them as also immune to further analysis or understanding. Or one might argue for some basic asymmetric metaphysical structure of time as grounding all of the asymmetries noted above. The idea of "branching" models, familiar from tense logics, is sometimes proposed as our clue to this fundamental structure of time.

Alternatively, one could seek some naturalistic account of the asymmetries, holding them to be founded on a pervasive asymmetry in time of physical processes as characterized by fundamental physics. Such an account, if successful, would go some way to resolving the mystery of the direction of time. But carrying out this reductivist program is not a simple task.

Several fundamental asymmetries occur in the world described by physics. Alleged lawlike time asymmetries present in weak interactions do not seem suitable for grounding the intuitive time asymmetries. More promising are the asymmetries of ENTROPY [2] increase in thermodynamics and that asymmetry of radiation in which we encounter outbound but not inbound spherically coherent patterns of wave radiation. No agreed-upon explanatory account for these asymmetries yet exists, although the mainstream of physical thought seeks an origin for them in deep facts about the cosmological structure of the universe.

How are these physical asymmetries of systems in time supposed to ground our intuitive temporal asymmetries? One can easily be misled by the familiar example, that of our using entropic facts to determine if the film of an entropy-changing process is being run in the correct time order, into thinking that the proposal is that we somehow determine the order in time of events in our experience by consulting entropic facts about the events, a claim that is surely false. But it is not such an epistemically motivated claim that the naturalist is making.

Rather, the claim is that the facts about the physical asymmetries fully account, in an explanatory way, for all of our intuitive asymmetries, such as having memories or records of the past and not the future or taking causation to be future directed. The analogy is often drawn to our use of the facts about gravity as a force to explain everything there is to explain about our intuitions about up and down spatial directions. Just as we now realize that "down" is just the local direction of the gravitational force, as it is said, we should also realize that "future" is just the local direction of time in which entropy is increasing for isolated systems.

It should be noted that it is not enough for such an account that there be a lawlike or quasi-lawlike correlation of the physical process with the intuitive temporal direction. The fact that some weak interaction processes are lawlike asymmetric with regard to left–right asymmetry does not mean that our intuitive distinction between left- and right-handed objects is somehow explanatorily grounded on the asymmetry of the weak interaction processes. For the naturalistic program to be plausible one would need a set of explanations that invoked the physical asymmetry and that accounted for the asymmetries of records, memories, and causation and that even explained the origin of our direct awareness of the time order of events in our experience, much as gravity's workings on the inner ear accounts for our ability to determine noninferentially which direction is downward at our location.

One important proposal for carrying out the naturalistic program has its origin with H. REICHENBACH [7]. The basic structure of the program is to argue that records of the past are systems in the world with surprisingly low "macroentropy" given their environments (such as the famous footprint on the beach whose sand grains have an order not possessed by the surrounding randomly distributed grains). The presence of this low macroentropy must, it is argued, be accounted for by means of a past interaction of the system with some outside system (such as the foot that pressed the footprint into the otherwise smooth beach). Such systems then serve as records of their past interactions. The fact that the explaining interactions are all in the same time direction, the direction we call the past, is accounted for by the physical asymmetry of entropic processes. Other asymmetries are then grounded on the asymmetries of records. This imaginative proposal has been subjected to skeptical criticism that notes, for example, high marcoentropy records (surprisingly disordered states) and the difficulties encountered in deriving the macroentropy asymmetry from the underlying physics of microentropy asymmetry.

Another imaginative proposal is that of D. Lewis. He analyzes CAUSATION [2; S] in terms of counterfactual conditionals and outlines our intuitive grounds for stipulating when such CONDITIONALS [S] are true. Considerations of the multiply correlated but physically spread-out consequences of a single local cause (such as occurs in wave spreading) leads, he claims, to a temporal asymmetry of our evaluation of the truth of counterfactual conditionals in cases such as this and hence to a temporal asymmetry in our notion of the causal relation.

Even were the naturalistic program successfully carried out, the issue of how to deal with our immediately sensed time of direct experience in a world of physically asymmetric time remains, as A. EDDINGTON [2] emphasized, problematic.

(SEE ALSO: *Philosophy of Physics,* and *Philosophy of Science* [S])

Bibliography

Boltzmann, L. "On Zermelo's Paper 'On the Mechanical Explanation of Irreversible Processes,' " in S. Brush, ed., *Kinetic Theory,* Vol. 2, *Irreversible Processes* (Oxford, 1966).

Davies, P. *The Physics of Time Asymmetry.* Berkeley, 1974.

Earman, J. "An Attempt to Add a Little Direction to 'The Problem of the Direction of Time,' " *Philosophy of Science,* Vol. 41 (1974), 15–47.

Eddington, A. *The Nature of the Physical World.* Cambridge, 1929.

Grünbaum, A. "The Anisotropy of Time," in *Philosophical Problems of Space and Time,* 2d ed. (Dordrecht, 1973).

Horwich, P. *Asymmetries in Time.* Cambridge, MA, 1987.

Lewis, D. "Counterfactual Dependence and Time's Arrow," in *Philosophical Papers,* Vol. 2 (Oxford, 1986).

Mehlberg, H. *Time, Causality, and Quantum Theory.* Dordrecht, 1980.

Reichenbach, H. *The Direction of Time.* Berkeley, 1956.

Sklar, L. "The Direction of Time," in *Physics and Chance* (Cambridge, 1993).

———. "Up and Down, Left and Right, Past and Future," in *Philosophy and Spacetime Physics* (Berkeley, 1985).

LAWRENCE SKLAR

TIME CONSCIOUSNESS. HUSSERL's [4; S] analysis of temporality proceeds at three levels: (1) objective (or the appearing) time of worldly events and objects; (2) "immanent" (or "internal") time of the acts and contents of consciousness through which worldly objects appear, such as the tones or sense impressions; (3) the temporal constitution of consciousness itself. Since all analyses take place within the constraints introduced by the method of phenomenological reduction, the "objectivity" of events analyzed and their actual temporal location are not the themes of Husserl's analysis. Rather, his concern is the elements involved in the very meaning of such events and objects, whether they exist or not. Husserl attempts to show how the temporality of the first level can be traced back to the second, and then how the second of these levels can be traced back to the ultimate or absolute foundation of the time-constituting flow of consciousness. In the lectures published as *Zur Phänomenologie des inneren Zeitbewußtseins (1893–1917),* Husserl concentrates on the second and third levels. His analyses focus on time as temporality—that is, as a dimension of the appearance of temporal objects and of consciousness.

He demonstrates how immanent temporal objects are all characterized by duration (*Dauer*) or temporal extension. All individual objects—be they events or things—last as unities over time. Be the span of their duration ever so small, their existence extends beyond merely punctual temporal location. Not all objects are necessarily temporal objects, however. Ideal objects such as mathematical propositions are not temporal, but the corresponding acts of grasping them are temporal and as such do have duration. As extended, the appearance of temporal objects is essentially characterized in terms of "now," "before," and "after," which correspond to the temporal modes of "present," "past," and "future." This holds even for past events or future events, which do not occur in the now, for their imagined or purported existence in the past still must involve a past or future now around which the just-having-been of its immediate past and the just-about-to-be of its immediate future are clustered, for no-longer or not-yet make sense only with reference to some past, present, or future, some real or imagined now.

Husserl points out, however, that the now is in turn also not a self-enclosed moment that can be conceived without reference to the other two fundamental dimensions of temporality. The now appears always with a temporal fringe or horizon. The now taken as a moment around which past and future coalesce is never strictly an isolated point; indeed, the very idea of time as a point is a merely limiting concept that is never experienced in itself. For conscious life every now also involves the consciousness of a having-been that has immediately preceded it and a not-yet that is about to become. Thus the "now" for consciousness is always an extended "living presence" that as the "originary temporal field" includes "no-longer" and "not-yet."

One of Husserl's primary contributions is his detailed discussion of the mode of the no-longer that is the immediate horizon for the now. Husserl departs from his teacher BRENTANO [1] in stressing that the awareness of this mode of the past, "retention," does not involve memory. MEMORY [5] is a making-present again what was no longer immediately present for consciousness; retention, by contrast, is the lingering of an impression that is no longer present as now but as just having-been, without yet having sunk off into nonpresence, so that it is a mode of impressional rather than representational consciousness. For instance, as one hears a melody, a note "runs off" into the retentional past as it is replaced by a new one, without, however, disappearing from consciousness, since it would otherwise be impossible to hear a melody as such. Similarly, there arises at each moment a new anticipation of the coming note (a "protention") emanating from the present, and that Husserl calls the "primal impression" to distinguish the way it is present from that of retentive or protentive impressional consciousness. Husserl's own analyses concentrate on the retentive aspect of perception. He shows how the "sinking back" or retention involves an interplay of sameness and difference.

As the perceptual content at each moment sinks back into the past, it sinks back in a determinate temporal position of before and after with regard to the moments that preceded and followed it. At the same time its position, along with those of its temporal neighbors, is constantly changing in regard to the continuously newly arising now of primal impression as it slowly sinks back into the nonpresence of forgetting. The former determinate aspect of temporal position and the possibility of coming back to it over and over in memory is the presupposition for the notion of objective time; the latter aspect makes clear how all time-consciousness, even of objective time, has an essentially subjective component.

The temporal modes of impressional consciousness pertain to the temporality of immanent temporal objects. Underlying them, however, is the temporality of consciousness itself. In attending to an immanent temporal object, one is aware of the threefold temporal intentional dimensions of the object in retention, primal impression, and protention. One's awareness of the past, for instance, is also itself a form of now-awareness, since it is taking place at a specific point in the present that one is aware of as different from that past and even from previous nows with regard to which the past had already been past before now, just as one's anticipation is an anticipation right now, one that itself will sink into the past at the next moment as the future becomes the present. At that point I may be aware of myself as now hearing what I am retentively aware of as just having anticipated. One constitutes not only a unity of an object through its appearances across time as one and the same object (vertical intentionality—*Längsintentionalität*, Husserl calls it), but also the unity of consciousness across the differences in objects that appear for consciousness as one and the same consciousness (horizontal intentionality—*Ouerintentionalität*). Moreover, this unified consciousness itself has an invariant temporal structure through which temporal objects and consciousness itself are constituted as unities. The name for this structure itself is "absolute primordially constituting consciousness," a constantly changing unity that is beyond change and, at least according to later manuscripts, is therefore best described as outside of time and as the ultimate ground for time-consciousness and the objects constituted through it and its modifications. (SEE ALSO: *Consciousness in Anglo-American Philosophy; Consciousness in Phenomenology: Husserl;* and *Consciousness in Phenomenology: Sartre* [S])

Bibliography

Bernet, R., I. Kern, and E. Marbach. *Edmund Husserl: An Introduction to His Thinking.* Evanston, IL, 1993. Chap. 3, sec. 2. Describes the development of Husserl's position on the nature of absolute time-constituting consciousness and provides a glimpse into the positions outlined in research manuscripts not included in the published volume.

Brough, J. "Husserl's Phenomenology of Time-Consciousness," in J. Mohanty and W. McKenna, eds., *Husserl's Phenomenology: A Textbook* (Lanham, MD, 1989). A clear introduction and overview.

Husserl, E. *Zur Phänomenologie des inneren Zeitbewußtseins (1893–1917). Husserliana,* Vol. 10, ed. R. Boehm. The Hague, 1966. Translated by J. Brough as *Concerning the Phenomenology of Internal Time Consciousness.* Dordrecht, 1990. The only extended treatment by Husserl of the issues associated with time-consciousness published up until now. The introductions by Boehm and Brough are helpful guides to understanding the construction of the text as published.

THOMAS NENON

TRACE. The notion of the trace has become a focal point of Continental philosophy's contestation of the tradition of Western metaphysics since PLATO [6; S]. Because the Greek philosophical tradition was construed by Martin HEIDEGGER [3; S] as a unity organized around the idea of being as presence, the preferred formulation for the trace is of "a past that has never been present." The phrase is found in Maurice MERLEAU-PONTY's [5; S] *Phenomenology of Perception,* where it describes the unreflective fund of experience on which reflection draws. Jacques DERRIDA [S] adopted it in "Violence and Metaphysics" to explicate the trace in the work of Emmanuel LEVINAS [S], who immediately introduced it into his own account.

Derrida has employed various strategies to show that the trace challenges conventional thought. For example, in *Of Grammatology,* when he introduced the concept of an originary trace or arche-trace, he underlined the fact that it represents a contradiction because a trace, which is ordinarily possible only as an effect, is here posited as an origin. The point is to problematize the language and procedures of transcendental philosophy, especially transcendental phenomenology, on which the thought of the trace nevertheless depends for its articulation. This was already Levinas's aim when he appealed to the trace in his account of the possibility of ethics in terms of the face of the Other. The trace is more than a sign of remoteness; it is an irrecuperable absence. Levinas was serving notice that the face surpasses the limits of phenomenology and yet can be approached only through phenomenology.

In "Différance," a lecture that summarizes many of his most important studies up to 1967, Derrida took the notion of trace from Levinas and joined it with that of other thinkers who, according to his account, serve to define our epoch, most notably Heidegger, SIGMUND FREUD (3; S), and Saussure. According to Heidegger, the trace of the ontological difference is effaced within Western metaphysics; it sinks without trace. Derrida makes Freud's failure to apply the effaceability of the trace to all traces a critical element of his reading, but at the same time he explicitly recognizes the unconscious as that which transcends transcendental phenomenology, just as the structure of delay in the sense of deferred effect *(Nachträglichkeit)* cannot be construed as a variation on the present. Finally, by examining what is implied in Saussure's account, Derrida concludes that the trace produces difference and infects the thought of pure identity.

Although in the 1960s it seemed that Derrida developed his account of the trace by gathering together the thought of each of these thinkers, he subsequently moved away from this largely parasitic approach. Most notably in *Cinders,* Derrida took the impossible thought of the trace to a different level by explicating it as ashes, with clear reference to the Holocaust. In this way the trace comes to define our epoch even more definitively. (SEE ALSO: *Supplement* [S])

Bibliography

Derrida, J. "La Différance," *Bulletin de la société française de philosophie,* Vol. 62 (1968), 73–101. Translated by Alan Bass as "Differance" in *Margins of Philosophy.* Chicago, 1982.

———. *Feu la cendre.* Paris, 1987. Translated by Ned Lukacher as *Cinders.* Lincoln, NE, 1987.

Levinas, E. "La Trace de l'autre," *Tijdschrift voor Filosofie,* Vol. 25 (1963), 605–23. Translated by Alphonso Lingis as "The Trace of the Other," in Mark Taylor, ed., *Deconstruction in Context* (Chicago, 1986).

ROBERT BERNASCONI

TRANSCENDENTAL LOGIC. The first aim of Edmund HUSSERL [4; S] in his early *Logical Investigations* was to provide an intentional explication of the proper sense of formal logic. In *Formal and Transcendental Logic* (1929) the problematic was resumed for two reasons: (1) as formal logic appears in the empirical sciences (and in all knowledge of experience) as the most general theory of judgments or connections between judgments, an inquiry is needed into how its normative function is to be understood—that is, how ideal a priori forms of reason can determine what is contingent and empirical in such a way that every positing of being, in abiding by logical laws, secures the necessary conditions of its rationality and truth; (2) formal logic cannot be reduced to the apophantic logic of predicative judgment because the apophantic categories of meaning (such as judgment, proposition, concept, truth) must themselves emerge from categories of objects in general—that is, from formal ontology. In Husserl's PHENOMENOLOGY [6; S] the ontological question of the sense of formal logic is at the same time a transcendental question. How can ontological status be assigned to empty formal objectivity? The region of being for the object in general cannot be independent of the subject, for otherwise phenomenology would be a form of logical Platonism. Rather, the object in general can acquire no being apart from the logical laws. The actual sense of formal lawfulness is therefore to be conceived genetically, in terms of a sense-bestowing transcendental subjectivity. In transcendental logic the logical formations arising in the active performance of judgment, as well as the many-leveled syntheses of judgment, are traced back through all the preceding levels of precategorical constitution and the basic occurrences of passive unification. Not eternal forms, but specific formal structures of reason (sources of habituality, as specific manners of intending) account for the fact that logical constructions have an enduring sense that reaches beyond the individual acts. These specific forms are sources of habituality and, as specific manners of intending, are identifiable at the level of intersubjective experience. Even though he was able to accomplish only a small part of the work required by the constitutive-genetic tasks in logic (in particular, the more basic evidence that grounds logical evidence), Husserl believed that transcendental logic, once completed, would be the final science clarifying all possible achievement under the idea of reason. Furthermore, the analyses pertaining to the formal theory of science would have to be supplemented with further analyses pertaining to a material doctrine of science; only this clarification would make possible the phenomenological insight into the determinability of the real through the ideal.

(SEE ALSO: *Judgment and Experience,* and *Psychology and Logic* [S])

Bibliography

Bachelard, S. *A Study of Husserl's Formal and Transcendental Logic.* Trans. by L. Embree. Evanston, IL, 1968.

Husserl, E. *Formal and Transcendental Logic.* Trans. by D. Cairns. The Hague, 1969.

Seebohm, T. "Phenomenology of Logic and the Problem of Modalizing," *Journal of the British Society for Phenomenology,* 19 (1988), 235–51.

PIERRE KERSZBERG

TRUTH. All mainstream theories of truth—correspondence, coherence, pragmatist—presuppose that 'truth' is the name of a substantive, explanatorily significant property. The nature of truth may be difficult to explain, but that truth has a nature is taken for granted. The thought seems to be that, just as a scientist might want to explain what it is that makes some substances acidic, so a philosopher will want to explain what makes true sentences (propositions, beliefs, etc.) true. However, there are alternative theories, now generally called deflationary, that challenge this preconception. For proponents of such views, there is no analogy between 'true' and terms such as 'acidic'. The predicate 'true' is an expressive convenience, not the name of a property requiring deep analysis.

Two factors incline philosophers toward deflationism: the existence of what seem to be insuperable objections to all traditional theories of truth and the thought that the behavior and significance of 'true' can be quite satisfactorily accounted for on a rather minimal basis. Indeed, because deflationary theories are so minimalist, it might be better to speak of deflationary views or approaches rather than theories.

An early version of such an approach to truth is RAMSEY's [7] redundancy theory, according to which "It is true that Caesar was murdered" means no more than that Caesar was murdered. Any difference is entirely "stylistic": for example, we may use "It is true that" to speak more emphatically. Because it stresses the use of 'true' in performing such special speech acts, this approach is sometimes also called the performative theory.

More recent views, such as QUINE's [7; S] disquotational theory, do not claim "that p" and "It is true that p" are synonymous. Rather, what matters about 'true' is given by certain logical equivalences. Thus, "All that glisters is not gold" is true if and only if all that glisters is not gold; "France is hexagonal" is true if and only if France is hexagonal; and so on. Appending "is true" to a quoted sentence is just like canceling the quotation marks ("disquotation"). Thus, 'true' offers a way of replacing talk about the world with logically equivalent talk about words. However, a move to the level of talk about words ("semantic ascent") gives us new things to generalize over (i.e., linguistic objects, sentences), thereby enabling us to express agreement and disagreement with sentences that we cannot specify—for example, because we do not know exactly what they are ("What the President said is true") or because there are too many of them ("Every sentence of the form 'P or not P' is true"). Accordingly, 'true' is an indispensable logical device.

The disquotational theory treats 'true' as a predicate of sentences. A similar account of the meaning and utility of the truth predicate can be given, mutatis mutandis, if we prefer to think of 'true' as predicated of propositions. The axioms of such a theory will be: the proposition "All that glisters is not gold" is true if and only if all that glisters is not gold, and so forth. Horwich's minimal theory takes this form.

Notice that while, on the redundancy/performative theory, to think of truth as any sort of property is, in Ramsey's words, just "linguistic muddle," on the disquotational and minimal theories we can see truth as a property, a complete theory of which is given by the appropriate equivalences. Of course, we cannot write this "theory" down, since it will have infinitely many axioms. But since these axioms share a common structure, we can indicate more or less what they are. (Only more or less because, without some restrictions on admissible substitutions, a schema like " 'p' is true if and only if p" will generate semantic paradoxes.)

TARSKI's [8] semantic theory, in its original form, can also be considered deflationary. For although Tarski defines "true-in-L" (where L is a particular formalized language) in terms of a generalized notion of reference (again for L), which he calls "satisfaction," he defines the relation of "satisfies" in a highly deflationary manner. However, though strongly influenced by Tarski's work, DAVIDSON's [S] view of truth is *not* deflationary. Davidson can sound like a deflationist, in that he denies the need for an analysis of truth and so rejects all traditional theories. But he insists that truth plays an indispensable explanatory role in the theory of meaning. He therefore concludes that we must accept the concept of truth as a primitive.

There are many objections to deflationism. Some, mostly rather technical, concern whether a deflationary account can even be given an adequate formulation. For example, disquotational truth, as described above, does not immediately apply to sentences involving indexical expressions ("I," "here," etc.) or to sentences of foreign languages. This latter problem is particularly significant, since the natural response is to expand the disquotation schema, allowing us to substitute on the right-hand side proper translations of foreign sentences quoted on the left: thus, "La France a huit côtés" is true if and only if France is octagonal. The question then arises as to whether we can explain "proper translation" without invoking a prior understanding of truth. A related problem arises for the minimal theory in connection with explaining the identity conditions for propositions.

However, perhaps the deepest source of skepticism with respect to deflationism is sheer incredulity in the face of its claim that truth is not a theoretically significant concept. Many (perhaps most) philosophers see truth as playing a crucial explanatory role in METAPHYSICS, EPISTEMOLOGY, PHILOSOPHY OF LANGUAGE [S], or even psychology. Deflationists have no master argument to prove them wrong. All they can do is to examine each purported explanatory use of truth and try to argue either that the explanation in question does not require a substantive notion of truth, that there is really nothing to explain, or that there is an alternative explanation that does not invoke truth at all.

" 'What is truth?' said jesting Pilate and would not stay for an answer." If deflationists are to be believed, he did not miss much.

(SEE ALSO: *Coherence Theory of Truth,* and *Correspondence Theory of Truth* [2]; *Performative Theory of Truth,* and *Pragmatic Theory of Truth* [6]; and *Propositions* [S])

Bibliography

Davidson, D. "The Structure and Content of Truth," *Journal of Philosophy,* Vol. 87 (1990), 280–328.

Field, H. "The Deflationary Conception of Truth," in C. Wright and G. McDonald, eds., *Fact, Science, and Morality* (New York, 1987).

Horwich, P. *Truth.* Oxford, 1990.

Leeds, S. "Theories of Reference and Truth," *Erkenntnis,* Vol. 13 (1978), 111–29.

Putnam, H. "On Truth," in L. Cauman et al., eds., *How Many Questions?* (Indianapolis, 1983).

Quine, W. V. O. *Pursuit of Truth.* Cambridge, MA, 1990.

Ramsey, F. "Facts and Propositions," *Proceedings of the Aristotelian Society,* supp. vol. 7 (1927), 153–70; repr. in D. H. Mellor, ed., *F. P. Ramsey, Philosophical Papers* (Cambridge, 1990).

Soames, S. "What Is a Theory of Truth?" *Journal of Philosophy,* Vol. 81 (1984), 411–29.

Strawson, P. F. "Truth," *Proceedings of the Aristotelian Society,* supp. vol. 24 (1950), 125–26.

Tarski, A. "The Semantic Conception of Truth," *Philosophy and Phenomenological Research,* Vol. 4 (1944), 341–75.

Williams, M. "Do We (Epistemologists) Need a Theory of Truth?" *Philosophical Topics,* Vol. 14 (1986), 223–42.

Wright, C. *Truth and Objectivity.* Cambridge, MA, 1992.

MICHAEL WILLIAMS

TRUTH IN HEIDEGGER. HEIDEGGER's [3; S] treatment of TRUTH [S] embodies two aspirations: (1) to pinpoint the specific phenomenon that goes by that name and offer a definitive analysis of it; (2) to show that it is not an isolated phenomenon but so deeply intertwined with LANGUAGE [4; S], history, awareness, and BEING [1] that any study of truth will lead into all the principal themes of thought.

The prevailing academic philosophy of Heidegger's youth had located the problem of truth within the theory of knowledge, while the theory of value was usually thought to deal with noncognitive questions. In particular, it was the judgment that could be true or false. Neo-Kantians, phenomenologists, and others debated about the conditions for the possibility of truth in judgments. In the 1920s Heidegger intervened critically in these debates. He rejected the doctrine of mental representations; he submitted such concepts as correspondence and adequation to critical analysis; he showed the weakness of most views of the "subject–object relation." It was not a Nietzschean perspectivism or SKEPTICISM [7; S] he was seeking, however, but a new kind of positive PHENOMENOLOGY [6; S]. The judgment (or, better, the statement, *Aussage*) does not represent a thing but discloses it, meaning (1) that the thing itself, not a mere intermediate principle, is being targeted and hit; (2) that the thing had been shrouded in concealment before the statement was made; (3) that the statement lets it be seen (i.e., overcomes the shroud so that the thing is accessible to us); (4) that some concealment of it nevertheless perseveres. The statement's power to communicate is grounded in this primordial power to disclose, and Heidegger claims that, when we call a statement true, what we mean is that it discloses. He encapsulates his point in an etymology: the Greek word *aletheia,* usually translated "truth," originally meant "unconcealedness." It follows that truth is always temporal or historical—an event of disclosure—not a timeless correspondence. There are no eternal truths.

Because Heidegger addressed himself first of all to an ongoing tradition of academic epistemology, it is not difficult to bring his thought into dialogue with later variants of analytic philosophy. It can well be asked whether his doctrine of disclosure is able to abandon entirely all reference to correspondence. If "*p* is true" means "*p* discloses," we can ask, Discloses *what*? Whether Heidegger can account for mathematical truth is another question that has had considerable discussion.

Being and Time opposed the epistemology of its day with the claim that neither the judgment nor the statement was the primordial locus of truth. They can be true only because humanity itself *(Dasein)* from the beginning discloses itself to itself, accomplishing therewith the disclosure of the world, the things of the world, and the very being of the self, the world, and the things. Statements and their truth are derivative from the "truth of *Dasein.*" In the decades after *Being and Time,* Heidegger put less emphasis on the theme of *Dasein,* yet he continued to insist on the derivativeness of "statement-truth." The things themselves, quite in advance of our statements about them, incorporated truth (i.e., unconcealedness) in their very being. More primordial still was the unveiling of being itself. Heidegger never neglected to point out the concealment of things that continued to shadow their unconcealment and the hiddenness of being that accompanied its unveiling. This linked the theme of truth to history, for every disclosure has an epochal limitation, and macrohistorical meditation can chart the limits of an epoch according to what is unveiled and what is left hidden.

Bibliography

Heidegger, M. *Being and Time,* trans. J. Macquarrie and E. Robinson. Oxford, 1967.

———. "On the Essence of Truth," trans. J. Sallis, in M. Heidegger, *Basic Writings,* ed. D. Krell. New York, 1977.

Kockelmans, J. J. *On the Truth of Being: Reflections on Heidegger's Later Philosophy.* Bloomington, IN, 1984.

Graeme Nicholson

TRUTHLIKENESS. Truth [S] is the aim of inquiry. Despite this, progress in an inquiry does not always consist in supplanting falsehoods with truths. The history of science is replete with cases of falsehoods supplanting other falsehoods. If such transitions are to constitute epistemic progress, then it must be possible for one falsehood better to realize the aim of inquiry—be more truthlike, be closer to the truth, or have more verisimilitude—than another. The notion of truthlikeness is thus fundamental for any theory of knowledge that endeavors to take our epistemic limitations seriously without embracing epistemic pessimism.

Given that truthlikeness is not only a much-needed notion but rich and interesting, it is surprising that it has attracted less attention than the simpler notion of truth. The explanation is twofold. First, if knowledge requires truth, then falsehoods cannot constitute knowledge. The high value of knowledge has obscured other epistemic values such as the comparative value of acquiring more truthlike theories. Second, if knowledge requires justification, then the notion of probability often takes center stage. There has been a long and deep confusion between the notions of subjective probability (seemingly true) and the notion of truthlikeness (similarity to the truth; Popper [6], 1972). This, together with the high degree of development of the theory of probability, obscured the necessity for a theory of truthlikeness.

Sir Karl Popper was the first to notice the importance of the notion (1972, chap. 10 and Addenda). Popper was long a lonely advocate of both scientific realism [7; S] and fallibilism: that, although science aims at the truth, most theories have turned out to be false and current theories are also likely to be false. This seems a bleak vision indeed and fails to do justice to the evident progress in science. Popper realized that the picture would be less bleak if a succession of false (and falsified) theories could nevertheless constitute steady progress toward the truth. Further, even if actually refuted by some of the data, the general observational accuracy of a false theory might be good evidence for the theory's approximate truth, or high degree of truthlikeness. That our theories, even if not true, are close to the truth, may be the best explanation available for the accuracy of their observable consequences (Boyd, 1983; Putnam [S], 1978, chap. 2).

Note that truthlikeness is no more an epistemic notion than is truth. How truthlike a theory is depends only on the theory's content and the world, not on our knowledge. The problem of our epistemic access to the truthlikeness of theories is quite different from the logically prior problem of what truthlikeness consists in.

Popper proposed a bold and simple account of truthlikeness: that theory B is more truthlike than theory A if B entails all the truths that A entails, A entails all the falsehoods that B entails, and either B entails at least one more truth than A or A entails at least one more falsehood than B (Popper, 1972).

This simple idea undoubtedly has virtues. Let the *Truth* be that theory that entails all and only truths (relative to some subject matter). On Popper's account the Truth is more truthlike than any other theory, and that is as it should be. The aim of an inquiry is not just some truth or other. Rather, it is the truth, the whole truth, and nothing but the truth about some matter—in short, the Truth—and the Truth realizes that aim better than any other theory. The account also clearly separates truthlikeness and probability. The Truth generally has a very low degree of (subjective) probability, but it definitely has maximal truthlikeness. Furthermore, the account yields an interesting ranking of truths—the more a truth entails, the closer it is to the Truth.

Popper's account also has some defects. For example, it does not permit any falsehood to be closer to the Truth than any truth. (Compare NEWTON's [5] theory of motion with denial of ARISTOTLE's [1; S] theory.) But its most serious defect is that it precludes any false theory being more truthlike than any other (Miller, 1974; Tichý, 1974). The flaw is simply demonstrated. Suppose theory A entails a falsehood, say *f*, and we attempt to improve on A by adding a new truth, say *t*. Then the extended theory entails both *t* and *f* and hence entails their conjunction: *t*&*f*. But *t*&*f* is a falsehood not entailed by A. Similarly, suppose A is false and we attempt to improve it by removing one of its falsehoods, say *f*. Let *g* be any falsehood entailed by the reduced theory B. Then *g*⊃*f* is a truth entailed by A but not B. (If B entailed both *g* and *g*⊃*f*, it would entail *f*.) So truths cannot be added without adding falsehoods, nor falsehoods subtracted without subtracting truths.

Maybe this lack of commensurability could be overcome by switching to quantitative measures of true and false logical content. Indeed, Popper proposed such accounts, but the problem they face is characteristic of the content approach, the central idea of which is that truthlikeness is a simple function of two factors—truth value and logical content/strength (Kuipers, 1982; Miller, 1978). If truthlikeness were such a function, then among false theories truthlikeness would vary with logical strength alone. There are only two well-behaved options here: truthlikeness either increases monotonically with logical strength, or else it decreases. But strengthening a false theory does not itself guarantee either an increase or a decrease in truthlikeness. If it is hot, rainy, and windy (h&r&w), then both of the following are logical strengthenings of the false claim that it is cold (~h): it is cold, rainy, and windy (~h&r&w); it is cold, dry, and still (~h&~r&~w). The former involves an increase, and the latter a decrease, in truthlikeness.

A quite different approach takes the likeness in truthlikeness seriously (Hilpinen, 1976; Niiniluoto, 1987; Oddie, 1981; Tichý, 1974, 1976). An inquiry involves a collection of possibilities, or possible worlds, one of which is actual. Each theory selects a range of possibilities from this collection—that theory's candidates for actuality. A proposition is true if it includes the actual world in its range. Each complete proposition includes just one such candidate. The Truth, the target of the inquiry, is the complete true proposition—that proposition that selects the actual world alone (*see* PROPOSITIONS [S]). If worlds vary in their degree of likeness to each other, then a complete proposition is the more truthlike the more like actuality is the world it selects. This is a promising start, but we need to extend it to incomplete propositions. The worlds in the range of an incomplete proposition typically vary in their degree of likeness to actuality, and the degree of truthlikeness of the proposition should be some kind of function thereof: average likeness is a simple suggestion that yields intuitively pleasing results. (For a survey, see Niiniluoto, 1987, chap. 6.) The framework can also be utilized in the analysis of related notions such as approximate truth or closeness to being true (Hilpinen, 1976; Weston, 1992).

There are two related problems with this program. The first concerns the measure of likeness between worlds. It would be a pity if this simply had to be postulated. The second concerns the size and complexity of worlds and the number of worlds that propositions typically select. Fortunately, there is available a handy logical tool for cutting the complexity down to a finite, manageable size (Niiniluoto, 1977; Tichý, 1974, 1976). We can work with kinds of worlds rather than whole words. The kinds at issue are specified by the constituents of first-order logic (Hintikka, 1965), a special case of which are the maximal conjunctions of propositional logic (like h&r&w, ~h&r&w, ~h&~r&~w). Constituents have two nice features. First, each depicts in its surface structure the underlying structure of a kind of world. And, second, like the propositional constituents, they are highly regular in their surface structure, enabling degree of likeness between constituents to be extracted. (The world in which it is cold, rainy, and windy [~h&r&w] is more like the world in which it is hot, rainy, and windy [h&r&w] than it is like the world in which it is cold, dry, and still [~h&~r&~w]. In the propositional case, just add up the surface differences.) Since every statement is logically equivalent to a disjunction of constituents, we have here the elements of a quite general account of truthlikeness, one that can be extended well beyond standard first-order logic (Oddie, 1986, chap. 5).

Not just any features count in a judgment of overall likeness. Such judgments clearly presuppose a class of respects of comparison. The possibilities specified by h&r&w and ~h&r&w differ in one weather respect and agree on two, whereas those specified by h&r&w and ~h&~r&~w differ in all three. But now consider the following two states (where ≡ is the material biconditional): hot≡rainy, and hot≡ windy. The possibility specified by h&r&w can equally be specified by h&(h≡r)&(h≡w); ~h&r&w by ~h&~(h≡r)&~(h≡w); and ~h&~r&~w by ~h&(h≡r)&(h≡w). Counting differences in terms of these new features does not line up with our intuitive judgments of likeness. Unless there is some objective reason for counting the hot-rainy-windy respects rather than the hot-(hot≡rainy)-(hot≡windy) respects, truthlikeness (unlike truth) seems robbed of objectivity.

This is the main objection to the likeness program (Miller, 1974). If sound, however, it would reach far indeed, for perfectly analogous arguments would establish a similar shortcoming in a host of important notions—similarity in general, structure, confirmation, disconfirmation, fit of theory to data, accuracy, and change (Oddie, 1986, chap. 6). The advocate of the objectivity of such notions simply has to grasp the nettle and maintain that some properties, relations, and magnitudes are more basic or fundamental than others. Realists, of course, should not find the sting too sharp to bear.
(SEE ALSO: *Philosophy of Science,* and *Confirmation Theory* [S])

Bibliography

Boyd, R. "On the Current Status of the Issue of Scientific Realism," *Erkenntniss,* Vol. 19 (1983), 45–90.

Hilpinen, R. "Approximate Truth and Truthlikeness," in M. Przelecki, K. Szaniawski, and R. Wojcicki, eds., *Formal Methods in the Methodology of the Empirical Sciences* (Dordrecht, 1976).

Hintikka, J. "Distributive Normal Forms in the Calculus of Predicates," in J. N. Crossley and M. A. Dummett, eds., *Formal Systems and Recursive Functions* (Amsterdam, 1965).

Kuipers, T. A. F. "Approaching Descriptive and Theoretical Truth," *Erkenntnis,* Vol. 18 (1982), 343–87.

———, ed. *What Is Closer-to-the-Truth?* Amsterdam, 1987.

Miller, D. "Popper's Qualitative Theory of Verisimilitude," *British Journal for the Philosophy of Science,* Vol. 25 (1974), 166–77.

———. "Distance from the Truth as a True Distance," in J. Hintikka, I. Niiniluoto, and E. Saarinen, eds., *Essays in Mathematical and Philosophical Logic* (Dordrecht, 1978).

Niiniluoto, I. "On the Truthlikeness of Generalizations," in R. E. Butts and J. Hintikka, eds., *Basic Problems in Methodology and Linguistics* (Dordrecht, 1977).

———. *Truthlikeness.* Dordrecht, 1987.

Oddie, G. "Verisimilitude Reviewed," *British Journal for the Philosophy of Science,* Vol. 32 (1981), 237–65.

———. *Likeness to Truth.* Dordrecht, 1986.

Popper, K. R. *Conjectures and Refutations,* 4th ed. London, 1972.

Putnam, H. *Meaning and the Moral Sciences.* London, 1978.

Tichý, P. "On Popper's Definitions of Verisimilitude," *British Journal for the Philosophy of Science,* Vol. 25 (1974), 155–60.

———. "Verisimilitude Redefined," *British Journal for the Philosophy of Science,* Vol. 27 (1976), 25–42.

Weston, T. "Approximate Truth and Scientific Realism," *Philosophy of Science,* Vol. 59 (1992), 53–74.

GRAHAM ODDIE

V

VAGUENESS. A term is vague if, and only if, capable of having borderline cases. All borderline cases are inquiry resistent. Bill Clinton is a borderline chase of 'chubby' because no amount of conceptual or empirical investigation can settle the question of whether Clinton is chubby. This is not vagueness in the sense of being underspecific. If the president's spokesman states that Clinton weighs between 100 and 400 pounds, reporters will complain that the assertion is too *obvious* to be informative—not that the matter is indeterminate.

Typically, borderline cases lie between clear negative cases and clear positives. Moreover, the transition from clear to borderline cases will itself be unclear. If a thousand men queue in order of weight, there is no definite point at which the definitely non-chubby end and the borderline chubby begin. This higher order vagueness ascends to higher levels: there is no definite point at which the definitely definite cases end and the indefinitely definite ones begin, and so on for unlimited iterations of 'definite'.

Vagueness is responsible for Eubulides' 2,400-year-old sorites paradox. This conceptual slippery-slope argument can be compactly formulated with the help of mathematical induction:

> Base step: A collection of one million grains of sand is a heap.
> Induction step: If a collection of n grains of sand is a heap, then so is a collection of $n - 1$ grains.
> Conclusion: One grain of sand is a heap.

Long dismissed as a sophism, the sorites gained respect in the twentieth century. Within the last twenty years, it has acquired a stature comparable to Eubulides' other underestimated paradox, the liar (*see* LIAR PARADOX [S]).

Eubulides may have intended the sorites to support Parmenides' conclusion that all is one. For one solution is to deny the base step on the grounds that there really are no heaps. Since a sorites paradox can be formulated for any vague predicate for ordinary things ('cloud', 'chair', 'person'), the solution only generalizes by a rejection of common sense. In any case, this radical position has been championed by a few contemporary metaphysicians. A less strident group hopes that the sorites will be rendered obsolete by science's tendency to replace vague predicates by precise ones.

C. S. PEIRCE [6; S] was the first to propose that logic be revised to fit vagueness. Peirce developed a form of many-valued logic (*see* LOGIC, MANY-VALUED [5]). 'Clinton is chubby' is assigned a degree of truth between 1 (full truth) and 0 (full falsehood), say 0.5. Truth values of compound statements are then calculated on the basis of rules. Disjunctions are assigned the same truth value as their highest disjunct. Conditionals count as fully true only when the antecedent has a truth value at least as high as the consequent. This undermines the induction step of the sorites. As the progression heads into the borderline zone, the consequent has a value a bit lower than the antecedent. Although a small departure from full truth is normally insignificant, the sorites accumulates marginal differences into a significant difference.

Supervaluationists deny that borderline statements have any truth value at all. Words mean what we decide them to mean. Since there has been no practical need to decide every case, our words are only partially meaningful. We are free to fill in the gaps as we go along. If a statement would come out true regardless of how the gaps were filled, then we are entitled to deem the statement as true. This modest departure from truth-functionality lets the supervaluationists count 'Clinton is chubby or Clinton is not chubby' as true even though neither disjunct has a truth value. Indeed, all the tautologies of classical logic will be endorsed by this principle. All the contradictions will be likewise rejected. This suggests a solution to the sorites paradox. For every precisification of 'heap' makes the induction step come out false.

Other forms of deviant logic, such as INTUITIONISM [S] and relevance logic, have been applied to the sorites. However, deviant logics have been criticized as an overreaction by the epistemic theorists. Instead of changing the center of our web of belief, they urge revision of our more peripheral beliefs about language. In particular, the epistemicists say that the data can be accommodated by the conservative hypothesis that vagueness is just a special form of ignorance—'Clinton is chubby' has an *unknown* truth value. The induction step of the sorites is plain false; there is an n such that n grains of sand makes a heap but $n - 1$ does not. Although the epistemic view is committed to hidden thresholds for any finite sequence, it is compatible with the absence of thresholds for infinite sequences. 'Shortest tall man' could be as empty as 'smallest fraction'. Since the meaning of a term covers infinitely many possible instances, the epistemic view is not committed to *semantic* thresholds. Nevertheless, it is committed to the principle that an F can be arbitrarily close to a non-F.

Epistemicism is frequently characterized as the view that the world is precise. However, epistemicists side with those who believe that vagueness and precision are solely features of *representations.* Those who believe that there are vague objects view the vagueness of language as reflective of a deeper, metaphysical phenomenon.
(SEE ALSO: *Philosophy of Language* [S])

Bibliography

Evans, G. "Can There Be Vague Objects?" *Analysis,* Vol. 38 (1978), 208.

Fine, K. "Vagueness, Truth, and Logic," *Synthese,* Vol. 30 (1975), 265–30.

Sorensen, R. *Blindspots.* Oxford, 1988.

Wheeler, S. "Megarian Paradoxes as Eleactic Arguments," *American Philosophical Quarterly,* Vol. 20 (1983), 287–95.

Williamson, T. *Vagueness.* London, 1994.

ROY A. SORENSON

VERIFIABILITY PRINCIPLE. The doctrines associated with the slogan that MEANING [S] is the mode of verification continued to develop in the last four decades of the twentieth century. While the exact formulation of the principle was itself controversial, the essential idea was to link semantic and epistemic concerns by letting the meaning of an expression be its role within an empirical epistemology. At the same time the fortunes of logical EMPIRICISM [2], the movement associated with verificationism, changed substantially as well. First, as philosophers who conspicuously did not identify themselves with logical empiricism moved to center stage, the movement as a separately identifiable phenomenon virtually ceased to exist. This did not dispose of verificationism, however, for often the later philosophers' views were strikingly similar to the logical empiricism that they supposedly replaced, just as the criticisms of logical empiricism were often pioneered by the logical empiricists themselves. The second major change in the fortunes of this view was the renewal of interest in the history of PHILOSOPHY OF SCIENCE [7; S], especially in the histories of the logical empiricists themselves. Now freed from the myopia that comes from being part of the fray, philosophers were able to explore the roots of logical empiricism, what held it together as a movement, which of its doctrines were central or peripheral, and even which views look more plausible in hindsight than they did before their systematic interconnection could be appreciated.

One root of verificationism lies in the increasing professionalization of both the sciences and PHILOSOPHY [S] around the turn of the century. The sciences tended to emphasize the importance of empirical investigation, to explore its scope and limits, and to deplore as metaphysical any claims not based on evidence. Correspondingly, many philosophers claimed for themselves a nonempirical source of knowledge concerning things higher or deeper than mere observation could reveal, that is, concerning metaphysics. Logical empiricism grew out of methodological discussions within science rather than philosophy, and many of its central proponents were trained in the sciences. True, logical empiricism made special accommodation for the a priori domains of mathematics and logic. But these were technical subjects of use within the sciences and for which there were increasingly well-developed modes of conflict resolution. Moreover, the way in which the accommodation was reached, namely through the logical analysis of LANGUAGE [S], especially the language of science, comported well with a basic empiricism and provided no comfort to traditional philosophy. A second root of verificationism lies in RUSSELL's [7] reaction to the paradox that bears his name (viz. a contradiction that arises when sets can contain themselves) and in WITTGENSTEIN's [8; S] further elaboration of a related idea. In order to avoid the paradox, Russell had restricted the grammar so that apparent assertions of sets containing themselves were no longer well formed. Similarly, Wittgenstein emphasized that some combinations of words were neither true nor false but just nonsensical; they were, he said, metaphysical. This seemed to offer the ideal diagnosis of the sought-after distinction: scientifically respectable claims were either empirically meaningful in virtue of having some appropriate relation to the observations that would be the source of their justification, or else they were true in virtue of the language itself; traditional metaphysics, by contrast, was simply unintelligible. Phrased in this way, the VERIFIABILITY PRINCIPLE [8] leaves as a separate question the issue of what the appropriate relation to observation would be.

It has also become clearer what the logical status of the principle itself is. Initially, these philosophers could imagine that they were saying something about language in general or about the language of science. But as it became apparent that there were alternative languages to be considered, it became obvious that the principle could be put as a proposal for a language or as an analytic or empirical claim either about a particular language or about a range of languages. Perhaps the dominant form of the principle is as a proposal for a language to explicate the linguistic practices that are already largely in place in the sciences. As a proposal, it is not a claim, and hence neither true nor false, but not thereby unintelligible. If the proposal is adopted, the corresponding claim about the language that has those rules would be analytic. There would also be the empirical claim that we had adopted such a language and even empirical claims about that language if it were specified as, say, the language that is now used in contemporary physics.

So construed, many of the objections that were first made to the principle (and which continued to be made through the period in question) can be seen to be wrongheaded. The most persistent of these criticisms is that the principle renders itself an unintelligible claim. Whether construed as a proposal, as an analytic claim, or as an empirical one, this is just a (willful) misunderstanding. The same can be said for the criticism that it renders all philosophy meaningless. Equally misguided is the repeated objection that the principle cannot be right because we can understand a sentence without knowing whether it is true. Obviously, the principle in no way denies this truism.

Potentially more serious is the idea that all attempts to specify the principle have failed and are thus likely to continue to do so. Reinforcing this idea are papers by HEMPEL [3] which, while they are not really histories, strike many readers as signed confessions of complicity in a series of disasters. In defense of the principle it must be said that, except for those immediately around Wittgenstein, complete verifiability was virtually never at issue. Even in the *Aufbau,* where the general question is raised many times, all but one formulation are much more liberal. Similarly, strict falsifiability was never proposed as a criterion of meaningfulness. Concerning the more fertile ground of confirmation and disconfirmation, the difficulties seem to have arisen because the formulations tried both to link semantic and epistemic concerns *and* to specify a complete theory of confirmation. This latter task is so difficult that we should not expect early success nor conclude from failure that the enterprise is misguided—any more than we give up physics simply because we still lack the final theory.

There were, of course, other sources of difficulty. Many attempts, such as AYER's [1], tried to apply a criterion of meaningfulness at the level of whole sentences even though those sentences could contain meaningless parts. More successful in this regard was CARNAP's [2; S] "Methodological Character of Theoretical Concepts" (1956), which applied the criterion at the level of primitive terms. In a paper that was famous despite being unpublished for many years, David Kaplan provided two counterexamples to Carnap's criterion. These examples were widely regarded as decisive, but Creath showed that one of the examples missed its mark and the criterion could be patched in a natural way so as to avoid the other. Less easily dismissed is Rozeboom's criticism that Carnap's criterion ties meaningfulness to a particular theory when it should apply only to the language. Finally, Carnap's criterion, like many others, seems to presuppose that the theory/observation distinction can be drawn at the level of vocabulary. There came to be general agreement that this presupposition is mistaken and distorts any criterion based on it. In fairness, it must be admitted that some theory/observation distinction is essential to a healthy empiricism and that Carnap was from the very beginning fully aware of the limitations of formulating the distinction in this way. Finding a satisfactory way is still an unsolved problem.

W. V. O. QUINE [7; S] is often associated with the demise of logical empiricism, and his "Two Dogmas of Empiricism" is often thought to have rejected verificationism decisively. It would be more accurate to say that he rejected the idea that individual sentences could be separately confirmed, but he did not resist linking meaningfulness with confirmation holistically construed. Indeed, his demand that behavioral criteria be provided for ANALYTICITY [S] to render it intelligible is exactly parallel to Carnap's demand for correspondence rules to render theoretical terms meaningful. Moreover, Quine's argument from the indeterminacy of translation to the unintelligibility of interlinguistic synonymy makes sense only if meaning and confirmation are somehow linked as in the verifiability principle.

So what then of this link between semantic and epistemic issues? At least there is much to be said for it. A theory of meaning should give accounts of meaningfulness (having a meaning), of synonymy (having the same meaning), and of understanding (knowing the meaning). The verifiability principle provides *a* way of doing these things not provided by simply identifying various entities as "the meanings" of expressions. Moreover, it provides *a* defense against wholesale SKEPTICISM [7; S] by tying what we know to how we know. And finally, it provides *a* way of dealing with the so-called a priori by making those claims knowable in virtue of knowing the meanings of the expressions involved. No doubt there are others ways, perhaps even equally systematic ways, of accomplishing these ends, and no doubt these

other paths should be investigated as well. But the basic idea behind the verifiability principle, namely that semantical and epistemic questions should be linked, is far from refuted, and its promise is far from exhausted.
(SEE ALSO: *Epistemology* [S], and *Semantics* [7; S])

Bibliography

Ayer, A. J. *Language, Truth and Logic.* London, 1936.

———. "The Principle of Verifiability," *Mind,* Vol. 45 (1936), 199–203.

Carnap, R. "On the Character of Philosophic Problems," trans. W. M. Malisoff, *Philosophy of Science,* Vol. 1 (1934), 5–19.

———. "The Methodological Character of Philosophic Problems," in H. Feigl and M. Scriven, eds., *The Foundations of Science and the Concepts of Psychology and Psychoanalysis* (Minneapolis, 1956).

———. "On the Use of Hilbert's ∈-Operator in Scientific Theories," in Y. Bar-Hillel et al., eds., *Essays on the Foundations of Mathematics* (Jerusalem, 1961).

Creath, R. "On Kaplan on Carnap on Significance," *Philosophical Studies,* Vol. 30 (1976), 393–400.

———. "Was Carnap a Complete Verificationist in the *Aufbau*?" *PSA 1982,* Vol. 1, 384–93.

Glymour, C. *Theory and Evidence.* Princeton, NJ, 1980.

Hempel, C. G. "Problems and Changes in the Empiricist Criterion of Meaning," *Revue internationale de philosophie,* Vol. 4 (1950), 41–63.

Kaplan, D. "Significance and Analyticity: A Comment on Some Recent Proposals of Carnap," in J. Hintikka, ed., *Rudolf Carnap, Logical Empiricist: Materials and Perspectives* (Dordrecht, 1975).

Quine, W. V. O. "Two Dogmas of Empiricism," *Philosophical Review,* Vol. 60 (1951), 20–43.

———. *Word and Object.* Cambridge, MA, 1960.

Rozeboom, W. "A Note on Carnap's Meaning Criterion," *Philosophical Studies,* Vol. 11 (1960), 33–38.

RICHARD CREATH

VIOLENCE. "Violence" is derived from the Latin *violentia,* "vehemence," which itself comes from *vis* ("force") + *latus* ("to carry") and means, literally, intense force. Violence shares its etymology with violate, "injure." "Violence" is used to refer to swift, extreme force (e.g., a violent storm) and to forceful injurious violation (e.g., rape, terrorism, war).

Violence has received some philosophical consideration since ancient times, but only in the twentieth century has the concept of violence itself been of particular concern to philosophers. Perhaps this is due to the exponential growth in the efficiency of and access to the means of violence in the modern era, to the unprecedented carnage the twentieth century has seen, or to the emergence of champions of nonviolence such as Mohandas Gandhi and Martin Luther King, Jr. Beyond clarifying the concept of violence, philosophical argument has turned to the moral and cultural justifiability of violence to achieve personal, social, or political ends.

Philosophers do not achieve consensus about the concept. Often, violence is taken to consist in overt physical manifestations of force. These may be on the scale of individuals (e.g., mugging) or of nations (e.g., war). In its primary use "violence" refers to swift, extreme physical force typically involving injury and violation to persons or property. There is increasing philosophical interest in a wider use of the term extending beyond the overtly physical to covert, psychological, and institutional violence. In this broader sense RACISM [7; S], SEXISM [S], economic exploitation, and ethnic and religious persecution all are possible examples of violence; that is, all involve constraints that injure and violate persons, even if not always physically.

Concerning the moral and political justifiability of using violence to achieve personal or social ends, again philosophers disagree. Some have taken violence to be inherently wrong (e.g., murder), while most have taken it to be an open question whether violence is normatively justifiable. Terrorism presents a special case. It is aimed at randomly selected innocent victims in an effort to create general fear, thus sharpening focus on the terrorists' cause or demands. This random targeting of innocents accounts for the near universal moral condemnation of terrorism, despite the dominant view that violence in general is not inherently wrong.

Arguments purporting to justify violence do not value it in itself but as a means to an end sufficiently good to outweigh the evils of the injury or violation involved. Often, such justifiable violence is seen as a necessary means to important ends; that is, the good achieved by justifiable violence could not be achieved without it. Arguments challenging the justifiability of violence tend to reject the claim to necessity, arguing for nonviolent means, or to deny the claim that violation and injury are outweighed by the ends achieved. Such arguments may be against violence per se or merely against particular violent acts.

Georges SOREL's [7] *Reflections on Violence* (1908) is the earliest extensive philosophical work devoted to the subject. While MARX [5] saw a role for violence in history, it was secondary to the contradictions inherent in collapsing systems. Sorel synthesizes Marx's proletarianism, PROUDON's [6] ANARCHISM [1] and BERGSON's [1] VOLUNTARISM [8], defending revolutionary trade unionism in its efforts to destroy the existing institutional order. Sorel advocates the violent general strike as the means of class warfare against the state and owners of industry.

In *On Violence* (1969) Hannah ARENDT [S] reviews the twentieth-century apologists for violence in an effort to explain the increasing advocacy of violence, especially by the new left. She questions Mao Zedong's "Power grows out of the barrel of a gun" and articulates the position that power and violence are opposites. For Arendt the extreme of violence is one against all while the extreme of power is all against one. Power is acting in concert with others while violence is acting with implements against others. Loss of power leads some to try to replace it with violence. But violence is the opposite of power and cannot stand in its stead. Arendt concedes that violence can be justified but insists that it is only in defense against clear, present, immediate threats to life where the violence does not exceed necessity and its good ends are likely and near.

Newton Garver's "What Violence Is" (1968) extends the discussion to covert, psychological, and institutional violence. According to Garver, "Any institution which systematically robs certain people of rightful options generally available to others does violence to those people" (p. 420). Despite his sympathy with nonviolence, Garver claims that it is not a viable social goal. Violence between nations may be reduced but not eliminated.

(SEE ALSO: *Pacifism,* and *Social and Political Philosophy* [S])

Bibliography

Arendt, H. *On Violence.* New York, 1969.

Cotta, S. *Why Violence? A Philosophical Interpretation.* Gainesville, FL, 1985.

Garver, N. "What Violence Is," in R. Wasserstrom, ed., *Today's Moral Problems* (New York, 1975).

Gray, G. *On Understanding Violence Philosophically.* New York, 1970.

Holmes, R. L. "Violence and the Perspective of Morality," in *On War and Morality* (Princeton, NJ, 1989).

Schaffer, J. A., ed. *Violence: Award Winning Essays in the Council for Philosophical Studies Competition.* New York, 1971.

Sorel, G. *Reflections on Violence* [1908], translated by T. E. Hulme and J. Roth. Glencoe, IL, 1950.

Wolff, R. P. "On Violence," *Journal of Philosophy,* Vol. 66 (1969), 601–16.

DUANE L. CADY

VIRTUE EPISTEMOLOGY. Virtue epistemology has a broad and a narrow sense. In the narrow sense the central claim of virtue epistemology is that, minor qualifications aside, knowledge is true belief resulting from an intellectual virtue. On this view the intellectual virtues are stable dispositions for arriving at true beliefs and avoiding false beliefs in a particular field. Put another way, the intellectual virtues are abilities of persons to reliably determine the truth. Plausible examples of such abilities are cognitive faculties such as vision and introspection, and cognitive habits such as careful evidence gathering. On this view knowledge is understood to be true belief arising from a reliable cognitive character.

In the broad sense virtue epistemology is the position that the intellectual virtues are the appropriate focus of epistemological inquiry, whether or not knowledge can be defined in terms of the virtues and whether or not the virtues can be understood as dispositions toward true belief. In this broader sense the intellectual virtues continue to be understood as character traits of cognitive agents, but it is left open whether such traits make the agent reliable or whether agent reliability is even relevant for the most important kinds of epistemic evaluation.

VIRTUE AND KNOWLEDGE

A major motivation for applying virtue epistemology to the analysis of knowledge is that the position explains a wide range of our pretheoretical intuitions about who knows and who does not. Thus suppose we think of a virtue as a faculty for believing the truth in a specific area and we think that knowledge derives from such abilities. This would explain why beliefs caused by clear vision, mathematical intuition, and reliable inductive reasoning typically have positive epistemic value and why beliefs caused by wishful thinking, superstition, and hasty generalization do not. The former beliefs are grounded in what are plausibly intellectual virtues, whereas the latter beliefs derive from intellectual vices.

Virtue epistemology also seems to provide the theoretical resources for answering important kinds of SKEPTICISM [7; S]. By making important kinds of epistemic evaluation depend on instancing the intellectual virtues, the approach potentially explains how justification and knowledge are possible for beings like us, even if we cannot rule out skeptical possibilities involving evil demons or brains in vats. The main idea is that actually instancing the virtues is what gives rise to knowledge, even if we would not have the virtues, or they would not have their reliability, in certain nonactual situations.

Perhaps most important, virtue epistemology promises a way of understanding the kind of normativity that is involved in justified belief and knowledge. As in ethics, a virtue theory in epistemology competes with purely consequentialist and purely deontological approaches. Virtue epistemology seems to provide a better account of epistemic normativity than either of these alternatives. Thus, until the early 1960s almost all of contemporary epistemology took a deontological approach, making justified belief depend on doing one's epistemic duty or perhaps following the right epistemic norms. But this kind of normativity will not turn true belief into knowledge. Consider the case of a meticulously dutiful believer who is also the victim of a Cartesian deceiver. Suppose that as a result of her predicament her beliefs about the world are massively false but that she occasionally forms a true belief purely by accident. Such a person has true belief that is justified in the deontological sense and yet still does not have knowledge. Virtue theory typically requires more than deontological justification and therefore can avoid this particular kind of problem.

An example of a purely consequentialist theory is process reliabilism, or the theory that a belief is justified just in case it is formed by a reliable process. But process theories are hampered by counter examples involving strange and fleeting reliable processes. Consider a person who has been given a clean bill of health but who suffers from a brain tumor, one effect of which is to reliably cause the belief that he has a brain tumor. This example shows that a belief can be formed by a reliable process and yet fail to be justified in any sense relevant for having knowledge. The problem, according to virtue theory, is that not all reliable processes are epistemically significant. But if we stipulate that knowledge must arise from the stable faculties (or virtues) of the believer, then this kind of counter example is avoided.

But even if virtue epistemology seems promising along these lines, the perceived intractability of traditional problems has led others to advocate a shift in the focus of epistemological inquiry. These theorists agree that the intellectual virtues should play a central role in epistemology, but they prefer to ask different questions and engage in different projects. Jonathan Kvanvig, for example, argues that the individual synchronic focus of traditional epistemology should be replaced by a social genetic approach and that such a shift is best achieved by focusing on the intellectual virtues. On such an approach questions such as whether *S* knows *p* at *t* are replaced by questions about cognitive development, the corporate nature of knowledge acquisition, and the cognitive impact of social structures on persons and communities.

Lorraine Code's topic is epistemic responsibility, or the responsibility to know well. Code thinks that such responsibility is related but not reducible to our moral responsibility to live well. James Montmarquet investigates the topic of doxastic responsibility, or the kind of responsibility for beliefs that can ground moral responsibility for actions. Both theorists emphasize the social and moral dimensions of epistemology, and both argue that a focus on the intellectual characters of persons is the most fruitful approach for investigating the relevant questions of responsibility.

Accordingly, virtue epistemology can be divided into two main camps. The first camp comprises philosophers who are interested in the traditional topics of epistemology such as the analysis of knowledge and the nature of epistemic justification. These philosophers argue that virtue epistemology provides new insights into old problems. (See Goldman, 1992; Greco, 1993; Plantinga, 1993; Sosa, 1991; and Zagzebski, 1993.) The second camp explicitly advocates a shift away from the traditional problems of epistemology and argues that virtue epistemology is the best vehicle for achieving the new focus. (See Code, 1987; Kvanvig, 1992; and Montmarquet, 1993.)

THE NATURE OF THE VIRTUES

As is the case with the moral virtues, the intellectual virtues may be given a consequentialist, a deontological, or a "pure virtue theory" account. Depending on the account that is adopted, one will get a different understanding of the nature of the virtues and a different sense of the importance of the virtues for an analysis of knowledge.

On a consequentialist account an intellectual virtue is a stable disposition to achieve some cognitive end, where that end is not to be defined in terms of the virtues themselves. For example, a common move is to define intellectual virtue in terms of TRUTH [S], so that an intellectual virtue is a reliable (i.e., truth-conducive) cognitive faculty or habit of the believer. Alternatively, one might give a deontological account of the virtues. Here an intellectual virtue is understood as a stable disposition to do one's duty, or perhaps to be guided by the right norms, where again duty and right norm are not to be understood in terms of the virtues themselves. Finally, on a pure virtue theory the virtues continue to be understood as stable dispositions of the cognitive agent, but such dispositions are not defined in terms of the good or the right. Rather, such notions are defined in terms of the virtues. For example, a pure virtue account might understand the epistemic good in terms of what the virtuous person would believe.

Other disputes concerning the nature of the intellectual virtues also have their analogs in virtue ethics. For example, virtue epistemologists differ over whether and how intellectual virtues involve the will, whether the virtues are subject to our control, and whether they are appropriate sources of praise and blame. (See especially Montmarquet, 1993; Plantinga, 1993; and Zagzebski, 1993.) There is also disagreement over the degree to which the intellectual virtues are social in nature and over the extent to which the intellectual virtues are analogous to the moral virtues. (See especially Code, 1987; Montmarquet, 1993; and Zagzebski, 1993.)

What all virtue epistemologies have in common is a focus on the stable dispositions (i.e., faculties, abilities, or habits) of epistemic agents and the attempt to understand important epistemic notions in terms of these dispositions. For example, a consequentialist like Ernest Sosa understands an intellectual virtue as a faculty for arriving at true belief and then defines both knowledge and justification in terms of belief caused by an intellectual virtue. Alternatively, a nonconsequentialist like Montmarquet understands virtues as qualities a truth-desiring person would want to have and then defines epistemic justification in terms of virtuous belief. In each case the more basic kind of epistemic evaluation concerns the character (or virtue) of the cognitive agent, and then further kinds of epistemic evaluation are understood in terms of these. (SEE ALSO: *Epistemology* [S])

Bibliography

Code, L. *Epistemic Responsibility*. Hanover, NH, 1987.

Goldman, A. "Epistemic Folkways and Scientific Epistemology," in *Liaisons: Philosophy Meets the Cognitive and Social Sciences* (Cambridge, 1992).

Greco, J. "Virtues and Vices of Virtue Epistemology," *Canadian Journal of Philosophy,* Vol. 23 (1993), 413–32.

Kvanvig, J. L. *The Intellectual Virtues and the Life of the Mind.* Savage, MD, 1992.

Montmarquet, J. A. *Epistemic Virtue and Doxastic Responsibility.* Lanham, MD, 1993.

Plantinga, A. *Warrant and Proper Function.* Oxford, 1993.

Sosa, E. *Knowledge in Perspective.* Cambridge, 1991.

Zagzebski, L. "Intellectual Virtue in Religious Epistemology," in E. Radcliffe and C. White, eds., *Faith in Theory and Practice* (Chicago, 1993).

JOHN GRECO

VIRTUE ETHICS. In 1930 C. D. BROAD [1] first proposed to divide ethical theories into two classes, teleological and deontological, thereby introducing a dichotomy that quickly became standard in ethics. (*See* CONSEQUENTIALISM, DEONTOLOGICAL ETHICS, and ETHICAL THEORY [S]). Teleological theories were defined as ones that hold that the moral rightness of an action is always determined by its tendency to promote certain consequences deemed intrinsicially good; deontological theories, as ones that deny this claim. Broad's dichotomy was widely accepted as being exhaustive, but in fact there are two fundamental classes of normative moral judgments that do not fit easily into it. First, it focuses on rightness or obligation, excluding moral judgments concerning what is admirable, good, excellent, or ideal. Second, it concerns only actions and their consequences, saying nothing about moral judgments concerning persons, character, and character traits.

The contemporary movement known as virtue ethics is usually said to have begun in 1958 with Elizabeth ANSCOMBE's [S] advice to do ethics without the notion of a 'moral ought'. Although her own critique of moral-obligation concepts (viz., that they have meaning only within religious frameworks that include the notion of a divine lawgiver) did not gain widespread acceptance among secular ethicists, her constructive proposal to look for moral norms not in duty concepts but within the virtues or traits of character that one needs to flourish as a human being quickly caught on. Soon thereafter philosophers such as Alasdair MacIntyre, Philippa Foot, Edmund Pincoffs, and many others began to articulate and defend a third option in normative ethics: one whose chief concern was not a theory of morally right action but rather those traits of character that define the morally good or admirable person.

Phrases such as "revival of" or "return to" often precede mention of virtue ethics in contemporary discussions, and it is generally true that questions about the virtues occupy a much more prominent place in ancient and medieval moral philosophy than in moral theories developed since the Enlightenment. But it is important to note that the conscious awareness of virtue ethics as a distinct way of theorizing about ethics arose from within contemporary Anglo-American ethical theory. Virtue ethics took root as a reaction against the underlying common assumptions of both teleological and deontological ethical theories and has achieved its greatest critical success as a protest against these accepted ways of doing normative ethics. Accordingly, one can view virtue ethics as having two complementary aspects: a critical program that presents a critique of the prevailing assumptions, methods, and aspirations of normative teleological and deontological moral theories; and a constructive program, in which an alternative virtue-oriented normative moral conception is developed and defended.

THE CRITICAL PROGRAM

At this first level virtue theorists are not necessarily committed to defending a full-scale alternative to existing ethical theory programs but rather to showing why such approaches are systematically unable to account satisfactorily for moral experience. Major criticisms made by virtue theorists against their opponents include the following.

Overreliance on Rule Models of Moral Choice. Utilitarians and Kantians, it is held, both mistakenly view universal and invariable principles and laws as being exhaustive of ethics (*see* KANT [4; S]; UTILITARIANISM [8]). But real-life moral exemplars do not simply deduce what to do from a hierarchy of timeless, universal principles and rules. They possess sound judgment skills that enable them to respond appropriately to the nuances of each particular situation in ways that go beyond mere mechanical application of rules.

Overly Rationalistic Accounts of Moral Agency. Traditional moral theorists, it is held, too often assign a merely negative role in the moral life for desires and emotions. However, morally admirable people are not simply people who do their duty, but people who do so with the right kinds of emotions. Additionally, though many teleologists and deontologists do acknowledge the importance of motives in ethics, they typically mislocate them in abstractions such as "the greatest happiness principle" or "the moral law" rather than in particular persons and our relationships to them.

Formalism. Mainstream teleological and deontological theorists tend to focus exclusively on conceptual analyses of their favored duty-concepts and then on logical arguments based on such analyses. Additionally, they tend to view moral questions as arising only when an individual agent is trying to decide what to do in certain problematic situations. These methodological commitments result in a view of morality that is impoverished and overly restrictive. Virtue theorists, on the other hand, are much more open to drawing connections between morality and other areas of life such as psychology, anthropology, history, art, and culture. Their long-term agent-perspective also enables them correctly to view moral deliberation and choice as involving much more than snapshot decisions.

THE CONSTRUCTIVE PROGRAM

In offering their alternative, virtue theorists face the fundamental task of showing how and why a virtue-oriented conception of ethics is superior to its act- and duty-based competitors. In what ways is moral experience better understood once virtue-concepts become the primary tools of analysis? Here one may distinguish two general tendencies: radical virtue ethics attempts to interpret moral experience and judgment without employing duty-concepts at all (or at least by claiming that such concepts are always derivable from more fundamental ones concerning good people—e.g., 'morally right' acts might be defined simply as those acts performed by moral exemplars); moderate virtue ethics seeks to supplement standard act approaches with an account of the virtues. The former approach tends to view teleological and deontological ethical theories as totally misguided; the latter sees them merely as incomplete. Major issues confronting constructive virtue ethics programs include the following.

Defining Moral Virtue. What counts as a moral virtue and why? Is there any plausible way to distinguish between moral and nonmoral virtues? How exactly do virtues relate to actions, reasons, principles, rules, desires, emotions? Are virtues beneficial to their possessors, and, if so, are they too self-centered to count as moral traits?

Justifying the Virtues. How can we establish the validity of those character traits defined as moral virtues, once the option of appealing to the value of the acts that the virtues tend to encourage is ruled out? Traditionally, moral virtues have been defined as traits that human beings need in order to live well or flourish. But does the idea of flourishing provide solid enough ground on which to base the moral virtues? Is it still possible to speak accurately of *a* single human function, or is human life more variously textured that the classical picture allows? How and why is evidence of flourishing necessarily evidence of moral virtuousness? On the other hand, if one declines to issue pronouncements about "the human *telos*" and instead opts for a softer, more pluralistic functionalism that seeks to define virtues in terms of different kinds of human purposes or practices, can one still arrive at a substantive notion of the virtues that holds that they are more than local cultural products?

Applying the Virtues. How do the virtues relate to one another in real life? Is there anything to the ancient "unity of virtues" thesis (which, on the Aristotelian model, views *phronesis* or practical wisdom as generating and uniting all of the moral virtues), or does it make sense to hold that a person might possess one moral virtue such as courage and nevertheless lack others? How many different moral virtues are there? Are some more fundamental than others? Can they be ranked in order of importance? Do virtues ever conflict with one another? What kinds of specific practical guidance do we get from the virtues, especially in cases where they appear to conflict with one another (e.g., honesty vs. kindness, love vs. fidelity)?

It should come as no surprise that radical virtue-ethics approaches have attracted far fewer followers than more moderate versions and that the critical program has had a much stronger influence on contemporary ethical theory than has the constructive program. Those who turn to late twentieth-century work in virtue ethics in hopes of finding greater consensus on either theoretical or normative issues than exists among ethical theorists elsewhere are bound to be disappointed. Still, it is no small sign of virtue ethics' success that contemporary ethical theorists of all persuasions are addressing questions of character, agency, and motivation as never before—and that there now exist greater realism and humility among contemporary philosophers concerning how ethical theory should proceed and what it might reasonably accomplish.

Bibliography

Anscombe, G. E. M. "Modern Moral Philosophy," *Philosophy,* Vol. 33 (1958), 1–19; reprt. in her *Collected Philosophical Papers,* vol. 3 (Minneapolis, 1981). The *locus classicus* of the contemporary genre.

Aristotle. *Ethica Nicomachea* [approx. 330 B.C.E.]. Translated by Terence Irwin as *Nichomachean Ethics.* Indianapolis, 1985. The most important classical source. See esp. bk. 2 for his definition of moral virtue; 1 and 10.6–9 on human flourishing; 6.5–13 on practical wisdom.

Broad, C. D. *Five Types of Ethical Theory.* London, 1930. See pp. 206–7 for Broad's division of ethical theories into deontological and teleological.

Foot, P. *Virtues and Vices.* Berkeley, 1978.

Flanagan, O., and A. O. Rorty, eds. *Identity, Character, and Morality: Essays in Moral Psychology.* Cambridge, 1990. Nineteen commissioned essays; see esp. part 5.

French, P. A., T. E. Uehling, and H. K. Wettstein, eds. *Ethical Theory: Character and Virtue.* Midwest Studies in Philosophy, Vol. 13. Notre Dame, IN, 1988. Twenty-nine commissioned essays.

Kruschwitz, R. B., and R. C. Roberts, eds. *The Virtues: Contemporary Essays in Moral Character.* Belmont, CA, 1987. Seventeen essays. The first anthology on the topic. Includes an extensive bibliography of relevant works published up to 1985.

MacIntyre, A. *After Virtue,* 2d ed. Notre Dame, IN, 1984. The most influential single book on the topic.

Philosophia, Vol. 20 (1990). Double issue on virtue, with special reference to Philippa Foot's work. Thirteen commissioned essays.

Pincoffs, E. L. *Quandaries and Virtues.* Lawrence, KS, 1986.

Slote, M. *From Morality to Virtue.* New York, 1992.

Statman, D., ed., *Virtue Ethics.* Edinburgh, 1996.

Wallace, J. *Virtues and Vices.* Ithaca, NY, 1978.

ROBERT B. LOUDEN

VOLUNTARY. *See:* RICOEUR, PAUL [S]

W

WITTGENSTEIN, LUDWIG JOSEF JOHANN (1889–1951). Of Wittgenstein's philosophical writings available in print, by far the greater part was published after the 1967 *Encyclopedia of Philosophy.* The year 1967 also saw the publication on microfilm of Wittgenstein's *Nachlass.* In addition to the *Nachlass* itself and the posthumously published material from it, there has become available since 1967 a considerable body of Wittgenstein's letters, records of conversations with him, and notes taken by students at his lectures. Altogether, vastly more material is available to the student of WITTGENSTEIN [8] than there was in the mid-1960s. The *Tractatus* and the *Philosophical Investigations* remain, however, the central works for anyone trying to understand Wittgenstein's philosophy. The other writings do give a far fuller understanding of how Wittgenstein's later thought developed; they make clear important continuities between earlier and later work that had been difficult to see earlier. The recognition of these continuities can, for example, be seen in several of the essays in Peter Winch (1969), including Winch's own introductory essay on the unity of Wittgenstein's philosophy. Hidé Ishiguro (1969), in that volume, established that Wittgenstein's connection between meaning and use was not new in his later philosophy. He had always tied meaning to use; what was new in the later work, Ishiguro argued, was the willingness to consider a great variety of different kinds of use besides stating of facts; and Winch notes also the importance in Wittgenstein's later work of the idea that what we call "stating a fact" can itself be many different sorts of thing. A very important continuity noted by Anthony Kenny (1973) lies in Wittgenstein's conception of PHILOSOPHY [6; S] itself, including the contrast he made between philosophy and natural science, and the central role he gave to descriptions (rather than proofs) within philosophy.

The material written in the late 1940s and just before Wittgenstein's death shows how Wittgenstein's thought developed after the completion of what was published as Part I of *Philosophical Investigations.* He mentioned to friends his intention (never carried out) of replacing much of what is in the last thirty pages or so of Part I with what is in Part II, along with related material (subsequently published as *Remarks on Philosophical Psychology* and *Last Writings on Philosophical Psychology,* Vol. 1). His comment helps make clear how he saw the investigations of psychological concepts that occupy so much of Part II of the *Investigations* and of the related manuscripts. He is not turning away from the central questions about language in the *Investigations* to new and unrelated topics. Those questions themselves led him repeatedly into detailed examination of such matters as how what is going on in our minds bears on whether we speak with understanding or rather only as parrots might. The late writings show also his concern with the question, important to him from the 1930s onward, how what is given in experience is relevant to the concepts we grasp. These issues are closely related also to the investigations in *Remarks on Colour* (1977), drawn from manuscripts from the last eighteen months of Wittgenstein's life.

Wittgenstein was greatly stimulated by G. E. MOORE'S [5] attempts to reply to skeptical arguments by asserting things he took it to be plain that he knew (for example, that the earth had existed for a long time) and by Moore's discussion of the paradoxical character of saying "I believe he has gone out, but he has not." Moore's paradox about belief provides a focus for some of Wittgenstein's discussions of psychological concepts in Part II of the *Investigations* and the related manuscripts. Moore's commonsense response to SKEPTICISM [7; S] provided the impetus for Wittgenstein's treatment of skepticism and knowledge in *On Certainty.* He criticized Moore for having misunderstood the concept of knowledge on the model of that of belief and doubt; and indeed *On Certainty* is to some degree continuous with Wittgenstein's other discussions of psychological concepts. But it also stands on its own as an investigation of how certainty forms a part of our various language games and of the role played in those language games by empirical propositions that are not questioned. Wittgenstein's methods in *On Certainty* have been applied by other philosophers in discussions of religious and ethical claims, but he himself does not attempt to apply general principles about doubt, certainty, or knowledge to ethics or religion. (Some of his views about ethics and religion, as well as about art and other topics, have been gathered from various manuscripts and published in *Culture and Value.*)

There is a group of questions about how Wittgenstein saw the relation between facts and the language games in which we are engaged and about how far his approach, in his later philosophy, involves some kind of idealism or relativism. Do facts exercise any sort of control on the character of our concepts? If there were people who engaged in language games very different from ours—if there were, for example, people who thought one could travel to the moon while in a dream—would we be in a position to criticize such people as fundamentally in error? Several of Wittgenstein's works published after 1967 are particularly relevant to these questions, including *On Certainty, Zettel* (a collection of remarks Wittgenstein had cut from various manuscripts, mostly from the late 1940s), and Wittgenstein's "Remarks on Frazer's *Golden Bough*" (included in Wittgenstein, 1993). Wittgenstein's discussions of mathematics also bear directly on the question how free we are in our development of concepts: what would we be getting wrong if our mathematics, or our logic, were very different? In these discussions Wittgenstein is frequently responding to Gottlob FREGE's [3; S] conception of objectivity in logic and mathematics.

RECEPTION OF WITTGENSTEIN'S PHILOSOPHY

Philosophers are far from agreement on how Wittgenstein's philosophical achievements can be assimilated or indeed whether they should be. There are many philosophers who regard Wittgenstein's influence as pernicious and who think that the best response to his philosophy is to ignore it. This view rests sometimes on the idea that his philosophy developed to meet his personal needs and is irrelevant to the genuine interests of contemporary philosophy. A second kind of response to Wittgenstein involves making a sharp distinction between, on the one hand, the important philosophical claims and arguments that are thought to be in his work or implied by it and, on the other, his own understanding of his philosophy as not involving disputable theses or explanations and as aiming to dissolve philosophical problems rather than to find the correct answers. If that distinction is made, it may then be held that we should simply ignore his views about philosophy (which it may also be held are inconsistent with his own practice) and should instead pay attention to the theses and arguments (on which, on this view, his reputation must properly rest). Philosophers who read Wittgenstein in this way do not agree among themselves whether the theses in question are true, the arguments sound; nor do they agree about what the extractible theses are supposed to be. Thus, for example, those who ascribe to him theses about the necessary conditions for a language disagree about whether these conditions include the necessity that a speaker of any language have been at least at some time a member of a community of speakers. A third distinct kind of response to Wittgenstein takes seriously his conception of philosophical problems as dependent upon our misunderstandings of the workings of our language; they arise when language is allowed to go "on holiday." And so any adequate approach to these problems depends on coming to see how we are led into them; it will not issue in solutions that leave unchanged our idea of the problems themselves. Finally, some elements of Wittgenstein's approach to philosophical problems, and his criticisms of standard philosophical moves in response to them, have also been treated as important and interesting by those who, like Richard Rorty, wish to see analytical philosophy replaced by some other kind of intellectual activity.

The philosophical disputes about Wittgenstein's work have been focused to a considerable degree on the issues discussed by Norman MALCOLM [5] in the original *Encyclopedia* piece, including the relation between meaning and use, the possibility of a private language, and the objectivity of rules. Much recent controversy has been inspired by the writings of Michael DUMMETT and Saul KRIPKE [S]. Dummett reads Wittgenstein as putting forward an antirealist theory of meaning; Kripke has argued that Wittgenstein in the *Investigations* presents a new skeptical problem and a skeptical solution to it. Responses to Dummett and Kripke have made clear the importance of understanding Wittgenstein's aims, his desire to show how our misconceptions can make something perfectly ordinary appear problematic; thus, it is the step in our arguments at which the ordinary first appears problematic which we fail to note, and to which we need to attend.

Bibliography

WORKS BY WITTGENSTEIN

Philosophical Remarks, ed. R. Rhees, trans. R. Hargreaves and R. White. Oxford, 1964; 2d ed., 1975.

Zettel, ed. G. E. M. Anscombe and G. H. von Wright, trans. G. E. M. Anscombe. Oxford, 1967; 2d ed., 1981.

On Certainty, ed. G. E. M. Anscombe and G. H. von Wright, trans G. E. M. Anscombe and D. Paul. Oxford, 1969.

Proto-tractatus, ed. B. F. McGuinness, T. Nyberg, and G. H. von Wright, trans. D. F. Pears and B. F. McGuinness. Ithaca, NY, 1971.

Philosophical Grammar, ed. R. Rhees, trans. A. Kenny. Oxford, 1974.

Remarks on Colour, ed. G. E. M. Anscombe, trans. L. McAlister and M. Schättle. Oxford, 1977.

Remarks on the Foundations of Mathematics, ed. G. H. von Wright, R. Rhees, and G. E. M. Anscombe, trans. G. E. M. Anscombe, 3d ed. Cambridge, MA, 1978.

Culture and Value, ed. G. H. von Wright, trans. P. Winch. Oxford, 1980.

Remarks on the Philosophy of Psychology. Vol. 1, ed. G. E. M. Anscombe and G. H. von Wright, trans. G. E. M. Anscombe. Chicago, 1980. Vol. 2, ed. G. H. von Wright and H. Nyman, trans. C. G. Luckhardt and M. A. E. Aue. Chicago, 1980.

Last Writings on the Philosophy of Psychology, ed. G. H. von Wright and H. Nyman, trans. C. G. Luckhardt and M. A. E. Aue. 2 vols. Chicago, 1982–92.

Werkausgabe. 8 vols. Frankfurt, 1989.

Philosophical Occasions, 1912–1951, ed. J. Klagge and A. Nordmann. Indianapolis, 1993. Contains all Wittgenstein's shorter published writings; some letters and records of lectures; also a full account of the Wittgenstein *Nachlass.*

Wienerausgabe, ed. M. Nedo. 22 vols. Vienna, 1993–.

The Published Works of Ludwig Wittgenstein, ed. H. Kaal and A. McKinnon. Electronic text database.

LECTURES AND CONVERSATIONS

Wittgenstein's Lectures, Cambridge, 1930–32, ed. D. Lee. Oxford, 1980.

Wittgenstein's Lectures, Cambridge, 1932–1935, ed. A. Ambrose. Totowa, NJ, 1979.

Wittgenstein's Lectures on the Foundations of Mathematics, Cambridge, 1939, ed. C. Diamond. Ithaca, NY, 1976; Chicago, 1989.

Wittgenstein's Lectures on Philosophical Psychology 1946–47, ed. P. T. Geach. Chicago, 1988.

Ludwig Wittgenstein and the Vienna Circle: Conversations Recorded by Friedrich Waismann, ed. B. F. McGuinness, trans. J. Schulte and B. F. McGuinness. Oxford, 1979.

WORKS ON WITTGENSTEIN

Anscombe, G. E. M. "The Question of Linguistic Idealism," in *From Parmenides to Wittgenstein* (Oxford, 1981).

Canfield, J. V., ed. *The Philosophy of Wittgenstein.* 15 vols. New York, 1986. Comprehensive collection of over 250 articles.

Cavell, S. *The Claim of Reason.* Oxford, 1979.

Conant, J. "Kierkegaard, Wittgenstein, and Nonsense," in T. Cohen et al., eds., *Pursuits of Reason* (Lubbock, TX, 1993).

Diamond, C. *The Realistic Spirit: Wittgenstein, Philosophy, and the Mind.* Cambridge, MA, 1991.

Dummett, M. *Truth and Other Enigmas.* London, 1978.

Goldfarb, W. "I Want You to Bring Me a Slab: Remarks on the Opening Sections of the *Philosophical Investigations,*" *Synthese,* Vol. 56 (1983).

———. "Kripke on Wittgenstein on Rules," *Journal of Philosophy,* Vol. 82 (1985).

Holtzman, S. H., and Leich, C. M., eds. *Wittgenstein: To Follow a Rule.* London, 1981.

Hacker, P. M. S. *Insight and Illusion: Themes in the Philosophy of Wittgenstein.* Oxford, 1972; rev. 2d ed., 1986.

Ishiguro, H. "Use and Reference of Names," in P. Winch, ed., *Studies in the Philosophy of Wittgenstein* (London, 1969).

Kenny, A. *Wittgenstein.* Harmondsworth, Middlesex, 1973.

Kripke, S. *Wittgenstein on Rules and Private Language.* Cambridge, MA, 1982.

Malcolm, N. *Nothing Is Hidden: Wittgenstein's Criticism of His Early Thought.* Oxford, 1986.

McDowell, J. *Selected Papers,* Vol. 1. Cambridge, MA, 1996.

McGuinness, B. F. *Wittgenstein—A Life: Young Ludwig: 1889–1921.* London, 1988.

Monk, R. *Ludwig Wittgenstein: The Duty of Genius.* New York, 1990.

Pears, D. F. *The False Prison.* 2 vols. Oxford, 1987–88.

Rhees, R. *Discussions of Wittgenstein.* London, 1970.

Shanker, S. G., ed. *Ludwig Wittgenstein: Critical Assessments.* 4 vols. Beckenham, Kent, 1986. Comprehensive collection of 104 articles.

Shanker, V. A., and S. G. Shanker. *A Wittgenstein Bibliography.* Beckenham, Kent, 1986. Covers primary sources and over 5,400 items on Wittgenstein.

Sluga, H., and D. Stern, eds. *Cambridge Companion to Wittgenstein.* Cambridge, 1996. Includes a full bibliography of Wittgenstein's writings and good selective bibliography of secondary literature.

Winch, P., ed. *Studies in the Philosophy of Wittgenstein.* London, 1969.

Wright, C. *Wittgenstein on the Foundations of Mathematics.* London, 1980.

CORA DIAMOND

WOLLSTONECRAFT, MARY (1757–97), has long been recognized as one of the most influential feminist theorists in history, largely through her *Vindication of the Rights of Woman* (1792). Late twentieth-century scholarship also began to explore her other texts and their significance.

Wollstonecraft's work is a product of the late ENLIGHTENMENT [2], emphasizing the need to achieve virtue and progress through development of reason and sensibility. It also reflects ideas of the Dissenters and political radicals who stood among the relatively few English supporters of the French Revolution. Wollstonecraft's early mentors were Richard PRICE and Joseph PRIESTLEY [6]. The circle with whom she continued to associate included writers and artists such as William BLAKE [1], Thomas PAINE [6], Henry Fuseli, and William GODWIN [3]. Like them, she opposed slavery, standing armies, and many elements of political patriarchy such as primogeniture, aristocracy, and probably monarchy. She shared their critique of the corrupting influence of political and social institutions structured around "unnatural distinctions" based on rank, property, religion, or profession.

Wollstonecraft's most distinctive and well-known contribution was to extend this analysis to demand an end to unnatural distinctions based on sex and family relations. As she wrote in the *Rights of Woman,* if observation could not prove that men had more natural capability for reason than women, they could claim no superiority over women and certainly no right to rule them. In analysis shaped by LOCKE [4; S] and ROUSSEAU [7; S] (but one that attacked Rousseau for his views on women), she concluded that education, experience, and the "present constitution of society," and not nature, created most observed character differences between men and women.

She argued that unnatural distinctions between women and men tended toward the same effects as other unjust power relations: they corrupt the character of all parties to the relationship, rendering the dominant party dependent on its power and making the subordinate party resort to cunning and unvirtuous strategies of self-preservation. In the case of women she pointed to the use of BEAUTY [1; S] as what might now be called a "weapon of the weak." Unlike more well-known democratic theorists of her era, she applied an antipatriarchal analysis commonly used on institutions such as government to the family itself.

She advocated altering the social practices such as dress, courtship, employment, and family relations that had given men power over women and kept both from virtue. She sought expanded work opportunities for women. She proposed development of a public school system educating girls and boys and children of different classes similarly and together, at least for the early years of their schooling, and wanted girls to study subjects that had been forbidden to them. Her final, unfinished novel, *Maria, or the Wrongs of Woman,* underscored the necessity of women's ability to support themselves, divorce, and have rights over their children.

Although most famous for her arguments on women's rights, other contributions are worth noting. Her *Vindication of the Rights of Men* (1790) was one of the first attacks on Edmund BURKE's [1] *Reflections on the Revolution in France,* and it engaged his work on the sublime and the beautiful, thus integrating aesthetics and politics in a critique of Burke's defense of monarchy, aristocracy, and pomp. Her further exploration of the French Revolution in the *Historical and Moral View of the Origin and Progress of the French Revolution* (1794) contains an underrated inquiry into the nature of political history and the relationship between ideals and human action. Wollstonecraft's *Letters Written during a Short Residence in Sweden, Norway, and Denmark* influenced the early generation of English Romantics, including COLERIDGE [2], Southey, Wordsworth, and Percy Bysshe SHELLEY [7] and his wife, Wollstonecraft's daughter, Mary Shelley.

Bibliography

WORKS BY WOLLSTONECRAFT

The Works of Mary Wollstonecraft, ed. J. Todd and M. Butler. New York, 1989. Includes all of Wollstonecraft's works (other than letters). Among the most important are:

Mary: A Fiction (1788).

A Vindication of the Rights of Men, in a Letter to the Right Honorable Edmund Burke (1790).

A Vindication of the Rights of Woman with Strictures on Moral and Political Subjects (1792).

An Historical and Moral View of the Origin and Progress of the French Revolution; and the Effect It Has Produced in Europe (1794).

Letters Written during a Short Residence in Sweden, Norway, and Denmark (1796).

Maria, or the Wrongs of Woman (post.).

WORKS ON WOLLSTONECRAFT

Poovey, M. *The Proper Lady and the Woman Writer: Ideology as Style in the Works of Mary Wollstonecraft, Mary Shelley, and Jane Austen.* Chicago, 1982.

Sapiro, V. *A Vindication of Political Virtue: The Political Theory of Mary Wollstonecraft.* Chicago, 1992.

Tomalin, C. *The Life and Death of Mary Wollstonecraft.* New York, 1974.

VIRGINIA SAPIRO

WOMEN IN THE HISTORY OF PHILOSOPHY. The standard twentieth-century histories of European philosophy do not include women as important, original contributors to the discipline's past. Some relegate a few to footnotes; most omit women entirely. Recent research, inspired by the influence of feminist theory, and by a renewed interest in the historiography of philosophy, has uncovered numerous women who contributed to philosophy over the centuries.

Women's representation in philosophy's history was not always as marginal as it came to be by the opening of the twentieth century. For example, in the seventeenth century, Thomas Stanley's history mentioned twenty-four women philosophers of the ancient world, while Gilles Ménage discussed some seventy, including women Platonists, Academicians, Dialecticians, Cyrenaics, Megarians, Cynics, Peripatetics, Epicureans, Stoics, and Pythagoreans. With respect to the moderns, the seventeenth-century treatises of Jean de La Forge and Marguerite Buffet provided doxographies of women philosophers. Even in the nineteenth century, when women were virtually being erased from the standard histories, Lescure, Joël, Foucher de Careil, and Cousin wrote special studies on female philosophers.

In recent years *A History of Women Philosophers,* volume 1, *600 BC–500 AD,* edited by Mary Ellen Waithe, has provided a detailed discussion of the following figures: Themistoclea, Theano I and II, Arignote, Myia, Damo, Aesara of Lucania, Phintys of Sparta, Perictione I and II, Aspasia of Miletus, Julia Domna, Makrina, HYPATIA [S] of Alexandria, Arete of Cyrene, Asclepigenia of Athens, Axiothea of Philesia, Cleobulina of Rhodes, Hipparchia the Cynic, and Lasthenia of Mantinea. In addition to the medieval and Renaissance philosophers discussed in the second volume of Waithe's *History* (HILDEGARD OF BINGEN [S], Heloise, Herrad of Hohenbourg, Beatrice of Nazareth, Mechtild of Magdeburg, Hadewych of Antwerp, Birgitta of Sweden, Julian of Norwich, Catherine of Siena, Oliva Sabuco de Nantes Barrera, Roswitha of Gandersheim, Christine de Pisan, Margaret More Roper, and Teresa of Avila), scholars have recently begun to focus attention on such humanist and Reformation figures as Isotta Nogarola, Laura Cereta, Cassandra Fidele, Olimpia Morata, and Caritas Pickheimer.

THE SEVENTEENTH CENTURY

In the early modern period women's initial published philosophical endeavors inserted argumentation into the largely literary genre of the *querelle des femmes,* or woman question. Thus, Marie de GOURNAY [S], adopted daughter of MONTAIGNE [5], in *The Equality of Men and Women* (1622) replaced persuasive force based on example with skeptical and fideistic arguments; Anna Maria van Schurman's *Whether a Maid May Be a Scholar?* (1659) and Sor Juana Inés de la Cruz's "Response to Sor Filotea" (1700) utilized scholastic models of argumentation to discuss woman's nature and her relation to learning. By 1673, when Bathsua Makin published *An Essay to Revive the Ancient Education of Gentlewomen,* an unbroken, explicitly acknowledged line of influence ran from Gournay through van Schurman to Makin. In the second half of the century, partly in response to the writings of ERASMUS [3], VIVES [8], and FÉNELON [3], a number of treatises on the education of girls appeared, stressing its importance for religion and society. Authors included the Port Royal educator Sister Jacqueline Pascal and Madame de Maintenon.

In the second half of the Age of Reason women also produced numerous works on morals and the passions, including the maxims of Marguerite de La Sablière, Marquise de Sablé, and Queen Christina of Sweden. Perhaps the most well-known seventeenth-century woman writer of moral psychology is Madeline de Scudéry, of whom LEIBNIZ [4; S] said that she had "clarified so well the temperaments and the passions in her . . . conversations on morals."

Another type of philosophical writing by women, the treatment of natural philosophy, begins to appear after 1660. In Paris Jeanne Dumée and, in England, Aphra Behn argued in defense of COPERNICUS [2]. But by far the most prolific female philosopher then was Margaret Cavendish, who published over a half dozen books on natural philosophy in which she advanced a unique combination of hard-nosed materialism together with an organic model of natural change and a denial of mechanism.

Of Anne CONWAY [S] Leibniz said, "My philosophical views approach somewhat closely those of the late Countess of Conway." Her metaphysical treatise argued against DESCARTES [2; S], SPINOZA [7; S], and HOBBES [4; S] in favor of a monistic vitalism. On the Continent Princess Elisabeth of Bohemia, whose letters to Descartes had exposed the weakness of the latter's published views on mind–body interaction and free will, discussed Conway's philosophy with a Quaker correspondent. Seventeenth-century England also produced Mary Astell, who in the appendix to the *Letters Concerning the Love of God* (1695) argued against occasionalism. In *A Serious Proposal to the Ladies, Part II* (1697), Astell offered women a manual for improving their powers of reasoning, a work that was influenced by Descartes and the Port Royal logicians. Damaris Cudworth Masham also argued against occasionalism in *Discourse Concerning the Love of God* (1696). In *Occasional Thoughts* (1705) she defended a number of Lockean views on knowledge, education, and the relative merits of reason and revelation (*see* LOCKE [4; S]). Masham also corresponded with Leibniz on metaphysical issues, especially his views on substance; yet despite this scholarly career, she stood in need of defense against the charge that the arguments addressed to Leibniz could not have been written by a woman. It was Catherine Trotter Cockburn who came to her defense. Cockburn wrote a number of philosophical works, including *A Defence of Mr. Locke's Essay of Human Understanding* (1702) and a vindication of the views of Samuel Clarke.

In France in the final years of the seventeenth century, Gabrielle Suchon published, arguably, the most ambitious philosophical text that had yet been written by a woman on the Continent: *Treatise of Morals and of Politics* (1693), which included book-length treatments of liberty, science, and authority. Excerpts of her work were published in the scholarly journals of the time, but since the *Treatise* was published under a pseudonym, Suchon fell into oblivion by the late eighteenth century. (Anonymous authorship similarly led to Conway's erasure.)

THE EIGHTEENTH CENTURY

In England Catherine Macaulay published a critical treatment of Hobbes's political philosophy and her magnum opus, *Letters on Education* (1790), to which Mary WOLLSTONECRAFT [S] explicitly acknowledges her debt in her own *Vindication of the Rights of Woman* (1792). By the end of the century Mary Hays's *Female Biography* (1803) demonstrated that English women were beginning to trace a history of feminist social and political philosophy that reached back about one hundred years to Mary Astell. At the turn of the century, with the growing professionalization of philosophy and placement of it over against the *belles lettres* and religion, women were producing philosophy stripped of its moorings within discussions of the woman question and theology, and written in journalistic style, as evidenced in Mary Shepherd's book-length treatments of causation, skepticism, and knowledge of the external world, with their attendant criticisms of such figures as HUME [4; S] and BERKELEY [1; S].

In Enlightenment France Anne Dacier published a translation and commentary for the writings of MARCUS AURELIUS [5] and entered the debate about the ancients versus the moderns in her *The Causes of the Corruption of Taste* (1714). Dacier's salonist friend, the Marquise de Lambert, published a number of works on morals, the passions, education, and woman's status, which continued to be published a century later. Sophie de Grouchy, Marquise de Condorcet, added to her translation of Adam Smith's *Theory of the Moral Sentiments* her own blend of rationalist ethics and moral sentiment theory in her eight letters on sympathy.

Prior to the French Revolution philosophy of education, in particular, critical responses to ROUSSEAU's [7; S] *Émile,* occupied a prominent place in women's philosophical writings, as exemplified in Louise d'Epinay's *The Conversations of Emilie* (1774) and the works of Mme de Genlis. In addition to her work on education Louise-Marie Dupin also left an extensive manuscript, *Observations on the Equality of the Sexes and of Their Difference,* which she dictated to her secretary, Rousseau. The French Revolution moved the issue of woman's education into the arena of the rights of a woman as a citizen. Perhaps the most famous of these treatises is Olympe de Gouge's *Declaration of the Rights of Woman* (1791).

In the area of natural philosophy there is no question but that Emilie Du Châtelet deserves recognition as an important figure of the eighteenth century. Her *Principles of Physics* (1740) and her letters on the "active force" controversy (1742) attempt to reconcile what she takes to be most useful in Newtonian mechanics and Leibnizian philosophy. Du Châtelet also published a *Discourse on Happiness* (1779) and essays on the existence of God, the formation of color, and grammatical structure.

By the end of the century French women were producing broad critiques of culture and the arts, as evidenced in the mathematician Sophie Germain's *General Considerations on the State of the Sciences and Letters* (1833) and Madame de Staël's *On the Influence of the Passions on the Happiness of Individuals and Nations* (1796).

Germany spawned two critical treatments of KANT's [4; S] views on women: the first by an unidentified "Henriette" and the second by Amalia Holst. In Switzerland Marie Huber's publications included three Enlightenment texts on the principles of natural religion: *The World Unmask'd* (English translation, 1736), *The State of Souls Separated from their Bodies* (English translation, 1736), and *Letters on the Religion Essential to Man* (English translation, 1738).

In Russia Catherine the Great's correspondence with VOLTAIRE [8] was published posthumously. Finally, in Italy Laura Bassi publicly disputed philosophical theses and published five lectures on natural philosophy; Maria Agnesi discussed logic, metaphysics, and Cartesian physics in *Philosophical Propositions* (1738); and Giuseppa Barbapiccola translated and wrote a critical introduction for Descartes's *Principles of Philosophy* (1731).

The information now available about women philosophers and ongoing research on this topic will provide us with a richer picture of philosophy's significant figures, topics, and styles of argumentation. It is to be hoped that future histories of philosophy will reflect this richer panorama of the past.

(SEE ALSO: *Feminist Philosophy* [S])

Bibliography

THE SEVENTEENTH CENTURY

Astell, M. *Letters Concerning the Love of God between the Author of the Proposal to the Ladies and Mr. John Norris* (London, 1695); *A Serious Proposal to the Ladies Part II: Wherein a Method is offer'd for the Improvement of their Minds* (London, 1697); *Some Reflections Upon Marriage* (London, 1700); *The Christian Religion as Profess'd by a Daughter of the Church of England* (London, 1705).

Behn, A. "The Translator's Preface," in B. le Bovier de Fontenelle, *A Discovery of New Worlds,* trans. A. Behn (London, 1688).

Cavendish, M. L., Duchess of Newcastle. *Philosophical and Physical Opinions* (London, 1655); *Orations of Divers Sorts* (London, 1662); *Philosophical Letters: or, Modest Reflections upon some Opinions in Natural Philosophy Maintained By Several Famous and Learned Authors of this Age* (London, 1664); *Observations upon Experimental Philosophy* (London, 1666); *Grounds of Natural Philosophy* (London, 1668).

Conway, A., Viscountess. *The Principles of the Most Ancient and Modern Philosophy* (Latin translation: Amsterdam, 1690; English retranslation: London, 1692; both reprinted: The Hague, 1982); *The Conway Letters,* ed. M. H. Nicholson and S. Hutton (Oxford, 1992).

Christina, Queen of Sweden. *L'Ouvrage de loisir* [ca. 1670–80] and *Les Sentiments héroïques* [ca. 1670–80], with *Réflexions diverses sur la Vie et sur les Actions du Grand Alexandre, Les Vertues et vices de Caesar,* and correspondence, in J. Arckenholtz, *Mémoires concernant Christine, reine de Suède,* 4 vols. (Leipzig, 1751–60).

Dumée, J. *Entretien sur l'opinion de Copernic touchant la mobilité de la terre* (Paris, n.d.); ms. ca. 1680, Bibliothèque Nationale Fonds français 19941.

Elisabeth, Princess of Bohemia. Her letters in: *Oeuvres de Descartes,* ed. C. Adam and P. Tannery (Paris, 1897–1913; rev. ed. 1964–74); N. Malebranche, *Correspondance, actes et documents 1638–1689,* ed. A. Robinet, Vol. 18 (Paris, 1961); *Papers of William Penn,* Vol. 1, ed. M. Dunn and R. Dunn (Philadelphia, 1981).

Gournay, M. le Jars de. *L'Egalité des hommes et des femmes* (Paris, 1622); *L'Ombre de la Damoiselle de Gournay* (Paris, 1626); *Les Advis ou Les Presens de la Demoiselle de Gournay* (Paris, 1634).

Juana Inés de la Cruz, Sor, *Carta athenagórica de la madre Juana Inés de la Cruz* (Puebla de los Angeles, 1690); *Fama, y obras póstumas del fenix de Mexico, Decima Musa, Poetisa Americana* (Madrid, 1700); *Obras completas,* ed. A. Méndez Plancarte [A. Salceda], 4 vols. (Mexico City, 1951–57).

Lettres, Opuscules et Mémoires de Mme. Périer et de Jacqueline, Soeurs de Pascal, ed. P. Faugère (Paris, 1845).

Maintenon, F. d'Aubigné. *Lettres sur l'éducation des filles,* ed. Th. Lavallée (Paris, 1854); *Entretiens sur l'éducation des filles,* ed. Th. Lavallée (Paris, 1854); *Lettres historiques et édifiantes adressées aux dames de St.-Louis,* ed. Th. Lavallée, 2 vols. (Paris, 1856); *Conseils et instructions aux demoiselles pour leur conduite dans le monde,* 2 vols. (Paris, 1857).

Makin, B. *An Essay to Revive the Antient Education of Gentlewomen* (London, 1673).

Masham, D. C. A *Discourse Concerning the Love of God* (London, 1696; French translation, 1705); *Occasional Thoughts in Reference to a Vertuous or Christian Life* (London, 1705); letters to Locke in *The Correspondence of John Locke,* ed. E. S. de Beer, 8 vols. (Oxford, 1976–85); letters to Leibniz in *Die Philosophischen Schriften von Leibniz,* ed. C. I. Gerhardt, 7 vols. (Berlin, 1875–90).

*Réflexions ou Sentences et Maximes morales de Monsieur de la Rochefoucauld, Maximes de Madame la marquise de Sablé. Pensées diverses de M. L. D. et les Maximes chrétiennes de M******* [Mme. de La Sablière] (Amsterdam, 1705).

Schurman, A. M. van. *Amica dissertatio inter Annam Mariam Schurmanniam et Andr. Rivetum de capacitate ingenii muliebris ad scientias* (Paris, 1638); *Opuscula, hebraea, graeca, latina, gallica, prosaica et metrica* (Leiden, 1648).

Scudéry, M. de. *Discours sur la gloire* (Paris, 1671); *Conversations sur divers sujets,* 2 vols. (Paris, 1680); *Conversations nouvelles sur divers sujets,* 2 vols. (Paris, 1684); *Conversations morales,* 2 vols. (Paris, 1686); *Nouvelles Conversations de morale,* 2 vols. (Paris, 1688); *Entretiens de morale,* 2 vols. (Paris, 1692).

Suchon, G. *Traité de la morale et de la Politique* (Lyon, 1693); *[Traité] Du célibat Volontaire, ou la Vie sans engagement, par Demoiselle Suchon* (Paris, 1700).

THE EIGHTEENTH CENTURY

Agnesi, M. G. *Propositiones Philosophicae* (Milan, 1738).

Barbapiccola, G. E. *I Principii della Filosopfia* (Turin, 1722).

Bassi, L. M. C. *Philosophica Studia* [forty-nine theses disputed for the doctorate] (Bologna, 1732); *De acqua corpore naturali elemento aliorum corporum parte universi* [theses for a disputation] (Bologna, 1732); the following appear in *De Bononiensi Scientiarum et Artium Instituto atque Academia Commentarii: De aeris compressione* (1745); *De problemate quodam hydrometrico* (1757); *De problemate quodam mechanico* (1757); *De immixto fluidis aere* (1792).

Cockburn, C. Trotter. *The Works of Mrs. Catherine Cockburn, Theological, Moral, Dramatic, and Poetical,* ed. T. Birch (London, 1751).

Dacier, A. L. *Réflexions morales de l'empereur Marc Antonin* (Paris, 1690–91; English translation: London, 1692); *Des Causes de la corruption du goût* (Paris, 1714).

D'Épinay, L. *Les Conversations d'Émilie* (Leipzig, 1774; Paris, 1781).

Documents of Catherine the Great: The Correspondence with Voltaire and the Instruction of 1767 in the English text of 1768, ed. W. F. Reddaway (Cambridge, 1931).

Du Châtelet, G. É. Le Tonnelier De Breteuil, Marquise. *Institutions de Physique* (Paris, 1740); *Réponse de Madame**** [du Châtelet] *à la lettre que M. de Mairan . . . lui a écrite le 18 février sur la question des forces vives* (Brussels, 1741); *Dissertation sur la Nature et la Propagation du Feu* (Paris, 1744); *Principes Mathématiques de la Philosophie Naturelle,* 2 vols. (Paris, 1756); *Réflexions sur le Bonheur* in *Opuscules philosophiques et littéraires, la plupart posthumes ou inédits* (Paris, 1796); essays in Ira O. Wade, *Studies on Voltaire with Some Unpublished Papers of Mme du Châtelet* (Princeton, NJ, 1947).

Dupin, L. *Portefeuille de Mme Dupin* (Paris, 1884).

Genlis, S. F. du Crest de Saint-Aubin, Comtesse de. *Adèle et Théodore ou lettres sur l'éducation* (Paris, 1782; English translation: London, 1783); *Discours sur la suppression des couvents de religieuses et l'éducation publique des femmes* (Paris, 1790).

Germain, S. *Oeuvres philosophiques de Sophie Germain, suivies de pensées et de lettres inédites* (Paris, 1879; 1896).

Gouges, O. de. *Les Droits de la Femme* (Paris, [1791]); *Oeuvres,* ed. Groult (Paris, 1986).

Grouchy, S. de, Marquise de Condorcet. *Lettres sur la Sympathie,* in *Théorie des Sentimens Moraux,* Vol. 2 (Paris, 1798).

Holst, A., *Über die Bestimmung des Weibes zur öhern Geistesbildung* (Berlin, 1802).

Huber, M., *Le monde fou préféré au monde sage* (Amsterdam, 1731); *Le systême des anciens et des modernes, . . . sur l'état des âmes séparées des corps* (London, 1731), both in English translation as *The World Unmask'd, or the Philosopher the greatest Cheat in Twenty Four Dialogues . . . To which is added, The State of Souls Separated from their Bodies . . . In Answer to a Treatise entitled, An Enquiry into Origenism* (London, 1736); *Lettres sur la religion essentielle à l'homme, distinguée de ce qui n'en est que l'accessoire* (Amsterdam, 1738; English translation, 1738).

Lambert, A. de. *Réflexions Nouvelles Sur Les Femmes par une Dame de la Cour de France* (Paris, 1727); *Lettres sur la véritable éducation* (Paris/Amsterdam, 1729); *Traité de l'Amitié, Traité de la Vieillesse, Réflexions sur les Femmes, sur le Goût, sur les Richesses* (Amsterdam, 1732); *Oeuvres complètes . . .* (Paris, 1808).

Macaulay, C. S. *Loose Remarks on Certain Positions to be found in Mr. Hobbes's Philosophical Rudiments of Government and Society* (London, 1767); *Letters on Education* (London, 1790).

Shepherd, M. *An Essay Upon the Relation of Cause and Effect, controverting the Doctrine of Mr. Hume . . .* (London, 1824); *Essays on the Perception of an External Universe* (London, 1827); "Lady Mary Shepherd's Metaphysics," *Fraser's Magazine for Town and Country,* Vol. 5, no. 30 (July 1832).

Staël, G. de. *De l'influence des passions sur le bonheur des individus et de nations* (Paris, 1796).

Wollstonecraft, M. *Thoughts on the Education of Daughters* (London, 1787); *A Vindication of the Rights of Men* (London, 1790); *A Vindication of the Rights of Woman* (London, 1792).

WORKS ON WOMEN PHILOSOPHERS

Albistur, M., and D. Armogathe. *Histoire du féminisme français,* Vol. 1. Paris, 1977.

Buffet, M. *Nouvelles observations sur la langue françoise . . . Avec les éloges d'illustres sçavantes tant anciennes que modernes* (Paris, 1668).

Cousin, V. *Jacqueline Pascal: Premières études sur les femmes illustres et la société du XVIIe siècle.* Paris, 1844. *Madame de Sablé: Nouvelles Etudes sur la société et les femmes illustres du dix-septième siècle.* Paris, 1854. *La Société Française au XVIIe*

Siècle d'après Le Grand Cyrus de Mlle de Scudéry. 2 vols. Paris, 1858.

Dronke, P. *Women Writers of the Middle Ages.* Cambridge, 1984.

Foucher de Careil, L. *Descartes et la Princesse Palatine, ou de l'influence du cartésianisme sur les femmes au XVIIe siècle.* Paris, 1862.

———. *Descartes, la princesse Elisabeth et la reine Christine.* Paris, 1909.

Harth, E. *Cartesian Women.* Ithaca, NY, 1992.

Joël, K. *Die Frauen in der Philosophie.* Hamburg, 1896.

King, M. L. *Women of the Renaissance.* Chicago, 1991.

Kristeller, P. O. "Learned Women of Early Modern Italy: Humanists and University Scholars," in P. Labalme, ed., *Beyond Their Sex: Learned Women of the European Past* (New York, 1980).

La Forge, J. de. *Le Cercle des femmes sçavantes.* Paris, 1663.

Le Doeuff, M. "Long Hair, Short Ideas," in *The Philosophical Imaginary* (Stanford, CA, 1989).

Lescure, M. de. *Les femmes philosophes.* Paris, 1881.

Ménage, G. *Historia mulierum philosopharum.* Lyon, 1690; English translation, 1702; new English edition by B. Zedler, Lanham, MD, 1984.

Merchant, C. *The Death of Nature: Women, Ecology, and the Scientific Revolution.* New York, 1980.

O'Neill, E. "Disappearing Ink: Early Modern Women Philosophers and Their Fate in History," in J. Kourany, ed., *Philosophy in a Different Voice* (Princeton, NJ, 1996).

Schiebinger, L. *The Mind Has No Sex? Women in the Origins of Modern Science.* Cambridge, MA, 1989.

Stanley, T. *A History of Philosophy.* 3 vols. London, 1687.

Waithe, M. E., ed. *A History of Women Philosophers.* 3 vols. Dordrecht, 1987–91.

Wilson, K., and F. Warnke, eds. *Women Writers of the Seventeenth Century.* Athens, GA, 1989.

EILEEN O'NEILL

WORLD. After phenomenologically "reading off" ontological categories directly from reality itself articulating into various domains, Martin HEIDEGGER [3; S] describes this articulation as a differentiation of "lifeworlds" by a pretheoretical, preworldly "original something" that does the "worlding." We first live in "categories" as in meaningful contexts in which we immediately operate interpretively and through which we mediately experience the things included in them. A "world" is not a thing or a sum total of things, but a preobjective, pretheoretical context of meaning already given in the immediate experience of factic life in accord with its interests and its tasks. Immediate experience is already worldly in its contextures of meaning.

Heidegger first retains the neo-Kantian division of values (the true, good, beautiful, holy) in differentiating lifeworlds into the scientific, ethical, aesthetic, and religious. But in 1919 he distinguishes the world-around of things, the world-with of others, and the self-world as their comprehensive "horizon of signification." Each world-context is intentionally correlated to its mode of interest: concern, solicitude, and care. We occupy the world because it occupies us. The world as milieu of meaning becomes the in-which of our very being; as the orienting context that gives things their sense and place, it is the with-which of our everyday preoccupation, preceding every objectifying perception of it. As a primary finding, I-am-already-in-a-world belies every Cartesian attempt to prove the existence of an "external world." World is already there in, through, and as immediate meaningfulness, which is the fundamental how of its being. The primary given is the world and not things, the primary presence is meaning and not objects.

First in 1923, Heidegger describes the environing world we get around in by way of the prepositional context and continuity of references of "in order to" and "for," and the thing encountered within such a world as something to-hand, handy, a tool. In *Sein und Zeit* (1927), the referential totality is ontologically defined as an implicative totality of appliance *(Bewandtnis)* or usage in which the handy is discoverable as such, the referential series of "fors" finds its terminus in a what-for that is no longer appliance but the "for-the-sake-of-which" of the entire series, the human *Dasein* itself, which understands itself in understanding its world. In analogy with linguistic usage, and in fact its precedent, tool usage in its means-end applications is understood in hermeneutical terms as a process of explicating the implications of a tradition of usage on the basis of an understanding familiarity with the meaningfulness of the world, its worldhood. To be in the world means to be precedented by its "present perfect a priori." *The* world as such thus becomes the overall context of mutually implicated referential contexts, from tool usage to social custom and cultural praxis to linguistic usage, in terms of which all things get explicated as meaningful to and for human being. It is our "hermeneutic situation," the constellation of presuppositions for all of our human projects.

In the later Heidegger, the world reappears on the level of being as its opening, clearing, and temporal space of play, the locus of the language "housing" ("its worlding").

How does world "world"? The course of 1928–29 introducing philosophy vis-à-vis world views takes its orientation from KANT's [4; S] antrophological sense of "world" as the "play" of life in its dispersive multiplicity, variability, chance, and destiny. As the manifold totality of human interests, "world is the name of the game that transcending Dasein as such plays." Exposed to its instability, human beings at risk in play naturally seek to find a hold for the stay of their dwelling on earth. In play, they "cultivate" the world to evoke the rules of leeway for the game of life, its ἦθος ('ethos': custom, usage of a habitat) responding to the "Why?" of the whole of being. Philosophy is this basic hold of a life transcending to its world-totality, and cultural "world-intuitions" are various holds schematizing a world in play, beginning with the mythical figuration that "wins" safe shelter from the overpowering whole of being.

Following this playful "poietic" line, the later Heidegger sites the artwork in a "contest" between the world that it opens and the "sheltering" earth from which it arises. The inauguration of a world is likewise glimpsed in domesticating things that "thing" (i.e., assemble) a world of interplay between earth and sky, the mortals and the godly. This interplaying quartet is Heidegger's replacement to "save" the world-play itself from its most dangerous contender, enframing technology, which "com-posit(ion)s" all uniformly into a secure "stand-by reserve."

(SEE ALSO: *Artworks, Ontological Status of in Heidegger; Fourfold, The*; and *Life-world in Husserl* [S])

Bibliography

WORKS BY HEIDEGGER

Die Kategorien- und Bedeutungslehre des Duns Scotus. Tübingen, 1916. Later in *Frühe Schriften.* Frankfurt, 1972, 1978. The *Ablesen* of categories.

Zur Bestimmung der Philosophie [1919]. Gesamtausgabe, Vols. 56–57, ed. B. Heimbüchel. Frankfurt, 1987. The early Freiburg courses of 1919. First use of *Es weltet.*

Die Grundprobleme der Phänomenologie (1919/20), ed. H.-H. Gander. Frankfurt, 1993. The early Freiburg course of Winter Semester 1919–20. Entry of the triad of *Umwelt, Mitwelt,* and *Selbstwelt.*

Ontologie: Hermeneutik der Faktizität. Gesamtausgabe, Vol. 63, ed. K. Bröcker-Oltmanns. Frankfurt, 1988. The early Freiburg course of Summer 1923. First reference to *Verweisungszusammenhang* and its *Zuhandene.*

Sein und Zeit [1927]. 16th ed., Tübingen, 1986. Translated by J. Macquarrie and E. S. Robinson as *Being and Time.* New York, 1962. §18: *Bewandtnis* distinguished from *Sich-umwillen,* the ultimate ground of *Weltlichkeit.*

Einleitung in die Philosophie. Gesamtausgabe, Vol. 27, to be edited by O. Saame. Freiburg course of Winter 1928–29. Unpublished typescript available at the Simon Silverman Phenomenology Center, Duquesne University. The world games inspire *Weltanschauungen.*

Vom Wesen des Grundes. Halle, 1929. Translated in a bilingual edition by T. Malick as *The Essence of Reasons.* Evanston, IL, 1969. History of metaphysical conceptions of the world.

Holzwege. Frankfurt, 1950. Especially the essay "Der Ursprung des Kunstwerkes" (1936), translated by A. Hofstadter as "The Origin of the Work of Art" in M. Heidegger, *Poetry, Language, Thought* (New York, 1971).

Vorträge und Aufsätze. Pfullingen, 1954. Especially the essays "Bauen Wohnen Denken" (1951) and "Das Ding" (1950), translated by A. Hofstadter as "Building Dwelling Thinking" and "The Thing" in M. Heidegger, *Poetry, Language, Thought* (New York, 1971).

WORKS ON HEIDEGGER

Biemel, W. *Le Concept du monde chez Heidegger.* Louvain, 1950.

Kisiel, T. *The Genesis of Heidegger's "Being and Time."* Berkeley, 1993.

Kockelmans, J. *The World in Science and Philosophy.* Milwaukee, 1969.

Vycinas, V. *Earth and Gods.* The Hague, 1961.

THEODORE KISIEL

WRIGHT, GEORG HENRIK VON, Finnish philosopher belonging to the Swedish-speaking minority, was born in 1916. He was a professor at the University of Helsinki from 1946 to 1948 and from 1952 to 1961, and, in between, at the University of Cambridge (1948–1951). Since 1961 he has been a research professor at the Academy of Finland.

Von Wright himself describes the main influence on his philosophy as coming from Eino Kaila, his teacher in Finland, as well as from Ludwig WITTGENSTEIN [8; S] and G. E. MOORE [5]. From Kaila stems his interest in formal matters and his use of logical methods. From Moore he may have gotten his unpretentiousness and unrelenting search for clarity. That Wittgenstein had a profound personal influence on von Wright is not in doubt—he was first Wittgenstein's student, then his successor as professor in Cambridge, and finally, with G. E. M. ANSCOMBE [S] and Rush Rhees, one of his literary executors—yet it is not obvious just how his philosophy has been influenced by Wittgenstein.

Throughout life von Wright has combined, to an extent that is not usual, two rather different approaches to philosophy, one the passionate commitment of the humanist, the other the detached objectiveness of the academic philosopher. The former approach has been exemplified by a number of books in Swedish such as *Thought and Prophecy* (1955), *Humanism as a Way of Life and Other Essays* (1978), and *Science and Reason* (1986). As a thinker of predominantly pessimistic views regarding the future of humankind, von Wright has won wide public acclaim in the Nordic countries, particularly in Sweden.

Internationally, however, it is for his academic work that von Wright is known. He has written on INDUCTION [4] and PROBABILITY [6; S] (*The Logical Problem of Induction* [1941], *A Treatise on Induction and Probability* [1951]), and on ethics (*The Varieties of Goodness* [1963]). But his main reputation lies in MODAL LOGIC [S] and theory of action.

In *An Essay in Modal Logic* (1951), von Wright developed his method of distributive normal forms and analyzed a number of modal systems, one of which is nowadays often referred to as the Gödel/Feys/von Wright system. In this work von Wright explicitly recognized the possibility of epistemic and doxastic logic (that is, logics in which the modal box operator is interpreted as "the agent knows that" and "the agent believes that"); these themes were later developed by von Wright's former student Jaakko Hintikka.

His paper "Deontic Logic" (1951) opened up the field of deontic logic and was the first in a long series of papers and books in which von Wright elaborated and deepened his analysis. One of his most important insights is that the study of deontic logic requires a logic of action as a basis (*Norm and Action,* 1963). He is unusual among early action theorists in letting his logic of action inform his philosophy of action and vice versa.

According to von Wright, to act is to interfere with the course of nature: to bring about a change, to bring about an event. This view has led him to question the relationship between action and causality; an explanation of human action in purely causal terms will always omit something important. In *Explanation and Understanding* (1973) this view drives him to an examination of practical syllogisms; they do not possess logical validity in the ordinary sense of the word, nevertheless they may be valid as explanations *ex post actu.*

Bibliography

Schilpp, P. A., and L. E. Hahn. *The Philosophy of Georg Henrik von Wright.* The Library of Living Philosophers, Vol. 19. La Salle, IL, 1989.

KRISTER SEGERBERG

Index

A

B

C

D

E

F

G

H

I

J

K

L

M

N

P

R

S

T

U

V

W

X

Y

Z